ENCYCLOPAEDIA OF
PAPUA AND NEW GUINEA

ENCYCLOPAEDIA OF
PAPUA AND
NEW GUINEA

VOLUME 1
A–K

General Editor
PETER RYAN

MELBOURNE UNIVERSITY PRESS

IN ASSOCIATION WITH THE

UNIVERSITY OF PAPUA AND NEW GUINEA

First published 1972
Printed in Australia by
Wilke and Company Limited, Clayton, Victoria 3168 for
Melbourne University Press, Carlton, Victoria 3053
Great Britain and Europe: ISBS Inc., London
USA and Canada: ISBS Inc., Portland, Oregon 97208
Registered in Australia for transmission by post as a book

ISBN 0 522 84025 6
Dewey Decimal Classification Number 919.5003

EDITORIAL ADVISORY BOARD

Editorial Assistants
Barbara Mary Ramsden, M.B.E., B.A. (*dcd* 1971)
Ellen Davies, B.Sc., M.Sc.(Melb.)
Alison Whitmore, B.A., M.A.(Victoria University of Wellington)

Design
Norman Quaintance

Production
Peter Jones

Cartography
John Collier

CONTENTS

The motif embossed on the front cover is based on a fretted turtle-shell carving from Bougainville.

PREFACE

It is now some five years since the preparation of this Encyclopaedia was undertaken jointly by Melbourne University Press and the University of Papua and New Guinea. Generous financial aid from various well-wishers has sustained it through this period, so full of activity yet with little to show for it until now.

Both the sponsors of the Encyclopaedia hope that it will prove so valuable that before long users will demand a new edition, to keep pace with change in an area of such extraordinarily rapid economic and social development. Only time and the candid opinions of readers will establish this, but against the possibility of a revised edition in a few years' time it is desired to begin now to gather in a systematic way all ideas for new articles or for more up-to-date or more accurate information, and all constructive criticisms which readers care to offer. They may be sent, addressed to the Encyclopaedia, to either sponsor; all suggestions are welcome, and all will be acknowledged.

J. T. GUNTHER
Vice-Chancellor
University of Papua and New Guinea

J. S. TURNER
Chairman, Board of Management
Melbourne University Press

December 1971

ACKNOWLEDGMENTS

An encyclopaedia during its compilation accumulates debts as a prodigal might through his life, and to acknowledge every one of them is almost as impossible as it would be to repay them. But this project never could have been completed without the help of scores of people who gave generously of their time and their special knowledge; grateful thanks are given to every one of them, whether they are mentioned by name or not.

Acknowledgment of a special kind is due to the members of the Editorial Board and to the individual contributors. All of them discharged their commitments to the Encyclopaedia in spite of many other calls and duties. The effort made and the pains taken by some of them far exceeded any reasonable definition of obligation.

The work suffered a sad blow with the death early in 1971 of Miss Barbara Ramsden. She was the doyenne of scholarly editors, whose learning, patience and scrupulous accuracy made her an example to all whose aspiration is to scholarship. Her contributions to the Encyclopaedia's early shaping were invaluable.

The heavy financial burden of the preparatory years was lightened by the assistance of The Reserve Bank of Australia, The Myer Foundation, Conzinc Riotinto of Australia Ltd, the Department of External Territories, The Ian Potter Foundation, Broken Hill Proprietary Company Ltd, The Commonwealth Banking Corporation, Mr Gordon Darling, Mr P. A. Ryan, Rheem Australia Pty Ltd, the National Bank of Australasia Ltd and the Australia and New Zealand Bank Ltd.

The following people or organizations gave help in ways too varied and numerous to describe in full, but their many services and kindnesses are gratefully acknowledged: Professor R. N. H. Bulmer, Mr D. S. Garden, Dr D. A. M. Lea, Professor J. A. Mabbutt, Mr A. J. Sweeting, Professor Gerard Ward, Miss Margaret Westwood, Mr R. W. Whitrod. The La Trobe Library, The Mitchell Library, The National Library of Australia, the T. P. N. G. Department of Information and Extension Services and the T. P. N. G. Bureau of Statistics.

INTRODUCTION

Neither knowledge nor history stands still obligingly while an encyclopaedia records them, frozen and motionless in some unreal instant of time. Even as the encyclopaedist writes, scholarly study and the movement of events are changing the material under his hand, just as a landscape changes hue while the artist paints it. Nowhere is this truer than in Papua New Guinea, where in some departments of life the rate of change is bewildering.

Moreover—it is today almost a cliché—Papua New Guinea is so varied, its parts and its people differ so much, that it sometimes seems difficult if not pointless to generalize about the place as a whole.

Are these valid arguments against the usefulness of an encyclopaedia such as this? By no means.

In the first place, although in political and social matters change is rapid indeed, the forces which carve the startling landscapes and the evolutionary processes which adapt the living creatures and plants of the region move at a more stately pace; but who will say that they are less significant? Again, past history does not change, however much our appreciation of it might alter; and even current events in changing situations are worth recording as the stuff of future history.

Secondly, the fragmented nature of the country is much exaggerated by superficial observers, who dwell upon the obvious facts of the several hundred languages or the rough and broken nature of much of the terrain. They overlook the equally powerful forces of nature and of history which make the country one. The fishes that swim in the seas around it and the birds that fly over it; the great mountain chain that articulates the land like the backbone of a body; the diseases which attack man and woman without the least distinction as to their language or their district; the obscurities of how mankind first came there and occupied the land, and the equal obscurities of his future in a world full of economic and political uncertainties—all these things and many others make it sensible to regard the area as a unity, and therefore to publish a compendious and authoritative work of knowledge about it as a whole.

In this spirit the Encyclopaedia was conceived and compiled, in the hope that it would prove just as useful and as interesting to the people who live in Papua New Guinea as to those who look at the land from the rest of the world outside.

Editorial policy has been that the Encyclopaedia as such has no opinions; individual contributors were asked to concentrate their space and their attention upon *facts*. Nevertheless they were not prohibited from offering an opinion clearly identified as such, when their expert knowledge entitled them to do so. Thus there will be found a small leavening in the factual lump, in the form of opinion offered in a moderate way in good faith.

For the same reason, slight differences of view upon similar topics may be found between one article and another, and no editorial attempt has been made to 'iron them out'. It seemed, indeed, to be a positive gain for the reader to have the benefit occasionally of more than one approach to a question upon which leading experts differ.

It was hoped that all articles would be within the grasp of the intelligent general reader. From time to time, where interest in a topic is likely to be fairly restricted, contributors have addressed themselves a little more to specialists. Nevertheless, the Encyclopaedia is not mainly for specialists, though it is hoped that the bibliographies which follow many of the articles will provide useful guidance to those who want to pursue a subject further and at a more expert level.

No attempt was made to impose a uniform style of writing upon the contributors. Consistency in formal usage has been sought, and efforts have been made to clarify the occasional obscurity or ambiguity. Sometimes a passage has been omitted, usually because an author has unwittingly dealt in repetition with matters covered at greater length elsewhere in the Encyclopaedia.

In the last stages of preparation for the printer, the name Papua New Guinea was adopted by the House of Assembly in Port Moresby as the unified name for the former Territory of Papua and the former Trust Territory of New Guinea. It was decided nevertheless to retain the original title of the *Encyclopaedia of Papua and New Guinea*, as being accurate and appropriate. After all, the work covers much history of the time when what became Papua was called British New Guinea, and when what became the Mandated Territory and then the Trust Territory was called German New Guinea; and when what is now West Irian was known as Dutch New Guinea. As the Encyclopaedia covers all these times and all these places, there was no point in changing to match a newly adopted national name.

For a different reason, the old name Territory of Papua and New Guinea, and variants of it, will be found to occur in a number of articles dealing with more or less recent affairs. This is simply because, with the printers ready to begin work, it was not practicable to make the changes. Therefore, it has been allowed to stand except in cases where it might be actually misleading or confusing.

Care also was taken in the terms used to describe the people who live there, and while a variety of words and phrases are employed by various authors, the particular meaning in any context is clear. Thus, in referring generally to the original native-born inhabitants, the adjectives or nouns 'indigenous', 'indigenous people', 'indigenes', 'native' may be used. 'Papuan' as a noun refers to an indigenous inhabitant of the former Territory of Papua and 'New Guinean' as a noun refers to an indigenous inhabitant of the former Trust Territory of New Guinea, unless the context clearly indicates otherwise.

The descriptive terms used for those who are not part of the indigenous population also need to be defined. The most all-embracing term used for them today is 'expatriate' (i.e. 'outside their own country'). They are also called frequently 'Europeans', meaning that they trace back ultimately to origins in Europe, though perhaps many generations ago. The great majority are Australians whose forebears came from the British Isles or from continental Europe. A minority have settled permanently in the country and regard it as their home; most are transients. As they are distinguished by their comparatively light complexions, they may also be called 'white men', 'the white community', and so on. In older documents the word 'Caucasian' may be found describing such people—a term now discarded. The Chinese form another group, upon whom there is a special article.

As a guide to indigenous peoples who were the subject of anthropological study up to 1970, a bibliography of the more important publications of reasonably ready access was prepared by Miss Susan Baume. Recent publications are listed as they appear in *Mankind in New Guinea*, a quarterly issued by the Department of Anthropology and Sociology of the University of Papua and New Guinea. Each bibliography is presented alphabetically under the name of the people concerned (e.g. ABAU, BAINING, CHIMBU, etc.).

Certain minor difficulties arise from the statistics. Different authorities collect and publish them sometimes upon slightly different bases or over different periods, or for different purposes. To bring every one of them to precise conformity was certainly beyond the resources of this—and probably any other encyclopaedia. In each article the figures most appropriate and authoritative have been used, and the source usually indicated.

Units of measurement are those most commonly in use for the particular purpose in the English-speaking countries today. Thus heights of mountains are given in feet and distances over the ground in miles. Measurements of scientific specimens are usually given in centimetres. Conversions to or from metric units can readily be made by use of the table in Volume 3.

As far as possible, names of places and natural features have been spelt according to the system followed by the Division of National Mapping, Canberra, in its 1:2,500,000 scale map of Papua New Guinea. Names which do not appear on that map have been spelt according to the most commonly accepted modern usage.

The main subject articles are arranged alphabetically through Volumes 1 and 2. A subject not regarded as sufficiently important to have its own main article, but referred to under another head or heads, may be located by consulting the Index in Volume 3.

The following two abbreviations appear, chiefly in the bibliographies which follow most articles:

ML: The Mitchell Library, Sydney
NLA: National Library of Australia, Canberra.

Any other abbreviations, except those of everyday general use, are explained within the text of the article where they are used.

P. R.

A

ABAL, Tei (1932-   ), Ministerial Member for Agriculture, Stock and Fisheries, M.H.A. for Wabag open electorate. Born in 1932 in Sakalis village, Western Highlands District, he received no formal education. For fourteen years he worked as a medical orderly at the Wabag Hospital, where he took charge of indigenous staff. He is president of the Wabag Native People's Club and a former Under-Secretary for Labour.

ABAU. People of the Central District. Reference: F. E. Williams, 'The Hornbill Feather in the Abau District', *Annual Report, Territory of Papua 1935-6.* Canberra, 1937.

ABEL, Charles William (1863-1930), missionary of the London Missionary Society in British New Guinea (later Papua) 1890-1917, Director of Kwato Extension Association and honorary L.M.S. missionary 1919-30, was born in London 25 September 1863. After an education distinguished more by sporting prowess than scholastic excellence, he left school at the age of sixteen and held a number of positions until he sailed to New Zealand in October 1881 to learn farming. This experiment soon failed, but in his attempt to find a satisfying career in New Zealand he gained some Maori friends and became deeply concerned about people of other races. He also decided to return to England and study to become a missionary. In 1884 he entered Cheshunt College and on successful completion of his training he was accepted by the London Missionary Society for their New Guinea mission. He spent one year after his ordination in medical training in London, sailing for New Guinea on 27 June 1889. He arrived in Port Moresby late in 1890. He then taught in the Port Moresby school while learning Motu, travelled to various mission stations with the Rev. James Chalmers [q.v.] and replaced him for a period at the Motumotu station. A deep friendship between the two developed at this time.

In July 1891 Abel finally left Port Moresby with the Rev. F. W. Walker to take up his main work in the Eastern Division. On 8 August they established their headquarters on Kwato Island, near Samarai. In August 1892 Abel married Beatrice Moxton. He took a keen interest in education and gathered children from the district into a boarding school at the station. He also involved local people in programmes of building and improvement of the station, including reclamation of the local swamp, a task completed in two years. His passion for cricket became an element of his educational programme. He believed that it could promote racial harmony and national unity.

Out of these early experiments Abel developed the idea of an 'industrial branch' in his mission as a means of building new and better conditions for the Papuan.

This scheme met with some opposition, particularly in those circles of the L.M.S. which saw it as a deflection from the evangelistic work of the missionary. Outstanding among these opponents was Dr W. G. Lawes [q.v.]. Several times Abel propounded the idea before the L.M.S. both in New Guinea and London and gained some support for particular aspects of the programme he was developing. When a deputation from the directors visited New Guinea in 1897 Abel spoke to them. Again while on furlough in England in 1900 he published a booklet on Kwato to gain further support. In March 1903 at the annual conference of the New Guinea District he read a paper on 'The Aim and Scope of an Industrial Branch of the New Guinea Mission', by which he won the support of all his brethren save Lawes. At this time part of his work was financed from money provided by one of the major benefactors of L.M.S. work in New Guinea, John Howard Angas of Adelaide. For nine months the Angas Industrial Mission had been in operation at Kwato, particularly in the fields of carpentry, house construction, boat building and furniture making. When on furlough in England in 1909, despite the caution of the L.M.S. about committing their limited funds to new projects, he gained support of his plan to extend his industrial work to include sawmilling. After a long debate about the supervision of copra production, a project aided by finance from an Australian group, in 1911 he began plantations on land given in trust to the mission. When another deputation from London came to an annual conference of the New Guinea District in 1916 with instructions to cut back all financial commitments and with proposals to disband the children's quarters and industrial branch at Kwato the parting of the ways had come.

Abel visited London in July 1917, resigned as a member of the L.M.S., became an honorary missionary and arranged for the properties of the station to be leased by the L.M.S. to the Kwato Extension Association for ten years.

The Association had as its first president Sir William MacGregor [q.v.] and its directorate included Sir George Le Hunte and Captain F. R. Barton [qq.v.], all of whom as previous Administrators of the colony had given support to Abel's experiments in education and industrial work. Sir Hubert Murray [q.v.] also gave his blessing to the Association, subsidizing it, since it was carrying out a native policy 'practically identical with that of the Government in the district', particularly in the field of 'industrial and agricultural education of the native'. In the early stages the venture struggled because of high prices for essential materials, food shortages and a slump in the copra market. The visit of the chairman of the Australian Committee in 1920 gave a boost to finance from this quarter. Wider support was won by Abel on two visits to America. As a result an auxiliary was formed, the New Guinea Evangelization Society, with a permanent council which organized capital from this source. By 1927 the Association was flourishing and control of its properties was handed over by the L.M.S. Abel was planning a new venture for the Fly River when the council called him urgently to America in 1929.

On his way back to Papua he made a visit to England, was involved in a motor accident, and died in London on 10 April 1930. He was survived by his widow and four children, Russell, Cecil, Phyllis and Mary.

As the founder of the Kwato Extension Association, Abel contributed significantly to the development of education in Papua. As a missionary, while expanding missionary methods in the educational and industrial fields, he shared the attitudes of his contemporaries about the traditional customs and culture of the people.

Abel Family Papers. University Library, Port Moresby; C. Abel, The Impact of Charles Abel. Port Moresby, 1968 (roneoed); C. W. Abel, *Kwato, New Guinea. 1890-1900*. London, 1900; ——— *Savage Life in New Guinea: The Papuan in Many Moods*. London, 1902; M. K. Abel, *Charles W. Abel: Papuan Pioneer*. London, 1957; R. W. Abel, *Charles W. Abel of Kwato: Forty Years in Dark Papua*. New York, 1934; Commonwealth of Australia, 'Report of the Royal Commission of Inquiry into the Present Conditions, including the Method of Government, of the Territory of Papua, and the Best Means for their Improvement', *Commonwealth Parliamentary Papers*, joint vol., 1907; London Missionary Society, Papers (M.L.).

                                               R. J. LACEY

(*See also* MISSIONS)

ABELAM. People of the Sepik River. References:
J. A. W. Forge, 'Notes on Eastern Abelam Designs Painted on Paper', in *Three Regions of Melanesian Art, New Guinea and the New Hebrides*. New York, Museum of Primitive Art, 1960.
——— 'Art and Environment in the Sepik', *Proceedings of the Royal Anthropological Institute*, 1965.
——— 'Learning to See in New Guinea', in *Socialization: the Approach from Social Anthropology*, ed. P. Mayer. London, 1970.
P. M. Kaberry 'The Abelam Tribe, Sepik District, New Guinea', *Oceania*, vol. 11, 1940-1.
——— 'Law and Political Organization of the Abelam Tribe, New Guinea', *Oceania*, vol. 12, 1941-2.
——— 'Political Organization among the Northern Abelam', *Anthropological Forum*, vol. 1, 1963-6.
R. Oxer, *The Socio-cultural Effects of Culture Contact and Land Shortage in the Wosera Census Division of the Sepik District*. Department of District Administration, Port Moresby, 1965 (roneoed).
J. Whiteman, 'Change and Tradition in an Abelam Village', *Oceania*, vol. 36, 1965-6.
——— 'A Comparison of Life, Beliefs and Social Changes in Two Abelam Villages', *Oceania*, vol. 37, 1966-7.
——— 'Magic in Saragum', *Oceania*, vol. 37, 1966-7.

ADMINISTRATIVE COLLEGE. The need to develop training facilities for Papuans and New Guineans to take up clerical and administrative positions in the public service was clearly recognized by the end of the 1950s. In 1961 a committee set up by the Minister for Territories recommended the establishment of a college to carry out a wide range of functions, from the running of general education courses at secondary and tertiary levels to legal training, policy workshops, training in extension techniques and the holding of seminars and conferences.'

Working from offices in Konedobu and the Port Moresby suburb of Saraga, the Administrative College began its training programme in 1964. Three years later the college moved to Waigani where buildings were erected on a site adjacent to that allocated for the University of Papua and New Guinea [q.v.]. Until the university had its own buildings many of its classes were held in the Administrative College rooms and the University Library also began there in shared accommodation. As both institutions developed, the Administrative College has resumed the full use of its facilities since 1969. By 1971 the college was training more than 600 students a year, including short courses, with a total of up to 340 in residence at any one time.

The main course programme operated by the college was organized as an executive development scheme to provide higher educational qualifications for officers in the public service. Each stage therefore includes basic general education together with specific vocational training and courses related to the current situation in Papua and New Guinea. The Stage 1 course is at Intermediate level, Stage 2 at the level of the Victorian Leaving Certificate, and the Diploma in Administration is at tertiary level. Officers enter at different levels according to the qualifications they have already achieved. Apart from these courses, vocational training has been provided through short courses for clerical workers and District Administration staff and through longer courses for magistrates and library assistants.

The college was originally under the supervision of an interim council which was advised by the

College Board of Studies and which made its recommendations to the Administrator and the Public Service Commissioner. The interim council has been replaced by an advisory body. In 1971 the organization of the college and its courses were under review by the Committee of Inquiry into post-secondary education and in the light of the decision by the House of Assembly that self-government should be achieved in the period 1972-6. Further expansion in the training of public servants is therefore expected.

ADMINISTRATOR AND LIEUTENANT-GOV-ERNOR. The title of Administrator (German, *Landeshauptmann*) was initially bestowed on the chief executive officer in both German New Guinea [q.v.] (1885) and British New Guinea [q.v.] (1888). The appointment was a means of maintaining closer control from the metropolitan capitals. After 1899 when Imperial administration finally replaced rule by chartered company (the New Guinea Company), the Germans appointed Governors. In British New Guinea the position of Lieutenant-Governor was created in 1895, the powers of Governor being still in effect exercised by the Governor of Queensland on behalf of both the British government and the contributing Australian colonies. After 1901, full powers were assumed by the Governor-General of the Commonwealth. It is believed that the title of Lieutenant-Governor was bestowed on Sir William MacGregor [q.v.] as an inducement to serve for a second term. The title remained in use in Papua, however, until 1940. This was in part due to the longevity of Sir Hubert Murray. His successor became merely Administrator which was the title employed in the Mandated Territory of New Guinea from the inception of Australian civilian control in 1921. In Murray's case the financial stringency which prevailed in Papua meant that his title was a relatively empty one. Whatever the formal nature of his powers, he had little scope for independent action without adequate internal revenues. Had the economy of Papua been more buoyant, Melbourne (and later Canberra) might have changed the title earlier. As it was, Murray frequently complained that he was treated like 'a clerk'. Since World War II there has been one Administrator for the two Territories, which have been administered as a single unit.

FORMAL POWERS

Administrative. Sections 13, 14 and 15 of the Papua and New Guinea Act 1949-68 read:
'13) There shall be an Administrator of the Territory, who shall be charged with the duty of administering the government of the Territory on behalf of the Commonwealth.
14) The Administrator shall be appointed by the Governor-General by Commission under the Seal of the Commonwealth and shall hold office during the pleasure of the Governor-General.
15) The Administrator shall exercise and perform all powers and functions that belong to his office in accordance with the tenor of his Commission and in accordance with such instructions as are given to him by the Governor-General.'
His administrative powers are therefore those vested in him by his Commission, by the instructions he receives from the Governor-General, and also any such powers as are conferred on him by the Statute Law of the Territory.
Legislative. Sections 49, 50, 54, 55 and 57, subsections (1) and (2) of the Act read:
'49) The House of Assembly may make rules and orders in respect of the order and conduct of its business and proceedings.
49A. The Administrator may, by message to the House of Assembly, declare that he is of opinion that the public interest requires special priority to be given to any specified business before the House (including business of which notice has been given in the House) and, where such a declaration is made, the Speaker shall, notwithstanding any rule, order or resolution of the House, cause that business to be given such priority in the proceedings of the House as an official member of the House requests.
50) A vote, resolution or proposed law for the appropriation of revenue or moneys of the Territory shall not be passed unless the purpose of the appropriation has in the same session been recommended by message of the Administrator to the House of Assembly.
54) (1) Every Ordinance passed by the House of Assembly shall be presented to the Administrator for assent.
(2) Subject to the next succeeding sub-section, the Administrator shall thereupon declare, according to his discretion but subject to this Act—
   (a) that he assents to the Ordinance;
   (b) that he withholds assent; or
   (c) that he reserves the Ordinance for the Governor-General's pleasure.
(3) The Administrator may return the Ordinance to the House of Assembly with amendments that he recommends.
(4) The House of Assembly shall consider the amendments recommended by the Administrator and the Ordinance, with or without amendments, shall be again presented to the Administrator for assent.
55) The Administrator shall reserve for the Governor-General's pleasure any Ordinance—
   (a) that relates to divorce;
   (b) that relates to the granting or disposal of lands of the Crown or of the Administration;
   (c) whereby a grant of money or of an interest in land is made to the Administrator;
   (d) that may not, in the opinion of the Administrator, be fully in accordance with the treaty obligations of the Commonwealth or with the obligations of the Commonwealth under the Trusteeship Agreement;
   (e) that relates to naval, military or air forces;
   (f) that relates to the sale of, or other disposition of or dealing with, land;
   (g) that relates to the employment of persons;
   (h) that relates to arms, ammunition, explosives, intoxicating liquor or opium;

(i) that relates to immigration, emigration or deportation;

(j) that relates to the Public Service;

(ja) that removes any matter or class of matters from the jurisdiction of the Supreme Court;

(jb) that makes provision affecting the practice or procedure of the Supreme Court;

(jc) that establishes, or provides for the establishment of, a court; or

(k) that contains a provision having substantially the same effect as a provision in an Ordinance, or in a part of an Ordinance, to which the Governor-General has withheld his assent or which the Governor-General has disallowed.

57) (1) Subject to this section, the Governor-General may, within six months after the Administrator's assent to an Ordinance, disallow the Ordinance or part of the Ordinance.

(2) The Governor-General may, within six months after the Administrator's assent to an ordinance, recommend to the Administrator any amendments of the laws of the Territory that the Governor-General considers to be desirable arising out of his consideration of the Ordinance.'

In addition, the Administrator has general powers to make regulations, conferred by various ordinances of the Territory. Under the Administrator's Council Ordinance 1960, he was required to seek the advice of the Council before using these powers, but did not have to accept such advice. This situation has changed in recent years (see below). In a similar manner, the Administrator has the power to issue specific legislative instruments such as proclamations and orders conferred by certain ordinances of the Territory.

Judicial. Certain ordinances give the Administrator judicial powers; on some matters he is the final arbiter.

CONSTRAINTS

The apparently wide discretionary powers of the Administrator are in fact constrained in a number of ways. Certain public corporations exist in the Territory, such as the Papua and New Guinea Copra Marketing Board, the Papua and New Guinea Coffee Marketing Board, the Papua and New Guinea Development Bank, the Papua and New Guinea Harbours Board, the Papua and New Guinea Electricity Commission and the Housing Commission. The powers and functions of these public corporations are defined by the ordinances that created them. Secondly, a number of Commonwealth departments and instrumentalities directly provide government services in the Territory. These include the Departments of the Army and Navy, the Department of Civil Aviation, the Department of Works ('CommWorks'), the Postmaster-General's Department, the Australian Broadcasting Commission and the Overseas Telecommunications Commission. Thus the Administrator is not in fact the chief executive of all the instruments of government which currently exist in the Territory.

In addition, the Minister for External Territories has the power to make appointments to the Territory Public Service (section 30 of the Act). Some of these powers were formerly delegated to a Public Service Commissioner rather than to the Administrator (Sir Hubert Murray as Lieutenant-Governor of Papua did have certain powers to make appointments). Under the Public Service Board Ordinance 1968, somewhat wider powers are now exercised by a Board of which the chairman is a former local officer, Sere Pitoi [q.v.]. Above all, however, the Administrator is constrained by the fact that he has no fixed term of appointment and must follow such instructions as are given him by the Governor-General as advised by the Minister. Taken together, these last three constraints provide the basis of the case that the Territory is 'excessively' under the control of Canberra.

CANBERRA CONTROL

As long as Papua and New Guinea is a dependent territory it must in the final resort be under 'Canberra control'. The extent and nature of such control have caused criticism. It has been the practice not to give a formal set of instructions to Administrators, for example, but to give them instructions from 'time to time as the necessity arises'. Circumstantial evidence suggests that there have been frequent necessities. Given the rapidity of change in the post-war years, a case can be made for such a practice. In political terms, however, it means that few conventions have been able to develop for the final making of decisions *within* the Territory. Mr Justice Kerr has argued that the Administrator is such a cipher that it is still possible to devolve power from Canberra to Port Moresby in such a way as to make his office the equivalent of *either* that of the Governor-General *or* to that of a strong President of the United States. Certainly this view is supported by a reading of the Act.

RECENT DEVELOPMENTS

Since 1970 it has been the declared policy of the Commonwealth government that the Administrator should pay increasing attention to the advice of ministerial office holders (ministerial members and assistant ministerial members) and to the views of the Administrator's Executive Council (AEC), particularly with regard to 'certain specified matters'. These matters are specified by ministerial regulation and could of course be amended in *any way* by the Minister for External Territories. Nevertheless, there seems some reason to see this as an almost irreversible devolution of power. Its significance affects the two major areas of the Administrator's activity: (1) administration and (2) legislation.

(1) Charged with administering the Territory, the Administrator was assisted by an Executive Council consisting of public servants until 1960, when that body was replaced by the Administrator's Council. This contained two elected (and one other non-official) members, but was largely an advisory body. Policy for the Territory was discussed within the smaller and wholly official Policy

and Planning Committee which was established in 1961. Although this made it possible to air opposing views, the Administrator was thus still in the last resort dealing with official subordinates. There was little *de facto* change after the inauguration of the House of Assembly [q.v.], the enlargement of the Council and the introduction of elected members as under-secretaries in 1964. The final report (1967) of the House of Assembly's Select Committee on Constitutional Development recommended the formation of a new Administrator's Executive Council, which should be the 'principal policy making body within the Territory'. This was set up in 1968; it contains a majority not merely of members elected to the House of Assembly, but of members elected (indirectly) by the House to sit in the AEC. With one exception, the Administrator's freedom to nominate elected members is restricted to such members as have already been nominated by the House Nominations Committee. The Executive Council comprises the Administrator, three official members, seven ministerial members and one elected member appointed by the Administrator. Six of the ministerial members are indigenous; the other six are expatriates.

Initially, these ministerial members shared responsibility with the permanent heads of 'their' departments, the Administrator being empowered to resolve any disputes which might arise. Since 1970, ministerial office holders have had in respect of certain specified matters 'full authority to make decisions, subject only to the AEC. These matters include the day to day running of their Departments excepting public service aspects', i.e. departmental heads are now their subordinate advisers on policy matters and the Administrator is no longer arbiter. In addition, despite its continued 'formal right to intervene' on any particular matter, the Minister stated in July 1970 that 'on many matters, powers of final decision have been handed over . . . [and] in future there will be no need to refer these matters to the Commonwealth Government'. The powers are listed in the annexes to his speech and can most succinctly be described negatively. The Commonwealth continued to be responsible for such matters as the judiciary, law and order, internal security, external affairs, international trade relations, defence and other matters administered directly by other Commonwealth departments. The net result is to make the Administrator's role more like that of the Governor-General. He continues to preside over the AEC, which has both statutory functions akin to those of the Governor-General's Executive Council and policy functions akin to those of Cabinet; but he is required in respect of these 'specified matters' to exercise his authority 'in accordance with the advice of the AEC and individual office holders'. On such matters, the official members of the AEC 'will be available to advise . . . but will take no part in decisions'. Similarly, his discretionary power not to refer matters to the AEC (section 19, subsection (2) of the Act) no longer exists with respect to these specified matters and it is officially claimed that, more generally, other matters are being increasingly referred to the AEC. A further indication of the changed situation is the creation of the position of Spokesman for the AEC to take over some of the functions previously performed by the senior official member, as well as certain new ones arising from the changes.

(2) In accordance with the changes in executive authority, the Minister at the same time announced that 'the Commonwealth' would not block legislation in the same areas as those for which ministerial office holders have final powers of decision. Since he also said that 'the right to withhold assent or to disallow will not be employed', it is perhaps fair to presume that this refers to both the Administrator's and to the Governor-General's veto power. The right to recommend amendments does not seem to be affected.

Although the formal powers of the Administrator have been reduced by the changes of 1970, his significance has actually been enhanced. Firstly, he was very much constrained in the exercise of his formal powers. Secondly, he is now the crucial man-in-the-middle on whom much of the future political development of the Territory rests. Aware of the policies of the Commonwealth and under some continued constraint to pursue them, he must simultaneously deal with ministerial office holders as power is increasingly devolved from Canberra to Port Moresby. It is scarcely conceivable that such a devolution can occur without some differences of opinion between Canberra and ministerial office holders. Much will therefore depend on the Administrator should such differences occur.

IAN GROSART

PAPUA (BRITISH NEW GUINEA)
Lieutenant-Governors and Administrators

Major-General Sir Peter Scratchley, Her Majesty's Special Commissioner. Appointed Nov. 1884. Established Port Moresby as seat of government. Died in office, 2 Dec. 1885.
H. H. Romilly, Deputy Commissioner from 2 Dec. 1885 to 26 Feb. 1886.
John Douglas, Her Majesty's Special Commissioner from 27 Feb. 1886 to 3 Sept. 1888.
William (later Sir William) MacGregor, Administrator of British New Guinea from 4 Sept. 1888 to 13 Mar. 1895. Lieutenant-Governor from 13 Mar. 1895 to 10 Sept. 1898.
F. P. (later Sir Francis) Winter, Acting Administrator from 1 Nov. 1898 to 23 Mar. 1899.
G. R. (later Sir George) Le Hunte, Lieutenant-Governor from 23 Mar. 1899 to 9 June 1903.
C. S. Robinson, Deputy and Acting Administrator from 9 June 1903 to 16 June 1904.
F. R. Barton, Administrator from 16 June 1904 to 9 Apr. 1907.
J. H. P. (later Sir Hubert) Murray, Acting Administrator from 9 Apr. 1907 to 18 Jan. 1909. Lieutenant-Governor from 18 Jan. 1909 to 27 Feb. 1940.
H. L. Murray, Administrator, Dec. 1940 to Feb. 1942.

During the period 1895-1940 the title 'Administrator' was used for temporary appointees who were either acting until a permanent appointment was made or acting in the absence of the Lieutenant-Governor.

MANDATED TERRITORY OF NEW GUINEA
Administrators

William Holmes* 20 Sept. 1914 to 8 Jan. 1915.
S. A. (later Sir Samuel) Pethebridge* 8 Jan. 1915 to 21 Oct. 1917.

S. S. Mackenzie (Acting)* 21 Oct. 1917 to 21 Apr. 1918.
G. J. Johnston* 16 Mar. 1918 to 1 May 1920.
Thomas Griffiths* 1 May 1920 to 21 Mar. 1921.
E. A. Wisdom 21 Mar. 1921 to June 1933.
Thomas Griffiths (Acting) 11 July 1932 to Sept. 1934.
W. R. (later Sir Walter) McNicoll Aug. 1934 to Dec. 1942.

* Military Administrator

TERRITORY OF PAPUA AND NEW GUINEA
Administrators

J. K. Murray* 11 Oct. 1945 to 30 June 1952
D. M. (later Sir Donald) Cleland† 23 Jan. 1953 to 8 Jan. 1967.
D. O. Hay 9 Jan. 1967 to 22 July 1970.
L. W. Johnson 23 July 1970 to —.

* At first administering 'south of the Markham River' only. The former military administration of the whole of the rest of the Territory was handed over to him on 24 June 1946.
† Acting Administrator from 10 Sept. 1951.

ADMIRALTY ISLANDS. People of the Bismarck Archipelago, north of New Guinea. References:

H. Damm, 'Hacken- und beilartige Geräte mit Schildkröteklinge und ihre Bedeutung im Wirtschaftsleben der Ozeanier', Leipzig, Museum für Völkerkunde, *Jahrbuch*, vol. 11, 1953.
————'Versuch einer Deutung der sogenannten Fetische von den Anachoreten-Inseln (Kaniet), Bismarck-Archipel', *Ethnologica*, vol. 2, 1960.
R. F. Fortune, 'Manus Religion', *Oceania*, vol. 2, 1931-2.
———— *Manus Religion*. Philadelphia, 1935.
M. Mead, 'Melanesian Middlemen', *Natural History*, vol. 30, 1930.
————'Living with the Natives of Melanesia', *Natural History*, vol. 31, 1931.
———— *Growing Up in New Guinea*. London, 1931.
————'An Investigation of the Thought of Primitive Children, with Special Reference to Animism', *Journal of the Royal Anthropological Institute*, vol. 62, 1932.
———— *Kinship in the Admiralty Islands*. Anthropological Papers of the American Museum of Natural History, vol. 34. New York, 1933-4.
————'The Manus of the Admiralty Islands', in *Co-operation and Competition among Primitive Peoples*, ed. M. Mead. New York, 1937.
————'Research on Primitive Children', in *Manual of Child Psychology,* ed. L. Carmichael. New York, 1946.
———— *Male and Female*. London, 1950.
————'Manus Revisited', Papua and New Guinea Scientific Society, *Annual Report and Proceedings*, 1953.
————'Twenty-fifth Reunion at Manus', *Natural History*, vol. 63, 1954.
————'Cultural Discontinuities and Personality Transformation', *Journal of Social Issues*, New York, Supplement Series, no. 8, 1954.
————'Manus Restudied', New York Academy of Sciences, *Transactions*, vol. 16, 1954.
———— *New Lives for Old*. London, 1956.
———— and T. Schwartz, 'The Cult as a Condensed Social Process', in *Group Processes: Transactions of the Fifth Conference, October 1958, Princeton, N.J.*, ed. B. Schaffner. New York, 1960.
H. Nevermann, 'Admiralitäts-Inseln', in *Ergebnisse der Südsee-Expedition 1908-1910*, II, A, Band 3, ed. G. Thilenius. Hamburg, 1934.
T. Schwartz, *The Paliau Movement in the Admiralty Islands, 1946-54.* Anthropological Papers of the American Museum of Natural History, vol. 49. New York, 1962.
————'Systems of Areal Integration: some Considerations Based on the Admiralty Islands of Northern Melanesia', *Anthropological Forum*, vol. 1, 1963-6.

ADULT EDUCATION. Despite the rapid growth of formal education in Papua and New Guinea over the past two decades, the majority of adults have had little or no schooling and even now fewer than half the children of school age attend school. Recent estimates show that fewer than one in four children of school age obtain a full primary education.

The actual spread of education has also been uneven; in particular the provision of schooling in some coastal areas is relatively much more extensive than it is in the Highlands Districts. Moreover, once schools have been established, the expectations of the community for further schooling rise so that the authorities are finding it difficult to correct existing imbalances, especially when trained teachers are in markedly short supply.

This pattern is common to many under-developed countries where, as in New Guinea, the provision of formal education and other aspects of development cause an increasing gulf between the young and the old, and between those who have long been in touch with the outside world and those who have only recently been contacted. The fact that most of the formal education and most of the business of government and industry are conducted in English, a foreign language, intensifies these problems.

Many consider that activities under the general name of adult education are vitally important in reducing the imbalances and tensions that result from such an uneven provision of formal education. Adult education offers hope for those who fail to find a place in the schools or who search unsuccessfully for jobs after primary school. Adult education may also channel into the educational process the energies and skills of organizations and individuals that would not normally undertake a teaching role in more developed societies.

All government departments are involved to some extent in providing adult education. Those most directly concerned are the Department of Information and Extension Services, the Department of Agriculture, Stock and Fisheries, the Department of Public Health, the Department of Social Development and Home Affairs, and the Department of Education. Their diverse activities in this field are co-ordinated through the Adult Education Council, the executive officer of which is the Principal Adult Education Officer in the Department of Education. Voluntary agencies also play a significant role.

At the District level the District Superintendent of Education, and more particularly the District Adult Education Committees which were introduced into most Districts during 1970-1, are responsible for fostering adult education. They identify community needs, determine priorities within each District, and help to form classes where appropriate. Regional Adult Education Officers have been appointed to extend the programmes and encourage greater participation by Local Government Councils, church voluntary and community bodies, and closer liaison with activities of other departments.

The Department of Education assists several projects in vernacular, Pidgin English [q.v.] and basic English, but the department's main direct involvement is in continuing education at the secondary level and vocationally oriented courses. The adult education section of the department includes a School of External Studies which provides courses leading to higher secondary, technical or certificate qualifications. Secondary courses are available to all who have completed a primary education to Standard 6.

Courses include all basic subjects—English, mathematics, history, geography, social studies, commerce, science, etc.—from Form I to Form IV levels of secondary education. Enrolments in 1970-1 exceeded 6,000, of whom approximately one-third studied by correspondence only, one-third in tutored groups with voluntary tutors, and one-third attended adult classes.

The School of External Studies in 1971 introduced courses in three stages for a post-secondary Certificate of Commerce awarded under the auspices of the Board of Commercial Studies. This certificate-level course is the first available to the general public by part-time studies (though Australian courses have been and are being studied by Papuans and New Guineans). It is designed to provide persons engaged in commercial procedures with a formal qualification. The certificate is regarded as suitable for the accountant of a small business or for the assistant to the accountant of a larger enterprise.

The third area covered by the School of External Studies is a support programme for apprentice studies. Apprentices indentured under the block-release system are required to complete theoretical studies by correspondence, or in classes organized by the School of External Studies, in the period between the annual full-time courses at a technical college. In 1971 some 220 students were enrolled in this way attending evening classes or block courses for up to eight weeks full-time study at the three centres of Lae, Rabaul and Port Moresby as part of the Technical Apprenticeship Scheme. Another 380 students were working in this scheme through correspondence courses.

Where there is a ready-made course such as that operated by a vocational centre or the School of External Studies, the adult education section directs inquiries to the institution concerned. Where no such course exists, the section, through the District committees, employs part-time instructors and collects fees. Ideally a programme of adult education should spring from the desires of the people. One successful vernacular literacy project of this kind, supported by the Department of Edu-

cation, is among the Atzera language group in the Morobe District. The course is organized by the Summer Institute of Linguistics [q.v.] and the Markham Local Government Council.

The Department of District Administration has an essentially educative task in most of its contacts with the public, particularly in less developed areas. Those activities shade into formal education in advisory services to Local Government Councils and in courses for newly elected councillors. Brief community training courses are given to representative village groups in special District centres. The department also operates over 700 women's clubs and assists sporting and other recreational groups with grants-in-aid to purchase equipment, establish recreational halls and similar activities. Since 1969 there has been a rapid expansion of the work of the department in running political education seminars for villagers and local government councillors.

The Department of Information and Extension Services is fundamentally an adult education institution, either providing a direct service through its radio stations broadcasting in English, Pidgin, Motu, Tolai (Kuanua), Kuman, Medlpa, Enga, Mid-Wahgi, Kiwai, Orokolo, Gogodala, Toaripi, Kerowo and other languages, through its film screenings, publications and libraries, or in its services to other departments. Such services to other branches of the Administration include training courses for extension workers, help with the design of visual material and aids, and research by surveys and other means into the effectiveness of Administration activities.

The Departments of Agriculture, Stock and Fisheries, of Forests and of Public Health all provide important adult education within their fields of interest. The approach adopted is usually the short residential course such as those provided for village farmers, forestry workers, and others. Instruction and advice in the course of patrol work is another method adopted by these departments, particularly the Departments of Health and Agriculture.

Employers in both the public and the private sectors are likely to offer more on-the-job training to employees. The banks and the Bougainville Copper Project [q.v.] have been especially active in this. Within the Administration the Public Service Board, mainly through its Administrative College [q.v.], provides a variety of courses, both formal and informal, of varying length, including high-level managerial courses for prospective Papuan and New Guinean executives.

The need for adult education is so large and the resources available from central government funds have been so limited that there has been a necessary reliance on many other sources. This support has come from the Army and the Churches, from Local Government Councils and the largest mining company. This may have advantages because it produces flexible programmes directly related to specific needs, but fragmented effort may cause overlapping and duplication. The need for greater co-ordination of adult education activities grew in the 1960s together with the awareness that the effectiveness of the formal school programme was hampered in communities where adult education was lacking.

AGENCY. Broadly speaking, the law understands as an agent one who acts on behalf of another, his principal, to establish contractual or commercial relations between that principal and a third party. For instance, a travel agent makes contracts between carrier and traveller, an employment agent between employer and employee, while an auctioneer accepts the offers of the highest bidders. The most important of such professional agents are the professional middlemen, factors and brokers, whose task relates to buying and selling on stock exchanges and commodity markets, generally defined as 'mercantile agents'.

The law of agency is thus a specific branch of the law of contract whose main purpose is to regulate both the internal relations between agent and principal, and the external relations between the principal and the third party.

The Territories of Papua and New Guinea derive their law of agency from three sources: English law, local legislation, and native custom.

The English law of agency is the creature of both the equitable and common law sides of the courts and, to a relatively small degree, it has been added to by legislation. Papua received the English law through the Courts and Laws Adopting Ordinance 1889-1951, which adopted English legislation in force in Queensland on 17 September 1888 and, by sections 3 and 4, 'the principles and rules of common law and equity that for the time being shall be in force and prevail in England'. The reception into New Guinea was achieved by the Laws Repeal and Adopting Ordinance 1921-1952, which adopted English legislation operative in Queensland on 9 May 1921 and the 'principles and rules of common law and equity that were in force in England' on that day. The fundamental qualification to this wholesale adoption of English law is that it is to be applicable only as far as local circumstances permit; to date the effect of this limitation has been minimal.

The second source of the law of agency in the Territories is local legislation and here there has been a great deal of activity. Sections 394 and 398 (VIII) of the Criminal Code (Queensland, adopted), untouched by subsequent amendments to that code, lay down the duties and liabilities of the agent with regard to property given to him for disposition and the proceeds thereof, while the Secret Commissions Act 1905 (Commonwealth, adopted) sections 4-7 of New Guinea lays down the standard of conduct required of the agent.

With regard to particular categories of agent the most important legislation is the Goods Ordinance 1951 and the Native Employment Ordinance of 1958-70, both of Papua and New Guinea. In sections 65-9 the former adopts the Factors Act 1889 of the Imperial Parliament as it relates to mercantile agents. It is important to note that section 76 of this ordinance specifically preserves the common law powers of the agent. The Native Employment Ordinance, in Part III sections 15-18,

lays down rules regarding the establishment of native employment agencies.

The third source of law is native custom. The Native Customs (Recognition) Ordinance 1963 of Papua and New Guinea permits recognition and application of native custom. Of especial interest is section 8(g) which refers to recognition in relation to 'a transaction which the parties intended should be, or which justice requires should be, regulated wholly or partly by native custom'. A qualification to this is section 6(b), (c) which denies the application of local custom 'if it is inconsistent with an Act, Ordinance or subordinate enactment in force in the Territory or part of the Territory' or 'its recognition or enforcement would result in the opinion of the court in injustice or would not be in the public interest'.

Native custom on agency, as with contracts generally, is at the moment very largely unknown. The courts, however, possessing the ability to deal in matters relating to local custom, are expected to make substantial contributions to this area of the law. As judicial bodies of 'first contact' with indigenous persons, the Local Courts could prove to be of especial importance in this regard.

G. C. Cheshire and C. H. S. Fifoot, *Law of Contract.* 2nd Australian ed., Sydney 1969; S. J. Stoljar, *Law of Agency.* London, 1961.

TERRITORY OF PAPUA AND NEW GUINEA LEGISLATION

Criminal Code (Queensland, adopted).
Goods Ordinance 1951.
Native Customs (Recognition) Ordinance 1963.
Native Employment Ordinance 1958-70.
Ordinances Revision Ordinance 1962.

TERRITORY OF PAPUA LEGISLATION

Courts and Laws Adopting Ordinance 1889-1951.

TERRITORY OF NEW GUINEA

Laws Repeal and Adopting Ordinance 1921-58.
Secret Commissions Act 1905 (Commonwealth adopted). R. G. L.

AGRICULTURAL EDUCATION in Papua and New Guinea had its beginnings in mission schools, although little agriculture was taught apart from manual work in the school garden. Notable exceptions included the Neuendettelsau Mission in New Guinea where lay brothers were recruited to specialize in agricultural training and animal husbandry to lift the productivity of village subsistence farmers. In Papua the teaching of agriculture by the missions [q.v.] was subsidized by the government, although the government itself attempted to organize agricultural education through the Native Plantations Scheme. Training consisted of practical demonstrations and experiments in tropical crops and new production methods. In New Guinea an agricultural school and demonstration plantation was established in 1928-9 on the Keravat River near Rabaul and it was here and at the botanical gardens in Rabaul that government agricultural training was carried on in the Trust Territory.

After World War II, training programmes in

Vudal Agricultural College, New Britain (top) The library (bottom) Spraying oil palm seedlings.

agriculture and farming for ex-soldiers were attempted. The Department of Education encouraged a rural bias in primary schooling and developed an agricultural emphasis at the Vunamami Education Centre near Rabaul. In 1952 the Department of Agriculture, Stock and Fisheries commenced training at the Mageri Centre near Bisianumu, not far from Port Moresby. Local students at Standard 5 level were given one or two years training to graduate as field workers or plant quarantine assistants, and Australian agriculture recruits were retrained in local tropical agriculture. A diploma-level agricultural college commenced at Vudal in 1965 and is now the major institution for agricultural education.

The Vudal Agricultural College is situated on six hundred acres of land on the Gazelle Peninsula, twenty-six miles from Rabaul. A sub-professional three-year course of practical and theoretical training in tropical agriculture is offered for Form IV school leavers. Scholarships are awarded by the Administration and private sponsors including banks operating in the Territory. The first nine diplomas were awarded in 1967 and by the end of 1970 a total of sixty-five students had graduated with the Diploma of Tropical Agriculture. The course is deliberately industry-based with a heavy loading towards practical work. It aims to produce diplomates who can fill a cross-section of positions within primary industry, including rural development officer, experimentalist, livestock officer, produce inspector, plantation manager assistant and bank agriculture officer. Business principles and farm management are kept central to the whole syllabus and third-year students are required to embark on practical farm projects of their own choosing where they can apply skills and principles to an actual field situation.

In 1970 130 students were in residence and facilities existed for expansion to a total intake of 180. Students are accepted from the British Solomon Islands Protectorate, Gilbert and Ellice Islands, and the U.S. Trust Territory of the Pacific.

In-service training of rural development officers is planned for the future and it is hoped that Vudal will also be able to provide specific post-diploma training courses according to the needs and activities of working diplomates.

In 1971 there was no faculty of agricultural science at the University of Papua and New Guinea [q.v.] and full professional training in agriculture was taking place at overseas universities.

A lower level of training in field-work is given at the Popondetta Agricultural Training Institute. In 1970 thirty-six students received certificates. Similar institutes are planned for Kapogere and Mount Hagen. Other opportunities for agricultural training are provided through vocational centres operated by the Department of Education for primary-school leavers and through the establishment of farmer-trainee positions in the Department of Agriculture, Stock and Fisheries. Approximately 1,500 positions are available for farmer trainees who are paid a small allowance to work

with agricultural field assistants. After a term of service as a trainee the place is taken by another potential farmer. Such training is usually specific to a particular industry, and it is assumed that if the trainee subsequently farms he will use the methods observed while a trainee.   B.B.

AGRICULTURE, INDIGENOUS. Most of the indigenous population live in rural areas and derive the bulk of their sustenance from the resources of their own well-defined local territories. The indigenous economies naturally reflect a wide range of environmental conditions, but most of them are based on some form of bush-fallow rotation (known also as 'shifting cultivation', 'slash and burn' and 'swidden horticulture'), with pig keeping, fishing, hunting [qq.v.], gathering, cash cropping and trade as subsidiary activities. For convenience, the economic activity can be divided into two main types.
(1) The lowland peoples who can be subdivided into:
   (a) The peoples of the lowland forest or savannah areas who practise a form of shifting cultivation dependent on having a long fallow under natural regrowth.
   (b) The peoples who usually live in swampy areas below 1,500 feet whose staple food is sago, extracted from the sago palm.
(2) The peoples who live between 4,000 and 7,000 feet in the intermontane valleys of the central cordillera.

LOWLAND SHIFTING CULTIVATORS

The bush-fallow system is widespread through the humid tropics where soils frequently have a low natural fertility. The long fallow period allows the natural vegetation to restore some essential plant nutrients to the soils and gradually allows the garden site to recover from exposure to the sun, erosion of the top soil, and infestation by weeds and insect pests. This method of cultivation has few harmful effects if the land is not used frequently, but deterioration of the soil has followed intensive cultivation in a few of the more densely populated areas. On the whole it is a system of land use which requires extensive areas of land and a low population density, but it does provide high yields in terms of labour input.

In the lowland forests, the practice is to cut a clearing, usually only between 0.2 and 0.8 of an acre but occasionally up to several acres, by felling the small trees and ring-barking or pollarding the larger trees, so that they will not obscure light. The felled trees and bush are trimmed to facilitate burning and a cleared area is left around the edge of the garden. The cut material is left to dry out and then burnt four to six weeks later. The first burn is never complete and the charred rubbish is heaped around stumps or made into piles and re-burnt. All the unburnable rubbish is piled in heaps, placed behind logs (often placed along contours to control erosion) or thrown over the fence which is usually erected around the garden to protect it

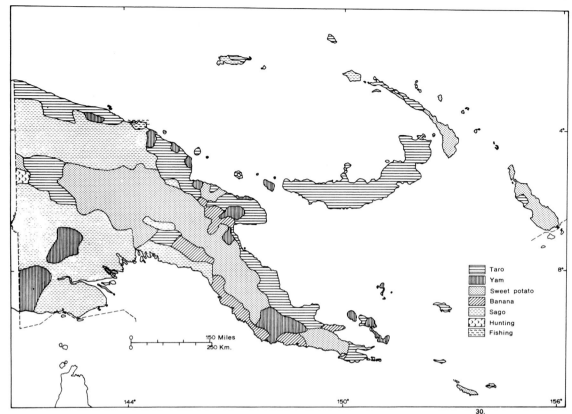

Principal food sources.

from pigs [q.v.] and wild animals. The garden is usually quite clean before planting starts.

Fire is thus the main agency in clearing the garden and the only tools used are normally an axe and a bush knife. Table 1 shows how few tools the indigenes have.

Crops are planted by making a small hole for each plant and sometimes roughly loosening the soil around the hole to give tubers and roots a better chance to develop. Apart from the bare hands, the only implement used is a simple digging stick often roughly made from a nearby tree, and

Table 1

IMPLEMENTS OWNED BY INDIGENES, 1961

	Number per 100 persons		
	Papua	*New Guinea*	*Papua-New Guinea*
Bush knives	30	44	40
Adzes and axes	31	39	37
Spades, shovels and forks	7	33	26

SOURCE: T.P.N.G. Bureau of Statistics, *Survey of Indigenous Agriculture and Ancillary Surveys 1961–2.* Port Moresby, 1963.

occasionally carved and decorated from the black *limbom* palm and used for many years.

Food crops. The staple food [q.v.] crops are yam, taro and occasionally cassava. Bananas are grown throughout the Territory and in some of the drier areas, particularly in the savannah lands and the dry parts of the Markham Valley (e.g. Kaiapit), they are the main food crop. Numerous varieties of all crops are grown and in any one area people can name many varieties of all the principal cultivated plants (*see* CROP PLANTS).

Taro, the most usual staple, thrives in a moist shady place and is propagated by cutting from the top of the corm or from small axillary or adventitious buds. Among some peoples such as the Baruya, the Mafulu and the Karam, taro is irrigated. In recent years, there has been a great decrease in taro cultivation in Bougainville and New Britain due to a blight caused by *Phytophthora colocasiae.* Yam flourishes best in areas with a deep, well-drained soil and with a definite dry season. Cassava is much more tolerant of a wide range of environmental conditions including drought and poor soils. It is easily propagated by planting stem cuttings and can be planted at any time of the year. Many other crops are interplanted and it would not be unusual for a half-acre garden to contain twenty or thirty different plant species (*see*

Table 2) and numerous cultivars of any one species.

After planting there is little work to be done apart from weeding, and this is usually left to the women. This task is only time consuming and difficult if the fallow period is short and if weeds, particularly *kunai* grass, have not been swamped by the previous forest fallow. Men do little in the gardens apart from making simple trellis for yam vines to climb up and repairing fences.

Harvesting naturally begins as soon as the first crops are mature for, with the exception of yam and, with special care, taro, it is not possible to store the crops. Thus in most areas families, usually the basic residential and economic unit, have two to six gardens at different stages of development so that at least one garden is producing food. Nevertheless there tends to be an agricultural cycle with peak periods of production. This is most clearly seen in the areas which grow yams. The main harvesting usually takes place at the beginning of the dry season. Most of the work is done with bare hands and a dibble stick, which is merely a pointed stick about five feet long and one and a half inches in diameter.

Table 2

SOME COMMON LOWLAND FOODS

	PIDGIN OR COMMON EUROPEAN NAME
STAPLE ROOT CROPS	
Colocasia esculenta	taro taro
Dioscorea alata	yam greater yam
Dioscorea esculenta	mami yam
Manihot esculenta	tapiok cassava
OTHER ROOT CROPS	
Alocasia macrorhiza	taro
Canna edulis	Queensland arrowroot
Cyrtosperma chamissonis	taro
Dioscorea bulbifera	patata aerial yam
Dioscorea nummularia	yam
Dioscorea pentaphylla	yam
Ipomoea batatas	kaukau sweet potato
Xanthosoma sp.	taro kong kong taro
Zingiber officinale	ginger
GREEN VEGETABLES AND LEGUMES	
Abelmoschus manihot	aibika
Allium spp.	anien onion
Amaranthus spp.	aupa
Arachis hypogaea	kasang peanut
Brassica chinensis	kabis Chinese cabbage
Brassica spp.	kabis
Cajanus cajan	pigeon pea
Celosia cristata	
Colocasia esculenta	taro
Deeringia amaranthoides	}kumu greens
Ficus wassa	
Ipomoea aquatica	
Nasturtium spp	cress
Psophocarpus tetragolobus	winged bean
Vigna sinensis	long bean
OTHER CROPS	
Ananas comosus	ananas pineapple
Capsicum spp.	chilli
Capsicum frutescens	lombo capsicum
Carica papaya	popo papaw
Citrullus vulgaris	melen water melon
Cucumis sativus	kukamba cucumber
Cucurbita maximima	squash
Cucurbita pepo	panekin pumpkin
Lycopersicon esculentum	tomato
Musa spp.	bananas
Oryza sativa	rice
Saccharum edule	pitpit
Saccharum officinarum	sugar
Zea mays	sweet corn

Agricultural calendar. Each garden has a productive life of from six months to about three years. An average sequence of activities would be something like this:
(1) Selection of garden site; often two years before the forest is cut a site is selected and rights of access to particular plots fixed.
(2) Cutting and clearing the forest, burning-off and the preparation of the garden; usually done during the dry season and may take from five weeks to three months.
(3) Planting of main crop takes from one day to several weeks depending on the gardeners' ability or desire to mobilize labour.
(4) Planting of minor crops may continue for about a year or more after the main planting.
(5) Harvesting begins after about three months in the case of some varieties of taro. Yams are the only garden crop which have a marked harvesting season. This is about six or seven months after planting and is usually timed to take place at the beginning of the dry season.
(6) The fallow; no further clearing takes place in the garden after about six months to three years. It is invaded first by weeds and bushes, then trees and finally, if the site is not used for about twenty years, by forest. Fallow periods depend on population pressures and alternative food resources, but they are rarely less than seven years and usually more than fifteen years.

Yields of gardens and individual plants vary considerably depending on environmental conditions, plant cultivars and agricultural practices. Yams for example were assessed by the Department of Agriculture, Stock and Fisheries to have a yield of 16.9 lb. per hole in Maprik, but the next highest yield was 9.5 lb. per hole in the Northern District. Most other areas in both Papua and New Guinea had yields of less than 7.5 lb. per hole. As a result of certain time-consuming practices, yams weighing more than 100 lb. have been grown by the Trobriand Islanders and the Abelam of the Maprik Sub-District.

The only comprehensive survey of yields to date is the *Survey of Indigenous Agriculture and Ancillary Surveys 1961-2*. Table 3 attempts to summarize the main features of that report.

Other sources of food. The gardens provide the bulk of the food but most groups obtain varying amounts of food from hunting and gathering in the forest. They also earn money by growing cash crops, washing for alluvial gold, selling artefacts or working for wages. With this money food is bought from trade stores.

Most gardeners keep some livestock such as pigs, chickens and occasionally goats and cattle. Pork is not a regular item of diet and is usually only eaten at feasts and on ceremonial occasions. Pigs are, however, an indication of wealth and prestige and by consuming excess production and household food waste, and foraging around the village and old gardens, they are a means of converting surplus food and waste into wealth and a meat reserve.

Many trees are planted around the villages,

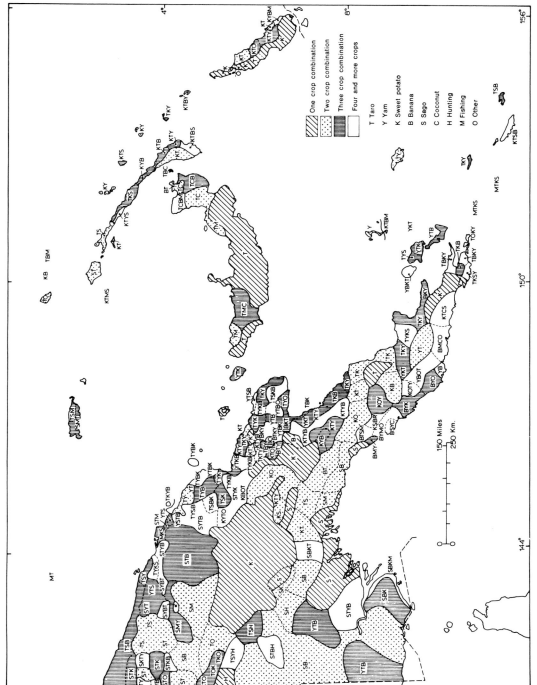

Food crop combinations.

Legend:

One crop combination
Two crop combination
Three crop combination
Four and more crops

T Taro
Y Yam
K Sweet potato
B Banana
S Sago
C Coconut
H Hunting
M Fishing
O Other

150 Miles
250 Km.

Table 3

AREAS AND PRODUCTION OF PRINCIPAL CROPS

April 1961 to March 1962

Crop	New Plantings during Year (1,000 acres)			Production (1,000 tons)			Ounces per Head per Day		
	Papua	New Guinea	Total	Papua	New Guinea	Total	Papua	New Guinea	Total
Banana	7.2	28.7	35.9	157	453	610	35.0	35.4	35.3
Sugar cane	2.6	5.3	7.9	96	211	307	21.4	16.5	17.7
Taro *Colocasia*	17.7	36.7	54.4	92	220	312	20.5	17.2	18.0
Taro *Xanthosoma*	0.5	5.6	6.1	10	136	146	2.2	10.6	8.4
Yam	8.0	10.4	18.4	91	142	233	20.3	11.1	13.5
Tapioca	0.6	2.3	2.9	16	36	52	3.6	2.8	3.0
Pineapple	0.2	0.2	0.4	2	3	5	0.4	0.2	0.3
Maize	4.5	32.9	37.4	15	46	61	3.3	3.6	3.5
Sweet potato	19.2	85.8	105.0	237	964	1,201	52.8	75.3	69.4

SOURCE: T. P. N. G. Bureau of Statistics, *Survey of Indigenous Agriculture and Ancillary Surveys 1961-2*. Port Moresby, 1963.

hamlets or homesteads and throughout the village lands. In the lowlands the coconut is the most important of all the supplementary foods. Other food-producing trees are the *tulip* tree, the betel-nut palm, the breadfruit tree, the *taun, Ficus copiosa, Pandanus* spp., *galip, Morinda citrifolia*, the papaw, and many tropical fruits such as citrus fruits, the mango, soursop, avocado, durian, custard apple and Malay apple.

THE SAGO EATERS

Over 100,000 sago-eating people live along the large rivers such as the Sepik, Fly and Idenburg and in the deltaic regions of the lowlands around Merauke, Waropen and the Purari Delta. Many small groups are found who, for part of the year, are mainly gardeners and for the rest of the year are dependent on sago gathering. Two interesting groups are the people of Lake Kutubu in the Southern Highlands who live at about 2,600 feet above sea-level and some people in the Torricelli Mountains of the West Sepik District who grow sago on the slopes of hills.

The sago palm grows in shallow freshwater swamps to a height of thirty to fifty feet and has a trunk twenty to thirty inches in diameter when mature. It grows in natural stands but the people also plant the palms in any swampy place from either shoots or seedlings. The only attention that the palm requires during its growth is the cutting back of the encroaching bush and the thinning of natural stands which are always very dense.

Each palm takes ten to fifteen years to mature. It produces only one inflorescence which rises in an enormous cluster straight from the top of the palm. The starch in the trunk is a reserve which would normally be used in the final flowering of the tree, so the palm is cut down just before flowering starts or in the early stages of flowering.

Preparation of sago. Men usually cut down the palm. They may then float the log back to the village or to some other convenient site for the extraction of the sago starch, or the processing may take place in the swamp. The cortex is stripped from the upper part of the log to expose the fibrous pith of the palm. From this point most of the processing is left to the women although men may occasionally help. Each woman sits cross-legged in front of a section of the log and pounds the pith with a blunt, adze-like instrument, which she swings in front of herself with a predominantly wrist action until the pith is like a fine fibrous sawdust.

The pulverized pith is placed in an inclined trough made from the leaf stalk of the sago frond. It is then saturated with water and pressed and kneaded into fibrous spaths of the coconut leaf which sieves the fine sago flour from the coarse pith. The water, with the sago flour in suspension, runs through the sieve and into a basin where the flour is collected by sedimentation. After about half an hour, the water is poured off and the flour is wrapped up and is either allowed to dry into a hard cake or is further processed into briquettes, biscuits or some other preparation. Each palm produces between two hundred and seven hundred pounds of sago flour.

Sago is not a seasonal crop and the palms can be cut and sago prepared in any month of the year. Some groups who are mainly gardeners process sago in times of shortages, or if they have seasonal crops such as yams, they collect sago when the garden staple is not available. Sago is a popular food and it is frequently an important component in many of the coastal trading relations, for example, the *hiri* of the Motu [qq.v.].

From a nutritional point of view sago is a poor food, for it has a high calorie content but virtually no protein or vitamins. Fortunately, the sago growers can obtain supplementary food from other sources to give them a more balanced diet. Most sago-growing areas are associated with rivers, lakes and channels in which fish can be caught. The people may also be able to catch freshwater prawns, crabs, ducks, wild fowl and crocodiles, or they may hunt the wallabies and cassowaries that live in the grasslands along the margins of the swamps, all of which are protein-rich foods. One source of food on the Sepik River is the may fly which suddenly, but regularly, swarms from the river and is collected and cooked in large quantities.

Sago eaters obtain their vitamin needs from a few small gardens on any available high ground such as levees, and from tree crops such as the coconut and breadfruit which grow around the villages. In the Gulf District and in the Waropen area of West Irian platform gardens ten feet high are built. Earth two feet deep is placed on the platforms and crops planted in the raised gardens. In lowlying areas around Merauke, the Marind build up long prismoid ridges, set out in parallel rows and divided by deep drainage ditches. Many of the food crops of Melanesia such as bananas and taro are tolerant of damp conditions and some other food plants, such as *Xanthosoma, Ipomoea aquatica, Nasturtium* spp. and water lilies (e.g. of the Chambri Lakes) grow in or near the water and provide green leaves or fruit.

THE HIGHLANDERS

In the Highlands the indigenous farmers have evolved methods of bush-fallow rotation where it is possible to cultivate the *Themeda-Miscanthus* grasslands which occur in intermontane valleys and tributary side valleys between 4,000 and 7,000 feet. Some settlements, such as those just below Mt Wilhelm, are at an altitude of 8,500 feet. Highland agriculture is different from lowland agriculture because the soil is tilled to eradicate grasses, there is widespread ditching, mulching and planting of a tree fallow, and finally there is usually a short fallow period followed by a long cultivation period with frequent re-cultivation before fallowing.

The food crops. The remarkable feature of the Highlanders is that they are almost entirely dependent on a single crop, the sweet potato, which is said to provide 85 per cent of the calorific intake in some areas. The sweet potato is propagated by means of leafy shoots and matures in four to eighteen months. Only a few tubers are removed at a time, and each plant is allowed to continue bearing for several months. The plant is sensitive to wet soil, drought and frost but the range of tolerance is wide. There has been some adaptation to different environments. For example, among the Central Dani of the Baliem Valley complicated drainage systems have been developed and in dry areas simple irrigation with bamboo pipes is practised.

Subsidiary crops are taro, sugar cane, banana, yam, maize, cassava, the Highland *pitpit* (*Setaria palmifolia*) and a wide range of green vegetables and legumes. In some areas such as the Vogelkop and Telefomin, taro is the main crop and among the Ok Sibil and the Karam people it is the main ceremonial crop. Where it is cultivated, it is often irrigated or grown in ditches.

Garden preparation. As Brookfield and Brown point out there are two basic methods of land preparation. 'In the first the whole land surface is turned over; in the second the land is trenched, the spoil from the ditches being thrown into the intervening beds.' There are, however, many modifications of these two systems. In the Baliem Valley and the Wissel Lakes gridiron ditches are dug and soil is thrown up to form island beds. The Enga of the Wabag area till the land and heap the loosened soil into circular mounds which they compost before planting crops. In some areas shallow drains are dug and the intervening land slightly ridged or made into small mounds. Various techniques have been developed for retaining soil. In the Chimbu District and many other areas a simple form of terracing is practised where saplings are placed across the slope at regular intervals and are pegged in position to form retaining walls about one foot high.

Cultivated land is usually enclosed because of the large number of domesticated pigs. Unlike the lowlands where enclosed areas may only be an isolated half-acre garden, extensive areas may be enclosed to include many contiguous gardens as well as some fallow land. On steep slopes fences may be supplemented or replaced by ditches, which are constructed primarily for drainage purposes.

The work of clearing and preparing the land is done by families although larger groups are formed for heavy tasks such as clearing grass. As in the lowlands there is a division of labour between the sexes (*see* Table 4).

The cultivation cycle. In the Highlands no clear agricultural cycle exists and any operation may be carried out at any time of the year. However, a certain agricultural periodicity occurs: land clearing, preparation and burning reach a peak in the latter half of the dry season. When a plot is cleared and planted it is allowed to continue bearing until the crop begins to decline in yield. It is then re-tilled, the ditches (if any) are cleared and a second crop is planted. Many gardens are cultivated in this way four or five times before they are abandoned to fallow. Sometimes there are short fallow periods between each re-cultivation.

Fallow periods vary considerably. On good land in areas of dense population gardens may be culti-

Table 4

Garden Tasks	Men	Women
Slashing of undergrowth	*	*
Clearing grass in Highlands	*	*
Cutting of trees	*	
Preparation for burning	*	
Burning	*	
Tilling of soil	*	
Final clearing of garden		*
Fence building	*	
Planting in Highlands		*
Weeding		*
Harvesting in Highlands		*
Carrying of harvested food		*
Cooking		*
Care and feeding of pigs		*
Killing and cooking of pigs	*	

vated, with intervals of short fallow, for from four to eight and even ten years, then fallowed (often under casuarinas in places like the Chimbu) for from five to twenty years. On the most valued land, the period under cultivation probably equals the period under fallow. In poor areas with comparatively sparse population, cultivation may only last for just over a year with fallows lasting over fifty years.

LAND USE AND POPULATION

The main areas of dense rural population are: the Highlands, particularly around Kundiawa, Wabag, Tari; around Maprik in the East Sepik District; and around Blanche Bay on the Gazelle Peninsula. Simple deterministic correlations with rainfall, soil fertility and disease are, however, inadequate to explain population distribution. While Rabaul and the area around Popondetta have fertile volcanic soils and are comparatively densely populated, some other areas with fertile soils are very sparsely populated. Examples are found in the Markham Valley and indeed the southern extension of the volcanic area of the Gazelle Peninsula itself is sparsely populated. In the Maprik area, on the island of Noemfoer in Geelvink Bay and in many areas of the Highlands a linguistic boundary often separates very different population densities. Only rarely is the present population related to, or even approaching, the carrying capacity of the land although there are possible exceptional areas around Kundiawa, Wabag, Maprik and Rabaul where real problems of over-population and land shortage seem to exist.

In the present context, more important than a crude measure of population density are measures of the annual area of garden land per head of population and the area of cultivated land. Various field studies indicate wide variation in the annual area of garden land per person. In the Highlands high values of 0.62 and 0.56 of an acre have been found for Korofeigu and Aiyura respectively but both areas have a marked seasonal rainfall. Usually values are around 0.2 to 0.3 of an acre per head per annum. The same is true of the lowlands although in the southern parts of the Maprik Sub-District values as low as 0.1 of an acre have been found. Here, however, garden crops are supplemented by sago, especially during a dietary lean

period. Among the sago eaters, who are dependent on gathering, fishing and trade, very little gardening land is available or used.

Few estimates have been made on the area of cultivable land in villages, but obviously such calculations vary depending on environmental factors such as soil, slopes, drainage, accessibility, rock, and so on. Also, cultural factors, such as settlement sites, taboo land, paths, roads and tree groves result in wide variations from village to village. Generally, however, the area of gardening land available is well above what is theoretically required (i.e. by multiplying the average area of garden land used per head per annum by the length of fallow period plus cultivation period). With a garden cycle of ten years each person needs say $0.25 \times 10 = 2.5$ acres. To date, figures below what appears to be a critical level have been found in the Wosera area south of Maprik and they may exist in part of the Chimbu and Wabag areas.

Some high occupational densities are set out in Table 5. Except on some islands or in coastal areas where people have access to marine resources or are on land of high initial fertility, most rural densities are well below these figures.

SOME RECENT CHANGES IN INDIGENOUS AGRICULTURE

Subsistence gardening, compared with social, demographic and political changes, has altered little from the pre-contact situation. There has been a general decline in gardening practices, but Europeans have wisely made few deliberate changes for generally the traditional systems of land use are better suited to local physical and economic conditions than anything yet devised to replace it.

Before actual contact was made by various administration exploratory patrols, steel tools and new crops, particularly those indigenous to intertropical America, were slowly disseminated. The effects of the introduction of steel have been discussed by Salisbury who found that labour-saving tools resulted in a labour surplus which could be channelled into new occupations such as work for wages, sport, cash cropping or larger ceremonial activities.

The process of plant introduction and dissemination accelerated as soon as the Administration brought areas under its control but generally the staple foods have not changed and introduced foods are mainly supplementary foods or relishes.

Within the subsistence gardens there is thus an increasing diversification of crops but also a decline in many of the traditional (and often time-consuming) horticultural methods needed to grow yam and taro. Intensification of land use has also been the direct result of increasing population and new forms of land use. However, cash cropping has caused the most dramatic changes since World War II. These changes are most significant in their economic context but they have also had far-reaching effects on traditional forms of organization and land use.

Indigenous planting of coconut in coastal areas

Table 5

RATIO OF POPULATION TO CULTIVABLE LAND

Locality	Approximate Population per Square Mile
Kapauku (Wissel Lakes)	500
Upper Chimbu	300–500
Kanusa	400
Central Dani (Baliem)	400?
Mae Enga	350?
Wosera (Maprik)	150–400
Laiapu Enga	150–300?
Huli	150?–300
Central Chimbu	100–300
Asaro	300

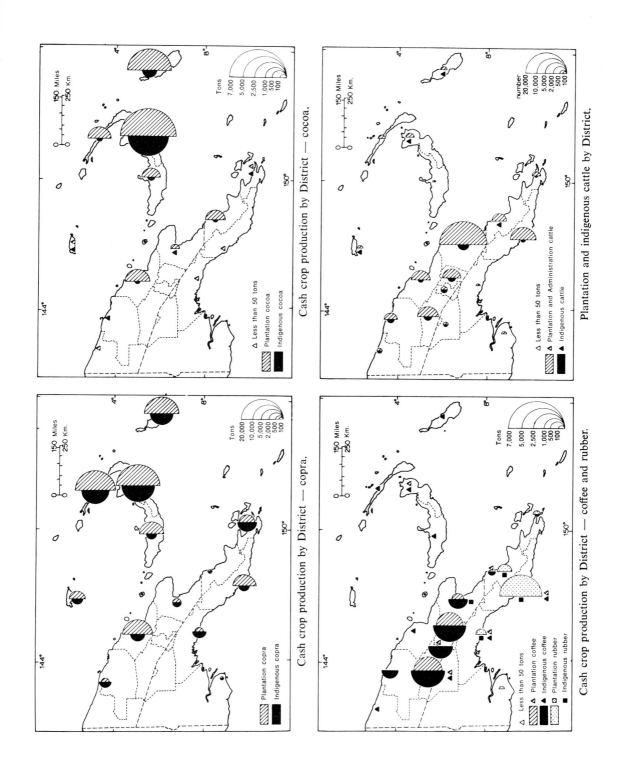

Cash crop production by District — copra.

Cash crop production by District — cocoa.

Cash crop production by District — coffee and rubber.

Plantation and indigenous cattle by District.

goes back to well before World War I and copra remains the principal cash crop. Other cash crops such as rubber and coffee were grown in some areas but attempts to establish indigenous plantings were unsuccessful because of problems of land tenure [q.v.], work organization, motivation and income distribution. Cheetham estimates that in 1939 only about one-quarter of all agricultural exports were produced by indigenous farmers. Since World War II, and particularly since 1956, indigenous smallholder production of cash crops has increased rapidly relative to the total production and has also become much more diversified. After copra, coffee, particularly in the Highlands, and cocoa, especially in the Gazelle Peninsula, are important. Rice, passionfruit, pyrethrum, rubber, tobacco, tea, oil palm and peanuts are of importance in some areas, and truck crops and fruits supply many local markets.

Cash cropping is almost certainly having its repercussions on traditional agriculture. It could be contributing to such things as a growth in individualism, a change in attitude to land tenure and village leadership and an increasing need for and dependence on money.

The response to commercial farming has been very uneven but interest in and success with cash cropping seem to depend on the following factors: the absence of any overt clash with indigenous systems of land tenure, a good indigenous leader, worthwhile recompense for their efforts, help and inspiration from the government and an incentive to obtain money.

POSSIBLE IMPROVEMENTS FOR INDIGENOUS AGRICULTURE

With increasing population and the desire to improve the living conditions of the people, agriculture must gradually become more sedentary and total productivity must increase. Commercial agriculture is the obvious answer but most areas will continue to have basically subsistence economies for many years. Also in some areas under stress of over-population, modern technology can offer only some palliatives which could operate within indigenous land-use systems.

The basic aims in improving indigenous agriculture are to improve the diet, facilitate production and preservation of foodstuffs, increase production and improve agricultural techniques. Ways in which these objectives could be obtained are:
(1) Upgrading staple foods.
(2) Introducing new food plants.
(3) Manuring the land or at least using mulches and green manures.
(4) More widespread soil conservation.
(5) Planting of fallows, particularly with legumes or trees for timber.
(6) Rotation of crops.
(7) Improving storage methods for crops that are storable.
(8) More intensive planting of food-producing trees.
(9) Improving hand implements and encouraging mechanization where possible.
(10) Making more intensive use of livestock.
(11) More encouragement of co-operatives or even collectives.

J. Barrau, *Subsistence Agriculture in Melanesia*. Honolulu, 1958.
——— 'Plant Introduction in the Tropical Pacific', *Pacific Viewpoint*, vol. 1, 1960.
H. C. Brookfield, 'Population Distribution and Labour Migration in New Guinea', *Australian Geographer*, vol. 7, 1960.
——— 'The Highland Peoples of New Guinea', *Geographical Journal*, vol. 127, 1961.
——— 'Local Study and Comparative Methods: An Example from Central New Guinea', *Annals of the Association of American Geographers*, vol. 52, 1962.
——— 'The Ecology of Highland Settlement', *American Anthropologist*, vol. 66, Special Publication, 1964.
——— and P. Brown, *Struggle for Land*. Melbourne, 1963.
R. M. Burnett, 'Some Cultural Practices in the Simbai Administrative Area, Madang District', *Papua and New Guinea Agricultural Journal*, vol. 16, 1963.
R. J. Cheetham, 'The Development of Indigenous Agriculture, Land Settlement and Rural Credit Facilities in Papua and New Guinea', *Papua and New Guinea Agricultural Journal*, vol. 15, 1962-3.
W. L. Conroy, 'Tradition and Trends in Agriculture', *Australian Territories*, vol. 2, 1962.
International Bank for Reconstruction and Development, *The Economic Development of Papua and New Guinea*. Baltimore, 1965.
D. A. M. Lea, 'The Abelam; A Study in Local Differentiation', *Pacific Viewpoint*, vol. 6, 1965.
——— 'Suggestions for the Improvement of Indigenous Subsistence Horticulture', *Papua and New Guinea Agricultural Journal*, vol. 18, 1966.
——— 'Staple Crops and Main Sources of Food' and 'Crop Combinations', in *An Atlas of Papua and New Guinea*, ed. R. G. Ward and D. A. M. Lea. Glasgow, 1970.
——— 'Activities Studies in New Guinea Villages', *Papua and New Guinea Agricultural Journal* (forthcoming).
——— 'Indigenous Horticulture in Melanesia: Some Recent Changes', in *Man in the Pacific Islands*, ed. R. G. Ward (forthcoming).
E. Messal and J. Barrau, *Food Plants of the South Sea Islands*. South Pacific Commission, Technical Paper no. 45. Sydney, 1953.
R. F. Salisbury, *From Stone to Steel*. Melbourne, 1962.
T. P. N. G. Bureau of Statistics, *Survey of Indigenous Agriculture and Ancillary Surveys 1961-2*. Port Moresby, 1963.
F. E. Williams, 'Practical Education: The Reform of Native Horticulture', Territory of Papua, *Anthropology Report*, no. 14. Port Moresby, 1933.

ACKNOWLEDGMENT

Maps from *An Atlas of Papua and New Guinea*, ed. R. G. Ward and D. A. M. Lea. Reproduced by courtesy of the editors, the copyright owner (the University of Papua and New Guinea) and the publishers (Wm Collins & Co. Ltd and Longmans Group Ltd).

D. A. M. Lea

(*See also* ECONOMY, INDIGENOUS; ETHNOBOTANY)

ALBERTIS, Luigi Maria d', (1841-1901), naturalist and explorer, was born at Voltri, near Genoa, on 21 November 1841, and died at Sassari, on Sardinia, on 2 September 1901. He followed Garibaldi from Sicily to Naples in 1860, and then travelled widely in Europe, before scientific curiosity, love of adventure and the desire to honour Italy through notable deeds led him to New Guinea. He spent most of 1872 in the Vogelkop—the 'bird's head' extremity of West Irian—with his countryman, the botanist Odoardo Beccari [q.v.]. In 1875, from Yule Island, he explored the Papuan coast and the lower Fly River. He returned to the Fly in 1876 and 1877.

His most famous exploit is the 1876 expedition, when he named the Victor Emanuel Range. He left Somerset, on the tip of Cape York Peninsula, on 18 May in the *Neva*, a steam launch borrowed from the New South Wales government. He was accompanied by Lawrence Hargrave, who later achieved fame as engineer, the seventeen-year-old Clarence Wilcox, a polyglot crew of South Sea Islanders, negroes and Chinese, a sheep and a dog. With only six inches freeboard, the *Neva* entered the Fly on 23 May under both Italian and British flags. For forty-five days they steamed upstream, stopping occasionally for collecting but were forced to retreat on 7 July by shortage of food, fever and the low water level.

But his chief importance lies in the scientific value of his collections of animals, especially mammals, birds, and insects, plants, and native artefacts and skeletal material. The specimens are housed in several institutions; the animals in the Museo Civico di Storia Naturale Giacomo Doria in Genoa, the plants in the Herbarium Universitatis Florentinae, Istituto Botanico (the Herbarium of the Istituto Botanico of the Università degli Studi) in Florence, and the National Herbarium of Victoria, Melbourne, and the anthropological material in the Florence Museum. The formal descriptions of his specimens were undertaken by a number of European specialists including Baron F. von Mueller of Melbourne, although d'Albertis was co-author with Count T. Salvadori of a couple of papers on the birds. Many animals and plants were named after him, including one of the birds of paradise, the red sicklebill (*Drepanornis albertisii*), d'Albertis' ringtail possum (*Pseu-*

docheirus albertisii), and the beautiful leguminous vine commonly called the d'Albertis creeper (*Mucuna novoguineensis*, synonym *M. albertisii*).

His book, *New Guinea: What I Did and What I Saw*, was published in both Italian and English in 1880. Its descriptions are wide-ranging and factual. Particularly revealing is d'Albertis' personal approach to the New Guinea situation. He sought 'ecstasy' in a land of 'primeval forests' where man was 'the unspoiled son of nature'. As a hunter, he relished bird-collecting. But he had little regard for the values of the native people. The cause of science could not allow the 'slightest repentance' for robbing villages, and for security it was necessary to inspire the islanders 'with a wholesome dread of approaching you'. He sought to inspire this dread through pretensions to sorcery and, on occasion, by force of arms yet, significantly, whereas the Fly expedition of 1876 met empty villages, that of 1877 encountered belligerent warriors. This voyage was unsuccessful and he returned to Europe in 1878. His claim to have travelled 580 miles up the Fly River in 1876 was disputed by Sir William MacGregor [q.v.] and later travellers criticized his high-handed ethnological collecting.

L. M. d'Albertis, *New Guinea: What I Did and What I Saw* (trans.). 2 vols, London, 1880; O. Beccari, *Nuova Guinea, Selebes e Molucche: diarii di viaggio.* Florence, 1924; H. M. Laracy, Italians on the Pacific Frontier (typescript, 1968; N.L.A.); G. Souter, *New Guinea: The Last Unknown.* Sydney, 1963.

HUGH LARACY

(*See also* EXPLORATION)

AMBO, George Somboba (*c.* 1921-   ), bishop, was born at Kurou village near Gona, Northern District of Papua, in about 1921. He was first trained as a primary-school teacher at St Aidan's College, Dogura, and later for the Church of England ministry at Newton College, also at Dogura. He was ordained in 1954 and consecrated bishop at St John's Cathedral, Brisbane. He is at present regional bishop for the Northern Papua Region of the Anglican Diocese of New Guinea. He is acknowledged to be a remarkable spiritual leader.

AMUCK. The Malay word *amok* was originally applied as much to the behaviour of a group as to that of an individual. The term was employed for the raiding parties in various parts of Malaysia and Indonesia, particularly the Buginese of the Celebes. As we use it today, it more often refers to the individual who, inflamed by some real or supposed insult, after a period of brooding 'runs amuck', attacks all in his path, and subsequently asserts that he had no motive and remembers nothing that has occurred. True amuck of this explosive variety has had its greatest concentration in and around Malaysia but is by no means confined to this area. Examples fulfilling all the essential criteria have been reported from such far apart places as India, Africa, Siberia,

Luigi Maria d'Albertis.

and Polynesia. Amuck is rare among Chinese, and it may well be that they do not greatly favour the employment of the device. Nevertheless, cases are reported from among migrants who are both ethnically and culturally Chinese. There is no doubt also that instances identical in all significant respects occur in European countries.

It is impossible to estimate the incidence of amuck in New Guinea, where it appears to be relatively uncommon at the present time, but by no means unimportant. Examples have been recorded from all parts, with a greater reporting from the Northern District, Fergusson and other islands of the D'Entrecasteaux group in eastern Papua, where there is an amuck tradition. The cases seen nowadays occur in healthy young adult males who have exhibited no other form of mental illness. They come from the labourer, village gardener, or artisan classes. Few have had any schooling, and all could be considered as only partially adapted to the new conditions of today. The young man is quieter than usual or goes bush for a few days, where he may be without food or shelter. There may be a history of some slight or insult. He may regain his normal composure or the condition may continue and remain unchanged, an abortive attack; or it may become worse, in which case suddenly, without anyone expecting such an immediate act at this particular point of time, he jumps up, seizes some spears or an axe, and runs around attacking everything animate or inanimate in his path. Yam houses or hospital property may be destroyed. Very shortly a number of people will be dead or wounded. In the early stages he shouts out that he is going to kill, and everyone endeavours to seek safety in flight. Most persons suddenly realize that the young man is suffering from amuck and that he will not be satiated and will continue in this way until overpowered or killed. They are now aware that he is suffering from a special form of insanity, *long-long* in Pidgin. The attack may be stopped by anyone brave enough to make the attempt. Usually the mania continues until the person is exhausted, overpowered, or killed. On recovery he usually says that he has no recollection of what happened.

Malaria, pneumonia [qq.v.], cerebral syphilis, encephalitis, epilepsy, heat-stroke, paranoid states, and cyclothymia have all been implicated in the past as conducive to the condition. Detzner gave an account of a type of explosive reaction he observed in which the individual armed with an axe or spear ran through the village and gardens attacking anyone near. He attributed such conduct to over-indulgence in betel-nut. This supposed relation to betel-nut was also referred to by Heim and Wasson, but it is doubtful whether such a mild stimulant, used widely throughout New Guinea, could be considered as primarily responsible for individual acts (*see* BETEL CHEWING). Although various drugs and diseases sometimes tend to increase irritability and in certain circumstances may act as aggravating factors,

the modern explanation of the condition points rather to individual idiosyncrasy and group expectations. In this view amuck is a standardized form of emotional release, accepted as such by the community as one likely to emanate from a person placed in an intolerable situation as a result of loss of face. Certain social structures associated with strong kinship ties and the tensions arising out of the consequent binding obligations have a definite influence on the frequency of amuck. Education and more powerful methods of social control probably diminish the incidence.

Superficially similar but distinct are the 'Wild-Man Behaviour' of Newman and the 'Collective Hysteria' of Reay. The wild-man episode is distinctly different in that the harmful component is lacking, and the rushing about and gesticulating is done in a more permissive environment. In the recurrent collective hysteria or so-called 'mushroom-madness' of the Minj area of the middle Wahgi Valley of the Western Highlands a man may appear to run amuck. He arms himself with whatever weapons he can find and goes around aggressively. He takes due care, however, not to injure anyone in the process.

Is the amuck person to be considered responsible for his actions? Where death, injury, or destruction of property have ensued the law requires that every case of amuck or pseudo-amuck be assessed on its merits. In the Territory the Queensland Criminal Code has been adopted, and the law relating to the excusatory effect of insanity under this Code follows but also goes beyond the common law rules formulated in the classical case of McNaghten. Wrongfulness is interpreted by Australian courts to mean 'wrong having regard to the everyday standards of reasonable people'. For the New Guinea person the reasonable people who make up his particular world are his own kin on the one hand and the rest of New Guinea population on the other. In addition, the Code adds a further ground of excuse; the alleged explosive reaction may result in depriving the sufferer of the capacity to control his actions. The closer the total picture corresponds to the classical description, the less likely is the individual to be legally responsible for his actions. If the preliminary brooding, explosive outburst, persistence without apparent reason, and alleged amnesia are present, and if the amuck is committed without motive or profit and is unlike any other form of mental illness or criminality, then it is unlikely that the man can be reasonably considered as criminally responsible.

A. Chowning, 'Amok and Aggression in the D'Entrecasteaux', in *Patterns of Land Utilization and Other Papers*, Proceedings of the 1961 Annual Spring Meeting of the American Ethnological Society, ed. V. E. Garfield. Seattle, 1961; H. Detzner, *Mœurs et coutumes des Papous* (translation of German ed. 1920). Paris, 1935; R. F. Fortune, *Sorcerers of Dobu*. London, 1932; D. J. Galloway, 'On Amok', *Far Eastern Association of Tropical Medicine: Transactions of Fifth Biennial Congress*. Singapore, 1923; R. Heim and

R. G. Wasson, 'La folie des Kuma', *Cahiers du Pacifique*, no. 6, 1964; P. L. Newman, ' "Wild Man" Behaviour in a New Guinea Highlands Community', *American Anthropologist*, vol. 66, 1964; M. Reay, 'Mushrooms and Collective Hysteria', *Australian Territories*, vol. 5, 1965; P. M. van Wulfften Palthe, 'Study of Amuck', *Nederlandsch Tidjschrift voor Geneeskunde*, vol. 77, 1933.

B. G. BURTON-BRADLEY

(*See also* POSSESSION, SPIRIT)

ANGAU (AUSTRALIAN NEW GUINEA ADMINISTRATIVE UNIT).

The war with Japan completely disrupted the peace time governments of both Papua and the Mandated Territory of New Guinea, and large sections of New Guinea were actually occupied by the Japanese for over three years. Australian civilians were either evacuated or enlisted in the armed forces, and the nucleus of a military administration was created in February 1942 with the raising of the New Guinea Administrative Unit and the Papuan Administrative Unit, combined on 10 April 1942 as the Australian New Guinea Administrative Unit (Angau), with H.Q. in Port Moresby. Since then the separate territories of Papua and New Guinea have had a unified administration.

The former operational commander in New Guinea, Major-General B. M. Morris, was appointed General Officer Commanding Angau in August 1942. More important, however, was the appointment of Brigadier D. M. Cleland [q.v.] as Deputy Adjutant and Quartermaster-General in March 1943. As Angau's principal staff officer he was the chief influence on the unit's organization and policy.

The main practical work of Angau fell upon officers who had been members of the pre-war civil administrations. In the field, the key post of District Officer (usual rank Major) was almost invariably held by a peace-time Resident Magistrate or District Officer. His subordinates at District H.Q. or at out-stations were usually members of the pre-war field staff. As Angau grew this experienced staff was supplemented, first by persons with New Guinea background in some other capacity, and later by officers and men who had no acquaintance with the Territories.

Angau had three main functions: operational; administrative; production.

Operational. These tasks included the recruitment and management of native labour to carry supplies for the army, and for other military work such as wharf labour, road-building and airfield construction; the conduct of propaganda campaigns among the indigenous people; the gathering of military intelligence by reconnaissance patrols in operational areas or in regions actually occupied by the Japanese. There was considerable actual fighting, involving not only Angau's European officers and non-commissioned officers but also the indigenous non-commissioned officers and constables of the Royal Papuan Constabulary, the police force under Angau command (*see* POLICE). Many other civilian indigenes helped in this work, and the casualties among them are not accurately known. Of Angau European personnel forty-six died on active service. The intelligence obtained by these scouts was of the highest value to Allied operational commanders, who could not have secured it in any other way.

Administrative. Attempts were made to continue the maintenance of law and order among the indigenous people and to guard their general welfare. Nominally, health services remained an Angau responsibility but these had been little more than embryonic in peace-time and almost ceased in the villages (*see* MEDICAL SERVICES, HISTORY). Medical attention to natives employed by the army was provided, and this rose to a good standard as the war proceeded. The quartering and rationing of refugees, and relief and rehabilitation in devastated areas recovered from the enemy, were substantial administrative tasks. The most important duty under this head, however, was the 'recruitment' of able-bodied male natives for service as army labour or as plantation workers. The later repatriation of these men was another administrative responsibility. Recruitment for the newly raised battalions of indigenous infantry was also entrusted to Angau; so was the control of civilians who were gradually permitted to return to Papua to manage plantations and similar undertakings.

Production. Copra and rubber, the chief strategic products of New Guinea, were in urgent demand. Angau was charged with securing maximum production of both, together with smaller items such as gum copal, manganese and timber (*see* COCONUT INDUSTRY; FORESTRY; TIMBER INDUSTRY). Many abandoned plantations were brought back to production, and substantial quantities of copra and rubber exported to Australia. Angau continued this work until May 1943, when the Australian New Guinea Production Control Board was set up under National Security Regulations. The Board was created as a result of pressure on the Australian government by plantation owners whom it enabled to resume operation of their properties. Although the Board was not responsible to the army, but to the Minister for External Territories, its Chairman was Brigadier Cleland, who remained Deputy Adjutant and Quartermaster-General in Angau. Moreover Angau was required to use its powers of compulsion to recruit plantation labour, and to keep it at work. Copra and rubber production thus remained inseparably connected with Angau's responsibilities, and the unit itself continued to supply timber and other products. The Board's production work was effective enough for rubber production in 1944 to exceed that of even the best peace-time year.

Conflict of functions. It was soon apparent that some of Angau's operational duties, e.g. the provision of all possible help to the fighting services, must conflict with important aspects of administration, e.g. the maintenance of native welfare. This conflict centred upon the army's ever-increasing demands for labour, which could not be reconciled with the necessity for a population with a finely balanced subsistence economy to keep most of its able-bodied men at home to grow food, to fish and to carry out other essential tasks. The Deputy Director of District Services and Native Affairs issued an order on 15 May 1942 stressing that the 'native population must be safeguarded'. He set a recruitment limit of 25 per cent of able-bodied males and warned field staff to watch for signs of hardship in the villages. The inherent conflict and a change of emphasis in policy are illustrated by General Morris's order of 20 August, which states that the needs of the fighting services must be met, 'even if a temporary sacrifice of native interests is involved'. During the Kokoda Trail fighting of 1942 native carriers had proved their remarkable effectiveness in bringing supplies forward and evacuating wounded, over mountainous jungle country so rugged that neither mechanical nor animal transport could be used. From that time onward the army's demands upon Angau for labour became constantly heavier. On 15 June 1942 an order had been made by New Guinea Force, the formation to which Angau was subordinate, under which any native might be conscripted to serve in any capacity anywhere in Papua or New Guinea. It was an offence for a native to refuse or neglect to sign a so-called 'contract of service' with the army, if ordered to do so by an appropriate Angau officer. Pay ranged from 5s to 15s (50c to $1.50) per month, with rations and bare personal necessities provided. At the end of October 1942 there were 7,914 natives under contract of service. In two months the number had doubled, to 16,050. By September 1943 it was 30,000, and by July 1944 it was 40,000. The Australian official war historian estimates that, at the peak, 55,000 native male adults—defined as male persons apparently over the age of fourteen years—were serving. This was more than the entire peace-time labour force; yet now large and populous parts of the Territories were occupied by the Japanese, so the increased burden fell upon about half the population. The effect in the villages was extensive hardship, including starvation, ill health, grossly increased infant mortality and a widespread malaise and loss of the desire to live. Though army demands for labour were often dictated by pressing operational necessity, they were inflated by lax administration which allowed the employment of large numbers of natives as officers' servants and in similar tasks. There appears to be no documentary record of Angau resisting army demands until April 1945, though earlier that year a senior officer from Land H.Q. in Melbourne had investigated the matter and was able to effect certain reforms, and to reduce the native labour force engaged upon more frivolous tasks in base areas. Angau's early attempts at repatriation of native labour were, according to Lucy Mair, not very effective.

Labour conditions. In 1942 conditions were uniformly bad. Rations, clothing, shelter and medical attention were all inadequate. Sickness rates among carriers on some important lines of communication were as high as 25 per cent, and 14 per cent was regarded as acceptable. The ration scale had been condemned as inadequate by the

Director of Army Catering in 1942 but was not improved until 1944, when the so-called 'New Guinea Force ration' was introduced. This was a plain but balanced diet and the health of carriers improved remarkably. Sickness rates dropped to 4 per cent. Adequate rest periods were not given and the official war historian reports instances of gross overwork of carriers right up to the end of hostilities. The Production Control Board, in spite of the protests of the Director-General of Medical Services at Land H.Q. and of Angau's Assistant Director of Medical Services, secured permission on grounds of economy to feed its labourers on the old ration scale; its work force continued to suffer beriberi and other deficiency diseases. However, for all employed natives medical attention improved markedly and the standard and extent of health services far exceeded even the best effort of the pre-war administrations. But in the villages medical services were still rudimentary. Though serious abuses were not widespread some European labour overseers did inflict assaults and arbitrary punishments on their indigenous workers, and Angau issued orders from time to time forbidding such practices. Labour supervision was put on a much sounder basis when Angau created a separate Native Labour Section in June 1943.

Other duties. As the Japanese fell back in New Britain, the Solomons and in northern New Guinea the attacking Allied forces, both Australian and American, usually went into action accompanied by specially selected Angau teams with local knowledge of the terrain and of the inhabitants. Both the European and the indigenous members of these teams performed bravely and effectively, assisting operations and reducing casualties. As soon as purely military operations allowed, the teams turned to the re-establishment of Australian government and to relief work. The people in areas occupied by the Japanese had suffered extreme hardship. Emergency rationing and medical attention were the first concerns, followed by the distribution of seeds and plants, gardening tools and other necessities, and assistance in the construction of shelter. Though the resources available were rarely equal to the full scale of the needs the work accomplished was of the highest usefulness and humanitarian importance.

When Brigadier Cleland returned to Australia to be demobilized early in 1945 the main burden of Angau's work was complete. On 30 October that year a provisional civil administration was set up in all that part of the Territories south of the latitude of the Markham River, to be extended as operations made this possible. Finally, on 24 June 1946, the provisional civil administration assumed control of the Gazelle Peninsula of New Britain, and the military administration of Angau ended (see PROVISIONAL ADMINISTRATION 1945-1949).

Conclusion. Angau was essentially an improvisation to serve the needs of war. It faced many difficulties, from shortage of supplies and personnel, lack of ships and air transport, to the problems of the suddenly shifting demands of armed services engaged in severe fighting. It did not have access to government at high policy level, but remained a subordinate unit under the command of New Guinea Force. It lacked expert staff of high professional qualification; indeed, after the death of F. E. Williams [q.v.] early in the war it did not even have an anthropologist. In matters of high policy or advanced technical expertise it depended on the advice of the somewhat remote Directorate of Research and Civil Affairs at Land H.Q. in Melbourne. The Directorate and not Angau was responsible for post-war planning, although in fact the employment of many former Angau men did result in considerable continuity in practice at the field level.

The unit's morale suffered from the conflict between the philosophies of the former Papuan and former New Guinea officers, from sharp divisions of feeling between those in the field and the H.Q. staff and from the pursuit of personal ends and petty vendettas, some of them carried over from peace-time. It had all those internal problems of any organization obliged to expand rapidly, for it grew from nothing in early 1942 to a large, complex and geographically scattered unit which in 1945 had some 300 officers and 1,400 other ranks. Nevertheless, it is scarcely conceivable that the Allies could have achieved local victory in New Guinea without Angau's management of supply and transport through the native work force. The Angau men and the Royal Papuan Constabulary, in operations either with normal military forces or on their hazardous special patrols, certainly performed some of the most impressive acts of personal gallantry in World War II.

Though sincere efforts were made it cannot seriously be maintained that Angau gave adequate attention to the broader administrative and governmental tasks. In its whole existence it probably did not spend $4,000 on native education. The official war historian has concluded that, during the war, the Australians drove the New Guinea people harder than they did themselves. If this is true, Angau was the driver. In his report of the Commission of Inquiry into the suspension of the civil administration of Papua, J. V. Barry gave the considered opinion: Angau 'was an essential and invaluable body to meet the urgencies [of the time] and it has, from the military viewpoint, been successful in its handling of native affairs, but the fact that it is a military unit has meant that when the supposed needs of the Army have conflicted with the welfare of the natives, Army requirements have triumphed'.

J. V. Barry, Report [to the Commonwealth Government] of Commission of Inquiry into the Suspension of the Civil Administration of the Territory of Papua in February, 1942. 1945 (roneoed); D. Dexter, *The New Guinea Offensives* (Australia in the War of 1939-1945). Canberra, 1961; G. Long, *The Final Campaigns* (Australia in the War of 1939-1945). Canberra, 1963; D. McCarthy, *South-West Pacific Area—First Year: Kokoda to Wau* (Australia in the War of 1939-1945). Canberra, 1959; L. P. Mair, *Australia in New Guinea*. Melbourne, 1970; P. A. Ryan, The Australian New Guinea Administrative Unit (Angau). Paper read at Second Waigani Seminar, Port Moresby, 1968 (roneoed).

PETER RYAN

ANTHROPOLOGICAL DEFINITIONS. The following are some of the terms most frequently used by professional anthropologists in accounts of the social life of New Guinea peoples:

Affines. Persons to whom an individual is related by marriage, e.g. the wife's brothers, the brothers' wives.

Age group. In many societies persons of the same sex and of approximately the same age are formally grouped into distinctive sets, which are usually formed at successive intervals. The age set is an organized group of age mates, youths or girls, men or women. An age set may pass through a series of stages each of which has a distinctive status and defined public duties to perform. Such stages are known as age grades.

Agnates. Persons descended in the male line from a common ancestor, i.e. patrilineal kin.

Avunculo-virilocal residence. Where a couple after marriage live close to the husband's mother's brothers, as in the Trobriand Islands, etc.

Bilocal residence. Where a couple after marriage live alternately, usually for about a year at a time, with the husband's relatives and the wife's relatives, as in Dobu, etc.

Bride-price (also called **Bride wealth**). In traditional New Guinea societies the wealth, foodstuffs, ornaments, valuables, etc., collected from the bridegroom's relatives and distributed among the bride's relatives; often the latter offer small return gifts. But once a money economy has been accepted the bride's parents tend to prefer cash to goods; moreover, they may demand a bigger and bigger amount and insist on spending it rather than giving a share to their kinsmen. Correspondingly, the bridegroom's kinsmen are often unwilling to part with their cash to help him, and he is forced to provide most of it himself. No portion of the bride-price, whether in a traditional or a Westernized marriage, ever goes to the young couple as a contribution to the expense of setting up the new household.

Clan. A unilateral descent group, patrilineal or matrilineal, within which the specific genealogical connections with the founding ancestor, real or putative, are unknown; many of the members are therefore unable to say exactly how they are related to one another. Often the clan has a name. The members may have a ritual relationship with some natural species or object, e.g. a bird or a plant, and are subject to a particular dietary taboo. A clan is said to be 'localized' when the adults of one sex, generally the men, live together as neighbours (the members of the opposite sex join their spouses at marriage and are hence scattered); it is said to be 'dispersed' when both sexes are scattered over a wide area. A clan may be divided into sub-clans (often the clan is then dispersed and the sub-clan localized), and the sub-clans into line-ages. Usually the clan is exogamous.

Cognates. Persons descended from a common ancestor. The descent may be traced through males, through females, or through males in one or more generations and females in the rest.

Cognatic group (also called **Non-unilineal group**). A descent group in which the connection with the founding ancestor is traced through males or females indifferently. It may or may not be exogamous. Where a society is organized on the basis of cognatic groups each person is potentially a member of more than one and can make a choice, limited though that choice may be. For instance, he may choose his father's group or his mother's; or he may choose the group of any of his four grandparents. He may even be allowed to change his membership later.

Corporate. A group, e.g. a clan, is said to be corporate if on certain defined occasions the members act as a single united body; for example, by coming together to take vengeance on an outsider for a wrong committed against one of themselves; by obeying the lawful commands of a leader; by holding property jointly; by performing regular ceremonies which other people attend only on sufferance or by invitation.

Cousins. Children of siblings of the same sex are said to be 'parallel' cousins, children of siblings of opposite sex 'cross' cousins.

Descent. A relationship mediated by a parent between a person and an ancestor, defined as a genealogical predecessor of the grandparental or an earlier generation. If descent is traced exclusively through one line it is said to be 'unilineal', 'patrilineal', when the line is of males, 'matrilineal' when of females. In some places descent is 'double unilineal', i.e. traced simultaneously through males for some purposes and through females for other purposes, as among the Ngaing of the Madang District. Where descent is traced through males and females indifferently it is said to be 'cognatic' or 'non-unilineal'.

Descent group. A kin group in which descent is a necessary criterion for recruitment.

Dowry. Wealth presented at marriage to the bride by her father. When dowry consists of land its management may be entrusted to the husband, but if divorce occurs the property goes back with the woman. On her death the children inherit.

Dual organization. Division of a society into halves, to one of which each person belongs. Recruitment may be on the basis of descent (*see* Moiety organization), residence, allocation by authority, or choice.

Exogamy. The rule by which a person is prohibited from taking a spouse from the same group as himself/herself. Usually clans, lineages, and moieties are exogamous.

Family. The need to define the varieties of family becomes evident when the use of the word in English is analysed. In common parlance 'family' may mean (a) a group composed of a married couple and their children, (b) a group of relatives with the same surname, (c) a person's patrilateral and matrilateral kinsfolk, (d) a person's ancestors, (e) a group of relatives and affines living as one household.

In anthropological literature the term 'simple', 'elementary', or 'nuclear' family refers to a group consisting of a father, a mother, and their children, whether or not they are living together. 'Polygynous family' refers to a group consisting of a man, his two or more wives, and their children. 'Extended family' refers to the group formed when two or more lineally related kinsfolk of the same sex, their spouses, and their children occupy a single dwelling or set of neighbouring dwellings and act together as a separate social unit; for example, a man and his wife, their married sons, and the son's wives and children; or a woman and her husband, their married daughters, and the daughters' husbands and children.

Filiation. The fact of being the child of a specified parent and hence related to that parent's kinsmen and having obligations towards them.

Incest. Sexual congress between persons related in specified prohibited degrees of kinship. The prohibited degrees differ widely from society to society. Marriage prohibitions and incest prohibitions do not necessarily coincide within the one society, and sexual relations may be tolerated between persons who are forbidden to marry.

Lineage. A descent group in which the members can give the specific genealogical connections with the founding ancestor; in theory each person is therefore able to say exactly how he is related to the rest. A lineage may be divided into segments each founded by an ancestor of a less remote generation. These units are referred to either as lineages themselves or as lineage segments. A large lineage segment may also be divided into small lineage segments each founded by an ancestor of a still less remote generation. Usually the lineage is exogamous.

Matrilateral. On the mother's side. Matrilateral kin: cognates on the mother's side.

Matrilineal. In the female line. Matrilineal kin: cognates who trace descent through females from a common ancestor.

Matri-uxorilocal residence. Where a couple after marriage live close to the wife's matrilineal kinsfolk, as in parts of New Ireland and Bougainville.

Moiety organization. The division of a society into halves on the basis of descent. Every person must belong to one moiety and usually the groups are exogamous, i.e. a member of one moiety is obliged to marry a member of the other. The division may be associated with reciprocal economic or ceremonial duties.

Neo-local residence. Where a couple after marriage move away from their relatives to a new locality.

Non-unilineal group. *See* Cognatic group.

Parish. The largest local group forming a political unit, i.e. the largest unit within which regular institutions exist for the maintenance of law and order; usually also the smallest war-making unit. As a rule the members combine for certain economic tasks, for feast-giving, and for certain religious ceremonies. Statistics are lacking, but probably the average New Guinea parish numbers 200-300 persons though some are smaller and a few have over 1,000.

Parish settlement. The collection of dwellings occupied by members of a parish. The houses may form a compact village, or they may be scattered over a defined area in a series of hamlets or small homesteads.

Patrilateral. On the father's side. Patrilateral kin: cognates on the father's side.

Patrilineal. In the male line. Patrilineal kin: cognates who trace descent through males from a common ancestor.

Patri-virilocal residence. Where a couple after marriage live close to the husband's patrilineal kinsfolk, as among the Orokaiva, etc.

Phratry organization. The division of a society, phyle, or tribe into three or more large groups each usually composed of several clans. The divisions may or may not be descent groups, and they may or may not be exogamous.

Phyle. A large group of people speaking the same language and practising the same customs but lacking political cohesion. The linguistic groups of New Guinea are best referred to as phylae rather than tribes; the term tribe suggests political cohesion.

Polygamy. The marriage of one person with more than one spouse. If a man has more than one wife the marriage is 'polygynous'; if a woman more than one husband it is 'polyandrous'.

Sib. There is no agreement about the meaning of this term, and its use has led to confusion. To some authors it is a synonym for patri-clan, to others it embraces the total number of cognates whom a person recognizes as kin.

Sibling. A brother or a sister.

Totem. The natural species, natural phenomenon, or object with which the members of a group, e.g. a clan, have a ritual relation. If the totem is edible the group members are forbidden to eat it. Often the group is named after its totem.

Tribe. *See* Phyle.

Uxorilocal residence. Where a couple after marriage live close to some of the wife's kinsmen.

Uterine kin. Persons descended in the female line from a common ancestor, i.e. matrilineal kin.

Virilocal residence. Where a couple after marriage live close to some of the husband's kinsmen.

IAN HOGBIN

ARAMBAK. People of the upper Karawari River, Sepik Districts. References:

J. A. W. Forge, 'Three Kamanggabi Figures from the Arambak People of the Sepik District', in *Three Regions of Melanesian Art, New Guinea and the New Hebrides*. New York, Museum of Primitive Art, 1960.

D. Newton, 'A Note on the Kamanggabi of the Arambak, New Guinea', *Man*, vol. 64, 1964.

ARAPESH. People of the East Sepik District. References:

R. F. Fortune, 'Arapesh Warfare', *American Anthropologist*, vol. 41, 1939.

———— *Arapesh*. Publications of the American Ethnological Society, vol. 19. New York, 1942.

———— 'Arapesh Maternity', *Nature*, vol. 152, 1943.

———— 'Law and Force in Papuan Societies', *American Anthropologist*, vol. 49, 1947.

M. Mead, 'The Marsalai Cult among the Arapesh, with Special Reference to the Rainbow Serpent Beliefs of the Australian Aboriginals', *Oceania*, vol. 4, 1933-4.

———— 'How the Papuan Plans his Dinner', *Natural History*, vol. 34, 1934.

———— *Sex and Temperament in Three Primitive Societies*. London, 1935.

———— *The Mountain Arapesh, I: An Importing Culture, II: Supernaturalism, III: Socio-economic Life, IV: Diary of Events in Alitoa, V: The Record of Unabelin*. Anthropological Papers of the American Museum of Natural History, vols 36-7, 40-1. New York, 1936-59.

———— 'Research on Primitive Children', in *Manual of Child Psychology*, ed. L. Carmichael. New York, 1946.

———— 'Early Influences that Mould the Arapesh Personality', in *Primitive Heritage*, ed. M. Mead and N. Calas. London, 1954.

———— 'The Arapesh of New Guinea', in *Cooperation and Competition among Primitive Peoples*, ed. M. Mead. New York, 1937.

ARCHBOLD EXPEDITIONS. The seven Archbold Expeditions of The American Museum of Natural History, New York, have been important in biological explorations in Papua and New Guinea and in West Irian. Sponsored and for the most part financed by Richard Archbold, a mammalogist and research associate of the American Museum who led the first three of them, these expeditions began in Papua in 1933-4 with a traverse from Yule Island on the south coast to the summit of Mt Albert Edward, 13,100 feet, and with work on the Oriomo River and Daru Island in western Papua. Archbold himself acted as mammalogist on this expedition, A. L. Rand as ornithologist and L. J. Brass as botanist, while C. J. Adamson saw to transport and supply. Transport on the main project was by pack-mules and -horses and indentured native carriers as far as Ononge in the Vanapa Valley, and beyond there by carriers alone, mainly local men. Mt Albert Edward was climbed twice from Gerenda Camp, 12,074 feet, situated at timberline at the head of the Chirima River. The botanical collections numbered 2,730 in all. Most of the specimens of flowering plants from higher altitudes were lost in transport to the coast. Although many of the plants remain to be identified in the necessarily slow process of revisional and monographic studies of the numerous taxonomic groups concerned, by December 1967 4 new genera and 321 new species had been described from the collections of the expedition.

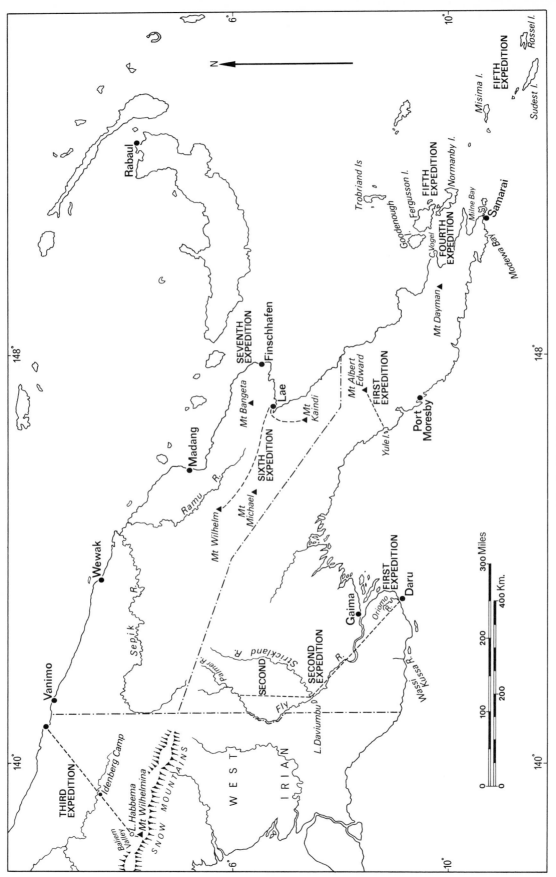

The Archbold Expeditions.

The Second Archbold Expedition, in 1936-7, worked principally on the Fly and Wassi Kussa Rivers in western Papua. Archbold had with him on this occasion Rand and Brass, G. H. H. Tate as mammalogist and L. H. Willis in charge of transport and supplies. The Administration supplied an escort of six armed native constabulary in the charge of Patrol Officer M. J. Healy for the upper Fly River, an uncontrolled area. A Fairchild amphibian aeroplane, piloted by Archbold and R. R. Rogers, was provided for reconnaissance and far-inland supply. The inland party, the aeroplane, and a coastal base at Daru were equipped with two-way radio. About sixty carriers plus collecting assistants and camp staff, were recruited, mainly from Fergusson Island. From Daru to a first base camp on the Fly, about 5 miles below Palmer Junction and 528 miles from the river-mouth, personnel and supplies were transported by the chartered auxiliary ketch *Maira*, 60 feet in length and drawing $5\frac{1}{2}$ feet of water when loaded. The aircraft was used for transport on to Black River Camp on the Palmer, 2 miles below the junction of the Black River. An advanced camp, at an elevation of about 2,500 feet near Mt Mabion, was established for approach to the high altitudes on the Dap Range at the head of the Palmer. Only some provisioning of this proposed base by parachutes and dump loads had been completed when the aircraft was lost at moorings in a sudden, very violent squall—*guba*—in Port Moresby harbour. This catastrophe forced the withdrawal of the advance party to Black River Camp and a five-day retreat down the river on rafts to Oroville gold-prospecting camp, 30 miles above D'Albertis Junction, where a relief boat met the party. Subsequent field-work on the Fly was carried out at Lake Daviumbu on the middle river, and at camps opposite Sturt Island and at Gaima on the lower river. The botanical collections numbered 2,590, from which 5 new genera and 215 new species have been described.

The Third Archbold Expedition, in 1938-9, was a joint project with the government of the Netherlands Indies and known officially as the Indisch-Amerikaansche Expeditie naar Nederlandsch Nieuw-Guinea. Basic transport was by a PBY-2 (Catalina) flying-boat, piloted by Archbold and Rogers and based at Hollandia; porterage was mainly by Dyaks recruited in Borneo. American scientific staff comprised Rand, Brass and W. B. Richardson, mammalogist. On the Netherlands side were L. J. Toxopeus, entomologist, E. Meijer Drees, forester, Ch. Versteegh, assistant to the forester, and a military covering party of fifty-six officers and other ranks commanded by Staff Captain C. G. J. Teerink. The principal areas of operation were the northern slopes of the Snow Mountains from the Baliem River to Lake Habbema, 10,580 feet, and Mt Wilhelmina, 15,585 feet, and the lowlands and mountains of the middle Idenburg River region. The big, heavily-populated high valley of the Baliem, which during World War II became known as the New Guinea Shangri-La, was discovered and explored. From 5,331 plant collections made by the American party, 5 new genera and 631 new species have been described.

An exceptionally important botanical find consisted of extensive forests of subantarctic beeches, *Nothofagus*, in the mountains. Similar forests had been encountered by the First Archbold Expedition, and *Nothofagus* had been collected on the south slopes of the Snow Mountains as early as 1913, but the identity of the trees, and the presence of the genus had gone unrecognized until the collections of the Third Archbold Expedition were studied.

The post-war expeditions of the series have been conducted under easier conditions and on a relatively modest scale. They followed an expedition to the Cape York Peninsula of Australia in 1948. In 1953 the Fourth Archbold Expedition to New Guinea, with Brass as botanist and leader, H. M. Van Deusen as mammalogist, G. M. Tate as general zoological collector, and K. M. Wynn as transport man, worked in eastern Papua on the Cape Vogel Peninsula, between Collingwood Bay and the crest of the central range at Mt Dayman, 9,800 feet, and on Goodenough Island. Transport was by small coastal vessels and local native carriers. From botanical collections numbering 3,445 and still largely unidentified, 50 new species have been described.

Brass, botanist and leader, R. F. Peterson, mammalogist, and L. J. Evennett, in charge of transport, were the members of the Fifth Archbold Expedition, in 1956 which confined its attention to the eastern Papuan islands: Normanby and Fergusson of the D'Entrecasteaux group; Misima, Sudest (Tagula) and Rossel in the Louisiade Archipelago; Woodlark; the Trobriands (zoology only); and Milne Bay and Modewa Bay (botany and invertebrates only) on the mainland. Transport was by small ships and carriers engaged locally. Botanical collections numbered 2,657, from which 1 new genus and 21 new species have been named.

The Sixth Archbold Expedition, again with Brass as botanist and leader, and with Van Deusen as mammalogist and J. D. Collins as transport man, operated in the Territory of New Guinea in 1959. Transport was partly by air, but a one-ton Land Rover and trailer and local native carriers were also used. Work was principally in the Eastern Highlands including the peaks of Mt Wilhelm (about 15,000 feet), Mt Otto (11,613 feet), Mt Michael (12,500 feet) and Mt Elandora (8,500 feet); in the Lae-Edie Creek area including Mt Kaindi (7,750 feet), and in the upper Markham Valley. Botanical collections totalled 3,635, from which 27 new species have been recognized.

After the sixth expedition Brass retired from active field-work. The Seventh Archbold Expedition, with Van Deusen as mammalogist and leader, operated on the Huon Peninsula in 1964. S. A. Grierson participated on this occasion as photographer and general zoologist, R. D. Hoogland as botanist, and K. McGowan was in charge of transport. Movement was by air, small boat, and local native carriers. After an initial period in the Pindiu area the expedition operated in the Rawlinson Range (to 7,430 feet) and in the Cromwell Mountains (9,500 feet) and adjoining high plains. In the later stages Van Deusen and Grierson worked in

AREK

the lowlands near Finschhafen while Hoogland established camp on the Sarawaket plateau, visiting the major peaks Bangeta (13,450 feet), Bolan (12,000 feet) and Sarawaket (12,500).

Richard Archbold and A. L. Rand, 'Results of the Archbold Expeditions. No. 7. Summary of the 1933-1934 Papuan Expedition', *Bulletin of The American Museum of Natural History*, vol. 68, 1934-5.
—— *New Guinea Expedition, Fly River Area, 1936-1937*. New York, 1940.
Richard Archbold, A. L. Rand and L. J. Brass, 'Results of the Archbold Expeditions, No. 41, Summary of the 1938-1939 New Guinea Expedition', *Bulletin of The American Museum of Natural History*, vol. 79, 1941-2.
L. J. Brass, 'Botanical Results of the Archbold Expeditions, IX. Notes on the Vegetation of the Fly and Wassi Kussa Rivers, British New Guinea', *Journal of the Arnold Arboretum*, vol. 19, 1938.
—— 'The 1938-39 Expedition to the Snow Mountains, Netherlands New Guinea', *Journal of the Arnold Arboretum*, vol. 22, 1941.
—— 'Results of the Archbold Expeditions. No. 75, Summary of the Fourth Archbold Expedition to New Guinea (1953), *Bulletin of The American Museum of Natural History*, vol. 111, 1956-7.
—— 'Results of the Archbold Expeditions. No. 79. Summary of the Fifth Archbold Expedition to New Guinea (1956-1957)', *Bulletin of The American Museum of Natural History*, vol. 118, 1959.
—— 'Results of the Archbold Expeditions. No. 86. Summary of the Sixth Archbold Expedition to New Guinea (1959)', *Bulletin of The American Museum of Natural History*, vol. 127, 1964.
A. L. Rand and L. J. Brass, 'Results of the Archbold Expeditions. No. 29. Summary of the 1936-1937 New Guinea Expedition', *Bulletin of The American Museum of Natural History*, vol. 77, 1940-1.
H. M. Van Deusen, 'The Seventh Archbold Expedition', *Bioscience*, vol. 16, 1966.

L. J. BRASS AND R. D. HOOGLAND

AREK, Paulus (1929-), M.H.A. for Ijivitari open electorate, was born on 3 December 1929 in Wanigela village, Northern District and educated in an Anglican mission and at Sogeri High School. He is vice-president of the Higaturu Local Government Council and president of the Northern District Workers' Association. He has travelled in the Pacific and in Australia on study tours and attended several conferences. He was chairman of the Select Committee on Constitutional Development, which presented its report to the House of Assembly in March 1971.

ARIAW. People of the Madang District. References:
J. Schebesta, 'Sprachengruppierung und Totemismus in der Potsdamhafen-Gruppe, Deutsch-Neuguinea', *Anthropos*, vol. 8, 1913.
—— 'Totemismus bei den Ariawiai, Neuguinea', *Anthropos*, vols 16-17, 1921-2.

ARMED FORCES. The main armed force in Papua and New Guinea is the Australian Army unit, the Pacific Islands Regiment (P.I.R.), with very small units of the Royal Australian Navy and the Royal Australian Air Force. (The police force, which is an armed constabulary, is not considered in this article. It is about 30 per cent bigger than the army.)

The P.I.R. consists of about 3,200 officers and men of whom some 2,600 are indigenous and the rest Australian. It is organized in two battalions, one of which is based in Port Moresby, where regimental headquarters and most of the staff and the support units are also located. The other battalion is based at Wewak on the north coast of New Guinea.

There is also a small citizen force unit, the New Guinea Volunteer Rifles.

History. The Pacific Islands Regiment has its origins in the wartime Papuan Infantry Battalion, raised in Port Moresby in June 1940. All its officers were Australians, as were most of its non-commissioned officers. It fought with distinction against the Japanese in the Owen Stanley Ranges. As the Pacific war continued, three more battalions were raised on similar lines in New Guinea (New Guinea Infantry Battalions) and a headquarters called Pacific Islands Regiment was created, with staff to administer all four battalions.

Units and sub-units fought with Australian and Allied troops in almost all parts of the Papuan and New Guinea theatre. When it was disbanded in 1946 the Regiment had been awarded eleven battle honours and twenty-three soldiers had been decorated. Some of its senior officers maintained that the battalions had never realized their full military potential, because they were so frequently split up into small and scattered detachments performing reconnaissance and similar duties for larger Australian and American units.

The raising of the New Guinea Volunteer Rifles was originally authorized on 4 September 1939. Its sub-units, comprising white people only, were small and scattered among the various centres, and could offer slight effective resistance to the Japanese invaders, though many notable feats of scouting and guerrilla warfare were performed by individual riflemen. The unit was disbanded in 1942, most of its members being absorbed into Angau [q.v.].

After World War II. The Pacific Islands Regiment was formed again in 1951, and its first battalion raised in Port Moresby in 1951-2. The second battalion was raised in Wewak in 1965. The basis of the Regiment's training is wide-ranging patrols of about company strength, undertaken at intervals over the whole of the New Guinea mainland and the more important islands. There is little activity involving the battalions as a whole. There is no artillery.

In the course of these exercises, 'civic action' is commonly undertaken, whereby some work useful to the local people is carried out, such as the construction of a bridge. This activity is arranged in close liaison with the Administration. It has been praised by some observers as helpful and sensible, and criticized by others because it can be misinterpreted as encroachment on the functions of the civil power.

Australian officers predominate, and present policy is to replace Australians in all ranks as quickly as possible. There are now about thirty indigenous commissioned officers, much of whose training has been at officer schools of high standards, outside the Territory. By May 1971, however, only one local man had attained the rank of major—E. R. Diro [q.v.]. The need for expatriate specialist officers and N.C.O.s will thus persist for a long while.

The Regiment is commanded by an Australian brigadier whose orders come from Army headquarters in Canberra, and not from the Administrator of Papua and New Guinea. Under the shadow of possible large-scale civil disorders arising from the activities of the Mataungan Association in the Gazelle Peninsula of New Britain, the Administrator was authorized in July 1970 to call upon the military for support. Such a move proved unnecessary, and the arrangement was revoked in May 1971.

The P.I.R. is accustomed to the use of air transport, and of helicopter support supplied by Australian units. These facilities are not under its own command. The RAAF maintains light transport capacity with Caribou aircraft.

The Papua and New Guinea Division of the Royal Australian Navy uses the once great naval base at Manus, in the Admiralty Islands, which has now been partly restored. Its craft are mainly light coastal patrol vessels. Most ratings are indigenous men, and several midshipmen and junior officers form the basis of the future officer corps.

The New Guinea Volunteer Rifles was also re-established in 1951. Since 1965 it has been multi-racial, and has its headquarters in Port Moresby with sub-units in various centres throughout the Territory.

The future. The whole cost of the armed forces in Papua and New Guinea is borne by the Australian government; to maintain them at present strength and efficiency is likely to be beyond the means of a newly independent local government, unless assistance is given. The role of the army after independence is a matter upon which observers speculate. However, there is no question that it is an efficient and well-disciplined force, although without its own artillery and air transport. To a notable extent tribal loyalties have been subordinated to *esprit de corps*, and even when they are in casual clothes off duty it is often easy to identify members of the Regiment by their impressive bearing and address. The regimental motto is 'To find a path'; what path is actually followed will depend largely upon wise and statesman-like decisions reached in mutual confidence by the Australian government and the new government of Papua and New Guinea.

N. E. W. Granter (ed.), *Yesterday and Today: an illustrated history of the Pacific Islands Regiment from its formation on 19 June 1940 until the present day*. Port Moresby, 1970; D. McCarthy, *South-west Pacific Area—First Year. Kokoda to Wau. (Australia in the War of 1939-45)*. Canberra, 1959; D. Dexter, *The New Guinea Offensives (Australia in the War of 1939-45)*. Canberra, 1961; R. J. O'Neill, 'The Army in Papua and New Guinea', *Canberra Papers on Strategy and Defence*, no. 10, 1971.   PETER RYAN

ART. The visual arts of New Guinea as a whole are extraordinary in their variety and in the number of objects produced. A great part of the population living in Highland areas has in recent times practised the visual arts only to a minor extent, but the people of the coasts and lowlands have created a vast mass of sculpture, paintings, and other objects. The variety of the art styles reflects the cultural diversity of the area.

THE STUDY OF NEW GUINEA ART

Relatively little attention has so far been paid to the art of New Guinea as a subject worthy of study in its own right. Most of the available information is to be found as incidental material in field reports by anthropologists and missionaries discussing material culture and religion. In actual studies of the art considerable attention has been given to the delineation of style areas. Such studies have been limited by incomplete surveying of the field, being dependent on the penetration of explorers beyond the coast. Another source of difficulty has been the inadequate reports of field collections. However, it appears that no large groups remain to be discovered in New Guinea, and while many fascinating discoveries have been made in the last few years among smaller groups, it seems unlikely that whatever small pockets of primitive cultures remain have any but the most rudimentary art styles.

The first important analysis was made by A. C. Haddon (1894), who distinguished several styles in Papua, the Trust Territory, and West Irian. Subsequently K. T. Preuss (1897-8) analysed the then German New Guinea into six areas. R. W. Firth (1936) added Mount Hagen to the Papua-New Guinea stylistic areas. A. A. Gerbrands (1950-1) and S. Kooijman (1961) have defined the stylistic areas of West Irian. F. Speiser (1936) analysed the art of the South Pacific generally into specifically art-form areas rather than ethnographically based ones. He defined (1) a 'primary style' not yet fully formed; (2) 'curvilinear style'; (3) 'the beak style' including figures with exaggeratedly long noses; (4) the '*korwar* style'; (5) the Melanesian 'Tami style' and (6) the '*malanggan* style' of New Ireland. The styles of New Guinea are subsumed under the primary style for the interior areas; the curvilinear style for the Trobriand Islands [q.v.], Gulf of Papua, Sepik (also Lake Sentani, Humboldt Bay and Geelvink Bay in West Irian); the beak style on the north-east coast, and the *korwar* style in the Trobriands; the Tami style dominated the coast from Astrolabe Bay to Huon Gulf.

Recent investigations have tended to re-define specific areas (Huon Gulf, Astrolabe Bay: Bodrogi 1959, 1961) to refine subdivisions of well-known areas (Lake Sentani: Kooijman 1959; Gulf of Papua: Newton 1961); or to integrate known areas with less known into broader assemblies (Sepik: Bühler 1960; Haberland 1964). In a few even more limited studies, stylistic areas have been treated in terms of single traits; e.g. shields (Sepik: Schmidt 1929); suspension hooks (Sepik: Schefold 1966); ceremonial houses (Sepik: Behrmann 1950-1).

Though almost nothing is known about the history of New Guinea art itself, discussions of art have formed part of the formation of theories of New Guinea history. Bühler and others (1962), indeed, consider that 'ethnological studies of art are essential for an understanding of the cultural history of Oceania, and future work in this field will have to rely to a considerable extent on such studies'.

Most studies so far have attacked the problems in terms of cultural diffusion or of autochthonous development. As early as 1888 Giglioli and Beccari suggested a relationship between the long-nosed masks of the Sepik and the elephant-headed Indian god Ganesha. Speiser elaborated on this theory in his discussion of the beak style; further suggesting that the *korwar* style derives from Khmer art, and the *malanggan* style from Indian sculpture. He regarded the curvilinear style as typically Papuan, and the Tami style as Melanesian.

The position of New Guinea art in theories of the widespread diffusion of early Chinese styles through the Pacific basin has been discussed by R. Heine-Geldern (1937) and Douglas Fraser (1968).

The sociological aspect of art in New Guinea has been largely ignored with the exception of studies by F. E. Williams (1940) and J. A. W. Forge (1967); and the socio-religious aspect has been discussed by C. Schmitz (1963). The personalities of Asmat carvers have been described by A. A. Gerbrands (1967).

THE PRESENT SITUATION

Sporadically over the last half-century, and with increasing volume over the last decade, sculpture and painting has poured out of the country in a flood that has now virtually come to an end. This has been the result of the activities of museum expeditions and local collectors. By now the more important and artistically productive cultures are, to all intents and purposes, completely stripped of any objects of pre-European vintage, and have little or nothing left even of more recent manufacture.

The future of New Guinea art in traditional styles is hard to foresee. Some communities, under the influence of mission censure or their own commercial ambition, have abandoned their arts completely. In other places a considerable amount of work is still being done, and it is probably fair to say that the cultures most productive in the past maintain an equal, or even greater, output. In occasional instances its quality is not far off that of the best work of the past.

How most of such work will be disposed of is uncertain. Production is much greater than necessary to satisfy the needs of the community and, while Administration encouragement of carving and painting as a possible source of income has been effective, marketing procedures are not.

There is a danger of considerable overstocking for the small tourist and curio market.

THE ARTIST

Art in New Guinea is predominantly the work of men; women are limited to crafts. Women make net bags and they paint some designs on bark-cloth garments (e.g. among the Orokaiva). Women also make the basic forms of pottery, but often the modelled or engraved decoration is added by men. In general women are debarred from looking at work in progress. They are supposed never to see the most important carvings and paintings, as these are for ritual use. However, much ceremonial (e.g. middle Sepik) requiring masks and other objects is staged for them or includes their actual participation; or they may be allowed to see paintings representing secret carvings (Waskuk or Kwoma).

While most men can execute necessary craft work, painting and carving are the work of recognized experts. The proportion of these to the total community is variable; in some groups (Waskuk, Yessan) it is now as high as 10-15 per cent of the adult male population; in others it is much less. Formerly the Waskuk were supposed to have one potter, one painter and one carver for each village. In no case does expertise lead to complete specialization; not only does an expert make utilitarian objects on demand, he also carries out normal agricultural and other tasks. The time occupied by carving and painting is hard to assess. A concerted effort apparently produces a huge area of bark-painting in a few days (Abelam); large slit-gongs may be completed in a couple of weeks (Hunstein Mountains); and smaller objects, even with sporadic work, may take only a few days. However, the total preparation for the ceremonies in which such things are used may take many years (Elema).

Qualification as an expert is variously acquired. In some cases its inception is personal inclination under the supervision of a recognized expert (Huon Gulf). Skill may be considered hereditary, and a man trains a son who shows aptitude; if not, his brother's son (Massim, Sepik); or it may be held to be innate, and only those born with the umbilical cord round their necks are capable (Mindököma). In other instances, qualifications are prescribed: skull-racks, *agibe*, are carved by homicides (Kerewa), and painted (i.e. re-vitalized) by old men, their 'fathers'; one type of sacred object is made by young men, another by the old (Hunstein Mountains); some carvings can only be made by men of the highest initiatory rank (Waskuk); a man carves masks for his maternal clan (Iatmül); makes masks for son, younger brother, brother's son (Elema); headmen are said to carve important house-posts, though actually experts do the work (Central District). Experts in magic make shields (Eastern Highlands).

Much large-scale work (Abelam façades; large Iatmül paintings; Sepik slit-gongs and house-posts) is carried out by assistants under the direction of a master responsible for the general design. For Elema masks, assistance is due from maternal uncles, trade partners, and interested bystanders in general. Elsewhere carvings are carried out individually; panels are painted by particular men and later incorporated in large assemblies (Waskuk, May River). Usually the master artist is also a leader in economic or political affairs, but in some recorded cases individual artists have an unusual personality, e.g. they may be epileptics.

Payment for commissions is probably universal. Little is known of the terms, but these probably correspond to the pattern for other craft services and, in the case of ceremonial objects, is subsumed in payments for the ceremony as a whole. The workers are sometimes provided with food during the progress of the work (Abelam, Elema, Telefomin).

MATERIALS AND TECHNIQUES

In recent times New Guinea artists have used virtually every available natural material except stone.

The material most used is wood, including white wood, *Vitex cofassus*, ironwood, *Intsia bijuga*, black palm, *Caryota* sp., and other tall palms. Sago pith, bamboos, and eccentric roots (Gulf of Papua) are also used.

Paintings are usually done on sago spathes (Sepik), but also on flat wooden shields (Huon Gulf). Bark-cloth (from *Ficus* sp.) is painted for garments (coastal Sepik, Huon Gulf, Astrolabe Bay, Orokaiva, Collingwood Bay, Gulf of Papua); and for dance standards (Saruwaged Range, Eastern Highlands). Bark-cloth is also stretched on cane frames to construct masks (Huon Gulf, Gulf of Papua), painted shields (Huon Gulf, Astrolabe Bay), and figures (Saruwaged Range, Gulf of Papua). Basketry masks (Sepik, Gulf of Papua), and figures (Sepik, Southern Highlands) are made, as well as small ornaments for lime tubes and flutes (Sepik).

Pigments consist in general of white (lime or ochre), reds from russet to pink (ochres, some burned), pandanus oil, vegetable scarlet, and black (charcoal and dark clay). This range is diversified locally. Ochres in buff, yellows, and orange are traded in compact lumps from Lake Chambri (middle Sepik). A semi-mineralized wood is burned to produce red (Abelam). Often it is rubbed on surfaces and produces the same effect (Hunstein Mountains). A green-grey ochre is rare (upper Sepik) and grey powdered soapstone is also used (Elema, Arapesh). Vegetable pigments include yellow (Wosera, Elema—from turmeric), red-brown (unspecified barks and leaves, Huon Gulf), scarlet (Waskuk), blue and green (Huon Gulf, Waskuk). The Waskuk scrape green bamboo to give their paintings a flock texture. A tree sap glazes the blacks (Wosera, Waskuk). Water is the usual medium, but vegetable oil is occasionally used (Waskuk).

Bone (human or cassowary femur) serves for incised daggers (Sepik) and spatulas, pig skulls and cassowary sterna for masks (lower Keram River).

Feathers are applied to wood panels (Keram River) to make mosaic pictures of human beings and animals. They are also built into huge constructions as mask-supporting head-dresses (Madang; Sepik delta; Lumi; Wosera).

Turtle-shell forms a base for masks and figures only in the Torres Strait, but small ornaments are made from it in many areas.

Clay is modelled for some small masks and figures (middle Sepik, Waskuk); and for vessels of various types (middle Sepik, Waskuk, Massim, Orokaiva, etc.). Coiling technique provides the base forms; designs are then engraved, or other details are modelled separately and applied before firing; painting is done after firing. For over-modelling features on basketry masks and skulls (Sepik, Gulf of Papua) the clay is powdered and puddled with oil.

Coconut shell is used for masks only on the Keram River, but many decorated utensils are made from it, such as containers and spoons, penis covers (upper Sepik), ceremonial whistles (Waskuk), charms (Gulf of Papua), and rattles resembling heads (middle Fly River). Gourds are used for masks (Eastern Highlands) and, rarely decorated, for penis covers (upper Sepik). In the middle Sepik they are more often used for lime containers, decorated with engraving, seeds, and shells. Bamboo tubes are also used as penis covers and lime containers, and, in many places, for tobacco smoking.

Trim is applied lavishly to carvings and to all kinds of other objects, including ornaments, weapons, and utensils. Skirts for masks are usually shredded sago leaf. Other materials attached for decorative effect include feathers; shells, including *Conus*, *Nassarius*, cowries, clam, mother-of-pearl, gold-lip, bailer, sea snail—either inlaid or attached; seeds, chiefly red *Abrus* and grey *Coix lacryma-jobi*—sometimes as a substitute for cowries; fur; human hair; animal vertebrae; frog and fish bones; complete dried lizards and birds; small rattan chains and bands; nut rattles; leaves, flowers, and fruits. Recent substitutes for some of these are unravelled wool, for hair, and buttons and beads, for shells.

In some places the main pre-European carving tools are still in use. The range includes stone adzes of varying sizes down to blades about two inches long for detailed work, sharpened boars' tusks and rat and bandicoot teeth—sometimes set in cane holders. For scraping, mussel (Sepik) and cockle (Gulf of Papua) shells are commonly employed; fine smoothing is carried out with rough leaves (Orokaiva). Bone gouges serve for grooving (Sepik, Huon Gulf), and borers are made of bird or fish bone (Sepik), or fish teeth (Gulf of Papua). Mallets are small, flat and carved (Sepik) or crude lumps of wood (Gulf of Papua).

Colour is mixed with its medium in small carved wooden bowls (middle Sepik), natural hollow stones (upper Sepik), or half coconut shells. Colours are not mixed together. They are applied with feathers (Abelam, Arapesh), chewed coconut, pandanus fibre, or areca husk. All four may be tied to a small twig (Waskuk, Elema).

Bark sheets are prepared with a wash of bread-fruit tree sap (Arapesh), followed with one of grey mud (Wosera), mineral grey (Arapesh), or black mud (Abelam).

While painting has hardly been affected by modern conditions—except that ochres can be traded over wider areas—the main work of carving is now generally done with metal tools, as it has been for varying periods in different areas. In some instances metal tools were available for a considerable time before formal contact with Europeans. They were obtained from shipwrecks (Kerewa) or trade with intermediary groups.

THE WESTERN SEPIK

A belt of country running from Bougainville Bay southwards through the Bewani Mountains and across the Sepik River to the Tirpitz Mountains is the home of a style with many local variants. Its basic design consists of two triangular forms connected at the apices or bases. It is found on a group of shields from Bougainville Bay itself, while a simple variant, with the triangles expressed as scrolls, comes from Lumi. A further group of shields from the Green River area, and along the Sepik towards the Yellow River, has such designs outlined by parallel ridges. Bark-paintings, engraved bamboo pipes, and hand-drums show similar designs that here include an S-shaped double spiral, also found on bark-paintings and shields from the hills of the upper May River.

Around Telefomin, and to the south and west of it, related designs appear not only on shields but also on large perforated boards used for house-entrances. These are used alone by the Telefomin and are combined with other boards to form façades by the Faiwolmin and Tifalmin. Façades of decorative carved boards are made by the Oksapmin and Wopkeimin.

THE HIGHLANDS

Carving and painting are hardly practised in the central Highlands apart from extremely simple designs painted on shields, while some fence boards have openwork elementary geometric designs. Only the barbs of ceremonial spears are carved with any elaboration. Belts, armlets, various small bamboo articles, and pottery ocarinas have incised or painted geometric designs. Ornamental lashing is used on the well-known Hagen axes. The most conspicuous efforts of the Highlanders, however, are reserved for personal decoration, mainly in the form of spectacular feather head-dresses. The southern Highlands are similarly barren of significant painting and sculpture. Shields are painted with geometric patterns, as are the boards of coffins. Some string figures of human beings are made, apparently as cult objects. The main carvings and paintings of the Highlanders just east of the Asaro River consist of shields with simple stylized patterns; and boards, *gerua*, exhibited at pig feasts. The latter may be small, worn on the head, or up to five feet long. They are thin silhouettes of human or animal figures painted with abstract designs.

Among the Fore, Yate, Kamano and Usurufa (Ramu-Purari divide) carving is limited to elaborate arrow-heads. Simple gourd masks are also made and figures of string for ceremonies. For secular occasions these peoples stage dramatic scenes using bark-cloth back-shields and standards mounted on poles. Some include naturalistic models of birds; most are painted with abstract designs representing natural objects or referring to mythology.

In a similar manner, the people of the valley systems of the Saruwaged Range construct life-size bark-cloth figures of birds, including cassowaries, and human beings, on basketry frames. Representing divinities, such effigies are exhibited in groups at initiation ceremonies. Other ceremonies demand the use of both similar figures and painted bark-cloth panels attached to poles strapped to dancers' backs. War shields are also painted with divine images. The main carved objects are small wood figures, sometimes used in sorcery, sometimes incorporated into the dance costumes. Other small carvings include head-rests and stools in human form (Azera). Large figure sculpture and house finials in abstract designs are reported from the Komba.

THE COASTAL AND LOWER SEPIK

The art styles of the Sepik coast, the islands off shore, the lower Ramu River and part of the hinterland between the Sepik and the Ramu form a closely interrelated group.

Carvings include a variety of figures, from small amulets to ancestral images up to ten feet high. Smaller figures, from the mouth of the Sepik, sometimes have real human skulls rather than carved heads. From the Ramu River come small figures of mothers carrying children. These are toys. Charms are also made in the form of flying foxes. Figures and masks are carved on ceremonial house-posts. A great variety of masks is made; as a rule they are used in pairs, male masks with long noses, female masks with short ones. Miniature masks are made for pectoral ornaments. Slit-gongs are carved, with squatting human figures as lugs at both ends. Ceremonial adzes are carved the full length of the shaft with masks and human and animal figures.

Many utilitarian objects are carved, including canoe prows with heads of animals, particularly crocodiles; bailers; paddles, including huge steering paddles; suspension hooks in human form; house ladders; flat bowls with incised designs and low reliefs of bats; betel mortars with human figures; head-rests; stools; weapons, including spear-throwers, spears, and shields engraved with several surmounted heads. Most carvings are simply painted in red with touches of black.

Paintings from this area are now rare but probably were common formerly. A few were collected early at Wewak, and ceremonial house fronts were lavishly decorated with paintings at Suain. At Bosngun, lower Ramu, the upper storeys of ceremonial houses are lined with bark-paintings, as are screens leading to inner sanctuaries. Bark-cloth loin cloths are painted with abstract patterns. The sails of sea-going canoes are painted with simple designs.

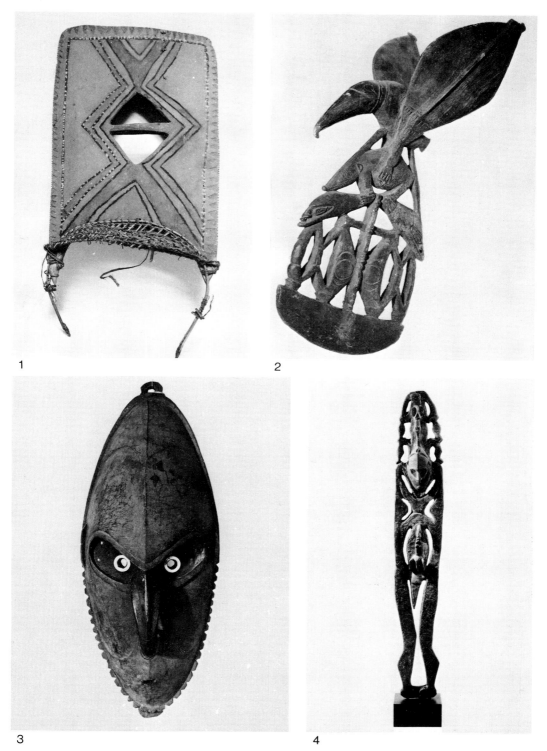

1

2

3

4

Fig 1. Wooden head ornament, *gerua*, painted in red, yellow, blue, grey-green; Eastern Highlands.
Fig 2. Wooden carving of bird, pig and men; Sepik coast.
Fig 3. Mask, Sepik coast (67 cm. high).
Fig 4. Ancestor figure, lower Sepik River (196.9 cm. high).

Between Murik and Awar huge feather head-dresses are made in the form of lanceolate panels with attached masks; this head-dress is often depicted on wooden figures.

Basketry is rare, though some large masks have been attributed to the area. Large figures of mythical boars are reported from Bosngun.

The best known feature of the group of styles is the depiction of greatly elongated noses, recurved to connect with the chest, navel, or penis. Second only in importance is the engraving of panels of tight geometrical pattern and bands of fret and zigzag. These occur on such flat surfaces as the side-planks of sea-going canoes, the waists of hand-drums, the sides of slit-gongs, and as detailing of most figures. All this work is often in a crisp and almost mechanically precise technique. Coastal Sepik styles extend to the first few villages up the Sepik itself. Some types of figures and masks are shared. Shields also correspond to coastal styles. At Singrin tall openwork silhouette figures are made of ancestors with animal attributes, the heads being in the round. From slightly further up river come small attenuated human figures with hands and feet connected with enormously elongated noses; they are possibly dance objects. At Kanduanum, on the border of the Iatmül area, there are long-nosed masks heavily decorated with boars' tusks and shells; though usually carved in wood, their base material is sometimes a human skull.

THE LOWER SEPIK TRIBUTARIES

Keram River carving has many similarities to that of the lower Sepik. Mask-like objects, similar to Kanduanum masks, are made of basketry panels with human skulls attached, the whole being coated with clay set with shells and tusks. Feather mosaics are made on wooden slabs, showing cassowaries, fish, and human figures. Some of great size are reported. They are in the same style as the bark-paintings that extend to Bosngun. At Kambaramba huge bark models of crocodiles are constructed for initiation. Little work comes from the Porapora area between the Keram and the coast, apart from house-posts carved with figures in a simple angular style; slit-gongs; small pig or cassowary bone masks; and staff-like figures with receptacles for skulls.

The chief carvings of the Yuat River (Mindö-köma people) include slit-gongs, shields, masks, large squatting figures used as house finials, suspension hooks, flute ornaments—figures of men and parrots—snakes used in sorcery, and personal ornaments. The human figures have almost spherical heads and round noses. Some animal figures and masks are covered with spikes, which appear in relief carving as serrated edges. They are also a feature of huge and intricate paintings of crocodiles carried out on assemblages of bark sheets.

From the bush on either side of the Yuat come a number of colossal human figures. The grass-landers east of the river also make small wood masks over-modelled with clay and shells; and modelled pottery traded to the river people.

THE MIDDLE SEPIK

The Iatmül, living along the middle Sepik River, work in styles that also extend to the lower Krosmeri and Karawari Rivers, Lake Chambri, and the Manambu to the west.

Virtually every object in daily use is carved and painted with abstract, human, or animal designs. The range includes suspension hooks, stools, bowls, paint palettes, mallets, adzes, pounders, head-rests, lime containers, lime spatulas, weapons —shields, clubs, spears, spear-throwers, bone daggers, canoe prows carved as crocodile or pig heads, sometimes with connected bird and human figures; canoe prow ornaments of bark sheeting, with attached masks; and paddles. Religious life is focused on large ceremonial houses that are themselves decorated with architectural carving: posts and beams have representations of mythological beings, including female seated figures at the foot of king-posts that extend through the gables and are capped with finials representing human figures and eagles. The gables themselves have large wood or basketry masks. Sacred mounds outside the houses are fenced with wooden ancestral figures or heads.

These houses are used as stores for the cult objects. Some of the most sacred are musical instruments, including slit-gongs with engraved ornamentation and carved lugs, flutes with attached carvings, hand-drums, drums and bowls to beat water, and percussion planks. Other carvings include ancestral figures, some over life-size, and often shown standing on suspension hooks. Masks are of several types: human faces in wood, some with elongated noses, *mei*; in basketry, with elongated noses; and large basketry masks, *awan*, with smaller ones attached. In a few instances the skulls of important men are incorporated into these masks. Basketry models of great size, representing pigs, crocodiles, birds and sawfish are also used as dance costumes.

Large paintings serve as racks for the display of skulls. Anthropomorphic stools are used in ceremonial debates. Skulls both of ancestors and raid victims have features modelled on them in painted clay. These are shown at initiation and mortuary ceremonies.

The Iatmül style is generally simple, and its frequent appearance of complexity is the result of painted or engraved linear patterning, either abstract or representing face-paint designs. Human, animal, and bird figures conform to standard naturalistic stylizations, with a concurrent use of highly stylized faces in low relief sculpture and painting. Some variations in the styles are discernible, corresponding to dialect divisions. The central and eastern Iatmül work tends to be lighter and more elegant than that of the western Iatmül, which has more massive and often rounded forms. Throughout, the craftsmanship of large carvings tends to be simple and even rough; that of small objects is frequently very refined.

Lower Krosmeri and Karawari River styles correspond closely to those of the eastern Iatmül, as do those of the Chambri. All have basketry masks

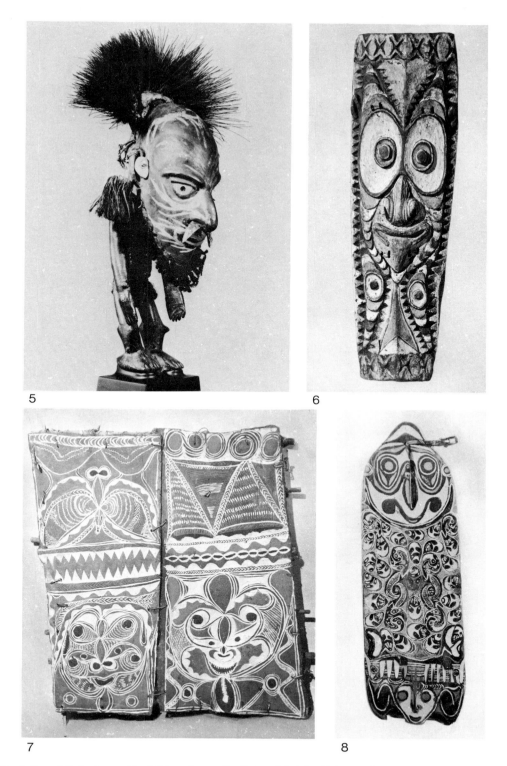

Fig 5. Sacred flute figure, Yuat River, lower Sepik (total height 50.8 cm., figure 34.9 cm. high).
Fig 6. Painted wooden shield, middle Sepik (137.2 cm. high).
Fig 7. Bark painting, red ochre, black and white paint; middle Sepik (82.5 x 73 cm.).
Fig 8. Openwork wooden board, black paint, light ochre, red ochre; middle Sepik (170.2 x 53.3 cm.).

with enormously elongated noses. Manambu carving (from Avatip, Malu, and Yambun) is closely similar to that of the Iatmül, though crude by comparison. Bark-paintings, sacred pottery vessels with modelled human heads, and pottery bowls resemble those of the Waskuk.

The southern villages of the Sawos, in the grasslands north of the Iatmül, share their range of objects and the more massive western style. Their most individual and striking works are large boards, the complex openwork carving of which shows a variety of bird and animal forms. The eastern Sawos specialize in the making of fine bowls, with intricate incised designs, for trade to the neighbouring river villages. The more northerly Sawos villages show, particularly in their bark-paintings, the influence of the southern Abelam style.

THE UPPER SEPIK

West of the Manambu, the hills and lowlands bordering the Sepik, up to the May River, are inhabited by a number of small groups whose styles, though widely differing, share a number of patterns and symbols.

The Waskuk, in the hills and swamps of Ambunti, are prolific carvers and painters. Ceremonial houses have ceilings lined with bark-paintings. The largely abstract designs represent mainly water or vegetation spirits. The several logs making up a ridge pole are carved, sometimes their entire length, usually with heads and birds on the protruding finials. Slit-gongs are carved at one end, often with human heads. For yam festivals a limited range of figures are carved; they include heads on posts, female figures, and stylized flat figures up to twelve feet high. Other ceremonial equipment includes flute ornaments, coconut shell whistles, carved adzes, and light openwork panels tied to the hair.

Other carved equipment is scanty apart from some lime-tube ornaments, figure-type suspension hooks, mallets, spears, shields, finely incised human bone daggers, spoon handles, and large sago stirrers. Pottery is an important product. Bowls and dishes are engraved with human, animal and abstract designs; pottery heads and large pots with modelled human features and figures are ceremonial objects.

Waskuk styles are bold, simple and massive. Both painting and sculpture show elements comparable to some used by the Abelam and Iatmül. Yasi (Yessan-Mayo) and Yaungget work is similar to that of the Waskuk.

The Ngala of Swagab village carve large slit-gongs terminating in human, animal and insect forms; fine gong beaters; large sacred masks not intended to be worn; masks surmounted with hook assemblies, like those of the Hunstein Mountains, for canoe prow ornaments; elaborate canoe prows; a few figures; and shields. Paintings closely resemble those of the Waskuk. Large pots are made but not decorated; and small pottery models of the big canoe prows are common.

The Wogamush, near the mouth of the April River, carve very large slit-gongs, up to twenty feet, terminating in heads of cassowaries or crocodiles and stylized insects; canoe prows; canoe prow ornaments with masks; hand-drums; shields; and slit-gong beaters. Finely engraved coconut shells are used as penis covers by homicides. The distinguishing mark of their work is the stylization of the human face and of the bird forms of the canoe prows. These latter are also common in Swagab. Senapian, a village close to those of the Wogamush, has a different language but shares the styles.

The Iwam, living further up the Sepik and along the middle May River, engage in little three-dimensional carving, apart from their canoe prows. These are openwork carvings of great variety. Some canoe prow ornaments have small full-length figures attached in place of the masks usual elsewhere. Paintings, made as individual units on individual sheets of bark, are assembled as door shutters and as linings for the interiors of houses. Shields are carved in low relief, as are the long terminals of slit-gongs. All Iwam art is based upon a limited number of abstract designs, symbolizing plant or animal forms, combined into intricate compositions.

THE SOUTHERN SEPIK

The belt of land extending from the April River across the Hunstein Mountains and the upper Krosmeri River to the upper Karawari River is inhabited by groups sharing related styles of carving. Their main feature is the use of concentric hooks converging on a central feature (usually a circle) and ranged along a central spine. Painting, apart from that applied to carvings, is unknown.

Among the Bahinemo of the Hunstein Mountains the hook complex is used not only in its simplest form but also as the central feature of large panel-shaped masks. A few old naturalistic masks also exist. Slit-gongs have their ends carved as stylized fish or sun symbols, scroll designs that are also carved on the widely-traded arrows. Sun symbols are carved on Hunstein Mountains shields, but those of the April River have human faces. Finials of rafters in the ceremonial houses resemble hornbill heads. Basketry is used for masks and flute ornaments.

The hook complex in its most elaborate form is found on the upper Karawari River in examples varying from small—used as personal charms—to colossal, terminating in human heads and legs. Most other carving and painting in the Karawari area follows middle Sepik models, including a unique group of wooden crocodiles up to twenty-five feet long.

From caves around Inyai, on a tributary of the upper Karawari, have come a quantity of carvings. These include a number of variations on the hook-complex style as well as large female figures in frontal positions with upraised arms. Traces of the hook style are also found as far east as the upper Yuat River.

THE NORTHERN SEPIK

The Abelam of the Prince Alexander Mountains and the plains south of them are immensely pro-

9

Fig 9. Clay bowl, black with traces of red paint; middle Sepik.
Fig 10. Painted clay head, upper Sepik (39.4 cm. high).
Fig 11. Painted wooden figure, southern Sepik (209.6 cm. high).
Fig 12. Wooden female figure, Karawari River, southern Sepik
        (168.3 cm. high).

10

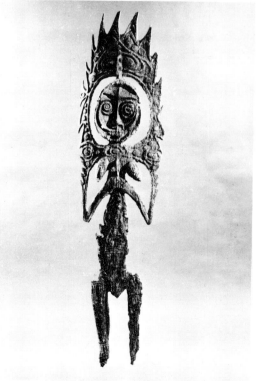

11   12

lific painters and sculptors, chiefly for ceremonial purposes. The main carvings are great numbers of human figures of various sizes in association with birds or pigs, many of them forming pole-like sculptures about twenty feet long. Others are large human heads. Reliefs of human figures, birds, and lizards are carved on plant roots, with some use of openwork. Small flat openwork panels are attached to the hair for ceremonials. Independent figures of animals and birds, including cockatoos, hornbills, snakes, lizards, and pigs are attached to the gables of ceremonial houses. Suspension hooks are carved, as are spears, hand-drums, and grave-posts. Slit-gongs are plain cylinders with a little engraving at the ends.

Though much carving is basically simple in its forms, all of it is given the appearance of considerable complexity and richness by total painting in black, white, red, and yellow, depicting all anatomical details, facial designs, and ornaments. Bark-paintings cover the entire façades of the ceremonial houses, showing tiers of ancestral faces, birds, and other designs. Such paintings are also used as settings for ceremonials. Inside the houses they frame displays of carvings and line the inner face of tunnels through which initiates must crawl. They are also used for large open-air displays before which more ceremonies take place. Basketry masks are also made for initiation, mainly in the form of hoods with more or less elaborate nose projections. Cassowary bone is carved for daggers, spatulas, knives, and hair ornaments. Some feather head-dresses of enormous size are made.

At least three areas of Abelam style are distinguishable corresponding to dialect differences. They are found respectively in the north, east, and south. The sculpture of the north tends to be based on simple bulky forms and has a great deal of detail painting over a red ground. The eastern style is notable for figures in which the human torso is replaced by clusters of vertical spikes or cockatoo beaks. The southern style tends to be markedly flatter on the frontal plane than are either of the other two; painting shows finer lines and areas of cross-hatching on larger fields of colour than occur with the other styles.

The southern Arapesh, to the west of the Abelam, copy their styles. The northern or mountain Arapesh have little painting, apart from a few bark panels. They decorate a few utilitarian objects, such as head-rests, bowls, and yam pounders, in imitation of those made by the coastal Arapesh around Dagua.

THE HUON PENINSULA AND GULF

The people of the Huon Gulf area have produced a great deal of sculpture, notable for its massive prismatic forms. These are embellished with a considerable amount of low-relief surface decoration, including geometrically stylized designs mainly in the form of serrated patterns and crescents.

Ceremonial houses have posts carved as kneeling or standing atlantes, external wall reliefs, carved rafter-ends, and gable-masks. The cults employed face-masks in wood and hood-masks of bark-cloth, the latter sometimes having wood-carved features attached. Among other ceremonial objects, drums and slit-gongs were decorated with relief carving. Flat dance staffs are topped with profile human or bird heads.

Much household equipment is carved, especially suspension hooks with the shanks as human figures, ladles, paddles, bailers, such tools as adzes, netting instruments, pestles, and mortars. The best known objects of this kind are the ovate bowls, occasionally in bird or fish form, in black wood with shallow relief decoration on the sides; and the small head-rests with human or animal figures as supporters. These head-rests and bowls, produced in the Tami Islands, are traded around the Gulf and to southern New Britain.

Minor objects such as turtle-shell ornaments, bamboo combs, gourd containers, and coconut-shell cups are also engraved with the usual range of designs.

Details of larger sculptures are picked out in colour, usually red and black on a white ground. Human figures and stylized forms are painted on shields of wood or bark-cloth. Abstract designs and fish forms are used on canoe planks, bark-cloth masks, dance hats, and loin cloths.

THE OROKAIVA AND THE KUKUKUKU

The large Orokaiva group seem, like the people north of them, to concentrate on dramatic performances rather than the visual arts. For these, however, some painted bark-cloth models and ornaments are made. Simple abstract patterns are painted on bark-cloth garments. A few large carvings of snakes are recorded, probably also intended for dance accessories. The mountain people of this area, including the Kukukuku, seem to be lacking in art apart from decorative lashings on their arrows.

THE MASSIM AREA

The northern part produces a great quantity of portable small carved objects, many of them for wide distribution in the course of the *kula* trading cycle. Most of them are made in the Trobriand Islands, including the bowls, betel mortars, and lime spatulas carved in innumerable variations on abstract forms, apparently derived from bird and animal figures. Larger carvings—no Massim works are on a big scale—include dance-paddles with two lunate panels connected by a bar grip. Others are several types of canoe splash-boards and decorative prow panels. These canoe carvings also appear to be distributed widely through the area in the course of trade. They are all richly ornamented in low relief with tightly packed, sweeping compositions of semi-abstract designs, based mainly on bird forms, but including the nautilus, body ornaments, and clouds. Such designs are also used for incised or relief decoration on clubs, rafters, paddles, and ceremonial axe handles. Independent figure sculpture was rare, although human figures were incorporated into rope-blocks and some suspension hooks.

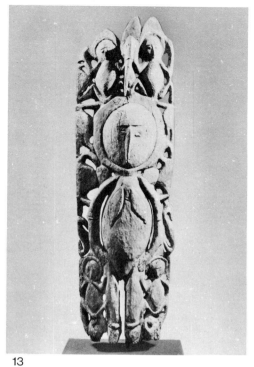

13

14

15

16

Fig 13. Painted wooden ancestor figure, northern Sepik (181 cm. high).
Fig 14. Carved wooden board, painted; northern Sepik (118 cm. high).
Fig 15. Carved wooden figure, Huon Peninsula (135 cm. high).
Fig 16. Carved black palm wood bowl, limed; Tami Islands, Huon Gulf (46.4 cm. long).

Work in other materials includes pyrographed lime gourds and elaborate turtle-shell lime spatulas.

Painting was limited to decorative designs on the gables of yam stores and an elaborate standardized design, perhaps of magical significance, on one type of war shield.

The southern Massim area, on the south coast and including the outlying islands, is less productive. It is possible, indeed, that much of the carving found there originated in the northern islands. However, the southern Massim do produce elaborate canoe carvings and spatulas with naturalistic human and animal figures.

THE CENTRAL SOUTH COAST

The Mailu, at the eastern end of this area, produce a great deal of pottery for trade decorated with bands of simple incised patterns around the rims. The projecting ends of rafters are crudely carved as birds; otherwise there is apparently no carving and no painting.

To the west the Koita and allied groups build ceremonial platforms, *dubu*, said to have originated among the Sinaugoro. The posts are carved with simple designs—rows of pyramids and some naturalistic reptiles—and the ends with human heads and stylized animals. Such designs also appear on the rafter-ends of private houses and are regarded as badges of the social groups.

The Roro, Mekeo, and Nara use such designs, and also elaborate feather head-dresses, as badges. Geometrically stylized birds, fish, and lizards are carved on the capitals of ceremonial house-posts, which may also have reliefs of human and animal figures, on the ends of poles and floor rafters, and the front ridge-pole. Planks under the ridge-pole and bordering the façade have similar designs. Little other sculpture exists, apart from a few figures of human beings and hornbills. Bark-cloth masks, *kaivakuku*, have a limited distribution and probably are derived from the Elema *kovave*, which they resemble.

THE GULF OF PAPUA

The Gulf of Papua may be subdivided into several stylistic areas with very considerable differences between them. They are those of the Elema, Purari, Urama, Kerewa, and Kiwai. The types of objects carved and decorated are few, and nearly all are ceremonial. Painting is virtually non-existent, and figure sculpture is rare. The commonest works are low-relief carvings on plane surfaces, usually oval boards, and masks of bark-cloth on basketry frames, sometimes with modelled bark-cloth attributes attached. Both are produced in enormous numbers. The main decoration is red, black, and white paint. In most areas there is a prevalence of sawtooth patterns and elaborate designs around eyes.

The chief Elema works of art are the basketry and bark-cloth masks associated with two ceremonial cycles, cults of bush and sea spirits. The bush spirits, *kovave* and other names, are represented by conical masks in which are embroidered and painted designs, with ears and beak-like mouths attached. The sea spirit, *hevehe* or *semese*, masks are lenticular panels up to twenty feet high; these too have added abstract designs, said to depict plants and other natural objects, and stylized features. This cycle also uses conical masks, *eharo*, surmounted by models of totemic creatures and mythological characters, some comic. The western Elema also have a colossal zoomorphic mask of unknown significance.

Woodcarving is confined among the Elema to a relatively few oval boards, *hohao*, on which stylized human figures are carved in relief. These boards are often bordered with chevron designs. The same stylization of the figure is occasionally carved on a block which is then roughly silhouetted to approximate a figure in the round. Elaborate stylized human faces are also carved on small V-shaped sling shields.

The Purari delta and Urama Island people have dome-shaped basketry masks with long protruding jaws, and small flat oval bark-cloth masks painted with axial spiral designs. The Urama make basketry masks with small round heads on immensely long necks. The Purari and Era River people also have huge basketry animals with gaping jaws, *kaiamunu*. These are their most sacred objects and figure largely in initiations.

Both Purari and Urama carve oval ancestral boards, *gope*, in great numbers. These have central reliefs of human faces. Those of the Purari almost invariably, and those of the Urama often, have chevron-band borders; the Urama boards as often have tight vertical designs of half-spirals. To the east the designs of boards from Wapo Creek consist of a characteristic heart-shaped face surmounting a series of disconnected pattern units. Both in the Era River and Wapo Creek areas there are large numbers of small silhouetted human figures of wood or bark made to stand on pig or crocodile skulls kept as trophies. A few large human figures are made in the Purari. As with the Elema, bark belts are intricately incised with the usual designs; and some combs are carved and incised. Drums are carved with gaping fish-like jaws with incised designs around them.

The Kerewa culture-area between the Bamu and Kikori Rivers is said to have been strongly influenced by the Kiwai but is much richer in art styles. Masks are of basketry, dome-shaped with elongated straight or looped noses. The commonest carvings are, again, the ancestral boards; a few are as much as nine feet long. The reliefs on them show full-length figures with disproportionately large heads, two such figures surmounted, or heads only. Silhouette half-length figures, *agibe*, have vertical projections between the arms and torsos to which human skulls are attached.

Large figures are known from the Bamu and Turama Rivers, a few being of colossal size. They were exhibited in initiation ceremonies in conjunction with large carvings of mythological animals and birds. As with the Wapo and Purari people, naturally deformed pieces of wood and bamboo were adapted as fantastic figures of men and animals and also for head-rests. Drums, of

17

18

19

20

Fig 17. Canoe prow, Massim area, probably Woodlark Island (121.9 cm. high).
Fig 18. Helmet mask of painted bark-cloth, cane, raffia; Gulf of Papua (95.9 cm. high).
Fig 19. Painted wooden ancestral board, *gope*; Gulf of Papua (128.9 cm. high).
Fig 20. Painted wooden board, Gulf of Papua (141.9 cm. high).

the Purari delta type, had longer jaws and similar engraving.

The Gogodara of the Aramia River have a style markedly unlike any other in the Gulf area. Its most prominent feature is the clan insignia, complex asymmetrical abstract designs, applied to most decorated objects. The most important of these are canoes and full-scale canoe models used in initiation, the carved prows showing crocodiles with heads protruding from their jaws. These have the insignia painted on the sides. Some house-beams have carvings similar to those of the canoes. Most other carvings are in very light wood. They include human figures with the insignia painted on their torsos. Tear-shaped or circular plaques of light wood are painted with the insignia, sometimes have small carved heads attached to the lower part, and are tied on conical woven hats. Drums, of exceptional size, have completely carved surfaces. Among the Gogodara the red, black, and white range of colour usual in the Gulf is extended with a variety of ochres and browns. Many objects are embellished with mother-of-pearl discs, *Abrus* seeds, and trophies of cut and shaped feathers.

The Kiwai Islanders, at the extreme west of the Gulf area, carve little beyond small silhouette figures used as pendants, and canoe splash-boards with reliefs showing curiously dispersed human features. Human figures are sometimes carved on house-posts, and small heads terminate digging sticks and paddles. A group of large, naturalistic male and female figures comes from the north bank of the Fly estuary, some with faces in the style of Torres Strait masks. Drums are engraved; combs have openwork designs.

Early writers record a certain amount of carving in the Kiwai mainland area around Daru, especially human figures—also carved on house-posts—and turtles from Mawata, Masingle, and Bampton Island; and large carved crocodiles from Masingle. None of this work has survived. Large male and female figures were also carved on the Binaturi River in the style of that region's well-known 'man arrows', which were traded in large numbers.

The coastal people make turtle-shell masks in fish and crocodile forms for use in funeral ceremonies. Such masks are also found in the western Torres Strait.

No painting beyond a single piece of bark collected by d'Albertis is known from the Fly River north of Kiwai Island. The only carvings appear to be the elaborate openwork crests for the shafts of middle Fly stone-headed clubs. Coconut-shell rattles, carved and given long rattan noses to resemble human heads, also come from this area. Drums and arrow shafts from the Fly River and the hinterland to the east are incised with simple geometric designs.

THE ADMIRALTY ISLANDS

Wood sculpture in the Admiralties (painting only exists as house decoration on Baluan) is largely the work of the Matankol people living around the coast of Manus Island. It is widely traded through the group and even beyond and generally is secular in intent. The main theme is the human figure, often associated with crocodile heads prolonging the human image or containing this in its jaws. The sculptures are mostly carved in a block-like convention and covered with red paint. Surface decoration consists of incised narrow lines of triangular patterns or small crosses in black and white paints. Some figures represent ancestors, others are used as door jambs or tops of house ladders. They may also form the legs of large beds, the terminals of which are large open scrolls combined with crosses and stylized birds. Large cylindrical slit-gongs have abstract designs on the barrel, with a human torso projecting from one end and legs from the other. Figures are also carved on lime spatulas and handles for coconut-shell spoons, though here stylized fish and openwork abstract designs also occur. Heads with long sprays of feathers attached are used as war charms. Spear-shafts are carved with human figures. Obsidian-bladed daggers have human or crocodile heads modelled on them in *Parinari* nut paste, as do combs. Net floats are carved as fish. Canoe prows also have the usual human and animal heads or openwork abstract designs. Hemispherical bowls are made in sizes varying from small to huge. They usually have feet and handles consisting of small human figures or very large scrolls. Small bowls are made in bird and animal forms.

Lime gourds have abstract pyrographed decoration. Oil containers are made of basketry with decorated *Parinari* paste coatings. Shell work includes engraved univalve shells, worn as penis covers, and *Tridacna* plates with attached openwork turtle-shell ornament, *kapkap*.

ST MATTHIAS GROUP

Carvings from this group are generally simple in form, based on the cylinder in the case of human figures, and covered with geometrical engraved patterns. Some human figures are known. A few are used as house-posts. Silhouettes of fish are carved, as are dance staffs in simple bird form. Canoe prows represent highly stylized birds. Men wear large flat decorative combs of bound wood slips and also incised shell penis covers.

NEW IRELAND

In north-western New Ireland a range of masks and other carvings collectively called *malanggan* [q.v.] are made for initiation and funeral festivals. The main types, each including several sub-types, are masks; large wooden heads; horizontal friezes; vertical figures to be planted in the ground; and huge vertical carvings. All these may include figures of birds, animals, fish, lizards, and cosmic symbols. Large areas are carved in openwork, and the main figures may be surrounded by slender vertical rods or crossing bands or be themselves crowned with openwork crests. Many are thus necessarily constructed from independently carved units. The carvings themselves are always covered with finely detailed painting in red, yellow, or

21

22

23

Fig 21. Wooden figure, Gulf of Papua (91.4 cm. high).
Fig 22. Ancestor figure, Admiralty Islands (74 cm. high).
Fig 23. Large carved wooden bowl, Admiralty Islands.

Fig 24. Ancestor figure, *uli*; New Ireland
(139.7 cm. high).

genitals. Smaller free-standing figures are often carved on the shoulders, in front of the body, or under the feet. Huge discs of worked fibre, emblematic of the sun, are also made for ceremonies. Skulls, modelled with a lime compound, are used in rain-making magic.

In the southern part of the island small chalk figures are carved for a funerary cult. They represent standing men and women, and have a little painting of details. Wooden masks, resembling those of the off-shore islands of New Britain, show simplified human features. There are several types of canoe prows, one a vertical comb in elaborate openwork, another a simpler beak-like form; their geometric details and painted designs are stylized natural elements. Paddles are incised and painted with similar designs. House-posts are carved with full-length or half-length human figures or geometric forms.

NEW BRITAIN

The large island of New Britain includes several distinct style areas. Masks of many types figure largely in all of them. Wooden masks are not often found, though a flat type with simply delineated features occurs in the Duke of York Islands and a helmet-like type in the Vitu Islands. Elsewhere they are chiefly made of bark-cloth or pith on frames. Some masks from the Gazelle Peninsula are made from the fascia of human skulls over-modelled and painted. The best known, however, are the conical bark-cloth type of the *Dukduk* society on the coastal Gazelle Peninsula. These are painted with a simple stylized human face. The style also appears in the human figures with upraised arms that are shown on the openwork boards carried as dance wands. Similar carvings are used as outrigger ornaments for ceremonial canoes, the prows of which, imported from the Duke of York Islands, are openwork grilles of closely spaced wooden bars.

Tufa and chalk human and animal figures are carved for the *Iniet* magico-religious society.

The Baining folk of the interior make a large variety of masks in bark-cloth, part of which is painted with geometrical patterns in black, brown, and the artist's own blood. There are two important forms. One is a helmet consisting of a circular panel on which are painted circular eyes; below this is a protruding muzzle with pendant lower lip. The other is an upstanding oval form. These are combined with other forms: the face type is sometimes added to a long horizontal body, while the vertical type is combined with long tubular projections front and back or may form the head of a slim cylindrical figure, up to thirty feet high, with only rudimentary arms and legs. Another type of dance-object is a huge bark-cloth hemisphere covering several men.

The Sulka, south of the Baining, have masks of frames covered with pith coloured a bright pink. These are often conical and show small human features under bulging brows; small carved attributes are attached. Other masks are cones supporting wide discs, the undersides of which are painted in serpentine designs. A dance head-dress

black and white face-paint designs, or with personal ornaments such as feathers, where appropriate. The richness of the effect is further enhanced by feather and fibre additions and seasnail opercula to denote eyes. In addition to individual figures in this style, there are also groups of figures set in model canoes, or in conjunction with huge fish representing mythological scenes.

Lesser carvings include small hornbill heads, which are carried in the mouths of dancers, and panels from house façades. Canoe prows are carved similarly to the masks. Small musical instruments have a little relief carving.

The most important works from central New Ireland are large funerary figures, *uli*, with massive crested heads and cylindrical bodies. The limbs are short and the hands often raised. The figures also have exaggerated breasts and male

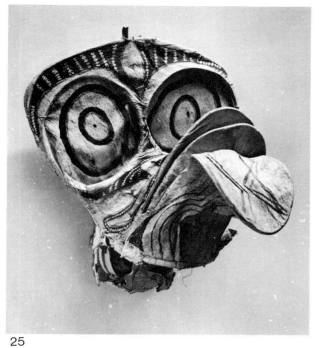

25

26

27

28

Fig 25. Bark-cloth mask (Baining), New Britain.
Fig 26. Two wooden dance figures (Sulka), New Britain (left, 107 cm. high; right, 145 cm. high).
Fig 27. Mask (Sulka), New Britain.
Fig 28. Wooden female figure, painted red, black, white; Western Solomons (121.9 cm. high).

consisting of a lanceolate painted panel is also made. The same patterns are also painted on the oval shields. Large carved canoe prows have human or animal figures surmounted by tall narrow panels. Small wooden ancestral figures are also carved.

The Vitu Islands have large conical bark-cloth masks with long triangles painted round the eyes.

The Nakanai in the middle of the island make a large variety of bark-cloth masks, ranging from simple hoods to representations of pigs and fish or huge spindle-shaped forms painted with designs similar to those of the Sulka, representing human faces. Funerary festivals include performances in which wooden carvings are manipulated for theatrical effects. Large painted bark-cloth cloaks are worn by mourners.

The shields of these coastal areas are long and narrow with cane bindings and incised stylized designs of human faces. The people of the mountainous interior make a peculiar type of shield from three parallel convex slabs joined together; the front surface is incised with registers of incised spirals.

Some wood carving is found in the Arawe Islands. It includes nearly life-size stylized human figures and extremely large elongated human heads.

The Kilenge area of Cape Gloucester is notable for several mask types, one carved and painted, others of coconut fibre over frames. A wide variety of objects is decorated with carved designs. These include adzes, shields, spears, betel mortars, pestles, drums, bullroarers, combs, coconut and gourd containers, canoes, paddles, floats, and sinkers.

Among the islands in the Vitiaz Strait posts and beams carved with human, fish, and crocodile figures are found in Rooke Island, as are canoes with decorated transverse prow boards and side planks. Masks and canoe prows from Siassi show strong influences from Tami, whence decorated bowls and other goods are frequently traded.

THE WESTERN SOLOMON ISLANDS

In Nissan small masks are made of painted palm spathe with long rectangular wooden ears. On Buka and Bougainville no face masks are made. However, at one initiation ceremony for boys, huge half-length human figures with upraised arms are worn like hoods by men impersonating spirits. At another ceremony smaller wooden figures of men, women, and birds are carried by the participants. Over-life-size figures of women are made for girls' puberty ceremonies and weddings. Like most work from the area, these are all painted black with touches of red and white. Wood or stone figures of fish are made for bonito magic.

Small flat U-shaped carvings with incised designs on the arms are made in the Telei area to be carried in dances. Long waisted dance clubs are made in Buka. The upper ends are carved in silhouette or relief with a standardized conventional figure: this is usually squatting with upraised arms and has a large face with a huge peaked coiffure. The figure is also carved on paddle blades, the side planks of canoes, and the sides of slit-gongs.

Few other objects are much decorated. Small coconut graters have some engraved designs, as do coconut-shell or bamboo lime containers. Large bulb-shaped hats of palm-leaf, worn by adolescent boys, are painted in red with decorative designs.

OUTLYING ISLANDS

The Western Islands of the Manus District and Nukumanu, east of Buka Island, several hundred miles away, are stylistically similar. They are the source of wooden standing human figures which vary in size from two feet to as much as sixteen feet in height. Such figures are distinguished by extreme simplicity, and the square section of the limbs. The triangular faces have combs placed transversely or laterally on the tops of the heads in Nukumanu, and square-cut beards in Kaniet Island. The Kaniet style moreover is elaborated with close notching along the edges in smaller carvings—handles of bowls, ceremonial adzes with human heads, combs, men's openwork carrying baskets—and the large openwork scrolls used as canoe prows in the Hermit group to the southwest. Lime spatulas with fine elaborate openwork scrolls are made in Kaniet.

WEST IRIAN

With a few, though spectacular, exceptions the cultures of West Irian are less productive of important sculpture or painting than those of Papua and New Guinea.

West of the Trans-Fly area live the Marind Anim groups, between the Merauke and Digul Rivers. Large numbers of objects are painted or engraved with concentric rectangles or ·opposed spirals. They include clubs, bullroarers, paddles, ceremonial staves, dwarf coconut-shell lime containers, charms, and decorative bark panels. Some canoes have similar designs along the sides, with prows carved in simple geometric forms. Ceremonial clubs have stone heads and the shaft terminates in a flat blade which is sometimes engraved and sometimes carved in openwork. The exceptionally large hand-drums have low-relief spiral designs. Large painted forked poles are used as skull racks or commemorative images. Posts of feast houses are carved in low relief with human and animal figures. A few simple bark face-masks are made.

The most important objects of the Marind Anim are enormous costumes, perhaps the most elaborate in all New Guinea. The wearers impersonated mythical heroes. The decorations include, among many other elements, quantities of figures of human beings, birds, reptiles, animals, fish, and crustaceans, as well as abstract emblems. Carved in light wood, they are often life-size. They are decorated with yellow paint and covered in dark blue, scarlet, and grey seeds.

North of the Digul River is the Mappi area, where there are large shields carved with angular

29

30

31

32

Fig 29. Commemorative poles (Asmat), West Irian.
Fig 30. Seated female figure (Asmat), West Irian (69.9 cm. high).
Fig 31. Painted wooden canoe prow, Geelvink Bay, West Irian (95.3 cm. high).
Fig 32. Wooden double figure from house-post, Lake Sentani, West Irian (70.5 cm. high).

geometric designs; spears with openwork panels below the points; and small openwork canoe prows. The styles are marginal to those of the area north and west, the Asmat country.

The Asmat are among the most prolific wood-carvers of New Guinea. Weapons include large numbers of shields with relief designs. Paddles have elaborately carved blades; the ends of the shafts, like the panels on spears, are often in openwork, or consist of human figures. The undersides of bowls and paint dishes, sago pounders, cylindrical head-rests, and bamboo horns are often completely covered with relief designs. Drums have both relief carving and large openwork handles running almost their full length. Canoe prows are adorned with elaborate openwork head-hunting symbols and human figures. Some independent standing or squatting figures of ancestors are made, but the most important carvings relate to funeral, head-hunting and initiation ceremonial; they are both complex and of colossal size. They include long pole-like carvings of crocodiles, with small human figures on their snouts, and the bodies entirely covered with low relief designs; long abstract openwork carvings combined with human heads and genitals; and heavy cylinders with human heads at either end. Model canoes with elaborate prows and holding figures of human beings and spirits reach a length of thirty feet. Commemorative poles, often twenty feet high, take the form of symbolic canoes with fantastically elaborated prows that include groups of human figures, the topmost one supporting a wing-shaped projection in openwork. Ceremonial house-posts take the same form.

Masks are simple basketry cones or netted hoods with attached wooden eye pieces. Bone is used for daggers and openwork nose ornaments.

Asmat carving of human figures in the round is naturalistic. Relief carving consists of highly stylized human figures or parts of the body, flying foxes, praying mantises, and various head-hunting symbols outlined in parallel ridges. Painting is confined to the decoration of carvings in red, black, and white.

The repertoire of sculpture from the Mimika area further along the coast resembles that of the Asmat. Drums, paddles, bowls, clubs, and head-rests are covered with relief designs, as are shield-like ceremonial objects. The designs, however, are in single, not parallel, ridges and tend to be based on groups of large intersecting arcs enclosing smaller geometric designs. They are occasionally in openwork, as are large canoe prows in the same style. Some large flat figures of cassowaries are made, and large standing ancestral figures in the round. Commemorative posts are similar to the poles of the Asmat but lack the symbolic canoe at the lower part. Like those of the Asmat, too, masks are woven, conical or hood-like with wooden eye pieces.

The Geelvink Bay area, on the north-west of the island, is best known for the style embodied in small figures, *korvar*, used by shamans—combination of square-cut figures with a wealth of tight openwork scrolls. The *korvar* themselves show squatting or standing human figures, often with the heads hollowed to accommodate ancestral skulls. These hold openwork scroll panels or intertwined snakes. The same configuration is used in miniature on small amulets. A few masks are made with the same face-style. Small human figures combined with scrolls are also used in head-rests. Canoe-prow ornaments have heads with panels of openwork scrolls. Drums, doors, and bamboo lime tubes are decorated with scroll designs. The area has several sub-styles, and the rare figures from the McCluer Gulf should be included in the same general style area.

The people of the Sarmi Coast, between Geelvink Bay and Humboldt Bay, produce several types of small canoe-prow ornaments, including simple naturalistic figures of birds and groups of conventionalized human heads.

Humboldt Bay, and Lake Sentani inland from it, have similar styles and a similar repertoire of objects, though those of Sentani are both more accomplished in execution and wider in range. Humboldt Bay sculpture is more block-like in its forms, with considerable crude painting in red, black, and white. Much of the sculpture of the area is essentially architectural. The pyramidal ceremonial houses have finials of human figures in wood (Humboldt Bay) or tree fern (Sentani). Poles projecting from the roof end in pig, fish, and bird figures. The posts of the houses of important men are carved with human figures and crocodiles, lizards in openwork, and the double spiral pattern characteristic of the area. Posts supporting floors or jetties also have their upper parts carved as human figures.

Smaller human figures are also carved as the prongs of suspension hooks, the handles of knives, the terminals of staffs, and on head-rests. Wooden bowls have stylized relief designs representing birds and reptiles. The double spirals and other patterns are found on many small utilitarian objects, such as coconut and gourd lime containers, mallets, bone daggers and spoons, bamboo tobacco containers, small drums, bamboo flutes, paddle blades, and large wooden hand-drums. Bark-cloth cloaks, worn by women or used as grave ornaments, are painted in two styles, one with variations on the double spiral, the other with free compositions of fish, flying foxes, lizards, birds, and vegetation. These paintings are also made in a coarser style in the villages of the Seko coast.

Spherical pottery bowls are made in Humboldt Bay, painted with bold designs representing totemic animals and fish.

THE TORRES STRAIT

The islanders of Torres Strait produced no painting but considerable carving and extraordinary works constructed from plates of turtle-shell.

No large-scale wood sculpture now exists, though carved house-posts and grave-posts are recorded. Canoes, traded from the Fly River delta, were refitted with carved decorations. A variety of small wood carvings included human figures, male and female, for garden magic; female figures for sexual magic; and very naturalistic fish, turtles, and dugongs for fishing magic. Wooden masks from the northern islands are in the elongated facial style of the Fly River area, with long noses and stretched pierced ear holes.

Turtle-shell masks, the most striking works of the area, are made in the western and eastern islands. Those of the west include face masks almost flat in section, bordered with openwork designs; figures of large fish, worn horizontally; and composites of crocodile heads with fish bodies, human faces and animal heads, and human heads surmounted by birds. These are often engraved with geometric designs and have feather trim and attached shells. The masks from the east are generally modelled to fit around the face and have beards of human hair.

Some large human figures were also made of turtle-shell; and there are records of huge figures of crocodiles, hammerhead sharks, and crabs in the same material.

Small stone figures were used as rain-making charms; other large stone carvings represent human figures and heads and fish skulls.

Minor wood carving includes two types of hand-drums of hour-glass and fish-mouth form; and dance staffs with superposed faces in relief. Stone tops are painted with designs representing dancers and masks. Bamboo smoking pipes are engraved with abstract and representational designs.

MAJOR COLLECTIONS OF NEW GUINEA ART

England

British Museum, London: collections made by Franks (Torres Strait, New Ireland); Malinowski (Trobriand Islands); Moyne (Sepik, Gulf of Papua); Cook Daniels (Gulf of Papua); Cranstone (Western Highlands).

University Museum of Archaeology and Ethnology, Cambridge: collections made by Haddon (Torres Strait, Gulf of Papua); Bateson (middle Sepik); Landtman (Kiwai).

France

Musée de l'Homme, Paris: collection made by *La Korrigane* expedition (Sepik); now partly dispersed by sale.

Germany

Museum für Völkerkunde, Berlin: collection made by Behrmann expedition (Sepik).

Museum für Völkerkunde, Frankfurt-am-Main: collection made by E. Haberland (Sepik).

Rautenstrauch-Joest Museum, Cologne: collections made by Schmitz (Markham area); Huon Gulf.

Museum für Völkerkunde und Vorgeschichte, Hamburg: collection made by Reche (Sepik).

Finland

National Museum, Helsingfors: collection made by Landtman (Kiwai).

Italy

Museo Pigorini, Rome: collection made by d'Albertis (Fly River); Trobriand Islands.

Museo Lateranensis, Rome: missionary collections (Sepik).

Hungary

Ethnographisches Museum, Budapest: collections made by Biró, Fenichel (Astrolabe Bay, Huon Gulf).

Netherlands

Instituut voor de Tropen, Amsterdam: West Irian; collections made by P. Wirz (Sepik, Gulf of Papua).

Museum voor Land- en Volkenkunde, Rotterdam: West Irian; collections made by Groenevelt (Sepik, Trobriand Islands).

Rijksmuseum voor Volkenkunde, Leyden: West Irian.

Switzerland

Museum für Völkerkunde, Basel: collections made by Bühler, Forge, Schuster, Speiser, D. Wirz (Sepik); P. Wirz (Gulf of Papua); New Ireland; Solomon Islands.

United States

Field Museum, Chicago: collections made by Lewis (Gulf of Papua, Trobriand Islands, Huon Gulf, Sepik, New Ireland, New Britain, Solomon Islands).

American Museum of Natural History, New York: collections made by Mead (Sepik, Admiralty Islands).

Museum of Primitive Art, New York: New Guinea in general; collection made by Rockefeller (Asmat).

Museum of Science, Buffalo: collections made by Black (Gulf of Papua, Massim).

University Museum, Philadelphia: Sepik.

Australia and Territory of Papua and New Guinea

Australian Museum, Sydney: collections made by Hurley (Gulf of Papua); Wauchope and Miles (Sepik); Solomon Islands; Admiralty Islands; New Britain; New Ireland.

Queensland Museum, Brisbane: collection made by MacGregor (Gulf of Papua, Torres Strait, Massim).

National Museum of Victoria, Melbourne: Robert Mond (Malinowski) collection (Massim —mainly Trobriand Islands); other material from the following areas: Sepik River, Huon Gulf and Markham Valley, Collingwood Bay, Gulf of Papua, New Britain, New Ireland.

Papua and New Guinea Public Museum and Art Gallery, Port Moresby: Papua-New Guinea in general, New Britain, New Ireland.

T. P. van Baaren, *Korwars and Korwar Style*. The Hague, 1968.

W. Behrmann, 'Die Versammlungshäuser (Kulthäuser) am Sepik in Neuguinea', *Erde*, vol. 2, 1950-1.

T. Bodrogi, 'Some Notes on the Ethnography of New Guinea', *Acta Ethnographica*, vol. 3, 1953.

——— 'New Guinean Style Provinces: the Style Province "Astrolabe Bay"', in *Opuscula ethnologica memoriae Ludovici Biró sacra*. Budapest, 1959.

——— *Art in North-east New Guinea*. Budapest, 1961.

A. Bühler, *Kunststile am Sepik*. Basel, Museum für Völkerkunde, 1960.

——— and others, *Oceania and Australia: The Art of the South Seas*. London, 1962.

B. Craig, 'The Houseboards of the Telefomin Sub-District, New Guinea', *Man*, new series, vol. 2, 1967.

H. Damm, 'Ethnographische Materialien aus dem Küstengebiet der Gazelle-Halbinsel (Neubrittanien)', *Jahrbuch des Museums für Völkerkunde zu Leipzig*, vol. 16, 1957.

W. H. Davenport, 'Sculpture of the Eastern Solomons', *Expedition*, vol. 10, 1967-8.

R. W. Firth, *Art and Life in New Guinea*. London, 1936.

J. A. W. Forge, 'Art and Environment in the Sepik', *Proceedings of the Royal Anthropological Institute*, 1965.

——— 'The Abelam Artist', in *Social Organization*. London, 1967.

D. Fraser, *Torres Straits Sculpture*. New York, 1959.

——— (ed.), *Early Chinese Art and the Pacific Basin*. New York, 1968.

A. A. Gerbrands, 'Kunststijlen in West Nieuw Guinea', *Indonesië*, vol. 4, 1950-1.

——— *Wow-Ipits: Eight Asmat Woodcarvers of New Guinea* (trans. from Dutch). The Hague, 1967.

——— (ed.), *The Asmat of New Guinea: The Journal of Michael Clark Rockefeller*. New York, 1967.

E. H. Giglioli, 'Note on a Singular Mask from Boissy Island, N. E. New Guinea', *Internationales Archiv für Ethnographie*, vol. 1, 1888.

E. Haberland, 'Zum Problem der "Hakenfiguren" der südlichen Sepik-Region in Neuguinea', *Paideuma*, vol. 10, 1964.

A. C. Haddon, *The Decorative Art of British New Guinea: A Study in Papuan Ethnography*. Royal Irish Academy, Cunningham Memoir no. 10. Dublin, 1894.

R. Heine-Geldern, 'L'art prébouddhique de la Chine et de l'Asie du sud-est et son influence en Océanie', *Revue des Arts asiatiques*, vol. 11, 1937.

J. Hoogerbrugge, 'Sentani-meer, mythe en ornament', *Kultuurpatronen*, vol. 9, 1967.

H. Kelm, *Kunst vom Sepik*. Berlin, 1966.

G. Koch, *Kultur der Abelam*. Berlin, 1968.

S. Kooijman, *The Art of Lake Sentani*. New York, 1959.

——— 'The Art Areas of Western New Guinea', in *Three Regions of Primitive Art*. New York, Museum of Primitive Art, 1961.

A. Krämer, *Die Malanggane von Tombara*. Munich, 1925.

H. Nevermann, *St. Matthias-Gruppe*. Hamburg, 1933.

——— *Admiralitäts-Inseln*. Hamburg, 1934.

D. Newton, *Art Styles of the Papuan Gulf*. New York, 1961.

K. T. Preuss, 'Künstlerische Darstellungen aus Kaiser-Wilhelms-Land in ihrer Bedeutung für die Ethnologie', *Zeitschrift für Ethnologie*, vols 29-30, 1897-8.

O. Reche, *Der Kaiserin-Augusta-Fluss*. Hamburg, 1913.

R. Schefold, *Versuch einer Stilanalyse der Aufhängehaken vom mittleren Sepik in Neu-Guinea*. Basel, 1966.

E. W. Schmidt, 'Die Schildtypen vom Kaiserin-Augusta-Fluss und eine Kritik der Deutung ihrer Gesichtsornamente', *Baessler-Archiv*, vol. 13, 1929.

C. A. Schmitz, *Wantoat*. The Hague, 1963.

F. Speiser, 'Uber Kunststile in Melanesien', *Zeitschrift für Ethnologie*, vol. 68, 1936.

F. E. Williams, *Drama of Orokolo*. Oxford, 1940.

ACKNOWLEDGMENTS

Figures by courtesy of: American Museum of Natural History, New York, no. 1; Museum für Völkerkunde, Basel, nos 2-3, 14, 22-23, 26, 28; Raymond Wielgus Collection, Chicago, nos 4-5, 21, 24, 30; Museum of Primitive Art, New York, nos 6, 10, 12-13, 16, 18-20, 29, 31-32; University Museum, Philadelphia, nos 7, 9; Collection of Mr Jay Leff, Uniontown, Pa., no. 8; Cleveland Museum of Art, no. 11; Ethnographic Museum, Budapest, no. 15; British Museum, London, no. 17; Field Museum of Natural History, Chicago, nos 25, 27.   D. NEWTON

(*See also* HANDICRAFTS INDUSTRY; MATERIAL CULTURE; MUSIC)

ASMAT. People of south-east West Irian. References:

A. A. Gerbrands (ed.), *The Asmat of New Guinea: The Journal of Michael Clark Rockefeller*. New York, 1967.

G. Zegwaard, 'Vrouwenruil bij de Asmatters', *Tijdschrift Nieuw Guinea*, vol. 15, 1954-5.

——— and J. H. M. C. Boelaars, 'De sociale structuur van de Asmat-stam', *Adatrechtbundels*, vol. 45, 1955.

AUSTRALIAN SCHOOL OF PACIFIC ADMINISTRATION (ASOPA). Sections 66 to 70 of the Papua and New Guinea Act 1949-70 provide for the establishment of an institution of this name to 'provide special courses for the education of officers and prospective officers of the Territory and of such other persons as are prescribed'. Its existence marks the official recognition after World War II that European skills need to be supplemented by special studies before expatriates can function effectively in a basically non-European environment. The subjects have varied over the years, but have essentially been the history, environment, contemporary institutions, policies, and developmental problems of the Territory. In recent years it has been accepted that indigenous officers can also benefit from such special studies at the school.

BEFORE WORLD WAR II

Initially Europeans in both Papua and New Guinea were trained on the job; this, because of the frequent staff shortages, all too often meant learning by doing. In his *Experiences of a New Guinea Resident Magistrate*, C. A. W. Monckton reveals (perhaps not always intentionally) the limitations of this approach for the training of resident magistrates in British New Guinea before World War I. In the last years of their rule the German authorities recognized this problem and established a number of courses for officials, planters, wives and others proposing to live in the German tropical colonies, including New Guinea. None, however, had time to demonstrate unequivocally before 1914 that 'theoretical' training could enhance efficiency in the field.

Advances in anthropology and the general discussion concerning mandated territories and 'trusteeship' in general, resulted in the establishment of a Chair of Anthropology at the University of Sydney in 1926, partly to instruct in applied anthropology cadets of the Department of District Services (cadet patrol officers) in the Mandated Territory of New Guinea. Commonwealth support was given, and between 1926 and 1940 some sixty cadets, after a probationary period in the field of twenty-one months, spent two terms at Sydney University. Lectures in anthropology, tropical medicine, criminal law, economic geography and mapping were not specifically designed for their needs, but specialized tutorials were provided and instruction on other relevant matters, such as recent developments in wireless, was sometimes given. Although no similar course was provided for officers of the Papuan service, individuals occasionally 'sat in' during their long leave. In general, however, Sir Hubert Murray defended the principle of on-the-job training. Nevertheless, his administration was one of the first to employ a government anthropologist.

AFTER WORLD WAR II

The war stimulated consideration of the problems posed by tropical territories; it also caused establishment of a military administration in both Territories. In 1945 the Army established the Land Headquarters School of Civil Affairs at Duntroon, Canberra, for the training of Angau [q.v.] personnel and in the same year the Australian Pacific Territories Research Council was established to explore, among other things, 'the research needs' of the two Territories. By the end of 1947, the school had been renamed, moved to Mosman, Sydney, taken over the functions of the Research Council, and a 'permanent' need for it had been recognized in principle by Cabinet by the statutory provisions of the Papua and New Guinea Act 1949-70.

PROBLEMS AND ACHIEVEMENTS

The working of the school has been affected by the disorganization of the war and the rate of change since. In particular, staff shortages in the field and the uneven flow of recruits made it difficult to establish any systematic training for personnel of the District Administration as a whole. Nevertheless, certain principles have been consistently pursued, namely that

(1) all official personnel should receive a general orientation course;
(2) patrol officers should receive an extended period of academic training after an initial period of field service before being appointed to positions of individual responsibility;
(3) some form of refresher course should exist for senior officers; and
(4) to this end, staff should engage in both teaching and research.

Above all, the results produced have been generally beneficial and have vindicated the case for specialized training of a 'theoretical' and 'applied-theoretical' kind. Acceptance of this has resulted in a proliferation of other institutions engaged in related activities, however; so that ASOPA today is one of several institutions and bodies pursuing this general objective. The emergence of the South Pacific Commission [q.v.], the Australian National University, the New Guinea Research Unit [q.v.], and the University of Papua and New Guinea [q.v.] have all reduced the significance of ASOPA as a research institution, although staff members have continued to research and have published their findings. Similarly, other journals have now replaced the school's *Monthly Notes*, later *South Pacific*. The need to localize the public service at a faster rate than was initially envisaged has meant that local officers have to date received much of their formal training at Territory institutions such as the Assistant Patrol Officers' School, Finschhafen; the Local Government Training Centre, Vunadidir; and the Administrative College [q.v.], Port Moresby. As indigenous officers have accumulated field experience and increasingly been recruited at higher levels of secondary education, training of a university type at ASOPA has presented fewer practical difficulties. Thus, since 1969, indigenous officers have predominated in the three-month course on local government practice and the same situation may soon occur in the more advanced local government course.

The existence of these courses on local government reflects the changed situation within the Territory and the fact that since 1963 expatriate patrol officers have been recruited on a six-year contract, rather than on a career basis, and no longer undergo a uniform course for patrol officers as such. Expatriate cadets now undergo an extended initial course of three to four months and such further studies, e.g. in local government, as seem warranted. Clearly this is not always satisfactory, but training needs must be weighed against staffing needs.

This problem of unfilled positions and rapid turnover within the Territory Administration, coupled with the rate and scope of change, has affected the proposed schemes for refresher courses for senior officers, which were conceived as a sabbatical break from daily pressures. The most striking success in this field was achieved between 1956 and 1963, when very senior officers, including departmental heads and District commissioners, from most departments were engaged in a series of 'workshop' sessions over several weeks, culminating in a report and recommendations on a single theme. These senior officers' courses considered the following problems: native economic development (1956); development of native local government (1957); education (1958); labour (1959); urbanization and urban problems (1960); community development (1961); and indigenous economic development and its relationship to social and political change (1963). Background papers were presented by the ASOPA staff, some of the senior officers and other specialists. There is little doubt that the courses were valuable. Once again, however, other institutions and bodies have subsequently held similar activities and some senior officers as well as ASOPA staff have participated in a series of seminars, wide-ranging or particular, organized by the Association for Cultural Freedom, the Council for New Guinea Affairs, the International Commission of Jurists, the New Guinea Research Unit, the Papua and New Guinea Society, and the University of Papua and New Guinea, as well as the Australian and New Zealand Association for the Advancement of Science.

OTHER ACTIVITIES

The primary concern of ASOPA has been with field administration in Papua New Guinea, and subsequently with local government, but two other areas have been of considerable importance.

The shortage of adequately trained teachers, headmasters and supervisors led in 1954 to the inauguration of a scheme for cadet education officers. From the first, it was recognized that such officers would require specialized training such as ASOPA gives, and various attempts were made to divide their training between ASOPA and teachers' colleges in N.S.W. From 1959 to 1966, the entire training for primary teacher trainees and from 1965 of junior secondary trainees in arts and science has been conducted at the school. Courses have also been provided for graduate cadets doing the University of Sydney Diploma of Education.

Secondly, as an Australian institution, and because the Department of Territories was at the time also responsible for the Northern Territory of Australia, increasing commitments have developed in the general field of Aboriginal affairs. In 1957 a one-year course for Northern Territory patrol officers began, which in 1970 was extended to an eighteen-month course for Aboriginal welfare officers, including officers from South Australia. Similarly in 1960, courses were organized to provide for the special needs of Northern Territory teachers-in-training.

These other major commitments have continued the existence of ASOPA and facilitated its continued involvement in and concern with the developmental problems of Papua New Guinea.

PRINCIPALS OF THE LAND HEADQUARTERS SCHOOL OF CIVIL AFFAIRS AND ASOPA

The officers who have directed the school from time to time are as follows: Lieutenant-Colonel J. K. Murray [q.v.], who was Chief Instructor of the Land Headquarters School of Civil Affairs from April to September 1945; and Lieutenant-Colonel (now Mr Justice) J. R. Kerr, who was Principal of ASOPA from April 1946 to August 1948. Principals thereafter have been A. A. Conlon [q.v.] (August 1948 to September 1949), C. D. Rowley (November 1950 to March 1964), and J. R. Mattes (March 1964-   ).   IAN GROSART

AWAR. People of the Madang District. References:
G. Höltker, 'Die Nubia-Awar an der Hansa-Bucht in Nordost-Neuguinea', Leipzig, Museum für Völkerkunde, *Jahrbuch*, vol. 20, 1964.
J. Schebesta, 'Ein paar erste Notizen über die Awarken in Neuguinea', *Anthropos*, vols 35-6, 1940-1.

AYOM. People of the Schrader Mountains. References:
M. Gusinde, 'A Pygmy Group Newly Discovered in New Guinea', *Anthropological Quarterly*, vol. 30, 1957.
———— 'Die Ayom-Pygmäen auf Neu-Guinea. Ein Forschungsbericht', *Anthropos*, vol. 53, 1958.
———— 'Somatological Investigation of the Pygmies in the Schrader Mountains of New Guinea', American Philosophical Society, *Yearbook 1957*, 1958.
———— 'Die heutigen Menschenrassen niedrigster Körperhöhe in biogenetischer Sicht', *Homo: Internationale Zeitschrift für die vergleichende Forschung am Menschen*, vol. 2, Supplement, 1959.
———— 'Somatology of the Ayom Pygmies of New Guinea', American Philosophical Society, *Proceedings*, vol. 105, 1961.

B

BAGITA, Alumu (1896-   ), policeman, was born at Mapamoiwa village near Samarai, Milne Bay District, in 1896. He was employed by Burns, Philp & Company in Samarai for four years from 1912. In 1916 he joined the police force, attaining the rank of sergeant after six years' service. For forty years he served in Port Moresby as a member of the Criminal Investigations Branch, in which position he earned a respected place in the community. He retired in 1966 after fifty years' service—the longest service rendered by a member of the Royal Papua and New Guinea Constabulary. During his police career he was awarded the British Empire Medal, the Australia Service Medal, and the Police Long Service and Good Conduct Medal besides several other awards. In retirement he is living in Port Moresby.

BAILMENT. This is the legal term to describe the act of delivery of goods or chattels for use—or some other agreed purpose—by the person to whom delivery is made. The person making the delivery is called the 'bailor', the recipient the 'bailee'. The delivery is made on a condition, express or implied, that the goods shall be restored by the bailee to the bailor, or that the bailee shall deliver them to some designated person after the purpose has been fulfilled.

The essence of bailment is to be found in the common law, its main principles being introduced to Papua by the Courts and Laws Adopting Ordinance 1889-1951 of Papua and to New Guinea by the Laws Repeal and Adopting Ordinance 1921 of New Guinea. The relevant provisions of these enactments adopt the rules of common law and equity 'for the time being' in force in England for Papua, and those in force in England on 9 May 1921-52 for New Guinea; though, in both instances, only so far as those rules are applicable to local circumstances.

At common law, the bailee is placed under a duty of care in respect of the goods. The nature of this duty may be fixed by the contract. If not, it will be implied from the character of the bailment. Where the contract can be presumed to be for the benefit of the bailor alone, e.g. in the 'bare' bailment where goods are delivered to the bailee to keep for the bailor's use, the bailee is liable only for his gross negligence.

A higher duty of care is required of the bailee where the bailment is for both his and the bailor's benefit, e.g. where goods are pawned or delivered as security for a loan or hired to the bailee. Here the bailee is bound to use reasonable care. Sometimes goods are lent gratis purely for the convenience and benefit of the bailee. In this case, he is bound to use the strictest care and diligence.

Transactions akin to bailment are known and practised among Papuans and New Guineans. Commonly the parties intend them to be governed by local usage. Where this is so, and where the usage meets the definition of 'native custom' (section 4 of the Native Customs (Recognition) Ordinance 1963), the courts are required to take the custom into account. This will be done where the parties intended that the transaction should be, or where justice requires it should be, regulated wholly or partly by native custom 'and not by law'. Account will also be taken of custom in relation to the reasonableness or otherwise of an act, default or omission by a person, or in relation to the existence of a state of mind of a person.

Elsewhere the Ordinance states plainly that the courts will not recognize or enforce a custom where to do so would not be in the public interest or where the custom is inconsistent with legislation in force in the Territory. One likely area of conflict between enacted law and custom is that of the sale by bailees of goods accepted by them for repair or other treatment but which, usually because of non-payment for their services, are not re-delivered to the bailor. This and similar situations are now regulated by the Unclaimed Goods Ordinance 1966. The bailee's right to sell is made subject to his observance of certain requirements of time and notice. Other important provisions deal with the recording and disposal of the proceeds of sale and detail the circumstances under which a buyer may acquire a good title. Special conditions are made applicable to the sale of motor vehicles.

The common law—so far as its rules are held to apply to Territory circumstances—creates exceptions to the general rule that bailees for reward are only liable for ordinary negligence. The 'common carrier', who holds himself out as willing to convey the goods of any person willing to pay him for the service, is strictly liable for any loss or damage to them. Hotel-keepers, as persons prepared to receive and entertain travellers, become insurers against loss of any goods entrusted to their care by guests. The extent of liability in either case may be varied by special agreement.

In a few instances, notably those of the carriage of goods by sea and carriage of baggage by air, the responsibilities, liabilities, rights and immunities of the bailees are defined by Commonwealth or Territory legislation.

Provisions aimed at safeguarding the welfare of native parties in certain commercial dealings, including 'job contracts', are contained in the Transactions with Natives Ordinance 1958-63.

COMMONWEALTH OF AUSTRALIA LEGISLATION
Civil Aviation (Carriers' Liability) Act 1959-66.

TERRITORY OF PAPUA AND NEW GUINEA LEGISLATION
Goods Ordinance 1951.
Hire-purchase Ordinance 1966.
Instruments Ordinances 1953.
Liquor (Licensing) Ordinance 1963-66.
Native Customs (Recognition) Ordinance 1963-69.
Pawnbrokers Ordinance 1951.
Sea-Carriage of Goods Ordinance 1951.
Transactions with Natives Ordinance 1958-63.
Unclaimed Goods Ordinance 1966.

TERRITORY OF PAPUA LEGISLATION
Courts and Laws Adopting Ordinance 1889-1951.

TERRITORY OF NEW GUINEA LEGISLATION
Laws Repeal and Adopting Ordinance 1921-52.

BAINING. People of the interior of the Gazelle Peninsula, New Britain. References:
G. Bateson, 'Further Notes on a Snake Dance of the Baining', *Oceania*, vol. 2, 1931-2.
J. Poole, 'Still Further Notes on a Snake Dance of the Baining', *Oceania*, vol. 13, 1942-3.
W. J. Read, 'A Snake Dance of the Baining', *Oceania*, vol. 2, 1931-2.

BANARO. People of the south-eastern Sepik. References:
R. C. Thurnwald, *Bánaro Society*. Memoirs of the American Anthropological Association, vol. 3. Lancaster, Pa., 1916.
———— 'Die Gemeinde der Banaro', *Zeitschrift für vergleichende Rechtswissenschaft*, vol. 38, 1920.

BANKERS' COLLEGE. The Papua and New Guinea Bankers' College represents the combined approach by the Australian banks to the training and education of indigenous bank staff in the Territory.

The administration of the College is through an Inter-Bank Committee on Staff Training in Papua and New Guinea which is comprised of executive officers of the following: Australia and New Zealand Bank Limited; Bank of New South Wales; Commonwealth Banking Corporation; National Bank of Australasia Limited; Papua and New Guinea Development Bank; and the Reserve Bank of Australia.

In 1966 the Inter-Bank Committee commissioned a research officer to investigate and report on the feasibility of the establishment of further education and training facilities. The research officer's report and recommendation provided, in broad outline, the basis on which the College is now operating. The first course to be conducted by the Bankers' College was held in Port Moresby in August 1965.

The main aims of the College are to give indigenous bank officers the opportunity to extend their general knowledge, particularly in regard to aspects and procedures of banking and to develop their competence in English. At the same time, it seeks to encourage interest in current affairs as well as to develop successful social and personal attitudes.

The long-term objective is to develop a well-trained cadre of Papuan and New Guinean bank officers and to provide an educational basis which will enable the more promising officers to embark upon advanced studies.

A three-level programme has been devised. Level 1 is the Elementary Banking Certificate, Level 2 the Advanced Banking Certificate and Level 3 the Basic Supervisory Certificate. The Level 1 syllabus requires the trainee to first attend a three-week residential induction course, at the conclusion of which he commences the Elementary Banking Certificate course. Syllabuses are constructed to provide the background necessary to bank staff as they progress through the various stages of their early careers in banking.

Since 1965, several residential induction courses have been held in Port Moresby with trainees coming from various centres in the Territory. The first students to enrol for the Elementary Banking Certificate course commenced their studies in May 1968.   JOHN WICKS

BANKING. With one exception, the banking system in Papua and New Guinea is an extension of the Australian system. The banks operating in the Territory are branches of Australian banks, responsible to head offices in Australia. The exception is the Papua and New Guinea Development Bank which has its head office in Port Moresby, was established under Territory legislation, and operates solely within the Territory (*see* Development Banking).

Banking is the most important part of any country's financial system. It is the pivot on which the processes of savings mobilization and of credit extension and creation revolve. In Papua and New Guinea the banking system developed initially to meet the needs of the expatriate planters and traders who formed the bulk of banks' customers. As the Territory's economy has become gradually more complex, and as Papuans and New Guineans have increased their role in the monetized sector of the economy, banks have tended to widen their horizons. They have taken increasing notice of the specific needs of the Territory and of its indigenous people. The commercial banks in the Territory have also joined forces with the central bank in a programme of financial education and in the training of Papuans and New Guineans as bank officers (*see* BANKERS' COLLEGE).

PRIOR TO 1942

Banking facilities were first provided in Papua when the Bank of New South Wales opened a branch in Port Moresby in May 1910 and one at

Samarai six weeks later. The only other bank in Papua prior to 1944 was a branch of the Union Bank of Australia Limited in Port Moresby from October 1910 to May 1916.

In German New Guinea, before World War I, banking facilities were provided by German trading firms which also handled the shipment and sale of produce. Upon Australian military occupation of New Guinea in 1914 the military administration set up its own bank to facilitate transactions by the troops and the civilian populace. Accounts were operable by cheque, and a savings bank section was opened. German currency remained legal tender and an issue of paper currency denominated in marks was printed by the military administration.

In April 1916, at the request of the Australian government, the Commonwealth Bank of Australia established a branch at Rabaul and took over the whole of the business of the 'Administration Bank' including its one thousand savings bank accounts. By proclamation, the Commonwealth Bank was given sole right to carry on banking business in New Guinea, and it began redeeming the German currency in circulation and replacing it with Australian notes and coin. To limit the demand for currency, Australian troops were paid by deposits to a savings bank account and savings bank agencies were opened at centres where troops were quartered.

The Commonwealth Bank started two more branches in New Guinea before World War II: Kavieng in May 1921—it closed in 1924; and Lae in December 1941—it closed six weeks later due to the arrival of Japanese forces.

In 1926 the Commonwealth Bank's monopoly in New Guinea ended with the arrival of the Bank of New South Wales which opened six branches in the following fifteen years. Its Lae branch, opened in November 1941, had only one month's longer initial life than the Commonwealth's.

In January 1942 all banks in both territories were closed owing to the Japanese invasion, and the bulk of the staff and records were evacuated.

POST-WAR

In October 1944, while Papua and New Guinea were still under army administration, the Commonwealth Bank of Australia opened a branch in Port Moresby. This was that bank's first branch in Papua. The Bank of New South Wales started reopening its branches in 1946 and, until 1953, these two were the only banks operating in the Territory. However, the Australia and New Zealand Bank Limited opened its first branch there in 1953, and The National Bank of Australasia Limited in 1957. Both have since opened more branches and agencies.

Following the transfer of the central banking functions of the Commonwealth Bank of Australia to the newly created Reserve Bank of Australia, a branch of the Reserve Bank was established at Port Moresby on 18 August 1960 (*see* Central Banking).

In July 1967 the Territory's first 'national' bank was formed when the Papua and New Guinea Development Bank was opened for business in Port Moresby (*see* Development Banking).

There is now an integrated banking system providing the following services:

Trading banking
Savings banking
Development banking
Central banking.

These are provided through a network, at 31 December 1969, of thirty-four branches and over five hundred agencies throughout the country. In addition, sub-banking facilities are provided at village level by over two hundred savings and loan societies.

LEGISLATION

Australian banking legislation extends to Papua and New Guinea and regulates operations there. The Reserve Bank Act 1959-66 establishes the functions and responsibilities of the Reserve Bank of Australia (*see* Central Banking); the Banking Act 1959-67 establishes the conditions under which banking business may be conducted and makes provision for the protection of bank depositors, supervision and control of credit by the Reserve Bank, mobilization of gold and foreign currency, and supervision of savings banks; and the Commonwealth Banks Act 1959-68 deals with the activities of the Commonwealth Banking Corporation and its constituent banks. In addition, the Papua and New Guinea Development Bank Ordinance 1965-68 of the Territory covers the operations of the Papua and New Guinea Development Bank which is also subject to the Banking Act 1959-67 of the Commonwealth.

Much of the business of banks relating to cheques, bills of exchange and promissory notes is conducted within the legal framework of the Bills of Exchange Ordinance 1951 of the Territory.

TRADING BANKING

Four trading banks operate in Papua and New Guinea:

Australia and New Zealand Bank Limited
Bank of New South Wales
Commonwealth Trading Bank of Australia
The National Bank of Australasia Limited.

These provide the normal services of trading banks: accept deposits, provide cheque facilities, make advances, give assistance in overseas trading and travel, provide safe custody facilities.

The main business of trading banks is the acceptance of deposits and the making of advances. There are two forms of deposits: deposits on current account, and fixed deposits, usually termed interest-bearing deposits. A deposit on current account is repayable on demand, usually by the customer presenting a cheque or cheques, or other bills of exchange, up to the amount on deposit. Current accounts offer a convenient means of receiving or making payments without the need to handle actual cash. Banks do not normally pay interest on current accounts, and they charge a fee for maintaining such accounts and for providing the associated services. Fixed deposits are lodged with a bank for a pre-elected period of three, six, twelve or twenty-four months, and interest is paid depending on the term. Fixed deposits have been a feature of importance in the Territory during recent years.

MAJOR TRADING BANKS—DEPOSITS

$ million

	Bearing Interest		Not Bearing Interest		Total
	Govern-ment	Other	Govern-ment	Other	
1961	0.014	4.832	0.462	9.082	14.390
1963	—	5.738	0.694	10.002	16.434
1965	—	11.312	0.930	12.538	24.780
1967	—	14.392	1.224	16.631	32.247
1968	—	15.318	1.428	19.313	36.058
1969	—	14.316	1.721	22.474	38.511

The trading banks do not maintain separate figures for deposits by Papuans and New Guineans but it is clear that the number of current accounts has been increasing significantly in recent years. This trend has been given impetus by the practice of the Papua and New Guinea Administration and some other employers of paying salaries directly to employees' bank accounts, and by the growing number of Papuans and New Guineans engaged in commercial activities.

Loans made by trading banks are mostly by overdraft. Under this system the bank sets a maximum limit up to which the borrower may draw; and interest is charged on the amount actually outstanding at the close of each day's business. Overdrafts technically are repayable on demand, but common practice is for the bank and its customer to agree upon a term within which the debt will be cleared. Terms are normally of short duration.

Trading banks are essentially short-term lenders, concentrating on providing finance for working expenses and preferring to leave capital provision of a longer-term nature to other financial institutions. Since April 1962, however, special

arrangements have existed to enable trading banks to develop new longer-term forms of lending. Under these arrangements, banks in Australia and in Papua and New Guinea can make fixed-term loans for capital expenditure for production in the rural, industrial and, to a lesser extent, the commercial fields, and to finance exports. Terms range from three to eight years or sometimes a little longer. Specific funds have been allocated for these term loans in Term Loan Fund Accounts established in the name of each trading bank with the Reserve Bank of Australia. These accounts are funded partly from the liquid assets of the banks and partly from each bank's Statutory Reserve Deposit Account with the Reserve Bank.

In April 1966 Farm Development Loan Fund Accounts were also established on a basis similar to that of the Term Loan Fund Accounts. From them, banks are enabled to make loans to rural producers, particularly small producers, for fixed terms up to fifteen years. Longer terms are possible in special cases.

Rates of interest for trading bank fixed deposits and advances in Papua and New Guinea are generally similar to those operating in Australia.

SAVINGS BANKING

Savings banks are simpler institutions with a more limited range of functions than trading banks. They exist primarily to encourage people to save money; they provide safe-keeping for savings and easy access to them; and they pay depositors interest on their savings. A savings bank is not concerned with commercial banking transactions nor with large firms. It provides cheque facilities to a very limited group of customers; all others operate with a passbook which must be presented each time money is deposited or withdrawn.

All four trading banks operating in Papua and New Guinea have affiliated savings banks:

Australia and New Zealand Savings Bank Limited
Bank of New South Wales Savings Bank Limited
The Commonwealth Savings Bank of Australia
The National Bank Savings Bank Limited.

These operate through a network of branches in the major towns. In addition, savings bank agen-

MAJOR TRADING BANKS—CLASSIFICATION OF ADVANCES*

At second Wednesday in July; $ million

	Agriculture, Dairying and Grazing	Manufacturing	Transport, Communication and Storage	Finance, Building Con-struction and Commerce	Other	Total
1961	2.14	0.21	0.28	2.01	1.13	5.75
1963	1.93	0.28	0.34	3.55	1.08	7.20
1965	2.07	0.56	0.47	4.71	1.84	9.65
1967	3.53	0.73	1.10	8.59	4.63	18.58
1968	3.98	1.47	1.41	9.58	6.70	23.14
1969	3.53	1.08	1.81	11.58	8.52	26.52

* By Territory branches, including term and farm development loans.

cies are conducted by the Territory Administration at sub-treasury offices throughout the country, by plantation owners or managers, by missions and by other private persons and traders. Savings bank agencies are also conducted at schools, some being organized by bank staff, some by teachers, and some by pupils themselves under supervision. At 30 June 1969 there were 86,693 school savings accounts operative with total balances of $404,482.

Savings bank deposits have grown significantly in recent years. At June 1969 there were 365,000 operative accounts conducted by Territory branches, with balances of $37.2 million. Of these, 325,000 were in the names of Papuans and New Guineans, almost 90 per cent of the total; their balances aggregated $14.9 million, approximately 40 per cent of the total.

SAVINGS BANKS ACCOUNTS

30 June	Operative Accounts	Balances $ million
1961	90,000	12.7
1963	125,000	16.1
1965	193,000	21.7
1967	286,000	29.8
1968	325,000	32.9
1969	365,000	37.2

All savings banks pay similar rates of interest on savings, calculated on the minimum monthly balance.

As savings banks in Papua and New Guinea are branches of Australian institutions, investment of their funds is handled mainly by their head offices. In terms of the regulations under the Banking Act 1959-67 savings banks are restricted in the types of investments they may make. In the Territory savings banks invest in securities issued by the Administration, and at the end of December 1969 their total investments in these securities were about $16 million. In addition, sums are advanced for housing to private home builders, to the Housing Commission, and to other organizations. Loans are also made to Local Government Councils.

DEVELOPMENT BANKING

Development banks, like trading banks, make loans to customers, and some also accept deposits; but they differ from trading banks in a number of ways. Usually, development banks are established to undertake the kinds of loans which might be desirable for the development of a country but which have features making them unsuitable for trading banks. A development bank often will make loans for longer periods or involving greater risk than would normally be acceptable to a trading bank. It is interested primarily in the developmental effects of the loan rather than in the security offered by the borrower.

In many countries, including Australia and Papua and New Guinea, governments have established development banks to provide finance

for ventures not well suited to traditional lenders and to provide a means of channelling government funds to nationally desirable enterprises. Until 1967 these functions were shared in the Territory by the Native Loans Board, the Ex-Servicemen's Credit Board and the Commonwealth Development Bank of Australia.

The Papua and New Guinea Development Bank was established under the Papua and New Guinea Development Bank Ordinance 1965, and commenced business on 6 July 1967. It is the only Territory-owned bank and its creation aroused considerable interest and enthusiasm among the Papuan and New Guinean people. The bank's formation followed a strong recommendation by the 1963 Mission from the International Bank for Reconstruction and Development. In its report, the Mission recommended 'that a Territory Development Finance Company should be organised to provide credit for the development program in amounts and on terms and conditions which meet the requirements of the Territory. The finance company could be organised as a private institution or as a government bank'. In the event, the Australian government chose the latter alternative.

The bank's main purpose is to stimulate development of the private sector by providing credit for primary production and for the establishment or development of industrial or commercial undertakings, particularly small undertakings. Finance may be made available for productive purposes only, by way of direct loan, hire purchase, guarantee of overdrafts, purchase of debentures, or by equity participation in enterprises. The bank also provides advice and assistance to promote the efficient organization and conduct of primary production or of industrial or commercial undertakings. To this end, it is gradually building up a staff of specialists including agricultural advisers and cost accountants.

The bank is empowered to carry on a wide range of banking business, including the acceptance of deposits from the public. However, it has not yet used these general powers.

To finance its activities the Papua and New Guinea Development Bank receives capital allocations through the Territory budget. By the end of 1969, $9 million had been provided in this way. Additional funds will be available from the absorption of the Native Loans Fund and Ex-Servicemen's Credit Fund. The bank also has power to borrow funds or to issue debentures or other securities.

The bank has its head office at Port Moresby, and it uses commercial bank branches and Administration officers throughout the Territory as agents for the acceptance of loan applications.

To 30 June 1969 the bank had approved loans totalling $7.7 million. In addition it had invested $1.6 million as equity in six local companies. These figures exclude loans taken over from the Ex-Servicemen's Credit Board and the Native Loans Board.

The Commonwealth Development Bank of Australia, a member bank of the Commonwealth

PAPUA AND NEW GUINEA DEVELOPMENT BANK—
TOTAL APPROVALS
To 30 June 1969

Classification	Number	Amount $000
Indigenes	961	1,500.8
Multi-Racial and Mixed Race	23	758.1
Non-Indigenes	233	5,439.2
Total Loans	1,217	7,698.1
Investments	6	1,622.5
Total Finance Approved	1,223	9,320.6

Of total approvals, $3.6 million was for commercial purposes, $3.0 million for rural, and $2.6 million for industrial.

Banking Corporation, also operates in Papua and New Guinea. It was the model on which the Papua and New Guinea Development Bank was based, and in most respects their functions, duties and responsibilities are similar. The 1963 Mission from the International Bank for Reconstruction and Development recommended that 'the Commonwealth Development Bank should discontinue its activities in the Territory when the new finance company [i.e. the Papua and New Guinea Development Bank] is established'. Since 1968, the Commonwealth Development Bank has undertaken no new lending operations in the Territory and its outstanding loans have been gradually reducing.

CENTRAL BANKING

Central banking, or the supervision and regulation of the monetary and credit system, is an accepted fact in most countries of the world. Central banks vary in form and in operating procedures, but there are certain basic features common to most. A central, or reserve, bank issues and distributes a country's legal currency, particularly the note issue, as required by the community; it acts as banker to the government, to other banks, and in some cases to other financial institutions, serving them in much the same way as a trading bank serves its customers; and it seeks to regulate the use of credit so that it contributes effectively to development and to the maintenance of reasonable stability within the economy as a whole.

Australia's central bank is the Reserve Bank of Australia, known before 1960 as the Commonwealth Bank of Australia. Under the Reserve Bank Act 1959-66, the Bank is required to exercise its powers in such a manner as will contribute to 'the economic prosperity and welfare of the people of Australia'. As Australia in this context includes the territories of Australia, the Reserve Bank has a responsibility also to the people of those territories, most of whom are in Papua and New Guinea.

Central banking functions and techniques are fairly clearly understood in developed economies. In Papua and New Guinea, however, the financial system is in a very early stage of development. The proportion of the people who do not form part of the monetized sector of the community is substantial, and many problems remain in the transition from subsistence to the money economy. Consequently, central banking must be viewed rather differently in Papua and New Guinea from Australia even though the one institution is responsible for both areas. For instance, lending policies which might be applied in the Territory would take specific account of Territory needs and conditions; new bank lending is not restricted by any general limitations of lending policy current in Australia.

The prime task of the central bank in Papua and New Guinea is to guide the development of a financial system suited to the needs of the country and its people. In particular, it has a responsibility to bring the indigenous people into financial institutions, from the grass-roots level to the more sophisticated levels of the financial system.

The Reserve Bank, through its Papua and New Guinea Division, is directing its main activities along several lines. It performs the normal banking functions of a central bank. It acts as banker to the commercial banks, to the Papua and New Guinea Administration, and to Commonwealth government departments in the Territory; it assists the Administration in floating domestic loan issues, manages the Inscribed Stock Registry on behalf of the Administration, and provides safe custody facilities for the public for government securities; it provides note issue and coin distribution facilities, undertakes economic research and periodically publishes statistics relevant to the Territory economy; and its Rural Credits Department provides seasonal finance to assist in the marketing of some primary products, notably copra and coffee.

The successful functioning of a financial system rests on its acceptance by the people it serves and their understanding of it. In association with the commercial banks the Reserve Bank conducts a campaign to improve the level of financial awareness in the community. The aims are to educate people in the significance of money and the operations of a money economy, to establish the connection between work, money and expenditure, and to clarify the concept of credit and the mutual responsibilities of borrowers and lenders.

The Bank has sought to widen the experience of Papuans and New Guineans in financial matters, and to provide better grass-roots facilities for saving and borrowing, by accepting responsibility for fostering savings and loan societies.

To assist in its consideration of Territory problems, the Reserve Bank has established an Advisory Committee on Central Banking in Papua and New Guinea. The Committee comprises a group of permanent residents, the majority being Papuans and New Guineans, which meets regularly with members of the Bank and the Territory Treasury to discuss local banking and financial matters.

Commonwealth of Australia, *Annual Reports, Territory of Papua*. Canberra.
—— *Report to the League of Nations on the Ter-*

ritory of New Guinea 1921-2 to *1939-40*. Melbourne and Canberra.
Commonwealth Bank of Australia in the Second World War, comp. by C. L. Mobbs, pp. 225-7, 298-304. Sydney, 1947.
H. C. Coombs, 'Pennies and Politics: A Reserve Bank in New Guinea', *New Guinea*, vol. 1, 1965-7.
C. C. Faulkner, *The Commonwealth Bank of Australia*, pp. 220-31. Sydney, 1923.
—— *Report to the United Nations on the Territory of New Guinea 1946-7*. Canberra.
R. R. Hirst and R. H. Wallace (eds), *Studies in the Australian Capital Market*. Melbourne, 1964.
R. F. Holder, 'Australia: Papua-New Guinea', in *Commonwealth Banking Systems*, ed. W. F. Crick. Oxford, 1965.
International Bank for Reconstruction and Development, *The Economic Development of the Territory of Papua and New Guinea*. Baltimore, 1965.
M. J. Phillips, 'Money and Banking in Papua and New Guinea', paper to Royal Institute of Public Administration. Port Moresby, 1963.
—— 'Unsatisfactory Trash—Monetary Transition in Papua and New Guinea', paper to Papua and New Guinea Society of Victoria. Melbourne, 1969 (roneoed).
Reserve Bank of Australia, *Report and Financial Statements*. Sydney (annual).
—— 'Statistics relating to the Territory of Papua and New Guinea', Supplement to the *Statistical Bulletin*. Sydney.
C. D. Rowley, *The Australians in German New Guinea 1914-1921*, pp. 47-65. Melbourne, 1958.
O. H. K. Spate, C. S. Belshaw and T. W. Swan, *Some Problems of Development in New Guinea*. Report of a Working Committee of the Australian National University. Canberra, 1953 (roneoed).
V. D. Stace, *The Pacific Islander and Modern Commerce*, South Pacific Commission, Technical Paper no. 54. Noumea, 1954.
J. R. Thomas and D. Ryan, *Report of a Survey on the Use of Money and of the Need for Credit by the Indigenous People of the Territory of Papua and New Guinea*. Commonwealth Bank of Australia, Sydney, 1959 (roneoed).
M. J. P.

(*See also* CURRENCY; FINANCIAL INSTITUTIONS)

BANKS, Charles Arthur, Col. the Hon. (1885-1961), company director, was born in New Zealand in 1885, of English parents, and was educated at Thames College, Auckland. He qualified as a mining engineer at the Thames School of Mines, but his career was interrupted by World War I, during which he served with the Royal Engineers in France. In 1916 he married Jean (Bunty), daughter of the Comte de Montalk.

In 1926 Banks was representing British gold-mining interests in Vancouver, Canada, when he met an Australian lawyer, William Addison Freeman, who had interests in Malayan tin mining. Together they formed Placer Development Limited, registered in Vancouver, with the object of examining and acquiring rights to alluvial mineral deposits anywhere in the world. From the outset the plan was to float separate operating companies, should prospects prove favourable, while retaining control in the hands of Placer directors.

By 1928 Placer had unsuccessfully tested several sites in North and South America. At this critical point in the company's fortunes Freeman heard that Guinea Gold of Adelaide had options to promising alluvial deposits in the Bulolo Valley, New Guinea. Placer quickly secured the rights to the area, though it lay some eighty miles inland over mountainous terrain and no road to the coast existed.

Test drilling by Placer in 1929 indicated a total recoverable gold content of £4 million, but extraction depended on the use of two large dredges. This seemed impossible when, in the same year, the government of the Mandated Territory was unable to raise sufficient funds to build a road. Banks refused to be discouraged and rallied the company by pointing to the possibilities of air transport (*see* CIVIL AVIATION).

He made detailed cost projections, based on the capacity of the new tri-motored Junkers G31 aircraft; these showed that, with the machines broken down into sections of suitable size, the venture was practicable. Accordingly, in 1930 Bulolo Gold Dredging Limited was floated as an operating company, with Banks as Managing Director; one third of the initial share issue was reserved for the Australian market.

Results at Bulolo during the 1930s exceeded all predictions, largely because of Banks' drive and organizing ability. Reserves of auriferous alluvium proved much greater than the original examination had revealed, so that by 1941 eight large dredges were in operation. These, together with equipment for three hydro-electric power stations and materials for an entire township, were flown in from Lae without a single mishap. In 1938 Banks was awarded the gold medal of the Mining and Metallurgical Society of America in recognition of this achievement; he also received an honorary doctorate from the Colorado State School of Mines.

Banks guided the reconstruction of the township and dredges at Bulolo after World War II; but gold production was dwindling, and diversification was necessary to utilize the company's assets. In 1952 the Australian government and B.G.D. in partnership formed Commonwealth New Guinea Timbers Limited, to manufacture high-grade plywood in the Bulolo valley; this has proved a very successful enterprise (*see* PLYWOOD INDUSTRY).

Banks also had a distinguished official career. During World War II he represented the Canadian Department of Munitions and Supply in London, in recognition of which he was awarded the C.M.G. in 1946. He served as Lieutenant-Governor of British Columbia from 1946 to 1950. At the time of his death in 1961 he was president of Placer Development Limited and of several subsidiary companies.
A. M. HEALY

(*See also* GOLDFIELDS)

BARNES, Hon. Charles Edward, cabinet minister. Mr Barnes is a member of the Australian Country Party and has held the Queensland seat of McPherson in the Commonwealth Parliament since 1958. He became Minister for Territories in 1963, and Minister for External Territories in 1968.

BARTON, Francis Rickman (1865-1947), soldier and administrator, was born at Fundenhall, Norfolk, England, on 4 January 1865, son of the Rev. Gerard Barton, described in the birth certificate as farmer, and his wife Elizabeth, née Hazard. He was educated at Norwich Grammar School and later in Germany. After three years' farming in the United States he entered Sandhurst from where he was posted to the West India Regiment as second lieutenant on 16 March 1889. On 1 November 1890 he became a lieutenant and on 23 May 1893 was appointed A.D.C. to the governor of Barbados. After promotion to captain on 1 October 1897 he arrived in British New Guinea in 1899 as private secretary to the new Lieutenant-Governor, G. R. (later Sir George) Le Hunte [q.v.]. From 13 November 1901 to 31 October 1903 he was commandant of the Armed Native Constabulary, and from 1 February 1902 to 16 June 1904 Resident Magistrate of the Central Division.

While on leave in Australia in 1904 he secured provisional appointment as Administrator of British New Guinea largely through the influence of Le Hunte, now governor of South Australia. Barton's rapid rise to eminence coupled with the suicide of the acting Administrator, C. S. Robinson [q.v.], a few days after his assumption of office made him many enemies and his term of office was marked by internecine feuds which almost wrecked the government. A Royal Commission appointed at Barton's own request investigated the state of the government late in 1906 and although little credence was given to allegations that he was dominated by Ballantine, the treasurer, his removal was recommended mainly on the ground that he had been guilty of gross favouritism in administering the public service. He was, however, given due credit for his protection of native rights.

Barton returned to London where, on 12 May 1908, he married Santa Carla, then aged sixteen, daughter of Alfred Tofft, a composer. Not long afterwards he was appointed finance member of the colonial government of Zanzibar and eventually first minister. In 1913 when the government of Zanzibar was reorganized, he retired and from then on lived quietly in England. During his retirement he published a translation of a Danish ornithological work and a book on nickel coinage. He died at Lustleigh in Devonshire on 4 October 1947.

Although Barton's administration was conspicuously unsuccessful the fault was not entirely his own. The protracted transfer of the Territory from British to Australian government caused all sorts of uncertainties and hesitations which made administration difficult. A stronger man might have been able to overcome these handicaps but Barton was the wrong man at the wrong time.

J. GIBBNEY

(See also BRITISH NEW GUINEA)

BATS. Most species of mammals of the New Guinea region are active only at night. However, even the casual observer living in the coastal towns soon becomes aware of the regular late afternoon flights of flying foxes or giant fruit bats as they leave their 'camps' on their nightly search for fruiting trees. Small bats often enter houses or are seen around street lamps in their pursuit of insects.

The Chiroptera or hand-winged mammals are divided into two suborders, the Megachiroptera which includes the fruit-, blossom-, and nectar-feeding bats, and the Microchiroptera. The latter group includes bats that are specialized to prey primarily on insects; however, there are species, although not in the New Guinea region, that eat fish, some that suck blood, others that have become fruit-eaters, and there are even species that prey upon other bats.

The New Guinea region is about midway along the great arc of islands stretching south-eastward into the Pacific Ocean from the Asian continent. Where the term 'New Guinea' is used without any qualification such as 'region' it means only the main island. The history of bats is a very ancient one, and their populating of the Indonesian islands and finally the Australian-New Guinean area has no doubt extended over millions of years. In the tropics most species have sedentary habits. It is therefore very likely that great natural disturbances such as violent cyclones have played a large part in the populating of new islands. Some species of flying foxes are known to wander, following the blossoming and fruiting seasons of certain trees in the equatorial forests. Actually very little is known about this search for food in the New Guinea region by the large fruit bats.

Because of the distance of New Guinea from the mainland of Asia one would not expect to find as large a bat fauna here as on the continent or on the large islands closer to the mainland. Surprisingly, a comparison with the bats from Borneo discloses the fact that, although New Guinea has only five families compared to Borneo's seven and twenty-four genera compared to twenty-nine, there are sixty-five species in New Guinea and sixty-four in Borneo. These five families are also found in Asia. Another family, the Megadermatidae, has evidently by-passed New Guinea, and is present in Australia. A second family, the Mystacinidae, is found only in New Zealand; the single genus may have been derived from either the Vespertilionidae or the Molossidae in Australia. When the bats of the Bismarck Archipelago and Buka and Bougainville of the Solomon Islands are added to the New Guinea list we have a total of twenty-seven genera and seventy-six species.

The family Pteropodidae includes not only the large flying foxes, one species of which, *Pteropus neohibernicus*, has a wing-spread of five and a half feet, but also a number of genera of long-tongued, nectar-feeding bats. With one known exception members of this family orient visually in the dark; the genus *Rousettus* also uses a form of acoustic orientation. Its flight is guided partly by the broadcast of sound waves and the interpretation of the resulting echoes from obstacles in its path, and partly by visual means (*Rousettus* has good, functional eyes). Even so, members of this genus have

A black flying fox, *Dobsonia moluccensis*, roosting under palm frond.

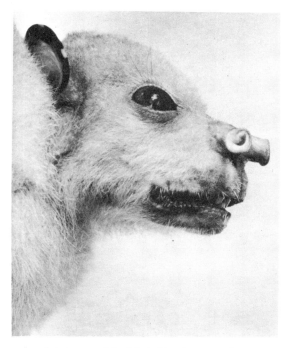

A tube-nosed fruit bat, *Nyctimene major*.

been caught in fine nylon nets strung near fruiting trees. This bat is frequently found in caves. Several species of *Pteropus* are netted by natives for food; a large *Pteropus neohibernicus* may weigh over three pounds and the meat is good eating. *Pteropus* usually roosts during the day-time in congregations or camps ranging from a few dozen individuals to many thousands. Late in the afternoon the camps break up and their members scatter throughout the rain forest to fruiting or flowering trees. Some *Pteropus* travel many miles to their favourite feeding grounds. *Pteropus* usually feeds in the canopy of the forest, while *Dobsonia*, the black flying fox which has the marked ability to hover, often feeds on the fruits of smaller trees beneath the interlaced branches of the canopy. *Dobsonia* often roosts in the dimly lit outer chambers of caves, and will even roost in rock crevices and hollow trees.

Until a few years ago, when collectors began using Japanese mist nets, nectar-feeding bats were considered uncommon. *Syconycteris* is now known to be one of the most common bats in New Guinea. This small (length of head and body, three inches) bat ranges from rain forest into the mossy forests of the higher mountains, and no doubt plays an important role in the cross-pollination of many plants. *Macroglossus*, a close relative, is found only in rain forest. Two other genera of small fruit bats, *Nyctimene* and *Paranyctimene*, are found throughout the lowland rain forests and oak forests of the lower mountains; *Paranyctimene* becomes more common with increasing elevation. In these bats the nostrils are set at the end of small tube-like facial outgrowths. The wing membranes and ears are covered with small yellowish-white spots. During the day these tube-nosed bats roost in trees, where they are very difficult to detect among the leaves.

The four families of Microchiroptera or little bats of the New Guinea region do not include any species with peculiar eating habits, they are all insect-eaters. Vampire bats are confined to the Americas, and no fish or bat-eating species have yet been found.

All of the bats of this suborder so far investigated orient in the dark by means of echo-location. Bats using this method send out short bursts of high-frequency sound waves; these waves, when reflected back to the bat from a solid object, are interpreted as obstacle or food. One has only to stand in complete darkness in the narrow passage of a cave which bats frequent to realize the efficiency of this method of orientation. Hundreds of bats swish past, but only rarely does a wing tip brush one's head or body. Bats are even known to locate prey on a leaf or branch.

Many of these small bats may be found during the day roosting in the limestone caves that are common along the long coastline. Other bats roost in hollow trees, under bark, or among the leaves of fan palms, to name but a few of the many hiding places. At dusk, when the swifts are going to roost, some species of bats emerge from their day-time roosts, and begin scouring the forests and the skies for their insect prey. But other bats wait until after dark before beginning their evening

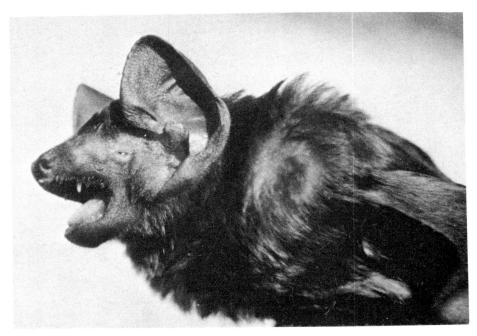

A rare insectivorous bat, *Philetor rohui.*

feeding. After many years of collecting, the basic bat fauna of the region is fairly well known, but there are always surprises when dealing with such secretive mammals. Mammal collectors hunt at night using powerful head lamps. At such times they see multitudes of bats in the forest but are able to secure relatively few of them. Occasionally collectors have accidental help. One expedition member found a small bat impaled on a spike of a lawyer cane vine; this was only the second record of this species in New Guinea. Another time a young boy noticed a tiny bat roosting in a crevice of the roof of his hut; this was the first record of *Murina* on the mainland. Other surprises are no doubt in store for students of the bats of this forested island.

Members of the family Emballonuridae can be recognized easily by the short tail that protrudes from the top of the membrane joining the hind legs. Some of these so-called sheath-tailed bats forage actively in the tree tops, others prefer open forest and clearings, and still others hunt along the coast. The bats in the family Molossidae have tails that project beyond the posterior margin of the interfemoral membrane. These free-tailed bats are rapid flyers, and usually patrol the air above the forest canopy for insects. The molossids usually roost in hollow trees.

Bats of the family Rhinolophidae are very common. All of these small bats have peculiar outgrowths on the face called nose leaves. They vary from species to species; some are relatively simple in structure, others are fantastically shaped. These nose leaves may have a great deal to do with the sending and receiving, in conjunction with the ears, of supersonic signals, but the details of this highly efficient and sensitive mechanism are still being investigated. It is known, for example, that in the genus *Hipposideros* the sounds are emitted through the nostrils, and that the bat can beam the signals in a narrow arc while in flight. Many other species that orient acoustically lack nose leaves.

The family Vespertilionidae has more species in the New Guinea region than any other except the family of fruit- and nectar-feeding bats. Superficially many of these small bats look very similar, and even the interested layman will have trouble distinguishing these simple-nosed bats. Less is known about the distribution and habits of the members of this family than of the other families of bats. It is therefore very important for residents to preserve in alcohol or formalin any small bat that is accidentally killed or brought to them. Museums are always anxious to receive such specimens. In these bats the long tail is completely contained in the large interfemoral membrane. Some species can extend this membrane below the body and literally scoop insects out of the air. Some collectors have used trout flies on a casting line to catch these bats; in many cases the bat was hooked by this membrane. Scientists have learned that bats have specific territories, that some hunt periodically during the night, others have maternity wards, and that bats harbour peculiar winged and wingless flies as ectoparasites. But in spite of all that is known there is still a great deal more to be learned about even the most common of New Guinea bats.

G. M. Allen, *Bats*. Cambridge, Mass., 1940.

K. Andersen, *Catalogue of the Chiroptera in the Collection of the British Museum*, vol. 1, Megachiroptera. British Museum (Natural History), 2nd ed., London, 1912.

T. D. Carter, J. E. Hill and G. H. H. Tate, *Mammals of the Pacific World*. New York, 1945.

D. R. Griffin, *Listening in the Dark: The Acoustic Orientation of Bats and Men*. New Haven, 1958.

K. F. Koopman and E. L. Cockrum, 'Bats', in *Recent Mammals of the World*, ed. S. Anderson and J. K. Jones, Jr. New York, 1967.

G. S. Miller, Jr, 'The Families and Genera of Bats', *United States National Museum*, *Bulletin* no. 57, 1907.

A. Novick, 'Orientation in Paleotropical Bats. II. Megachiroptera', *Journal of Experimental Zoology*, vol. 137, 1958.

R. F. Peterson, *Silently, By Night*. New York, 1964.

G. H. H. Tate, 'Results of the Archbold Expeditions: Nos. 23-4, 36-8, 46', *American Museum Novitates*, no. 1035-6, 1140-2, 1204, 1939-42; 'No. 35, 39-40, 47-8', *Bulletin of the American Museum of Natural History*, vol. 78, 80, 1941-2.

H. M. Van Deusen and R. F. Peterson, 'Chiroptera of New Guinea', *Natural History*, vol. 67, 1958.

E. P. Walker, *Mammals of the World*, vol. 1. Baltimore, 1964.

HOBART M. VAN DEUSEN

BECCARI, Odoardo (1843-1920), naturalist and explorer, was born at Florence on 16 November 1843 and died there on 25 October 1920. In contrast with d'Albertis [q.v.] he was a professional scientist, studying at the Universities of Pisa and Bologna and at Kew Gardens, London, and his sojourns in New Guinea were part of a much wider pattern of travel and research. He had visited Borneo in 1865-7 and Abyssinia in 1870 before spending seven months in New Guinea, mostly on the Vogelkop, with d'Albertis in 1872. He travelled in the Indonesian islands of Ambon, Kai, Aru, Celebes and Java, before returning to New Guinea. Between January and July 1875 he explored the Vogelkop and Geelvink Bay area, and from November 1875 to March

Odoardo Beccari, 1879.

1876, commissioned by the Dutch authorities, he explored the north coast as far as Humboldt Bay in the man-of-war *Soerabaia*.

Beccari's monuments are his bird of paradise collection in the Museum at Genoa, the breadth of observation in his writings, his discovery of the largest flower in the world (*Amorphophallus titanum*) in Sumatra in 1878, and his theory of the origin of species. He rejected the evolutionary theory of 'natural selection through chance variations' advanced by Darwin and Wallace. Rather, arguing from the apparent stability of species he observed in Borneo and elsewhere, he maintained they had developed from the response of organisms to their environment during a 'Plasmative Epoch'. By this he meant a time before hereditary characteristics had become sufficiently dominant in them to limit adaptability.

O. Beccari, *Wanderings in the Great Forests of Borneo: Travels and Researches of a Naturalist in Sarawak*; trans. by E. H. Giglioli. London, 1904; —— *Nuova Guinea, Selebes e Molucche: diarii di viaggio*. Florence, 1924; —— and J. F. Rock, *A Monographic Study of the Genus Pritchardia*. Memoirs of the Bernice P. Bishop Museum, vol 8. Honolulu, 1921.

HUGH LARACY

BEETLES (Coleoptera) are numerous in species throughout the tropics, and are especially abundant in New Guinea. Where the term 'New Guinea' is used without qualification such as region it refers to the whole main island. It would be difficult to estimate the number of species of Coleoptera in New Guinea, but it might easily exceed 50,000. Most major families are represented, so there are probably far more than fifty families of beetles on the island. Beetles are among the most conspicuous and abundant of the insects, and include some of the largest species. They inhabit nearly all types of environments, although very few are parasitic. Many are associated with forests, feeding on leaves, fruit, flowers, fungi, boring in living or dead wood, stumps, roots, soil, living in streams, ponds, etc. Others are predacious, scavenging or coprophagous. The New Guinea beetles are dominantly Oriental in relationships, although a number of Australian genera are also represented. Many genera occurring in Queensland are actually centred in New Guinea and have extended into nearby areas.

The ground beetles (Carabidae) constitute a large predacious family, many species living in moss on tree trunks. The tiger beetles, also predacious as both adults and larvae, are considered a subfamily of Carabidae. They occur on banks, paths and tree trunks, but are not very numerous in New Guinea.

Water beetles, some predacious and some scavengers, belong to several families. The Dytiscidae are predacious, as are the Gyrinidae (whirly-gig beetles); the Hydrophilidae are primarily scavengers.

The rove-beetles (Staphylinidae) are predacious, but often occur in decaying plants or other decom-

posing materials. They have short wing-covers and
are active fliers. Some in the lowlands are quite
large, showy and sometimes metallic, and fly short
distances above the ground making a fair noise.
Dermestidae are scavengers living in cadavers,
birds' nests, museum specimens, hides and the
like. Ciidae live mainly in fungi and dead wood.
Coccinellidae (Fig. 1d), the lady-bird beetles, are
numerous and varied. They are mostly predators
on scale insects and their relatives, but the genus
Epilachna includes pests of potato, tomato and
related plants. The Discolomidae and Propalticidae are minute beetles of little-known habits,
often resembling coccinellids and occurring in
litter or under bark. Colydiidae (Fig. 1a) are of
diverse form and varied habits, but often occur
on or in dead wood.

Tenebrionidae (darkling beetles) vary greatly
in form, size and habit. They are often black, but
may be metallic green or purple. They are primarily scavengers in dead wood. Elateridae, the
click-beetles, jump by snapping the articulation
of pro- and meso-thorax. Some large species commonly come to lights at night, particularly in the
mountains. Their larvae are generally found in
dead wood or in roots, but some of them are predacious upon other wood-boring beetle larvae.
Buprestidae are wood-borers as larvae and generally metallic and often very beautiful as adults.
Lampyridae (fire-flies) have representatives in New
Guinea, which sometimes swarm with synchron-
ous flashing of light, particularly at low altitudes.
Their relatives, the Cantharidae (Telephoridae)
or soldier beetles and the Malachiidae, are much
more numerous in New Guinea, particularly at
higher altitudes, where the largest known species
of the family is found.

The Scarabaeidae, including Melolonthinae,

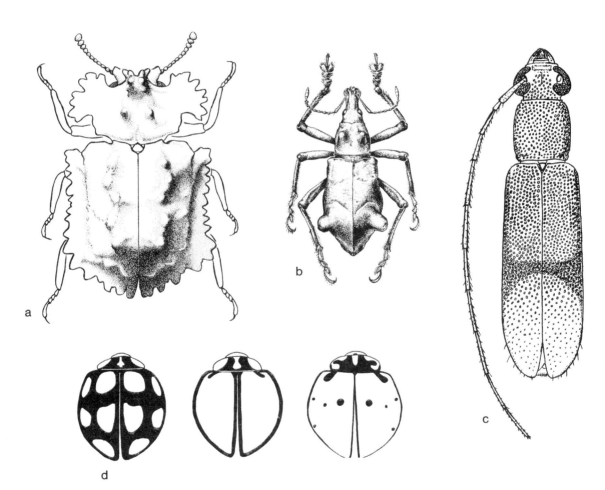

Fig 1. (a) *Dryptops phytophorus* (family Colydiidae) from north-east New Guinea, dorsum covered
with lichen growth, 10 times; (b) *Gymnopholus vetustus* (family Curculionidae) from north-
east New Guinea, 1.8 times; (c) *Tethionea cheesmanae* (family Cerambycidae) from
northern New Guinea, 14 times; (d) *Harmonia testudinaria* (left and middle) and *H. basi-
notata* (right) (family Coccinellidae) from north-east New Guinea, 4 times.

Rutelinae, Dynastinae (rhinoceros beetles), Cetoniinae and other subfamilies, are well represented. Many of the species are night-fliers, but the Cetoniinae are active day-fliers and are generally of bright metallic colours. The wing-covers of two or three species are widely used for forehead decorations by men in the Highlands. Lucanidae, the stag beetles, include some spectacular species with long mandibles in the males, but New Guinea is relatively poorer than South-east Asia in this group. The Passalidae, generally black, oblong and flattish, are as a rule grooved above and somewhat hairy, often bearing large mites on their bodies. They live in and feed on dead wood when it becomes fairly well decayed. Some of the species are quite large.

The Bruchidae (pea weevils) are poorly represented in the New Guinea region. Chrysomelidae (leaf-beetles) are extremely abundant in species and individuals and there may be 3,000 species in the New Guinea region. They feed upon nearly all types of higher plants. The larvae may feed on the surface of leaves, within leaves as miners, in crowns, stems and petiole bases, or on or in roots. The adults almost always feed on leaves, sometimes making numerous small holes (pinholes or shot-holes), or eating away parts of or the entire leaf. Most of the species are quite small, but some reach more than three-quarters of an inch in length and may be brightly coloured. Members of the subfamily Eumolpinae are usually root-feeders as larvae (Fig. 2), and feed on young leaves as adults, many of them on new cacao leaves. Members of the subfamily Hispinae feed primarily on monocotyledons, particular palms, rattans, canes, grasses and gingers. They include *Promecotheca*, a serious coconut pest, and also many common species in Pandanus.

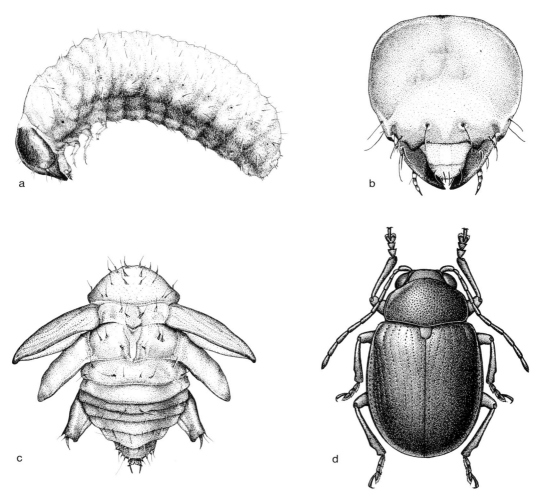

Fig 2. *Rhyparida coriacea* (family Chrysomelidae) from north-east New Guinea, about 4 times
(a) Larva, side view; (b) Larval head, front view; (c) Pupa, dorsal view; (d) Adult.

The Cerambycidae (long-horned beetles) are also extremely numerous in species, and range in size from small to extremely large. As a rule the antenna is longer than the body (Fig. 1c). One of the most spectacular species is *Batocera wallacei*, a heavy-bodied species some four inches long, blackish with a pair of long white stripes. Larvae in this family are wood-borers in living or dead trees or logs, and the adults may feed upon bark. There are probably about 2,000 species in the New Guinea region.

The Curculionidae (weevils or snout-beetles) include the largest assemblage, perhaps the largest family, of insects. They are particularly well represented in New Guinea, where they may number some 5,000 species. They vary greatly in size and appearance. They are primarily associated with forests, living in stumps, logs, stems, leaves, fruit and seeds. Some types closely resemble certain leaf-beetles, and both are mimicked by certain spiders which have relatively hard shiny black bodies. The weevils vary in size from half an inch or so to one-quarter inch in length. Some of the largest are the Araucaria weevil (*Vanapa*) and the *Gymnopholus* weevils (Fig. 1b), the latter often carrying gardens of algae, fungi, lichens, liverworts and mosses on their backs. The Brenthidae, relatives of the weevils, have fairly large jaws pointing forward. The Anthribidae have the jaws pointing downward, and often have long antennae. The bark-beetles (Scolytidae and Platypodidae) are smaller and more cylindrical. All of these are wood- or bark-borers.

ACKNOWLEDGMENTS

The figures are reproduced from R. Bielawski, *Pacific Insects*, vol. 6, 1964 (1d); J. L. Gressitt, *Proceedings of the Hawaiian Entomological Society for 1954*, vol. 15, 1955 (1c); ——— *Pacific Insects*, vol. 9, 1967 (2a, b, c, d); ——— and J. Sedlacek, *Pacific Insects*, vol. 9, 1967 (1b); G. A. Samuelson, *Pacific Insects*, vol. 8, 1966 (1a).
                                                J. L. GRESSITT

BETEL CHEWING. This custom is widespread throughout New Guinea. The total geographic area of the habit appears on the globe as a crescent extending from Africa to the north and northwest of Australia. Madagascar and Tanzania on the east African coast, India, Pakistan, Ceylon, southern Tibet and southern China, Formosa, Micronesia, the Philippines, Vietnam, Thailand, Malaysia, and Melanesia as far as the island of Tikopia are all included. At the present time some two hundred million people chew betel. Extension is limited by agricultural factors and competition with other long-established tension-reducing agents. Thus to the north there is opium and to the east kava. In the south the Australian Aboriginal is no horticulturist—and the betel vine needs a lot of attention. Betel chewing demands three basic items—betel pepper, areca nut, and lime. In New Guinea the custom is more common in the coastal regions but is by no means confined to them. There are certain Highlands regions favourable to the growth of the nut, and

indigenous traders are beginning to bring in all the ingredients, which nowadays are often on sale in the Highland towns. There is no doubt that the habit is spreading. The Highlands are still unsophisticated, nevertheless, and in general the people have not been greatly influenced by such customs as smoking and drinking alcohol. Betel chewing would seem to be in its initial phase and is not yet firmly established. This is in marked contrast to other remote areas, such as the Trobriands. At the same time, here and there on the Papuan coast, where the influence of certain missionary groups is strong, the custom has been virtually eliminated. Occasionally one comes across a few older people who are non-chewers. Betel chewing was introduced after they had grown up, and they never succumbed. In general, however, it may be said that where chewing is practised, everyone engages in it from the earliest years. There is a parallel with cigarette smoking in European societies. The child steals the betel-nut and hides in the garden. His (or her) father or other appropriate authority catches him *in flagrante delicto* and may punish him, though usually without much enthusiasm.

The items are the betel leaf or fruit (*Piper betle*, Linn.), the areca nut (*Areca catechu*, Linn.) and slaked lime processed from coral, sea shells, or mountain lime. The cultivated species of the areca palm and the betel vine are almost always used. Only rarely do people chew nuts of the wild species of areca; as well as leaves, fruits, and stems of the wild species of the betel vine. Old people without teeth select soft immature nuts.

Ripe areca nuts are slightly larger than a large cherry and brownish in colour; like nutmeg, they are hot and acrid and have aromatic and astringent properties. Chewers may enclose the nut in a betel leaf along with a little lime; or the lime may be applied directly to the inside of the cheek with the aid of a spatula; or the bean of the pepper may be dipped directly into the lime before chewing. These various combinations are put between the teeth and the cheek wall, pressed with the tongue, and sucked. The mucous membrane thus irritated gives local pleasure, which is reinforced by the action of the mixture as a cerebral stimulant.

A betel set consists of a wooden box or metal case for the areca nuts, knives for cutting them, and a hollow gourd or bamboo container with dipping stick or spatula for the lime. Usually all are nowadays contained in a plastic travelling bag. The spatula and container are often carved or otherwise ornamented.

The nicotine-like properties of the alkaloid arecoline, the active principle of the nut, are responsible for the euphoria. These, combined with an essential oil, account for the stimulant effect. Arecoline also acts on the parasympathetic nervous system to produce contraction of the pupils and increased secretion of tears, sweat and saliva. A feeling of well-being, good humour, and an increased capacity for work are typical, together with a suffused appearance, and red-coloured saliva. The beginner undergoes an initial phase not unlike that of a person new to smoking. He may experience dizziness, vertigo, nausea, and cold perspiration. The taste is burning and acrid, there may be a feeling of constriction in the throat, and complaints are made of a sore tongue. Soon habituation is established, and the unpleasant symptoms diminish. Hunger, tiredness, and irritability disappear; and a feeling of well-being spreads over the entire body. One of the most highly prized effects is the pleasant odour imparted to the breath. Consciousness remains unimpaired. Nervous complications are rare and are described as cases of betel-nut addiction and betel-nut psychosis (Burton-Bradley).

Attitudes to betel chewing are determined largely by social circumstances. To the culture-bound alien the practice is 'filthy'. It is contrary to reasonable standards of hygiene, and the widespread spitting of abundant red-stained saliva is disgusting because property may be damaged. Contrariwise, the reaction of the culture-bound indigene is that it sweetens the breath, drives away care, and promotes goodwill. Indigenous people constantly aver that the offering of betel-nut is a sign of good manners. They say that it engenders harmony, particularly when one meets somebody for the first time. As might be guessed, the person of mixed race tends to adopt an intermediate position, and his reaction tends to be ambivalent—he may chew in private but not in public.

There can be no question that betel chewing is firmly embedded in the social life and customs of the people. Holmes has pointed out the part played by betel-nut in bride wealth and betrothal among the Namau and the Ipi of western Papua. Among the Orokaiva a girl making her debut after first menstruation holds a club or spear in one hand and a bunch of areca nuts in the other. Many groups offer betel-nut to the dead and to spirits as propitiatory offerings. It is also used in magic to ward off illness and to control the movements of shoals of fish. Among the masked dancers of the Baining in New Britain betel chewing is so important that for five days prior to a feast they may eat nothing else. During the celebration chewing is continuous. Chewing also occupies a vital place in the ceremonial life of the Binandere-speaking peoples. Among these a person who has achieved a certain status may rattle his lime stick against the top of the gourd, a privilege denied to others; and he alone is permitted to ornament his gourd with beeswax and red seeds. Among other groups rattling a lime stick serves to indicate that a man wishes to make known his emotional state. Seligman noted that a Mekeo could stop quarrels by scattering lime from his gourd. The red mixture of betel-nut and lime may also serve as a cosmetic. The Aiga are said to be fond of streamers of thin areca palm spathe attached to tags of their hair.

Medical opinion accepts that there may be a relationship between betel chewing and oral cancer, though Atkinson and others state that the picture is by no means clear.

L. Atkinson, I. C. Chester, F. G. Smyth and R. E. J. ten Seldam, 'Oral Cancer in New Guinea', *Cancer*, vol. 17, 1964; B. G. Burton-Bradley, 'Papua and New Guinea Transcultural Psychiatry: Some Implications of Betel Chewing', *Medical Journal of Australia*, vol. 2, 1966; E. W. P. Chinnery, 'Piper methysticum in Betel Chewing', *Man*, vol. 22, 1922; H. Detzner, *Mœurs et coutumes des Papous* (translation of German ed. 1920). Paris, 1935; H. B. Guppy, *The Solomon Islands and their Natives*. London, 1887; J. H. Holmes, *In Primitive New Guinea*. London, 1924; W. Krenger, 'Kulturgeschichtliches zum Betelkauen', *Ciba Zeitschrift*, vol. 7, 1939-42; L. Lewin, *Phantastica: Narcotic and Stimulating Drugs*. London, 1964; C. G. Seligman, *The Melanesians of British New Guinea*. Cambridge, 1910.

B. G. BURTON-BRADLEY

BEVAN, Theodore Francis (1860-1907), explorer, was born in London on 14 October 1860. After working in a merchant's office in the City he sailed for New Zealand and then toured Australia. In 1884 he visited Port Moresby three weeks after the establishment of the protectorate of the south-eastern part of the island by Britain. On a second visit in 1885 he sailed eastwards along the coast from Port Moresby, spending three weeks in Milne Bay; and on a third visit in August 1885 sailed westwards to the Gulf, spending a fortnight at Motu Motu. In 1886 he went prospecting in the Astrolabe Range and then in 1887, with the offer of a launch by Robert Philp, of Burns, Philp and Co., explored the Gulf, reaching the Aird Hills on his first trip, and exploring the Aird River system on his second. His explorations, with a good deal of self-congratulation and acrimony, he described in his book, published in 1890.

T. F. Bevan, *Toil, Travel, and Discovery in British New Guinea*. London, 1890.

FRANCIS WEST

(*See also* EXPLORATION).

BIRDS. New Guinea and the nearby Melanesian islands (Bismarck Archipelago, Solomon Islands) together have one of the richest and most varied bird faunas in the world. There are approximately 860 species recognized so far compared with about 650 known from Australia, about 800 from North America and some 1,100 from the whole of Eurasia. Peculiar to the region are some of the most remarkable birds. Examples are the small, exquisitely plumaged kingfishers [q.v.] (e.g. *Ceyx*, *Tanysiptera*), lorikeets (*Charmosyna*), jewel-thrushes (*Pitta*) and emperor-wrens (*Todopsis*), whose metallic tints and brilliant reds, blues and yellows, rival those of the well-known birds of paradise [q.v.]; the great harpy-eagle (*Harpyopsis*) which is a primitive relative of the Philippine monkey-eating eagle (*Pithecophaga*); the comical hornbill (*Rhyticeros*) with its grunting call, noisy 'swooshing' flight and communal roosts; the magnificent crested goura pigeons which are the size of a small turkey and are the largest pigeons in the world. At the other extreme are the pygmy parrots (*Micropsitta*) which, as small as a white-eye (*Zosterops*), have stiff tail feathers that are used as a prop as the birds perch to feed on tree trunks. Other notable kinds are the tail-waving pied torrent lark (*Pomareopsis*) whose only established relative is the Australian magpie lark (*Grallina*), and an aberrant brown forest crow (*Gymnocorvus*) with a most un-crow-like plaintive call.

The New Guinea region is also a major, sometimes the only, centre of diversity for a number of families—the birds of paradise, bower birds, cassowaries, honeyeaters, kingfishers, megapodes, parrots, pigeons [qq.v.], pachycephalids and flower-peckers—many of which show striking endemism and numerical and ecological dominance there. The immediate affinities of these families beyond New Guinea lie overwhelmingly with the Australian bird fauna; indeed a number of groups, namely the birds of paradise, bower birds, honey-eaters, cassowaries and pachycephalids, are confined almost entirely to the Australo-Papuasian avifaunal region (or Australian-New Guinea area).

ZOOGEOGRAPHY

It is now generally accepted by bird geographers that the Australasian avifaunal region comprises the following subregions:
(1) Moluccan—the Indonesian islands east of Weber's Line (*see* Fig. 1). This is an area of historic geological instability, of severe tectonic activity during the Tertiary period, and with an impoverished fauna compared with that of Borneo to the west and Papuasia to the east.
(2) Papuasian—(a) New Guinea; (b) Northern Melanesia, including the Bismarck Archipelago and the Solomon Islands. This subregion is referred to as Papuasia or the New Guinea region in the ensuing text.

(3) Australian—Australia, Tasmania and off-shore islands.
(4) New Zealand—including Norfolk and the Kermadec Islands.
(5) Polynesian—(a) Micronesia, including Palau, the Marianas, Caroline, Marshall and Gilbert Islands; (b) Central Polynesia, including Fiji, Tonga and Samoa; (c) Eastern Polynesia, comprising all the islands east of 165°W., such as the Society, Tuamotus and Marquesas; and (d) Southern Melanesia, including the Santa Cruz Group, Banks, New Hebrides, Loyalty Islands and New Caledonia.

New Guinea is the heart-land of the Papuasian subregion. According to Mayr it includes the whole mainland, the western Papuan islands (Kofiau, Misool, Waigeo, etc.) in the west; in the north, the islands of Geelvink Bay, also Manam and Karkar Islands, but excludes Long and Rooke Islands; in the east it includes Woodlark Island and the D'Entrecasteaux and Louisiade Archipelagos; in the south the border goes through Torres Strait and includes the Aru Islands but not the Kei Islands nor any of the outliers of the southern Moluccas. These are its boundaries wherever it is referred to in the following text.

The total number of species recorded for New Guinea is some 670 made up as follows: breeding land and freshwater birds, approximately 570 (dominant families listed in Table 1)—of these some 190 species are shared with Australia; sea birds, 28—few of which (including the reef egret and beach stone curlew) are so far known to breed

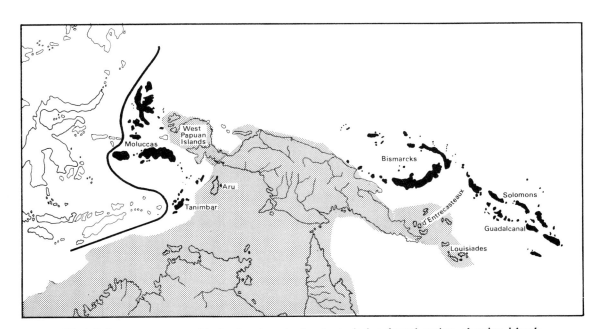

Fig 1. Relevant zoogeographical subregions in the Australasian faunal region, showing islands of the Moluccan and Northern Melanesian Provinces (black) in relation to the Papuan continental shelf (stippled to the 600-foot isobath), Weber's Line of faunal balance, and the wider water-gaps of the Polynesian region.

Table 1

BIRD FAMILIES STRONGLY REPRESENTED IN THE PAPUASIAN SUBREGION

Family	New Guinea (Species)	Bismarck Archipelago (Species)	Solomon Islands (Species)	Total Endemic Species
Pigeons (Columbidae)	45(18)*	20(5)	20(6)	29
Parrots (Psittacidae)	46(33)	14(5)	11(5)	42
Kingfishers (Alcedinidae)	24(13)	10(2)	8(2)	16
Cuckoo-shrikes (Campephagidae)	15(8)	5(nil)	8(2)	9
Old world flycatchers (Muscicapidae)	56(32)	15(7)	13(9)	49
Flower-peckers (Dicaeidae)	11(11)	1(1)	2(2)	14
Honeyeaters (Meliphagidae)	65(45)	9(5)	9(7)	56
Bower birds (Ptilonorhynchidae)	11(9)	—	—	9
Birds of paradise (Paradisaeidae)	38(36)	—	—	36

* Figures in parentheses are endemics.

in the New Guinea region; palaearctic migrants, over 40 (including mostly northern shore birds, several hawks, two terns, one cuckoo, one nightjar, two swifts, one swallow, two wagtails, one warbler, one flycatcher and one shrike) (see Table 4); and 27 regular migrants from Australia and New Zealand (including one ibis, one falcon, three or four shore birds, six cuckoos, two nightjars, three kingfishers, one bee-eater, one roller, one pitta, two swallows, two cuckoo-shrikes, two flycatchers and one drongo). Several of the latter are represented by resident races in New Guinea

also, namely *Tanysiptera sylvia*, *Eurystomus orientalis* and *Dicrurus hottentottus*. If subspecies are added there is a total of about 1,640 forms: some 1,540 breeding land and freshwater birds, about 30 sea birds, about 40 palaearctic migrants, and about 30 migrants from Australia and New Zealand.

An analysis of the affinities of all genera of New Guinea birds shows that the Australo-Papuasian element outweighs the Oriental element, 46 per cent against 35 per cent. Asian forms such as bulbuls, fringillid finches, emberizids, vultures, tits and woodpeckers are absent, and hornbills, leaf warblers (*Phylloscopus*) and shrikes (*Lanius*) are represented by single species only. There is, moreover, a high proportion of endemism and typically Papuan elements that are not endemic, comprising about 45 per cent of all genera in New Guinea. It is important to bear in mind, however, that the great majority of these endemics have austral rather than oriental affinities (see below). There are two sub-endemic families in New Guinea: the birds of paradise (Paradisaeidae) with 38 species, plus two in the Moluccas and four in north-eastern Australia, of which two occur also in lowland New Guinea; and the cassowaries (Casuariidae) with three species of which one, *Casuarius casuarius*, is also found in North Queensland and one, *C. bennetti*, in New Britain. Other families centred in the region have been mentioned above.

Table 2 shows the number of endemic genera, species and subspecies for New Guinea compared with those for the main island groups of the Bismarck Archipelago and for Bougainville Island. Although birds are highly mobile animals, most species, particularly land forms on tropical islands, tend to be quite sedentary. Mayr has pointed out

Table 2

COMPARISON OF ENDEMIC FORMS BETWEEN NEW GUINEA, THE BISMARCK ARCHIPELAGO AND BOUGAINVILLE ISLAND

	Non-Passerines			Passerines			Total Species (Excluding Pelagic Birds)
	Endemic Genera	Endemic Species	Endemic Subspecies	Endemic Genera	Endemic Species	Endemic Subspecies	
New Guinea	28	102	401	50	215	792	about 650
New Britain	—	9	7	2	4	13	150
New Ireland	—	1	2	—	4	6	103
New Hanover	—	—	1	—	—	3	73
Duke of York Group	—	—	—	—	—	—	45
Admiralty Islands	—	—	4	—	1	9	43
St Matthias Group	—	—	8	—	2	8	38
Djaul Island	—	—	—	—	1	4	18*
Tabar Islands	—	—	—	—	—	4	14*
Lihir Group	—	—	1	—	—	3	18
Tanga Islands	—	—	—	—	—	1	9*
Feni Islands	—	—	1	—	—	1	35
Bougainville Island	—	—	3	—	1	7	115

* Passerines only.

that of the 265 species which are known from that part of New Guinea which is opposite New Britain, only about 80 species have a representative on New Britain. In other words, the 45-mile-wide stretch of water which separates the two islands has prevented the crossing over of 75 per cent of the New Guinea species. Furthermore, a large number of distinctive subspecies (geographical races) have evolved on most of the small islands adjacent to the New Guinea mainland.

Northern Melanesia. (1) Bismarck Archipelago and Admiralty Islands. In passing from New Guinea through New Britain and New Ireland to the Solomons group, poorer bird faunas of Papuan affinity are encountered progressively. As shown in Table 1, the bird fauna of the Bismarck Archipelago is substantially poorer than that of New Guinea, and endemism is not nearly so striking. The number of land and freshwater species so far recorded for New Britain alone is 138. Furthermore, the honeyeaters (Meliphagidae), the largest family on mainland New Guinea with 65 species, are represented there by only nine species, five of which belong to the widespread south-western Pacific genus *Myzomela*. Only New Britain has endemic genera: a warbler, *Ortygocichla*, whose nearest relative appears to be *Trichocichla* of Fiji, and a honeyeater, *Vosea*. Moreover, few islands—New Britain, New Ireland, Manus, St Matthias and Djaul—have developed endemic species. The total number of endemic forms (species and subspecies) in the Bismarcks is only about 80 compared with some 1,190 in New Guinea. It is also noteworthy that the proportion of passerine bird species (nearly all of which are forest dwellers) to non-passerines (which include the freshwater birds) is almost 1 to 2 whereas on mainland New Guinea it is about 1 to 1. This comparison emphasizes the limited opportunities available in time and space to forest-dwelling birds for colonizing these islands across water barriers.

An analysis of the bird fauna of New Britain indicates that its affinities lie with New Guinea. Even so, the following Australo-Papuasian families have no representative there or elsewhere in the Bismarcks and Solomons: Aegothelidae (owlet-nightjars), Maluridae (wren-warblers), Orthonychidae (log-runners), Falcunculidae (shrike-tits), Grallinidae (magpie-larks), Cracticidae (butcher-birds), Neosittidae (Australian nuthatches), Climacteridae (Australian treecreepers), Ptilonorhynchidae (bower birds) and Paradisaeidae (birds of paradise). Of the bird species present (migrants, endemics and several wide-ranging species excluded), the following have their eastern limits in the Bismarck Archipelago: one cassowary, *Casuarius bennetti*; one hawk, *Henicopernis longicauda*; four pigeons, *Ptilinopus rivoli*, *Ducula spilorrhoa*, *Gymnophaps albertisii* and *Macropygia nigrirostris*; three parrots, *Lorius hypoinochrous*, *Cacatua galerita*, *Micropsitta pusio*; one kingfisher, *Tanysiptera sylvia*; one pitta, *Pitta erythrogaster*; one cuckoo-shrike, *Lalage leucomela*; one grass-warbler, *Cisticola exilis*; four fly-catchers, *Rhipidura rufiventris*, *Myiagra alecto*, *Monarcha chrysomela* and *Monachella muelleriana*; one sunbird, *Nectarinia sericea*; four honeyeaters, *Myzomela cruentata*, *M. eques* and *M. nigrita* and *Philemon novaeguineae*; one finch, *Lonchura spectabilis*; and one crow, *Corvus orru*.

But there appears to have been some immigration from, or exchange with, the Solomons and the following species, which are widespread in the Solomons, have their western limits in the Bismarck Archipelago: three pigeons, *Ducula pistrinaria* (also on off-shore islands but not the mainland of New Guinea), *D. rubricera* and *Columba pallidiceps*; and one parrot, *Geoffroyus heteroclitus*.

The avifauna of the central ranges of New Britain and southern New Ireland is still largely unknown and as recently as 1958 E. T. Gilliard made the first collection of birds from the Whiteman Range in New Britain. On the summit of this range, low altitude cloud (moss) forest occurs at 5,000 feet. There Gilliard discovered a new genus and species of honeyeater, *Vosea whitemanensis*, a new species of thicket-warbler, *Cichlornis grosvenori*, and a new subspecies of leaf-warbler, *Phylloscopus trivirgatus moorhousei*.

(2) Solomon Islands. Treatment herein of the birds of the region is confined in the main to Australian-administered Bougainville Island. Like the Bismarck Archipelago, the Solomon Islands possess a bird fauna which is much poorer than that of New Guinea. There are about 150 species of land and freshwater birds, including migrants, in the Solomons. Bougainville, which has the richest bird fauna in the archipelago, has 97 of these. If shore birds—mainly northern migrants—are added, the Bougainville total is 115 species (*see* Table 2).

Only two genera, the owl *Nesasio* and the pigeon *Microgoura*, are endemic to the Solomons; the latter is apparently closely related to *Trugon* in New Guinea. Of the approximately 55 species endemic to the Solomons, 32 are found on Bougainville as follows: three raptores (Accipitridae), one of which, *Accipiter albogularis*, is also represented by an endemic race on the Feni Islands; one rail (Rallidae); two pigeons (Columbidae); four parrots (Psittacidae); one coucal (Cuculidae); two owls (Strigidae); two kingfishers (Alcedinidae); one pitta (Pittidae); one cuckoo-shrike (Campephagidae); six flycatchers (Muscicapidae); one whistler (Pachycephalidae); one flower-pecker (Dicaeidae); two white-eyes (Zosteropidae); two honeyeaters (Meliphagidae); two starlings (Sturnidae); and one crow (Corvidae). Only one of the above species, a mountain honeyeater, *Melilestes bougainvillei*, is endemic to Bougainville; but there are five subspecies endemic to that island: one rail, one kingfisher, two flycatchers and one white-eye. An additional five endemic subspecies are races of species not confined to the Solomons.

As in New Guinea, predominant families in the Solomons are Columbidae, Psittacidae, Alcedinidae, Campephagidae, Muscicapidae and, to a lesser extent, Meliphagidae. Nearly all Solomons genera of these families also occur in New Guinea.

Nevertheless, some of the links forged by the Solomons in the chains of relationships within the Australo-Papuasian bird fauna are independent of New Guinea. The scarlet robin (*Petroica multicolor*) and corellas (*Cacatua* spp.), for example, are represented by resident species in both Australia and Bougainville Island but not New Guinea; the little corella (*C. sanguinea*), which has been recorded from New Guinea, may only reach that island as a visitor.

ECOLOGY

Bird habitats in the New Guinea region may be grouped into three main categories: water, including both marine and fresh water; grasslands; and rain forests and associated vegetation, which harbour the majority of bird forms.

Water. Water birds are relatively poorly represented in the region. Terns, frigate-birds, and wading birds (stone-curlews, sand pipers, whim-brels, dotterels, and herons and egrets of various species) are frequent along marine shores, but many are over-winterers or itinerant visitors, and only six of the 28 sea birds found in New Guinea are known to breed there.

Freshwater birds are rather more diversified, having had scope for development on the extensive water ways of the Fly and Sepik River systems, the Purari delta, and the Meervlakte in western New Guinea. Endemics are represented by the genera *Zonerodius* (Papuan tiger bittern), *Megacrex* (a flightless giant rail), and the species *Anas waigiuensis* (Salvadori's teal) and *Gymnocrex plumbeiventris* (bare-eyed rail). By far the greater number of freshwater species are, nevertheless, widespread forms occurring also in Australia and beyond.

The predominant groups of swamp birds in the region are herons and bitterns (Ardeidae) with 15 species on mainland New Guinea, ducks and geese (Anatidae) with 13 species, and rails, crakes and

White egret (*Egretta alba*).

(left) Grass owl (*Tyto longimembris*). (right) Blue-breasted pitta (*Pitta erythrogaster*). (bottom) White-flanked flag-bird (*Parotia carolae*).

water-hens (Rallidae) with 18 species. Relatively few of these forms reach the Bismarck Archipelago and Bougainville Island, and only the nankeen night heron (*Nycticorax caledonicus*), black duck (*Anas superciliosa*), purple swamp hen (*Porphyrio porphyrio*), and the rails *Rallus philippensis*, *Porzana cinerea* and *Amaurornis olivaceus* are widespread: they occur on most large islands. On the other hand, several rails, such as *Rallus insignis* which is endemic to New Britain and *Nesosclopeus woodfordi* on Bougainville, do not extend to New Guinea.

Grasslands. There are three main types of grassland habitat: *Eucalyptus-Melaleuca* woodland; anthropogenous grassland; and alpine meadowland. Only two species, the brown quail (*Synoicus ypsilophorus*) and tawny grass-bird (*Megalurus timoriensis*), are found in all three. The northern Melanesian archipelagos peripheral to eastern New Guinea have only anthropogenous grasslands which, though more impoverished, carry a bird fauna similar to that of their counterpart on mainland New Guinea.

Eucalyptus-Melaleuca woodland is confined to low altitudes in the Trans-Fly and Port Moresby areas on the southern coast and the Hydrographers Range-Cape Vogel area on the north-eastern coast. Some 35 species are peculiar to it, most of which are representatives of species that are widespread in Australia. Characteristic forms are the zebra dove (*Geopelia striata*), blue-winged kookaburra (*Dacelo leachii*), black-faced cuckoo-shrike (*Coracina novaehollandiae*) and black-backed butcher-bird (*Cracticus mentalis*). There are minor avifaunal differences between the Port Moresby and Trans-Fly woodlands which are separated by the rain-forested lowlands along the Gulf of Papua. The former, with 17 woodland species, has seven peculiar to it, e.g. the green-fig bird (*Sphecotheres*) and yellow-tinted honeyeater (*Meliphaga flavescens*). The latter, with a greater number of such forms (28) presumably because of proximity to Australia, has 18 species confined to it, e.g. the wedge-tailed eagle (*Aquila audax*), grey-crowned babbler (*Pomatostomus temporalis*), Australian magpie (*Gymnorhina tibicen*), and the noisy and little friar-birds (*Philemon corniculatus*, *P. citreogularis*).

Anthropogenous grasslands, found throughout all man-settled parts of New Guinea but most widespread in mid-mountain valleys, possess an impoverished bird fauna in which widespread palaearctic species predominate, namely the pied chat (*Saxicola caprata*), the king quail (*Excalfactoria chinensis*), an owl (*Tyto longimembris*), the Schach shrike (*Lanius schach*) and Richards pipit (*Anthus novaeseelandiae*). The dearth of variety in the grassland bird fauna reflects its relatively recent origin. Only one group of weaver finches, the mannikins (*Lonchura*), have expanded and diversified there: ten species are known, five of which are localized endemics. Similarly, the white-shouldered wren (*Malurus alboscapulatus*) has separated into a large number of races, some of which have still to be defined.

Alpine meadow-lands, which are basically natural grasslands on mountain peaks above the tree-line between 9,500 and 13,500 feet altitude, carry a similarly impoverished bird fauna that, by contrast, is relatively rich in endemics. Not only are endemic races of mannikins, the island blackbird (*Turdus poliocephalus*) and brown quail found there, but also endemic species and genera, namely the alpine pipit (*Anthus gutturalis*), snow quail (*Anurophasis*) and alpine fire-tail finch (*Oreostruthus*). A further endemic species, Archbold's robin (*Petroica archboldi*), lives among rocks and talus slopes above the grass-line at 12,800 to 13,700 feet in the Snow Mountains of western New Guinea.

Rain forests. The vast primary rain forests and associated vegetation hold the core of the Papuasian avifauna. Some 45 per cent of the land and freshwater birds are confined to primary forest alone and another 25 per cent live at least partly in this habitat, i.e. 70·5 per cent of the region's avifauna are essentially rain-forest forms. Of endemic species, 65 per cent are confined to primary rain forest while a further 25 per cent are partially primary, partially secondary forest forms. In these forests in lowland New Guinea, the distribution of birds is such that an observer may see 15 to 20 species at once and up to 30 in several hours in and around a single flowering or fruiting food tree. Foraging in the canopy will be several large and noisy lories (*Chalcopsitta*, *Pseudeos*, *Trichoglossus*) or pigeons (*Ducula*, *Ptilinopus*), and the ubiquitous honeyeaters (*Myzomela*, *Meliphaga*), and friar-birds (*Philemon*) which chase each other as much as insects or blossom; there also, the red, white and black flycatcher, *Peltops*, will perch on the topmost bare twigs waiting to make a sudden sally after insects flying past. Attracted by all the hubbub, flycatchers (*Monarcha*, *Poecilodryas*) and fly-eaters (*Gerygone*) will pass through the lower, shaded branches, along with itinerant birds of paradise (*Paradisaea*, *Manucodia*). Towards the ground, babblers (*Garritornis*), forest kingfishers (*Alcyone*, *Tanysiptera*), fantails (*Rhipidura*) and wrens (*Todopsis*, etc.) usually dart or flutter about, and foraging on the forest floor will be occasional jewel thrushes (*Pitta*), vine-wrens (*Crateroscelis*) and megapodes (*Talegallus*, *Megapodius*). The same phenomenon is just as striking, though manifested by fewer species, in the montane forests. There flowering food trees, often species of Elaeocarpaceae and Cunoniaceae, attract lorikeets (*Charmosyna*) and large honeyeaters (*Melidectes*, *Melipotes*) as well as the small (*Myzomela rosenbergii*), and at lower levels, a host of flycatchers and robins (Muscicapidae)—whistlers (Pachycephalidae) and scrub-wrens (*Sericornis*), all of which gather frequently in loose feeding flocks.

The seemingly uniform expanses of rain forest, which support this varied bird fauna, are in reality a complex of biotopes, as indicated by three major partitions in forest habitat (Table 3). The primary partition is altitudinal. The great mountain ranges in the region, one of the main factors controlling the distribution of the biota through their influence on temperature, rainfall and hence

Table 3

EXAMPLES OF BIRD DISTRIBUTION IN FORESTS IN EASTERN NEW GUINEA*

Altitude (Feet)	Stratum	Forest Habitats	
		Primary Formations	Secondary Formations
0	Canopy	Ducula pinon Probosciger aterrimus Rhyticeros plicatus Peltops blainvillii Mino anais Philemon meyeri Seleucidis melanoleuca	Ptilinopus superbus Reinwardtoena reinwardtii Trichoglossus haematodus Geoffroyus geoffroyi Eurystomus orientalis Mino dumontii Cracticus cassicus Meliphaga versicolor
	Midstages	Ptilinopus magnificus Micropsitta pusio Ceyx lepidus Tanysiptera galatea Gerygone chrysogaster Monarcha guttula Pitohui kirhocephalus Cicinnurus regius	Ptilinopus magnificus Macropygia nigrirostris Cacomantis variolosus Lalage leucomela Rhipidura leucothorax Dicaeum geelvinkianum Meliphaga analoga Manucodia ater
500	Floor	Casuarius casuarius Talegallus fuscirostris Goura spp. Trugon terrestris Pitta spp. Ptilorrhoa caerulescens Pitohui cristatus	Chalcophaps indica Centropus menbeki
2,000	Canopy	Ducula zoeae Gymnophaps albertisii Opopsitta diophthalma Psittrichas fulgidus Pachycare flavogrisea Chaetorhynchus papuensis Drepanornis albertisii Ailuroedus melanotis	Ptilinopus superbus Macropygia amboinensis Trichoglossus haematodus Hemiprocne mystacea Coracina caeruleogrisea Myzomela adolphinae Phonygammus keraudrenii Paradisaea raggiana
	Midstages	Micropsitta bruijnii Clytoceyx rex Tanysiptera danae Sericornis arfakianus Tregellasia leucops Melanocharis longicauda Toxorhamphus poliopterus Amblyornis subalaris	Macropygia nigrirostris Chalcites meyerii Aegotheles insignis Todopsis wallacii Cacomantis variolosus Meliphaga mimikae Diphyllodes magnificus
4,000	Floor	Casuarius bennetti Gallicolumba jobiensis Otidiphaps nobilis Crateroscelis murina Ptilorrhoa castanonota	Erythrura trichroa
4,500	Canopy	Ducula chalconota Gymnophaps albertisii Charmosyna pulchella Psittacella madaraszi Coracina montana Neositta papuensis Astrapia stephaniae Paradisaea rudolphi	Ptilinopus rivoli Macropygia amboinensis Neopsittacus musschenbroekii Peltops montanus Pachycephala modesta Myzomela rosenbergii Melidectes rufocrissalis
	Midstages	Aegotheles albertisii Ifrita kowaldi Sericornis perspicillatus Peneothello cyanus Ptiloprora guisei Melanocharis versteri Loria loriae Amblyornis macgregoria	Cacomantis pyrrhophanus Phylloscopus trivirgatus Gerygone ruficollis Machaerirhynchus nigripectus Melipotes fumigatus Melidectes torquatus Zosterops novaeguineae Lophorina superba
7,000	Floor	Aepypodius arfakianus Rallicula forbesi Gallicolumba beccarii Amalocichla incerta Ptilorrhoa leucosticta Crateroscelis robusta Sericornis nouhuysi	Pomareopsis bruijni (streams) Erythrura trichroa
7,500	Canopy	Charmosyna papou Psittacella picta Petroica bivittata Pachycephala schlegelii Daphoenositta miranda Melidectes belfordi Pteridophora alberti Archboldia papuensis	Reinwardtoena reinwardtii Neopsittacus pullicauda Melidectes belfordi
	Midstages	Chalcites ruficollis Eurostopodus archboldi Sericornis papuensis Peneothello sigillata Eulacestoma nigropectus Ptiloprora perstriata Paramythia monium Cnemophilus macgregorii	Rhipidura brachyrhyncha Rhipidura albolimbata Melipotes fumigatus Pycnopygius cinereus
10,000	Floor	Casuarius bennetti Rallicula forbesi Amalocichla sclateriana Crateroscelis robusta Sericornis nouhuysi	Oreostruthus fuliginosus

* All species are allocated to the ranges and habitats in which they are most frequent.

general environment, have had the effect of 'zoning' the avifauna altitudinally. Each zone in any one area is characterized by a particular suite of species (*see* Table 3). Correlated with 'zoning', there is also a gradual decrease in the number of forest bird species with altitude, for example from about 260 species at the 0 to 1,500-foot level to about 110 above 7,500 feet in New Guinea alone.

Some species are confined to very narrow altitudinal belts, such as the goura pigeons (*Goura*) and twelve-wired bird of paradise (*Seleucidis*), which are usually found in lowland alluvial forests between 0 and 500 feet; also Wilhelmina's lorikeet (*Charmosyna wilhelminae*), the spotted fly robin (*Peneothello bimaculatus*) and the striped gardener-bird (*Amblyornis subalaris*), which are known only from between 2,000 and 4,000 feet; and the dark vine-wren (*Crateroscelis nigrorufa*),

the shieldbill bird of paradise (*Loboparadisea*) and the white-flanked flag-bird (*Parotia carolae*), which are confined to mid-mountain forests between 4,000 and 6,200 feet. Other species are more ubiquitous altitudinally, namely the giant cuckoo-dove (*Reinwardtoena*), mountain pigeon (*Gymnophaps*), harpy eagle (*Harpyopsis*) and fantail cuckoo (*Cacomantis pyrrhophanus*), which range through almost the whole gamut of forested altitudes, or the southern log-runner (*Orthonyx*), Papuan king parrot (*Alisterus chloropterus*) and Schlegel's whistler (*Pachycephala schlegelii*), which are essentially montane species with altitudinal ranges of almost 7,000 feet. Still others occur at particular altitudes in one part of their range and at different altitudes elsewhere. For example, Wallace's owlet-nightjar (*Aegotheles wallacei*), the white-faced robin (*Tregellasia leucops*) and spotted cat-bird (*Ailuroedus melanotis*), widespread species in mid-mountain forests throughout New Guinea, are represented by outlier lowland populations in the region of the Fly River mouth. It is clear that the altitudinal ranges of many species are affected by food requirements, for which the length of food chains may serve as a useful correlating concept. In general, the most widely ranging forms are raptores (long or complex food chains) and fruit-eaters such as pigeons and parrots which have to forage for preferred flowering and fruiting trees (short or simple chains). Insect-eaters, with chains of medium length and complexity, are the most altitudinally sedentary forms.

In addition, there is a well-marked discontinuity in the composition of the forest avifauna between 4,000 and 5,500 feet. There many bird groups have their upper or lower limits. Below these levels, predominant components of the bird fauna are pigeons (Columbidae), cockatoos and large loriine parrots (Psittacidae), kingfishers (Alcedinidae), a hornbill (Bucerotidae), a number of endemic cuckoos (Cuculidae), pittas (Pittidae) and many small honeyeaters (Meliphagidae). Above, the fauna has a different make-up: the most prominent forms are small lorikeets (Psittacidae), scrub-wrens (Sylviidae), robins (Muscicapidae), whistlers (Pachycephalidae), berry-peckers (Dicaeidae, excluding *Dicaeum*), nuthatches and creepers (Neosittidae, Certhiidae), birds of paradise (Paradiseaidae), bower birds (Ptilonorhynchidae) and large honeyeaters (Meliphagidae). Even in the eastern archipelagos, there is evidence of a similar discontinuity in distribution, but often at lower altitudes (3,000-4,000 feet) because of the 'land-mass' effect. In the poorer bird faunas of these islands, however, the break is between species rather than between genera and higher taxa. On Bougainville Island, for example, *Ptilinopus solomonensis*, *Rhipidura drownei* and *Pachycephala implicata* replace *Ptilinopus viridis*, *Rhipidura rufifrons* and *Pachycephala pectoralis* above about 3,000 feet.

In New Guinea, the discontinuity in distribution appears to be correlated with changes in the floristic composition of the vegetation rather than intrinsic differences in the ability of species to live at particular altitudinal levels. The primary rain forest, though zoned altitudinally like the bird fauna, comprises a diverse lowland and 'oak' (*Lithocarpus*, *Castanopsis*) hill flora of predominantly palaeotropic affinities below 4,000-5,500 feet, and a montane flora dominated by antarctic beech (*Nothofagus*), podocarps, myrtles and laurels of southern hemisphere affinity above. These correlations bear on the origin of the region's avifaunal elements (*see* below).

The secondary partition distinguishes between primary forest on the one hand and secondary forest and forest edges on the other. Secondary and edge forests are the densely tangled formations, rarely of great height, which are responsible for the misconception of the impenetrability of jungle. While the great majority of forest birds in the region are essentially primary forest forms, many of them move into secondary growth at one time or another. Others are virtually confined

to such habitat, namely the cuckoo-doves (*Macropygia*), the brush cuckoo (*Cacomantis variolosus*), white-eyes (*Zosterops* spp.) and the superb bird of paradise (*Lophorina superba*). Species adapted to life in secondary forest have, in general, wider altitudinal ranges than their counterparts in primary forest, undoubtedly because of the greater uniformity of the habitat with altitude; food plants (e.g. Euphorbiaceae, Urticaceae spp.) of the secondary forest are also relatively ubiquitous altitudinally.

The tertiary partition is the segregation of different forms to different strata (levels) within the rain forest at any altitudinal level (*see* Table 3). For example, most parrots, the hornbill, fruit-eating pigeons of the genera *Ducula* and *Ptilinopus*, and friar- (*Philemon*) and wattle-birds (*Melidectes*) are as a rule confined to the forest canopy; many passerines such as the thick-heads (Pachycephalidae) and flycatchers (*Monarcha*, *Rhipidura*), and non-passerines such as the owlet-nightjars (*Aegotheles*) and paradise-kingfishers (*Tanysiptera*) are species of the middle and lower stages of the forest interior; others, such as the pigeons (*Goura*, *Henicophaps*, *Gallicolumba*) and log-runners (Orthonychidae), live on the forest floor. Preference for a particular vegetation stratum has even played a role in separating related species. Thus in the scrub-wrens (*Sericornis*), there are three sibling species which invariably forage at different levels in the forest wherever they are altitudinally sympatric (i.e. geographically overlapping) along the central New Guinean cordillera, usually between 4,500 and 7,500 feet; the buff-faced (*S. perspicillatus*) moves in the main near the forest canopy, the Papuan (*S. papuensis*) through the forest midstages, and the noisy (*S. nouhuysi*) in the forest floor shrubbery. A similar segregation, based in this case on display requirements, is found in the three closely related genera of flag birds of paradise; the enamelled bird (*Pteridophora*) courts from the highest branches of a tall forest tree, the superb bird (*Lophorina*) performs in the forest midstage, while the flag birds (*Parotia*) dance on clearings on the forest floor.

MOVEMENTS

Movements in species of the Papuasian-breeding land bird fauna are as a rule very local, as indicated (a) by bird banding (under the auspices of CSIRO, Australia) in eastern New Guinea and (b) by the degree of subspeciation throughout the region. Banded individuals of many lowland rain-forest species, such as the spot-winged monarch (*Monarcha guttula*), rufous shrike-thrush (*Colluricincla megarhyncha*) and plumed honeyeater (*Oedistoma iliolophus*), have been re-trapped month after month over a period of years at one banding site, yet never recorded at an adjacent station only three or four miles away. Even though blossom- and fruit-feeders—lorikeets, pigeons and some honeyeaters—often flock conspicuously in food trees from time to time, thus giving the impression of marked nomadism, their latitudinal and altitudinal movements appear in fact to be rarely great. In lowland New Guinea, where major geographical barriers or even breaks in habitat are lacking, the high levels of subspeciation can only reflect marked sedentary behaviour (see Fig. 3). Some species, e.g. those with few or no subspecies (*Chalcophaps stephani, Eclectus roratus, Dacelo gaudichaud, Monarcha manadensis*), apparently move more widely than the many passerines and other forms with a greater number of subspecies (*Arses telescophthalmus, Colluricincla megarhyncha, Ptilinopus coronulatus, Trichoglossus haematodus*). By this estimation, the satin monarch (*Monarcha manadensis*), monotypic on mainland New Guinea and represented widely in the peripheral archipelagos, appears to be a species which wanders rather extensively.

Breeding freshwater birds are subject to greater fluctuations in numbers and movements because of the seasonal changes in their habitat in wet and dry seasons. Individuals of many species—ducks, egrets, herons, cormorants, ibises, etc.—are known to commute between New Guinea, Australia and other island groups.

All seasonal migrants present in the New Guinea region are non-breeding and use the region for over-wintering. They include both marine and land immigrants from both the northern and southern hemispheres, examples of which are given in Table 4.

BREEDING

Breeding in most bird species occurs in response to local conditions (e.g. food availability) and as a consequence is correlated with climatic variation. In temperate latitudes where there are well-marked seasonal changes in day length, temperature and rainfall, breeding takes place over well-defined periods, usually once a year. In the New Guinea region, the only climatic factor showing equivalent annual alternation is rainfall, and even then its variation is relatively slight in montane areas. How the breeding periods of the birds of the region are correlated with the environmental regime is still barely known. The breeding data available at present have been gathered largely

from the gonad condition of collected birds, rather than from direct observations of breeding. They suggest firstly that many species of land birds breed spasmodically throughout the year (though an individual pair may breed only once in that time), and secondly that there are general peaks of breeding in these species in the austral spring and early summer months. Evidence for associating these peaks with the seasonal climatic variations, e.g. the onset and fall-off of rains in New Guinea, is somewhat conflicting. Whereas the breeding peak has been linked with the onset of the north-west monsoon in north-western and south-eastern New Guinea, it coincides with the end of the south-east monsoon in the Lake Kutubu area of southern New Guinea. Much further study is needed of the breeding cycles of individual species throughout their ranges before the environmental correlations can begin to be comprehended.

Frequency of breeding bears on the maintenance of bird numbers. As frequency of breeding may tend to be maximized in the New Guinea region, because of the seasonal uniformity of the environment, predators (reptiles, raptores, rodents, man) and clutch size theoretically play an important role in regulating bird numbers. In this respect, and even though it may merely reflect seasonal uniformity in the availability of food, the relatively high proportion of species having a known clutch size of only one or two eggs seems significant. Examples are numerous pigeons and parrots, and many passerine species, notably in the birds of paradise, bower birds, flycatchers and honeyeaters. By contrast, Australian representatives of some of the New Guinea passerines with such small average broods have clutches of between two and six eggs at temperate latitudes, e.g. the scrub-wrens (*Sericornis*), grey shrike-thrush (*Colluricincla harmonica*), magpie-lark (*Grallina*), white-breasted wood-swallow (*Artamus leucorhynchus*) and honeyeaters (*Meliphaga*).

REGIONAL VARIATION AND EVOLUTION

In birds, spatial isolation of local populations is the primary environmental promoter of speciation and evolution. In the New Guinea region, the major isolating mechanisms are the latitudinal barriers of sea water between islands and the altitudinal barriers of mountain ranges on islands (see Fig. 2); these are indubitably responsible for the richness of the region's avifauna in species and races. As land birds, particularly forest passerine species, tend to avoid water gaps, the effect of sea-water barriers, especially between small and adjacent island groups, is simple and dramatic; each island has its own suite of endemic races and species. The astonishing, partially heterogynic variation in the golden whistler (*Pachycephala pectoralis*) between small islands in the south-western Pacific graphically illustrates this phenomenon. On islands between the Admiralty group and Bougainville Island, this whistler and the northern fantail (*Rhipidura rufiventris*) are represented by no less than seven and six races respec-

Table 4

SOME OVER-WINTERING MIGRANTS IN THE NEW GUINEA REGION

Breeding Region	Marine and Shore Species	Land Species
Palaearctic	Puffinus leucomelas Charadrius spp. Numenius spp. Tringa spp. Calidris spp. Sterna hirundo Stercorarius pomarinus	Accipiter soloensis Cuculus saturatus Chaetura caudacuta Hirundo rustica Motacilla spp. Locustella fasciolata Muscicapa griseisticta
Austral	Oceanites oceanicus Haematopus ostralegus	Stiltia isabella Eudynamis taitensis Halcyon sanctus Merops ornatus (in part) Eurystomus orientalis (in part) Lalage sueurii Coracina novaehollandiae Myiagra spp. (in part)

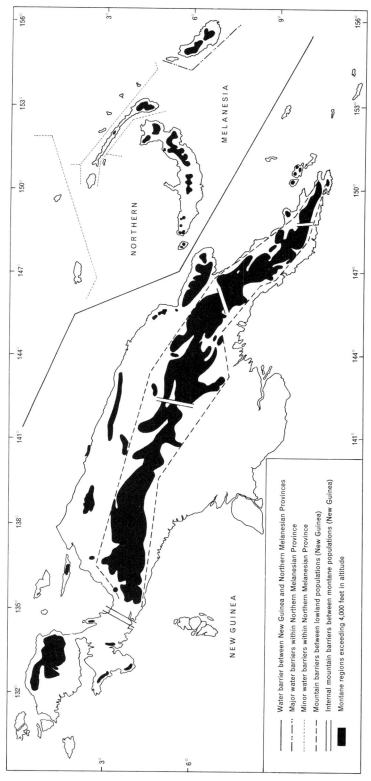

Fig 2. Physical barriers to avifaunal interchange.

NEW GUINEA

NORTHERN

MELANESIA

Water barrier between New Guinea and Northern Melanesian Provinces
Major water barriers within Northern Melanesian Province
Minor water barriers within Northern Melanesian Province
Mountain barriers between lowland populations (New Guinea)
Internal mountain barriers between montane populations (New Guinea)
Montane regions exceeding 4,000 feet in altitude

Victoria crowned pigeon (*Goura victoria*).

tively. Even more striking is the diversity in the pied monarch (*Monarcha manadensis*) super-species: four or five species of the group are represented there, one replacing another on adjacent islands and each differing from the others by well-marked variations in the amount of black and white on different parts of the body and tail. By contrast, more itinerant species such as water birds, e.g. the nankeen night heron (*Nycticorax caledonicus*) and the reef egret (*Egretta sacra*), and free-flying birds, e.g. the whiskered tree swift (*Hemiprocne mystacea*), are represented by only one or two races throughout the region.

The regional mountain ranges have a more complex influence on local evolution: not only do they effectively separate low altitude populations along their opposite scarps, but their intervening valleys also isolate many montane populations on high mountain massifs (*see* Fig. 2). Both effects are seen predominantly in the great central cordillera of mainland New Guinea. Running the

length of the island and rising to 10,000 feet or above in many parts, this mountain system forms an almost impassable barrier between the biological communities of the tropical and lower subtropical levels which occur for more than 1,000 miles along each of its sides. Only around the ends of the wall and through a gap in the isthmus south of Geelvink Bay are tropical species linked to each other, and then by often relatively attenuated connections. As a result, not only do many lowland allopatric (i.e. geographically replacing) forms on opposite sides of the cordillera differ from each other at racial and species level, but also each is linked to the other by clinal gradients in the differing characters or by isolated intermediate populations in the classical 'ring' species arrangement. A simple example is the pattern of variation in the pinon imperial pigeon (*Ducula pinon*) of the lowland rain forests between 0 and 1,000 feet. Central southern populations between the Fly River and Gulf of Papua have plain dark grey shoulders while those along the Sepik River on the opposite side of the central cordillera have shoulders marked with conspicuous pale scallopings. These forms are connected at each end of the island by intermediate populations which grade gradually in their shoulder markings from one extreme form to the other. More complex variation in similar sequence is found in the variable pitohui (*Pitohui kirhocephalus*) which is represented throughout the lowland regions and off-shore islands by approximately 20 recognized races, some strikingly distinct in black and chestnut and others weakly defined by subtle variations in grey and dull chestnut.

Sharper steps in the character gradients of some of the 'ring' species groups have led to the discrimination of allopatric species. Two of the most striking examples of this in New Guinea are the three crowned pigeons (*Goura*) and three lowland species of 'true' birds of paradise (*Paradisaea*). *Goura cristata* in western New Guinea has a uniformly grey crest and partly maroon back, *G. scheepmakeri* in southern and south-eastern parts a similarly grey crest but grey or black back, and *G. victoria* in northern New Guinea a white-tipped crest and grey or black back. *Paradisaea apoda*, with yellow plumes and a brown female, is found in south-western New Guinea, *P. raggiana*, with red plumes and brown female, in southern and eastern New Guinea, and *P. minor*, with yellow plumes and white-breasted female, in northern New Guinea. A remarkable feature of the latter 'ring' is the approach, even partial overlap, of two extreme forms of *P. raggiana* and *P. minor* across gaps in the Wahgi-Baiyer divide in eastern central New Guinea.

With increasing altitude above about 4,000 feet, the continuity of the biota is progressively broken up by mountain topography (*see* Fig. 3). Bird populations become more isolated locally and fewer in number; and in them speciation proceeds at a theoretically more rapid rate. The alpine avifauna, rich in endemic species and races, lives literally on islands of grassland and moor amid a sea of lower altitude forested habitat. At mid-montane altitudes (5,000-9,500 feet), there are many species groups with chains of allopatric forms strung out along the New Guinean ranges. Examples are the superb (*Lophorina*) and astrapia birds of paradise (*Astrapia*) at racial and species level respectively: each of these genera is represented by endemic forms on every isolated or semi-isolated high mountain range throughout the island. Broad gaps of tropical lowland between the ranges signify major zoogeographical disjunctions. The most striking of these are between the central cordillera, the mountains of the Huon Peninsula, the northern Sepik ranges, and the Arfak Mountains of the Vogelkop (*see* Fig. 2). Montane genera are invariably represented by different races or species on each of the separated mountain systems. Even within the main central cordillera there are several broad gaps which cut through at approximately 4,000 to 5,000 feet altitude. These lie at the immediate headwaters of the Strickland River and its gorge in central New Guinea, the Tauri-Watut watershed in eastern New Guinea, and the Keveri grasslands north-west of Mt Suckling in the Owen Stanley Range. Though these gaps are low enough to permit, or to have permitted, the passage of elements of the lowland bird fauna through to the opposite sides of the island, they appear at present to play a more significant role in separating the montane fauna on either side of them. The Strickland gorge area, for example, which descends in parts to about 2,500 feet in the heart of the central cordillera, would appear to constitute the minor but significant zoogeographical barrier that has been predicted by some ornithologists to lie between the Telefomin and Mt Hagen mountains.

Three major phases of altitudinal speciation may be distinguished in montane New Guinean birds: (a) latitudinally allopatric forms; (b) altitudinally allopatric but latitudinally sympatric forms, or species pairs, which may still compete ecologically; and (c) closely related, fully sympatric species. Examples of latitudinally allopatric forms have been given above. Present distribution patterns and environmental conditions explain their evolution. Examples of phase (b) are the *Pachycephala schlegelii-P. soror*, *Ptiloprora perstriata-P. guisei*, *Melidectes belfordi-M. rufocrissalis*, *Astrapia stephaniae-A. mayeri*, *Amblyornis macgregoriae-A. subalaris*, and perhaps *Sericornis perspicillatus-S. arfakianus* species pairs. A factor that has probably contributed incipiently to their development is the phenomenon of clinal increase in size with increasing altitude (Bergmann's rule). Increase of size with altitude is exhibited in many montane species, notably the glossy swiftlet (*Collocalia esculenta*), stout-billed cuckoo-shrike (*Coracina caeruleogrisea*) and bare-eyed honeyeater (*Melipotes fumigatus*). Examples of phase (c) are the other species of scrub-wrens (*Sericornis*) and flag birds of paradise (*Lophorina, Parotia* and *Pteridophora*) whose sympatry and ecology have been summarized above under 'Ecology'.

Because phases (b) and (c) represent older levels of speciation the following model, based on reconstruction of the more recent palaeo-environment of New Guinea, is tentatively put forward to explain

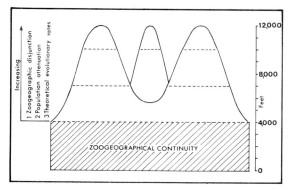

Fig 3. Altitudinal zonation of life zones showing increasing fragmentation with altitude.

their evolution. Current evidence indicates that the New Guinean mountain systems were thrown up in late Tertiary to Pleistocene times (less than 10 million years ago). Major climatic events to which the mountains have been subjected since then have been the temperature oscillations of the Pleistocene with its several (three or four) glacial epochs. These oscillations are believed to have had the effect of alternately depressing and expanding the life zones, like a concertina, in glacial and inter-glacial periods respectively. At the height of glaciation, it is estimated that the ice caps on the mountain ranges descended to approximately 11,500 feet and the tree-line to about 8,000 to 9,000 feet; today the snow-line lies at some 15,500 feet and the tree-line at about 11,000 to 13,000 feet. From the aspect of speciation, these climatic fluctuations appear to have had the important consequence of bringing about the union and separation of montane populations in alternating sequence: during periods of altitudinal contraction of the life zones, montane populations would tend to merge on lower, less-dissected terrain, and during periods of zone expansion, the populations would tend to separate on higher less-connected massifs. When populations of originally common origin re-met after a period of such separation (during which the processes of speciation and evolution would have been operating in isolation), they would have tended either to re-unite or to remain discrete, depending upon the extent to which they had diverged. Evidence of reunion is probably at best reflected today in the altitudinal character gradients in some montane bird species; that of separation appears to be manifest in the species pairs of phase (b); and that of partial separation would seem to be represented by detectable degrees of introgressive hybridization, as between *Astrapia stephaniae* and *A. mayeri* on the northern slopes of Mt Hagen, and between *Melidectes belfordi* and *M. rufocrissalis* in various parts of their range. Such altitudinal introgression is otherwise rare in the New Guinea region. For re-meeting populations to remain discrete, isolating mechanisms such as marked morphological or ethological differences of the kind exemplified in the bowers of *Amblyornis macgregoriae* and *A. subalaris* would have to be developed relatively rapidly. Ecological competition would operate also to keep the populations apart and, in turn, induce altitudinal if not latitudinal sympatry.

Moreover, because the life zones on small, outlying mountain systems are usually altitudinally depressed (land-mass effect), it might be expected that populations from high central and lower peripheral mountain ranges would have impinged on each other at slightly different mean altitudes whenever and wherever they re-met. This, together with ecological competition, is thought to have caused members of the species pairs of phase (b) to 'slide' over or under one another altitudinally. The distribution of the black-backed honeyeater (*Ptiloprora perstriata*)–rufous-backed honeyeater (*P. guisei*) species pair may be interpreted as evidence of such sliding. *P. perstriata* is distributed over a wide altitudinal range (4,000-10,000 feet) in western New Guinea where *P. guisei* is absent; eastwards, it is confined to progressively higher altitudes until, in the Owen Stanley Range, it is only found between 9,000 and 11,000 feet. *P. guisei* replaces *P. perstriata* at lower altitudes in eastern New Guinea, being found between 4,000 and 7,000 feet in the western parts of its range and extending up to 8,000 feet in the east. That the land-mass effect has itself played some part in these postulated developments is indicated by the occurrence of those species centred in the higher, central mountain massifs at the higher levels in almost all cases where their distribution overlaps that of the opposite member of their pair. Notable examples of this relationship are *Ptiloprora perstriata-P. guisei*, *Astrapia mayeri-A. stephaniae*, *Melidectes belfordi-M. rufocrissalis* and *Amblyornis macgregoriae-A. subalaris*.

The altitudinally sympatric species of phase (c) appear to comprise mainly forms whose evolution has been subject to a longer series of environmental fluctuations than the two or three alternations needed to bring about phase (b).

ORIGIN AND HISTORY

New Guinea. The island's marine and freshwater birds, with their generally migratory or nomadic behaviour, comprise part of an essentially cosmopolitan fauna that shows few significant regional characteristics. The relatively impoverished Papuasian representation of this fauna merely reflects the limited opportunities available to water birds in such a well-forested, mountainous region.

By contrast, the land bird fauna, with its richness in numbers, diversity in forms and high proportion of endemics, is almost unique: the greater proportion of it is elsewhere represented only in adjacent Australia. The basic stocks of this fauna are believed to have entered Australo-Papua from Asiatic regions in late Mesozoic (to early Tertiary) times (60-80 million years ago), and to have subsequently diversified there in isolation. Whatever their nature, whether according with steady-state concepts or resulting from continental junctions, land links between south-eastern Asia and Australo-Papua apparently existed then in sufficient continuity to have allowed a rather free faunal exchange.

Reconstruction of the history of the land bird fauna is nevertheless complicated by the presence in New Guinea of five distinct eco-geographical faunal units, each of different or partially different origin. The composition of each of these units has been summarized (*see* 'Ecology' above). The overall congruity of the *Eucalyptus-Melaleuca* woodland unit with the woodland bird fauna of northern Australia at species level indicates that this element arrived in New Guinea from Australia relatively recently. Passage was probably afforded by land bridges that appear to have linked Australia and New Guinea during the glacial epochs of the Pleistocene period (less than one million years ago). It seems likely that the above-mentioned faunal differences between the

Port Moresby and Trans-Fly areas can be attributed to different immigratory pathways at different times.

The impoverished anthropogenous grassland unit, as implied above, is disharmonic and comprises a very high proportion of recently arrived, colonizing bird species from diverse sources, both internal and external to New Guinea. As a unit it may be regarded as having originated with the advent of indigenous man. The alpine meadowland unit has similarly diverse geographical affinities. Nevertheless, its much higher proportion of endemism at racial, species and generic level indicates that it has had a longer history of itinerant colonization, probably dating back to the time when the central mountain ranges were raised towards the end of Tertiary times.

That the distinction between the lowland and montane rain-forest fauna units has zoogeographical as well as ecological significance is only just beginning to be appreciated. Analysis of all forest genera in New Guinea shows that 57 per cent are lowland-centred, 33 per cent montane-centred, and 10 per cent represented approximately equally well in both units. The affinities of the lowland-centred and ubiquitous forest genera break down as follows: palaeotropic or endemic with palaeotropic affinities, 41 per cent; Australo-Papuan or endemic with Australo-Papuan affinities, 55 per cent; cosmopolitan, 4 per cent. Those of the montane-centred and ubiquitous genera are: palaeotropic or endemic with palaeotropic affinities, 15 per cent; Australo-Papuan or endemic with Australo-Papuan affinities, 82 per cent; cosmopolitan, 3 per cent. In other words, the lowland fauna has sub-equal representation of palaeotropic and Australo-Papuan elements while the montane fauna is overwhelmingly Australo-Papuan.

The faunal affinities of the montane fauna, moreover, lie not with the bird fauna of northern Australia, but with that found in moister eastern and south-eastern Australia. Despite the distance between montane New Guinea and the humid forests of mid-eastern Australia on the one hand and the proximity of lowland New Guinea to Cape York on the other, there are almost as many genera common to the former two regions as there are to the latter. The number of allopatric genera shared by montane New Guinea and humid eastern Australia also seems significantly high, e.g. *Aepypodius* (New Guinea)-*Alectura* (Australia) in the megapodes; *Melidectes* (New Guinea)-*Anthochaera* (Australia) in the honeyeaters; *Pomareopsis* (New Guinea)-*Grallina* (Australia, though widespread there) in the magpie-larks; *Crateroscelis* (New Guinea)-*Oreoscopus* (Australia) in the vine-wrens; and *Amblyornis* (New Guinea)-*Prionodura* (Australia) in the bower birds. Furthermore, the few species reckoned to represent generalized (i.e. primitive) types by the scant studies that have compared evolutionary relationships between rain forest and related Australian dry country forms on the one hand, and between related forms at different altitudes in New Guinea on the other, are in many cases confined to the subtropical rain forests and associated formations in eastern Australia and montane New Guinea. Such supposedly generalized types are in *Acanthiza*, the Papuan thornbill (*A. murina*) in New Guinea and, probably, the mountain thornbill (*A. katherina*) in Queensland; in *Gerygone*, the brown fly-eater (*G. mouki*) in eastern Australia; in the *Pachycephala pectoralis* superspecies, Schlegel's (*P. schlegelii*) and Sclater's (*P. soror*) whistlers in New Guinea; in birds of paradise, the cnemophiline birds of paradise in New Guinea; in bower birds, the satin (*Ptilonorhynchus*), regent (*Sericulus*) and golden (*Prionodura*) bower birds in Australia; and in Cracticidae, the butcher-birds (*Cracticus*) in Australia and New Guinea.

All of the genera and species mentioned above belong to those families which are thought to have been among the basic stocks of the Australo-Papuan land bird fauna. Many of the relationships quoted are at generic level which suggests that they have considerable antiquity. Considered together, these data favour the view that the great divided arc of subtropical-type rain forest extending from montane New Guinea to eastern Australia represents the ancestral environment for many, perhaps basic elements, of the Australo-Papuan land bird fauna. This concept, which needs much more corroborative data before it can be accepted, has been previously given little credence for two reasons in particular. One is the not inconsiderable immigration of bird forms that is believed to have occurred in wave after wave from New Guinea to Australia during more recent geological history, thus explaining most of the avifaunal links between the two lands. The other stems from the widely held opinion that the forest flora of New Guinea has, as a whole, had a different (relatively recent palaeotropic) origin from that of Australia, thus ruling out the concept of joint ancestral habitat.

The only opportunities of any significance for faunal interchange between New Guinea and Australia after continental continuity was broken by sea towards the end of Tertiary times appear to have occurred during the Pleistocene period. At that time, the lowering of sea-level during the several glacial maxima is believed to have re-established land connections. There are indications, nevertheless, that these land bridges have played a less important role in the overall history of the region's rain-forest bird fauna than has been previously supposed. Firstly, it appears that the interchange of rain-forest elements across the connections may have been relatively limited: plant geographers have concluded that climatic conditions during the relatively dry glacial epochs would have favoured migration of eucalypt woodland at the expense of rain forest. Secondly, the estimated evolutionary rates in Australian birds during the Pleistocene period appear to be too slow to account for the degree of difference between many related Australian and New Guinean groups. The differences are often at generic and superspecies level. Thirdly, many of the rain-forest forms that seem to have drifted into Australia from New Guinea during Pleistocene times have penetrated no further south than north-eastern Queensland. Examples are presumably the northern wompoo (*Ptilinopus magnificus assimilis*), eclectus parrot (*Eclectus*), palm cockatoo (*Probosciger*), double-eyed fig-parrot (*Opopsitta diophthalma marshalli*), frill-necked flycatcher (*Arses telescophthalmus*), tawny-breasted honey-eater (*Xanthotis chrysotis*), trumpet bird (*Phonygammus*) and magnificent rifle-bird (*Ptiloris magnificus*). There is evidence that perhaps the main route used by these species ran from the southern Fly River area across Torres Strait to the region of Cape York Peninsula: for stranded, as it were, in small pockets of rain forest through the Trans-Fly plains are some ten species whose nearest other stations are Cape York Peninsula and the foothill forests of the central New Guinean ranges. *Sericornis beccarii*, *Microeca griseoceps*, *Tregellasia leucops* and *Ptiloris magnificus* are among the species involved.

It appears likely that there were several periods of maximum opportunity for faunal interchange between New Guinea and Australia during the Pleistocene, coinciding with the glacial epochs. The above-mentioned species, all confined to pockets of rain forest on Cape York Peninsula, are probably examples of only the most recent movements into Australia. Some possible examples of earlier drifts are the other species of rifle-birds (*Ptiloris*), the flycatcher *Arses kaupi*, and the other races of the wompoo pigeon and fig-parrot; and also the rainbow lorikeet (*Trichoglossus haematodus*), fern wren (*Oreoscopus*), grey-headed robin (*Heteromyias cinereifrons*), barred cuckoo-shrike (*Coracina lineata*), bridled honeyeater (*Meliphaga frenata*), the cat-birds (*Ailuroedus crassirostris*, *A. melanotis*), and the bower birds *Prionodura* and *Sericulus*. Keast has even asserted that colonization in successive waves by New Guinean rain-forest species across Torres Strait has been the main way in which *new* flycatchers have been added to the Australian bird fauna. Movement in the reverse direction, i.e., from Australia to New Guinea, appears to have been minimal, but may be represented by the butcher-birds (*Cracticus*), a log-runner (*Orthonyx*), the flycatchers *Monarcha trivirgata* and *Rhipidura rufifrons*, some members of the golden whistler (*Pachycephala pectoralis*) superspecies, a tree-creeper (*Climacteris*) and the varied honeyeater (*Meliphaga versicolor*). For a number of these species, e.g. the cat-birds, spectacled flycatcher (*Monarcha*), log-runner, golden whistler group, bridled honeyeater and golden bower bird (*Prionodura*), it is nevertheless virtually impossible to determine whether drifting took place from New Guinea to Australia or in the reverse direction or both ways at different times, or whether it has, in fact, occurred at all.

Apropos the presumed palaeotropic affinities of the New Guinean rain forests, current data indicate that these forests comprise two basic floral elements, one essentially low altitude, the other montane. These elements meet at about 4,000 to 5,000 feet throughout New Guinea, at a level that coincides significantly with the abrupt change in composition of the forest bird fauna. As has been inferred (*see* above), the lowland and hill rain forests are predominantly palaeotropic in origin. The montane forests, on the other hand, with their preponderance of southern hemisphere elements, have closer affinity with the subtropical rain forests of eastern Australia; they appear, in fact, to represent surviving remnants of an austral rain-forest flora that was much more extensive in Australia during Tertiary times (10-70 million years ago). Available palaeobotanical data, for example, indicate that those groups of antarctic beech (*Nothofagus*) and conifers (*Podocarpus*) that are today found only in montane New Guinean (and New Caledonian) subtropical rain forests were distributed widely in southern Australia during the Tertiary.

From these palaeo- and bio-geographical correlations, the following brief and tentative reconstruction of the history of the Australo-Papuan bird fauna has been pieced together. It seems that during early and middle Tertiary times, when continuous land appears to have extended from Australia to southern New Guinea or what there was of it, the basic stocks of the Australo-Papuan bird fauna had the opportunity to establish themselves and to diversify primarily in the then widespread subtropical rain forests. Principal components of the bird fauna were progenitors of the honeyeaters, loriine parrots, pachycephalids, birds of paradise and bower birds, cracticids, and many flycatcher (Muscicapidae) and warbler (Maluridae, Sylviidae) groups. From the later middle Tertiary, a gradual deterioration of climate commenced, and towards the end of that period, New Guinea was cut off from Australia by sea and its central mountain ranges raised. Isolation by sea has continued on and off to present times. In response to these events, the ancestral elements of the bird fauna, together with the subtropical rain forest, apparently withdrew or became confined to refuges along the eastern seaboard of Australia and in montane New Guinea. In Australia, some elements of the bird fauna presumably began to adapt to cooler and probably drier conditions by exploiting niches in the developing sclerophyllous flora, e.g. *Phaps* and its allies, Platycercinae, *Amytornis*, *Acanthiza*, Epthianuridae, *Anthochaera* and related large honeyeaters, and Cracticidae. At the same time (Miocene onwards), it seems that a trickle of palaeotropic forms commenced to flow into New Guinea, continuing up until the present, across islands up-folded between the Sunda and Sahul Shelves. Palaeotropic forest elements probably entered New Guinea in the same way. The island stepping-stones, usually low in altitude and strung out along the equator, in all likelihood afforded selective passage to lowland rain-forest forms. This would offer some explanation for the present mingling of palaeotropic and Australo-Papuan forest faunas at low altitudes in New Guinea and the apparently pristine composition of the latter in montane regions.

Northern Melanesia. The relatively impoverished bird faunas on the islands and archipelagos peripheral to northern and eastern New Guinea have been derived mainly from New Guinea by colonization across the sea. The geography of the region, and patterns of distribution and variation in some apparently recent arrivals, suggest that the main route of ingress ran from north-eastern New Guinea through New Britain and New Ireland to the Solomons, rather than directly from eastern New Guinea to the Solomons via the D'Entrecasteaux and Louisiade archipelagos. Even so, representative populations of many stocks in the Solomons are more distinct and diverse, and thus probably older, than those in the Bismarcks. One such example is the relationship between the cuckoo-doves, *Reinwardtoena crassirostris* (Bougainville)-*R. browni* (New Britain)-*R. reinwardtii* (New Guinea). The evolutionary isolation offered by the Solomons to arriving forms is strikingly exemplified by the sea-eagle (*Haliaeetus*): *H. leucogaster* extends without appreciable variation from India to Australia, New Guinea and the Bismarcks, but is represented in the Solomons by the distinct *H. sanfordi*.

The origin and affinities of the bird faunas on the islands of the Bismarck Archipelago surrounding New Britain may be summarized as follows. New Ireland and New Hanover represent the origin of the main part of the land bird fauna in four different groups of islands: (1) the Admiralty and St Matthias islands, which are outlying islands with a typically peripheral fauna (impoverished, but with a high proportion of strongly modified forms); (2) the islands lying off the north-east coast of New Ireland (Tabar, Lihir, Tanga, and Feni groups), which like (1) are oceanic but differ in having only slightly differentiated endemic forms; (3) the Duke of York islands which are not oceanic and lack endemic forms; and (4) Djaul Island which is possibly not oceanic and has a comparatively rich fauna with many strikingly modified endemic forms. The zoogeographical differences between the four groups of islands have apparently resulted from unequal possibilities for avian colonization and from differences in the geological history of the four groups of islands.

BIRDS AND MAN

Barely emancipated from a stone-age culture and still living close to his natural environment, indigenous Melanesian man has an affinity with native bird fauna beyond the ken of western society. His understanding of local bird life varies from all-embracing comprehension to surprising ignorance. He may know the walking pads and favoured fruit of the cassowary, the precise times of egg-laying in local megapodes and every bird of paradise display tree within ten miles; or he may have no idea whatever of the small passerine birds that flutter past him every day. At the root of his understanding is the value of birds to him. Thus, in a region away from the sea where protein is scarce and communal *singsings* the main form of social entertainment, birds with meat and plumes claim his almost undivided attention. Cassowaries are of pre-eminent importance as, apart from the feral pig, they are the only ubiquitous large wild animal in the region. A single bird will furnish a meal of meat for a whole village, and its bones can be used in implements such as spear-heads and its feathers in head-dress adornment. Cassowaries consequently figure prominently in local mythology in many parts of New Guinea. Of lesser value are the smaller 'meat' birds, such as megapodes, large pigeons, cockatoos and hornbills. The eggs of megapodes, laid in heaps of forest-floor debris or in ground warmed by volcanic activity, are also harvested regularly in many parts of Papuasia. In some areas, agricultural activity is geared to the movement of the more obvious migratory birds. Thus in parts of the central Highlands, sweet potato gardens are planted when the bee-eater (*Merops ornatus*), known locally as the 'fine-weather bird', arrives from Australia. Plumes from birds of paradise, particularly the black central tail feathers of the Stephanie astrapia (*Astrapia stephaniae*), are highly prized for adornments to *singsing* head-dresses. Of even greater value in some Highland areas are the feathers of the harpy eagle (*Harpyopsis*), a bird associated with the ghosts. So strong is this belief that some of the peoples sacrifice pigs [q.v.] when they kill one of these eagles. Hornbills, cockatoos and cassowaries are often kept as village pets, though the latter are usually butchered for meat when they are large enough.

Knowledge of birds varies from man to man and from area to area. Older men are usually found to have a more detailed understanding of the local bird fauna than younger men who, drawn to the main towns and becoming familiar with shot guns, are in many areas beginning to lose the kind of acquaintance with the natural environment that comes from following traditional hunting methods. On the regional level, it is generally found that the peoples in the Highlands of New Guinea and on outlying islands have a better knowledge of local bird faunas than some lowland peoples such as those who live by fishing rather than hunting. The Buin people of Bougainville Island, for example, know every local species by a name that is derived from the sound of the species' call or song, e.g. *kakata* for the corella, *Cacatua ducrops*, and *tui* for the flycatcher, *Myiagra ferocyanea*.

Indigenous man's impact on the bird fauna is being felt in three different ways: from hunting, from the introduction of feral animals, and from the clearing of natural habitat (i.e. forest). The traditional hunting methods using bow and arrow, and snare, are now being replaced by the more efficient shot gun. This, together with the growth of population in many areas, has brought about increased hunting pressure all over the region. Species affected are mainly game and plume birds. Presumably as a consequence of shooting, large pigeons, especially those with sedentary habits like the great crowned pigeons (*Goura*) and several of the larger parrots, e.g. Pesquet's parrot (*Psittrichas fulgidus*), have become rare almost to the point of extinction over large parts of their range. Yet despite the intensity of hunting, the birds of paradise—particularly the sought-after species, the Stephanie astrapia and red and yellow kumuls (*Paradisaea raggiana* and *P. minor* respectively) —do not yet appear to have been seriously depleted in numbers. One reason for this may be the polygynous breeding system developed in the more gaudily plumed species, and the breeding capacity of uncoloured males.

There are three main feral animals: the cane toad (*Bufo marinus*), a deer (*Cervus timorensis*) and the pig (*Sus scrofa*). All operate to disrupt the ecology of natural habitats. Cane toads, found around lowland towns and adjacent areas, not only eat small reptiles, insects, etc., that are normally taken by birds and small mammals, but may also poison some of the larger animals that prey on the toads themselves. *Cervus timorensis*, confined so far to certain parts of lowland southern New Guinea, and the ubiquitous pig root and forage destructively on the forest floor ruining the environment for the smaller ground-dwelling and -feeding native fauna. About towns and villages, feral and domestic cats (*Felis catus*) also take their toll of small birds and other native fauna.

Deprivation of forest habitat, whether through clearing or burning for garden, village or hunting, has the most serious effect of all on the forest bird fauna. The vast anthropogenous grasslands of the mid-mountain valleys in eastern New Guinea testify to this. Two birds of paradise, the blue bird (*Paradisaea rudolphi*) and the white-fronted flag-bird (*Parotia lawesii*), are among those species threatened by loss of forest in these valleys. Though they occasionally select display trees or bowers in secondary growth, both birds apparently depend for survival on large stretches of primary forest on gently sloping or flat land surfaces between 3,500 and 6,000 feet altitude.

Indigenous man, especially where he lives close to his natural environment, is readily and sympathetically responsive to the need for nature conservation [q.v.]. Indeed, tracts of forested land are maintained in the Tari Valley (as sacred groves of the sun) and, elsewhere in New Guinea, tracts of primary or tall secondary forest are left intentionally as hunting or fauna protection preserves. Nevertheless, indigenous man is at present confronted by two cardinal obstacles that he will have to overcome if his endeavours for nature conservation are to be at all effective: one is the tendency for the juggernaut of technological progress to overwhelm his thinking; the other is his predisposition to regard nature conservation as a local rather than a regional or national need.

ZOOGEOGRAPHY

R. A. Falla, 'The Australian Element in the Avifauna of New Zealand', *Emu*, vol. 53, 1953.
I. C. J. Galbraith and E. H. Galbraith, 'Land birds of Guadalcanal and the San Cristoval group, Eastern Solomon Islands', *Bulletin of the British Museum (Natural History)*, Zoology, vol. 9, 1962.
E. T. Gilliard and M. Le Croy, 'Results of the 1958-1959 Gilliard New Britain Expedition. 4. Annotated list of birds of the Whiteman Mountains, New Britain', *Bulletin of the American Museum of Natural History*, vol. 135, 1967.
A. Keast, 'Australian birds: their zoogeography and adaptations to an arid continent', in *Biogeography and Ecology in Australia*, ed. A. Keast, R. L. Crocker and C. S. Christian. The Hague, 1959.
——— 'Bird Speciation on the Australian Continent', *Bulletin of the Museum of Comparative Zoology at Harvard College*, vol. 123, 1961.
E. Mayr, 'Borders and subdivision of the Polynesian region as based on our knowledge of the distribution of birds', *Proceedings of the Sixth Pacific Science Congress*, vol. 4, 1941.
——— 'The origin and the history of the bird fauna of Polynesia', *Proceedings of the Sixth Pacific Science Congress*, vol. 4, 1941.
——— *List of New Guinea Birds*. New York, 1941.
——— 'The birds of Timor and Sumba', *Bulletin of the American Museum of Natural History*, vol. 83, 1944.
——— 'Wallace's Line in the Light of Recent Zoogeographic Studies', *Quarterly Review of Biology*, vol. 19, 1944.
——— *Birds of the southwest Pacific*. New York, 1945.
——— 'Fragments of a Papuan Ornithogeography', *Proceedings of the Seventh Pacific Science Congress*, vol. 4, 1953.
A. L. Rand and E. T. Gilliard, *Handbook of New Guinea Birds*. London, 1967.
F. Salomonsen, 'Some remarkable new birds from Dyaul Island, Bismarck Archipelago, with zoogeographical notes', *Biologiske Skrifter*, vol. 14, 1964.
E. Stresemann, 'Sauropsida; Aves', in *Handbuch der Zoologie*, ed. W. G. Kuekenthal and T. Krumbach. Berlin, 1927-34.

ECOLOGY

R. Archbold and A. L. Rand, 'Results of the Archbold Expeditions. No. 7. Summary of the 1933-1934 Papuan Expedition', *Bulletin of the American Museum of Natural History*, vol. 68, 1934-5.
——— and L. J. Brass, 'Results of the Archbold Expeditions. No. 41. Summary of the 1938-1939 New Guinea Expedition', *Bulletin of the American Museum of Natural History*, vol. 79, 1941-2.
J. M. Diamond, 'Preliminary Results of an Ornithological Exploration of the North Coastal Range, New Guinea', *American Museum Novitates*, no. 2362, 1969.
J. Kikkawa and W. T. Williams, 'Altitudinal Distribution of Land Birds in New Guinea', *Search*, vol. 2, 1971.
E. Mayr, *List of New Guinea Birds*. New York, 1941.
——— *Birds of the southwest Pacific*. New York, 1945.
A. L. Rand and L. J. Brass, 'Results of the Archbold Expeditions. No. 29. *Bulletin of the American Museum of Natural History*, vol. 77, 1940-1.
A. L. Rand and E. T. Gilliard, *Handbook of New Guinea Birds*. London, 1967.
R. Schodde and W. B. Hitchcock, 'Contributions to Papuasian Ornithology. 1. Report on the Birds of the Lake Kutubu Area, Territory of Papua and New Guinea', *CSIRO Division of Wildlife Research*, *Technical Paper*, no. 13, 1968.
E. Stresemann, 'Dr. Burgers' ornithologische Ausbeute im Stromgebiet des Sepik', *Archiv für Naturgeschichte*, vol. 89, 1923.

MOVEMENTS

L. W. Filewood, 'A New Guinea Jungle Banding Station', *The Australian Bird Bander*, vol. 9, 1971.
A. L. Rand and E. T. Gilliard, *Handbook of New Guinea Birds*. London, 1967.

S. D. Ripley, 'A Systematic and Ecological Study of Birds of New Guinea', *Bulletin of the Peabody Museum of Natural History*, vol. 19, 1964.

BREEDING

R. Archbold and A. L. Rand, 'Results of the Archbold Expeditions. No. 7. Summary of the 1933-1934 Papuan Expedition', *Bulletin of the American Museum of Natural History*, vol. 68, 1934-5.
——— and L. J. Brass, 'Results of the Archbold Expeditions. No. 41. Summary of the 1938-1939 New Guinea Expedition', *Bulletin of the American Museum of Natural History*, vol. 79, 1941-2.
A. H. Miller, 'Seasonal Activity and Ecology of the Avifauna of an American Equatorial Cloud Forest', *University of California Publications in Zoology*, vol. 66, 1963.
A. J. North, *Nests and eggs of birds found breeding in Australia and Tasmania*. Australian Museum, Sydney, 1901-14.
A. L. Rand and E. T. Gilliard, *Handbook of New Guinea Birds*. London, 1967.
S. D. Ripley, 'A Systematic and Ecological Study of Birds of New Guinea', *Bulletin of the Peabody Museum of Natural History*, vol. 19, 1964.
R. Schodde and W. B. Hitchcock, 'Contributions to Papuasian Ornithology. 1. Report on the Birds of the Lake Kutubu Area, Territory of Papua and New Guinea', CSIRO Division of Wildlife Research, *Technical Paper*, no. 13, 1968.

REGIONAL VARIATION AND EVOLUTION

T. W. E. David, *The Geology of the Commonwealth of Australia*, ed. W. R. Browne. London, 1950.
J. M. Diamond, 'Preliminary Results of an Ornithological Exploration of the North Coastal Range, New Guinea', *American Museum Novitates*, no. 2362, 1969.
I. C. J. Galbraith, 'Variation, Relationships and Evolution in the *Pachycephala pectoralis* superspecies (Aves, Muscicapidae), *Bulletin of the British Museum (Natural History)*, Zoology, vol. 4, 1956.
E. T. Gilliard, *Birds of Paradise and Bower Birds*. London, 1969.
——— and M. Le Croy, 'Birds of the Victor Emanuel and Hindenburg Mountains, New Guinea. Results of the American Museum of Natural History Expedition to New Guinea in 1954', *Bulletin of the American Museum of Natural History*, vol. 123, 1961.
A. Keast, 'Bird Speciation on the Australian Continent', *Bulletin of the Museum of Comparative Zoology at Harvard College*, vol. 123, 1961.
E. Löffler, 'Pleistocene Glaciation in Papua and New Guinea', *Zeitschrift für Geomorphologie* (forthcoming).
E. Mayr, *List of New Guinea Birds*. New York, 1941.
——— *Systematics and the origin of species, from the viewpoint of a zoologist*. New York, 1942.
——— *Birds of the southwest Pacific*. New York, 1945.
——— and E. T. Gilliard, 'Altitudinal Hybridization in New Guinea Honeyeaters', *Condor*, vol. 54, 1952.
A. L. Rand and E. T. Gilliard, *Handbook of New Guinea Birds*. London, 1967.
F. Salomonsen, 'Some remarkable new birds from Dyaul Island, Bismarck Archipelago, with zoogeographic notes', *Biologiske Skrifter*, vol. 14, 1964.
R. Schodde and J. L. McKean, Ecological distribution of the bower-birds *Amblyornis subalaris* and *A. macgregoriae* in south-eastern New Guinea and their evolution (unpublished).

ORIGIN AND HISTORY

D. Amadon, 'Taxonomic notes on the Australian butcherbirds (family Cracticidae)', *American Museum Novitates*, no. 1504, 1951.
M. G. Audley-Charles, 'Mesozoic Palaeogeography of Australasia', *Palaeogeography, Palaeoclimatology, Palaeoecology*, vol. 2, 1966.
W. J. Bock, 'Relationships between the Birds of Paradise and Bower Birds', *Condor*, vol. 65, 1963.
R. L. Crocker and J. G. Wood, 'Some Historical Influences on the Development of the South -Australian Vegetation Communities and their bearing on Concepts and Classification in Ecology', *Transactions of the Royal Society of South Australia*, vol. 71, 1947.
R. A. Couper, 'Southern hemisphere Mesozoic and Tertiary Podocarpaceae and Fagaceae and their palaeogeographic significance', *Proceedings of the Royal Society*, series B, vol. 152, 1960.
P. J. Darlington, *Zoogeography: the geographical distribution of animals*. New York, 1957.
T. W. E. David, *The Geology of the Commonwealth of Australia*, ed. W. R. Browne. London, 1950.
I. C. J. Galbraith, 'Variation, Relationships and Evolution in the *Pachycephala pectoralis* superspecies (Aves, Muscicapidae), *Bulletin of the British Museum (Natural History)*, Zoology, vol. 4, 1956.
——— and E. H. Galbraith, 'Land birds of Guadalcanal and the San Cristoval group, Eastern Solomon Islands', *Bulletin of the British Museum (Natural History)*, Zoology, vol. 9, 1962.
J. Gentilli, 'Foundations of Australian Bird Geography', *Emu*, vol. 49, 1949.
E. T. Gilliard, *Birds of Paradise and Bower Birds*. London, 1969.
M. F. Glaessner, 'Isolation and Communication in the Geological History of the Australian Fauna', in *The Evolution of Living Organisms*, ed. G. W. Leeper. Melbourne, 1962.
R. Good, 'On the geographical relationships of the angiosperm flora of New Guinea', *Bulletin of the British Museum (Natural History)*, Botany, vol. 2, 1960.
D. A. Herbert, 'Tropical and sub-tropical rainforest in Australia', *Australian Journal of Science*, vol. 22, 1960.
——— 'Ecological Segregation and Australian Phytogeographic Elements', *Proceedings of the Royal Society of Queensland*, vol. 78, 1966.
A. Keast, 'Bird Speciation on the Australian Continent', *Bulletin of the Museum of Comparative Zoology at Harvard College*, vol. 123, 1961.
H. J. Lam, 'Materials towards a study of the flora of the island of New Guinea', *Blumea*, vol. 1, 1934.
E. Mayr, 'The origin of the bird fauna of Polynesia', *Proceedings of the Sixth Pacific Science Congress*, vol. 4, 1941.
——— 'Timor and the Colonization of Australia by Birds', *Emu*, vol. 44, 1944.
——— 'Fragments of a Papuan Ornithogeography', *Proceedings of the Seventh Pacific Science Congress*, vol. 4, 1953.
——— and D. L. Serventy, 'A Review of the Genus *Acanthiza*, Vigors and Horsfield', *Emu*, vol. 38, 1938.
R. Melville, 'Continental drift, mesozoic continents and the migration of the angiosperms', *Nature*, vol. 211, 1966.
I. D. Ripper, 'Global Tectonics and the New Guinea-Solomon Islands Region', *Search*, vol. 1, 1970.
F. Salomonsen, 'Some remarkable new birds from Dyaul Island, Bismarck Archipelago, with zoo-

geographical notes', *Biologiske Skrifter*, vol. 14, 1964.

R. Schodde, Notes on the taxonomy and relationships of the grey-brown species of the genus *Gerygone*, Gould (unpublished).

R. L. Specht, 'The geographical relationships of the flora of Arnhemland', in *Records of the American-Australian Scientific Expedition to Arnhem Land. Vol. 3*, ed. R. L. Specht and C. P. Mountford. Melbourne, 1958.

D. Walker, 'The Changing Vegetation of the Montane Tropics', *Search*, vol. 1, 1970.

J. T. Wilson, 'Hypothesis of Earth's Behaviour', *Nature*, vol. 198, 1963.

MAN AND BIRDS

R. N. Bulmer, 'A primitive ornithology', *Australian Museum Magazine*, vol. 12, 1957.

———— Men and birds in New Guinea: an anthropologist's comments on problems of nature conservation in the Central Highlands. Unpublished mimeo version of talk given to the New Guinea Society, Canberra, 14 May 1961.

———— 'Why is the cassowary not a bird? A problem of zoological taxonomy among the Karam of the New Guinea Highlands', *Man*, vol. 2, 1967.

W. B. Hitchcock, 'Wildlife resources in New Guinea', *Proceedings of the Regional Conference on the Conservation of Nature and Natural Resources in Tropical S. E. Asia, Bangkok, 1965*. Morges, Switzerland, 1968.

A. L. Rand and E. T. Gilliard, *Handbook of New Guinea Birds*. London, 1967.

ACKNOWLEDGMENTS

Figs 1 and 3 are adapted from Galbraith and Galbraith (1962) and Schodde and Hitchcock (1968), respectively.

RICHARD SCHODDE AND W. B. HITCHCOCK

BIRDS OF PARADISE. It is common knowledge that the birds of paradise, family Paradisaeidae, are among the most magnificently plumaged birds in the world. The name has an incongruously fanciful origin. The first specimens to reach Europe, of the greater (*Paradisaea apoda*) and king (*Cicinnurus regius*) birds, which were received by the navigator del Cano from the Rajah of Batjan in the early 1500s, were made up by natives who, as was their way, cut off the feet. This gave rise to the myth that the birds lived and flew forever in the 'highest sky', the female incubating the egg on the hollowed back of the male; so they became known as birds of paradise.

The birds of paradise are almost entirely confined to the New Guinea mainland and off-shore islands, where eighteen of the twenty genera and thirty-eight of the forty-two known species occur. Outside New Guinea, two species are confined to the Moluccas, and four (one manucode and three rifle birds) are found in eastern Australia; two of the latter occur also in New Guinea. There are no species known from the Bismarck Archipelago, Admiralty Islands, or Solomon Islands.

Comprising some of the most highly evolved forms of passerine birds, the group is more closely related to the bower birds than to crow-like birds as was previously supposed. Birds of paradise, like bower birds, have developed specialized patterns of arena behaviour in display, accompanied by an extraordinary variety of plumages which are flaunted to advantage in fantastic displays by adult males. In comparatively unspecialized forms, such as MacGregor's bird (*Macgregoria pulchra*) and the manucodes (genera *Manucodia* and *Phonygammus*), which are apparently monogamous and exhibit conventional avian display patterns, the sexes are similarly plumaged. The males assist in the brooding and feeding of young, and are dark, often glossy black with crisped feathers, without any of the remarkable colours or plumes found in other members of the family.

Advanced forms are the 'true' birds of paradise (*Paradisaea*), the magnificent bird (*Diphyllodes magnificus*), and the flag birds (*Parotia*), in all of which arena behaviour is complex, and the males are gaudily and bizarrely plumaged, polygynous, and do not participate in nest-building or the feeding of young. Most paradisaeas congregate in groups to perform on nearly horizontal bare branches of chosen trees of the forest canopy. There, amid clamorous cawing, up to twenty adult males will dance or perch shivering in concert on the branches with bodies horizontal and plumes flung upward from under the wings over the back in two curving shimmering sprays. Young males and females keep as a rule to the outskirts of the arena while adult males are in attendance. The displays of two paradisaeas, the blue bird (*P. rudolphi*) and hooded bird (*P. guilielmi*), differ in that the male at the height of his performance hangs beneath the branch and surrounds himself with a pulsating aura of breast plumes.

The erect stems of saplings in a circular space in low secondary bush from which all undergrowth has been cleared is the display area for the magnificent bird. Each 'bower' is the property of a solitary male; he displays while perched on the saplings, spreading his yellow back cape and pulsating his deep emerald green breast shield. Flag birds, though they make similar display clearings in the forest, are unique in performing their displays on the ground. In display, the male spreads his velvet black or chestnut and white flank plumes around his body like a skirt or umbrella, vibrates his flag-like head plumes in various directions, and proceeds to prance in half circles around the bower on stiff legs.

Birds of paradise vary in size from six inches long in the king bird (*Cicinnurus regius*) to at least forty-four inches in the black sicklebill (*Epimachus fastosus*), though such measurements are not strictly comparable because of the extraordinarily long tails of some species. The ribbontail (*Astrapia mayeri*), for example, is a small iridescently green-black bird about the size of a thrush, but its tail, with two white central streamers up to forty inches long, is the longest in the world for the size of the bird. This bird of paradise was the last species to be described, in 1939, and even now is known for sure only from a small triangle of mountainous highland in central east New Guinea near Mount Hagen.

The diversity of plumages between adult males of different species of birds of paradise is un-

Magnificent bird of paradise (*Diphyllodes magnifica*), male.

paralleled in any other avian group. Not only do the colours vary, from metallic green-black and blue tints in the manucodes, superb bird (*Lophorina superba*), astrapias, and rifle birds (*Ptiloris*), to scintillating reds in the king and antenna birds (*Cnemophilus macgregorii*) and filmy saffron in the twelve-wired bird (*Seleucidis melanoleuca*) and some paradisaeas, but the plumes are often extraordinarily modified through adaptation to different display patterns. Examples are the flank plumes, which are wire-like and swathed in saffron in the twelve-wired bird, and flat and metallic black in the sicklebills (*Epimachus*); the central tail feathers which are also wire-like and tipped with metallic green in the king bird, and elongate expanded plumes in the astrapias; and the crown plumes which comprise a pair of elongate shafts with blue-white enamelled plates in the enamelled bird (*Pteridophora alberti*) and six flag-tipped wires in the flag birds. In one species, the tonsured bird (*Diphyllodes respublica*), the crown is bare of feathers and the exposed skin coloured brilliant blue.

Such diversity has led to the suggestion that the birds of paradise have evolved from a variety of unrelated birds. There is, nevertheless, compelling evidence that the group is monophyletic. Common themes run through the plumages, exemplified by the dull or duller plumaged females which, in many species, are barred on the breast. A number of homologies appear evident, moreover, in the gaudily plumed males. The side breast and flank feathers in the sicklebills, twelve-wired bird, king bird, and members of the genus *Paradisaea*, all used in display, may have a common genetic basis; likewise, the wire-like tail pendants in the magnificent bird, king bird, and genus *Paradisaea*; and perhaps the metallically tinted gorgets of the rifle birds, flag birds, superb bird, and enamelled bird.

Other evidence comes from common muscle and bone patterns of the head which, in conjunction with plumage and behavioural characteristics, has clarified the lines and direction of evolution in the family. Three species together stand apart in having unspecialized skulls which in structure resemble those of other passerine groups, such as the starlings, and are adapted to allow generalized insect- and fruit-eating. These species, the satin bird (*Loria loriae*), the shieldbill bird (*Loboparadisaea sericea*), and antenna bird, which are grouped in the subfamily Cnemophilinae, are thought to represent the ancestral stock from which both the true birds of paradise, subfamily Paradisaeinae, and bower birds have evolved and diverged. But whereas the cnemophiline birds of paradise are sharply distinct from bower birds in cranial features, they are linked to the true birds of paradise by MacGregor's bird in these characters as well as by jaw muscle patterns. The skull and jaws of paradisaeine birds are specially modified to permit the probing of crevices and grasping of insects by a powerful pincer action of the bill, as is revealed by the ossification of the nasal region and fusion of the mandibular rami. Though the Cnemophilinae have at times been placed with bower birds, they have never been known to construct bowers. The three species are undemonstrative in behaviour and occur in the more remote mountain forests.

That birds of paradise are recently evolved is indicated particularly by relatively frequent hybridism and the almost complete confinement of the family to New Guinea. Hybridism is well-known and documented; no less than sixteen described 'species' have been shown to be individual hybrid forms between different species and even genera. From such hybridism it is inferred that not only are the behavioural, physiological, and genetic differences between the species not as great as their diverse plumages indicate, but also that evolutionary divergence is still young and somewhat incomplete. Concerning confinement to New Guinea, it seems inconceivable that such a highly developed group of birds should be restricted to the region, unless it had evolved only recently with little time to disperse. Even within New Guinea dispersal and distribution patterns are apparently still developing. The great majority of species, twenty-six, including all primitive forms, occur in the mountain forests of the interior. These forests, dominated by trees of the genera *Podocarpus* and *Nothofagus* (antarctic beech), and of the families Cunoniaceae, Escalloniaceae, Lauraceae, Monimiaceae, and Myrtaceae, all of which have affinity with the floras of the southern continents, are also centres of diversification for the closely related bower birds in both New Guinea and Australia. The lowland New Guinea rain forests of Malesian affinity (*see* MALESIA), by contrast, support few species, including some of the most highly evolved forms such as the king bird, twelve-wired bird, and species of *Paradisaea*, as well as all manucodes. Thus it may be concluded that the birds of paradise originated in the cool mountain forests of New Guinea and that their history since has been one of expansions and evolution towards lower ground.

All members of the family are forest dwellers and arboreal feeders, spending much of their time in the mid and upper forest stages where they eat insects and fruit. The sicklebills (*Drepanornis* and *Epimachus*) use their long decurved bills for probing their food from crevices, epiphytes, and matted vegetable debris on tree trunks and branches.

Each species, moreover, fills its own particular niche at particular altitudes. At heights from sea-level to about 1,600 feet in eastern New Guinea, for example, the paradisaeas are found in tree crowns, the king bird in the forest undergrowth and midstage, and the twelve-wired bird in primary swamp and alluvial forest. Between the altitudes of 3,000 and 5,000 feet the magnificent bird occurs in mixed forest along the river valleys, the blue bird is confined to primary oak (*Lithocarpus-Castanopsis*) forest, while in the secondary growth and disturbed forest about native gardens, the red (*Paradisaea raggiana*) and lesser (*P. minor*) birds may be found. In the river gullies above about 5,000 feet, the superb bird replaces the magnificent, but does not extend above 6,500-8,000 feet. On mountain slopes above 6,500 feet, where the oaks are replaced by antarctic beech forest little disturbed by gardening, the red and blue birds give way to the Stephanie astrapia (*Astrapia stephaniae*), Meyer's sicklebill (*Epimachus meyeri*), and satin bird. The sicklebill extends to 10,000-10,500 feet, near the tree line, but at 8,000-9,000 feet, where the cloud forest dominated by podocarps and species of Myrtaceae replaces the beech, the Stephanie astrapia and satin birds are replaced by the ribbontail and antenna birds, respectively. MacGregor's bird is known to prefer the sub-alpine shrubberies bordering alpine grasslands at the tree line, between 10,000-11,500 feet.

The voices of the birds of paradise are often the antithesis of their resplendent plumages, the harsh crow-like cawings of the paradisaeas being particularly discordant. Some calls, nevertheless, are arrestingly characteristic, such as the strange hissing whistle of the ribbontail, uttered as the bird flies with streaming tail from tree to tree, or the staccato machine-gun-like rattle of Meyer's sicklebill, barked during display.

All species, except the king bird and cnemophiline birds, build cup-shaped nests constructed of sticks and/or herbaceous and woody tendrils, bark, and leaves, and lined with finer vegetable material. They are usually placed in the fork of a tree branch well above the ground. Cnemophiline birds build domed nests and the king bird uses hollows in small trees. The eggs vary from grey-white to usually pink, pale reddish-brown, or buff in ground colour, and are often beautifully marked with dark grey-brown to reddish spots and streaks. Clutch size varies from one egg—most birds of paradise—to two—king bird, rifle birds, superb bird, and all manucodes.

Some species, particularly those of the genus *Paradisaea*, suffered from plume hunters when, at the height of the millinery trade in feathers between 1880 and 1920, some twenty to eighty thousand skins reached the European markets every year. The export of bird of paradise plumes from New Guinea, at least the Australian-administered territories, is now prohibited by law, and there are severe penalties for killing birds of paradise with fire-arms.

W. J. Bock, 'Relationships between the Birds of Paradise and the Bower Birds', *Condor*, vol. 65, 1963; E. T. Gilliard, *Birds of Paradise and Bower Birds*. London, 1969; E. Mayr, 'Birds of Paradise', *Natural History*, vol. 54, 1945; —— Family Paradisaeidae, in *Check-list of Birds of the World*: A Continuation of the Work of James L. Peters; ed. by E. Mayr and J. C. Greenway, Jr, vol. 15. Cambridge, Mass., 1962; A. L. Rand and E. T. Gilliard, *Handbook of New Guinea Birds*. London, 1967; R. Schodde, 'About the Kumul', *Wildlife in Australia*, vol. 3, no. 2, 1965-6.

ACKNOWLEDGMENT
Photograph by E. T. Gilliard.

RICHARD SCHODDE

BLACKWOOD, Francis Price (1809-1854), Royal Navy officer, was born 25 May 1809, second son of Vice-Admiral Sir Henry Blackwood. He entered the Navy in 1821 and served in H.M.S. *Arachne* and *Alligator*, becoming a captain in 1838. He was then placed in command of a surveying expedition and in H.M.S. *Fly* explored the south-eastern coast of New Guinea between 1842 and 1845. He also surveyed the central and north-eastern parts of Torres Strait and explored about 150 miles of the coast of New Guinea to the north and east of Torres Strait. He died on 22 March 1854.

D. C. Gordon, *The Australian Frontier in New Guinea 1870-1885*. New York, 1951.

FRANCIS WEST

BOGIA. People of the Madang District.
Reference:
J. Schebesta, 'Terms Expressing Relationship in the Language of Dagoi and Bonaputa-Mopu, New Guinea', *Anthropos*, vols 35-6, 1940-1.

BOISMENU, Alain Marie Guynot de (1870-1953), one of the Congregation of Missionaries of the Sacred Heart in British New Guinea (Papua) 1898-1945, was born the eleventh child of an aristocratic Breton family at St Malo, France, on 27 December 1870. In his youth he planned to become a missionary and at the age of sixteen he entered Sacred Heart Congregation, taking his vows on 4 October 1888. He was ordained priest on 10 February 1895. After a short period as a teacher and professor in training establishments he was appointed to the British New Guinea mission. He embarked at Genoa on 8 September 1897 and arrived at Port Leon, Yule Island, on 25 January 1898, to begin a ministry which lasted almost continuously for the next forty-seven years.

Within a fortnight of his arrival, on 11 February 1898, this young man of twenty-eight, with little pastoral and no missionary experience, was appointed counsellor to Archbishop Navarre [q.v.], the Vicar Apostolic of British New Guinea, pro-Vicar General and Superior of the mission. This meant that, in effect, he was the chief executive of the mission since Navarre was in a state of almost continual ill-health and the Vicar General and Superior, Father André Jullien, was visiting Europe at the time seeking new funds for the rapidly expanding mission. Two years later, on 18 March 1900, Father de Boismenu was consecrated in Paris as coadjutor bishop to Navarre. He succeeded him as Vicar Apostolic of British New Guinea in January 1908, when Navarre retired. Bishop de Boismenu himself retired towards the close of World War II, in January 1945. He then went to live in retirement in the green valley of Kubuna, where he died on 5 November 1953, having lived and worked in Papua for nearly fifty-six years.

Since he served as a member of Navarre's episcopal council from within the first few weeks of his arrival at Yule Island in 1898 and then became coadjutor and finally bishop himself until 1945, de Boismenu was always in a position of influence and authority within the mission. In the first few decades he was largely responsible for transforming Navarre's pioneer mission into a more highly developed structure able to cope with the expansion of activities from the coast and the Mekeo plain into the mountains. In February 1898 de Boismenu encouraged the development of an approach and organizational structure based on plans developed by André Jullien as a result of his experience in New Guinea. This was a break from the structure that Navarre had developed on the basis of his experience in European parish churches. Under this new arrangement the mission was organized into a number of districts. Each district had its head-station or centre under a director, who had local responsibility over the community of mission priests and brothers and converts in his district. There was also a definition of central responsibilities. All pastoral matters in the district were referred by the director to the bishop, all matters concerning religious affairs were referred to the superior of the mission. Financial affairs in the districts were co-ordinated under a central bursar to whom the directors referred in matters of local finance. This structure allowed for more precisely defined central administration, but also for the growth of variety in the districts where there could be adaptations of policy and structure to local circumstances. It also marked a change from a pattern of single stations, with a local missionary evangelizing a small local population, to the development of district centres where comparatively larger communities could grow and from which missionaries could move around to evangelize a wider population. The training of local catechists was essential for the success of this system. At a meeting of the episcopal council in March 1908 de Boismenu developed certain aspects of this system a stage further, particularly in relation to finance. In 1893 the mission had reserve funds in Sydney of 100,000 francs, but by 1900 these were exhausted. Local revenues were not providing sufficient for the demands made by the costly extension of their work into the mountains. By 1900 Oba Oba had been established as the centre of the Kuni district and by May 1905 Popoli had become the centre of the Mafulu district, both largely developed as a result of explorations by de Boismenu. In the reorganization of financial administration in 1908 the office of the bursar was defined more precisely. With the bishop and the superior he was to control all financial affairs. His responsibilities also included the management of livestock and of the two coconut plantations of Kevori and Maeaera totalling approximately a thousand acres. To rationalize financial administration, the directors of centres sent all requests for supplies and equipment to the bursar and he made at least two visits a year to each district to assess the situation. This new financial system, devised by de Boismenu, gradually produced results. By 1909 the deficit was reduced, revenue being 63,000 francs and expenditure being 66,500 francs. However, unlike his contemporary, Mgr Louis Couppé, Vicar Apostolic of New Britain from 1890 to 1923, who developed extensive plantations as an economic basis for his mission, Mgr de Boismenu ran his mission on a shoestring budget. For instance, in 1913 only 10,000 francs out of a total revenue of 73,000 came from plantations, the remainder coming from overseas funds and donations. His approach was dictated not only by the restrictions which the Papuan terrain placed on plantation development and the tight control the Administration exercised over the leasing of land, but more significantly, by his views on the role of the mission and the need for strict economy in the management of its material establishments. Perhaps this policy made it more possible for these missionaries to grow close to their Papuan congregations.

To rationalize the administration of the mission further he also instituted, about this time, an annual reporting system. Each July directors of districts assembled key members of their team to prepare a district report on a questionnaire he had devised. These district reports were then examined by the bishop, assembled into an annual report and used as the basis for further policy developments.

Under his administration the missionary districts and activities were greatly expanded. In 1898, when de Boismenu arrived, there were five districts covering 8,000 people of whom 2,400 were baptized Catholics, while 800 children were attending the mission's schools. By 1945 there were eleven districts covering 65,000 people and the mission counted 23,500 people as adherents and had an enrolment of 7,000 pupils in its schools. After the restoration and expansion programme began in 1908 the mission spread into new centres in Onongge (1913), Port Moresby (1915), Toaripi (1927), and Samarai (1932). As soon as he assumed responsibility as coadjutor in 1900 he joined the last stages of what he and Navarre saw as the 'spheres of influence' battle.

When Australia assumed control over Papua de Boismenu carried the battle into Australian religious and political circles. In October 1904 he went as the official representative of New Guinea to a congress of the Catholic Church held in Melbourne. There he tried to win the support of the Australian hierarchy for the mission's battle to extend its territory. Then in December 1907 a letter was written by representatives of the London Missionary Society, Anglican and Methodist missions to the Prime Minister, Alfred Deakin, protesting at a suggestion made by the Royal Commission into Papua for a relaxation of the 'spheres of influence' arrangements. In reply to this de Boismenu wrote a letter stating the views of the mission on the issue. The closing remarks of this letter to Deakin gave the key to understanding his position: 'I respectfully request the Government of the Territory not to support a plan in this country which would tend to impede the missionaries' free activity and to destroy the peoples' religious liberty'. This and other evidence suggests that de Boismenu and his fellow French missionaries brought to this conflict a special sensitivity and interpretation moulded by the heated divisions between Church and State current in France at the time.

In a pastoral letter of 1 November 1908 to his missionaries de Boismenu laid down basic principles of policy in relation to their work. He felt that, despite vigorous missionary endeavour up to that time, the Christians of Papua did not live in a way that was distinguishable from that of their fellow-countrymen. He therefore laid down broad lines to guide the missionaries in achieving this object. He wished them, without neglecting the others, to concentrate their greatest efforts on building up 'a group of young serious Christians who would form a focus of Christian life in each village'. The formation of this Christian elite became the basis for his educational policy too. In 1911 he stressed that his objective was 'to have finally, not simply Christians, but a Christian community (une chrétienté)'. By 1932, in a circular letter dated 25 July, he was refining pastoral methods in order to give the missionaries guide lines for dealing with the wide range of religious situations that had developed by that time. As early as 1908, to ensure a uniform basis for religious teaching, he had a catechism, already in the Roro language, translated into other vernaculars. Along with his stress on the need for thorough grounding in vernacular and a clear understanding of local life and customs, it seems clear from much of his writing that he was antagonistic to customs such as dancing and polygamy and that he saw Papuans as children. The religious culture and way of life that he was attempting to implant was not only contrary to many aspects of indigenous life, but was influenced very much by the background of French Catholicism from which he and most of his missionaries came.

De Boismenu laid the foundations of his educational policy in a set of regulations for schools which he released in October 1908. By these regulations a 'school visitor' was appointed with full authority for organizing and directing schools, particularly in the field of secular education. He was to make biennial visits to each school, conduct examinations, check pupil registers, develop programmes and methods for teaching secular subjects and report annually to the bishop as a means of applying and developing this policy and programme. Gradually the various teaching functions of priests, brothers and sisters were defined and a system of various types and levels of schools was evolved. In a pastoral letter of 3 December 1913, on 'Christian education in schools' de Boismenu stressed the importance of an adequate general education to supplement the basic work of religious education in mission schools. He also stressed the importance of English language in the curriculum, if graduates from mission schools were to play an adequate role in the colonial society. By his stress on teaching English in his schools he anticipated the growing concern of the Administration about this aspect of education.

The bishop was also responsible for the development of another important area of education. In his pastoral letter 'on the need for indigenous assistance' of 12 February 1918 he suggested the necessity for turning into a formal educational programme the existing practice whereby mission priests and brothers gathered local assistants to teach them the trades needed for the building and maintenance of mission stations. In 1919 Father E. van Goetham, a school visitor, began an arts and crafts centre at the central school on Yule Island. Soon after Father P. Fastre taught some of the people in the Mafulu district how to plant and cultivate coffee and rice. In 1923 de Boismenu stressed the need to introduce professional trade training into the educational system. August 1924 saw the establishment of a technical school at Yule Island, for a full course of technical training. A similar scheme of craft education was begun for girls. By 1932, forty-eight graduates of this and other technical schools were employed by the Administration and private enterprise, while sixteen worked for the mission itself. By the following year ninety-two students were attending these institutions at various centres throughout the mission. In both general and technical education the mission had the support of government grants and subsidies.

De Boismenu hoped that young graduates from this system of technical education would become a Christian elite in the general community. He also devised plans for an indigenous elite in the more religious aspects of mission life. Navarre had attempted to establish special schools for the training of Papuan catechists. These had failed for a number of reasons. In the extension of his original education programme in 1913 de Boismenu made plans for special programmes to train catechists. Finally in 1916 he established a special training school for them at Kevori. His episcopate also marked a gradual expansion in the numbers of catechists from nine in 1908 to 219 in 1933. He also laid down principles to guide their work.

This period saw also the beginning of an indigenous priesthood. In 1918 Joseph Tavrino was sent to Europe to continue studies after special training at Yule Island, but he died in Marseilles at the age of twenty-two in 1922. Louis Vangeke [q.v.], born in Beipa in 1905, went to Madagascar in 1928 for his studies. He returned to Papua an ordained priest in 1937. Attempts had been made in 1920 to found an indigenous congregation of brothers, but this proved unsuccessful. More successful was de Boismenu's foundation in April 1918 of the Handmaids of Our Lord, an indigenous sisterhood. In 1921 he brought to Papua Sister Marie Thérèse Noblet who, until her death in January 1930, did much to develop this congregation. Its headquarters were established at Kubuna, where in 1935 de Boismenu brought a group of Carmelite nuns from France and the Philippine Islands to found the first contemplative monastery in New Guinea.

Mgr de Boismenu, in his lengthy and productive episcopacy in Papua, laid solid foundations for the expanding mission. His personality and outlook made a deep impression upon his people. Perhaps the most fitting assessment of this remarkable man is that from James McAuley, who knew him during his last years of retirement: 'I would nominate him as the person in my experience who most completely exemplified "greatness" —an inspiring force of mind and will, large views, courage, intense affections and complete self-abnegation, cheerfulness, candour, a noble simplicity utterly devoid of pretension. And behind these qualities something more, as all his associates knew: a rare sanctity and unerring spiritual discernment'.

Australian Annals of Our Lady of the Sacred Heart, 1889—, Kensington, N.S.W.
British New Guinea, *Annual Report* 1898-9 to 1905-6.
Commonwealth of Australia, 'Report of the Royal Commission of Inquiry into the Present Conditions, including the Method of Government, of the Territory of Papua, and the Best Means for their Improvement', *C. P. P.*, joint vol., 1907.
———— *Annual Report, Territory of Papua 1906-7* to *1939-40*. Melbourne and Canberra, 1908-41.
A. Dupeyrat, *Papouasie: Histoire de la Mission, 1885-1935*. Paris, 1935.
———— *Papuan Conquest*. Melbourne, 1948.
———— *Mitsinari: Twenty-one Years among the Papuans*. London, 1954.
———— and F. de la Noe, *Sainteté au Naturel: Alain de Boismenu, évêque des Papous*. Paris, 1958.
B. Grimshaw, *Adventures in Papua with the Catholic Mission*. Melbourne, 1912.
J. McAuley, 'My New Guinea', *Quadrant*, vol. 5, no. 3, 1960-1.
Missionaries of the Sacred Heart, Archives. Diocese of Bereina, Kairuku (formerly Vicariate Apostolic of Yule Island).
A. Pineau, *Marie-Thérèse Noblet, Servante de Notre-Seigneur en Papouasie 1889-1930*. Issoudun, 1938.
R. J. LACEY

(*See also* MISSIONS)

BOLUMINSKI, Franz (1863-1913), German administrator, was born in 1863 at Lessen in the district of Graudenz in West Prussia. After serving as a sergeant with the German troops in East Africa he found employment with the New Guinea Company in 1894, and was stationed at Astrolabe Bay. In March 1899 he transferred to the colonial service and was posted to New Ireland to open the station at Kavieng in the following year. He was promoted to the rank of district officer (Bezirksamtmann) on 9 November 1910. He died at Kavieng in 1913. Boluminski ruled his district with the methods he had learnt as a sergeant in East Africa, demanding absolute obedience from the local people. He was regarded with awe rather than affection. But he appears to have had a paternalistic interest in their welfare and within the limitations of his method was a conscientious and devoted official.   MARJORIE JACOBS

(*See also* GERMAN NEW GUINEA)

BOUGAINVILLE. People of the Solomon Islands, east of New Guinea. References:
B. Blackwood, 'Report on Field Work in Buka and Bougainville', *Oceania*, vol. 2, 1931-2.
———— *Both Sides of Buka Passage*. Oxford, 1935.
———— 'Treatment of the Sick in the Solomon Islands', *Folklore*, vol. 46, 1935.
———— 'Field Work in Bougainville', in *Custom is King*, ed. L. H. Dudley Buxton. London, 1936.
W. H. Howells and D. Oliver, 'Microevolution among the Bougainville Populations', Tenth Pacific Science Congress, Honolulu, *Abstracts of Symposium Papers*, 1961.
E. Ogan, 'An Election in Bougainville', *Ethnology*, vol. 4, 1965.
———— 'Nasioi Marriage', *Southwestern Journal of Anthropology*, vol. 22, 1966.

(*See also* BUIN; SIWAI)

BOUGAINVILLE.   People of the Solomon 1768), French officer and navigator. After serving in the French Army in Canada Bougainville became a naval officer and in 1766 he sailed with the *Boudeuse* and the *Etoile* into the Pacific to the Tuamotus and Tahiti, where he was the second European visitor. Thence via Manua Islands and Tutuila in the Samoan group, Bougainville rediscovered the Solomon Islands which Quiros had found and then skirted the Great Barrier Reef of Australia. Sailing north he reached New Guinea at the Louisiade Archipelago, probably discovering Rossel Island which Torres [q.v.] may have seen from Tagula. He worked his way to Choiseul and Buka, all of which he named, and discovered Bougainville itself. He anchored off New Britain for refreshment and then went on to New Ireland, whence he sailed via the Dutch East Indies back to France.

J. C. Beaglehole, *The Exploration of the Pacific*. 3rd ed., London, 1966; A. Sharp, *The Discovery of the Pacific Islands*. Oxford, 1960.   FRANCIS WEST

(*See also* DISCOVERY)

BOUGAINVILLE ‚ COPPER PROJECT.   The copper mine on Bougainville Island is by far the largest developmental project ever undertaken in Papua New Guinea. Apart from its sheer magnitude it presents many features of unique interest in technique, economics and social and political relationships, and its progress will have far-reaching consequences throughout the whole country.

OPERATIONS

The mining company is Bougainville Copper Pty Limited incorporated in Papua New Guinea, and a member of the Conzinc Riotinto group of companies. Its operations are centred at Panguna, in the central mountain range of the island (*see* BOUGAINVILLE DISTRICT).

C.R.A. Exploration Pty Limited began to investigate the Panguna area in 1964, and shortly after began drilling. Following good results, the programme was expanded to include metallurgical testing, exploratory underground adits and engineering studies, leading ultimately to establishment of ore reserves estimated at a minimum of 1,000 million short tons of 0.48 per cent copper and 0.32 dwt gold per ton.

An economic feasibility study completed in mid-1969 resulted in the decision to proceed. The Bechtel-Western Knapp Engineering joint venture was appointed as engineering and construction manager, and major construction began in July 1969.

The ore will be mined by open-cut methods and will be treated in a conventional concentrator with a nominal capacity of 90,000 short tons per day. The resulting concentrate, of 30 per cent copper will be pumped in slurry form through a 16-mile pipeline to the port of Anewa Bay, which has been established on the east coast. There it will be filtered and dried ready for export.

Other supporting facilities are two townships, a 135MW steam power station, mine haul roads and equipment, and an access highway from mine to port. This 16-mile highway involved the excavation of 13 million cubic yards of material and is a major engineering achievement.

The company-owned town on the mine site at Panguna will accommodate about 3,000. Arawa, an open town, is being erected on the east coast and initially will have a population of some 8,000, with considerable room for further growth.

Bougainville Copper will invest, in all, about $400 million before production begins, and known ore resources will last at least thirty years.

It is planned to begin commercial production of copper concentrate in 1972, though pre-stripping in the open cut commenced in November 1970. By 1972 eight years will have been spent in exploring and investigating the deposit and in constructing the mine facilities.

The major part of the first fifteen years' production has been sold in advance to Japanese and European smelters. Average annual production will be 160,000 short tons of copper in concentrate and 500,000 ounces of gold.

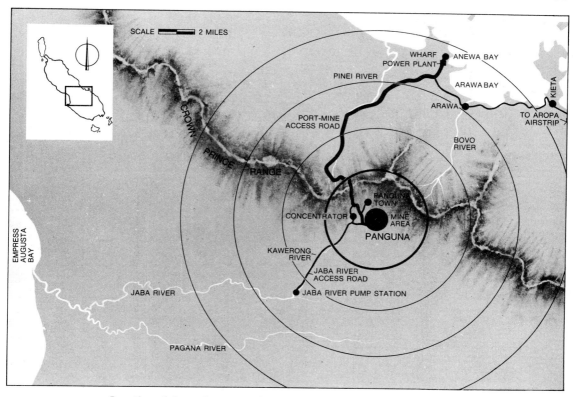

Location of the various operations of Bougainville Copper Pty Limited.

Geology. The Panguna deposit is a porphyry copper type. Copper-gold mineralization with small amounts of silver and molybdenum is associated with a group of acid to intermediate igneous rocks which have intruded a pre-existing sequence of andesitic volcanics. The intrusives, and the host rocks near the contacts, are mineralized in zones associated with pervasive alteration. Faulting and intense fracturing, particularly of the andesitic rock, are features of the mineralized area. The orientations of intrusives and quartz veining appear to be controlled by pre-mineralization fault-joint patterns in the intruded rocks.

The discovery resulted from investigation of old gold prospects which had been worked in the 1930s, and in which copper had been reported by government geologists. The surface extent of the copper mineralization was defined by geochemical drainage and soil and chip sampling of exposures in creeks.

The host rock, the Panguna andesite, a sequence of andesite volcanics of Oligocene to lower Miocene age, is intruded by a series of diorite-granodiorite rocks. These are regarded as co-magmatic and there appears to be a tendency for the younger members to be more porphyritic and quartz-rich, and to occur near the margins of the main intrusion. The main intrusion is the Kawerong quartz diorite, which is typically a pink hornblende diorite. The quartz content varies from *nil* to about 10 per cent, and hornblende forms 15 to 25 per cent of the rock. Marginal differentiates, or facies of the quartz diorite, some of which are late stage, include biotite diorite, biotite granodiorite, leucocratic quartz diorite and quartz feldspar porphyries.

As expected in a high sulphur-type porphyry copper deposit, chalcopyrite is the dominant primary copper mineral, being accompanied in places by bornite and a little molybdenite and silver. Gold content varies sympathetically with the copper, and pyrite is widely distributed. Chalcopyrite occurs principally in the Panguna andesite, in and about the leucocratic quartz diorite, and in the biotite diorite.

Mineralization occurs mainly in quartz veins which normally contain the chalcopyrite in a central zone with quartz crystals growing inwards from the straight vein walls. Chalcopyrite also occurs disseminated in the Panguna andesite and in the quartz and biotite diorites.

Oxidized and secondary zones occur. The oxidized zone ranges from *nil* to 260 feet in thickness, and averages about 100 feet. The base of the zone may be defined mineralogically by the upper limit of chalcocite, the downward limit of the minerals malachite cuprite and limonite, and the upper limit of chalcopyrite or bornite.

Secondary enrichment is restricted, generally being confined to areas of combined high topography and relatively high grade mineralization. The maximum known thickness of the secondary zone is 250 feet.

The evaluation drilling programme involved more than 200 holes with a total footage of some 240,000 feet.

Mining. Mine planning began early in 1966, and the two basic alternatives of underground block caving and open-pit mining were studied. Economic analysis favoured the latter method.

Detailed investigation of open-pit mining followed. This entailed analysing the economic consequences of changes in the various factors subject to management control, namely:

pre-production stripping,
pit output,
concentrator throughput,
cut-off grade and hence head grade,
waste to ore ratio.

These variables were altered subject to the independent parameters which affect the economics of the project. The parameters considered were:

the distribution of mineralization within the rock mass,
marketing constraints,
operating and capital costs,
metal prices.

Continual reassessment of the various factors took place as more information became available from the exploration programme; computer and operations research techniques were used.

The physical problems and the costs of an open-pit operation in the highlands of Bougainville were studied in parallel with the economic analysis. Methods were evolved for clearing jungle cover, removing unconsolidated overburden and determining stable pit slopes; the latter are much affected by the highly fractured nature of the rock mass, the seismic environment with frequent earthquakes, and a high rainfall.

Geotechnical studies were important, as the results affected not only pit slopes, but also the stability of waste dumps, haul roads and all other fill structures. As the presence of underground water is critical to slope stability and the whole area has abundant underground water supplies, exhaustive studies were made into the behaviour of the water-table. Two horizontal adits, Panguna and Western, were driven into the orebody to assess the reliability of diamond drilling as a sampling method. Both adits were pre-drilled by horizontal diamond drilling to allow comparison between the drill-core assays and the bulk samples obtained as each heading advanced. In addition, several raises were developed coaxially with surface diamond-drill holes to check earlier evaluation drilling. Underground development totalled 12,500 feet horizontally plus a further 1,800 feet of vertical rising. It established that diamond-drill core assays gave a conservative prediction of orebody grade. It also provided material for metallurgical testing. After completion of tests, both adits were closed.

The basic criteria which emerged from studies were:
a mine excavation rate of 159,000 short tons a day,
a waste-to-ore ratio of 0.68,
concentrator throughput of 90,000 short tons a day.

Mining and concentrating operations were based on working three 8-hour shifts a day and twenty-one shifts a week.

Mining equipment of the largest possible size will be used:

Shovels six 17-cubic yard electrics
Trucks thirty-six 100-ton
Drills five 9⅞-inch diameter electric rotary.

Metallurgy. Metallurgical assessment of the orebody began in mid-1966 at the Metallurgy Research Laboratories of the Zinc Corporation Limited at Broken Hill, using drill cores from Bougainville. The tests showed that the primary sulphide copper and gold values were particularly amenable to recovery by flotation, with the ability to achieve about 90 per cent copper flotation recoveries at head grades as low as 0.15 per cent copper at coarse grinds of 40-50 per cent minus 200 mesh and high flotation pulp densities of up to 45 per cent solids. Concentrate grade was strongly correlated with head grade, varying from approximately 33 per cent copper at head grades of about 0.7 per cent copper and above, down to 25 per cent at 0.25 per cent copper.

Gold and silver recoveries were also strongly correlated with head grade and tended to be in the range of 70-80 and 40-50 per cent, respectively. Molybdenum and magnetite also are present, but production of concentrates will not be pursued at this stage.

Engineering of facilities and services began in mid-1966. The first need was a temporary access road from the base camp on the east coast near Kieta to support the exploration and drilling programme. Until early 1967 the camp at Panguna was supplied by helicopter.

Construction of the access road was made difficult by the instability of the volcanic tuff covering the Crown Prince Range. Lack of a good port site on the west coast meant that the permanent access road had to lead from the east coast, where there was a good port site at Anewa Bay.

Logistical problems have been critical throughout, requiring efficient assembling and interaction of thousands of components. Most of these (including key personnel and operatives) had to be imported. Approximately 500,000 shipping tons of goods will have been delivered to the island by start-up time, in the face of inadequate facilities for unloading and bottlenecks caused by the scarcity of lay-down areas.

A major bottleneck—lack of road access from port to mine—was eliminated early in 1971. The temporary track to Panguna (winding often in hair-raising fashion through the precipitous Crown Prince Range), which has been used since early 1967, was replaced by a new two-lane highway 24 feet wide and having a maximum gradient of

The mountain section of the access highway put through the Crown Prince Range by Bougainville Copper Pty Limited to connect the mine and the port. The old access track can be seen to its right.

12 per cent (compared with up to 27 per cent in mountain sections on the old track).

This highway, which was built with design and construction running concurrently, involved over 13 million cubic yards of excavation. It was built despite recurring land slides and mud flows, which often led to re-design and at times required the contractor to return to the tops of cuttings to start excavation again. At one point where a hairpin occurs, the height of the cut from the bottom road level to the top of the cut above the upper road is 750 feet.

The port at Anewa Bay is 16 miles from the mine site. It will accommodate ships up to 40,000 deadweight tons. The permanent wharf was ready for imports in the last quarter of 1970, and in 1971 work proceeded on construction of the filtering, drying and load-out facilities for the export of copper concentrates.

Also at Anewa Bay is the huge (by Papua New Guinea standards) 135MW oil-fired steam turbine power station, which is one of the critical items in the project. It is more economic to transmit power at 132kV from Anewa Bay to Panguna than to pump fuel oil over the Crown Prince Range.

With flat land a rarity in the Panguna area two towns were required. Personnel engaged on critical or stand-by activities in the mine area are housed at Panguna where the total population of the town will be about 3,000, including families. The much larger town at Arawa on the east coast has been built in conjunction with the Administration of Papua New Guinea. Planning provides for a population of over 8,000 people and includes the development of commercial and administrative facilities for a major city centre. It will become Administration headquarters for Bougainville District.

Other vital roads include mine-haul roads, the Jaba River access road and the existing road from Anewa Bay to Kieta, the present administrative capital of the island.

The Jaba River road will pass through 7½ miles of very rugged terrain along the pipeline from the water pumping station near the junction of the Kawerong and Jaba Rivers to the concentrator.

When C.R.A. Exploration Pty Limited commenced operation on Bougainville there was no internal communication system on the island, and the only external link was a poor quality H.F. link from Kieta to Rabaul which operated for a limited time on certain days. The project required a completely integrated communication system between its centres of operation on the island, and telex and voice connections to the international communication system.

The Administration's Department of Posts and Telegraphs decided to install a high quality tropo-scatter-microwave system to cover internal communications on Bougainville and to connect Bougainville to the international communication system via the SEACOM cable at Madang. As this system would not be operational until 1971, Bougainville Copper installed an interim system of three main centres of operation coupled together by a U.H.F. radio link. At the same time, the off-island H.F. radio link between Kieta and Lae has been updated by the Posts and Telegraphs Department, part of the cost being contributed by Bougainville Copper Pty Limited.

Engineering was a race against time. Delay in start-up meant delay in the cash flow needed for repayment of the large international loans, including $220 million from a group led by the Bank of America. Because of the remote and undeveloped area, the major part of the capital expenditure has been devoted to non-productive, or support, facilities.

Pre-production. The problem of scarce suitable land in Panguna Valley has been solved by extensive clearing, stripping and benching. By shovel and truck about 35 million tons of pre-production material must be moved. Total clearing for mine facilities and stripping of the orebody in the pre-production pit area involved over 600 acres of tropical rain forest and dense undergrowth. Larger trees were first poisoned, followed by spraying of the undergrowth from a helicopter. After standing for about four months the area was cleared by a modified logging technique known as 'Hi-lead yarding'. After felling, the trees were assembled with rubber-tyred log skidders into heaps for burning. The wet conditions were substantially overcome with large axial flow fans and injection of fuel oil into the base of the fire.

The next stage was 'hydraulicking' to remove unconsolidated volcanic ash and weathered worthless rock. A further 25 million cubic yards were scheduled to be removed by hydraulicking which hoses away material pushed to the monitors by crawler-dozers. Each monitor is capable of jetting 2,500 gallons per minute through a 2½-inch nozzle at a pressure of up to 100 p.s.i. The impact of a water jet at this pressure itself only punches a hole in undisturbed ash, but once broken up by bulldozers the material rapidly forms a slurry. The dislodged material goes into fast-flowing mountain streams.

Conventional mining operations at Panguna began with the mine pre-stripping operation in November 1970. At this stage, the first Euclid R-105 dump trucks and P & H 17-cubic yard shovels were put into action. As the waste rock to be removed before ore is exposed becomes harder, it is necessary to drill and blast—drilling by rotary drilling, common to most pits and carried out by five Bucyrus Erie drills, and blasting, for which the primary explosive will be a low metal-content ammonium nitrate water-resistant slurry.

Economical pre-production in the Bougainville environment must take account of oxidation if ore is left lying on the bench, and of extensive maintenance and repair facilities.

Ore is delivered to the primary crushers via 80-foot wide haul roads for the final stages of processing on the island.

Ore treatment. The final stages in the production of saleable copper concentrates involve upgrading the ore by crushing, grinding and flotation to obtain a concentrate containing about 30 per cent copper. The concentrate is then pumped through

Bougainville Copper Pty. Limited is developing Papua and New Guinea's largest ever mining operation. By start of production in mid-1972 the Company will have spent about $400 million in establishing one of the world's largest copper mines.

The ore will be taken from the Panguna open pit by shovels and trucks and processed to a concentrate containing 30% copper.

The copper concentrate will then be pumped in a pipeline to the Company's port at Anewa Bay on the east coast of Bougainville. From there it will be exported to customers in Europe and Japan.

1. OPEN PIT MINING, PANGUNA

The Panguna copper mine is an open pit. The ore, of approximately ½% copper, will be extracted by digging a large hole with huge shovels. Giant trucks will carry away 100 tons at a time, some of which is waste and some copper-bearing ore.

2. PRIMARY CRUSHING

The ore to be treated goes first into a machine which prepares it for concentrating by crushing it to a smaller size. The Panguna concentrator handles 90,000 short tons of ore each day.

3. COARSE ORE STOCKPILE

After primary crushing the ore is taken by conveyor belt to the stockpile. From here the concentrating process begins its three stages—fine crushing, grinding and flotation. Considerable electric power is needed for concentrating.

4. FINE CRUSHING

Fine crushing consists of two further stages to reduce the size of the ore. Secondary crushing reduces the ore from pieces less than 8 inches to pieces of less than one half inch.

5. SCREEN HOUSE

The screen house checks the size of the ore. Any pieces greater than one half inch are returned to the crushing process before further screening.

6. FINE ORE STORAGE

To feed the concentrator with a consistent supply, fine ore will be stored in a large shed that can hold 80,000 short tons.

7. CONCENTRATOR—GRINDING

The second stage in concentrating is the grinding of the fine ore until it becomes fine particles—like sand. Grinding at Panguna will be done in eight ball mills which will use about 20,000 tons of iron grinding balls a year.

8. CONCENTRATOR—FLOTATION

Flotation separates the valuable copper and other minerals from the rock by agitating the fine ore in water containing chemicals. The concentrate produced contains about 30% copper. Tailings, which are left over after flotation, are not wanted and are disposed of.

9. CONCENTRATE PIPELINE OVER MOUNTAINS

The concentrate mixed with water is then pumped in a steel pipeline over the Crown Prince mountain range to the port at Anewa Bay. The pipeline is buried under the shoulder of the mine-port road.

10. CONCENTRATE FILTERING AND DRYING

The final process before shipment is to reduce the water content of the concentrate. This is done at the port by vacuum filtering and rotary kiln drying. The concentrate at this stage is almost dry.

11. CONCENTRATE STORAGE

Near the wharf is a shed to hold 60,000 short tons of concentrate. From this stockpile will be drawn the loads of concentrate to be shipped.

12. SHIPMENT OVERSEAS

The ship loading machine can put 1,000 tons of concentrate per hour into a ship's hold. The average shipment to the overseas buyers will be approximately 20,000 tons.

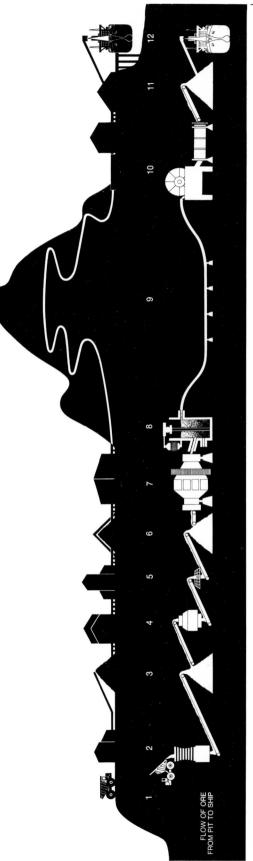

FLOW OF ORE
FROM PIT TO SHIP

The production of copper concentrate.

a 5½-inch diameter pipe in slurry form, at a pressure of up to 2,400 p.s.i., from the concentrator at the mine site to the export port at Anewa Bay 16 miles away. After filtering and drying to about 7 per cent moisture content, the concentrate is ready for despatch by bulk ore carriers to smelters overseas.

The sulphide ore is amenable to flotation, and the only major problems envisaged are of continuous handling of vast tonnages through the concentrator. A total of 90,000 short tons of ore will be treated daily, 24 hours per day, seven days per week throughout the year. The initial target is an average annual production of 160,000 short tons of copper in concentrates, including 500,000 ounces of gold.

Because flat open ground is scarce in the Panguna Valley, the only operation carried out there will be primary crushing to minus 8 inches by two 54-inch gyratory crushers. The ore will be transported to the concentrator in a nearby valley by a covered coarse-ore conveyor. There, further stages of crushing and screening reduce the ore to minus ¼ inch, ready for grinding in eight single-stage ball mills, each 18 feet in diameter and 21 feet long. These mills will be among the largest in the copper industry, and require a total of 34,000 horsepower, and over 20,000 tons of grinding balls per year.

Flotation will be achieved in a two-section plant, containing 224 flotation cells of 300 cubic feet and 117 cells of 100 cubic feet. Total nominal flotation capacity will then be 79,000 cubic feet, which is more than five times the capacity of all the Broken Hill underground mines combined. The principle behind flotation is to grind the ore to fine particle size to release the valuable minerals from the rock, and then agitate it in water to which collecting and frothing reagents have been added. The mineral particles then rise with the froth and the waste material will sink. A product of higher mineral grade is thus obtained.

The possibility of leaching the waste dumps for selected oxide and secondary ore materials has been studied. Scarce dump space and frequent heavy rain and local flooding are problems, but study continues.

The principal technical details of the concentrator are:

Average work index	10.4
Economic optimum grinding power consumption at a grind of 50 per cent-200 mesh	5.8 kWh/short ton
Economic optimum flotation time	18 minutes
Total power consumption	13 kWh/short ton
Total ball consumption	1.2 lb./short ton
Flotation reagents	S 3501, 0.015 lb./short ton Frother, 0.09 lb./short ton Lime, 1.15 lb./short ton

Human and political relations. In its exploration years the company encountered many difficulties in establishing its presence satisfactorily, but at least it gained first-hand knowledge and contact with the local people and their customs before embarking on a heavy construction programme. Nevertheless, the impact of the project when it began in earnest in mid-1969 was inevitably large on a relatively undisturbed community based principally on a village subsistence economy. The company has tried to minimize disturbance and to plan its operations in accord with the developing sense of nationhood in Papua New Guinea.

Security of tenure was obtained through a legal agreement with the Administration which imposed obligations on both parties. The company was issued with a special mining lease for an initial forty-two years with provision for two extensions of twenty-one years. The House of Assembly ratified this agreement in August 1967.

Probably the major political problem was the acquisition of sufficient land for construction. There is a strong tie between the people and their land, and it was not surprising that the Bougainville people, who had been quite sheltered from contact with a western-type industrial society, would have difficulty in comprehending the project. Under the agreement, the Administration is responsible for acquiring sufficient land for the reasonable needs of the company.

From the start, company officers have explained the ramifications of the project. Priority also has been given to easing and eliminating associated social strains in recruitment, employee relationships, integration, localization and communication.

Policy seeks social integration which gives a local person some option on how fast he wants to go along this course; employment opportunities with good standard conditions (i.e. accommodation, meals, canteens, married quarters); training and education programmes in a variety of occupations plus unbonded apprenticeship, cadetship and scholarship schemes; localization of the work force, meaning positive encouragement to Papuans and New Guineans to move up to higher positions in the company; compensation for disturbance, etc., plus resettlement, help and advice on re-establishment and on new business ventures; encouragement to local people to increase their equity in the project; sale to the Administration of 25 million shares at par, equal to 20 per cent of the equity in Bougainville Copper Pty Limited, to be held on behalf of the people of Papua New Guinea.

B. B.

ECONOMIC ASPECTS

The mining industry in Papua New Guinea made a substantial contribution to economic activity in the small monetary sector in the decade prior to World War II. The industry at the time was concerned almost exclusively with mining gold which by 1939-40 accounted for some 75 per cent of the country's $8 million export earnings. After the war the industry at first recovered rapidly, but rising costs and the depletion of known gold deposits eventually caused a decline in both relative and absolute terms. In 1965-6 mining and quarrying together contributed only 1 per cent of gross monetary sector product at factor cost; and gold, which still continued to dominate mineral production, accounted for only 2 per cent of the total value of exports.

However, the importance of mining in the economy should increase dramatically in the 1970s, when the Bougainville copper project begins exporting copper concentrate in 1972. As a result Papua New Guinea will rank among the more important of the world's producers of copper and gold. In addition, there is the possibility that the Bougainville project may be followed by other large-scale copper mining ventures. In particular, the exploration being undertaken by the American corporation, Kennecott, in the Western District and by Carpentaria Exploration, a subsidiary of M.I.M. Holdings Limited, in the East and West Sepik Districts may result in further mining operations. The search for other minerals such as lead, zinc, silver, iron and bauxite has also intensified.

Mining operations will be conducted by Bougainville Copper Pty Limited, which was incorporated in Papua New Guinea in 1967. The two largest effective equity interests in this company will be held by Conzinc Riotinto of Australia Limited (44.67 per cent) and New Broken Hill Consolidated Limited (22.33 per cent). In addition, under the terms of an offer written into the Mining (Bougainville Copper Agreement) Ordinance of 1967, the Administration is purchasing on behalf of the people of Papua New Guinea 20 per cent of the ordinary share capital of the operating company.

Not only will the project operate on a very large scale, but it will also be extremely capital-intensive. The total capital cost to the company of establishing the operation is expected to exceed $350 million, while the production work force will be only about 2,300. This implies a capital-labour ratio considerably greater than that of any existing industry in Papua New Guinea. The finance for the initial capital expenditure is coming in part from the company's equity resources of $125 million, and in part from overseas borrowing. The principal component of the latter is a Eurodollar loan of up to $220 million.

In addition to the investment being undertaken by the company, the Administration is spending nearly $46 million in the period 1969-72 on its share of the development of the new mining town of Arawa and other public works and services directly and indirectly related to the project. The Australian government is lending $20 million to help meet the Arawa component of this expenditure. (The Administration is also borrowing abroad to finance its 20 per cent equity interest in the company.)

Sales contracts have been signed for the first fifteen years of production. During this period the major markets for the exports of copper concentrate will be Japan, West Germany and Spain. The copper will be sold at the free world price, but for the most part with a guaranteed floor price of U.S.30c per pound. The life of the mine should, however, be considerably longer than the duration of these initial contracts. Estimating from the planned rate of production and known reserves only, it will be about thirty years. **Direct impact of the project.** The direct contribution of the project to economic activity in Papua New Guinea may be viewed as occurring in two distinct phases, the construction period, 1969-72, and the subsequent exporting period.

The capital formation being undertaken by Bougainville Copper Pty Limited in the period from 1969 to 1972 is probably greater in real terms than all the private fixed investment which occurred throughout the monetary sector of the economy in the previous nine years. If private investment in ancillary industries and public investment connected with the project are also taken into account, it is clear that the project involves a very substantial increase in the capital stock of the country. It is, moreover, an increase which for the most part does not involve a current real cost to the country—in the sense of a reduction in the availability of goods and services for other purposes—since it is being financed almost completely by capital inflow from abroad.

A large proportion of the initial capital expenditure is, in fact, being spent on imports of capital equipment and materials. The principal suppliers of these items are Australia, the U.S.A. and Japan. The major expenses incurred locally, and hence the major forms of income generated locally, are the wages and salaries of the construction work force. The Administration estimated that in 1969-70 this work force would reach 6,830, of whom 2,950 would be indigenes and 3,880 expatriates. Together with rough estimates of prevailing wage rates, these figures suggest an annual construction payroll of about $30 million per annum. In 1968-9 total wages and salaries for the whole of the economy amounted to only $140 million. However, because of large differences between average wages paid to expatriates and indigenes, as much as 80 to 90 per cent of the construction payroll could be accruing to expatriates, the majority of whom are temporary immigrants.

The project will begin to contribute to the country's export earnings in 1972. The size of this contribution will be determined largely by the world price of copper which historically has shown marked instability. However, in terms of 1968-9 mineral prices, the contribution should average between $160 million and $170 million per annum or about 2.5 times the total Papua New Guinea exports for 1968-9 ($65 million).

The net direct impact of the project on the balance of payments as a whole will be considerably smaller than the contribution to exports. The project will be directly responsible for substantial debit entries in the international accounts. These will include the cost of imported inputs such as the forged iron balls needed for grinding the ore; interest payments on the overseas debt incurred in establishing the project; repayment of this debt; and profits remitted abroad.

The domestic income generated directly by the company's mining operations will be dominated by public revenue in the form of dividends, income tax, royalties, rent, indirect taxes and services charges. For the first three years of operations the company has been granted an income (company) tax holiday. Thereafter, it will be allowed to write off immediately and in full against income the capital expenditures it incurred in establishing the project. Consequently, the company is unlikely to start paying company tax until some six or seven years after mining operations begin. Nevertheless, assuming a copper price of U.S.55c per pound (the average 1968-9 price), the Administration has estimated that it may still receive about $33 million per annum from the project in the interim period 1973-7. Subsequently, when company tax does come into effect, the company will pay not only the normal rate of tax (currently 22.5 per cent), but also special additional tax which will eventually raise the overall effective rate of tax towards 50 per cent of taxable income. As a result, at a copper price of U.S.55c per pound total public revenue accruing to the Administration from the project could reach $50 million per annum.

Of the private income payments generated directly in Papua New Guinea by the mining operations the most important will be wages. However, because of the relatively small production work force (which will reflect the capital-intensive nature of the mining operations) these should in total be considerably less than the annual public revenue generated by the mining operations and also considerably less than the construction payroll. Moreover, at least in the early years of operations, by far the larger proportion of wage payments is likely to be received, as in the case of the construction payroll, by expatriates.

Effects on rest of economy. Relative to its size and to existing levels of economic activity in Papua New Guinea, the Bougainville project by itself can be expected to provide only a small immediate stimulus to the expansion of the private, non-mining sectors of the economy through purchases of locally produced material inputs and through induced demand for consumer goods. In this respect, it has much in common with the various examples of other large-scale, capital-intensive, foreign-owned and -controlled, export industries which have been introduced into less developed countries with only limited effects on overall economic development in the countries concerned. Such industries have been seen as enclaves of progress in primarily subsistence-oriented environments.

The reason for expecting only a small direct stimulus—only small pecuniary external economies or spillover effects—from the Bougainville project lies mainly in the nature and magnitude of the various inputs required for the production of concentrate. With the obvious exception of the ore itself, these do not match well with the country's capacity to supply them. Thus the complex capital equipment and the intermediate goods

necessary for production, which will form such a large part of the initial construction cost and operating cost respectively, will have a high import content because the country lacks the know-how, the economies of scale and the resource base to be able to produce them competitively. Furthermore, the low labour input requirement of the mining operations means that additional consumer-good demand stemming from wage payments will be small in relation to the total level of consumer demand in the country.

Pecuniary spillover effects will be increased if further processing of the concentrate (e.g. smelting) is eventually undertaken in Papua New Guinea. However, by late 1970 no such plans had been announced. A decision by the operating company will depend on a variety of factors including future movements in overseas processing costs and mineral prices; transport costs; the availability and cost of skilled workers, material inputs and power; the availability and cost of finance; a solution to problems of waste disposal; and markets for by-products. Only some of these factors will depend on future developments in Papua New Guinea.

The effects of the project on the rest of the economy are not, however, likely to be confined to the limited repercussions for domestic demand created by the input requirements of the project. Several more indirect influences can be identified.

First, despite some temporary disruption to the labour market during the construction phase, the project should in the long run contribute to the supply of skilled labour available to other firms and industries. The project work force will contain a proportionately large skilled and semi-skilled element in both the construction and production periods. In the beginning this is being supplied for the most part by expatriate workers hired from abroad; but Bougainville Copper Pty Limited is training indigenes gradually to replace expatriates in the more skilled and responsible areas of employment. In 1970, for example, the company planned to spend in excess of $500,000 on scholarships and training. Accordingly, since some degree of labour turnover may be expected, a stream of trained indigenes, having skills sufficiently general to be employed outside the project, should eventually become available to other industries. Because of the small size of the total production work force, however, the magnitude of this stream will not be large relative to the probable future requirements of the economy as a whole.

Secondly, the fact that a large international corporation has chosen to undertake an expensive long-term investment in Papua New Guinea may well be improving the investment climate. This applies particularly to the mining sector where the Bougainville success has probably helped to encourage further exploration which could lead to other mining ventures. In addition, even in sectors quite remote from copper mining, Bougainville Copper's example may be improving the confidence of other potential foreign and local investors in the economic prospects of the

An indigenous apprentice in the machine shop at Panguna.

country. Such a phenomenon is, of course, difficult to quantify. It may nevertheless be of considerable importance in the otherwise uncertain atmosphere which inevitably exists at this stage of the country's political and economic development.

Finally, the potentially strongest influence on the rest of the economy lies in the large public revenue that will be generated by the project. For the years 1969-70 to 1981-2 as a whole—the construction period and the first decade of operations—official estimates indicate that at a copper price of U.S.55c per pound the project will directly yield an excess of public receipts over public expenditure or a net contribution to Administration revenue of $248.9 million. This is equivalent to an average annual sum of about $19 million or nearly 13 per cent of total Administration receipts from all sources in 1968-9. Given that there will be no offsetting adjustments in other sources of revenue (e.g. a reduction in the Commonwealth government grant), the Administration's command over resources will be increased substantially. Depending on how the additional funds are used, they could contribute significantly to the promotion of growth elsewhere in the economy.

This third point should be qualified in one major respect; namely, the size of the fiscal gain will be heavily dependent on the world price of copper. The latter will be a direct determinant of the receipts from company tax, dividends and royalties. If the past instability of this price continues then, notwithstanding the floor price of U.S.30c per pound in the company's sales contracts, internal revenue will become much more exposed to short term fluctuations. More generally, the likelihood that the economy will be relying very heavily for its export earnings on one commodity noted for its price instability means that the level of economic activity throughout the economy could become more susceptible to cyclical movements, transmitted both through the public sector and more directly. M. L. T.

The Bougainville mine has a life of at least thirty years based on present reserves, and from a modest beginning, the project has gone far towards conquering the difficulties of access, terrain and climate; it has overcome large engineering problems and it has put together a successful financing and marketing package. It is a leader in the world extractive industry, backed up by competent management and sophisticated techniques. It can be expected that it will completely overcome the physical problems of mining copper on Bougainville. Its major test is in the realm of human relationships—political, economic, social, cultural and environmental. To these it is applying experience, sound personnel and community management and enlightened policies.

B. R. Stewardson, 'The Bougainville Copper Agreement', Paper presented to Section 24 of the 42nd ANZAAS Congress, Port Moresby, 1970 (roneoed); T. P. N. G., *House of Assembly Debates*, vol. 2, pp. 2250-4. Statement delivered by the Assistant Administrator (Economic Affairs), Mr A. P. J. Newman, M.H.A., Port Moresby, March 1970; M. L. Treadgold, 'Bougainville Copper and the Economic Development of Papua-New Guinea', *Economic Record*, vol. 47, 1971.

TERRITORY OF PAPUA AND NEW GUINEA LEGISLATION

Mining (Bougainville Copper Agreement) Ordinance, 1967.

BOUGAINVILLE DISTRICT is the easternmost District of Papua New Guinea. It lies within the area bounded by the equator and latitude 8°S. and by longitudes 154°E. and 160°E. It is a District of islands dispersed over a large expanse of sea in which the land masses cover 3,550 square miles or a mere 2 per cent of the total area. The islands may be grouped for convenience into two divisions: the larger islands of Bougainville and Buka plus their smaller satellite islands; and the lesser coral island groups of Nuguria (or Fead), Green (or Nissan), Kilinailau (or Carteret), Tauu (or Mortlock) and Nukumanu (or Tasman). Bougainville and Buka have a total land area of 3,475 square miles; the land area of the island groups is only 75 square miles.

For internal administrative purposes the District is split into three Sub-Districts of approximately equal area. The Buka Passage Sub-District includes Buka, northern Bougainville and the island groups; the Buin Sub-District covers the southern and south-western sections; and Kieta Sub-District covers the eastern section of Bougainville.

In Buka Passage Sub-District headquarters are at Hutjena; there are patrol posts at Tinputz and Kunua and a base camp at Hanahan. Buin Sub-District headquarters are at Buin; there is a patrol post at Boku and a base camp at Konga. Headquarters for Kieta Sub-District are at Kieta and there is a patrol post at Wakunai. The District headquarters are also at Kieta.

Local Government Councils have been established throughout most of the District since 1958. At 30 June 1970 there were seven councils operating and 415 villages with a combined population of 55,278 were included in the council areas.

DISCOVERY AND HISTORY

The discovery of the islands in the Bougainville District began in 1616 when the Dutch navigators le Maire and Schouten [qq.v.] sighted the Tauu Islands. It continued with the discovery of the Nukumanu group by another Dutchman, Tasman

[q.v.], in 1643. Over a century elapsed before any more discoveries were made. In 1767 the Englishman Carteret [q.v.] discovered Kilinailau and sailed close to Buka, which he called Winchelsea Island. Discovery was completed in the following year when the French navigator Bougainville [q.v.] sighted the island which now bears his name.

Apart from the occasional sperm whaler who dropped anchor off the shore and traded hoop-iron and manufactured articles for fresh food, no real contact was made with the islands of this area until some time between 1860 and 1865 when recruiters looking for labourers for the plantations of Queensland and the more advanced Pacific islands turned their attention to the Solomon group. By 1875 Bougainville and Buka had become part of the labour recruiters' territory and they so remained until Germany gained possession of the islands in 1886.

About 1880 the new interest shown by the European powers in the political and strategic importance of the Pacific Islands began to affect the Solomons. In 1886 Germany and Britain, who had already demarcated their respective spheres of influence in eastern New Guinea, agreed to delimit their respective spheres in the Solomons. Under the agreement Germany took possession of the northern Solomon Islands which included Buka, Bougainville, Choiseul and Santa Isabel, and Britain gained control of the remainder. The agreement of 1886 was short lived and in 1899 Germany agreed to transfer its Solomon Islands possessions south of Bougainville to Britain as one of the conditions for Britain's withdrawal from Samoa. After the agreement was ratified in 1900 Germany added Bougainville and Buka to the Bismarck Archipelago for administrative purposes.

In the early years of German control the main contacts with the newly acquired possessions were made by representatives of the German Neuguinea-Kompagnie who traded with and recruited labour from the islands. Buka Islanders in particular were much sought after as labourers for the plantations of New Britain and as recruits for the local police force.

By 1902 the first trading posts and plantations had already been established on the Nuguria, Nukumanu, Kilinailau and Green Islands by the trading and planting company of E. E. Forsayth [q.v.], founded by 'Queen Emma'. In this year the first Europeans, members of the Catholic mission of the German Solomon Islands (Society of Mary), more popularly known as the Marist mission, settled on Bougainville at Kieta. Three years later the German administration established its first government station also at Kieta. In 1907 the first European plantation enterprise was started on Bougainville by the Bismarck Archipelago Trading Company.

When German administration ended in 1914 one-third of the area had been brought under control, the first overland exploration of the southern part of Bougainville had taken place, the Marist mission had extended its influence to Buin in the south and Buka in the north, and a

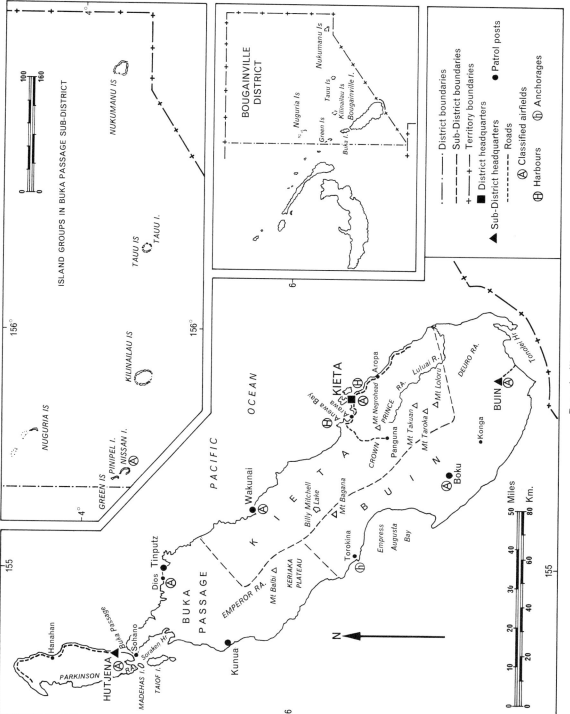

ISLAND GROUPS IN BUKA PASSAGE SUB-DISTRICT

BOUGAINVILLE DISTRICT

—·—·—·— District boundaries
— — — — Sub-District boundaries
+ + + + Territory boundaries
■ District headquarters
▲ Sub-District headquarters
● Patrol posts
Ⓐ Classified airfields
—— Roads
Ⓐ Harbours
Ⓗ Anchorages

Bougainville District.

number of Europeans had established plantations, mainly on the east coast of Bougainville.

Between 1914 and 1921 the area was under Australian military occupation. Control then passed to Australia through the League of Nations mandate covering the Territory of New Guinea and the area was placed under the authority of a District officer located at Kieta and became known as the Kieta District. Additional government posts were established on the Terei coast and at Buka Passage, and systematic census and exploratory patrols were instituted. By the time World War II began most of the District had been brought under effective government control.

In the period between the two World Wars mission activity continued to expand. The Marist mission extended its influence over most of Bougainville and Buka and entered the Green Islands. In 1921 the Methodist Missionary Society of New Zealand came to Bougainville. It was followed by the Seventh Day Adventist mission in 1924. The mission bodies established schools and provided all education within the District. They also made valuable contributions to health services by establishing and staffing hospitals and first aid centres.

During this period the plantation industry also expanded. By 1940 expatriates had established sixty-one plantations in the District on a total area of 69,950 acres of which 30,257 acres were under crop. Most of the acreage was under coconuts but small areas of cocoa, coffee, rubber and kapok had also been planted. Plantation production for the year ending 30 June 1940 was 10,508 tons of copra, 21 tons of cocoa and 20 tons of coffee.

During World War II the Japanese gained control of the District. They landed on Bougainville early in 1942 and by October 1944 had 42,000 troops on the island. Bitter fighting took place between Japanese and Australian troops from December 1944 until the Japanese surrendered in August 1945.

Civil administration was re-established in the District on 15 May 1946. District headquarters were set up at Sohano where they remained until 1968 when they were transferred back to Kieta. In the immediate post-World War II period the efforts of the Administration and of private enterprise were concentrated on repairing the damage caused by the war but the work was hampered by lack of staff, finance, materials and transport. By 1947 the missions had returned; Chinese stores had been re-opened at Kieta and Buka; and twelve plantations were in the process of being restored to working order.

Over the last ten years there has been continued progress in the fields of social, political and economic development with the indigenous people playing an increasingly active role. The accelerated pace of development has not been without incident, social and political tensions have increased, and these have manifested themselves in a number of ways on both Buka and Bougainville. The economic future of Bougainville District appears bright. Already an important copra and cocoa producing area, it is soon to become the centre of a multi-million dollar copper mining industry.

TOPOGRAPHY AND DRAINAGE

Bougainville is an elongated north-west to south-east trending island, 130 miles long and of varying width from 20 to 40 miles. The topography of the island is dominated by a backbone of mountains and hills which run for most of its length and cover approximately half of its area.

Beginning in the north the Emperor Range, a line of rugged mountains between 4,000 feet and 7,000 feet high extends in a south-south-east direction for 25 miles where it terminates at Mt Balbi, a dormant volcano whose summit (8,502 feet) is the highest point on the island. South-east of Mt Balbi, the active volcano Bagana (5,730 feet) and the extinct volcanoes Billy Mitchell, Numa Numa and Reini separate the Emperor Range from the Crown Prince Range which is a sinuous line of steep-sided mountains extending south-eastwards for 50 miles. The highest point in this range is Mt Negrohead (5,502 feet). To the south-west of the Crown Prince Range are two north-westerly aligned rows of volcanoes; Mt Takuan (7,385 feet) and Mt Taroka (7,240 feet) are the highest peaks in this section. With the possible exception of Mt Loloru all of these volcanoes are considered to be extinct. South of, and extending in a south-easterly direction from the Takuan-Taroka volcanic area is the 20-mile long Deuro Range, a series of hills less than 2,500 feet high.

South of the Emperor Range and Mt Balbi lies the Keriaka plateau, an elevated and ancient, eroded raised coral atoll with a karst landscape of closely spaced sink holes and deep valleys separated by saw-tooth ridges up to 400 feet high. The plateau dips gently westwards from 4,000 feet at its inland margin to 100 feet on the west coast.

Another plateau of uplifted coral with a maximum elevation of 300 feet forms the lowland area in the north of the island. This is a younger area and its surface still shows the topographic features of the original reef complex.

In the main the mid-altitude and lowland areas of Bougainville consist of sloping volcano-alluvial fans and plains. These are most extensively developed in the south where the Buin plain covers over 350 square miles. Volcano-alluvial fans have formed at the base of each Bougainville volcano. They are composed of volcanic mud flows and ash falls interspersed with stream deposits derived from volcanic material. Surface configuration of the fans varies considerably from undulating country with low ridges and shallow radiating valleys to dissected areas with valleys incised to depths of up to 800 feet below the original surface level. Usually the middle slopes show the maximum dissection. These fans extend over a wide altitude range from sea-level to 3,000 feet.

Extending outwards and formed of alluvial material derived from the volcano-alluvial fans are extensive areas of alluvial plains. Deep river entrenchment often occurs along their inner margins where streams are contained in narrow terraced flood plain valleys up to 1,000 feet wide and 80 feet below the general level of the plain. Towards the coast stream entrenchment diminishes and ultimately disappears. Unimpeded by high banks the rivers meander freely across the plains frequently overflowing their channels and flooding the surrounding countryside. On their outer margins the plains either terminate in swamps or extend to the coast as narrow tracts of swampy flood plain up to a mile wide.

The coastline of Bougainville shows a number of diverse topographic features. On the north coast is the raised coral reef complex which forms cliffs up to 300 feet high. On the northern sections of the west and east coasts emerged coral platforms 5 to 15 feet above high-water mark are common. With the exception of limited areas where hilly country comes right down to the coast and forms well-drained steeply ridged areas, such as at Kieta, the rest of the Bougainville coastline is characterized by narrow beach-ridge barriers rising 5 to 10 feet above high-water mark, spaced 200 to 500 feet apart and aligned parallel to the shore. The sand-ridge line is not continuous but is broken by narrow tracts of alluvial flood plain through which the main rivers flow to the sea. Extensive areas of swamp, varying in width from 2 to 8 miles, also occur around this section of the coastline. Nearly all the swamps are found behind the beach ridges which impound them in the embayments between the alluvial plains or the base of the hills.

The numerous rivers of Bougainville rise in the mountainous or hilly regions of the island where they flow as shallow torrents in deep gorge-like valleys, some of which, on the flanks of volcanoes, may be up to 1,500 feet deep. They remain deeply entrenched as they cut through the volcano-alluvial fans. In this section the streams are usually less than 20 feet wide and 1 foot deep. As they flow across the alluvial plains the rivers widen and deepen and by the time they reach the sea may be up to 300 feet wide and 8 feet deep. All the rivers are short, most being less than 20 miles long. The Luluai River, which is 45 miles from source to mouth, is the longest river in Bougainville.

Buka Island is 35 miles long and 9 miles wide and is elongated in a more northerly direction than Bougainville from which it is separated by the narrow half-mile-wide Buka Passage. The main topographic feature on Buka is the Parkinson Range in the south-west of the island which rises to a maximum height of 1,654 feet, a southerly extension of which can be traced south of Buka on the smaller islands of Madehas, Taiof and Tanwoa. The second topographic component is a raised coral reef complex which forms cliffs up to 300 feet high along the north and east coasts of Buka and also forms Sohano Island which is situated at the south-west end of Buka Passage. This raised reef is a continuation of the raised reef of northern Bougainville. Much of

the drainage on Buka is underground and surface streams are mostly found in the Parkinson Range.

Fringing, patch and discontinuous barrier reefs and coral islands abound in the seas around Bougainville and Buka. They are best developed off the west coast of Buka, in Machin Bay south of Sohano and along the east coast of Bougainville.

GEOLOGY

Bougainville and Buka Islands are part of a massive pile of volcanic material bordering the Planet Deep from 28,500 feet below to 8,500 feet above sea-level.

The oldest rocks exposed on Bougainville Island are the Kieta volcanics which form the Crown Prince and Deuro Ranges of southern Bougainville and outcrop over an area of 950 square miles. The formation is considered to consist of the products of a number of ancient volcanoes and contains andesitic and basaltic lavas, agglomerate and tuff, and conglomerates, sandstones and siltstones derived from volcanic material. The age of the formation is not definitely known but is thought to be Oligocene to lower Miocene. The maximum thickness of the unit is also unknown but is probably greater than 5,000 feet.

Equally old is the Buka formation which outcrops over 64 square miles and forms the Parkinson Range on Buka Island and the hilly areas of the near-shore islands of Madehas, Taiof and Tanwoa. It consists mainly of sandstone and siltstone composed of volcanic material with subordinate agglomerate, tuff and basaltic lava flows. The maximum thickness of this formation is probably greater than 1,600 feet.

In central Bougainville the Kieta volcanics are locally overlain by a lower Miocene reef limestone, the Keriaka limestone which outcrops over a roughly rectangular area of 100 square miles on the western side of Bougainville, where it forms a south-westerly tilted plateau on the southern side of Balbi volcano. Smaller outcrops also occur on the eastern side of the island. This formation has a maximum thickness of at least 4,000 feet.

In the northern part of central Bougainville volcanic rocks of uncertain age outcrop over an area of 38 square miles. These rocks, referred to as unnamed volcanics, are mainly dacitic, andesitic and basaltic lavas, agglomerates and tuffs.

The younger volcanic rocks on Bougainville, which outcrop over more than half of the island, are known collectively as the Bougainville group. This group includes nine formations, each of which comprises the products of an easily identifiable volcano or group of volcanoes. From north to south these formations are the Tore, Balbi, Numa Numa, Billy Mitchell, Bagana, Reini, Bakonovi, Takuan and Taroka volcanics. Also included in the group are the Emperor Range volcanic beds which are the volcanic products of unspecified volcanic centres. The rocks of this group consist predominantly of andesitic lavas, agglomerates, tuffs and sedimentary rocks derived from volcanic materials. Their age ranges from

Pliocene or possibly Miocene to the present day. The maximum thickness of this unit is 8,000 feet.

A reef complex is exposed on the northern and eastern coasts of Buka, the north coast of Bougainville and on Sohano Island. It also occurs as isolated outcrops on the west coast of Buka. This formation which is known as the Sohano limestone consists almost entirely of a richly fossiliferous, whitish limestone of Pleistocene age. The maximum observed thickness of this formation is 290 feet.

Alluvium of Quaternary age covers lowlying coastal areas where it forms deltaic, swamp and beach deposits. The greatest expanses of this material are found on parts of the west, east and south-east coasts of Bougainville. Beach deposits containing both volcanic and organic detritus occur around much of the Bougainville coastline; and sand, composed mainly of pulverized coral, occurs on the small off-shore coral islands.

Much of Bougainville and Buka is covered by ash ejected by the Bougainville volcanoes. The ash deposits vary in thickness from less than one inch to several feet. It is best preserved on ridge tops as it has generally been eroded from steep slopes and deposited in valleys as alluvium. The ash is of andesitic composition and probably ranges in age from Pleistocene to Recent.

Igneous intrusions occur within the Kieta volcanics, the unnamed volcanics and the Emperor Range formation. They vary in size from small dyke and plug-like bodies to larger and more irregular masses. The smaller intrusions are of porphyritic microdiorite and the larger contain a variety of rock types including diorite, granodiorite, monzonite, syenite and granophyre. Sulphide mineralization is associated with most intrusions, and gold and copper with a few such as those at Kupei and Panguna south-west of Kieta.

Contact metamorphic rocks of the hornfels type are found in the metamorphic aureoles around most of the diorite intrusions, and also in and around the cores of eroded volcanic centres. Low grade regionally metamorphosed lavas, agglomerates and tuffs occur within the Kieta volcanics and the Buka formation.

Bougainville and Buka Islands lie in a zone of intense volcanic and seismic activity, although they show little evidence of tectonic movements at the present time. Faulting is of major importance and two possible major faults can be seen on the geological map of the islands. One is on the west coast of Buka and parallel to the Parkinson Range and a second on the south-west side of the Crown Prince Range in central Bougainville. There is little evidence of folding in the region; dips are less than 15° and appear to be largely depositional. Tectonic warping has occurred on Bougainville and is indicated by the attitudes of both the Keriaka and Sohano limestones. Evidence of major subsidence and uplift of at least 4,000 feet is also indicated by the Keriaka limestone.

The Solomon Islands in general and Bougainville in particular lie in a region of high seismicity. Most of the earthquakes are shallow to intermediate in depth with foci less than 125 miles.

Earthquakes sufficiently intense to be felt by observers are common in the southern half of Bougainville but rare in the northern part.

The volcanoes of Bougainville, which are stratovolcanoes, are of two types: those which have cones surfaced with blocky lava flows, e.g. Bagana and Takuan, and those in which lava flows have played a subordinate role in cone formation, e.g. Balbi and Loloru. The former type of volcanic cone is symmetrical with steep, straight slopes, of the order of 25°; the latter type has a rugged summit area below which extensive debris slopes form a concave outline with an inclination decreasing from 20° at the top to 6° at the base.

With the exception of Bagana, Balbi and Loloru, the volcanoes of Bougainville are extinct. Bagana is the most active volcano in Papua New Guinea. Its activity was first recorded in 1887 and it has probably been more or less continuously active ever since. Its most recent manifestations of activity include powerful explosive eruptions in 1948 and 1952 and the emission of lava flows in 1946-7, 1952 and 1963-5. Balbi and Loloru are considered to be dormant volcanoes. The last eruption of Balbi is reputed to have occurred between 1800 and 1850; it is not known when Loloru last erupted. Both volcanoes have solfataric zones on their summit areas and hot springs on their flanks.

A crescent-shaped crater lake, Lake Loloru, has been formed in the crater of Loloru volcano. The water level in the lake is at about 4,500 feet which is 1,500 feet below the highest point of the volcano. Another crater lake, Lake Billy Mitchell, has formed in the centre of the extinct Billy Mitchell volcano. The water level in the lake is at 3,500 feet and the highest point on the rim of the crater is 5,028 feet above sea-level.

CLIMATE

The District has a wet tropical climate, with the climatic year divisible into two major wind seasons: the north-west season (December to April) during which the area is under the influence of the north-west monsoons, and the south-east season (May to November) when the area is under the influence of the south-east trades. The winds of the south-east season are stronger, more persistent and less variable in direction than those of the north-west season. The major wind seasons are separated by a change-over period of unpredictable and variable wind conditions, which lasts for about six weeks and occurs twice in the year. Each of the seasonal winds is warm and moist and both bring rain.

The average rainfall for the District as a whole is over 100 inches. It varies from a relatively low 75 inches (75 rainy days) at Baniu plantation on the north coast of Bougainville to a high 199 inches (232 rainy days) at Boku in the south-west of the island. It is probable that still higher rainfalls may occur in the highland areas.

The north-west season produces approximately the same amount of rainfall throughout the islands but in the south-east season the northern part of the area receives less than half the rainfall of the southern portion. This rainfall variation is caused by the mountains of southern Bougainville inducing instability in the warm moist winds which results in heavy precipitation in southern Bougainville and produces a lee effect to the north. Rainfall is, therefore, much more evenly distributed throughout the year in the south than it is in the north which has relatively drier conditions in the south-east season.

The equatorial position and maritime influences on these islands produce an equable temperature regime. The mean annual temperature in the lowlands is 80°F. and the difference in the monthly means between the hottest and coldest months is only 3°F. The mean monthly maximum temperature rises to 87°F. and the mean monthly minimum temperature falls to 74°F. giving a range of 13°F. The highest daily temperatures recorded vary from 90 to 98°F. and the lowest daily temperatures from 58 to 72°F. Kieta and Buin have consistently lower minimum temperatures than Sohano. This difference is caused by the proximity of Kieta and Buin to mountain slopes down which cold air masses (katabic winds) descend. No meteorological observations are available from the highland areas of the District, but it may be assumed that the normal lapse rate conditions apply (i.e. 3.5°F. drop in mean temperature for every 1,000 feet ascent). Diurnal temperature ranges can be expected to increase with altitude. Under the prevailing strong maritime influence there is no frost risk at any elevation.

Relative humidity is uniformly high and constant throughout the year rarely falling below 75 per cent or rising above 86 per cent. The difference between the 9 a.m. and 3 p.m. relative humidity readings for any one day is never greater than 2 per cent. This also indicates clearly the strong maritime influence on the island. Day length [q.v.] varies only about 40 minutes through the year, and in conjunction with uniform cloudiness results in little seasonal variation in the hours of sunshine.

SOILS

The soils of the District are formed from either volcanic material or coral limestone.

Ash soils, derived from volcanic ash, make up half the soils of the District. They are concentrated around volcanic centres in the central mountainous and hilly regions of the island, except in areas of extremely rugged and dissected terrain where the soil has been stripped off the steeper ridges by erosion leaving bare rock faces, boulder debris or very shallow soil covering. The ash soils fall into two textural groups, grey fine sands and brown loams. The former occur on the gentler slopes of Balbi and Bagana volcanoes. One of the outstanding features of these soils is their resistance to erosion.

Ash covered soils are found on the periphery of the ash soils. Here thicknesses of ash up to 3 feet deep form brown loams overlying a variety of buried older sands and clays.

Acid clay soils occur on steeper slopes and ridges where the ash cover has been thinner and more easily removed. They are of two types: a brown clay with a varying depth from 24 to 40 inches and a red friable clay with a depth of from 40 to 70 inches.

Terra rossa soils are also found in areas from which the ash overlay has been removed by moderate erosion. They occur on ridges, plains and in depressions. These soils are largely ash-derived but overlie weathered coral into which they merge at depths varying from 1 to 6 feet.

Rendzinas are coral-derived soils which may be contaminated with wind-blown sand and volcanic ash. They cover youthful coral platforms 5 to 15 feet above high-water mark. They are shallow soils which merge into weathered coral at depths from 12 to 15 inches.

Swamp peats occur in areas which are permanently inundated to depths greater than 4 feet. These organic soils are composed of a vegetative layer at least 1 foot thick.

Swamp soils are found in swampy situations which are permanently inundated by at least 6 inches of water. The soils have no profile development apart from a peaty surface horizon. They are neutral grey-brown sands or clays.

Mangrove soils are found only on tidally inundated flats. They are either shallow, strongly alkaline, brown peaty sands or neutral to moderately alkaline dark or very dark greyish-brown sands. These soils show no profile development and vary in depth from 6 to 18 inches.

Alluvial soils include relatively unstable soils derived from water-borne sediments which occur on alluvial plains subject to flooding for short periods. They have no profile development, apart from an organic surface layer. They may be sands, loams or clays, shallow or deep, dark brown or greyish-brown usually mottled below the humic layer.

Littoral soils derived from both wave and tidal sorted sands, form beach ridges along parts of the coast. White sands occur on the outermost ridges, and brown sands which represent an older and more stable soil are found further back. Local concentrations of black minerals may occur in the white sands.

VEGETATION

Lowland tropical rain forest, which grows on all well-drained land from sea-level to 2,000 feet, is the climax vegetation cover on 63 per cent of the land area of the District. It is an evergreen multi-layered forest with an irregularly closed tree canopy 100 to 115 feet tall through which scattered emergents may grow to 130 feet. Below the canopy a lower storey of trees rises to 50 feet. A dense shrub layer 15 to 20 feet tall and a patchy ground cover complete the forest structure. This forest is usually exceedingly rich in plant species in all storeys, but under special environmental conditions certain species may predominate. In general the trees have straight trunks and are high branching; many have well-developed buttress roots. Palms are common in the lower tree and shrub layers. Epiphytes are plentiful but climbers such as rattans and lianes are rare.

Lower montane forest, which covers 24 per cent of the area, becomes the climax vegetation in the zone between 2,000 and 4,000 feet above sea-level. This evergreen forest is less complicated than the lowland forest. The straight-trunked trees are of medium height and often have buttress roots. Many tree ferns grow in the lower tree and shrub layers, but palms, with the exception of stilt-rooted types, are rare or absent. Grasses and ferns are characteristic of the herb layer. Epiphytes, including numerous ferns, club mosses and mosses, are common to abundant. Climbers are rare to common.

Upper montane vegetation becomes dominant above 4,000 feet, where the climax vegetation is a palm-pandanus combination which grows to about 65 feet high and is characterized by an abundance of palms in the canopy and pandanus in the lower storey. Tree ferns are common in the scattered shrub layer; the herb layer consists mainly of grasses and ferns. A layer of mosses covers 70 per cent of the ground. Thin woody climbers, including bamboo, are present. Epiphytes, consisting predominantly of small ferns and mosses, are abundant, orchids are common. On steep slopes the pandanus in the lower storey are replaced by bamboo thickets. Pockets of low forest occur in more sheltered positions. Mountain scrub and grasses are of minor importance and occur only at high altitudes on the upper slopes and peaks of some volcanoes.

Swamp vegetation grows on 9 per cent of the land area. More or less stagnant swamps are covered either with a floating mat of grasses, coarse sedges, herbs and ferns up to 6 feet high which are anchored in organic mud, or with *Phragmites-Saccharum* grasses 8 to 15 feet high. Areas under permanently flowing water and areas which are frequently flooded carry open tall swamp forest in which *Terminalia brassi* trees up to 140 feet tall are the dominant tree species. Tidally flooded areas in sheltered embayments have a cover of mangrove forest dominated by species of *Rhizophora* and *Bruguiera*, which grow from 50 to 80 feet high.

Grassland is of very little importance. Minor areas of *Imperata-Themeda* (*kunai*-kangaroo) grasses form a dense cover up to 4 feet high in the north-western part of Bougainville.

Plantations and gardens have replaced the natural vegetation in many areas of the lowland rain forest zone, and secondary growth in all stages of regeneration, from colonizing grasses and scrub to tall secondary tree growth, may be seen on abandoned garden sites.

FAUNA

Knowledge of the fauna of the District is incomplete, but there is enough data available to indicate that it is diverse and varied.

Butterflies are plentiful and at least four families, the papillons, danaids, nymphs and lycaenids, are represented in this area. Most of the butterflies are large and brightly coloured, and many are beautifully marked. Other insects are numerous; some, such as the malaria-carrying mosquito, are dangerous to man, others affect agricultural crops.

Over 145 species of fish have so far been identified from the Bougainville-Buka waters. Among the important game fish are bass, barracuda, crevally, tuna, bonito and mackerel.

Amphibians are represented by many species of frogs of varying sizes and habitats from the large river frogs to the tiny leaf-burrowing and leaf-dwelling species.

Reptiles include the estuarine crocodile, species of gecko, skink, goanna, tree snake and ground python. None of the land snakes are venomous.

There is a wonderful profusion of birdlife; at least sixty-five species of birds have been recorded from the region. Sea birds, shore birds and land and freshwater birds are all represented.

The largest mammal in the region is the wild pig. Other mammals include species of possums and many rodents such as tree rats, flying fox and bats.

POPULATION

The total population of the District as at 30 June 1970 was 85,794 persons. Of these 4 per cent of the population are non-indigenous.

The non-indigenous population is made up of 3,263 Europeans, 142 Asians and 113 persons of mixed-race ancestry, of whom 83 per cent reside in the Kieta Sub-District where most are associated with the Bougainville copper project [q.v.]. No figures are available on the male to female or child to adult ratios for the non-indigenous population.

The indigenous population numbers 82,176 persons, of whom less than 6 per cent live in the urban or town areas. As is the case with the non-indigenous sector of the population, most of the town-dwelling indigenous people (approximately 80 per cent) live in the Kieta Sub-District. Many of these people are not local but have come from other parts of Papua New Guinea to work in Bougainville.

Most of the indigenous people (77,793) live in villages and hamlets scattered throughout the District. The sex ratio of the non-urban population is 1 female to 1.1 males; and the child-adult distribution is 1 child to 1.01 adults. The average annual population increase is estimated to be 3 per cent.

Population density for the District as a whole is 17 persons per square mile, but the population is not evenly distributed. The heaviest densities are found on the north-east coast of Buka where densities on village land may reach over 300 people per square mile. The Buin, Kieta and Boku areas also have pockets of heavy population concentration. Areas such as the swampy sections of the west and south coasts and the very rugged parts of the mountainous interior of Bougainville are virtually unpopulated.

THE INDIGENOUS PEOPLE

The most striking physical characteristics common to the people of Bougainville and Buka Islands are the coal black colour of their skins and the extreme curliness of their hair, but apart from the lowlands people being taller and of better physique than the mountain dwellers, other morphological characteristics are variable.

Nineteen different languages are spoken on Bougainville and Buka. These can be grouped into two main categories, the Austronesian languages of which there are eleven and the Non-Austronesian languages of which there are eight. The Austronesian speakers occupy Buka Island and the off-shore islands west of Buka; on Bougainville they are concentrated in the north, along the west coast around Empress Augusta Bay and in two isolated pockets on the central east coast. The Non-Austronesian speakers occupy the rest of Bougainville Island. Except in very rugged terrain each language group tends to be concentrated in one relatively compact area separated from other groups by tracts of unoccupied land. Within the two main language categories many of the languages are closely related in both vocabulary and structure; also many of the Austronesian languages contain some Non-Austronesian elements. The number of persons speaking a particular language varies considerably; the smallest group has less than 200, the largest 12,000 speakers.

Looked at broadly, traditional culture appears to be relatively uniform on the technological, economic and sociological levels. Weapons and tools are very much alike everywhere. All groups are subsistence agriculturalists and use similar cultivation methods. Descent is reckoned matrilineally throughout the area. A more detailed examination reveals many cultural differences between groups. These are most apparent if the Austronesian speakers of Buka are compared with the Non-Austronesian speakers of southern Bougainville.

After almost seventy years of increasing European contact most of the people of the District can no longer be regarded as primitive. The white man's laws have outlawed head-hunting and cannibalism and both practices have disappeared. Modern technology has introduced new tools and materials, which have altered gardening, hunting, fishing and house building techniques. Administration influence extending back to the period of German rule has led to changes in village size and siting. Smaller villages and hamlets have been amalgamated to form larger units and villages have been relocated for administrative ease and to take advantage of transport and other facilities. Many of the traditional religious beliefs appear to have been abandoned and replaced by Christianity. Initiation rites have died out.

Improved transport, better education, and the growing use of Pidgin English [q.v.] as a common language are helping to break down the small insular traditional groupings. The individual family is the basic social unit and loyalties to the larger traditional social units are weakening. Increasing involvement in the modern cash economy especially in cash cropping is placing strain on the traditional land use and land inheritance systems.

The attitude of the indigenous people to change is ambivalent and they are torn between desire for social, political and economic development and fear and distrust of the changes which such development may bring. The formation of the anti-Administration Hahalis Welfare Society on Buka in 1961 was largely an expression of dissatisfaction with Administration policies and efforts in promoting development. So also was the appeal made to the United Nations delegation at Kieta in 1962 that Australia be forced to relinquish the administration of Bougainville to the United States. The continued opposition to the Bougainville copper project indicates the fear and distrust with which many indigenous people regard attempts of the Administration and expatriate private enterprise to promote economic development which they feel is just another ruse by which the European will exploit the local people and their resources for his own ends.

AGRICULTURE

Most indigenous people in the District grow the bulk of their own food using a traditional system of bush-fallow cultivation (see AGRICULTURE, INDIGENOUS). The average amount of land used for gardening is 0.4 acres per head per annum.

The type of land chosen for garden sites varies from area to area. Coral reef flats are used on Buka and on the northern Bougainville coast. In the hilly sections of northern Bougainville broad ridge tops and gentle upper slopes are chosen and valley floors are avoided. The people of east and west central Bougainville prefer to cultivate stream terraces; those on the southern and central east coast choose hillsides. In the Buin area inland plains and plateaux are favoured, while along the coast beach ridges and coral platforms are cultivated.

Cultivation is based mainly on the tuberous root crops, sweet potato, taro and yam. Sweet potato is the most widely distributed and is the main staple crop over all of the region with the exception of small taro-dominant areas on the western side of Bougainville. Taro is an important secondary staple in northern and central east Bougainville, while yam is an important secondary food in the central east and south-east areas of the island.

Subsidiary foods include sugar-cane, papaw, bananas, breadfruit and coconuts. Introduced vegetables such as tomatoes, maize, beans, are grown in most lowland gardens and potatoes and cabbage in the higher areas. Sago which grows in freshwater marsh and swamp is an important food, especially in times of other food shortages.

The subsistence cultivator obtains additional foods by hunting, gathering and fishing if these resources are available. Many groups also keep pigs and poultry.

Commercial agriculture is the most important component in the District's cash economy and although its relative importance will lessen with the beginning of copper production it will remain the major source of income for most indigenous people and for many expatriates.

The two major agricultural products are copra and cocoa. Production for the year ending 30 June 1969 was 21,647 tons of copra and 6,290 tons of cocoa which represented 12 and 23 per cent respectively of Papua New Guinea's total production of these crops. Indigenous cash croppers produced 35 per cent of the copra and 17 per cent of the cocoa and expatriate plantation enterprises produced the remainder. Numerous small cash-cropping units are scattered throughout the District and are rarely more than a few acres in size. The eighty-one plantations are mainly concentrated along the north and east coasts of Bougainville and have an average size of over 500 acres. However, the two largest plantations in the District each contain over 5,000 acres. The cash-cropping unit is usually worked by a man and his family; the large plantation is invariably a large company-owned enterprise employing managerial staff and large numbers of labourers. Total employment on Bougainville plantations in 1969 was 5,138. Details of cash-cropping and plantation acreages and production are set out in the table.

INDIGENOUS PRODUCTION YEAR ENDING 30 JUNE 1969

Crop	Growers	Area Planted Acres	Area Bearing Acres	Production to Nearest Ton
Coconuts	7,510	53,519	27,393	6,282
Cocoa	5,581	13,206	7,574	1,050
Coffee (Arabica)	62	37	16	—
Coffee (Robusta)	489	386	260	5
Rubber	47	94	94	—

EXPATRIATE PRODUCTION YEAR ENDING 30 JUNE 1969

Crop	Total Area Under Crop	Area Bearing Acres	Production Tons
Coconuts	36,131	29,774	15,365
Cocoa	25,479*	19,061	5,240

* 22,177 acres or 87 per cent of cocoa trees are interplanted with coconuts.

Large acreages under immature crops will greatly increase the copra and cocoa production in the future.

Not shown in the figures are the large amounts of fresh fruit and vegetables, which are produced by the cash croppers and sold within the District. The production of these crops is also expected to increase greatly over the next few years.

The total value of agricultural production for the year ending 30 June 1970 was in excess of $7 million.

MINING

The Kieta goldfield was proclaimed in 1930 after lode gold had been discovered near Kupei about 9 miles south-west of Kieta. Later, gold was also found at Panguna and Moroni 3 miles south-west

of the Kupei occurrence. Gold mining on a small scale began in the Panguna-Kupei area in 1934. The available tonnages of ore were small and the unpredictable nature of the structure of the lodes did not support expensive underground development. Eventually the mines became uneconomic and were closed down in 1941. During the time of operation the mines produced 1,789 ounces of gold and 89 ounces of silver. After World War II alluvial gold was worked at several localities in the Crown Prince Range. None of these alluvial prospects produced much and activity ceased in 1959. The total gold production for the field to this date was 2,282 fine ounces valued at $48,020.

After the Kupei mine was abandoned in 1941, little or no prospecting was done until 1964. In late 1963 C.R.A. Exploration Pty Limited applied for and was granted a special prospecting authority to search for minerals in the District (see BOUGAINVILLE COPPER PROJECT).

Other useful rocks and minerals occur in the District but will be only of relatively minor importance. These include mineral sands, limestone and road metals.

FORESTS AND TIMBER

Bougainville has very good timber resources. Forty-three per cent of the District is forested and approximately half of this is exploitable. The remainder is impossible or uneconomic to exploit because of rugged terrain or permanently swampy conditions. Generally the higher yielding forests occur on well-drained plains, volcano-alluvial fans, low altitude uplands with gentle to moderate slopes and occasionally in swamps with through drainage. The forests encircle the central mountain ranges but occur predominantly on the south-eastern end of Bougainville Island.

The main millable timber trees are: taun, brown terminalia, calophyllum, red silkwood, vitex, erima and terminalia species. Other less abundant timber trees are satin ash, yellow hardwood, grey canarium, celtis, cheesewood, white silkwood, dysoxylum, cryptocarya, white beech, New Guinea rosewood and amoora.

As yet the timber resources of the District have hardly been touched. The first attempt at establishing a large-scale lumbering enterprise began in 1963 when a large timber lease at Tonolei in southern Bougainville was put up for tender. The lease of approximately 110,000 acres was estimated to contain 500 million super feet of saleable timber. Logs were exported from the lease in the middle sixties, but continuing production, marketing and financial difficulties led to the abandonment of the enterprise in 1970. There is a possibility that production will recommence in the near future but probably on a smaller scale and mainly to supply the local market.

In 1970 three small sawmills were operating in the District producing timber for local use.

LIVESTOCK

The livestock industry is of little importance in

the District. Cattle, 439 head, of which 328 are dairy animals, are kept as small herds on plantations and mission stations, but they do not constitute a separate industry. An attempt is being made at present to establish small cattle herds in indigenous communities, but the number of cattle involved is small. In 1969 only 47 cattle were owned by indigenous people.

Pigs assume local importance in a number of indigenous communities; some are sold but most are kept for ceremonial purposes and are eaten only on special occasions. Small numbers of pigs, goats and horses are also raised on plantations and mission stations.

FISHING

Fish abound in the seas around the reefs and islands of the District and are an important source of food for the coastal people, but no large-scale fishing industry has developed.

SECONDARY INDUSTRY

The District contains thirteen factories employing a total labour force of 153 people and having a product value of $415,662. The factories, which are relatively small, include a general engineering factory, a motor repair works, three bakeries, two aerated waters factories, three sawmills, two joinery works and one non-government generating plant.

The numerous copra and cocoa processing units which are located on plantations and near cash-cropping ventures are not counted secondary industries for statistical purposes.

TRANSPORT

There are 780 miles of vehicular roads in the District, of which 550 miles are suitable for heavy or medium to light traffic. The rest are suitable only for four-wheel-drive vehicles. Good roads are found along the north and east coasts of Buka, in the Aropa-Kieta-Panguna area of east Bougainville, and around Buin, Konga and Boku in the south and south-west. Road links between Buin and Konga have been completed and a further linkage between Boku and Moratanoa is proceeding. A link between Boku and Panguna which is a possible development in the near future will give Bougainville its first trans-island road. Work is also proceeding on the north-east and north-west road systems which will link the plantations along the coasts. Throughout the District there are over 1,000 miles of foot-tracks connecting indigenous settlements.

There are seven licensed aerodromes in the District at Kieta, Buka, Buin, Boku, Wakunai, Dios and Nissan. Several regular passenger flights link Buka and Kieta with Port Moresby, Rabaul and Lae, and a weekly flight links them with Honiara in the British Solomon Islands.

Small coastal ships from Rabaul call regularly at the many good anchorages which are located on the west coast of Buka and the coast of Bougainville between Soraken and Tonolei. There are no anchorages on the east coast of Buka and only one on the west coast of Bougainville at Torokina. The main ports for the District are Kieta and the new port on Anewa Bay.

OTHER SERVICES

Official post offices have been established at Buin, Buka, Kieta and Panguna, and a post office agency is located at Tinputz. There is a manual telephone exchange at Kieta. To provide communications for the new copper industry towns of Arawa, Panguna and an unnamed industrial town, three new post offices and four new telephone exchanges will be built in 1970-1.

A radio telegraph control centre and an Administration broadcasting station are operating at Kieta.

All power supplied in the District is diesel generated. The Electricity Commission maintains diesel generating plants at the main centres in the District. Missions, plantations and smaller settlements supply their own power. A 135 MW steam power station is being erected at Anewa Bay to supply the power for the copper mining industry.

There is no large-scale reticulated water supply in the District. The high rainfall ensures an adequate supply of water for tank storage.

The health facilities of the District are provided mainly for indigenous people. There are twenty-two mission and six Administration hospitals, which with the exception of the Administration hospital at Panguna supply public ward accommodation only. Numerous maternal and child health centres and several aid posts are strategically placed throughout the District. A leper colony run by the Marist mission has been established at Torokina.

There are 125 primary schools in the District with a total primary enrolment in 1970 of 13,951, including 132 non-indigenous pupils. Eighty of these schools are run by the Marist mission, eighteen by the United Church (Methodist) and ten by the S.D.A. mission; the remaining seventeen are Administration schools.

The District has four high schools, two of which have been established by the Marist mission and two by the Administration. Total secondary enrolment in 1970 was 1,009, including two non-indigenous pupils. Six vocational schools, three mission and three Administration, have a total enrolment of 327 indigenous pupils.

THE LESSER ISLAND GROUPS

The Nuguria (or Fead) group lies about 125 miles north of Buka and contains fifty-two low coral islets which form two coral atolls about 11 miles apart. The total land area of the group is approximately 2 square miles.

The Green (or Nissan) group, approximately 45 miles to the north-west of Buka, is an elliptical atoll containing three islands. Pinipel, a coral island one and a half miles to the north-west, is included in the group for administrative purposes.

The Kilinailau (or Carteret) group is about 43

miles north-west of Bougainville and consists of seven islands on an almost circular atoll-type reef 8 miles in diameter.

The Tauu (or Mortlock) group is some 120 miles north-east of Bougainville and consists of twenty-three low coral islets on a ring-shaped atoll reef. The southernmost island Tauu is the largest. The total land area of the group is 205 acres.

The Nukumanu (or Tasman) group which is about 250 miles north-east of Bougainville contains forty small islands on a reef 7 miles wide by 11 miles long. Nukumanu which has an area of 1 square mile is the largest island in the group.

The combined population of the island groups in 1968 was 4,244, over half of which (2,500) lived on the Green group.

The inhabitants of these islands show marked cultural and racial variations from group to group. The people of the Nukumanu Islands are almost pure Polynesian, those of the Nuguria group are mainly Polynesian, and the Tauu Islanders are Polynesian with admixtures from New Britain, Manus and the Caroline Islands. The Nissan people are Melanesian. On the Kilinailau Islands Buka migrants have apparently displaced an earlier Polynesian population.

Between 1885 and 1907 expatriate-owned coconut plantations were established on all the island groups. Today the only expatriate plantation is on the Nuguria Islands.

There are no regular transport services and, with the exception of Nissan Island which has an air strip, the only contact with the islands is by boat.

'Bougainville Timber to Become Available—Tonolei Timber Area', *Australian Timber Journal*, vol. 29, 1963; B. Blackwood, *Both Sides of Buka Passage*. Oxford, 1935; Commonwealth of Australia, Bureau of Mineral Resources, Geology and Geophysics, 'Geology of Bougainville and Buka Islands, New Guinea', *Bulletin No. 93, Bulletin No. PNG 1*, 1967; CSIRO, 'Lands of Bougainville and Buka Islands, Territory of Papua and New Guinea', *Land Research Series*, no. 20, 1967; H. B. Guppy, *The Solomon Islands and their natives*. London, 1887; D. L. Oliver, *Studies in the Anthropology of Bougainville, Solomon Islands*. Papers of the Peabody Museum of American Archaeology and Ethnology, vol. 29, nos 1-4, Cambridge, Mass., 1949; ——— *A Solomon Islands society: kinship and leadership among the Siuai of Bougainville*. Cambridge, Mass., 1955; ——— *The Pacific Islands*. New York, 1961.   J. P. REYNOLDS

BOVEN-BIAN. People of south West Irian.
Reference:
J. van Baal, 'Een en ander over de bevolking van het Boven-Bian-gebied (Zuid-Nieuw Guinea)', *Tijdschrift voor Indische taal-, land- en volkenkunde*, vol. 80, 1940.

BOWER BIRDS, family Ptilonorhynchidae, are among the most advanced groups of passerine birds in the world. Like the birds of paradise [q.v.], they are endemic to and characteristic of the Australian-New Guinea area, where they are confined to mainland New Guinea and Australia. Including

non-bower-builders (cat birds), there are five genera and eleven species in New Guinea and six genera and nine or ten species in Australia. The New Guinea complement comprises two cat birds, *Ailuroedus*, Archbold's bower bird, *Archboldia*, four maypole or gardener birds, *Amblyornis*, two regent birds, *Sericulus*, and two species of the genus *Chlamydera*, Lauterbach's and the fawn-breasted bower bird.

Resembling large thrushes and 8 to 15 inches long, bower birds are remarkable for their bower-building habits and specialized displays. These activities, which are performed exclusively by male birds, appear to have evolved in response to the need for territory domination, including the spacing of the population, the attraction of females, and the development and synchronization of the sexual processes in both sexes prior to breeding. Bower-building itself may have originated as a displacement activity that is fundamentally allied to nest-building, resulting in a behaviour pattern that has become ritualized and permanent in the course of evolution of the species. Even the posturing movements of males in the bower with various objects held in the bill, such as performed by Archbold's bower bird and the chlamyderas, can be suggested as displaced courtship feeding.

Available evidence, at least for the New Guinea bower-building species, suggests that males are polygynous and, in the several months preceding breeding, set up contiguous territories in which each competes with neighbouring males for itinerant females. Such an arrangement follows the same, if less specialized, pattern of arena behaviour found independently in other birds such as the sandpipers, pheasants, cotingas, and the birds of paradise. Mating, as far as is known, occurs in the bower, and the female subsequently attends solely to nest-building and the rearing of young. Freed from such domestic duties, mature males devote themselves entirely to the intricacies of bower displays. Furthermore, because of promiscuous polygyny, the males with more attractive (elaborate) bowers and displays mate with more females, enforcing natural selection to operate in the direction of more complex display behaviour. It has been inferred from such circumstances that bower birds and birds of paradise are evolving at more rapid rates than other bird groups, an hypothesis which seems to be supported by the extraordinary variety of bower structures and associated behaviour.

But whereas evolution in birds of paradise is proceeding actively in the direction of gorgeous and bizarre plumages, it is leading in bower birds to increased complexity of bower structure, at the expense of plumage colour. The most brilliantly plumaged bower-builders, the regent birds, construct bowers only infrequently, and those that they finish are simple rough avenues of sticks. The adult males are resplendently patterned in orange-yellow and black; the females are brownish. The other New Guinea species to build a relatively unspecialized bower is Archbold's bower bird. Both sexes are black but the mature males of apparently both known subspecies have brilliant golden crests.

The bower, usually adorned with snail shells and blue berries, is a five-foot-wide mat of fern fronds. Described in 1940, this species was the last in the family to be discovered; it is still known only from isolated areas in the central Highlands of the Territory of Papua and New Guinea and the Snow Mountains of West Irian.

The maypole or gardener birds construct more complex bowers, towers of sticks built up around a central pole, usually the trunk of a small sapling. All are uniformly brown birds, though the adult males in three of the species sport orange-yellow erectile crests. Of the better known species, that with the most brilliant crown crest, *Amblyornis macgregoriae*, builds the simplest bower, a central tower of sticks surrounded by a circular runway constructed of moss and vegetable matting. In *A. subalaris*, which has a smaller crest and is confined to south-eastern New Guinea, the central stick tower is extended from the top on one side into a verandah-like shelter. An open area in front of the bower is strewn haphazardly with flowers, berries, and other brightly coloured objects. *A. inornatus* from the Vogelkop constructs the most complex bowers in the genus, and is uncrested. The tower is entirely roofed over, with a low entrance on one side. In front of the entrance, small heaps of coloured objects, for example fruit, are arranged in neat order. A fourth species of the genus, *A. flavifrons*, is known only from a series of four adult male trade skins from an unknown locality presumed to be somewhere in West Irian.

Species building the most elaborate bowers of the avenue type belong to the genus *Chlamydera*. The males have brown, female-type plumage, and are uncrested except for three species confined to Australia which bear erectile lilac nuchal plumes and build less elaborate bowers than their New Guinea relatives. The chlamyderas give the impression that the focal point of the display ritual has been transferred almost entirely from plume colours to bower decoration in order that sombre plumage can be used to protect the males from predators in the open habitat where they live. One New Guinea species, the fawn-breasted (*C. cerviniventris*), constructs a simple avenue raised on a basal platform, and adorns it with greenish flowers and fruit. The other, Lauterbach's (*C. lauterbachi*), builds a more elaborate structure with an inner avenue set within an outer avenue at right angles. Stones and reddish and greenish-blue berries are used for ornamentation.

It has been suggested that the bower bird family is a heterogeneous grouping of forms of diverse origin. One reason for this is the inclusion of cat birds, which are more conventional in behaviour in so far as the males do not build bowers and are apparently monogamous, assisting in nest-building and the feeding of young. Cat birds are heavy in build and have strong bills. The sexes are similar, all are bright greenish above; one is fawn below (white-eared cat bird, *Ailuroedus buccoides*); two are coarsely mottled below (spotted, *A. melanotis*). They are undoubtedly the least specialized members of the family. Their vernacular name comes from the extraordinary whining calls of the spotted cat bird group which occurs in both New Guinea and eastern Australia.

Yet there is little doubt that bower birds are a relatively homogeneous group of similar origin, the nearest relatives of which are the birds of paradise. Evidence for similar origin comes from the conformity of body structure and cranial anatomy, geographical distribution, and habitat preferences in cat birds and bower-builders, from incipient bower-building behaviour in a species like the cat-birds, the tooth-billed bower bird (*Scenopoeetes dentirostris*), of north-eastern Queensland, and from the presence of erectile crests in most species of bower-builders. These crests, varying from large golden-orange head and nape capes in the regent birds to short lilac nuchal plumes in Australian chlamyderas, appear to be homologous in all cases; they are all raised, flicked, and shaken in similar patterns of bower display. Even in the advanced uncrested New Guinea species of *Chlamydera* it is likely that the crests have been lost rather than that they were never present, because in display the unadorned back of the head of the male is still twisted and flicked at the female. Evidence for relationship with the birds of paradise comes from the barred female plumages of such relatively unspecialized bower birds as the satin (*Ptilonorhynchus violaceus*, in Australia) and regent birds, which bear a remarkable resemblance to the female plumages of most birds of paradise, and from the similarity in body and cranial structure between bower birds and some of the more primitive birds of paradise (subfamily Cnemophilinae). The bower bird skull has a number of peculiar features, such as the large lachrymal, which seem to permit strong grasping by the bill with a delicate control of movements; these functional properties appear to be associated with snail-eating in some species and bower-building habits and displays.

Although not meritorious songsters, most bower-builders are accomplished in mimicry which they use to advantage in bower displays. They also give forth an extraordinary array of chuckling, growling, hissing, and whistled notes when so performing.

All species are essentially fruit-eaters and, with the exception of cat birds and the chlamyderas, feed in or near the forest canopy. The fruit diet is occasionally varied with insects. Two species at least, Archbold's and the tooth-billed bower birds, eat snails, which they break open on a special stone near the bower.

Nests vary somewhat between species groups in the family. Though cup-shaped and constructed of vegetable fibres in all, those of the cat birds are large bulky obvious structures, whereas those of true bower-builders are much smaller and better hidden. The eggs are still more variable and support the relationships between the species groups indicated by plumage and bower types. Those of avenue bower-builders are spotted or streaked with olive to blackish-brown markings, whereas those of the maypole-builders, including *Prionodura* in north-eastern Queensland, are unmarked.

Cat birds, including the tooth-billed bower bird, also have unmarked eggs.

Except for the species of *Chlamydera*, all members of the family live in essentially primary rain forest. Those in New Guinea are confined largely to cool mountain forests above altitudes of 1,600 feet, where they are rather shy and far less obtrusive than most birds of paradise. Only the two cat birds occur at all regularly at lower altitudes, to which one, *A. buccoides*, is confined. As is the rule in bird distribution in New Guinea, each species has its particular altitudinal range; indeed, in south-eastern New Guinea, two species of maypole-builders replace each other at different altitudes.

When the plumage characteristics and bower designs of all bower birds are viewed against present geographical distribution and ecological preferences, some conception is gained of the geographical origin and direction of evolution in the family. The unspecialized cat birds are found throughout New Guinea and along the eastern coast of Australia; the single member of the group which builds a bower, the tooth-billed bower bird, is confined to montane north-eastern Queensland. Of the unspecialized bower-builders, Archbold's bower bird is confined to the central New Guinea mountains; the satin bird is found in coastal eastern Australia; and the regent birds are disjunct in New Guinea and central eastern Australia. The maypole-builders, though most diversified in New Guinea, are represented also by a single member in north-eastern Queensland, *Prionodura newtoniana*, which, on account of its bright plumage and relatively unordered bower, appears to be the least specialized in the group. The most advanced bower birds, the species of *Chlamydera*, are widespread in grasslands and savannahs throughout New Guinea and over much of Australia. Thus it appears that the arc of cool rain forest extending from the New Guinea mountains down the eastern seaboard of Australia, with its diversity of the more primitive bower bird forms and greater number of species, represents the centre of origin of the family and the ancestral habitat. From this environment, the chlamyderas have adapted successfully to life in dried environments and become much more wide-ranging in the Australian-New Guinean area than other species.

W. J. Bock, 'Relationships between the Birds of Paradise and the Bower Birds', *Condor*, vol. 65, 1963; E. T. Gilliard, 'The Evolution of Bowerbirds', *Scientific American*, vol. 209, 1963; ——— *Birds of Paradise and Bower Birds*. London, 1969; A. J. Marshall, *Bower-birds, their Displays and Breeding Cycles*. Oxford, 1954; E. Mayr, Family Ptilonorhynchidae in *Check-list of Birds of the World*: A Continuation of the Work of James L. Peters; ed. by E. Mayr and J. C. Greenway, Jr, vol. 15. Cambridge, Mass., 1962; A. L. Rand and E. T. Gilliard, *Handbook of New Guinea Birds*. London, 1967.   RICHARD SCHODDE

BREWING INDUSTRY. The brewing industry of the Territory of Papua and New Guinea began in 1952 when a small brewery, with a capacity of about two hundred and fifty thousand gallons per annum, was established at Port Moresby by Australian interests. Another small brewery of about the same size was started at Lae in 1957, but both suffered from import competition and in neither case did output reach capacity. In 1957 a Dutch firm with interests in Malaya bought a controlling interest in the Port Moresby brewery and increased capacity about three times, doubling the capital invested, but the problem of import competition increased at the end of the decade. At this time, the Australian government was offering incentives to stimulate exports and Australian firms were able to earn tax rebates by raising their exports to the Territory. The local breweries also suffered certain disabilities compared with their competitors in Australia. Being small they were unable to achieve the economies of scale of the large Australian breweries. The low wages were little advantage in an industry as capital-intensive as brewing and, in any case, they were offset by the higher salary and housing costs of the skilled expatriate employees. Further, while imported draught beer came in steel returnable kegs which were free of duty, it was levied on the bottles, crown seals, hops and labels for local beer. Freight on beer between New Guinea ports was about equal to that on imports into the same ports from Australia. Imports of canned beer captured the Highlands market because of the saving in weight for air freight and elimination of breakage. Local production was too small for a local canning line to be economic.

Brewers in Papua-New Guinea claimed that the difference between local excise of 55 cents a gallon and import duty of 75 cents was not enough to compensate for higher costs of production and applied for more tariff protection. This was finally granted in 1963 when import duty was raised a further 20 cents. Half the market had been traditionally held by imports. In November 1962 the licensing laws were changed to allow indigenes to drink and the market expanded.

The immediate effect was a large increase in imports but as this was temporary and, as the change in duty had effect, the local industry was able to expand output. In 1965 the Lae brewery was brought under the same control as the one in Port Moresby, and a $2 million programme was put in hand to expand the Port Moresby plant to two million gallons per annum and Lae to one million gallons. This was completed in 1967. Production was then expected to be close to capacity. The Treasurer announced a 10 cent a gallon increase in excise in the budget for 1967-8 and expected to raise $250,000 with it, but did not increase the import duty.

The main features of the brewing industry thus far have been four: massive investment—the largest investment of any single manufacturing industry in New Guinea in the 1960s; rapid growth in the 1960s, quadrupling the output of the industry in four years; small growth in employment because of the capital-intensive nature of the industry—total employment in 1967 was about two hundred and fifty; and considerable dependence on imports—hops, sugar, bottles, cartons and crown tops were imported and only labels, water, power and labour were supplied locally. Plans were in hand to reduce this import dependence by manufacturing crown seals, bottles and cartons locally, although they would be made from imported materials. These prospective developments illustrate the role of protection in stimulating domestic production. In the long run, the sugar will be produced in New Guinea and the brewing industry will be able to rely chiefly on domestic sources of supply. Market penetration is incomplete; it is estimated that only about 15 per cent of the population of over two million is within the reach of regular supplies of liquor. But beer drinking is becoming more popular with indigenes who are within reach and a major growth in the market can be confidently predicted.   R. K. W.

BRITISH NEW GUINEA. The area now called Papua was known until 1906 as British New Guinea. Its status was curious and at times confused, being designated at first a Protectorate and then a Colony. Responsibility for its administration was at different times spread between the Imperial government and various Australian colonies and this fact, together with New Guinea's remoteness from the scenes of major international interest, did little to promote positive development or effective government.

GOVERNMENT

The Protectorate. The British Protectorate in New Guinea began in November 1884 and continued until September 1888. Previously, other forms of British official influence had followed British missionaries, traders and explorers to the island, and Royal Navy captains had reluctantly declared war on some villages to 'revenge' attacks by Papuans on British subjects. In 1877 the British High Commission for the Western Pacific was established with headquarters in Fiji. One of its objectives was to take over from the Navy the protection and supervision of Britons in the Pacific, but it was not intended to extend British sovereignty in the islands. The Commission was not effective in New Guinea, where it was first represented in 1878 when Sir Arthur Gordon, the High Commissioner, appointed as Deputy Commissioners both the Queensland Magistrate on Thursday Island and the commander of the naval vessel, H.M.S. *Sappho*. In 1881 H. H. Romilly [q.v.] was officially ordered by the Commission to visit 'various parts of New Guinea and to inspect New Britain and New Ireland thoroughly', a task which Gordon described as 'an ambulatory mission of inspection of British Beachcombers'. In 1883 Romilly, equipped with more specific instructions, was centred at Port Moresby [q.v.]. His lack of power and dependence on inadequate local transport reinforced criticism of the Commission which had extinguished 'the assured jurisdiction of the Navy [while] its own powers, especially among the more remote islands, remain in abeyance from the impossibility of exercising them'.

The criticism came from Australian interests which were pressing for the extension of British control. This pressure, suspicion of German activities in New Britain, and perhaps also hopes of using the islands as recruiting grounds for labour for the Queensland sugar plantations, all led to an abortive annexation by Queensland. Its Premier, Sir Thomas McIlwraith, sent the Thursday Island police magistrate, H. M. Chester, to annex New Guinea in 1883. When the British government refused to ratify this annexation Australians were indignant. The British Colonial Office, however, realized that some action would eventually have to be taken, and R. G. W. Herbert viewed increasing European interest in New Guinea as 'one of those growths which cannot be arrested'. In 1884 Britain and Germany agreed on several questions, including the division of east New Guinea between them, though both countries were really more interested in the settlement of African problems than in the acquisition of Pacific territory. The British flag was raised in New Guinea at Port Moresby twice in 1884: unofficially on 23 October by Romilly, who had mistaken his instructions from the High Commission, and officially on 6 November by Commander Erskine of the Royal Navy.

The Protectorate was represented on the spot by a Special Commissioner responsible directly to the Colonial Office. The first Commissioner was Major-General P. (later Sir Peter) Scratchley [q.v.], whose term was from 1884 to 1885; he was succeeded by John Douglas (1885-8). Scratchley had a staff of six British officers; under Douglas the civil service remained almost as diminutive. Disputes about paying for the Protectorate continued almost throughout its existence. The Australian colonies refused to accept full responsibility and Britain showed little interest. At the 1887 Colonial Conference agreement was eventually reached on a ten-year plan suggested by Sir Samuel Griffith, Queensland Premier, whereby Britain was to pay £18,000 for the purchase and maintenance of a vessel if the colonies found £15,000 annually for administration. The Protectorate had little effective power, relying on the Royal Navy to enforce its decisions.

Romilly, with his British background, was passed over for the appointment in favour of Scratchley, who had served Australian colonies, especially Victoria, as defence adviser for many years. Although he had well developed ideas about colonial rule—for instance intending 'to appoint a tribal chief in each district, who was not only to be a trustee for the lands, and responsible for the conduct of the inhabitants in his district, but also an official vested with government authority'—he had little time to test his ideas. He was detained from January to August 1885 in Australia seeking some assurance of finance for his government. Three months after his belated arrival in New Guinea he died of malaria on 2 December 1885.

Romilly was temporarily in charge until 27

February 1886 when the Colonial Office, realizing that 'something was necessary to please Queensland', superseded him by a former Premier of that colony, John Douglas. As Douglas was told that his position was only temporary he had little incentive to lay down any definite lines of policy. The debate about finance continued.

British control was not greatly extended during the Protectorate, although in a few villages Papuans who seemed to have authority were given official recognition. Penetration by government officers into new areas usually followed the requests of traders who sought protection against Papuan hostility and who wanted firm titles to the land they used. The British government, keenly conscious of land ownership problems in Fiji, delayed decisions in the lack of definite advice about the willingness of the original owners to sell. Commander Erskine in his proclamation of 1884 had assured Papuans that their land would be secured to them, but Douglas was eager to acquire considerable areas for future settlers.

The missionaries generally opposed such land alienation. Disputes developed between the London Missionary Society and the government, notably with Anthony Musgrave, the Government Secretary [q.v.]. Musgrave was indignant about the high death roll amongst the South Sea Islands assistant missionaries, and he blamed the mission for neglecting its officers. The mission leaders, notably William Lawes and James Chalmers [qq.v.], resenting the coming of the government, tended to treat its criticism as impertinent.

Explorers received some aid from the government, both Romilly and Douglas agreeing with Scratchley's idea that 'no exploring party should act independently of the Government'.

In general, the four years of the Protectorate achieved little; it was an interim stage marred by disputes within and without the territory. Government officials, Papuans and private settlers alike expected changes when British sovereignty was declared in September 1888.

The Colony. British New Guinea existed as a colony from September 1888 to March 1902, with an uneasy prolongation to September 1906 when the Australian government finally assumed responsibility for the area, renamed Papua. There were three distinct periods in these eighteen years. From 1888 to 1898 the colony was controlled by the ten-year agreement between Britain and the Australian colonies. From 1898 to 1902 it existed by temporary expedients until the Royal Letters Patent of March 1902, which provided for formal acceptance of responsibility by the new Commonwealth government of Australia. These Letters Patent, however, were not followed by any measure declaring precisely how Australia was to control the territory, or how the internal administration was to be organized. The third period from March 1902 to September 1906, when an Australian Act was finally proclaimed, was distinguished by both lack of decision in Australia and by disputes within the New Guinea administration.

Control was divided between the usual machinery of a British Crown Colony with the administration directly responsible to the British Colonial Office, and an anomalous power of supervision by those Australian colonies which contributed to the upkeep of the new colony. It was successively controlled by Dr W. (later Sir William) MacGregor (1888-98); G. R. (later Sir George) Le Hunte (1899-1903); C. S. Robinson (1903-4); F. R. Barton (1904-6) and J. H. P. (later Sir Hubert) Murray from 1906 [qq.v.].

All dispatches were liable to be considered by the Governor-in-Council in Queensland, and any matter which went beyond ordinary administration could be referred to the Governor-in-Council in any other colony which contributed to the costs of British New Guinea. The Governor of Queensland, Sir Anthony Musgrave, initiated a formal argument about the extent of his power both vis-à-vis the elected government of Queensland and also in relation to MacGregor, then Administrator. Distrusting McIlwraith's motives where New Guinea was concerned, Musgrave argued that he should not have to consult the Queensland cabinet. Musgrave died in 1885, unsatisfied by explanations of how the system was to work. MacGregor was more worried when Sir Arthur Palmer, acting as Administrator of Queensland, argued that Queensland should have almost sole control of New Guinea. Although Palmer was probably acting as mouthpiece for McIlwraith, MacGregor's fear of Queensland's political intervention proved exaggerated, especially after the political alliance between his friend, the liberal Griffith, and McIlwraith in 1890. The Queensland government helped MacGregor in framing ordinances and in auditing the colony's accounts, but interfered very little with his policies. New South Wales and Victoria, while continuing payments for administration throughout the ten years, exercised no supervision whatsoever until 1898. The only serious clash MacGregor had was a largely personal one with Sir Henry Norman, the Governor of Queensland who followed Palmer. The quarrel led to MacGregor's threatening to resign in 1890, 1893 and 1894 and to his claim that Norman 'at heart . . . thinks nothing of the coloured man. I fear it is so with many old India men'. MacGregor survived the clash, Norman's opposition merely delayed some of his measures, and MacGregor agreed to stay for a second term in the colony.

The strength of Australia's latent supervisory powers was shown at the end of his second term when Australian pressures defeated MacGregor's plan to grant large land and other concessions to a British company, the British New Guinea Syndicate. After opposition by private Australian interests, including the firm of Burns, Philp & Co., the Premiers of Queensland (T. J. Byrnes), N.S.W. (Sir George Reid) and Victoria (Sir George Turner) combined to defeat the support given by MacGregor and the Colonial Office to this British firm.

Within New Guinea the Administrator, before making most decisions, had to consult Executive and Legislative Councils although he had the power to overrule both in exceptional cases. The Legislative Council had at least two but not more than five members, while the Executive Council in addition to the Administrator had at least two members nominated by him. Neither Council offered any significant opposition to the policies of MacGregor. Debates were very restricted, every measure being passed unanimously except for one vote cast against an ordinance to restrict Chinese immigration. This vote was made by the only member of either Council who was not a government officer, the local manager of Burns, Philp. The Councils were dominated by the three senior officials, the Administrator, the Chief Judicial Officer and the Government Secretary. The indigenous people were not represented on either Council.

MacGregor divided the colony into areas controlled by resident officers and subdivided these areas as control extended, hoping to connect the divisional centres 'by stations for government agents who would be Magistrates for native affairs'. He at first split the colony into two divisions, Western and Eastern, with headquarters respectively at Mabadauan and Samarai [q.v.]. He appointed government agents to two districts within the Western Division, Mekeo and Rigo. Changes were made as government control extended, as more men became available, or as the need arose to supervise gold-mining expansion. In November 1889 the Western Division was reduced in size when a new Central Division was proclaimed with headquarters at Port Moresby. The new Division included Mekeo and Rigo. In 1892 the eastern region was reduced in size when the Louisiades were made a separate South-eastern Division with headquarters at Nivani. Previously in this area government officers on the goldfields had exercised limited jurisdiction. In 1893 the headquarters of the Western Division was moved to Daru. Government agents were appointed to Cloudy Bay for short periods in 1889-90 and 1894-5, and in the same area a temporary travelling agent was installed from 1896-8, his chief function being to assist the miners in the ranges of the Central Division. The gold rush to the Mambare led to the appointment of a government agent in the north at the end of 1898. Soon after MacGregor left separate Northern and North-eastern Districts were proclaimed.

Control from these few government centres was not very effective, and most of the colony was under no firm authority. MacGregor had few government officers, less than sixty Europeans under him in all his ten years, of whom he lost almost half through death (twelve), resignation (fourteen), or dismissal (three). MacGregor wanted men who were versatile: 'All government officers must be prepared to do anything they can to further the public service. The question as to whether a given duty was within the scope of an officer's special duty is one which is seldom given a hearing to. A man that does all that he can is sure to find advancement when an opportunity offers'. He was, however, disappointed with many of his staff, writing in 1889: 'I have no man I can depend on to do a thing "thoroughly" and I have no man I can depend on to execute a task promptly'. His chief supporters were Francis Winter [q.v.], the Chief Judicial Officer, and those of his magistrates who shared his sympathy with Papuans, such as Frank Lawes, John Green and Charles Kowald.

All his officers were apparently members of the British Colonial Service, though the Queensland government had to concur in all appointments and claimed some control over them. All applications for transfer or promotion were in practice referred to London.

After 1902, under MacGregor's successor Le Hunte, dispatches were sent only to the Commonwealth government, but not to the Colonial Office or to Queensland. The two Councils continued unchanged, but gained more power because Le Hunte, through his enforced absences in Australia seeking funds, had to rely on them more than had MacGregor. The Executive Council, which met 118 times in the ten years 1888-98, met 104 times in the next three years. Forty men joined the Colonial Service between 1889 and 1903, most of them after the Commonwealth formally accepted financial responsibility in March 1902.

The Papua Act was not followed by any measure declaring how Australia was to control the territory, nor how the internal administration was to be organized. The slow passage of the Bill through the Commonwealth Parliament—introduced on 15 July 1903, it was not finally enacted until November 1905, and not proclaimed until September 1906—provides a measure of Australian apathy towards Papua. The debates show general ignorance of Papuan problems and include almost no discussion of the aims of Australian policy. They say little about how to achieve the broad objectives set out by the Prime Minister, Edmund Barton, in 1903: 'We should try to encourage the settlement of white people with a constant regard to the promotion of the welfare of the natives, and the avoidance of oppression and tyranny towards them'. To finance administration the Commonwealth government supplied from 1901 an annual grant of £20,000.

On 9 June 1903 C. S. Robinson, who had replaced Winter as Chief Judicial Officer, became acting Administrator. Robinson's brief rule ended with his suicide in June 1904, after a public furore about the handling of the raid on the Goaribari people who had murdered the missionaries Chalmers and Tomkins [qq.v.].

In February 1904 Alfred Deakin, the Australian Prime Minister, had selected an Englishman, F. R. Barton, to replace Robinson. Barton was unable to command the general support of his staff and their clashes led to a virtual standstill of administration while 'a dozen men, senior officials among the fifty or so who comprise the entire "establishment" watched one another's activities with suspicion and malevolence'.

Hubert Murray, who arrived in the colony as Chief Judicial Officer in August 1904, became one of Barton's main critics. Veterans of the service were divided. The ageing Government Secretary,

Musgrave, had no time for Barton, a feeling which Barton reciprocated, while the Treasurer, Ballantine, strongly supported and influenced Barton. Ballantine and Murray clashed bitterly. All these disputes were highlighted by the Royal Commission of 1906, the report of which largely accepted Murray's views.

In succession to Barton, Murray was appointed acting Administrator of Papua in 1907, but not before Deakin had sought the return of Sir William MacGregor and also made certain offers to Staniforth Smith [q.v.]. Murray's appointment, the beginning of an unbroken period of over thirty years in office, meant that it was now possible to look forward to stable and progressive government, both sadly lacking since 1898.

R. B. JOYCE

NATIVE POLICY

The Protectorate. The development of an effective native policy under the Protectorate was impeded by the ill-defined jurisdiction of the Special Commissioner. Scratchley was enjoined in his instructions to protect the persons and lands of the natives and to 'inspire their confidence and acquire their good-will'. But he could make no laws affecting them, and he was uncertain whether he could legitimately punish them or intervene in inter-tribal disputes.

In practice, however, the Special Commissioner's main responsibility was to protect the lives and property of visiting Europeans and teachers of the London Missionary Society. Consequently, both Scratchley and his successor, Douglas, continued to apply 'commodore justice', that is, the burning or bombardment of villages whose inhabitants were believed to be implicated in attacks on non-natives. They recognized that this policy obstructed the establishment of friendly relations but could see no alternative. They lacked the staff to supervise the whole coast and outlying islands, and it seemed that they were not empowered to appoint native officials who might exercise delegated autho.ity amongst their own peoples.

From the beginning of British contact with New Guinea officials recognized that the activities of European traders often provoked native attacks. In 1884 both officials and missionaries expressed concern about the possible influence on administration of the 'unfit government of Queensland', to quote the words of Sir Arthur Gordon, the British High Commissioner for the Western Pacific. They feared that, unless they found some means of protecting the rights of the natives, unscrupulous traders would seize land and property and abduct labour for the Queensland plantations. This sentiment induced Scratchley to proclaim that priority would be given to administration of, for, and by the natives, as far as possible.

Commodore Erskine, in proclaiming the Protectorate along the coast, had selected a native 'chief' at each landing place and had given him an ebony staff as an emblem of office. He told each chief that he should report to officials any

complaints against Europeans or other natives, and that he should restrain his own people from direct retaliation. This policy was encouraged by Lawes and Chalmers, the pioneer L.M.S. missionaries, upon whom Erskine relied for the selection of suitable chiefs, who generally proved to be mission adherents. To some extent this policy was continued after 1884, though it quickly became clear that few native leaders possessed authority over their fellows sufficient to make the system work. More direct methods were then tried. Even in Hanuabada, the 'great village' at Port Moresby, the chief proved to be an ineffectual nonentity, and officials simply issued instructions at village gatherings—on one occasion, with the threat that non-compliance would mean stoppage of the water supply.

Nevertheless, from 1886 to 1888 a few government officers tried to employ natives in a semiformal way within the administration. At Kerepunu, near Port Moresby, when John Douglas was Special Commissioner, he intervened in a feud and appointed several prominent native assessors to determine the reparations to be paid by the offending group. Amongst the Kiwai in the west Hugh Milman introduced the idea, borrowed from the Torres Strait islands, of appointed chiefs having defined executive and judicial powers and being supported by village policemen, but Douglas remained convinced that he lacked the formal authority to establish such institutions officially.

Simultaneously, in the eastern part of the Protectorate, where European traders were most active and most insistent on protection, the burning and shelling of villages continued.

Generally, native administration under the Protectorate was notable for great confusion over policy and for arbitrary action by individual officials. But the experience did compel some preliminary assessment of the problem of administering indigenous societies which appeared, in the then state of anthropological knowledge, to be anarchic groups quite lacking any notion of government.

The Colony. William MacGregor arrived in British New Guinea as its first Administrator on 4 September 1888. He looked forward, as in Fiji, to gaining the support of native leaders in New Guinea, and to incorporating them into the administrative structure; but the immediate need to impose law and order, and the nature of social organization in the colony, gradually frustrated this hope.

His first task, as he saw it, was pacification. In the year preceding his arrival there had been a series of attacks on Europeans in an area stretching from Port Moresby to the Louisiades. He believed that the natives respected only one thing, armed force, on the assumption that this was the main sanction within and between native societies themselves. He thought that strong punitive action saved lives on both sides, in the long term, by compelling permanent native submission. Especially during his first two years, MacGregor personally led police expeditions to disturbed areas in the eastern part of the colony.

Nevertheless, he wished to avoid the indiscriminate application of mass sanctions which had occurred under the Protectorate. Accordingly, as for example in the case of the murder of Captain, Ansell, of the *Star of Peace*, at Chad's Bay in 1888, he tried to enlist the aid of influential natives in isolating and apprehending the culpable individuals or groups. This case ended with the public execution of the four convicted murderers at different points along the coast, and MacGregor later claimed that this had ensured the lasting co-operation of all the neighbouring peoples and the rapid extension of peaceful administration.

His basic policy centred on preventive rather than punitive action; and he patrolled unusually large and coherent communities like Aroma with a substantial force in order to deter the natives from aggression. It is worth noting that all the Christian missions supported him in both methods of pacification.

At the same time MacGregor was trying to achieve an alliance between government and native authority by conferring official rank on natives who appeared to be leaders. He knew that few men under Papuan social conditions exercised individual authority, but at first he hoped that government recognition and support would strengthen their hands. To this end many natives were designated 'government chiefs', and surrounding communities were enjoined to obey them and to submit grievances through them; but the paucity of European staff and the haste of patrols meant that the selection of chiefs was usually arbitrary and often ill-judged.

Three main factors militated against this attempt at 'indirect' administration. First, contact between chiefs and government officers was so infrequent that the former derived neither enhanced prestige nor increased authority from the appointment, and they either lost interest or were ignored by their own people. Secondly, the chiefs had no clearly defined or statutory functions, and were vague about their responsibilities. Thirdly, government law, for example against feuding and witchcraft, was often unpopular and it proscribed the very activities which had been the props of traditional leadership.

Not surprisingly, the institution failed to work as intended. In 1891-2 many chiefs were found to have concealed or even to have committed what the government regarded as offences. Amongst the Kiwai of the Western Division, where conditions had seemed most promising, two chiefs who had been given minor judicial powers had used their office to browbeat fellow natives and to augment their own property. MacGregor's disillusionment was bitter and profound, and he complained that the country had never produced a leader 'capable of uniting two contiguous glens'.

But not all the problems arose from indigenous social organization. MacGregor's officials, drawn from the ranks of almost anyone reasonably literate and willing to serve, were often impatient and sometimes brutal. Some of them conspicuously lacked the humane qualities which enable a man to confer on equal terms with primitive peoples. They responded well only to the punitive and autocratic opportunities of administration.

MacGregor himself was sometimes over-zealous and hasty in upholding the pre-eminent authority of government. For example, he recognized in 1892 that the people of the Trobriand Islands had a system of genuine chieftainship, but in 1896, acting on advice from the newly established Methodist mission, he deliberately humiliated the paramount Trobriands chief and compelled his public submission. Moreover, both the mission and MacGregor expressed disapproval of polygamy although this was the basis of the chief's relatively wide authority.

In 1889 MacGregor had set up a Native Regulations Board on the Fiji model, to frame in simple terms laws relating specifically to natives. Originally the Board was to have included native representatives, but none was ever appointed. Its functions were largely confined to proscribing practices such as sorcery and adultery which were thought to be dangerous or undesirable. This set a precedent of central dictation and reduced the scope of local flexibility in the vital sphere of customary law.

In 1892 a system of Village Constables was instituted under the native regulations. These men had a statutory responsibility to report law-breakers to the government. By 1898 MacGregor was regularly appointing as Village Constables ex-members of the Armed Native Constabulary, a force which he had established in 1890. Such men had a better grasp of law and order and usually spoke some Police Motu which had been developed within the Constabulary as a lingua franca. In consequence, most Village Constables lacked traditional standing in their villages; the poorer ones proved totally ineffective and were frequently replaced; the better ones became adept at balancing the demands of government and those of the village, often to their own advantage.

When MacGregor retired in 1898 he named the Armed Native Constabulary and the Village Constables as the most valuable institutions within his administration; but in reality they represented the abandonment of the original ideal of consultation with the indigenous people.

The trend towards reliance on compulsion by European officials became most pronounced in the period 1898-1906. Le Hunte, who was Lieutenant-Governor from 1898 to 1903, was a weak man who exercised little control over punitive administration. His successors were temporary Administrators lacking metropolitan guidance or direction, for Australia made no effective provision for the colony's government until 1906, after Britain transferred control by the Letters Patent of March 1902.

The result was that officials often led police parties on expeditions of indiscriminate reprisal. The most notorious instance was the action against the Goaribari in 1904. This incident, and protests by missionaries, impelled the Australian government in 1906 to establish a Royal Commission to report on future administration; but the

Commission tended to concentrate on prospective economic development by white settlers, and clearly regarded a progressive native policy as subordinate.

By 1906, when Australia made proper provision for the government of the colony, the office of government chief had been abolished even in name, and native administration had become little more than a simple police operation, the Village Constables being supported and supervised by European magistrates who made visits at irregular intervals, accompanied by parties of the Armed Native Constabulary.   A. M. HEALY

EUROPEAN ENTERPRISE

At the time of Britain's proclamation of a Protectorate over the south-eastern coasts of the island of New Guinea in November 1884 the European economic stake in the region was very small. Activity was limited to the presence of a handful of individuals—representatives of the London Missionary Society stationed at Port Moresby, a handful of beachcombers, a few traders, pearl and bêche-de-mer fishers, occasional labour recruiters, and from time to time some gold prospectors.

During the four years of the Protectorate, 1884-8, this picture did not change greatly. Burns, Philp & Co. appointed their trading agent, and a group of prospectors were at work on Sudest Island. The German firm Deutsche Handels-und Plantagen-Gesellschaft der Südseeinseln sought trading facilities which the Special Commissioner, Sir Peter Scratchley, felt obliged to refuse because of doubts as to his power to control foreigners. An English syndicate anxious to engage in trade and to establish plantations met a similar refusal. The Special Commissioners had criminal jurisdiction over British subjects but they had no power to make regulations governing such matters as land transactions, and they were therefore anxious to discourage settlers. They were concerned in particular with the problems of law and order posed by small and often disreputable traders, 'reckless, unscrupulous, brutal and piratical . . . a thorn in my side', said Scratchley.

With annexation in 1888 Europeans could at last obtain firm titles to land, legislation could be enacted to control relations between settler and native, and law and order could gradually be extended to provide a framework within which development could take place. And official policy as laid down under the administration of Sir William MacGregor, while concerned that European enterprise should not have an adverse impact on native interests, was in favour of the expansion of such enterprise. The Crown reserved for itself the sole right to acquire land from natives, but bound itself, when exercising that right, to ensure that the land in question was not required for the vendors' own purposes. Land so acquired could then be made available to settlers. The Crown could grant land in fee simple and conditions were laid down for the employment by Europeans of native labour under one-year contracts backed by a penal sanction. At first MacGregor was opposed to the alienation of large tracts of land to Europeans but he encouraged the small settler. Later he sought large-scale investment also.

Even so the scale of European development remained small. Though exports jumped from £5,943 in 1888-9 to £76,435 in 1904-5, the main item was gold which represented almost three quarters of the total export figure at the end of the period.

By 1906 the European population stood at slightly less than seven hundred. They were a mixed collection of people: administrative officials recruited often from the local white community, missionaries, traders and storekeepers, small planters who formed the beginning of a settled white community, and the more transient prospecting population, hard drinking and often disorderly, but facing with courage extraordinary hardships in such fields as the Yodda Valley. The social origins of this population varied widely. It included Englishmen of good family, Australians of working class origin, wanderers—runaway seamen, escaped convicts and others, many of whom lived a beachcombing existence. This admixture of elements gave the British New Guinea scene the same kind of flavour as in European communities throughout the South Pacific.

Mining. South-eastern New Guinea had attracted prospectors well before the declaration of a British Protectorate. A minor gold rush in 1878 had aroused a temporary Australian clamour for British annexation, but the rush petered out very quickly. Prospecting activities on Sudest Island between 1884 and 1888 expanded immediately after the annexation of British New Guinea—the number of miners jumped within a few months from two hundred to about eight hundred—and were followed by the larger-scale enterprise of the British New Guinea Gold Mining Company. This company sought for a few years to develop reef mining on Sudest Island but it finally suspended operations in 1900. On the mainland the Yodda Valley became the main centre of mining activity after 1895, though this field was limited to alluvial operations. The other main field was that on Woodlark Island which was worked by companies rather than by individual alluvial miners. The Woodlark Island Gold Mining Company, the Kulumadau Woodlark Island Gold Mining Company, and the Woodlark Ivanhoe Gold Mining Company—succeeded by the Murua Syndicate—employed between them over a hundred native miners by the time of the transfer to Australian control (*see* GOLDFIELDS).

Gold exports during the first ten years of British New Guinea were valued at £103,592.

Agriculture. While mining dominated the export economy of British New Guinea, the foundations were laid under MacGregor's administration for the export of those agricultural products which were to outstrip gold exports by the end of World War I. After some degree of pessimism in the early years about the availability of land for settlement, MacGregor moved to a policy first of encouraging small settlers and then of actively seeking to interest large investors in the agricultural prospects of British New Guinea. His efforts were not very successful, and at the end of his administration his plan to provide up to 250,000 acres for a plantation for the British New Guinea Syndicate ran into colonial opposition and was abandoned, as was a similar proposal of the Hall Sound Company a few years later. Less than seven thousand acres were granted to Europeans during MacGregor's period of office of which only about three thousand were for agriculture. On these grants a beginning was made in the production of what were to become the country's staple exports—copra and rubber. Copra, exported to the value of £550 in 1888-9, was exported to the total value of almost £20,000 over British New Guinea's first decade. Rubber first appeared as an export item in 1895 but after early expansion—rubber exports increased from £27 in 1894-5 to £3,683 in 1897-8—it suffered a temporary decline towards the end of the period. Coffee and tobacco were being grown experimentally by 1906 (see COCONUT INDUSTRY, COFFEE INDUSTRY, RUBBER INDUSTRY).

In addition to the small European-owned plantations which produced this development, the Administration itself established and maintained several small experimental coconut plantations.

Commerce. Though small traders had operated on New Guinea's coasts well before 1888, annexation was followed by a considerable expansion. In addition to gold and agricultural exports pearl-shell, bêche-de-mer and sandalwood were important exports. Pearl-shell [q.v.] ranked second in the list of exports in the first ten years of British New Guinea's existence. Collected almost entirely in the eastern seas, its value was £8,468 in 1897-8 and over the whole decade it was exported to the value of £28,024. Bêche-de-mer was third on the list of exports for the same period, £25,005, and was followed by sandalwood, £21,235. In other words, the trade goods collected by coastal traders formed a much greater proportion of exports than did the agricultural products copra and rubber. In his Annual Report for 1897-8 MacGregor surveyed the future prospects of the territory and saw agriculture as the basis of the country's economy, but he looked to an increase in native production to augment that of Europeans.

Trade was at first largely in the hands of small traders, but with Burns, Philp & Co. coming to occupy an overwhelmingly dominant position. In addition to its own trading activities, its pre-eminent position in shipping meant that the small traders disposed of their goods through Burns, Philp and became in effect little more than their agents.

Samarai was the main port and by 1906 it handled over three times as much trade as Port Moresby. Imports for the goldfields and most exports were channelled through this centre which, with its hotels and its three stores, had become by 1906 British New Guinea's nearest approach to a town.   J. D. LEGGE

Correspondence dealing with the British Protectorate in New Guinea and with the period of joint British and Australian control of the colony, including correspondence between the Administrator or Lieutenant-Governor and the Governor of Queensland, is housed in the Commonwealth Archives Office, Canberra.

British New Guinea, Protectorate, *Report* 1884-5 to 1888.
———— Colony, *Annual Report* 1889-9 to 1905-6.
———— Colony, Legislative and Executive Council Records (C. O. 436/1-3).
———— Colony, *Government Gazette*, vols 1-19, 1888-1906.
C. B. Fletcher, *The New Pacific: British Policy and German Aims.* London, 1917.
G. S. Fort, *Chance or Design? A Pioneer Looks Back.* London, 1942.
H. J. Gibbney, 'The Interregnum in the Government of Papua, 1901-1906', *Australian Journal of Politics and History*, vol. 12, 1966.
Great Britain, Colonial Office Records, original correspondence, New Guinea, C. O. 422/1-15, C. O. 418/14, 19, 27, 32, 38, 46.
J. A. La Nauze, *Alfred Deakin*, vol. 2, ch. 20. Melbourne, 1965.
J. D. Legge, *Australian Colonial Policy.* Sydney, 1956.
L. Lett, *Papuan Gold.* Sydney, 1943.
W. MacGregor, Diary, 4 vols, 1890-2 (N.L.A.)
L. P. Mair, *Australia in New Guinea.* Melbourne, 1970.
W. P. Morrell, *Britain in the Pacific Islands.* Oxford, 1960.
J. H. P. Murray, *Papua or British New Guinea.* London, 1912.
M. Roe, A History of Southeast Papua to 1930. Thesis, Australian National University, Canberra, 1962.
'Report of the Royal Commission of Inquiry into the Present Conditions, including the Method of Government, of the Territory of Papua, and the Best Means for their Improvement', *C. P. P. 1907*, joint vol.
H. H. Romilly, *The Western Pacific and New Guinea.* 2nd ed., London, 1887.
———— *From my Verandah in New Guinea.* London, 1889.
D. Scarr, *Fragments of Empire: A History of the Western Pacific High Commission 1877-1914.* Canberra, 1967.
P. Scratchley, *Australian Defences and New Guinea*, comp. from the papers of Sir Peter Scratchley by C. Kinloch Cooke. London, 1887.
G. Souter, *New Guinea: The Last Unknown.* Sydney, 1963.
J. P. Thomson, *British New Guinea.* London, 1892.
F. J. West, *Hubert Murray: The Australian Pro-Consul.* Melbourne, 1968.

(*See also* GERMAN NEW GUINEA)

BROADCASTING. There is no local ordinance dealing with the Territory's dual broadcasting service. The Papua and New Guinea Service of the Australian Broadcasting Commission (A.B.C.) operates under the Australian Broadcasting and Television Act 1942-69, and the Administration Broadcasting Service is licensed under the Australian Wireless Telegraphy Act 1905-67. Each operates independently of the other and both spend public money. It is expected that they will merge and will come under the control of a Papua and New Guinea broadcasting authority.

HISTORY

In the 1930s Amalgamated Wireless (A/asia.) Ltd maintained a Coastal Radio Service which provided communication facilities for shipping, Administration patrols, exploratory expeditions and survey parties. This company also maintained inter-island links, gathered weather information for official collation, inaugurated a radio link with Australia, and provided air-radio contact for Mandated Airlines on the first Australia–Papua and New Guinea service. Small transmitters up and down the coast formed a communications network. Pedal wireless was used by shippers, missions, mining camps and various patrols. These people clamoured for news and information and on 25 October 1935 Amalgamated Wireless opened the Territory's first broadcasting station.

The first station, 4PM Port Moresby (medium-wave, 250 watts), sold advertising, but a two-hour daily schedule with Sunday a silent day and low power precluded profitable operation. Amalgamated Wireless subsidized the service until the economic pressures of a world war and shortage of manpower forced its closure on 19 December 1941. The technical equipment was handed over to the Australian Army for use against the Japanese invaders. The station fertilized no ancient cultures, but it did feature indigenous groups, and the first to broadcast in the Territory was the London Missionary Society Poreporena Choir led by John Spychieger. Other programmes consisted of records, transcriptions, news and a weekly play broadcast live. It was a beginning.

In 1943 General Douglas MacArthur requested a radio station for the armed forces to foster troop morale in Papua. There was an Australian reluctance to an American-controlled broadcasting station on Australian territory in case continuing rights were sought to broadcast *Voice of America* material when hostilities ceased. The Australian government would provide the station, it would be jointly operated with the Americans, and programmes would be on a 50–50 basis. A 500 watts transmitter was installed, the Australian Army erected the buildings in twelve days, and Station 9PA Port Moresby was opened by General MacArthur on 26 February 1944. It was predominantly an A.B.C. operation. Police Motu sessions were introduced for the Papuans, and a choir from a Port Moresby village broadcast regularly.

When the Allied forces moved north in 1944, 9PA was taken over by Army Amenities, the call-sign was changed to 9AA, and among other tasks it helped to bridge the gap between serving Papuans and their villages on the coast. Police Motu became a focal point in 9AA transmissions. The first indigenous announcer was Morea Hila whose pop song *Raisi Mo* swept the coast.

When the war ended various Australian interests were anxious to secure a broadcasting franchise in the Territory but the Australian government considered it would be unwise to allow diverse interests to broadcast and requested the A.B.C. to provide a broadcasting service. Meanwhile 9AA provided an interim service.

THE PAPUA AND NEW GUINEA SERVICE OF THE A.B.C.

The A.B.C. acquired the Army Amenities station 9AA, restored the call-sign to 9PA and commenced its Papua and New Guinea Service on 1 July 1946.

There were economic, technical, cultural and administrative problems to be overcome. The indigenous listeners were illiterate, many had no knowledge of happenings outside their immediate environment, and there was a linguistic problem involving more than 700 languages and dialects. The A.B.C. looked to the Administration for assistance.

The Special Services Division of the Department of Education, already broadcasting material in Police Motu from the interim service, agreed to organize and deliver to the microphone all programmes for indigenous listeners. This arrangement, in various forms, continued for sixteen years, and it was not until 1962 that the A.B.C. became fully operative in programmes for indigenous listeners.

Station 9PA Port Moresby remained on its original 500 watts power for sixteen years. The only expansion in that period was the provision, in 1948, of a 2 kilowatts short-wave station located in Port Moresby, which relayed 9PA programmes and extended its coverage.

In 1962 a 2 kilowatt medium-wave station, 9RB Rabaul, was commissioned to originate programmes for New Britain and the adjacent New Guinea islands. In the same year 9PA Port Moresby increased power to 2 kilowatts, short-wave VLT increased to 10 kilowatts, and a year later another 10 kilowatt short-wave station, VLK Port Moresby, greatly extended 9PA programme coverage.

By 1963 the Papua and New Guinea Service of the A.B.C. was heard throughout the Territory but there were reception gaps. These were reduced in 1971 with the provision of medium-wave transmitters and shared studio facilities with the Administration Broadcasting Service stations at Madang and Lae. These A.B.C. stations, 9MD Madang and 9LA Lae, each on 2 kilowatts, collect area material and can originate programmes, but their main purpose is to relay the national programme from Port Moresby.

The expatriates obtained a balanced fare of news, information, sport and entertainment. Programmes for the indigenes were more difficult. Until 1956 the A.B.C. tried to combine the roles of a national, regional and local service from one station, and broadcast in eight languages. These have long since been reduced to English, Police Motu and Pidgin, with the Rabaul regional substituting Kuanua for Police Motu. There are magazine-type sessions, news, current affairs, talks, sport, information and entertainment, each handled by its relative area announcer. The pattern is Australian and the main object is to cater for nation-wide needs. Analysis indicates 40 per cent of programmes for indigenes, 30 per cent for expatriates, and the remainder general interest.

In the late 1950s the Administration wanted broadcasting to counter social unrest on the Gazelle Peninsula of New Britain, and offset the demographic and political pressures from adjoining Dutch New Guinea (now West Irian). They wanted broadcasting to *communicate* with the indigenous people, to explain government policies in social and economic fields, and work for an acceptance of those policies through understanding. The A.B.C. was urged to become more active in the Territory, to increase stations and provide regional identification in programmes.

The A.B.C. agreed on the need for additional stations, but stations for work among the indigenous people did not come within the orbit of the A.B.C. It was not the role of the A.B.C. to operate as an instrument of communication for the purpose of the Administration, and in the way the Administration thought best. That was a problem for the Administration and its Department of Posts and Telegraphs.

THE ADMINISTRATION BROADCASTING SERVICE

The Australian government reluctantly agreed to Administration broadcasting in Rabaul and in other areas as 'an interim measure until the A.B.C. is in a position to proceed with its own development'. Shortwave station 9BR Rabaul (now on 10 kilowatts) opened on 19 October 1961 and won immediate acceptance from the Tolai people who resisted any suggestion that it close down when the A.B.C. opened its Rabaul regional station. This station's success laid the foundation for what was to become the Administration Broadcasting Service.

Deteriorating relationships between the Netherlands and Indonesia, the existence of a regional broadcasting service in adjoining Dutch New Guinea, and a campaign to woo border Papuans from listening to Radio Ambon and Radio Macassar, resulted in the Administration abandoning its development plan to concentrate on those areas where demographic and political pressures might arise. In 1963 Radio Wewak (10 kilowatts) commenced in the Sepik area, Radio Kerema (now 2 kilowatts) in the Gulf District of Papua, and in 1965 Radio Daru (10 kilowatts) in the Western District of Papua. These stations filled a communications gap in areas adjoining Dutch New Guinea.

Development was now concentrated upon the densely populated areas or areas with special local problems. In 1965 Radio Goroka (now 2 kilowatts) served the Eastern Highlands, and in 1966 Radio Mount Hagen (now 2 kilowatts) served the Western Highlands. Then in 1967 came Radio Milne Bay (now 10 kilowatts), and Radio Bougainville in the northern Solomons (transmitting power 10 kilowatts) in 1968. Radio Madang and Radio Morobe followed in 1971, each on 2 kilowatts. All Administration broadcasting stations operate on the short-wave band. Further stations are planned for Popondetta, Kundiawa, Mendi, Kavieng, Kimbe, Vanimo and Manus Island.

A broad programme policy enunciated by the 1961 Broadcasting Services Committee gave priority to obtaining an understanding and acceptance of what the government is trying to do. It recommended that programmes should, among other requirements, assist and supplement the work of field extension officers by arousing interest and helping to influence attitudes. Administration broadcasting is an extension service of government.

Programmes are related to existing levels of comprehension. The network principle does not apply. Each station concentrates on the local lingua franca and supports it with the major area languages. Programmes ignore the expatriates and avoid any suggestion of an Australian image. Staff recruitment from the locality served by each station provides an empathy for people at village level.

'Programme for People' is a generic term because the purpose of Administration broadcasting is to involve people in the process of government and encourage them to participate in their own development. There is music, news, information and talks, and extension programmes ranging from health, agriculture, education, patrol movements, village hygiene, the law, employment opportunities and general notices, to a news coverage of House of Assembly meetings, with translations into area languages.

Each Administration broadcasting station is a communicator. Its aim is to be the base of the information pyramid at village level.

IAN K. MACKAY

(*See also* EDUCATIONAL BROADCASTING)

BROMILOW, William Edward (1857-1929), Methodist missionary in British New Guinea (later Papua) 1891-1908, 1920-4, was born at Geelong 15 January 1857, the son of Thomas Bromilow. He was educated at Grenville College, Ballarat, matriculating at the age of fourteen and later taught at Queenscliff State School. At the age of twenty-one he became a probationer in the Methodist Church and served at Rupanyup in the Wimmera. While there he volunteered for work in the mission field. In April 1879, after marriage to Harriet Lilly Thomson and ordination, he sailed from Sydney on the *John Wesley* to serve in Fiji for ten years. Like many of his contemporaries, Bromilow acquired his skills, attitudes and first experience as a missionary in another Pacific field before working in New Guinea. Bromilow states that in his case this was particularly so with regard to the methods he adopted for learning the local language and for translating the Scriptures.

He returned to Victoria and after two years' circuit work he once again volunteered for mission work, this time to lead the Australian Methodist team setting out to begin a new venture in southeastern British New Guinea. Accompanied by the Rev. George Brown [q.v.], who as General Secretary of the Mission Board had negotiated the establishment of this mission with Sir William MacGregor [q.v.], the London Missionary Society and the Anglican Church, he arrived at Samarai in a chartered vessel, *Lord of the Isles*, on 3 June 1891. The party also included the Rev. S. B. Fellows, the Rev. J. T. Field, the Rev. J. Watson, G. H. Bardsley, and twenty-two South Sea Island teachers from Fiji, Samoa and Tonga. They took with them most of their basic equipment and supplies.

Because of its central position and the prestige of its inhabitants among their neighbours, Dobu Island in the D'Entrecasteaux group was chosen as headquarters. From this centre Bromilow directed the mission's work as chairman of the district.

He remained for seventeen years at Dobu. During this period mission stations were established in strategic centres in the D'Entrecasteaux Islands, the Louisiade Archipelago, the Trobriand Islands and Woodlark Island; boarding schools for girls and boys and a training institution for local teachers and pastors were also founded. In 1892 Mrs Bromilow established a group of Australian Methodist mission sisters.

In 1908 Bromilow and his wife retired from Papua for health reasons. During the period from 1908 to 1920 Bromilow occupied various suburban circuits in Sydney but also played a prominent role in the administration of Papuan and Pacific work by serving on the Mission Board, particularly as clerical treasurer between 1913 and 1920. During this time he received a D.D. degree from Aberdeen University in recognition of his New Guinea translation work. Because of staff shortages in the post-war years he offered his services specifically for translation work. In July 1920 he arrived in Ubuia, the new headquarters of the Papuan mission, where he served as chairman of the district until his final retirement from the field in 1924. Besides devoting his time to the work of preparing a translation of the Bible in the Dobuan language he supervised further developments in the mission. The headquarters were moved from Ubuia to Salamo. The Rev. M. K. Gilmour succeeded him as chairman and under his leadership Salamo became a complex administrative, training and welfare centre. During this period Bromilow welcomed the formation by the Administration of Village Councils in the area.

During his retirement he completed his translation work. The Dobuan Bible was published in 1927. He served on the executive committee of the Mission Board, from which he resigned for health reasons about a year before his death. He died in Sydney on 24 June 1929. He was survived by his wife and daughter.

Certainly as a pioneer missionary of the Methodist Church Bromilow must rank with George Brown in significance, since in every respect he was the founder of the Methodist mission in British New Guinea. For this work he seems to have been particularly well chosen. He established harmonious relations in the field between his own mission and that of the L.M.S., as well as with successive heads of government, particularly Sir William MacGregor, Sir George Le Hunte and Sir Hubert Murray [qq.v.]. His deep interest in language and his skills in translation meant that he came close to the people and could communicate effectively with them. He developed a strong faith in what he termed the spiritual, intellectual and practical capacity of the Papuan. He held to the view that 'Papua afforded a unique field for the government and development of an inferior race upon altruistic lines, before less ideal forms had spoiled the opportunity'. His linguistic ability and diplomacy meant that, early in his work, he was admitted to membership of the *kula* [q.v.] ring, while he and his family became members of a Dobuan clan. In his second term of service he withdrew from the *kula* on the grounds that it had deteriorated into 'little more than a mere ordinary trading concern'. Because of his own religious and moral training he tended, like so many missionaries of his age, to make a stern assessment of many of the values and customs of the Papuan people. The attitudes he had formed in Fiji about the persistence with which old superstitions and practices 'coarsened and polluted the Fijian soul' were carried over into his Papuan work. This attitude to local custom was borne out clearly in an address he gave at the meeting of the Australasian Association for the Advancement of Science in 1912. He was an acute recorder of traditional custom and at the same time an active and stern agent in its destruction, wherever it conflicted with his own particular moral standards.

His outstanding achievement was his translation work. The Dobuan language was selected by him as the lingua franca for the Methodist Mission in British New Guinea. By 1908 he had published a New Testament. This was revised in 1925, two years before the publication of his Dobuan Bible. His publications included some papers on the life of the people and his autobiography. The latter contains valuable information on his mission work and also on contemporary administration and society. It was published posthumously in 1929.

British New Guinea, *Annual Report* 1889-90 to 1905-6; W. E. Bromilow, *Vocabulary of English Words with Equivalents in Dobuan (New Guinea), Fijian and Samoan, with a Short Dobuan Grammar.* Geelong, 1904; —— 'Some Manners and Customs of the Dobuans of S.E. Papua', *Report of 12th Meeting of A'asian Assoc. Adv. Science, 1909.* Brisbane, 1910; —— 'Dobuan (Papua) Beliefs and Folklore', *Report of 13th Meeting of A'asian Assoc. Adv. Science, 1911.* Sydney, 1912; —— 'New Guinea', in *A Century in the Pacific,* ed. J. Colwell. Sydney, 1914; —— *Twenty Years among Primitive Papuans.* London, 1929; Commonwealth of Australia, *Annual Report, Territory of Papua 1906-7* to *1923-4.* Melbourne and Canberra, 1908-25; Methodist Church of Australasia, Overseas Missions Papers (M.L.).

R. J. LACEY

(*See also* MISSIONS)

BROWN, George (1835-1917), Methodist missionary in New Britain 1875-80, General Secretary for Foreign Missions of the Australasian Board of Missions of the Methodist Church 1887-1908, was

George Brown.

born 7 December 1835, the son of George Brown, barrister, at Barnard Castle, near Durham, England. He was educated at a small private local school and after a brief round of occupations he eventually ran away to sea in 1850. He then spent five years in Canada and after a rather unsettled period in England went to New Zealand in 1855. Here he came under the influence of the Wesleyan Church and in 1860 he was accepted for missionary work. On 2 August 1860 he married Miss S. L. Wallis, the daughter of a New Zealand Wesleyan missionary. His ordination followed in Sydney on 10 September just before he left for his appointment in Samoa, where he arrived in October 1860. In the next fourteen years he devoted himself to the building of churches, and to linguistic, educational and health work. He also became involved in the inter-clan war that was shaking Samoa at the time and gained some standing as a peacemaker.

Soon after leaving the Samoan mission he presented a recommendation to a meeting in Sydney of the Executive Committee of the Board of Missions in September 1874, on the establishment of a mission in New Britain. His recommendation was adopted by the Board and the next months were spent in preparation for this new establishment. He travelled around Australia seeking financial support and while in New Zealand obtained information about a possible site from members of H.M.S. *Blanche* which had recently returned from a survey in waters around the Bismarck Archipelago. After recruiting teachers from Fiji and Samoa he landed at Port Hunter, Duke of York Island, on Sunday 15 August 1875. During the next five years he pioneered the establishment of this first European missionary work in the area, founding mission stations and churches in the Duke of York Islands, the Gazelle Peninsula region of New Britain and New Ireland. By the time Brown withdrew from the mission on 4 January 1881 there were ten stations in the Duke of York area, including the head-station of the District, Port Hunter, seven in the Gazelle Peninsula and four on New Ireland. Until he was joined

by the Rev. Benjamin Danks [q.v.] on 2 December 1878, Brown was the only European missionary at work. He had to rely, therefore, on the effectiveness of mainly Fijian teachers and ministers for the spread and continuity of mission work. This reliance on the South Seas Island teachers becomes more obvious when it is realized that Brown's stay in the area during these five years was far from continuous. He was away for either health or business reasons from August 1876 to August 1877 and from May 1879 to March 1880.

During these five years in the Bismarck Archipelago he was a witness and sometimes a protagonist in important events in the history of the area. In February 1878 he witnessed and investigated the effects of a volcanic eruption in Blanche Bay. In April of the same year one Fijian minister and three teachers were murdered by local Tolai people in the hill country between Kabakada and Malaguna in the Gazelle Peninsula. Faced with the fears of his teachers and of the small European trading community about their safety Brown directed and took part in a punitive expedition between 16 and 23 April against the local people involved in the murders. As a result a number of Tolais were killed and several villages burnt down. Brown held to the view that this action was necessary for self defence and security. He wrote in his diary: 'I confess that I felt well pleased to see that such swift retribution had followed that barbarous act'. This action caused a storm of reaction in the Methodist Church in Australia, the Pacific and overseas. It was the subject of investigation by his own Church, by Captain Purvis of H.M.S. *Danae* for the British Admiralty, and by Captain von Werner of the corvette *Ariadne* for the German Imperial authorities. He also appeared before Sir Arthur Gordon, the Western Pacific High Commissioner, and Sir John Gorrie, Chief Judicial Commissioner in Fiji, in November 1879. These investigations cleared him of criminal charges and his action was thus vindicated by both church and state authorities. During a third period of residence in the area, from March 1880 to January 1881, he assisted and rescued many of the immigrants who had been brought to Port Praslin in southern New Ireland as part of the abortive and tragic scheme planned by the Marquis de Rays [q.v.] for the foundation of the free colony of New France. In the same period, on 13 April 1880, the first steps towards the foundation of a local church were taken with the appointment of the first local preachers. They were Peni Lelei of Duke of York Island, Ilaita Togimamara of New Britain, and Petero Topiliki of New Ireland.

On retiring from the chairmanship of the New Britain mission district Brown served in a number of administrative and clerical posts in Sydney until taking up his appointment as General Secretary of Missions in April 1887. He remained in this office until April 1908 when he retired from public duties. In his twenty-one years as General Secretary many important developments occurred in Methodist mission activities in the South-West

Pacific and particularly in New Guinea. His first task as General Secretary was to take part in and then direct a series of investigations into mission and other affairs in Tonga; he was particularly concerned with the consequences of the actions of the Rev. Shirley Baker and the establishment of a break-away church, the Free Church.

Meanwhile in August 1889 the Australasian Board of Missions considered an invitation that had come from Sir William MacGregor [q.v.], the Administrator of British New Guinea, for the Methodist Church to enter the mission field in this colony. The General Conference of May 1890 in Sydney directed George Brown to visit the area and report on the feasibility of establishing a mission. He reached Port Moresby on 9 June and had discussions with Sir William MacGregor, members of the London Missionary Society, especially the Rev. W. G. Lawes [q.v.] and the Rev. Albert Maclaren of the Anglican Church. An agreement about spheres of influence was worked out between these missionaries under the guidance of the Administrator and later approved by the relevant mission boards. In company with MacGregor and other officials he visited many areas along the south-east coast and in the island region east of this coast, where his mission would operate. He left Port Moresby on 14 August. With the Rev. W. E. Bromilow [q.v.], the first chairman of this new district of the British New Guinea mission and a group of European and South Sea Island missionaries, George Brown landed at Dobu Island on 13 June 1891 to supervise the foundation of the mission. A month later he visited the New Britain mission to inspect the work being done there. During this visit he had discussions with the Imperial German official, Herr Schmiele, on mission affairs, one of which referred to lines of demarcation between the activities of the Wesleyan missionaries and of the Catholic Missionaries of the Sacred Heart who had come to the Gazelle Peninsula in 1882. This discussion resulted from a decision of the Colonial Department of the German Foreign Office communicated to Brown in a letter of 13 January 1891. Rather than approve his suggestion that the Catholic missionaries work in New Ireland alone while the Wesleyan mission occupied the whole of the Gazelle Peninsula, the Foreign Office decided that both should be free to operate in the Gazelle Peninsula. The Catholics were to concentrate their activities in the southern valleys and lowlands and the Wesleyans in the northern tablelands. This decision was welcomed by the Wesleyans at the 1892 meeting of the New Britain district committee. Perhaps George Brown's attempts to have a broader and more rigidly defined policy of spheres of influence had been affected by the gentlemen's agreement reached in British New Guinea in June 1890.

As General Secretary George Brown paid three more official visits to the New Guinea and New Britain mission districts from May to September 1897, in July and August 1899 and in October and November 1905. During these visits, besides having discussions with Methodist missionaries about their work and planning new developments,

he also took the opportunity of meeting leaders of other missions, such as the Rev. James Chalmers of the L.M.S., Mgr Navarre M.S.C. and Pastor J. Flierl of the Lutheran Mission [qq.v.]. Also as the result of a resolution of the General Conference of 1901 he investigated and then supervised the establishment of a new mission district in the British Solomon Islands in May 1902.

His *Autobiography*, based on his prolific journals, letters and writings, was published in 1908. In the same year he was placed on the supernumerary list of his church. His last years, spent in Sydney, were devoted to writing and giving addresses to such gatherings as meetings of the Australasian Association for the Advancement of Science, where he contributed a number of papers over the years. He died on 7 April 1917 and was survived by his wife, two sons and three daughters. For his work of translating the Gospel of St Mark into the Duke of York language, in co-operation with other missionaries, he was granted an honorary D.D. degree.

Obviously in his work as the pioneer of the New Britain mission and founder of the mission in British New Guinea, he made an important and unique contribution to the development of missionary activity in both New Guinea and Papua. As General Secretary of the Mission Board for twenty-one years he guided and shaped the broad lines of policy. In his time, because of his experience with the peoples of the Pacific and his methodical recording of their customs and cultures, as well as his constant field-work in natural history, he was recognized as a foremost authority on the anthropology and natural history of the area. As a missionary his greatest gifts were as an executive, a pioneer and an organizer. He established and guided the development of the structural frame work and the institutions of missionary activity. It is in this area that his missionary achievement was quite remarkable.

G. Brown, Papers and Correspondence (M.L.).
——— 'Notes on the Duke of York Group, New Britain and New Ireland', *Journal of the Royal Geographical Society*, vol. 47, 1877.
——— 'A Journey along the Coasts of New Ireland and Neighbouring Islands', *Proceedings of the Royal Geographical Society*, new series, vol. 3, 1881.
——— 'Papuans and Polynesians', *Journal of the Anthropological Institute*, vol. 16, 1887.
——— 'Life History of a Savage [of New Britain]', *Report of 7th Meeting of A'asian Assoc. Adv. Science, 1898*. Sydney, 1898.
——— 'Notes of a Recent Journey to New Guinea and New Britain', *Report of 7th Meeting of A'asian Assoc. Adv. Science, 1898*. Sydney, 1898.
——— 'Some New Britain Customs', *Report of 8th Meeting of A'asian Assoc. Adv. Science, 1900*. Melbourne, 1901.
——— 'Presidential Address—The Pacific, East and West', *Report of 9th Meeting of A'asian Assoc. Adv. Science, 1902*. Hobart, 1903.
——— *A Brief Account of Methodist Missions in Australasia, Polynesia and Melanesia*. Sydney, 1904.
——— *George Brown D.D., Pioneer Missionary and Explorer: An Autobiography*. London, 1908.

——— *Melanesians and Polynesians. Their Life Histories Described and Compared.* London, 1910.
——— 'The Conceptional Theory of the Origin of Totemism', *Report of 13th Meeting of A'asian Assoc. Adv. Science, 1911.* Sydney, 1912.
——— 'Languages', in *A Century in the Pacific,* ed. J. Colwell. Sydney, 1914 .
——— and B. Danks, *A Dictionary of the Duke of York Language, New Britain Group; also a grammar.* Sydney, 1882 (duplicated).
J. W. Burton, *The Pioneer. The Story of Dr George Brown.* Sydney, n.d.
B. Danks, 'New Britain' in *A Century in the Pacific,* ed. J. Colwell. Sydney, 1914.
C. B. Fletcher, *The Black Knight of the Pacific.* Sydney, 1944.
Methodist Church of Australasia, Overseas Missions Papers (M.L.).
R. J. LACEY

(*See also* MISSIONS)

BRUNY D'ENTRECASTEAUX, Joseph-Antoine
Raymond (1739-1793), French naval officer, in command of the *Recherche* and the *Espérance* was searching for the missing La Pérouse during 1791-3. In June 1793 he came to the Louisiade Archipelago which he skirted on the north side. He discovered and named the Trobriand Islands and the islands which are named after himself.

A. Sharp, *The Discovery of the Pacific Islands.* Oxford, 1960.
FRANCIS WEST

(*See also* DISCOVERY)

BUIN. People of the southern tip of Bougainville,
Solomon Islands. References:
J. Köhler, 'Zu den Ausführungen Thurnwalds über die Verwandtschaftsnamen der Bewohner von Buin', *Zeitschrift für vergleichende Rechtswissenschaft,* vol. 23, 1910.
——— 'Recht auf den Salomoinseln und dem Bismarckarchipel nach Thurnwald', *Zeitschrift für vergleichende Rechtswissenschaft,* vol. 29, 1913.
H. Thurnwald, 'Woman's Status in Buin Society', *Oceania,* vol. 5, 1934-5.
——— *Menschen der Südsee: Charaktere und Schicksale.* Stuttgart, 1937.
——— 'Ehe und Mutterschaft in Buin', *Archiv für Anthropologie,* vol. 24, 1937-8.
——— 'Jenseitsvorstellungen und Dämonenglaube des Buin-Volkes', in *Beiträge zur Gesellungs- und Völkerwissenschaft. Professor Dr. Richard Thurnwald zu seinem achtzigsten Geburtstag gewidmet.* Berlin, 1950.
R. C. Thurnwald, 'Reisebericht aus Buin und Kieta', *Zeitschrift für Ethnologie,* vol. 41, 1909.
——— 'Das Rechtsleben der Eingeborenen der deutschen Südseeinseln, seine geistigen und wirtschaftlichen Grundlagen', *Blätter für vergleichende Rechtswissenschaft und Volkswirtschaftslehre,* vol. 6, 1910.
——— 'Ermittlungen über Eingeborenenrechte der Südsee', *Zeitschrift für vergleichende Rechtswissenschaft,* vol. 23, 1910.
——— *Forschungen auf den Salomo-Inseln und dem Bismarck-Archipel.* Berlin, 1912.
——— 'Pigs and Currency in Buin', *Oceania,* vol. 5, 1934-5.
——— 'Stone Monuments in Buin', *Oceania,* vol. 5, 1934-5.
——— *Profane Literature of Buin, Solomon Islands.* New Haven, 1936.

——— 'The Price of the White Man's Peace', *Pacific Affairs,* vol. 9, 1936.
——— 'Alte und neue Volkslieder aus Buin', *Zeitschrift für Ethnologie,* vol. 73, 1941.
G. C. Wheeler, 'Sketch of the Totemism and Religion of the People of the Islands in the Bougainville Strait (Western Solomon Islands)', *Archiv für Religionswissenschaft,* vol. 15, 1912.
——— 'Totemismus in Buin', *Zeitschrift für Ethnologie,* vol. 46, 1914.

BUKAWA. People of the north coast, Huon Gulf,
Morobe District. References:
S. Lehner, 'Bukaua', in *Deutsch Neu-Guinea,* R. Neuhauss. 3 vols, Berlin, 1911.
——— 'Märchen und Sagen des Melanesierstammes der Bukawac', *Baessler-Archiv,* vol. 14, 1930-1.
——— 'Die Naturanschauung der Eingeborenen im nordöstliche Neu-Guineas', *Baessler-Archiv,* vol. 14, 1930-1.
——— 'The Balum Cult of the Bukaua of Huon Gulf, New Guinea', (translation of section of part IV, Bukaua, by S. Lehner in R. Neuhauss, *Deutsch Neu-Guinea,* Bd III, 1911), *Oceania,* vol. 5, 1934-5.
——— 'Sitten und Rechte des Melanesierstammes der Bukawac', *Archiv für Anthropologie,* vol. 23, 1935.
——— 'Einige Gedanken zum Kapitel "Frauenkauf" bei den Eingeborenen im Huongolf, Nordosten Neuguineas', Gesellschaft für Völkerkunde, Leipzig, *Mitteilungsblatt,* vol. 6, 1935.
——— 'Zur Psychologie des Melanesierstammes der Bukawac', *Archiv für Anthropologie,* vol. 24, 1938.
——— 'Zur Naturanschauung des Melanesierstammes der Bukawac', *Archiv für Anthropologie,* vol. 24, 1937-8.
H. Zahn, 'Die Jabim', in *Deutsch Neu-Guinea,* R. Neuhauss. 3 vols, Berlin, 1911.
——— 'Erzählungen und Sagen der Jabim', *Baessler-Archiv,* vol. 4, 1913-14.
——— 'Lehrbuch der Jabêm-Sprache (Deutsch-Neuguinea)', *Zeitschrift für Eingeborenen-Sprachen,* 21. Beiheft. Berlin, 1940.

BURKITT'S LYMPHOMA. The cancer that has
become known by this name is the commonest form of childhood cancer in Africa. It has two unusual features: a high incidence of jaw tumours and an unusual distribution of cases.

Outside Africa, New Guinea appears to be the only country where there is a significant incidence in children. At the present time there is worldwide interest by pathologists in the unique features of this disease.

Special qualities of the disease. The interest in Burkitt's lymphoma arises from the observations that in Africa (1) it has unusual geographic distribution depending on altitude and humidity, which reflect a temperature barrier and suggest mosquito transmission; (2) there is an exceptionally high incidence of jaw tumours; (3) there is an interesting and often dramatic form of regression following treatment with chemotherapeutic agents; and (4) evidence is accumulating which suggests that the lymphomas may be induced by a virus which may be mosquito transmitted in areas of high incidence.

This cancer certainly offers a greater opportunity than most for some effort towards the solution of its aetiology.

The disease commonly begins as a tumour of the jaw, sometimes involving several or all quadrants, but may also present as an abdominal tumour in kidneys, ovaries and retroperitoneal tissues. In contrast to other forms of lymphoma, less than 1 per cent of African patients had enlarged lymph-glands and the spleen and lungs were never seriously affected.

Distribution of the disease. The distribution corresponds closely to areas where the average rainfall is at least 20 inches and where the mean temperature of the coolest month is at least 60°F. The lymphoma occurs rarely and sporadically in countries outside tropical Africa, New Guinea, and Colombia, but it is only in Africa and New Guinea that it represents the commonest form of childhood malignancy. Most people who have studied it claim it as a distinct type of cancer associated with characteristic lymphoid cells 20 to 30 μ in diameter. The morphology of Giemsa-stained impressions has been described in detail and the electron microscopy morphology of the cultured lymphoblasts has been presented in many publications. Most, but not all, of these cultured-cell lines contain 'herpes-like' particles.

Leukaemia in African children is rare, although the adult forms of the disease apparently occur as commonly as in European countries. It has been suggested that Burkitt's lymphoma is the African biological equivalent of leukaemia elsewhere. This idea, however, conflicts with the view that Burkitt's lymphoma is a specific tumour and is rejected by Burkitt because the British type of leukaemia appeared in Kenya with roughly the same frequency as in Britain.

Attention has been drawn to a possible association in New Guinea and Africa between malarial infection and Burkitt's lymphoma. The distribution of the maximum incidence of the latter is similar to that of malaria [q.v.], and a relationship between the two at the cellular level has been emphasized. However, this association needs examination in New Guinea, as no cases of Burkitt's lymphoma have been recorded in children living around Port Moresby, yet the third commonest cause of admission to hospital among children in this area is malaria.

The probable role of viruses. It is now commonly agreed that mosquitoes are the most likely vectors of the inducing agent and on theoretical grounds viruses are implicated. Investigation suggests that arboviruses are most unlikely candidates, but consideration (from virus isolation studies) must be given to reovirus 3, herpes simplex, *Mycoplasma* sp., enteroviruses and the herpes-like particles seen in cultured Burkitt's cells. The evidence now favours reovirus 3 because

(1) reovirus 3 isolates are specifically associated with Burkitt's lymphoma, but enteroviruses, herpes simplex and herpes-like viruses are demonstrated in non-Burkitt-type tumours with equal frequency;
(2) reovirus 3 is the only one of the agents listed that has so far been isolated frequently from mosquitoes and blood;

(3) reovirus 3 has been shown to induce the formation of murine lymphomas with a picture startlingly similar to that of Burkitt's lymphoma;
(4) the murine lymphoma has been shown to contain a complement-fixing antigen of reovirus 3, which is also present in the cultured cells of Burkitt's lymphoma biopsy specimens from New Guinea, but not in the cultured cells from a patient with myeloid leukaemia, nor in other murine lymphomas; and
(5) the herpes-like particles so frequently seen in cultured cells of Burkitt's lymphoma have now been seen in the cultured leucocytes from healthy humans without known malignant disease, as well as in cultures of non-Burkitt tumours. Cultured lines of Burkitt's lymphoma have been obtained without these virus-particles, antibody to which appears in a high percentage of the population in the U.S.A. The herpes-like particles are therefore probably 'passengers'.

It is not yet known whether a 'helper' virus operates with the reovirus 3, or whether reovirus 3 and a herpesvirus act jointly to induce malignancy or whether all of the circumstantial evidence above is purely fortuitous. For this reason alone, the New Guinea lymphomas should be examined in an attempt to clarify their epidemiology and aetiology.

Incidence in New Guinea. Although accurate assessment of incidence is rendered difficult because of differences of opinion with regard to diagnosis, it is probably safe to say that of more than fifty cases recorded in the Territory, only three were in the Highlands, despite the fact that more than half the population live at high altitudes. Between 1958 and 1969 sixty-seven Burkitt's tumours were reported, but only thirty-nine cases of leukaemia in children. Thus Burkitt's lymphoma was more common than leukaemia and represented more than 20 per cent of the total childhood malignancies. Therapy with cyclophosphamide in New Guinea seems to support the observations made by Burkitt and others in Africa. At present, numbers so treated have been small.

The tumour is more common in the wet northern part of the island than in the drier southern part. This observation suggests that, as in Africa, it is rainfall and altitude—and hence temperature—dependent, but further studies are needed before conclusions are made. No cases have been recorded in the area near Port Moresby, where the rainfall admittedly is 33 inches per annum, but which has a very long dry period.

These observations obviously demand further study in an effort to reveal some common factor or factors operating in both Africa and New Guinea. As the interesting picture of its geographical pathology is emerging, combined studies for virus and antibody in patients, healthy individuals, vertebrates, intermediate hosts and arthropods are called for.

D. Burkitt and D. H. Wright, 'Geographical and tribal distribution of the African lymphoma in Uganda', *British Medical Journal*, vol. 1, 1966; N. F.

Stanley, 'The aetiology and pathogenesis of Burkitt's African lymphoma', *Lancet*, vol. 1, 1966.

N. F. STANLEY

BURTON, John Wear (1875-1970), missionary and administrator, was born in Yorkshire on 7 May 1875. He entered the Methodist ministry in New Zealand in 1897, after completing his theological education at Prince Alfred College, Auckland. His missionary experience was gained in Fiji where he served for nine years, 1902-11, taking a special interest in the Indian population, particularly the indentured workers. From 1914 to 1924 he was the Conference Overseas Mission Secretary for Victoria and Tasmania. During this period he gained an M.A. honours degree in philosophy at the University of Melbourne and developed within his office a new department as Secretary for Literature and Home Organisation. For the next twenty-one years, until his retirement in May 1945, he served as General Secretary for the Methodist Missionary Society of Australasia. In 1931 he became President of the N.S.W. Conference and in 1941 he was appointed Secretary-General of the Methodist Church of Australasia. The last office he held was as President-General of his church from 1945 to 1948. In these offices he contributed much to the development of his church's missionary policy for New Guinea as well as in other parts of the Pacific. He also negotiated with government departments on mission policy issues. For eleven years, 1931-42, he assisted in the shaping of wider missionary thinking as Chairman of the National Missionary Council. One of his major contributions to the New Guinea missions was as a writer and publicist, and he was editor of the *Missionary Review* 1922-45, as well as being a regular contributor. He was one of the first two Australian Commissioners to the South Pacific Commission, from 1947 to 1950. He lived at Wahroonga, near Sydney, until his death on 22 May 1970.

His son is J. W. Burton, Reader in International Relations, University College, London, since 1963, and formerly Secretary, Department of External Affairs, Canberra, 1947-50.

J. W. Burton, *Our Task in Papua*. Aust. ed., London, 1926; ———'Notes on Communications in the Mandated Territory of New Guinea', in *The Australian Mandate for New Guinea*, ed. F. W. Eggleston. Melbourne, 1928; ———'The Australian Mandate in New Guinea', in *Studies in Australian Affairs*, ed. P. Campbell, R. C. Mills and G. V. Portus. Melbourne, 1930; ——— *Missionary Survey of the Pacific Islands*. London, 1930.

R. J. LACEY

BUSAMA. People of the west coast, Huon Gulf, Morobe District. References:
H. I. Hogbin, 'Local Government for New Guinea', *Oceania*, vol. 17, 1946-7.
——— 'Sex and Marriage in Busama, North-eastern New Guinea', *Oceania*, vol. 17, 1946-7.
——— 'Shame: a Study of Social Conformity in a New Guinea Village', *Oceania*, vol. 17, 1946-7.
——— 'Native Trade around the Huon Gulf, North-eastern New Guinea', *Journal of the Polynesian Society*, vol. 56, 1947.
——— 'Native Christianity in a New Guinea Village', *Oceania*, vol. 18, 1947-8.
——— 'Pagan Religion in a New Guinea Village', *Oceania*, vol. 18, 1947-8.
——— 'Government Chiefs in New Guinea', in *Social Structure: Studies Presented to A. R. Radcliffe-Brown*, ed. M. Fortes. Oxford, 1949.
——— *Transformation Scene*. London, 1951.
——— *Kinship and Marriage in a New Guinea Village*. London, 1963.

BUT. People on the coast, west of Wewak, Sepik Districts. References:
A. Gerstner, 'Zauberei bei den But-Leuten an der Nordküste Neuguineas', *Anthropos*, vol. 32, 1937.
——— 'Der Yams-Anbau im But-Bezirk Neuguineas', *Anthropos*, vol. 34, 1939.
——— 'Die Handflügler in Glauben und Brauch der Wewäk-Boikin-Leute Neuguineas', *Anthropos*, vol. 46, 1951.
——— 'Jagdgebräuche der Wewäk-Boikin-Leute in Nordost-Neuguinea', *Anthropos*, vol. 47, 1952; vol. 53, 1958.
——— 'Der Geisterglaube im Wewäk-Boikin-Gebiet Nordost-Neuguineas', *Anthropos*, vol. 47, 1952.
——— 'Aus dem Gemeinschaftsleben der Wewäk-Boikin-Leute, Nordost-Neuguinea', *Anthropos*, vol. 48, 1953.
——— 'Die glaubensmässige Einstellung der Wewäk-Boikin-Leute zu den Krankheiten und deren Heilung (Nordost-Neuguinea)', *Anthropos*, vols 49-50, 1954-5.
——— 'Der magische Meuchelmord im Wewäk-Boikin-Gebiet (Nordost-Neuguinea)', *Anthropos*, vol. 58, 1963.

C

CALENDARS. A calendar is usually defined as a method of distributing time into periods adapted to the purposes of social life. It is the system according to which the beginning and length of years, and the subdivisions of the year, are fixed. Calendars, among other things, enable a society to decide when events are to take place and to make preparations ahead.

There has been some discussion as to whether the peoples of Papua and New Guinea described by early travellers, missionaries, and anthropologists had true calendars. The question really revolves around the interpretation of data collected in the field. Such data are sometimes misleading because either they rested on insufficient empirical observations or they were supplied by informants whose conceptual systems had already been disrupted by the introduction of the European calendar and the disappearance of those activities that kept traditional time-reckoning in use, e.g. the pagan festivals forbidden by Christian missions [q.v.]. Allowing for such difficulties, it is safe to say that the communities of Papua and New Guinea had, and still have, true calendars that serve three major purposes: ascertaining the right time for gardening work, arranging festivals, and organizing trading expeditions.

To plan anything beforehand the indigenes have to gear their calendars to natural clocks independent of human activities. Clocks resorted to most frequently are: the appearance and disappearance of stars and constellations (usually the Pleiades), the direction of the rising sun between and at solstices, lunations, monsoons and the directions of prevailing winds, the appearance of the palolo worm (the marine annelid *Eunice viridis*) (*see* WORMS, MARINE), and the flowering habits of certain trees. In many cases observations of some of these phenomena serve as additional checks upon a calendar that is basically lunar.

The recognition of an annual unit of time, named and conceived as such, does not seem to be common. In general the season is the largest unit of practical significance, for this is directly connected with monsoons and the gardening cycle. Some calendars distinguish, within the annual cycle, four seasons, e.g. Torres Strait; others only two, e.g. New Britain. The second unit of some significance for traditional calendars may be described as a month. It is not necessarily a lunar month. In some areas, e.g. the Maenge country in New Britain, this unit is identified with the flowering of certain trees and overlaps lunar months.

Where both lunar months and solar year are basic to the calendar some adjustment has to be devised so that the lunar and solar years never get more than a month out of step. In most calendars this problem of intercalation is solved, when necessary, by doubling a particular lunar month or allowing one month's interval between two named months, e.g. Wogeo. On this basis it has been suggested that the periodic doubling of the *milamala* festival in the Trobriands was not haphazard but rather a regular means of inserting an intercalary month into the annual cycle (cf. Leach). It is now too late to check the hypothesis. It has also been reported that the calendar of the Mae Enga is so arranged that solar time-reckoning and lunar time-reckoning are kept in perfect harmony by introducing an additional month every thirty-nine years (cf. Meggitt). Unfortunately, empirical evidence in support has not been produced. Such adjustment problems do not occur where the calendar is geared to other natural clocks, e.g. the flowering habits of plants. Astronomical observations then serve from time to time as a check.

L. Austen, 'The Seasonal Gardening Calendar of Kiriwina, Trobriand Islands', *Oceania*, vol. 9, 1938-9; ——— 'A Note on Dr. Leach's "Primitive Calendars" ', *Oceania*, vol. 20, 1949-50; G. Brown, *Melanesians and Polynesians*, pp. 331-2. London, 1910; A. C. Haddon (ed.), *Reports of the Cambridge Anthropological Expedition to Torres Straits*, vol. 4, *Arts and Crafts*, pp. 225-8, 'Seasons'. Cambridge, 1912; H. I. Hogbin and P. Lawrence, *Studies in New Guinea Land Tenure*, pp. 54-8. Sydney, 1967; E. R. Leach, 'Primitive Calendars', *Oceania*, vol. 20, 1949-50; B. Malinowski, 'Lunar and Seasonal Calendar in the Trobriands', *Journal of the Royal Anthropological Institute*, vol. 57, 1927; M. J. Meggitt, 'Mae Enga Time-Reckoning and Calendar, New Guinea', *Man*, vol. 58, 1958; M. Panoff, 'The Notion of Time among the Maenge People of New Britain', *Ethnology*, vol. 8, 1969. MICHEL PANOFF

CAMPBELL, Alexander Malcolm (*c.* 1856-1928), Resident Magistrate in British New Guinea and Government Secretary, Papua. His early career is difficult to trace accurately, but he is thought to have been a schoolteacher in South Africa, to have enlisted in the Cape Mounted Rifles in 1881 and to have deserted in 1883. Soon afterwards he applied for a position in Fiji, and was employed in the Fijian Customs service. In about 1889 he entered the service of the Kingdom of Tonga as Collector of Customs, where he assisted Basil Thomson in the work of reorganization after the deportation of the Rev. Shirley Baker. In 1890 he was appointed Assistant Minister for Finance and Minister for Foreign Affairs in the Tongan cabinet, serving at the same time as an officer of the Royal Guards. Campbell's financial work made him some enemies and in 1894 he defended himself successfully against a malicious charge of theft. Shortly afterwards he resigned from the Tongan service and went to New Guinea, where he entered the government service of British New Guinea as Resident Magistrate, South-Eastern Division, on 4 July 1896.

He remained in charge of the South-Eastern Division until 29 January 1902 when he exchanged posts with M. H. Moreton of the Eastern Division whose increasing age made it necessary to transfer him to somewhat lighter duties. Campbell then served in the Eastern Division until his promotion to the position of Government Secretary following the retirement of Anthony Musgrave [q.v.] on 30 June 1908. Soon after his appointment Campbell threatened to resign because the appointment of M. Staniforth Smith [q.v.] as Administrator under the Lieutenant-Governor had reduced the position of Government Secretary from second to third in the hierarchy, but he was eventually prevailed upon to remain. He retired from the service on 6 May 1914 and settled in Caloundra, Queensland, where he died of malaria on 22 January 1928. Campbell never married and died intestate. His total assets at death amounted to £40, but before his retirement he made a gift in Port Moresby of what must even then have been a valuable library.

Thomson in his description of Tonga speaks of Campbell as a reliable and competent administrator. Monckton [q.v.] alleges that he had an absurd passion for administrative minutiae. His management of the Papuan government service was competent but quite undistinguished.

C. A. W. Monckton, *Last Days in New Guinea, Being Further Experiences of a New Guinea Resident Magistrate.* London, 1922; B. H. Thomson, *Diversions of a Prime Minister.* Edinburgh, 1894; *British New Guinea Government Gazette; Papuan Times,* 18 February, 6 May 1914; *Tongan Gazette,* 25 July 1890; Fiji, Central Archives: CSO 83/1703, WPHC 1889/89, 1891/81, 1894/37; South Africa, Government Archives, Capetown: D/D 7/48.

H. J. GIBBNEY

CAPITAL AND INVESTMENT. The economy of the Territory of Papua and New Guinea is unusual in its very heavy dependence on expenditure in the public sector, because of the scale of Australian aid, and in the importance of the subsistence sector as a source of income. Both these aspects of the economic organization of the country are apparent in the pattern of investment and capital formation. Government and its instrumentalities have in the past been by far the greatest contributors of fixed capital formation in

the economy, and non-monetary investment within the subsistence sector is also a very much more important source of capital formation than most people would imagine possible.

In tracing the sources of capital and investment the simple division into private and public investment is insufficient. The subsistence sector is an important source of both private and public investment, but requires separate treatment because of the nature of the investment. Monetary private investment is better understood if subdivided into new foreign investment, new local investment, and re-investment, as the factors determining the flow of each type are not always the same. Finally, public sector monetary investment is of such size that it requires separate consideration.

Subsistence sector investment. As with most components of subsistence sector accounting, the determination of a meaningful value is a difficult and uncertain process.

Non-monetary investment derives from the utilization, without immediate reward in cash or kind, of part of the surplus labour available within the subsistence sector. Examples of non-monetary private investment are the labour of clearing new land and planting it with slow maturing tree crops such as coconuts, cocoa or oil palm, when that labour is contributed without payment, and whether for the worker's own ultimate benefit, on his own holding, or for the benefit of friends, relations, or outside institutions such as missions. Where the labour is partly rewarded, as by the provision of food during the working period, the non-monetary investment is that component of the labour that is not rewarded; for example, if a man contributes a whole day of labour to the building of a mission school, and receives from the mission a midday meal valued at ten cents, where the going rate for casual labour in the area is sixty cents a day, the non-monetary investment contribution might be calculated at fifty cents worth of labour.

Non-monetary public or community investment is the unpaid labour contributed to the construction of community or public works and facilities, such as roads, tracks, airfields, schools and rest houses. In both community and private investment of this kind there may also be subsistence goods contributed to the work or to the labourers engaged in the work but, as this is quite impossible to estimate, only the labour component is considered in detail.

In compiling the National Income Estimates for Papua and New Guinea an attempt was made to estimate the value of non-monetary community investment and private investment for the year 1962-3, and from these figures projections have been made for other years on the basis of variations in subsistence sector population. The methods adopted, and the limitations of the data, are discussed in detail in the full edition of *National Income Estimates for Papua and New Guinea 1960/61-1962/63,* ch. III, pp. 50-7, published by the Department of Territories, Canberra, in 1964. However, it must be remembered that as the figures are derived solely from estimates of labour contributed, it is not possible to distinguish between the precise uses to which the labour was put; work on maintenance of public works, as well as on new construction and replacement, is included (Table 1).

Table 1

NON-MONETARY COMMUNITY INVESTMENT, REPLACEMENT AND MAINTENANCE 1962–3

	Work Days Contributed	Value of Unpaid Contribution, $
Village or tribal works	15,360,000	9,216,000
District roads, rest houses, airfields, etc.	25,950,000	15,522,000
Council works	7,440,000	4,462,000
Total	48,750,000	29,200,000

NOTE: For an explanation of the derivation of these figures, see pp. 50–3 of the source publication.

SOURCE: Department of Territories, *National Income Estimates for Papua and New Guinea, 1960/61–1962/63*, table 3.9. Canberra, 1964.

In the estimates of non-monetary private investment in *National Income Estimates* some detail is given, with separate figures for the main components of indigenous agriculture, such as coconuts, cocoa, other tree crops, expansion of subsistence gardens, manufacture of canoes, fish traps, tool handles, etc. In all cases the monetary component of investment, where it exists, has been excluded. In Table 2, however, only total figures for indigenous agriculture, and for contributions to mission gardens and works, are given.

Table 2

NON-MONETARY PRIVATE INVESTMENT, REPLACEMENT AND MAINTENANCE 1962–3

	Value, $
Indigenous agriculture	2,720,000
Mission gardens and works	5,740,000
Total	8,460,000

NOTE: For an explanation of the derivation of these figures, see pp. 50–1, 54–7 of the source publication.

SOURCE: Department of Territories, *National Income Estimates for Papua and New Guinea, 1960/61–1962/63*, table 3.10. Canberra, 1964.

The capital stock contributed by the subsistence sector is a very important factor in the total economy of the Territory, as comparison of Tables 1 and 2 with Table 3 will show. Moreover, a considerable proportion of that contribution, although non-monetary in origin, is used for production in the monetary sector of the economy. Examples of this part would be the non-monetary investment in indigenous agriculture devoted to the planting of cash crops, and much of the non-monetary community investment devoted to roads, tracks and airfields, etc. The capacity for such investment is dependent on there being a genuine surplus of labour within the subsistence sector. As the economy becomes more sophisticated and participation in the monetary sector increases, this surplus will increasingly be attracted to other uses, and the importance of non-monetary investment will decrease (*see* SUBSISTENCE ECONOMY).

Monetary sector—private investment. Apart from the subsistence sector contribution, private investment in the monetary sector takes three forms: new foreign investment, new local investment from cash savings, and re-investment of profits earned in the Territory.

New foreign investment has been a very important factor in the development of the productive resources of the country. Historically it played a large part in introducing the Territory to world markets and establishing an exchange economy, first through the establishment of trading stations and initial processing of primary products, then through the establishment of plantations under foreign ownership. Based on these activities, and on the government activities accompanying them, a demand gradually developed for other local goods and services, and in this field foreign investment has also played a major part. In recent years new foreign investment has been particularly significant in mineral prospecting, and in the establishment of a large copper mine in Bougainville (*see* BOUGAINVILLE COPPER PROJECT).

Local investment from cash savings, whether by expatriates or by indigenes, has to date been much less important, though quantitative assessment is a very difficult matter. Until the late 1960s high personal cash incomes were received, in the main, only by expatriates, and a substantial proportion of savings from such incomes flows out of the country before being invested. Indigenous people have saved substantial sums, certainly running into tens of millions of dollars. Of this an unknown, but probably decreasing, proportion is hoarded in coin; substantial sums are invested in agriculture, and to a lesser extent in small businesses, particularly in the retail and transport service industries; several millions are invested in co-operative societies [q.v.] and savings clubs, etc.; savings bank accounts in the names of Papuans and New Guineans at 30 June 1969 totalled a little over $15 million (*see* BANKING; FINANCIAL INSTITUTIONS). However, up to 1969 indigenous investment in manufacturing or service industries represented a very small proportion of the total.

Re-investment of profits, whether corporate or individual, has been and remains a particularly important source of private investment. It is difficult to make any estimate of the amounts involved from year to year, but the T. P. N. G. Bureau of Statistics, Port Moresby, has prepared estimates for businesses incorporated or registered as foreign companies in the Territory. The first year for which these figures are available is 1967–8, and the revised figures for that year (issued in October 1970) indicate that of $31,918,000 inflow of

Table 3

GROSS DOMESTIC CAPITAL FORMATION 1960-1 TO 1965-6

Monetary Sector only

Item	1960–1	1961–2	1962–3	1963–4	1964–5	1965–6
	$	$	$	$	$	$
PRIVATE FIXED CAPITAL FORMATION						
Private	11,190,000	11,126,000	12,419,000	13,458,000	19,469,000	29,244,000
Missions	564,000	674,000	591,000	607,000	844,000	791,000
Total	11,754,000	11,800,000	13,010,000	14,065,000	20,313,000	30,035,000
PUBLIC FIXED CAPITAL FORMATION						
Administration	12,356,000	12,051,000	16,546,000	21,577,000	26,555,000	28,846,000
Electricity Commission				704,000	2,303,000	4,079,000
Local Government Councils	205,000	283,000	435,000	512,000	605,000	888,000
Commonwealth entities	3,284,000	4,656,000	4,300,000	6,496,000	7,037,000	17,696,000
Total	15,845,000	16,990,000	21,281,000	29,289,000	36,500,000	51,509,000
INCREASE IN VALUE OF STOCKS	3,151,000	−664,000	901,000	2,854,000	8,373,000	5,219,000

SOURCE: Commonwealth of Australia, *Report to the United Nations on the Territory of New Guinea, 1967–8*, p.403. Canberra, 1969.

direct, private, overseas investment into these companies, $8,923,000 or 28 per cent was re-investment of profits.

No serious attempt has yet been made to assess the value and ownership of the capital stock of the Territory economy, though this would make an interesting and instructive exercise. However, some idea of the current level of investment in certain types of capital stock can be gained by examination of the depreciation claimed on tax returns. For the year ended 30 June 1966 these claims totalled $8,661,000 which, on the basis of a very rough average of 5 per cent, would suggest a capital stock in the hands of private resident individuals, partnerships, trusts, companies, and including dwellings whether owner occupied or let, amounting to about $170 million. However, it must be emphasized that this figure refers only to items such as plant, machinery, buildings and business transport equipment. A large part of productive investment in agriculture, for instance investment in the clearing and planting of land on estates, would not be included in this figure.

Missions [q.v.] are also a significant source of capital formation in the private sector. The official estimates of the gross national product prepared by the Department of External Territories give a figure of about $800,000 for private fixed capital formation by missions for both 1964-5 and 1965-6 (Table 3). However, contributions to mission capital formation from the subsistence sector, in the form of free labour and other supplies, would be very much more than this, as indicated in Table 2.

Monetary sector—government investment. With the rapid increase in size of the Australian grant, and in direct Australian government expenditure in the Territory, the total gross domestic capital formation in the public sector has grown substan-

tially in recent years. The official estimates of gross national product indicate an increase in total public fixed capital formation from $15.8 million in 1960-1 to $51.5 million in 1965-6.

Public fixed capital formation takes a number of forms. In addition to the non-monetary contribution from the subsistence sector, there is the contribution by the Administration itself, by the Electricity Commission, by Local Government Councils, and directly by Australian Commonwealth departments and instrumentalities, among others Defence, Civil Aviation, and Broadcasting (*see* ECONOMIC POLICY). Table 3 gives details for recent years.

E. K. F.

CARGO CULTS. This is a general name for a large number of religious cults peculiar, and indigenous, to New Guinea and the rest of Melanesia. By a cult religion is meant one that is intense, short-lived, and relatively small-scale. Cargo cults can also be described as millennial and messianic. Many religions promise some sort of reward or perfect life to come. Millenarian religions predict that the perfect state of affairs will arrive on earth after a definite, and usually short, lapse of time, perhaps even imminently. Messianism indicates that the religion was founded and/or is run by a messiah, a prophet. These New Guinea cults have been called 'cargo' cults because they all have the peculiar feature of including the arrival of cargo as the signal and substance of the millennium. The Pidgin word *kago* is close in meaning to 'ship's cargo', and is used to refer to any sorts of goods that are found in a trading store, and to jeeps, aeroplanes, telephones, ships—in short Western treasure. It has struck scholars as intriguing that cargo has become an integral part of a religious cult; Westerners are apt to separate the spiritual domain of religion from that of material concerns. Not so the Melanesians.

Cargo cults usually begin with a Melanesian assuming the role of a prophet. He indicates that the present time of troubles will come to an end and be followed by the millennium. The ancestors will return to join the living, bringing with them in ships or aeroplanes abundant cargo so that material well-being will be enjoyed by all. Present wrongs will at last be righted; for example, skin colours will change, or the white men will be expelled. Usually the prophet desires to separate his faithful sheep from the faithless goats. He does this by judging faith by works. He commands the making of adequate preparations for the millennium: sometimes social reorganization, sometimes economic reorganization, new religious rites, the construction of jetties or airstrips to receive the dead and the cargo, the construction of new planned villages including accommodation for the prophet and the returning spirits, the disposal of produce and wealth to show faith. The faithful must adhere to the regimen or otherwise they will not be saved, perhaps, even, the millennium will not come.

The unique and even spectacular features of the cults (e.g. the large-scale construction of jetties or airstrips to receive cargo) have gained them worldwide publicity. The regimen imposed, the destruction of pigs and crops, or the resettlement, sometimes wreaked a certain amount of havoc in the areas where they occurred. This is perhaps the main reason why the official attitude towards them has always been one of disapproval.

HISTORY

One of the first manifestations now regarded as a cargo cult is the Tuka movement of Fiji, which began in 1885, disappeared for a time, and recurred after World War II. Other principal cults are the Milne Bay Prophet Movement (1893); the Baigona Movement (1912); and the Taro Cult of Fiji (1914). After World War I there was the Vailala Madness (1919) and then a series of cults too numerous to list. When the Japanese swept across the Pacific a wave of cargo activity preceded them and continued for some time after their arrival. Typical of these was the Mansren Myth in the west of what is now West Irian. Traceable back to 1867, prophecy and cult activity seem to have gone on intermittently in this area until in 1942 in a flurry of activity a prophet organized whole villages in imitation of an army with officers and dummy equipment. Despite a massacre by the Japanese the Mansren cultists continued to be active. Since World War II the principal cults have been the Naked Cult of Espiritu Santo; the John Frum Movement of Tanna; Masinga (or Marching) Rule of Malaita, Solomon Islands; and a movement in Manus, Admiralty Islands.

Two of the best-documented cults, which can serve as illustrations, are the Vailala Madness of Papua, and the cults among the Garia of the Madang District. As to the former: in 1919 it came to the attention of the Australian authorities that among the people living in the Gulf Division of Papua there were 'reports . . . that their ancestors were about to return in the guise of white men, by steamer, or, according to one version, by aeroplane, and would bring with them a large cargo of European goods of every kind. These goods, it was said, were actually the property of the natives, but were being withheld from them by the whites. The latter, however, would soon be driven out of the country. The leaders of the movement, who claimed to have received messages to this effect from the spirits, ordered the people to suspend all work and prepare feasts of welcome. Platforms were built and loaded with presents of food. The leaders, and some of their followers, imitated European manners and customs in various ways, some ludicrous or pathetic. The leaders drilled their own "police boys." At a certain time each day they would sit, dressed in their best clothes, at the tables, decorated, European fashion, with flowers in bottles, which had been set up to entertain the returning spirits. . . .

'A feature of the Vailala movement was a violent reaction against the native religion. The leaders ordered their followers to abandon all traditional ceremonies and destroy the ritual objects associated with them, and they met with an enthusiastic response' (Mair).

'The anthropologist on the Papuan government staff [F. E. Williams] referred to the mass hysteria with which the movement was accompanied. "Great numbers were affected by a kind of giddiness; they lost or abandoned control of their limbs and reeled about the villages, one man following another until almost the whole population of a village might be affected at the same moment. While they indulged in their antics the leaders frequently poured forth utterances in 'Djaman', or 'German', a language composed mostly of nonsense syllables, and pidgin-English which was almost wholly unintelligible" ' (Hogbin).

Summing up the position in 1947, L. P. Mair writes 'By now the "cargo cult" has appeared in every administrative district of the mandated territory, and even in the highlands which have only known the white man for fifteen years. . . . The common characteristic is the insistence on the cargo of European goods to be sent by the ancestors, and the disappearance of the white man and his rule. Underlying the cargo myth is the idea that all trade goods have been manufactured in the spirit world by the ancestors as gifts for their descendants, and are misappropriated by white men. The prophet of one of these movements, who was named Batari, scored a strong point on one occasion when a crate marked "battery" was unloaded from a ship—but not delivered to him. In every case, the leaders order native economic activities to be suspended. No gardens need be made, since the ancestors will provide all the food required—but only to those who have shown their faith by not growing any for themselves. For the same reason all the pigs are killed and eaten. The people spend their time preparing to welcome the ancestors; sometimes this involves special songs and dances. In the highlands, where it would be both unrealistic and beyond the scope of the people's imagination to expect a ship, they make airstrips and decorate the borders. . . . On Karkar Island the root-conception of the natives' entry into the kingdom from which the whites have debarred them was expressed in the belief that the whole island would be turned upside down, and those who survived would have white skins.

'Usually there was some attempt to set up a rival "government." The leader of the movement would often be a village official, but if he was not he would disregard the luluai's authority. He drilled his own "police boys," sometimes with dummy rifles made of wood, and on some occasions set up an "office," where he sat in imitation of the government official, pathetically surrounded by the paraphernalia of writing'.

For further descriptive material the original works should be consulted, and especially that of Lawrence on the Garia. He there describes five successive cargo movements over seventy-odd years, and an especially intense period from 1944 to 1949 when at least ten outbursts of cargo activity are recorded.

SOCIOLOGY

Originally these cults were explained as a kind of bizarre aberration, a kind of temporary delusion—hence Vailala 'Madness'. This view is clearly behind Williams's remarks, for he elsewhere indicates that his ire was raised by the people's foolish behaviour. It seemed hard to reconcile these movements with the rational behaviour of everyday life. There can be few scholars who take this explanation seriously today, which is not to say that it is not held by anyone. However, as the cults were appearing in similar form all over the western Pacific islands it became less and less plausible to talk of delusion and irrationality; too many societies were involved.

A slightly better theory emphasized the role of the white man and of native-white relations in the cult ideology, and suggested they were some kind of reaction to contact with the white man. In such a vague formulation this hypothesis led nowhere. It did not explain why the cults came about long after contact had begun, or how it happened that they occurred in areas where the white man had never been seen. However, as a general line of inquiry it has been persisted with, and most subsequent theories are specifications within this framework. Yet it was not sufficient to explain the cults by indicating how the natives admired the white man's power and material goods but abhorred his selfishness, racism, and boss attitudes. For besides spreading widely, the cults displayed considerable similarity across vast distances. It would be incredible that widely scattered native societies should react to the intrusion of the white man in such similar ways as starting a cult with a particular set of beliefs built into it. Certainly no one would suggest that native experi-ence of the white man has been homogeneous throughout Melanesia; yet native reaction in its cult expression has been strikingly homogeneous.

To a certain extent progress on the theory of the cults was hindered by the difficulty of getting to see one happening. Mostly anthropologists and government officials heard of them only when they had been going on for some time or were already over. This made it very difficult to test those hypotheses which attempted to specify in greater detail the mechanisms behind the cult. Indeed, only three anthropologists seem to have been around while there was still cult activity to follow and investigate. These are Jean Guiart, K. O. L. Burridge, and P. Lawrence. To them we are indebted for much of the progress that has been made towards a satisfactory explanation.

However, these authors' explanations vary greatly in quality. Guiart sees the beginnings of a Melanesian nationalism in the cults. He stresses the way their ideology promotes unity among the natives against the whites; and how missionaries, businessmen, and government officials are all seen as 'them'. Burridge explains the cults largely in terms of myth and aspirations. He indicates that certain myths dealing with the origin of man and society have become fused with aspirations for the power and wealth of the white man. He thinks the history of the formation of this 'myth-dream' is the prehistory of the cargo cult. And that the role of the prophets is to translate this myth into concrete action. This is a hazardous process and one attempt follows another; trying to implement the same myth, but each in its own way. Failure of one prophet leaves intact the myth-dream itself; only the implementation has failed.

It is perhaps only with the work of Lawrence, published as recently as 1965, that a fully developed and fleshed-out model of what goes on in a cargo cult has been presented. He not only dispels the idea that they are in any way bizarre behaviour, he goes so far as to indicate that cargo cults are perhaps even typical Melanesian religions, special mainly in their specific syncretic formula and in the paraphernalia of their ritual. His analysis has to be placed alongside that of Cohn on mediaeval millenarianism, which tends to show that cargo cults are pretty typical of millenarian religions too. Thus the initial sense that they were bizarre is dispelled as our experience broadens. There remain the specific sociological and historical questions of why the cargo cults came when they did and spread as they did.

Following the general line of other thinkers, Lawrence accepts that they are a product of Western contact and clash. The Melanesians live in materially poor societies with a very great deal of reciprocity and mutual exchange. While property is not unknown, monopoly of any goods or means is unknown. Then came the white man; powerful, a bit arrogant, extremely wealthy, with many desirable goods and a seemingly miraculous means of getting ever more. Yet he kept himself very much to himself and shared none of his wealth or his secrets with the people. Such wages as he paid were meagre and not enough to induct the employees into the white man's social or economic world. However, one gift the white man did extend, and that was his religion. Missionaries, either before or after the trade ship, spread all over the Pacific trying to sell Christianity. Of course, that being their tradition, they attempted to be persuasive; but here and there the resort to bribes—housing, jobs, medicine, and even direct money payments—helped along the work of God. This is sensible enough since the natives were intrigued by Christianity—they noted all the white men going to the churches—as a possible clue to the white man's secrets.

In this situation, quite a number of native hypotheses came forth. One was that the white men were gods. But if they were, they weren't benevolent since they didn't pass on their wealth and benefits. The white men could be another but wealthy tribe. Yet they hardly had a social system that was intelligible to other people. How did the white men get the goods? From heaven? Were they perhaps pirates intercepting goods destined for the natives? Who were the missionaries? Renegades, perhaps, intent on helping the natives? Con men, perhaps, sent to mislead and dupe the natives into abandoning their quest for shares in what the white men had. If the goods came from the gods then the gods should be manipulable by the usual rituals. If this doesn't yield the goods then the rituals may be the wrong ones, and here the offerings of the missionaries may provide some clue as to which rituals are correct. How do the spirits of the dead come into all this? The return of the dead is not a new element in Melanesian religion, but something of the old blended into the new vision of the apocalypse. The expectations of the apocalypse have broadened because of contact; a whole range of new and desirable objects has been added to the inventory along with the spirits. Another new and distressing element is the occasional prediction that the skins of black men will turn white. Complete fulfilment and dignity can only come when one takes on the whole colour of one's colonizer—and he becomes his true colour, black. Here the white man's racism has been directly incorporated into the black man's world view.

The cargo cult, then, has a clear enough rationale. Given a society whose religious organization is loose and ephemeral rather than doctrinaire and institutionalized, the cargo cult is reasonable enough. The differences among the cults can be explained by different prophets and propagators, different degrees and levels of contact. The spread can be explained by the hypothesis that white-black relations were similarly structured all over Melanesia. The cult then provided a model for a solution in any area. It must have been transmitted from one area to another by gossip, travellers, missionaries, officials, newspapers, etc. One would expect places where white-black relations have been differently structured to show different development. There remains the baffling problem of why wave after wave of cult activity should occur, in the same areas, with different prophets and slightly different doctrines.

Our expectation would be that once bitten by the cult bug the natives would be twice shy of entering into such cataclysmic upheavals again. Lawrence suggests that the lack of a linear chronology, a vision of history stretching behind them and in front of them, makes this explicable: 'The most perceptive knew, of course, that within the span of the previous three or four generations there had been five major attempts to explain and get control of the new situation, and that as each attempt failed it was succeeded by another. Beyond this, however, they regarded each attempt at explanation—each cargo belief or myth—as in itself a separate and complete "history" of the world. It bore no relation to earlier attempts at explanation, which were all in error and had been, as it were, erased.'

Our appreciation of their situation is different, i.e. temporarily linear, and only by teaching them our language can we introduce them to our vision. Melanesia has a welter of unwritten languages and dialects with no body of literature and very few people speaking each tongue. It seems inevitable—even if regretted by some—that some lingua franca will have to be taught and that English is the obvious choice. People have a right to remain in their religion, but they also have a right to know why others regard their religion as damaging. Unfortunately, there seems little doubt that English education will be indoctrination in Western cosmology too; there seems little we can do about this. But it seems a price that may be worth paying for forestalling further devastation from the cults. The Westerners are the intruders; theirs is the responsibility to restore these societies to a viable mode of existence. Once having dangled the carrot of wealth and trade goods under their noses it becomes our responsibility to put it within their reach. Having jumbled up their needs and expectations, we have to find some way of giving them access to our world, should they want it.

At the time of writing, the main flush of cargo activity seems to have died down, although reports of new ones keep coming in. There were cults during the war that predicted the arrival of Roosevelt or the King of England; lately we have heard of cultists who were saving up to buy President Johnson.

There are many elements in the colonial legacy. Cargo cults help make us acutely aware of some of them. The white men brought a racism which degraded the black man and made him ashamed of himself. The white man brought a religion which said it offered the keys to the kingdom, but in the upshot the black man was excluded and deprived of what he wanted, as before. We Westerners live in a society convulsed by the 'revolution of rising expectations'. In Melanesia that took the form of the following Garia prayer:

'O Father Consel, you are sorry for us. You can help us. We have nothing—no aircraft, no ships, no jeeps, nothing at all. The Europeans steal it from us. You will be sorry for us and send us something.'

The problem is: expectations once raised cannot be scaled down again.

K. O. L. Burridge, *Mambu*. London, 1960.
—— *New Heaven, New Earth*. Oxford, 1969.
N. Cohn, *The Pursuit of the Millennium*. London, 1957.
A. Dewey, The Marching Rule and Its Anthropological Perspective. Honours Thesis, Harvard University, 1950.
H. I. Hogbin, *Social Change*. London, 1958; 2nd impr., Melbourne, 1970.
I. C. Jarvie, 'Theories of Cargo Cults', *Oceania*, vol. 34, 1963-4.
V. Lanternari, *The Religions of the Oppressed* (translation from Italian). New English Library ed., London, 1965.
P. Lawrence, *Road Belong Cargo*. Melbourne, 1965.
I. Leeson, *Bibliography of Cargo Cults and Other Nativistic Movements in the South Pacific*. South Pacific Commission, Technical Paper no. 30. Sydney, 1957.
L. P. Mair, *Australia in New Guinea*. Melbourne, 1970.
M. J. Meggitt, 'Uses of Literacy in New Guinea and Melanesia', *Bijdragen tot de Taal-, Land-, en Volkenkunde*, vol. 123, 1967.
T. Schwartz, *The Paliau Movement in the Admiralty Islands, 1946-54*. Anthropological Papers of the American Museum of Natural History, vol. 49. New York, 1962.
S. Thrupp (ed.), *Millennial Dreams in Action*. The Hague, 1962.
P. M. Worsley, *The Trumpet Shall Sound*. London, 1957; 2nd ed., New York, 1968.   I. C. JARVIE

CARSTENZ, Jan (*fl.* 1623), Dutch navigator, was sent by Governor van Speult of Amboyna, in command of two yachts, the *Arnhem* and the *Pera*, to extend Dutch discoveries in Australia and New Guinea. In 1623 he followed the south coast as far as Torres Strait, but failed to find his way through. He saw the snow-covered mountains which bear his name, but a landing party was savagely attacked, and Carstenz turned towards Australia.

J. C. Beaglehole, *Exploration of the Pacific*. 3rd ed., London, 1966; G. Souter, *New Guinea: The Last Unknown*. Sydney, 1963.   FRANCIS WEST

(*See also* DISCOVERY)

CARTERET, Philip (*fl.* 1766), English naval officer, sailed with the Hon. John Byron in the *Tamar* and the *Dolphin* on the expedition which went through Magellan Straits in 1765 and thence via the Tuamotus and the Gilberts to Batavia in the Dutch East Indies. In 1766 he sailed in company with Wallis in the *Dolphin* in command of the sloop *Swallow*, through the Straits of Magellan into the Pacific, but the two ships became separated. Wallis discovered Tahiti, but Carteret, his ship in bad condition, reached Masafuera and there, after sighting Pitcairn and the Tuamotus, rediscovered Santa Cruz in the Solomons. Turning north-west he discovered Buka and then watered his ship in New Britain at St George's Bay where Dampier [q.v.] had done likewise. He sailed on past New Ireland, thence to the Dutch East Indies and via the Cape of Good Hope back to England, on the way meeting Bougainville [q.v.], whose ship overtook him.

J. C. Beaglehole, *The Exploration of the Pacific*. 3rd ed., London, 1966; A. Sharp, *The Discovery of the Pacific Islands*. Oxford, 1960.   FRANCIS WEST

(*See also* DISCOVERY)

CASSOWARIES. Known by the Pidgin name *muruk*, cassowaries, family Casuariidae, are represented in the New Guinea region by the three known living species. They are members of the superorder Ratitae, a group of large flightless birds that also includes emus, ostriches, rheas, with a flat raft-like sternum, vestigial wings, and powerful legs for running. These birds are confined generally to open grassy plains on the southern continents of the world. Cassowaries differ in that they occur entirely within tropical latitudes and are adapted to life in tropical and tropical-montane rain forest. There they feed on fallen fruit on the forest floor, and have a characteristic horny casque on the head which they apparently use to break their way through forest undergrowth.

All species are thick-set birds varying from $3\frac{1}{2}$ to 6 feet high, with uniformly blackish body plumage. Their necks, bare of feathers, are brightly coloured and often wattled. The presence and form of the wattles are diagnostic of species, and variations in skin colour are characteristic of races within a species. The shape of the crown casque also differs between species, being triangular in two (*Casuarius bennetti* and *C. unappendiculatus*), and blade-like in the third (*C. casuarius*). Males are smaller than females.

In the New Guinea region the smallest species, *C. bennetti*, is the most wide-ranging, occurring from sea-level to altitudes of 10,000 feet over mainland New Guinea and New Britain. Of the two larger species, *C. unappendiculatus* is confined to lowland New Guinea north of the central cordillera, while *C. casuarius* is more widespread in lowland southern, eastern, and western New Guinea and extends to north-eastern Queensland.

Cassowaries are monogamous. Though usually shy and retiring, they can become aggressive when breeding. The eggs, which are green and coarsely granular, are laid directly on the forest floor and are incubated by the male.

All species have been prized by the New Guinea native as food; parts are used as tools or in weapons, e.g. claws and bones in spear-heads; and the feathers are used as ornamentation. They figure prominently in folk-lore. The young are commonly kept as pets.

E. Mayr, *List of New Guinea Birds*. New York, 1941; A. L. Rand and E. T. Gilliard, *Handbook of New Guinea Birds*. London, 1967.

    RICHARD SCHODDE

CATTLE INDUSTRY. The cattle industry in Papua and New Guinea is based entirely on introduced breeds. The country lies to the east of

Wallace's Line [q.v.], which divides the flora and fauna of Asia from that of Australia. Early settlers in Papua and New Guinea thus found no indigenous cattle, the Asian and Indonesian breeds not having found their way east of the Indonesian island of Bali.

The first introductions of cattle took place in the late nineteenth century when German missionaries and the Neuguinea-Kompagnie imported cattle from Siam (Thailand), the then Dutch East Indies (Indonesia) and South Australia. The Siamese cattle were a Zebu breed indigenous to that country, while those from the Dutch East Indies were very likely either Javanese or Sumatran cattle which originated from the Banteng (*Bos javanicus* (= *B. sondaicus*)) and Zebu breeds. The Australian cattle were of the Jersey and Guernsey breeds.

The administration of British New Guinea (Papua) [q.v.] recognized the dangers of importing cattle from South-east Asia, as this would risk the introduction of Texas fever, surra and rinderpest. In fact, as early as 1900, the German administration was faced with the problem of restricting the spread of Texas fever (babesiosis) which flared up in cattle on the Gazelle Peninsula. It is interesting to note that the German authorities found that 'the animals imported from Asia (Siam) and the Dutch Indies show a greater power of resistance (to Texas fever) than those obtained from South Australia'.

At the turn of the century there were approximately 250 head of cattle in the country. By 1940 the Territories of Papua and New Guinea had nearly thirty thousand head, based mainly on breeds such as Jersey, Guernsey, Australian Illawarra Shorthorn and Beef Shorthorn introduced from Australia. Most were run on coconut plantations, primarily to keep down the growth of grass and herbage under the coconuts. It was pointed out by M. Staniforth Smith [q.v.], responsible for agricultural administration in the Territory of Papua in 1921, that it required 120 labourers to maintain one thousand acres of coconuts where cattle were not used, but only sixty labourers for the same area when cattle were grazed under the coconuts.

Some 1,500 head of these cattle were used for draught purposes, especially by German missionaries along the north coast of New Guinea. As late as 1964 there were still a few draught oxen of Zebu origin at the Lutheran mission plantation at Heldsbach, near Finschhafen. Some of these animals weighed nearly 2,500 lb. and stood almost six feet high at the shoulder.

There was, in effect, no real cattle industry in Papua and New Guinea before World War II. The raising of cattle was a secondary interest to coconut plantation owners. In addition to the function of cattle as 'grass cutters', some were used to provide meat and milk for plantation staff. No real disease control procedures were followed, husbandry methods were haphazard and no organized marketing of produce was considered.

World War II caused a striking reduction of cattle numbers in Papua and New Guinea. The first post-war figures, in 1950, showed that there were then only 4,100 head in the Territories of Papua and New Guinea.

Immediately after the war a start was made to develop a viable cattle industry.

By the early 1950s the Australian Administration had established four livestock breeding stations in the Territory of Papua and New Guinea. These stations began breeding selected types, to boost the number of suitable cattle available to the private sector of the industry.

Progress was relatively slow, however, with the cattle industry still mainly a subsidiary activity on coconut plantations. As the policy of the Administration turned to active encouragement of the pastoral industry large areas of land made available as pastoral leases were taken up for grazing beef cattle. The introduction of free veterinary and advisory services and a scheme to subsidize freight costs on imported cattle further encouraged the industry, and by 1964 cattle numbers in the Territory were back to the pre-war level of thirty thousand head. The industry turned more to raising cattle for beef and dairy products.

During this time, the Dutch administration in West Irian concentrated on the introduction of cattle to the indigenous people, there being no real development of a large-scale pastoral industry. The Dutch imported cattle to government-owned breeding stations, and distributed the progeny of these cattle to the indigenous people on a share breeding contract. In general, one bull and three cows were issued on loan, on the condition that after five years, six head were to be returned to the government, all other animals becoming the property of the indigenous breeders. The Indonesian administration has carried on this programme, and there are at present some four thousand head of cattle in West Irian, the majority around Merauke.

The island of New Guinea lies wholly within the humid tropics, and experiences generally high temperatures with little daily or seasonal variation, and high humidities. Such conditions cause a considerable climatic stress in cattle. This fact, together with transport and communication difficulties, a scarcity of experienced labour, and the distance from a source of supply of cattle and farm equipment, has made the task of developing a productive industry a challenging one. However, cattle numbers have continued to increase rapidly and 1966 figures showed 44,700 head in the Territory of Papua and New Guinea.

The Territory, by virtue of its relative geographical isolation, has remained free from the major cattle diseases, such as foot and mouth disease, rinderpest, haemorrhagic septicaemia and contagious bovine pleuro-pneumonia. The Australian Administration is carrying out active eradication programmes for brucellosis and tuberculosis and has restricted the incidence of the cattle tick (*Boophilus microplus*) to small areas in the Territory of Papua (*see* LIVESTOCK PESTS).

The 'old world' screw-worm fly (*Chrysomya bezziana*) is present in Papua and New Guinea and poses some problems of management. In general, the incidence of this parasite has made intensive management procedures necessary, in order to maintain closer supervision of individual animals.

It has been estimated that there are between 8.5 and 9.5 million acres of grassland in the Territory of Papua and New Guinea which could be used for cattle raising. These grasslands result from the indigenous peoples' hunting [q.v.] methods, which include regular burning to flush out small game, hence many grassland areas are in different stages of development. Of this available area, only some 160,000 acres were being used for grazing in 1966.

One of the problems facing the pastoral industry, and other agricultural pursuits, is the existing indigenous land tenure [q.v.] system. The concept of individual ownership of land does not traditionally exist in Papua and New Guinea. Land generally belongs to a group or clan, with rights of land use differing from place to place. The inheritance of usage rights follows a complicated pattern, and as a result ownership is difficult to establish. This problem is, however, being resolved, with the indigenous people being encouraged by the Administration to demarcate land owned by different groups and to establish land usage rights.

The greatest areas of suitable grasslands, and the areas of greatest potential, are the open grasslands of river valleys such as the Markham-Ramu Valleys, and the Highland valleys of the Wahgi and Asaro River systems. It is here that the pastoral industry has assumed greatest importance. Other areas with potential are the south coast of Papua with its somewhat drier eucalypt savannah country, and the highly productive north coast of New Guinea, where the climate makes for ideal pasture growth.

There is only a small indigenous population in the areas, such as the Markham-Ramu Valleys, where the large-scale pastoral industry has naturally been established. In thickly populated areas efforts to expand the industry must be made through the indigenous land-holders, in two ways: where possible, introduce cattle into subsistence farming systems; and establish economic farm units on either a mixed farm or a pastoral basis. The governments of West Irian and of the Australian Territory have lately tried to do this, primarily through the establishment of government cattle stations which breed suitable types of cattle for sale to the indigenous people, and train prospective farmers in basic cattle husbandry.

The fact that Papua and New Guinea had no indigenous cattle has made efficient extension of the industry extremely difficult. The average indigenous farmer has had no previous contact with any of the larger domestic animals. He has no concept of cattle husbandry, no knowledge of

Brahman-cross breeders in the coastal savannah country of southern Papua.

cattle grazing habits or of grassland capacity, and some fear of the animal itself. The basis of the expansion must therefore be the adequate training of indigenous farmers, and the use of the most productive breeds of cattle under existing climatic conditions.

Experience and research have shown that some Zebu (*Bos indicus*) blood is necessary in cattle in Papua and New Guinea as only a small percentage of animals of the 'European' breeds of cattle (*Bos taurus*) adapt to the continuous high temperatures. Certainly there is a wide range of climatic conditions in the country, ranging from the high temperatures in the lowlands to the more pleasant Highland environment, which is very similar to a typical temperate climate. However, even in the Highlands an infusion of Zebu blood has proved advantageous, especially under poor management conditions. These findings are in line with those of current Australian research, which have shown a greater resistance by Zebu breeds to the effects of both internal and external parasites, and an ability to withstand greater heat stress.

Research carried out by the Australian Administration in the Territory of Papua and New Guinea has shown better reproductive and growth performances in Zebu-cross cattle, both Africander and Brahman, than in cattle of European breeds. It should be noted, however, that under conditions of nutritional stress the Zebu breeds—and to a certain extent Zebu-cross cattle—will fail to conceive while they have a calf at foot. While not making for high productivity in terms of reproductive performance, this characteristic provides a natural safeguard against breeder mortality under poor management, and may thus be advantageous in the early stages of the development of a cattle industry in the indigenous community.

Recent figures for imports of beef and milk products indicate a ready market for the products of a local cattle industry. For example, in 1965-6

A Brahman heifer exhibited at the Port Moresby Agricultural Show.

total beef consumption in the Territory amounted to 49,000 carcass equivalents, of which some 45,000 carcass equivalents were imported in the form of fresh, chilled and frozen beef, and canned goods. In 1965 consumption of beef by expatriates was about one-third of indigenous consumption. On the other hand, expatriate consumption is mainly in the form of fresh beef, whereas indigenous consumption is mainly canned beef. The proportion and quantity of fresh beef consumed by the indigenous population is rising rapidly. In 1962-3 only 6 per cent of total fresh beef supplies were consumed by indigenes, whereas by 1964-5 this proportion had risen to 28 per cent. Present indigenous per capita beef consumption is estimated to be 5.3 lb. per annum.

Marketing services for the beef industry at present are adequate. Abattoirs operated by the Australian Administration handle slaughter beef in the main centres, while small privately owned slaughter floors, licensed by the Administration, operate on farms in more isolated areas.

One factor essential to the viability of the beef cattle industry is the development of adequate distribution services. It would be reasonable to assume that, once assured of regular and substantial supplies of fresh beef, local meat traders would be willing to develop wholesale meat handling facilities.

The prospective market for dairy products is equally encouraging. Total imports of milk to the Territory of Papua and New Guinea in 1965-6, in the form of fresh, evaporated, condensed and powdered milk, were equivalent to 1.1 million gallons. In addition, some 157,000 gallons of fresh milk were produced locally. While the total replacement of powdered and evaporated milk imports is unlikely, the replacement of 30 per cent would provide a market for a further 300,000 gallons of fresh milk.

Per capita consumption figures for milk are not accurately known. Indigenous consumption would, however, be very low. An increase of 3,500 head of dairy cattle would enable substantial replacement of imports but any major expansion of the industry would depend on increased milk consumption by the indigenous people. Such an expansion could perhaps best be achieved by their participation in the dairy industry.

Expansion of the dairying industry will necessitate the development of adequate distribution facilities. There are at present some six major dairy farms in operation in the Territory, all close to the main towns. Milk is packaged on the farm and delivered direct to the retail stores by the producer.

The Australian government in 1963 requested the International Bank for Reconstruction and Development to send a mission to Papua and New Guinea to undertake a survey of economic potential. The Mission reported in 1964, and in the agricultural sphere proposed 'a program whereby the skilled manpower of the Department of Agriculture . . . would be concentrated on agricultural and livestock programs in areas with greatest promise in human and physical resources'.

With the need for this concentration of effort in mind, the Mission proposed an initial expansion of the cattle industry in the non-indigenous sector, where a better knowledge of production techniques would allow for more efficient development in the early stages. The ultimate aim of the livestock programme was for the establishment of a beef cattle industry at a rate which would bring a tenfold increase in cattle herds to a total of 300,000 head in ten years, of which indigenous operators would have 150,000 to 200,000 head. The commencement of a dairying industry in the Highlands was also proposed.

Provision of agricultural credit was considered by the Mission to be basic to the proposed development programme and the Mission gave detailed recommendations, including the setting up of a Territory Development Finance Company.

The Australian government and the Administration of the Territory have indicated a broad acceptance of the recommendations of the Bank Mission 'as a working basis for planning in the Territory'.

Another Mission from the Bank visited the Territory in 1967 to review progress made and to examine in broad terms possible avenues of I.B.R.D. assistance.

The Administration's proposals for future cattle development, while based on those made by the 1964 Bank Mission, will take a number of other factors into account. Such factors include the views expressed by the 1967 Mission, changes in the character of the economy since the report of the 1964 Mission and a somewhat reduced availability of breeding stock from Australia. However, the Administration's proposals aim at achieving an overall rate of development as close as possible to that proposed by the Mission. The Administration is therefore planning for the Territory cattle herd to be increased as rapidly as possible to a total of 300,000 head, and in such a way that by the time this figure is reached, two-thirds of this number will be owned by indigenous operators.

On an estimated take-off of 15 per cent, the proposed target of 300,000 head would provide an annual kill of 45,000 carcasses. The Bank Mission was of the opinion that 'an expanded local output of 45,000 head should be easily absorbed by partial replacement of current imports, and by increased consumption likely to result from the expanding economy, the changing dietary habits of the people and the expected increase in population'. Certainly, local supplies would rise to a level which would permit complete replacement of imported chilled and frozen beef. The basic marketing problem will be one of adjustment of imports to local production and consumption trends.

Plans for the future development of the cattle industry are thus ambitious, but within the capabilities of the Administration and the people. The wide extension of the cattle industry among indigenous farmers should stimulate the use of fresh beef in rural areas, as local authorities and traders become interested in marketing. The indigenous agricultural cash economy is based at present on export crops and the income is spent largely on imported consumer goods, including beef. There is little, if any, re-investment. Indigenous investment in the cattle industry and near self-sufficiency in beef will thus increase the secondary benefits derived from export crops, and will be an important contribution towards the ultimate goal of economic viability for the country.

J. L. Anderson, 'A Project in the Development of Cattle adapted to a Tropical Environment', *Papua and New Guinea Agricultural Journal*, vol. 14, 1961-2.
—— 'The Development of a Cattle Industry in the Territory of Papua and New Guinea', *Papua and New Guinea Agricultural Journal*, vol. 14, 1961-2.
Commonwealth of Australia, *Annual Report, Territory of Papua 1906-7, 1907-8, 1921-2 to 1925-6, 1947-8*. Melbourne and Canberra, 1908, 1923-7, 1949.
—— *Report to the League of Nations on the Administration of the Territory of New Guinea 1928-9, 1929-30*. Canberra, 1930-1.
—— *Report to the United Nations on the Administration of the Territory of New Guinea 1947-8, 1948-9*. Canberra, 1949-50.
Department of National Development, *Resources of the Territory of Papua and New Guinea*. 2 vols, Canberra, 1950-1.
B. Essai, *Papua and New Guinea: A Contemporary Survey*, pp. 120-5. Melbourne, 1961.
Germany, Colonial Office, Annual Report on the Development of the German Protectorates in Africa and the South Sea for the years 1900-01, 1901-02 —German New Guinea and the island spheres of the Caroline, Pelew and Mariana Islands (translation; typescript in N.L.A. and Commonwealth Archives).
R. C. Hutchinson, 'Milk Production in New Guinea', *New Guinea Agricultural Gazette*, vol. 7, February 1941.
International Bank for Reconstruction and Development, *The Economic Development of the Territory of Papua and New Guinea*, pp. 18-19, 32-4, 43-5, 48, 122-43, 146-7, 173, 186-8, 379-82. Baltimore, 1965.
T. P. N. G. Administrator, *Economic Development of Papua and New Guinea*. Port Moresby, 1967 (mimeographed).

D. J. PURDY

CENTRAL DISTRICT. The cliche that 'Port Moresby is not Papua New Guinea' is equally true when 'Central District' is substituted for 'Papua New Guinea'. Containing Port Moresby, Papua New Guinea's administrative capital and largest urban centre, the Central District displays a complex social and economic plurality. This results in part from the establishment of a modern colonial city in an area from which access to the outlying portions of the District, and to the rest of Papua New Guinea, is difficult.

TOPOGRAPHY

For approximately 140 miles from Cape Possession in the west, south-east to Hood Point and then for about 130 miles due east to Baibara village, the narrow Central District extends along the south-

Central District.

eastern coast of the New Guinea mainland. The inland dimensions do not match its east-west extent. The distance from the coast to the crest of the Chapman, Wharton and Owen Stanley Ranges, which mark the northern boundary of the District, can vary from as little as fourteen miles in the Cloudy Bay area to as much as sixty-eight miles from Cape Suckling which lies between Kairuku and Galley Reach.

The Central District is in a zone of subsidence and drowned estuaries such as Hall Sound, Galley Reach, Fairfax Harbour, Bootless Inlet, Hood Lagoon, Marshall Lagoon and Cloudy Bay. The fringing and barrier reefs also result from subsidence.

Landforms result largely from folding and subsequent erosion and deposition. Towering peaks include the 13,400-foot Mt Victoria, Papua's second highest mountain, lying on the crest of the Owen Stanley Range.

The main ranges have a foothill zone which, in the western and central sections of the District, rises from undulating plains to ridges and plateau formations at 3,600 feet with locally spectacular relief, seen in the 2,000-foot escarpment of the Astrolabe Range fourteen miles inland from Port Moresby. Having descended from the main range through foothills, including the Sogeri plateau, a downfold or trough is encountered. This is separated from the coast by an upfold in the form of a relatively low range of hills. From the upland areas the many rivers have transported large quantities of alluvial material to form the fluvial plains that separate the coastal hills from the foothills of the main range. Inland from Hall Sound in the Kairuku Sub-District the westward-flowing Biaru and southward-flowing Angabunga Rivers have developed an extensive plain. The Angabunga traverses this plain in a large meandering channel whose instability poses a major problem for construction engineers pushing the Hiritano Highway west from Port Moresby to Bereina.

The largest swampland areas occupy the lower reaches of the Vanapa and Laloki-Brown River systems. The lower reaches of the Kemp Welch and other major rivers eastward have flat to undulating plains extending inland beyond the point at which the coastal hills are breached.

The coastal hills are an irregular formation lying more or less parallel to the coast. In the western part of the District they tend to lie inland and are breached by Hall Sound and Galley Reach which occupy wide, transverse downwarps in the formation. In the Port Moresby area they rise to 1,200 feet and extend to the coast. Some minor cliffing occurs here, both on shore and on the small off-shore islands which are outliers of the coastal hills. Separating the higher ridges are undulating valleys and plains which in the Port Moresby area accommodate expanding suburbia and the airport. These hills continue through the eastern part of the District and form prominent peninsulas between Mayri Bay, Millport Harbour and Port Glasgow.

The littoral plains consist of tidal flats, some non-tidal estuarine flats and beach ridges. Frequently between the sandy beach ridges and the coastal hills there are poorly drained swampy areas. These flats and ridges constitute a very small proportion of the total land surface of the District, being most extensive in the drowned estuary areas, for example around Hall Sound, Galley Reach, Hood Lagoon and Cloudy Bay, but the villages on this coast contain a significant part of the population.

Sedimentary rocks predominate with andesitic volcanics evident over a wide area of the northern foothills and main ranges, especially in the main rubber-growing areas of the Sogeri plateau and Galley Reach. Older basic volcanics outcrop between Kapa Kapa and Kwikila east of Port Moresby. Metamorphic rocks flanking the volcanics contain minerals and many intrusions of gabbro. Before World War II some 81,000 tons of copper ore were extracted from the foothills of the Astrolabe Range and some 2,000 tons of manganese ore were mined from the metamorphic series flanking the basic volcanics near Kwikila. There has been a revival of interest in the copper-bearing lenses to the east of Port Moresby, not only in the previously mined deposits near Sapphire Creek on the Sogeri road but also some forty miles further east at Boku.

CLIMATE

The north-west to south-east alignment of landforms between Cape Possession and Hood Point, which is parallel to the direction of the prevailing winds, makes the coastal section of this part of the District the driest area in Papua New Guinea. Port Moresby has an annual average rainfall of 40 inches, and the narrow coastal strip from Cape Possession to Hood Point receives less than 60 inches. With increasing altitude inland, rainfall rises to an estimated average of 140-200 inches per year along the crest of the main range. East of Hood Point, where the alignment of the ranges changes to west-east the coastal area becomes progressively wetter. Abau has an annual average rainfall of 90 inches.

Rainfall is markedly seasonal in distribution, with two contrasting regimes evident. These broadly coincide with the differing alignments of landforms to the west and east of Hood Point. The western area experiences maximum rainfall in the north-west season, December to April, with a pronounced dry when the south-east trades prevail.

	Port Moresby	Abau
	Rainfall in inches	
January	6.99	6.47
February	7.57	6.53
March	6.64	8.72
April	4.22	9.31
May	2.50	10.33
June	1.26	9.27
July	1.10	10.04
August	0.66	8.10
September	1.04	5.71
October	1.38	4.46
November	1.91	4.93
December	4.42	5.72
Total	39.69	89.59

To the east of Hood Point maximum rainfall is experienced during the south-east season, March to August. The average monthly rainfall figures for Port Moresby and Abau neatly point up this contrast.

The coastal areas of the Central District, in common with the rest of the south coast of Papua, experience an annual range of maximum temperature of approximately 7°F. In Port Moresby the range is from 82.1°F. in August to 89.8°F. in December.

VEGETATION

Those peaks of the main range rising above the tree line at approximately 11,000 feet, for example Mt Victoria and Mt Albert Edward, have alpine shrubs and grasses clothing their upper slopes. Above 3,000-3,500 feet are the mountain forests which differ from tropical lowland forests in that they have a simpler two-tier structure. Species such as beeches, oaks and podocarps, or southern hemisphere pines, are predominant. The plank buttresses, woody vines and palms typical of the lowland forests are absent at these higher altitudes. However the edible pandanus, so important in the Highlands Districts, also occurs here and contributes to the diet of the people in the Goilala Sub-District. In this fairly densely populated Sub-District which lies in the mountain forest zone, considerable areas of forest have been replaced by grassland.

The lowland areas range from tidal flats, through freshwater swamps and well-drained river plains to hill slopes with shallow, stony soils. Additionally, rainfall in the lowland area ranges from 40-150 inches.

Dense stands of mangrove clothe the saltwater and brackish tidal estuaries and the sheltered muddy shores. Nipa palms, which line the banks of the tidal reaches of rivers, give way to sago palms where the water changes from brackish to fresh. Sago also grows in the shallow, seasonal freshwater swamps of the District, whilst the deeper parts of the permanent swamps support herbaceous growth rather than trees.

The seasonally dry coastal hill and foothill zones have savannah vegetation in which eucalypts and kangaroo grass up to three feet high are dominant, making the area appear very similar to parts of northern Australia.

The seasonally dry area also contains some deciduous forest. In re-entrants, valley heads and bouldery valley floors of the savannah area are patches of predominantly deciduous forest, while partially deciduous forest occurs in those parts of the coastal hill and foothill zones where the seasons are less pronounced. Much of the foothills, lower mountain slopes and better watered river plains are covered by a three-layered rain forest in which the canopy or upper layer, 100 to 120 feet high, is topped with occasional emergents. Beneath this is a second layer of trees reaching about 75 feet and a third layer of trees 30 to 40 feet tall. This lowland rain forest contains a number of commercially useful trees.

THE PEOPLE

The variations in language, social organization and appearance of various groups within the District are considerable. Along the coast from Cape Possession to a little east of Cape Rodney Austronesian languages are spoken. Austronesian languages extend a considerable distance inland in the western section and include the Mekeo and Gabadi groups. There is another fairly deep incursion from near Kapa Kapa east to Cape Rodney to include the Sinaugoro and other Austronesian languages. Between these two large areas in a narrow strip along the coast from Galley Reach to Kapa Kapa live the Motu [q.v.] people whose Austronesian language was pidginized and used in pre-European times as a trade language during the *hiri* [q.v.] trading expeditions. It was later adopted by the Royal Papuan Constabulary as Police Motu [q.v.]. The population of the remainder of the District, including the coast east of Cape Rodney, speak non-Austronesian or Papuan languages which are inter-related and belong to the South-east New Guinea Phylum (*see* LANGUAGES).

The mountain-dwelling groups, such as those in the Goilala Sub-District, the mountain Koiari people in the area traversed by the Kokoda Trail, and the people inland from Kwikila between the Kemp Welch and Amawai Rivers, live in small hamlets and grow taro and sweet potato as their staple food under a system of shifting horticulture. In the lowlands where the dry season becomes important, the staple changes to yams and bananas. Settlements in these lowland areas are larger than those of the mountain dwellers. The coastal peoples, of whom the Motu and Hula are the most reported, depend very largely on fishing with quite limited gardening. As a result relationships developed between the coastal groups and the inland peoples, such as the Koita, for the exchange of fish for yams, bananas and other garden produce. This can still be observed in villages such as Kapa Kapa. The closeness of the relationships between these groups is well illustrated by the Hanuabada [q.v.] complex of villages in which, even in pre-European times, both Austronesian-speaking Motu and non-Austronesian-speaking Koita people lived.

The Motu coastal area is a food deficient region because of the dry conditions, and the rapidly expanding indigenous urban population have to pay high prices at Koki Market for staples largely replaced by imported rice, bread and biscuits from expatriate-owned trade stores.

The 1966 Census estimate of the population in the Central District was 146,331 and with an area of 12,000 square miles, this makes it the eighth most populous in Papua New Guinea and, after the Southern Highlands, the second most populous in Papua. Approximately 30 per cent of the District's population were in Port Moresby, and the remainder scattered along the coast. Large inland concentrations surround the administrative posts Tapini, Woitape and Guari in the Goilala Sub-District and the Kwikila area of the Rigo Sub-District.

Of the total expatriate population of 34,669 in Papua New Guinea in 1966, 11,638, or one-third, were in the Central District, most residing in Port Moresby. Expatriates constituted 8 per cent of the population, a higher proportion than in any other District.

Over one hundred plantations and the industries of Port Moresby attract workers to the District, many of whom are transported and accommodated by their employers. Many employers prefer male workers; and in 1966 there were 76,853 males and only 57,840 females in the indigenous population of the District. Non-indigenes showed a similar preponderance of males, 6,747 compared with 4,891 females. The composition of the indigenous population, in urban areas at least may be changing. The special enumeration of Port Moresby in 1970 showed that since 1966 the female population had increased by 40.2 per cent compared with a 28 per cent increase in the male population. Increasingly migrants see their stay in Port Moresby as long term and bring their dependants. This tendency is at present most marked among migrants from coastal Papua, probably because of long association with Port Moresby, and the ease and relatively low cost of movement to the town. Many of the single workers come from the Highlands, but more are now accompanied by their women and children.

In April 1970 a special census of Port Moresby, covering a slightly larger area than in 1966, revealed that the population had risen to 56,206, 42,616 indigenes and 13,590 non-indigenes. The average annual rate of increase of 9 per cent in the non-indigenous population outstripped the 7 per cent of the indigenous population.

OUTSIDE INFLUENCES

The earliest known European contact was on the island of Mailu at the eastern end of the District. Here, on 25 August 1606, there was a confrontation between the men of Mailu and those of Torres [q.v.], whose muskets and cannon shattered the world of these island people. Torres took possession of the country for the King of Spain and abducted fourteen children who apparently spent the remainder of their days in Manila.

Subsequent callers included Yule [q.v.] in 1846, and Moresby [q.v.] in 1873. The year before, the London Missionary Society had put Rarotongan missionaries in the westernmost Motu village of Manu Manu at the entrance to Galley Reach. Malaria took its toll, so in the hope of a healthier environment, as well as a better anchorage, the London Missionary Society moved the Rarotongans to Port Moresby in 1873. European settlement in Papua began with the arrival in November 1874 of the Rev. W. G. Lawes [q.v.].

From this time outside influences began to encroach directly and continuously on the population of the District and Papuans became engaged in administrative, mission, plantation and other enterprises.

Proclamation of the British Protectorate by Commodore Erskine at Hanuabada on 6 November 1884, was followed by the arrival in 1885 of the Special Commissioner to New Guinea, Sir Peter Scratchley [q.v.]. He chose Port Moresby as the seat of government on the grounds that it was the only permanent European settlement, was comparatively healthy, and had a fine harbour close to Cooktown in northern Queensland.

The first post outside Port Moresby was a base camp set up at Sogeri in late 1885, and closed within a few months. The next, established at Rigo in 1888, remained operational until 1960 when Kwikila was made the Sub-District centre. It administered the area along the lower reaches of the Kemp Welch River, where the area of land alienated for plantations was sufficiently great to cause J. H. P. Murray [q.v.] to close the area to European settlement in 1908.

In September 1890 an administrative centre was opened on the site of the present agricultural station at Epo in the Mekeo area of the present Kairuku Sub-District. Here too was considerable European settlement, with the Catholic mission from Yule Island pushing inland through the Mekeo to Mafulu, just west of Woitape.

In 1904 the Mekeo station was replaced by a new post at Kairuku on Yule Island. Administration presence returned to the Cloudy Bay area when, in 1911, Abau Island became headquarters of the new East Central Division. Such off-shore posts were a feature of early Papuan administration.

Between 1911 and 1946 no new administrative posts were established within the present Central District, although patrols covered much of the District, albeit superficially in some areas.

In 1946 a station was opened at Naoro on the Kokoda Trail to settle wartime compensation claims and help rehabilitation. It was closed in 1947. In 1948, in the densely populated Goilala area, Tapini station was opened with sub-district status. The area was previously only visited by patrols from Kairuku.

Incorporation of East Central in Central District in 1950 gave the latter boundaries which closely approximate those it has today. In 1957 Sogeri, Marshall Lagoon and Guari Patrol Posts were all established. Woitape Patrol Post was established in 1958 and in the following year Margarida, at the eastern end of the District. Bereina was established in 1961 and immediately made Sub-District headquarters. In 1965 Abau Sub-District headquarters transferred from Abau Island to Marshall Lagoon which was renamed Kupiano. In the same year Sogeri Patrol Post passed from the control of the Department of District Administration to the Royal Papuan Constabulary, and in 1966 Kairuku and Abau Patrol Posts were closed.

MISSIONS

The number of London Missionary Society stations steadily increased along the coast, especially after the arrival in Port Moresby in 1877 of the Rev. James Chalmers [q.v.]. Two South Sea Islands missionaries were settled at Kairuku in November 1875, but they were withdrawn in September 1876

following the murder of two Europeans in Hall
Sound several months earlier. On returning five
years later the London Missionary Society found
that Kairuku had been pre-empted by the Roman
Catholic Mission of the Sacred Heart. Thus the
village of Delena, just south of Hall Sound, became
the site for renewed mission activity which still
continues there. Several weeks prior to the return
to the Kairuku area, Chalmers had settled Polynesian pastors in the eastern villages of Hula,
Kerepuna and Aroma.

The London Missionary Society at Delena had
attracted and held very few converts by 1930.
Until this time most mission workers were non-
indigenous, but the increasing use of Papuan
pastor-teachers and the local language heightened
the impact of the mission in the Delena area from
1931 on.

Throughout the Motu, Hula and Aroma areas
the London Missionary Society became well established with pastor-teachers providing some elementary education. The training of these pastor-
teachers, first undertaken at Metoreia, the mission
headquarters at Hanuabada, was transferred to
Vatorata near Kapa Kapa in the 1890s.

The reception and early influence of the mission
varied. In 1881 eight of the Kalo missionary community were massacred, while in 1906 the Delena
mission house was no protection for the assistant
resident magistrate for the Kairuku area, for he
was killed in it by local people. The Polynesian
influence remains in songs, basket and mat weaving and in words now part of the vernaculars. The
other major influences were education and health
services. The Administration did not enter education directly until after World War II, but as early
as 1884 a visitor to Hula reported that children at
the mission school could read and write. A great
majority of the Papuans now in senior positions
received much or all of their education in mission
schools.

The Catholic Mission of the Sacred Heart began
work from Kairuku in 1885, and penetrated a
considerable distance into the hinterland from its
off-shore base. The earliest long penetration was
through Kubuna to Mafulu. Construction of mule
or packhorse tracks has continued, with the
Woitape-Kanosia link being completed in 1970.
This allows the movement of cattle to and from
the coast, and improves earning prospects for the
Woitape people, especially when the now imminent
Hiritano (literally 'land *hiri*') Highway reaches the
Kanosia area.

The influence of the mission's Filipino lay
workers was soon seen in rice plantings at Beipa
mission station, and subsequent attempts were
made to develop a major rice industry in the
Mekeo area.

The Sacred Heart mission also was interested in
both health and education. An early graduate of
their educational system was Bishop Louis Vangeke [q.v.], and of the first three Papuan university
graduates two were from the Sacred Heart mission
area in the Kairuku Sub-District. The Catholic
mission is the only mission in the District with
extensive post-primary educational facilities. It

has high and vocational schools at Bereina,
Kairuku, and at Bomana near Port Moresby.

These two long-established missions exercised a
pervasive influence over part of the western inland
area and the coastal fringe from Cape Possession
as far east as Cape Rodney. In the remaining
inland areas and along the coast from Marshall
Lagoon to the Mailu area mission influence was
minimal. The Seventh Day Adventist mission
began working at Bisiatabu on the Sogeri plateau
in the late 1920s, and established its influence
along the Kokoda Trail. It also moved into villages around Marshall Lagoon in the 1930s.

Another 'gap' in the District was filled by the
Kwato mission which in 1934 moved into the
Cloudy Bay hinterland. The long term result of
this was the resettlement nearer the coast at Amau
of the inland groups known as the Keveri and
Dorevaidi. Amau was the Kwato headstation in this
area.

The influence of the missions was, and still
remains, considerable, as nearly all social activities
at the village level are organized by the church, and
traditional feasts have been transmuted into festivals associated with such celebrations as Christmas
and Easter. Villages chosen as mission head-
stations experienced great changes.

MINERS, TRADERS AND PLANTERS

The first prospectors in the District arrived in
1878 to investigate reports of gold along the
Laloki River about ten miles inland from Port
Moresby. No payable quantities were found.

In 1896 Sir William MacGregor [q.v.] noted
that there were 400 men in the Central Division
prospecting on the St Joseph (Angabunga), Vanapa, Brown and other rivers. Although the Yodda
field near Kokoda was not proclaimed until July
1900, gold started coming out in 1895-6. A satisfactory though formidable access was pioneered
by Sir William MacGregor, giving Port Moresby a
land link with the goldfield and its administrative
post, Kokoda. Fortnightly mail services to the
Northern Division used this route during the first
decades of this century, and it became famous as
the wartime Kokoda Trail of 1942.

The short-lived Keveri goldfield inland from
Cloudy Bay was declared in 1904. It too attracted
large numbers of miners whose contacts with the
local inhabitants were mainly unfriendly.

The Astrolabe Mineral Field was declared in
December 1906. Copper ore was exported from
that year until 1922, and in only six of these years
did exports exceed 1,000 tons. In 1922 the New
Guinea Copper Company established a smelter on
the shores of Bootless Inlet. A wharf and railway
which ran inland for seven and a half miles to
Dubuna mine together with an aerial tramway
connecting the Laloki mine to the railway were
constructed. For the next four years blister and
matte copper were exported. In 1925-6, the peak
year, 7,025 tons of matte and 173 tons of blister
copper worth £124,262 were exported. Financial
difficulties led to the company's collapse in 1927.

Pearl-shell [q.v.] and bêche-de-mer attracted a

cosmopolitan group to the coastal area in the last quarter of the nineteenth century, including 'Malays' who apparently came from the Surabaya area of Java. Trading bases and smokehouses were established along the coast. There was considerable interaction between these fishermen-traders and the coastal villagers with the latter exchanging shell, bêche-de-mer or coconuts for trade goods. Other villagers working on the boats, in the stores, or in smokehouses received cash or trade goods for their efforts.

Sandalwood also brought outsiders, especially to the Galley Reach area where cutters, backed by the firm of Burns Philp & Co. Ltd, worked in the 1890s and early 1900s.

Inland on the Sogeri plateau and at the head of Galley Reach large areas were alienated, which now accommodate the greater part of Papua New Guinea's rubber industry. Most of the remaining plantation land was coastal, although the lower reaches of river valleys, for example those of the Kemp Welch, Bomguina, Robinson and Mamai Rivers, were also popular. Some individuals started planting coconuts during the last decade of the nineteenth century with rubber becoming the other major crop during the early part of this century, but the major developments were by companies, the largest of which was the British New Guinea Development Company. It began in Papua in 1910 and is now a subsidiary of Burns Philp. Its interests spread from Hisiu west of Galley Reach to Robinson River in the east and included coconuts, rubber and sisal.

By 1926 eighty-six plantations had been established and the acreages of the three main crops were coconuts 12,566, rubber 6,089, and sisal 3,560. Coconuts and rubber survive, but sisal has long since disappeared. The principal sisal growing areas were the British New Guinea Company's holdings at the head of Fairfax Harbour and Bomana. Some was also grown at Rigo. Exports of sisal reached their maximum value in 1917-18 at which time just over 6,000 acres had been planted in the Central Division.

The plantation companies also experimented with cotton, principally in the Galley Reach-Hisiu area from about 1910 to 1930, and planted about a thousand acres. In the face of pests and other difficulties it was abandoned.

In the depression of the 1930s many small plantations failed and ownership passed to big companies.

WORLD WAR II

Although land fighting only occurred along the thin ribbon of the Kokoda Trail between Kokoda and Itikinumu plantation on the Sogeri plateau, and bombing was restricted to the immediate Port Moresby area, World War II saw great disturbance of the District's population. Hanuabada and other villages were evacuated to both the eastern and western Motu areas, and Motu songs today evoke memories of the dislocation of those times. All able bodied men were liable to be pressed into war service.

Several hundred thousand troops were staged in the Port Moresby area. An extra wharf was constructed on Tatana Island which was linked to the mainland by a causeway. Roads were driven inland to the five hastily constructed airfields and the camps which stretched for many miles. After the war most of these roads were abandoned, but restoration has occurred in valleys occupied by the newer suburban developments.

The road linking Port Moresby with the Laloki copper mine, seventeen miles inland, was extended up to Ower's Corner on the Sogeri plateau from where the Kokoda Trail became a foot-track. Another temporary road was driven eastwards along the general alignment of the present Rigo road by United States Army engineers. Designed as another springboard for troop movements over the Owen Stanley Range, it followed the east bank of the Kemp Welch to Laruni village at the foot of the main range. After the war this temporary link soon disappeared to be reconstructed to all-weather standard by 1965. The section north of Kwikila has not been restored.

POST-WAR DEVELOPMENTS

In 1944 some army buildings at Sogeri were taken over as a centre at which the first of the Administration's teachers received their training. In 1947 technical training was started at Idubada, Port Moresby. However, until 1960 emphasis was on primary education. Nevertheless Sogeri Secondary School had presented candidates for the Queensland Junior examination from 1958 on. In the development of the educational system the presence of the administrative capital within its area gave the Central District a distinct advantage. The table shows that the District is favoured by the unequal distribution of resources devoted to education.

SCHOOLS AND ENROLMENTS AT 30 MAY 1970

	Central District	Total Papua	Total Papua New Guinea
Primary-'T' schools	123	471	1,557
Enrolments	20,527	60,957	206,405
Primary-'A' schools	14	21	63
Enrolments	2,907	3,661	8,853
Territory high schools	8	18	59
Enrolments	2,782	5,817	17,785
Multi-racial high schools	1	1	3
Enrolments	474	474	928
Technical schools	1	2	3
Enrolments	346	440	1,575
Vocational schools	9	20	61
Enrolments	523	1,046	3,140

Enrolments in Primary-'T' schools (Territory curriculum) in 1966 as a percentage of the six- to twelve-year-old population was: Papua New Guinea 49 per cent, rural Central District 67 per cent, and Port Moresby 116 per cent. This latter figure suggests that many non-urban and five- and thirteen-year-old children were enrolled in Port Moresby's primary schools. Expressing the numbers in Standard 6 in 1970 as a percentage of children enrolled in Standard 1 in 1965, the Papua New Guinea figure was 49 per cent, rural Central

District 51 per cent and Port Moresby 92 per cent. The proportion of 1969 Standard 6 children accepted in high school for Papua New Guinea as a whole in 1970 was 40 per cent, in rural Central District 44 per cent and in Port Moresby 57 per cent. Thus the Central District population has received the cumulative educational benefits of early mission activity followed by a disproportionate share of the Administration's educational effort.

Compulsory planting of cash crops by Papuans, enforced by the Administration from 1918 under the Native Plantations Ordinance, was not particularly successful, and the planting of tree crops became important only after World War II. In 1969 it was estimated that Papuan planters in the District had 26,000 acres under coconuts and 1,800 acres under rubber. The coconuts, which are widely dispersed along the coast, have not been cropped intensively. In 1969 only 1,374 tons of copra were produced, compared with 4,500 tons from a similar acreage in the Milne Bay District and 2,156 tons from 10,000 acres in the Gulf District. Fresh nuts sold at Koki Market in Port Moresby would not account for the difference.

Planting of rubber by Papuans is comparatively recent. The major areas are Bomguina, inland from Cape Rodney, Margarida, and Bakoiudu inland from Bereina. The Cape Rodney scheme, which involved resettlement on Administration land, has not progressed very satisfactorily to date. Some of those granted blocks were nearby villagers anxious for land for their descendants rather than for immediate cash crops. The Bakoiudu resettlement scheme involves the northernmost members of the Kuni people who in 1961, under the influence of the Catholic mission, moved south from the rugged sections of their homeland to the more gently undulating foothills which rise from the Mekeo plain. The land occupied was 40,000 acres made available by an influential Kuni man in the Bakoiudu area. This scheme has encountered some difficulties during its development with tensions arising from conflicts between group and individual interests. Nevertheless the rubber is being tapped, and processing undertaken by a co-operative society.

Production of fresh food for the Port Moresby market has not received detailed study, though there have been surveys of Koki Market. People with access to land from Mekeo to Hula along the coast and into the foothills beyond Sogeri and up the Kemp Welch River have the opportunity to cultivate specifically for the market or to sell any surplus. Many of the village people living in the area served by the Rigo, Sogeri and trans-Brown River roads have increased their acreage under cultivation and regularly journey to Port Moresby to sell bananas, yams, taro, sweet potato or other fruits and vegetables at Koki Market where the bulk of the produce is purchased by Papuans and New Guineans. Motorized canoes from both the western and eastern sections of the District also bring produce to the market. The Hula fishermen, most of whom operate from peri-urban village bases are the main suppliers of fresh fish.

Some expatriate landholders in the same areas also produce food crops as well as poultry, eggs and milk. This produce is sold through the large trading firms in Port Moresby or sold on contract to the large residential institutions in the town, for example the army barracks, the hospital, and educational institutions such as the University of Papua and New Guinea and the Administrative College.

The stimulant betel or areca nut, is also produced in large quantities for the Port Moresby market, with the Mekeo area being the principal area of supply. So lucrative is the trade that growers charter aircraft in addition to the usual coastal vessels and outboard-powered canoes to bring the nuts to Port Moresby. While it is necessary for Papuans and New Guineas to go to Koki to obtain their traditional fresh foods, betel-nut sellers are ubiquitous being found in front of many trade stores, in villages such as Hanuabada and at major transport pick-up points. This trade is concentrated in the hands of people from the Mekeo, and although there have been no detailed studies of the trade it would appear that many of the sellers are long-term town dwellers to whom supplies are sent from their home areas. If this is so the betel-nut trade is in marked contrast to the fresh food trade in that it possesses middlemen. The bulk of the produce sold in Koki Market is handled by the grower who, in many cases, comes to town as much for social as economic reasons (see BETEL CHEWING).

Another significant group of producers supplying the fresh food market are plantation labourers, and a small number of Goilala and Kerema people occupying unused land in the Sogeri and Waigani swamp areas. The plantation labourers cultivate sweet potatoes, taro, peanuts and sugar on unused land on the plantations where they work and bring their produce to town on Saturdays and Sundays. For many of them this supplementary income greatly exceeds their earnings as labourers.

The co-operative movement flourished in the early 1950s along the coast (see CO-OPERATIVES).

Agricultural activity centres around copra and rubber. In 1969 there were 125 expatriate-controlled rural holdings with 43,000 acres under crop and 45,500 acres of pasture. The year's output from the fifty-two properties producing copra was 6,134 tons. A further forty plantations produced 4,658 tons of rubber, which was more than 80 per cent of Papua New Guinea's output. Coffee and cocoa are very minor crops in the District.

The plantation work force in 1969 was 6,400, largely Highlanders. Many of these men move directly from plantations to Port Moresby. Others having been repatriated, leave their villages not to return to a plantation but rather to come to town. Increasing numbers are paying the air fare from the Highlands or Lae to come to Port Moresby.

The plantations, faced with declining prices, particularly for rubber, and uncertainty concerning the future, are not expanding plantings to any marked extent; acreage may well contract. Some plantations, lacking skilled management and the long-term confidence necessary to replant with high-yielding stocks, are likely to go out of production because of falling profitability in the face of rising wages.

Cattle are also raised on expatriate holdings and given the large areas of grassland in the Central District and the large Port Moresby market, the beef cattle industry is, understandably, one which the Department of Agriculture, Stock and Fisheries is encouraging. In 1969 there were 8,500 head on these properties, mainly in the Port Moresby Sub-District. This number equals that in Madang District and is only exceeded by Morobe District total of 26,000.

Papuan participation in the cattle industry is slowly increasing, and in mid-1971 680 head of cattle were being run by Papuans in the District. Goilala Sub-District has the largest number of Papuan-owned cattle, though they have to be walked in and out.

Indigenous cash cropping is gradually expanding.

Some fifteen sawmills operate in the Central District. Most are small operations concentrated between Galley Reach and the Sogeri plateau. The only large enterprise, Pacific Island Timbers, has its major operation in the Kupiano-Cape Rodney area.

A known forestry potential of 635,000 acres has been assessed in the District. A further 435,000 acres are believed to have economic potential, but require detailed assessment. Thus a possible one million acres, or 14 per cent of the District's total area, carries timber which may be exploitable. Of those areas thoroughly investigated the Aroa timber area, some fifty miles north-west of Port Moresby and between the Vanapa and Aroa Rivers, contains approximately 61,000 acres suitable for harvesting. The Abau timber area, between Cloudy Bay and Margarida and extending from the coast to the foothills of the Owen Stanley Range is estimated to contain some 215,000 acres suitable for harvesting. The former is an attractive source of supply for Port Moresby, while the latter has an acreage which makes contemplation of export markets possible. However, purchase of timber rights is not always easy, and neither is attracting entrepreneurs with the necessary finance and know-how.

COMMUNICATIONS

The national daily newspaper, *South Pacific Post*, is published in Port Moresby and the Australian Broadcasting Commission has its main station there. The newspaper and, to a large extent the Australian Broadcasting Commission, reach chiefly English-speakers (*see* BROADCASTING).

In addition to the District network of plantation wharves, timber loading points, etc., sea transport for most of the south coast of Papua focuses on Port Moresby, which is now Papua New Guinea's second largest port in terms of value of trade after Lae. Exports are greatly exceeded in value by imports. For example in the year ended 30 June 1969 imports at $53.5 million were almost six times the value of exports at $9.4 million.

About 25 per cent of the cargo tonnage is to or from other ports in Papua New Guinea with Lae being the principal partner, while the remaining 75 per cent involves direct movement to or from overseas.

The air network is the other communications system in which Port Moresby is a principal node. As the only airport in Papua New Guinea equipped to handle jet aircraft Port Moresby has primacy in the air transport system (*see* TRANSPORT). There are twenty-three airfields in the District of which only ten can accommodate aircraft as large as a Skyvan. The remaining thirteen are restricted landing grounds which can only be used by light aircraft for limited commercial operations or private flights.

PORT MORESBY

The town has largely developed as a function of its position as the administrative capital. From a foreign foundation, with a fence to divide the indigenous inhabitants from the non-indigenous enclave, Port Moresby's attitudes have gradually changed until now the official policy is residential integration in new housing developments. Nevertheless the outsider's first likely impression is well described in Oram's words, 'that Port Moresby is an Australian town. There is a congested central business district near the harbour and a number of low density suburbs laid out on an Australian pattern with small shopping centres. The town is designed for people who follow a prosperous and car-oriented way of life. Indigenous areas are largely out of sight.' Recognition that the fringe of unplanned village-type settlement is no short-term phase, as the majority of these settlers are not returning to the rural areas and, further, that they do not have the financial capacity to build to the standard required, has led to official acceptance of no-covenant housing areas in Port Moresby.

The special enumeration of 1970 showed Port Moresby to have a population of 56,200, an increase of 33 per cent on the 1966 Census figure.

The indigenous population consists of three or four elements. The original inhabitants, the Motu and Koita, occupy their traditional land in housing that varies according to the level of income of the owner. The feeling of security resulting from land ownership has led many of these people to outlay considerable sums on their housing, and the provision of access roads and essential services such as piped water, garbage disposal and electric light have made possible a rising level of satisfaction.

The other Papuans and New Guineans in Port Moresby are migrants, some of whom occupy government-built houses in the suburbs of Hohola, Kaugere, Ward's Strip, Gordon Estate and Waigani. They are mainly public servants and some better paid employees of private enterprise, and represent a large part of the indigenous elite. Families in these suburbs have as neighbours people from many other parts of the country. Officials and members of nationally oriented trade union and political organizations such as the Pangu Party live in these suburbs.

Still other migrants live in approximately forty settlements which are language-group communities. Some of these settlements, on Motu or Koita land, result from arrangements between the landowners and the migrants. Probably traditional trading ties have been invoked in making these arrangements, as Papuans from Hula to Kerema are the groups involved. These were among the earliest migrants to Port Moresby and access and essential services have been provided to some of their settlements which closely approximate the traditional villages with a fairly normal sex composition.

Most migrant settlements, however, have been established without permission on Administration or indigenously owned land and the settlers, feeling insecure, spend little on their dwellings and the government authorities do not provide access or essential services. This type of settlement is the fastest growing within the urban area and poses the greatest problems, in terms of development and control, for the newly elected Port Moresby Town Council.

Quite large numbers of the Papuans and New Guineans living in Port Moresby occupy what is best described as institutional accommodation which ranges from the superior quarters of the army, police and centres of learning through the domestic quarters of non-indigenous suburbs to the labour 'compounds' of various enterprises operating in the town.

At the 1966 Census 57 per cent of Port Moresby's indigenous population was of Central District origin and a further 25 per cent had come from the Western, Gulf and Milne Bay Districts. Port Moresby is easily accessible to the residents of these Districts and offers the opportunity of a cash income and some maintenance of traditional kinship ties.

New Guinea contributed 14 per cent of Port Moresby's indigenous population in 1966, and of these about 40 per cent came from Morobe District, the closest New Guinea District and the one possessing the best air link with Port Moresby. Observations suggest that migration from Highlands Districts has increased more rapidly than that from the rest of Papua New Guinea since 1966. There is increasing use of Pidgin English [q.v.] as a lingua franca in the town.

The former male-only move into towns is starting to give way to a more balanced movement with increasing numbers of women. Between the 1966 Census and the 1970 enumeration the male over-eighteen population increased by 33 per cent compared with a rise of 48 per cent in the over-eighteen females. This suggests a commitment to long-term residence in Port Moresby.

The modern, even multi-storey, buildings of the central business area, the expanding commercial centre in Boroko, the traffic congestion and the plethora of pleasure craft in Port Moresby harbour all provide testimony to prosperity. However this wealth is unevenly distributed, being largely concentrated in non-indigenous hands. In the public sector the majority of senior positions are occupied by non-indigenes. Similarly the private sector is dominated by non-indigenes, with large Australian companies such as Burns Philp supplemented by a recently arrived, but fairly fast growing, Chinese [q.v.] business community which has opened a large number of businesses in the Port Moresby urban area. There are fewer than ten indigenous permanent enterprises in Port Moresby, and the need for a vigorous localization policy has been recognized by the public service.

In 1966 40 per cent of the employed work force were in government jobs. In turn the government demand for facilities such as accommodation, generates a great deal of construction employment and associated manufacturing. The high-income government employees attract and support retailing and service facilities as well as manufacturers of consumer goods, and Port Moresby has become the main industrial centre in Papua New Guinea. The diversity and number of secondary and tertiary enterprises is indicated by the fact that the *Handbook of Papua and New Guinea* (6th ed., 1969) has an eight-page business and professional directory for Port Moresby.

Being the capital Port Moresby is the site of many institutions which meet national needs. Post-secondary educational institutions include the University of Papua and New Guinea [q.v.], the Administrative College [q.v.], a teachers' college, the Posts and Telegraphs training college and the Electricity Commission's training centre. Additionally the Papua and New Guinea Army Command, the 1st Battalion of the Pacific Islands Regiment and the Recruit Training Centre, situated in or near Port Moresby, have an establishment of almost two thousand men. All these institutions, catering for citizens from all parts of the country, are significant centres of change, and their graduates the emerging elite of Papua New Guinea.

Port Moresby's rapid growth over the past fifteen years has resulted in a shortage of land in the central business district and the government office area at Konedobu and there is severe traffic congestion between these centres and the residential suburbs. The Administration engaged consultants to prepare a comprehensive plan for Port Moresby's development over the period 1970-90. The major proposal of the plan was the relocation inland of the main business and government centres. They are to occupy the broad valley which accommodated the wartime Ward's Strip. The establishment of no-covenant suburbs near main transport routes and the removal of the airport to an off-shore site some fifteen miles west of the town were integral features of the proposal. The Administration has agreed to all proposals except removal of the airport, and the first government buildings will be started at the new site in 1972.

The provision of services such as roads, water and electricity for Port Moresby is a major burden for the Administration. The electricity supply comes from two hydro-plants, one of which is underground, on the Laloki River (*see* ELECTRIC POWER). The town water supply has also involved major capital works to purify and pipe water from the Laloki River.

As stated, Port Moresby is not the Central

District, but as the colonial capital it is the centre from which administrative unification has begun. It also offers maximum educational and economic opportunities for many of those seeking to move out of the traditional rural subsistence economic systems, and it contains the largest concentration of non-indigenous people in Papua New Guinea; from here ideas are diffused to the homelands of the migrants.

The aspirations kindled by experiences in Port Moresby will not be easily satisfied in many rural areas of the Central District which are either inaccessible or lack commercially exploitable land or other resources. For some this may mean migration, an already accelerating phenomenon. For others improved communications, loan funds and extension assistance by the various Administration agencies to develop their land may prove a solution.

W. M. Barclay, 'The Kairuku Joint Venture', *Journal of the Papua and New Guinea Society*, vol. 3, 1969.
C. S. Belshaw, 'Port Moresby Canoe Traders', *Oceania*, vol. 23, 1952.
———— *The Great Village*. London, 1957.
H. C. Brookfield, *Pacific Market Places*. Canberra, 1969.
P. Chatterton, 'A History of Delena', *Journal of the Papua and New Guinea Society*, vol. 2, 1968.
———— 'The Story of a Migration', *Journal of the Papua and New Guinea Society*, vol. 2, 1969.
———— 'Interlude between two worlds: Hanuabada in the 1930's', *Journal of the Papua and New Guinea Society*, vol. 4, 1970.
CSIRO, 'Lands of the Port Moresby-Kairuku Area, Territory of Papua and New Guinea', *Land Research Series*, no. 14, 1965.
T. E. Dutton, 'Linguistic Clues to Koiaran Pre-History', paper read at Second Waigani Seminar, Port Moresby, 1968 (roneoed).
R. A. Fink, 'Moresby's Race Relations', *New Guinea and Australia, the Pacific and South-east Asia*, vol. 1, 1965.
O. Gostin, 'Resettlement, Cash Cropping and Social Change Among the Kuni at Bakoiudu, 1961-71', paper read at Fifth Waigani Seminar, Port Moresby, 1971 (roneoed).
H. Jackman, 'Sir Peter Scratchley: Her Majesty's Special Commissioner for New Guinea', *Journal of the Papua and New Guinea Society*, vol. 3, 1969.
J. V. Langmore, 'Contractors in Port Moresby', *New Guinea Research Bulletin*, no. 16, 1967.
———— and N. D. Oram, 'Port Moresby Urban Development', *New Guinea Research Bulletin*, no. 37, 1970.
N. D. Oram, 'Social and Economic Relationships in a Port Moresby Canoe Settlement', *New Guinea Research Bulletin*, no. 18, 1967.
———— 'Culture Change, Economic Development and Migration Among the Hula', *Oceania*, vol. 38, 1968.
———— 'Land and race in Port Moresby', *Journal of the Papua and New Guinea Society*, vol. 4, 1970.
———— 'The Development of Port Moresby, What and Whose are the Problems?', *Search*, vol. 1, 1970.
G. Smith, 'Urban Pressure on Education in the Central District of Papua', *Papua and New Guinea Journal of Education*, vol. 7, 1971.
I. Stuart, *Port Moresby Yesterday and Today*. Sydney, 1970.
T. P. N. G. Administration Office of the Economic Adviser, *Central District Draft Economic Development Programme*. Port Moresby, 1969.
T. P. N. G. Division of District Administration, *Population Statistics: Port Moresby Urban Area*. Port Moresby, 1970 (roneoed).
M. W. Ward, 'The Rigo Road', *New Guinea Research Bulletin*, no. 33, 1970.
———— 'Urbanisation', *New Guinea and Australia, the Pacific and South-east Asia*, vol. 5, 1970.

J. RUMENS

CHALMERS, James (1841-1901), missionary of the London Missionary Society in British New Guinea 1877-1901, was born at Ardrishaig, Argyllshire, Scotland, on 4 August 1841 and educated at an elementary school at Glenaray and later at grammar school. From the age of fourteen he was employed in a lawyer's office in Inveraray until he decided before he was twenty that he wished to be a missionary. During 1861 he joined the Glasgow City Mission and then in September 1862 he was sent by the L.M.S. to Cheshunt College for training. He left his mark there with his industry, individuality and leadership qualities. On 17 October 1865 he married Jane Hercus and two days later was ordained a minister of the Congregational Church. In April 1866 he left England in the mission ship *John Williams* for his first post at Rarotonga in the Cook Islands. He arrived at his destination on 20 May 1867 after a hazardous voyage which included two shipwrecks, one at Niue (Savage Island) where he first met the Rev. W. G. Lawes [q.v.] in January 1867. His journey was completed in a brig commanded by William Henry ('Bully') Hayes the blackbirder. Hayes appears to have been touched briefly by Chalmers' warm personality. In Rarotonga Chalmers not only acquired the name *Tamate* by which he was known for the rest of his life, but also spent the next ten years tackling the problems of a community which had been under the influence of Christian missions for several decades. Principally, he developed the training facilities for Rarotongan mission teachers who were playing a significant role in L.M.S. work in the Pacific and opposed the consumption of alcohol, 'this engine of Satan', in the community. For years he had 'longed to get amongst real heathen and savages' and so rejoiced when he was assigned to work in New Guinea. He arrived in Port Moresby in October 1877.

During his first nine years' work Chalmers travelled extensively along the coastal areas of British New Guinea as far west as Orokolo and eastwards as far as the China Strait. In some areas he also travelled further inland than had white men to this time. This extensive travelling and exploration familiarized him with the terrain and people and introduced many New Guinea communities to the European in a peaceful way because of Chalmers' personality and outlook. His bent for zestful and colourful writing and his sense of drama helped to publicize both the L.M.S. work and the country and people of New Guinea, particularly in this early productive period. His main missionary activities were centred on the south-eastern end of the country at South Cape where he helped to build up a mission station among the Suau people.

Soon after his return to New Guinea from his first furlough Chalmers began work, late in 1887, at the Motumotu station west of Port Moresby near the Lakekamu River. He was to devote much attention to the development of this station and gradually more and more of his efforts and attention were drawn to spreading and developing L.M.S. activities in the Gulf region. After a brief visit to Samoa and Rarotonga in 1890 he began his Fly River mission work by establishing his headquarters in 1892 on Saguane Island near Kiwai Island. The Fly River area became the centre of his activities for the rest of his life. This consolidation reached a new point when he was joined by the young Rev. Oliver Tomkins [q.v.] early in 1900. By taking over the responsibilities of the Torres Strait region Tomkins allowed Chalmers to concentrate more of his efforts on the Fly River area. However, this new stimulus to extension was short-lived. When Chalmers and Tomkins arrived near Goaribari Island in the Aird River area on 7 April 1901 they found themselves in a tense, hostile situation. Next day Chalmers went on shore at Dopima to negotiate with the people, but both he and Tomkins were murdered.

His missionary work in New Guinea was dogged by personal loss and tragedy. His first wife died in Sydney in 1879. In 1888 he married Elizabeth Harrison, a widow who had been a friend of his first wife. She died in October 1900 at Daru after a long illness. By April 1901 his own health was in a state of decline and entries in his diary reveal that he was in very low spirits. Despite this ill health and depression and the constant warnings he received from fellow missionaries and government officers about the Goaribari people, he determined to visit them as part of a plan for establishing a string of stations along this coastal area.

Chalmers' great volume of descriptive, ethnographic and personal writings reveals a man of great enthusiasm and energy, who lived up to the ideals he set of a missionary being in close contact with the people and a constant support to his teachers in the field. His approach to his task was different to that of his famous co-missionary, the Rev. W. G. Lawes. Thus their contributions were different. While the scholarly Lawes contributed much to the knowledge of indigenous languages and cultures in the Port Moresby region, Chalmers left a more extensive record of aspects of the people he contacted. These extensive contacts also meant that Chalmers laid foundations for the establishment and spread of British administration in the area. He welcomed limited British intervention, since he thought it could provide an adequate protective shield for the people. He, like Lawes, assisted in the early establishment of this administration from 1884, because of his experience and knowledge.

His attitudes, methods and personality marked him as one of the most paternal and attractive pioneer missionaries in New Guinea.

British New Guinea, *Annual Report* 1884-5 to 1900-1.
J. Chalmers, Letters (M.L.).
———— *Adventures in New Guinea*. London, 1886.
———— 'New Guinea, Past, Present, and Future', *Proceedings of the Royal Colonial Institute*, vol. 18, 1886-7.
———— 'On the Manners and Customs of Some of the Tribes of New Guinea', *Proceedings of the Philosophical Society of Glasgow*, vol. 18, 1886-7.
———— 'Explorations in South-Eastern New Guinea', *Proceedings of the Royal Geographical Society*, new series, vol. 9, 1887.
———— 'History and Description of the Pottery Trade. A Papuan Enoch Arden', in *Picturesque New Guinea*, ed. J. W. Lindt. London, 1887.
———— *Pioneering in New Guinea*. London, 1887.
———— *Pioneer Life and Work in New Guinea, 1877-94*. London, 1895.
———— 'Toaripi (Motumotu Tribe of the Gulf of Papua)', *Journal of Anthropological Institute*, vol. 27, 1898.
———— 'Notes on the Bugilai, British New Guinea', *Journal of the Anthropological Institute*, vol. 33, 1903.
———— 'Notes on the Natives of Kiwai Island, Fly River, British New Guinea', *Journal of the Anthropological Institute*, vol. 33, 1903.
———— and W. W. Gill, *Work and Adventure in New Guinea, 1877 to 1885*. London, 1885.
———— and S. MacFarlane, *British New Guinea Vocabularies*, ed. R. N. Cust. London, 1888.
———— and S. H. Ray, 'Vocabularies of the Bugilai and Tagota Dialects, British New Guinea, and a Note on West Papuan Dialects', *Journal of the Anthropological Institute*, vol. 27, 1898.
C. Lennox, *James Chalmers of New Guinea: Missionary, Pioneer, Martyr*. London, 1902.
London Missionary Society, Papers. (M.L.).
R. Lovett, *James Chalmers, His Autobiography and Letters*. London, 1902.   R. J. LACEY

(*See also* MISSIONS)

CHAMBRI. People of the Sepik River. Reference: M. Mead, *Sex and Temperament in Three Primitive Societies*. London, 1935.

CHAMPION, Herbert William (1880-   ), administrator, was born at Kaiapoi, New Zealand, on 8 August 1880, son of Charles James Champion, an English migrant, and was educated at Canterbury College, Christchurch. He went to British New Guinea in private employment and then joined the public service of British New Guinea as Postmaster in Port Moresby. With the change to Australian control and the resignations which followed the findings of the Royal Commission of 1906 Champion became Treasurer, in which post he incurred the displeasure of Atlee Hunt [q.v.] but the praise of Hubert Murray [q.v.], and on the latter's recommendation succeeded Campbell [q.v.] as Government Secretary in 1913. Champion remained in this position, acting on occasion as Administrator during Murray's absences, until the suspension of civil administration in 1942. He was considered as a possible successor to Hubert Murray in 1940.

F. J. West, *Hubert Murray: The Australian Pro-Consul*. Melbourne, 1968. The official records of Champion's administrative career are in the Commonwealth Archives Office and printed in *Commonwealth Parliamentary Papers*.

FRANCIS WEST

CHAMPION, Ivan Francis (1904-   ) government officer, was born at Port Moresby on 9 March 1904, the eldest son of H. W. Champion, Papuan Government Secretary from 1914 to 1940. He was educated at Port Moresby European School (1911-14); Manly (N.S.W.) Public School (1915); Southport (Queensland) School (1916-22), and was prominent in rowing, swimming, football and cricket. At thirteen he attempted to join the Royal Australian Navy but was rejected because of bad eyesight. He joined the Papuan Public Service in November 1923 as clerk, was appointed Patrol Officer in May 1924 and posted to Kerema. In 1925 he was transferred to Kambisi Police Camp, Central Division, under Assistant Resident Magistrate Charles Henry Karius. From December 1926 to January 1928 Champion accompanied Karius on the North-West Patrol, crossing New Guinea from the Fly to the Sepik, the most ambitious piece of exploration carried out in Papua and New Guinea to that date. He was appointed Assistant Resident Magistrate in 1928, and was officer-in-charge at Kambisi from 1928 to 1929. Between 1930 and 1936 he served at various posts: Ioma, 1930-31; Misima and Trobriand Islands, 1932-34; Misima (as Acting R.M.) 1935; Rigo, 1935.

In April 1936, accompanied by C. J. Adamson, Patrol Officer, he set out as leader of the Bamu-Purari Patrol, which was a follow-up to the Strickland-Purari Patrol of J. G. Hides [q.v.], and which traversed the present Southern Highlands District. From November 1937 to January 1940 he was in charge of the exploration of the Southern Highlands from Lake Kutubu Police Camp. He was Acting Resident Magistrate, Kikori, from January to June 1940; Acting Resident Magistrate, Misima, 1940; Assistant Resident Magistrate, Rigo, 1941; Acting Resident Magistrate, Misima, from December 1941 to February 1942.

In July 1940 he was rejected as medically unfit for the A.I.F., again because of his eyes. However, he was appointed sub-lieutenant in the Australian Navy (R.A.N.V.R.) in February 1942, mainly because of his extensive knowledge of the Papuan coast and of navigation and surveying. He was promoted lieutenant in June 1942, and was commanding officer of H.M.A.S. *Laurabada*, the former administrative vessel of the Lieutenant-Governor of Papua. He rescued the remnants of the Australian Rabaul garrison from Jacquinot Bay on the south coast of New Britain in April 1942, was commanding officer of the Coastwatchers' vessel *Paluma* in September-December 1942, and official pilot of all Allied vessels from Milne Bay to Oro Bay, December 1942-January 1943. He was with U.S. Navy hydrographic vessel *Sumner*, and was pilot to Allied vessels in the Buna operations. From August 1943 to the end of hostilities he commanded the *Laurabada* on

survey operations in Huon Gulf, Dreger Harbour, at Cape Gloucester, Seeadler Harbour and in Torres Strait.

After the war he was appointed District Officer, Western District, in November 1945. He became Assistant Director of District Services and Native Affairs in the combined Papua and New Guinea Administration in July 1946, and was Acting Director from 1949 to 1951. He was in charge of operations at the disastrous Mount Lamington volcanic eruption January-March 1951. In July 1952 he was appointed Chief Commissioner of the Native Land Commission, and in 1963 Senior Commissioner, Native Land Titles Commissioner. He retired in February 1964.

Champion was awarded the Gill Memorial Medal of the Royal Geographical Society in 1938, the John Lewis Gold Medal in 1953, and was appointed O.B.E. in 1953. He was an Official Member of the Legislative Council from 1951 to 1963.

He published *Across New Guinea from the Fly to the Sepik* in London in 1932, a book which was republished in Melbourne in 1966.

J. P. SINCLAIR

(*See also* EXPLORATION)

CHILD GROWTH AND DEVELOPMENT. The growth pattern of the child of Papua and New Guinea is as diverse and varied as its geography, people and their culture. Wide geographical variations in the island are associated with, and are no doubt causally related to, the wide diversity of human physique, and this in turn to the influence of the environment on child growth and development from birth to maturity.

Average birth weights vary from a world record low of 2.4 kg. in the sago-eaters of the Sepik to over 3.3 kg. in the infants of well-nourished Highland mothers on a rice and meat diet. These all fall short of the average for Caucasian infants. The lower weights and the variations between different populations may be attributed to a complex of nutritional, racial and disease factors.

After birth, growth in all societies is rapid and either parallels or exceeds the rate of growth of the Caucasian child. This is probably due to the unregimented feeding schedule and the outstanding lactational performance of the mother.

Beyond 4 to 6 months, however, the unsatisfactory weaning diet and the tendency to rely too much on breast milk as the sole source of calories and protein results in a sharp break in the continuity of the growth curve. Substantial differences occur, from the relatively satisfactory growth rates of the urban child to the very slow rates of some Highland and Sepik populations. These differences in growth curves of both height and weight continue throughout the growth period, reaching a maximum divergence just prior to the adolescent spurt. At this stage the height of the European child of 10 years is not reached until the age of 11 years in urban populations, 14 years in the average coastal child and 16 or 17 years in Highland children. Final adult height in males varies from an average of 59 to 67 inches, the slower-growing child reaching his final adult size at 22 to 25 years, compared with 18 years in the European male child.

Skeletal and sexual development is correspondingly delayed, the mean age of menarche varying from less than 14 years in urban girls to over 18 years in the Highlands.

Dental development, however, is comparatively uninfluenced by variation in growth rates. Deciduous eruption, which is constant throughout the region, is closely similar to that of other world populations. The eruption of permanent teeth is earlier on average than Caucasians and is only slightly affected by environmental circumstances which delay growth. Eruption times of deciduous and permanent teeth, therefore, offer a method of determining age when birth records are unavailable.

The cause of the slow growth pattern is clearly related to the lack of dietary protein in the village. Supplementary protein feeding has been shown to accelerate growth in height and weight in both the toddler and the school-age child. The rate of growth and development of the urban child, with his high protein intake, indicates that the child of Papua and New Guinea has a relatively normal growth potential. It is possible, however, that the slow growth pattern may to some extent be determined genetically and that adaptation to the protein-deficient environment may have occurred in the past through natural selection of slow-growing children and hence shorter adults through a high childhood mortality.

Dietary improvement in the villages through the growing of better sources of protein, improved infant feeding practices, and the purchase of tinned meat, fish and milk, are all influencing the traditional growth pattern. The secular trend towards faster childhood growth, earlier sexual development and taller adult height, which has occurred in Western societies over the past 150 years, may now be observed in some societies in Papua and New Guinea.

K. V. Bailey, 'Growth of Chimbu infants in the New Guinea Highlands', *Journal of Tropical Pediatrics and African Child Health*, vol. 10, 1964; L. A. Malcolm, 'Growth and development in New Guinea—A study of the Bundi people of the Madang District', Institute of Human Biology, monograph series no. 1, Madang, 1970; —— 'Growth of the Asai child of the Madang District of New Guinea', *Journal of Biosocial Science*, vol. 2, 1970; R. F. R. Scragg, 'Birth weight, prematurity and growth rate to thirty months of the New Guinea native child', *Medical Journal of Australia*, vol. 1, 1955; M. L. Wark and L. A. Malcolm, 'Growth and development of the Lumi child in the Sepik district of New Guinea', *Medical Journal of Australia*, vol. 2, 1969.   L. A. MALCOLM

(*See also* CHILD HEALTH)

CHILD HEALTH. Papua and New Guinea is a young, rapidly developing country; 97 per cent of the population lives in rural areas, often in very remote areas. The terrain is harsh, and communications poor. Mainly because of physical and geographical factors, there are about seven hundred cultural groups, each with their own language, customs, and traditions, often living in almost complete isolation, and in very unsophisticated surroundings. They have no knowledge of disease or germs, and rely on magic and sorcery for the explanation of sickness and disease. The population is also young, 50 per cent are under the age of fifteen years.

The problems of child health. These problems are many. Lack of reliable statistics make it difficult firstly, to determine what are the most urgent problems; and secondly, to gauge the effect of current public health measures. Because of wide geographic and ethnologic variations, statistics can only be applied locally, and it is quite impossible to draw general conclusions from data obtained from one particular area.

The infant mortality rate varies between 50 per 1,000 in Port Moresby, to over 300 per 1,000 in the more unsophisticated areas. Where basic health services such as malaria eradication and maternal and child health care have been successful, the infant mortality rate is approximately 70 per 1,000. The toddler mortality rate is estimated to be between 10 and 30 per 1,000.

There is no accurate picture of illness in the villages and rural areas, although studies of local morbidity patterns are in progress.

Hospital statistics suggest that the commonest causes of death in children under the age of ten years are, in order of frequency: pneumonia [q.v.], gastroenteritis, prematurity, malnutrition [q.v.], meningitis, whooping cough, and malaria [q.v.]. It is unfortunate that nearly all the mortality and morbidity figures available are related to hospital statistics, which obviously bear little relation to the true morbidity picture (*see* DISEASE PREVALENCE (MORBIDITY)).

Obstetric care. It is estimated that there are about 90,000 births annually in Papua and New Guinea, and about half of these occur without any medical assistance—or even long-range supervision.

Modern thinking is emphatic that the proper care of the mother during pregnancy and labour is essential to ensure a healthy newborn baby and infant. Child care, therefore, begins with the care of the mother during pregnancy and labour.

Although conditions do not permit all mothers to have their babies in hospital, emphasis is placed on the value and importance of regular antenatal examinations during pregnancy. In this way the mother's health is safeguarded and complications that could occur during labour recognized and anticipated. Mothers are immunized against tetanus, since the antibodies so produced will protect the neonate against tetanus. In some remote areas traditional midwives are given a simple training in hygiene, and taught to recognize the danger signs during labour.

The mission medical services and the Department of Public Health supervised 33,000 deliveries during 1967.

Care in the village. Child health programmes

involve three basic principles: education, prevention, and cure, and if a balanced child health programme is to be developed, full weight must be given to each. Because of the predominantly rural population a hospital orientated service is inappropriate. Curative medicine is not enough, and the educational and preventive aspects of child health are equally if not more important. Infants and children must be seen regularly—in clinics, in schools, and in the homes, if the curative and preventive aspects of child health are to be given their proper emphasis. Child health programmes must therefore operate at a village level, and reach the child in his home, and in his community.

But to reach the child in his village presents big problems owing to the poor communications, and difficult country. In many areas, the customs of the people do not bring them together in villages, but in small groups that tend to be scattered over a wide area. An effective child health service depends on regular visits of health staff, and attendances of mothers and children; but the frequency and quality of the service provided often depend on the availability of transport and communications.

For the reasons given above, the maternal and child health service is a field service, and the basic health unit is the village clinic.

The first maternal and child health clinics were begun in 1931 when the Methodist Mission established a clinic at Malabunga in New Britain. In 1947 the London Missionary Society commenced a similar clinic in Port Moresby.

In 1948 the Maternal and Child Health (M.C.H.) service was established as a separate section within the Department of Public Health with a staff of one doctor, one sister, and an interpreter. In 1967 the service had six doctors, and a staff of 140 local and expatriate sisters, and 191 mission stations were reporting regularly on the maternal and child health work they carried out.

In 1967 the Administration had 690 village clinics operating from 38 fixed clinics, and the missions had 2044 village clinics operating from 198 fixed clinics. About 55 per cent of the children of the country were seen regularly or irregularly.

Maternal and child health work in the Territory is quite unlike infant welfare work in Australia, where only well children attend. In Papua and New Guinea no attempt is made to segregate sick from well children for two reasons; firstly, the M.C.H. worker is often the only medical worker in the area, and the mothers often walk for many hours with their children to reach the clinic; and secondly, if child health is to be practised properly, the treatment of sickness must not be separated from prevention and education.

The curative and preventive aspects of clinic work consist of a general immunization programme against tetanus, whooping cough, diphtheria, tuberculosis, and poliomyelitis, together with talks and demonstrations on hygiene, nutrition, and the general care of children.

Understanding social and community problems is of vital importance, but is often difficult because of language difficulties, and failure to appreciate and understand local customs can ridicule the M.C.H. staff in the eyes of the local people.

Family life and the social conditions of the family play an important part in the growth and development of the child, both for good and ill. For this reason, and particularly in urban areas, children are visited in their homes, and child health in the context of family life becomes important. Home visiting in rural areas is just as important, but is more difficult since houses are scattered, and as a result home visiting is time-consuming and uneconomic in staff.

It has been said that in an underdeveloped country, advice and help on nutrition should form a major part of M.C.H. work. Papua and New Guinea, with its major problems of under-nutrition and malnutrition is no exception, and teaching mothers and families the correct use of local foods is very important. Where possible demonstrations showing the correct preparation of food are given. Breast feeding—usually for prolonged periods—is almost universal, and every effort is made to preserve and maintain this custom. Unfortunately it is a fact that with increasing contact with Western ways and methods breast feeding is becoming less common, and the feeding bottle is the fashionable method of feeding babies in urban areas.

Clinics are held regularly—usually monthly—sometimes in a village, or at a central point to which mothers and families come. Maternal and Child Health staff may travel by car, canoe, boat, or light aircraft. At one particular centre, the sisters travel by air, and the clinic, lasting several days, is held on the airstrip. During this period, some eight hundred mothers and children attend, some walking six to eight hours to reach the clinic.

Care in schools and missions. In 1967 there were over 200,000 children in primary schools, and in the urban areas some schools have over a thousand students.

Schools in rural areas are often small, and these are visited regularly by the Maternal and Child Health staff as part of their regular village clinic programme. In the urban areas of Lae, Port Moresby, and Rabaul special school medical teams visit the local schools. During 1967 mission and Health Department workers examined 64,000 school children, and gave 187,000 treatments.

The work of the various missions deserves special mention for the part they play in child health, and 196 mission stations send in regular monthly reports on their maternal and child health work. Mission workers carry out programmes similar to that of the Department of Public Health, often working in extremely isolated conditions, carrying health services to communities that would otherwise be without any help or assistance. In order to help the missions in their work, the Department of Public Health gives financial assistance to sisters and nurses carrying out field work.

Child health specialists. Because a unified approach to child health is so important the Department of Public Health has developed the concept of area Child Health Specialists, paediatricians who are responsible for the management and development of an area involving a population of 80,000 to 200,000.

The specialist is in charge of the children's ward at the Base Hospital, where the bulk of the admissions are acute infectious illnesses and nutritional disorders.

However, other and equally important aspects of his work involve visits to isolated mission and Administrative outstations to advise, and for consultations; to plan and evaluate preventive measures and campaigns; to carry out surveys, and to collect vital statistics. The specialist must also teach, carrying out a continuing education programme of lower grade workers. In this way the doctor is able to practise child health in its fullest sense—education, prevention, and treatment.

Welfare services. Child care not only involves optimal growth and development and the prevention and treatment of disease, but must also protect the child from the stresses and strains within the community and family.

Between 1900 and 1962 various regulations and ordinances made provision for mothers and children who were deserted, for the care of babies where the mother died; and payments were made to provide minimum assistance where guardians were unable to care for children.

In 1962 the Child Welfare Ordinance became the first comprehensive piece of legislation concerned with the care and welfare of children in the Territory. Under this ordinance a Child Welfare Council was appointed to advise the Director of Child Welfare (Department of District Administration), who administered the ordinance. This ordinance, and the setting up of the Child Welfare Council were brought about mainly through the efforts of Dr Joan Refshauge who was the first Assistant Director, Maternal and Child Health, in the Department of Public Health.

The Child Welfare Council interests itself in a wide range of subjects: child-minding centres; children's courts; destitute, neglected and incorrigible children; adoption and employment of children; and indeed in any matter that may affect the well-being of the children in the community.

The care of children is influenced indirectly in many other ways, mothercraft lectures to school girls and women's clubs, and the women's clubs themselves are an important medium through which instruction and help is given to mothers on the care and upbringing of their children. The steadily rising standard of education is also an important factor in improving the social standards of the community, which in turn improves the health and well-being of children.

Finally, in considering child health in Papua and New Guinea it is essential to appreciate and be aware of the effect a Western way of life and Western medicine has on the lives of the people,

and particularly on the health of their children. Such far-reaching changes imposed on the many different cultures will have consequences that are difficult to foresee, and which may affect the health of children in ways far removed from the original intentions.   D. P. BOWLER

(*See also* MEDICAL SERVICES, HISTORY)

CHILD REARING AND SOCIALIZATION.

The first anthropologists to investigate child rearing in New Guinea on a comparative basis—Mead, Hogbin, Wedgwood—were struck by the great diversity, and further work has only confirmed the initial impression. Everywhere, so far as we know, babies are normally suckled for more than a year and girls are expected to assume adult responsibilities much earlier than boys. Apart from these, few generalizations can be made to which there are not conspicuous exceptions, even though there are not many detailed studies to compare. The fullest data come from a relatively limited area, notably the East Sepik District and islands north and east of the New Guinea mainland. Information on traditional systems is increasingly difficult to obtain because of the spread of Western attitudes and practices. Even where European contact is recent, the societies investigated are usually under government control, which removes the constant threat of enemy attack and thus gives children considerably more freedom than they enjoyed when warfare was endemic. The following description can give only a general impression of how children were—or are—brought up prior to the introduction and acceptance of alien theories about hygiene, discipline, and education.

It should also be remembered that even within a single society there is never absolute uniformity of opinion and behaviour. Children may be indulged in one family and neglected in another, parents may quarrel over questions of discipline, and the children of one family may receive differential treatment according to birth order, sex, individual personality, or simple favouritism. Diversity in such matters is not peculiar to Western civilization.

CHILD REARING

Early infancy. In most traditional societies the infantile death rate is high. Young babies are treated with the greatest care and surrounded by taboos until it seems clear that they will survive. If a baby dies within a few days of birth it is usually buried without ceremony and not mourned; the occurrence is too common. The mother often remains in seclusion with the child at least until the umbilical cord has dropped off and the skin begun to darken. Their emergence may be marked by a ritual welcoming of the baby into the community. His life is still precarious, however, and the parents must think constantly of his interests. The mother is usually forbidden sexual intercourse at least until the child is walking well, a prohibition that prevents her becoming pregnant too soon and so depriving the child of a milk supply for which there is no substitute. She must avoid exposing the child to the sun or taking him near places haunted by spirits, which are particularly likely to attack infants. It is often believed that the child's soul, sometimes localized in the fontanelle, is loosely attached at first, and nothing must be done to drive it away, such as startling or striking the infant or permitting it to cry excessively. Babies are almost always fed on demand for some months, and distracted or lulled with jogging or songs if they cry from other reasons than hunger.

Feeding. In some societies another woman feeds the baby until the mother's milk appears, and later he may be suckled by any woman who has milk if his mother is absent. Elsewhere the milk of another woman is considered dangerous, or women feel that they have only enough milk for one child and none to share. If the mother alone can feed the child, she either stays home for some time while other women perform her garden work or carries him everywhere in sling or net bag. The mother generally seems to enjoy suckling the infant, and it is a long-drawn-out process during which the child is fondled and talked to. In a few societies, as Mundugumor, babies are regarded as something of a nuisance to be fed and placated as quickly as possible, and returned to their baskets. As the child grows older, he is allowed to go for increasingly long periods without milk, and the mother tends to be more casual about suckling, sometimes not holding or looking at the child. If a child is frightened or ill, however, the breast may be offered primarily for the sake of comfort, and both mother and child revert to the earlier pattern. The use of dummies is very rare, though the Mbowamb employ one soaked in salt. Where betel is chewed, babies are given the rind to suck as a mechanical pacifier and teething aid. But most commonly a child whose mother is absent is pacified with solid food.

Although babies are normally suckled at least until they are walking well, solid food is usually added to the diet in the first few months. In Kurtatchi prechewed taro is given from the day of birth, but most peoples wait until the baby is three to five months old or has his first teeth. Premasticated starchy foods, sugar water, and coconut milk are typically the first foods. These are supplemented as the child grows older and acquires more teeth. Most peoples forbid some foods to small children on the assumption that these will cause sickness or stunt growth. Children are always forbidden to eat any foods taboo to their kin groups but, unlike their elders, are not normally expected to abstain from staple foods in mourning for dead relatives. On the whole, there are relatively few distinctions between the child's and adult's diet; a two-year-old usually eats what the rest of the family eats, simply washing it down with a swallow of mother's milk. Occasionally the chewing of betel-nut is also introduced in infancy, though most societies discourage both chewing and smoking until at least six, and often until adolescence.

Caring for the baby. In many societies contact with the blood shed in childbirth, the aura of which is thought to cling to the new-born child, or even contact with the infant himself, is considered dangerous to masculinity. The father may consequently avoid touching his child for periods that range from a few days or weeks to the extreme in Wogeo of one year. Men may also consider it degrading to be soiled by a baby or to be seen carrying one, or women may believe men incompetent to look after babies. It is not uncommon for the care of small infants to be entirely in the hands of women, who may also specialize in treating childhood ailments, though men may be called in to perform growth magic or deal with serious diseases. But once the baby is a few months old he may spend almost as much time with his father as with his mother. Masculine attitudes vary from society to society, but offspring are a source of pride in most. The father and grandfather care for the baby and play with him while the mother is working, and they usually draw the line only at cleaning up after him. Rarely are men reported to be sterner disciplinarians than women. Even where fathers spend relatively little time with their babies, a man may be constantly mindful of his child—providing food, observing taboos and making sure that his wife does so as well, sponsoring ceremonies, and even arranging a betrothal. If the father has more than one wife, and the women are friendly, they are likely to share the baby-sitting.

In addition to the parents, aunts or grandmothers who live nearby normally help care for the baby; and so may older siblings. A child of eight or more is usually considered capable of minding an infant for hours at a time. The baby-sitter is usually a girl, unless the baby has only brothers of the right age, but in many societies boys enjoy playing with babies as much as girls do. In some societies, however, babies are not entrusted to the care of a child, or even to that of adults other than the closest kin. Here babies grow up accustomed only to the narrow family circle. The observable consequences of these different attitudes are the older child's reactions to outsiders or strangers, though timidity also varies with age and personality. Sometimes parents deliberately teach children to fear strangers, who are equated with enemies. By contrast, the parents may teach the baby to extend kinship terms at an early age, and persuade him to accept strangers by identifying them as 'aunts' or other trusted relatives.

There are notable differences in the treatment accorded children who are frightened or in pain. Older children are rarely coddled unless they are really ill. Among two- to three-year-olds, prolonged crying fits and real temper tantrums are not only common but tend to be ignored. Furthermore, even among peoples who treat young babies with the greatest tenderness, adults may delight in teasing older ones to tears. In some areas, as among the Orokaiva, little boys are deliberately frightened so that they will eventually become courageous, and parents elsewhere may invoke bogey men to keep a small child out of dangerous places; but in many societies the teasing and false tales have no aim other than to amuse adults.

Headbinding, southern New Britain.

Appearance and adornment. Many groups have well defined standards of beauty, and even a new-born child may be appraised in such terms. Women may attempt to mould the infant's features by the shaping of the skull with the fingers, pinching up the bridge of the nose, or flattening the ears to the head. It is unlikely that the pressure is great or continuous enough to have any effect. But in south-west New Britain, where a highly elongated skull is the ideal, babies have their heads bound with bark-cloth immediately after birth, and the binding is renewed every day for at least three months. The motive is purely aesthetic, and the results are per-manent. In a few other areas, notably on Bougain-ville, the lobes of the ears and septum of the nose may be pierced in infancy, and cicatrization may be begun then, on the assumption that these actions are less painful to a baby. Circumcision is also occasionally carried out in infancy. It is more often assumed, however, that such mutilations should be delayed until the child is older and stronger.

In some regions neither children nor adults wash regularly, though a baby may be bathed for cool-ness on a hot day. On the coast babies are usually bathed frequently, and it has often been noted that people otherwise careful not to shock or upset a baby will douse him with cold water, ignoring his howls. They may be concerned only with ap-pearance, but the motive is often hygienic, and older children may be allowed to go dirty. Simi-larly, the oils and pigments sometimes rubbed on a baby's skin may be designed to strengthen it or to give protection against the sun rather than simply to improve its appearance, and the pen-dants and bracelets he wears may be intended pri-marily as amulets.

Adults often delight in adorning babies and even dressing them in miniature grown-ups' cos-tume for special occasions. Though usually naked until they are about six, children may wear neck-laces and armbands, and have designs painted on their faces and bodies, from earliest infancy. As the hair grows it may be trimmed, dyed, or adorned in various ways, though small children have their hair cut short to prevent severe louse infestation.

Walking. During the suckling period, the child learns to walk and talk. Walking is usually en-couraged by adults, who hold him erect, guide his first steps, and set up stakes to which he can hold. Parents boast of the precocious walker and recite spells to speed up the retarded. Only the Wogeo are known to try to prevent crawling and to dis-courage walking until a child is old enough to look after himself, at about two. Elsewhere the parents are glad to be partially relieved of the burden of carrying.

Once the baby is able to move around freely,

there are specific dangers to be avoided. Different groups are nervous about different things; the Sengseng are careless about letting babies get into fires and allow the smallest infants to play with sharp knives; but they guard constantly against falls. Some peoples teach babies to swim as soon as they can walk, and others keep them away from the water. Manus babies are trained very young to be physically adept and then are left to their own devices; Wogeo babies are watched at all times.

Talking. Speech seems to be encouraged in all societies. The mother in particular usually talks constantly to the baby, imitating and responding to his babbling, and often saying words and simple phrases over and over. As the child grows older, he may be told to repeat the phrases. Sometimes the phrases are sung, and babies may learn to carry a tune before they can talk intelligibly. Baby talk, in the strict sense, is rarely used by adults, though many people teach babies special easy-to-pronounce terms for 'mother' and 'father'. The Kove of New Britain pronounce words in a childish fashion, as by substituting *t* for *s*, in speaking to babies, but such behaviour is rare. Children often have difficulty in pronouncing all the sounds of their language correctly before the age of six or so, and usually adults ignore their mispronunciations, assuming that these will disappear with age. Mistakes in terminology are usually corrected at once, but grammatical errors may be tolerated. Whatever the attitude of adults, older children often mock mistakes and stammering, and small children are frequently reported to be shy about talking in front of strangers.

Toilet training. While caring for a young baby an adult may try to anticipate his intentions and place him aside to avoid being soiled by faeces. Serious toilet training does not usually take place until the child can walk and talk. He is simply expected to leave the house to urinate; but he may need an escort to the place set aside for defecation, especially if he goes after dark, and he may also need help in cleaning himself. He is expected to avoid soiling the house at some period between two and three, and toilet training is usually accomplished gradually and without noticeable difficulties. After a period of instruction and explanation, the child may be scolded or slapped if he has an accident, especially if he dirties clothes or a sleeping mat or misbehaves in front of a visitor. Toilet training usually focuses on defecation; urine is often equated with water, and urination may be treated casually unless or until the child is taught to feel shame about exposing the genitals.

Ceremonial in infancy. Throughout this period the baby's parents are concerned with his health and development. Magical devices of various sorts—amulets, spells, the observation of taboos, the placation of spirits—may be used to ensure that he grows up normally; and each stage of development may be marked ceremonially. Often the full set of rites is carried out only for a first-born child, on the assumption that subsequent children will benefit as well. In those coastal areas where hereditary rank exists, upper-class children are usually the focus of more ceremonies than those of lower class. A man who is rich or powerful, or aspiring to high status, often sponsors particularly numerous or elaborate ceremonies in honour of his child.

Many of these ceremonies are what Oliver calls 'introduction rites'. The *naven* ceremonies of the Iatmül are a famous example. These are carried out when the baby does something significant, or has something done to it, for the first time. In addition to emergence from seclusion, ceremonies may mark the first haircut, the appearance of the first tooth, the first trip to the gardens, the first visit to a strange village, and a variety of other occasions. They may also be held when a child has recovered from any illness. Occasionally, as in *naven* and the Siuai baptism, the ritual is most elaborate, but often it is slight, though the child is normally adorned and displayed, and the ceremony is assumed to be of some direct benefit to him. These occasions also serve to cement relations between the child's various kinsmen and typically demand exchanges of wealth and a feast.

The bestowal of a name may also be marked by ceremonial. An outstanding example is found among the Mbowamb, where naming marks the child's real acceptance into his clan. It is delayed until the members are sure that he will survive. In some other areas an adult names a child after himself (or herself) before or shortly after its birth; the same name may be used for either sex. This person then assumes certain responsibilities towards his namesake. The whole question of naming is complex; children are often given several names, sometimes commemorating their ancestors, and the child himself may be forbidden to say his 'true' name. Names given in infancy are not necessarily permanent, and often a child receives a new one at a puberty ceremony.

Weaning. The child is usually considered ready for weaning at between eighteen months and three years of age, though he may occasionally be suckled for five years if the mother does not become pregnant. Some older children are said simply to wean themselves, or the mother may be able to persuade the child that further sucking is babyish without having to employ forcible means. If the mother becomes pregnant when the child is between one and two she may have to use drastic measures, especially where continued suckling is thought to harm the older child or the foetus. She either puts a repulsive or bitter substance on her breasts, or the child is sent to stay with relatives for a week or two. Sometimes a child weaned forcibly may seem permanently alienated from his mother. Children being weaned appear particularly likely to have temper tantrums, but whether these are the result of weaning or simply tend to occur at the same age is uncertain. Thumb- and finger-sucking are rare and seem to bear no relation to age at weaning; they can be observed in unweaned babies when the mother is within reach. Nakanai (Lakalai) parents punish thumb-sucking as a reflection on themselves, saying that onlookers will conclude that the child is underfed. Arapesh children play with their lips after weaning and throughout childhood in what may be a variant on thumb-sucking.

Weaning generally marks the transition from infancy to childhood. Unless the child is the last-born, it is also likely to produce a degree of separation from the mother, who turns her attention to the new baby. Jealousy of the baby, while often considered normal, is sometimes repressed by the parents' insistence that siblings must love one another; and sometimes, so long as it is only expressed verbally, regarded as just amusing childish behaviour. The three-year-old is likely to spend more time with other children and less under the constant surveillance of his parents. They may consider it time to begin his education.

SOCIALIZATION

Attitudes towards education. The absence of rigid discipline and identifiable schools has struck many commentators on village life, but it is incorrect to conclude that children automatically grow up conforming to the standards of the group. Some societies place a high value on formal instruction; the Wogeo, for example, believe that it is literally sinful not to teach a child the ways of the ancestors. By contrast, the Manus boy is taught only to observe a few restrictions and then is allowed to spend a carefree childhood bearing little relation to adulthood. Most societies fall between these extremes. Instruction is begun at various ages, depending on local theories about the development of intelligence. Some peoples feel that it is futile to expect rational behaviour or to impart moral instruction before the ages of eight or nine. Younger children are not held responsible for offences, though their parents may be expected to keep an eye on them or to pay for damage. Elsewhere a seven-year-old may own property, have his opinions listened to solemnly by adults, and contribute to the work and food supply of the community. He might be severely punished for striking a sibling, refusing to share food, or stealing.

Regardless of age, however, similar kinds of things are usually taught. At the earliest, the child must know which objects, areas, and people are dangerous; whom he can trust; and whose food is safe to eat. He must learn to cope with his environment and handle simple tools, weapons, and fire. He should know the properties of common plants and animals and be able to collect and prepare such foodstuffs as shellfish. He must be instructed to observe taboos. Knowledge of the spirit world is likely to be hazy; the parents are only concerned with protecting the child from supernatural dangers and with preserving the mysteries from non-initiates. Admission to full knowledge comes only with adulthood.

Social education. The first social virtues inculcated often have to do with property, including food. Usually generosity is highly valued, and children may be urged or forced to share food almost from babyhood. Attitudes towards other sorts of property differ. In Manus, where children are not taught to be generous, they are so constantly warned and punished for touching goods belonging to others that all property is safe in their presence. Elsewhere the discipline is not so severe, and adults may have to hide valuables where children cannot see them. In Wogeo a small child is given any fragile object it cries for; in Sengseng, wanton destruction of property, including garden crops, is tolerated even in six-year-olds. But generally speaking a child is told not to touch the property of others lest he damage it and so arouse anger or provoke a demand for payment, or lest he be called a thief. He may be told that people will condemn him or his parents, or practise sorcery against him. Often only the fear of sorcery can prevent boys from stealing sugar-cane or coconuts; it is a rare society which instils real respect for property in children.

Children are also taught proper behaviour towards kin and the duties they owe to the kin group as a whole. This is a slow process, and small children are often not expected to observe all the prohibitions that inhibit relations between certain categories of kin. Incest regulations are usually rigidly enforced from the beginning, and children are strongly discouraged from engaging in anything approximating to sexual behaviour with forbidden kinsmen. Where child betrothal is practised children may also have to avoid certain affines. Children learn the kinship terminologies early in societies in which they are normally used in address and reference, beginning with the words for 'mother' and 'father'. Parents concentrate on establishing favourable relations with people who will be the child's major sources of support later in life, such as his brothers, the members of his clan, or his closest neighbours, and may force him to refrain from quarrelling or fighting with any of these. On the other hand, striking a parent is often regarded with amusement rather than outrage.

Where warfare is endemic a certain amount of male aggressiveness must be tolerated if the people are to survive. Some Highlands groups seem to encourage boys to be bullies, ruthless even towards their kinsmen. Usually, however, they are allowed to display such traits only in dealing with members of other clans or residents of other villages. Within his own group, a boy may be allowed to compete with others but not actually to fight. In some societies even competitiveness is discouraged lest the loser bear a grudge. It is noteworthy that rivalry rarely remains friendly in this part of the world, but adults do tend to compete with each other, more or less overtly, and the children often mimic the adult patterns without being taught them. The Arapesh are virtually unique in trying to muffle all expressions of competitiveness and aggressiveness in boys as well as girls. In almost every other society boys are afforded considerable opportunities for developing initiative and independence in at least some spheres, even when they are not specifically trained for warfare. Adults typically allow boys plenty of freedom, cheer on their exploits against outsiders, offer no sympathy for minor injuries, and teach them to use weapons. In Iatmül little boys are helped to kill prisoners, but in most societies actual experience of killing and active participation in warfare is delayed until a man is fully grown. Boys simply play at fighting.

Juvenile tendencies to violence are almost always restricted by the demand that respect be shown to elders (usually excluding grandparents, who are treated with freedom) and, where an upper class exists, to its members. Older men are often adept at sorcery and the use of spears, and may have uncertain tempers. If they are powerful leaders, 'big men', or hold hereditary high rank, their persons may actually be surrounded by taboos. Insistence on respect for those who possess special knowledge is intensified if there are secret societies, restricted men's houses, and rigorous initiation rites; children may be threatened with death at the hands of men or spirits if they trespass on the sacred areas. Older women, who are unlikely to be threatening figures, are rarely accorded the same respect as men, except in those few areas where they may be suspected of witchcraft. Children of both sexes must be careful not to antagonize the parents of potential spouses, and obedience to elders is a highly esteemed trait, as adults constantly remind their own children.

Methods of education. As the foregoing statements indicate, different approaches are used to produce conformity to adult norms. Some peoples try never to strike a child and only do so when seriously provoked; others, like the Kwoma, subject him to constant cuffs and kicks and occasional beatings. The Wogeo reason even with a very small child, explaining just why he should behave correctly, and the Nakanai point out the probable consequences of his actions and expect him to react accordingly; but the Busama feel that small children are incapable of understanding, and they tend to employ force instead. Although bribery, in the form of food, is occasionally offered, a child who behaves correctly may get little reward but the knowledge of adult approval. The child who is particularly attentive to a parent or old person may be repaid with the teaching of special knowledge and with substantial gifts if the kinship system permits.

On the whole, children are more concerned to avoid censure than to acquire rewards. Good behaviour is induced by accounts of the probable retaliation of those offended, who may withdraw support and aid, refuse to consider the child as an affine, or actually attack him with physical weapons or sorcery. He sometimes realizes that the danger is in being caught and may be prepared to evade the rules in secret. Through constant repetition, the parents may also inculcate a strong sense of shame at misbehaviour in a child. Sometimes the parents emphasize their own shame at the child's actions; in an area where shame frequently leads to suicide this can be a powerful sanction. Ridicule may be employed freely, though children may be warned not to ridicule others lest they alienate them completely. Parents may use standard epithets ('idiot!' 'bush demon!' 'hardhead!') with children, or may curse them and threaten mayhem. Since threats are often not carried out, and parents rarely consider it necessary to maintain a consistent attitude, many children simply run away to the bush or go to stay with a relative till the parent's anger has cooled. Punish-

ment is almost entirely in the hands of the parents and other senior kin, and they are likely to resent it strongly if anyone else strikes the child. Sometimes the parents threaten to summon a village 'big man' or one of the masked figures which, in some societies, chase and beat non-initiates; but such threats are usually idle, as the child soon discovers. There are only a few societies in which adults believe that the spirits of the ancestors punish misbehaviour by bringing sickness to the child or to members of his family. Where such a belief is held, the threat of supernatural wrath may strongly impress an older child who has seen the affliction of others explained in these terms.

When infants cry adults seek to distract them; when older children lose their tempers a diversion of attention may also be employed. The child is persuaded to attack things, as by chopping a tree rather than hitting people, and he grows up to be a man who chops down his house when he is offended. As an alternative, he may simply be permitted to scream and roll on the ground; Arapesh boys may do this even in adolescence. These devices are employed only where interpersonal violence cannot be tolerated by the society.

Where hereditary rank exists, an upper-class child may be pampered because people are reluctant to chastise him, and he may also have the right to order other children around. At the same time, such a child may be expected to be particularly well behaved and is constantly reminded to live up to his obligations. Wedgwood found upper-class children in Manam to be more courteous, generous, and honest than others. The children of chiefs and important men may similarly be expected to provide examples.

Although most parents want their children to conform to community norms, the spoiled child is by no means unknown. Sometimes a recalcitrant child is regarded as simply unable to learn for one reason or another, but there are also parents who are amused by the stubbornness, independence, or aggressiveness of their children and tolerate these traits at whatever cost to community relations. There also exist parents who are simply unable to cope with a strong-minded child, and some who are blinded by affection to behaviour that may scandalize the neighbourhood. Occasionally other kinsmen intervene if the parents are unwilling or unable to discipline a child, but in some societies no one else would dare to usurp the parent's prerogatives, and the child grows up relatively free from restraint. Other adults find some relief in prophesying a bad end for him.

Apart from moral qualities, children must also be taught such techniques as food production, house-building, and the manufacture of various artefacts. Such teaching is always the primary responsibility of the parent of the same sex, though an expert at such specialties as canoe manufacture or weather control may teach a nephew or more remote relative, especially if he has no son of his own or is paid for the job. Much is learned by a child's simply trailing along, partly for amusement's sake, observing, and trying tasks for himself. Detailed instruction is sometimes given, however, with the adult demonstrating, explaining, and guiding the child's hands. Children are usually encouraged to help with small tasks even when they may actually be a hindrance, on the assumption that they will only learn by doing.

General knowledge is usually passed on informally. Much information is volunteered, but children are usually encouraged to ask questions, and parents may test their fund of information by questioning them in turn. Knowledge is esteemed, and children are normally eager to learn and anxious to display their learning. A certain amount of information is imparted by story-telling, which is practised particularly at night and during the rainy season. Some of the stories are purely entertainment, though among the Massim it is believed that listening to stories aids growth. Many stories point a moral, teach the rules of traditional behaviour, describe the spirit world, explain the origin of natural features and human customs, and sometimes give the sacred history of the child's own clan. Among the Iatmül a spell is recited over a child to help him remember the clan legends. In Wogeo children are constantly enjoined to follow the example of the hero children described in the myths. Some myths may be too sacred to be revealed until the child is initiated, but otherwise there is usually no special category of children's tales or censorship for children's ears. The Manus are apparently peculiar in not telling stories to children, saying that they do not enjoy them.

Play. Childhood is by no means only a time for instruction; children, especially the younger ones, typically pass most of the day in play. The size and composition of the play group varies with the local residence patterns, but at least one companion is usually available, and ties of friendship may be forged that last into adulthood. In most areas a wide choice of diversions is available. Both the sea and the bush offer numerous amusements, and at the same time the opportunity to practise hunting, paddling canoes, and other useful skills. Formal and elaborate games, accompanied by rhymes, are often performed particularly on moonlight nights. During the day, children romp and scuffle, dance and sing, and imitate adult activities—playing 'house' or pig-hunt, engaging in a ceremonial exchange, carrying out an elaborate mortuary rite. They may also pretend to be the evil spirits and witches whom they genuinely fear at night. Certain games and toys are particularly common: 'stilts' of half-coconut shells, leaf whirligigs and puzzles, spinning tops made of a fruit pierced with a stick, swings of bark loops or vines, string figures—cat's cradle—contests in which darts are thrown at a rolling disc, and, in a few coastal areas, surfboards. Perhaps because they usually have real babies to play with, little girls rarely own a doll, but girls between two and four, too young to be trusted with an infant, often carry around an object such as a smooth stone and treat it as a baby.

Some games such as mock combat with miniature weapons and shooting at insects with toy bows, or preparing meals on improvised hearths, definitely train for adulthood. So, in different ways, do riddles and guessing games. While amusing themselves, the children acquire physical skills and manual dexterity, and may exercise their imaginations and develop social awareness. They are bound to learn standards of interpersonal behaviour—perhaps that the strong can bully the weak, perhaps that co-operation is necessary if the games and enterprises are to be successful and enjoyable. Boys typically continue to pass their days in play until adolescence, roaming in groups, while the growing girl gradually spends more time helping her mother with the work of the household and has less and less opportunity for diversion with her contemporaries.

Sex in childhood. Although babies are usually treated almost exactly alike, regardless of sex, children begin to show appreciation of their separate roles by the age of five or so. Adults may begin to tease very small children about their marital prospects and often remind them of taboos on matters which would affect their sexual development. Emotional behaviour is gradually conditioned by the society's expectations and demands. Whereas the Nakanai expect boys to be stoical and girls to be volatile, the Arapesh permit only boys to weep and indulge in fits of rage. The Wogeo and Siuai reproach girls for any display of violence, reserving such behaviour for boys, while the Sengseng teach baby girls to chase and beat boys in anticipation of the later courtship patterns. Children also impose some restrictions on themselves, identifying with adults of their sex and refusing to play inappropriate roles in games. If necessary adults may forbid little girls to mimic men's ceremonies. By seven or so boys often begin to sleep apart from their mothers and sisters, though they are usually still forbidden to enter ceremonial structures. It is rare for small children to be aware of sexual discrimination; most parents want children of both sexes and give them equal attention. As they grow older it is usually made clear to the girl that her life will be more restricted and drabber than her brother's. As children approach puberty they are likely to be held to standards of modesty in dress and behaviour and often seem to adopt these of their own accord. A few notably prudish societies like the Manus demand great modesty even of young children. Rigid standards are sometimes imposed even where adults wear no clothes; Kwoma girls, for example, are taught to sit with their legs together and Kwoma boys are adjured not to stare at or react publicly to the sight of female genitals. Almost universally children learn to seek privacy, or darkness, for defecation and sexual activities, and not infrequently for eating, which has complex connections with sex in many societies.

Attitudes towards childish sexual activity vary greatly. Because children usually go naked for years, are thoroughly aware of the facts of life at an early age, and are permitted to hear and use bawdy language, it is sometimes thought that they have complete sexual freedom, inhibited only by the incest taboos. In fact, children lead relatively free sex lives in only a few scattered coastal areas. Most people seem to believe that sexual activity in childhood will stunt growth, and a number of groups, especially in the Highlands, regard all contact with females as potentially dangerous to males. Adults in these societies often manage to frighten most boys out of attempting copulation prior to marriage. Masturbation in the young may be regarded tolerantly, but in some societies it is condemned because it is thought to lead to a precocious interest in sex. Especially along the Fly and Sepik Rivers, life in the men's houses may involve a good deal of homosexuality, often ritual in nature and sometimes believed necessary to promote growth in boys. Active homosexuality involving children is rarely reported for other areas, even those in which boys are discouraged from heterosexual relations for many years. Among the Busama, who prohibit premarital intercourse, an old woman gives a girl sexual instruction after her first menstruation. In other societies, the girl may be initiated by her husband. Constant chaperonage may ensure premarital chastity, especially where child betrothal is practised and a girl is supervised by her prospective parents-in-law.

Where premarital sexual relations are permitted, techniques are almost always learned from older children and from observation rather than from direct instruction by an adult. A parent may teach love magic to a growing son, or warn a daughter against it, but rarely do members of the same family discuss sex freely among themselves. Copulation between an adult and a child is usually strongly disapproved, and children, sometimes after a considerable period of experimentation, are typically initiated into intercourse by older and more experienced children. In some societies in eastern Papua girls are allowed to receive boys at night in their parent's house, and in parts of the Highlands free courtship is carried on for years in the boys' houses, but more often, young lovers must arrange a secret rendezvous in the bush, and the girl is at least careful to preserve her reputation.

Ceremonial in childhood. Some societies hold no rituals for children between those marking birth and puberty, and a few, particularly in the Massim, do not even mark puberty formally. Other societies continue to perform introduction rites, especially for first-born children or children of high rank. These may mark such events as the first participation in a dance, first catch of game, and first harvesting of a crop planted by the child. Often the decorative mutilations, such as tattooing, tooth-blackening, and ear-piercing, take place (or, in the case of tattooing, are begun) prior to puberty, and they may be the occasion for ceremonies honouring each child who undergoes them. The assumption of adult clothing may also be a formal occasion marking a step in the child's maturation. In only a few societies are all children or all boys involved in a series of rituals which begin in childhood and culminate, years later, in initiation [q.v.] into adult society. Where such rituals demand seclusion, as in northern Bougainville, they may effectively remove the boys from contact with females for a long period. In most

cases seclusion is relatively brief. Although the children being initiated are often exhorted to abide by the rule of the society, they seem rarely to receive any systematic instruction except in ritual matters: the nature and use of bullroarers or sacred flutes, the manufacture of masks, and myths.

Achieving adulthood. Girls are usually considered marriageable after their first menstruation, which, contrary to popular belief, tends to occur somewhat later in New Guinea than among Europeans. In the period prior to this the girl has learned and become used to performing the tasks of an adult. Indeed, by the age of nine or ten, she often is able at least to make leaf skirts, cook a meal, help in the gardens and plant a few crops, and care for a baby all day. By puberty she usually has a garden of her own and can manufacture all the standard woman's goods. She is urged to be industrious, obedient, and good-tempered so that she will be sought in marriage [q.v.]. Child betrothal is common, and the engaged girl usually spends at least part of the time with the groom's family, although the marriage is not usually consummated until the girl is physically mature. She may nevertheless be expected to observe the decorum proper to a married woman. By contrast, unmarried girls in many societies are granted a great deal of freedom to travel around, dance, and conduct love affairs. This freedom ends at marriage, and girls may consequently try to extend the relatively carefree period as long as possible. Most marriages are arranged, and the girl often has little choice. Unless she is married very young, she is usually well able to assume her adult role, though in some groups she may still need instruction about the processes of childbirth.

Boys tend to marry somewhat later than girls and, as has been noted, are not usually expected to settle down to steady work as soon. They are often adept at hunting and fishing long before they spend much time in gardening. By late adolescence a boy should be able to perform all the everyday masculine tasks. He may still not control wealth, though he may be the nominal owner of a pig and some shell 'money', both of which are cared for by others. He too may be expected to marry at the desire of his parents, though he may have more choice than a girl. As a child he was taught a few simple spells to, for example, keep away rain, lure octopus, or attract a girl temporarily; now he is admitted to the repertoire of garden and hunting magic, serious love magic, and spells to protect property and cure disease. Before he is ready to marry the principal secrets of the men's house, if any, are revealed to him. Nevertheless, in many groups learning still continues well into adulthood. Only long after marriage does a man become a specialist at carving or curing; only in his forties, perhaps, admitted to the inner rites of a secret society; only when about to become a father himself taught the spells to ensure the growth of his children; and only when his own father is about to die instructed in the last special knowledge. In many societies, fully grown and married men often announce 'I am but a child' in recognition of the fact that acquisition of knowledge and the gradual assumption of responsibility is a gradual process and that full maturity may come only with middle age.

G. Bateson, *Naven*. Cambridge, 1936.
B. Blackwood, *Both Sides of Buka Passage*. Oxford, 1935.
H. I. Hogbin, 'A New Guinea Infancy', *Oceania*, vol. 13, 1942-3.
———— 'A New Guinea Childhood', *Oceania*, vol. 16, 1945-6.
———— *Kinship and Marriage in a New Guinea Village*. London, 1963.
B. Malinowski, *The Sexual Life of Savages in North-Western Melanesia*. London, 1929.
M. Mead, *Growing Up in New Guinea*. New York, 1930.
———— *Sex and Temperament in Three Primitive Societies*. London, 1935.
D. L. Oliver, *A Solomon Island Society*. Cambridge, Mass., 1955.
H. Powdermaker, *Life in Lesu*. London, 1933.
G. F. Vicedom and H. Tischner, *Die Mbowamb*, vol. 2, 3 vols. Hamburg, 1943-8.
C. Wedgwood, 'The Life of Children in Manam', *Oceania*, vol. 9, 1938-9.
J. W. M. Whiting, *Becoming a Kwoma*. New Haven, 1941.

A. CHOWNING

CHIMBU. People of the Chimbu District. References:
H. C. Brookfield and P. Brown, *Struggle for Land*. Melbourne, 1963.
P. Brown, 'Chimbu Tribes: Political Organization in the Eastern Highlands of New Guinea', *Southwestern Journal of Anthropology*, vol. 16, 1960.
———— 'Chimbu Death Payments', *Journal of the Royal Anthropological Institute*, vol. 91, 1961.
———— 'Non-agnates among the Patrilineal Chimbu', *Journal of the Polynesian Society*, vol. 71, 1962.
———— 'Anthropology and Geography', *Pacific Viewpoint*, vol. 3, 1962.
———— 'From Anarchy to Satrapy', *American Anthropologist*, vol. 65, 1963.
———— 'Enemies and Affines', *Ethnology*, vol. 3, 1964.
———— 'Marriage in Chimbu', in *Pigs, Pearlshells, and Women: Marriage in the New Guinea Highlands*, ed. R. M. Glasse and M. J. Meggitt. Englewood Cliffs, N.J., 1969.
———— 'Chimbu Transactions', *Man*, new series, vol. 5, 1970.
———— and H. C. Brookfield, 'Chimbu Land and Society', *Oceania*, vol. 30, 1959-60.
———— and G. Winefield, 'Some Demographic Measures Applied to Chimbu Census and Field Data', *Oceania*, vol. 35, 1964-5.
C. Criper, 'The Chimbu Open Electorate', in *The Papua-New Guinea Elections 1964*, ed. D. G. Bettison, C. A. Hughes and P. W. van der Veur. Canberra, 1965.
R. F. Salisbury, 'Despotism and Australian Administration in the New Guinea Highlands', *American Anthropologist*, vol. 66, Special Publication, 1964.

CHIMBU DISTRICT. In the deep, folded valleys and on the precipitous spurs and ranges of the 2,260 square miles of the Chimbu District live over 187,000 people, the highest population density of any of the eighteen administrative Districts of Papua and New Guinea. In terms of land area, only Manus District is smaller than Chimbu; by contrast, the largest of the Districts, Western, has an area of 37,700 square miles but a population of only 65,000. Indeed, the press of the expanding Chimbu population on land resources is becoming serious in some areas.

The Chimbu District extends southwards from the watershed along the Ramu-Wahgi divide to the downfall of the Tua River towards the Gulf of Papua across the New Guinea-Papua border. The most densely inhabited part of the District is the northern, above the junction of the Wahgi and Asaro and particularly in the valleys and on the valley walls and spurs of the Chimbu and Koro Rivers draining down from the Mt Wilhelm massif. On these valley walls and interfluvial spurs between the levels of 5,000 and 7,000 or more feet are great densities of population. Southwards, where the Wahgi and Asaro Rivers join to form the Tua, the population is much lower, possibly because of poorer soil resources but perhaps also because of other factors, including the incidence of malaria.

Climatological records in the District have not been taken for a sufficient length of time to provide reliable averages. It is probable that the average annual rainfall of such stations as Kundiawa and Kerowagi is about 100 inches with a maximum or several monthly maxima in the November-March season. Day temperatures at these stations may reach 80°F. but fall to 50°F. or less at night, and above the altitude of these stations day and night temperatures will both decrease. Above the high rain forest comes the moss forest and then the alpine grassland. In the latter, night temperatures may be low enough for ice to form at night on exposed water surfaces.

Throughout the District diurnal temperature differences are more significant than seasonal. It is an exaggeration, but not an unreasonable one, to say that at these altitudes 'there is summer every day and winter every night'.

Formally declared a District on 1 July 1966, Chimbu is wholly contained by the great central range system of mainland New Guinea. It is a fiercely beautiful District, steep and broken, inhabited by powerfully built, virile people. From 1951 to 1966, it was administered as a division of the Eastern Highlands District, but efficient administration of so large an area from one headquarters station at Goroka proved to be impossible and led to the splitting off of the western part of the Eastern Highlands and the establishment of the new Chimbu District, with headquarters at Kundiawa. There are five sub-districts: Kundiawa, Chuave, Kerowagi, Gumine and Gembogl, with a patrol post at Karimui and base camps at Sinasina, Kup and Nomane. There are almost 600 miles of vehicular roads in the District—most of them suitable only for four-wheel-drive traffic—and some 90 per cent of the District population is within a few hours drive of Kundiawa.

Although densely wooded centuries ago, much of the District is today grass covered, the forests having fallen under the intensive cultivation methods of a population so dense in places that

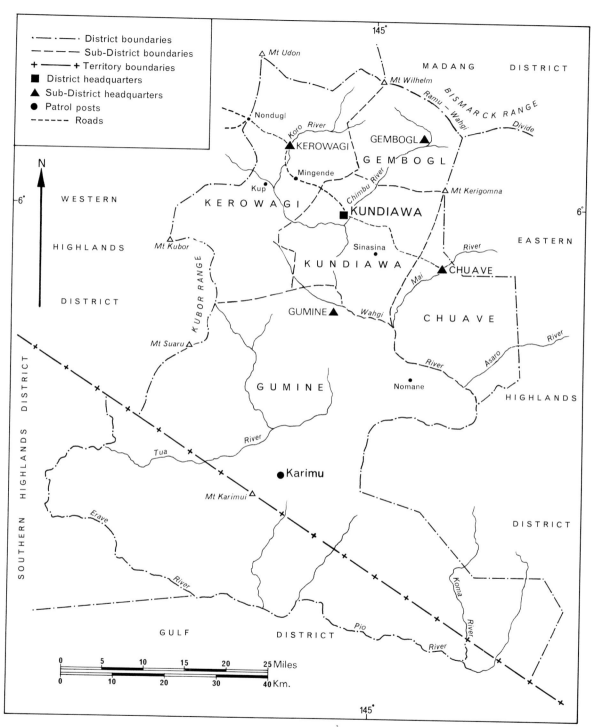

Chimbu District.

their gardens may be seen clinging to steep slopes that would be scorned as garden land in other parts of Papua New Guinea. This intense cultivation has also driven most of the fauna into the highest, least accessible country; the meat-hungry Chimbu will eat anything remotely edible, and the cassowary, wild pig, cuscus, tree kangaroo, snake and the iguana are today seldom seen throughout most of the District.

Like all the Highlands people, the Chimbu are predominantly subsistence farmers, growing many varieties of sweet potato as their staple food. Meat seldom appears in their diet, and then most usually at times of ceremony and festival, when the people gorge on the most preferred food, pork. It has been estimated that the pig population of the Chimbu is greater than the human. Hundreds, even thousands, of pigs will be slaughtered at necessarily rather infrequent times of great social significance.

The people of the Chimbu River valley gave the District its name. When the first explorers walked through this valley, they were greeted with cries of 'Chimbu!' by the painted, plume-decked warriors. 'The term *Chimbu* is actually the cheer of satisfaction, amazement or exhilaration', reported Assistant District Officer A. A. Roberts in 1935, 'it may be better described as the local Hurrah!'. The name has persisted to this day.

HISTORY

The origins of the Highlands people, including the Chimbu, are a mystery. Many theories have been developed by different authorities; some hold that the present-day Chimbu people have only been living in their high valleys for some three hundred years; other estimates vary widely. It has been suggested that the ancestors of the Chimbu were driven into this land from the west, from the Sepik, after repeated defeats in war. What does appear certain is that some previous race of people, about whom we know almost nothing, lived in the valleys of the Chimbu District long before the present tribal groups occupied them (*see* PREHISTORY). Implements of stone—pestles, mortars, axe-heads, clubs—have been found throughout the entire length of the Highlands, from the Arona Valley near Kainantu through to Mount Hagen and beyond. The Highlanders of today know nothing of these ancient stone objects, of their manufacture nor their origins. It is interesting to speculate on the uses to which pestles and mortars were put by those long-vanished stone-workers, for there were no major grain crops in the Highlands when the first explorers came. It has been suggested that they were used to grind dyes for decoration or adornment.

The recorded history of the Chimbu people began in 1933, for the Chimbu tribes and clans had no written languages and kept no records. They lived the traditional strife-filled life of the Highlander, completely remote from the world outside. When the first explorers walked through their land in 1933, the Chimbu tribes were as much astonished as any of the other Highlands people first contacted by this same expedition.

Lutheran mission parties and Administration patrols began probing into what is now the Eastern Highlands District as early as 1922; the prospector, Ned Rowlands, entered the Ramu headwaters in 1928 looking for gold, and found it on the Ornapinka River. This find had far reaching effects. Insignificant in itself, Rowlands' discovery was sufficient to interest the Edie Creek goldminers. They raised the sum of £302 and commissioned Michael J. Leahy and Michael Dwyer [qq.v.] to walk into the Upper Ramu and trace the source of Rowlands' gold. But Leahy and Dwyer commenced their search from Lihona Lutheran mission station, just 10 miles to the west of Rowlands' Ornapinka find. Instead of the Upper Ramu, they walked down the Dunantina, a tributary of the great Purari River system flowing to the south through the Central Range to the Gulf of Papua. Caught up in the Purari system, they walked right across the island, proving that the interior of the mainland, thought to be an empty waste of mountain, was in fact heavily populated.

Later that year the two prospectors explored the valleys of the Bena and the Asaro and in October 1932 Leahy was commissioned by Major Harrison, General Manager of the Wau-based New Guinea Goldfields Limited, to lead another prospecting party to the Bena. It was as a result of this 1932 expedition that the company and the Mandated Territory Administration decided to mount a joint patrol to the west to explore a huge grassed valley seen by the 1932 party, which we now know as the Wahgi.

Leahy, his brother Dan, and the company surveyor Ken Spinks made up the European personnel of the company party; the Administration was represented by J. L. Taylor [q.v.], Assistant District Officer, and a detachment of police.

This big expedition, the most significant ever made in Papua and New Guinea, left the newly established police post in the Bena on 28 March 1933. They were eighty-six strong, seven of the number being armed police. On Monday, 3 April, they reached the Chimbu River.

The expedition passed straight through the Chimbu to the Wahgi and further west. Only a small number of Chimbu District people were contacted, but they were friendly and brought in ample quantities of sweet potato to trade for steel and shell. The expedition established a base at Mt Hagen in the Western Highlands, and for some months explored from that base. In August, Taylor and Spinks walked back through the Wahgi and the Chimbu to the Bena camp to repatriate carriers. On this return visit, Taylor and his police were twice forced to open fire on attacking bands in protection of their carriers.

The twentieth century quickly overtook the people of the Chimbu District. The boundaries of the Morobe District were extended to the Sepik watershed to include the newly penetrated Highlands valleys. The Christian missions very soon showed their keen interest in the new lands in a practical manner. A party of Catholic priests of the Divine Word Mission (S.V.D.) led by Father Schaefer visited Kerowagi late in 1933 from the station at Bundi in Madang District. In February and March 1934 another S.V.D. party led by Father William Ross [q.v.] walked through the Chimbu and on to Mt Hagen; they chose a site for a station at Wilya, but returned to Mingende in the Chimbu, and built their first station there. Soon afterwards a station was established at Denglagu.

The Lutherans were the very first to approach the fringes of the Highlands and it was natural that they would early seek to establish stations there. A big Lutheran party, over one hundred strong, entered the Chimbu in 1934 and later that year the Revs W. Bergmann and Zimmerman founded the Lutheran station at Ega and built an airstrip there. By early March 1935, the Lutheran Junkers F13 aeroplane, 'Papua', was landing at Ega, and at the other three Lutheran stations that were by this date established in other parts of the Highlands. By the end of June 1935, the Lutherans and the Catholics were operating a total of ten stations manned by Europeans and seventy-four by local people between Kainantu and Mt Hagen.

In 1935 the Administration opened two base camps in the Chimbu, the principal one near the Ega aerodrome at the present site of Kundiawa, and the other at Goromei. 'The Chimbu Valley is in a state of constant inter-tribal warfare', says the Annual Report of the Mandated Territory for 1934-1935, 'and on two occasions during May, while the officer was absent on patrol, about 500 natives took part in spectacular fights within view of the Chimbu-Wahgi Post.'

The Administration was forced into the Chimbu Valley by the murder of two S.V.D. missionaries, Father Morschheuser and Brother Eugene, in December 1934 and January 1935, near Gogolme. Coming after the murder of Assistant District Officer Ian Mack near Kainantu in 1933, and of the prospector MacGrath, near Finintegu in 1934, the murder of the two missionaries spurred the Administration into establishing the Chimbu base camps, and led to the declaration of the Highlands as an 'Uncontrolled Area', closed to all Europeans except the armed patrols of the Administration, and to the prospectors and missionaries already on the scene, these latter under severe movement restrictions including the curtailment of the activities of the many small locally staffed mission posts.

After the death of the missionaries, order was restored in the Chimbu Valley by J. L. Taylor and A. A. Roberts, with some bloodshed. Daniel Leahy assisted in this work, as did Patrol Officer George Greathead. As the decade of the thirties drew to its end, patrols of the Administration visited most parts of the Chimbu District, gradually introducing the government's law and with some success bringing the warring tribes under a degree of control. Much of the work was directed by three notable officers: A.D.O. William Kyle and Patrol Officer Leigh Vial (both killed during World War II) and Patrol Officer Ian Downs.

The beginnings of the present road system were constructed during these years. By 1938 almost 20,000 of the Chimbu District people had been formally censused and brought under strong government influence. By 1940, the figure was in excess of 31,000. A number of important fight-leaders had been appointed *luluais* and were actively assisting the efforts of the officers in their respective tribal areas. Much remained to be done, but substantial progress had been achieved by the Administration and the missions when war broke out in the Pacific.

The war had little direct effect upon the people of the Chimbu. No Japanese land forces ever penetrated there, although there was some aerial activity. Probably the most significant effect was the evacuation of all the white missionaries and an inevitable lessening of Administration patrolling activity. Civil administration was restored in 1946 and in 1947 and 1952 the uncontrolled areas and lands alienation restrictions were relaxed under proper controls, permitting the rapid development which began shortly after and which has continued to the present day. The forties and fifties saw the establishment of most of the new mission and Administration stations of today, and the beginnings of cash cropping, local government and commercial development. As the new stations were set up the rate of patrolling increased until by the end of 1957 the whole of the Chimbu District had been brought under full government control.

CULTURE

The most important linguistic and cultural group in the District is the Kuman, the people of the Upper Wahgi, Chimbu and Koronigl Valleys who have given the District its name. Indeed, this is one of the largest language groups in all of Papua and New Guinea; some 120,000 people speak Kuman as their mother tongue. But it must not be thought that the Kuman were a peaceful, united people; fighting was their chief preoccupation.

They are divided into tribal groups, each consisting of clans and sub-clans who generally recognize a common tribal territory. Some of these tribes are large—over 4,000 people—and many of the clans, too, are of considerable size. Warfare between tribes occurred on a significant scale and there were often hostilities between clans and smaller groupings of the same tribe. The Kuman fought for reasons common among Highland cultures: individual and group prestige, 'pay-back', and in this densely populated country, for land. Most fighting was between individuals or small groups and sprang from the theft of women and pigs, from fear of sorcery, from disputes over the ownership of land and food-trees. The warriors fought with long spears, clubs, axes of stone and with the bow and arrow; the favourite tactic was ambush and stealth: there was no chivalry among the Kuman. Alliances of tribes and clans for a specific war-like purpose were common, but such alliances were seldom lasting: the allies of today could well become the enemies of tomorrow.

Traditionally, Kuman women occupied an inferior place in everyday life, and some of the characteristic Highlands male-female antagonism was evident. Marriage was invariably arranged (although the girl was allowed the refusal of her intended marriage partner) and was regarded as cementing relationships between groups. After marriage, the Kuman husband and wife lived with their male and female children respectively in separate households. The young wife was immediately involved in the hard physical labour in the family gardens that would be her lot until the end of her life.

Polygyny was practised extensively and divorce, with its property complications, perhaps involving the return of portion of the original bride-price payments, often resulted in clan warfare. Nowadays there are few plural marriages because of mission influence. Younger married couples are beginning to abandon the rigid male-female household separation of the past, and are setting up common domicile. The introduction of the rule of law, the cessation of organized tribal fighting and the impact of western civilization—and in particular its economic system—are having far-reaching effects upon the Kuman people. Money is now a most significant item, mostly replacing the fur, teeth, shell and plumage of the old ceremonial exchanges, although the pig has retained its importance to the people.

The process of change has undoubtedly been accelerated by the Highlands Labour Scheme, introduced by the Administration in 1949 to control and regulate the employment of Highlanders as plantation labourers on the coast. Many thousands of young Chimbu men have thus experienced life outside their crowded valleys, on their return bringing with them new concepts, new awareness. Even today between 1,500 and 2,000 Chimbu men leave the District each year under the protection of the Scheme. This experience of the outside world has had its effect in another way: because of land pressures many Chimbu people have left their homes for the urban settlements on the coast, in particular Lae and Port Moresby, where they settle in what are often squalid shanty settlements.

Like all the Highlands people, the Kuman and the other Chimbu tribal groups love to deck themselves with paint, shell, fur and plumes. The bird of paradise is particularly valued. Parties of Chimbu plume buyers have for many years travelled into neighbouring Districts, seeking the superb plumes that are used to such striking effect at times of festival and ceremony. So eagerly have these beautiful birds been hunted and trapped by the Chimbu people that it is only in the lightly populated Mt Karimui country that they survive in any great number.

AGRICULTURE

Sweet potato remains the staple food of the Chimbu people, and so efficient are they in its production, in fenced, drained gardens intensively prepared, that modern agricultural techniques have not been able to effect any worthwhile yield increase. Other important subsistence crops include yams, taro, bananas, sugar-cane, maize and a variety of beans and greens. Fine European-type vegetables are nowadays grown.

The cash economy of the District is almost totally dependent upon coffee, which makes it vulnerable to movements in the world market. In contrast to the Western and Eastern Highlands Districts, where there are large expatriate-owned coffee estates, virtually all the coffee of the Chimbu District is grown by the people, in village coffee groves. These are usually very small; it is estimated that some 10,000 acres are under 7 million coffee trees, worked by approximately 55,000 growers. The production of processed coffee in 1971 was in excess of 10 million pounds per year.

The marketing of coffee is extremely competitive. So many coffee buyers roam the Chimbu roads in four-wheel-drive vehicles that the competition ensures a fair price to the grower. Prices fluctuate widely, according to the state of the international coffee market; in 1971 prices paid to growers ranged from 17 to 24 cents or more per pound of parchment at the village (see COFFEE INDUSTRY).

There are four processing factories in the District, two of which are owned by the Chimbu Coffee Co-operative Ltd, the largest indigenously owned business enterprise in Papua and New Guinea, and the only co-operative society in the District. During 1970, the co-operative processed almost 2,600,000 pounds of coffee. Coffee buying is not controlled, and buyers from the Western and Eastern Highlands freely enter the Chimbu District, often with long-term forward contracts to satisfy, and usually offer the growers prices that the co-operative cannot match. This led to an erosion of the business position of the co-operative that assumed crisis proportions in 1970. Daily operations are controlled by a general manager who is answerable to a board of fourteen elected directors; as a result of the 1970 crisis an efficient and experienced expatriate has been appointed general manager, with increased powers and responsibilities, and it is hoped that the co-operative will now be in a position to attract an increasing percentage of District coffee production in future years.

A secondary cash crop of increasing importance is passionfruit. Annual production has varied, with a recent peak of 88,000 pounds, but with the planting of some 1,300,000 seedlings in 1969 and 1970 production is expected to increase. The entire crop is sold to Cottees and is processed at the modern factory at Goroka (see PASSIONFRUIT INDUSTRY).

Another cash crop of limited importance is pyrethrum (see PYRETHRUM INDUSTRY). Some 80 tons are produced each year in the high country where coffee does not thrive. A small quantity of tobacco is grown, and there is a possibility of further development in this field.

In the Western and Eastern Highlands cattle production is fast becoming significant. In these Districts there are enormous expanses of grassed valleys and rolling ridges, well suited to the grazing of cattle. The Chimbu, with its heavy population and very limited open land, is not so favoured although the people are keenly interested in raising cattle and officers of the Department of Agriculture, Stock and Fisheries are assisting them to establish small projects. Currently, Chimbu people own 600 head of cattle.

THE CHRISTIAN MISSIONS

We have seen that the Catholic and Lutheran missions were very early established in the Chimbu District, and mission influence in many spheres remains profound. There are presently forty mission stations in the District, of the following denominations: Catholic 17, Lutheran 9, Anglican 2, Seventh Day Adventist 5, New Tribes 2, Swiss Evangelical Brotherhood 3, Independent 2. Although many of these stations are small, they provide apart from religious guidance and instruction many essential services in the medical and infant welfare field, and particularly in education. Between them, the major missions operate thirty-nine primary schools with an enrolment of 5,600. By contrast, Administration schools educate a total of 3,700 pupils at the primary level. The Administration is ahead of the mission effort at the secondary and technical level: 343 pupils as against 178 educated by the missions.

The Highlands in general are lagging behind most of the coastal Districts in education, less than a third of the village children having access to schools. The Department of Education recognizes the problem and is striving to provide more. Insufficient teachers rather than finance is the limiting factor.

The Administration plans to establish a vocational centre near Kerowagi in 1972, and a secondary school at Chuave the following year. The Kerowagi High School was commenced in 1968 and should be completed in 1973.

LOCAL GOVERNMENT

There are seven Local Government Councils in the District, covering 95 per cent of the Chimbu population. In common with all Local Government Councils the Chimbu councils obtain their revenue from head tax—at rates set by each council—and from Administration special purposes grants. Tax rates vary according to the economic circumstances of particular areas; rates for adult males in 1971 were applied within the range $2 to $10. The total tax revenue raised by all councils in 1969-70 amounted to $265,172. Administration grants, plus loans, amounted to $171,271.

Council effort in past years was primarily devoted to the provision of rural social services in the fields of health and education, but more recently the trend has been to spend the bulk of council income on the construction and upgrading of roads and bridges upon which the economic life of the District depends. The following details of major expenditure by Chimbu councils in 1969-70 illustrate this trend:

Health	$36,739
Education	$39,946
Transport	$37,595
Roads and bridges	$137,556

This council involvement has been recognized by the Administration with annually increasing grants under the Rural Development programme.

To rationalize the operations of the councils on roads and bridges, the Chimbu Councils Services Unit has been formed, under an experienced expatriate manager, to carry out all building construction and maintenance work and operate a garage-cum-workshop for member Councils. The unit also operates a District ambulance and a duplicating service. Equipment available includes two heavy four-wheel-drive trucks, a D4 bulldozer, a grader and a front-end loader.

Chimbu councils are still dependent upon expatriate advisers for their efficient functioning, but they are each year accepting more responsibility and they are in the process acquiring new confidence. The lack of formal education of the big majority of the elected councillors is a major limiting factor. The councillors are looked upon by most of the Chimbu people as simply a replacement for the government-appointed *luluai* of pre-council days; few village people have as yet any true appreciation of the role of the councillor as the elected representative of the people rather than an agent of central government. But each year sees an improvement in the overall operations of the councils.

SOCIAL DEVELOPMENT

Welfare officers of the Department of Social Development and Home Affairs are now active in the District. A welfare training centre has been established and will be in operation in 1972. Women's clubs are functioning and endeavour to improve the status of women in this generally male-dominated society. An Administration radio station is to be established, working in local dialects as well as in English and Pidgin English [q.v.].

The Department of Business Development is fostering blanket-weaving as a cottage industry in the Chimbu. The wool must be imported from Australia; all efforts to establish a viable wool industry in Papua and New Guinea have been unsuccessful. Simple wooden looms are employed, and the colourful, beautifully woven blankets produced in many District centres and villages find a ready sale to tourists. Both men and women are engaged in the industry on a self-employed basis after a brief period of training by the department's officers.

HEALTH

The population has steadily increased over the past forty years. There is little doubt that the incessant tribal fighting of the old days resulted in many deaths; infant mortality, too, was high. With no medical services of any kind, the sick and wounded died.

Today, both the Administration and the missions provide health services, down to the village aid post level: no Chimbu need suffer without assistance. There is a base hospital at Kundiawa, and the District has access to the big, modern regional base hospital at Goroka, in the Eastern Highlands, where a full specialist staff is available. There are also four smaller hospitals, and ninety-four aid posts throughout the District, with supporting staff.

The medical problems of the Chimbu are common to all the Highlands Districts: injury—particularly neglected injury—infection, worm infestation, dysentery, respiratory ailments, child-birth complications, some leprosy, malaria and tuberculosis and, increasingly, venereal disease. Malaria, leprosy and tuberculosis [qq.v.] are being attacked by specialist units of the Department of Public Health, and maternal and infant welfare services have been extended throughout the District. The Chimbu Local Government Councils have assisted greatly in medical work by the provision of buildings, transport and money.

INDIVIDUAL LEADERS

The cultural pattern of traditional Chimbu life ensured that only those individuals of outstanding strength, skill and merit attained authority and standing in their communities. In the economic field the same factors seem to apply. In general, Melanesian society has produced few outstanding entrepreneurs. This is certainly true of the Chimbu, but the people are acquisitive and to an increasing degree economically motivated, and the business leaders of the future, usually store and commercial vehicle proprietors, and coffee producers on a larger than normal scale, are gradually coming to the fore. In the political arena, Chimbu politicians are becoming effective in the Territory's House of Assembly [q.v.].

Of all the Chimbu men of recent times, probably the late Kondom [q.v.] was the most outstanding. Forceful, intelligent and far-sighted, Kondom—who was killed in 1966 in a car accident—did more to advance his people than any other individual.

EXPATRIATE ACTIVITY

The majority of the Europeans in the Chimbu District belong to missions or the Administration. European commercial activity has always been severely limited by the acute pressure on available land, which has made it very difficult to establish any business or agricultural activity on a large scale. Most development has taken place in Kundiawa in small retail trading, garages and workshops, warehouses and bakeries.

Land pressures remain the most acute problem facing the District, and must increase with the steady growth of the population. The problem has been discussed for many years. A number of Chimbu have migrated to urban centres in other parts of the Territory, most of them unlikely ever to return, and Chimbu farmers with their families have taken up oil-palm blocks at Cape Hoskins in New Britain. The Karimui area of the District is very lightly populated, and it is expected that some of the surplus Chimbu population will eventually settle there. The Ramu grasslands of the Madang District, too, appear likely to absorb part of the Chimbu population overflow, provided the social and political problems can be overcome. Resettlement for many of the Chimbu appears to be certain in the years to come, for these vigorous people seem likely to continue to increase.

H. C. Brookfield and P. Brown, *Struggle for Land*. Melbourne, 1963.
R. M. Glasse and M. J. Meggitt (eds), *Pigs, Pearlshell and Women*. New Jersey, 1969.
M. J. Leahy and M. Crain, *The Land that Time Forgot*. London, 1937.
J. Nilles, 'Digging-sticks, spades, hoes, axes and adzes of the Kuman people in the Bismarck mountains of east-central New Guinea', *Anthropos*, vols 37-40, 1942-5.
———'Natives of the Bismarck mountains, New Guinea', *Oceania*, vol. 14, 1943-4; vol. 15, 1944-5.
———'The Kuman of the Chimbu region, central highlands, New Guinea', *Oceania*, vol. 21, 1950-1.
———'The Kuman people: a study of cultural change in a primitive society in the central highlands of New Guinea', *Oceania*, vol. 24, 1953-4, pp. 1-27, 119-31.
R. F. Salisbury, *From Stone to Steel*. Melbourne, 1962.
C. Simpson, *Adam in Plumes*. Sydney, 1961.
J. P. Sinclair, *The Highlanders*. Brisbane, 1971.
G. Souter, *New Guinea: The Last Unknown*. Sydney, 1963.
JAMES SINCLAIR

CHINESE. In 1966 there were 2,935 Chinese and part-Chinese living in the Territory of Papua and New Guinea. The Chinese were 9 per cent of the non-indigenous population of the Territory and 0.01 per cent of the total population. Before World War II, the Chinese constituted a far larger proportion of the non-indigenous population. Their importance in New Guinea is greater than the figures might suggest. Unlike the majority of the non-indigenous population, the Chinese are not expatriates who spend a relatively short period of their life in New Guinea without any intention of remaining permanently. With the exception of a handful of Australian Chinese, all the Chinese in the Territory regard it as their home where they wish to remain for the rest of their lives. The more established nature of the Chinese and part-Chinese community is evidenced by a ratio of 125 men to every 100 women which is below that for the rest of the non-indigenous population and, also, by the large proportion of Territory-born Chinese and part-Chinese. Over 80 per cent of them were born in the Territory and many are fourth-generation settlers.

BEFORE 1942

For several hundred years Chinese and other Asian traders and seafarers had visited the island of New Guinea. These visitors established no settlements and when, in 1884, both Britain and Germany annexed portions of the eastern half of the island, only a handful of Chinese were in the area. Until the late 1950s, Chinese settlement in the eastern half of the island was almost entirely confined to the former German Protectorate which Australia administered from 1914. In 1889 Papua (then British New Guinea) adopted legislation which, until the end of the century, prevented Chinese working on the goldfields. This discouraged Chinese immigration since gold was Papua's main economic attraction. In 1898, Papua adopted Queensland legislation restricting Chinese

Table 1

CHINESE POPULATION OF PAPUA AND NEW GUINEA 1947–66

Year	Papua				New Guinea			
	Chinese	Chinese–Europeans	Chinese–Indigenous	Total Non-Indigenous	Chinese	Chinese–Europeans	Chinese–Indigenous	Total Non-Indigenous
1947	5	26*	n.a.	3,239	1,769	274*	n.a.	6,200
1954	4	—	14	6,313	2,192	45	368	11,442
1961	24	13	13	9,794	2,295	242*	266	15,536
1966	273	18	9	14,377	2,182	56	397	20,292

* Accuracy of this figure is in doubt. It appears to include Chinese–Indigenous.
n.a. not available.

migration to the Territory, and this was supplemented by the application of the 'white Australia policy' when Australia took control of Papua in 1906. Although skilled Chinese tradesmen were admitted to Papua to work as indentured labourers for short periods after this, the numbers were very small. According to the 1954 Census there were only four Chinese, and a slightly larger number of part-Chinese, in Papua.

By contrast to the Papuan situation, the Germans in north-eastern New Guinea encouraged the immigration of Chinese and other non-Europeans. This was to provide labour for the plantations on the mainland of German New Guinea and later, when this ceased to be an economic proposition, to provide the skilled labour necessary for building and other tasks. In 1889 the Germans brought the first indentured Chinese labour to New Guinea and the importation of indentured labour continued until 1901. Before 1889, a small number of independent Chinese were established in New Guinea. Their numbers increased during the German administration so that by 1914 there were 1,377 Chinese in New Guinea—nearly half of the total non-indigenous population. Throughout the preceding years there had been an extensive turnover in the Chinese population with many departing for or arriving from China, sometimes by way of Singapore. This high turnover and the predominance of male immigrants was typical of Chinese migration; it was, essentially, economically motivated. By 1914, however, there were the beginnings of a stable community for a number of Chinese who ran small businesses and plantations and who had settled in New Guinea with their Chinese or indigenous wives.

In 1914 an Australian Expeditionary Force occupied the part of German New Guinea which now constitutes the Territory of New Guinea. The

Australian military administration of New Guinea which continued until 1921, generally followed what were thought to be the procedures and regulations of the German administration. One change made by the military administration, which was of significance to the Chinese, was the alteration of their legal status from non-indigenous natives to 'Europeans'.

The wartime disruption of shipping prevented Chinese entering and leaving the Territory and, to this extent, forced a degree of stabilization on the Chinese community, though a decline in the Chinese population of nearly 3,000 between 1921 and 1931 suggests that it was only partial. A major factor influencing the departure of Chinese was the introduction, by the Australian Administration, of restrictions on Chinese entry to the Territory which prevented the families of Chinese joining them permanently in New Guinea. From 1917 the military administration had restricted the entry of Chinese residents. The Australian civil administration which commenced in 1921 adopted the Australian immigration legislation and regulations which allowed only temporary entry of Chinese, and then under extremely restrictive conditions. The two main categories of Chinese allowed temporary admission were wives and children of existing residents (who, after ten years' separation from the husband, were allowed in for periods up to three years) and skilled tradesmen who were admitted under indentures for three years. Missionaries were another main category of Chinese allowed temporary entry. The increase in the numbers of Chinese after 1931 was a result of the increasing numbers of Chinese born in New Guinea and the arrival of wives and children entering the Territory for short visits.

The expressed purpose of the Australian Administration in adopting these measures was to discourage the settlement of Chinese in New Guinea. This policy, which was directly contradictory to that pursued by the Germans, had as its stated rationale the protection of indigenous interests. However, the additional economic measures which were adopted to discourage the Chinese appeared to be designed to protect the European settlers and companies from Chinese competition. Although, under the Germans, the Chinese had been unable to acquire freehold land for agriculture, they had been able to obtain thirty-year leases on small areas of 120 acres. Under the Australian Administration the Chinese were

Table 2

CHINESE POPULATION OF NEW GUINEA 1890–1940

Year	Chinese (including Chinese–Indigenous)	Chinese–European	Total Non-Indigenous
1890	114	—	548
1914	1,377	n.a.	2,708
1921	1,424	2	3,173
1931	1,179	n.a.	4,142
1933	1,449	—	5,216
1940	2,061	n.a.	6,498

n.a. not available.

unable to acquire agricultural land even on lease-hold. Chinese were not issued with professional recruiting licences until just before World War II, and an ordinance was introduced which prevented a trade store being licensed to operate within two miles of another store or of the boundaries of plantations—which often had their own European-run store. The legal basis for much of this discrimination against the Chinese lay in their permanent status as aliens. Foreign-born Chinese were ineligible for naturalization while those born in the Territory were required to adopt their father's Chinese nationality.

In 1914 nearly half the Chinese were employed as artisans, while labourers and businessmen each constituted 15 per cent of the male population and the remainder were planters (2 per cent), engineers, seamen, cooks and so on. Following the period of enforced stabilization, there had been by 1921 a large increase in the proportion of Chinese who were self-employed and who were in commercial (29 per cent) and agricultural activities (13 per cent). Figures are not available to show the extent to which the various restrictions instituted after 1921 altered the Chinese occupational patterns but the most likely effect was to increase the proportion employed as tradesmen such as builders, shipwrights and tailors.

Socially, the Chinese were a middle group distinct from both the Europeans and indigenes. Regarded as inferior by the Europeans they were required to live in separate 'Chinatowns' and to use separate hospitals and gaols. No schooling facilities were provided for the Chinese. Though the Chinese did not merge with the indigenous society, their contacts with the indigenes were probably far closer than either had with the Europeans. In the period between 1928 and 1940, nearly 25 per cent of Chinese men who married took indigenous wives, while the comparable figure for Europeans was less than 2 per cent. It was the relations of the Chinese with the indigenes, rather than the lack of European or Chinese women, which caused this greater rate of intermarriage. The Chinese and European groups also differed in their treatment of mixed-race children. Whereas the Chinese-indigenous child was reared by both his parents and became part of the Chinese community, it was far more usual for the rearing of the European-indigenous child to be left to his indigenous mother or the missions.

The social and economic disabilities experienced by the Chinese emphasized to them their group distinctiveness and the necessity of self-help if they were to improve their position in New Guinea. Thus the Chinese organized and supported their own schools for which they obtained Chinese and European teachers with the help of the Catholic and Methodist missions. In the absence of secondary schools, children could complete their education only when the family could afford to send them overseas. Most went to China though, in the 1930s, a few children were also sent to Australia.

With the outbreak of war in the Pacific, European women and children were evacuated from New Guinea. No provision was made for the evacuation of Chinese women and children and, when the Japanese invaded New Guinea, only a minority on the mainland managed to escape to Papua whence they were evacuated to Australia. The majority were placed by the Japanese in detention centres and were used as a source of labour. No exact figure for Chinese casualties is available, but in the Rabaul area 10 per cent died.

AFTER WORLD WAR II

In the immediate post-war period the Administration made few policy changes affecting the Chinese. One concession granted was that those Chinese who had been resident in New Guinea on temporary permits when the Japanese occupation took place were allowed to remain and were not repatriated to China. In 1951 the New Guinea-born Chinese were allowed to change their legal status from aliens to Australian Protected Persons. They could now vote, marry, and change their occupation and their place of residence without being required to notify the authorities. But this change in status was not accompanied by the removal of major economic and social discrimination. The Chinese after the war were allowed to acquire agricultural land, but as Chinese they were restricted in the area which they could own and were required to live and work on their plantations. Differential pay scales for Chinese and 'Asians' on the one hand and 'Europeans' on the other continued within the public and private sectors of the economy. Physical segregation also remained with separate 'Asiatic' hospitals, schools, residential and business areas and even prisons being provided for the Chinese and other Asians and for mixed-race people. From the mid-1950s these more overt forms of segregation of Chinese from Europeans were gradually eliminated as part of a general change in Territory race relations. The gradual improvement in the social standing of the Chinese vis-à-vis the European population is indicated by the increasing frequency of intermarriage.

In the post-war years, the Chinese family's economic and sentimental links with China and Hong Kong have been increasingly replaced by links with Australia. Although China, Hong Kong and, more recently, Singapore still attract visitors on holidays, few of the New Guinea Chinese would seriously consider living in these places. Contacts with Chinese in other places, such as West Irian, are extremely limited. Many of the young Chinese now receive part of their secondary and tertiary education in Australia. This has been an important influence in the change of Chinese attitudes and values, both in general and concerning Australia. Not all cultural changes are of recent origin. Before the war for example, many Chinese were Christians and now the majority are mainly Catholics, Methodists or Lutherans. Despite various cultural changes, Chinese is still spoken although the younger generation cannot read or write it. Cantonese is the lingua franca in New Guinea, where the major Chinese languages are Sze Yap and Hakka.

The legal status of the Chinese was altered significantly in 1957 by the decision that Chinese who had been born in New Guinea or had arrived by 1921 would be allowed to apply for Australian citizenship. Following this decision, citizenship was gradually extended to those Chinese who had entered the Territory on a temporary basis before the war and also to those of mixed race. The Chinese community had been campaigning for these alterations. However, probably of greater significance in causing the changes was the relaxation in 1956 of Australia's own laws concerning the immigration and naturalization of non-Europeans, and concern about the loyalty of the New Guinea Chinese. This concern over their loyalties was associated with the dispute between Indonesia and Holland over the possession of West New Guinea.

Australian citizenship has enabled the Chinese to bring their non-European wives and dependants to settle in the Territory. In addition it has allowed them to move freely to Australia and its various territories including Papua. With this change in legal status, legal and administrative discrimination against the Chinese was no longer practicable. The new Australian citizens were able to acquire land on the same basis as Europeans and were given equal pay. One example of concurrent change in the private sector was that Chinese were accepted as members of the New Guinea Planters' Association.

Before 1957 the largest Chinese community was in Rabaul, and Lae and Madang also had large populations of Chinese. Following the granting of Australian citizenship, large numbers of Chinese migrated from New Guinea into Papua. Port Moresby at first attracted many, but the coastal areas of Papua as well as the New Guinea Highlands, West New Britain and Bougainville are now attracting Chinese from the older centres. Economic reasons underlie this migration; the Chinese are seeking areas where there is greater scope than in the older centres for a trade store or general business.

Figures from the 1966 Census showed that approximately half the Chinese male workforce was involved in either the wholesale (10 per cent) or retail trade (40 per cent) where the majority owned their own businesses. Apart from commerce, agriculture (12 per cent), manufacturing (10 per cent) and construction (9 per cent) are the major industries employing Chinese. Except for a few individuals with professional training such as teachers, the public service has not attracted many Chinese. Previous experiences of discrimination have increased their preference to be self-employed rather than work for the Administration or European firms. In 1966 one-third of the Chinese men who worked were either employers or self-employed.

While the Chinese make up nearly 25 per cent of the non-indigenes in commerce and over 27 per cent of those in the retail trade their importance is increased by virtue of the large number who own their own businesses. The indigenes involved in commerce outnumber the non-indigenes by five to one, but the Chinese and European stores account for a volume of trade out of proportion to their numbers involved in commerce. The typical Chinese store is a 'trade' store catering for indigenous customers and carrying a wide range of stock from foodstuffs to textiles and hardware. The Chinese share of commerce is large but difficult to estimate with accuracy. Certainly virtually all the non-indigenous trade stores are Chinese owned. The exceptions would be plantation stores and the occasional trade store run by the large companies such as Steamships Trading Company Limited. The Chinese are concentrated in the town areas outside which there are many hundreds of indigenous-owned trade stores. Many of these latter have only a small volume of trade and are operated inefficiently.

Since World War II the concentration of Chinese in trade has increased and is now at a higher level than in 1921. Apart from the operation of discriminatory measures, the occupational choices of older Chinese were limited by lack of education; either they could not afford to go overseas for their education or it had been disrupted by the war. Limited capital also restricted the options available. The increasing indigenous participation in a money economy, and the growth of urban populations dependent on buying rather than producing their foodstuffs, has greatly increased the scope for retail businesses. Hard work, sometimes involving fourteen or more hours a day, has contributed to the success of the Chinese in running trade stores in New Guinea. But two other very important factors are the organization of the businesses and the methods used to obtain capital. Apart from indigenous assistants, most Chinese stores employ only members of the family. This keeps the overheads low since members of the family may not be paid for the overtime they work. Furthermore, family shareholders or partners may consent to a large proportion of the profits being put back into the business rather than being distributed. Many of these stores would be uneconomic if they had to replace family members with salaried employees. Another important factor associated with the Chinese concentration in business is the ability of the community to organize unsecured loans which provide members with capital to start or expand their businesses. Although some Chinese have become very wealthy there are some wage earners who find it a struggle to support and educate their families. Nevertheless, most of them have an income comparable to that of Europeans.

Whether the Chinese will continue their concentration in commerce is difficult to predict. A majority of the younger Chinese now obtain at least some of their secondary schooling in Australia. Because they have a better education than their parents and broader experiences at school and elsewhere, the long and often dull work in a trade store does not appeal to them. While some are turning to more specialized types of retailing, an increasing number are finding employment which utilizes their professional or skilled training. In addition to changes within the Chinese community, there are external forces which will influence Chinese participation in the retail trade. Many of the factors which attracted the Chinese to running trade stores, such as the relatively small amount of capital, and the limited formal education and knowledge of English which are necessary, make these stores the logical starting point for indigenes wishing to gain a greater share in commerce. This was recognized in February 1971 when the Administrator's Executive Council approved proposals which would allow preference to be given to indigenous applicants when issuing licences for new trade stores and other small businesses.

The relations between the Chinese and indigenous population are of great importance to future developments. These relations are highly complex and cannot be described as simply 'good' or 'bad'. Marriages between Chinese and indigenes are now uncommon. Apart from intermarriage, personal relations are hard to assess but there is no real evidence to suggest that Chinese generally 'get on' less well with indigenes than do Europeans. In developing countries the non-indigenous trade-store owner is often accused of exploitation. In the Territory an ordinance restricting the giving of credit to indigenes was designed to prevent such a situation. Since the major cash crops are harvestable for long periods of the year and only small numbers of Chinese are buying from producers, the incidence of exploitation is low. The main opportunity for exploitation in the Territory is plain overcharging. While cases do occur this practice is not confined to Chinese storekeepers, nor is it possible to make other than impressionistic comments about its incidence. However, the strong competition between Chinese storekeepers operates against overcharging. Hostility to storekeepers may often arise from an inadequate appreciation of their costs and overheads. Though of doubtful validity, a belief that exploitation occurs could, in the future, operate to the disadvantage of the Chinese in New Guinea.

In a period of increasing political activity the Chinese have remained relatively inactive. The various Chinese clubs which exist in the larger centres occasionally represent the community in dealings with the Administration but their main concerns are welfare and social activities for the Chinese and non-Chinese community. In Rabaul two Chinese trusts use the income from property they own to support several schools for Chinese and non-Chinese. More recently, a scholarship scheme was organized to pay the fees of over fifty indigenous children attending high school. The attaining of Australian citizenship and differences of opinion within the Chinese community have to date prevented the emergence of a 'Chinese' political party or strong pressure group. Their small numbers make many Chinese feel that, as Chinese, they are powerless to influence political developments. Some individuals have been active though, relative to the Europeans, their numbers have been small. At the 1968 House of Assembly elections a few Chinese and part-Chinese were candidates; of these, one part-Chinese was successful. More Chinese and part-Chinese have stood, and with some success, for the various multi-racial Local Government Councils. At present, the president of the Local Government Association is a part-Chinese. In other spheres of political activity a Chinese was campaign manager for a successful indigenous candidate and another Chinese organized the United Political Society.

Unlike many other non-indigenes, the Chinese wish to have a permanent future in the Territory which they regard as their home. Developments within the next few years will determine the feasibility of these hopes.

P. Biskup, 'Foreign coloured labour in German New Guinea', Journal of Pacific History, vol. 5, 1970; Commonwealth Bureau of Census and Statistics, Census of the Commonwealth of Australia, 1921-1961. Canberra (five yearly); Commonwealth of Australia, Report to the United Nations on the Territory of New Guinea. Canberra (annual); 'Interim and Final Report of Royal Commission on Late German New Guinea', Commonwealth Parliamentary Papers, vol. 3, 1920-1; C. D. Rowley, The Australians in German New Guinea 1914-1921. Melbourne, 1958, ch. 5; T. P. N. G. Bureau of Statistics, Population Census, 1966. Port Moresby; C. A. Valentine, 'Social Status, Political Power and Native Responses to European Influence in Oceania', Anthropological Forum, vol. 1, 1963.

CHRISTINE INGLIS

CHINNERY, Ernest William Pearson (1887-   ), administrator and anthropologist, was born 5 November 1887 at Waterloo, Victoria. He was educated at various Victorian schools and Christ's College, Cambridge. In 1909 he joined the Papuan service and as a magistrate served from 1911 until 1921, with a break for war service with the Australian Flying Corps. He then worked as adviser on labour to New Guinea Copper Mines, and later joined the Mandated Territory Public Service as government anthropologist, from 1932 being also Director of District Services and Native Affairs. In 1938 he became Director of Native Affairs in the Northern Territory and retired in 1946. He published a number of anthropological papers and reports on New Guinea.   FRANCIS WEST

CIVIL AVIATION. The early history of aviation in New Guinea is unique. The development of air cargo was so rapid that more freight was lifted by air in the small region Lae-Wau-Bulolo in the late 1920s and early 1930s than was flown by all the rest of the world's airlines combined. Even the U.S.S.R. and the U.S.A. could not challenge the New Guinea cargo airlift until the mid-1930s. The New Guinea experience was the first true demonstration of the value of the aeroplane in the service of man anywhere on earth.

The success achieved by the aviation pioneers in New Guinea before World War II was due largely to geography. The combination of jungle, rivers and mountains made it almost impossible, certainly impracticable, for the Administration to invest relatively enormous capital sums in the construction of roads to the goldfields area, though the goldfields were within a hundred miles of the coast. Had the economy of the interior been based on any other 'crop' but gold, the development of the highly sophisticated airlift would have been economically impossible.

The alternative to the 90 or 100 miles per hour aeroplane was the 800 yards per hour indigenous porter, who consumed a considerable proportion of his load in food to maintain his muscles, who was prey to disease and terrain, and who was unmarked by any deep enthusiasm for his task. In the New Guinea operation everything was flown to the goldfields—flour, people, iron roofing, tobacco, pianos, the first horses ever transported by air anywhere in the world, even entire 3,000-ton gold dredges.

The techniques evolved in this massive airlift were studied and followed in the development of air cargo transport throughout the world. They are known to have greatly influenced the German military organization of air transport for World War II. They did as much to prove to the world that the aeroplane was neither a toy nor a luxury as the pioneering long distance flights of Lindbergh and Kingsford Smith, with which they were contemporary.

The first recorded aviation connection with Papua New Guinea was a proposal made by Count Zeppelin and the Grand Duke of Hesse in 1913 for the employment of balloons and later zeppelin airships in the exploration and exploitation of the island. The Dutch, Germans and British were to be committed to the extent of 3 million marks. World War I ended the idea.

The first aircraft to reach the area were a BE2A from the Australian Army's Central Flying School at Point Cook and a Farman flying-boat previously owned by the Sydney businessman Lebbeus Hordern, which were sent with the Australian army and navy contingents which occupied German New Guinea in 1914. The pilots were Captain Eric Harrison, an Australian pioneer pilot with a European reputation and one of the first two instructors at Point Cook, and one of his pupils, a Melbourne doctor named G. P. Merz, who was the first Australian pilot killed in action in Mesopotamia in July 1915. Neither aircraft was actually flown and both were returned to Australia in the original crates.

In 1916 a Swedish scientist and pioneer aviator, Dr E. Mjoberg, requested permission to use aircraft for survey work, but Hubert Murray [q.v.] refused. The following year, Fathers Garin and Bourgade joined the French Air Force intending to apply their future flying skills to mission work in Papua. Garin was killed but Bourgade was the fourth-ranking French ace alive when war ended (twenty-six victories). He came to Yule Island in 1921 and died there in 1924, and his grave is always visited by French warships in the area. He never flew after the war, but he may have witnessed the first flight in Papua New Guinea.

Captain Frank Hurley, the Australian explorer and cameraman, brought an expedition to Yule Island in 1922 which employed aircraft in the exploration of parts of Papua, as he relates in *Pearls and Savages*. The first flight was made by a Curtiss Seagull seaplane of American manufacture at ten on the morning of 5 August 1922. The pilot flew for about half-an-hour over Port Moresby and the bay. The press referred to the aircraft as a 'seaboat' and described the utter astonishment of the indigenous population.

There is no doubt about the identity of the pilot who was Captain Andrew Lang, the first commander of No. 4 Squadron, Australian Flying Corps. Lang was later a wartime test pilot and was killed in 1924. Associated with him in this enterprise was a mechanic named Hill, and both were kept hard at work maintaining the aircraft under very primitive conditions. The expedition also included a number of Australian scientists, one being E. W. P. Chinnery [q.v.].

There is some doubt about the types of aircraft flown. Hurley refers to one Seagull and a Fleetwing seaplane (American) which Hordern had provided in 1921, but he also refers to two Seagulls, while the main photograph of the aircraft used by the expedition shows one Seagull and a Short Shrimp (British), a very rare type of which only three were built. The records of the Short firm prove that a Shrimp was sold to Australia and official Australian records show its loss in Rose Bay later. Presumably all three types, perhaps all four machines, were used.

Hurley recognized the danger inherent in being first into the Papua area where turbulent atmospheric conditions and extreme humidity, with great weather build-ups through the day, were a constant menace to operational capability and to life. Forced landings at any distance from Port Moresby must have meant death by natural forces or at indigenous hands. However, the Seagull was flown over the delta country and up the Fly River, at one stage being based at Daru.

The first flight made from the Australian mainland to Papua New Guinea was captained by the Chief of the Air Staff, Royal Australian Air Force, Group Captain (later Air Marshal Sir) Richard Williams, the first Australian-trained pilot. He was accompanied by co-pilot Flight Lieutenant I. E. McIntyre and an engineer, Flight Sergeant L. J. Trist, who was to have a notable career in Papua New Guinea. They used a DH50A powered by a 250 horsepower Siddeley Puma engine because, being of low compression, it could use the ordinary automobile fuel available in the islands. Leaving Point Cook on 25 September 1926, they flew to Thursday Island (where the flight was almost abandoned when busybodies in Parliament and in the press claimed there was too much danger) and thence to Daru, Yule Island, Port Moresby, Samarai, Morobe, Lindenhafen, Rabaul (engine overhaul), Nissan, Kieta, Shortlands, Gizo and Tulagi.

The R.A.A.F. men spent nineteen days at Tulagi replacing the engine and then flew home to reach Point Cook on 7 December, the flight recording 127 flying hours. This flight has never received the credit due to it, for it was one of the first long distance flights which demonstrated that aircraft could be used for any distance. The intent of the flight was not for records but for study of the meteorological and flying conditions, and the siting of water and land aerodromes for future

R.A.A.F. and civil needs. McIntyre was killed soon afterwards. Almost exactly a year later Squadron Leader (later Air Vice-Marshal) E. C. Wackett led two Supermarine Seagulls (not related to the 1922 aircraft) on a similar type of flight which included Lae.

While Williams was organizing and actually flying, the civil aviation story of Papua New Guinea began, and the credit must go to C. J. Levien [q.v.], a former District officer, who was one of the main personalities connected with the discovery and opening of the Morobe goldfields in the mid-1920s. Levien saw that the only solution to the problem of transport was the aeroplane, though he was rather over-optimistic in believing that a Lae-Wau service could prosper at a rate of twopence per pound.

About the same time, late 1926, Charles Kingsford Smith and two associates (Hitchcock and Anderson) had arrived in Sydney from Western Australia, where Smith had been one of the original pilots flying the first Australian airline service for West Australia Airways from December 1922. Smith brought over two Bristol Tourers, for which he sought adequate occupation, and when Burns Philp & Co. Ltd suggested they might be well used in New Guinea he inspected maps and photographs and geographical information about the area. His quick decision was that it could not be done, for the country was too bad for regular services with available aircraft. He then used the Tourers for his round-Australia flight that led to the trans-Pacific pioneer flight. No Australian operator was interested; Qantas was flying regular services in Queensland and pioneer services were operating between Adelaide and Sydney. Larkin was in fact approached by Levien who was told that at least £10,500 would be needed to start a service into the goldfields.

In November 1926 the Morobe District Miners' Association cabled the Australian Prime Minister (S. M., later Lord, Bruce) in London a number of grievances and asked for an inquiry at government level. The cable included the information that there were 150 miners and 2,500 indigenous labourers in the goldfields area.

Levien was a director with the largest of the Australian-based mining companies, Guinea Gold No Liability of Adelaide. He was not the only party with aircraft in mind to solve the transport problem of getting materials and men from the coast to the mountain goldfields, but he was the main figure. The discoverer of Edie Creek, W. G. Royal, together with R. L. Clark, both directors of Bulolo Exploration Co. Ltd, had ideas for the operation of two amphibious aircraft, a proposal which in the long run might have been best. Levien contacted them to discuss the whole idea of aviation and used their enthusiasm to force his own idea through with his own board in Adelaide. The company asked that a landing ground be prepared at Salamaua where there were then only two houses, but that airfield was not built until 1929, though A.W.A. installed radio communications there in 1927.

The first aircraft bought for the New Guinea operations was a DH37 previously owned by the Civil Aviation Branch of the Department of Defence, which two New Guinea identities, Holdgate and McKenzie both later associated with Guinea Gold, bought without having the capital to operate it. They made offers to several pilots: to a nineteen-year-old named Arthur Affleck they offered £1,500 a year and all living expenses, but he just did not believe them. They contacted an R.A.A.F. officer, E. A. Mustard (who later dropped the final d), without success, but six months later when he was instructing as a civil employee at Essendon they were more successful. The DH37 biplane was powered by a 275 horse-power Rolls-Royce Falcon and boasted a cockpit capable of taking two passengers, as well as the usual pilot cockpit. It was the first aircraft to be given a VH (Australian) registration number, and the first to fly on civil operations in Papua New Guinea.

Mustar was a fine pilot with a first-class record in war and peace; he had won a Distinguished Flying Cross with No. 1 Squadron in Palestine. On attachment to R.A.N. ships he had helped to site areas for future airfields in Papua New Guinea and Queensland in 1925. Most important, he also had some idea of administration which his main rival-to-be quite lacked. He was assisted by a very able engineer, also a wartime product, who was specially released by the civil aviation authorities to join him, A. W. D. Mullins.

The operation began as Guinea Gold Air Services until it was realized that the country's law

E. A. Mustar.

did not permit such an operation by a 'no liability' company. Guinea Gold then registered a subsidiary in Adelaide, Guinea Airways Ltd, or G.A.L., which took over the aircraft, stores, spares and ground equipment. Of the 20,000 £1 shares, 10,100 were allotted to the parent company.

Meanwhile, another Australian air force pilot had been thinking that New Guinea offered opportunities. Ray Parer had won the Air Force Cross, had attracted some attention in the England-Australia 'race' of 1919 by starting too late to win anything and then taking seven months to reach Australia after much bad luck and near-disaster, and had spent the post-war period largely in barnstorming. In a sugar farmer from Queensland named Gallet he found the backer he needed, and they floated the Bulolo Goldfields Aeroplane Service. The Commonwealth refused any aid in the form of aircraft, so they had to buy a DH4 from the Larkin airline. Powered by a 375 horsepower Rolls-Royce Eagle, the DH4 was a wartime veteran, not a post-war civil design as the DH37. F. S. Briggs had made the first flight across Australia to Perth in one, and Lindbergh had flown others with the ill-fated U.S. airmail operated by the U.S. Army Signal Corps. It was a poor aircraft for the job, there was no engineering backing for the enterprise, and while Parer was a pilot who would take any risk, he was not an organizer.

The two organizations competed to be first into Lae. Aircraft had to be shipped to Rabaul and then flown to Lae after assembly. Parer could not at first raise money to get his DH4 on the ship which took the DH37, and when finance was available the ship was in Townsville loading sixty donkeys to cover the available deck space. The DH37, though in the original manufacturer's case, was almost wrecked in a cyclone.

On the same ship was W. J. Duncan, a civil aviation officer sent to watch the start of operations. He stayed less than six months and a permanent successor was not appointed for seven years in spite of the great development of aviation. Duncan was no desk man; he walked over the jungle trails to locate the routes over which the aircraft would fly. Later he returned to start a local air service in Rabaul.

When the ship arrived at Rabaul on 15 February 1927 pieces of the DH37 were passed ashore along a line of natives but, as Mustar watched, the case on deck collapsed around the fuselage. He was a lucky man.

Mustar solved the airstrip problem when he found the local gaol officer was an old wartime friend, who ordered the prisoners to level a stretch of ground at Matupi. Mustar and Duncan went to Salamaua by ship and thence to Lae to arrange affairs there. On 30 March Mustar and Mullins flew to Lae—four hundred miles of single-engined flying, mostly over the sea, with no other aircraft in the area to search for them. He picked up the Lae strip by a big tree on a hill that was known for years as the pilot identification. When they landed, Mullins said he had given himself up for dead three hours ago.

The arrangements were primitive. Fuel was tossed ashore from ships in forty-five gallon drums and guided to the beach by natives. Levien could not meet the DH37 because he was under the shadow of a murder charge at Wau; later he went to Rabaul, where he was acquitted.

Mustar made the first operational flight to Wau with Holdgate and Mullins on 17 April, but in two attempts the experienced Holdgate was unable to guide the pilot to the landing place. Mustar tried next day with a miner named Taylor who was instantly successful.

There were no aids to navigation, air-to-ground radio was not yet developed, no ground lighting systems, just a levelled area to land on. The mountainous jungle was a death-trap from wild natives and natural hazards. The Lae-Wau flight took only fifty minutes, but it was a lonely time for the pilot. Mustar was very glad when Parer arrived, for this meant quick aid in trouble. Yet conditions on the ground were such that for many months Mustar was happiest and more free of worry when actually flying.

The DH37's three seats located the pilot at the rear and he communicated with male passengers by kicking their bottoms and with female customers by slapping the fuselage. All three heads were open to the winds. By modern standards the single engine was anything but reliable.

To dissuade traffic to Wau rates were originally set at £33 8s 4d per passenger and 1s 6d per pound for cargo, while the trip back to Lae was priced at £10. Everybody wanted to get to Wau. The service settled down to lift rice by the ton, food, pipes for the mine sluices, hydraulic equipment, and the obvious necessities and amenities for the European population. The DH37 transformed life on the goldfields.

While Mustar fretted that the one aircraft could not handle the Lae-Wau traffic, Parer was in bad luck as usual. The DH4 got to Rabaul without cyclonic or other troubles but crashed on the test flight. Gallet broke his collarbone in the first air crash in New Guinea, a dubious distinction. Parer had no engineering assistance, but managed with help from a Japanese shipwright, Gallet and a local identity Lexius Burlington, generally known as Burlington Bertie, whom in gratitude he took on the flight to Lae on 23 June. Parer now settled down to a successful period with all the work he could handle. He later introduced a DH9, with an engineer named Moss who soon died of blackwater fever, as by then the DH4 was largely unserviceable. He and Charles Pratt made the two first flights between Port Moresby and the goldfields on 12 January 1928. He later ran an operation with the name Morlae Airlines and introduced a Fokker F VII. In 1930 he found another backer to start Pacific Air Transport, but he was never formidable opposition for Guinea Airways.

Within months of the inauguration of Lae-Wau operations a Melbourne merchant named Nott backed P. H. (Skip) Moody (who had wanted to fly the Tasman) to form Airgold with a Ryan monoplane. Trist, who left the air force to join Moody as engineer, also flew as a pilot and ended his career in a fatal crash flying for Guinea Airways. Nott lost £20,000 in this venture, partly because he allowed himself to be talked into buying unsuitable aircraft, Farmans, and Avros, against Moody's wishes. Moody wanted a DH50, a very suitable aeroplane. There was big money to be made; in thirty-five days Moody earned £3,000 at 1s per pound.

The real basis of the New Guinea operation was Guinea Airways. The Edie Creek goldfields organization tried to get into aviation late in 1927 with an Avro 504K, and Royal brought up a great pilot in Jerry Pentland to fly a DH60 and a DH Moth as Mandated Territory Airways from February 1928. A pilot named Shortee started a one-aircraft operation at Salamaua.

Like Parer, all these people made money because of the number of Guinea Airways aircraft which went unserviceable; they were plagued by this unserviceability for years, though they always had a good engineering organization. Sometimes only one aircraft would be flying out of five or six. Pilots and engineers were hired from Australia, including Alan Cross, who was to succeed Mustar as manager, and I. H. Grabowsky, who also became manager.

It was the introduction of the right type of aircraft which established Guinea Airways and proved Mustar's quality. He had read of the Junkers family of all-metal, stressed aircraft, which were unequalled. They were developed in Germany and Sweden regardless of the Versailles Peace Treaty and designed for massive airlift operations. It took a great deal of courage to defy popular prejudice against Germany, but Mustar went there in September 1927 and bought a W34 at the then very high price of £8,000. It could lift a ton. The American and British aircraft industries refused to help him with alternative designs.

By the end of 1928, Guinea Airways had two

I. H. Grabowsky.

W34s operating in a service unequalled anywhere in the world. The W34 had a useful load greater than its own empty weight, and cruised at 100 miles per hour. In 1928, though only one Junkers was flying from April until the end of December, more tonnage was lifted in New Guinea (by the various operators) than by all the established Australian airlines, and the latter enjoyed £66,475 subsidy while not a penny was paid in New Guinea. Australian airlines were subsidized until World War II, while New Guinea operators not only were not subsidized, but had to pay for many tasks which the Commonwealth covered in Australia. The New Guinea success was due to the absence of any competitive transport system, there being available maximum payloads from firms and persons who had the maximum ability to pay—a situation possibly unique in the world. Guinea Airways reaped the harvest because it was the only aviation firm with adequate capital backing and was run by men who had vision as well as operational ability. No real control was exercised over these operations until May 1930, when the Administrator was empowered to exercise certain powers under the Commonwealth Air Navigation Regulations, but there were no trained staff provided to police them.

The Bulolo goldfields prospered only because there was an air service network, but for large-scale development dredges were required. Mustar was ill in 1929 and joined Vacuum Oil Company in Australia until Placer Development Company, a large mining concern with international operations, became active in the Bulolo Valley. Mustar was brought back to provide air support with the then fantastic idea of flying 3,000-ton dredges piecemeal into the goldfields. Nothing like this had ever been attempted. Mustar was laughed at by the American and British aircraft manufacturers, but Junkers had the G31, costing £30,000 with three engines and a capacity of 3 tons. The Placer executives could not believe it when Mustar returned; by late 1930 Junkers and Mustar won. Cross, who was managing Guinea Airways, was sent to Germany to buy a G31 and within months of the first G31 operation to Bulolo on 31 March 1931, Bulolo Gold Dredging (a Placer subsidiary) had two G31s in service, actually flown and maintained by Guinea Airways under contract. The opposition was dumbfounded on 27 November 1931 when the G31, overloaded to 6,870 pounds payload, flew a 12-foot-long tumbler-shaft weighing nearly 3½ tons into Bulolo. Grabowsky, the pilot, had sixty minutes' fuel for the forty-five minute flight.

The ambivalent attitude of the Guinea Gold directors to aviation allowed the smaller operators in Papua New Guinea to depress the rates for cargo. Guinea Airways was not allowed to fight the issue properly and the smaller airlines forced rates down to a few pence per pound. Cross and others wanted to create a New Guinea monopoly, not because this would make more money for the Adelaide parent firm but because it would allow adequate development and provide a massive airlift for the goldfields. Constant attempts to get the

Loading a Guinea Airways' three-engined Junkers in the early 1930s.

Administration to build roads provided the main political conflict for the industry.

Yet the smaller operators did provide good services. Holden brought in a Canberra DH61 in 1931, and after he died (and Guinea Airways bought 51 per cent of his company's shares) Ford monoplanes were introduced.

There were many highlights such as Moody's first commercial flight from Australia to Rabaul in a DH80 Puss Moth seaplane in October 1931. Bond flew a bullock waggon from Sydney to New Guinea in a Junkers. The first horses to be flown as cargo anywhere in the world were three Suffolk Punch medium draught-horses a G31 took from the coast to Wau for £35 each on 23 September 1933. In 1934 Lae and Wau were the world's busiest airports. On 12 April 1934 Sid Marshall made the first non-stop New Guinea–Australia flight, from Port Moresby to Cooktown in his Westland Widgeon carrying, much against his will, 400 letters. Guinea Airways was the first airline in the world to provide free insurance for passengers—only for Europeans and up to £500. From 1934, it was probably the first to provide what are now known as commodity rates for certain types of cargo.

Problems included the Administration's decision (2 July 1930) to impose a 10 per cent duty on all machinery including aircraft. This was bitterly fought by the airlines, which rightly claimed that without them the goldfields could not create the wealth for the Administration to tax. Guinea Airways estimated that in the mid-1930s the aviation industry provided £250,000 a year for the Administration, but the tax remained.

Though New Guinea was a world leader in aviation, the Commonwealth provided no civil aviation controllers until 1934. In July 1930 J. A. Collopy inspected the country for the Department of Defence, which still controlled Australian civil aviation, but he did not remain. Guinea Airways had a system of 'smoke boys', indigenous personnel who lit fires when they saw an aircraft nearing an airfield. Later, the same boys became control officers at each end of airstrips, Guinea Airways providing a board with a metal handle to show white or green. The Department's first permanent officer, Max Allen, arrived at Salamaua in 1934, and had to secure quick permission from Melbourne to ignore Australian standards or the whole operation would have stopped. This attitude prevailed, sensibly, until the 1950s. It even allowed the transport of indigenous people in aircraft without seats until a disastrous crash near Port Moresby in 1948. In the 1930s, natives were carried at so much a pound, not at a rate per person. On one occasion, a Guinea Airways' G31 was loaded with fifty-four bush natives and four Europeans.

The commercial aspects went ahead in spite of

official attitudes. From 1932 Guinea Airways operated a service for passengers between Port Moresby and the goldfields with a six-seat Junkers F13. There was long trouble over mails: the airlines carried local airmail free until the Administration stepped in. Miners would simply hand packages of gold to pilots, with no receipt and just a verbal indication of destination. In July 1934 Charles Ulm and G. U. (Scotty) Allan flew the first mail from Melbourne (24 July) to Lae (27 July) in *Faith In Australia*, and were appalled to find themselves coming out of clouds with mountains above them. They at once recognized the grim law of Papua New Guinea flying, which still holds, 'No see—no fly'. They brought 28,000 letters up and took 19,300 back, but the Government did not grasp the opportunity of starting a regular service between Australia and Port Moresby and Lae.

A significant entry into aviation came in January 1933, when W. R. Carpenter & Co. Ltd decided it would be cheaper to fly its own goods and brought in two DH83 Fox Moths, which carried 500 pounds each. In August 1934 the firm bought a DH84 Dragon, an able biplane which allowed rates to be cut on the Port Moresby-goldfields run.

In January 1936 the Australian government at last called for tenders for a weekly service between Sydney and Salamaua or Rabaul, and W. R. Carpenter & Co. Ltd was the successful tenderer. The service to Rabaul began on 30 May 1938, with a subsidy of £12,115 a year, and operated until war stopped it on 13 February 1942. It was temporarily restored as far as Port Moresby in February and March 1943, but Carpenter never again resumed the service.

When war began in 1939, Guinea Airways was operating two Ford AT5s, two Ford AT4s, four Junkers G31s, and twelve other aircraft. Other operators in Papua New Guinea had fleets totalling twenty-three aircraft of less total payload in all than the Guinea Airways fleet. Freight rates had gradually gone down to twopence per pound because of this competition. Guinea Airways might have won its case for monopoly, but in the late 1930s international affairs preoccupied the Australian Federal Cabinet. In retrospect, the very low rate was probably beneficial, regardless of the other possible benefits of monopoly.

Internal airmail contracts were held by Guinea Airways, Holden's Air Transport, W. R. Carpenter & Co. Ltd, Parer's Pacific Air Transport, Mandated Airlines and Stephens Aviation at various periods between 1933 and 1939, but in 1939 the main contracts were held by Guinea Airways and Mandated Airlines.

Other civil operations had been progressing meanwhile. The Lutheran missionaries began the story of mission aviation in February 1934 when they introduced a Junkers F13, flown by a German named Loose who had disagreed with the Nazis. This Junkers made 135 flights in the first four months, but it was obviously underpowered with its 280 horsepower engine. The mission based it at Finschhafen and cleared other strips inland.

The Roman Catholic mission began flying at Alexishafen about the same time with a smaller Klemm 25.

An interesting sidelight in June 1928 was the arrival of a Fairchild floatplane with a scientific party. Flown by an American, Richard Peck, and co-operating with a ketch, the aircraft worked in the Fly River area and was the first aeroplane to visit Madang.

In 1935 Stuart Campbell, representing H. Heming and Partners of London, flew two DH Dragons for a survey of all the goldmining areas and then contracted to make aerial maps for Guinea Airways, using one of their W34s flown by A. A. Koch. The mosaics he made were probably the first made anywhere, and certainly the first in Australasia. Campbell subsequently flew a Short Scion from Sydney to Lae for Hemings, an experience which he described as 'cruel' because of the unsuitability of the aircraft.

The old days ended on 21 January 1942, when the Japanese mounted a massive raid on Salamaua, Bulolo and Lae. They destroyed twenty aircraft and most of the hangars. Civil flying was ended, except for the evacuation of civilians from the war areas.

Guinea Airways had already formed a big operation in Australia, pioneering the route from Adelaide north through Alice Springs to Darwin, using the very modern American Lockheed Electra airliners. When Lae was bombed the organization retreated to Adelaide, hoping to return to New Guinea when the war ended, but this was not permitted by the Labor government of the day.

Qantas had developed fast in the late 1930s and in partnership with Imperial Airways was operating an Empire Airmail Service to London, as well as a big network in Queensland. In 1944 Qantas bought out the Carpenter aviation interests, which allowed it to start a weekly service to Lae on 2 April 1945, mail being subsidized on a pound-a-mile basis. Rabaul was included from 15 January 1947.

The war gave Qantas its opportunity to consolidate within Papua New Guinea. In April 1942 Father Glover, a mission pilot who had been evacuating people from the Mount Hagen area, went to Melbourne to seek government help. Qantas was ordered in and two DH86 four-engined airliners were used to evacuate the Hagen area. Qantas also operated for the military to Port Moresby, provided a considerable troop transport capability, and attracted world-wide attention with their 'bully beef bombers'. These were Lodestars which dropped supplies to troops in New Guinea right in the fighting zones. Qantas also operated Empire flying-boats into Port Moresby and in general played a big part in supplying the whole New Guinea war zone.

Guinea Airways was a victim of post-war politics, but Qantas quickly developed a fine network of services within and to Papua New Guinea. It was nationalized when the Commonwealth took over all shares in the company, and the area was used partly as a training ground for Qantas captains; flying in command of smaller aircraft in Papua New Guinea was fine training for mainline captains. Qantas was finally restricted to overseas operations and the government domestic airline, Trans-Australia Airlines, took over the network.

With the Japanese raid of 1942 a great chapter in world aviation history ended. The pioneers had to take aircraft of very marginal safety standards into tiny jungle and mountain clearings which were hardly airstrips at all, often uphill on landing, downhill taking-off. During take-off, natives would be holding the wings while the engines revved up, to allow the pilot something like full power to get off. The early Junkers had a bad tendency to sway when landing and the first aircraft with brakes of any sort were the G31s. Pilots were nervous during their first flights in the 1920s and early 1930s, and had to evolve special techniques.

Mustar served as a group captain in the wartime R.A.A.F. and was officer-in-charge of Airmen's Records at the Department of Air after the war. He now lives in Melbourne. Parer took part in the MacRobertson Air Race to Melbourne in 1934 but his habitual bad luck, though it did not force him out of the race, kept him weeks later than other competitors. He then took the Fairey Fox up to New Guinea, and just before the war bought a Boeing freighter which crashed in October 1939. He died in Queensland on 4 July 1967.

AIRCRAFT AND PERSONNEL IN NEW GUINEA, JULY 1935

Lae

Guinea Airways Ltd: 2 DH Fox Moths, 1 Ford AT5, 2 Junkers W34s, 1 Junkers G31, 2 DH61s being assembled, 1 Junkers F13 and 2 DH Moths all unserviceable.

Bulolo Gold Dredging Ltd: 2 Junkers G31s, 1 Junkers G31 unserviceable (all flown and serviced by Guinea Airways Ltd). Manager: I. H. Grabowsky; pilots 11, engineers 23.

Private Owner: S. D. Marshall, Westland Widgeon. (Marshall was working for Guinea Airways Ltd as an engineer.)

Wau

Pacific Aerial Transport Co.: 1 Junkers W33, 1 DH Moth, 1 Fairey 111F, 1 Simmonds Spartan, 1 DH Moth and 1 Fokker FV11 both unserviceable. Manager: K. F. Parer; pilots 3 (including Ray Parer), engineers 4.

Salamaua Aerial Services: 1 Avro Avian unserviceable. Pilot-engineer 1.

Salamaua

Holden's Air Transport Services: 1 Waco 10T, 1 Avro Avian, 2 DH50As. Manager: T. F. O'Dea; pilots 5 (including O'Dea), engineers 6.

W. R. Carpenter & Co. Ltd: 1 Fox Moth, 2 Dragons. Pilots 2, engineers 2.

Malahang

Lutheran mission: 1 Junkers F13. Pilot: Fritz Loose, engineer 1.

Sek

Roman Catholic mission: 1 Klemm Swallow L25. Pilot 1.

GUINEA AIRWAYS LTD

	Tons	Passengers	Revenue £ Gross
1928–9	434	869	44,006
1929–30	949	2,047	72,756
1930–1	1,146	1,995	67,922
1931–2	3,947	1,607	95,619
1932–3	3,980	3,856	77,695
1933–4	6,044	7,398	111,203
1934–5	6,102	9,721	114,465
1935–6	6,476	12,137	137,729
1936–7	6,705	11,869	96,134
1937–8	8,408	12,120	92,541
1938–9	8,804	11,626	102,576

NOTE: In this period the per-pound cargo rate was reduced from 10.61 pence in 1928–9 to 4.31 pence in 1932–3, and to 1.94 pence in 1937–8, and rose to 2.07 pence in 1938–9.

ALL OPERATORS IN PAPUA NEW GUINEA

	Tons	Passengers
1930	1,343	2,390
1931	2,987	3,278
1932	3,930	4,904
1933	6,059	8,923
1934	7,769	12,647
1935	8,479	15,930
1935–6	9,769	15,943
1936–7	10,912	11,718
1937–8	11,417	12,247
1938–9	12,082	12,909
1939–40	10,491	15,433
1940–1	8,864	12,995

A *History of Aviation in New Guinea* by James Sinclair had not been published when this article was completed. There is no other complete reference work, but the veteran Guinea Airways pilot and manager, I. H. Grabowsky, while employed by the Department of Civil Aviation for the purpose in the late 1960s, wrote a quarry of historical data on aviation in Papua New Guinea in 1927-8 and 1930-5. Some two thousand pages of foolscap typescript are available to the approved student.

A. H. Affleck, *The Wandering Years*. Melbourne, 1964.
E. B. Bremner, *Frontline Airline*. Sydney, 1944.
S. Brogden, *The History of Australian Aviation*. Melbourne, 1960.
F. Clune, *D'Air Devil*. Sydney, 1942.
E. H. Fysh, *Qantas At War*. Sydney, 1968.
———— *Wings To The World*. Sydney, 1970.
J. Godwin, *Battling Parer*. Adelaide, 1968.
D. M. Hocking and C. P. Haddon-Cave, *Air Transport in Australia*. Sydney, 1951.
F. Hurley, *Pearls and Savages. Adventures in New Guinea*. London, 1930.
I. L. Idriess, *Gold-dust and Ashes*. Sydney, 1933.

STANLEY BROGDEN

CLELAND, Donald Mackinnon (1901-   ), administrator, was born on 28 June 1901, son of E. D. Cleland. Educated at Guildford Grammar School, W.A., he was called to the Bar in Western Australia in 1925. He served in the Second A.I.F.

from 1939 to 1945, in 1943 being appointed Deputy Adjutant and Quartermaster-General of Angau [q.v.]. With the rank of brigadier he remained its principal staff officer until 1945. During this time he also held the position of Chairman of the Australian New Guinea Production Control Board, which was responsible for the production in Papua of strategic materials, chiefly copra and rubber. Cleland was Chairman of the State Executive of the National Party of W.A. 1936-9, Vice-President of the Liberal Party of W.A. 1945. He was Administrator of Papua and New Guinea from 1952 to 1967. He was appointed C.B.E. in 1945 and knighted in 1961.

CLIMATE AND WEATHER. Since Papua New Guinea lies wholly within the tropics, it is commonly thought that constant high temperatures and uniformly heavy rains are characteristic of the whole country. This is very far from the truth, and a visitor travelling by air could quite easily, with but an hour or so between locations, find himself successively in the parched dryness of Port Moresby, beneath a torrential downpour in steamy Lae, and shivering in the clear cold air of a night in the central Highlands.

Climate and weather in Papua New Guinea are greatly influenced by topography. Clearly, where there are great mountain ranges, some of which approach the snow line, the elevation of a place will tell a great deal more about its temperature than its latitude. The height and directional trend of ranges will also greatly modify the basic wind systems, altering their directions and affecting the amount of water vapour which is precipitated as rain in any one locality.

Two examples illustrate how marked this local influence may be: the Vitiaz Strait, between the Huon Peninsula and the western end of New Britain, displays perhaps the most spectacularly turbulent seas in New Guinea waters, because the prevailing winds are 'funnelled' between the high mountains on either side of the strait; the Owen Stanley Ranges behind Port Moresby run parallel in this area to the north-west monsoon and the south-east trade wind, so these wind-streams are not forced to rise and drop their moisture, and the Moresby country has all the appearance of a dry savannah, an annual rainfall of only 39 inches, and strongly marked wet and dry seasons, with the rain coming largely from local thunderstorms. This is quite unlike the conventional notion of the 'hot wet tropics'.

For such reasons, the broader generalizations of this article should not be applied too rigidly to any particular area without more detailed local information. In the articles on each of the eighteen administrative Districts some notes on weather and climate have been included wherever possible. Even within one District, however, there may be startling variations. In Morobe District, for example, it is possible in the course of a single day's walk to pass from the hot dry floor of the Markham Valley into the cool, moist climate of the high mountains which flank it.

Temperature and humidity. These are the most constant elements in the pattern of climate of Papua New Guinea, and for any given place the range is much smaller than is usual in the temperate zones; summer and winter seasons cannot be said to exist. Both the annual and the daily temperature ranges show this uniformity, which is more even on the coast than in the Highlands. A daily range of about 15°F. is common on the coast, and about 20°F. in the mountains up to 5,000 feet.

Temperatures above 100°F. such as occur commonly in Australia are unusual in Papua New Guinea. In Port Moresby the highest temperature recorded in a 24-year period was 97.4°F. and Lae has recorded 101.7°F., but both these figures are untypically high. For Port Moresby, a range between 72 and 88°F. is roughly to be expected over a year.

Relative humidity is high in all places, a range of 70-85 per cent covering the whole country, with the lowland areas in the top of the range (about 75-85 per cent). This higher relative humidity, together with generally higher temperatures, produces in the lowlands the discomfort often associated with the tropics. The Highlands, with considerably lower night-time temperatures and somewhat lower relative humidity are usually more congenial to expatriates.

Sunshine. There has been little accurate recording of sunshine outside Port Moresby, which has a mean daily figure for sunshine of 6.9 hours throughout the year. This figure is far from typical of the country as a whole, which is probably one of the cloudiest places in the world. In many parts of the extensive mountainous areas, cumulus cloud cover is likely to increase during the day. Certain mountain peaks are so habitually under cloud that it is a positive rarity to have them in clear view. Cloud is a severely limiting factor upon air transport, on which much of Papua New Guinea is dependent.

Winds. As would be expected just south of the Equator, the south-east trade wind and the north-west monsoon are the main regular air currents. In spite of the traditional difference in name between 'trade wind' and 'monsoon' these airstreams are basically of the same type—convergent streams blowing from the subtropical high pressure zone in each hemisphere towards the inter-tropical front, the low pressure belt of heated ascending air currents with surface calms and variable winds, that lies under the vertical sun and moves as that sun appears to move. The trade and the monsoon expand and contract in turn as the inter-tropical front (and the vertical sun) move north and south across the Equator with the seasons. The south-east trade blows from about May to October, and the monsoon from approximately December to the end of March. There are short seasons of comparative calm (when the inter-tropical front lies across New Guinea) in between the two seasons. Tropical cyclones (hurricanes) do not often affect the area. However, local thunderstorms of sometimes frightening severity occur with great frequency in the mountains, and quite often in the lower country and around the coasts.

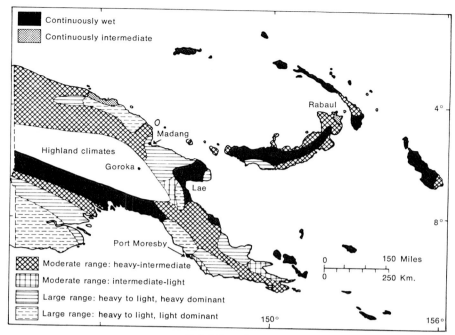

Legend:
- Continuously wet
- Continuously intermediate
- Moderate range: heavy-intermediate
- Moderate range: intermediate-light
- Large range: heavy to light, heavy dominant
- Large range: heavy to light, light dominant

Rabaul

Madang

Highland climates

Goroka

Lae

Port Moresby

0   150 Miles
0   250 Km.

Rainfall regimes.

The effect of the high mountains greatly distorts the theoretical simplicity of the pattern of trade wind and monsoon, and local systems of considerable regularity appear. A marked example of this occurs on the lower Markham River near Lae. Almost throughout the year the wind blows from the north-west at 9 a.m. and changes to south-east at 3 p.m., a fact greatly used by native canoemen in earlier times for sailing up and down the Markham before the wind.

Rainfall. The main airstreams are heavily moisture-laden because of their warmth and the availability of water in the oceans over which they flow, but where and when they will deposit their burden as rain is very largely determined by topography. As already noted, the lie of the land makes Port Moresby a comparatively dry place, with an aver-

age rainfall of about 39 inches per year, and strongly marked wet and dry seasons. At the other extreme, most of Bougainville District, comprising islands exposed to the winds and containing high mountains to lift and cool the moist airstreams, has rain almost throughout the year; much of Bougainville receives 180 inches annually.

However, considerable variations can occur from year to year. Port Moresby experienced one year of severe drought when only 23 inches fell and serious hardship occurred. In another year, 72 inches were recorded. Some areas regularly receive 200 inches per year, chiefly the south coast of New Britain, and a wide sweep of country which begins at the head of the Gulf of Papua, and strikes north-westerly towards the centre of the main island, south of the great central cordillera. Indi-

	Jan.	Feb.	Mar.	Apr.	May	June	July	Aug.	Sept.	Oct.	Nov.	Dec.	Annual Average
Port Moresby													
Mean temp. (°F.)	81.6	81.0	80.9	80.3	80.3	79.0	78.4	78.8	79.7	81.2	81.6	81.9	80.3
Rainfall (inches)	7	8	7	7	2	2	1	1	1	1	2	6	46
Lae													
Mean temp. (°F.)	81.3	81.4	81.0	80.0	79.2	77.8	76.7	76.9	77.8	79.0	80.0	80.7	79.3
Rainfall (inches)	11	9	12	15	16	16	20	20	18	14	13	13	180
Rabaul													
Mean temp. (°F.)	81.3	81.5	81.6	81.7	81.8	81.3	80.8	80.9	81.9	82.3	82.2	81.7	81.6
Rainfall (inches)	15	10	10	10	5	3	5	5	3	5	7	10	88
Madang													
Mean temp. (°F.)	80.7	80.5	80.8	81.1	81.5	81.3	81.1	81.1	81.4	81.6	81.3	81.1	81.1
Rainfall (inches)	12	12	15	17	15	11	8	5	6	10	13	14	138
Goroka													
Mean max. temp. (°F.)	78.5	77.9	78.1	77.8	78.8	77.2	76.5	77.2	78.3	78.9	78.9	78.1	78.0
Mean min. temp. (°F.)	59.0	59.1	59.5	59.1	58.3	56.6	56.1	57.0	57.0	57.0	57.5	58.6	57.9
Rainfall (inches)	9	10	10	8	9	2	2	3	5	6	6	10	76

vidual falls recorded in a single 24-hour period have been as high as 21.6 inches at Pondo on the west coast of the Gazelle Peninsula. It is quite likely that there have been falls of up to 30 inches in 24 hours.

Much remains to be learnt about the climate and weather of Papua New Guinea, not only about local variations but also about some of the broader elements. There is still a shortage of stations making regular observations in the field, and many of those which do exist are recent, without the long recording period necessary to establish reliable information. For the high mountains, above 6,000-7,000 feet, almost no detailed rainfall records are available. This situation should improve markedly, as more and more Papuans and New Guineans acquire the necessary technical training to collect and interpret information.

H. C. Brookfield and D. Hart, *Rainfall in the Tropical Southwest Pacific*. Canberra, 1966; Commonwealth Bureau of Census and Statistics, *Official Year Book of the Commonwealth of Australia*. Canberra, 1970; R. G. Ward and D. A. M. Lea (eds), *An Atlas of Papua and New Guinea*. Glasgow, 1970.

ACKNOWLEDGMENT

Map from *An Atlas of Papua and New Guinea*, ed. R. G. Ward and D. A. M. Lea. Reproduced by courtesy of the editors, the copyright owner (the University of Papua and New Guinea) and the publishers (Wm Collins & Co. Ltd and Longmans Group Ltd).

COCOA INDUSTRY. Cocoa was introduced into New Guinea soon after 1900, but there was only small commercial development of this crop under German administration. The position changed little under early Australian civil administration and in 1923 total exports of cocoa beans amounted to only 83 tons worth $7,468.

The Australian government subsequently took steps to encourage the industry. The Papua and New Guinea Bounties Act 1926 was passed, which provided for a subsidy of about 1 cent per pound on cocoa beans and shell produced, commencing January 1927 and extending over a ten-year period. The Customs Tariff (Papua and New Guinea Preference) Act 1926 was also passed, providing for duty-free importation into Australia of a wide range of commodities including cocoa beans. After World War I a series of field research projects were initiated by the Department of Agriculture, Stock and Fisheries at the Keravat demonstration plantations in New Britain.

While copra prices were at low levels during the 1930s there was some interest in cocoa growing but it remained a small industry. In 1940 the total output of cocoa beans amounted to only 210 tons. By 1941 only 1.6 million trees had been planted. Most of these were in New Britain, with small areas in Bougainville, in the Madang District and in New Ireland. Until after World War II indigenous participation in cocoa growing was negligible.

Damage to cocoa trees during World War II was severe and it was estimated by officials that about two-thirds of the pre-war trees were destroyed.

Following World War II the world cocoa market developed favourably for producers. There was a quick recovery of demand with the re-entry of Western Europe into the market and with the expansion of demand in North America. World production on the other hand responded sluggishly and a period of sustained high prices followed. This stimulated new interest in the industry both in Papua and New Guinea and in other parts of the world, notably Africa, and new planting was undertaken on a large scale.

Picking cocoa.

COCOA INDUSTRY

185

After 1950 the industry expanded rapidly in Papua and New Guinea. The total area planted rose from around 8,000 acres in 1951 to almost 150,000 acres by 1965. This post-war expansion was due principally to development of estates by expatriates. Indeed, post-war investment by Europeans in Territory primary production has been greatest in this industry. In 1965 the 435 European and Chinese plantations accounted for almost 80 per cent of the total area of cocoa trees. In that year these estates produced over 14,000 tons of raw beans or about 74 per cent of total cocoa bean production. Indigenous smallholders had planted about 31,000 acres of trees which yielded over 5,000 tons of beans, or 26 per cent of total output.

Cocoa estates are an important source of employment for indigenous labour. A precise measurement of this cannot be given because employment data are available only for the coconut and cocoa industries combined—due to the practice of interplanting the two crops on estates—but some indication of the extent of indigenous employment can be gained from the fact that, in 1965, estates producing one or both crops employed over twenty-six thousand or 58 per cent of those employed in primary production and 29 per cent of the total indigenous work force (see COCONUT INDUSTRY).

Export earnings from this crop have risen fast and in 1964-5 realized $7 million. This growth, however, has not been without fluctuations. In 1965-6, for example, earnings fell to only $4.4 million due to the fall in world prices and to the effects of the disease 'die back'. After World War II cocoa rapidly achieved a prominent position among the country's export industries. From 1959 to 1964 it held second position to copra and although it has run third, after coffee, since 1965, it has contributed very substantial export earnings during this whole period.

The natural habitat of the cocoa tree is the tropical lowland rain forest. The bulk of the world's crop is produced at altitudes below 1,000 feet and within 10° of the equator. It is grown where annual rainfall is above 50 inches and commonly below 200 inches per annum. The tree prefers a soil of a porous clay loam type. These growing conditions are encountered in the low altitude coastal areas of the New Guinea mainland and islands, particularly in New Britain. Relatively few areas of Papua have been found to be suitable. In 1965 there were well over 100,000 acres of estate cocoa in New Guinea but only 11,618 acres in Papua, mostly on the coastal lowlands of the Northern District around Popondetta. In New Guinea the most important location was New Britain with 48 per cent of the estate area of Papua and New Guinea, and producing over one-half of its cocoa in that year. Other important locations were Bougainville, with 16 per cent of the area, and the Madang and New Ireland Districts, with 13 per cent and 11 per cent respectively.

Cocoa tree planting by indigenous smallholders follows a similar pattern. In 1964, 54 per cent of

their trees were located in New Britain, mainly on the Gazelle Peninsula, 17 per cent in Bougainville, 13 per cent in the Northern District of Papua, especially around Popondetta, while the Madang District accounted for 8 per cent. This pattern has, in fact, been encouraged by the Administration, which has promoted cocoa development where large-scale production is possible, so that an economically efficient system of central processing can be used.

Cocoa is grown both as a sole crop and in combination with coconuts. Where cocoa is grown solely, it is customary to clear the ground and plant shade trees, Leucaena glauca. About six months later cocoa tree seedlings are established in the plantation. In Papua and New Guinea interplanting with coconuts has proved to be the most popular technique and about 70 per cent of the total area of plantation cocoa has been established in this way. In most instances cocoa seedlings were planted beneath well established coconut trees which provided an effective leaf canopy. Where new interplanted plantations were developed, coconut palms were usually planted three years before the cocoa seedlings.

There is at present no shortage of land suitable for cocoa growing although the most accessible areas are now fairly well developed. Some areas of coconut stands may still be underplanted although, in general, this has already been done where the soils are most suitable. There are other large areas, for example, along the littoral of the mainland, the Northern District of Papua, and on the islands, especially New Britain and Bougainville, which could be used for cocoa growing. This land, however, is generally in sparsely settled areas at some distance from marketing centres and development would be expensive.

The most important production problem in the industry is 'die back', a fungal disease. This has seriously affected current production and future prospects on a large number of estates and smallholdings in the Gazelle Peninsula. There are other diseases, e.g. black pod, and some pests, e.g. capsids, and various weevils and beetles, but their effects have been less serious than those of 'die back'.

Estates process their own cocoa and except in the Gazelle Peninsula of New Britain also purchase and process smallholder production. The greatest number of indigenous producers is found among the Tolais of the Gazelle Peninsula and in 1953 the Administration established the first of a number of central fermentaries which are now organized, on behalf of the producers and in collaboration with native Local Government Councils, as the Tolai Cocoa Project. In 1966 these fermentaries processed a substantial proportion of the smallholder cocoa produced in the area.

The Territory Administration has been actively involved in the development of the industry. The Department of Agriculture, Stock and Fisheries has conducted a programme of research into many aspects of cocoa production, such as improved breeding and selection, agronomy, vegetative propagation and disease control, at the Keravat

Agricultural Experiment Station in New Britain. The extension service of the Department has been largely instrumental in the expansion of indigenous participation in cocoa growing through promotional activities in the villages. The Department has also supplied technical assistance to both estates and smallholders. It has been active in the distribution of planting material to smallholders and in administering the system of registration and inspection of smallholdings. It has been heavily involved also in the organization and operation of the Tolai Cocoa Project. Other departments of the Administration have also promoted development directly or indirectly. Officers of the Department of Native Affairs (now the Department of District Administration) assisted village promotional work, particularly in the 1950s. This department and that of Public Works have also contributed through road-building programmes, etc.

Territory cocoa is generally sold abroad through agents on growers' accounts overseas. Most estate owners prefer to ship cocoa to the consuming countries and sell there as prices, net of delivery charges and selling commission, have exceeded those obtainable at Territory ports.

DESTINATION AND VALUE OF COCOA EXPORTS

Country of Destination	1956–7		1965–6	
	$	%	$	%
Australia	695,142	75	1,174,074	26
Belgium	—	—	427,741	10
Canada	—	—	20,580	—
Finland	—	—	4,468	—
France	—	—	82,612	2
Germany, Fed. Rep.	—	—	315,151	7
Italy	—	—	39,287	1
Japan	—	—	145,599	3
Netherlands	—	—	202,902	5
Philippines	—	—	24,184	1
South Africa	—	—	20,040	—
Sweden	—	—	19,236	—
United Kingdom	227,750	25	733,550	17
U.S.A.	1,190	—	1,225,253	28
Others	278	—	—	—
Total	924,360	100	4,434,677	100

SOURCE: T. P. N. G. Bureau of Statistics, *Oversea Trade 1956–7, 1965–6.* Port Moresby.

In recent years Territory cocoa has been sold widely on world markets. Whereas in 1957 there were virtually only two buyers of Territory cocoa, Australia and the United Kingdom, by 1965-6 the number of buyers had increased. In that year the United States of America was the most important purchaser and, in addition to Australia and the United Kingdom, several other countries were buying in substantial quantities, e.g. Belgium, the Federal Republic of Germany, the Netherlands and Japan.

Australia does not now offer the Territory preferential entry for cocoa, but in view of the ease

with which output has found markets in the post-war period this has been no cause for concern. Export duty was levied on cocoa in the Territory from 1953 to 1959. This duty was based on the f.o.b. value and was calculated on a sliding scale according to the assessed value per ton.

New Guinea cocoa belongs botanically to the Trinitario group. It is reported to have come from Ceylon and Java at the turn of the century though some may have come from Venezuela. The Trinitario group produces a 'flavour' cocoa that is well regarded in the trade.

The Territory was a late starter in cocoa production, and is by world standards still a relatively minor producer. In the year ending June 1965 output was 20,000 tons, only 1.3 per cent of world production.

However, as currently immature trees in the Territory come into bearing and as young bearing trees reach their yield potential, there is likely to be a substantial growth in Territory production during the 1970s, despite the anticipated effects of 'die back'. In 1964 roughly 47 per cent of all trees were immature (49 per cent on estates and 42 per cent on smallholdings), and it is thought probable that production will exceed 30,000 tons by 1975.

The future expansion of the industry depends, in the short run, on planting which has already taken place. Longer run expansion is heavily dependent on trends in the world market. The high prices of the 1950s stimulated planting in Papua and New Guinea. Statistics for estates, the most important producers in the past, indicate that planting from 1955 to 1963 averaged about 10,000 acres per annum. There was also extensive new planting in other parts of the world over this period, especially in African countries.

From 1959, as these new trees came into bearing, world market conditions began to deteriorate and prices fell heavily over the next few years until in 1962 they reached the lowest level since 1947. There was some recovery and stability up to 1965, but in that year a record world crop reduced prices, this time to by far the lowest level since World War II. Recovery followed in 1966 and since then price levels have remained reasonably attractive to producers.

Early in the 1960s world producers believed that a serious situation of excess capacity was developing in the industry. They attempted unsuccessfully to organize an international agreement for the crop, then to operate a producers' alliance in order to stabilize and, if possible, to improve the market. When the 1965 price collapse occurred fresh efforts were made towards an international agreement, but with the subsequent recovery hopes of successful negotiations with consuming countries were again dashed.

As a producer of 'flavour' cocoa which has not been in heavy supply on the world market the Territory has been in a relatively favourable position. In fact, the Territory is the only world producer which is now expanding production significantly. However, the market for 'flavour' cocoa has been limited to a fairly stable 7-10 per cent of world demand over the past thirty years and this proportion seems unlikely to increase.

The fluctuating market of the early 1960s appears to have had some influence on recent new plantings, at least on estates. From 1962-3 planting diminished from about 10,000 acres to only 6,349 acres in 1963-4 and 7,058 acres in the following year, and the proportion of trees planted as replacements, as distinct from new plantings, has been higher since 1962.

The 1963-4 Mission from the International Bank for Reconstrucion and Development assigned a high priority to the cocoa industry in its recommendations for the economic development of the Territory. It recommended an average annual target rate of planting on estates and smallholdings combined of 14,500 acres for the late 1960s. This is a somewhat higher rate than the average recorded from 1955 to 1962, the time of greatest activity in the post-war period.

The Mission advocated the participation of indigenous and European farmers in this expansion. In the short run, that is up to 1970, a relatively heavy reliance on estates for development was envisaged at 9,000 acres annually. The participation of smallholders, which was regarded as taking somewhat longer to organize, was to increase gradually to a point where, from 1970 onwards, they would provide the main impetus for expansion through new planting, 9,500 acres annually at their peak. New plantings on estates were expected to stabilize at a lower total level of about 6,000 acres in the early 1970s.

Since the visit of the Mission the severe fluctuations of the world market have made cocoa a less attractive investment proposition. The recent reductions in new estate plantings outlined above bear witness to this. New planting recorded for 1964-5 and 1965-6 was substantially below the targets recommended by the Mission.

These factors have persuaded the Administration to adopt somewhat more conservative expectations of export income from cocoa up to 1970 and to lower somewhat the targets for new plantings in the decade to 1975.

Department of Territories, *Cocoa in Papua and New Guinea*. Canberra, 1958.
F. A. O. United Nations, *Agricultural Commodities—Projections for 1970, Commodity Review* 1962 special supplement. Rome, 1962.
——— *Cocoa Statistics* (quarterly), vol. 1—, 1958—. Rome, 1958—.
——— *Commodity Review 1963-6*. Rome.
——— *Monthly Bulletin of Agricultural Economics and Statistics*. Rome.
International Bank for Reconstruction and Development, *The Economic Development of the Territory of Papua and New Guinea*. Baltimore, 1965.
Reserve Bank of Australia Rural Liaison Service, *Commodity Notes for Papua-New Guinea*. Sydney, 1962-6.
R. T. Shand, 'The Development of Cash-Cropping in Papua and New Guinea', *Australian Journal of Agricultural Economics*, vol. 7, 1963.
——— 'Trade Prospects for the Rural Sector' in *New Guinea on the Threshold*, ed. E. K. Fisk. Canberra, 1966.
T. P. N. G. Administrator, *Economic Development of Papua and New Guinea*. Port Moresby, 1967 (mimeographed).
——— Bureau of Statistics, *Production Bulletin*, Part 1: Rural Industries, 1958-9—. Port Moresby.
——— *Quarterly Summary of Statistics*. Port Moresby.
——— Department of Agriculture, Stock and Fisheries, *Annual Report*. Port Moresby.
D. H. Urquhart, *Cocoa*. London, 1955.
R. T. S.

COCONUT INDUSTRY. The coconut palm is most suited to tropical areas, and successful cultivation is located within 20° of the equator. It is primarily a lowland crop, preferring altitudes of less than 1,000 feet. It thrives in a warm climate with minimal diurnal variation in temperature. The ideal mean annual temperature is around 85°F. and the crop does not flourish below 70°F. From 50 to 90 inches of rainfall are considered adequate, though higher levels are acceptable so long as there is good soil drainage. The palm has a high sunlight requirement, is not suited to cloudy areas and is retarded by shade. It will thrive on a variety of soils, ranging from rich volcanic soils to saline sandy soils found along sea-shores, but it requires good drainage. The tree commences to bear in the sixth year, produces substantial yields by the seventh and eighth years, and is in full production by the fifteenth year. It remains in its prime until roughly the fortieth year, after which yields decline though production may continue for as long as eighty years.

In the Territory of Papua and New Guinea the coconut palm is grown on the coast and lowlands of the mainland and on the islands. It was grown by the coastal indigenous population as a source of food long before substantial contact with Europeans commenced late in the nineteenth century.

Before European settlement traders had plied around the islands and mainland coastline and bartered goods for the crop. Between annexation and the end of the century the first plantations were established by Germans in the Gazelle Peninsula and elsewhere. By 1914 it was estimated that 76,849 acres had been planted in New Guinea, of which 31 per cent were in bearing. During World War I the area planted increased to about 134,000 acres. After World War I German plantations were expropriated and most were sold to Australian ex-servicemen on tender.

In Papua the most significant period of acreage expansion occurred between 1907 and 1926 when the area planted rose from less than 5,000 to a little over 50,000 acres. From 1927 until World War II there was virtually no further planting; indeed some decline in total acreage took place during the 1930s and by the end of 1940 there were only about 45,000 acres under crop. By contrast, in New Guinea during the late 1920s and in the 1930s, acreage increased from around 178,000 acres in 1927 to over 260,000 acres in 1940.

Before 1930 the coconut industry was dominant in the market sector of the economy. It was the

Removing the meat from the coconut preparatory to drying, New Britain.

main source of export income for both territories; it was the chief source of cash income for indigenes both as producers and as employees on estates; and it was the most important attraction for outside investors. During the 1930s its contribution to export income was overshadowed by gold earnings, partly because gold output increased and partly because the world economic depression drastically reduced the price of, and earnings from, coconut products. With a temporary recovery in prices, total output in Papua and New Guinea reached a pre-World War II peak in 1936-7 with over 90,000 tons of copra exported at a value of almost $3 million.

Initially, marketed output consisted wholly of the indigenous contribution. Later, however, the indigenes' share of the total decreased, partly because European estates came into bearing and partly because of a lack of sustained new planting in the villages. During the period of low prices in the 1930s there was some loss of interest in the marketing of copra amongst the indigenous population. One estimate placed the proportion of indigenous-produced copra in New Guinea exports at only 3-4 per cent for 1934-5.

At the outbreak of World War II there were more than 300,000 acres under coconuts on estates in Papua and New Guinea. In Papua, with

45,000 acres, the estates were mainly in what were then called the Eastern, Central and South-Eastern Divisions, with 54, 22, and 14 per cent respectively. In New Guinea, with 260,000 acres, almost one-third were planted on New Britain, 30 per cent on New Ireland, 11 per cent on Bougainville and 10 per cent on Manus and nearby islands, with the remaining less than 20 per cent located along the mainland littoral. This distribution did not change greatly up to 1967.

In 1941 one-half of the plantations were 400 acres or less in size, but accounted for only 18 per cent of the total area planted. Only 10 per cent of the plantations were over 1,000 acres, but these were almost one-third of the total area.

The industry suffered severely in World War II, particularly in New Guinea. In Papua the military administration under Angau [q.v.] kept many plantations in production. In New Guinea, however, there were substantial losses in buildings and equipment and large numbers of indigenous- and plantation-owned trees were either destroyed during the hostilities or suffered through neglect. An official report estimated that about 25 per cent of coconut bearing areas in New Guinea were destroyed during the war. Many plantations were rehabilitated after the war with compensation paid by the Australian government, but in some cases the damage or deterioration was too severe for rehabilitation to be attempted.

Marketed output of coconut products of all kinds from the Territory of Papua and New Guinea did not regain pre-war levels until 1954. Since then, expansion has continued on a moderate scale. In 1967-8 the total quantity marketed was estimated to have reached 122,000 tons copra equivalent with a value of $22.6 million. Since World War II planting on estates has been slow. It was estimated that in 1968 total estate acreage was 270,000 acres, still less than the acreage reached before World War II. It was also estimated for the same year that indigenous people owned 322,000 acres, some 54 per cent of the estimated total area in the Territory. However, a large proportion of indigenous production was used to meet subsistence requirements and did not reach the market. Of the 122,000 tons of copra equivalent marketed in 1967-8, it was calculated that indigenous producers sold only 36,000 tons or 30 per cent. Plantation yields for Papua and New Guinea as a whole were 0.39 tons per acre in 1964-5. Highest yields were recorded on Bougainville—0.51 tons per acre, and New Britain—0.42 tons per acre.

The Administration has given substantial help to the industry through research, extension and marketing activities. Research on coconut production is being undertaken at the Lowlands Agricultural Experimental Station at Keravat on New Britain. Extension officers of the Department of Agriculture, Stock and Fisheries provide technical advice to estates and smallholders. The Administration has been involved in export marketing through the Copra Marketing Board (*see* section below) and in administering the levy on exports used to build up a stabilization fund, the Copra Fund (*see* section below). In some instances it has also provided marketing services for smallholders. Purchases have been made directly from the producer where the incentives for private enterprise have been too weak. Assistance in marketing has also been offered through the encouragement of grower organizations such as rural progress societies and co-operatives.

Copra is the main coconut product exported from Papua and New Guinea. There were a number of desiccated coconut factories in operation in the 1930s and exports in this form rose from about 100 tons in 1927-8 to a peak of 3,658 tons in 1939-40. Following a suspension of production during World War II exports recommenced and rose to over 1,500 tons in 1950-1. In 1953-4, however, the Australian government banned imports of desiccated coconut for health reasons. Territory factories then ceased production but in 1968 a new factory was opened at Rabaul.

A copra crushing mill was opened near Rabaul in 1952 and coconut oil was exported for the first time. Output increased to 26,000 tons ($7.6 million) in 1960. Since then, export volume and value have fluctuated somewhat below this level. In 1966-7 Territory exports of coconut products were: copra, 63 per cent; coconut oil, 33 per cent; and oil cake and meal, 4 per cent.

Before World War II the overseas marketing of copra was largely organized by several large trading and shipping companies in the two Territories. A few individual plantation owners sold through agents or directly in Australia and overseas. In 1943 the Australian-New Guinea Production Control Board was established by the Australian government to secure the maximum production of copra and other commodities for the Allied war effort. After the war this Board continued to control copra marketing because the industry was of such importance to the economy; in 1952 it was replaced by the Copra Marketing Board.

An agreement was concluded between the United Kingdom and Australian governments, with effect for nine years from March 1949, for the sale to the United Kingdom of all copra produced in excess of the domestic needs of Australia and the Territory itself. Since termination of the contract copra has been sold on the world market, but the United Kingdom has been the most important purchaser of coconut products since World War II. In 1966-7 it bought almost all the coconut oil and 56 per cent of the volume of copra and, in all, about 66 per cent of the value of all coconut exports. Australia, where copra is admitted duty-free, has been the other significant buyer and, in 1966-7, purchased about one quarter of the total value of exports, almost exclusively as copra. West Germany absorbed the balance of all exports of coconut oil, meal and cake in 1966-7, while Japan was a minor market for copra.

Despite the recent slow growth of production, and the diversification into other export industries such as coffee and cocoa, the coconut industry is still the most important primary industry. At its post-war peak it provided two-thirds of total export income. In recent years, however, its relative importance has declined, providing only 30 per cent in 1966-7 and 40 per cent in the previous year. While the industry remains important to the Territory, it is a minor producer by world standards. The total output in 1965-6 was only 3 per cent of world production.

Future prospects for the industry until 1975 depend largely upon planting which has already taken place. It is expected that marketed output will continue to increase and an official source estimates that output will rise from 122,000 tons copra equivalent in 1967-8 to about 166,000 tons in 1974-5, a rise of 36 per cent in seven years. Little of this increase is expected to come from plantations, where recent plantings have barely kept pace with replacement needs. The indigenous contribution, however, is expected to double within this period to about 72,000 tons which, if achieved, will be 43 per cent of total marketed output.

World market prospects are not particularly encouraging owing to competition from a range of other oils and synthetics. This competition will probably prevent prices from rising substantially other than on a short term basis. These prospects are expected to deter large-scale expansion on plantations, but may still be attractive enough to encourage further expansion of smallholder acreage. The Administration's agricultural programme emphasizes the encouragement of smallholder planting and aims at an annual planting rate more than double that of plantations. If targets are achieved there should be an expansion of output into the 1980s, with a continued rise in the relative importance of the smallholder contribution.

COPRA MARKETING BOARD

This Board was established in 1952 by the Papua and New Guinea Copra Marketing Board Ordinance 1952-67, to replace the board which had been set up as a war-time measure in 1943.

Under the provisions of the 1952 Ordinance the Board may purchase and sell copra and retains the right to be the sole authorized exporter. It buys for export from growers or agents at ports of concentration and is empowered to determine the purchase price of copra it buys. The Board, appointed by the Minister for External Territories, has six members including a chairman, two representatives of New Guinea copra producers and one of Papua producers, the Director of the Department of Agriculture, Stock and Fisheries, and one other member. It buys copra under a system of grade and ownership markings and takes delivery ex ships' slings or at a Board warehouse. Most indigenously produced copra is bought by the Board from co-operatives but individuals can negotiate privately.

The price paid by the Board is decided commercially, on a modified 'pool' principle. Tentative prices are declared, from which are subtracted costs of handling, administration, etc. Final prices are determined later on actual trading results, and the surplus is distributed *pro rata* among delivering producers.

COPRA FUND

As a reaction to highly variable prices before World War II, provision was made for levying an export duty on copra exports from Papua and New Guinea. This was to finance a reserve fund for stabilizing returns to the industry. Doubts concerning the future of copra prices persisted during and immediately after World War II and the levy was first applied in 1946. It was calculated on a sliding scale, according to the value per ton exported.

The Copra Fund, currently administered under the Customs (Copra Industry Stabilization) Ordinance 1959-60, received contributions from the levy until 1959, when the levy was discontinued. The Fund, however, has continued to grow with dividends accruing to it from investments and, in June 1967, contained almost $9 million.

The Copra Industry Stabilization Board, which administers the Fund, has five members: two representatives of New Guinea copra producers, one of Papua producers and two other members. The 1959-60 Ordinance empowers the Board to declare bounties to producers and in 1966-7 total payments of about $225,000 were made, at $2 per ton. Up to 1969 it had not been necessary to use the resources of the Fund for any stabilization scheme.

Bureau of Agricultural Economics, *An Economic and Cost Survey of the Copra Industry in the Territory of Papua and New Guinea*, Bulletin no. 9. Canberra, 1953.

Commonwealth of Australia, *Annual Report, Territory of Papua 1906-7* to *1940-1, 1946-7* to *1960-1*. Melbourne and Canberra, 1908-62.

———— *Report to the League of Nations on the Administration of the Territory of New Guinea 1921-2* to *1939-40*. Melbourne and Canberra, 1923-41.

———— *Report to the United Nations on the Administration of the Territory of New Guinea 1946-7—*. Canberra, 1947—.

R. E. P. Dwyer, 'A Survey of the Coco-nut Industry in the Mandated Territory of New Guinea', *New Guinea Agricultural Gazette*, vol. 2, 1936.

F. A. O. United Nations, *Production Yearbook 1967*. Rome, 1968.

E. C. Green, 'The Agricultural Aspect of the Coconut Industry in the Mandated Territory of New Guinea', *New Guinea Agricultural Gazette*, vol. 2, 1936.

W. C. Klein, 'A Comparison in Colonial Development: Trade in Australian and Dutch New Guinea', *Asiatic Review*, new series, vol. 33, 1937.

R. T. Shand, 'The Development of Cash Cropping in Papua and New Guinea', *Australian Journal of Agricultural Economics*, vol. 7, 1963.

———— 'The Coconut Industry', *New Guinea*, vol. 1, 1965.

———— 'Trade Prospects for the Rural Sector', in *New Guinea on the Threshold*, ed. E. K. Fisk. Canberra, 1966.

M. Staniforth Smith (comp.), *Handbook of the Territory of Papua*. Melbourne, 1907; 2nd ed., 1909; 3rd ed., 1912; 4th ed., 1927.

T. P. N. G. Administrator, *Programmes and Policies for the Economic Development of Papua and New Guinea*. Port Moresby, 1968.

T. P. N. G. Bureau of Statistics, *Quarterly Bulletin of Oversea Trade Statistics, June 1967*. Port Moresby, 1967.

TERRITORY OF PAPUA AND NEW GUINEA LEGISLATION

Customs (Copra Industry Stabilization) Ordinance 1959-60.

Papua and New Guinea Copra Marketing Board Ordinance 1952-67.   R. T. S.

COELENTERATA (Cnidaria). The lowest group of invertebrates which display a definite pattern of organization of the tissues are assembled in the phylum Coelenterata (also called Cnidaria). The phylum is composed of some ten thousand species, including such familiar forms as the jellyfishes, sea anemones and corals, nearly all of which are marine. Many of the species are brightly coloured, and combined with their radial symmetry, create a beauty that is surpassed by few other animals. They are of slight economic importance; some coral is used for jewellery and decorative art, the stings of certain jellyfishes and siphonophores occasionally injure bathers, and people on some Pacific islands eat jellyfishes.

The phylum is divided into three classes: Hydrozoa, containing the inconspicuous hydroids and hydromedusae; Scyphozoa, which are essentially the jellyfishes; and Anthozoa, a very large class containing the sea anemones and corals.

The members of the phylum Coelenterata are characterized by a hollowed-out gastrovascular cavity, which opens at one end to form the mouth, and a circle of tentacles developed around the mouth. These tentacles aid the capture and digestion of food. All coelenterates, although basically tentacular and radially symmetrical, are divided into two structural types: the polyp or sessile form, and the free-swimming medusoid form. The polypoid form is characterized by a cylindrically stalked body, the upper or oral end bearing the mouth and tentacles, while the opposite or aboral end is attached, for example, sea anemones. The free-swimming medusoid form is umbrella-shaped, with the convex side upward and the mouth located in the centre of the concave under-surface.

Class Hydrozoa contains approximately three thousand seven hundred species, but because of their small size and relative inconspicuousness, the layman is largely unaware of their existence. A considerable part of the marine growth attached to rocks, shells and wharf piles, and usually dismissed as sea-weed, is actually composed of hydrozoan coelenterates. Hydrozoans display either the polypoid or medusoid structure, while some species pass through both stages in their life history.

Class Hydrozoa is divided into four orders, of which only two are described here. The order Siphonophora, which includes the familiar *Physalia* sp. (Portuguese man-of-war) and *Velella* sp. (the purple sail), exist as pelagic colonies composed of modified polypoid and medusoid individuals, the majority displaying a remarkable degree of polymorphism. The tentacles of *Physalia* are strewn with nematocysts (stinging cysts), and an accidental encounter with a large colony can be a painful and even dangerous experience for bathers. Siphonophorans are largely tropical and subtropical in their distribution, but members of the genus *Physalia* are commonly found in cooler waters.

Order Hydrocorallina is divided into two sub-orders, Milliporina and Stylasterina. Both these suborders are characterized by their ability to secrete a calcareous skeleton. Both are colonial polypoid hydrozoans with either an encrusting or upright growth form, attaining considerable size and often brightly coloured. They are tropical to semi-tropical in distribution, the genus *Millipora* being common on the coral reefs in the New Guinea region.

Class Scyphozoa is composed essentially of those coelenterates commonly referred to as jellyfish. The medusoid stage is the dominant and conspicuous individual in the life cycle, the polypoid form being restricted to a small larval stage. In addition, scyphozoan medusae are generally larger in size than the hydromedusae. Locomotion of this animal is by pulsations produced by the contraction of the powerful coronal muscle fibres, which tend to move the animal upwards

towards the surface. When contraction ceases, the animal slowly sinks. Horizontal movement is by wind and currents.

Scyphozoans are present in all waters from the Arctic and Antarctic to the tropics. Many inhabit coastal waters, becoming a nuisance on bathing beaches because of their size and sting. The average diameter of the umbrella-shaped bell ranges from ¾ to 16 inches, although the bell of *Cyanea arctica* from the Arctic Ocean reaches up to seven feet in diameter. The colour of scyphomedusae is often very striking; the gonads and other internal structures, which may be orange, pink, or other colours, are visible through the colourless or more delicately coloured bell.

Class Anthozoa, containing over six thousand species, is made up of either solitary or colonial polypoid coelenterates in which the medusoid stage is completely absent. Many of the familiar marine coelenterates such as the sea anemones, corals, sea fans, and sea pansies belong to this class. The anthozoan polypoid stage differs considerably from the hydrozoan polypoid stage. The mouth leads into a tubular pharynx that extends more than half-way into the gastrovascular cavity. The gastrovascular cavity is divided by longitudinal septa into radiating components, the edges of the septa bearing nematocysts.

Class Anthozoa is divided into two subclasses: Alcyonaria or Octocorallia, characterized by eight pinnately branched tentacles and eight single complete septa; and Zoantheria or Hexacorallia, characterized by a few to many tentacles, never eight.

Subclass Alcyonaria is composed of a small number of forms which include the sea pens, sea pansies, sea fans, whip corals and pipe corals. The alcyonarian corals are similar to the subclass Zoantheria in general structure, but differ in that they always possess eight tentacles which are pinnate; corresponding with the eight tentacles there are always eight septa. Only one syphonoglyph (feeding groove) is present. The alcyonarian corals are colonial coelenterates, the polyps being small and connected by a mass of tissue containing amoebocytes (wandering amoeba-like cells), which are responsible for secreting skeletal material. The skeleton may be composed of separate or fused calcareous spicules, or horny material, which becomes an integral part of the tissue supporting the colony.

Subclass Zoantheria is divided into five orders: Actinaria, containing the sea anemones; Madreporaria or Scleractinia, containing the stony corals; and three small orders, Zoanthidae, Antipatharia and Ceriantharia.

The sea anemones, belonging to the order Actinaria, are solitary polyps, larger and heavier than the hydrozoan polyps. They are very brightly coloured and spectacular with colours of white, green, blue, orange, red, or a combination and commonly inhabit coastal waters throughout the world, being particularly abundant in tropical waters. They feed on various invertebrates, the larger species even capturing fish, the prey being paralysed by the stinging action of the nematocysts. Although sea anemones are essentially sessile animals, some species are able to change position by slowly gliding on the pedal disc, by floating, or by walking on the tentacles.

The order Madreporina is composed of the stony or madreporite corals, which are commonly referred to as the reef-building corals. Unlike the sea anemones, madreporite corals produce a calcium carbonate skeleton. This calcareous skeleton, the possession of which constitutes the marked distinction between a coral and a sea anemone, is secreted by the lower half of the column as well as by the basal disc, producing a skeletal cup called a theca within which the polyp is immovably fixed. The madreporite corals also do not possess a syphonoglyph.

Some of the madreporite corals may be solitary, such as the mushroom-coral, genus *Fungia*, which is well represented in the coastal waters around New Guinea. The polyp of this genus may reach up to 10 inches in diameter. The majority of madreporite corals are colonial with very small polyps averaging 0.4 to 1.2 inches in diameter. Some of the madreporite coral genera represented in the waters of the New Guinea area include: *Galaxea, Goniastrea, Goniopora, Hydnophora, Merulina, Montipora, Pocillopora, Porites, Seriatopora, Stylophora, Turbinaria.*

Reef-forming corals owe their solidity and extensive dimensions to the fact that they represent, for the most part, imperfectly separated coral skeletons or coralla of a great number of closely associated sea anemone-like polyps. The majority of clusters arise from the repeated fission of a single polyp.

The actual proportion that the growing corals bear to the aggregated reef-masses is very small. The polyp that lays the foundations of these vast reefs cannot survive the long exposures and evaporating action of the sun that would be inevitably associated with their growth at a plane of high elevation. We thus find the living corals on these reefs lying entirely out of sight at a lower depth on the outer margin of the reef.

Thus, the characteristic structure of the larger reef-masses typified by a relatively large, dead and weathered central core associated with a comparatively small and narrow peripheral zone of living coral is very common. Those reefs in which growing coral is developed almost uninterruptedly over extensive areas, are very rarely laid bare at low tide.

Coral reef-building polyps are practically confined to the seas of the tropics, as limited by the parallels of latitude of 23° 30′ north and south of the equator. The main determining factor in their distribution is a uniformly high temperature, which, in the coldest months should not fall below 68°F.

The highest elevation at which corals are found growing is about that of ordinary low-water mark. From here downwards, to a depth of approximately 200 feet, represents the generally recognized range of reef-coral growth. The most luxuriant coral growth, however, is limited to a depth of around 100 feet.

The solid coral-rock, which represents the chief constituent of all reef-masses is composed exclusively of the broken-down and subsequently reconsolidated, calcareous elements of the peripherally growing corals. The species that contribute the most are the more fragile and rapidly growing species upon which wave action exerts its greatest force.

Coral reefs have been divided into three universally recognized categories. Firstly there is the lagoon island or atoll. These are characterized by vast rings of coral reef, on the outside of which are the large breakers and on the inside a calm expanse of water. The contour of these atolls may vary considerably in form, from an almost perfect circle to every conceivable pattern of irregularity. Secondly there is the barrier or encircling reef, which characteristically is a vast reef fronting a land mass, with the outer margin of the reef abruptly descending into very deep water. The third type is called a fringing or shore reef which appears to differ little from the barrier-type reefs, but the absence of an interior deep-water channel, and the close relation of their horizontal extension with the probable slope of the adjoining land beneath the sea, present essential points of difference. All three types of coral reefs are commonly found around the shores of the New Guinea region.

W. Saville-Kent, *The Great Barrier Reef of Australia.* London, 1893.

R. R. PYNE

COFFEE INDUSTRY. Coffee was introduced to New Guinea during the German administration late in the nineteenth century. It was grown experimentally on agricultural stations and by missions, but commercially on only a small scale up to World War II. However, after World War II and particularly during the 1950s, commercial development of the crop was rapid, owing to the high world prices which prevailed until about 1957.

Coffee is a tolerant crop in terms of climate, soil and topography. It has been planted in areas where annual rainfall is at times below 30 inches and in others where it exceeds 110 inches. Robusta and Arabica varieties can be grown on a wide variety of soils, varying in acidity, parent material, depth and nutrient content. There are varieties successful on lowland areas and others suited to high altitudes. Trees can be established on flat land and on steep slopes. The main areas used for coffee in the Territory are in the Highlands at altitudes of 3,000-6,500 feet. Particular concentrations are in the Goroka-Kainantu Valleys, in the vicinity of Wau, in the Wahgi Valley, on the Mount Hagen Plateau and at higher altitudes on the Huon Peninsula. In these areas Typica or Bourbon varieties of Arabica coffee are grown, yielding a 'mild' bean which is favourably regarded by the market. Small areas of Robusta varieties have also been planted in the lowland coastal areas of the Territory, particularly around Popondetta, Milne Bay, Madang, and in the Sepik District.

Coffee is grown both as an estate and as a smallholder crop. The area planted by estates rose from 370 acres in 1951 to 12,229 acres by March 1965. In that year there were 261 estates with 7.9 million trees of which 62 per cent were in production and the remainder immature. From 1954 to 1965 the rate of increase in estate acreage was steady, averaging about 1,000 acres per annum. Estates are located principally in the Western and Eastern Highlands. In 1965 they employed 5,146 indigenous workers, or some 13 per cent of all employed by private industry in primary production. Non-indigenous investment in coffee was estimated to have been over $14 million by 1966, of which a little over $2 million was in processing mills and such facilities.

The Department of Agriculture, Stock and Fisheries estimated that indigenous smallholders had planted 12.2 million trees by June 1964, about 64 per cent of all coffee trees in the Territory at that time. Most smallholders are in the Eastern and Central Highlands and in the highland areas of the Huon Peninsula. Others are in the Northern, Milne Bay, Madang, Sepik, New Ireland and Central Districts. Most smallholdings are operated by unpaid family labour, though some of the larger producers do hire labour. The substantial capital value of these coffee gardens comes primarily from the investment of unpaid family labour. Little monetary investment was made—or needed—by smallholders.

Since coffee beans tend to ripen unevenly harvesting usually consists of a number of selective pickings during the year. On plantations the ripe cherry is processed by the so-called 'wet' method, whereby, after pulping, it is fermented, washed and dried to produce 'parchment', a stage at which the beans still retain the parchment skin. Beans are then hulled, polished, graded and bagged ready for export. Most smallholders process the cherry to the parchment stage in the village, although some sell their coffee as cherry. Smallholder coffee is purchased by European traders, plantations, indigenous producer co-operatives, the Administration and, in a few instances, by missions.

The Administration has spent a large amount of money in support of the industry. Estates and smallholders alike have benefited from the provision of roads to facilitate transportation and marketing, though villagers themselves make a substantial contribution to the construction of feeder roads from villages. The Department of Agriculture carried out promotional work in villages, particularly during the 1950s, to stimulate smallholder development, and also provided technical assistance both to smallholders and to estates.

Where the output from smallholders was insufficient to attract private enterprise on the marketing and processing side, which often occurred in the early years of production, the Administration provided these services as an initial encouragement to village producers. When output expanded these operations were generally handed over to private enterprise or to co-operatives.

Plantations generally transported their own coffee, but there was considerable development of public road transport to serve smallholder coffee development. Private buyers and co-operatives, associated with coffee factories, set up buying points to which smallholders carried their coffee. In many instances, especially in the early years, villagers travelled long distances to reach a buying point. As output expanded, however, the number of these buying points grew and transport required less labour.

DESTINATION OF COFFEE EXPORTS 1965-6

Principal Countries of Destination	Million lb. Green Beans	% of Total Exports
Australia	10.7	44
Netherlands	3.2	13
Germany, Fed. Rep.	3.1	13
United Kingdom	2.7	11
United States	2.7	11
Canada	0.7	3
Japan	0.6	2
New Zealand	0.5	2
Total—all countries	24.2	100

SOURCE: T. P. N. G. Bureau of Statistics, *Oversea Trade 1965-6*. Port Moresby.

This table shows that while almost half the coffee exported in 1965-6 was bought by Australia, the remainder was sold to a considerable number of other countries, with the United Kingdom, the United States and Western European countries being prominent customers.

Opinion has varied as to how the quality of Territory coffee compares with that of other countries. However, through the early 1960s most New Guinea coffee has attracted prices similar to those paid for mild Arabicas of medium to good quality from Kenya and Tanganyika.

In Papua and New Guinea Arabica beans are graded in two systems. The first is on the basis of bean size and appearance (A, B, C, etc.), primarily to meet the requirements of coffee houses who sell whole beans. The second system is based on the proportion of sound beans (X, Y, etc.) mainly to suit instant coffee manufacturers for whom appearance is not important. In 1963-4 about 40 per cent of the Arabica was A and B grades, 9 per cent was C, PB and E grades, 29 per cent X grade, 15 per cent Y grade and 6 per cent inferior T grade.

Coffee has been one of the fastest growing industries since World War II. It has risen in importance from 1 per cent of total exports in 1955-6 to 18 per cent in 1965-6. However, by world standards the Territory is a late starter and a small producer. In 1963-4, for example, production was about 0.2 per cent of world output.

Before 1958 the total annual production was low, since trees planted after World War II were still immature. Whilst output was small there was no difficulty in disposing of the coffee on the Australian market. However, after 1959 the Aus-

Grading coffee beans in processing factory, Goroka.

tralian market was not able to absorb the rapid growth in output.

An approach was made to the Australian Tariff Board for special assistance which would enlarge the Territory's share of the Australian market. Such assistance was recommended by the Tariff Board and granted by the Australian government in 1962. Raw coffee from the Territory was subsequently admitted duty free, while import duties were imposed on raw coffee from other sources. This assistance effectively gave first preference to Territory coffee in the Australian market.

In addition, provision was made for the remission of duty on coffee from other areas, to importers fulfilling conditions as follows:

(a) to those importing 25 per cent of their requirements from the Territory, partial remission.

(b) to those importing 30 per cent or more of their total requirements from the Territory, total remission.

In 1965, after a tariff review, condition (a) was abolished, but the provisions under condition (b) were retained.

Duties were also applied to processed coffee imported into Australia. This was intended to protect Australian processing firms using Territory coffee and thereby to stimulate the use of Territory coffee in Australia.

These tariff provisions were of considerable assistance to producers. First, they provided an assured market for a considerable volume of Territory output. Second, they succeeded in raising the share of the Australian market held by Territory producers. Of the total Australian imports of raw coffee the proportion from the Territory rose from 26 per cent in 1961-2 to 35 per cent in 1964-5. Furthermore, the duties on imports of processed coffee led to the desired expansion of processing facilities within Australia, and the share of the instant coffee market held by Australian manufacturers increased from 80 per cent in 1962-3 to about 90 per cent in 1964-5.

The scope for sale of Territory coffee is of course limited, even with these special arrangements. First, a large proportion, about one-half in 1960-1, of the Australian demand is for Robusta coffee, little of which is yet produced in Papua and New Guinea. Second, the country is unable to produce all the varieties of Arabica demanded by the Australian market, and this limits the quantities which can be absorbed in Australia. It is unlikely that the Territory could expect to supply much more than one-third of the Australian coffee market, unless the production of Robusta coffee expands substantially.

On present trends, the Australian market will expand less rapidly than Territory production over the next few years, with the result that by 1970-1 it may absorb less than 40 per cent of the output. Fortunately, the Territory has been able to find overseas markets for the excess production up to the end of 1967. However, it may not be possible to retain these markets in the 1970s.

Rapid expansion of coffee exports came at a time when the world market situation was beginning to deteriorate. Prices, which had remained buoyant in the decade to 1957, fell sharply to 1963 when they reached their lowest level since 1949.

As a direct result of the collapse of the world market Papua and New Guinea became subject to the International Coffee Agreement, which commenced to operate formally in 1965 though it had previously been accepted informally. The Agreement contained export quotas designed to regulate the annual quantity marketed internationally. It assigned producers the task of adjusting production to these quotas, e.g. through programmes of tree eradication and agricultural diversification. It also recommended ways in which world consumption could be expanded.

The Territory was classed with Australia under the Agreement. No export quota is required for the Territory as long as the combination remains a net importer. While this situation continues Territory coffee is freely marketable. However, it is expected that by the early 1970s, when a higher proportion of trees come into bearing, Australia and Papua and New Guinea will become a net exporter. It will then become necessary to apply for a quota. If there is no great improvement in the world market situation, it will undoubtedly be difficult for the Territory to obtain a sizeable allocation in the world market.

Meanwhile the prospect of becoming a net exporter has already made it necessary for the Administration to discourage further planting of coffee trees, and has effectively brought the growth of a promising young industry almost to a halt. Actually, no new areas of land were released to Europeans after January 1959. The Administration has also ceased to encourage smallholders and though some planting still continues, indigenous expansion has also been largely checked.

Barring a radical change in the market outlook, the only likely long term growth will be a slow expansion of Robusta coffee production on the coastal lowlands for the Australian market. There will, however, be a continuing growth in production due in part to increasing yields on young plantations, in part to new areas being planted on leases obtained before 1959, and in part to some new areas being planted by smallholders whose activities cannot be fully controlled by the Administration. Recent export levels and trends in output suggest that production in the Territory could rise to 18,000 tons by 1971.

Bureau of Agricultural Economics, *The Coffee Industry in Papua-New Guinea*. Canberra, 1961.
F. A. O. United Nations, *Agricultural Commodities—Projections for 1970. Commodity Review* 1962 special supplement. Rome, 1962.
——— *Commodity Review, 1963-5*. Rome.
——— *Monthly Bulletin of Agricultural Economics and Statistics*, vols 1-15. Rome, 1952-66.
——— *The World Coffee Economy*. Commodity Bulletin series no. 33. Rome, 1961.
Reserve Bank of Australia Rural Liaison Service, *Commodity Notes for Papua-New Guinea*. Sydney.
R. T. Shand, 'Trade Prospects for the Rural Sector', in *New Guinea on the Threshold*, ed. E. K. Fisk. Canberra, 1966.
Tariff Board, 'Report on Coffee 1962', *Commonwealth Parliamentary Papers*, vol. 10, 1962-3.
——— 'Report on Coffee, Tariff Revision 15th July, 1966', *Commonwealth Parliamentary Papers*, 1966.
T. P. N. G. Bureau of Statistics, *Oversea Trade, 1955-6—*. Port Moresby, 1957—.
——— Bureau of Statistics, *Production Bulletin*, Part 1: Rural Industries, 1958-9—. Port Moresby.
——— Bureau of Statistics, *Quarterly Bulletin of Oversea Trade Statistics, 1956—*. Port Moresby, 1956—.
——— Bureau of Statistics, *Quarterly Summary of Statistics*. Port Moresby.
——— Department of Agriculture, Stock and Fisheries, *Annual Report 1963-4*. Port Moresby.
'T. P. N. G.—The Economy in the Sixties', *Current Affairs Bulletin*, vol. 39, 1966-7.
V. D. Wickizer, 'International Collaboration in the World Coffee Market', *Stanford University, Food Research Institute Studies*, vol. 4, 1963-4.

R. T. S.

COMMISSIONS, COMMITTEES OF INQUIRY AND SPECIAL REPORTS.

The following is a chronological list of special investigations held in Papua New Guinea.

1884 Western Pacific Royal Commission, *Report*. Brisbane, 1884; Victoria, *Parliamentary Papers*, vol. 3, 1884.

1885 Royal Commission appointed to inquire into the circumstances under which labourers have been introduced into Queensland from New Guinea and the other islands, *Report*. Brisbane, 1885.

1886 *Report on British New Guinea from data and notes by the late Sir Peter Scratchley*, by G. Seymour Fort. Melbourne, 1886; Victoria, *Parliamentary Papers*, vol. 2, 1886.

1904 Royal Commission on the affray at Goaribari Island, British New Guinea, on 6th March 1904, *Report*. Sydney, 1904; *Commonwealth Parliamentary Papers*, vol. 2, 1904.

1905 *British New Guinea*, report by the Secretary of the Department of External Affairs, Atlee Hunt. Melbourne, 1905; *Commonwealth Parliamentary Papers*, vol. 2, 1905.

1907 Royal Commission of inquiry into the present conditions of Papua, *Report, with minutes of evidence*. Melbourne, 1907.

1918 Commonwealth of Australia, Parliament, *Report from the Joint Committee of Public Accounts upon Papua oilfields*. Melbourne, 1918.

Inter-State Commission of Australia, *Report on British and Australian trade in the South Pacific*. Melbourne, 1918.

1919 *Report by the Lieut.-Governor of Papua to the Minister for Home and Territories on an article on 'Three Power Rule in New Guinea' by Rinzo Gond*, by J. H. P. Murray. Port Moresby, 1919.

1920 Royal Commission on late German New Guinea, *Interim and Final Reports*. Melbourne, 1920; *Commonwealth Parliamentary Papers*, vol. 3, 1920-1.

1922 Commonwealth of Australia, Department of Defence, *Report by the Minister of State for Defence on the military occupation of the German New Guinea Possessions*. Melbourne, 1922; *Commonwealth Parliamentary Papers*, vol. 2, 1922.

1924 Royal Commission on the Navigation Act, *First report, Appendix 3*, report by the Assistant Director of Navigation on the effect of the Navigation Act on the Territories of Papua and New Guinea. Melbourne, 1924; *Commonwealth Parliamentary Papers*, vol. 2, 1923-4. *Second report, 1925*. Melbourne, 1925; *Commonwealth Parliamentary Papers*, vol. 2, 1925.

Report on administrative arrangements and matters affecting the interests of natives in the Territory of New Guinea, by John Ainsworth. Melbourne, 1924.

1925 *The forest resources of the Territories of Papua and New Guinea*, report by C. E. Lane-Poole. Melbourne, 1925; *Commonwealth Parliamentary Papers*, vol. 2, 1925.

1927 Royal Commission on the Edie Creek (New Guinea) Leases, *Report*. Canberra, 1927; *Commonwealth Parliamentary Papers*, vol. 4, 1926-8.

1930 The oil exploration work in Papua and New Guinea, *Reports, 1920-9*, by the Anglo-Persian Oil Company. 4 vols and 2 atlases, London, 1930.

1938 Commonwealth of Australia, Parliament, Committee appointed to investigate a new site for the administrative headquarters of the Territory of New Guinea, *Report*. Canberra, 1938; *Commonwealth Parliamentary Papers*, vol. 3, 1937-40.

1939 Commonwealth of Australia, Committee appointed to survey the possibility of establishing a combined administration of Papua and New Guinea, *Report*. Canberra, 1939; *Commonwealth Parliamentary Papers*, vol. 3, 1937-40.

1944 Australian New Guinea Administrative Unit (ANGAU), *Report on the activities of ANGAU in respect of Native Relief and Rehabilitation in the Territory of Papua and the Mandated Territory of New Guinea*, February 1941-1944. Port Moresby (roneoed).

Australian New Guinea Administrative Unit (ANGAU), Conference of officers of Headquarters and officers of Districts Staff, Port Moresby, 7-12 February 1944, *Papers and discussions*. 3 vols, Port Moresby (roneoed).

1945 Commonwealth of Australia, Department of External Territories, Commission of Inquiry under the National Security (Inquiries) Regulations and the National Security (General) Regulations into the circumstances relating to the suspension of the civil administration of the Territory of Papua in February 1942 (Commissioner J. V. Barry), *Report*. 1945 (roneoed).

Commonwealth of Australia, Committee appointed by the Minister for External Territories, *Compensation to the natives of Papua and New Guinea for war injuries and war damage*, report. Canberra, 1945 (roneoed).

1947 *Public Service of the Provisional Administration of Papua and New Guinea*, report by C. J. Buttsworth. 1947 (roneoed).

Report to the Minister for External Territories with comments from heads of departments on the provisions suggested in the Buttsworth report, by J. K. Murray. 1947 (roneoed).

1948 T. P. N. G., *Report of the Economic Development Committee of the Provisional Administration*. 7 September 1948 (roneoed).

T. P. N. G., *Report of the Social Development Planning Committee of the Provisional Administration*. 23 July 1948 (roneoed).

1949 Royal Commission to inquire into certain transactions in relation to timber rights in the Territory now known as Papua-New Guinea, *Report*. Canberra, 1949; *Commonwealth Parliamentary Papers*, vol. 48, 1948-9.

1950 to date. United Nations Trusteeship Council, *Report of Visiting Mission to the Trust Territory of New Guinea*, 1950, 1953, 1956, 1959, 1962, 1965, 1968 and 1971. New York (three yearly).

1952 T. P. N. G., Customs Inquiry Committee (Chairman S. J. Butlin), *Report to the Minister for Territories*. Canberra, 1952.

1957 *Report of an Investigation into the Desirability and Practicability of the Introduction of Local Government into the Territory of Papua and New Guinea, 1956*, by J. R. Winders. Port Moresby, 1957.

1959 Commonwealth of Australia, Commission of inquiry into the Navuneram incident, New Britain (Commissioner A. H. Mann), *Report*, vols 1-7 minutes, vol. 8 Commissioner's report. Canberra, 1959; vol. 8 only, *Commonwealth Parliamentary Papers*, vol. 4, 1959-60.

1962 T. P. N. G. Legislative Council, Select Committee appointed to inquire into and report upon the political development of the Territory (Chairman J. T. Gunther), *Interim report 1962. Second interim report 1963*. Canberra, 1963; *Commonwealth Parliamentary Papers*, vol. 13, 1962-3. No final report was issued.

1963 T. P. N. G., Liquor Commission, *Report of a Committee appointed by the Administrator, 23 July 1962*. Port Moresby, 1963.

1964 Commonwealth of Australia, Department of Territories, Commission on higher education in Papua and New Guinea (Chairman Sir George Currie), *Report*. Canberra, 1964.

T. P. N. G. Chief Electoral Officer, *Report of the Chief Electoral Officer on the House of Assembly election, 1964*. Port Moresby, 1964.

1965 International Bank for Reconstruction and Development, Mission on the economic development of Papua and New Guinea, *The economic development of the Territory of Papua and New Guinea*. Baltimore, 1965.

T. P. N. G. House of Assembly, Select Committee on constitutional development (Chairman John Guise), *Interim report 1965. Second interim report 1966. Final report 1967*. Port Moresby, 1967; Canberra, 1968; *Commonwealth Parliamentary Papers*, session 1, vol. 7, 1967-8.

1967 T. P. N. G. Department of Information and Extension Services, *Economic development of Papua and New Guinea*. Port Moresby, 1967.

T. P. N. G., Distribution Committee appointed for the purpose of redistributing the Territory of Papua and New Guinea into electorates, *Report* to his Honour the Administrator. Port Moresby, 1967.

T. P. N. G. House of Assembly, Select Committee on the conduct of the Administration towards Andree Margaret Bellaard, *Report* together with minutes of proceedings, 24 April 1967. Port Moresby, 1967.

1968 T. P. N. G. Chief Electoral Officer, *Report of the Chief Electoral Officer on the House of Assembly Election, 1968*. Port Moresby, 1968.

T. P. N. G. Department of the Administrator, *Programmes and policies for the economic development of Papua and New Guinea*. Port Moresby, 1968. *Review of progress*, 1968-9 and 1969-70.

1969 T. P. N. G. House of Assembly, Select Committee on House of Assembly procedures, *Interim report. Final report. Supplementary report*. Port Moresby, 1969.

T. P. N. G. House of Assembly, Committee of privileges, *Report* relating to the matter raised by Traimya Kambipi, M.H.A. on 17 June 1969. Port Moresby, 1969.

Commonwealth of Australia, Department of External Territories, Advisory Committee on education in Papua and New Guinea (Chairman C. J. Weedon), *Report*. Canberra, 1969.

T. P. N. G., Commission of Inquiry into local government and other matters in the Gazelle Peninsula of East New Britain, *Report*. Port Moresby, 1969.

T. P. N. G. House of Assembly, Select Committee on constitutional development (Chairman Paulus Arek), *First interim report 1969. Second interim report 1970. Final report 1971.* Port Moresby, 1971.

1970 T. P. N. G., Board of Inquiry investigating rural minimum wages, minimum wage-fixing machinery and related matters, *Report*. Port Moresby, 1970.

T. P. N. G., Commission of Inquiry into electoral procedures, *Report*. Port Moresby, 1970.

(*See also* SOURCES FOR HISTORY)

COMMUNICATIONS. The people of the Territory of Papua and New Guinea traditionally possessed many means of communication, a number of which are still in use today. Simple oral methods, which include calling or yodelling, are practised especially among Highland peoples (*see* LANGUAGES, CALL). News of a helicopter crash on a cloud-covered mountain-top near Goroka in 1970 was first conveyed to the authorities many miles away and several thousand feet below by yodelling. Oratory is well developed among Papuans and New Guineans and few major decisions are made without much speech-making and discussion. Songs are often composed to commemorate special events. In a largely pre-literate society, rumour is an important means of spreading news. Reports of events, and the fears sometimes associated with them, often become magnified as news passes from mouth to mouth.

In some situations dancing can be a means of communicating information. For example, a war party may indicate its intentions to the residents of a village by the dances it performs as it approaches. Aggressive intentions may also be conveyed by the type of adornment worn by the intruders.

Fire or smoke are also used in the transmission of messages. Since fire is sacred, charcoal is sometimes used to place objects or places under a taboo. Plants are used in many ways: as calendars [q.v.] to indicate times for particular agricultural tasks; as number signals, for example, knotted leaves or vines are frequently carried by messengers to mark the number of days to a special event (*see* COUNTING AND NUMBERS); as taboo signs; as totem identification; and to convey other ideas. A betel nut with tooth marks in it may be an invitation for people to join in a fight.

Shells may be used to signify certain events. For example, among the Sengseng in New Britain a special kind of sea shell displayed by a man who has killed exonerates his action. Another kind is always carried by a messenger bringing news of a death to indicate the truth of his message. Mourning and grief can be shown by special clothing or adornment.

Many musical instruments are used to convey messages. Best known of these is the *garamut*, a large slit-gong made from a hollowed tree trunk. Other percussion instruments include drums made from wood and animal skins, tree roots and signal boards. Wind instruments, which include bamboo and water flutes, horns, shells and gourds, are particularly used for ceremonial occasions or on trading expeditions to warn of the trade party's approach. Blasts on conch shells may broadcast news of special events such as deaths.

Traditional methods of communication continue to be used today for traditional matters. For example, at a village near Goroka the preparation of traditional dress for a *singsing* demands the playing of specific tunes on sacred bamboo flutes. Taboo signs are frequently placed on gardens, trees and other property. However, introduced forms of communication are having increasing impact througout Papua and New Guinea. Radios are now found in many villages and programmes are broadcast in local languages as well as Pidgin English [q.v.], Police Motu [q.v.] and English. Many of the stations have excellent recordings of indigenous music, although they are played too rarely. Letters pass readily through mails and by hand between urban or plantation workers and relatives and friends in their villages. A Pidgin newspaper is published once a week.

A postal service (originally by surface) has operated in Papua since the later years of the nineteenth century. Before 1900 Queensland stamps were used. The first British New Guinea stamps issued in 1901 featured the Motuan *lakatoi*, or large trading canoes. The first radio-telegraph station was established at Port Moresby about 1912 and gave telegraphic communication to Thursday Island, Cooktown and Townsville. Under good conditions regular communications could also be established with Brisbane, Sydney, Darwin, Timor, Java and German New Guinea. Postal and telegraphic services also operated in German New Guinea up to 1914.

From these early beginnings the range and type of facilities for communications as well as the volume of messages transmitted have increased to cover Papua and New Guinea comprehensively. Carriage of mail by air became common with the introduction of air transport in the 1930s. Today the main means of business and personal communications within the Territory are postal services, telephone and radio-telephone services, and telegraph and telex services.

The Administration provides a full range of mail and postal services, although there are no house-to-house deliveries by postmen. Mail is delivered through private bags, private boxes and poste restante. There are registration and cash-on-delivery parcel services and provision for air letters and air parcels. Twenty-six post offices are operated by staff of the Department of Posts and Telegraphs, nineteen agency offices by field staff of the Department of District Administration, and forty-four offices are operated under contract, usually in conjunction with a private business.

There are frequent airmail services within the Territory and to Australia. Surface mail to Australia is despatched at approximately weekly intervals. Within Papua and New Guinea mails are conveyed principally by aircraft, but small ships and road transport are also used if they are quicker.

The Universal Postal Union Conventions apply to Papua and New Guinea. Under one of them literature for the blind is exempted from all postal charges.

In recent years the Posts and Telegraphs Department has issued special postage stamps [q.v.] of philatelic interest to mark important occasions or anniversaries, and to illustrate the fauna, flora, traditional art and buildings.

Except for about 120 telephones in Bulolo, Morobe District, all internal telephones and radio-telephone services are owned and operated by the Posts and Telegraphs Department. All external telephone and radio-telephone circuits are owned and operated by the Australian Overseas Telecommunications Commission.

A continuous telephone service is available at all main centres, and limited services operate at a number of minor urban centres. A trunk-line service is available at some twenty urban centres, and there is also a phonogram service at most major centres.

A major four-year $20 million capital programme to expand and improve telecommunications in the Territory began in 1968. A loan from the International Bank for Reconstruction and Development (World Bank) of over $6 million provided about 43 per cent of the total cost, 26 per cent will come from the Department of Posts and Telegraphs, and the remainder will be advanced by the government. The programme will provide 10,000 more lines in the local telephone exchange service, automatic telephone exchange equipment at thirty-five locations and the necessary increase in associated subscriber plant, telephones and radio outstations. The most important and costly part of the project is the virtual replacement of the long-distance toll and telegraph network with one of much greater capacity. A microwave 'backbone' route on the main island with a basic capacity of 300 channels will link the principal towns (Port Moresby, Lae, Madang, Goroka and Mount Hagen), and there will be spurs to other centres and off-shore islands. Fourteen main repeater stations are now being built on the mountain ranges of the main island at altitudes as high as 12,000 feet above sea-level. This programme should provide first-class links between the main centres, the Highlands, New Britain and Bougainville by 1972.

The Seacom cable terminal at Madang now has high-quality telephone circuit links with Lae.

Thus these two towns already enjoy first-class communications to Australia, Europe and North America. In 1972 all other major towns will have the same facility.

In 1971 there were some seventy-three telex machines in the Territory: forty-three in Port Moresby, twenty in Lae and ten in Bougainville. Subscribers include the Administration and a number of large commercial organizations. Capacity will be greatly increased in the next few years and by 1975 is expected to meet most telex demands.

The Department of Posts and Telegraphs maintains a residential college in Port Moresby to provide in-service training to international standards in telecommunications and postal services. Depending on the particular training need, courses for communications trainees vary from six months to two years; postal trainees undertake training lasting from one to three years and, in addition, undertake special advanced courses. Radio and telephone technician courses range from three to five years full time and selected trainees undertake block training to qualify as senior technicians. Some staff members receive advanced specialist training in Australia.

Commonwealth of Australia, *Annual Report of the Territory of Papua for 1967-1968*. Canberra, 1969; —— *Report to the United Nations on the Territory of New Guinea for 1967-1968*. Canberra, 1969; F.-J. Eilers, *Zur Publizistik Schriftloser Kulturen in Nordost-Neuguinea*. Siegburg, 1967.   MARION W. WARD

COMMUNITY MEDICINE. The health services of the Territory of Papua and New Guinea are the responsibility of the Department of Public Health which in addition to its own services makes use of those provided by mission organizations. Medical activities are administered within the framework of the Health Department and the eighteen Districts and seventy-three Sub-Districts of the Territory. The Sub-District hospitals and most of the District hospitals provide integrated promotive-preventive-curative health programmes for their communities. These are the centres from which all District health services emanate. At the Sub-District level there is a rapidly increasing participation by Local Government Councils in the provision of health services. Over 1.8 million of the 2.3 million people are now under local government influence. At each of the base hospitals—Port Moresby, Lae, Rabaul and Goroka —and at some of the District hospitals—Mount Hagen, Wewak, Madang—various specialist clinical services are provided. The child health specialists, in particular, are involved with the preventive and promotive aspects of health as well as clinical care.

More or less parallel with Administration medical services are the activities of the various missions, described later.

SUB-DISTRICT HEALTH SERVICES

These come close to the 97 per cent of the population living in rural areas in some eleven thou-

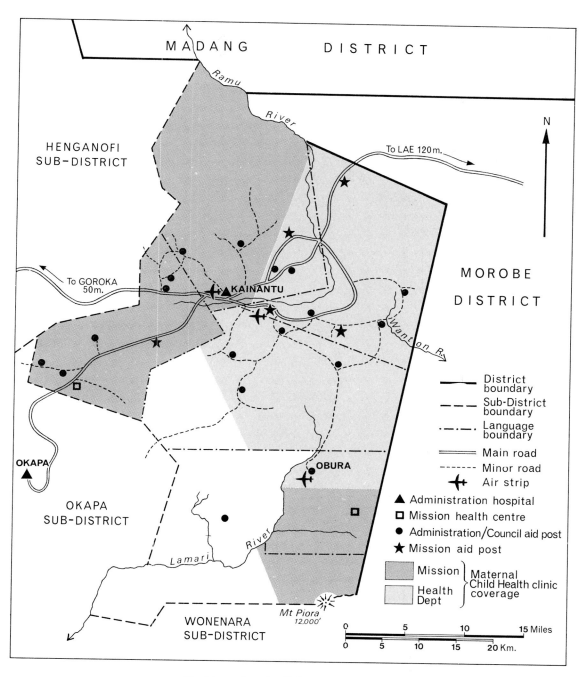

Health services for Kainantu Sub-District.

sand villages. Very few of these have more than a thousand people and some, as in the Chimbu District, are scattered hamlets of one or two households only. The average village population is one to three hundred. The immediate needs of the villages are provided by a network of aid posts, groups of which are supervised from health centres, Sub-District hospitals or District Health Offices.

The actual services and staff provided at the Sub-District level vary from place to place. A good example of one of the better serviced areas is the Kainantu Sub-District of the Eastern Highlands. The structure of the services in this Sub-District is typical but communications are especially good and the coverage better than in most other areas (see Map).

Kainantu is the gateway by road to the Highlands. The highway from the Markham Valley is the major route by which malaria, tuberculosis and venereal diseases have access to almost half the country's population. The Sub-District's population of almost 50,000 is found in 180 villages scattered over nearly 1,200 square miles. The area is divided into seven census divisions, four of which follow the main language groups. The principal cash crop is coffee and the staple is sweet potato. The main centre is the town of Kainantu with a population of 1,200 of whom 120 are expatriates.

There are eighteen aid posts administered either by the Local Government Councils or the Department of Public Health and five mission aid posts. Together with the hospital at Kainantu and two mission health centres this gives a ratio of approximately one health unit per two thousand people.

Four mission groups actively participate in the health work of the Sub-District; two administer health centres. One of these is being extended in association with the Local Government Council and the other provides an extensive ambulatory (out-patient) service for leprosy patients in addition to general services.

Maternal and child health clinics are conducted by both mission and Public Health Department units and together they make services available to over 75 per cent of the population.

The Sub-District hospital has 100 beds and an average of 150-200 new in-patients and 500-700 new out-patients each month.

A training centre has been established at Kainantu where medical assistants, medical students, and resident medical officers spend a considerable period of training in community health practice.

The Eastern Highlands District Malaria Service unit is also based at Kainantu and undertakes the field training of four categories of workers.

AID POSTS

Aid posts are the smallest and most peripheral health units. They, together with maternal and child health clinics, provide health services in the villages. Aid posts have been established to provide initial medical care for groups of between 500

and 3,000 people, involving over 1,250 aid post orderlies throughout the country. With improved communication networks, aid posts have been closed in some areas such as the Gazelle Peninsula of New Britain, while new ones are still being established in the more recently opened up areas of the Southern Highlands.

The aid post orderly is a base grade health worker who, after a primary education of 0-6 years, attended a training school for eighteen months to two years in which he acquired sufficient basic health knowledge to enable him to:
(1) maintain an aid post and provide simple curative treatments for the commonly occurring diseases of the country,
(2) recognize complications which require further treatment at a health centre or hospital,
(3) conduct domiciliary treatment for endemic diseases such as leprosy and tuberculosis [q.v.].
(4) regularly patrol a group of villages, usually 3-10, recognizing obvious diseases as well as poor hygiene such as an obviously polluted water supply or poor latrine facilities,
(5) assist various medical patrols such as malaria eradication, anti-tuberculosis and maternal-child health clinics,
(6) report epidemics such as gastroenteritis, whooping cough, malaria [q.v.], or deaths of an unusual nature in his area.

Aid post orderlies may be employed by Local Government Councils, by missions or directly by the Public Health Department. Most are part-time workers, few speak English and experience has shown that they need regular supervisory visits and opportunities for refresher courses of training, if they are to do effective work.

HEALTH CENTRES

Health centres are responsible for the health services of communities of ten to twenty thousand people. In a well staffed health centre there is a medical assistant or male nurse in charge, with one or two maternal and child health nurses, a health education orderly, an aid post orderly supervisor and a variable number of hospital orderlies according to the volume of out-patients and in-patients. Most of the mission centres are staffed by expatriate female nurses.

A medical assistant is 'a community health worker trained to administer a health centre and its field services, and to work with individuals, councils and other groups to develop a sense of personal and community responsibility for health'.

Village work is the main activity of health centre staff. They conduct village clinics which deal particularly with young children and antenatal mothers, school health services, aid post supervision, environmental sanitation projects such as improved housing and provision of clean water supplies, nutrition projects in association with the Department of Agriculture, Stock and Fisheries, e.g. fish ponds and peanut crops, and gather information on local customs and beliefs about health, hygiene and disease that will enable more effective health education to be carried out.

The extent to which these services are provided depends on the number of trained staff available. They handle out-patients and short-term in-patient cases such as acute respiratory and alimentary tract infections, malaria and normal obstetric deliveries. Long-term or complicated cases are referred to the nearest base hospital.

SUB-DISTRICT AND SMALLER DISTRICT HOSPITALS

Of the fifty-five rural Sub-Districts only fourteen have a doctor and a further twenty-five have a medical assistant as the head of the local health team. The distribution of these hospitals is shown on the map. The officer in charge is assisted in the conduct of the hospital by a group of hospital orderlies and sometimes one or two trained nurses, usually for maternal-child health work.

The hospital orderlies are of two types: general wardsmen and 'specialists'. The former do the routine patient care and dispensing of treatment under the supervision of a senior orderly or trained nurse. The latter group have shown aptitude for special skills and have become theatre, X-ray, laboratory and store orderlies. Most of the 'specialist' orderlies and a few of the general wardsmen have had some formal training at a base hospital but the rest have learnt their work 'on-the-job'. Only a few of the orderlies are female and they are used in the obstetric and children's wards. In some areas 'nursing aides' are now being trained. These are girls who may not have completed their primary education and are given a year's hospital training aimed:

to produce a good practical nurse in the hospital situation;

to help her become a better wife, mother and villager.

Hospital orderlies are no longer being recruited, their place being taken by the increasing number of graduates from the Territory's five schools of nursing which are providing more highly skilled nursing staff for rural hospitals. Most of them are used in maternal and child health work. There is usually a maternal and child health unit attached to the Sub-District hospital and it is concerned with the running of the nutrition and obstetric wards as well as the village community health, school health and family planning clinics.

The medical assistant performs much of the hospital management activities and together with the doctor is responsible for the rural health service administration of aid posts, health centres and immunization patrols. They also act as advisers on health matters to Local Government Councils.

LARGE DISTRICT AND REGIONAL HOSPITALS

Specialized clinical services are confined to these hospitals whose distribution is shown in the map.

Formerly their patients were drawn from the immediate area of the hospital with a smaller number of referrals coming from outlying hospitals. However, in recent years more patients are coming direct to base hospitals from peripheral areas.

Each of the regional hospitals has a specialist surgeon and physician and Port Moresby, Rabaul and Goroka provide specialist gynaecological and obstetric services. Port Moresby, Goroka, Mount Hagen, Madang and Wewak each have a child health specialist and Port Moresby, Lae and Rabaul each have an ophthalmologist. Mount Hagen and Wewak also have specialist physicians and Madang has the services of a surgeon specializing in leprosy reconstruction. There is a small radiotherapy unit at Port Moresby. Limited specialized pathological services are available at regional centres.

MISSION MEDICAL SERVICES

In the past some missions played a leading part in providing medical services and at present their principal spheres of work are:
(1) maternal and child health where they provide over half the services,
(2) staffing of leprosy and tuberculosis hospitals, many of which are owned by the Administration (see Map),
(3) participation in epidemiological and statistical studies,
(4) general medical work, operating from a health centre or a hospital with or without a surrounding network of aid posts. Mission health centres and hospitals tend to be in the more isolated areas of the country and serve populations which are generally much smaller than those served by Public Health Department units with equivalent staff establishments (see MISSIONS).

The Northern District of Papua, with a population of approximately sixty thousand, is a good example of the extent to which missions participate in the medical work of a District. Here they conduct a general hospital with a doctor in charge, staff an Administration tuberculosis hospital and run five health centres and five aid posts. An expatriate trained nurse is in charge of each health centre, serving an average population of less than five thousand. Together these sisters conduct over half the maternal and child health clinics in the District.

Mission hospitals with doctors and places where mission sisters are in charge of hospitals which serve as Sub-District hospital-health centres are shown on the map.

THE ROLE OF LOCAL GOVERNMENT COUNCILS

With increased incomes and greater awareness of the role that they can play in providing health services many of the Local Government Councils have taken over the administration of aid posts and health centres. These functions include construction and finance of buildings and water supplies, employment of personnel, payment of salaries, purchase of equipment and in some areas a role on hospital management committees. For many of these activities they receive subsidies from the Department of Public Health. All councils have been encouraged to establish health committees to initiate and co-ordinate

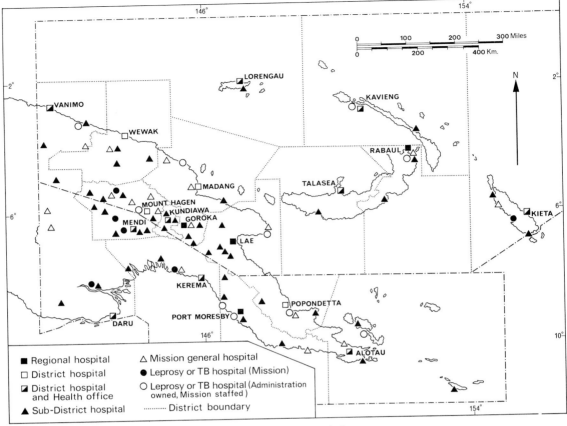

Distribution of hospitals.

health matters in their area and a senior health worker from the Health Department acts as adviser to the committee. Other health information relevant to the area is disseminated at general council meetings.

In line with the 1965 report of the International Bank for Reconstruction and Development no more base hospitals are being constructed by the Health Department. In some areas, such as Mount Hagen and Popondetta, the Local Government Councils and the general community have been responsible for establishing their own hospitals, for which the Public Health Department provides staff and supplies.

FINANCIAL ASPECTS

In 1967-8 $15,250,000 were spent on all health programmes in the Territory. This was 11 per cent of the total Territory budget, excluding contributions by Commonwealth departments but including the annual Commonwealth government grant. This represents $6.5 per head of the population.

In the last decade there has been a 300 per cent increase in Administration expenditure on health. Over the next five years to 1972-3 it is estimated that an average of $16.7 million will be spent annually on health services. Within the Health Department budget an increasing appropriation for community health programmes is being made, although the proportion of the total Territory budget devoted to health has been reduced from about 20 per cent in the immediate post-war years to 8.4 per cent in the Five Year Plan for 1968-9 to 1972-3.

The functional distribution of current expenditure for 1967-8 was as follows:

	%
Medical Services	58.5
Community Health	31.6
(includes maternal and child health, and preventive medicine programmes)	
Medical Training	5.1
Administration	4.3
Medical Research	.5
	100.0

In 1967-8 the Administration made charges for the first time for public hospital services at three regional hospitals. Treatments for children's immunizations and certain diseases such as leprosy and tuberculosis were exempted from payment of this 'fee for service'. Some missions have been charging for curative services for several years.

The charge at Port Moresby, Lae and Rabaul is 20 cents for an out-patient treatment and two dollars for an admission, irrespective of the length of stay in hospital or the treatment received.

It is expected that by making charges the out-patient loads at base hospitals will be reduced as patients will favour the free peripheral clinics. There will almost certainly be an extension of the 'fee for service' principle in Administration hospitals in the future. ANTHONY J. RADFORD

(*See also* MEDICAL SERVICES, HISTORY)

COMPANY LAW. The basis of company law in the Territory of Papua and New Guinea is the Companies Ordinance 1963-68 which is modelled on the uniform Company Acts introduced into the Australian States and the other Australian territories in 1962 and 1963. The present Territory legislation, which came into operation on 1 July 1964, replaced separate but virtually identical pre-war ordinances in Papua and New Guinea. The former legislation was based on the English Companies (Consolidation) Act 1908 and the New South Wales Companies Act 1899 and it inevitably proved inadequate to meet changing social and economic conditions.

The present legislation provides for the incorporation of six different types of company. These are as follows: public companies limited by shares; proprietary companies limited by shares; companies limited by guarantee; companies limited both by shares and by guarantee; unlimited companies in which liability is not limited to unpaid calls on shares and the members are in effect guarantors of the company; and no-liability companies, a class restricted to mining companies the members of which are not liable for unpaid calls on shares although on failure to pay calls the shares may be forfeited and sold.

Special provision is made for two further sub-categories. Firstly, there are companies formed for the purpose of providing recreation or amusement, or promoting commerce, industry, art, science, religion, charity, pension or superannuation schemes or any other object useful to the community and which do not intend to distribute profits among members. Such a company may obtain a licence from the Administrator directing that it be registered without the word 'Limited' in its name and it is then normally exempted from the requirement to lodge annual returns of directors, managers and secretaries and to publish accounts. Secondly, the Administrator may declare investment companies which then become subject to certain restrictions on borrowing, investment, underwriting, holding shares or debentures in other investment companies and buying or selling raw materials or manufactured goods. They are also required to adopt certain special accounting procedures.

Provision is made in the Ordinance for the registration of foreign companies which have previously been incorporated elsewhere. Such registration is required within one month of the foreign company's establishing a place of business or commencing to carry on business in the Territory. The company must have a registered office in the Territory and an agent who is personally responsible for compliance with the Ordinance by the company. It is required to lodge with the Registrar of Companies a copy of its balance sheet once a year and an annual return and on application by a member resident in the Territory must keep a branch share register at its Territory office.

The differences between the 1963 legislation and the former law are extensive. The principal changes may be listed as follows.

Prospectus safeguards. A prohibition is included against invitations to the public to subscribe for shares in or debentures of a company or to lend money to a company unless a prospectus containing certain statements and particulars has first been signed by or on behalf of the directors or proposed directors and registered with the Registrar of Companies. Criminal as well as civil liability is imposed for untrue statements or wilful non-disclosure in a prospectus.

End of separate registration. It is no longer necessary to register a company separately in Papua and in New Guinea if business is to be carried on in both Territories. The former maximum fee payable on registration ($150) has been removed, registration fees now being based on nominal share capital with no upward limit.

Alteration of company's objects. Under the former legislation there was a requirement that all special resolutions altering the provisions of the memorandum of association with respect to the company's objects should be ineffective until confirmed by the Supreme Court. The new legislation substitutes provisions for service of notice of the proposed resolution on the members, the trustees for debenture holders or debenture holders, and they may then apply to the Court for cancellation of the resolution.

Premium on issue of shares. Moneys received as premium on an issue of shares are to be treated as capital and cannot be distributed as dividends except as a bonus share issue.

Preference shares. Provision is made for the issue of redeemable preference shares and for a limited power, subject to a resolution confirmed by the Court, to issue shares at a discount.

No issue of share warrants. A prohibition has been placed on the issue of share warrants. The repealed legislation had allowed the issue of such warrants which were transferable by delivery with the result that the company's share register might not fully disclose all its members.

Company's disposal of shares. A company may no longer purchase, deal in or lend money on its own shares or provide financial assistance for the purchase of shares in itself or any holding company. The transfer or allotment of shares in a company to its subsidiary is also prohibited.

Time restriction on grant of option to take up shares. The Ordinance also prohibits the grant of options to take up shares extending beyond five years except by way of redemption of debentures.

Restrictions on issue of debentures. More detailed provisions have been included for the issue of debentures, the keeping of a register of debentures, the appointment and qualifications of trustees for the debenture holders and the contents of debentures and trust deeds issued to secure debentures.

Unit trusts protection. The holders of unit trusts and similar interests are now protected by the insertion of provisions requiring trust deeds and the trustees appointed thereunder to be approved, stipulating the covenants which must be included in such deeds and requiring the keeping of certain registers and the furnishing of certain returns to the Registrar.

Issue and transfer of shares. More elaborate provisions for the issue of share certificates and the transfer of shares are made. These include a requirement that a company must have ready for delivery the appropriate share certificate or debenture within two months of initial allotment or one month of transfer.

Directors. A public company must have at least three directors of whom at least one must be a natural person ordinarily residing within the Territory and another a natural person ordinarily residing within the Territory or Australia. A proprietary company must have at least one director who is a natural person ordinarily residing within the Territory.

No person may be named as a director or proposed director in the memorandum or articles of a company, or in a prospectus or a statement in lieu of prospectus, unless he or his authorized agent has signed and lodged with the Registrar a written consent to act and has taken up or agreed to take up any qualification shares required by the articles. No undischarged bankrupt or person convicted of certain offences may act as a director or take part in the management of a company except with the leave of the Court. A further prohibition is placed on the appointment or reappointment as a director of a person of or over the age of seventy-two except where such a person is appointed or reappointed by a three-fourths majority of members voting at a general meeting of which special notice has been given.

Specific provisions are included which require directors to disclose any interest in contracts or proposed contracts with the company and requiring them to act honestly and diligently. Directors and other officers are prohibited from making use of information acquired by virtue of their position so as to gain an improper advantage for themselves or to cause detriment to the company. Although similar sections were not contained in the repealed legislation the common law has always provided protection against fraudulent directors. Subject to a number of exceptions, prohibitions are imposed on a company (a) making a loan to or providing a guarantee or security for one of its directors or a director of a 'related company', (b) paying directors remuneration free of or varying with the rate of income tax, (c) making payments to directors as compensation for loss of office or in connection with retirement or

the transfer of any part of the company's property, and (d) exempting officers or auditors from or indemnifying them against legal liability for negligence, default or breach of duty or trust.

Registers of officers and members. A register of directors, managers and secretaries must be kept at the company's registered office and be available there for inspection by members and the public. Returns giving particulars of directors, managers and secretaries and changes in such particulars are required to be lodged with the Registrar. The repealed legislation only required a return and register of directors and managers in the case of a company not having a capital divided into shares.

As well as keeping a register of members at its registered office as was required under the repealed legislation, a company with more than fifty members is required to keep an index to the register and the register is now required to show details of every allotment of shares.

Annual returns, balance sheets, and profit and loss accounts. Certain additions are made to the particulars in the annual return required to be lodged with the Registrar by a company having a share capital. However, there is included a limited exemption from the requirement to furnish a list of members in favour of certain companies having more than five hundred members.

The new Ordinance requires that a company not having a share capital should now make annual returns.

Also inserted are detailed requirements of material to be included in balance sheets and profit and loss accounts, the imposition of a duty on directors to take reasonable steps to ensure compliance with these requirements and a specific requirement for companies to send copies of the profit and loss account, balance sheet and auditor's report to all persons entitled to receive notice of general meeting—usually all shareholders—at least seven days before the date of the meeting.

Companies Auditors Board. A Companies Auditors Board is set up to effect and control the registration of company auditors and liquidators in accordance with qualifications and restrictions detailed in the Ordinance. The repealed legislation made no provision for the registration of either auditors or liquidators. This innovation is accompanied by detailed provisions for the appointment and remuneration of auditors, their powers and duties and the contents of their reports which are required to be laid before the company at each general meeting.

Inspection on application and special investigation. The repealed legislation contained provisions for the appointment by the Administrator of inspectors to examine the affairs of a company on application by the holders of one-fifth of the issued capital; or, in the case of a company not having a share capital, by one-fifth of the members; or, in the case of a banking company, by the holders of one-third of the issued capital. The present legislation preserves these requirements for banking companies and companies not having a share capital, but in other cases enables application to be made by not less than two hundred members, by the holders of not less than one-tenth of the issued capital or by holders of debentures holding not less than one-fifth in the nominal value of debentures issued.

Provision has now been added for four types of special investigation which do not require application by any specified proportion of members or debenture holders: (a) a general investigation after declaration of the company by notice in the *Gazette* where the Administrator is satisfied that an investigation is desirable for the protection of the public, shareholders, creditors or unit trust holders or that it is in the public interest that allegations of fraud or misfeasance should be investigated or that for any other reason it is in the public interest that an investigation should be held, (b) an investigation to determine the true persons financially interested in the success or failure of a corporation or able to control or materially influence its policy, (c) an investigation into the ownership of shares or debentures of a corporation or the circumstances under which shares or debentures have been acquired or disposed of, (d) an investigation ancillary to one being conducted in an Australian State or another Territory.

Inspectors appointed to conduct any of the above types of investigation have wide powers to take possession of books and documents, to examine on oath the company's officers and agents and to investigate 'related companies'. Investigations can lead to the prosecution of delinquent company officers, to civil actions for damages for fraud or other misconduct in the promotion, formation or management of a company or to the winding up of the company. A company can also appoint its own inspectors by special resolution.

There is now specific statutory provision enabling a member of a company—or, after a report by an inspector, the Secretary for Law—to apply to the Court for relief against oppressive conduct in the affairs of the company.

Arrangements and reconstructions. Provision is made for compromises and arrangements between a company and its creditors or members or any class of them to be approved by the Court after a meeting of the creditors or members has by a three-fourths majority in value and a simple majority in number agreed. This type of provision has been liberally construed and enables a company to effect a complete reorganization of its share capital or to amalgamate with another company.

Take-over and compulsory acquisition. Detailed requirements are inserted for take-over offers including various notices and statements which must be given by both the offeror and offeree company and for the compulsory acquisition of the shares of dissenting shareholders after nine-tenths in value of shareholders have accepted a take-over offer.

Receivership. A prohibition has been placed on undischarged bankrupts, auditors or officers of the company, mortgagees or officers of a mortgagee corporation and persons not registered as liquidators being appointed or acting as receivers. A statement of affairs must be submitted to a receiver. Certain additions are made to the information and returns required to be lodged by the receiver with the Registrar and there is provision for certain debts to be paid in preference to principal and interest due under the debentures.

Alternative to receivership. The Ordinance introduces an entirely new procedure of official management as an alternative to receivership or liquidation. This concept is new in Australia although well tried in South Africa. It enables an insolvent company to obtain a moratorium from its creditors and continue trading in the hope that solvency will be restored. The directors or an unsatisfied judgment creditor in an amount of not less than $500 may initiate a meeting of creditors before whom is placed a statement of the company's affairs certified by the directors. Where the creditors consider that the company is unable to pay its debts, but that if it were placed under official management there would be a reasonable probability of its being able to do so, they may by special resolution place the company under official management for a period of up to two years, appoint an official manager, determine his remuneration and appoint a committee of management representative of the creditors and the members of the company. The directors then cease to hold office and the official manager assumes control of the company. He is required at six-monthly intervals to place before the creditors and members at a joint meeting a statement of the company's assets and liabilities and to report generally to those meetings. The committee of management assists and advises the official manager where he requests such assistance and advice and generally acts as a watch-dog over the interests of the creditors and members.

Legal proceedings against the company cannot be commenced or continued during the period of official management except by leave of the Court. If at any time the official manager forms the opinion that continuance of the official management will not enable the company to pay its debts, he is required to call separate meetings of members and creditors to consider the voluntary winding up of the company. At the expiration of the period fixed in the initial resolution the official management automatically determines; by then, if the official management has achieved its end, the company will again be solvent.

Liquidations. Part X of the new legislation deals in 103 sections with the winding up of companies. Its provisions are far more detailed than those of the equivalent part of the repealed legislation which contained a mere eighty-five sections. The repealed legislation still governs liquidations commenced before 1 July 1964. There are now three types of liquidation: (a) winding up by the Court, (b) members' voluntary winding up, (c) creditors' voluntary winding up.

The provisions in the repealed legislation for a winding up subject to the supervision of the Court have no equivalent in the new Ordinance. A company may now be wound up under an order of the Court where (a) it has so resolved by special resolution, (b) default is made in lodging the statutory report or holding the statutory meeting, (c) it does not commence business within a year from its incorporation or suspends its business for a whole year, (d) the number of members is reduced in the case of most proprietary companies below two or in the case of public companies below five, (e) the company is unable to pay its debts, (f) the directors have acted unfairly or unjustly, or where (g) an inspector has reported that a winding up is desirable because the company is unable to pay its debts or it is otherwise in the interests of the public, shareholders or creditors.

The Ordinance prescribes who may present a winding up petition. If the Court makes a winding up order on the hearing of the petition an official liquidator is appointed. The liquidator takes control of the company's property and seeks to realize its assets and pay its debts in accordance with a system of priorities set out in the Ordinance. He is required to lodge reports and accounts with the Court and the officers, or former officers, of the company are required to submit to the liquidator a statement of the company's affairs. The Court has power to examine persons considered capable of giving information on the company's affairs. The creditors and shareholders may appoint a committee of inspection which can give directions to the liquidator. Certain dealings with a company's property before the commencement of the liquidation may be set aside where there is an element of fraud or undue preference. When the liquidator has realized all the company's assets or so much as can be realized without needlessly protracting the liquidation, he applies to the Court and an order is then made releasing him and dissolving the company.

Both types of voluntary winding up are initiated by the company's passing a special resolution which must be lodged with the Registrar and advertised. A members' voluntary winding up is designed for use in the case of a solvent company. Before the passing of the winding up resolution the directors or a majority of them make a written declaration that they have formed the opinion after inquiry that the company will be able to pay its debts in full within a period not exceeding twelve months. There are penalties for making such a declaration without reasonable grounds and there is a presumption that an offence has been committed where the debts are not paid within the period stated in the declaration. In this type of winding up the liquidator is appointed by the company in general meeting. If it later appears to the liquidator that the company will be unable to pay its debts within the declared period there is provision for converting the liquidation into a creditors' voluntary winding up. If no declaration of solvency is made the winding up is from the outset a creditors' one and a meeting of creditors must be called for the day or the day following that on which the winding up resolution is to be proposed. A statement of the company's affairs is laid before the creditors' meeting and the creditors may nominate the liquidator and appoint a committee of inspection. In either type of voluntary winding up, if there is no liquidator acting the Court may appoint one and the Court may, on cause shown, remove a liquidator and appoint a replacement.

Meetings of the company and, in the case of a creditors' winding up, of its creditors, must be called by the liquidator each year and a final meeting is called when the affairs of the company are fully wound up. A return of the meeting and accounts are then lodged with the Registrar and three months later the company is automatically dissolved. In the case of all three types of liquidation the liquidator is required to keep proper books of account and is subject to the control of the Court. Every six months he is required to lodge accounts with the Registrar of Companies who may have them audited. All invoices, orders, letters, etc., issued by the company must bear the words 'In liquidation' after the name of the company. The Ordinance defines numerous offences which can be committed by past or present officers of companies in liquidation or by persons inducing an appointment as liquidator, falsifying or destroying books or records, failing to keep proper books or being parties to fraudulent trading.

Concealed assets. Although on dissolution following a liquidation there should be no further assets of the company as these will normally have been sold by the liquidator, it sometimes happens that assets are later discovered. The new legislation now provides that these vest in the Registrar who may dispose of them and account for the proceeds to the Treasurer. The Court may also within two years of dissolution declare the dissolution void. As in the repealed legislation the Registrar has power to strike defunct companies off the register after giving notice.

L. C. B. Gower. *The Principles of Modern Company Law.* 2nd ed., London, 1957; W. E. Paterson and H. H. Ednie, *Australian Company Law.* Sydney, 1962; G. Wallace and J. McI. Young, *Australian Company Law and Practice.* Sydney, 1965.

TERRITORY OF PAPUA AND NEW GUINEA LEGISLATION
Companies Ordinance 1963-68.
Companies (Undischarged Bankrupts) Ordinance 1966.

P. J. C.

CONIFERS, as a class of plants, include the familiar pines, spruces, firs and cedars of the Northern Hemisphere together with a rather different group from the Southern Hemisphere. Kauri pine, Huon pine, cyprus pine, hoop pine, none of which are pines in the strict sense of the genus *Pinus*, all occur south of the equator. The southern conifers exhibit rather different cone structures from those of the Northern Hemisphere.

The conifers are of particular interest to plant geographers because the modern flowering plant is generally thought to have evolved from plant forms which are referable to the conifers. Certain of the conifers still extant are described as living fossils and this has been said of the *Araucaria* forests of the Bulolo Valley.

Araucaria hunsteinii, the klinkii pine.

In the Northern Hemisphere the conifers form a vegetation zone across Europe, Asia and North America. Plant species other than conifers are rare in these forests. The southern conifers occur through normal forest communities as scattered trees usually not exceeding 50 per cent of the number of trees per acre; often they are much scarcer. Only on high mountains do conifers become frequent and contribute to the appearance of the vegetation. The *Araucaria* forests are exceptional in that individual trees tower above the closed canopy of rain forest.

Ecologically the conifers are found at all altitudes. Some species have a broad altitudinal tolerance; others are restricted to narrow zones. No conifers are known from the dry monsoon types of forest or from savannah communities, but one or more species are components of other vegetation types up to an altitudinal limit of woody growth.

The conifers of New Guinea have been classified into six genera in three families, namely:

Araucariaceae	Araucaria
	Agathis
Cupressaceae	Papuacedrus
Podocarpaceae	Dacrydium
	Podocarpus
	Phyllocladus

De Laubenfels (1970) considers that *Podocarpus* should be dissected into several genera and that one species formerly included in *Dacrydium* is the type of a new genus *Falcatifolium*.

Economically the conifers provide the raw material for the plywood industry based in Bulolo and other species provide high-grade sawn timber. To sustain and increase the softwood resources of the Territory extensive plantations of *Araucaria cunninghamii* and *A. hunsteinii* have been established at Bulolo (*see* FORESTRY). *Agathis* spp. have been grown experimentally as individual trees with considerable success. However, under plantation conditions insect pests could be a problem.

Family Araucariaceae. The cone-shaped fruits of this family are reminiscent of the Lebanon cedar, *Cedrus* and to a lesser extent the woody cones of the true pines, *Pinus* sp. This family today is restricted to the Southern Hemisphere on both sides of the Pacific basin. *Agathis* is confined to Malaysia, the western and southern Pacific, with *Araucaria* in South America but not New Zealand.

The genus *Araucaria* was first reported from New Guinea by von Mueller (1887) from among the very earliest collections of plants sent from Papua. Beccari [q.v.] (1877) also collected *Araucaria* on the Vogelkop peninsula in West Irian. In both localities *Araucaria cunninghamii* occurs. This species has the widest geographic distribution of the *Araucaria* species, extending from the Vogelkop to eastern Papua and south to northern New South Wales.

In north-east New Guinea, then Kaiser Wilhelmsland, a series of three coarsely broad-leaved species were described in succession. Two of these were from virtually the same locality; the third was not too far distant. The names, in order of publication, are *Araucaria hunsteinii* K. Schum.

(1889), *A. schummaniana* Warb. (1900) and *A. klinkii* Laut. (1913). These names have been shown to apply to a single botanical entity for which the correct name is *Araucaria hunsteinii* K. Schum. with the trade name of klinkii pine.

This is the timber of most of the Bulolo and Jimi Valley pine forests. *A. hunsteinii* is of restricted distribution; it is not found east of the Waria River, nor west of the foothills of the Sepik fall of the Western Highlands. The tree is very conspicuous as it towers out of the canopy layer of rain forests. In certain localities where cloud is frequent the *Araucaria* crowns are lost to the old man's beard lichen, *Usnea*.

The cones of *Araucaria hunsteinii*, while not as large as those of the Australian species *A. bidwilli*, are of considerable size and many weigh up to 2 lb. Seeds fall freely from the tree; the cone does not fall entire. In the plantation work by the Department of Forests at Bulolo large quantities of de-winged seed is stored under refrigerated conditions. Seed rapidly loses viability unless it is refrigerated, but the seed from cold stores can be sown at any time and will germinate satisfactorily.

The second genus in the family Araucariaceae, *Agathis* is somewhat of an enigma. Some authors regard *Agathis* as a genus of a few widely distributed and somewhat polymorphic species. Other authors write of many species with narrow geographic ranges. In New Guinea at least four entities are recognizable. In an endeavour to improve botanical knowledge of the species a collection of growing plants has been established in the botanic gardens at Lae. In the Sepik basin and in parts of West Irian *Agathis labillardieri* occurs. This species has been used as a source for the resin, dammar. *Agathis alba*, as understood here, is a very massive tree with a thick trunk and heavy crown. This species is usually found in hill country up to 6,000 feet. Dammar has been obtained near Lumi from what appears to be this species.

On the island of New Britain there is a species not yet botanically named. The foliage, although characteristically *Agathis*, is clearly distinct from the New Guinea mainland material. It is reminiscent of species from New Caledonia.

The fourth entity is a tree from the vicinity of Sogeri in Papua. This species may have affinity with the north Queensland species *Agathis palmerstonii* or may possibly be a form of *Agathis alba*.

The wood of *Agathis* is generally known as kauri pine and is valued in the trade. Natural regeneration is poor and experiments with plantations have not been successful. Seedlings were being planted in existing forest by Dutch foresters at Biak, but the success of these experiments is not known.

Family Cupressaceae, which includes the Cupressus trees of temperate latitudes, has a single representative in New Guinea. This tree was originally placed in the genus *Libocedrus* but the botanist Li (1953) created a new genus *Papuacedrus* for the local tree. Several species have been described but it is now considered that these differ only in foliage characteristics due to the exposure or altitude of the location in which the plant is growing. The species is *Papuacedrus papuanus*. The juvenile foliage is very attractive. The leaves are tightly adpressed to the twigs with narrow succedent wing-like leaf blades, the undersides of which are a pale silver-grey. Young trees are commonly planted in *singsing* grounds throughout the Western Highlands. Seedlings are collected wild from the forest. Other species planted are *Eucalyptus deglupta* with attractive green and pink bark, *Podocarpus archboldianus* with the young foliage pale brown, *Nothofagus grandis* with red young foliage and *Araucaria cunninghamii*, the latter probably because of its stature.

The bark of *Papuacedrus* is extensively used as a walling material for Highland houses and for bark belts for men. A grove of *Papuacedrus* trees on Mt Kaindi near Wau were all killed when the bark was removed for housing. The timber is valuable but nothing is known of the problems associated with growing this species under plantation conditions. As it occurs naturally between 7,000 and 10,000 feet above sea-level it could be a useful reforestation species for the denuded grasslands of the Highlands above the limits of economic agriculture.

Family Podocarpaceae occurs throughout the Southern Hemisphere with species extending north of the equator, particularly in Asia and the northwest Pacific. The treatment here does not follow that of de Laubenfels (1970).

Three genera of this family, *Dacrydium*, *Phyllocladus* and *Podocarpus* occur in the flora. The genus *Dacrydium* is represented by four species; a fifth is possibly referable to this genus, but is placed in a new genus, *Falcatifolium*, by de Laubenfels. *Dacrydium nidulum* is the correct name for the tree usually reported from New Guinea as *Dacrydium elatum*. This species tolerates a variety of soil conditions including poor acid soils. *Dacrydium nidulum* is sometimes found in almost pure stands, probably because the edaphic factors of the locality are such that few other species can survive. This is the case on the sandstones on Normanby Island. The young trees have soft, pendulous leafy shoots. There is a record that missionaries who were at Sattelberg before 1914 used the species for Christmas trees. *Dacrydium novo-guineense* is a species from the mountains above 5,000 feet. The third species, *Dacrydium xanthandrum*, is widespread from Borneo and the Philippines to the Solomon Islands. It occurs in the mountains between 3,000 feet and 10,000 feet above sea-level. The fourth species, *Dacrydium beccari*, occurs in West Irian and on Tagula Island as the variety *rudens*.

Dacrydium nidulum is a significant timber tree when occurring near centres of population; otherwise this genus is of little economic significance.

The genus *Falcatifolium* has been created by de Laubenfels to accommodate a small group of plants previously referred to *Dacrydium*. *Falcatifolium papuanum* is found as an understorey tree of the high mountains of the Owen Stanley Range.

Species of the genus *Phyllocladus* are remarkable in that the leaf-life structures (phyllodes) are in fact expanded shoots. There are only a few species in this genus of which only *P. hypophyllus* occurs in New Guinea. The form of this tree varies from a large forest tree at about 5,000 feet altitude, where it is used for timber production, to a forest-margin shrub at the upper limits of woody vegetation. Throughout the range leaf size varies. The cones in *Phyllocladus* are developed in the notches of each phyllode.

The genus *Podocarpus* includes at least twenty species in New Guinea. Several distinct sections are recognizable and these have been raised to separate genera by de Laubenfels. *Podocarpus* is treated here in the broad sense.

Section *Nageia* is distinct in that the leaves are very broad with fine, longitudinally parallel venation. In many respects the leaves resemble *Agathis*. The species may be readily distinguished by examining the terminal bud which is pointed in *Podocarpus* but rounded in *Agathis*. The common tree known as *Podocarpus blumei* is frequently mistaken for *Agathis*. De Laubenfels considers this species to be identical with *Podocarpus wallichianus* from India. Trees of this species may sometimes be common locally. The timber is of high quality. In the same section is *Podocarpus vitiensis* with acicular bilaterally flattened leaves. This species is distributed from the Moluccas to Fiji. The seeds are relatively large and red when ripe. Section *Dacrycarpus* includes the species of *Podocarpus* with *Dacrydium*-like leaves. The species of this section are frequently misidentified as *Dacrydium* by foresters. The commonest and most widely spread species is *Podocarpus imbricatus*. This tree exhibits remarkably polymorphic foliage. Adult trees have araucarioid foliage of numerous spirally arranged short acicular leaves. Juvenile foliage is bilateral and distichous. This foliage type may persist on trees 60 to 80 feet tall and only change to the mature form when the tree crown emerges through the canopy. Sometimes very young growing shoots have exceedingly tightly adpressed scale leaves giving cord-like new shoots. This tree is also known as *Podocarpus papuanus*. The wood is of high quality and frequently cut by Highland sawmills. At high altitudes a second species of this section *P. compactus* is common. Although short in stature this tree dominates the subalpine shrubbery from altitudes of 12,000 feet to the tree line. There are several other species of section *Dacrycarpus* but most are rare.

Quite distinct by their foliage are the podocarps with laterally flattened, parallel-sided leaves. One species, *Podocarpus amarus*, the black pine, has a globular fruit with the seed completely surrounded by the fleshy scale. This species is placed in the section *Sundacarpus*. The wood of this tree is a useful timber.

The section *Endocarpus* includes ten or more species in New Guinea. Several of these are widespread geographically. The fruit consists of a globular seed seated in a fleshy peduncle which is red to purple when ripe. There is an altitudinal succession apparent in New Guinea from the lowland species *P. neeriifolius* occurring between sealevel and 5,000 feet through *P. archboldianus* from

Cycas circinalis (left) Male plant with the developing cone from which pollen is shed; (right) Female plant with the specialized leaves called sporophylls on which the ovules develop. After fertilization the ovules become seeds.

5,000 to 8,000 feet with *P. pilgeri* and *P. brassii* in the upper levels. Both the leaves and the tree generally become smaller with increasing altitude. The wood is useful. The bark of the species included in this section is generally fibrous and appears to be spiralled around the trunk.

Botanically akin to the conifers are two groups of plants which are locally significant in New Guinea. The cycads of which two species occur, *Cycas circinalis* and *C. rumphii*, are more primitive in structure. *C. circinalis* is a single-stemmed plant with a crown whorl of pinnate leaves. From the centre of the crown develops a male cone, looking somewhat like a pineapple without the crown leaves, or individual shoots which spread between the leaves and become almost pendulous. These shoots develop one, or sometimes several, ovoid structures which are the seeds. Each shoot is technically a female sporophyll. *C. circinalis* is common in dry savannah situations near Port Moresby, the Markham Valley, Bulolo and elsewhere.

On some Pacific islands the seeds may be used for food. Prolonged cooking or washing is necessary to remove a cyanogenetic glucoside. Cattle suffer from a condition known as 'staggers' if allowed to feed on *Cycas* fronds. To kill the plants poison must be used, because they are fire resistant. Due to their somewhat similar appearance *Cycas circinalis* is sometimes confused with the Australian blackboys *Xanthorrhoea* spp. which do not occur in New Guinea.

Cycas rumphii is rarer and occurs only on rocky or coral coasts. The plants usually have many stems, the leaves are very large and dark green. It is sometimes grown as a garden ornamental in coastal towns.

The second group of plants related to the conifers are the Gnetaceae. This family exhibits many of the structural features which characterize conifers but also shows features associated with the flowering plants. The only genus *Gnetum* (the g is silent) includes two species of trees and some twenty-eight species of lianes. Both the trees and three to four lianes occur in New Guinea. The trees are important to the indigenous people because the bark provides fibre for string, the leaves are eaten as a green vegetable (*tulip*) and the seeds can be boiled and eaten. In Java boiled *Gnetum* seeds are pounded into a paste which is used to make *krupok*—thin cakes fried in oil. At least one of the lianes is reputed to have a poisonous sap.

J. T. Bucholz and N. E. Gray, 'A Taxonomic Revision of *Podocarpus*. Parts 1-13', *Journal of the Arnold Arboretum*, vols 29-43, 1948-62; W. Dallimore and A. B. Jackson, *A Handbook of Coniferae and Ginkoaceae*, rev. S. G. Harrison. London, 1966; H. Li, 'A Reclassification of Librocedrus and Cupressaceae', *Journal of the Arnold Arboretum*, vol. 34, 1953; J. D. de Laubenfels, 'A Revision of the Malesian and Pacific Rainforest Conifers, I, Podocarpaceae, in Part', *Journal of the Arnold Arboretum*, vol. 50, 1969; F. Markgraf, 'Gnetaceae', *Flora Malesiana*, series 1, vol. 4, 1951; E. D. Meijer, 'The genus *Agathis* in Malaysia', *Bulletin du Jardin Botanique*, series III, vol. 16, 1940; R. G. Robbins, 'Montane Formations in the Central Highlands of New Guinea', in *Proceedings of the Symposium on Humid Tropics Vegetation, Tjiawai (Indonesia) December 1958*. UNESCO, 1961; T. P. N. G. Department of Forests, *The Forests and Forest Conditions in the Territories of Papua and New Guinea*. Port Moresby, 1957; J. S. Womersley, 'The Araucaria Forests in New Guinea', in *Proceedings of the Symposium on Humid Tropics Vegetation, Tjiawai (Indonesia) December 1958*. UNESCO, 1961.

ACKNOWLEDGMENT

Photograph of *Araucaria hunsteinii* by courtesy of CSIRO.

J. S. WOMERSLEY

CONLON, Alfred Austin (1908-1961), intellectual, administrator and medical practitioner, was born at Paddington, N.S.W. and educated at Fort Street Boys' High School and the University of Sydney, where he graduated in Arts in 1931, and in Medicine twenty years later. In 1942, after a period in which he studied law, engaged in private study, and was concerned in student affairs, he became chairman of the wartime Prime Minister's Committee on National Morale, and soon afterwards Director of Research for the Army at Land Headquarters, Melbourne, with the rank of major. He was later appointed to the staff of the Commander-in-Chief, General Sir Thomas Blamey, as Director of Research and Civil Affairs with the rank of lieutenant-colonel, later colonel. From 1948 to 1949 he was Principal of the Australian School of Pacific Administration at Mosman, Sydney.

His influence on Papua and New Guinea was considerable in the period 1942-9. During World War II the Australian Army administered the Territories through Angau [q.v.], but high policy was laid down by the Commander-in-Chief, who drew his advice mainly from Conlon and his unit. Conlon also enjoyed a close personal relationship with the Prime Minister, John Curtin, and the Minister for External Territories, E. J. Ward [q.v.]. Much progressive and useful work was set in hand by the officers of the Directorate, in fields so diverse as law, animal husbandry, agriculture, education and colonial administration generally, all at a much higher level of expertise than was ever attempted by the peace-time government. Conlon's influence was decisive in the framing of legislation for the provisional civil administration which took over Papua and New Guinea when military operations ceased in 1945, and he secured the appointment of J. K. Murray [q.v.] as the first post-war Administrator.

The creation of the Australian School of Pacific Administration was also largely his work. This school was designed to give Administration officials a much higher standard of training than any hitherto available. Conlon's short period as principal was not a happy one, and from 1951 until his death in 1961 he practised medicine in Newcastle, Melbourne and Sydney.

His knowledge and interests were of unusual breadth, and his friends and associates were drawn from every profession and academic discipline. His foresight in New Guinea affairs was uncommon, and he frequently remarked in the 1940s that Australia could expect a bare twenty years to solve the problems facing it in New Guinea. The poet A. D. Hope wrote that Conlon had once said to him that if you were a jump ahead of other people, and never let them catch up with you, then you could get things done. Such an attitude led to administrative methods which were unorthodox and sometimes ineffectual, and which earned him considerable unpopularity. This, together with his shunning of personal publicity, has led to his importance being under-estimated. Gavin Long, in his concluding volume of the official War History, is unfair to the Directorate of Research and Civil Affairs.

Conlon died in Sydney on 21 September 1961, leaving a wife and one son.

Alfred Conlon: A Memorial by some of His Friends (Published for limited circulation). Sydney, 1963; G. Long, *The Final Campaigns* (Australia in the War of 1939-1945). Canberra, 1963.

P. A. RYAN

A. A. Conlon (right), with the Hon. E. J. Ward (second from right) in Papua in 1944.

CONTRACTS. The law of Papua and New Guinea regards certain agreements as binding upon the parties who enter into them. These agreements are usually called contracts and the body of legal doctrine relating to them derives from three main sources: English law, local legislation, and native custom.

The law of contracts in England is the product of the courts and the legislature. It was developed partly by the courts which administered the common law, partly by the Court of Chancery which administered equity, and partly by enactment of parliament. The historical reasons for this are not important in the context of Papua and New Guinea but what is important is that each territory has received as a component of its basic law the various elements which constitute the English law of contracts.

This has been accomplished in Papua by the Courts and Laws Adopting Ordinance 1889-1951 which adopted English legislation in force in Queensland on 17 September 1888 and the 'principles and rules of common law and equity that for the time being shall be in force and prevail in England' (sections 3, 4). In New Guinea the Laws Repeal and Adopting Ordinance 1921-52 adopted English legislation in force in Queensland on 9 May 1921 and the 'principles and rules of common law and equity that were in force in England' on the same day (sections 14, 16). Included in the body of English law thus imported to Papua and New Guinea was the law of contracts. However, the English law on the subject was not taken over in its entirety. It was received only so far as applicable to local circumstances but the practical effect of this limitation has been negligible.

Both territories adopted certain Queensland statutes as part of their basic law. New Guinea also adopted a number of Acts of the Commonwealth of Australia and Papuan Ordinances. The situation is further complicated by the fact that several imperial enactments apply of their own force to Papua, as a former British colony, but not to New Guinea. However, these complications are not significant for the law of contract because most of this legislation deals with other branches of the law.

The imported English law of contract has been modified and supplemented in some important respects by local legislation, especially since Papua and New Guinea came to have a single legislature in 1951. Some of this legislation, such as the Goods Ordinance 1951 which codifies the law relating to the sale of goods, simply re-enacts English legislation. Other Ordinances, however, have effected drastic changes in the imported law. For instance the Transactions with Natives Ordinance 1958-63 provides that a contract to which a native is a party 'is unenforceable as against any party thereto unless the contract is in writing and contains the full names and residences of every party thereto and what is to be done under the contract by each of those persons' (section 6 (1)). There are, however, important exceptions such as certain job contracts and other contracts the consideration for which passing to or from a native or natives does not exceed $100 (section 6 (2)). The Ordinance defines a job contract as 'a contract for the performance of a piece of work

by a native or natives other than a contract which creates the relationship of master and servant between the parties or two or more of them' (section 4). If an action is brought on a contract to which a native is a party the court may, 'whether the contract has been completely executed by all the parties thereto or not, ignore the terms of the contract and give such a verdict as the Court considers equitable' (section 8).

The Native Employment Ordinance 1958-70 of Papua and New Guinea also limits freedom of contract where a native is a party. This Ordinance prescribes in detail the terms which must be included in contracts of service for labourers recruited to work outside their home areas.

Other important Ordinances which impinge upon the law of contracts are the Hire-purchase Ordinance 1966, the Hire-purchase Agreements Ordinance 1951, and the Statutes of Frauds and of Limitations Ordinance 1951. The Hire-purchase Ordinance 1966 sets out the requirements of a valid hire-purchase agreement and specifies the powers of the owner of goods on hire if the hirer defaults. It repeals the Hire-purchase Agreements Ordinance 1951 which nevertheless continues to govern agreements entered into before the commencement of the 1966 Ordinance. The Statutes of Frauds and of Limitations Ordinance 1951 is a re-enactment of English legislation which provides that certain contracts, including a contract for the sale of an interest in land, be evidenced by writing before becoming enforceable.

The third substantial component of the law of contracts is native custom. The Native Customs (Recognition) Ordinance 1963 provides for the recognition and enforcement of native custom by the courts in certain cases and one such case is in relation to 'a transaction which the parties intended should be, or which justice requires should be, regulated wholly or partly by native custom' (section 8 (g)). This provision enables the courts to enforce certain agreements which would not be valid contracts according to the law imported from England. If an agreement is valid according to the native custom appropriate to the case then it is, as a general rule, enforceable though it would not be valid at common law.

For instance, English law insists that all contracts other than those contained in documents called deeds be supported by consideration. In other words, each party must be able to show that by entering into the agreement he either confers a benefit upon the other party or brings some detriment upon himself. However, if a relevant native custom regarded an agreement as valid though unsupported by consideration a court in Papua or New Guinea would be at liberty to apply the custom and enforce the agreement, thus ignoring the rules of the imported law.

It must be noted that the opportunity of the courts to apply section 8 (g) is limited by subsections (b) and (c) of section 6 of the Ordinance which provide that a native custom shall not be applied if 'it is inconsistent with an Act, Ordinance or subordinate enactment in force in the Territory or a part of the Territory' or 'its recognition or enforcement would result, in the opinion of the court, in injustice or would not be in the public interest'.

The customary component of the law of contracts is to a very large extent unrecorded and no attempt has been made to ascertain whether there are customs relevant to this branch of the law which are generally recognized as binding throughout the Territory. However, the Local Courts—established by the Local Courts Ordinance 1963-66 have extensive jurisdiction in matters arising out of and regulated by native custom and the recorded decisions of these courts, and of the Supreme Court which entertains appeals from them, may in time make it possible to define customary contractual rules with more precision and to ascertain the extent of their operation throughout Papua and New Guinea.

At present most litigation concerning contracts is decided by reference to the imported English law and local legislation. However, native custom will undoubtedly become more significant now that it has been recognized as a source of law and the courts have been enjoined to apply it.

P. S. Atiyah, *An Introduction to the Law of Contract*. Oxford, 1961; G. C. Cheshire and C. H. S. Fifoot, *The Law of Contract*. 2nd Australian ed., Sydney, 1969; J. R. Mattes, 'Sources of Law in Papua and New Guinea', *Australian Law Journal*, vol. 37, 1963-4; G. H. Treitel, *The Law of Contract*. 2nd ed., London, 1966.

TERRITORY OF PAPUA AND NEW GUINEA LEGISLATION

Ordinances Revision Ordinance 1962.
Native Customs (Recognition) Ordinance 1963.
Native Employment Ordinance 1958-70.
Statutes of Frauds and of Limitations Ordinance 1951.
Transactions with Natives Ordinance 1958-63.

TERRITORY OF PAPUA LEGISLATION

Courts and Laws Adopting Ordinance 1889-1951.

TERRITORY OF NEW GUINEA LEGISLATION

Laws Repeal and Adopting Ordinance 1921-52.

R. S. O'R.

CO-OPERATIVES. During World War II, contact with servicemen displaying great material wealth and reflecting the organization and techniques of industrial countries prompted indigenous group economic activities in many parts of the Territory of Papua and New Guinea, often using money earned working for the armed forces or received as war damage compensation. In the Trust Territory of New Guinea these groups called themselves *kampani* (Pidgin for 'company') and in Papua, 'co-operative society'—the use of this term probably came about through the efforts of a missionary in the Northern District who preached Christian co-operation in pre-war days. The indigenous people's desire to undertake such ventures was also stimulated by a few private expatriates in Port Moresby.

In May 1947 the Administration recognized the existence of an indigenous co-operative movement. The task of guiding and assisting it was vested in the Director of the then Department of District Services and Native Affairs. A special Co-operative Section, later known as Registry of Co-operative Societies, headed by a Native Affairs officer who had studied co-operatives and other native economic activities in West Africa, was set up in the Department, and a small team of officers started to investigate the ramifications of the co-operative movement and its future possibilities.

From the outset, self-help was encouraged and the Registry confined itself to investigating potential, providing legal status, advising management, offering information on markets, teaching bookkeeping and co-operative principles, and explaining meeting procedures. The Co-operative Societies Ordinance 1950 was enacted, based on the New South Wales Co-operation Act, but this proved too comprehensive and cumbersome for Territory conditions, and a much simpler law, Native Economic Development Ordinance 1951, was therefore passed. This Ordinance made possible the formation of co-operatives by peoples at all levels of development, and provided adequate protection, corporate status and limited liability until progress should make necessary more advanced legislation. Indigenes only were permitted to form co-operatives under this Ordinance.

In the early stages, the desire of almost every group was to operate a retail store. This appeared to be due, firstly, to the wish to eliminate the middleman—though the people did not fully understand his function in the distributive cycle or the work that has to be done to earn his profit; secondly, to the desire for enhancement of village prestige; thirdly, to convenience. The Registry has tried to change this emphasis on retail trading to an interest in the more balanced type of producer-consumer enterprise. It has also collaborated with the Department of Agriculture, Stock and Fisheries to bring about diversification of cash crops and has encouraged other commercial activities. Commencing in the Central and Gulf Districts, the co-operative movement gradually spread and now has secondary and tertiary organizations in fourteen of the eighteen Administration Districts.

Co-operatives operate according to the Rochdale principles: (1) voluntary membership; (2) democratic control—one member, one vote; (3) restriction of interest on share capital—co-operative legislation restricts dividends on share capital to 6 per cent; (4) distribution of surplus as dividends on the value of members' purchases; (5) political and religious neutrality; (6) goods sold at market prices; and (7) active education in co-operation. The Administration confines itself to providing extension services and ensuring that co-operatives work according to their rules and observe the Ordinance.

The co-operative movement in Papua and New Guinea is an apex structure. At the bottom are the primary co-operatives, nearly all of them in rural areas, which are mostly multi-purpose ones, buying and, where necessary, processing produce such as copra, coffee, rice and peanuts, and operating retail stores. These primary co-operatives, known as societies, are independent legal entities, wholly owned and controlled by indigenous people, with an annual general meeting as the supreme authority and an elected board of directors controlling routine activities. The most common share unit is $10.

Most primary co-operatives join together at area or District level to form secondary organizations known as associations, which undertake inspections and audits of their member co-operatives. The associations join together to form regional tertiary organizations known as unions which, together with certain service co-operatives such as Co-operative Security Society Ltd, Co-operative Shipping & Freezer Society Ltd and P.N.G. Co-operative Investments Ltd, join together to form the top co-operative body in Papua and New Guinea, the T.P.N.G. Federation of Co-operative Unions Ltd. The Federation wholly owns the Co-operative Wholesale Society Ltd which, with main branches at Lae, Port Moresby, Rabaul and Samarai (and later on elsewhere), imports or otherwise obtains goods for sale to primary co-operatives. The Federation operates the secretariat for the whole of the Papua and New Guinea co-operative movement and renders some special services to societies, associations and unions, such as the preparation of taxation returns.

Outside the co-operative apex structure, but in many instances parallel to it, are several service co-operatives. The Central Co-operative Finance Society receives interest-bearing deposits from co-operatives and lends money to co-operatives to expand their present trading or service activities and/or to undertake new activities. Lending could be to enable acquisition of fixed assets, stock-in-trade, equipment, etc. The Co-operative Security Society insures vessels and selected fire risks of co-operatives. Several co-operative shipping societies operate vessels carrying goods, produce and passengers. At Moveave in the Gulf District a sawmill is being operated by a co-operative which also markets copra and runs a trade store. In the 1950s two tradesmen's co-operatives undertook house building contracts at Port Moresby but went into liquidation because of management problems. A co-operative owns and operates a coconut plantation in the Manus District and two co-operatives have been formed on the Gazelle Peninsula, East New Britain District, to buy coconut plantations and convert them into settler blocks for members. A co-operative fishing society on Yule Island, Central District, has undertaken a crayfish processing and marketing venture jointly with an expatriate entrepreneur.

A recent development has been the establishment of traders' wholesale co-operatives which supply bulk consumer goods to members who own and run their own trade stores. This departure from co-operative ownership and management of retail trading caters for the emerging individual indigenous entrepreneur.

From 1950 on co-operatives known as rural progress societies have been initiated by the De-partment of Agriculture, Stock and Fisheries, with the prime object of meeting a development need for the processing and marketing of produce, as well as providing an institution in which indigenous farmers can be educated in technical skills and managerial know-how. Rural progress societies are only established where indigenous communities wish to pool their resources to undertake an agricultural venture which necessitates the purchase of relatively costly equipment such as a processing plant, or for the provision of marketing services. These societies are registered under the Co-operative Societies Ordinance and an agricultural extension officer is appointed as adviser under section 11 of the Ordinance. Rural progress societies do not act as producers themselves but are an adjunct to rural community development and are centres for the diffusion of agricultural extension services. Credit sales of produce by growers to their rural progress societies and deliberately conservative first payments for produce, followed by significant payments or rebates, are avoided. The rules of rural progress societies are similar to those of other co-operatives.

The following figures show the growth and present state of the co-operative movement, including the rural progress societies:

Table 1

TURNOVER OF PRIMARY CO-OPERATIVE SOCIETIES

Year	Retail Trading	Copra	Other	Total
	$	$	$	$
1956–7	1,079,796	734,840	240,462	2,055,098
1957–8	879,364	494,720	130,234	1,504,318
1958–9	881,556	594,366	158,906	1,634,828
1959–60	1,124,838	1,046,172	153,892	2,324,902
1960–1	1,366,474	865,844	131,500	2,363,818
1961–2	1,350,142	784,654	92,958	2,227,754
1962–3	1,401,760	746,274	139,740	2,287,774
1963–4	1,393,380	810,692	314,218	2,518,290
1964–5	1,703,946	712,176	1,433,602	3,849,724
1965–6	2,044,860	914,586	2,150,359	5,109,805
1966–7	2,012,897	770,466	2,191,061	4,974,424
1967–8	2,197,326	725,772	2,455,320	5,378,418

SOURCE: T. P. N. G. Registry of Co-operative Societies

Apart from a fall in turnover in 1957-8 and 1958-9 and a static situation between 1960 and 1964, the co-operative movement's turnover has made steady progress, with a spectacular rise in 1965-6. Primary products accounted for about half of total turnover throughout and three-fifths in 1965-6, almost entirely made up of tropical products that are subject to wide market fluctuations over which producers have no control. Most indigenous producers do not yet fully understand the market mechanism and, with very few exceptions, still function in their traditional subsistence economy with cash cropping as a subordinate activity to acquire goods not obtainable in any other way. Unfavourable market trends will frequently cause some indigenous producers to return to entirely subsistence production.

Because of fluctuating world market prices for primary produce statistics of annual turnover are not a true indicator of co-operative development and it is more useful to look at other indicators of growth, such as capital formation.

Table 2
GROWTH IN THE CO-OPERATIVE MOVEMENT

Year	Members (Primary Societies Only)	Capital (Primary Societies Only)	Total Reserves (All Co-operatives)
	$	$	$
1956–7	64,035	766,662	n.a.
1957–8	61,733	851,036	n.a.
1958–9	72,730	886,170	n.a.
1959–60	71,651	963,770	n.a.
1960–1	74,140	1,026,448	286,624
1961–2	78,203	1,154,790	316,766
1962–3	85,451	1,228,790	362,094
1963–4	85,900	1,288,720	423,874
1964–5	94,083	1,562,374	533,282
1965–6	102,120	1,823,091	680,785
1966–7	109,488	2,063,221	750,472
1967–8	109,366	2,330,487	827,306

n.a. not available

NOTE: In 1967–8 there were 316 primary societies, 14 secondary associations, 6 service associations, and 1 tertiary federation.
SOURCE: T. P. N. G. Registry of Co-operative Societies.

The reserves of the co-operative movement have risen from $282,492 in 1960-1 to $655,921 in 1965-6 and investments from $143,896 to $839,574 (Federation and Security Society not included).

Sound development and growth of the co-operative movement have been hampered by the low level of general education and lack of knowledge of basic economics and business among the indigenous people. An educational programme has been set up, therefore, aimed at employees, directors and members of co-operatives as well as Registry staff, and a Co-operative Educational Centre has been established at Port Moresby. The educational programme of this Centre and the experience gained overseas by Registry officers and indigenous members of the co-operative movement have brought about a greater knowledge among co-operative employees and Registry staff. This, together with the rapidly rising level of general education among the indigenous people, has helped to prepare Papuans and New Guineans for senior positions in the co-operative movement and the Registry.

The figures quoted in the tables do not show the intangible benefits of co-operative development, such as the spread of business management, knowledge and skill. Of the thousand students who have already attended the Co-operative Educational Centre and of the others who have gained knowledge and experience as directors and employees of co-operatives, many have established businesses of their own or taken up responsible positions in private enterprise. Fifteen of the thirty-eight elected indigenous members of the House of Assembly in 1966 have been or are associated with co-operatives.

Other factors, such as the constraints of custom and status and the extended family system, presented difficulties during the early years of co-operative development. Traditional religious and social customs, closely integrated with the use of land and systems or methods of agricultural practice, frequently hinder the indigenous people's movement from subsistence to cash production and retard co-operative development. The close collaboration between the Registry of Co-operative Societies and the Department of Agriculture, Stock and Fisheries, the rising level of education, and a growing culture contact and familiarity with modern commerce, have made possible a rapid advance in the co-operative movement in recent years. Papuans and New Guineans are beginning to acquire the skills needed to manage the more complex types of co-operatives that are constantly being formed to provide the services needed by the people.

It has always been recognized in Papua and New Guinea that co-operatives are very much a form of business enterprise in which the people who supply the capital and organize activities are also the suppliers and/or customers, and that, in general, economic or commercial services provided by co-operatives are the same as those supplied by private firms. At the same time, efficient co-operatives give the people the satisfaction of supporting an undertaking in which they have a stake as part-owners and in which they are associated with others sharing common interests, common problems and a common background. For this special reason and because co-operatives have often provided services in areas that have not attracted other forms of business organization, the co-operative movement has received the support of many indigenous people. Its future success will depend upon its continuing ability and capacity to make the best use of resources and to meet the needs of the people.

Since the above was written there has been further growth of the co-operative movement. During 1968-9 primary co-operatives had 129,343 members, $2,582,757 subscribed capital, $1,687,817 reserves and $6,411,963 turnover. Statistics for 1969-70 and 1970-1 are expected to show further increases.

Significant steps have been taken to further co-operative education and training. In 1970 a statutory body, the Co-operative Education Trust, was established and legislation was enacted to levy co-operatives for the purpose of co-operative education and training. The Trust, on which indigenes have majority representation, administers the Co-operative College which has been established near Port Moresby as part of a three-year joint project by the indigenous co-operative movement, the government and the United Nations Development Programme, involving an expenditure of $900,000.

T. P. N. G. Registry of Co-operative Societies, *Annual Report 1947-8* to *1965-6*. Port Moresby, 1949-67; —— *The Co-operative Movement in Papua and New Guinea*. South Pacific Commission, Technical Paper no. 42. Noumea, 1953.   H. H. JACKMAN

COPYRIGHT LAW. The law protects authors—and their assignees—of original literary, dramatic, musical or artistic work against the reproduction, or substantial reproduction, of those works. Generally, copyright enures for the duration of the author's life and until fifty years after; or, if the work was not published during his lifetime, until fifty years after the date on which it was first published.

Until 1969 the substantive basis of copyright law in Papua and New Guinea, as in Australia, was supplied by the British Copyright Act 1911. That Act was adopted by the Commonwealth Copyright Act 1912-1963 which provided for its extension to such territories as the Governor-General, by proclamation, declared. In 1941 the Act was proclaimed to extend to Papua, New Guinea and Norfolk Island.

In May 1969 the Copyright Act 1968 came into operation. The Act makes certain substantial changes to the former legislation. Rights given to authors, composers and creative artists are confirmed and the rights are extended to cover new means of reproduction such as television broadcasting and multi-copying and tape-recording appliances; they also meet the considerable changes which have occurred in the film and sound-recording industries and those in library administration.

The legislation enabled Australia to become a party to at least two international agreements on copyright: the Brussels revision in 1948 of the Berne Convention for the Protection of Literary and Artistic Works and the Universal Copyright Convention of 1952. A notable advantage of adherence to the Universal Convention will be to allow Australian book publishers to have a readier access to the United States market. The new law applies to the territories of the Commonwealth.

Other significant features of the Act are the abolition of registration and the avoidance of any overlap between copyright and industrial design protection. The copyright term has been slightly lengthened by calculating the commencement of the fifty-year period from the end of the calendar year of the author's death or first posthumous publication.

The British Act of 1911 set up an 'imperial copyright area' which was to be co-extensive with the whole of what was then the British Empire. This is now an inappropriate concept and, in the case of original literary, dramatic, musical or artistic work that is published, has been replaced by the criterion of Australian 'place of first publication' or the author's status as an Australian citizen, protected person or resident at the time when the work was first published; in the case of original unpublished work, by the criterion of Australian citizenship, protection or residence at the time when the work was made—or, if the work extended over a period, where the author was thus 'qualified' for a substantial part of that period. Regulations under the Act extend copyright protection to other countries and to international organizations.

A copyright tribunal has been established to arbitrate on disputes relating to royalty payments on recordings, to make determinations of equitable remuneration to be paid to copyright owners in works sound-recorded or filmed or adapted—or, in the case of sound-recordings for the making of a record embodying the record, and to make orders confirming or varying any proposed licensing schemes referred to it. It is not yet known whether the tribunal will be peripatetic; if not, it could prove to be a less convenient forum than its predecessors—especially where the parties to a dispute are resident in distant places like Papua and New Guinea. Questions of law arising before the tribunal are referable to the High Court.

To date copyright practice in Papua and New Guinea has been of negligible proportions. This does not mean that the indigenous population is indifferent to the unauthorized reproduction of its original works. On the contrary, the available evidence suggests that in many areas the imitation —without compensatory payment—by one group of the songs, or totemic or tattoo designs of another results in ill-feeling and sometimes in acts of violent redress. The Native Customs (Recognition) Ordinance 1963 recognizes and enforces custom but not where it is inconsistent with legislation.

A developing concern in sections of the community about the political, economic and cultural implications of independence is likely to be matched by an increased awareness in the Territory's authors and craftsmen of the law's protective interest in their works.

Attorney-General's Department, *Report of the Copyright Law Review Committee, 1959.* Canberra, 1960; Commonwealth of Australia, *Gazette,* no. 187, 1941, p. 2078; —— *Parliamentary Debates (H. of R.),* vol. 55, 1967, pp. 2327-35; R. W. Williamson, *The Ways of the South Sea Savage,* pp. 140-2. London, 1914.

COMMONWEALTH OF AUSTRALIA LEGISLATION
Broadcasting and Television Act 1942-69.
Copyright Act 1913-63.
Copyright Act 1968.
Designs Act 1906-68.
Patents, Trade Marks, Designs and Copyright Act 1939-53.
Commonwealth Statutory Rules, 1941, p. 1131.
Copyright Regulations.
Copyright (International Protection) Regulations.

TERRITORY OF PAPUA AND NEW GUINEA LEGISLATION
Native Customs (Recognition) Ordinance 1963.

COUNTING AND NUMBERS. Different groups in the Territory of Papua and New Guinea have used a wide variety of devices and techniques, as well as systems of numeration or counting, to tally and, less frequently, record quantities of goods and multiples of people, animals, shells, or days until a meeting or ceremony is due. It is as yet impossible to provide a comprehensive guide to the counting systems of Papua and New Guinea or to provide a key to their geographical distribution as Galis has done for West Irian. Readers who wish to inquire into the system employed by specific populations, or into the distribution of a particular method or device, should consult the bibliography below. This article is confined to a survey of the kinds of tallying, recording and counting systems used, and examples are provided only of each major type.

TALLYING DEVICES

The most frequently used tallying devices are probably the counter's fingers and/or toes, together with those of his friends where he cannot carry ten or twenty in his head and start again as each set of tallies is exhausted. Many people also check off numbers on their bodies by proceeding from the fingers of one hand, up one arm, across the body and down the other side. Other, less personal, methods of tallying and recording quantities include cutting notches in a stick, piling sticks or stones together, or tying knots in lengths of twine. Each notch, stick, stone or knot then represents a certain number of units of whatever is being counted.

Among the Metlpa, Western Highlands, a small length of bamboo is added to those already hanging horizontally from a man's neck each time he gives a partner eight to ten *kina* shells in ceremonial exchange (*see* MOKA). The Parevavo, inland from the Gulf of Papua, tie a knot in a length of twine for each man killed in battle and unravel the knots as each death is avenged. Some Chimbu groups reputedly kept scoreboards in red pigment on the walls of rock shelters, one mark for each important man who died in battle. The Elema, Gulf of Papua, keep a positive and negative tally of men killed ('ours' on the right, 'theirs' on the left) by sticking pieces of *selo* (the hard outer covering on the stalk or midrib of the frond) into either side of a stripped sago palm frond. They used a similar device, with *selo* pieces variously shaped, to record the different kinds of earthenware pots and quantities of sago that they exchanged with their Motuan partners in the *hiri* [q.v.].

KINDS OF NUMERICAL SYSTEMS

The traditional counting systems of Papua and New Guinea have never been systematically collected, nor thoroughly classified, except for a few restricted areas. An early attempt was made by Ray to classify them according to language type. His general system of classification seems now to have had serious doubt cast upon it, although no body-counting systems, as distinct from finger and/or toe-counting systems, have so far been recorded as being in use among speakers of Austronesian languages.

Abstract and finger-counting systems. The British

employ a variety of systems with different numerical bases to express different kinds of quantities: e.g. amounts of money, distances and weights are all measured in terms of separate sets of bases. Similarly, some groups in Papua and New Guinea employ different systems for different kinds of calculations. The Siuai, southern Bougainville, at one recorded extreme, employ a decimal system but with a separate set of terms to denote each number according to which of forty categories the item(s) being counted come(s) under. Other groups employ different bases according to what is being counted (*see* below, Keraki-Gambadi-Semariji, Enga, Mailu and Duke of York Group systems), and it is common for calendars [q.v.] to have a numerical base unlike that in daily use for other purposes.

The most frequently occurring kinds of numerical systems are those with bases of two, five and ten. The Kiwai, Western District, count as follows:

1 *nau*
2 *netewa*
3 *netewa nau*
4 *netewa netewa*, etc.,

in a perfect binary system. Curiously, however, and unlike many other binary counters, they also have three special sets of suffixes which they attach to nouns, pronouns and verbs respectively to indicate whether they refer to one, two, three or more (some, many, all, etc.) actors or objects in a sentence.

The Kuman, Chimbu District, also count in twos, although at five they sometimes break the system ('two then two then something') to say 'one hand', and at ten, 'two hands', as in a base-five system—which has a binary base for numbers not divisible by five.

Most of the recorded counting systems with a base of five are really only quinary for numbers not divisible by ten or twenty. They are, in fact, vigesimal (that is, base-twenty) or decimal (base-ten, e.g. Domara, Sinaugoro) systems, counted internally in fives, and not infrequently, as with the Kuman, with a binary system for numbers not divisible by five.

The Wedau people, Milne Bay region, employ a base-five system—ten is expressed as 'hands two are finished'—until twenty, when they say 'one man is dead', and their system is thus truly vigesimal. The Suau, also Milne Bay, employ a similar system, except that they have a special word for ten that is not derived from five on the way to twenty, after which they continue to count by twenties. The Kamano, Eastern Highlands, employ a vigesimal system, with the numbers not divisible by five made up according to a binary system, although they do not have a single term for each number. They tend rather to describe the number they are up to with such expressions as 'hand two finish five finish two take' for seventeen and 'hand two finish hand one leave out' for nineteen.

There are some counting systems in Papua and New Guinea that are of the perfect decimal kind: there is a distinct term, not derived from any earlier numbers, for every number from one to ten inclusive. Several such systems are used by the island dwellers of far eastern Papua. However, most decimal systems are of the imperfect decimal type: some of the numbers between one and ten are constructed by multiplying or adding earlier numbers, or by subtracting from a later one. Six in Motu, Central District, is expressed as 'twice three', and eight is 'twice four', while nine is 'twice four and one'. The Hula, also Central District, compound six and eight as do the Motu, while seven is expressed as 'unit less than double four' and nine is 'unit less than one ten'. Near by, at Domara, an imperfect decimal system is employed, in which the numbers from six to nine are based upon those from one to four:

1 *ombua* (-*bua*=only)
2 *awa*
3 *ais'eri*
4 *taurai*
5 *ima*
6 *lili-omo*
7 *lili-awa*
8 *lili-ais'eri*
9 *lili-ataurai*
10 *nana* or *nana-om*
20 *nana-awa*, etc.

The Sinaugoro, of the same general area, employ a similar system except that their term for six, *imaima-sebona* ('five-one'), is directly built upon the word for five, *imaima*, as are seven, eight and nine.

Some of the base-five, -ten and -twenty counting systems may not consist of purely abstract numbers so much as the names of fingers, hands, toes and feet required to indicate a certain number. The pattern varies considerably, and some of the systems that contain such expressions as 'one hand finished' for five are used without the counter actually ticking off his fingers as he goes.

There are a few systems with numbers that are wholly abstract, with bases not anatomically derived. The Bine, Western District, count in threes:

1 *iepa*
2 *neneni*
3 *nesae*
4 *nesae iepa*
5 *nesae neneni*
6 *nesae nesae*
7 *nesae nesae iepa*
8 *nesae nesae neneni*
9 *nesae nesae nesae*, etc.

The Kewa, Southern Highlands, sometimes employ a tetradic, base-four, system, and sometimes one of several variant body-counting systems (*see* section below). The Mailu, Central District, who normally count in tens, count certain foods—taro, sweet potatoes and fish—in groups of four, and similarly with coconuts that are counted for a feast. The people of the Duke of York Group, also count usually in tens; but they count coconuts, taro and yams by fours, and have a special set of terms for counting shell money (*diwara*) in quantities of sixty. The Kapauku of the Wissel Lakes count between one and sixty according to a decimal system, and then in sixties, a fact that has been

adduced as evidence for a connection between them and the ancient Babylonians, who employed a similar system.

The Keraki, Western District, who normally count in fives, employ their Gambadi and Semariji neighbours to count their annual yam harvest for them, which the latter groups do in a base-six system. When they reach 1,296—i.e. one *dameno* of six *tarumba*, each consisting of six groups or *peta* of thirty-six yams—the counters start again. The Gambadi-Semariji system, then, does not appear to be a perfect six-base system in that it has not been recorded as operating in multiples of one *dameno* (*see* section Modulus systems below).

The Enga, Western Highlands, normally work in tens but employ a special system when counting pigs in the *te* [q.v.] ceremonial exchange. Then they count two pigs at a time, in twos to four, and then to four again and eight, then ten, when they employ a special set of terms for counting pairs of pigs by fours to about fifty, when counting starts again. This special pig-counting system contains no terms to express odd numbers and is known only to a comparatively small number of men.

Body-counting systems. Many groups employ systems in which each successive number is indicated by the counter pointing to, touching or calling the name of a particular point on his own or another's fingers, arms, body or head. Most, but not all, of these systems seem to have an odd number as their base, with the same body parts on either side of the counter's nose or forehead being indicated in reverse order on the way up to, and then down from, the centre point. One mild exception to the rule is the body-counting system employed by some Elema, who proceed from the thumb of one hand, across the fingers, to the shoulder (ten) on the same arm, whence counting proceeds again on the fingers.

Again, the list of body-counting systems here is not exhaustive. The Jibu, Western District, count to a base nineteen; the Namau, Gulf, to twenty-three or twenty-five; the Telefomin, West Sepik, to twenty-seven; the Gende, northern Chimbu, to thirty-one; and different groups of Kewa to thirty-five in the south and forty-seven in the east and west. Another Kewa system has been recorded with a base of forty-four.

The east and west Kewa system, the one with the highest recorded base, is presented below, with the vernacular terms for the various body parts translated into English. The other body-counting systems generally miss out some of the places at which a Kewa counter points:

1	little finger	47
2	ring finger	46
3	middle finger	45
4	index finger	44
5	thumb	43
6	heel of thumb	42
7	palm	41
8	wrist	40
9	forearm	39
10	large arm bone	38
11	small arm bone	37

12	above elbow	36
13	lower upper arm	35
14	upper upper arm	34
15	shoulder	33
16	shoulder bone	32
17	neck muscle	31
18	neck	30
19	jaw	29
20	ear	28
21	cheek	27
22	eye	26
23	inside corner of eye	25
	between eyes	
	24	

After the mid-point has been reached, the Kewa qualify the names of the body parts on the other side with the word *mendaa*, 'another of the same'. One Kewa unit, forty-seven, is *paapu*, 'around the body parts'.

In some cases people who employ body-counting systems can point without hesitation to the place where a number higher than the base would normally be indicated. They are able to carry the base in their heads, and count out high numbers by going through several revolutions on a single body. Other people seem to require several bodies to count out numbers larger than the base, as they can carry this only in physical form. They seem to have no expression for multiples of 'one man finished', or the base. Several body-counting systems seem not to have bases. They are of the modulus type of counting system.

Modulus systems. The counting systems outlined above have been described as having bases. When they reach a certain number counting starts again, and the previous total is carried either verbally or in physical form. A Kewa counter, for example, must start from the beginning again once he reaches forty-seven, but if, say, he passes from his own body to a neighbour's, or says 'one *paapu* and little finger' for forty-eight, he is in fact not simply starting all over again but carrying forty-seven—and may later carry multiples of it—as he proceeds. The east and west Kewa then may count in multiples of forty-seven just as those people who employ a decimal system of numeration count in tens; unless, of course, the Kewa counters cannot carry one *paapu* verbally nor pass from one body to another, i.e. try to indicate the number of *paapu* so far counted either verbally or through pointing to the number of completed revolutions around the human body.

Some counting systems have a modulus rather than a base. The hour-hand on a clock, for example, can never proceed beyond twelve. It cannot show whether it is morning or night or what day, week, month or year it is. Once it reaches twelve it starts again; it cannot carry or otherwise indicate the total number of times it has passed twelve. Because it cannot carry multiples of twelve, the hour-hand on a clock is referred to as having a modulus of twelve.

Although the mathematical distinction between a modulus and a base is clear-cut, it is not always apparent just how a particular counting system operates. Some body-counting systems have no re-

corded multiples for 'one man finished' or 'around the body parts', although the very act of proceeding from one body to the next may be a way of carrying that number visually if not verbally, i.e. the observer can see that the counter has proceeded from one body to another. The existence of modulus systems, or of counting systems with a physically present or visual, but no verbal, base may explain why some writers have assumed that particular groups in Papua and New Guinea cannot count beyond a certain number.

The Huli, Southern Highlands, for example, count in fifteens—but not by indicating body parts—until they reach fifteen fifteens, 225, when they start again. They have no way of expressing multiples of 225, although more than 225 units of a single kind of object may be physically present. The Huli counting system therefore has a base of fifteen and a modulus of 225, at least verbally. Similarly, the absence of a set of terms to denote multiples of one *dameno*, 1,296 yams, would indicate that the Gambadi-Semariji counting system has a base of six and a modulus of 1,296. When 1,296 is reached, then counting starts again. The only doubt here is whether the Gambadi-Semariji can or cannot, in fact, compose multiples of one *dameno* but have simply never had occasion to do so, perhaps because they can see, if not describe, how many multiples of one *dameno* have been counted when they use this counting system.

The Daribi of the Karimui area employ a body-counting system with a modulus and perhaps a higher, physically present, base. They count in twos, *me si, me si* ('and two, and two') around their bodies, or with counting sticks as tally markers, to a total of between twenty-six and thirty and have no terms to denote the total, or any intermediate totals, between two and thirty. Their counting system has a verbal modulus of two, although it is arguable that this system is really a binary adding system with the progressive totals physically indicated if not verbally expressed.

Finally, the Karam-speaking people from near Aiome in the mountainous inland of the Madang District usually count on their bodies to a total of twenty-three on the first time across and may then turn back to count to twenty-two each time they cross from the little finger of one hand to the other; they do not count the last finger of one circuit when they begin the next, it is counted only once. When in a hurry the Karam may divide their labours, so that one man groups the objects he is counting in pairs, saying *omngar o, omngar o* ('these two, these two') as he goes, while an assistant records the growing total on his body. The first man tallies with a modulus of two while the second counts to twenty-three, and then to a base of twenty-two, again using a combination modulus- and base-type system.

Generally, then, most peoples have always been able to count or tally as high and as exactly as they needed to survive—through being able to calculate how much food to store, to celebrate, to pay or collect their debts, or to check on what they owned. There was not so much a limit to counting as a limit to the goods and quantities that needed to be counted or that particular groups of people wanted to measure. Neighbouring groups sometimes used disparate systems, and tended to have developed their systems to different heights, depending upon what they felt required counting.

Today some systems, e.g. the binary, and some methods of tallying, e.g. body counting, are too cumbersome to be used for most non-traditional kinds of calculations. Where once a binary counter just said 'many' after ten, precision may now be required. Thus the decimal system of abstract numbers, in its Pidgin English [q.v.], English, or sometimes newly developed vernacular version, is increasingly employed for the sake of brevity and accuracy.

SURVEYS

K. W. Galis, 'Telsystemen in Nederlands-Nieuw-Guinea', *Nieuw-Guinea Studiën*, vol. 4, 1960.
T. Kluge, *Die Zahlbegriffe der Australier, Papua und Bantuneger nebst einer Einleitung über die Zahl; ein Beitrag zur Geistesgeschichte des Menschen* (microfilmed typescript). Berlin, 1938.
———— 'Völker und Sprachen von Neu-Guinea', *Petermanns Geographische Mitteilungen*, vol. 88, 1942.
S. H. Ray, *Linguistics*, vol. 3 of *Reports of the Cambridge Anthropological Expedition to Torres Straits*, ed. A. C. Haddon. Cambridge, 1907.
E. P. Wolfers, 'Do New Guineans Count?', *Institute of Current World Affairs Newsletter* EPW-18, New York, 26 April 1969.

PARTICULAR COUNTING AND TALLYING SYSTEMS

H. Aufenanger, 'Etwas über Zahl und Zählen bei den Gende in Bismarckgebirge Neuguineas' *Anthropos*, vol. 33, 1938.
———— 'The Ayom Pygmies' Myth of Origin and Their Method of Counting', *Anthropos*, vol. 55, 1960.
G. Brown, *Melanesians and Polynesians*, pp. 292-5. London, 1910.
S. and R. Bulmer, 'The Prehistory of the Australian New Guinea Highlands', p. 59, *American Anthropologist*, vol. 66, Special Publication, 1964.
D. J. de Solla Price and L. Pospisil, 'A Survival of Babylonian Arithmetic in New Guinea', *Indian Journal of History of Science*, vol. 1, 1966.
P. Fillery, 'Preliminary Considerations when Teaching Number in the Waiye Area of the Chimbu District', *Papua and New Guinea Education Gazette*, vol. 3, 1969.
K. J. Franklin, *The Dialects of Kewa*, pp. 31-5 (Linguistic Circle of Canberra). Canberra, 1968.
K. and J. Franklin, 'The Kewa Counting Systems', *Journal of the Polynesian Society*, vol. 71, 1962.
D. L. Oliver, *A Solomon Island Society*, pp. 62-3, 100-1. Cambridge, Mass., 1955.
S. H. Ray, *A Grammar of the Kiwai Language, Fly Delta, Papua*, pp. 12-13, 70. Port Moresby, 1932.
W. J. V. Saville, *In Unknown New Guinea*, pp. 193-4. London, 1926.
H. Strauss and H. Tischner, *Die Mi-Kultur der Hagenberg-Stämme in östlichen Zentral-Neuguinea: Eine religions-soziologische Studie*, pp. 7-8. Hamburg, 1962.
R. Wagner, *The Curse of Souw*, p. 245. Chicago, 1968.
F. E. Williams, *Papuans of the Trans-Fly*, pp. 225-7. Oxford, 1936.
———— 'Natives of Lake Kutubu, Papua', *Oceania Monograph* no. 6, pp. 33-4. Sydney, 1940-2.

EDWARD P. WOLFERS

COUTANCE, Louis Ruault, the first European, after Torres [q.v.], to land on the Papuan coast, sailed along the southern coast of Papua in 1804 in the 130-ton brig *Adèle*. Coutance, a former French Navy officer, had left Mauritius in June 1803 to try to establish trade between Mauritius, Sydney and South America on behalf of some Mauritian merchants. After selling a cargo of liquor in Sydney Coutance went on to Chile, where he filled the *Adèle*'s holds with salmon and copper for Mauritius. On his return voyage across the Pacific Coutance touched at the Marquesas Islands, Nassau Island in the Northern Cook Group, which no European had previously seen, and several islands in the southern Solomons. In May 1804 he sighted Rossel Island in the Louisiade Archipelago of Papua, and in passing to the south of this he discovered a small, low, wooded island east of Rossel which he named after his ship. Continuing westward, occasionally in sight of the Papuan coast, Coutance eventually reached the Great Barrier Reef. Being unable to find a passage through this to Torres Strait, he turned north hoping to find one between the New Guinea mainland and the Louisiades. This brought him into the Gulf of Papua where, after skirmishes with some natives, a landing was made on a small reef island to get wood and water. This was the first European landing on Papuan soil since Torres in 1606.

Continuing northward for five days, Coutance came to 'a superb river' at the head of the gulf, where he replenished his water after a few menacing natives were driven into the bush by musket shots. Convinced now that he would not find a passage to the northern side of New Guinea, Coutance sailed south again and this time succeeded in passing through Torres Strait, thus becoming the first Frenchman to do so. On returning to Mauritius Coutance wrote a report on his voyage for the French government. Although some officials found it interesting, no account of the voyage was ever published. However, in 1808 a young naval officer, Louis de Saulces de Freycinet, borrowed the report to help him prepare a chart of Australia and New Guinea for an atlas to accompany the official account of Baudin's voyage. The atlas was published in 1811, and thanks to Coutance, Freycinet gave a more accurate idea of the Papuan coastline than previous cartographers had done. In an explanatory note Freycinet said: 'Islands, coasts, banks and reefs marked R-C . . . are discoveries made in 1804 by Captain Ruault Coutance, commanding the French ship *Adèle* . . . I have taken from the manuscript journal of that officer many valuable details.' Freycinet's information and the details on his chart were subsequently incorporated in the hydrographic works of A. J. Krusenstern and others. In June 1827 the French explorer Dumont d'Urville made a point of searching for and fixing the position of Coutance's Adèle Island at the eastern extremity of the Louisiades. It is still marked as such on present-day charts. British naval surveyors gave the name Coutance Island to a small island between Keppel Point and Cape Rodney in the 1870s when all the 'islands, coasts, banks and reefs marked R-C' on Freycinet's map were carefully investigated.

A transcript of Coutance's report is in the Mitchell Library, Sydney (MS. B1190).

ROBERT LANGDON

CROCODILES. Two species of crocodiles are found in the New Guinea region.

The most widely distributed is the estuarine or salt-water crocodile, *Crocodylus porosus*, a species found from the northern coast of Australia through the Indo-Malayan Archipelago to the coast of India and eastward from New Guinea through the Bismarck Archipelago and Solomon Islands to Fiji and beyond.

Although largely restricted to coastal waters, the estuarine crocodile may be found well out to sea or up in the fresh-water reaches of many of the rivers. It is the world's largest crocodile, but, although specimens approaching thirty feet in length have been recorded, few individuals exceeding twenty feet are ever seen. This crocodile is responsible for numbers of deaths and maulings among the native population.

The estuarine crocodile is most conveniently distinguished from the only other crocodile in the area, the New Guinea marsh crocodile, *Crocodylus novaeguineae*, by the large scales on the neck. In the estuarine crocodile there is a group of four or six enlarged horny plates which are separated from the skull by an area of small granular scales. This area is about as long as the group of plates, whereas in the marsh crocodile, there is an almost continuous series of enlarged horny plates between the skull and the large plates on the back. Another important distinguishing feature lies in the belly scales, which are much smaller in the estuarine crocodile than they are in the marsh crocodile.

The marsh crocodile is found largely in the lowland fresh-water reaches of most river systems of the main island, as well as being abundant in most of the lowland lakes, swamps and marshes. It is particularly plentiful in such larger rivers as the Sepik, Ramu, Fly and Digul. The marsh crocodile averages only six to seven feet in length, although occasional specimens of about twelve feet are reported.

Estuarine crocodile *Crocodylus porosus*, showing neck-scales.

Both crocodiles build nests of mud, leaves and other litter, a short distance from water. The marsh crocodile lays about thirty eggs towards the end of the dry season, while the estuarine crocodile may lay up to sixty eggs, also at the end of the dry season. The females of both species are reported to guard the eggs until they hatch, six to nine weeks after being laid. Crocodiles feed on reptiles, water birds and mammals which come to water to drink or bathe.

The skins of both species fetch high prices, and hunting in recent years has reached such intensity that most populations have been decimated. Current protection measures include the licensing of all hunters and a ban on the buying, selling and export of skins over twenty inches in belly width—which corresponds to a live body length of eight to nine feet—in an attempt to conserve the larger breeding stock. However as the only study made on the marsh crocodile's habits indicate that breeding females average only five feet in length, the above protection laws may be of dubious value in the conservation of this species.

The decline of crocodile populations is shown clearly in the following total values of skins exported from the Territory of Papua and New Guinea.

Year	Export value ($)
1962-3	689,000
1963-4	906,000
1964-5	856,000
1965-6	1,001,000
1966-7	736,000
1967-8	509,000

This dramatic reduction in export values occurred during a period when unit skin prices were increasing.

L. D. Brongersma, *The Animal World of Netherlands New Guinea*. Groningen, 1958; A. Loveridge, *Reptiles of the Pacific World*. New York, 1945; ——— 'New Guinean Reptiles and Amphibians in the Museum of Comparative Zoology and United States National Museum', *Bulletin of the Museum of Comparative Zoology*, vol. 101, 1948; W. T. Neill, 'Notes on *Crocodylus novae-guineae*', *Copeia*, no. 1, 1946; N. de Rooij, *The Reptiles of the Indo-Australian Archipelago*. 2 vols. Leyden, 1915-17.   H. G. COGGER

CROP PLANTS. Many indigenous plants are used by village people in their daily life for food, domestic materials, clothing and spiritual and medicinal needs. The most important are those which are involved in the pattern of subsistence agriculture. It becomes difficult to distinguish a crop, in which a considerable number of plants of one kind are grown together, from the occasional garden plant or the gathering of edible produce from plants of the forests.

The crops discussed do not include by any means all plant species found in native gardens or used by the villager or nomad from the forest. No such enumeration exists, nor can one be prepared. Almost any indigenous plant has some use. The stinging tree, a species of *Laportea* (*Dendrocnide*)

is used as a counter-irritant to spur flagging muscles at the end of a hard day's trek. Toxic plants such as *Derris* and *Gnetum latifolium* are traditional suicide materials. *Evodia hortense* and *Aralia ficifolia* are shrubs with aromatic leaves used in dance festivals. *Acorus calamus* a herb with aromatic rhizome occurs from the Mediterranean to New Guinea. It is used as a cure for lung congestion and is also a reputed contraceptive. *Caldesia parnassifolia* is reputed to cause sterility in both human females and pigs. There is no end to this story of ethnobotany among the wild and semi-domesticated plants. The more notable species of each category are considered. Where the term 'New Guinea' is used without qualification such as 'region' it means the whole main island.

CROPS

Cocoa (*Theobroma cacao*). The genus *Theobroma* includes about twenty-two species confined to the tropical regions of America. *Theobroma cacao* is the only species of commercial importance. The plant is of ancient cultivation in Central America. Cocoa beans were first brought to Europe by Columbus. A number of botanical varieties of *Theobroma cacao* are recognized and these interbreed readily to give fully fertile hybrids. Three main types are recognized in commercial production: Criollo of Central American or Venezuelan origin, Forastero of Amazonian origin, and Trinitario, originally from Trinidad but covering the wide range of hybrids between Criollo and Amazonian Forastero. Trinitario-type hybrids are of great importance in cocoa breeding. The only consistently recognizable entities are clones.

Cocoa is a strictly tropical crop. Purseglove (1968) gives as the limits of cultivation the latitudes 20° N. and S. of the equator and the optimum area within 10° of the equator and at altitudes below 1,000 feet. Many types of soil are good for cocoa: soils of volcanic, igneous or marine sediment origin are suitable. Richness in potassium and phosphorus and a just acid pH are desirable attributes. (*See* COCOA INDUSTRY.)

Coconut, Copra (*Cocos nucifera*). The coconut is one of the most useful plants known to man and certainly the most useful of the palms. The fronds yield thatching material, are plaited for baskets and finely split along the pinnae for decoration; the trunk is used for house posts, wharf piles and other building purposes; the flower stem when developing can be cut to yield a strong flow of sugar-containing sap which is, by fermentation, converted to toddy; the fruits when unripe yield coconut milk as a drink and the soft meat as coconut cream; mature fruits yield copra; the husk fibre can be spun into ropes, woven into matting, bags, etc.; the shell may be carved into bowls, spoons and ornaments, or burnt to produce the finest medicinal charcoal; the dry endosperm can be further dried as copra or grated as desiccated coconut.

The original home of the coconut is not known precisely but the available evidence suggests a South Pacific or Melanesian origin. Corner (1966) states that there are more than 6 hundred million coconut palms producing an annual harvest of about 3 million tons of copra. Throughout Asia and the Pacific there are many varieties of the coconut palm, tall palms and dwarf palms; the fruits may be orange red, ochre yellow or green when ripe; some have a fragrant endosperm. The proportions of husk, shell and meat vary in different varieties. The endosperm or white meat of the coconut may be dried by exposure of halved nuts to the sun so that the meat contracts from the shell and may be readily removed. Hot air or smoke may be used in a special drying house called a copra dryer. The different techniques for drying produce grades of copra which command different prices.

Coconut oil is extracted from copra for soap manufacture or edible fats. The remaining dry coconut meal may be used for stock feed. (See COCONUT INDUSTRY.)

Coffee (*Coffea arabica* and *C. canephora*, family Rubiaceae). The genus *Coffea* contains many species distributed through tropical Africa, the islands of the Indian Ocean and tropical Southeast Asia. The only species used commercially are *Coffea arabica* which produces about 90 per cent of the world's coffee, *C. canephora* (Robusta coffee), about 10 per cent and a very small quantity (none in Papua New Guinea) from *C. liberica*. The use of coffee as a beverage is of recent origin; it was reported in Cairo in 1510 and in Constantinople about 1550. This coffee was derived from Arabia and Ethiopia. *Coffea arabica* occurs wild at an altitude of 4,500 to 6,000 feet in Ethiopia. Two botanical varieties are recognized, var. *arabica* and var. *bourbon*. Within these varieties are many horticultural variants and hybrids. Some of these are named as cultivars and used extensively for commercial production, e.g. Blue Mountain which originated in Jamaica, Kents from Mysore in India, Mundo Novo from Brazil, etc.

Coffea arabica is an upland species of the equatorial belt (Ethiopia to latitude 9° N.). Commercial production is in similar latitudes both north and south of the equator and at altitudes of 3,000 to 6,000 feet.

Coffea canephora was formerly called *Coffea robusta*; hence the common name. This species originates in the African equatorial forest zones from sea-level up to 5,000 feet. Botanically the plant can be distinguished from *C. arabica* by its larger leaves. Propagation of both *Coffea* species is by seeds from selected clones.

Coffea liberica, grown sometimes in Malaya is not planted commercially in New Guinea. (See COFFEE INDUSTRY.)

Passionfruit (*Passiflora edulis*). The cultivated purple passionfruit is a relatively recent introduction. Only since 1955 has there been any extensive cultivation as a cash crop. *Passiflora edulis* does best in the Highlands. A mutation which has a larger fruit with yellow skin, *Passiflora edulis* var. *flavicarpa*, does better in the lowlands but pollination is erratic.

P. edulis is native to Brazil and was widely introduced in England during the nineteenth century,

being first grown as a flowering ornamental in 1810. In cool temperate countries the plant is grown mainly as an ornamental. In the subtropics and tropics fruit is produced for the pulp which is used in cordials and flavourings.

In the Highlands villagers have been encouraged to produce passionfruit to supply pulp-extracting plants which have been established at Mount Hagen and Goroka. The vines are grown over *Casuarina* trees in association with garden regeneration (see PASSIONFRUIT INDUSTRY).

In addition to the species of economic importance, the granadilla (*Passiflora quadrangularis*) is widely grown in lowland areas for the large fruit. The skin is pale golden cream at maturity. The pulp is used in fruit salads and it is said to resemble stewed apple. The green fruit may be boiled as a vegetable.

The shape of the fruit is sometimes irregular, being constricted in the middle or terminally due to imperfect pollination. The granadilla is best grown over a strong trellis or tree.

Tacsonia mollissima is a recent introduction to areas above 8,000 feet where it has become naturalized. The fruit is offered for sale on the roadside at Daulo and Tomba in the Highlands. The fruit is of high quality but cannot be carried far because the skin bruises very easily.

Peanut or groundnut (*Arachis hypogea*). The peanut is unusual in that the plant flowers above ground, and the developing fruit is then buried in the soil by elongation of the inflorescence stem. The fruit matures below ground-level.

Peanuts are used either raw or roasted as a foodstuff. Peanut oil is obtained by crushing or chemical extraction of mature seeds with a suitable solvent.

Peanuts were used by early South American people. Seeds have been found throughout the continent, e.g. at excavations dated 800 B.C. in coastal Peru. As with so many crops of American origin, Columbus and his men introduced peanuts to Europe. They were probably introduced to New Guinea after 1900 and to the Highlands after 1946. Two general varieties are recognized: Spanish Red and Virginia Bunch. In Africa there is a great diversity of cultivated forms but only a few have been introduced to Papua New Guinea.

The peanut bushes grow as erect plants up to 2 feet in height.

Pyrethrum (*Chrysanthemum cinerariaefolium*). Pyrethrum flowers contain an insecticide. First the dried powdered flowers were used, but later an extract was developed, first in Europe then in America. In World War II the use of pyrethrum extract increased enormously. *Chrysanthemum cinerariaefolium* occurs as a wild plant on the Dalmatian coast of Yugoslavia. Most commercial production comes from Kenya but in the last twenty years pyrethrum growing has been widely fostered by the Administration in the Highlands of Papua New Guinea. Stafford Allen have established an extracting plant at Mount Hagen. The concentrated extract is shipped to the United Kingdom for further refining.

In the equatorial tropics pyrethrum thrives best

between 6,000 and 9,000 feet where flowering and a high content of pyrethrins are obtained. Periods of cold weather below 60°F. are required to stimulate flower production. The active substances occur in the flower heads which are picked by hand when freshly opened. At this stage there is an obvious relationship to garden chrysanthemums. After picking, the heads are dried and transported to the extracting plant. Small village growers sell their production to buyers who transport the flowers to the central factory.

Plants are propagated vegetatively as are other chrysanthemums. Clonal lines giving good flower production and a reasonable yield of pyrethrum are used (*see* PYRETHRUM INDUSTRY).

Rubber (*Hevea braziliensis*). A variety of plants produce in the bark a latex which dries to an elastic, and more or less translucent, substance. Among the more notable are *Ficus elastica*, *Castilla elastica*, *Manihot glaziovii*, *Funtumia elastica* and *Landolphia* spp. and, most notable of all, *Hevea braziliensis*. The latter is the wild rubber tree of the Amazon. In Papua rubber was introduced before 1930; in New Guinea by German agriculturalists. Trees of German origin still exist on Aropa plantation, Bougainville, and probably elsewhere.

The latex of *Hevea braziliensis* flows as an opaque, thin white liquid from any wound to the bark. Commercial production is obtained by causing latex to flow from bark freshly cut in a V-shaped formation on the lower part of the trunk. The latex is collected into cups on individual trees then bulked in buckets and tanks. On arrival at the plantation factory the latex is thinned with water and a coagulant (formic or acetic acid) added. Coagulation occurs in shallow tanks and the latex is collected on a series of flat plates. The coagulated latex may be removed from the plates as a curd-like sheet from which free water is mechanically squeezed by a series of rollers. This sheet is then placed into a smoke house for curing. Curd natural rubber sheet is pale brown, and translucent to almost transparent. The sheet rubber is baled for export.

Much research has been done toward improving the yield of latex from the trees by grafting sound root-stocks to high-yielding stems and desirable crown characteristics. Propagation is also effected by using clonal seed.

The bark grows over the tapping panel and may be reworked after a suitable interval (Purseglove reports ten years for bark renewal in Malaya).

Ficus rubber, *Ficus elastica* was planted by German agriculturalists in Bougainville, on the Gazelle Peninsula and near Madang but there does not appear to have been any commercial production (*see* RUBBER INDUSTRY).

Sugar-cane (*Saccharum officinarum*) Most botanists and plant geographers agree that New Guinea is the botanical home of the sugar-canes and further, it is probable that the indigenous people, by selection from wild forms, brought into cultivation the numerous varieties which are today grown all over the world. (*See* SUGAR INDUSTRY.)

Saccharum officinarum, *S. robustum* and *S.*

edule are probably only variations on a theme. *S. officinarum* includes all the noble canes grown for the high sugar content of the sap. *S. robustum* is the wild sugar-cane or *pitpit* of river banks. Some of these canes contain sap with a low sugar content. It is probable that some wild forms at least have been brought into the *S. officinarum* complex. The stem of the wild form is extensively used for building, fencing, etc. *S. edule* is cultivated throughout the lowlands for the abortive flower spike which does not burst through the leaf sheath. This flower spike is eaten either boiled or roasted. It is known colloquially as *pitpit*, a name also applied to the building material from *S. robustum* and to the vegetative shoots of *Setaria palmifolia*.

Tea (*Camellia sinensis*, family Theaceae). The genus *Camellia* includes a number of ornamental flowering shrubs native to tropical and subtropical Asia. *C. sinensis* provides the tea of commerce. Tea has long been grown in China and used as a beverage for 2,000-3,000 years. It was possibly used even earlier for medicinal purposes. Tea is made from the young leaves which are plucked, withered, rolled, fermented and dried (black tea); green tea is made by steaming and then drying the leaves.

Two principal varieties are recognized—China tea, *Camellia sinensis* var. *sinensis*, and Assam, *C. sinensis* var. *assamica*. Numerous hybrids are known between these varieties. Tea seed is used extensively for propagation. Seed is collected from gardens of selected clones. Single internode cuttings may be used in propagating beds. (*See* TEA INDUSTRY.)

Tobacco (*Nicotiana tabacum*). Purseglove (1968) remarks that the cured leaf provides a pleasurable and habit-forming narcotic used for smoking, chewing and snuffing. At the time of Columbus the use of *Nicotiana tabacum* was restricted to the New World. It is now history how the use of tobacco was taken to the Old World by returning Spaniards and Englishmen.

The leaves of the tobacco plant contain alkaloids of the nicotine group. These chemicals may be ingested or absorbed through the lungs to afford the user the mild narcosis associated with smoking, chewing tobacco or taking snuff.

Tobacco is indubitably of South American origin and did not occur outside the New World before the mid-sixteenth century. In Malaysia it was introduced probably a century later. By 1700 Dampier was able to supply all the tobacco his crew required when their ship touched Java. A little later two centres in the Philippines and one in Java became exporting points for tobacco. It is probable that tobacco reached New Guinea early in the eighteenth century. Certainly by the time of extensive European exploration tobacco was well established in the lowlands and the technique of drying and smoking tobacco leaf was well known.

The plant *Nicotiana tabacum* is grown as an annual from seed. In many villages it would appear that young tobacco plants establish at random and are then husbanded. Production of tobacco experimentally and as a small commercial operation is now established in the Goroka Valley. The necessity to maintain rigorous controls in growing and preparing the leaf may handicap the development of tobacco growing for export. Quite a lot of tobacco is produced for sale in small quantities in local markets.

ROOT CROPS

Kaukau or sweet potato (*Ipomoea batatas*) is an annual or perennial slender-stemmed plant; its root tubers sustain most of the indigenous population. The introduction of sweet potato to the Pacific and Melanesia is complex and to date there has been much postulation but little proof. The weight of evidence points to an origin in America although others favour Africa. Sweet potato was in the western limits of Melanesia in 1650 as evidenced by specimens in Rumphs Herbarium Amboinense, perhaps brought by Spanish and Portuguese from America. Sweet potato may have been introduced to Melanesia through Indonesia, and also via Polynesian migrations. It has been shown that the New Guinea sweet potato varieties come within the range of variability of the same plant in South America and are presumably a portion of this population which has adapted with local somatic or genetic variations to its great altitudinal ranges— from sea-level to 8,000 feet.

Throughout its range of altitude sweet potato is planted from cuttings in some form of mound. Production of 3 to 6 tons of tuber per acre is average after a growing season of three to six months. At higher altitudes the production is much lower and the time to maturity up to twelve months. Above 7,000 feet the plants are liable to be severely damaged by frost.

Mounding for sweet potato cultivation is general; the mounds take various forms from square or rectangular plots about ten feet square to domes or beehive shapes. In all cases rotting vegetation is dug in during the preparation of the mound and drainage ditches prepared around the mounds. Harvesting is usually by burrowing in from the side or from above to remove individual tubers. Throughout New Guinea sweet potato is a constant source of food. No one from the village leaves for work without several pieces of sweet potato in his bag for a midday snack.

Tapioca or cassava (*Manihot esculenta*). The root tubers are an important food and carbohydrate source in many parts of the tropical lowlands and cassava is a regular item of food in areas having a seasonal drought. However, almost all native gardens have some cassava which is retained for use in times of sweet potato or taro shortage.

Cassava is of American origin and is probably an introduction of some antiquity to New Guinea. The Portuguese are credited with bringing cassava to Africa in the late 1500s, and probably Spaniards or Portuguese introduced the plant to the Philippines about the same time or later. From the Philippines this plant spread throughout South-east Asia.

Many cultivated varieties contain cyanogenetic glucosides in the tuber. This substance is poisonous unless destroyed by heat during preparation or removed by repeated washing. Tubers which store well tend to be high in the poisonous glucoside. So called sweet tubers, which are low in glucoside, do not store well.

Taro (*Colocasia esculenta*) exists in a great number of varieties most of which grow best in shade. The plants develop a large rhizome at or just below the surface of the ground. From this, leaf stalks arise and carry a large sagittate leaf. Plants are propagated by cutting off the leaf-bearing apex of the rhizome and planting this. The base of the rhizome is used in cooking and may be baked or boiled.

Other related aroids of minor use are *Alocasia macrorrhiza*, probably native to New Guinea but little used except perhaps in time of famine.

Cyrtosperma chamissonis, the swamp taro, is found mainly on coral atolls which have a freshwater swamp or lagoon. The fibre of the leaf stalk is of very fine quality for weaving. Propagation is by cuttings as for *Colocasia*.

Xanthosoma spp. are plants of South American origin which have been introduced in recent times. They are not widely used in New Guinea where taro and sweet potato are most common.

Yam (*Dioscorea esculenta* and *D. alata*). Although six species of yam which produce edible tubers occur in New Guinea only two are regularly planted. These are *D. esculenta* and *D. alata*. Others are gathered wild and used in times of garden famine. Yam is a climbing plant which is grown most successfully in light friable soil with strong stakes up to 15 feet in height to support the plants. In certain parts of Polynesia and Melanesia great cultural emphasis is placed on yams and gardening techniques have been developed to produce giant tubers. Yam, unlike sweet potato, is a seasonal crop but the tubers, also unlike the sweet potato, may be stored in well-ventilated specially constructed yam houses.

Yams are prepared by baking, boiling or by grating into an oven and dehydrating.

VEGETABLES

A great variety of vegetables are used. It is impossible to record all species and varieties here but the following notes give an outline as to what may be found.

The Europeans introduced many of their vegetables to New Guinea. Among them were the shallot (*Allium ascalonicum*), which is commonly grown and used by native people up to an altitude of at least 7,000 feet. The onion (*Allium cepa*) is a very recent introduction. Only in a few localities do the plants form acceptable bulbous bases and these do not store well. Cabbage, cauliflower, chinese cabbage and turnip (*Brassica* spp.) have been introduced for cultivation for sale to Europeans. Village people have acquired a taste for cabbage and chinese cabbage. The chilli (*Capsicum frutescens*) in its many forms has been widely introduced. Native use is small, cultivation being mainly for sale. Bird's eye chillies are being grown in commercial quantities for export after drying. Indian corn or maize (*Zea mays*) is a widespread post-European settlement crop which has spread throughout New Guinea. The cobs are eaten boiled or roasted as in *Saccharum edule*. There appears to be no indigenous use of the dried seed as a source of meal or flour.

A great diversity of leafy greens are used by village people.

Abika (*Abelmoschus manihot*) is a common plant in most lowland native villages. The leaves are used as a green vegetable. Flowering is rare, largely because the bushes are kept in a vegetative state to ensure abundant leaf production. The leaves are seriously attacked by beetles and other leaf-eating insects.

Amaranth (*Amaranthus tricolor* and *A. hybridus*) occurs in a diversity of forms particularly in Highlands gardens.

Bamboo shoots are rarely used as food but the stems are of considerable importance in domestic uses for carrying water, cooking food, building, and making bows.

Banana flowers. The male bud of the *Musa* is cut after all female flowers have set fruit. The bud is boiled and used as a vegetable. In Malaysia some varieties of bananas are grown principally for the flowers.

Beans. The common bean (*Phaseolus vulgaris*) provides many of the cultivated table beans for domestic consumption in temperate countries. These include the french bean, haricot bean, kidney bean, runner bean, etc. In New Guinea the village people grow only the french bean or runner bean and the produce of these is mainly for sale at town markets. The plant is of American origin and appears to have come to New Guinea with European settlement.

The lima bean (*Phaseolus lunatus*) in a wild form is naturalized in some localities in New Guinea. Great care is needed in using the beans of the wild form as these contain dangerous quantities of a cyanogenetic glucoside which on digestion releases hydrocyanic acid. Prolonged boiling with changes of the cooking water will make the beans safe. The most frequent cause of fatalities among young children is the unripe bean which resembles and is mistaken for the pod of the garden pea. The lima bean of commerce is a selected form of this plant which lacks the toxic substance.

The winged bean (*Psophocarpus tetragonolobus*) is of some antiquity in village gardens and certainly pre-dates European settlement. The original source of this plant may have been South-east Asia or even the New Guinea region.

Throughout the Highlands and many lowland areas of New Guinea *Psophocarpus* is a common garden plant. The beans are eaten as a green vegetable, or dried and the seeds boiled. Leaves and young shoots may be eaten as a pot herb. The plant also produces a tuberous root which is used as a vegetable.

There is considerable confusion in the botanical literature regarding the correct names to be applied to the cow pea (*Vigna sesquipedalis*) and its relatives. In the tropics the usual form grown has cylindrical fruits up to 40 inches in length. This is the common kanaka bean or Markham bean of New Guinea. The agricultural forms of the cow pea, which is usually referred to as *Victa sinensis*, have been introduced on experimental stations and may have been planted in native gardens.

The Markham bean is used fresh much as french beans are.

Begonia leaves of various species are used in parts of the Highlands as a green vegetable.

Cucumber (*Cucumis sativus*). The semi-mature or mature fruits are extensively eaten, particularly by children. There are many cultivated forms but little selection appears to be practised by villagers. The mature fruit becomes bitter and is not favoured by Europeans.

Evodia hortense. The leaves, which have a strong aniseed scent, are worn at *singsings* and also boiled and used as flavouring.

Ferns of various species of the genera *Asplenium*, *Athyrium*, *Cyclosorus*, *Diplazium*, *Pteris* and others are gathered, and usually cooked.

Figs (*Ficus dammaropsis* and other species) provide leaves in which meat is wrapped for cooking. As far as is known, fig fruits are little used. The leaves of some species are boiled.

Gourds. Many species are involved; the shoots and tendrils of *Cucurbita pepo* are used as a green vegetable. Summer squash, winter squash, pumpkin and ornamental gourds are cultivars of this species.

The bitter gourd (*Momordica charantia*) is extensively used in South-east Asia as a flavouring in curries. The only use reported in New Guinea is of the red pulp which surrounds the seed. The vine naturalizes and forms dense mats of foliage which eliminate other growth; it is therefore used as a cover crop but tends to climb. The green fruits are used in Chinese cooking.

The bottle gourd (*Lagenaria siceraria*) is used by the indigenous people for smoking pipes and as a container for water and lime.

The snake gourd (*Trichosanthes cucumerina*) is sometimes erroneously referred to as snake bean or New Guinea bean. Fruits can attain a very large size, 6 feet or more in length. They tend to coil so a weight is hung to the tip of the developing fruit to keep it straight. This plant is widely grown in the lowlands and young fruits appear in local markets. However, it is probably of minor significance in the pattern of food intake.

Luffa spp. (*Luffa acutangula* and *L. cylindrica*) are little used in New Guinea although they grow well.

Oenanthe javanica, a weedy herb found in wet places throughout New Guinea up to 8,000 feet, is used as a green vegetable.

Palms, *Arenga* and probably other species, are used by cutting out the growing shoot and eating it raw or cooked.

Pea (*Pisum sativum*). The garden pea is a very recent introduction to the Highlands areas where it is grown largely for market. In the Chimbu and Western Highlands Districts peas also seem to be used by villagers uncooked as an incidental food.

Pueraria lobata is first reported in literature as 'a wild legume with large fibrous tubers . . . found all over Melanesia but . . . eaten mainly in time of famine'. Further reports suggest that this plant is cultivated quite deliberately in various regions of the central Highlands between Kainantu in the east and the Wissel Lakes in the west. *Pueraria lobata* may have been more significant in the past as a subsistence crop than it is today. The plant grows as a perennial trailing or climbing thin-stemmed liane. Tubers are produced over a period of time so that large tubers may be harvested and the small tubers remain to mature over several years. The tubers are described as 'stronger' than sweet potato.

Rungia klossii is an acanthaceous plant widely grown in the Highlands areas. It has a number of very marked forms varying from compact, oval-leaved plants to spreading, etiolated plants with very narrow leaves.

Setaria palmifolia is a grass grown in the Highlands for the compact vegetative shoots which are eaten steamed or roasted.

Watercress and other *Nasturtium* spp. are gathered and used as vegetables.

FRUITS

Avocado or alligator pear (*Persea americana*) appears to have been introduced into New Guinea from tropical America since 1920. The pulp of the large fruit is high in edible oil and has a consistency not unlike butter. The fruit is an acquired taste for Europeans but is little used by indigenous people. In Java where the plant was introduced by Dutch agriculturalists, *Persea americana* is now widely naturalized. The Javanese show little interest in the fruits as a food.

There are many cultivated varieties which bear their fruit at different times of the year. Careful selection of varieties can lead to a fruiting season of eight months or more.

Production in the Territory is entirely home garden or for local sale.

Banana (*Musa acuminata, M. balbisiana* and hybrids). The edible cultivated bananas belong almost entirely to an assemblage of hybrids or polyploids based upon two species, *Musa acuminata* and *M. balbisiana*, the fruits of which develop parthenocarpically, i.e. without pollination. The exceptions are the Fe'i bananas.

The parents of the cultivated bananas occur from Samoa in the east to India in the west. It is probable that parthenocarpy, hybridity and polyploidy developed individually in a number of separate centres. Native peoples, by selection and propagation, have grown plants with seedless edible fruits for a very long time. The vegetative propagation of a banana sucker ensures that the genetic material remains unaltered. However, variation does occur in the vegetative growing cells which can lead to change; this is somatic variation. Thus a wide variety of bananas with edible fruits have developed. If the parents be denoted as A for *M. acuminata* and B for *M. balbisiana* the cultivars may be ascribed to sets of polyploids on general characteristics of growth, leaf arrangement, bunch size and finger shape and size. The basic chromosome number in both parents is 11, hence:

Diploids, 22 chromosomes may be: AA AB BB

Triploids, 33 chromosomes: AAA AAB ABB BBB

Tetraploids, 44 chromosomes: AAAA ABBB

(The missing tetraploid combinations, if occurring in nature, are rare and do not contribute to the edible bananas.)

The *M. acuminata* series, characterized by AA, AAA or AAAA, are the sweet bananas of commerce. The starch bananas used generally for cooking and known in some parts of the world, but not consistently, as plantain, are the hybrids involving AB, AAB, ABB and ABBB becoming progressively more starchy in that order. Polyploid *M. balbisiana* do occur but the fruit is inedible. The leaves of polyploid *M. balbisiana* are used in Malaya for high quality wrapping materials.

Bananas are an important seasonal staple diet in many parts of New Guinea and elsewhere are used as a supplementary food. The leaves are everywhere used for shelter, wrapping and as food plates. Most of the New Guinea cultigens are of the hybrid *M. acuminata-M. balbisiana* series. The triploid and tetraploid *M. acuminata* polyploids of the Cavendish and Gros Michel types are recent introductions.

Throughout the lowlands, jungle clearing results in an immediate crop of young banana seedlings. These arise from the dormant seed of several wild species of *Musa* which occur as plants in forest clearings and open places. The fruit skin of *Musa schizocarpa* peels back at maturity; this ensures that flying fox will find the ripe fruits. *M. angustigemma* and *M. macleayi* belong to the *Australimusa*, a series from which the Fe'i bananas of the Pacific have developed. This series, with a basic chromosome number of ten, is quite distinct from that characterized by the *M. acuminata-M. balbisiana* series (*Eumusa*). The former have an erect bunch, usually with pink trunk sap. Cultivars frequently have very few, but very large, fruit to the stem. The flesh is usually yellow or orange and may be used raw or cooked.

Bananas have been described as the largest herbs in the world. Pride of place in this must go to *Musa ingens*, a mountain species, which occurs throughout north-east New Guinea between 5,500 and 6,500 feet above sea-level. This plant will attain a height from ground-level to leaf tip of 60 feet. The bunch of very tightly packed fingers has been weighed at 150 lb. Fruits are edible and suckers produced only after the main stem has died.

Breadfruit (*Artocarpus altilis*) is indigenous to New Guinea. The fruits of wild trees contain seeds which are eaten either boiled or roasted like chestnuts. The Polynesian breadfruit which is seedless is a selection propagated vegetatively. There is a possibility that the seedless form is a hybrid involving *A. mariannensis* from Micronesia.

Captain Cook and other travellers in Polynesia brought back descriptions of the tree from which 'bread itself is gathered as a fruit'. West Indian planters hoped that it would provide a staple food for their slaves and an expedition under Lieutenant William Bligh was sent for its collection. Bligh in the *Bounty* arrived in Tahiti in October 1788. On the return journey, mutiny broke out near the Friendly Islands and Bligh and eighteen of his men completed their crossing of the Pacific in a small open boat. The mutiny attracted world-wide interest, not only in itself, but also in the breadfruit. Bligh returned to Tahiti in 1792 and successfully carried breadfruit plants to Jamaica.

Breadfruit had already reached eastern Malaysia before the Bligh epic; it reached Penang about 1802, Malacca in 1836 and has now been carried throughout the tropics.

The tree itself is very handsome and often used as an ornamental. It is usually relatively short lived and the large leaves can be unsightly when fallen. The leaf shape is very variable, from entire to deeply laciniate. Some forms appear almost pinnate.

Duku or langsat (*Lansium domesticum*), one of the best of the native fruits of Malaya, have only recently been introduced and are not yet widely grown. The fruit are produced in bunches below the leaves and when ripe the thin skin is translucent whitish-brown. The ripe fruit fall to the ground; they should be collected frequently and may be eaten fresh. The smooth pulp around the seeds is of a very pleasant flavour. Seedless varieties occur in which the fruit, though smaller, is better for eating.

Durian (*Durio zibethinus*). This Malayan tree is a recent introduction. A single tree at Keravat, which was planted some time in the 1930s, flowers but has never produced fruit. The tree may be self-sterile and require cross-pollination. It is also suggested that bats are the pollinators in Malaya and Borneo where the genus *Durio* is indigenous. If so, the right bat may be absent from New Guinea, in which case the several trees in the botanic garden at Lae, which are now reaching flowering size, will also fail to fruit. The structure of the fruit of *Durio* is considered to be a fundamental clue to the evolutionary biology of flowering plants.

Five corner (*Averrhoa carambola*) was brought to New Guinea so long ago that it has become naturalized, or it is indigenous, to at least some of the eastern islands. The tree attains moderate height. The attractive pale pink flowers and the orange fruits are nearly always present. The fruit is acid sweet, and may be boiled or used in fruit cup. Local people often eat it raw.

A close relation, the bilimbi (*Averrhoa bilimbi*), is a smaller tree. The fruits resemble green cucumbers and develop on the branches and the trunk of the tree. This species is almost certainly indigenous to the eastern island archipelago. The juice from the fruit will remove stains from clothing.

Grapefruit (*Citrus paradisi*) have been introduced into a few villages and grown largely for sale to Europeans. The fruit is of inferior quality to that grown in temperate regions.

Guava (*Psidium guyava*) is an introduced tree which can become a serious weed problem if naturalized. This appears to be happening in the Bulolo Valley. The fruit varies in quality. A good strain produces a large juicy fruit which is lemon-yellow when ripe with reddish or yellowish pulp. The seeds are numerous and tend to be gritty. The pulp may be eaten fresh or preserved. Children often eat the unripe fruits.

There are other related species, including the strawberry guava (*Psidium cattleianum*), but these are of little more than botanical interest at present.

Hog plum (*Spondias dulcis*) is an indigenous tree of which there are garden selections bearing yellow-orange fruit with a layer of pulp surrounding the large seed. In season the fruit from selected trees may be sold in markets. The fruit of the forest tree are generally eaten by pigs and cassowary. There are other species in Central America which have more palatable fruit and should perhaps be introduced to New Guinea as village fruit trees.

Jack fruit (*Artocarpus heterophyllus*) is of ancient cultivation in India and Africa but probably originated in the Indo-Malayan region. It is of very recent introduction to New Guinea. Trees fruiting in the botanic gardens at Lae proved of interest to local people but the fruit, which has a pungent odour, did not appeal. As far as is known there are no groups of native people in New Guinea who use the jack fruit as a food.

The related chempadak is naturalized near Talasea, introduced presumably by the Germans. It is not much used as a food.

Laulau or malay apple (*Eugenia malaccensis*) and the related species of rose apple (*Eugenia aquae* and *E. jambos*) and Java apple (*E. javanica*) provide several edible village fruits. In Malaya and Thailand the species are cultivated for the fruit, which is sold, but in Papua New Guinea it is rare to see the fruit in the markets. Trees are found in most of the lowland villages but the quality of the fruit is very variable. *E. malaccensis* is showy when in flower. The purple stamens fall to give a complete carpet below the trees. The fruit is seriously infested by the larvae of fruit fly and attacked by flying fox (*Dobsonia* and other genera). The brazilian cherry (*Eugenia uniflora*) is sometimes grown in plantation gardens for the acid sweet, aromatic fruits.

Lime, mouli or sipora (*Citrus aurantifolia*). Several varieties of limes are widely grown in New Guinea. If the 'sour mouli' of the north-eastern part of New Guinea is introduced then this was before the earliest European settlement. The first explorers reported limes in the villages. The form of *Citrus aurantifolia* grown throughout north-eastern New Guinea is superior to that of Papua. The latter is similar to the plant widespread in Java and Malaya. The fruit tend to be small, hard and green at maturity whereas the north coast varieties have larger fruit, yellow and juicy when ripe.

Mango (*Mangifera indica*) is the most popular fruit among millions of people in South-east Asia. It has been introduced only in limited areas of Papua New Guinea. Good fruit setting requires a definite dry season; hence the Port Moresby area, Gazelle

Peninsula, Northern District and the Markham Valley are the main producing areas. Elsewhere the tree grows well as a shade tree but rarely fruits.

The mango may have been introduced before European settlement. There are only a few varieties grown in the country, and undoubtedly more could be introduced. There are several wild species. Their fruit, which has a strong turpentine taste, is eaten by villagers.

Mangosteen (*Garcinia mangostana*), probably originating in the Malay Peninsula, has been known in cultivation for a long time. The fruit is described as the most delectable of all tropical fruits. The trees grow slowly; they are densely branched with a crown of large glossy green leaves. The red flowers appear singly within the crown and develop into a fruit which is purple-black, with four fleshy calyx lobes at the base and the remnants of the four to seven wedge-shaped stigmatic lobes at the apex. The rind is cut through with a sharp knife and the top removed to expose the five to eight segments of creamy-coloured pulp. In most fruit only one segment will have a seed. This should be carefully kept and planted as soon as possible. The seed appears to develop parthenocarpically as male trees do not normally occur. 'Seedlings' therefore reproduce the characters of the parent tree.

There are a number of native species of *Garcinia* in New Guinea but none have a palatable fruit. The yellow latex of two species in Thailand and India is the source of colouring for gamboge paint.

Nutmeg (*Myristica fragrans*). The genus *Myristica* contains many species but only two, *M. fragrans* and *M. argentea*, provide nutmeg and mace. While the original home of *M. fragrans* is unknown it is possible that it originates in the Malaysian region, perhaps Banda. The fruit produces two useful products, the red aril which encloses the seed is dried to be sold as mace and the seed itself provides the spice, nutmeg. The husk may be boiled in sugar syrup to make sweetmeats and jellies.

Nutmeg and mace contain myristicin, a poisonous narcotic, hence the spice and mace must be used sparingly.

Commercial production of nutmegs was tried in West Irian, but in Papua New Guinea interest is very low. Nutmeg trees have been introduced to most agricultural stations. There is considerable variety in the stock now available and care should be taken to select only the best for future plantings.

Orange or sweet mouli (*Citrus sinensis*). In parts of New Guinea an orange, which was probably introduced by German settlers, is grown in the villages. The fruit does not colour well and has a moderately thick skin and poor flavour. Propagation is by seed.

A wild orange (*Citrus papuana* and related species) occurs throughout lowlands. The fruit is quite inedible being mainly pith with a small central dry pulp. This species may have some value as a tropical root stock. The fruit are yellow when ripe. An unidentified citrus from the Gogol Valley near Madang has bright orange fruit. This plant has not been brought into cultivation.

Papaw (*Carica papaya*) probably originated in South Mexico and Costa Rica. It is now widespread in all tropical parts of the world. Throughout lowland New Guinea the plant is completely naturalized and is among the first wave of light-demanding pioneer species which germinate after clearing of forests. Seed is apparently distributed by birds or flying fox (*Dobsonia* and other genera) and remains dormant until exposed to light.

Plants are separately male and female, rarely hermaphrodite. The ripe fruit is used fresh; unripe fruit may be boiled. The whitish juice from the cut surface of green fruit contains papain which is a proteolytic enzyme used in meat tenderizing, manufacture of chewing gum, cosmetics, in tanning of hides, etc.

Village production of fruit is for local consumption or market sale.

Pineapples (*Ananus comosus*) appear to be relatively recent in New Guinea; they were probably introduced during the days of German administration. The fact that the Pidgin word for pineapple is the botanical name testifies to German influence. Two forms of the pineapple are widely grown. The smooth skin or queen pineapple produces very large fruit and grows well in seasonally dry climates. The flavour in this variety is probably inferior to that of the rough skin pineapple which is widely grown in areas of higher rainfall.

Pineapples are best propagated by the side shoots or slips which develop at the base of the parent plant after fruiting. Each erect shoot produces only one fruit then dies back. Pineapples grown at higher altitudes, up to 5,000 feet, are smaller than on the coast but often sweeter and of superior flavour.

The leaf fibre is used in the Philippines, southern China and Formosa for weaving into a high quality cloth.

Pomelo (*Citrus grandis*) was apparently introduced by the Germans in a number of areas; it is not the successful fruit it is in Malaya. The best fruit come from the Gazelle Peninsula. Propagation by seed has brought about a number of varieties none of which come true from seedlings.

Rambutan (*Nephelium lappaceum*) is one of the best-known fruit trees in Malaysia; it has been introduced only recently to New Guinea where the fruit has already proved popular among local people. The tree bears characteristic red fruit which are covered in soft wavy spines. The seed is surrounded by a layer of white pulp (aril). This is the edible portion. Selected varieties have the seed almost free from the pulp which is eaten raw. There are many varieties, some with aromatic seed pulp, others with thick but rather tough pulp layers. The best have not yet been introduced to New Guinea.

Closely related is the Chinese litchi (*Nephelium litchi*) which grows in a subtropical climate and the indigenous *Pometia pinnata*. This latter species is an important forest timber tree. There is a selection, now quite widely cultivated, which has fruit the size of a small apple. In these the seed pulp is much enlarged and edible. The popularity of this fruit varies greatly. Local people in Lae do not collect the edible fruit from trees planted in the botanic garden, but will eat the wild fruit from the nearby forest.

Rozelle or rosella (*Hibiscus sabdariffa*) is an annual or sometimes bi-annual plant. Two varieties exist, one a much-branched undershrub with red or green stems; the red or yellow calyx is edible at fruiting. The other variety is erect, scarcely branched and with fibrous, spiny inedible calyces.

The red acid succulent calyces are boiled with sugar to produce a drink or made into jellies, jams or sauces.

It is not widely grown, and more as an ornamental than a food plant. The fibre-producing variety is not known in New Guinea.

Soursop or sapsap (*Annona muricata*) is a medium-sized tree with very dark green foliage of South American origin. It appears to have been introduced at the time of German settlement, perhaps earlier. The large green fruit soften at maturity. The pulp can be eaten straight from the fruit, or the seeds and surrounding fibres removed by sieving. The creamy liquid which remains is excellent as a base for fruit drinks or may be frozen as an ice-cream. Other species of *Annona* have been introduced and one, the sugar apple, *Annona squamosa*, is naturalized on the dry hills around Port Moresby. These are of little use.

Tamarind (*Tamarindus indica*) is apparently of African origin, introduced into India and South-east Asia. In New Guinea it is a fairly recent introduction, probably since 1920. It does best in semi-arid tropical regions but will grow in monsoon regions in well-drained soil. The tree does not fruit in continuously wet climates.

The fruit is a pod with fleshy walls. The seeds are embedded in brown pulp which is pleasantly tart. It is used to make sherbert and cooling drinks, and to season curries, etc. The seeds, properly cleaned, can be roasted or boiled.

The tree is the source of a number of medicinal preparations in India, but it is planted mainly as a shade tree in Papua New Guinea. There are good specimens in Port Moresby.

FRUITS USED AS NUTS

A variety of fruits which have a large kernel are used as nuts, although few, if any, can be stored as almonds, walnuts, etc., can be.

Aila, or the Pacific chestnut (*Inocarpus edulis*), is common throughout the lowlands. It is often found near water and the large fruit have a spongy, fibrous husk which is clearly adapted to dispersal by water. The seed is eaten after the husk is broken away either by force or by burning.

Barringtonia edulis and other species are used in the Gazelle Peninsula and Solomon Islands areas.

Breadfruit (*Artocarpus altilis*). The seeds of the wild breadfruit are collected, often after the fruit have been torn apart by flying fox. They may be roasted or boiled.

Candle nut (*Aleurites moluccana*) may be eaten after roasting but it is more often used as its name implies. The nuts are placed on top of one another on a sharpened sliver of bamboo and burnt as a candle.

Finschia chloroxantha is a member of the family Proteaceae and a close relative of the Queensland macadamia nut. It grows wild in the lowland and mid-mountain forests. The flowers are spectacular, resembling hanging spikes reminiscent of slender *Banksia* inflorescences. The fruit develop after flowering and attain a diameter of 1½ inches. The ripe fruit fall and are collected from the ground. The hard shell is usually broken by burning but sometimes stones are used to crack the nut. In season large piles of shells may be seen in villages having access to these trees. It may be possible to cultivate the trees for commercial production of the nuts, which are larger than macadamia nuts. It would be necessary to select thin-shelled varieties.

Galip nut (*Canarium indicum*), probably the most delectable of all tropical nuts, is relished by native people and Europeans. In season large quantities are sold in the markets in Rabaul and Madang. The galip tree is actually a large forest tree exceeding 100 feet in height. However, young trees will carry good crops and wherever space is available it is a tree to be recommended. The purple fruit have a thin layer of pulp and a very hard inner shell. Skilled operators can readily break it to expose the kernel. The kernel may be eaten raw, or blanched and fried in butter and salt. *Canarium indicum* and several other species, all of which produce edible nuts, occur from Malaysia to the Pacific.

Java almond (*Terminalia catappa*) is a tree of coastal situations. The fruit contains a small edible nut which is used by village people.

T. solomonensis is a tree which occurs in the Solomons area and appears to have been brought to the eastern islands of New Guinea. The outer portion of the fruit is soft and fleshy, and eaten like a plum. The seed is not eaten.

Karuka or marita (*Pandanus* spp.). Various species of *Pandanus*, particularly *P. julianetti* and *P. brosimos*, produce oily seeds which are extensively eaten. The fruiting head consists of an aggregate of syncarps. Each syncarp is a very fibrous cover for the several seeds. The fruit break up on drying into the syncarps, but the latter can only be opened by force, or by smoking or heating. The fruit are stored in the rafters of Highlands houses and become smoked and dried. In this state the kernels are preserved for an appreciable time. Throughout the Highlands, *Pandanus* is at least fostered and in some places actually planted. Large groves in forest areas are in part natural, but man has certainly encouraged them.

There is another section of *Pandanus* which produces an elongated cylindrical fruit with very small syncarps (*Pandanus conoideus*). Each syncarp has a small amount of red flesh surrounding the fibrous portion enclosing the seed. The syncarps are boiled so that the fleshy portion comes away to make a type of soup.

The botany of *Pandanus* in New Guinea can best be described as confused.

The plant is of considerable importance as a provider of food and also of shelter. The leaves are sewn together edge to edge to make rain capes, roofing, sleeping mats and canoe sails. Split leaf blades are folded and woven into baskets. From sea-level to the limit of forest vegetation species of *Pandanus* occur and are put to use.

Mangrove fruits (*Bruguiera* and *Rhizophora* spp.) are not really nuts; the part eaten is the developing shoot from the seed of these mangrove trees.

Okari nut (*Terminalia kaernbachii*) and the related species *T. impediens* provide an edible nut of quality. The trees are generally large and fruit sporadically. The nuts are purple-red when ripe. The thick husk has to be forcibly broken to expose the kernel. The nut may be eaten raw or roasted, and contains oil of high quality as an edible fat.

Palmyra palm (*Borassus flabellifer*), well known throughout Africa and South-east Asia is found in only a few localities in New Guinea. On the Sepik River groves of the palms occur on headlands projecting into the river. It has been suggested that these occurrences are on old camp sites of the Malay bird-of-paradise hunters who came to the north coast before Europeans discovered the island. *Borassus* fruit could have been carried in dugout canoes and planted at the camp sites.

Pangium edule. The seeds from the fruit of this tree are used. Corner writes 'one of Nature's monsters. It is a poisonous tree with ungainly fruit suggesting a stomach crammed with big seeds'.

The seeds, like all parts of the tree, contain cyanogenetic glucosides which release hydrocyanic acid on digestion. The seeds can be rendered safe for eating by boiling for an hour or more, or baking. However, it is more usual to crush the seeds and leave them enclosed in a bag in running water for a day or more, then boil them well. The tree often grows on stream and river banks.

The hard dry seed coats with the interior hollowed out are used extensively for dance rattles either as a cluster tied to the wrists or waist, or on a string down the dancer's back.

Trichosanthes spp. Seeds of the several species of *Trichosanthes* may be collected and dried rather as the Chinese dry melon seeds. The whole fruit is also used in times of necessity.

Tulip or 'two-leaf' (*Gnetum gnemon*). The Pidgin name for this plant alludes to the paired leaves. Throughout lowland New Guinea the young foliage of this tree is used as a green vegetable. To a lesser extent the seeds are collected and boiled. In Java boiled seeds of *Gnetum* are beaten into a paste and then dried as a type of krupok.

AGRICULTURAL COVER CROPS

Calopogonium mucunoides is an American plant now widely introduced in the tropics to suppress weeds in plantations. Initial growth is very rapid and produces a dense mat of foliage. Palatability to stock is reduced because of hairs on the leaves and stems. The pods are relatively short, blunt at the apex, and hairy.

Centro (*Centrosema pubescens*) is an American plant widely introduced throughout the tropics as a cover crop in plantations to suppress undesirable species. The flowers are pale blue and relatively large. The long, narrow, flattened pod is pointed at the apex; it is not hairy.

This plant is often used in mixed cover crops with *Calopogonium muconoides* and *Pueraria phaseoloides*.

Tropical kudjea (*Pueraria phaseoloides*). This South-east Asian plant is now planted widely throughout the tropics for cover cropping and green manure. The flowers grow in an erect raceme; they are pink, blue or white; the pod is narrow and elongate but, at least when young, hairy.

This plant is used both to suppress undesirable growth and for fodder.

BEVERAGES

Toddy. The sap collected from the inflorescence of the coconut palm is fermented into a toddy on the Mortlock and Tasman Islands. Elsewhere in New Guinea the practice is not known. In Papua there have been suggestions of toddy brewing on the lower Fly River.

Kava drinking is not known in New Guinea, although the plant from which the active principle is extracted is said to occur near the Fly River. There are species of *Piper* native to New Guinea, which are closely related to *Piper methysticum*, the yangona plant of Fiji and the classical raw material of kava.

MISCELLANEOUS CROPS

Cinnamon (*Cinnamomum zeylanicum*). Most agricultural stations have one or more trees of *Cinnamomum zeylanicum*. There is no commercial production of cinnamon bark in the Territory. *Cinnamomum culilawan* is a large forest tree with highly aromatic bark. The aromatic oil is almost entirely eugenol and has no commercial significance. Another closely related tree, *Cryptocarya massoia*, is the source of massoy oil. Commercial interest in this oil exists, but supplies of the tree are very limited.

Ginger (*Zingiber officinale*) is grown in a small way as a commercial crop. Other species of *Zingiber* are used by villagers for flavouring food and for curing colds. The flowers and young fruit are sometimes eaten as a snack.

Hydnocarpus anthelminticus has been introduced to a few agricultural stations in Papua New Guinea. At Bubia, 7 miles from Lae on the Highlands Highway, there is a line of trees by the roadside. The large velvety fruit contain seeds which yield an oil similar in chemical composition to chaulmoogra oil, formerly used to treat leprosy.

Job's tears (*Coix lacryma-jobi*) is a grass occurring wild and semi-cultivated. The large whitish-grey seeds are used to ornament headbands, etc., and are also used in necklaces of assorted seeds produced for sale to tourists. There is a possibility that the grain may have been crushed for flour. If this practice did exist it appears to have died out.

Sago palm (*Metroxylon sagu*) of New Guinea is an important source of food for people living in swampy areas. Two forms of the palm occur: one has spiny leaf bases, the other is spineless. The former is sometimes referred to as *M. rumphii* but, as both forms can be raised from a seed collection from one fruiting specimen, there can be no valid botanical distinction warranting two separate names.

Sago palm grows with an underground stem from which leafy shoots grow vertically. Growth is slow. After four to five years a trunk begins to form with an aggregation of leaves toward the apex. As the trunk grows upward to 25 feet or more starch builds up in the fibrous part of the trunk. This starch is really reserve food material for the developing flower head which appears when the trunk reaches maximum height. This is usually about fifteen years from the first development of the leafy sucker. The inflorescence develops and flowers, eventually producing fruit. In *M. sagu* these are about 1 inch in diameter. *M. bougainvillense* has fruit up to 4 inches in diameter; these are the ivory nut of commerce.

If the sago as prepared by local people (*see* FOOD) is further washed and allowed to settle, a very white, arrowroot-like, starch can be prepared. Many missionaries use this for children's food when they are cut off from other supplies.

The yield of starch from any one palm is very variable. Some palms which never produce an inflorescence have been known to yield 900 lb. of crude sago, but the average yield is much lower.

Tangket (*Cordyline terminalis*) is an erect-stemmed leafy plant which is deeply involved in indigenous culture. It is used widely to mark the boundaries of gardens and land. Highland people wear the leaves tied in a bunch so as to cover the buttocks. Wild forms of the plant occur in the forest and there is a large array of cultivars in gardens. Plants are propagated by cuttings. The roots produce a large underground tuber which can be used as a source of starchy food. Use of *Cordyline* tubers has now almost disappeared in favour of sweet potato and taro. (*See* TANGKET.)

Turmeric (*Curcuma* sp.) occurs wild in the lowland forests and is also found in the anthropogenous grasslands of the Highlands. The underground rhizome is very persistent. The presence today of these plants, often closely aggregated together, must be a remnant of native gardening. *Curcuma*, widely used in South-east Asia as a colouring for rice, is little used in New Guinea.

Vanilla (*Vanilla planifolia*), probably the only orchid of agricultural significance, has a continually growing stem with aerial roots produced at each node. The roots attach themselves to whatever support is offered. In commercial plantations *Vanilla* is grown on shade trees. The plants ascend, then sprawl, and hang down in loops. The flowers are produced in succession on short spikes, and are cream, and reminiscent of a miniature *Cattleya* orchid. Pollination is frequently ineffective unless done by hand. The developing fruit or vanilla beans are green and attain a length of about 8 inches and diameter of about half an inch. At maturity the pods are picked and cured to induce fermentation which produces vanillin, the flavouring of commerce. Vanilla essence is an alcoholic extract of vanillin from vanilla pods. This has largely been replaced by synthetic vanillin.

I. H. Burkhill, *A Dictionary of the Economic Products of the Malay Peninsula*. 2 vols, Singapore, 1966; E. J. H. Corner, *The Natural History of Palms*. London, 1966; E. E. Henty, 'A manual of the grasses of New Guinea', T. P. N. G. Department of Forests, *Botany Bulletin*, no. 1, 1969; J. W. Purseglove, *Tropical Crops, Dicotyledons*. 2 parts, London, 1968.

J. S. WOMERSLEY

CROWN. The Crown is the executive government of the country and exercises central government functions. Papua is a Crown colony owned by the Crown in right of the Commonwealth of Australia. New Guinea is not a Crown colony and is not owned by the Crown in right of the Commonwealth of Australia. By international law, treaties are executed by the Crown in right of the Commonwealth. Under the relevant treaty (annexed to the schedule of the Papua New Guinea Act) the United Nations vested in the Crown in right of the Commonwealth the function of administering New Guinea as a trust territory. Therefore, the Crown in New Guinea operates as an agent and not as a principal, but this does not affect its legal status and all common law doctrines attaching to the Crown apply to the Crown in right of New Guinea, save in so far as they are modified either expressly or by necessary implication by statute. For example, criminal proceedings before the Supreme Court are commenced in the name of the Crown, e.g. *The Queen* v. *Ebulya*. Similarly, the Crown would be immune from criminal proceedings, unless statute provided otherwise. J. LeMAIRE

CRUSTACEA. The class Crustacea, which with the classes Insecta, Arachnoidea and others forms the phylum Arthropoda, contains about forty thousand known species; however, the actual number of species of Crustacea is probably much higher as many surely remain to be discovered. The group itself is divided into eight subclasses, the best known of which are the Branchiopoda—with the orders Cladocera (water fleas), Anostraca (fairy shrimps), and others; the Ostracoda, the Copepoda, the Cirripedia—with five orders, of which the Thoracica (barnacles), and Rhizocephala are best known; and the Malacostraca. The subclass Malacostraca is composed of twelve orders, among which the Mysidacea, Cumacea, Isopoda, Amphipoda, Stomatopoda, and Decapoda are the more important.

The body length of adult Crustacea varies from less than a millimetre in some Copepoda, Ostracoda and Cladocera to more than two feet in some spiny lobsters, the antennae not included. In the Japanese giant crab, *Macrocheira kaempferi*, the distance between the tips of the fully extended chelipeds may attain ten feet.

The crustacean body is divided into segments, the number of which may vary from less than ten, in some Ostracoda, to more than forty, in some Branchiopoda. In some parasitic groups, like the Rhizocephala, the body is so degenerate that no segmentation is visible at all; the crustacean nature of such groups is only shown by their larvae. In principle each segment of the crustacean body bears two articulated appendages, but here too a great diversity is shown: some appendages are slender walking legs, others are leaf-shaped and flattened, some end in pincers, others in flagellae; sometimes the appendages are strongly reduced and may even be entirely absent. The head bears the eyes, which are composite and sometimes stalked, and two pairs of antennae. The appendages of the posterior cephalic segments are the so-called mouth-parts, used for the intake and processing of the food. The appendages of the thorax and abdomen are usually used for locomotion and respiration. The whole body and the appendages are covered by an exoskeleton of chitin, which in the larger species is usually more or less strongly calcified. In the higher Crustacea a shield-shaped carapace covers the cephalothorax; in crabs this carapace is practically the only part of the body that is visible in dorsal view.

The Crustacea produce eggs, which in most groups are carried by the female until they hatch. The development as a rule passes through various larval stages. Growth is through moulting. The larvae often are so different from the adults that originally they were considered to represent distinct species and even genera. Only in recent years have zoologists succeeded in raising several of the higher Crustacea from the egg to the adult stage and in this way the true relationship between the larva and the adult form has been established with certainty.

The habits and habitats of Crustacea are as diverse as the animals themselves. Among the Crustacea there are free-living and sessile forms, planktonic species and bottom-dwellers, commensals and parasites. In the parasites the body is very often strangely deformed, part of or the entire segmentation is lost and the animal may become sac- or sausage-shaped, as in many Rhizocephala; or the body may become enlarged and so aberrant in shape that the animal can hardly be recognized as a crustacean, as in some parasitic Copepoda. Non-parasitic sessile forms are found among the Cirripedia. Here too the shape of the body is such that the animals, e.g. the barnacles and goose-barnacles, are hardly recognizable as Crustacea; many of the early authors therefore classed them with the Mollusca, and only when the larvae became known were they definitely placed with the Crustacea. Even the habitat of the sessile forms shows great differences: many barnacles live intertidally, or even slightly above high tide level, others may be found in the deep sea; floating objects like pieces of driftwood or ship's hulls often form the substrate for barnacles, while certain species are only to be found on other animals like whales, manatees, turtles, crabs, etc. The habitats of the non-sessile forms are likewise extremely diverse: these species inhabit the sea, but also brackish and fresh waters, while some groups such as the Isopoda terrestria are adapted to terrestrial life, being encountered even in deserts. Marine Crustacea are found down to depths of 10,000 metres (22,500 feet), while some freshwater Copepoda have been taken at altitudes of more than 13,000 feet above sea-level. Crustacea can be found in practically all types of fresh water. For example, many crustacean groups form part of the peculiar cavernicolous fauna which lives in the complete darkness of subterranean waters; in many of these creatures the body has lost all colour, the eyes are reduced or absent, and the appendages are very long and slender. Some forms are found in hot springs.

A number of Crustacea live in association with other animals. The best known of such commensals is the pea-crab, *Pinnotheres* which can be found in the mantle cavity of bivalve molluscs, a phenomenon noted by ancient Greek and Roman authors. Other species of Crustacea are found within ascidians and holothurians, in or on sponges, corals and echinoderms, etc. The crab *Hapalocarcinus* and the shrimp *Paratypton* cause corals to grow a gall-like formation, in which these crustaceans live. Recently a most interesting association between fish and some species of shrimp was discovered: fishes let themselves be cleaned by the shrimp which walks all over the body of the fish picking off parasites, growths, etc., even entering the branchial cavity and the mouth without being harmed by the fish.

Practically all major crustacean groups are well represented in New Guinea. The seas around the island contain an abundance of forms hardly surpassed anywhere else in the world. The marine Crustacea form part of the Indo-West Pacific fauna, which ranges from the east coast of Africa, including the Red Sea, to southern Japan, northern Australia and Polynesia. The animal life in this area is richer in species than that of any other marine zoogeographic area, while within it the Indo-Australian province is again the richest. The great variety of habitats along the coast of New Guinea, like coral reefs, sandy and rocky beaches, mud flats, mangroves, etc., also contributes to the overwhelming number of species of Crustacea found there. The freshwater Crustacea are also well represented, several freshwater species showing an interesting affinity to the Australian freshwater fauna.

Of the eight subclasses of Crustacea, the Cephalocarida, Mystacocarida, and Branchiura have so far not been reported from New Guinea. The suborder Cladocera (water fleas) of the subclass Branchiopoda is rather common in fresh waters both in the lowlands and in the mountains; most species are cosmopolitan or have a wide distribution in the Indo-West Pacific area. Ostracoda have been reported both from salt and fresh waters. Most of the freshwater species seem to be endemic to the island. Of the saltwater species little is known. The same is true for the marine Copepoda, which are very plentiful in the plankton of the seas around the island, but have so far been little studied. Also the freshwater Copepoda have received but relatively little attention. Like the Cladocera they have been found both in lowland waters and high up in the mountains at altitudes as high as 5,000 feet. A rather great percentage of the freshwater Copepoda seem to be endemic, some species are cosmopolitan, one is restricted to New Guinea and the northern part of Australia, while one of the endemic species belongs to a genus (*Calamoecia*) that otherwise is only known from Australia and New Zealand.

The Cirripedia (barnacles and goose barnacles) can be found in a great variety of habitats along the coasts. All the species are sessile marine forms. They live attached to floating and fixed substrates, mostly in the littoral and sub-littoral zones, but some forms occur in deeper waters, even in the deep sea. In this group there are also parasites, like the Rhizocephala.

Of the subclass Malacostraca the orders Syncarida, Thermosbaenacea, and Spelaeogriphacea are not known from New Guinea. All the other orders are present, although only very few records of some have been published. The Stomatopoda can be found on sandy and muddy bottoms, but also in coral-reef areas; they are well represented in the New Guinea fauna. Isopoda and Amphipoda are not rare in the seas around the island. Terrestrial Isopoda are found all over the island, even at high altitudes. In the Wissel Lakes area of central West Irian, at an altitude of 5,000 feet, not only terrestrial Isopoda, but also terrestrial Amphipoda have been encountered. Terrestrial Amphipoda were also found at an altitude of 12,000 feet on Mt Wilhelm in the Bismarck Range in the north-east.

The best known order of Crustacea is that of the Decapoda, which includes prawns, lobsters and crabs. Prawns are represented by a great number of species, the ranges of which extend from the deep sea to lakes and streams high up in the central mountain range. Many hundreds of species of marine prawns inhabit New Guinea waters, some only a few millimetres long, e.g. some Pontoniinae; others, like several penaeids, attaining sizes of more than 250 millimetres. Where the sea bottom is flat, and consists of mud and sand, as along the south-west coast, Penaeidae are found plentifully, and eventually may become of commercial importance. A host of small prawns and shrimps can be found in the coral-reef areas; many are delicately and often brilliantly coloured, like the Gnathophyllidae, Pontoniinae, etc. The fresh waters at practically all altitudes are inhabited by numerous species of palaemonid and atyid prawns. Those of the family Atyidae as a rule are small, but many Palaemonidae, especially species of the genus *Macrobrachium*, may attain considerable sizes and are caught for food by the native population. No true lobsters, *Homarus*, occur in New Guinea, but there are slipper lobsters, Scyllaridae, and spiny lobsters or marine crayfish, Palinuridae. The latter are represented by various species of *Panulirus* that are hunted by the natives in the coral-reef areas; the feasibility of commercial exploitation of these animals has recently been investigated along the south coast of Papua.

The freshwater crayfishes form one of the most interesting groups of Crustacea of the island. They belong to the family Parastacidae and occur not only in lowland streams and lakes, but also ascend

The freshwater crayfish, *Cherax communis*; Paniai Lake, Wissel Lakes area, West Irian.

into the mountains as shown by the rich parastacid fauna found in the Wissel Lakes of West Irian at an altitude of about 5,000 feet. The crayfish fauna of these three lakes is extremely rich both in individuals and in species; at present eight species have been described from there, but this number is likely to increase. The crayfishes are so abundant in the lakes that there is an intensive fishery for these animals which form the main source of animal protein for the native population. The family Parastacidae has a most remarkable discontinuous distribution, being restricted to the southern hemisphere and occurring there only in a few widely separated places, southern South America, Madagascar, Australia, New Guinea and New Zealand. The New Guinea species—about a dozen are known now—all belong to the genus *Cherax*, which also occurs in Australia. In New Guinea these crayfishes are only found south of the central mountain range, in rivers and lakes that empty into or are connected with either the Arafura Sea or the Gulf of Papua. The genus *Cherax* also occurs on Misool Island and in the Aru Archipelago, both situated on the shallow Sahul Shelf which connects New Guinea with Australia. The distribution of the Parastacidae thus gives a clear indication of the close faunal connection of New Guinea with Australia.

The decapod suborder Anomura also is well represented. The best known forms are the hermit crabs, Paguridea, all species of which, except *Birgus*, have the soft abdomen hidden in an empty gastropod shell which they carry around and in which they can withdraw when danger threatens. Hermit crabs are plentiful on the coral-reefs, in the mangroves and other marine habitats. The land hermit crabs of the family Coenobitidae are true terrestrial animals, and only go to the sea at the time their eggs hatch. The most remarkable of these Coenobitidae is the huge robber crab, *Birgus*, which attains a body length of about 300 millimetres; it feeds on coconuts, fruit of *Pandanus* and *Canarium* trees, etc., and has been observed climbing coconut palms. Whether it is capable of opening a coconut by itself is still unknown. The species occurs on a number of small islands around New Guinea; its range extends far into the Indian and Pacific Oceans.

Also among the true crabs (Brachyura) of New Guinea there are genuine terrestrial species like those belonging to the family Gecarcinidae; and some species of Grapsidae may be found far away from water. Freshwater crabs occur all over the island up into the mountain ranges. Most of these are species of Potamonidae, but recently a freshwater species of hymenosomatid crab was discovered in the mountains of Papua at an altitude of about 5,500 feet. Marine crabs are represented by a bewildering number of species. The diversity is especially great in the coral-reef areas, where there are many species of very different shape, size and colour; for example, the often long-legged spider crabs, Majidae, many of which camouflage themselves with pieces of algae that they attach to the dorsal surface of the body and legs; very rough, coral rock-mimicking crabs like *Daldorfia*; the beautifully coloured *Carpilius*, *Carpilodes* and other xanthids; the curious shame-face or box crab, the shell of which resembles a coconut in some species, giving the genus its Latin name *Calappa*; the delicately tinted *Trapezia* that live only on coral branches, and numerous other interesting forms. Crabs also occur on the muddy and sandy shores, some species in groups of very numerous individuals like the fiddler crabs, *Uca*, and the soldier crabs, *Myctiris*. The crustacean fauna has so far received relatively little attention and many interesting discoveries can still be expected.   L. B. HOLTHUIS

CURRENCY. The system of Papua and New Guinea is that operating throughout the Commonwealth of Australia; Australian notes and coin are legal tender in the Territory. The Reserve Bank Act 1959-66 of the Commonwealth (sections 5, 36) provides that Australian notes are legal tender; Australian coinage is legal tender in terms of the Currency Ordinance 1965 of the Territory. Small quantities of New Guinea coinage also circulate as legal tender. British coins may also be used as legal tender in terms of the Currency Ordinance (section 21), but such coins are no longer seen.

New Guinea 'holey coins'. From left, top then bottom: penny, threepence, sixpence, shilling.

1936 Edward VIII penny.

Until 1964, in parts of coastal New Britain, the use of gold-lip shell, *Pinctada maxima*, was permitted in place of legal tender under the New Guinea Currency Coinage and Tokens Ordinance 1922-60 section 7(2). Its exchange rate was fixed at twelve shillings ($1.20) a pair. This shell is still used in trading though it is no longer legal tender. Shell moneys still play a significant part in some areas of the Territory, though mostly as status symbols or associated with ceremonial exchanges. An exception is the *tambu* shell money (*Nassarius callosa*) of New Britain which is still used alongside currency for trading in the local market as well as for ceremonial and status purposes (*see* KULA, ROSSEL ISLAND CURRENCY).

Specimen of five mark note issued by Australian authorities in New Guinea, 1914.

The Reserve Bank of Australia conducts a note issuing branch at Port Moresby from which banks in that area draw their requirements; other bank branches requisition either their point of administrative control in Australia or their Port Moresby office. Coin, which is the responsibility of Commonwealth Treasury, is distributed by the Reserve Bank of Australia in Port Moresby and by the Commonwealth Trading Bank, as agent, at other main centres. Foreign exchange regulations of the Commonwealth apply, requirements of foreign exchange being provided by the central bank through Territory branches of the trading banks. There are no restrictions on payments or currency transfers between the Territory and Australia. The Territory has no separate reserves of gold and foreign exchange, but relies on Australia's reserves; nor does it quote separate exchange rates with other countries.

Australian currency has circulated in Papua since that Territory was brought within the currency arrangements of the Commonwealth by the Currency Ordinance 1911 of Papua. In New Guinea, however, a variety of coinages has circulated.

German currency in New Guinea. Until the establishment of the Commonwealth Bank of Australia in Rabaul in 1916 German currency was the legal tender. German currency notes, silver coins of half, one, two and five marks denominations, and copper coins of one, two and ten pfennigs denominations circulated side by side with smaller quantities of British and Australian coins.

Following the occupation of German New Guinea [q.v.] in September 1914 the Australian military administration arranged for the printing and issue of an emergency issue of paper money. On the standard that one mark equalled one Australian shilling, an issue to the value of £2,600 ($5,200) was made, denominated in five, ten, twenty and fifty marks. The notes were simply printed on poor paper and circulated with the German paper money and coins.

From 30 June 1916 the importation of further German currency was forbidden and the process of withdrawal of German currency and its replacement by Australian was commenced. However, German currency continued in use for a considerable period despite difficulties in setting its value in terms of Australian currency. Finally, in December 1920, the use of German currency was prohibited, except that coins in the possession of native people were exempted. So far as the native population was concerned, marks and shillings were freely interchangeable and both were accepted. German marks were still common in the Rabaul area in the late 1930s.

New Guinea coinage. In 1928 steps were taken to introduce low value coinage of special design. Coins of penny and halfpenny denominations were designed by Robert Law of the Melbourne Mint. They were about the size of an Australian shilling (10c) and sixpence (5c) respectively but with plain edge and a hole in the centre. The coins were of nickel alloy and the designs were based on New Guinea native art. It was hoped that the reproduction of native art on the coins would have an 'additional appeal to the native mind', making the coins a rival to tobacco which still served as currency in much of the hinterland.

During 1929, 62,670 pence and 24,590 halfpence were minted. The coins were well received by numismatists but not by local traders. At the time, it was the custom in New Guinea to roll shillings into *fuses* of 100 coins (£5). These fuses, enclosed in paper wrapping, were passed from person to person without the contents being checked. As the new pennies were the same size as a shilling they could easily be incorporated in fuses without being readily detectable. For this reason, traders declined to handle the new pennies—the halfpenny hardly circulated anyway—and both coins were withdrawn.

In 1935 another more successful attempt was made to provide distinctive coinage for New

Guinea. During 1935 and 1936 silver shillings, nickel-bronze sixpences and threepences, and bronze pennies were struck at the Melbourne Mint. These were designed by Kruger Gray along the lines of Law's original conception and all coins had the hole in the centre. This perforation is said to have been for the purpose of facilitating carriage of the coins by the native people; the idea being that a piece of string, wire, etc., could be passed through the centre of the coins which could then be slung around the neck of the owner. Further issues of these coins were made until 1945 when the minting of New Guinea coinage ceased. It is interesting to note that 360,000 pennies struck in 1936 were the only coins minted in Australia bearing the imperial cipher of Edward VIII, E.R.I.

Following the decision for joint administration of the two territories of Papua and New Guinea after World War II, no further issues of New Guinea coinage were made. The total issue, excluding the pence and halfpence minted in 1929, was 12,059,120 coins totalling $964,312.

NEW GUINEA COINAGE—MINTINGS

Year Minted	Denomination	No. of Pieces
1929	1d	62,670
	½d	24,590
1935	1s	1,500,000
1936	1s	600,000
	6d	400,000
	3d	1,200,000
	1d	360,000
1937	1s	1,360,000
1938	1s	600,000
	1d	360,000
1943	1s	1,007,120
1944	1s	1,808,000
	6d	128,000
	3d	496,000
	1d	240,000
1945	1s	2,000,000

Decimal currency 1966. Australian decimal currency was introduced within Papua and New Guinea at the same time as in Australia, 14 February 1966. A Papua and New Guinea Currency Conversion Commission was established under the Currency Conversion Ordinance 1964 to plan the change-over and promote the efficient introduction of the new currency. The transition was successfully and smoothly accomplished and the new currency has been accepted by the indigenous population. Quantities of the old coinage will continue to circulate for some time, but practically all notes denominated in pounds and shillings had been withdrawn by the end of 1966-7 as had the bulk of coins with no exact equivalent in decimal coins, halfpence, pence and threepence. Decimal notes are available in denominations of one, two, five, ten and twenty dollars; coins in denominations of one, two, five, ten, twenty and fifty cents.

Currency in circulation. It is possible only to estimate the volume of currency in circulation in Papua and New Guinea. Accurate statistics of currency sent to the Territory for use by banks, and of currency returned by banks to Australia for destruction or other reasons, are available only since 1946. Amounts of currency movements to and from the Territory by travellers or other persons or institutions are unrecorded. Accordingly the following estimates should be regarded as subject to possible error of up to 5 per cent.

ESTIMATE OF AUSTRALIAN CURRENCY IN CIRCULATION
$ million

End of	Notes	Coin	Total
December 1955	2.8	2.0	4.8
December 1960	4.2	3.1	7.3
December 1962	6.8	3.7	10.5
December 1964	9.8	4.8	14.7
December 1966	13.8	5.7	19.5
December 1968	19.7	6.7	26.4
December 1969	24.2	7.2	31.4

Hoarding. Stories concerning the hoarding propensities of the Papuan and New Guinean people are numerous. In recent times, currency hoards have been variously estimated as high as $30 million.

Certainly, village people over the years have hoarded substantial quantities of currency, mostly coinage. The lack of convenient facilities for savings, the general misunderstanding and sometimes mistrust of banks, and traditional attitudes towards holding and storing valuables, including shell money and the like, all have contributed to this practice. Co-operative societies, savings and loan societies, the extension of banking agencies, and the general financial development of the community have helped to start a disgorgement of hoards in some areas. However, hoarding is a problem; but many of the estimates of hoarding are extravagant.

At the end of December 1969 the total Australian currency in circulation in Papua and New Guinea was estimated at about $31.4 million, of which $24.2 million were notes and $7.2 million were coinage. In the post-war period, net imports of notes into the Territory have totalled just on $22 million and of coin about $6 million. In addition small amounts of New Guinea coinage are still in circulation. These latter are of relatively little significance as most of those issued have found their way over the years into coin collections, tourist souvenir collections, wartime keepsakes, or to Asian ports for illegal sale for silver reclamation.

There is evidence suggesting that hoards total not less than $1 million. Certainly, when the figures for currency supply are considered they could not be as high as $10 million. Somewhere between these two extremes lies the truth. A reasonable estimate might be $4-5 million; much of this, while technically hoarded in that it has been removed from the money stream, still plays a part in ceremonial exchanges and wealth displays.

A separate currency for the Territory. From time to time the general question of a separate currency for Papua and New Guinea has been raised in the press or in the legislature. No strong body of opinion has emerged, however, in favour of such a change. The 1963 Mission from the International Bank for Reconstruction and Development in its report considered 'whether there were economic factors which would suggest an independent monetary and banking system'. It concluded that 'a separate monetary system would not be to the economic advantage of the Territory. The inclusion of the Territory in the Australian monetary area has the substantial advantages of unlimited access to foreign exchange (within the framework of the Australian regulations) and complete freedom of payments between the Territory and Australia. These factors are of paramount importance from the point of view of confidence of the foreign investor'.

When the decision was taken to introduce decimal currency into Australia, it was necessary to decide whether Papua and New Guinea would follow suit or whether it would take the opportunity to introduce its own currency. In his speech on 11 June 1964 on the Second Reading of the Currency Bill 1964 in the House of Assembly the Treasurer said: 'It is elementary that working as we are towards the independence of the Territory of Papua and New Guinea a local currency will be introduced at some time or other'. However, the Administration decided that the interests of the Territory were best served by the retention of Australian currency.

The economic factors to be considered in relation to a separate currency include the costs of minting, printing, distributing and replacing currency, the acceptance of the currency by the populace, the effect of a change on investors' confidence, the backing for the currency and the investment of the assets backing. These, in Papua and New Guinea's case, would be further influenced by the relationship of any new currency to Australian currency, the fate of the common monetary area with Australia, and the effect if any on the annual Commonwealth grant to the Territory. In the event of an independent Papua and New Guinea these considerations are likely to be outweighed by immeasurable factors such as the degree of national prestige offered by a separate currency and the desire for greater local control of the monetary system.

Commonwealth of Australia, *Annual Report, Territory of Papua 1927-8, 1948-9, 1951-2* —. Canberra, 1929, 1950, 1953 —.
——— *Report to the League of Nations on the Administration of the Territory of New Guinea 1936-7.* Canberra, 1938.
——— *Report to the United Nations on the Administration of the Territory of New Guinea 1947-8* —. Canberra, 1949 —.
C. C. Faulkner, *The Commonwealth Bank of Australia*, pp. 220-31. Sydney, 1923.
T. Hanley and B. James, *Collecting Australian Coins*, pp. 206-9. Sydney, 1966.
International Bank for Reconstruction and Development, *The Economic Development of the Territory of Papua and New Guinea*, pp. 366-8. Baltimore, 1965.
C. D. Rowley, *The Australians in German New Guinea 1914-1921*, pp. 62-7. Melbourne, 1958.
Royal Mint, *Annual Reports of the Deputy Master and Comptroller*: Fifty-ninth, 1928, Appendix XI, Report of the Deputy Master of the Melbourne Branch, 1928. London, 1929.
Sixtieth, 1929, Appendix X, Report of the Deputy Master of the Melbourne Branch, 1929. London, 1930.
Sixty-sixth and Sixty-seventh, 1935, 1936, Appendix XIII A, D, Reports of the Deputy Master of the Melbourne Branch, 1935, 1936. London, 1937.
C. W. Tomlinson, *Australian Bank Notes 1817-1963.* Melbourne, 1963.
T. P. N. G. Currency Conversion Commission, *Annual Report 1964-5* to *1966-7.* Port Moresby, 1965-7.
——— House of Assembly, *Debates*, vol. 1, nos 1-15, 1964-7.   M. J. P.

(See also BANKING)

D

DAMPIER, William (1651-1715), British naval officer and ex-buccaneer, was sent by the Admiralty in 1699 in command of the *Roebuck* to explore the unknown east coast of New Guinea and Australia. He sailed round the Cape of Good Hope via Timor to the north coast of New Guinea, discovering Massau and Emira in the Bismarck Archipelago, thence along the east and south coasts of New Ireland, missing St George's Channel which he called a bay, but sailing through the strait between New Britain and New Guinea, which he named but which is now called by his name.

A. Sharp, *The Discovery of the Pacific Islands.* Oxford, 1960.

FRANCIS WEST

(*See also* DISCOVERY)

DANI. People of West Irian. References:
M. Bromley, 'A Preliminary Report on Law among the Grand Valley Dani of Netherlands New Guinea', *Nieuw-Guinea Studiën*, vol. 4, 1960.
———— *The Phonology of Lower Grand Valley Dani.* The Hague, 1961.
K. F. Koch, 'Marriage in Jalemo', *Oceania*, vol. 39, 1968-9.
D. O'Brien, 'Marriage among the Konda Valley Dani', in *Pigs, Pearlshells, and Women: Marriage in the New Guinea Highlands*, ed. R. M. Glasse and M. J. Meggitt. Englewood Cliffs, N.J., 1969.
———— and A. Ploeg, 'Acculturation Movements among the Western Dani', *American Anthropologist*, vol. 66, Special Publication, 1964.

DANKS, Benjamin (1853-1921), Methodist missionary in New Britain 1878-86, was born at Wednesbury, near Birmingham, on 12 February 1853. He moved to Melbourne with his parents in 1863 and went to school in that city. At sixteen years of age he entered the firm of John Danks, brass founders, of which his uncle was the founder. Danks learnt the trade of brass founding and worked in the firm for nine years. In 1878 he was accepted by the Victoria and Tasmania Conference of the Wesleyan Methodist Church and entered Wesley College, Melbourne, for training as a minister. After three months of study he was asked to join the Rev. George Brown [q.v.] in the New Britain mission. Danks accepted the call and shortly afterwards married Emma Watsford, the daughter of the Rev. John Watsford. In September 1878 he was ordained in Sydney and embarked for the mission field shortly afterwards. Danks arrived at Port Hunter, Duke of York Island, in December 1878. The mission was suffering from the adverse effects of press criticism following George Brown's punitive expedition against Talili and his followers on New Britain. Danks sustained Brown by his loyal support although privately he noted his misgivings at Brown's action.

He served the mission from 1878 to 1886, for about eighteen months on Duke of York Island and for the remainder of his term at Kabakada on the coast of the Gazelle Peninsula opposite to Watom (Man) Island. From May 1879 to March 1880 Danks was the sole European missionary in New Britain and it was due to his efforts alone that the mission survived a period of severe crisis. It was in this period that Brown had to answer his critics in the Australian colonies and to face an official inquiry in Fiji. In the Bismarck Archipelago Danks tried to counter the work of European labour recruiters amongst the indigenous people and in doing so incurred the enmity of resident traders engaged in the traffic.

Danks was associated with developments in the colony of the Marquis de Rays [q.v.] in New Ireland. In April 1880 he accompanied Brown to Likiliki (Metlik) on the south-eastern coast and helped in the evacuation of sick and distressed colonists to Port Hunter. Here Danks helped to nurse the colonists back to health. In 1882 Danks took part in the negotiations between Thomas Farrell, Emma Forsayth [q.v.], Captain Rabardy and Dr A. Baudouin by which the last of the colonists at Port Breton on New Ireland were repatriated to Sydney in one of Farrell's ships.

Danks did important work in language study, first of all in collaboration with the Rev. George Brown in the compilation of a dictionary of the Duke of York Island language and then with the Rev. R. H. Rickard [q.v.] in work for the dictionary of the Blanche Bay dialect.

Danks was associated indirectly with the events surrounding the murder of the German naturalist Kleinschmidt and two of his colleagues on Utuan Island, Duke of York Group, in April 1881. He was invited by Farrell to co-operate in the punitive expedition launched against the Utuan natives by the local European community. Danks refused although he agreed later on that there had been no alternative to the action taken. Danks and his teachers provided medical assistance to the wounded following the action.

Danks was a man of strong views on the affairs of the mission and on the behaviour of his fellow

Europeans in the region. These views were expressed in the prolific correspondence which he
conducted with his superiors in the Australian
colonies. As a source of historical knowledge
these and his journal are important.

Danks returned to Australia in 1886 and was
attached to the New South Wales Conference on
deputation work and then he was appointed minister to the Hamilton circuit in Victoria. In 1891 he
was appointed secretary of the Foreign Mission
Department of Victoria and in 1898 he was appointed organizing secretary for the Board of Missions in Sydney. After a short term as minister at
Lewisham in Sydney he retired in 1914. He died
in 1921.

G. Brown and B. Danks, *Dictionary of the Duke
of York Language, New Britain Group; also a gram-
mar.* Sydney, 1882 (duplicated); B. Danks, 'Burial
Customs of New Britain', *Journal of the Anthropo-
logical Institute,* vol. 21, 1892; ——— *Our Mission
Fields.* Wesleyan Methodist Missionary Society, Syd-
ney, 1897; ——— *A Brief History of the New Britain
Mission.* 2nd ed., Sydney, 1901; ——— *In Wild New
Britain: The Story of Benjamin Danks, Pioneer Mis-
sionary,* from his Diary; ed. W. Deane. Sydney, 1933;
Methodist Church of Australasia, Overseas Missions
Papers (M.L.); Methodist Church, Papers (M.L.).

NOEL GASH

DARIBI. People of the Chimbu District.
References:
R. Wagner, *The Curse of Souw.* Chicago, 1968.
——— 'Marriage among the Daribi', in *Pigs, Pearl-
shells, and Women: Marriage in the New Guinea
Highlands,* ed. R. M. Glasse and M. J. Meggitt.
Englewood Cliffs, N.J., 1969.

DAY LENGTH. Most of the familiar horticultural plants, whether economic crops, ornamental
flowers, fruit trees or forest plantation trees are
species or adaptions from species which occur in
the wild either north (the majority) or south of
the tropics. Under tropical conditions, particularly
within the equatorial tropics bounded by 10° N.
and 10° S. latitude, many of these plants either
do not grow, grow in an unusual manner, fail to
flower or fail to fruit. Typical examples are stone
fruits, apples and pears. These will grow but fail
to produce normal fruit no matter at what altitude
they may be grown in an attempt to achieve temperate growing conditions. Cauliflowers produce
either no head or only a small one; onions, with
the exception of one or two varieties, do not
'bulb'.

The reasons for this anomaly do not lie with
temperature but with the length of day. Many
plants which originate in temperate latitudes
produce their flowers with the onset of spring to
summer, when days are lengthening. Fruit development occurs during the autumn when days are
shortening, presaging the onset of winter which
is a resting period for plants.

Within the tropics day length exhibits quite a
different pattern, with little variation throughout
the year and very short periods of twilight and
dawn. The graph shows the variation throughout

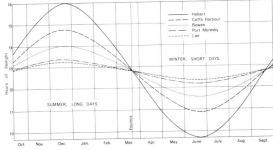
Length of daylight.

the year of hours of daylight at Lae, 7° S., Port
Moresby, 9° 30' S., Bowen, 20° S., Coffs Harbour,
30° S., and Hobart, 43° S. There is little appreciable variation at Lae, only 48 minutes, and at
Port Moresby 1 hour 13 minutes. The extreme
shown in the graph is Hobart, with a variation
in day length of 6 hours 20 minutes.

Plants growing naturally in the tropics are
adapted to uniform length of day; if they are
grown in temperate latitudes, the short days of
winter must be compensated for by use of artificial
light, to achieve optimum growth. Some species
are more adaptable than others in this respect.

J. S. WOMERSLEY

DEER. Two species of introduced deer are
recorded from the Territory of Papua and New
Guinea: rusa, *Cervus timorensis,* and axis deer,
Axis axis. Small populations of rusa exist in
separated locations at Port Moresby, the Gazelle
Peninsula of New Britain and the Hermit Islands
of the Admiralty group. A larger population in
the plains of the Trans-Fly River area adjoins
that of Merauke in West Irian. Axis deer exist in
small numbers on the outskirts of Madang.

Except in the Trans-Fly area, the deer are not
in sufficient numbers to allow significant hunting;
they are only shot occasionally for food or sport.
The Port Moresby area. In general the rusa deer
in this region are distributed in the area bounded
by the Vanapa River and Galley Reach on the
west, by the edge of the rain forest on the lower
slopes of the Owen Stanley Range on the northern
or inland side, and by the Kemp Welch River to
the east. It is probable that the deer were introduced by Australians in the first decade of this
century.

The habitat for the deer in this area consists of:
The Coastal Hill Zone with ridges, lowlands
and some alluvial plains; a low rainfall area
covered mainly with grassy savannah.

The Swamp Zone, which appears to hold the
greatest concentrations of deer at the present
time. Along the edges of the swamps extensive
areas of deer-cover and food develop around the
permanent or seasonal standing water; for example, Waigani swamp.

The Alluvial Plains Zone; for example, along
the Brown River from the bridge at Karema

through to Galley Reach, which contains many deer. The area consists of tall evergreen forest with extensive grassy patches, particularly associated with the swamps and meandering river channels and round-waters.

The Foothills Zone, comprising most of the Astrolabe Range, which is covered mainly with savannah but has a slightly increased rainfall compared with the coastal plains. Deer are regularly reported throughout this zone in small numbers.

The Sogeri Plateau of the Upland Zone, where there are irregular patches of savannah distributed through the tall evergreen forest. Deer are frequently seen in the cleared areas.

Gazelle Peninsula, New Britain. In the annual report on German New Guinea for 1900-1, it is recorded that on Credner Island, in St George's Channel off Kokopo, 'there are also a few red deer, presented to the Government by the Governor'.

The deer now established in the plantations and adjacent forest around Kokopo are rusa deer. In the 1950s they were commonly seen on the roads and close to most of the stations during mornings and evenings. The limits of distribution appear to have been between Cape Gazelle on the east and Varzin and Toma on the west.

With the establishment of cocoa plantings beneath the extensive coconut stands, and the consequent greater activity in and around the accessible portions of the peninsula, a marked decline in the deer has been noted over the past ten years. At the present time only small numbers of deer are rarely reported in areas which once carried hundreds.

The Hermit Islands of the Admiralty group. A pair of rusa deer from a zoo in Australia were released in 1909 on Maron Island. These walked via a sandy strip to Arkeb Island. The descendants of this pair subsequently built up to considerable numbers.

When Arkeb and Maron Islands were developed, mainly by clearing for coconut, deer were transferred or driven by hunting to Luf Island which is all scrub. The number on Luf was estimated to be several hundreds in 1953.

The Trans-Fly area of Papua. Rusa deer are present in large numbers west of the Fly River in Papua, having crossed from Merauke in West Irian. Local reports put their introduction to Merauke at about 1920.

Numbers have greatly increased from the late 1950s to the present time. In Papua the main concentration is on the large plains between the Bensbach and Morehead Rivers. Deer are occasionally shot in small numbers throughout the whole of the lightly forested and scrubby area south of the Fly River, where the native population is sparse. They are occasionally shot as far north as Boset near the intersection of the Fly River with the border, some 120 miles from the coast; at the few settlements such as Suki Lagoon and Maderi Plantation on the south bank of the Fly; as far east as Daru Island; and in the islands in the mouth of the Fly River estuary.

In 1969 the Department of Agriculture, Stock and Fisheries began an ecological investigation of the deer in this area to determine the density, distribution and spread of the population, the significance of parasites and disease, and the potential value of the herds as a source of meat.

The Madang area. Deer were introduced into Madang by the Germans before World War I. Small numbers have been reported on the outskirts of the township, along the coastal roads and in the adjoining coconut plantations. These have been tentatively identified from skins and skulls as axis deer. Virgin country consists of tropical rain forest, and the deer feed where the forest is cleared to native gardens or plantations. The deer hide in the dense *Ficus* plantations during the day, coming out to graze at night and in the early morning.

A. Bentley, *An Introduction to the Deer of Australia*. Melbourne, 1967; ———— and M. C. Downes, 'Deer in New Guinea, Part I', *Papua and New Guinea Agricultural Journal*, vol. 20, 1968-9; M. C. Downes, 'Deer in New Guinea, Part II', *Papua and New Guinea Agricultural Journal*, vol. 20, 1968-9.

M. C. DOWNES

DEFENCE. So long as Australia holds the United Nations Trusteeship for New Guinea, and Papua is an Australian territory, the Australian government is responsible for the defence of both Papua and New Guinea. This responsibility may change as self-government or independence is obtained, although it is likely that the costs of maintaining armed forces [q.v.] and defence facilities, and the need to concentrate on other social and economic development, will prompt the government to seek or accept Australian defence help, physically or financially.

Until independence, the Territory is within the ambit of the security treaty between Australia, New Zealand and the United States (ANZUS), and also—technically at least—the South-east Asia Treaty Organization (SEATO). The latter is unlikely to have any bearing on the Territory; the effect of the former will depend on the circumstances prevailing at any given time. There is no automatic Treaty response. After independence, ANZUS would not apply to the Territory, but it could be held to apply to Australian forces operating there.

Defence forces and arrangements are provided by governments to meet existing or potential external or internal threats to national security. They are also part of the apparatus of government, reassuring the government and the people that the nation is capable of defending itself and of maintaining internal law and order in extreme situations. All these aspects apply to Papua and New Guinea.

There is no visible external threat to the Territory. Situations which Papua and New Guinea might conceivably have to meet in the future include attempts by some later Indonesian government to acquire the Territory or to persuade it to join West Irian within Indonesia; a 'liberation' movement, possibly assisted from outside, to do the same, or to create a single state for the whole island; pressure by large external powers (e.g. the Soviet Union or Japan) to obtain favoured access to natural resources, either on land or off shore, or to existing or potential strategic facilities such as the former naval base at Manus in the Admiralty Islands. Manus is currently the head-quarters of the Papua and New Guinea division of the Royal Australian Navy, and will presumably be the main depot for the New Guinea navy. It is also possible that a major power might seek to obtain the use of a small island on which to erect its own facilities.

The major threat to the security of Papua and New Guinea is internal. The unequal distribution of people and natural resources, physical separation by land formations or by sea, and contrasting social and cultural patterns are leading to moves for separate states, or for differential rates of progress to self-government and independence. As the central government is developing, it may well feel impelled at some stage to use force to prevent the separation of part of the Territory. Neither Australia nor the United Nations is likely to agree that some parts of the Territory should achieve self-government before others. If the Territory were to break up into several small states, only a minority would be viable; the others would either continue dependent on external subventions (not necessarily only from Australia) or be forced to reduce government services drastically. Further, local politicians do not always realize that the possession of profitable natural resources is not of itself sufficient to ensure an effective political system, an equitable distribution of wealth, or balanced social development. Natural resources also have a tendency in due course to become exhausted.

Whatever the degrees of regional autonomy within the independent state which it is planned Papua and New Guinea will become, no central government is likely to feel that it can afford the separation of part of the state, especially a well-endowed part.

TERRAIN IMPLICATIONS

The massive cordillera extending from the border with West Irian to the south-east corner of the island varies in width from 50 to 150 miles, ranges up to 14,700 feet in height, and limits communications and thus cohesion between Papua and New Guinea. Dense jungle, heavy rainfall, swiftly flowing and rarely navigable rivers, as well as language differences, tribal limitations and low living standards add to the problems of creating a sense of common national identity, mutual physical and economic support, and joint action against internal or external threats.

The long border with West Irian can be patrolled during the dry season, from time to time, but is still very vulnerable to penetration, just as the long coastline and numerous islands make incursions comparatively easy. During the wet season, much of the border is impassable.

Where the terrain is rugged or covered with dense jungle hostile action from outside is more difficult, but defence is equally hampered by inadequate communications. As radio links are developed, more helicopter pads or light-aircraft landing strips are built, and roads are extended, the government will be more able to detect and deal with any external infiltrations or internal subversive activities. There are already a remarkable number of airfields and landing strips, nearly 400; the great majority take light aircraft only.

DEFENCE PROCUREMENT

Except for the daily necessities of food and drink, virtually none of the material requirements of modern armed forces are produced in Papua and New Guinea. Vehicles can be serviced, and barracks, roads, bridges, etc., can be built, but arms, ammunition, equipment and transport must all be imported. Some very small craft are being built which could be used for defence if necessary, but the patrol boats at present in use were built in Australia. The lack of virtually any industrial back-up for defence—which will take a good many years to overcome—means that without external help only the simplest defence measures are possible, and even these could not be sustained for very long.

Technical skills are, however, being developed within the Territory. The Department of Posts and Telegraphs, for example, conducts a five-year training course for radio and telephone technicians. Other technical training is provided at technical schools, colleges, vocational centres and through apprenticeships in industry. Some of these skills will in the future become available for defence communications or logistical support activities.

DEFENCE NEEDS

The difficult terrain, the extensive maritime nature of much of Papua and New Guinea, and the problems mentioned above suggest that the primary defence requirements are an adequate intelligence system and communications facilities; ground troops capable of patrolling the whole area on foot, or with fast transport to points of insurgency or infiltration; and naval patrol craft in adequate numbers. If there were a major security problem, internally or externally produced, the present level of indigenous forces would be inadequate to cope with it. This of course may never occur. But there does need to be built up, within the Territory, a capacity for rapid deployment by air, helicopter, light transports and possibly one or two heavy transports with a small paratroop capability.

Peter Hastings, *New Guinea: Problems and Prospects.* Melbourne, 1969; T. B. Millar, *Australia's Defence*, 2nd ed. Melbourne, 1969; R. J. O'Neill, 'The Army in Papua-New Guinea', *Canberra Papers on Strategy and Defence*, no. 10, 1971.

T. B. MILLAR

DENTAL COLLEGE. Planned development of dental services in Papua and New Guinea began in the mid-1950s and necessitated the introduction of training programmes for indigenous personnel. The 1954 W.H.O. Dental Health Seminar, held in Wellington, New Zealand, had added stimulus to the idea of establishing a dental section within the Department of Public Health to provide emergency treatment on demand and this was set up in 1955. The Williams Report, 1958, had proposed a comprehensive free dental health service in the schools and recommended the training of indigenous people. This service was established in 1959 using available expatriate staff.

Early training programmes included sending two students to Fiji in each of the years 1955, 1960 and 1961 to undertake the training course for assistant dental officers at the Central Medical School in Suva (renamed the Fiji School of Medicine). This provided four graduates. However, the course was not entirely satisfactory for Territory conditions; the programme was abandoned and a course for dental officers was developed within the Territory. In 1960 the Port Moresby Dental College was formally established at the Dental Section, Port Moresby General Hospital.

The original aim of the College was to train dental assistants along the lines of the New Zealand Dental Nurse course. The syllabus provided a two-year course to fit graduates for field work: fillings, extractions, periodontal treatment and dental health education for school children. The first intake consisted of four students taught by two part-time lecturers from the dental service—the senior dental officer and the oral surgeon. Rapid expansion occurred in 1962: new premises were acquired, a full-time principal was appointed and a secondment scheme was introduced whereby two New Zealand tutor sisters from the Dental Nurse Training School joined the staff. Annual intake soon rose to about fifteen, but in the last four years has levelled off to approximately eight students, usually entering with a Form IV pass. This course had provided seventy-eight graduates by the end of 1970. In Papua and New Guinea, most dental assistants are eventually posted to Sub-Districts where, as well as their commitment to the school service, they form the first point of contact in the treatment of dental disease for the adult population. Consequently, the course also trains students in emergency treatment (relief of pain), selected general treatment and referral for adults. Regional dental officers regularly inspect these auxiliary dental operators to ensure that standards are maintained and to provide in-service training and clinical assistance.

The training of dental technicians commenced late in 1962. A course of two and a half years, later extended to three, was provided in the mechanics of the commonly required prosthetic procedures—construction, repair and maintenance of artificial teeth and the fabrication of preformed dental restorations. This group forms a second cadre of dental auxiliaries and works under the direct supervision of a dental officer. Originally the entry standard was Form I but is now generally Form III. There were nineteen dental technician graduates by 1970.

In 1966 nine students entered the newly established dental officer course at Form III level. In 1969 entry level was raised to university preliminary year and in 1970 to Science I at the University of Papua and New Guinea [q.v.]. A total of thirteen students were training as dental officers in 1971. Dental officers take a four-year course which is designed to provide professional operators capable of independent practice in all branches of dentistry, occupying administrative positions in the Dental Health Service, directing and co-ordinating the activities of dental auxiliaries, entering private practice and leading a developing dental profession. As these graduates enter the service expatriate field officers will be phased out. It is expected that they will be capable of specializing and of teaching in the training institutions. The first four graduates entered the service in 1970.

Although a six-month course for dental orderlies has been proposed for several years, there was no formal training up to 1971 because money and facilities were lacking; this had also prevented the establishment of refresher courses for dental assistants.

The content of the courses offered by the Dental College has generally been adapted to meet the Territory's requirements at three levels: dental officer, dental assistant and dental technician. The courses have been organized in different ways to integrate areas of training for these levels, both within the College and in co-operation with the Papuan Medical College. It is hoped that this association will continue with the newly established Faculty of Medicine at the University of Papua and New Guinea. It will become even closer if a combined Faculty of Medicine and Dentistry is established; this was recommended by the Currie Commission (1966) and the investigations called for by the Ministerial Member for Public Health in his speech at the first graduation ceremony for dental officers (October 1970).

T. P. N. G. Department of Public Health, *Report and Plan for the Establishment and Development of a Public Dental Health Service in the Territory of Papua and New Guinea, 1958* [J. F. Williams], Port Moresby, 1958.

P. B. BARNES

DENTAL HEALTH. It has long been believed that people living in primitive conditions and existing on a diet of natural foods enjoy immunity from the common dental ailments, dental caries, periodontal disease and malocclusion. Early explorers and later health administrators and even epidemiologists were glowing in their reports of the excellent dentitions and well developed jaws of the indigenous people living in many such communities in the Pacific. New Guinea was no exception and when moderate to severe dental disease was encountered it became usual to blame the betel chewing habit for such departures from what had been accepted as normal.

Actually, early reports usually overstated both good and bad dental health and it is necessary to understand more about these conditions to find the reason for the exaggeration.

DENTAL CARIES

Dental caries or tooth decay is particularly prevalent in highly developed countries today. However, it seems certain that the disease has always existed everywhere, possibly to only a slight extent. Supporting evidence for this statement is abundant from skeletal material, various old to ancient reports, and from modern studies of races which have shown recent increases in caries or are reaching the point at which such changes might be expected. Moreover, the weight of evidence clearly indicates that major changes have occurred as man's food has taken more and more indirect roads from primary production to the dinner table. These indirect pathways, associated more and more with refining and preservation, have monotonously accompanied major increases in caries.

What has been much less recognized is that what might be termed endemic levels of the disease undoubtedly varied from race to race and from region to region, or even from village to village. There is not so much evidence of this though hints of it are constantly appearing in research reports.

Groups of people still in a period of low prevalence are of immense value to a full understanding of the 'endemic' caries picture, and there is a growing amount of evidence to suggest that these basic racial or regional differences remain, though in a far less obvious state, even after massive increases in the disease.

Two factors have had an important bearing on errors of assessment of dental health in Papua New Guinea. On the side of good dental health, evidence from groups with negligible caries, disregarding other dental diseases, has led to generalizations that are not valid and over optimistic. On the other hand, evidence from groups with moderate prevalence of caries has led to dismayed reports of a complete breakdown in dental health, because observers have failed to consider the fact that complete lack of services, associated with moderate disease prevalence, can present a far worse superficial picture than comprehensive services, associated with extremely high disease prevalence.

What has been found in Papua New Guinea, among groups with no change of diet, is a range of prevalence from a remarkable nil to an also remarkable, for a primitive group, 30 per cent of all teeth carious. This latter is about half the rate likely to be found in highly developed countries.

These facts clearly demonstrate that both the generalization claiming excellent dental health, again considering caries only, and that claiming high caries prevalence were wrong.

Research has revealed much more of interest than the *range* of caries prevalence. In terms of carious teeth *per person*, six distinct groups have been discovered with 0, 1, 2, 3, 7, 7 decayed teeth per person respectively. For the last two groups, with the same number of decayed teeth, it is important to realize that, besides a simple count of carious teeth, differentiation is possible between the surfaces of teeth most often attacked. It has been shown that in the 0, 1 and 2 groups the disease was mostly in the grooves and pits of teeth; in the 3 and one of the 7 groups mostly on surfaces facing cheek and lips; the remaining group had caries mainly between the teeth.

These caries prevalence levels seem to be associated with diet in a way which is not yet clear. Staple foods for Papuans and New Guineans are sago, sweet potato, and a complex of taro, yams and bananas. The first of these is typical of swampy areas and the last of coastal strips, while the sweet potato diet is typical of Highland areas. There seems to be a transition between the taro, yam, banana complex and the sweet potato diet as medium altitudes are reached and these diets present a variety of mixtures of the Highland and coastal staples.

The Highland diet is associated with the group which has 7 carious teeth per person affecting, mainly, surfaces facing cheek and lips. This is especially so in the Western and Eastern Highlands and the Chimbu Districts and accounts for an estimated 800,000 people. However, in the Southern Highlands, for an estimated 150,000 people, the group is that having about 3 teeth carious per person. It is not clear whether there is a significant difference between the diets of the two areas.

The coastal diet for an estimated 800,000 people is consistently associated with the group having 1 tooth carious per person, while the transitional diet for an estimated 250,000 relates to the group with 2 teeth carious per person. These two groups together account for most coastal and subcoastal populations on both main and other islands.

Sago staple diets result in the same division into two groups as the sweet potato diets and in a more dramatic way. An estimated 20,000 people living on this type of diet in the south-west of Papua account for the other group having 7 teeth carious per person (caries between the teeth), while about 150,000 in the Sepik River valley in the north-east, having a very similar diet, have either no caries at all or an almost negligible prevalence.

The discovery of the latter group is unique for either modern or ancient times and has led to interesting studies of how prevalence may be related to the environment. A comparison of these caries-free villages with others in similar country which do have the disease will be of special research interest since diet in both groups comes from their immediate environment without refinement. This means that any relationships discovered between caries and food or soil have a much better chance of being meaningful than in an environment where the diet includes imported and refined foods.

PERIODONTAL DISEASE

Probably, if caries is one of the most prevalent diseases of modern man, periodontal disease is *the* most prevalent known to either modern or ancient man. Whereas caries has a modern history of steady increase associated in one way or another with changing environments, abundant periodontal disease seems to have been always with us. Less well known to the average man than caries because of its chronic and insidious nature, this disease includes mild to severe inflammation of the soft tissues surrounding the teeth and all stages of destruction of soft and hard tissue supports of the teeth, terminating in wholesale tooth loss. The disease is closely associated with age, usually becoming severe in the mid-thirties and -forties and, in degrees from extremely mild to very severe, it has always and in every race attacked nearly all mature adults. It is usual to find that 40-50 per cent of adults have severe forms of this disease, though the figures available are less than those for caries.

Whereas a crude statement of dental health in terms of caries would place Papuans and New Guineans in the extremely fortunate class compared with other races, such a statement in terms of periodontal disease would place them, probably, in a less favoured group with a prevalence above the average. Forty-five to 70 per cent of adults with severe forms of the disease have been reported; by the age of twenty-two the average Papuan or New Guinean has significant periodontal disease, and by thirty-five has it in a severe form.

Very often older Papuans and New Guineans have no teeth remaining and all 32 have been lost due to periodontal disease. This has led to errors in popular assessment of dental health, because caries is usually blamed in such cases and the insidious periodontal disease continues its ravages without attracting the attention it should.

MALOCCLUSION

This term is used for any severe disharmony in jaw or tooth relationships and seems, like caries, to have become more frequent in modern times. Among primitive peoples probably less than 10 per cent, often much less, suffered from this condition, whereas in highly developed, racially mixed populations 40-50 per cent prevalence is not unusual.

Papuans and New Guineans in villages have not suffered this increase in malocclusion and usually fall in the range of nil to 5 per cent prevalence. The impression obtained here by layman or dentist is the same, that of a race of people with large, well developed jaws and even, well positioned teeth.

OTHER FEATURES

The betel and smoking habits. These habits, and particularly the former, have been popularly associated with various oral and general diseases. Smoking is found throughout the population, whereas the betel habit is prevalent only in coastal regions and at low altitudes.

So far there is no evidence to associate either habit with caries or periodontal disease. There is some evidence of an association between these habits and cancerous or so called pre-cancerous lesions of the mouth and it is possible that smoking is the more active of the two in relation to pre-cancerous lesions (*see* BETEL CHEWING).

Morphology. Shape of teeth and size of jaws may well be worth study in terms of genetic background and may be of importance in general studies of racial origin as well as in relation to dental pathology. To date it is known that very distinct and easily measurable differences do exist (*see* PHYSICAL ANTHROPOLOGY).

Oral cancer. As with other races which have enjoyed the benefits of modern medicine only recently, it has been a common experience for central hospitals to receive patients suffering from massive tumours, particularly adamantinomas, carcinomas and sarcomas. While these late cases are usually the result of failure to seek early treatment, there is some evidence to suggest that oral cancer accounts for a much higher percentage of all cancer than in most highly developed countries.

PRINCIPLES OF DENTAL HEALTH

The village Papuan or New Guinean with, usually, a low prevalence of caries, high prevalence of periodontal disease and no malocclusion problem is progressively being replaced by an urbanized successor who has abandoned traditional diets for a highly refined and often unbalanced one. This is only one aspect of the emancipation of urbanized people from the traditional customs and discipline of the village.

Similar racial groups have shown a great increase in caries in such altered conditions. Evidence is already available in the main towns of Papua New Guinea where some groups now have a prevalence very close to that of Australia, and far higher than has been found so far in village groups.

No less important is the effect development is likely to have on periodontal disease, though the effect will probably be indirect. As the prevalence is already higher than average it is unlikely to increase with more urbanization and refined diets. However, with improvement in health services life expectancy has increased. This means that, if periodontal disease caused major to total loss of teeth in the relatively short-lived villager, the same level of disease will have a far worse effect on the much longer-lived urban dweller, in terms of years without effective teeth.

Again, the prevalence of malocclusion is likely to be increased by marriage between various groups of Papuans and New Guineans and by intermarriage with other racial groups. This increase will also be accentuated by premature loss of deciduous teeth from caries, and by the possibility that habits such as thumb-sucking and lip-biting will develop in an urbanized society.

Thus the effects of social change are potentially

harmful in the three major areas of dental disease. Will it be possible to maintain reasonable dental health in the face of those increases?

The Territory has plans both for the education of dental personnel and for the provision of services. These are based on a team concept with division of labour between professionals and several types of auxiliaries, the skills of each type being specifically adapted to the problems peculiar to the country. Part of the plans provides for routine regular care for school children which, of itself, should reduce disease prevalence, if efficiently maintained.

At the same time a bill providing for fluoridation of all existing or future reticulated water supplies is in existence and this will help to combat caries at the most vulnerable points—the developing cities.

However, it is as near to certain as any biological event can be that major increases in dental disease will occur and the real hope for preservation of reasonable dental health in the Territory, to say nothing of improvement, is for preventive and control methods to proceed hand in hand with the provision of treatment for established disease.   D. E. BARMES

DETZNER, Hermann (1882-196?), German army officer, was born at Speyer, Austria. He served in the Cameroons and in 1914 arrived in German New Guinea with the rank of lieutenant as a surveyor in the Landwehr. In 1914 he was on the Papuan border near Mt Chapman, but did not surrender after war broke out and German New Guinea capitulated, instead remaining in the bush until he gave himself up at the end of the war. In these four years, by his own account published in Germany in 1920, he made three attempts to reach neutral Dutch New Guinea, and he claimed that in the course of the second expedition, from the Saruwageds to Mt Hagen, he had discovered the central Highlands valleys. But his descriptions of land and people are vague and sometimes inconsistent, and he himself disowned the book in part in 1932. The probability, in spite of the argument which has taken place, is that his account of the Highlands was based on other people's accounts of parts of the interior.

H. Detzner, *Vier Jahre unter Kannibalen*. Berlin, 1920; G. Souter, *New Guinea: The Last Unknown*. Sydney, 1963; J. Flierl, *Forty-Five Years in New Guinea*, tr. M. Wiederaenders. Columbus, Ohio, 1931.
                                    FRANCIS WEST

DIRO, Edward Ramu (1943-   ), army officer, was born on 14 December 1943 in Boku village, Rigo Sub-District, Central District. He attended the mission school in Boku, Kila Kila High School in Port Moresby, Sogeri High School, and the Slade School, Warwick, Queensland, where he attained the Queensland Senior. He entered the Officer Cadet School of Australia in January 1963 and the following December graduated as a commissioned officer (2nd lieutenant) in the Australian Army. He

Major E. Diro.

has been a platoon commander in the Royal Australian Regiment and the Pacific Islands Regiment, company second in command, battalion adjutant and staff officer. He was promoted to the rank of captain in 1967 and on 3 May 1971 he became the first Papuan or New Guinean to be promoted to the rank of major. At present he is Officer Commanding C Company, 1st Pacific Islands Regiment.

DISCOVERY. Joao de Barros, the Portuguese chronicler, writing in the second quarter of the seventeenth century in the fourth of his *Decadas da Asia* informs us that in 1526 Jorge de Meneses, the Captain-designate of the Moluccas, whilst *en route* to take up his appointment was blown past Halmahera and down towards 'islands judged to be 200 leagues from the Moluccas', inhabited by people called Papuas, and that in a port named Versija he awaited the change of wind and then sailed for the Moluccas. It has usually been assumed that de Meneses, by this accident of navigation, discovered New Guinea, though whether this is actually so is by no means certain. It is possible that he went no further than Waigeo, a name not very far removed from the Versija of de Barros' account, or to one of the other islands off West Irian, but the possibility exists that he did in fact discover what was later to become known as New Guinea, and certainly from that time onwards a strip of coastline, as opposed to 'islands', running from east to west and located to the east of the Moluccas or Spice Islands was shown on contemporary Portuguese charts.

New Guinea was, however, already known to the Portuguese, albeit indirectly and in a confused and limited way. On a chart prepared between 1513 and 1520 by Francisco Rodrigues, pilot to the first expedition dispatched by Albuquerque from Malacca to the Moluccas between November 1511 and December 1512 under the command of Abreu and Serrao, the inscription 'Islands of *papoia* and the people of them are *cafres*' (black) is applied to a large island in the approximate region of Gilolo (Halmahera Island), and seems to reflect confused information on both Gilolo and New Guinea. In 1512 Rodrigues did not get any further east than Amboina, at the eastern end of Ceram, and Banda Island. Serrao reached the Moluccas. Rodrigues may have obtained information of the 'Islands of *papoia*' from the lost Javanese pilot's chart he copied and which Albuquerque referred to in a letter to the King of Portugal of 1 April 1512. Alternatively he may have obtained it in Malacca from indigenous traders; from Serrao, who sent information concerning the Moluccas back to Malacca in 1513; from Miranda who visited Banda in 1513 and 1514 and may have got as far as the Moluccas, returning to Malacca in 1515; or from Coelho, who took two junks to Ternate in 1515.

Tome Pires, writing in his *Suma Oriental* at Malacca between July 1512 and January 1515, on information derived from sources presumably similar to those of Rodrigues, notes that 'people come to Banda from a great many outside islands to buy Banda cloth, from *Bato Ymbo* (Gilolo) to *Papua*, from *Papua* to the Moluccas, and many other islands', that 'The *nore* parrots (*papaguaios*) come from the island of *Papua*, which is about eighty leagues from Banda. Those which are prized most come from the islands called *Aru*', and that 'in the island of *Papua*, which is about eighty leagues from Banda, there are men with big ears who cover themselves with them'.

The Portuguese chronicler Diogo do Couto remarks that the word Papuas means *negros* or people of dark skin pigmentation 'in the language of the natives', whilst Antonio Galvano, sometime Governor of the Moluccas, writing in his *Tratado* of 1563, remarks that the Papuas as a people were so named by the people of the Moluccas because of their dark complexion and frizzled hair.

That New Guinea had long been known to the indigenous inhabitants of island South-east Asia, and that trade contact existed, would hardly be surprising in view of their proximity. The suggestion has even been made, though with scant evidence and perhaps an excess of nationalist fervour, that New Guinea is referred to in the Indian *Ramayana* (*c.* 300 B.C.), and may have been vaguely known to India in the period of Indianization in South-east Asia during the first centuries of the Christian era.

It has also been argued that at least part of West Irian lay within the imperial bounds claimed for the Javanese empire of Majapahit (1293–c. 1515) in the fourteenth century chronicle, the *Nagarakertagama*, of the monk Prapança, and although the most reliable evidence would seem to indicate that this Javanese empire was by no means as large as Prapança wishfully suggests, and that the *Nagarakertagama* is essentially a statement of geographical knowledge, it is fairly clear that trade contact existed between Java and West Irian. It is possible that some trade suzerainty was exercised by Java over the New Guinea coastal settlements, perhaps even indirectly through rulers of the Moluccas, who may have acknowledged Majapahit and claimed suzerainty themselves over coastal West Irian and the offshore islands.

Portuguese contact with New Guinea both before and after de Meneses' uncertain discovery seems to have been slight or non-existent, but Castanheda, the Portuguese chronicler, records that in 1534, when the rulers of Ternate, Tidore and Batjan allied to drive out the Portuguese, they sought the aid of the four 'Papua rajahs' of Vaigama (Waigama, Misool), Vaigue (Waigee), Quibibi (Gebe) and Mincimbo (?). What is particularly interesting is the fact that the first three kingdoms named are all islands off West Irian and not part of the land mass itself, and the application of the name Papua to them is perhaps further evidence that the land of the Papuas was really primarily the off-shore islands rather than New Guinea proper.

The certain discovery and initial exploration of New Guinea proper was due to the presence of Spaniards in the Moluccas. Spain and Portugal had both had ambitions to enjoy the known and reputed trade and riches of the Spice Islands and Cathay and to spread the Catholic faith in the Orient, and whilst the Portuguese had directed their efforts to rounding the Cape of Good Hope and approaching the East by way of India and Malacca, the Spaniards, originally impressed by Columbus' extreme claim that Cathay could be reached by a short Atlantic crossing, had consequently begun to acquire an empire in the hitherto unknown Americas. Not content with the Americas Spain had supported the Portuguese Fernao de Magalhaes (Magellan) in his successful attempt to prove that South America could be rounded, and his attempt to demonstrate that the Spice Islands could be reached by sailing no great distance westwards across the Pacific.

Against the background of a complex series of Papal bulls relating variously to the recognition and delimitation of the spheres of expansion of the Catholic nations of Spain and Portugal, these two powers, apparently regarding the bulls as implied grants or donations of the earth's surface, had jointly agreed at the Treaty of Tordesillas in June 1494 to a line of demarcation laid down 370 leagues west of the Cape Verde Islands, the hemisphere to the west of which would appertain to Spain, that to the east to Portugal. The determination of such a line was virtually impossible with the cartographical knowledge and navigational techniques available, and the league, which could have been either one of three Italian miles or one of four Italian miles, was not defined.

At the time the question of the antipodal line in Asia was not raised, and in any case the circumference of the earth was unknown and estimates of it varied. The arrival of the Portuguese in the East, however, followed by Magellan's claim, based amongst other things upon an underestimate of the circumference of the world and the width of the as yet unknown Pacific, that the Spice Islands lay within the Spanish hemisphere, and his subsequent voyage, focused attention upon

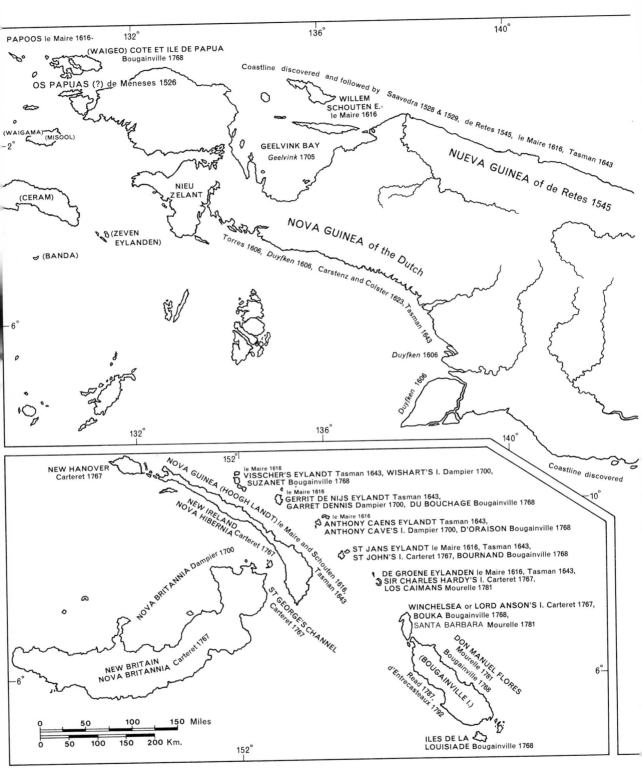

The discovery of New Guinea.

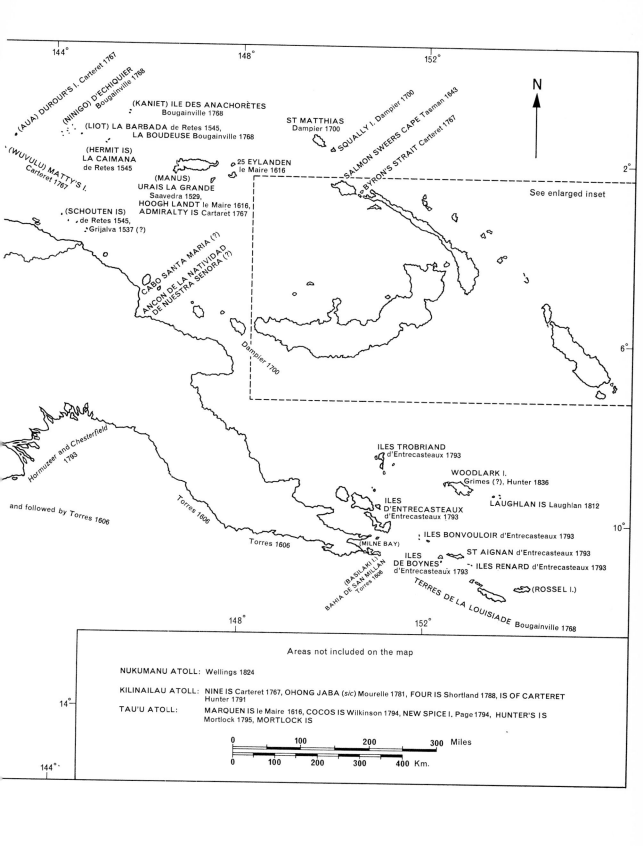

(AUA) DUROUR'S I. Carteret 1767
(NINIGO) D'ECHIQUIER Bougainville 1768
(KANIET) ILE DES ANACHORÈTES Bougainville 1768
(LIOT) LA BARBADA de Retes 1545, LA BOUDEUSE Bougainville 1768
(HERMIT IS) LA CAIMANA de Retes 1545
(WUVULU) MATTY'S I. Carteret 1767
(MANUS) URAIS LA GRANDE Saavedra 1529, HOOGH LANDT le Maire 1616, ADMIRALTY IS Cartaret 1767
(SCHOUTEN IS) de Retes 1545, Grijalva 1537 (?)
25 EYLANDEN le Maire 1616
ST MATTHIAS Dampier 1700
SQUALLY I. Dampier 1700
SALMON SWEERS CAPE Tasman 1643
BYRON'S STRAIT Carteret 1767

N

See enlarged inset

CABO SANTA MARIA (?)
ANCON DE LA NATIVIDAD DE NUESTRA SENORA (?)

Dampier 1700

Hormuzeer and Chesterfield 1793

and followed by Torres 1606

Torres 1606

Torres 1606

ILES TROBRIAND d'Entrecasteaux 1793
WOODLARK I. Grimes (?), Hunter 1836
ILES D'ENTRECASTEAUX d'Entrecasteaux 1793
LAUGHLAN IS Laughlan 1812
ILES BONVOULOIR d'Entrecasteaux 1793
(MILNE BAY)
ILES DE BOYNES d'Entrecasteaux 1793
ST AIGNAN d'Entrecasteaux 1793
ILES RENARD d'Entrecasteaux 1793
(BASILAKI I.)
BAHIA DE SAN MILLAN Torres 1606
(ROSSEL I.)
TERRES DE LA LOUISIADE Bougainville 1768

2°
6°
10°
14°

144° 148° 152°
148° 152°
144°

Areas not included on the map

NUKUMANU ATOLL: Wellings 1824

KILINAILAU ATOLL: NINE IS Carteret 1767, OHONG JABA (sic) Mourelle 1781, FOUR IS Shortland 1788, IS OF CARTERET Hunter 1791

TAU'U ATOLL: MARQUEN IS le Maire 1616, COCOS IS Wilkinson 1794, NEW SPICE I. Page 1794, HUNTER'S IS Mortlock 1795, MORTLOCK IS

0   100   200   300   Miles
0   100   200   300   400   Km.

the antipodal line and its position. The Portuguese, although adamant in their claim to the Spice Islands, were certainly doubtful as to their position in relation to the antipodal line; but in fact, irrespective as to which league value was applied, the Spice Islands did lie within the 'Portuguese hemisphere'. New Guinea, however, lay predominantly within the 'Spanish hemisphere' since the alternative antipodal *demarcaciones* fell in either 135°02′E. or 140°14′E. of Greenwich, and more probably the former. Magellan and del Cano, like many of their successors, were subjected to favourable winds and currents, and underestimated the width of the Pacific, thereby favouring the Spanish case, and contributing to the subsequent cartographical demonstration of a narrow Pacific with New Guinea lying at no great distance from the Americas. Pigafetta, who accompanied Magellan, reported information obtained that the Papuas were gold-bearing, and this itself provided encouragement for the Ophirian conjectures of the day.

The Junta of Badajoz of April-May 1524 failed to reach any significant agreement on the question of the Spice Islands, but in 1529, at the Treaty of Saragossa, Charles V of Spain, in need of money and deterred by the failure of his expeditions to find a return sailing route from the Spice Islands to the Americas, pledged his claim to the Spice Islands for 350,000 ducats pending the determination of the position of the Tordesillas demarcation. In the interim a provisional demarcation was agreed upon lying 17°E. of the Spice Islands. In fact the Spaniards occupied the Philippines despite both Tordesillas and Saragossa, but since Portugal had no ambitions there the fundamental purpose of the treaties was not infringed.

The dispatch by Hernan Cortes of Spanish expeditions under Juan Garcia Jofre de Loaysa (Loyasa) in 1525 and Alvaro de Saavedra in 1527 had established a Spanish presence in the Spice Islands, but Saavedra, who had found the remnants of the deceased Loaysa's expedition entrenched on Tidore under Hernando de la Torre, was himself unsuccessful in two attempts to make the return voyage across the Pacific, and eventually the survivors capitulated to the Portuguese.

Saavedra left the Moluccas on 3 June 1528 in the *Florida* on the first of these attempts to return to the Americas. Passing to the north of Halmahera, his expedition came down to 'an island of Papuas', a large island, well populated by frizzy-haired, black and naked inhabitants who provided the Spaniards with food. Here the expedition was detained for almost a month by contrary weather, after which Saavedra headed south and then east and came to an 'island' the coastline of which he followed for some 100 leagues, passing other islands *en route*, and afterwards coming to another island where he remained for three days and where three hostile indigenes, described as 'black, frizzy-haired and ugly', were captured. Leaving this island Saavedra then sailed for some 250 leagues to an island in 7°N. inhabited by a hostile, light-coloured, bearded people. Heading north to 14° the contrary winds forced the expedition to

abandon their objective and return via one of the Ladrone Islands and Mindanao to the Moluccas.

On 3 May 1529 Saavedra made yet another attempt to return to the Americas and followed the same route as in the year previously, as far as the island where he had taken the three prisoners. Fifty days and 200 leagues out from the Moluccas the expedition reached the 'island of Paine', rested for some five weeks and then resumed their journey, arriving two weeks later at an island which they named Urais la grande in 1°40′S. Heading to the north-east against unfavourable winds, they came to five islands, one larger than the others, inhabited by dark, bearded people clad in cloaks of palm leaf. Further to the north-east, they came to three low islands in 9°30′N., and to three other islands in 11°30′N. In 26°N. Saavedra died, and in 31°N. the expedition was forced to abandon its attempt to reach the Americas and returned to the Moluccas.

On both expeditions Saavedra appears to have come down through the islands of West Irian, to have followed the New Guinea coastline eastwards to the Admiralty Islands, and to have discovered Manus (Urais la grande) on his second expedition, Murai being the name of an island off the south-west coast of Manus. Beyond the Admiralty Islands Saavedra's expeditions had encountered islands in the Carolines, Marshalls and Ladrones.

In 1542 another Spanish attempt to win a position in the Spice Islands was made when Mendoza, Viceroy of Mexico, in contravention of Saragossa and a royal prohibition, dispatched Ruy Lopez de Villalobos to the Spice Islands. In August 1543 Villalobos ordered Bernardo de la Torre from the Moluccas in the *San Juan* to return to New Spain with a report to Mendoza, but in the summer of 1544 de la Torre returned, having been unable to make an easterly passage in such southerly latitudes as he remained in against contrary winds and currents. Whether or not Bernardo de la Torre sighted New Guinea is not certain, although Gallego and Quiros were later to refer to such a claim having been made and deny it, mentioning a Cabo de la Cruz as a place named by de la Torre.

In March 1545, Iñigo Ortiz de Retes was dispatched in the *San Juan* in another attempt to reach New Spain and, although unsuccessful, he followed the northern coast of New Guinea eastward via coastal islands to a point in 5°S. where contrary winds forced him to head northwards and return to Tidore by way of the north coast of West Irian, and he applied the name Nueva Guinea to the land which he had coasted. *En route* he appears to have encountered the Schouten Islands, the Hermit Islands (La Caimana), Liot-Ninigo (La Barbada) and other islands, although precise identifications are not possible.

In an account of Villalobos' expedition written by Escalante, the Emperor Charles V's factor, the author refers to what must have been the Schouten Islands as the islands where 'there was lost a ship of the Marquis del Valle (Cortes) in which there came as Captain Grijalva, whom the sailors murdered', and Galvano and others record how in 1537 Hernando de Grijalva left Peru on Cortes' orders, and how his crew mutinied in 29°S., headed for the Spice Islands, were wrecked in the area of the Schouten Islands, captured by indigenes, 'black, with fuzzy hair whom the people of the Moluccas call Papuas', and ultimately sold to the Portuguese.

Within a few years charts began to appear which laid down the northern New Guinea coastline sighted by Saavedra and de Retes, exaggerated in size, with a nomenclature that may be attributed to de Retes, terminating to the east at about latitude 5°S., near the Ancon de la Natividad de Nuestra Señora (Bay of the Birth of Our Lady), or Cabo Santa Maria as it was later known to the Dutch, which may be the same as Cabo de la Cruz. New Guinea is variously shown as an island, with a hypothetical southern coastline, or as a promontory of the vast antipodean continent conceived in classical antiquity and developed by sixteenth century cosmographers, the belief in which had been temporarily reinforced by Magellan's discovery of Tierra del Fuego, which was presumed to be another promontory of it.

The accession of Philip II to the Spanish throne in 1556 brought a change of policy which culminated in the occupation of the Philippines by the expedition of Miguel Lopez de Legazpi and Fray Andres de Urdañeta and the subsequent discovery of the North Pacific return route. The occupation of the Philippines satisfied Spanish longing for a foothold in Asia, and largely diverted their attention from the Spice Islands, permitting increased attention to be directed towards the Central and South Pacific. Urdañeta, who had previously accompanied Loaysa, had proposed the Papuas or Nueva Guinea as the object of the expedition, and indeed believed this to be the objective when the expedition set sail.

In 1567 Alvaro de Mendaña was dispatched from Peru to search for 'islands and a continent' reputed to lie in the South Sea. The object of the search, referred to as 'Western Isles' or 'Islands of Solomon', was a vague geographical concept consisting of Terra Australis or a vast antipodean continent, with off-lying islands; lands mistakenly believed to have been visited by Marco Polo to the south-east of Java (Lucach, Beach, Java Major, Java Minor, etc.); lands supposedly in the area reported to Ludovico di Varthema; possibly indirectly acquired Portuguese reports of Australia; the Ophir of King Solomon; rich Pacific islands reputed to have been known to the Incas; and New Guinea in particular, perhaps conjoined to Terra Australis with which legends of gold had already come to be associated. It was separated from Peru by a considerably underestimated Pacific. In fact the expedition discovered the archipelago named, shortly after the return of the expedition to Peru, the Islands of Solomon, lying immediately to the east of New Guinea, and visited Santa Ysabel, Malaita, San Cristoval, Guadalcanal, the Nggela Group, and other smaller islands, sighting in the distance the New Georgia Group (Arracifes/San Nicolas) and Choiseul (San Marcos).

Subjected to similar favourable wind and current conditions, and limited in their navigational techniques as Magellan and his successors had been, Mendaña's expedition underestimated the distance sailed across the Pacific, but by virtue of the underestimate of its width they were able, correctly but for the wrong reasons, to assume the proximity of their discoveries to New Guinea, even though only the western half of New Guinea's north coast had been discovered. Indeed, in the last stages of the expedition, before it was forced to return to Peru, it was unsuccessfully argued by some *expedicionarios* that they should proceed to New Guinea for refreshment.

Within twenty years of the return of the expedition to Peru charts began to appear which laid down these discoveries with an exaggerated size, in close proximity to the eastern extremity of an enlarged western half of New Guinea, and usually at an even shorter distance from Peru than Mendaña's expedition had underestimated them as lying, in a Pacific of considerably underestimated longitudinal dimensions.

In 1595 Mendaña returned to colonize the archipelago but discovered the island of Santa Cruz, where he established an abortive and short-lived colony and where he died. The colony was then abandoned and some of the survivors reached the Philippines, but the expedition had arrived at a more accurate estimate of the width of the Pacific, and correctly concluded that the Solomons must be further east than Santa Cruz. More importantly, perhaps, in this context, it was on this expedition that the chief pilot, Pedro Fernandez de Quiros, became obsessed with the idea of discovering the austral continent and of saving the souls of its inhabitants from perdition.

In 1606 Quiros was back in the South-west Pacific, bent on this quest and in command of his own expedition. Crossing the Pacific, and making a more accurate estimate of the distance travelled than he had in 1595, he discovered the New Hebrides, and assumed the island of Espiritu Santo (Malekula) to be part of the supposed austral continent. Here he became separated from his second in command, Luis Vaez de Torres [q.v.], who sailed around the island, headed south-west to 20° 30' S. and then north-west, and came upon the south coast of eastern New Guinea which he correctly identified as New Guinea. Contrary winds prevented him from rounding the eastern extremity of New Guinea, and he was forced to run westwards along the south coast, eventually reaching the Moluccas, Ternate and Manila. Exactly which route Torres followed along the south coast of New Guinea and through the strait which bears his name, and whether or not he actually sighted Australia, is a subject for what is at times rather vexed academic conjecture and debate. Certainly he was in the Louisiade Archipelago, followed much of New Guinea's southern coast, and charted Basilisk (Basilaki) Island and Jenkins Bay (Bahia de San Millan).

Although the Spanish authorities seem to have

attempted to keep secret the results of Torres' voyage, charts were published during the first quarter of the seventeenth century which laid down the southern coastline of New Guinea with Torres' nomenclature. Map 16 in the Duchess of Berry Atlas of 1615-23, which omits the Solomons discoveries of 1568, although applying the name Ilhas de Salamao, but includes the discoveries of 1595 and 1606, is perhaps a classic, with its demonstration of the north-eastern coastline supposedly sighted by de Meneses (Papuas), the northern coastline sighted by Saavedra and de Retes, and the southern coastline sighted by Torres.

The Van Langren Globe of c.1625 shows a slightly different form, as well as demonstrating the Solomons discoveries of 1568 with the Southern Solomons (Guadalcanal and the New Georgia Group) which had not been circumnavigated, shown as projections of a northern promontory of the Terra Australis. On the eastern side of this promontory is also incorporated Quiros' reputedly continental discovery of Espiritu Santo, the cartographer having failed to appreciate that this was an island, and that Torres had passed to the south of it *en route* to the south coast of New Guinea. These two cartographic demonstrations of Torres' New Guinea discoveries may be typical of a larger body of similar maps, but, although a tradition of maps delineating Torres' southern New Guinea coastline appears to have continued into the eighteenth century, as is shown by a chart of New Guinea's southern coastline in the *Suite du Neptune françois* of 1700 and a map by Vaugondy in de Brosses' *Histoire des Navigations* of 1756, the results of Torres' voyage and his demonstration of the insularity of New Guinea seem to have been little known outside Spanish circles and, perhaps, to have been little known or been largely forgotten there. Quiros' expedition, however, virtually marked the end of the period of Spanish exploratory activity in the South-west Pacific, and the next phase was one of Dutch activity.

Following the voyages to the East of Houtman in 1595 and 1597 and the successful return of van Neck's fleet in 1599, the Dutch were encouraged in their ambitions to replace the Portuguese in the East. In 1602 Vereenigde Oost-Indische Compagnie or Dutch East India Company was formed, and by 1607 the Dutch were already in a significantly powerful position in the East Indies.

From the East Indies it was inevitable that they, like the Portuguese cosmographer Erédia who had sought in 1601 to lead an expedition to the south-east of Java, would look towards New Guinea and to the south-east of Java, to the area in which late sixteenth century charts—following the *Dieppe portolanos*, which may reflect an indirectly acquired Portuguese knowledge of Australia—had laid down a large promontory of the Terra Australis mistakenly identified with lands in South-east Asia visited by and reported to Polo.

As early as 1602 the Dutch sent the yacht *Duyfken* to Ceram to inquire about Nova Guinea, under Willem Cornelisz Schouten and Claes Gaeff, who returned with a perhaps misunderstood report that the Portuguese were active on the south-west coast of New Guinea.

In 1605 the *Duyfken* was dispatched from Banda under Jan Lodewijkszoon Roossengin and Willem Jansz with the object of exploring Nova Guinea and Terra. Australis. During 1606, a few months before Torres' appearance in these waters, the expedition had followed the south coast of New Guinea eastwards, and had headed south to discover the west coast of the Cape York Peninsula of Australia, without determining the certain existence of a passage between New Guinea and Australia. Indeed, for the Dutch both New Guinea itself and the Great Southland of Australia, following the discovery of the western coastline of the latter by Hartog in 1616, and further discoveries of its western and southern coastlines, continued for some time to be referred to jointly as Nova Guinea.

In 1623 the *Pera* and *Arnhem* were dispatched from Amboina under Jan Carstenz [q.v.] and Willem Colster to follow up the *Duyfken*'s discoveries and, following the south coast of New Guinea eastwards, they also headed south to 17°8′S. without determining whether or not New Guinea was separate from Australia. Here they became separated, the *Pera* returning to Amboina, the *Arnhem* continuing westwards to discover the extremity of Arnhem Land. In his log-book Carstenz refers to Ceram being named de Papues on some charts.

In June 1615 a private Dutch expedition of the Zuid Compagnie of Australische, led by Schouten and le Maire [qq.v.], left Holland to round Cape Horn and cross the Pacific westwards to the Spice Islands, intending, by taking this route, to defeat the Dutch East India Company monopoly and to discover Terra Australis from the east. Misled by the current cartographical underestimate of the width of the Pacific, by the underestimate of the position of the Western Pacific discoveries of the Spaniards westwards from Peru, and by their own more precise determination of distance travelled, Schouten and le Maire, justifiably concerned that they might fall beneath the south coast of an eastern promontory of Nova Guinea and become embayed upon a lee shore, headed north-westwards into lower latitudes in the Western Pacific to discover Ont(h)ong Java, Tauu (Marquen), the Green Islands, (de Groene Eylanden), St John's Island (Ambitle of the Feni Islands, St Jans Eylandt), and the north-eastern coastline of New Ireland which they identified as part of New Guinea (Nova Guinea) and charted as Hoogh Landt.

Following the east coast of New Ireland north-westwards, le Maire and Schouten discovered the Tanga Islands, the Lihir Group, the Tabar Islands, took the passage between New Ireland and New Hanover to be a bay, rounded the north end of New Hanover without sighting Mussau to the north, and passed to the south of Manus, (charted as Hoogh Landt) the largest of the Admiralty Islands previously discovered by Saavedra, through the archipelago of small islands off its southern coast (25 Eylanden). Following the New Guinea coast westwards, they passed the Kumamba Islands, came to Biak or Willem Schouten Eylandt, sailed across the mouth of Geelvink Bay which, in bad weather, they were not able to determine but which they seem to have charted as open coastline, came to the small islands northwest of Waigeo (Papoos) and passed around the northern end of Gilolo and down to Batavia.

In 1643 Abel Janszoon Tasman [q.v.] sailed from Batavia to circumnavigate the Great Southland of Australia, Nova Hollandia. Passing to the south of Australia, and by way of Van Diemen's Landt (Tasmania) and the western coast of New Zealand, he came up to the Tonga Group to join what he thought was the route of le Maire, when in fact he was to the west of it. Misled by his chart to fear that the Fiji Archipelago might be Quiros' Espiritu Santo and supposed antipodean continent he, like le Maire and Schouten, headed northwards to avoid a possible lee shore on the Australian continent below Nova Guinea and made the same landfalls in the Northern Solomons and New Ireland area as le Maire, naming Tanga (Anthony Caens Eylandt) Lihir (Gerrit de Nijs Eylandt) and Tabar (Visscher's Eylandt). Rounding New Hanover's northern tip (Salmon Sweers Cape), he sailed south between the Vitu Islands and the Willaumez Peninsula on the north coast of New Britain which he may be regarded as having discovered, and followed the coast of New Guinea westwards, assuming New Ireland, New Hanover, New Britain and New Guinea to be one continuous land mass.

By the end of the seventeenth century some of the cartographical problems associated with the Pacific had come to be appreciated. New Guinea was represented in either the traditional Spanish or the new Dutch form or a combination of both. The Solomons presented a special problem. Their proximity to New Guinea was known, but the immense width of the Pacific was now more accurately understood. In this much wider ocean, the difficulty was to place the Solomons in New Guinea waters, and also at what was believed to be their distance from Peru, a distance greatly underestimated by the early navigators. Their frequent re-drawing in what was still considered to be the central Pacific was often only partial, and limited to the large island of Santa Ysabel and a few diminutive neighbours, the other discoveries of 1568 in the Southern Solomons, as laid down in earlier Spanish charts, having disappeared in the period when they were absorbed as promontories of the reputed austral continent in proximity to Quiros' reputed continental discovery. It was the more accurate Dutch charts which became the accepted models for the representation of New Guinea and Australia.

In 1644 Tasman was again dispatched, this time to determine whether or not a passage existed between Nova Guinea and Nova Hollandia (Australia), and, if so, to sail through to the east and follow the east coast of Nova Hollandia southwards to Van Diemen's Landt, which he was

to circumnavigate, and then complete the circumnavigation of Nova Hollandia. In fact, he failed to find the strait between New Guinea and Australia, and although he made a significant exploration of the north and north-west coasts of Australia, his exploration of New Guinea's southwest coasts seems to have revealed little that was new, much as Roggeveen, who crossed the Pacific westwards to New Ireland in 1722, appears to have contributed little that was new to knowledge of northern New Guinea. In about 1645 Maarten Gerritszoon Vries made a voyage for the Dutch East India Company from Batavia along the north coast of New Guinea as far as New Hanover and then headed for the Marianas, but little else is known of his voyage including whether or not he made any new discoveries.

As early as 1599 English traders had expressed their ambitions towards 'the Est Indies and other islandes and cuntries thereabouts'; at the Anglo-French peace talks of 1600 the English had demanded the right to trade in 'the rich and goulden land of Sumatra—Java Major—Java Minor—Os Papua and the Longe Tracte of Nova Guinea and the Isles of Solomon', and on the last day of that year the English East India Company was licensed. Although New Guinea was to be mentioned in other proposals, English activity in the East Indies was unsuccessful at first, and it was not until 1699 that effective further action was taken by the English.

That year the Admiralty dispatched William Dampier [q.v.] in command of the *Roebuck* to explore the unknown east coast of New Guinea and New Holland. Heading eastwards off the north coast of New Guinea, he came to Mussau and Emira (St Matthias and Squally Islands) off New Hanover in the Bismarck Archipelago, which he seems probably to have discovered, if Vries had not already done so. Following the eastern coasts of New Ireland and New Britain southwards, without realizing that New Hanover, New Ireland and New Britain were separate islands, naming them collectively Nova Britannia, and assuming that the strait between New Britain and New Ireland was a bay which he named St George's Bay, he passed the Tabar Islands (Wishart's Island), the Lihir Group (Garret Dennis Island), and the Tanga Islands (Anthony Cave's Island), and St John's Island, discovered the strait between New Britain and New Guinea (Dampier's Passage), and then returned westwards along the north coast of New Guinea, noting and naming various islands, to pass between New Guinea and Waigeo. Further English interest in the Pacific was to follow Anson's voyage of 1740-3, and in 1744 Campbell suggested the English colonization of Nova Britannia in his edition of Harris's *Navigantum atque Itinerarium Bibliotheca*, whilst Charles de Brosses, in his *Histoire des Navigations* of 1756, recommended a French settlement there.

Meanwhile, in 1705, the Dutch yacht the *Geelvink*, in company with an Indonesian-built vessel, was dispatched to explore the south-eastern part of New Guinea. According to Burney the *Geelvink* crew discovered the large bay on the north coast of West Irian which now bears the name Geelvink Bay. Some contemporary and later cartographers, however, assumed that the *Geelvink* had sailed along the north coast of New Guinea to the eastern extremity, and they plotted a northern coastline of New Guinea immediately to the south of Dampier's Nova Britannia. The *Geelvink* discovery of Geelvink Bay was apparently little known to cartographers. Earlier navigators such as Tasman and Dampier had noted the absence of proximate coastline in the area south of the Schouten Islands, and cartographers in some cases showed New Guinea as divided by a hypothetical passage or channel, sometimes described as conjectural, which had its origin in this uncertainty concerning the area of open sea to the south of the Schouten Islands and the earlier Dutch knowledge of McCluer Gulf obtained by the *Arnhem* in 1623, with the name Papua applied to the land to the west and the name New Guinea applied to the greater land mass to the east. Bougainville, in 1768 whilst off Geelvink Bay, assumed from the state of the tides and currents that a strait might exist there without knowing from the available cartography what did exist. As late as the last decade of the eighteenth century most cartographers continued to leave the area of Geelvink Bay blank, or to lay down a hypothetical channel, and one of the earliest cartographers to lay down the bay with any accuracy was Rochette in 1803.

An account of the *Geelvink*'s voyage had appeared in a work by Nicolas Struyck in 1753, accompanied by a chart to demonstrate the then known parts of north-western New Guinea, but it seems to have been Alexander Dalrymple who really drew attention to the *Geelvink*'s discovery in a chart in his *Collection of Plans* of 1781, based on a Dutch manuscript chart of the *Geelvink*'s track, and who ultimately dispelled the idea of a *Geelvink* coastline at the eastern extremity of New Guinea.

The voyage of Jacob Roggeveen westwards across the Pacific in 1722, which in its latter stages followed the general route taken by Schouten and le Maire from New Ireland to the East Indies, appears to have contributed nothing to the increase of knowledge of New Guinea's northern coastline.

In 1767 Philip Carteret [q.v.] sailed west across the Pacific in the *Swallow*, searching for the austral or antipodean continent, to rediscover and later recognize Santa Cruz, to rediscover but fail to identify part of the Solomons, Malaita and Ndai, and to discover Kilinailau Atoll (Carteret's Nine Islands) and Buka (Winchelsea or Lord Anson's Island). Beyond he rediscovered the Green Islands (Sir Charles Hardy's Island), rediscovered and recognized St John's Island, and came upon 'what Dampier had named Nova Britannia'. At Dampier's St George's Bay Carteret heeled the *Swallow*, and then, prevented by contrary winds from following Dampier's route through Dampier's Passage, sailed northwards to discover St George's Channel between what he now renamed New Britain and New Ireland.

Following the western side of New Ireland northwards, he came to what he named Byron's Strait and New Hanover. Passing south of the Admiralty Islands, as he named them, he sighted and may indeed have been the discoverer of Aua (Durour's Island), and Wuvulu (Matty's Island), and then passed the Schouten Islands to arrive in Batavia at the end of the year.

In the following year the French navigator Louis de Bougainville [q.v.] came westwards across the Pacific to rediscover the New Hebrides, and to attempt to determine whether or not New Guinea was separated from New Holland. Deterred by the Great Barrier Reef, he headed north to come upon the Louisiade Archipelago and, after unsuccessfully attempting to head westwards in the doubtful belief that a passage might exist between New Guinea and Australia, to round Rossel Island which Torres may not have sighted. Sailing towards the north, he passed the New Georgia Group in the Solomons, and navigated what was to become known as Bougainville Strait between Choiseul (San Marcos) and Bougainville Island, the latter being a new discovery. Continuing north-westwards, he passed Bouka (Buka), as he named it from a word much used by the indigenes who came off in canoes, and came to New Ireland, known to him only as it was described by Dampier, that is, as Nova Britannia. Heading northwards, and noting that there was some evidence that a strait might exist in the area of St George's Channel, he passed the Feni Islands (Bournand Island), the Tanga Islands (d'Oraison Island), Lihir Island (du Bouchage Island), Tabar Island (Suzanet Island), all previously discovered by the Dutch. Passing north of Mussau and Emira, which Bougainville recognized as the St Matthias and Squally Islands of Dampier, he now came to Kaniet (Ile des Anachorètes), with Sae beyond, which he recorded for the first time if he did not discover them. He then passed the Ninigo Group (d'Echiquier), and Liot (la Boudeuse) and, proceeding south-westwards, sighted what may have been Wuvulu; islands which may already have been discovered by Saavedra, de Retes or Vries. Following the New Guinea coast westwards, he passed between Waigeo (Côte et Ile de Papua) and New Guinea, and arrived at Boero (Buru) in the Indies.

It was Lieutenant James Cook who was to make the next contribution to knowledge of New Guinea, for it was in 1770 during his first voyage of 1768-71 that, having crossed the Pacific eastwards, having circumnavigated New Zealand and proved that this was not part of an antipodean and antarctic continent, and having explored and charted the east coast of Australia, thereby determining the east-west limits of the Pacific, he sailed northwards towards the eastern entrance of the Torres Strait. One of Cook's objectives was to determine whether or not New Guinea was separated from New Holland (Australia). Aided by de Brosses' *Histoire de Navigations* of 1756 with its charts depicting, in the cartographical tradition derived from Torres, New Guinea separated from New Holland, and further aided by the chart in Alexander Dalrymple's *Account of the Discoveries made in the South Pacific Ocean, Previous to 1764* of 1769, which laid down Dalrymple's approximate reconstruction of Torres' route between New Guinea and Australia, he succeeded in circumventing the problems of the Great Barrier Reef and the myriad shoals and reefs of the Torres Strait, to discover, not perhaps the best, but certainly a navigable passage between New Guinea and Australia.

In his *Account of the Discoveries made* Dalrymple had argued, on the basis of a superficial similarity between a chart of the Solomon Islands of 1596 by de Bry and Dampier's chart of Nova Britannia, and on the false assumption that the reported proximity of the Solomons to New Guinea was more reliable than the reported latitudes of the archipelago, that the Solomon Islands must be the same as Nova Britannia. However, it was the French geographer Buâche, who in 1781 postulated the correct thesis that the Solomon Islands of Mendaña in 1568 must be the same lands as those coasted by Carteret and Bougainville, and in 1769 by Surville, who had sailed via the Philippines, Bashees and north-eastern limits of the Solomons from Pondicherry *en route* to Peru.

In 1781 the Spaniard Francisco Antonio Mourelle (Maurelle), *en route* from the Philippines to the Americas by an unsuccessful South Pacific route, recognized the Ninigo Islands as the group Bougainville reported. He then came to Los Hermitanos (the Hermit Island), which he appears to have been the first navigator to report, but which may have been La Caimana of de Retes, perhaps also seen by Saavedra, and then passed Sae, Kaniet and Manus, to sight and discover what seems probably to have been Tench Island to the north-north-east of New Hanover. Continuing southeastwards he came to St John's Island (Feni Islands) and the northern perimeter of the Solomons. He called the Green Islands, Los Caimans; Buka, Santa Bárbara, and Bougainville's north coast, Don Manuel Flores. Kilinailau he mistook for 'Ohong Jaba of the French charts', (Tasman's Othong Java).

At this stage Dalrymple appears to have abandoned his identification of Nova Britannia as the Solomons, but in 1790 he returned to his assertions with the same dogmatism which he had applied to his belief in a vast antipodean and antarctic continent until Cook had disproved it in his second Pacific voyage of 1772-5. That Dalrymple did this is interesting in terms of the fact that one of the ingredients to his belief that New Britain and New Ireland could be identified with early Spanish charts of the Solomons was the erroneous belief that the *Geelvink* had explored a coastline to the south of New Britain, a belief which he had himself dispelled in 1781 with his publication of a chart showing the actual *Geelvink* discoveries.

In 1787 an American merchantman the *Alliance*, commanded by Thomas Read, came north from the east coast of Australia in an attempt to develop a new tea-trade route to China via the South Atlantic and around Australia, to reach the Western Solomons and to follow the west coast of Bougainville northwards. His voyage, in fact, disproved one current assumption following Bougainville's voyage, that the island which now bears his name and which he had only coasted to the eastwards of, was the eastern limit of New Guinea. However, the voyage was not reported internationally, and Read appears to have contributed nothing to contemporary European cartographical knowledge.

La Pérouse, dispatched from France in 1786 on a voyage of quite incredible ambitions, was instructed, among other things, to explore the Louisiade coast of Bougainville (i.e. the Louisiade Archipelago) and 'an island to the north-west of the Terre des Arsacides (i.e. the Solomons as seen by Surville) which was seen by Bougainville in 1768' (i.e. Bougainville Island). His disappearance after leaving Botany Bay in 1788, and what we know to have been the shipwreck of his expedition on Vanikoro, marked the end of an expedition which might have contributed considerably to knowledge of the area.

In 1788 Lieutenant John Shortland, *en route* to China from the colony at Port Jackson following its establishment by the First Fleet, passed along the southern limits of the Solomons and through the Shortland or Bougainville Strait without recognizing the group as such. Naming the whole New Georgia, he named the Treasury Islands just south of Bougainville, described Kilinailau as the Four Islands, and mistakenly assumed that these were not the same as the Nine Islands of Carteret. From Kilinailau he headed north and west towards the Pelew Islands, and to Canton.

Fleurieu, the French geographer, now took up the question of the identity of the Solomons, and in his *Découvertes des François* of 1790 he firmly identified the discoveries of Carteret, Bougainville, Surville and Shortland as the Solomon Islands discovered by Mendaña in 1568, and attempted an identification of the particular islands reported by Mendaña's expedition. Carteret's Nine Islands and Shortland's Four Islands he regarded, incorrectly, as different, and, ignorant of Read's voyage, he left the west coast of Bougainville blank. Dalrymple on the other hand, in a chart in his *Memoir concerning the Passages to and from China* of 1782, had shown the east coast of Bougainville Island and the Louisiade coastline of Bougainville as the eastern and south-eastern coastal limits of New Guinea.

In 1791 Captain Hunter left Port Jackson in the *Waaksamheyd* to secure supplies in Batavia. Heading north-westwards from Sikaiana (Stewart's Islands), which he had discovered, he sailed past Bradley's Shoals and Ontong Java (Lord Howe's Group) in the Solomons, failing to recognize the latter as an earlier Dutch discovery. He then passed Kilinailau, which he identified with some reservation as the Nine Islands of Carteret. To the south he observed Buka and Bougainville and the strait between them, passed the Green Islands, headed through St George's Channel between New Ireland and New Britain, and then past the Admiralty Islands to reach Batavia on 27 September 1791. In the same year Captain Edwards of the *Pandora*, dispatched to the Pacific to apprehend the Bounty mutineers, returned westwards via the Torres or Endeavour Strait, sighted New Guinea, discovered the Murray Islands and foundered on the Great Barrier Reef, the survivors subsequently reaching Timor by small boat.

Yet again in 1792, the French navigator Antoine d'Entrecasteaux was in the Western Pacific in search of la Pérouse and on a voyage of exploration. Amongst other things he was required to explore the Solomons in detail, and in July he followed the southern coastlines of the Western Solomons north-westwards, past the Island of Mono, the Shortland Islands, and then followed and charted the west coasts of Bougainville Island and Buka. Passing through St George's Channel, after sighting the Green Islands and after a brief stay at Carteret Harbour in New Ireland, d'Entrecasteaux arrived at Amboina, and then continued south along the west coast of and around New Holland to New Zealand, the Friendly Islands, New Caledonia and back again to the Solomons. From Santa Cruz he passed via San Cristoval, Guadalcanal and the southern coastline of the New Georgia Group, sailed south to 11°30'S. and then headed westwards towards the Louisiade coastline of Bougainville. Coasting the northern side of the Louisiade Archipelago, he confirmed the already expressed suspicion that what Bougainville had seen from the south was not a coastline but a chain of islands, and dispelled completely the erroneous belief that the *Geelvink* had discovered a coastline in this area. In the Louisiade Archipelago d'Entrecasteaux discovered the Renard Islands (Iles Renard), Misima or Eruption (Saint Aignan), the Deboyne Islands (Iles de Boynes), the Bonvouloir Islands (Iles Bonvouloir), the D'Entrecasteaux Islands, the Trobriand Islands (Iles Trobriand), all in June 1793. Passing through Dampier's Strait, he followed the west coasts of New Britain and New Ireland northwards, arriving at the Admiralty Islands in July, where he died, the remainder of the expedition then proceeding to the Dutch East Indies.

In 1793 the *Hormuzeer* and *Chesterfield*, *en route* to Timor, passed through the Torres Strait. According to their tracks as laid down on Flinders' charts of 1802-3 and on Chart 26 (a) in Norie's *The Country Trade or Free Mariner's Journal* of 1837, which well reflects the cartographical knowledge of east New Guinea and its off-shore islands at that time, they explored, charted, and may have made some actual discovery of coastline along the south coast of New Guinea in the area of Deception Bay in the Gulf of Papua.

In 1794 the English Captain Wilkinson in the *Indispensable* and the American Captain Page in the *Halcyon* sailed north from Port Jackson through the Solomons between Rennell and Bellona Islands, between Guadalcanal and San Cristoval, to come upon what seems likely to have been the Tauu Islands, but to which Wilkinson gave the name Cocos Islands, and to which Page appears to

have given the name New Spice Island.

In 1795 James Mortlock in the *Young William*, passed north through the Solomons to sight Tauu Atoll, to record its position with accuracy and to grant it yet another name, Hunter's Islands, presumably in the mistaken belief that these were the islands sighted and identified with reservation as the Islands of Carteret by Hunter in 1791. Krusenstern, a Russian hydrographer, added yet another name to the group by calling them the Mortlock Isles. In his *Carte Systématique* in 1824-7 he duplicates the group as Is de Mortlock in one position and Marqueen I. or Is Cocos in another close by, whilst Butler's *Chart of the Western Part of the Pacific Ocean* of 1800 presents yet another form of the general confusion associated with these northern atolls.

In 1802 the French privateer the *Adèle* was in the waters off east New Guinea (*see* COUTANCE); in 1811 the *Union* of Calcutta passed through the same area; and Duperrey, the French navigator, in the *Coquille* and accompanied by Dumont d'Urville, was in the same area in 1823. In 1812 Captain Abraham Bristow of the *Thames* cruised extensively in the Buka/New Ireland area, as he had done in 1808 in the *Sarah*, when he passed along the northern route of the Louisiade Archipelago by a new route to Dampier Strait which was reported in Purdy's *Oriental Navigator* of 1816. In July 1812 he appears to have charted for the first time the Boang Island (Day's Island) of the Tanga Islands, the Oraison of Bougainville, who failed to realize that what had appeared to be one island, Malendok, was in fact two.

It appears to have been in the same year, 1812, that the next discovery was made in the area, when David Laughlan, master of the *Mary*, discovered the Laughlan Islands slightly to the east of Woodlark Island. In 1822 the whaler *Abgarris* reported Abgarris Island in a position where, in 1826, Captain Renneck of the *Lyra* reported a group of islands and banks which may be identified as Nuguria to the east of New Ireland and north of Kilinailau.

The only significant and distinct atoll or island group distant from but within the modern political boundaries of Papua-New Guinea was Nukumanu. This appears to have been discovered by Captain Wellings in 1824, and may subsequently have been seen by Captain Thomas Beckford Simpson of Sydney in about 1845, thereafter to be known to some geographers as Simpson's Coral Islands. In 1826 Dumont d'Urville was in the Pacific and, having sailed from Fiji south to the Solomons, sighted and was reputed to have discovered Cannac Island between the Laughlan Islands and Woodlark, although it seems likely that this had already been sighted previously.

By the second quarter of the nineteenth century it is perhaps true to say that the general outline of New Guinea was fairly well known, the major islands off shore had been discovered, rediscovered and reasonably well charted, and most of the small islands worthy of note within the area had been discovered. There was certainly quite considerable activity in the eastern areas of

New Guinea and the Northern Solomons by this time, and as the *Colonial Magazine and Commercial Maritime Journal* for 1841 remarks: the 'Solomon Islands have become better known, from the many English and American whalers that have anchored in the bays of the various islands'.

In 1830 the American Morell was in the Kilinailau and Buka area in the *Atlantic* in search of bêche-de-mer, and in 1834 he was back again in the *Margaret Oakley* on the west coast of Bougainville. Many voyages, however, have obviously been lost to record, particularly American whaling and other commercial voyages which were commercial by nature, secret by interest, and outside the mainstream of European hydrographic recording.

The first certain report of the discovery of Woodlark Island, Kulumadau, is that of Captain Hunter of the *Marshall Bennett*, who recorded in the *Nautical Magazine* for July 1840 that its position had been reported by Captain Grimes of the *Woodlark* of Sydney, and that he himself had come upon it in September 1836, whilst sailing from the Laughlan Islands (Louisiade Archipelago). He also noted the four islands of the Marshall Bennett Islands, commenting that these were erroneously laid down on the charts as three in number, thus indicating their prior discovery. The Louisiade Archipelago was still very inadequately explored, however, as Chart 26 (a) in Norie's *Country Trade or Free Mariner's Journal* of 1833 indicates.

J. Burney, *A Chronological History of the Voyages and Discoveries in the South Sea or Pacific Ocean.* 5 vols, London, 1803-17; C. Jack-Hinton, *The Search for the Islands of Solomon, 1568-1838.* Oxford, 1968; A. Sharp, *The Discovery of the Pacific Islands.* Oxford, 1960; ——— *The Discovery of Australia.* Oxford, 1963.

C. JACK-HINTON

DISCRIMINATORY LEGISLATION. Discriminatory laws of some kind are to be found in most legal systems; this article is concerned with legislation that discriminates against race or colour.

It must be remembered that the Territory of Papua and the Mandated Territory of New Guinea were administered separately until 1945 and were subject to different legislatures until the cessation of civil government in February 1942. In an article of this length it is impossible to treat the Territories separately. Examples are taken from both but in most cases similar legislation would have been in force in the other Territory.

Discriminatory legislation of the type we are discussing falls generally into two classes, punitive or protective. Legislation which imposes a penal sanction where under the general law the remedy would be a civil action or no action at all, is punitive legislation. Legislation which although discriminatory, has as its main purpose the protection of the indigenous population, is protective or paternalistic. This, of course, is a rough delineation only as some laws fall within both categories.

Labour legislation. Legislation regulating the use of labour was originally protective, later fell into the category of punitive, and is now once more protective.

The Letters Patent of 8 June 1888 relating to British New Guinea (later Papua) required the Legislative Council of the Possession to establish a law providing 'that no deportation of Natives be allowed, either from one part of the Possession to another, or to any place beyond the Possession, except under such conditions as may be established by order of Ourselves in Our Privy Council or by some law of the Possession, which has been reserved for signification of Our pleasure, and assented to by Ourselves in Our Privy Council'.

Effect was given to this condition by Ordinance no. 3 of 1888. Under this ordinance the Possession was divided into districts and natives could be required to work only within their own district. The reason for this enactment was the danger seen to the native in moving him from his own home district as he would then be liable to attack by hostile people. This danger was thought to have been overcome by contact, and Ordinance no. 3 of 1892 allowed employers to move natives from their home district, but did not allow them to be taken outside the Possession except in the way provided by the ordinance. By Ordinance no. 3 of 1893 imprisonment was imposed as a punishment for natives who failed to take up service after entering an agreement or deserted after taking-up employment.

Imprisonment of the employee, or a fine to the amount of two months' wages for failing to carry out the terms of employment remained part of the labour legislation until the Native Labour Ordinance 1946 of the Territory of Papua and New Guinea. Today the employer of native labour is in the same position as any other employer, in that he can bring a civil action for breach of contract where appropriate.

The original ordinance in Papua, then, restricted employment because of the physical danger to natives moving freely through the Territory. When these dangers ceased to exist, the geographical limitations imposed by the ordinance were relaxed and it was not long before punitive provisions were written into the legislation. Natives were liable to imprisonment (*inter alia*) for breaking the contract of employment by running away, for refusing to work and even for failing to show ordinary diligence. These provisions have long been repealed. Legislation governing the employment of natives is still discriminatory but protective.

Criminal legislation. The Criminal Procedure Ordinance 1889 of Papua (adopted in New Guinea) provided in effect that trials of indictable offences should be by a judge sitting alone. The Jury Ordinance 1907 (Papua) and the Jury Ordinance 1951 (New Guinea), provided that the trial of a person of European descent charged with a crime punishable by death should be held before a jury of four persons of European descent.

This obviously discriminatory legislation could possibly be justified by the difficulty of finding a jury of natives who understood the procedure and rules of evidence of our courts, but this does not justify juries for Europeans. These ordinances were repealed by the Jury Ordinance (Repeal) Ordinance 1964. All trials of indictable offences are now held before a judge or judges sitting alone and deciding both fact and law.

The Native Regulation Ordinance 1908 (Papua) and the Native Administration Ordinance 1921 (New Guinea) provided for courts to deal solely with offences by, or disputes between, natives. The Native Regulations and the Native Administration Regulations made under these ordinances provided for the jurisdiction of these courts which were presided over by Magistrates of Native Matters or Native Affairs. The regulations set out offences and punishments to be awarded. Some offences under the regulations were also offences under the general law but with a smaller penalty, but some offences were novel in a sense that they were not offences under the general law, e.g. sorcery and adultery.

The Native Regulations and Native Administration Regulations were both protective and punitive. Protective in the sense that they took into account the fact that the Administration was imposing a sophisticated law on an unsophisticated people and that offences that were quite serious according to European standards were not serious according to the native standard. (Indictable offences could be heard before magistrates presiding over these special courts with jurisdiction limited to award punishment up to six months.) The regulations were also punitive in that they created offences if the act was done by a native that were not offences if done by a European, e.g. adultery.

The Native Regulations and the Native Administration Regulations are still in force in the Territory but the special courts have been abolished and offences under the regulations are tried by Local Courts, which are courts having a general though limited jurisdiction over all people in the Territory.

The criminal legislation that was perhaps the most obviously discriminatory was the White Womens Protection Ordinance 1926 of the Territory of Papua. This ordinance, as the name implies, and despite the protection given by the Criminal Code, made provisions for the punishment for sexual offences against European women. The punishments imposed by this ordinance were very harsh, e.g. indecent assault was punishable with life imprisonment with up to three whippings as opposed to the punishment under the Criminal Code of two years imprisonment; offences against native women would be punishable under the Code. By the Native Offenders Exclusion Ordinance 1930 natives convicted of an offence of an indecent nature against a white woman were excluded from the towns of the Territory. The first ordinance was repealed in 1958, the latter in 1962.

Land legislation. From the original occupation, Territory laws dealing with the acquisition of land have always been discriminatory, protecting the native's rights to his land.

The proclamation by Commodore Erskine of the Protectorate in 1884 declared that 'No acquisition of land whensoever or howsoever acquired within the limit of the Protectorate hereby established,

will be recognised by Her Majesty'. The Letters Patent establishing the Possession required the Legislative Council 'to establish a law providing that no purchase of land within the Possession be allowed to be made by private persons, except from the Administrator, or other authorised officers of the Government, or from the purchaser from him'.

The second Ordinance of the Possession, no. 2 of 1888, prohibited any person from purchasing land, or any interest in land, from any native. Natives were also forbidden to sell land and any such transaction was declared null and void. The Administrator could, however, purchase land in the public interest after satisfying himself that the land was not required, or likely to be required for native use. The Crown Land Ordinance 1890 allowed waste and vacant lands not used or likely to be required by the natives to be taken into possession by the Crown as Crown lands.

All native rights in land existing in British New Guinea at the time of the annexation, and in the Territory of New Guinea after the assumption of control by Australia as Mandatory, were recognized by the law, and it has been possible for natives to part with their rights only in accordance with protective land legislation which has been enacted.

By the Land Ordinance 1962 an ordinance that applies to both Territories, provision is made for acquisition of land by the Administrator by compulsory process only after very stringent enquiries and proper notice, etc., have been given.

Conclusion. The foregoing is a short summary of some of the more important discriminatory legislation which has applied in Papua New Guinea. Other legislation has discriminated, e.g. the divorce law, where in Papua a native although married in accordance with the law could not come before the divorce courts. But nearly all discriminatory legislation with the exception of some protective legislation, has now disappeared, this trend culminating in the Discriminatory Practices Ordinance 1963-69. By this ordinance it is an offence generally for a person to be discriminated against by reason only of his race or colour.   J. R. MATTES

DISEASE PREVALENCE (MORBIDITY). As a practical approach to this involved subject of morbidity in the Territory of Papua and New Guinea the most important contributions to the present knowledge of disease patterns will be described according to six available sources of information. These are historical sources, patrol reports, hospital admission records, epidemiological reports of notifiable diseases, special hospital studies, and special field surveys.

HISTORICAL SOURCES

Old *Annual Reports* of British New Guinea (now Papua) reveal that smallpox in epidemic form had scourged German New Guinea in 1894 and evidence suggested that twenty-five years earlier the disease had visited what is now called the Northern District of Papua.

The annual *Reports to the League of Nations on the Territory of New Guinea* mentioned severe outbreaks of dysentery on the goldfields with case mortality rates in excess of 50 per cent. The goldfields are no longer characterized by widespread dysentery nor by such fearful case fatality rates.

In the 1924-5 *Report* of the Health Department, Territory of New Guinea, it was stated that up to 50 per cent of indentured labourers showed signs of beriberi. Beriberi today is an extremely rare disease.

The activities of the Australian Hookworm Campaign extended to Papua because at that time it was believed that the very prevalent hookworm infestation of Papuans must be causing severe debilitating anaemia. These early reports, such as that of Sweet in 1924, were very optimistic of the final benefits to result from the eradication campaign.

The annual reports from both Territories during the first forty years of this century indicated that yaws was very common in almost all areas. In 1939-40, 65,906 injections of N.A.B. for yaws treatment were given in the Mandated Territory. Post-war and prior to the anti-yaws campaign of universal penicillin injections, yaws [q.v.] was still very common. Thus in 1959 Lake found that 13 per cent of the population of 1,294 South Wapi people in the Sepik had infectious yaws lesions.

PATROL REPORTS

Since the days of very early contact, Administration and medical patrols have visited both remote and near villages, assembled and examined the people, and subsequently reported their findings to the health authorities. From this source it became known that goitre was prevalent on the Huon Peninsula, on Karkar Island, on the east bank of the Lamari River, on the south side of the Wahgi Valley near Mount Hagen, and inland on Bougainville.

Perusal of the voluminous patrol reports in Department of Health files also shows that tinea imbricata (*Grilli* or *Sipoma*) is a lowland disease. This is true also of filariasis [q.v.] and its most obvious manifestation, elephantiasis, whereas leprosy [q.v.] cases are scattered irregularly at all altitudes.

These patrol reports also indicated that tropical ulcer was found over the whole country but with its highest prevalence in the lowlands. Unfortunately, interpretation of patrol reports must be very guarded because often the old, the sick, and the truculent did not come for examination and their absence could distort the picture.

HOSPITAL ADMISSION RECORDS

Amongst the best sources of morbidity statistics for Papua and New Guinea are the annual *Hospital Disease Statistics* issued by the Department of Public Health. These statistics give a detailed count of the cases discharged from Administration hospitals each year. The information is derived from hospitals and not from the whole community and it may well be a biased, incomplete count of all the cases existing in the community served by the hospitals. For example, people living near a hospital will be more frequently admitted than those who must travel far to seek admission. Any sex difference in the prevalence rates for various diseases may merely reflect different community attitudes towards hospital attendance by the different sexes. Despite the lower standard of diagnosis attained in the small remote hospitals as compared to that attained in the large base hospitals, all the statistics have been amalgamated in this annual publication.

Pneumonia [q.v.] emerges the most common cause of admission to Administration hospitals. The next commonest reason for admission is malaria [q.v.]; then, in sequence of decreasing prevalence, gastroenteritis, skin infections, bronchitis, lacerations and contusions, tropical ulcer, tuberculosis, dysentery, upper respiratory tract infections, influenza, inflammatory diseases of the eye, anaemias, and malnutrition [q.v.]. There are, however, significant differences between the regions in the prevalence of certain diseases. Thus, tropical ulcer is most commonly a cause of admission in the predominantly lowland parts of the Territory of New Guinea and least commonly in Highlands hospitals. In the Highlands, tuberculosis admissions are rare, but gastroenteritis and dysentery comprise a higher proportion of admissions than in the other areas.

In Fig. 1 the overall and inter-regional characteristics of the disease prevalences are indicated by the hospital statistics of admissions.

It was formerly believed that appendicitis, peptic ulceration, and coronary occlusion did not occur in the indigenous people. However, it is now recognized that all three of these conditions do have a definite though very low incidence.

From the health administrator's viewpoint, hospital bed occupancy may be a more significant criterion in grading the importance of different diseases than the mere numbers of admissions. In 1966-7, 1,651 beds were daily occupied by tuberculosis sufferers and 1,349 by leprosy sufferers. The next most important disease, if estimated by the criterion of bed occupancy, was pneumonia, for which there was a daily average bed occupancy of 490.

EPIDEMIOLOGICAL REPORTS OF NOTIFIABLE DISEASES

From every Territory hospital each month is radioed a report of the number of cases of notifiable communicable diseases seen by the medical staff in either the hospital or the surrounding community. These reports are collated in the Department of Public Health headquarters in Port Moresby to provide a continuing record of the status of each area for these notifiable diseases. This reporting system enables the health authorities to observe and take action appropriate to the development, spread or disappearance of foci of epidemic diseases such as poliomyelitis, meningitis, whooping cough, measles, influenza, gastroenteritis, dysentery, typhoid and the venereal dis-

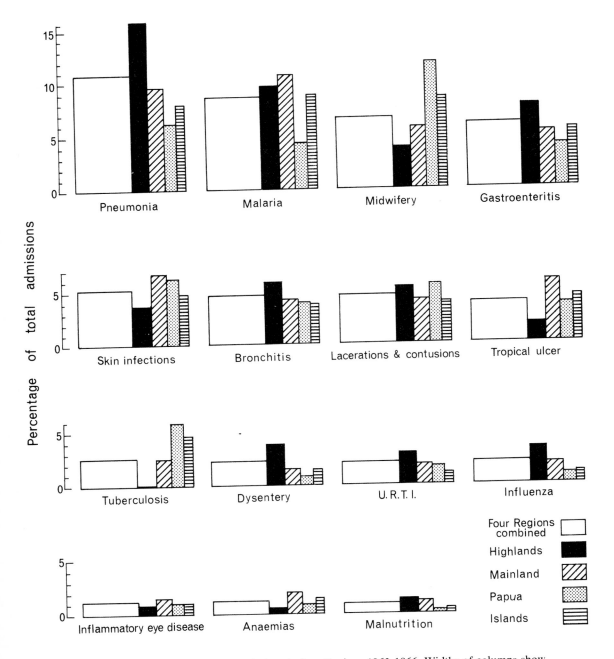

Fig 1. Leading causes of hospital admissions in four Regions 1963-1966. Widths of columns show ratio of total admissions in each Region to total admissions of four Regions.

NOTE: For the purposes of public health administration Papua and New Guinea were divided into four geographical Regions until 1970. The Regions consisted of the following areas; Highlands—the Highlands of the Territory of New Guinea plus the Southern Highlands; Mainland—the remaining mainland area of the Territory of New Guinea; Papua—the Territory of Papua minus the Southern Highlands; Islands—the islands of the Territory of New Guinea.

eases, particularly gonorrhoea and venereal granuloma.

Childhood diseases. From these reports it is known that poliomyelitis occurs from time to time in epidemics chiefly affecting young children, but that rare sporadic cases also occur in intervening periods. Whooping cough is reported somewhere every month, but periodically severe epidemics visit different areas and the case mortality rate in children under three years of age may reach as high as 7.5 per cent.

Infectious hepatitis causes sporadic disease amongst indigenous people, but epidemics are common amongst the children and young adults of the expatriate, mainly Australian, community.

Measles, like whooping cough, is present somewhere all the time, but usually is a fairly mild disease. However, on occasions it has been serious. The epidemic in the Eastern Highlands in 1961, when it affected the Okapa Hospital kuru orphans, many of whom were malnourished, resulted in four deaths amongst thirty-nine cases.

Mumps, chickenpox and rubella are all reported periodically in epidemic form from various parts of the Territory but are not usually associated with serious morbidity or mortality.

Miscellaneous infections. Influenza visits Papua and New Guinea from time to time. When it does, there is increased prevalence of acute bronchitis and pneumonia with increased mortality in the community, especially at higher altitudes amongst adult males.

Diphtheritic disease of the upper respiratory tract is rare.

Meningococcal meningitis or septicaemia are reported sporadically from all parts of the country.

Bacillary dysentery is very steadily reported from the whole area, but especially from the Highlands. Although epidemics of true dysentery do occur from time to time, large outbreaks of diarrhoeal disease usually represent gastroenteritis. Often no causative bacterial organism can be isolated from these gastroenteritis cases and they are presumed to be viral infections. Gastroenteritis epidemics show no preference for any particular altitude.

Typhoid is usually reported as sporadic cases, but small epidemics of four or five cases have infrequently occurred in institutional, village, and urban areas.

Anthrax, although recognized in pigs in the Highlands, has never been diagnosed in an indigenous Territorian.

Venereal disease. Gonorrhoea is steadily reported from all areas with greatest prevalence in the lowlands. There appears to be a trend towards much greater prevalence of gonorrhoea and venereal granuloma in the urban communities where up to 10 per cent of some examined groups of labourers have been found suffering from venereal disease. Gonorrhoea and venereal granuloma affect more males than females, because prostitution is often the infection source. More than a decade ago Scragg showed that in the New Ireland area gonorrhoea was an important cause of sterility.

Lymphogranuloma venereum is only occasionally reported. Syphilis is treated in a separate article.

Scrub typhus. Scrub typhus cases, which occurred in epidemic outbreaks amongst troops during World War II, are now reported only two or three times a year. This disease is usually contracted by working or camping in the site of old overgrown native gardens where the infected mites maintain the rickettsial cycle independently of man with the aid of rodents or marsupials in the area. The infected mite bites man, who subsequently develops an eschar at the site of inoculation, tender regional lymph nodes, fever, headache and in severe cases signs of meningitis or encephalitis or pneumonia. The indigenes living locally are often immune but visitors must protect themselves with the mite repellant dibutyl phthalate. Cure with chloramphenicol or the tetracyclines is rapid. No other form of typhus exists in the Territory.

SPECIAL HOSPITAL STUDIES

Detailed study of a hospital admission series in certain hospitals has been rewarding. For instance, it was known that about 2 per cent of hospital deaths in Papua and New Guinea were due to chronic renal disease but careful investigation, especially by Cooke and Champness, has shown that the commonest form of chronic renal disease is amyloid. Another clinical study by Douglas has indicated the unusually high prevalence of lobar pneumonia amongst young adults admitted to hospital. The majority of these cases are due to pneumococcal bacterial infections. Hospital studies by Maddocks have also shown that Reiter's disease is the most common cause of polyarthritis, at least in the Port Moresby area. This disease is characterized by an arthritis, skin rash, iritis or conjunctivitis, urethritis and balanitis. A diagnostic feature of Reiter's disease is the limping painful heel with characteristic radiological changes in the os calcaneum. Probably the disease is transmitted venereally.

Bites, stings, etc. Snake bite studies were originated by Campbell after caring for many cases admitted to the Port Moresby General Hospital. Sea-snake bite is rare but bite by death adder, Papuan black or taipan is fairly common, especially in Papua. Death adder bite occurs more widely, being found in New Britain as well as on the main island. Victims of snake bite variously manifest symptoms of muscular paralysis or haemorrhage (*see* SNAKES).

Stonefish (*Synanceja trachynis*) poisoning, which occurs sporadically along the coast, is caused by the penetration of the bather's foot by the poisonous dorsal spines of the shallow-bottom-dwelling stonefish; the victim suffers intense pain and the limb remains swollen for several days. The pain can be relieved by the injection of emetine along the wound. Occasional admissions to hospital also occur for shark bite and stingray wounds. Cone shell bites have caused critical illness but are rare events (*see* VENOMOUS MARINE ANIMALS).

Food poisoning from eating marine foods occurs occasionally. The ingestion of some un-identified species of red fish has occasionally caused a peripheral neuritis which has taken several weeks to clear. One episode of eating turtle meat in New Ireland resulted in seventeen admissions for gastroenteritis with five deaths. A similar episode occurred near Samarai and re-sulted in seven deaths.

No admissions for poisonous spider bite ever occur but occasional persons are treated for scor-pion or centipede stings. Occasional admissions do occur for crocodile bite and pig bite.

Pig-bel: necrotic enteritis. The study of enteritis necroticans began with the recognition of the clinical condition amongst Highlands hospital ad-missions. Murrell has described this disease, some-times called 'pig bel'. It usually develops as a gastroenteritis amongst people who have eaten pig from a pig feast. Some cases are more severe because segments of small bowel may become gangrenous. Such cases often die. If survival occurs the subject may sometimes develop symp-toms due to the failure of normal absorption of nutrients from those segments of gut which had been affected by the necrotizing enteritis. Murrell found that cases had a better prognosis when given intravenously a serum containing clostri-dial antitoxin. This disease is not confined to the Highlands (*see* PIGS).

Amoebic dysentery. Amoebic dysentery and liver abscess, well described by Burchett for the West-ern Highlands, have been recognized in hospitals throughout the Territory. However, it is less than ten years since it was reported that genital amoe-biasis was not rare, at least in male Highlanders. Sometimes the transfer of infection is by sodomy. The intestines of 10 to 15 per cent of the popu-lation harbour the causative pathogen *Entamoeba histolytica*, but most of these people are free of disease symptoms.

Microbacterial ulcer. The disease caused by *Mycobacterium ulcerans* was studied by Reid in a series of thirteen hospital admissions. He found the disease most often presented from amongst the population living along the Kamusi River in the Northern District of Papua, but other cases came from the Western District. The condition was usually seen in children and produced ex-tensive ulceration of the skin. Dapsone and strep-tomycin both may control the condition, but often wide surgical excision and skin grafting are neces-sary to effect a cure.

Perinatal disease in infants. Knowledge is scant about the causes of foetal death or of death dur-ing the first week of life. Most of what is known is derived from hospital studies. In a series of 113 perinatal deaths Vines and Dudley found that complications of delivery—including dispropor-tion, foetal malposition, and other causes of pro-longed labour—accounted for 27.4 per cent. Of this number only 22 per cent of the mothers had attended an antenatal clinic for two or more months. Placental and cord conditions, including placenta praevia and accidental haemorrhage, caused 12.4 of the deaths, while toxaemia of

pregnancy and immaturity each accounted for 9.8 per cent. Birth injuries caused only 6.2 per cent, and 2.7 per cent were due to congenital malfor-mations. Other maternal causes of perinatal death included anaemia, chronic nephritis, cervical scarring, prediabetes, essential hypertension, and cor pulmonale. Other foetal or newborn causes included haemolytic and haemorrhagic diseases of the newborn, postnatal asphyxia, and atelectasis and pneumonia. Nevertheless, 11.5 per cent of deaths were classified as cause unknown.

In this series with an overall death rate of 34.4 per 1,000 live births both twin pregnancy and first pregnancy status increased the probability of peri-natal death.

Cancer. A register of all persons admitted to Territory hospitals suffering from any tumour is maintained. All registered cases are followed up to document the course of the disease. From this source it is known that skin tumours predominate and that tumours of the oral cavity are next most common. The table below summarizes the regis-tered tumour distribution as compiled by Booth for the year 1967.

Malignant Tumours	Tumours Confirmed 1967	Per cent
Skin	63	17.4
Oral cavity	47	13.0
Female genitalia	39	10.8
Lymphoma	35	9.7
Digestive tract	31	8.6
Liver primary	25	6.9
Leukaemia	23	6.4
Breast	12	3.3
Respiratory system	12	3.3
Soft tissue	10	2.8
Male genitalia	9	2.5
Malignant bone	9	2.5
Urinary system	8	2.2
Thyroid	5	1.4
Eye	4	1.1
Nervous system	—	—
Metastases, unknown primary	20	5.5
Tumour, unknown origin	10	2.8
Total	362	

Special Interest		
Hydatidiform mole	16	
Salivary gland and sweat gland	6	
Primary jaw	7	
Cystic hygroma	5	
Soft tissue	10	
Other	8	
Total	52	

All malignant skin tumours appear to be rarer than in Australia. Squamous cell carcinomata are the most frequently seen, with only about a quar-ter as many melanomata of the skin, while rodent ulcers are only about a quarter as frequent as melanomata.

Cancer of the mouth mainly arises in the buc-cal mucosa. Development of oral cancer is be-lieved causally related to the widespread custom of chewing betel-nut with lime. Certainly the whitish thickened oral mucosa called oral hyperkeratosis which is often a precursor of cancer is frequently due to the betel-nut chewing habit.

About half of the digestive system cancers detected originated primarily in the liver.

Probably most females with genital cancer do not attend Territory hospitals for treatment. The present registry figures show that cervical cancer comprises about 40 per cent of this group, ovarian cancer about 35 per cent, vaginal or vulval cancer about 20 per cent. Only about 3 per cent of malignant female genital organ tumours arose primarily in the body of the uterus. It is likely that cancer of the breast is less common than in Australia. It has been suggested that the prolonged lactation practised by Territory women reduces the occurrence of breast cancer.

SPECIAL FIELD SURVEYS

Most of the rest of our knowledge of the pattern of morbidity in Papua and New Guinea is derived from special field surveys. Some of these surveys have merely presented a picture of the disease pattern at a moment in time.

The report edited by Hipsley and Clements covers an extensive survey of five different ecological zones made in 1947. This survey did not find evidence of gross protein malnutrition nor of vitamin deficiencies but reported that decline in body weight began very early in adult life, especially for women. No scorbutic changes were found, and less X-ray evidence of rachitic changes than in Australian infants. The survey demonstrated the wide distribution of hookworm infestation but could not show a relationship between hookworm infestation and anaemia in the population.

In 1955 Mann and Loschdorfer conducted an ophthalmological survey. They showed that trachoma was very common throughout the Territory, that it was usually very mild, and that its highest prevalence and severity was seen in New Britain, over 80 per cent of the population affected, and New Ireland.

Surveys for diabetes mellitus have been conducted by Price and Hingston, and Price and Tulloch. Diabetes mellitus is extremely uncommon in rural areas but is not so rare in some highly urbanized indigenous population groups in Port Moresby. However, even in the highly urbanized groups the prevalence is still far lower than amongst Australians.

Blood pressure levels. Between 1963 and 1966 Vines conducted a cross section random sample survey in three of the four medical administrative Regions of the Territory—Mainland, Highlands, Islands. This survey confirmed the report by Maddocks and Rovin that blood pressure amongst most male indigenes does not rise progressively during adult life. Women aged forty-five years and older did have a significant rise in their blood pressure but it was very small in comparison with that of Londoners. It is not surprising then that essential hypertension, a very common disease in

Western civilization, is practically never diagnosed amongst indigenous Papuans and New Guineans.

The random sample survey also showed that amongst Mainland urban dwellers blood pressures tended to rise with age. This finding is compatible with Maddocks' discovery that blood pressures do rise in the older adults amongst the highly urbanized Papuans living in Hanuabada Village, Port Moresby.

In Western society serum cholesterol values tend to rise with advancing age but this is not the case in Papua and New Guinea. The difference can probably be explained as due mainly to lower intake of fat but it is also known that malarial infection is associated with lower serum cholesterol levels. For example, Mainland Region males aged 30 to 44 years have a mean serum cholesterol level of 162.9 grammes per 100 c.c. whereas in the Islands Region, where malaria control work has been carried out for a long time, the corresponding mean value is 189 grammes per 100 c.c. It is interesting to note that urbanization raises the serum cholesterol level and for Mainland Region males the mean level was 29 grammes above their village counterparts.

Anaemia. The same survey also measured haemoglobin values in the Highlands, Mainland and Islands Regions. The results are shown in Fig. 2.

The grossly anaemic character of the Mainland Region population is obvious. This Region is also characterized by the most intense malaria transmission of the three under comparison. The Islands Region is at least as free of anaemia as the Highlands Region. This is probably a recently acquired characteristic, due to the far better health coverage in the Islands where malaria control work has been well established for over five years. Haemoglobin studies done in lowland Papua indicate that much of that Region must also be severely anaemic like the Mainland Region of New Guinea. Much of the anaemia is due to malarial infection but the pallor of the red cells seen under the microscope suggests that some is due to iron deficiency. In pregnant women folic acid deficiency anaemia is fairly common too.

Worm infestations. The random sample survey also covered the distribution of the various worm infestations. It was found that the prevalence of hookworm infestation was lowest on small atolls and islands, 48 per cent; highest in the lowland rain-forest situation, 90 per cent; still high in the Highlands, 78 per cent; but decreased in prevalence in communities living above 6,000 feet altitude. This survey agreed with the 1947 Nutrition Survey's inability to demonstrate that hookworm infestation causes anaemia in indigenous populations of the Territory.

The roundworm, *Ascaris*, was more prevalent in the Highlands, 50-60 per cent, than in most lowland areas, 15-30 per cent. The amount of morbidity attributable to this worm is uncertain. Occasionally a heavy infestation causes acute bowel obstruction or intussusception. It is not known to what extent larval migration of *Ascaris* is responsible for bronchitis or pneumonia. The large pig population in the Highlands may ac-

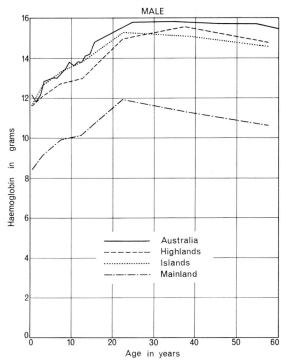

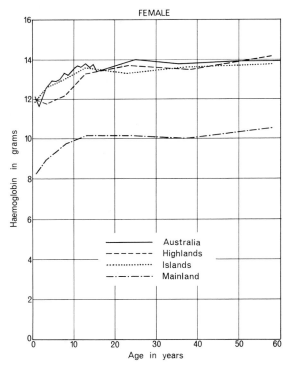

Fig 2. Mean haemoglobins by age. Comparison of Australia and three Regions.

count for the high *Ascaris* infestation rate of that area.

Threadworm (*Enterobius vermicularis*) infestation has been demonstrated in 30 per cent of children under five years of age. This prevalence was found by the single examination of each subject's perianal skin using the adhesive cellulose tape technique. It is probable that repeated examination would reveal at least double this rate of infestation. No definite morbidity can be ascribed to these infestations and the same can be stated of the very common whipworm (*Trichuris trichiura*) infestation.

Liver disease. Enlargement of the liver has been studied periodically ever since Peters in 1957 found an association between liver enlargement and spleen enlargement in people of the very malarious Fly River and Milne Bay areas of Papua. However, he also reported that enlargement of the liver was found at a 4 per cent prevalence level amongst late teenagers of the malaria-free Wabag Highlands area. This suggested that significant numbers of cases of liver enlargement are not due to malaria. In the Sepik, Schofield later reported that some cases of enlargement of both liver and spleen in older women persisted and were associated with anaemia despite the introduction of vigorous malaria control measures. Vines' random sample survey confirmed these findings and emphasized that the highest prevalence of enlarged livers is in women in malarious areas where over 60 per cent of those over forty-five years old have hepatic enlargement.

Cirrhosis of the liver is diagnosed on clinical grounds about seven times more frequently amongst Highlands hospital admissions than in the other regions of Papua and New Guinea. However, this is a clinical diagnosis and Blackburn in 1966 reported that in none of his series of 158 Highlanders suspected of having cirrhosis on clinical grounds could the diagnosis be confirmed by the results of liver biopsy. Instead, 90 per cent of biopsied livers showed a focal inflammation about the bile ducts but this inflammation was not causing the liver enlargement.

Serum protein levels. Many surveys have dealt with the serum protein patterns of people of the Territory. Serum albumin levels tend to be low. The increase in the globulin fraction of the serum is principally due to the increase in immunoglobulins. A typical adult male New Guinean would have a total serum protein level of 7.5 grammes per 100 c.c., consisting of 3.8 grammes of albumin and 3.7 grammes of globulin. Those people with enlarged spleens due to malaria tend to have lower serum albumin levels and higher serum globulin levels than the rest of the community. Although the geographical distribution of malaria is important in explaining the serum protein pattern it is not by any means the only important infection influencing it. Liver disease and nutritional status are also important factors in determining the serum protein pattern.

Malnutrition. Since Hipsley and Clements in 1947 first drew attention to the onset of decline in weight early in adult life for both sexes, several workers have revealed other evidences of malnutrition. In 1956 Ivinskis identified cases of nutritional oedema in pregnant and lactating Highlanders. The following year, Venkatachalam and Ivinskis reported kwashiorkor cases amongst both Highlands and lowlands children. Such children have an oedematous body and face, wasted buttocks, dry reddish sparse hair, may have a skin rash, and are apathetic.

Oomen and Malcolm in 1958 suggested that in lowland New Guinea there tended to be a pattern of gross under-nutrition on a relatively balanced diet resulting in wasted marasmic individuals, whereas in the Highlands caloric intake may be sufficient but the low protein content of the sweet potato staple, together with the absence of protective animal foods, endangered the intake balance and could result in kwashiorkor. However, Bailey reported that even in the Highlands, in hospital practice, there were more than four marasmic children to one suffering from kwashiorkor.

The random sample survey by Vines showed that amongst adults urbanization is associated with greater deposition of subcutaneous fat, higher serum albumin levels, higher serum cholesterol levels and bulkier individuals.

Goitre. The prevalence of goitre and of iodine deficiency has not yet been fully charted but the work begun by McCullagh, continued by Hennessey, and refined finally by Buttfield and Hetzel, has identified iodine deficient populations on the Huon Peninsula and in the Highlands. It has been demonstrated that injection with iodized oil can reduce goitre sizes and prevent the development of new cases (see GOITRE AND CRETINISM).

Parotid enlargement. Chronic bilateral enlargement of the parotid glands, whereby the subjects appear to be suffering from mumps, is a very prevalent condition. It is most common in the Highlands and hinterland areas and least common in the coastal areas. The condition reaches its peak prevalence between the ages of five and fifteen years, with over 50 per cent of that age group affected in both the Highlands and other parts of the mainland of the Territory of New Guinea. It is most common amongst sweet potato and sago eaters. Venkatachalam caused the enlargements to disappear by high protein feeds and considered that protein malnutrition underlay the condition. However, Farago attributed it to a physiological adaptation to a bulky unrefined starchy diet. Vines' sample survey supported the latter explanation since the highest prevalence of the condition is not during the known periods of severest protein lack, under five years of age and the reproductive phase of female life, and it is not more common amongst females than males.

Eye diseases. Vines' random sample survey found that senile cataract was most prevalent in the Highlands and least in the islands of the Territory of New Guinea. Pterygium, a leash of vessels growing over the cornea enclosed in a fold of conjunctiva, was most common in females, associated especially with the paler skinned indigenes and most common in situations where exposure to ultra-violet irradiation is very great. Defective colour vision was rarer amongst indigenes than amongst Europeans. Approximately 0.8 per cent of the population had functional blindness, defined as 6/36 visual acuity or worse in the better eye.

Ear disease. The same survey established that between 2 and 5 per cent of the population have a chronic purulent discharge from one or both middle ears. The Highlands had the lowest prevalence of this condition and the islands of the Territory of New Guinea the highest. Mild deafness was about eight times more common in children of the Territory than in Australian children. Deafness became very common in old people and affected more males than females. Much of the deafness is due to middle ear disease.

Mental disease. Mental illness is poorly understood and its extent ill defined. However, Cawte, Cuthbertson and Holland in 1967 reported an eight-fold greater prevalence of referred mental disorder amongst immigrants to the Gazelle Peninsula than amongst the local Tolai population. This suggests that the breakdown of traditional village life associated with emigration places increased mental stress upon indigenous people (see MENTAL HEALTH).

Miscellaneous. Tetanus, more common in Papua and New Guinea than in Australia, was frequently seen amongst newborn infants in certain areas of the country. In 1961 Schofield estimated that tetanus accounted for 61 neonatal deaths per 1,000 live births in the Maprik area of the East Sepik District. He subsequently demonstrated that immunization of pregnant women against tetanus results in the protection of the newborn.

Rhinoscleroma is an uncommon disease which up to date has only been recognized in the Western Highlands. It is due to a specific bacterial infection, which manifests itself by tumour formation first in the nose, then nasopharynx, but eventually may involve and obstruct larynx and trachea.

The modified Kahn-Laughlen serological test, widely used in other countries as a screening test in the detection of syphilis [q.v.] has limitations in Papua and New Guinea. It has been found that over 30 per cent of subjects tested give a positive Kahn-Laughlen test, yet until recently no syphilis had been detected in the local population. Yaws infection, due to a spirochaete almost identical with that which causes syphilis, would be expected to confer a positive Kahn-Laughlen test on any individual but it is now a rare disease. Many false 'positive results' from this test must be due to malarial or other infections.

Aid posts are the only other source of information on the morbidity pattern. The men staffing aid posts have had a minimum of formal medical education but examination of their records makes it clear that scabies and burns are much more prevalent in the Highlands than in lowland areas.

ABSENT DISEASES

Some diseases are significant because of their absence from the Territory of Papua and New Guinea. Important amongst these are smallpox and rabies, both of which occur in neighbouring Indonesia, El Tor cholera, which in 1962-3 broke out in adjacent West Irian during the South-east Asian pandemic, plague and yellow fever.

The common beef and pork tapeworms, *Taenia saginata* and *Taenia solium* respectively, do not infest the indigenous population, hydatid disease is not present, and trichinosis does not occur despite the prominence of pigs in the culture of the people. Schistosomiasis has never been reported.

K. Booth, 'Folic-Acid-Deficient Megaloblastic Anaemia associated with Child-bearing in Papua', *Medical Journal of Australia*, vol. 1, 1967.

P. M. Burchett, 'Amoebiasis in the New Guinea Western Highlands', *Medical Journal of Australia*, vol. 2, 1966.

I. H. Buttfield and B. S. Hetzel, 'The Aetiology and Control of Endemic Goitre in Eastern New Guinea', *Papua and New Guinea Medical Journal*, vol. 9, 1966.

R. A. Cooke and L. T. Champness, 'Amyloidosis in Papua and New Guinea', *Papua and New Guinea Medical Journal*, vol. 10, 1967.

———— and R. B. Rodrigue, 'Amoebic Balanitis', *Medical Journal of Australia*, vol. 1, 1964.

C. C. Curtain and others, 'A Study of the Serum Proteins of the Peoples of Papua and New Guinea', *American Journal of Tropical Medicine and Hygiene*, vol. 14, 1965.

E. H. Hipsley and F. W. Clements (eds), *Report of the New Guinea Nutrition Survey Expedition 1947*. Sydney, 1950.

I. Maddocks and L. Rovin, 'A New Guinea Population in which Blood Pressure appears to Fall as Age Advances', *Papua and New Guinea Medical Journal*, vol. 8, 1965.

I. Mann and J. Loschdorfer, *Ophthalmic Survey of the Territories of Papua and New Guinea 1955*. Port Moresby, 1955.

A. V. G. Price and J. A. Tulloch, 'Diabetes Mellitus in Papua and New Guinea', *Medical Journal of Australia*, vol. 2, 1966.

D. S. Pryor, 'The Mechanism of Anaemia in Tropical Splenomegaly', *Quarterly Journal of Medicine*, new series, vol. 36, 1967.

F. D. Schofield, A. D. Parkinson and A. Kelly, 'Changes in Haemoglobin Values and Hepatosplenomegaly produced by Control of Holoendemic Malaria', *British Medical Journal*, vol. 1, 1964.

R. F. R. Scragg, *Depopulation in New Ireland: A Study of Demography and Fertility*. Port Moresby, 1957.

W. C. Sweet, 'The Activities of the Australian Hookworm Campaign', *Medical Journal of Australia*, vol. 1, Supplement, 1924.

T. P. N. G. Department of Public Health, *Hospital Diseases Statistics 1960-1*—(annual). Port Moresby.

A. P. Vines, Epidemiological Sample Survey. Department of Public Health Report. Port Moresby, 1967 (typescript).
                                                   A. P. VINES

(*See also* MEDICAL DEMOGRAPHY).

DISTRICT ADMINISTRATION.

The Territory is divided into eighteen administrative Districts, which vary widely both in area and population. Manus is the smallest District in terms of actual land area and population. The largest District in terms of population is the Western Highlands and in terms of area, the Western District. The latter is also the most sparsely populated, although important segments of the population of Milne Bay District are dispersed over a wide area. The most densely populated District is Chimbu in the Highlands.

The number and boundaries of Districts have changed considerably since the late nineteenth century. Following World War II greater stability has prevailed and the two main reorganizations occurred in 1951, when the Central Highlands District was divided into the Eastern, Western, and Southern Highlands Districts, and in 1966, when Sepik became East and West Sepik, New Britain became East and West New Britain, and Eastern Highlands became Chimbu and Eastern Highlands. District boundaries do not coincide with any traditional social groupings and are essentially the result of administrative convenience and tradition, although attempts have usually been made to recognize existing patterns of social organization. A detailed article on each District is provided under the individual District name.

Initially, the administration of Districts (known as Divisions in Papua until 1951) was a relatively simple matter handled by a patrolling District Officer (Resident Magistrate in Papua) with perhaps a patrol officer or two, and a clerk. In 1921, the Annual Report of the Mandated Territory of New Guinea described the principal duties of District officers as being the care and welfare of the natives; opening of the Territory by patrols; and strict enforcement of the laws, particularly in native matters. Opening up the Territory continued to be an important function in many areas even into the fifties and sixties. In 1970, there was still a total area of 670 square miles (in the Western Highlands and West Sepik Districts) which was classified as not being fully under administrative control; the figure in 1950 had been 65,146 square miles. Despite this emphasis given to the establishment of control, the administration of Districts has become more intensive and complex since World War II and the inauguration of more positive policies of welfare and development.

Most Districts are too large for such policies to be effectively administered from a single headquarters and they have been progressively divided into Sub-Districts, of which there were seventy-nine in 1969. Each Sub-District has its own headquarters station and in a number of Districts there are as many as half a dozen of these. Even Sub-Districts may be too large or difficult in one way or another for fully effective administration to be based exclusively on a single station. Accordingly, they may contain patrol posts and base camps, the distinction between them being that base camps are only manned part-time as the situation demands. In the Madang District, for example, there are four Sub-Districts. Madang Sub-District has two patrol posts and a base camp; Ramu has three patrol posts and two base camps; Bogia has one patrol post; and Saidor has neither a patrol post nor a base camp. Thus officers of the central administration are based throughout the Territory, facilitating their access to village officials or Local Government Councils. In 1949, there were seventy-seven

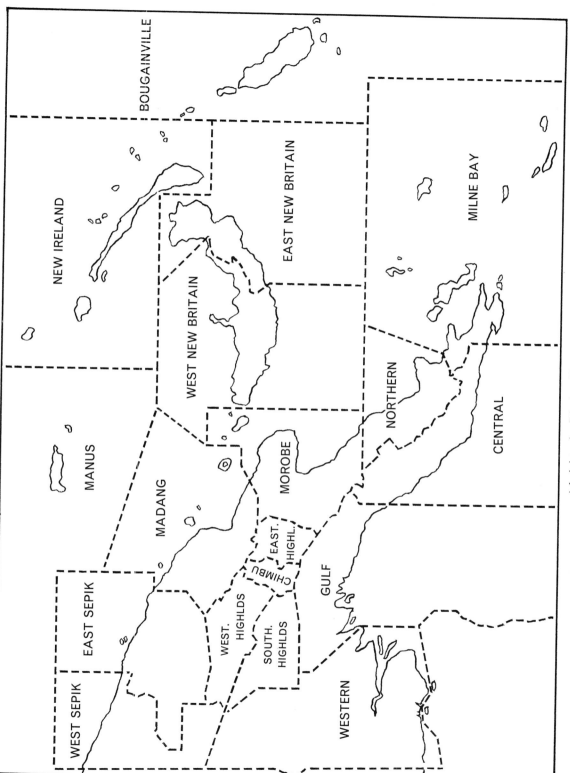

BOUGAINVILLE

NEW IRELAND

EAST NEW BRITAIN

MILNE BAY

WEST NEW BRITAIN

MANUS

NORTHERN

CENTRAL

MADANG

MOROBE

EAST SEPIK

EAST.
HIGHL.

CHIMBU

WEST SEPIK

WEST.
HIGHLDS

SOUTH.
HIGHLDS

GULF

WESTERN

Administrative Districts, November 1969.

government stations of all kinds and by 1969 their total number had more than doubled.

Before 1950 there were no Local Government Councils, and District administration was based ultimately on village officials. The system varied slightly between Papua and New Guinea, but in essence the Village Constable (Papua) and the *luluai* (New Guinea) were government-appointed headmen. Nevertheless, villagers could by a variety of means secure the appointment of the man of their choice, if they so desired, and he might or might not be a man they respected. On the initial establishment of control, administrations tended to appoint the existing 'fight-leader' or some other prominent warrior. Pacification meant, however, that some other criterion of selection had to be devised and this was difficult. In areas where development occurred, as on the Gazelle Peninsula (near Rabaul), the office was generally valued and often tended to become hereditary in a particular family. Where villagers could see less advantage in contacts with the Administration, they often shielded their real leaders from the unwanted task and put forward 'rubbish men', sometimes successfully. In an attempt to improve its channels of communication and make itself less dependent on a single man, the Papuan Administration sometimes appointed so-called 'village councillors'. These never officially met in any council and their significance varied much from place to place. On the New Guinea side, all *luluais* had *tultuls* to assist them. In some areas, where the Germans had introduced them, paramount *luluais* exercised an areal jurisdiction over a number of *luluais*. Australian attempts to promote this office in other areas were not often successful and little serious attempt was ever made to introduce the similar office of Government Chief in Papua. After 1950, these offices were progressively abolished as elected Local Government Councils were introduced, although former office-holders sometimes remained influential either as councillors or as men behind the council.

The complexity of District administration is in part due to the growth in the number of specialist officers. These are unevenly distributed. Some departments are barely represented outside of Port Moresby, some are heavily represented in some Districts only, and some are organized on a regional basis. There is no uniform definition of 'region', however, and the Department of Forests recognizes Papua, New Guinea and the New Guinea Islands; whereas the Department of Public Works recognizes Papua, New Guinea Islands, New Guinea Mainland, Highlands East and Highlands West. The Department of Public Health until 1970 was organized in terms of regions and now by administrative Districts. Naturally the demands on particular departments and the nature of the services they perform very largely determine the pattern of their organization. The net result, however, is that it is difficult to generalize about specialist services in a 'typical' District. At Sub-District level or below, few specialist departments are permanently represented, apart from Public Health and Education.

In addition to the specialists, there are generalist officers who perform administrative duties at various levels, together with 'agency functions' for those specialist departments which are not directly represented at their particular level of operations. These are the so-called *kiaps*. After World War II they belonged to the Department of District Services and Native Affairs; after 1956, to the Department of Native Affairs; after 1964, to the Department of District Administration; and since 1969, to the Division of District Administration within the Department of the Administrator. These were the men who carried out the initial exploration of the Territory and brought the people under administrative control. They maintained law and order before the advent of regular police officers and police stations in the area. They were magistrates of the Local Courts and District Courts. They introduced basic services such as postal and radio communication, roads and airstrips. They patrolled and maintained contact with village officials, before introducing local government and acting as advisers to the new councils. In the sixties, they were responsible for political education and community development, together with a variety of welfare and social services. They also had an important role as the eyes and ears of the Administration and were for a long time virtually the central administration's sole source of information concerning the villagers, their numbers, hopes, fears, and likely reactions to proposed changes.

In the 1970s *kiaps* (i.e. field officers of the Division of District Administration) still perform all or some of these functions in many areas, but their tasks are complicated (although potentially facilitated) by the existence of specialist officers in the field and the fact that some 90 per cent of the population is now under elected Local Government Councils. Increasingly, therefore, their role has become one of filling the interstices and making the system work. There is a need for an administrative framework within which specialist officers and councils can operate; the centre needs information; and the people still need assistance to maximize their overall benefit from those innovations which might have relevance for them. In particular, the new positive policies of overall development can only work with the active co-operation, participation, and initiatives of villagers themselves. All field officers must therefore engage more often in political or bargaining relationships (whether explicit or implicit). They must stimulate the release of local resources and to some extent direct, without stifling, various types of self-help activity.

In the period under review, District administration in New Guinea has faced two types of problems: (1) both the new policies and the new structures of local government required the development of a new relationship between the central administration and villagers to replace the simple hierarchical or 'command' pattern of organization which, in broad terms, operated in the days of village officials; and (2) there was a growing need for co-ordination between officers of the central administration operating within Districts. Such co-ordination is the responsibility of the District Commissioner and at Sub-District level, of the Assistant District Commissioner (known as the Assistant District Officer before the reorganization of 1964).

The District Commissioner (an office created in 1950) is the personal representative of the Administrator in each District. Within it, he is the principal executive officer; responsible for peace and good order; and the efficient conduct of all public business. Nevertheless, specialist officers remain responsible to their own departments in matters of policy and must look to them for the advancement of their careers. Between 1955 and 1964, this applied also to generalist officers; since District commissioners belonged to the Department of the Administrator and not to the Department of Native Affairs. In essence, District commissioners were expected to produce co-ordination, without being able to command it, except in times of emergency. The need for co-ordination became particularly apparent after the adoption of the Territory's first five-year plan and in 1965 led to the establishment of District Co-ordinating Committees. These are chaired by the District Commissioner, with his deputy as executive officer and representative of the Department (later Division) of District Administration. The Departments of Public Health, Education and Agriculture are also represented by their senior District representative. In some Districts, other locally significant departments (e.g. Forests) are also represented and the committee has the power to co-opt other advisers, as agenda items require. The objective is to develop a 'District team', which can reach agreement on priorities and evolve a co-ordinated approach to developmental problems. Where disagreements persist, however, they can only be finally resolved on an inter-departmental level.

In 1971, legislation was passed which provides for the establishment of area authorities. This followed growing demands for local and non-official participation in the making of decisions at District level. A minimum of two-thirds of the membership of these area authorities will consist of members of Local Government Councils and it has been officially stated that, where established, the area authority will (amongst other things) replace the District Co-ordinating Committee as the body setting priorities in the rural development programme. It should be stressed that there may be more than one area authority in a District and that where there is only one, it need not cover the whole of the District. However, it is not envisaged that area authorities will straddle District boundaries. Thus area authorities will certainly have an important impact on District administration, as currently practised. In particular, the District commissioners (and local members of the House of Assembly) have the right to attend and speak at meetings, but do not have a vote nor can they be counted towards a quorum.   IAN GROSART

J. K. McCarthy, *Patrol into Yesterday*. Melbourne, 1963; L. P. Mair, *Australia in New Guinea*. 2nd ed., Melbourne, 1970; C. A. W. Monckton, *Some Experiences of a New Guinea Resident Magistrate*. 2 vols, London, 1927; J. H. P. Murray, *Papua or British New Guinea*. London, 1912; ——— *Papua of Today*. London, 1925; R. S. Parker, 'The Growth of Territory Administration', in *New Guinea on the Threshold*, ed. E. K. Fisk. Canberra, 1966.

DIVINATION. The need for a sense of order and control appears to be a basic feature of human existence. Men everywhere would like to understand the past, especially in so far as it bears on the present; they would like to control the future; and they would like also to plan, decide, and act unimpeded by the uncertainty and ambiguity that so often complicate human affairs. Divination—practices designed for communication with esoteric or extraordinary sources about past and future events—is one of the means whereby people, particularly those without science, try to extend knowledge beyond everyday limits and so gain in confidence, self-assurance, and determination.

Divination may at times be directed to nothing more vital than the location of lost possessions, as Fortune showed in his observations on Manus diviners and mediums, but often it will be found to centre on a society's fundamental concerns. In New Guinea its most important applications have to do with sorcery and death. Among tribal peoples death is not generally looked upon only as an individual or family misfortune; the death of anyone other than the very young or very old is interpreted as a loss to the entire social group. Such catastrophes cannot be philosophically accepted as 'natural' or inevitable; for always one may ask: Why this particular person at this particular time? As many New Guineans see it, the only acceptable conclusion is that, with a few possible exceptions, death is caused by the malevolence of sorcerers.

In these circumstances divination emerges as a procedure whereby an otherwise unanswerable—or, in any event, heavily charged—question: Who is guilty? can be answered without anyone's having to assume responsibility for doing so. Indeed, it would appear that there are times when even though most persons are thinking along certain lines and would like to commit themselves, no one is willing to come out and say so; it is then that a diviner, acting as a neutral vehicle through which information is relayed, may catalyse action by saying precisely what everyone wants to hear. Thus ultimate responsibility for the difficult or awkward decision as to who is to be charged with a death may rest not with any individual but with a culturally sanctioned technique and a source of information outside and beyond the range of ordinary social intercourse.

As might perhaps be expected, very often it is the dead man's ghost or corpse which is somehow the source of information. The dead man may signal—whistle, twitch, defecate—when confronted with the sorcerer or his name; he may even speak directly to a kinsman, as Williams was told in western Papua.

A divination rite observed among the Gimi, an Eastern Highlands people living south-west of

Lufa, began almost immediately after the death of a middle-aged man and was predicated on his co-operation. The sinister course of this man's illness—severe abdominal distension, lingering coma, and death, probably from cancer and intestinal obstruction—left no doubt in anyone's mind that he had been the victim of a sorcerer, which in the Gimi scheme of things meant someone in an enemy village; so that it was incumbent on his kinsmen to identify the guilty party and take revenge. The corpse lay in a large hut surrounded by dozens of kinsmen and neighbours. A tuft of hair from the head was fastened near the tip of a war arrow which was placed point down in a bamboo tube. The man performing the rite, an affinal kinsman living in the dead man's village, assisted by two others, blew thick draughts of pipe smoke on to the tube; he then inhaled deeply and repeatedly until he passed into a trance-like state. Eventually his hands began to tremble as the tube, with the arrow rattling violently inside, seemed to vibrate of its own accord. Now a younger kinsman of the deceased turned to the corpse and whispered that it must help them identify the sorcerer. As he softly spoke the names of suspects the arrow rattled even more excitedly; the ghost was trying to reply. Had the young man lighted on the name of the sorcerer, the arrow should have leaped from the tube; but on this occasion they were not to be successful. In former days it would have been incumbent on these men to reach a decision, but now that warfare has been abolished, they are perhaps less driven to identify a killer on whom it would be difficult to take proper revenge.

In this connection it is worth noting that ghosts themselves are sometimes believed to be responsible for illnesses and deaths. In the Western Highlands Kyaka diviners, using techniques also demanding the use of arrows, seek to identify ancestral ghosts responsible for illness and also to learn why they are angry and how they can be appeased. In contrast, Kyaka women diviners invoke ghosts of their agnatic kinsmen for information about diverse misfortunes—suggesting that ancestral ghosts are conceived as sources of power that are at times harmful, at other times benevolent.

Finally it may be remarked that, divorced from their immediate contexts, methods of divining can be and have been looked upon simply as cultural phenomena that diffuse from one area to another, much as might a technique, say, for making arrows or pots. But there is this important consideration that should be borne in mind: not only the form of a divining technique but also its essential meaning and function may change as it diffuses. Mead describes, for instance, how new divining techniques reaching the Arapesh of the Sepik were remodelled to accord with the spirit of Arapesh culture. To understand divination in a particular place, therefore, it must be considered in proper context.

In conclusion, divination practices are understandable as culturally sanctioned procedures for making vital decisions in the face of little or no knowledge—procedures that, as Park has phrased it, have the effect of 'stamping with a mark of special legitimacy' actions bearing on fundamental concerns of human social existence.

R. N. H. Bulmer, 'The Kyaka of the Western Highlands', pp. 144-6, in *Gods Ghosts and Men in Melanesia*, ed. P. Lawrence and M. J. Meggitt. Melbourne, 1965; R. F. Fortune, *Manus Religion*. Philadelphia, 1935; L. Glick, 'Medicine as an Ethnographic Category: The Gimi of the New Guinea Highlands', *Ethnology*, vol. 6, 1967, pp. 50-1; M. Mead, *The Mountain Arapesh, II: Supernaturalism*. Anthropological Papers of the American Museum of Natural History, vol. 37, pp. 433-7. New York, 1939-41; G. Park, 'Divination and Its Social Contexts', *Journal of the Royal Anthropological Institute*, vol. 93, 1963; F. E. Williams, *Papuans of the Trans-Fly*, pp. 356-7. Oxford, 1936.   LEONARD B. GLICK

DOLPHINS AND WHALES. The dolphins, porpoises and whales, the most aberrant of all mammals [q.v.], are highly adapted for life in their aquatic environment. They are found in all oceans and seas, and a few species inhabit the fresh waters of some of the large rivers of Asia and South America. They are classified in the order Cetacea, and the living species are contained in two very distinct suborders, the Odontoceti (toothed whales) and the Mysticeti (baleen or whalebone whales). If we allow for some exceptions in the embryonic stage, the mysticetes do not have teeth, and are characterized by the possession of baleen or whalebone plates suspended from the upper jaws with which they filter out the small marine organisms on which they feed.

Very little has been published on the whales and dolphins of the waters of Papua New Guinea and only a dozen species have been recorded to date, but it is fairly certain that some others known from Indonesian and Queensland waters will be found eventually in the area.

A number of the cetacea known from Papua New Guinea waters are fairly well-known species of wide distribution in the Pacific as well as other oceans. These will be treated more briefly than those that are either of restricted tropical occurrence or that occur in particular abundance in the area.

Toothed whales, including dolphins (Odontoceti). Of the dozen species known at present the most frequently sighted are some of the 'ocean' or 'spotted dolphins' belonging to the genus *Stenella*. The taxonomy of this group has been described as 'being in a chaotic state', so pending further revision the names used here for these and also for the other cetacea will follow the list of scientific names compiled by Hershkovitz (1966).

The spinner dolphin, *Stenella longirostris*, occurs throughout the waters of Papua New Guinea and is especially abundant along the north coast of New Guinea through Manus and New Britain to the southern part of the Solomon Islands. Frequently it can be seen in large schools of several hundred, and sometimes schools containing thousands of these spectacular animals may be sighted. Their habit of leaping vertically from the water while rotating rapidly on their long axis has given the popular name to this species. Frame counts

(top) Spinner dolphin, *Stenella longirostris*, from Astrolabe Bay, New Guinea.
(bottom) Bottlenosed dolphin, *Tursiops truncatus*, rear, caught off Queensland but occurring in waters of the Territory. Front, *Sotalia borneensis* also caught off Queensland but likely to occur in waters of the Territory.

of several movie sequences taken near New Guinea show that they can spin at rates of six or more revolutions per second although the method of achieving this and the function of the performance is far from clear. Sometimes in a large school, several spinners may be seen in the air at once but more usually isolated individuals emerge suddenly from apparently random positions in the group, spin rapidly and then fall back with a splash. This ceases when the school is actively on the move.

Spinner dolphins are relatively small, reaching about 6 feet in length, and in summer the cows are often seen accompanied by calves little more than 2 feet long. The body is slender while the beak is proportionately very long and armed with about 50 peg-like delicate teeth in each side of the upper and lower jaw, making 200 in all.

The body colour is dark slate above (without spotting) and creamy white below with a distinct dark band running back from the eye to the base of the fin which is also dark in colour. There is a well-developed dorsal fin which tapers posteriorly and can be distinguished from the more hook-shaped fin of other *Stenella* species in the area. In some schools the underside appears to have a distinct orange-pink or reddish tinge but it is difficult to tell whether this is a lighting effect on the normally creamy surface. Those with the latter colour darken rapidly through pink to reddish after death, but there have been no reports of a mixture of cream and pinkish living individuals within the same school.

It is still at least possible that there are two kinds of spinner dolphin present, in which case the second is probably *S. roseiventris* which Hershkovitz regards as a synonym for *S. longirostris*. Certainly Solomon Island natives who hunt dolphins distinguish two forms for which they use separate names, but there is as yet insufficient material to determine the status of these varieties.

Formerly, spinner dolphins were hunted from Nova village, Buka Passage, for meat and for the teeth which were used for currency. Today this still occurs farther south in the Solomon Islands on Malaita. However, the species remains abundant in the region and it is recorded from warmer waters in the Atlantic and Indian as well as the Pacific Ocean. Off California there is evidence from fish otoliths in stomach contents that the spinner dolphin feeds regularly in waters 800 feet or more below the surface.

A larger 'spotted dolphin' provisionally identified as *Stenella dubia* has no general common name but is known as *unubolu* to many Solomon Islanders. It has a similar distribution in the region and is almost as abundant as the spinner. *S. dubia* grows to 8 or 9 feet in length, is proportionately more solidly built with shorter and stouter beak than the spinner and has a distinct partial hook at the rear edge of the dorsal fin. There is an area of dark grey, sometimes with a bluish tinge extending from the beak, over the back of the head and dorsal side of the body, as an elongate saddle-shaped region ending about a foot behind the fin. The dorsal side of the tail peduncle is therefore somewhat lighter and is a greyish colour matching that of the sides and most of the underside. All or part of this lighter area may be dappled with spots of dark grey. The distribution and density of dappling is quite variable even between individuals in the same school. There is similar variation in the presence or absence of whitish lips and white tip to the beak. These latter features therefore seem less likely to be helpful in diagnosing *Stenella* species than has been believed previously.

On occasion, individuals in a school of *S. dubia* will leap above the sea but they tend to emerge much more obliquely than the spinner. Their movement follows an arc in which they may show slow rolling or sometimes no rotational movement at all so, even at a distance, there is little difficulty in distinguishing the leaps of this species from that of the spinner dolphin.

The teeth in this species are fewer (about 140 total) but markedly larger than in the spinner. They are twice as valuable to the natives who particularly prize this species in areas where hunting still occurs. Stomach contents indicate that squid is the main item of diet although fish are sometimes taken. The size of embryos in different seasons suggests that calving occurs in early spring.

The bottlenosed dolphin, *Tursiops truncatus*, occurs in all oceans ranging from cool temperate to subtropical and tropical waters and has been the species most intensively studied in oceanaria, where they have proved particularly suitable for training as performing animals. Television sequences and films have made the appearance of this species familiar to a very large public. It is more heavy bodied and larger (up to 10 feet in length) than the preceding species with a relatively shorter though well-defined beak, below which the lower jaw projects slightly. Teeth are considerably larger than in the two preceding species, measuring ⅜ inch in diameter, but the total number present is reduced to about eighty to ninety erupted. The fin is well developed and concave posteriorly. Colouration is predominantly lead grey above, shading to light grey at the sides and ventrally. Differences in colour and average size between the populations in various seas have often been reported but the conservative view is to regard these as part of a single species with possibly some subspecies of which that found in the New Guinea region is regarded as *T. truncatus aduncus*.

These dolphins travel in small schools of from three or four to a dozen or so and are fairly common along the north coast of New Guinea. It seems likely that they occur throughout the area.

The Irrawaddy dolphin, *Orcaella brevirostris*, reaches about 7 feet in length, has a very rounded and completely beakless head with a distinct and surprisingly mobile neck for a cetacean. The flippers are large and blunt while the fin is small, roughly triangular and situated more than half-way back along the body. The colour of those in waters of the Territory is light brown above merging to cream or dark cream below. There are less than twenty teeth in each side of the upper and lower jaws and in older animals these are usually bluntly rounded. These dolphins swim relatively slowly but are capable of much more twisting and flexing of

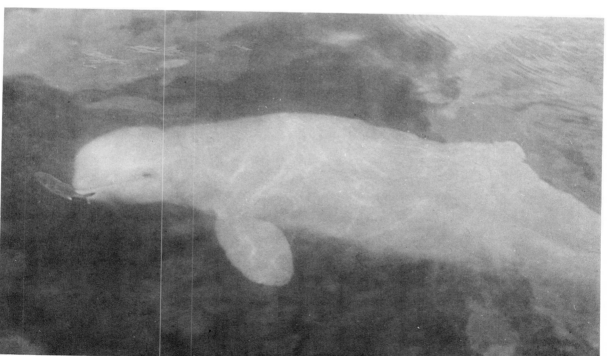

(top) 'Spotted' dolphin provisionally identified as *Stenella dubia* from Rabaul, New Guinea.
(bottom) Irrawaddy dolphin, *Orcaella brevirostris*, from Cairns but known in the Gulf of Papua.

the body than most other species. The combination of their size, colour, blunt head and over-all appearance has led to this species at a distance being confused with dugongs [q.v.].

As its name suggests, the Irrawaddy dolphin was first described from animals collected in the Irrawaddy River. Until recently it was thought to be confined to a region between the Bay of Bengal and Borneo including a number of rivers in which it may be found some hundreds of miles from the sea. Recently published data record sightings throughout Indonesian coastal waters to the north coast of West Irian while specimens accidentally caught in fishing nets in the Gulf of Papua extend the known range to the waters of the Territory, and others have been seen off the Queensland coast to south of Cairns. The species therefore has a much more extensive range than formerly believed but has so far not been recorded off the north coast of New Guinea or in waters further east. Throughout its distribution the marine populations have been seen within a mile or so off shore, travelling in small groups of about half a dozen or less. So far as is known, the species is exclusively a fish-eater.

The false killer whale, *Pseudorca crassidens*, grows to about 18 feet in length, is usually entirely black in colour with a blunt beakless snout which projects slightly beyond the lower jaw. The flippers are small slender and tapering while the fin is small with a concave posterior margin. There are approximately ten large teeth in each side of the upper and lower jaws and they are circular in cross-section.

This species is seldom sighted at sea but large schools have stranded at scattered points along the coasts of all the main oceans from the latitudes of northern Europe to those of Capetown and New Zealand in the south. It is clearly a very widely distributed species and has been captured between Papua and Australia and sighted north of New Guinea.

The killer whale, *Orcinus orca*, is a large species in which males may reach 30 feet in length and females about 18 feet. The blunt head has a very slight depression above the snout demarcating a vestigial beak but the most striking feature especially in large males is the very high, steeply triangular fin from 2 or 3 feet up to 6 feet in height. This and the conspicuous colour pattern of black dorsally, except for a light saddle behind the fin, and prominent creamy white patch above the eye and along the underside extending upwards as a sharply defined patch on either side of the tail peduncle, make this whale easy to recognize. It has large rounded flippers and large teeth, ten or more in each side of the upper and lower jaw, which are oval in cross-section.

Killer whales are widely known from all oceans and have a probably exaggerated reputation for voracity, speed and fierceness. While they are known to prey on seals, penguins and smaller cetacea, they also eat squid. There are dramatic reports of pack attacks on large whales but doubtful evidence that this occurs unless the whale is already injured or sick, and there is no conclusive evidence

that they have attacked man. Specimens in captivity respond as well as dolphins to their trainers and training programmes. In Papua New Guinea waters the most frequent sightings reported are those from off the coast of north-west New Guinea.

Risso's dolphin, *Grampus griseus*, is of moderate size reaching about 12 feet with rounded forehead and only a very slight indication of a beak. It has a distinctive prominent fin tapering backwards along its leading edge and concave to almost vertical with a posteriorly recurved tip. The flippers are narrow and moderately long. The colour is grey above, shading darker over the tail and top of the flippers, then merging gradually to light grey or creamy white along the underside. Teeth are large but confined to the lower jaw where three to seven may occur towards the tip of each side. Food appears to be squid and cuttlefish only.

The pilot whale, *Globicephala melaena*, is a well-known species in which the adult males sometimes exceed 25 feet in length but the females are smaller. The top of the head is a large blunt structure bulging forward above a slight depression indicating the margin of an ill-defined beak. The fin has a long base but is relatively low except in adult males and it slopes upwards gradually from the front, to end in a concave hinder margin. The flippers are long, narrow and pointed. Most specimens are black all over except for a paler anchor-shaped marking on the throat and occasionally a lighter saddle on either side behind the fin. There are ten teeth on either side of each jaw confined towards the anterior region. Squid and cuttlefish form the main food.

This highly gregarious species occurs in large schools sometimes containing hundreds of individuals of varied sizes, and mass strandings of entire schools are well known from many parts of the world ranging from the north Atlantic to Australia, Tasmania and New Zealand. Regional differences in flipper size, skull proportions and colour markings have often been described but the conservative view is to regard these as races within *G. melaena*.

Pilot whales have been observed basking or feeding on many occasions in Astrolabe Bay and specimens from there have been brought to oceanaria in Australia.

The pigmy sperm whale, *Kogia breviceps*, grows to about 10 to 12 feet in length. The bluntly rounded upper part of the head is much larger and extends well beyond the end of the lower jaw. There is a small more or less triangular fin a little behind the middle of the back. The colouration grades from dark grey or black above to lighter or even creamy grey below. Teeth are slender, curved backwards and confined to the lower jaw where nine to fourteen occur on each side.

These small whales are seldom seen alive and the distribution is therefore deduced from strandings which are normally of single specimens rather than of schools. They appear to occur in temperate and tropical waters in all oceans and one stranding has been recorded from Bogia on the north coast of New Guinea.

The sperm whale, *Physeter catodon*, is the larg-

Pilot whales, *Globicephala melaena*, basking in Astrolabe Bay, New Guinea.

est and best known of the toothed whales. Males grow to 60 feet but females are less than 40 feet in length. The relatively enormous barrel-shaped head overhanging a long narrow lower jaw bearing up to about thirty large teeth on each side, has been illustrated many times because this whale formed the main quarry of the great Yankee whaling fleet in the nineteenth century and the species still forms a very significant part of the present world catch of whales. Some were caught in New Guinea waters last century although this area was never a major whaling ground. Isolated individuals and small schools are today a not uncommon sight over deeper waters where they search for the giant squid that forms the major part of their diet. They occur in all oceans, but polar waters are penetrated by large males only.

Bottlenosed or beaked whales of the family Ziphiidae appear to be unrecorded from the New Guinea region. Very little is known about most species in this group but it would be surprising if those recorded in other tropical waters are totally unrepresented in the area.

There are several other small odontocetes which have been collected or recorded in Indonesian waters on the one side and Queensland waters on the other, suggesting a high probability that they will be located eventually in Papua New Guinea waters. These include the rough-toothed dolphin, *Steno bredanensis*; the Bornean white dolphin *Sotalia borneensis*; and the broad-beaked dolphin, *Peponocephala electra=Lagenorhynchus electra*.

On the other hand the southern right-whale dolphin, *Lissodelphis peroni*, listed from New Guinea early last century appears to be distributed in temperate and cool temperate waters, and its occurrence in New Guinea waters needs confirmation.

Baleen or whalebone whales (Mysticeti). These large filter-feeding cetacea in general spend most of their lives in cold to temperate waters of all oceans moving briefly into subtropical and sometimes tropical waters during the breeding season. However, the major part of each population remains farther from the equator than the waters of Papua New Guinea and those that do occur are probably mainly stragglers.

The humpback whale, *Megaptera novaeangliae*, is the only baleen whale positively identified in New Guinea waters. Females may grow to 50 feet in length and males to about 47 feet. They can be distinguished by their very large flippers (up to 15 feet in length), small dorsal fin, prominent throat grooves and frequent habit of breaching almost completely clear of the water. During such leaps the huge flippers are strikingly evident and the black dorsal surface is usually clearly demarcated from the white below, although there is considerable variability in the amount of white present. Humpbacks occur singly, in pairs or in small groups and females at these latitudes are often accompanied by newborn calves. They migrate annually to and from the feeding grounds in Antarctic waters where they were formerly hunted. They were also caught from land stations in Australia, New Zealand and Norfolk Island. Following severe depletion they have been given total protection. Prior to their decline, humpbacks were occasionally seen as far north as the Gulf of Papua and sometimes as far past the Solomon Islands as New Britain, but there is little evidence relating to their presence along the north coast of New Guinea.

Rorquals of the genus *Balaenoptera* including blue, fin, sei, Bryde's and minke or little piked whales have all been recorded from Indonesian waters but so far none have been identified specifically from New Guinea waters. The appearance and biology of these whales together with humpbacks have been described extensively in many publications dealing with the Antarctic Ocean and with whaling in general.

R. J. Harrison and J. E. King, *Marine Mammals.* London, 1965; P. Hershkovitz, 'Catalog of Living Whales', *United States National Museum Bulletin* no. 246, 1966; J. R. Norman and F. C. Fraser, *Giant Fishes, Whales and Dolphins.* London, 1948; E. J. Slijper, *Whales.* London, 1962.   W. H. DAWBIN

DUGONG. This (*Dugong dugon*) is the only living species in the family Dugongidae, which together with the three species of manatees (Trichechidae) of the tropical and subtropical parts of West Africa and eastern North and South America, comprise the mammalian order Sirenia. The sirenians are highly adapted to an aquatic, usually marine, mode of life.

Dugongs are found along shallow tropical and subtropical coasts, around islands, and in suitable estuaries from the Red Sea and East Africa, through India, Ceylon and Malaya, and Indonesia to Australia and New Guinea. Despite their apparent wide natural distribution they have become increasingly rare in areas where they were once abundant.

In northern Australia, where the dugong is legally protected from slaughter, except by the Aborigines, they are still commonly found. In New Guinea the known range of distribution is from the Eilanden River in West Irian, around the Papuan coast and through the New Guinea islands, with small numbers being found around Manus Island, New Ireland and Bougainville.

The coastal Motu-speaking people in the Central District of Papua in particular have a strong tradition of dugong hunting, the Motu name for dugong being *rui*, while the Pidgin English name is *bulmakau bilong solwara* or *bonon*. The dugongs were prized for their flesh, oil, hides, and the small ivory tusks which were used for ornamental purposes. Spears and nets are the main methods of capture. In the Trobriand and Manus Islands the very strong three- to six-inch mesh nets are woven from pandanus palm leaves, while in the Siassi Islands the bark of a tree is used.

Dugong hunting is still practised today in many areas. With the mechanization of canoes and the use of more efficient nets and weapons the number of dugongs appears to be decreasing, although no detailed statistics are available. As development progresses year by year the desire to hunt

the dugong is decreasing, although no conservation measures have been introduced.

The dugong is a spindle-shaped creature with flipper-like fore-limbs, no hind-limbs or dorsal fin, and a horizontally notched tail. By nature it is a sluggish animal, though if disturbed it can swim very fast. The average length ranges between six and nine feet and it weighs between three and four hundred pounds. The skin is tough and practically hairless except around the mouth.

Dugongs in general are gregarious, living together in twos or threes. Their sight is poor, the eyes small and located on the side of the head, but they have very acute hearing even when submerged. Dugongs are air-breathers, coming to the surface every two or three minutes, although they have been known to remain submerged for up to sixteen minutes.

Mating is said to occur in very shallow water but the frequency of breeding is not known. Usually one young is born at a time. The young is suckled by the female from two mammae located on the chest. The female dugong is said to hold herself vertical and clasp the young with her fore-limbs to the mammae.

Dugongs are one of the few remaining aquatic herbivores, thriving on many different types of aquatic vegetation, the main species being the *Zostera*-like sea-grass, *Posidonia australis*. Their powerful muscular lips, armed with stiff hairs and bristles, are well adapted for dealing with all but the toughest vegetable matter.

G. C. L. Bertram and C. K. Ricardo Bertram, 'The Dugong', *Nature*, vol. 209, 1966; S. Jones, 'The Dugong *Dugong dugon* (Müller)—its present status in the seas around India with observations on its behaviour in captivity', *International Zoo Yearbook*, vol. 7, 1967; L. Engel and the Editors of *Life, The Sea.* Life Nature Library, New York, 1963; W. Saville-Kent, *The Great Barrier Reef of Australia.* London, 1893; E. P. Walker and others, *Mammals of the World*, vol. 2. Baltimore, 1964.

R. R. PYNE

DUTCH NEW GUINEA. The western half of New Guinea was administered by Holland from 1828 until 1962, when control was assumed by the United Nations for a short period, before handing over to Indonesia in April 1963. Elsewhere in the Encyclopaedia the area is referred to as West Irian.

EXPLORATION AND GOVERNMENT

The arrival of the first Europeans in east Indonesian waters in the early part of the sixteenth century had little impact on western New Guinea. A few fitful attempts to find profitable trade in New Guinea by the Dutch East India Company served to confirm the Company's belief that only trouble could be obtained from the island's inhospitable shores. The Company was satisfied to conclude treaties with the potentates of Ternate, Tidore, and Batjan in eastern Indonesia which in effect burdened these rulers with 'protecting' the western tip of New Guinea and its off-shore islands from foreign intrusion.

The first Western attempt at effective occupation was made by Lieutenant John Hayes in 1793. Hayes had a small wooden fort built near present-day Manokwari, raised the British flag, proclaimed himself 'Governor of New Albion', and declared the whole northern coast of New Guinea annexed to the British Crown. But Hayes's ambitious scheme failed to receive official support and quickly collapsed.

In 1826 ill-founded rumours that the British were establishing a post in south-west New Guinea spurred the Dutch into activity. It led to the founding of a settlement, Merkusoord, at Triton Bay, the building of a fort, Fort du Bus, and a formal act of annexation on 24 August 1828 which claimed for the Netherlands Crown the territory from the 141st meridian east longitude in the south to the Cape of Good Hope (Cape Yamarsba) on the north-west of the Vogelkop. The Dutch held on precariously for a few years but had to abandon Fort du Bus in 1836. During subsequent decades their activity was once more limited to occasional coastal expeditions, the placing of markers with the royal coat of arms, and the appointment of 'chiefs'.

Repeated complaints in the early 1890s by the Administrator of British New Guinea, Sir William MacGregor [q.v.] about incursions of Tugeri (Marind) head-hunters and his accusation that the Netherlands was evading its sovereign duties once more forced the hand of the Dutch. First they made an abortive attempt to place a border post in Tugeri territory at Selirika (Sarire); then they agreed to a more natural boundary at the Bensbach River—described in the Anglo-Dutch Convention of 1895—and, finally, they set up administrative posts at Manokwari and Fakfak in 1898, followed by the founding of Merauke in 1902.

Most of Dutch New Guinea at this time was still *terra incognita*, only the coastline and a few rivers had been charted. In 1906, however, Governor-General J. B. van Heutsz sent Captain H. Colijn to advise him on what should be done with this totally neglected part of the Dutch colonial empire. Colijn's report, which urged systematic exploration of the entire territory before other steps could be taken, led to the formation of four military patrols which from different directions made a concerted effort at exploration between 1907 and 1915. But for the outbreak of World War I the central cordillera would have been forced to part with its mysteries. Nevertheless, the results of these expeditions were impressive as shown by the elaborate report, *Verslag van de Militaire Exploratie*, and the magnificent map, *Schetskaart van Nieuw Guinea* (scale 1:1,000,000).

Scientific explorations meanwhile began to play an important role. A Dutch expedition under H. A. Lorentz reached the snowfields of Wilhelmina Peak in November 1909; a performance repeated by the 1912-13 expedition under A. Franssen Herderschee. Also in 1913, a British expedition under Dr A. F. R. Wollaston reached the snowline of the Carstensz mountains. In December 1921 the Wilhelmina Peak was climbed from the north via the Mamberamo by an expedition under Captains J. A. van Overeem and J. H. G. Kremer. On the way, this expedition entered the Swart valley, close to the Baliem. This area was not visited again until the 1950s. A lull in exploratory activity after 1921 was broken in the mid-thirties by the search for oil initiated by the Nederlandsch Nieuw Guinee Petroleum Maatschappij (NNGPM), Netherlands New Guinea Oil Company. The NNGPM lent a helping hand in aerial surveys of the Carstensz mountains and an expedition under Dr A. H. Colijn in 1938 was able to make a quick thrust which reached what probably was one of its highest peaks, the Nga poeloe (16,500 feet). Also explored during 1937-8 was the Wissel Lakes area at the western end of the central cordillera with its large Kapauku population. Finally, in the region south-west from Hollandia, the third Archbold expedition provided new information and led to the discovery, from the air, of the densely populated Grand Valley of the Baliem. However, there still remained a sizeable sector of the central mountains upon which European explorers had never set foot.

The bursts of great exploratory activity in the 1907-15, 1920-2 and 1935-8 periods were rarely followed by the establishment of administrative control. Dutch authority, therefore, remained almost exclusively limited to the coastal fringes and the more easily accessible parts of the interior. As late as 1937 the number of inhabitants claimed to be under administrative control was 200,000. This may seem a respectable total on the basis of the 1930 population estimate of 330,000 but by 1937 this figure had been raised to 466,000, still some 250,000 short of more reliable post-World War II figures. A handful of Dutch officials—fifteen in 1937—manned the main posts at Hollandia, Sarmi, Serui, Manokwari, Sorong, Inanwatan, Ajamaru, Fakfak, Japero, Mappi, and Merauke. Subordinate (Indonesian) officials were in charge of some fifty smaller stations. As practically all missionary and educational activities outside the major centres were also carried out by east Indonesians these men, and their wives, bore the brunt of extending Dutch colonial rule.

As far as administrative organization is concerned, one must first make a distinction between that part under direct rule—the south-eastern sector, since 1901—and the remainder which continued to be ruled indirectly under the Sultan of Tidore. In actual fact, rule by Tidore was a legal fiction and amounted to being direct rule *de facto*.

In terms of administrative structure, eastern Indonesia generally followed the pattern of Java with a division into residencies and their respective subdivisions, the *Afdelingen* (under Assistant Residents) and *Onderafdelingen* (under *Controleurs*). The south-eastern part briefly formed an *Afdeling* under an Assistant Resident but in 1913 was demoted to being an *Onderafdeling* of the *Afdeling* Tual, Kai Islands, which was part of the Residency of Ternate. In the remaining part there were originally two *Afdelingen*, headed by

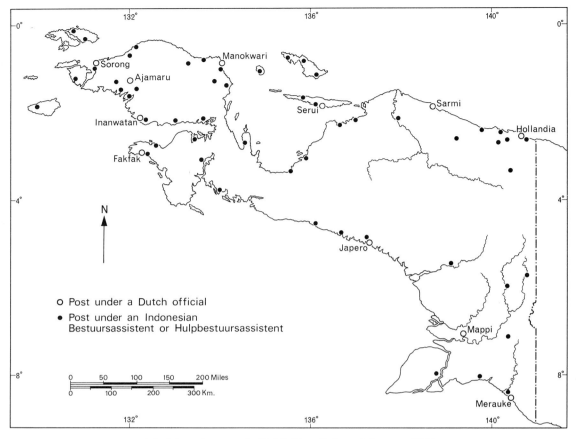

Administrative posts in Dutch New Guinea, 1 January 1937.

Assistant Residents. These formed part of the Residency of Amboina, with the exception of a brief period of optimism following the conclusion of the military explorations when Dutch New Guinea formed a Residency of its own under Resident C. Lulofs.

In the absence of qualified local staff, as was the case in Java, there also existed for the territories outside Java a special Dutch *hulpcorps* (auxiliary corps) composed of *Gezaghebbers* and *Candidaat-Gezaghebbers* who did not possess the qualifications required for the regular Dutch administrative corps. With Dutch New Guinea 'the last waggon on the train' and one of the most undesirable outposts, the majority of its *Onderafdelingen* were headed by such officials. The *Onderafdelingen* themselves were divided into *Districten* under Indonesian officials who after 1929 had the titles of *Bestuursassistenten* and *Hulpbestuursassistenten*.

The practical problems faced in administering the territory were overwhelming. There was first the poor, time-consuming, connection between the Resident's headquarters in the Moluccas and the various officials within the enormous area of his jurisdiction. In practice, this meant that proper guidance and supervision was absent, especially in the New Guinea periphery. There existed an additional problem of attracting and keeping qualified personnel; few were eager to serve in 'the Devil's own country'; most considered an assignment to New Guinea, or even the Moluccas, a punitive transfer. The calibre of administration, then, was almost entirely dependent upon the whims of a succession of poorly trained local officials. The absence of a strong community opinion among the Papuans and their fatalistic acceptance of the intruders left free reign, moreover, to potential abuses and malpractices. Indeed, to several east Indonesian officials and evangelists, the primitive Papuans were just barely human. A fourth problem faced by the administration lay in the field of taxation. Given the almost total lack of a money economy it could be argued that it was better to do without levying taxes. Taxation—frequently paid in kind—was seen as the only way, however, of forcing Papuans to contribute in a modest way to the export of products. In tax-delinquent areas officials silently engaged in the practice of forcing the people to deliver their products to them. The officials then auctioned the goods off to the highest bidder, most often a Chinese trader, with the producer receiving what was left after taxes had been paid. This unsatisfactory practice obviously played into the hands of those eager to supplement their income.

The extension of administrative control was greatly helped by the activities of the Protestant and Catholic missionary organizations. Missionaries often preceded the flag and were in effect seen as 'the government' by the local population. They made 'laws', laid down regulations, and administered justice. This situation continued even after the arrival of officials, most of whom were more than willing to leave the arduous tasks mentioned above to those whose residence there was longer and whose familiarity with the language and customs of the Papuans was far greater than theirs. It was only when the calibre of administrative personnel improved in the 1930s that the 'illegal' interference of the missionaries in administrative and judicial affairs began to create friction and led to the gradual 'usurpation' of powers by the administration.

In summary, the minimal effect of the pre-World War II administrative efforts appear to have been well stated by one of the Assistant Residents in 1937 when he remarked that in the administered parts of Dutch New Guinea 'The greatest practical result of our administration is, apart from the existence of peace and order, that the people have become accustomed to the payment of taxes and—if there is sufficient inspection and supervision—the regular performance of corvée'.

NATIVE ADMINISTRATION

The pre-World War II Dutch colonial administration was minimal and superficial. Posts were not established at Manokwari and Fakfak until 1898. Subsequent pacification occurred mainly along the coasts and some of the major rivers. The piecemeal development was due partly to the colonial administration's lack of interest in the remote and inhospitable region, but also to the fact that both the land and people almost defied establishment of a modern administration. In most of the coastal areas the Papuan population—small in numbers to begin with—lived in tiny and widely scattered pockets. Only in the west, in the Radja Ampat Islands and the Onin Peninsula, were there rulers with some sort of authority over wider areas. Elsewhere, to establish contact, the administration almost literally had to reach down to the level of individual Papuan families and small kinship groups which were cajoled into settling in more accessible areas, in villages laid out and built according to the officials' decisions and regulations. Not surprisingly, the villages often remained empty shells, occasional places of rendezvous rather than community centres. Contributing to the empty artificiality of native life was the missionaries' concern with eliminating all traces of paganism. Early officials also prohibited native dances and destroyed some of the symbols of traditional beliefs such as the *karawari* houses (*haus tambaran*, Pidgin English for spirit house) found in the Humboldt Bay area.

To create a viable administration was made even more difficult by the fact that in this highly segmented society authority was only lightly institutionalized. Given the administration's total ignorance of Papuan cultures, it was no wonder that officials remained oblivious to the existence of men with some type of authority. Administrative policy, then, was highly opportunistic: appointed as 'chiefs' were those who happened to speak a few words of the lingua franca, bazaar Malay, or drew attention to themselves in other ways. The authority of these men was minimal, but officials still held them responsible for the collection of taxes and organization of *corvée*. The position of village chief, then, was an unenviable one. Chiefs were 'hired and fired' almost at will and it was only when Papuan society became better known and the calibre of officials improved in the 1930s that men with some authority were discovered in formerly chiefless areas.

The administration of justice suffered from similar problems. One of the cornerstones of Dutch colonial policy in Indonesia was the concept of *adat* law which prescribed that indigenous peoples should be left to enjoy their customary rules and regulations, as long as these did not clash with the general requirements of (Western) equity and humanity. To officials in Dutch New Guinea to whom Papuan administration of justice appeared either absent or at most approaching an informal, loose, type of arbitration, the whole concept of *adat* law was senseless. They administered justice by going through the motions of paying attention to native custom and making the proper reference to the Dutch penal code while deciding the case on the basis of what they deemed equitable. This was especially significant since, with the dearth of administrative personnel, officials combined police, administrative, and judicial powers. Officials continued to comment on and complain about the Papuans' susceptibility to intimidation and the unreliability of their evidence. Nor were the *dorpsrechtbanken*, village tribunals, which were being established in the late 1930s, of any greater benefit. Too formalistic and too alien, they remained as lifeless an institution as the village chieftainship. The saving grace in all this was that most disputes about land, women, dowries, etc., continued to be dealt with informally outside the administration on the basis of the *tjara adat*, customary manner, of the Papuan communities.

Land and labour problems brought about by European involvement were few. Neither the very gradual pace of development, nor the very few and generally small estates, nor the colonization efforts by Eurasians caused much trouble. Understandably, however, friction about land tenure did occur in those few areas in which Eurasian colonists settled. Generally speaking, officials and settlers had only the vaguest notion of Papuan customary land rights. They remained unfamiliar with the fact that uncultivated lands frequently were the inalienable possession of traditional genealogical groups and that the strongly individualistic nature of the Papuans made lands cultivated by them their personal property. Although Papuans were not unwilling to let Eurasian and other colonists use their land, they did not consider this a long-term right. Government-approved leases to colonists, on the other hand, generally ran for a period of twenty years (*see* LAND TENURE).

If development on even a modest scale had taken place the major labour problem would have been a shortage of workers. Economic conditions being what they were, the need for labourers was met easily from available resources within each region. Even so, it should be noted that the one estate worthy of the name—Waren-Seri which belonged to the Japanese Nanyo Kohatsu Kaishu (Society for the Development of the South Seas)—attracted labourers from all around the Geelvink Bay area, taking about half the labour available. Government-sponsored labour recruitment was not practised because the supply of free labour filled the demand; moreover, if the need arose use of Java's inexhaustible supply would have been preferable to employers. In labour legislation there was no uniformity in pre-war Indonesia. Different laws applied to various regions and to the type of work performed. Nor did the government set minimum wages, relying instead upon supervision and recommendation of a reasonable wage.

In the field of native welfare, a great neglect of medical care contrasted with a somewhat brighter picture in the educational field. Facing a seemingly insurmountable task, health measures originally were limited strictly to the major European posts. Only when a virulent venereal disease threatened the Marind tribe with extinction in the early 1920s did the government place a small medical staff in Merauke. From then on, it also was instrumental in vaccinating the coastal people under administrative control against smallpox. The main effort during the 1920-41 period, however, was limited to carrying out investigations of the main diseases prevalent among Papuans. And even this effort was superficial in that no data were gathered on births and mortality, including infant mortality.

In education, direct participation by the government in establishing schools was very limited. In 1937, for example, there were only five public schools. At this time, however, the government provided subsidies to 133 mission schools while the *Binnenlandscholen*, Interior Schools, subsidy regulation permitted the establishment of simple *beschavingsscholen*, 'civilization' schools, in the still unadministered interior. The total number of pupils in subsidized and unsubsidized schools at this time was 15,200. The rigorous curtailment of expenses from 1931 onward, however, sharply reduced educational progress. And in the whole of the country the only 'higher' education available to Papuan graduates of the three-year *volks-school*, 'folk school', was the single two-year *Ver-volgschool*, continuation school, which enabled further training at the teacher-evangelist institute at Miai on the east side of Wandamen Bay. Still,

the educational development laid the basis for post-World War II expansion and the entry of Papuans into new fields. It also raised new expectations which could not be filled. It was G. J. Held who first noted in the late 1930s that the desire for education had an almost exclusively materialistic motivation. The subsequent outbreak of messianic movements occurred where most of the educational effort had been concentrated. Finally, the fact that the government left practically the whole educational task to missionary organizations resulted in those areas which were unlikely to provide converts—such as Kaimana and the Radja Ampat Islands, in which there were some 15,000 Muslims—being entirely neglected.

EUROPEAN ENTERPRISE

Dutch New Guinea, competing for attention with other parts of Indonesia such as Java and Sumatra, attracted very little European enterprise. Next to nothing happened economically until the 1930s when the beginnings were made in large-scale exploration and experimentation.

Ignoring the intermittent visits of Western explorers and Dutch East India Company officials and traders and the more regular *prahu* trade carried on by East Indonesians, the first European concern which indirectly included New Guinea in its contacts was the Nederlandsche Handel Maatschappij, Netherlands Trading Society. Its representative in Menado (North Celebes) was Deyghton & Co. which sent vessels to the Geelvink Bay area to exchange tobacco and textiles for bêche-de-mer, massoi, and copal. Later, the Ternate trading house of Van Renesse van Duyvenbode, founded in 1830, joined in this trade. Bird of paradise skins became another important product during the subsequent period. Friction within the Van Renesse van Duyvenbode concern led in 1892 to the formation of another company, the Nieuw Guinea Handel Maatschappij N. V., the New Guinea Trading Company Ltd. The company maintained a trade store in Mansinam, a small island off Manokwari.

The inclusion of Dutch New Guinea in the shipping network of the Koninklijke Paketvaart Maatschappij (KPM), Royal Navigation Lines, after 1892 brought the floating shops of Chinese traders on board these liners to various coastal towns. Some activity by the government also led a number of Chinese traders to establish stores in the more settled parts. Following restrictions on the hunting of birds of paradise, some of these men leased land for coconut cultivation. Such leases, mainly in the Sorong, Radja Ampat, and Fakfak region totalled slightly over two thousand acres in 1940.

The Maatschappij Kelapa, Coconut Society, which leased land between Merauke and Okaba, was founded in 1919. It was the only Dutch company engaged in European enterprise during this period. Shortly before its liquidation in 1932, the company sold the 692 acres of its lease known as Kolam Kolam to the Roman Catholic Mission at Merauke. The Mission employed Papuan missionary labour and made Kolam Kolam into a reasonably well run estate with a production of about 150 tons of copra a year in the early 1950s.

The arrival of German planters from the former German New Guinea brought considerable activity in the early 1920s. Leases for coconut plantations were acquired in the Hollandia and Sarmi areas and copal concessions at the Tor (east of the Mamberamo) and in the Waropen, near Nabire and Weinami. German settlers subsequently formed the trade and estate company Phoenix which took over the Wanggar copal concessions and the estate Waren-Seri near Momi, some forty-five miles south of Manokwari. Phoenix also briefly operated the government-owned sawmill at Kokas in the Onin Peninsula. In spite of laudable efforts, the company failed. It had to give up the sawmill operation and sold its concessions at a considerable loss in the early 1930s. By 1939 only seven German-operated estates with a combined acreage of less than 1,500 remained.

Much commotion but little result was achieved in the late 1920s and 1930s by the efforts of some Eurasians in Java to found a new home in Dutch New Guinea. The two organizations active in the effort were the Vereeniging Kolonisatie Nieuw Guinea (VKNG), Colonization of New Guinea Organization, and the Stichting Kolonisatie Nieuw Guinea (SIKNG), Colonization of New Guinea Foundation. A motley crowd of several hundred colonists did arrive and settled near Lake Sentani in the Hollandia area and around Manokwari. But these efforts at *kleinlandbouw*, small-scale agriculture, which had been unsuccessful in Java, faced even greater obstacles in New Guinea and were—apart from some individual exceptions—a dismal failure.

The first more significant attempt at estate agriculture was made by the Nanyo Kohatsu Kaishu (NKK), Society for the Development of the South Seas, a Japanese firm registered in Macassar in 1931. The NKK opened an office in Manokwari and was the company which took over the copal concessions and the Waren-Seri estate from Phoenix. It employed from four to five hundred Papuan labourers and several Indonesian overseers and experimented with cotton and jute growing. Production in 1940 amounted to 8 tons of coconuts, 32 tons of cotton, 184 tons of jute and 54.5 tons of dried cassava roots. Lack of success was unimportant to NKK as the main reason for its presence was not economic.

However, the presence of NKK did stimulate the Netherlands Indies government into exhibiting a greater concern for New Guinea. The Gouvernements Rubber Onderneming (Government Rubber Estate) Ransiki was set up on a fertile plain south of Manokwari, just north of the Japanese lease at Momi, in 1938. Several dozen acres were brought under cultivation and planted with rubber and oil palm. The same year saw the establishment in Amsterdam of the Nederlandse Maatschappij voor Nieuw Guinea (Negumij), Netherlands Company for New Guinea, by some fifteen major concerns with extensive estate, shipping, trade, and banking interests in Indonesia. The

company's main purpose was to explore the potential for estate agriculture. Selected as exploration area was the Grime-Sekolie plain west of Lake Sentani where an experimental station was set up near Genjem in October 1941.

The 1930s also saw the first major mining activities. The costly exploration for gold in the south-east by N. V. Mijnbouw Maatschappij Nieuw Guinea (Mining Company New Guinea Inc.) in the years 1936-9 was unsuccessful. The discovery of oil and gas seepages in the Vogelkop (Bird's Head) area, however, brought not only major investment but promising results. A contract between the Netherlands Indies government and the Nederlandsch Nieuw Guinee Petroleum Maatschappij—a joint venture of Dutch Shell (BPM), Standard Oil, and Far Pacific Investments —was concluded in 1935. In the following years the 24,710,000 acres exploration area granted to the company was mapped by means of aerial photography and drilling was begun in the Vogelkop. Labourers employed by the NNGPM numbered about four thousand in 1938 including almost eleven hundred Papuans. Significant amounts of capital goods—cement, machinery, etc.—entered Dutch New Guinea for the first time. Oilfields were discovered at Klamono, south-east of Sorong, in 1936 and at Mogoi and Wasian, some thirty miles inland from Bintuni Bay in the south-eastern portion of the Vogelkop, in 1939. Although the Japanese were able to ship out small quantities of oil during 1942-4, production did not begin officially until late 1948.

MISSIONS

Missionary activity began in 1855 with the arrival at Mansinam of the German missionaries J. G. Geissler and C. W. Ottow. Both men were students of the Rev. J. Goszner in Berlin whose attention had been drawn to New Guinea by the Dutch Reformed minister O. G. Heldring. Under Heldring's influence the newly formed Utrechtsche Zendingsvereeniging, Utrecht Mission Society, sent its first missionaries to assist Geissler and Ottow in 1862. This mission society carried on the work of the Gosznerscher Missionsverein from then.

Missionary efforts were long without result. Goszner's philosophy that missionaries should build an independent livelihood in the community in which they were working was ill-suited to Dutch New Guinea and although the Papuans tolerated the missionaries they were not interested in their message. The first and almost only converts were the children of slaves whom the missionaries freed from bondage. However, following the great smallpox epidemic in the first decade of the twentieth century, a dramatic reversal of missionary fortunes occurred. The gradual establishment of administrative control in the Geelvink Bay area, the inclusion of the territory in the inter-island network of the Koninklijke Paketvaart Maatschappij and the activities of the small band of Papuan evangelist-teachers had set the stage for the changed attitude of the Papuans.

Working in close co-operation with the Utrecht Mission Society and providing it with East Indonesian evangelists and teachers was the Indische (since 1935 Moluks Protestantse) Kerk, the Dutch Reformed State Church in Indonesia. A 1933 estimate put the number of Protestants of the Utrecht Mission Society at almost 46,000; those of the Moluccan Protestant Church at 5,140.

Catholic missionary work was initiated by the Jesuit Father Le Cocq d'Armandville near Fakfak on the Onin Peninsula in 1894 but ended in 1896 with his untimely death. In 1902, however, the apostolic prefecture, elevated to a vicariate in 1920, of Nederlandsch-Nieuw Guinea (Netherlands New Guinea)—including Dutch New Guinea and the Moluccas—was set up with headquarters at Langgar in the Kai Islands. The prefecture was assigned to the Dutch branch of the Missionaries of the Sacred Heart. Work began in Merauke in 1905 but not until 1920 were the first converts made among the fierce Marind tribe. In 1933 the number of Catholics—found almost exclusively in the south—was estimated at 7,100.

The original separate areas of Catholic and Protestant missionary activities were retained by a government-imposed demarcation line until 1927. But even after this date the government usually opposed *dubbele zending*, double missionary activity, because it considered it detrimental to peace and order. The gentlemen's agreement of 1937 permitted entry of the various missions into each other's areas if there was a demand among the population for instruction in the other faith. The Moluccan Protestant Church had become active meanwhile in parts of the south and the Catholics in the Fakfak area. The latter region was allocated to the Franciscan Order which also began to pay attention to the area. A Catholic missionary penetrated the wild hinterland of Hollandia in the late 1930s laying the foundation for post-World War II Catholic successes in the Waris-Jaffi region.

Missionary efforts cannot be separated from those of pacification. In many cases, missionaries preceded the flag and were, in effect, the only 'government' known to the people. The medium *par excellence* was the three-year *volksschool* and, in more primitive areas, the *beschavingsschool*, 'civilization' school, whose main purpose was to establish contact, bring people to abandon their nomadic existence, and teach pupils neatness and order. Missionary education in other parts of Indonesia most often existed alongside government schools. In Dutch New Guinea, however, the early missionary foothold and the flimsy nature of the administrative apparatus led to an exclusively missionary effort. Mission schools received a government subsidy when they met government standards. More stringent application of the subsidy regulations in the 1930s threatened the continuation of many low quality mission schools. However, several adaptations in the regulations were made to take into account New Guinea's special circumstances. The most significant one was the *Binnenlandscholen*, Interior Schools, subsidy regulation which freed schools in the hinterland from being bound by the general regulations and proved to be a special stimulus for the setting up of *beschavingsscholen*. An important contribution to the spread of *Moluks Maleis*, a version of bazaar Malay, was made by the missionary organizations as this medium was employed in most of the folk schools.

The following (1937) figures illustrate the significance of the educational effort borne by the missionary organizations.

Denomination	Number of Schools		Estimated no. of pupils
	Subs.	Unsubs.	
Utrecht Mission Society	98	64	9,200
Moluccan Protestant Church	8	70	900
Missionaries of the Sacred Heart	27	111*	5,100
	133	245*	15,200

* Of which 20 were *beschavingsscholen*.

In spite of the expansion of missionary education, the number of European missionaries remained quite small. In 1933, for example, the Protestants had a European staff of thirty-nine, including eighteen wives of missionaries, a doctor and a nurse, while in 1937 the Catholics had seventeen pastors, four sisters, and two brothers. The actual teaching and evangelizing, therefore, was done mostly by non-Europeans. Many of these men were recruited from (Protestant) Ambon and the Sangihe and Talaud Islands, off northern Celebes, in the case of the Protestant missions, and from the (Catholic) Kai Islands in the case of the Catholic mission. The Utrecht Mission Society, however, partly because of its earlier start, was able to make deliberate effort to train Papuan personnel. As early as 1905 it sent some twenty Papuan youngsters to Depok in Java and, subsequently, to Tobelo on Halmahera in the Moluccas. In 1918 it initiated a training school at Mansinam which was expanded into a regular teacher-evangelist training institute at Miai in the Wandamen in 1923. The long-term results and implications are clear from the fact that of the 266 Papuan folk teachers in the whole of the country in 1947, 221 belonged to the Utrecht Mission Society.

The delegation of the main pioneering task to non-European teachers put a tremendous burden on these poorly paid, ill-supervised, and often minimally trained persons. Their position in the village, however, was one of almost unlimited prestige and power and lent itself to abuse. In many respects the teachers reflected the zeal and dogmatism of the European missionaries and insisted upon a rigid, unquestioning acceptance of discipline. While some adaptation to traditional beliefs and cultural expression was attempted by the Missionaries of the Sacred Heart, those of the Utrecht Mission Society and the Moluccan

Protestant Church traditionally drew a sharp line between Christianity and paganism. They insisted upon the destruction of pagan relics and art objects and outlawed traditional dances. Life—although neat, well ordered, and safe—became deadly monotonous. Moreover, in the absence of social and economic development in the country as a whole, the only entrance into the 'new world' for graduates of the simple 'folk schools' was the limited opportunity to become missionary teachers. Under these circumstances, the employment of 'folk school' graduates began to pose a problem as early as the 1920s.

L. N. van Asperen, *Zending en Zendingsonderwijs op Nederlandsch-Nieuw-Guinea*. Leyden, 1936.
R. Broersma, 'De Koopvaardij in de Molukken', *Koloniaal Tijdschrift*, vol. 23, 1934.
K. W. Galis, 'Geschiedenis', in *Nieuw Guinea*, ed. W. C. Klein, vol. 1. The Hague, 1953.
H. Geurtjens, 'De Katholieke Missie op Nieuw Guinee', in *Nieuw Guinee*, vol. 1. Molukken-Instituut, Amsterdam, 1935.
A. Haga, *Nederlandsch Nieuw-Guinea en de Papoesche Eilanden*. 2 vols, The Hague, 1884.
B. J. Haga, *Memorie van Overgave van Bestuur van den Aftredenden Resident der Molukken*. Ambon, 1937.
F. J. F. van Hasselt, 'De Zending op Nieuw Guinee', in *Nieuw Guinee*, vol. 1. Molukken-Instituut, Amsterdam, 1935.
L. de Jong, *Onderwijs Verslag over Nieuw-Guinea* (Report to the Director of Education). Kotabaroe, 1948.
W. C. Klein (ed.), *Nieuw Guinea*. 3 vols, The Hague, 1953-4.
F. T. Marijn, 'Het Werkvolkvraagstuk in Australisch en Nederlandsch Nieuw-Guinea', *Koloniale Studiën*, vol. 22, 1938.
Nederlandsch Indië, Departement van Oorlog, *Verslag van de Militaire Exploratie van Nederlandsch-Nieuw Guinea, 1907-15*. Weltevreden, 1920.
Nieuw-Guinea, Adatrechtbundels, vol. 45, 1955.
Nieuw Guinee. 3 vols, Molukken-Instituut, Amsterdam, 1935-8.
Joh. Rauws, *De Zending op Nieuw Guinea*. The Hague, 1919.
C. C. F. M. le Roux, 'De Exploratie', in *Nieuw Guinee*, vol. 1. Molukken-Instituut, Amsterdam, 1935.
C. Schumacher, 'Exploratie', in *Nieuw Guinea*, ed. W. C. Klein, vol. 3. The Hague, 1954.
J. Verschueren, 'Zuid Nieuw Guinea 35 Jaren onder Missie invloed', *Koloniale Studiën*, vol. 24, 1940.
P. W. van der Veur, *Search for New Guinea's Boundaries, from Torres Strait to the Pacific*. Canberra, 1966.
A. Wichmann, *Entdeckungsgeschichte von Neu-Guinea*. 3 vols, Leyden, 1909-12.

PAUL W. VAN DER VEUR

DWYER, Michael Ignatius (1898-   ), prospector, accompanied M. J. Leahy [q.v.] on the famous expedition of 1930 which, from Edie Creek, pushed into the Eastern Highlands of the Mandated Territory of New Guinea and then rafted down the Purari River to the south coast of Papua. He now lives in Queensland.

M. J. Leahy, Diaries (N.L.A.); —— and M. Crain, *The Land that Time Forgot*. London, 1937; I. J. Willis, *An Epic Journey: The 1930 Crossing of New Guinea*. Unpublished paper, University of Papua and New Guinea, 1969.

FRANCIS WEST

(*See also* EXPLORATION)

E

EASTERN HIGHLANDS DISTRICT. At the end of World War II the whole of the main Highland area of both Papua and New Guinea was administered as one unit, the Central Highlands District. Though this was an appropriate unit while civil administration was being re-established and almost the whole area was still uncontrolled, its size militated against effective local administration. The original District was therefore distributed in five parts in September 1951. In Papua the Southern Highlands District [q.v.] was established and the western sector of the Papuan Highlands was joined to the Western District [q.v.]. In New Guinea the westernmost sector was added to the Sepik District (*see* SEPIK DISTRICTS, EAST AND WEST) while the large remaining heavily populated area was formed into two new districts, the Western Highlands and Eastern Highlands Districts [qq.v.].

In June 1966 a further readjustment of boundaries was made. The Chimbu Sub-District and parts of the Southern Highlands and Gulf Districts of Papua were joined to form the Chimbu District [q.v.], the remaining easterly area retaining the old title of Eastern Highlands District with which this article deals.

The District has a population of 225,000 and an area of approximately 5,000 square miles. While one of the smallest of the country's eighteen Districts it has, after Chimbu District, the second highest population density, 45 persons per square mile.

Its central location and its proximity to the chief mainland ports of Lae and Madang with their developed hinterlands ensured that it would be the first contacted Highland area and the first to undergo economic development.

The District is divided into six Sub-Districts: Goroka, Kainantu, Okapa, Henganofi, Lufa and Wonenara, all administered from settlements of the same name. Goroka is the District headquarters and only it and Kainantu are towns of any size and diversity. While the area and population directly administered from Goroka has diminished as a consequence of the redrafting of District boundaries, there has been greater development within the District and the developing importance of Goroka as an entrepôt for the Highland areas to the west.

PHYSICAL SETTING

Except in the west the District is generally bounded by natural features. To the north the Bismarck Range abutting the Ramu and Markham Valleys forms the border; to the east it runs along the steep, forested Kratke Range which also cuts across the centre of the District; to the south it follows the country falling along the Lamari River to the Purari River. To the west the District boundary follows the lower Wahgi-upper Tua Rivers in part but elsewhere follows a generally north-south line, an artificial but convenient administrative separation from the populated areas of the Chimbu District.

The whole area consists of highland valleys, hills and ranges, generally varying from 5,000 to 9,000 feet but with some mountains rising to 12,000 feet. In the south and north the land surface falls to less than 1,000 feet above sea-level.

Of the Highland areas the District has the driest climate although this is only relative, for no rainfall station shows less than an average annual fall of 68 inches (Henganofi). The normal range varies from 75 inches at Goroka to 100 inches at Lufa with low annual rainfall variability. The limited number of recording stations all lie between 5,000 and 7,000 feet so that it is impossible to state whether rainfall increases with altitude on mountains and ranges. However, rainfall records for the Upper Ramu catchment near Kainantu indicate that such an increase, if it exists, would be slight. The increasing ground and vegetation dampness at higher altitudes results most probably not from greater rainfall but from lower rates of evaporation. This has been estimated to be of the order of 50 inches per annum at Goroka and less than 20 inches above 10,000 feet.

Monthly rainfall follows a seasonal pattern, with a wet season from December to early April having mean monthly falls of about 8-12 inches. A dry season follows, with monthly falls in the general range of 2-4 inches. The months of April-May and October-November tend to be transitional.

Temperature ranges are most equable. At Goroka the maximum temperature for the whole year is 78°F. There is little seasonal variation in mean temperature or in extremes and for a ten-year period the highest maximum on record was only 85°F. with a lowest minimum of 50°F. At 8,500 feet ground frosts are reasonably common and at 10,000 feet probably occur on about 50 per cent of the days in the year.

At Goroka mean humidity varies from 87 per cent at 9.00 a.m. to 57 per cent at 3.00 p.m. Associated with this is the typical cycle of cloud movements found in the Highlands. In the early

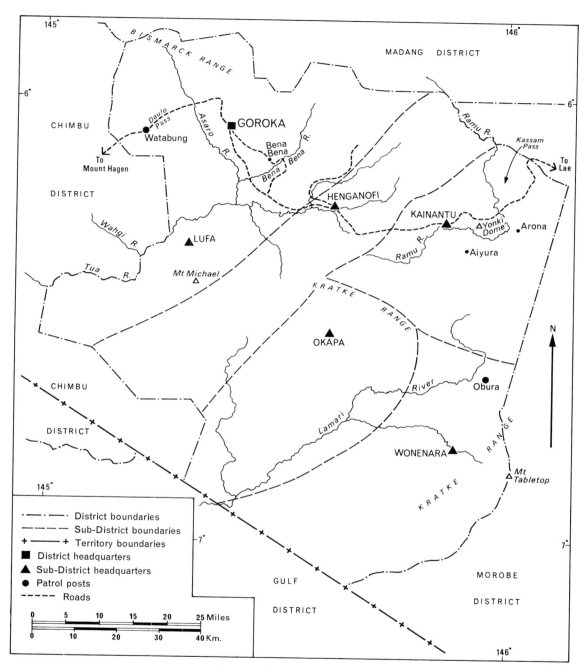

Eastern Highlands District.

morning valley slopes and bottoms are submerged in fog with higher hills and ranges protruding into clear sunlight. As the day progresses the fog lifts from the valleys and clouds begin to bank up on the ranges frequently with associated local convectional storms. Towards evening the cloud extends from the ranges to the valleys and with cooling sinks by morning to the valley bottoms. This cycle of afternoon cloud and storm on the ranges and morning fog in valley bottoms, where airstrips are located, makes the maintenance of flight schedules difficult.

The landscape has been formed from the effects of this climate on the surface geology. While the oldest rocks date back to Palaeozoic time the present landscape is almost wholly related to processes operating since the major uplift of older land masses which took place in late Pliocene to early Pleistocene times.

The action of high rainfall on this greatly increased uplift relief caused considerable weathering and erosion. The material carried away was deposited as large alluvial and colluvial fans on which for instance the town and airstrip of Goroka now stand, and as lacustrine beds seen for instance in the area around Aiyura. Where the process of erosion acted on lower, softer materials (e.g. siltstone) hill and valley form became less rugged, stream energy decreased and eventually resulted in large areas of hilly uplands and valley systems as seen on the road to Okapa.

Although there is some evidence of pre-Pleistocene intrusive activity at Yonki Dome and near Okapa, the District did not undergo the major Pleistocene volcanism that occurred to the west, although light ash showers settled over it. Towards the end of the Pleistocene glaciers formed on the highest mountains as a result of the last ice age, leaving today cirques, vestigial traces of moraines and small lakes on Mt Michael (11,900 feet) and Mt Tabletop (12,000 feet).

Possibly nowhere else in New Guinea has the original vegetation been as much modified by man as in the Highlands. This is particularly so in this District where human activities in combination with a somewhat drier climate resulted in a more precarious ecological balance.

Nearly all areas below 8,500 feet are or have long been used for subsistence agriculture and hunting. Consequently the chief form of vegetation apart from actual gardening is short to tall grassland and low shrubby regrowth. Generally the taller grasslands, dominated by *Miscanthus* sword grass, form part of the garden-cycle area. Elsewhere large areas lie under short grasslands with *Themeda* dominant and these have been assumed to be caused by a combination of human interference, soil and climatic features (*see* GRASSES). They tend not to be used at present except for hunting. The old custom of planting *Casuarina* trees around and in gardened land has been intensified in the last decade, and is gradually bringing a more wooded appearance. It is believed that prior to the coming of man these grasslands were under a mixed forest of oak and beech, but only small remnants of this older vegetation still exist.

Where remnants of forest survive below 9,000 feet the species composition is mixed but less diverse than in lowland rain forest, and is classified under the general title of lower montane forest. In places the forest is rich in conifers [q.v.] and below 7,500 feet contains much oak (*Castanopsis*). Between 7,000 and 9,000 feet oak gives way to beech (*Nothofagus*). Above this to 10,000-12,000 feet lies a region of mostly stunted mossy montane rain forest which in turn at higher altitudes merges into subalpine forest and scrub. The highest vegetation type consists of natural alpine tussock grassland which occurs on some mountains above 11,000 feet.

The only other major vegetation types found in the area are the swamp grasslands and herbaceous bog communities found in poorly drained areas at all altitudes.

HISTORY

Archaeological research (*see* PREHISTORY) suggests that man entered the eastern Highlands at the conclusion of the cool Pleistocene glaciation. However, the earliest confirmed date for human habitation is 11,000 years before the present and the evidence indicates that these people lived in caves and rock shelters, and found subsistence as hunters and gatherers. The presence of pigs has been dated back 6,000 years. The best evidence for a long established permanent system of agriculture comes from the Western Highlands District where old drainage channel networks and gardening implements have been dated as 2,500 years old.

The first Europeans to visit the area found a population who practised a form of short fallow agriculture using sweet potato as the main staple. The gardens were fenced and drained by a rectangular lattice of ditches, pigs were common and stone axes, digging sticks and bows and arrows were the main subsistence implements. People lived in small villages and hamlets or in nearby gardens in circular houses constructed from poles, thatch and woven sword grass with earthen floors.

Initial European contact with these people was made from Salamaua, the Bulolo area and Madang. As the District was the closest to these centres it naturally was the first Highland area of contact.

The first European claiming to have entered the Highlands was a German army surveyor, H. Detzner [q.v.], during World War I, but his claim remains unsubstantiated. In 1927 a Lutheran missionary, the Rev. L. Flierl, crossed the Bismarcks and traversed the Asaro and Bena Bena River area, establishing the pre-war Highland contact pattern in which Christian mission and gold prospecting penetration either preceded or accompanied the spread of government influence (*see* CHIMBU DISTRICT).

During the latter half of the 1930s the real spread of government influence through the District was commenced from stations opened at Bena Bena (later shifted to Henganofi) and Kainantu (Ramu police post), Goroka itself not being established until 1939. At the opening of World War II most of the northern populated areas were under partial government influence with somewhat closer contact around Kainantu. Elsewhere only a few areas had been penetrated by patrols. Initial contact experiences were variable, depending largely on the personal qualities of the European and his indigenous associates. Despite a few deaths on both sides, contact and pacification were in general peaceable.

During World War II the District was governed by a military administration, Angau [q.v.], and to a limited extent was used as a rest centre and provider of fresh vegetables for the forces. Despite intense fighting in the nearby Ramu and Markham Valleys the District was almost untouched directly by the war. The indirect effects of the war were enormous. Pre-war development marked by lack of funds, personnel and even interest, changed to a post-war policy of intensive development. The utility of aircraft in overcoming supply problems in remote and rugged interior regions had finally been demonstrated.

Upon the restoration of civil administration the extension of control, carried out solely by the Administration, proceeded rapidly. Missionaries, prospectors and others were not permitted to enter new areas until they were declared 'unrestricted'. The greater portion of the unpacified sections of the District lay to the south and all of these were 'derestricted' between 1960 and 1965.

ECONOMIC DEVELOPMENT

Economic development commenced in the north, particularly around the Goroka and Kainantu basins, partly because land with the highest agricultural potential lay in that region.

Internal transport and links to seaports were both needed. A series of feeder roads to the local hinterlands of the two main centres Goroka and Kainantu were built. These developed closer contacts between the Administration and the local populace and hastened social development. The roads were constructed largely by hand, involving large numbers of people in a project directly useful though foreign to them. These roads provided the link with the airstrips where supplies were received from the coast. Until the mid-1960s all passenger traffic and supplies not locally available were flown into the District. Madang, the closest seaport and a 40-minute flight in a DC3, became the main supply centre and cargo flown to Goroka alone reached a peak of 10,000 tons per annum before road haulage to the coast became economic.

Roads and airstrips were constantly upgraded and extended; local road networks were linked each to the other, new roads and airstrips were constructed in the south of the District and most importantly a main route, the Highlands Highway, linked the District to the seaport of Lae. Despite major construction difficulties, particularly on the Daulo Pass (8,500 feet) to the west of Goroka and on the Kassam Pass linking the highland valleys with the lowland Markham Valley, it was possible by the mid-1950s to travel by vehicle from Goroka eastward to Lae and westward to Mount Hagen. However road construction was such that cargo

trucking from the coast was more expensive and less reliable than air transport. In the early 1960s considerable effort and expenditure upgraded the highway so that transport became economic. Air cargo decreased rapidly and Lae became the main seaport, adversely affecting the growth of Madang. This transport system made it possible to establish a cash-cropping industry in the District.

The first and main cash crop to be introduced was Arabica coffee, planted initially on expatriate estates on land of high potential near Goroka and Kainantu. An agricultural experiment station was established at Aiyura to investigate problems of agronomic practice in coffee production. As well as providing a profitable enterprise for a limited number of European settlers this development demonstrated coffee culture and production to the indigenous population. The intention was to minimize land alienation and promote indigenous smallholder production.

By 1969 expatriate estates covered 4,900 acres of which the great bulk had been planted during the 1950s and early 1960s; 87 per cent of this planted area was under mature trees and annual production was 2,300 tons of green beans compared with 2,000 tons for 1968. When all alienated areas are brought to maturity production is likely to stabilize at below 3,000 tons per annum.

Production of coffee by indigenous people on smallholdings is still increasing rapidly. In 1968 9,000 acres of mature trees were producing 2,900 tons, and by 1969 this had increased to 4,900 tons from 9,700 acres (see COFFEE INDUSTRY).

While coffee is by far the most important cash product, other specialized crops are grown. These include pyrethrum (see PYRETHRUM INDUSTRY), passionfruit (see PASSIONFRUIT INDUSTRY), peanuts, truck crops for local and coastal consumption, and experimental plantings of tobacco made by an expatriate company on the Asaro River.

Livestock production is also being encouraged to increase protein supply and to replace imports. In 1969 there were 1,100 head of cattle run by indigenous owners on small cattle projects, and a further 3,500 head on 12,500 acres of expatriate and Administration holdings.

Forest potential is not great, yet high population density and economic growth create considerable demands for timber. Forestry is mainly concerned with reafforestation of the large grassland areas chiefly with klinkii (Araucaria) pine species and eucalypts, and the tapping of existing forest resources, generally at high altitudes, for local consumption. There are four sawmills with a daily log input potential per shift of 28,000 super feet, logs being felled from six permit areas covering 19,000 acres.

Development of primary industry has been paralleled by growth in service industries and administrative infrastructure, based particularly on Goroka. As the major transport and commercial centre and distributor for air passenger traffic, it is in a key position for growing tourist activities. Goroka also serves Districts to the west and the rate of development of its service functions substantially exceeds those of centres in other Highlands Districts. The growth of Goroka as an entrepôt is likely to continue at least until a highway is constructed linking areas west of it directly with Madang.

Kainantu provides functions similar to Goroka's but on a more modest scale. It is likely to undergo a period of growth in the near future from development of the upper Ramu hydro-electric scheme designed to provide power for the Highlands, Lae and Madang. It has also been suggested that the future capital of an independent New Guinea might be established at Arona, near Kainantu, and this would inevitably lead to considerable additional growth in Kainantu Sub-District.

While growth in the cash sector is impressive, there is a severe spatial imbalance at Sub-District level. For instance 98 per cent of expatriate coffee production comes from Goroka and Kainantu Sub-Districts, and the same areas contain 99 per cent of expatriate-owned cattle. The same order of distribution applies to production from the indigenous sector, yet these two Sub-Districts cover only approximately half the population and area of the District. This imbalance, common in Papua New Guinea and developing countries generally, stems partly from the distribution of natural resources and partly from a policy of concentrating development to optimize gain from limited resources.

SOCIAL AND POLITICAL DEVELOPMENT

The rapidity of social change in the Eastern Highlands is considerable by both Papua New Guinean and world experience. Change in an effective sense commenced only one generation ago. A broad indication of its extent can be inferred from the effect of direct and indirect agencies of development such as schooling and employment.

Social change began with contacts, including trade, with the first explorers and settlers. Trade within the Highlands and to the coast was a feature of the existing neolithic society, chiefly with pearlshell [q.v.] and other sea shells. Early trade between Europeans and indigenes consisted of exchanges of shell, salt and other trade goods including steel axes and knives for foodstuffs, local building materials and labour. The utility of steel implements was rapidly recognized and these quickly became prized trade items. As the District economy became cash oriented, barter for European goods was largely replaced by the gradual introduction of trade stores and other retail and wholesale establishments. By 1968 there were 1,100 trade stores operating in the District with an average turnover per head of population of $1.50 and a gross turnover of approximately $300,000 per annum.

The cash to support this activity comes from cash cropping and employment. The District was the first Highland area to be tapped for coastal plantation labour after World War II. Male labour was recruited under the Highlands Labour Scheme for two-year contracts on the coast. The scheme not only provided the first chance for many indigenes to gain a cash income but provided their first wider experience of the country, its towns and

European culture. It was also a major force in the spread of Pidgin English [q.v.]. The scheme was designed to provide employment in a protective environment suitable for the first contact experiences of subsistence farmers.

As the District and its population developed, employment increased and became more diverse. By 1968 nearly 11,000 District inhabitants were in employment, 4,200 working within the District and 6,600 outside. A further 3,100 indigenous persons from other Districts were also employed in the District. Of the total adult male population of the District only 15 per cent are in employment, but this figure must be extended as a result of a high labour turnover and the effects of indirect employment through cash cropping.

Employment tends to be largely restricted at present to labouring and trade activities, because of lack of educational opportunity. In 1970 there were seventy-eight primary schools in the District with an enrolment of 10,000 indigenes together with a further three secondary schools with 1,200 students, three technical or vocational schools with 300 pupils, and one teacher training college at Goroka. In all approximately 17 per cent of school age children in the District actually attend school and of these the ratio of boys to girls is almost four to one.

Another major, direct agency for social development is health services. There are six Administration hospitals in the District, one in each Sub-District, the main establishment being at Goroka. In addition the Administration runs a number of maternal and child health centres and clinics and the various missions also conduct medical centres. Local Government Councils have recently begun to provide social services. Until 1962 governmental rule was direct and hierarchical. Village officials called *luluais* and *tultuls* were appointed to help carry out the orders of the Administration, and in 1962 they numbered 1,900. In 1970 their numbers had been reduced to 72 as a consequence of the progressive establishment of Local Government Councils in nearly all areas of the District. By 1970 seven councils had been formed. The Asaro-Watabung, Goroka and Henganofi councils were established in 1962-3 and the Kainantu, Lufa and Okapa councils in 1965-6. The last council to be established was the Lamari in 1967. Of the total population, 97 per cent are covered by councils and 103,000 persons are enrolled as actual electors.

The income of councils is dependent on taxes and Administration grants. The less developed areas to the south-east, such as Lamari, set a tax rate of only $0.50-1.50 per man, whereas Goroka Council levies a rate which varies from $6-10. Although newer councils have relatively low tax rates, total council expenditure and revenue for the District is the highest in Papua New Guinea. In 1970 total revenue reached $1,130,000 made up equally from recurrent revenue (e.g. taxes, charges) and nonrecurrent items (e.g. grants, borrowings). Expenditure was apportioned as follows: 22 per cent to education, health and welfare, 43 per cent to transport and communications, 11 per cent to development of water supply and agriculture and the remainder covering general services, maintenance, interest, etc.

The councils are multi-racial and controlled by 309 representatives. Professional advice is supplied by the Administration, especially to the newer councils. A ward system is used for elections, and on average one councillor represents approximately 320 people, providing not only close councillor-elector contact, but also an understanding of electoral procedures.

The District is represented by seven members in the House of Assembly [q.v.]. Six of these are from the open electorates of Daulo, Goroka, Lufa, Henganofi, Okapa and Kainantu, and one represents the Eastern Highlands regional electorate.

PROSPECT

The majority of the population are still basically subsistence cultivators who, through employment and cash cropping, have marginal and intermittent direct contacts with the cash sector of the District economy. The people in the more developed north in general have considerably higher incomes than those in the south. This results not only from the self-reinforcing aspect of economic growth in the north but also from the lack of areas of high potential in the south. Barring large mineral finds in the south this north-south differential may increase and lead eventually to local, and because the situation is common to other Districts, to wider political problems.

J. McALPINE

EAST NEW BRITAIN DISTRICT. Until 1966 the island of New Britain was administered as a single District. From that time it has been divided into two Districts, East and West New Britain, with the headquarters of East New Britain at Rabaul.

The East New Britain District covers about 7,000 square miles, approximately half the land mass of the island, and has a long coastline on the south of the island and a comparatively short one on the northern side. On its northern perimeter it includes the islands of the Duke of York Group.

TOPOGRAPHY

Coasts and boundaries. Montagu Harbour, almost midway along the south coast of New Britain, is the south-western corner of the District boundary. Nearby the considerable Ania River reaches the sea from its headwaters in the Nakanai Ranges. A track, first followed in 1929, joins Montagu Harbour with Commodore Bay on the north side of New Britain. East of Montagu Harbour the fringing reef is not continuous and there are marshy flats at the heads of the bays and along such streams as the Melkoi a few miles west of Cape Beechey. Eight miles further east the Torlu River forms a delta as it reaches the coast. At Drina, south-west of Cape Cunningham, there is an anchorage behind the reefs where plantations have been established. Cape Cunningham North is the eastern end of a peninsula that lies between Drina

River and Jacquinot Bay where the extensive Palmalmal plantations are. There are coastal reefs off shore. At the head of Jacquinot Bay is Pomio, the Sub-District headquarters. Cape Jacquinot is the western point of Waterfall Bay where the large Esis and Beg Beg Rivers have their mouths and where the cone Kwoi rises 1,800 feet to the north-east. Coral patches are numerous near the Mocklon Islets and the reef is almost continuous from nearby Rondahl Harbour to Cape Orford. Here the coast turns north and there are steep cliffs forming a corner bastion as the Nakanai Mountains slope steeply to the sea. At Crater Point, eight miles further on, the coast begins its deep indentation to the north-west which is the beginning of Wide Bay. The island of New Britain is here at its narrowest for the shores of Open Bay on the other side of the island, are but twenty miles distant. The Nakanai Mountains drop to a height of 1,000 feet in this isthmus which separates the Gazelle Peninsula from the remainder of New Britain. The head of Wide Bay is called Henry Reid Bay and here the Mavlo and Powell Rivers form a delta. At Tol Plantation nearby many Australian soldiers were executed after they had surrendered to the Japanese in 1942.

The northern side of Wide Bay is very steep as the high ranges of the Baining Mountains come close to the shore and remain so until Cape Archway is reached. The cliffs then give way to rough beaches as Sumsum Bay is approached but the coast is an inhospitable one. At Put Put (Rugen Harbour), some 15 miles further northward, there is a harbour but suited only to small vessels. Plantations border both sides of the harbour.

A geographical change occurs here. At Put Put the raised coral limestones which rise thousands of feet to form the central range are no longer seen. Instead there is the heavy debris of volcanic pumice and soil—the result of Rabaul eruptions. Eight miles north of Put Put the Warangoi River enters the sea from its headwaters in the Baining Mountains and the Varzin hills south of Kokopo. Some twelve miles from the Warangoi River is reef-fringed Cape Gazelle, the easternmost point of New Britain. The quadrant formed by Kokopo-Warangoi River-Cape Gazelle is comparatively flat and lowlying and contains extensive plantations.

From Cape Gazelle to Kokopo the coast proceeds generally west. Kokopo, the second largest town in the District is also the headquarters of the Sub-District of that name. From Raluana, about five miles from Kokopo, the coast turns west-north-west and the point may be considered the southern headland of Blanche Bay. Along the shores of the Blue Lagoon the coast is steep and arched with cliffs. The extinct cone of Vulcan, which erupted from the sea in 1937, lies on the south side of Blanche Bay while its northern side is enclosed by the Crater Peninsula with its line of volcanic cones. These are the Mother (Kombiu) and her North and South Daughters (Towanambatir and Turanguna). The peak Palagiagia overlooks the extinct crater Rabalanakaia, while the active volcano Matupi is near the foreshore. The lowlying island of Matupi is almost beneath the

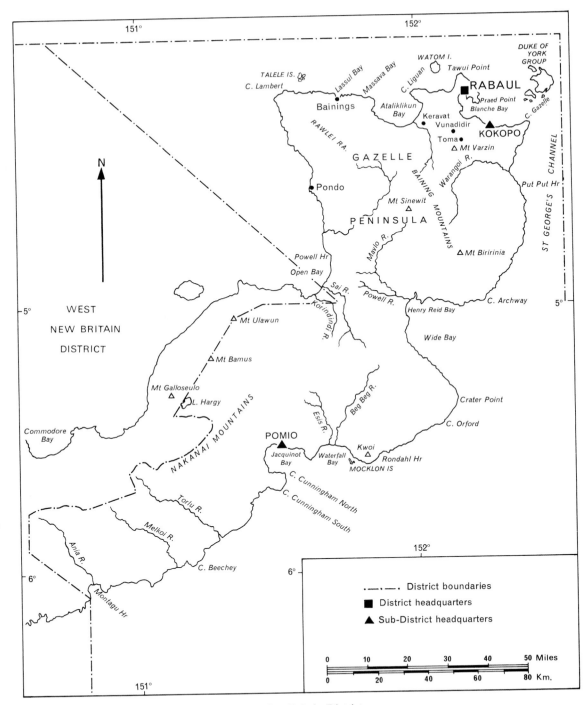

East New Britain District.

smoking volcano and joined to the mainland by a narrow causeway.

Praed Point lies at the foot of the South Daughter and marks the northern entrance to Blanche Bay. The large village of Nodup is on the northern side of the Crater Peninsula and from there to Tawui Point the coast is bold with cliffs 150 feet high.

The Duke of York Group lies about 18 miles east-north-east of Rabaul and 12 miles from the western coast of New Ireland, about midway across St George's Channel. Low-lying and heavily populated, the group's largest island is Duke of York Island; others include Mioko, Utuan, Ulu and Makada. The small Credner (Pigeon) Islands lie between this group and Blanche Bay.

From Tawui Point, the most northerly cape in New Britain, the coast turns south. Kabagada Point is the western limit of Talili Bay and from here to Cape Liguan the shore is rocky with isolated coral patches. Watom Island lies 4 miles west of Tawui Point while Urara Island is about 5 miles west-north-west of Cape Liguan. The cape marks the eastern point of Ataliklikun Bay which has some 25 miles of coastline; near its head is the mouth of the Keravat River. The western point of Ataliklikun Bay is near the Ramandu River, some 15 miles further on. From here the coast runs westward for 20 miles until the north-west point of the Gazelle Peninsula is reached at Cape Lambert.

The shore is known as the Baining coast and only the shallow indentations of Massava and Lassul Bays break its straight line. There is a chain of reefs off shore enclosing the Talele Islands a few miles north-east of Cape Lambert, and while the native population of the Baining coast is sparse, plantations edge its whole length. Cape Lambert to Open Bay forms the west coast of the Gazelle Peninsula. This 60 miles contains some plantations but few villages. A chain of off-shore reefs extends as far as the head of Open Bay with breaks in it where the plantations of Seraji, Stockholm and Pondo are located. Some 12 miles south of Pondo is the Toriu River; at the northern head of Open Bay there is Powell Harbour (Tavanatangir), a narrow inlet, one of the very few on the eastern side of the peninsula that offers shelter for ships. The southern extremity of Open Bay is Rangambol Point and within its reaches are the Sai and Korindindi Rivers, both having their rise in the narrow isthmus that separates the Gazelle Peninsula from the rest of New Britain. About 4 miles up the Korindindi River begins the boundary between East New Britain and West New Britain Districts [q.v.], the line running north-west to the mouth of the river so that it bisects Open Bay. From that point on the Korindindi the District boundary runs westwards to Mt Ulawun (the Father volcano, 7,546 feet), thence to the summit of Mt Bamus (the South Son, 7,376 feet), and on to within a few miles west of Mt Galloseulo (3,484 feet) which is located in the adjoining District of West New Britain. The boundary then continues along the centre of the island until it turns south and south-east to meet the coast near Montagu Harbour.

Mountains. There are four main mountain systems in the District.

The Nakanai Mountains run almost the entire length of New Britain, creating a rugged barrier between the north and south coasts of the island. The Nakanai Range in the western part of the District is part of this central backbone. Broken and rugged, limestone peaks reach their greatest height of 7,000 feet about 20 miles north-west of Crater Point on the south coast. There are several peaks exceeding 6,000 feet and many between 4,000-5,000 feet.

The magnificent active cones of Ulawun (the Father) and Bamus (the South Son) are part of the Bismarck volcanic belt which includes the Matupi volcano and the extinct cones of Blanche Bay. Mt Ulawun is separated by a valley from the central chain of the Nakanai Mountains and 28 miles south-west of it is Lake Hargy, a crater lake. The range loses height as it reaches the isthmus between Open and Wide Bays. Basically it is composed of uplifted limestone with granite outcrops occurring in it. In the Ulawun area there are heavy volcanic deposits.

The Baining Mountains of the Gazelle Peninsula extend from the isthmus over almost the entire central and south-eastern parts of the peninsula. The greatest height is reached at Mt Sinewit at 8,000 feet in the centre of the peninsula, and Mt Biririnia (7,900 feet). The Gazelle Peninsula is upfolded from the northern side of Wide Bay to Cape Lambert and the coral is tilted towards the sea as it rises steeply to form limestone scarps; tertiary rocks appear as the under-core of older formations. From Mt Sinewit north-eastwards this raised series of reefs continues until it disappears beneath the volcanic deposits of the Blanche Bay volcanoes. The Rawlei and Gavit Ranges, located in the Cape Lambert and Baining coast areas, are part of the Baining Mountains.

South of Blanche Bay a series of low ranges rise from the coast to extend behind Kokopo, where their greatest height is reached at Mt Varzin (Vunakorkor 2,600 feet). Where the hills end abruptly at Blanche Bay they form steep slopes and there are low cliffs overlooking the shallow beaches at Kokopo. The country levels in the Vunakanau-Toma area where a considerable plateau is formed about 1,200 feet above sea-level. The southern escarpment overlooks the Warangoi Valley at Vunadidir.

The coastal range on the northern side of Blanche Bay from Praed Point to Tawui Point and the western part of Talili Bay is part of the volcanic arc that runs from New Guinea along the north coast of New Britain. Thermal springs occur in the Rapindik area nearby.

Rivers. The mountainous terrain and heavy rainfall give rise to many rivers although there are no significant streams between the northern shores of Ataliklikun Bay, on the west, and Kabanga Bay, facing St George's Channel, on the east. The Ania, Melkoi, Esis and Beg Beg are the largest rivers in the south-eastern part of the District while the Mavlo, Sai and Korindindi drain the narrow isthmus between Wide and Open Bays. The Toriu, on the west coast of Gazelle Peninsula, has its headwaters in the Baining Mountains near Mt Sinewit. In the northern part of the peninsula are the considerable rivers, the Keravat, flowing north-west from the Baining Mountains, and Warangoi, which reaches the sea a few miles north of Put Put Harbour. The Warangoi has its headwaters in the central Baining massif with tributaries from the Varzin hills flowing into it.

CLIMATE, SOILS AND VEGETATION

The general climate follows that of other coastal parts of Papua New Guinea. The north-west monsoon may be expected in November and continues until March, when there is a break until the south-east trade winds commence in May. Because of the District's central mountain system rainfall varies, with the highest falls in the south-west coastal areas. The average annual rainfall in the Rabaul area is 96 inches, and at Kokopo slightly less; in parts of the Duke of York Group, within 20 miles of Rabaul, it rises to 119 inches per annum. The average rainfall increases greatly as one proceeds west along the south coast of the island. At Jacquinot Bay it is over 190 inches.

In the coastal and hinterland areas humidity is high and afternoon and night rain is frequent at higher altitudes.

On the coast and in the hinterland of the northern part of the Gazelle Peninsula soils are of pumice and clay with occurrences of Quaternary volcanic rocks—the result of volcanic eruptions. This volcanic debris is also seen in the areas near Mt Ulawun. The soils here are probably the most fertile in the Territory.

As has been noted, the core of the Nakanai and Baining Mountains is predominantly limestone, the result of a tremendous coral upfolding; however, metamorphic and granitic rocks occur in this basic formation and the whole is covered by a heavy overlay of soil except at extreme altitudes.

Heavy rain forest is usual in the District except above 5,000 feet and covers even the most steep and broken slopes. There are no significant grass plains although *kunai* grass is common on otherwise bare patches. Mangrove swamps are also common in delta and lowlying coastal areas.

The vegetation pattern in general follows that of Papua New Guinea but there are considerable stands of *kamarere*, a tree similar to the giant Australian eucalypts, on the Korindindi River flats. Other timbers include the red cedar, the New Guinea walnut, *taun* and the hardwood kwila.

In the coastal and hinterland areas coconut palms are in abundance, and the staple foods of the indigenous people, taro, sweet potatoes, bananas and almost all other tropical vegetables and fruit are grown without difficulty. The large plantations of coconuts and cocoa, owned by both expatriates and indigenous people, are proof of the fertility of the soil.

EUROPEANS AND INDIGENES

The island of New Britain was so named by William Dampier [q.v.]. However, he did not dis-cern that New Ireland and New Britain were separate and called the strait of water dividing them St George's Bay. In 1767 another Royal Navy captain, Philip Carteret [q.v.], discovered the strait and called it St George's Channel. Carteret made another discovery—that there were active volcanoes in the area now known as Blanche Bay. Sighting the Mother and Daughter peaks he recorded that there were large clouds of smoke and dust rising behind them. It is probable that he was witnessing one of Matupi's eruptions. In 1872 Captain Simpson, in H.M.S. *Blanche*, discovered Blanche Bay and dropped anchor in that part of it which now bears his name, Simpson Harbour, and on which Rabaul [q.v.] was established in 1910. (Rabaul means 'the mangrove'.)

Traders and missionaries had long preceded government in the Gazelle Peninsula. In 1872 an Englishman established a trading station at Port Hunter, in the Duke of York Group, and in 1873 the German firm of Godeffroy set up trading stations in the Blanche Bay area.

In 1878 Emma Forsayth [q.v.] later known as 'Queen Emma' settled at Mioko in the Duke of York Group and established coconut plantations. By 1884, when the Germans took possession of the colony, the annual export of copra had reached 2,000 tons. In 1875 the Rev. George Brown [q.v.], pioneer Methodist missionary, established his church at Molot, in the Duke of York Group, and in 1896 the Catholic mission set up its head-quarters at Vunapope, a few miles from Kokopo.

The largest tribal group in the District is the Gunantuna or Kuanua—more generally known as the Tolai [q.v.]. The Tolai people are believed to have come from New Ireland some centuries ago and are now settled on the northern part of the Gazelle Peninsula and on the Duke of York islands. A virile race, they had no difficulty in defeating the original people of the area and taking possession of their land. At the time of the Tolai invasion the coastal fringe and hinterland of that part of the Gazelle Peninsula were owned by the original tribes—the Baining and some of the Sulka. The timid and rather pygmy-like Baining people were no match for Tolai war clubs and sling-shots, they were driven off their lands to take refuge in the inland areas. Until the beginning of the present century they remained the prey of the conquering Tolai. Those Baining that were not killed in the frequent Tolai raids were taken prisoner, later to be eaten or used as slaves.

Only once did the Baining show hostility, and that was not against the Tolai but against white missionaries. In 1904 the Baining attacked the Catholic mission station, St Paul's, in the Massava Bay area and killed several of the nuns and brothers. The Tolai were pleased to assist the government in punishing the murderers and joined in the hunt which followed. Even today the mark of the oppressed clearly shows on the Baining; in the face of a Tolai his confidence leaves him and he becomes timid. The close-knit social organization of the Tolai had historical and traditional advantages and to a great degree the people have maintained them.

They had a well-developed system of traditional currency long before the advent of the white man, and it still exists. It is a shell currency called *dewara* or *tambu* and the original shells are obtained by trading with the people of Nakanai, some 180 miles down the north coast of New Britain. With the pointed ends of the shells filed off the resulting small rings are bleached and then threaded on string. Each ring, about a quarter of an inch in diameter, was carefully counted and as a result the Tolai people could count up to thousands. This shell wealth was stored in village treasury houses and a record of individual ownership recorded by knotted cords. Here it remained under the custody of the *agala*, or *luluai*, the village chiefs. The owner of much *tambu* was highly respected; the man who had none was a pauper. *Tambu* suffered no fluctuations; its value today is the same as it was in 1884. The social organization of the Tolai was largely controlled by a system of secret societies, the memory and fear of which still exists.

Good agriculturists and skilled fishermen, the Tolai people, as a tribal group are the wealthiest of all in Papua New Guinea. Almost all the copra and cocoa produced by the indigenous people in the District comes from the extensive groves and plantations cultivated by the Tolai on their own land. Another source of revenue is the production and marketing of vegetables. Despite these advantages the Tolai people are not happy. At the time of writing (1971) the race is torn by dissension (*see* below).

The Baining, Timoip and Mokolkol comprise the remainder of the indigenous people of the Gazelle Peninsula. Numerically they are few, being approximately 9,000 people as against the 68,000 Tolai.

The Baining occupy the foothills of the Rawlei Range and the land south-west of Ataliklikun Bay. They are probably the descendants of the first Negrito migrants to reach New Guinea and its islands. Other Baining villages are located north and south of the Warangoi River. The minor tribe of Timoip have their habitations in the hinterland west of the Rawlei Range.

The smallest group of people, known as the Mokolkol, are located in the narrow isthmus between Wide and Open Bays. For many years nothing was known of them except for their sudden raids on the coastal hamlets of the area when they would attack, kill and disappear into their jungle fastness. All efforts by the Administration to trace these bushmen failed. They became a legendary terror and were regarded by their coastal victims as devils from another world. Exploratory patrols could find no signs of their habitations and for years it was thought that they were nomads. In 1951 a patrol succeeded in reaching two of their round houses and eventually managed to make peaceful contact with these wild people. It was then found that they numbered less than fifty. Still primitive, the Mokolkol are now a peaceful people.

The population of the Pomio Sub-District, although less than a quarter (21,187 persons) of the Gazelle Peninsula, shows a far greater diversity in tribes and languages than the northern part of the

District. Excluding administrative classifications, they may be divided into seven principal groups. They are:

Sulka: with habitations north of Wide Bay and on the coastal area near Cape Orford.
Mengen (East): occupying the coast and hinterland from Cape Orford to Jacquinot Bay.
Mengen (West): from Jacquinot Bay to Lau, south-west of Cape Cunningham.
Kol: an inland and mountain people in the country north of Pomio and east of Mt Ulawun.
Mansong, Melkoi and Mamusi: whose villages are located in the western part of the District from the coast to the central range.

POPULATION

In 1966 when the last census for the Territory was recorded the population of East New Britain was: indigenous males 60,068 and females 44,819; non-indigenous males 2,785 and females 2,258; total 109,930; giving a density of 15 persons per square mile. The 104,887 persons recorded as indigenes included visitors and workers from other Districts of the Territory and may be regarded as temporary residents who have their homes outside East New Britain.

From figures supplied by the Department of District Administration the true local indigenous population number 98,597 (*see* Table 1). The difference between the two totals (6,290) represents indigenous employees from other parts of Papua New Guinea and temporarily resident expatriates.

Table 1

Sub-District	Children		Adults		Persons
	Male	Female	Male	Female	
Rabaul	16,337	15,302	15,631	12,951	60,221
Kokopo	4,684	4,153	4,527	3,825	17,189
Pomio	4,723	4,573	6,175	5,716	21,187
Total	25,744	24,028	26,333	22,492	98,597

Of the 77,410 indigenous people living in the Rabaul and Kokopo Sub-Districts, 68,500 are Tolai people and the remaining 8,910 of the Baining, Timoip and other tribes.

Distribution of non-indigenous urban population at 1966 was estimated as: Rabaul Sub-District 4,317; Kokopo Sub-District 665; and Pomio Sub-District 65.

ADMINISTRATION, HEALTH AND EDUCATION SERVICES

East New Britain District is divided into three Sub-Districts: Rabaul and Kokopo, both on the Gazelle Peninsula, and Pomio, the western part of the District. Base camps have been established at Lassul Bay, Reimber, Tawui, Toma and on Duke of York Island, all on the Gazelle Peninsula. The District headquarters and representatives of all government departments are at Rabaul. Each Sub-District is under the charge of an assistant District commissioner.

There are three Local Government Councils in the District. Both the Baining and the Mengen Councils are multi-racial. The largest Local Government Council, Gazelle Pensinsula, which covers the Tolai people, excludes non-indigenes and remains an all-indigenous council. The Rabaul Town Council has been proclaimed but no elections have yet been held. Together the councils cover approximately 74,000 persons—about 74 per cent of the District's population.

Health services include the large and fully equipped base hospital at Nonga in Rabaul, where there is also a school of nursing. Some 180 nurses have graduated here and post-graduate courses are also conducted. There are smaller hospitals conducted by the Department of Public Health at Pomio and Butuwin and four Rural Health Centres located through the District. A fifth centre is to be opened in the Duke of York Group in the near future.

A community health centre is maintained at Rabaul and a dental section travels regularly to villages in the District. Domiciliary treatment is given to 336 leprosy patients at their villages and to some tuberculosis cases; serious cases of tuberculosis being treated at Nonga hospital. Maternal-child welfare clinics visit all villages and there are thirty-nine aid posts established in native communities. The Administration medical and nursing staff in the District number 279.

The missions maintain generous health facilities. The Catholic mission maintains a large general hospital at Vunapope (263 beds) and there are hospitals at all of its main outstations. Both the United Church and the Seventh Day Adventist missions maintain and operate both hospitals and clinics.

The people of the Gazelle Peninsula benefited from the early arrival of missions there, in so much as they were the first to receive some schooling. Simple as it was, the opportunity for that education was welcomed by the people and their enthusiasm has never waned.

Educational establishments in the District number 131 with a total enrolment of 25,482. A breakdown of this figure by type of establishment is given in Table 2. In addition the Department of Agriculture, Stock and Fisheries maintains an agricultural college at Vudal, near Rabaul, and the Department of District Administration conducts a training centre for local government clerks at Vunadidir.

ECONOMIC DEVELOPMENT

The land within the arc directly affected by volcanic eruptions in the Gazelle Peninsula is the most fertile in the Territory. Extensive coconut plantations were established by the Germans in the Blanche Bay and Kokopo areas before 1914 and since then the Australians have extended the plantings. In the 1930s it was found that the climate and pumice soils were suitable for cocoa and that the trees could be successfully grown under the shade of the coconut palms. World War II interfered with the development of cocoa production but since 1946 large plantings have been made.

The Tolai people were quick to realize the value of cash crops and with the encouragement of the Administration they began to plant cocoa in 1951. At the same time they greatly extended their coconut groves.

In 1968-9 East New Britain District produced approximately one-quarter of Papua New Guinea's copra and nearly half its cocoa. By far the greater part of these crops was produced in the fertile belt in the northern part of the Gazelle Peninsula.

A feature of Rabaul is the large vegetable, fruit, fish and fowl market controlled by the Local Government Council. The market is open six days a week to sell produce grown by the Tolais. Annual turnover is estimated to be $3 million, and it is the largest concern of its kind in the country.

There are 171 holdings of land in the District, under freehold or leasehold to expatriates and missions, covering 171,526 acres. Of this, 62,503 acres are not presently utilized because of soil, terrain or for other reasons. The total area alienated constitutes only 3.8 per cent of the total land of the District but of this 136,700 acres are located in the volcanic arc around Blanche Bay and the northern end of the Gazelle Peninsula. There can be little doubt that over-alienation of land has occurred in the past in that part of the Gazelle Peninsula.

Although the District has valuable timber assets these have not been fully exploited, mainly owing to the stands being in steep and mountainous terrain.

The fishing potential is considerable but has not been developed commercially, although the native people fish for domestic and local market needs.

Rabaul, on Simpson Harbour within Blanche Bay, is the District's only port. For the year 1969-70 cargoes handled at Rabaul were: 255,000 tons discharged; and 333,000 tons laden.

Table 2

EDUCATIONAL ESTABLISHMENTS, 1970

Type	Administration		Mission		Total	
	Number	Enrolment	Number	Enrolment	Number	Enrolment
Primary-'T'	26	8,415	78	11,825	104	20,240
Primary-'A'	3	769	3	283	6	1,052
Secondary-'T'	3	1,371	5	1,322	8	2,693
Secondary-'A'	1	251	—	—	1	251
Technical	2	422	1	25	3	447
Vocational	3	264	2	134	5	398
Teachers' colleges	—	—	4	402	—	402

NOTE: 'T' denotes curriculum adopted for the Territory; 'A' denotes Australian curriculum.

The District is served by three airfields: Rabaul (Lakunai) for heavy aircraft; Palmalmal (Jacquinot Bay) for medium aircraft; and Tol (Wide Bay) for light aircraft.

A network of roads laces the northern part of the Gazelle Peninsula. From Rabaul a sealed road runs to Kokopo and another partly sealed to Keravat, skirting Talili and Ataliklikun Bay. The system includes many vehicular roads that serve the Warangoi Valley and the Toma-Vunakanau plateau.

THE POLITICAL SITUATION

As this is written, in 1971, there is grave dissension between a considerable number of the Tolai people, their fellow countrymen and the Administration. Such unrest is not new, for it has existed below the surface for many years, but it has now been clearly brought to light by the rise to power of the group known as the Mataungan Association, which may be freely translated as the 'Look ahead' party. The aims of the Mataungan were first expounded by one of its founders, Oscar Tammur, a Tolai and member of the House of Assembly, a few years ago, and since then its objectives appear to have changed. Starting with the demand that the Tolai should not be incorporated into the multi-racial council which had been proclaimed, the Mataungan changed its target until it reached its present position of opposition to many government policies—particularly the Administration's past and present methods of dealing with land.

It is necessary to look at the past in order to perceive more clearly the situation as it now exists in the Gazelle Peninsula. Land disputes between the local people and Europeans have their origin as far back as 1878 when Emma Forsayth established a trading station in the Duke of York islands. Trading was then based on a simple barter system; the natives brought their coconuts to the trader where they were exchanged for salt, steel tools and other trade goods. This sort of trading had existed for some years and except for the actual trading sites, no significant land had been acquired from the native owners for, in the Gazelle Peninsula at least, the white man did not plant large areas of land for himself; plantations as we know them now did not exist. However, Emma Forsayth purchased land from the native owners and by the time the German government had formally settled in the new colony her family business headquarters and adjoining planted areas were firmly established at Ralum, on Blanche Bay. Ultimately her claims to the land were officially recognized, and for the first time, land became a factor in the relationship between the white man and the native people of the Gazelle Peninsula.

There were, of course, to be many other factors but none of them so important as land. Time and education have enabled the local people to accept new concepts but the problem of land remains largely unsolved.

It was not long before the people realized that the white man's idea of land ownership differed from their own traditional *vunaterai*. There were

frequent disputes and killings but the government had the force to ensure law and order. And there was no general objection by the Tolai to selling additional land to the newcomer; there were even advantages, for the presence of the white man at least guaranteed peace. Also, land was plentiful and much of it was unused. Land continued to be sold and most of it was disposed of with the full consent of the owners, though some purchases were objected to.

Despite his loss of land the Tolai still had plenty of it. The first census of the people of Blanche Bay showed a total of 20,500 persons, and it was not thought that the population would grow to three times that in sixty years.

In the meantime the Tolai were to see the sudden departure of the Germans in 1914 and the advent of the Australians who, twenty-eight years later, were removed by the Japanese, and although the Australians were to return, the Tolai had seen that the white man, like themselves, was vulnerable to force. It was to be remembered.

Keeping the promise of democratic rule, the Administration established the first Local Government Councils in the Gazelle Peninsula in 1951. For the first year there was no objection to the new system; on the contrary, it appeared as if the entire Tolai population would welcome the councils with enthusiasm. But a minority of villages strongly opposed the introduction of councils and they received the support of some white men who wanted no change in the old methods of administration. The first physical clash occurred in 1953 and resulted in victory for the anti-council groups, then numbering less than 2,000 people, for they succeeded in getting the principle of 'voluntary participation' adopted by the government. Thus no group could legally be forced to join a council. They could remain outside even if their villages were in a council area; the choice would be theirs.

The anti-council group regarded this 'freedom of choice' as a chink in the government armour, and they were quick to exploit it. By argument, threat and force they gained additional adherents to their ranks. The result was a far more serious riot in 1958 when police were forced to protect themselves against anti-council demonstrators and two men of the attacking party were killed. For almost eleven years the Tolai situation remained quiescent, and the Administration took pains to keep it that way. In addition to not pressing entry into councils, the government was generous in giving schools, aid posts and other assistance to the dissentient groups, but these tactics satisfied nobody. The anti-council groups regarded it as a permit to canvass for further supporters, while the council people thought it grossly unfair that the opponents of councils should be given benefits free while the supporters of government policy should have to pay for them through council taxes. Mistaking the apparent calm for permanent peace, the Administration decided to proclaim the Tolai Gazelle Peninsula Council multi-racial in 1969.

There was immediate objection by some Tolai and the Mataungan Association was formed to lead the protest. The core of the objectors was said to be centred at Matupit and the leaders at the time were Oscar Tammur, M.H.A., Torumit, Toeriken, Tomat and John Kaputin [q.v.]. Mataungan's influence (but not necessarily support) was shown when only 25 per cent of the eligible voters went to poll in the elections for the multi-racial council in May 1969. Since in previous elections some 50 per cent of the roll had voted, it was evident that many voters had abstained because they supported the Mataungan or feared Mataungan threats. The Administration believed the latter reason to be the correct one. The election resulted in four non-indigenous seats in a total of forty-two. The preponderance of indigenous councillors elected did not satisfy the Mataungan which vigorously protested that the election of non-indigenes to the council, no matter how few their number, would mean that the indigenous councillors would be dominated by them. 'The white man is too clever', said Oscar Tammur, 'his will is too great and the Tolai will abandon their traditions and become "half-castes"—imitation white men with all their good customs gone for ever.'

The Mataungan also claimed that the election was invalid because the people had never properly been told what a multi-racial council meant and therefore the new type of council had been foisted upon them. Despite all arguments to the contrary the Mataungan adhered to these views. In an effort to settle the matter, the Administration proposed that a referendum be held among the Tolai. Such a vote would necessarily be a secret one, in view of threats that had been made against those who disagreed with the Mataungan. The Mataungan insisted that the referendum should be an open one with the voters lining up behind their respective leaders. Naturally, this was unacceptable to the Administration and to the rest of the Tolai people.

The Mataungan's specific opposition to the formation of a multi-racial council was in many ways puzzling, for there had been no public demand by any of the Tolai that the membership of the House of Assembly should be restricted to indigenes; councils comprising representatives of all races had been accepted with enthusiasm throughout the Territory; of the 145 Local Government Councils then established in the Territory, 114 were multi-racial. 'The Tolai are different from other people', said Tammur, and there appeared to be some truth in what he said. Ultimately, the Administration withdrew the proclamation and for the time being, at least, abandoned the idea of a Gazelle Peninsula multi-racial council. The decision was the only one possible, but it left a rift between the Tolai people.

Encouraged by some political support from Australia, the Mataungan looked for fresh fields to conquer. It was announced that an independent marketing organization would be set up in order to obtain better prices for Tolai copra and cocoa. In 1951 the Tolai had been encouraged by the Administration to plant cocoa and to enlarge their coconut groves. Although some senior officers in the government were less than keen about the people planting cocoa on land held under traditional tenure, the Tolai people welcomed the

scheme and it was widely supported. In order to build fermentaries large sums of money were borrowed from a bank and the loan repaid by deducting a small percentage from the price paid to the grower for his cocoa beans. The councils, aided by the Administration, operated the scheme and it worked successfully. Non-indigenous businessmen, mostly Chinese, saw opportunities in this, and by offering slightly higher prices for the Tolai cocoa beans, because the percentage for repayment of the loan was not deductible, attracted a great deal of business from the council fermentaries. An appeal by the Tolai people that a law should be passed prohibiting council growers selling to private fermentaries was refused by the Administration and consequently the business of the council fermentaries declined. In addition to cocoa the Tolai produced thousands of tons of copra, this being processed by the growers. In 1970 the Tolai people produced some 12,000 tons of copra valued at $1.8 million and some 4,200 tons of cocoa valued at $1.6 million.

To date the proposed Mataungan marketing project has not been established and it is difficult to see how better prices may be obtained for copra and cocoa. The prices paid for cocoa are based on world market prices and copra is sold to the Copra Marketing Board, so the Tolai producer receives the same prices as the expatriate planter. The Mataungan Association announced its third aim when the Administration proposed settling selected Tolai farmers on land it had acquired in the Vudal-Keravat area. It had already subdivided the land and was preparing to offer it for lease to the farmers when Tolai squatters occupied the area. When eviction orders were served on them the squatters refused to leave and they were supported in their refusal by the Mataungan. The Mataungan based their support for the squatters on the claim that the land had never been legally acquired by the government and therefore it was still indigenously owned. Although never announced, the probable real point here is that while the Administration was prepared to give the people the use of the land, it was to be given under lease, the white man's way, and not given to the Tolai to be used under their traditional system of land tenure.

'The white man has stolen our land!' was the cry of the Mataungan, a cry calculated to attract some of the Mataungan's erstwhile opponents amongst the Tolai, for even if a man supported the multi-racial council, he might well support the Mataungan if the return of land was to be its policy. While the lawless methods of some Mataungan leaders and followers must be condemned, it must be admitted they had grounds for discontent. According to a well-informed estimate, the area originally occupied by the Tolai people in the northern part of the Gazelle Peninsula covered approximately 424 square miles (278,180 acres). Since the acquisitions by Emma Forsayth, nearly half this land has been alienated leaving the Tolai with approximately 143,000 acres, or little more than 2 acres per head for subsistence gardening and future cash cropping; and the population is increasing. The alienated land can be accounted as follows:

	Acres	Percentage of Tolai land
Freehold land	52,000	18.7
Leasehold land	21,500	7.7
Occupied Administration land	12,960	4.7
Vacant Administration land	41,200	14.8
Native reserves	7,490	2.7

However, even if it were possible to return all alienated land to the Tolai it would not remove the problem of land shortage. A rapidly multiplying people must often be prepared to move when their original lands are insufficient, and this must apply to the Tolai. While most of the land alienated in the past was honestly and legally acquired there have been a few transactions that are open to doubt. And there have been some foolish and stiff-necked actions by the Administration in meticulously adhering to the white man's legal concepts and ignoring traditional custom in land matters. An example occurred in 1937 when Vulcan Island erupted and caused a great new area to rise from the sea in Blanche Bay. The eruption killed over 500 Tolai people who lie buried under the land that was thrown up. While the new land was still hot the remaining people occupied the area. The Administration at once issued a declaration of government ownership, despite claims that the native people owned it according to their custom. After World War II the people renewed their claims and eventually the court awarded the land to the Administration on a technical point. In spite of the most careful explanation the Tolai claimants could not understand the decision and there was bitterness and hatred growing when at last the government relented and gave the land to the people; had it done so in the first place gratitude may have replaced the bitterness.

In recent years the Administration has shown itself willing to deal logically and humanely with Mataungan demands, even to the point of stepping aside and letting the opposing Tolai factions find a solution. A party known as Warmaran, wholly composed of Tolai members, attempted to confer with the Mataungan but was refused. The Mataungan continued to stage calculated acts of lawlessness, such as assaults against police and upon Tolai who had not joined its ranks, incidents which widened the breach between themselves and the rest of the people.

Thus, in mid-1971, without reasonable dialogue, hopes of a negotiated settlement seem to be deadlocked.

J. Andrews, 'Landforms of New Britain', *Australian Geographer*, vol. 7, 1957-60; A. L. Epstein, *Matupit: Land, Politics, and Change among the Tolai of New Britain*. Canberra, 1969; D. Fenbury, 'Those Makolkol!', *New Guinea and Australia, the Pacific and South-east Asia*, vol. 3, 1968; R. Parkinson, *Dreissig Jahre in der Südsee. Land und Leute, Sitten und Gebräuche im Bismarckarchipel und auf den deutschen Salomoninsel*. Stuttgart, 1907; R. F. Salisbury, *Vunamami: Economic Transformation in a Traditional Society*. Melbourne, 1970.

J. K. MCCARTHY

ECHIDNAS, or spiny anteaters, together with the platypus form one of the most puzzling groups of living mammals. They are the only mammals classified in the subclass Prototheria and in the order Monotremata—mammals having a well-developed cloaca, or body cavity with a single opening to the exterior, into which the intestinal, urinary and reproductive organs empty. The echidnas and platypus are also the only mammals that lay eggs. This and other anatomical features characteristic of the reptiles have led some scientists to place these 'quasi-mammals' in the class Reptilia. Another writer calls them mammals by definition and not phylogeny. The platypus builds a nest in a burrow for the reception and hatching of eggs, while the echidna incubates its single egg, rarely two or three, in a simple infolding of the abdominal wall. It is not a pouch in the sense of the term marsupium which is present in many marsupials. The echidna is often called a porcupine but this is a misnomer; porcupines belong to the order Rodentia and do not occur in the Australian-New Guinean area. Where the term 'New Guinea' is used without any qualification such as 'region' it means the whole main island.

The fossil record is very incomplete. No fossils have been found in New Guinea; however, fossils of the living genera are known from the Pleistocene Epoch of Australia. The discovery of still earlier fossil ancestors of the living monotremes would be one of the most exciting events in the history of Australian palaeontology. The current hypothesis is that their ancestors reached the Australian-New Guinean area late in the Triassic or in the Jurassic Period (possibly 200 million years ago), and evolved into generalized monotremes. It has been suggested that the living monotremes are remnants of a once much larger radiation of this subclass of mammals. Anatomically the monotremes have many primitive characters, but they are highly specialized for the lives they lead. *Tachyglossus*, the short-beaked echidna, is found in both Australia and New Guinea. *Zaglossus*, the long-beaked echidna, although found as a fossil in Australia, lives at present only in New Guinea and on Salawati, an off-shore island. Although there is good habitat for the platypus in southern New Guinea there are no records of this mammal having crossed the Torres Strait from Australia.

Tachyglossus aculeatus, the only species of the genus, has a very wide distribution in Australia, including Tasmania, but it is limited in New Guinea mainly to the country south of the east-west cordillera. Recent reports, however, show that it has penetrated this central range in several places in north-eastern New Guinea, and it is now found on several river systems that flow to the north coast. *Zaglossus* has a known distribution from eastern Papua to the island of Salawati, just off the west coast of the Vogelkop in West Irian. The habitats of the short-beaked echidna include the savannah woodlands of the outwash plains south of the central ranges, and the gallery forests along the river courses. In those areas where *Tachyglossus* has extended its range into the mountains it lives in rain and oak forests. *Zaglossus*, on the other hand, is primarily an inhabitant of the mid-montane and high mountain forests. These are the forests where the cloud cover forms regularly each morning during most of the year; the mossy covering of the trees is characteristic of these humid forests. There may well be some overlap at the lower elevations in the ranges of these two echidnas in the north-east, but as yet there are no examples of this.

The front feet of spiny anteaters are highly modified for digging. Elongated, curved claws are developed on certain toes of the hind feet for scratching among the body spines, and presumably for grooming—the second toe in *Tachyglossus*, the three middle toes in *Zaglossus*. Echidnas are known hosts for fleas and ticks. The diet of anteaters varies with locality and food availability, but consists largely of ants and termites, and sometimes other insects. The tongue is covered with a sticky mucus from enlarged salivary glands, and may be extended several inches beyond the beak when feeding. The insects are mashed between the base of the tongue and the hard palate. Echidnas do not possess teeth. They are primarily nocturnal, but are occasionally active during the day. Vision is relatively poor, but the senses of smell and hearing are well developed. It is not known what natural enemies the echidnas have, but, as is usual in New Guinea, man exerts heavy hunting pressure. Trained dogs are used to locate *Zaglossus*. The echidna takes refuge by digging among the roots of trees or under rocks, but up to twenty pounds of meat and fat reward the patient hunter.

Tachyglossus is not a large animal, but when the spines are erected the appearance of size is greatly enhanced. Adults from Papua average about seventeen inches in total length (maximum,

twenty inches); the females seem to be larger than the males. The average adult weight is about five pounds. *Zaglossus* is a larger and heavier animal. Total length of adults averages about twenty-four inches (maximum, thirty inches); the weight, about twelve pounds (maximum, twenty pounds). Again, the few data indicate that females are slightly larger and heavier. The almost straight beak of *Tachyglossus* averages nearly two inches in length; the strongly decurved beak of *Zaglossus*, four inches (maximum, about five inches).

Zaglossus is covered with yellowish-white barbless spines up to two inches in length, but a thick covering of black, occasionally brownish, hair effectively hides most of the spines except on the nape of the neck, the sides, and rump. A number of specific names have been proposed for the various populations of long-beaked echidnas in New Guinea. These names have been based in large part on colour of hair and spines and on the presence or absence of claws on the toes. There is probably but one variable species of this echidna in New Guinea, its scientific name is *Zaglossus bruijni*. The New Guinea *Tachyglossus*, in contrast, has relatively little hair, and the usually black-tipped spines are very conspicuous. Unlike the loose quills of porcupines, echidna spines are firmly anchored in muscle tissue. Spines are absent in both echidnas on the under-surface of the body. The tail is reduced to a short stub. External ears are present but concealed by the hairs and spines.

The egg has a tough, rubbery covering rather than a hard shell. It is incubated in the abdominal pouch for perhaps ten days. Milk glands empty at two distinct areas in the pouch—there are no teats, and the young feeds on a thick pinkish-white milk. The young, which is born naked, is kept in the pouch for several weeks; after this it is left in the den while the female forages. Echidnas breed only once a year. Males have a short, sharp spur on the inner surface of the ankles. The function of these spurs and the associated glands is unknown. Studies are being made on *Tachyglossus* in Australia, but there are few data on the life history of the long-beaked echidna in New Guinea.

There are several records in Germany of *Zaglossus* having lived in captivity for over thirty years. But the record for longevity goes to a *Tachyglossus* that lived in the Philadelphia Zoological Gardens for forty-nine years, five and a half months. Its age at death was certainly more than fifty years. However, we have no information on longevity under natural conditions.

G. M. Allen, 'Zaglossus', *Memoirs of the Museum of Comparative Zoölogy at Harvard College*, vol. 40, 1912; L. S. Crandall, *The Management of Wild Mammals in Captivity*, Chicago, 1964; P.-P. Grassé (ed.), 'Ordre des Monotrèmes', in *Traité de Zoologie*, vol. 17, Mammifères, Paris, 1955; J. K. Jones, Jr, 'Monotremes', in *Recent Mammals of the World*, ed. S. Anderson and J. K. Jones, Jr, New York, 1967; G. T. MacIntyre, 'Foramen Pseudovale and Quasi-mammals', *Evolution*, vol. 21, 1967; G. G. Simpson, 'The Principles of Classification and a Classification of Mammals', *Bulletin of the American Museum of*

The long-beaked echidna, *Zaglossus bruijni*.

Natural History, vol. 85, 1945; E. Troughton, *Furred Animals of Australia*, 9th ed., Sydney, 1967; H. M. Van Deusen and G. G. George, 'Results of the Archbold Expeditions. No. 90 Notes on the Echidnas (Mammalia, Tachyglossidae) of New Guinea', *American Museum Novitates*, no. 2383, 1969; E. P. Walker, *Mammals of the World*, vol. 1, Baltimore, 1964.

HOBART M. VAN DEUSEN

ECONOMIC PLANNING. During recent years the Australian government has paid considerable attention to economic planning for the Territory of Papua and New Guinea, preparing an integrated development programme to advance the Territory towards viability and to improve the living standards of the people. In 1963 the International Bank for Reconstruction and Development (I.B.R.D.) was asked to send a Mission 'to undertake a general review of the economic potentialities of the Territory and to make recommendations to assist the Australian government in planning a development program designed to expand and stimulate the economy and thereby raise the standard of living of the people'. The Mission's report was presented in 1964, and the government broadly endorsed its approach and accepted the proposals for increased production 'as a working basis for planning in the Territory'.

The report set out production and other targets for the principal export crops, timber products, and beef cattle. It also dealt with the other sectors of the economy, made a number of policy recommendations designed to achieve the proposed programme and provided some broad estimates of the necessary expenditure. Among its recommendations was a proposal that an economic adviser be appointed with a small professional staff to undertake planning responsibilities. This appointment was made in late 1965, followed by the appointment of several professional and other officers to form an Office of the Economic Adviser. The Economic Adviser reports directly to the Administrator [q.v.], and has the following principal responsibilities:

to prepare and maintain a co-ordinated development plan for the Territory;

to review and evaluate progress in the implementation of the development plan and recommend proper action and change;

to review progress in the private sector and recommend ways and means of accelerating and strengthening private development.

In accordance with another recommendation of the Mission a Co-ordinator of Transport was appointed in 1967. In 1970 the Co-ordinator of Transport became head of a new Department of Transport.

When he was appointed the Economic Adviser became a member of the Central Policy and Planning Committee, the then principal advisory body, consisting of the Administrator as chairman, the two Assistant Administrators, the Treasurer and the Director of District Administration. That Committee has now been replaced by the Inter-departmental Co-ordinating Committee of all departmental heads. It meets either in full or as a more limited group, depending on the subjects for discussion.

The other principal committees of officials with responsibilities for economic planning are:

the Budget Sub-Committee, presided over by the Treasurer, which advises the Administrator on all matters relating to the annual estimates;

the Works Consultative Committee, presided over by the Treasurer, which formulates the draft annual works programme;

the Land Development Board, now presided over by the Economic Adviser, which advises on land development, and settlement and land use patterns;

the Manpower Committee, chaired by the Secretary for Labour, whose primary task is to advise on future manpower strategies and policies in the public service and private enterprise. The Committee is supported by a special Manpower Unit which has been established in the Department of Labour.

In addition, special committees with varying memberships, under the chairmanship of the Economic Adviser, meet to discuss problem economic areas and to assist in formulating and reviewing the development programme.

At the District level, District Co-ordinating Committees have been established to participate in formulating District development plans and to hasten their application with more effective inter-departmental co-operation. The Committees are functioning, and machinery is being developed for integrating their activities more effectively into overall planning. By late 1970 draft programmes had been prepared for all Districts but were not yet available for general publication.

Contact between the Administration and the Papua and New Guinea House of Assembly [q.v.], on economic development as on other matters, is maintained through the Administrator's Executive Council, by debates and questions in the House of Assembly, and through frequent discussions with individual members. The Economic Adviser is not a member of the Administrator's Executive Council but attends meetings when required. There is a standing committee of the House of Assembly on economic development.

Contact is maintained with the Commonwealth Department of External Territories and through that Department with other Commonwealth and overseas bodies. In particular, arrangements have been made for joint work on a number of technical, economic, and statistical matters.

It has been one of the functions of the Economic Adviser to encourage and assist planning within the departments and agencies of the Administration. This has been done in the committees described above and by liaison with the officers responsible for planning throughout the Administration. Particularly close contact is maintained with the Treasury because of that Department's responsibility for overall financial planning, and with the Bureau of Statistics which has greatly extended its activities in recent years.

At first, planning was concentrated largely on

a medium-term programme for the public sector, because of its high relative importance in the economy, the greater amount of information available, the need for at least a provisional programme to serve as a base for administrative decisions, and the direct relevance of public expenditure and performance to indigenous economic activity, especially in agriculture. The first step was to revise the agricultural, forestry and other production targets suggested by the I.B.R.D. Mission, in the light of more recent experience and reassessed future prospects, and then to estimate the cost of achieving these targets in terms of finance, manpower and other resources. This was done in close consultation with the departments concerned and on the basis of information supplied by them. At the same time, the contributions required from the 'non-economic' departments to support the programme and maintain a reasonable rate of progress in the fields of health, education and services generally were estimated and included in the programme.

This work is co-ordinated with annual budgets and works programmes through the preparation by departments of annual 'physical performance' statements alongside their financial estimates for the year. These statements set out in the most precise terms possible the actual activities contemplated by the departments; for example, details of extension activities to be undertaken by the Department of Agriculture, Stock and Fisheries, school enrolments in the various categories, numbers of hospital admissions, areas of land to be purchased. This information was first compiled in a comprehensive budget statement in 1966-7 under the heading 'Expenditure and Physical Performance'. The intention was to convert the 1966-7 budget into an explicit one-year economic programme, before the preparation of a longer-range plan. The procedures used for the one-year estimates were then adapted for the preparation of the medium-term programme.

In November 1966, preceding the normal Treasury Instruction regarding the preparation of estimates for the following financial year, departments were asked by the Economic Adviser to review their physical performance in 1965-6, indicate their estimated performance in 1966-7 and to project their expected performance in each year to 1969-70. They were to show the implications of the programme for finance, recruitment and housing, and demands on other departments, including works and capital purchases. This information was used as a basis for the 1967-8 estimates and for the formulation of provisional public sector programmes and production and other targets. These were then summarized in *Economic Development of Papua and New Guinea*, first issued as a paper presented to the House of Assembly in June 1967.

This was not an integrated development programme, as much of it was in general terms, and the treatment of the non-agricultural private sector was slight. Its purpose was to give 'a progress report on the economy and planning by the Administration rather than a settled programme for implementation'. The paper did, however, 'introduce the broad elements of a development programme for analysis and public discussion' on the basis of tentative production and other targets, and it gave a brief analysis of the problems and constraints likely to affect development. The tentative production targets, for the most important export commodities and beef cattle, extended for the most part to 1974-5.

The financial, manpower, capital and other requirements of the tentative programme were discussed in general terms. The underlying detailed work was done by the Office of the Economic Adviser and in the departments, to ensure that the draft programmes were physically and financially feasible, that the activities proposed for departments were consistent with programme requirements, and that appropriate priorities for capital works and other expenditure had been adopted. Work on these aspects remains a continuing process in view of changing requirements and prospects and, in particular, of the need to adjust the draft programme to budgetary and manpower developments.

After the publication of *Economic Development* it was decided to revise the provisional programme again, extend the budgetary and manpower, etc., aspects to 1972-3, concentrate attention on certain areas such as transport and housing, and above all to take full account of the private sector component of the manufacturing and service industries which hitherto had been dealt with only in a sketchy fashion. The overall balance of payments, national income and other general implications were to be assessed, taking advantage of the results of the 1966 Census and other additional statistical information that was becoming available. An attempt was also to be made to place the provisional programme in its longer-term perspective.

This work proceeded and resulted in the publication in September 1968 of *Programmes and Policies for the Economic Development of Papua and New Guinea*. The provisional development programme provided in considerable detail a possible course of economic progress between 1968-9 and 1972-3, and envisaged the expenditure of nearly $1,000 million by the Administration over that period. Allowing for modifications that would be needed from time to time in the light of changing circumstances, the proposed objectives and targets of the programme were endorsed by the Commonwealth government as a basis for planning, subject to similar endorsement by the Territory House of Assembly.

The Commonwealth government also recognized that the development programme would require increased Commonwealth financial contributions. In his speech on the programme in the House of Representatives on 10 September, 1968, the Minister for External Territories stated: 'On the basis of mutual co-operation between the Government and the House of Assembly and the people of the Territory, the Government is prepared to assist in this way the achievement of the programme if the House of Assembly indicates that it is prepared progressively to increase the Territory's financial self reliance by raising the level of Territory revenue and loan receipts as much as practicable over the period of the programme.'

In November 1968 the proposed objectives and targets of the programme were endorsed as a basis for planning by the House of Assembly, which at the same time formally declared that it was prepared to accept financial commitments in the terms of the Minister's statement.

Reviews of progress under the programme were produced as White Papers issued with the 1969-70 and 1970-1 budgets. In October 1970, because of major developments in the previous two years, particularly the beginning of a large-scale copper-mining venture in Bougainville, the original programme was being revised and consideration given to the extension of the programme period to 1974-5. It was proposed to complete this work and table the revised programme in the House of Assembly early in 1971. A. W. McC.

(See also ECONOMIC POLICY; PUBLIC ADMINISTRATION)

ECONOMIC POLICY is difficult to define in detail. Official announcements tend to specify major items of policy, but can rarely explain more than a small part of the intricate decision-making of which total economic policy is composed. The following is an attempt to show, in addition to the main stated lines of policy, the lines upon which these more detailed decisions are made. The view presented is, therefore, that seen from within the government department concerned.—Note by Editor.

GOVERNMENT POLICY

The Australian government's basic policy for the Territory of Papua and New Guinea, as expressed in the Governor-General's speech at the opening of the second House of Assembly on 4 June 1968, is to develop the country for self-determination.

The government has made it clear that it regards political autonomy as incompatible with extreme economic dependence and its stated aim is to help develop a viable economy as soon as possible. Underlying this policy is the premise that the development of the Territory's physical and human resources will help to make it more self-reliant and, at the same time, provide a rising level of welfare for the people.

The five-year economic development programme, published in September 1968, provides guide lines for the development proposed for the period from 1968 to 1973.

The programme envisages expenditure by the Administration of about $1,000 million over the five-year period and puts emphasis on raising productive capacity, especially in agriculture, on strengthening infrastructure and on secondary and higher education and vocational training. Much of the investment proposed is relatively

long-term and will bear fruit only in the years beyond 1973.

A major aim of the programme is to provide Papuans and New Guineans with growing opportunities for employment in both the private and the public sectors and for developing their capacity to manage their own enterprises and to assume positions of responsibility in administration and business.

Certain broad principles are applied in promoting these economic objectives. First, it is intended that development of both human and physical resources should proceed in a balanced fashion. This does not necessarily imply that increases in expenditure should be evenly spread over a large number of different administrative functions or geographical regions. Development policies often require attention to be concentrated on key functions or key regions during a particular period. In education, for example, at an earlier stage of development major emphasis was placed on universal primary education. In recent years the focus has shifted to secondary, technical and tertiary education to advance the date when cadres of trained indigenes can man senior posts in administration and industry. And economic expenditure has for the most part been concentrated in a number of key areas where favourable conditions enable investment, e.g. oil palm or tea production, to yield outstanding results over relatively short periods. At the same time it is government policy to see that less favoured districts are allocated adequate resources from Territory revenues to generate and maintain some momentum of local development and to avoid a widening gap between more and less advanced regions.

Another major principle is the setting up and enforcement of standards appropriate to the stage of development and the current and prospective availability of resources. This can often raise problems, especially because of the important role played by Australian expatriates in the economy. Expatriates are accustomed to and maintain levels of income and expenditure considerably in excess of those appropriate to a relatively under-developed country like the Territory.

This applies particularly in the fields of wage policy and in the provision of facilities and services by the public sector. The question asked at each turn is: Is this the standard of wages, of accommodation, etc., which a self-governing Territory, standing as far as possible on its own feet economically, would be able to support? It is necessary to face the situation that standards set by these criteria are in many cases well below those adopted in Australia or by Australian expatriates in Papua and New Guinea.

Another major principle is that of advancing indigenes to positions of increasing responsibility. Attention must be focused on the subsistence sector of the economy in which the majority of indigenes are employed and on methods of drawing subsistence producers into the market economy.

This requires co-ordinated action on a number

of different fronts. Financial incentives, and attractive consumption goods on which to spend additional earnings, must be available to encourage subsistence producers to turn to cash cropping or to contemplate paid employment on plantations or elsewhere. Technical assistance is provided by the extension services to guide emergent cash croppers in problems of production and marketing and in their access to equipment, materials and credit for a cash cropping operation. Educational facilities, health services, and improved communications are all prerequisites for progress towards this objective. The government favours the extension of co-operatives, especially in fields where they have proved successful, e.g. agricultural marketing and processing and the operation of retail establishments.

FISCAL POLICY

The fiscal policy conforms to the basic objective of moving towards increasing economic self-dependence. In the revenue field it endeavours to generate as rapid a growth in taxation and other revenues as is consistent with the maintenance of incentive for fast expansion in the private sector and with equity between different classes of taxpayers. At the same time, it is government policy to ensure that the development programme is not frustrated in essential features by lack of funds.

In recent years the Commonwealth grant has continued to rise, but locally raised revenues have paid for a gradually increasing proportion of total Administration expenditure.

Increased Commonwealth financial contribution to Territory revenues will be needed during the five-year development programme and the government has expressed its readiness to assist in this way, subject to an indication by the House of Assembly that it is prepared to increase the country's financial self-reliance by raising the level of Territory revenue and loan receipts as much as practicable during that period. The House of Assembly has adopted the programme on this basis.

The tax structure reflects the dual nature of the Territory's economy: the existence side by side of a primitive subsistence sector and a quite sophisticated market economy largely dominated by expatriates. Relatively low levels of personal and company tax aim at maintaining incentive to investment in the private sector. The allocation of budgetary expenditure follows the line of priorities in the five-year development programme. It gives special emphasis to activities which contribute to the development of the Territory's physical and human resources, to the advancement of the local people, to growth in domestic wealth and welfare, and to reduced dependence on external aid.

BANKING AND INVESTMENT

Banking policy in the Territory is governed by Australian banking legislation and administered by the Reserve Bank of Australia. The Bank en-

sures that policies formulated to serve the needs of the Australian economy are modified in such a way as to promote the government's policy in the Territory in the light of local conditions. Where necessary the Bank's guide lines on credit policy in Papua and New Guinea are separate and distinct from those applying to the Australian economy (*see* BANKING).

Four Australian trading banks have branches in the main centres and their affiliates or subsidiaries operate savings banks.

In addition the government set up the Papua and New Guinea Development Bank with a special mandate for channelling credit to native producers. In doing so the Bank pays more regard to the productive potential of individual investment proposals than to the amount and quality of security offered by intending investors. The Bank commenced business in July 1966.

Rapid development of the Territory's economy requires a much higher level of investment in both the public and private sector than can at present be sustained from its own resources. In the public sector the gap is mainly filled by the Australian grant. The government also aims to attract assistance from international bodies such as the International Bank for Reconstruction and Development, the United Nations Development Programme, Unesco, etc.

Development in the private sector depends largely on an adequate inflow of capital. The government favours such an inflow and seeks to promote it through appropriate taxation and other policies. At the same time it ensures that investment proposals are consistent with its development policy and that they accord with the wishes of the Territory people.

Generally the government encourages investment proposals which will assist in developing the country on a sound and balanced basis, provide opportunities for local people to participate in projects, provide employment and training for local people, involve maximum processing in the Territory, and lead to the provision of basic services such as roads and ports.

Particular emphasis is placed on the provision of opportunities for local people to participate in the ownership and management of projects, especially those using natural resources. The objective is to avoid a situation where an excessive share of local enterprise is owned or controlled by expatriates. Participation can be achieved in a number of ways and no hard and fast rules have been laid down on how it is to be done. In some important cases the government has itself taken a share in the equity of major enterprises either directly or through the Papua and New Guinea Development Bank. In some other cases opportunities have been offered for local people to take up equity in enterprises by direct purchase of shares.

Recent arrangements for the establishment of some major enterprises reflect these policies. One example is the Nakanai oil palm project in West New Britain which the Administration owns jointly with a foreign investor experienced in the growing and processing of oil palm. In the case of the Bougainville copper mining project the agreement between the Administration and Bougainville Copper Pty Limited provides for an option by the Administration to participate to the extent of 20 per cent in the equity of the enterprise; it includes a formula under which after an initial tax holiday the Company will escalate its annual tax payment to 50 per cent of profits in addition to making a number of other payments to the Administration.

TRADE AND INDUSTRY

Imports have for long exceeded exports by a wide margin. This imbalance provides a measure of the country's inability to finance from its own resources its current level of expenditure on goods and services.

Development plans for agriculture, forestry, fisheries and mining aim at increasing export potential by stimulating expansion of existing industries and the creation of new ones. More recently the government has placed additional emphasis on the encouragement of import replacement industries which in the long run can help to contain the growth in import demand.

Export products are internationally promoted through publications, exhibitions and trade fairs [qq.v.]. Territory interests are kept before international conferences and organizations when international commodity problems are under consideration and Territory representatives have taken part in such meetings.

Most products are accorded duty free entry into Australia. In addition, the Territory has been granted special concessions in the Australian market under which preferential access is given to some important export commodities including coffee, plywood and rubber (see OVERSEAS TRADE).

WAGES AND MANPOWER

The objective of promoting a steady rise in the people's welfare, while increasing economic self-reliance, determines the wage policy, which is to maintain wages [q.v.] in the private sector at a level which will not discourage investment, especially in the export industries which compete in world markets. A minimum rural wage is set by the Administration. The government is less directly involved with setting private sector wages in urban areas but encourages discussions and negotiations between employers and employees on wage issues.

In the Public Service, wages for local employees and for expatriates are determined by different factors. Expatriate wages must be sufficient to attract an adequate supply of essential skills. As most expatriates come from Australia the supply price is closely related to, but necessarily above, Australian wage and salary scales. Wages of Papuan and New Guinea employees, however, have been fixed after arbitration at a level adequate to cover the reasonable needs of employees, having regard to the Territory's capacity to pay.

It is the government's policy to recruit where necessary additional skilled expatriates so that programmes designed to accelerate economic and social development should not be impeded by lack of suitable local manpower. This may necessitate a greater short-term dependence on expatriate skills to ensure the success of longer-term plans for faster progress towards economic self-reliance and greater indigenous development.

The longer-term manpower programme provides education and training programmes designed to increase the supply of local people qualified for jobs at all levels. The Administration does not recruit expatriates for jobs when sufficient local manpower is available. The replacement of expatriates by indigenous employees within the public sector will be a matter for special attention by the Localization Unit recently set up in the Territory's Public Service Board.

REGIONAL DEVELOPMENT

Government policy aims to increase the involvement of regional and local authorities in the process of economic decision making. It favours measures for greater local self-help and for increasing local revenues and thereby adding to the resources available for development. It also aims at involving increasing numbers of local people in local economic and political affairs.

The government favours projects which in the short and medium term show the best promise of adding to economic development, especially in export earning or import saving industries. To that extent development will not be spread evenly over all regions, just as industrial development cannot be spread evenly over all actual or potential industries.

ECONOMIC SECTORS

Primary industries. The major policies for primary industry derive from the overall objectives set out earlier. In agriculture, livestock, fisheries, forestry and mining the government aims to diversify and increase production, to reduce the Territory's dependence on a narrow range of primary export commodities, and to add to its capacity to procure from abroad the resources required for development of a viable economy. In addition, the development of primary industry is seen as an important step in the absorption of indigenes into the market economy and in raising their levels of income and welfare. In agriculture and fisheries the aim is to expand local food production both for subsistence and for sale, to improve the native diet, to prevent undue rises in food prices, and to reduce import requirements. Sound policies for economic husbandry and exploitation of resources are an important objective in all primary industries. Wherever possible the processing of local raw materials is encouraged as well as opportunities for the training and employment of indigenes in the processing establishment.

In agriculture the government's objectives are pursued in the following ways. Increased production is encouraged at the village level where there is a sufficient concentration of indigenous population in areas of good potential and with adequate communications. It is in these areas that a major agricultural extension effort is planned to expand commercial production. Where land of good potential exists in areas apart from existing populations, these opportunities for special development projects will be exploited through planned smallholder development.

Agricultural development depends heavily on the expansion of tree crops which take a relatively long time to mature. Finance for this purpose has not been easily obtainable in the past, especially for indigenous producers, because the loan terms required are longer than those usually granted by trading banks. Availability of longer-term credit from the Development Bank is intended to provide a substantial stimulus to the planting of tree crops by local people.

For crops which require substantial investment in processing facilities, e.g. tea and oil palm, government policy calls for a close association between expatriate interests owning a nucleus estate and processing facilities, and native smallholders, in which the smallholders' production is either bought from them or processed for them at a reasonable price by the nucleus estate factory.

In forestry, the immediate objective is to raise the supply and quality of forest products both for local use and for overseas markets. In the long term, production targets for a permanent forest estate are to be achieved by the establishment of integrated forest industries involving all aspects of logging, sawmilling, veneer and plywood production, in association with an export woodchip, or a local paper pulp, industry.

Secondary industry. The government's policy provides for the encouragement of manufacturing industries, to reduce the economy's dependence on a limited range of primary export products and to reduce the need for imports of manufactures. With population poised for possible rapid increase, manufacturing industries will become increasingly significant as employers of labour.

Secondary industries are being encouraged through tax concessions under a pioneer industries scheme, and by recent legislation to strengthen the Territory's tariff machinery; serviced sites are to be made available for industrial purposes. High priority is also placed on programmes to raise the level of skills in the work force through secondary and technical education and through the training of apprentices. Service industries in the transport, building and construction fields will be encouraged, as well as secondary industries producing simple consumer goods such as clothing, footwear and processed foods, for the rapidly growing local market (*see* INDUSTRIALIZATION).

TRANSPORT AND COMMUNICATIONS

The inadequacy of the transport system is one of the main obstacles to Territory development. The domestic market is divided into small areas and transport charges on goods are high. Inaccessibility also hinders integration of isolated tribes into the wider social community and into the market economy. The broad objectives of the transport programme are therefore to:

develop a minimum system of efficient and reliable inter-regional land and sea communications,

reduce transport costs,

service planned development projects, especially in the primary industries, and service planned and expected urban growth,

facilitate rural development and the penetration of the subsistence economy.

Special emphasis is placed on the need for close integration between different modes of transport and for the justification of individual projects by detailed cost benefit studies.

High priority has been given to the development of telecommunications, financed partly by a loan from the International Bank for Reconstruction and Development.

PLANNING UNDER THE FIVE-YEAR DEVELOPMENT PROGRAMME

The five-year development programme gives expression to the objectives and basic policies of the government and sets targets for the various sectors. The programme preserves the essential free-market character of the economy. While expenditures in the public sector will be programmed with the aim of reaching the targets set by the plan, the government has not proposed to take additional powers for directing the planning of the private sector. The aim is to establish an economic climate attractive to investors both from within the Territory and from outside, and to offer a range of incentives to entrepreneurs and employees to work effectively towards the achievement of the programme.   G. O. GUTMAN

Since the above article was written there have been important developments in the Australian government's Papua New Guinea policies. Rapid progress with the devolution of policy making functions has accompanied some significant changes in the programmes and actual content of economic policy.

In Port Moresby in July 1970 the Prime Minister (John Gorton) announced in a major speech: '. . . there are further steps now short of self-government but towards self-government which I feel should be made . . . We believe that the time has come when less should be referred to Canberra for decision and more should be retained for decision by the Administrator's Executive Council and by the Ministerial Members who for the most part make up that Council.'

Since then Papua New Guinea's constitutional relationships with Australia have been modified by the transfer of a number of important functions to ministerial members of the Administrator's Executive Council. The transfer was subject to the understanding that policies should continue to develop in conformity with the broad scheme contained in the Papua New Guinea economic development programme of 1968.

Thus while the broad framework remains, decision making functions within it have to varying degrees been vested in elected representatives. Such devolution is seen as a continuing process. In March 1971 the House of Assembly accepted recommendations of its Select Committee on Constitutional Development which set an approximate timetable for constitutional development and proposed preparation of a programme for full internal self-government in the period 1972 to 1976 (i.e. the lifetime of the next House of Assembly). This proposal was endorsed by the Australian government. Implementation of this programme will depend on the state of public opinion and the policies of the political leaders who emerge after the 1972 House of Assembly elections.

New economic measures over recent years have specifically aimed at accelerating indigenous involvement in the management and direction of commercial and economic affairs as well as promoting greater indigenous participation directly or indirectly in the ownership of new enterprises.

The Department of Business Development, created in 1970 with an indigene as its first departmental head, is charged with the special function of encouraging indigenous involvement in all phases of business. It promotes indigenous participation in enterprises through the co-operative movement and also by providing advice and training for individual businessmen. The department collaborates with other government agencies, notably the Development Bank.

Other steps to accelerate indigenous development include the Business Licences Ordinance of 1971 which provides for preference for indigenes in the licensing of new trade stores, the prevalent form of small retail business in Papua New Guinea. Another measure provides for restraints on immigration to prevent an influx of expatriates into types of employment for which trained local people are available.

A major new institution, the Papua New Guinea Investment Corporation, has been set up for the specific purpose of ensuring an appropriate component of Papua New Guinea equity in major investment projects. Where funds are not locally available in the hands of indigenous investors, the Corporation can step in and take up, by way of an option or otherwise, a proportion of the equity with a view to disposing of it later to local shareholders.

Economic policy management continues to be guided by the major principles referred to in the main article. The Administration has on the whole succeeded in maintaining standards appropriate to the Papua New Guinea environment and to its economic capacity in dealing with the ever-present pressures for higher wages and increased expenditures on more elaborate infrastructure and social provisions.

The other broad principle calling for concentration of economic efforts to produce a properly balanced and optimal development has also been broadly observed. Nevertheless the gradual emergence of the House of Assembly as a vocal representative body will generate occasional pressures on the Administration to divert resources from more productive avenues towards areas less well endowed with natural resources so that residents may obtain their due share of government expenditures. In Papua New Guinea as elsewhere such claims will need to be considered and in some instances deferred to.

Changing economic circumstances rather than political pressures have called for some important modifications of the 1968 economic development programme and led to the adoption by the House of Assembly of a revised programme in September 1971.

The most significant new development was the Bougainville copper project [q.v.] scheduled to come into production in mid-1972. This project will more than double the gross value of Papua New Guinea's exports and make a substantial contribution to national income and government revenues. With the possibility of other important mining projects and major fisheries and forest-product ventures being launched as well as potential expansion of tourism, the economic future of Papua New Guinea now appears less heavily dependent than earlier on the export of a small range of traditional tropical plantation products.

The outlook for these traditional crops (especially copra, cocoa, coffee and rubber) is perhaps marginally more uncertain even than it appeared some years ago. Substantial increases in production in other tropical developing countries and the threat of substitutes (especially for vegetable oil and rubber) are important factors. In addition the world-wide rise in interest rates has reduced the attractiveness of the heavy investment needed to bring slow maturing plantation crops to the profit-earning stage.

Furthermore Britain's accession to the European Economic Community (E.E.C.) could deprive Papua New Guinea of preferential access to a market which traditionally has taken something like a quarter of her exports. The Australian government has made strong and continuous representations on Papua New Guinea's behalf to both Britain and the members of the E.E.C. to impress on them the unique nature and importance of her case for continued access to the U.K. market. There are some grounds for hope that from these representations arrangements will emerge which will prevent serious damage to Papua New Guinea's export trade.

In keeping with the policies of fostering indigenous participation as well as economic growth, emphasis is being placed on the development of crops such as tea and oil palm which lend themselves to a system of 'nuclear' settlement with a large number of smallholders grouped around a technologically advanced processing facility.

A paramount fact of Papua New Guinea's economic situation remains the preponderance of agriculture as a form of livelihood for the great majority of its people. Extension of cash cropping and the availability of paid employment are essential if subsistence producers are to be integrated more fully into the modern economy and enjoy rising living standards. Global economic trends militating against excessive reliance on traditional plantation crops have directed attention to the development of new crops for export as well as increased production for the home market.

The more rapid growth of manufacturing industries especially those processing primary products for export (e.g. timber) will help to diversify employment opportunities for the growing work force.

Outside the rapidly expanding natural resource industries (mining, forestry, fisheries) the centre of gravity of economic effort is likely to move towards import saving production in both the primary and secondary sectors with more attention devoted to the production of export-orientated manufacturing.

The second five-year development programme now in preparation will be placed before the House of Assembly during 1972-3 and will aim to delineate new policies in response to these shifting economic trends both within the rapidly developing economy of Papua New Guinea and in the wider world beyond.

(*See also* ECONOMIC PLANNING; FINANCIAL INSTITUTIONS; PUBLIC FINANCE)

ECONOMY, INDIGENOUS. The quantitative and qualitative analysis of primitive economic systems is still in its infancy. The main reason is the absence of money as a generally accepted medium of exchange. Without such a common measure of value it is difficult to examine the rationality of choices or decisions. Time, the universally scarce factor, may be taken as a measuring rod. Salisbury did this successfully for the Siane. Yet to use time as a unit of measurement poses certain problems; it does not take into account the different amount of energies and skills invested on different occasions in the same unit of time. A further complicating variable in the study of under-developed societies is the entanglement of purely economic transactions with the complex of social ties that often channel the movement of goods and services. Economic transactions no doubt pervade the social life of primitive peoples, and economic difficulties constantly face them. Yet hardly any of their activities or relationships are guided by purely economic considerations, i.e. the maximization of material gains; these form only one strand in the total nexus of socio-economic activities. Accordingly much information relevant to the study of isolated primitive economies can be extracted from general ethnographic and anthropological literature.

In discussing the operation of small economies in New Guinea it is essential to distinguish between 'traditional' and 'modern' systems. The basic difference between the two is that the former were isolated and stagnant whereas the latter are integrated and geared to growth. One distinction is important particularly with reference to reports of large surplus production and shrewd indigenous entrepreneurs operating in

the traditional economy. These reports may give the impression of a history of economic development even prior to European contact. A flexible socio-political system of rule by 'big men' certainly encouraged individual thrift and enterprise, yet from the point of view of the total economy it simply meant a periodic re-allocation of control over input and output of a volume of productive resources that was in the long run stable and fixed. Life in the pre-contact era must have proceeded without any major economic or social changes. A limited mastery over the physical environment had been achieved, and with the technological knowledge and the technical equipment available the standard of living could not be improved. Moreover, there was no alien civilization near at hand from which borrowings might have been made.

TRADITIONAL

Most economic activities were associated with agriculture. Each area had its staple crop: in the Highlands this was mainly sweet potatoes, along the coast usually taro or yam. Shifting cultivation was practised with extensive periods of bush fallow. Coconuts, bananas, and other nuts, fruit, and vegetables were grown wherever climate and soil permitted. Environmental conditions determined whether or not indigenes supplemented their cultivation with hunting and fishing [qq.v.]. In the sphere of animal husbandry the people mainly concentrated on raising pigs [q.v.]. These, like human beings, feed largely on root crops, which in turn have to be cultivated. Crafts were on the whole developed only to a rudimentary level (*see* MATERIAL CULTURE).

Land. Agricultural pursuits formed the basis of most pre-contact economies. Accordingly, land tenure and inheritance were of vital importance. Rights to land were in most cases vested in social groups. A man could cultivate a certain plot of land by virtue of his membership of the particular kin-group that controlled it. Systems of land tenure and inheritance differed from area to area (*see* LAND TENURE). In some places, for instance among the Wain of the Lae Highlands, a man had rights not only in the land belonging to his paternal relatives but also in that belonging to his maternal relatives. Which rights he invoked depended on where he decided to live. If he settled patri-virilocally he rarely claimed his maternal land rights; on the other hand, he was at no disadvantage if he happened to live among his mother's kin. Other peoples, like the Chimbu of the Highlands, studied by Brookfield and Brown, placed greater emphasis on land inheritance in the patrilineal line of descent. But even among them there were several kin-groups to which a young man could attach himself and so he had a choice as to where to exercise his claims to land. In many Melanesian societies descent and inheritance were matrilineal. But even in these it was often possible for a son to cultivate some of the land vested in his father's relatives if he gave a large feast for them or handed over valuables or distributed shell money at one of their important mortuary rites. There was thus much flexibility in the traditional pattern of land rights. This was facilitated by the absence of population pressure on land. Salisbury suggests that it might be argued that the balance between population and available resources in any one area was in fact the result of conscious planning. He cites as an example one of the Siane clans, members of which in 1953 recognized that they had reached the maximum population density possible; consequently some of them were migrating, offering as excuse that lineage strips at home were too small and too few. The availability of large areas of uninhabited bush land made for frontier societies. In pre-contact days warfare was probably the most important means by which major areas of land were transferred between social groups. This enabled families who found that they had exhausted landed resources within their home area to shift to other places and exploit different ground. More often it was a case of the 'big man' trying to gather a following to help in the cultivation of land and increase the supply of available manpower rather than of men fighting over, or moving in search of, cultivable land.

Production planning. All creation of wealth started with the cultivation of crops (*see* AGRICULTURE, INDIGENOUS). This was the first labour investment any young man had to make. He may have inherited one or more pigs or acted as custodian for some, but in order to feed his family and his animals he had to grow food. Much production was carried on for specific ends. The Trobriand Islanders of Papua, the Kapauku of West Irian, and other peoples distinguished between certain kinds of yams as appropriate for ceremonials and others for normal food. Moreover, cultivators frequently allocated the produce of certain plots at the time of planting. A man might plan one plot to produce food to be given to his affinal kin, another to his wife to dispose of as she thought fit, another to provide for his family's consumption, and yet another to feed the people he expected to help him build a house or a canoe or clear another area of bush. The beneficiaries were informed at the time of planting that the produce was destined for them. Thus within the limits set to output by climate and soil conditions the recipients were able to plan their own cultivation as well as the arrangements for large feasts. There was, indeed, a considerable element of planning in traditional agriculture, though it frequently went wrong. Pospisil relates how a number of dry years caused the Kapauku to relax their precautions and disregard the weather factor in their choice of new garden lots. They planted most of their sweet potatoes in the lowlands, expecting more dry weather. But the next year proved to be so wet that all the crops in the valley gardens rotted and the people almost starved. This clearly indicates the extent to which agricultural output was subject to forces beyond the cultivator's control. It also emphasizes the necessity to plan for a surplus in normal years as protection against possible drought or flood.

Labour. Many of the subsistence crops required comparatively little labour, and there was thus much unused manpower potential. All societies in the area practised some division of labour based on sex. Men coped with most of the physically heavy and dangerous work such as clearing bush, making fences and boundaries, fighting, hunting, and so on; while women concentrated on the lighter tasks such as weeding, harvesting, and household duties. Children were trained at an early age to perform the tasks appropriate to their sex. Thus economic practices, probably the result of trial and error, were handed down from generation to generation. For instance, the Mount Hagen people discussed by Gitlow knew that land may be replanted when a certain kind of tree had reached a height of approximately ten feet. Similarly, the Kapauku cultivated their valley gardens intensively by means of drainage ditches, composting, and crop rotation. Often they were able to take three or four harvests from the one plot. By contrast, they took only a single harvest from their slope gardens, which they simply cleared by fire and cultivated without fertilizer. Many indigenes were aware of the advantages of rotating crops: greens were often followed by corn, taro, or bananas and then by sweet potatoes. They seemed to have worked out what was the most effective system of cultivation possible within the limits set by their environment and technology.

Traditionally most peoples organized their agricultural activities at the level of the primary household. Yet there was extensive reciprocal assistance at irregular intervals for tasks that required strenuous or tedious work, such as bush clearing, or those that had to be completed within a short period of time, such as harvesting or house building. The Busama, discussed by Hogbin, explained the need for mutual aid in preparing garden land by saying, 'Felling the bush alone is like trying to empty the sea with a canoe bailer—it never ends'. Siane men of the Eastern Highlands also had reciprocal labour arrangements: they usually visited their mother's brothers or sister's sons during the *roi* and nut seasons and helped in harvesting. Such assistance was reciprocated when their own crop was due. These mutual-aid arrangements often gave rise to limited trade and exchanges. Siane owners of *roi* trees tended to visit kinsmen who owned nut trees, from whom they received nuts; subsequently the nut owners visited the *roi* owners and received oil.

In other societies master-client relationships were used to secure labour. Parkinson describes how the shrewd Tolai [q.v.] 'big man' encouraged his followers to plant large areas. He had to reward them with either shell money or food, but made a handsome profit when he finally sold the total output for shell money. Among the Kapauku labour was employed on a contract basis and paid in shell money. The customary price for making a *peka*-sized garden—one *peka* equals about 900 square metres—was two Kapauku cowries. In their contractual transactions the Kapauku always stated the price for the accomplishment of a specific task, never for a unit of working time. If, for instance, a man agreed to build a fence and it was destroyed by pigs before he had been paid he could not expect to receive payment.

A number of possibilities were thus exploited to organize labour. In all traditional New Guinea societies some household members provided at least part of the work force. Among many peoples additional labour was arranged reciprocally, among some in master-client relationships, and in a few by contract (see SOCIAL STRUCTURE).

Capital and entrepreneurship. The indigenous capital asset that required most labour and materials was probably the canoe. Cultivators handled only very primitive tools in their agricultural activities: sharp pieces of bamboo, pointed sticks, and stone axes or adzes were often all they used. Stone axe blades chipped easily, were quickly abraded by sharpening, and had an average life of no more than eighteen months. This high rate of replacement could still be met by a little labour. The Siane took six man-days to produce one stone axe, their most important tool.

Owing to the low level of technology capital requirements were limited. Consequently there was no annual net addition to the stock of assets; replacement of tools was practically the only investment in productive equipment. The lands, associated with comparatively little labour input for subsistence production and capital replacement, made entrepreneurship the main limiting factor in the supply of output. These are the conditions responsible for the existence of 'primitive affluence' as described by Fisk. In these circumstances organizing ability and entrepreneurship must be regarded as important factors of production. Most of the settlements had one or more 'big men'. Recognition as a leader depended on prominent participation in feasts and ceremonial exchanges as well as on the possession of other qualities of leadership. A flexible social system with emphasis on achieved as opposed to ascribed social status provided the background to the exercise of entrepreneurship by capable men. However, not all 'big men' were entirely self-made. In many societies the heir to a rich man was in a favoured position. But if he proved to be negligent or careless, his fortunes were soon dissipated. In fact no leader was ever secure.

Economics and politics. The low level of technical knowledge made almost impossible the production of unusually elaborate items of food, clothing, or shelter. Consequently, 'big men' could hardly consume any different quality or quantity of goods from those consumed by their followers, in spite of the fact that as leaders they controlled the economic resources of land, pigs, and such valuables as feathers and shells. Hoarded wealth did not in itself carry prestige nor attract a following. It was the distribution of wealth and the extension of credit that did this. A wealthy creditor not only became a political leader and legal authority, he was also regarded as among the most moral of individuals. This stress on egalitarian living was often reinforced by fears

of magic. A 'big man' tempted by conspicuous consumption was afraid to arouse jealousy because of the possibility of sorcery being directed against him.

The lack of opportunity to acquire durable consumer goods or to invest in the creation of new and additional productive assets therefore led 'big men' to invest their wealth in scarce valuables and to build up a following by making loans to young people. The real skill of the traditional entrepreneur was expressed in his ability to strike the right balance between his accumulation of valuables and his redistribution of goods. If he spent too much on valuables he was bound to lose influence in his society; on the other hand, if he dissipated too much of his wealth he lost respect and went bankrupt. The Tolai 'big man' had to be a shrewd operator: he had to accumulate shell money and simultaneously display generosity towards his followers.

Economics and religion. Economic activities and religious beliefs were frequently interdependent. Among the Tolai, for instance, thrift was supported by supernatural sanctions. These people believed that it provided the passport to a happy afterlife. On the other hand, the leader was also expected to finance and organize large ceremonials and religious festivals. He occupied a key economic position and translated this into the sphere of religion and rituals. Accordingly, the Tolai 'big man' was also the master of his local group of the *Dukduk,* a male cult that represented the central theme in Tolai philosophy. Every man of ambition was an entrepreneur; ceremonial and its marked exchange character forced him to be. If a young man was about to be married, or if the death of an important elder was imminent, the nearest kin had to plan ahead by planting large food gardens so as to have sufficient crops not only to feed the necessary helpers in the performance of marriage or mortuary rites, but also to offer lavish hospitality to a wide circle of visitors. Thus religious ceremonies provided some of the occasions for large-scale feasting and redistribution of wealth.

Consumption. In most traditional societies the composition of the productive unit differed radically from that of the unit of consumption. The Kapauku had 'gardening units', composed of the simple or polygynous family of the landowner, which were responsible for productive activities, whereas the people who shared a common residence, often several families, planned consumption in common. They placed great emphasis on the intake of sweet potatoes, their staple diet. Hunger was conceptualized as a state of being without sweet potatoes in the stomach. Consequently eating pork, greens or any other food did not in their eyes alleviate hunger; only a dish of sweet potatoes could do that. This emphasis on the consumption of the staple crop resulted in the size of the cultivated area being determined by the number of people who lived together rather than by the number making up the 'gardening unit'. The Kapauku were compelled by custom to share food with their friends and relatives. Therefore, to avoid extensive sharing, a man who had some delicacy usually tried to hide it and consume it secretly.

The stress of reciprocity was often sanctioned by religious beliefs. The Busama were convinced that illness would follow if they were to eat any meat from a pig they had themselves raised. Accordingly when a household slaughtered an animal the pork was given away. The distribution without expectation of immediate return was of paramount importance for nutrition. Fresh meat deteriorates quickly in the tropics. The owner had no way of preserving pork and therefore gave it away in the expectation of a countergift. This general method of exchange ensured that in time individuals obtained roughly equal shares. It necessarily implied the notion of credit.

Specialization, barter and trade. All barter or trade is based on some specialization unless for ritual reasons identical articles are exchanged. Often the natural resources of neighbouring areas differed. The Busama, for example, had more agricultural land than they required to meet immediate needs. These villagers, therefore, produced quantities of taro for export. Other villages in the area possessed large swamps where surplus sago was grown; yet other villages specialized in pottery or woodcarving. There were thus some economically interdependent regions within which the population exchanged products. In some places soil variations were so great that a certain variety of one and the same crop flourished only in strictly limited localities, thereby encouraging barter or trade.

The pattern of exchanges varied from the highly personal relations between kula [q.v.] partners in the Trobriand Islands [q.v.] to the largely impersonal and contractual market transactions of the Kapauku and the Tolai who have a system of shell currency almost equivalent to Western money.

It is difficult to analyse the price-formation process in primitive economies. The Siane had a relatively fixed equivalence of one salt cake for one pig. When a Siane clan had publicly received a presentation of roi oil it behoved them to give value for what had been presented to them and return an equivalent. If the initial donors regarded the amount as insufficient they expressed dissatisfaction. This usually led the initial recipients to add to what they had given rather than risk the loss of future supplies of roi oil. In some instances the return was expected immediately but in others the settlement may have been delayed for years. Among the Suau of Milne Bay all transactions were registered either as credits or debts, as also were the pigs speared and the portions distributed. At the periodic pig feast some men obtained payment for past credits, others incurred fresh debts to be settled at a future date, perhaps after five years. Accounts were memorized and return gifts always expected and usually effected. In this way barter was conducted to the mutual satisfaction of the parties. Return gifts were sometimes more valuable than the initial presents. In such cases the man's intention was to show off his wealth and stress his generosity. In contrast with these personal economic exchanges the Kapauku Papuans, the Tolai, and other societies employing shell money had largely impersonal economic dealings. Market exchange with shell money as the medium frequently occurred between strangers who met once to conclude a single transaction. Since ultimate social advantage and prestige could be achieved only through the medium of becoming wealthy, trading was largely profit-motivated with few other considerations. The Tolai had chains of markets linking the coastal settlements with the interior of the Gazelle Peninsula, where middlemen acted as intermediaries. At the Kapauku pig market trading was often conducted by complete strangers. Men invested shell money in pigs and chickens with the hope of breeding the animals and selling their offspring. At times when supply was good in relation to demand, and prices consequently low, shrewd businessmen bought commodities such as bundles of salt, or pigs, as a speculation. At Tolai markets too, prices fluctuated in the short run as a result of changes in supply and demand. Besides, the closer the relationship between parties to a transaction the less profitable it was for the initiator. When a Busama acquired a string bag from a fellow villager he always gave twice what he paid to a more distant relative on the north coast. A rich Kapauku political leader was frequently offered commodities for prices lower than normal, either because the seller expected favours, or because he was afraid the rich man might demand payment of a debt. Accordingly, 'big men' were able to buy several pigs from followers, or even from outsiders, at less than the customary or even the market price. Though all traditional trade articles appear to have had a customary price, actual rates differed from the norm not only because of changes in supply and demand but also because of the social status of the parties. Nevertheless, the customary price remained an ideal, a moral and fair price that ought to be asked and paid. Paying the right price meant security for both parties to the contract. This security, however, was obtained at the expense of the possible greater profit to one of them had a higher or lower price been offered.

Shell money, credits, savings, investment and interest. In most of New Guinea shells acted as valuables. Being highly desired, they were usually a liquid asset. Yet the exchange value differed according to age, size, texture, regularity of shape, and colouring. Among the Abelam some shells were kept as heirlooms and called by the name of the owners' totem. Fine specimens were stored with care and much admired for their smoothness and shape. Shells were given away at marriage, at the birth of a child, and at death; a small one was handed in compensation for adultery; a man who wished to injure someone sent a shell to a sorcerer in another village to engage his services. Yet shells hardly ever facilitated everyday exchanges among the Abelam, nor were market values of other commodities expressed in them. Their significance lay in the social and ceremonial sphere rather than in economics. In these circumstances the employment of shells in certain exchanges did not mean they were being used as money, i.e. as a medium of exchange and as a measure and store of value. In contrast, societies such as the Kapauku, the Tolai, and the Rossel Islanders must be regarded as having had highly monetized economies even in pre-contact days (*see* ROSSEL ISLAND CURRENCY). The Kapauku cowrie money (*Cypraea* sp.) came in various denominations with a fixed equivalence between the different types of shells: one *tuanika mege* equalled five *kawane*, and one *dege bomoje* was equivalent to three *tuanika mege* or fifteen *kawane*. These shells were not found in their own area, all were acquired through trade from peoples on the coast. Consequently the amount in circulation was limited. Pospisil believes that in pre-contact days the number of cowries in circulation remained the same; those lost or destroyed through wear and tear about equalled importations. The value of the currency was generally stable and fixed by its scarcity. Similarly the Tolai used shells (*Nassarius callosa*) as money, called *tambu*, which were not available in their own area. Tolai from the eastern part of the Gazelle Peninsula had to undertake dangerous and costly trips two hundred miles along the coast to obtain them through trading or fighting. This fact limited the supply of shells. *Tambu* consisted of pierced shells threaded on string and was counted in numbers of individual shells, or in fathoms—measured from fingertip to fingertip when both arms were outstretched—or fractions thereof. It was durable and could easily be kept as small change for the purpose of daily purchases. Larger quantities were stored in the form of coils made by winding strings of *tambu* —about 100 to 500 fathoms—around a circle of bamboo. The whole was then covered with pandanus leaves. The Tolai, like the Kapauku, paid with shell money for most of the goods and services derived from outside the household. They clearly distinguished between purchase and barter —they had different words to denote the two types of transaction—and an overwhelming amount of goods was exchanged through sales. Barter operated according to certain rules on spheres of exchange, which limited the free movement of goods. In contrast, shell money was accepted as a general means of settling transactions. Only money enabled a Kapauku or a Tolai to marry, to gain prestige, to become a political leader and legal authority, and to secure for himself a happy afterlife. 'Big men' often started their careers with borrowed shell money and subsequently became large-scale creditors themselves. Both peoples were familiar with the concept of interest. But they did not believe that time was money. Consequently, the amount of interest bore no relationship to the duration of the loan and was stipulated at the time the credit was given; among the Tolai it was usually 20 per cent. If a man refused to pay a debt he was thenceforth marked, and no one would lend him anything in future. The Tolai 'big man' acted as banker for his followers by storing all their accumulated wealth of *tambu,* and thereby offered a place for safe deposits as well as chan-

nels for reinvestment. Bankers could utilize at least part of the deposits to finance such activities as planting large food gardens so as to sell the crop or to invest in the distribution of articles with a view to collecting payment, including some profit, at a special function. In some instances the banker became too extravagant and used up too much of the stock of *tambu* in his care. If found out in his lifetime he was immediately discredited. More often his fraudulent activities remained undiscovered till after his death, when his kinsmen scrutinized his assets. In societies with shell currencies savings were usually kept in this form. The Kapauku distinguished between two kinds of savings: shell money for requirements and tabooed shell money destined to be inherited by sons. The Tolai, on the other hand, placed more emphasis on redistributing the accumulated stock of a deceased man at the mortuary rites. The distribution of the hoarded *tambu* at rituals and ceremonies appears to have been the only way in which the vast majority of the accumulated Tolai wealth at any one time was actually used. The Kapauku invested a major part of their wealth in raising pigs, always with a view to holding a pig feast at which a large number of the total stock was slaughtered and consumed. Accordingly their pre-contact economy passed through four-year pig-cycles, starting and finishing with a pig feast and high monetary income, and with a period in between made up of two years of reinvestment and two years of breeding and fattening the growing animals, with occasional slaughter of male pigs and sales of piglets to outsiders.

Accounts of the operation of shell money economies throw into relief the similarities with modern capitalism. At the same time, they emphasize the basic difference between the two polar economic systems. The development of capitalistic economies has been marked by trade cycles, yet throughout there has been a growth trend. In contrast pig cycles have hardly brought about any economic expansion. Primitive peoples, even those who used money, were halted in their progress by their limited technology. There was thus no net addition to the stock of capital assets and consequently no improvement in the standard of living.

MODERN

First contact with the wider cash economy offered indigenes two new economic opportunities: they could sell their produce or their labour. The first European traders in the area sought mostly shell —turtle, trochus, etc.—and later coconuts. Recruitment of New Guineans for work on plantations in other Pacific areas, such as Samoa and Queensland, started almost simultaneously with external trade. The 'primitive affluence' of pre-contact days made many young men reluctant to volunteer for labour migration. In order to secure supplies of workers some blackbirders made deals with indigenous 'big men', offering steel tools and other desired articles for permission to abduct young men. The attractiveness of the new goods induced many leaders to become parties to these unsavoury deals. In exchange for steel axes, knives, guns, ammunition, and such-like articles natives were prepared to give almost anything they had. The immediate effect of this external trade on the traditional economy was to induce a more efficient use of available resources; for instance, all fallen coconuts were carefully collected rather than left about sometimes even to rot, as had been previous practice. The coastal people, the first to be approached, were quick to realize the strategic position they occupied. The possession of guns increased the power and influence of 'big men', who were often also war leaders. This enlarged the size of political units, by enabling a few men to wield greater power and influence over more people. The monopolistic 'big men' resented any attempts by traders or missionaries to establish direct contact with peoples from the interior.

For some years traditionally produced commodities—coconuts, sandalwood, turtle-shell— were the only items sold to the newcomers. Then the Europeans realized that large areas of land for plantations could be bought for only a few trade articles. Before long the natives concerned began to regret these sales.

The new plantations needed labour. Most were situated in coastal regions where the people had alternative opportunities to acquire trade goods and were therefore reluctant to accept employment. Consequently workers had to be recruited from further afield and fed by their new employers. This created an additional demand for locally produced food. The foreign cash crop ventures also set an example to the indigenes, who soon expanded their cultivation for the purpose of selling the surplus. Colonial administrators in the area actively sponsored and encouraged natives to plant more coconuts. New economic opportunities were thus extended over a wider range of activities as well as over a greater number of people (see COCONUT INDUSTRY).

European planters produced not only copra but also experimented with several other crops, such as cotton, coffee, cocoa, and rice. Natives did not have the necessary expertise to copy these experiments. Accordingly coconuts were practically their only cash crop until after World War II, when the Australian authorities organized large-scale extension programmes and instructed and supervised the cultivation of a variety of crops.

Land. Most of the Territory's increasing cash produce is derived from perennial tree crops. Allocation of a continuously increasing area to long-term tree cultivation is therefore necessary. Land tenure hence plays a vital part in economic expansion. Among many peoples ownership of land is vested in groups. Corporate control is suitable for the traditional shifting cultivation and facilitates the pooling of financial resources to invest in costly capital items; but in the long term it presents an obstacle to economic growth. The overlapping claims of various clans and subclans often cause uncertainty as to the rights of each, in particular with respect to lands planted with cash crops. Perennial trees tend to freeze

land titles and thereby eliminate the flexibility that was part of traditional land tenure. But as long as there is ample land available the allocation of titles presents little problem.

However, the extension of cash cropping in districts where there has been considerable land alienation and where the population is growing rapidly has already produced pressure on land resources, and in the most developed regions disputes have become frequent and often insoluble. Cash cropping has not only introduced additional strains in the large kin units by creating a profit motive for individual members, but it has also strengthened the tie between fathers and sons who usually operate their cash ventures jointly. This is particularly apparent in matrilineal societies with patri-virilocal residence. Many Tolai men would like to leave their property to their sons, who assist in accumulating it, rather than to their sisters' sons, who frequently grow up in another parish and never offer any help. Yet according to customary law the nearest uterine relative, rather than the son, has the right to inherit all wealth. As a result much unofficial cultivation takes place by young men who, encouraged by the father, grow cocoa and coconuts on his lands. They sell the crops secretly to Chinese traders and deposit the cash received in their own savings bank accounts. As soon as the present elders die it is likely therefore that strife will occur between the sons on the one hand and the uterine kin on the other. Previously a Tolai who wanted to stake a claim to some of his father's property had to help his paternal kin arrange a lavish mortuary feast at which he generously distributed shell money to all and sundry. Attacks by missionaries on feasting and traditional exchanges may have serious social and economic consequences.

The hindrances to economic growth caused by the system of corporate land-holding, particularly by a matrilineal descent group, will become more and more apparent as land shortage becomes acute. The Australian Administration has attempted some reform of indigenous land tenure by legalizing conversion of holdings to individual titles, and by offering long-term leases to some individuals under secure conditions of tenure on resettlement schemes. Neither of these attempts has as yet gone far enough to offer any great relief to the problem of land tenure. By 31 March 1967 only 42,533 acres had been allocated for resettlement, of which no more than 1,717 blocks totalling 37,168 acres had been taken up by leaseholders. The resettlement projects occupy less than .1 per cent of the total area of unalienated lands. Yet these new possibilities for cultivators indicate the trend of change. At Silanga mission-sponsored resettlement scheme the cultivators decided jointly to make their cash crops subject to patrilineal inheritance rather than continue their traditional matrilineal system; each son is to get an equal share of his father's property. Settlers say that 'there are two ways for working at Silanga: one for the gardens where they all work together, and one for the cocoa, each one for himself. This is the new way because they get money for cocoa and each one takes his own money'. Enterprising men want to be able to realize the full value of their work. However, conversion to individual titles necessitates the agreement of all members of the group which by custom has a claim to the land. This probably accounts for the slow process of land reform; since December 1964 when the Land (Tenure Conversion) Ordinance came into operation only 153 titles and approximately 5,000 acres have been officially granted to individuals.

Labour. The introduced steel axes have in a very brief period almost entirely replaced those of stone. The latter, once carried habitually by most male adults, have been relegated to display in men's houses. Steel tools have considerably reduced male labour requirements for cultivation. One Siane ward group was estimated to have spent 1,000 man-days on land improvements when working with stone tools as compared with only 620 man-days when using steel equipment. In earlier times Siane men spent as much as 80 per cent of their time on subsistence work; the new steel technology has reduced this proportion to half. By contrast, female labour remained unaffected by the introduction of new tools; Siane women still devote 82 per cent of their days to subsistence activities. Remoteness prevented Siane men from reinvesting the saved time by producing for the market. Instead they spent longer on ceremonials and political manoeuvrings. However, some of the more accessible peoples began cash cropping soon after first contact. Copra, the first indigenous cash crop and still the Territory's major export—in 1964-5 it contributed about 25 per cent of the total produce sold abroad—requires little labour. It is in fact a lazy man's produce. Other tree crops, such as cocoa, coffee and rubber, are more time consuming but not very much so. This accounts for the resistance to growing one-season crops, like grain or millets, which require periodical digging up of soils. Cultivators normally like to clear the ground and inter-plant subsistence food with perennial trees until the latter provide too much shade. This practice facilitates a steady extension of production by indigenes for sale in open markets. Traditional labour organization still provides the bulk of work required on small holdings, though there is an increasing emphasis on contract labour. Some Tolai now employ men from more backward areas and pay them pitifully low wages.

Capital and investment. The few tools normally needed for small-scale primary production are easily acquired. A Siane man has to work only twelve days to secure one steel axe, which lasts for about twelve years. The acquisition of more expensive capital items such as tractors was at first facilitated by the traditional corporate ownership of assets. This was instanced by the Erap Mechanical Farming Project, where 426 people contributed to raise $1841.40 for their first tractor. Similarly, many large Tolai trucks were bought by most members of a matrilineage pooling their savings. However, they soon discovered that joint ownership of capital assets was a different matter from joint ownership of land. In subsistence cultivation it was easy for each partner to exercise his rights to land without his interests clashing with those of the others. This is not so in the case of vehicles, where continuous maintenance and periodic overhauls are necessary. Consequently many a truck was stranded waiting until the owners could pool more money to pay for necessary repairs. There is now a trend towards individual ownership of capital items. This in turn creates a financial problem. Few individuals have sufficient resources to acquire a costly asset themselves. Most people distrust intra-societal loans because they suspect that the borrower will rely on kinship obligations when the creditor wants repayment of the loan. Therefore there is a need to familiarize them with new forms of economic organization, such as fixed shareholding and limited liability.

Many tree crops, like cocoa, coffee, copra, and rubber, have to be processed before they can be exported. The more elaborate the processing, the more costly the machinery. The Tolai Cocoa Project, one of the biggest native-owned and controlled enterprises, was started in 1955 and is vested in the Gazelle Local Government Council. It operates eighteen fermentaries for which a total outlay of $544,000 was necessary. A commercial bank made this amount available under guarantee from the Administration. Almost 75 per cent of this loan was repaid within twelve years. The Project's Board of Management is now composed of seven men, six Tolai council members and a European agricultural officer. Although it was started by active Administration participation it is now largely under indigenous control. Similarly the Kerema Bay Rubber Project was at first actively sponsored by the authorities, who provided a factory costing about $5,000, but the production of latex has now been handed over to indigenous control. Such large-scale indigenous ventures are still few and far between, probably because of the type of organization and management problems.

Most indigenes prefer to invest their money in small trade stores. As many as 5,849 licences to operate shops had been issued by 1966, and others were operating without official recognition. The traditional system of trade exchanges with delayed reciprocity provided the basis for modern shop trade. But as most supplies have to be obtained from external sources and require immediate cash payment many a small store gets into financial difficulties. The social ties between an indigenous shopkeeper and his customers are responsible for the high proportion of credit sales. In turn this accounts for the mushroom growth and decline of trade stores in native settlements.

So far all indigenous investment has been in agricultural and processing and servicing industries. The very nature of these ventures protects them from foreign competition though they are still subject to competition from local Europeans. In contrast, manufactured articles would have to compete with imports from advanced industrial economies.

Entrepreneurship and politics. Europeans provided an example for indigenous enterprises. The higher a native's degree of education, and the longer his period in employment, the more ready he is to accept innovations. This vanguard sets an example to fellow villagers. Such men are also a channel for the redistribution of wealth among those who continue their traditional work. In many cases men who make their wealth through modern trade spend some of it on pigs for feasts and heirlooms for exchange. This expenditure on traditional items provides income for others not directly concerned with modern business. In Ware, discussed by Belshaw, many enterprising men are among the most active in trade exchanges and the most wealthy in heirlooms. Success in new cash ventures is also tied up with traditional social status. Not all Tolai who were in employment blossomed out as modern entrepreneurs; only those who on their return home managed to get themselves accepted as lineage elders have in fact become rich. These elder-entrepreneurs translated their strategic political position into economic advantage for themselves, while simultaneously redistributing part of their accumulated wealth along traditional channels. This throws into relief the interaction between forces of social continuity and of change in the process of economic development.

Traditional 'big men' were leaders not only in the economic but also in the political sphere. Similarly indigenous entrepreneurs, the modern 'big men', take an active part in formal politics. Most indigenous members of the present House of Assembly are comparatively wealthy business men. This is true also of members of the Local Government Councils. But not all entrepreneurs compete for political positions. Some are too occupied with making money; others act as powers behind the throne rather than occupy it themselves.

Expenditure and savings. The availability of new consumer goods, together with ready cash derived from the sale of labour or crops, resulted in a widening of the indigenous expenditure pattern. The more urban the population the greater the quantity of purchased articles, though twist tobacco, cheap tinned fish or meat, and rice appear to have reached even the remotest peoples. Yet native produce is so readily available that bought food is regarded by most as a luxury. Prior to contact, natives were only scantily dressed. Now most people possess at least a few items of introduced clothing: women wear loin cloth and blouse, men dress in shirt and loin cloth or shorts. Some of the wealthier natives dress like Europeans. Housing also is changing; fibro-cement houses with corrugated iron roofs are replacing the old huts with thatched roofs. The new bungalows are rare in the more remote areas but are beginning to be common in developed regions such as the Gazelle Peninsula. Household chattels are still rare. Only the most sophisticated villagers have much furniture and household equipment. Fears of sorcery and witchcraft militate against extreme economic differentiation expressed in terms of different standards of living. The richer may have small luxuries, but they refrain from being ostentatious in order not to arouse the jealousy of others. Similarly young Siane men, who in the 1950s returned from spells of plantation labour, distributed more than half their accumulated acquisitions to their kin and friends. This emphasis on egalitarian living has important economic consequences. It results in a high elasticity of demand for most purchased articles and leads to a continuous redistribution of incomes from the rich to the poor. Furthermore, it encourages a high rate of savings, which provide finance for investment and in turn can be employed to speed up economic growth.

In June 1966 total indigenous bank savings amounted to about $9,200,000. This means average savings over the whole population of approximately $7.50 per adult. The uneven distribution of wealth necessarily means a considerable range in the amounts of cash saved. Some natives also have cash hoards. There is thus a reasonably large fund available for profitable investment.

Markets and trade. In most areas indigenes were quick to respond to the increased demand for their food crops, and many markets have been set up. Most commodities are over-supplied, and sellers have to take back at least part of their produce. Villagers could supply considerably greater quantities of fresh vegetables, particularly their staple crops of taro and sweet potatoes, if the demand could be increased. In spite of this surplus prices are uniform and rarely change in reply to changes in demand. There is very little competition among vendors. Many sellers are women, who regard market trade as a social occasion as well as an economic enterprise. They are frequently satisfied to cover just the expense of visiting the market place and regard any extra as windfall profit. 'Primitive affluence' accompanied by socially integrated sellers may explain the lack of competition apparent in the local markets. Natives are not accustomed to seeking out the highest bidder even in their sales of cash crops to expatriates. Ware people prefer a standardized relationship with one firm for selling their copra rather than moving from one buyer to another. They prefer security in trade to greater risk, possibly associated with higher gains.

Cash is now widely used, not only in interracial trade but also in exchanges between natives. In many areas it has supplanted such valuables as cowrie shells and feathers. Some people, like the Tolai, cling to their traditional shell currency. *Tambu* is still used for payment in intra-Tolai trade and circulates freely at Rabaul market.

The flexible social systems of pre-contact New Guinea peoples provided a fertile field for economic improvements. 'Big men' constituted the prototype for modern entrepreneurs. Capital formation was at first facilitated by the traditional pattern of corporate ownership of assets. In turn capital formation is undermining the very system that helped to create it. As the pace of economic growth increases it is likely to have a revolutionary impact on social organization.

W. E. Armstrong, 'Report on the Suau-Tawala', Territory of Papua, *Anthropology Report*, no. 1. Port Moresby, 1922.
C. S. Belshaw, *In Search of Wealth*. American Anthropological Association, Memoir no. 80, 1955.
H. C. Brookfield and P. Brown, *Struggle for Land*. Melbourne, 1963.
R. G. Crocombe and G. R. Hogbin, 'The Erap Mechanical Farming Project', *New Guinea Research Unit Bulletin*, no. 1, 1963.
A. L. Epstein, 'The Economy of Modern Matupit', *Oceania*, vol. 33, 1962-3.
T. S. Epstein, *Capitalism, Primitive and Modern: Some Aspects of Tolai Economic Growth*. Canberra, 1968.
E. K. Fisk (ed.), *New Guinea on the Threshold*. Canberra, 1966.
A. L. Gitlow, *Economics of the Mt Hagen Tribes*. New York, 1947.
G. R. Hogbin, 'A Survey of Indigenous Rubber Producers in the Kerema Bay Area', *New Guinea Research Unit Bulletin*, no. 5, 1964.
H. I. Hogbin, *Transformation Scene*. London, 1951.
―――― and P. Lawrence, *Studies in New Guinea Land Tenure*. Sydney, 1967.
G. Jackson, 'Cattle, Coffee and Land among the Wain', *New Guinea Research Unit Bulletin*, no. 8, 1965.
P. M. Kaberry, 'The Abelam Tribe, Sepik District, New Guinea', *Oceania*, vol. 11, 1940-1.
P. A. Kleintitschen, *Die Küstenbewohner der Gazelle-Halbinsel*. Hiltrup bei Münster, 1906.
B. Malinowski, *Argonauts of the Western Pacific*. London, 1922.
―――― *Coral Gardens and their Magic*. 2 vols, London, 1935.
R. Parkinson, *Im Bismarck Archipel*. Leipzig, 1887.
―――― *Dreissig Jahre in der Südsee*. Stuttgart, 1907.
L. Pospisil, *Kapauku Papuan Economy*. New Haven, 1963.
O. van Rijswijk, 'The Silanga Resettlement Project', *New Guinea Research Unit Bulletin*, no. 10, 1966.
R. F. Salisbury, *From Stone to Steel*. Melbourne, 1962.　　　T. S. EPSTEIN

(*See also* AGRICULTURE, INDIGENOUS)

EDUCATIONAL BROADCASTING for community and adult education is shared by the Australian Broadcasting Commission (A.B.C.) and the Administration radio stations. Both services provide news of current events and information on aspects of development in the Territory; the A.B.C. operates mainly in English, the Administration radio stations in lingua franca and vernaculars. The potential audience for this type of educational extension service is far greater than for broadcasting specifically for schools since less than one-third of the total population in 1970 had attended school of any sort or at any level. English-medium broadcasting is restricted to the educated minority and there is no reliable assessment of the actual coverage, much less the effectiveness of broadcasting for informal education.

The A.B.C. is responsible for broadcasting within the formal school system. Until 1964 broadcasts to the schools of the Territory were selected from those produced in the six states of Australia. These programmes were designed for Australian children working to a syllabus which presupposed an Australian environment. Consequently, in Papua and New Guinea they were of use only to those few schools whose pupils' mother tongue was English and which used an Australian-type syllabus. At the end of 1964 a permanent supervisor of education was appointed to the Papua New Guinea branch of the A.B.C. to provide school broadcasts for the Territory. Within five years a small staff had increased the schedule of new productions to over 300 per annum for an audience which was estimated to include 90 per cent of the Territory's primary schools.

The isolation of many village schools and the low educational standards of many primary teachers make broadcasting a very important part of education. The same two factors also limit its effectiveness. To ensure that adequate supporting material is available in all schools for each broadcast makes large demands on production and postal services. To use broadcast programmes effectively as a part of classroom teaching, or even to maintain the radio and rig the aerial to secure regular reception, is not easy for teachers who may themselves have received little education beyond primary school.

Effective school broadcasting requires a training programme. Lectures and demonstrations are given at teachers' colleges on the use of school broadcasts and two- or three-day instruction courses are held at District centres. Indigenous producers are trained as part of studio operation and workshops have been organized for indigenous artists. Scripts for some of the earlier English teaching programmes were written by the Commonwealth Office of Education but now scripts are generally written by practising teachers in Papua and New Guinea.

It may easily happen in Papua and New Guinea that a whole year will pass without anyone whose mother tongue is English entering a classroom. There is therefore a particular value in the English medium of the broadcast lesson. Most formal broadcasting for schools is the teaching of English from Standards 1 to 6. Programmes of health education, religion, music and current events are also provided for primary schools. Social studies broadcasts provide information in dramatized form about the Territory, South-east Asia and Australia, and stimulate awareness of Papua New Guinea as a developing nation. Most schools broadcasting is aimed at the primary grades, but secondary-school broadcasting is expected to grow substantially in the 1970s and there is a special programme for teachers.

'Teachers World' is prepared by the Department of Education and broadcast three times a week; it attempts to bridge the gap between headquarters and the teacher in the school. The programme provides news about the development of teachers' associations and provides a medium for explanation and discussion of educational policy. It also conveys ideas from one school to another and thus links teachers in remote parts of the Territory with their colleagues.

The School Broadcast Advisory Committee is the policy-making body for educational broadcasting, and also determines priorities for future productions and assesses the existing programmes. It comprises representatives of the agencies operating schools, teachers, members of the Education Department and the A.B.C. A Commission of Inquiry into television was appointed in 1965 and, although its recommendations were not implemented, the use of educational television in the Territory is continually being considered.

(*See also* BROADCASTING)

EDUCATION, HISTORY AND DEVELOPMENT.

Education presents many problems in a country made up of several hundred different language groups, with people living in scattered settlements separated from each other by rivers and mountain ranges. The problems and achievements of current educational policy can only be appreciated in relation to the history of educational development in the Territory. A past of schooling only on the coast for many decades before modern education reached the Highlands gives rise to the present imbalance of educational opportunity. The dispersion of educational effort among more than sixty mission authorities, which established low-level schools for evangelistic purposes and in response to village pressures, underlies the tension between local and national views of educational planning. The concentration on primary education and the extension of literacy [q.v.] in English, with a concurrent neglect of high-school education until the 1960s, explains the need for a rapid build-up of secondary- and tertiary-level institutions.

EARLY MISSION EDUCATION

Throughout the period 1873-1946, education was almost solely the responsibility of the religious missions [q.v.]. Between 1873, when the London Missionary Society (L.M.S.) placed teachers at Port Moresby, and 1899, when the Marist Mission Society was established at Kieta in Bougainville, various Protestant and Catholic missions had established separate or overlapping spheres of interest in both Territories.

The purpose which directed all the activities of the missions was the preaching of the gospel and the conversion of a primitive people from pagan beliefs to the Christian faith. Education was seen as a means to this end, in general to provide moral and Christian training, and in particular to train catechists, evangelists, pastors and teachers. The organization, amount, content and quality of education were determined largely by this purpose (see EDUCATION, MISSIONS).

The typical organization of education by missions was to provide village schools in the out-stations in all areas for which a teacher could be found; a boarding school for boys (sometimes also for girls) at the head-stations—that is, where a European missionary lived; and advanced train-

ing centres for pastors and teachers at the mission's central station or some other important location. For example, the advanced training school for the L.M.S., which served the whole of the south coast apart from the Yule Island-Mekeo area, was first at Port Moresby, then later at Vatorata, inland from Kapa Kapa; the advanced training school for the Neuendettelsau Society of the Lutheran Church, which worked in the Morobe District of New Guinea, was established at Kai and later at Heldsbach.

The amount of time devoted to education was limited. It was common, in Papuan and New Britain schools at least, for children to attend school for only four days a week so that work in family gardens would be less disturbed. In head-station schools where there were boarders, it was almost invariable that the afternoons were devoted to gardening to provide food for all. There are many early references to the difficulty of maintaining regular attendances and, in particular, the difficulty of keeping girls at school for long. As was natural enough in a mission school, a considerable part of the time was given to religious exercises and especially to the imparting of religious knowledge, so that the time spent on secular education was quite limited.

Successful preaching and teaching depended upon adequate communication with the indigenous people. One of the first tasks of the missionaries was the translation of scriptures into the vernaculars of their areas. The Rev. W. G. Lawes [q.v.], the pioneer L.M.S. worker in Papua, was able to report in early 1875, 'I have printed a sheet alphabet with the small amateur press, as the first step toward giving the people the Word of God'. By 1877 Lawes had produced his first book written in Motu which consisted of 'reading lessons, the Ten Commandments, an epitome of Old and New Testament history and thirteen hymns'. In 1879 Benjamin Danks [q.v.] of the Methodist Mission Society made his first educational materials from flattened kerosene tins on which he painted the alphabet, the multiplication table and some short sentences. He commented, 'So began the present educational system of New Britain'. By 1882 he had translated into the language of Duke of York Island the Gospel of Saint Matthew, a short life of Christ, a catechism and a dictionary of 4,000 words. From the printing press of the Neuendettelsau mission in 1906 came primers, first readers, hymn books and Bible histories, and vernacular papers for the churches.

While religious subject matter was the principal object of translation and of teaching, elementary instruction in reading, writing, arithmetic and geography was commonly given. Most classes were taught in the vernaculars, although the more senior students were instructed in English in some Papuan schools and in German in the Catholic and Methodist schools of New Britain.

The choice of a language of instruction posed one of the most vexing problems in education in both Papua and New Guinea. The missionaries believed that the language of a people was too precious a heritage to be despoiled or neglected, that it was the only means of communication with the natives' innermost being, that it was 'the shrine of the peoples soul'. Following this principle, the language of preaching and teaching must be the local vernacular. However, faced with such a multiplicity of distinctive languages [q.v.], the missionaries were forced to attempt to establish common vernaculars by the practical need to economize on effort and money in producing printed literature. Motu, the language of the Port Moresby area, was spread much further east and west by the L.M.S.; Yabem (Jabim) was used in the coastal stations of the Neuendettelsau mission on the Huon Peninsula, while Kâte was used in the hinterland and both languages were being used by those who were not native speakers. The Methodist and Catholic missions in New Britain and New Ireland used the Kuanua language of the Blanche Bay area far more widely than it appeared originally; the Anglican mission, operating in north-eastern Papua, used the Wedau language of its coastal headquarters outside its original limits on the coast, and also in the hinterland where it was previously unknown. The strong argument used by the missions to justify the introduction of a common vernacular into areas where it was unused was that similarities of structure, if not of vocabulary, of most vernaculars made them easier than a European language, such as English or German, for native speakers to learn. The entrenched interest in vernaculars thus developed by the missions made them reluctant to fulfil the wishes of their respective administrations to teach in English or German, and it became the universal practice to teach basic literacy in the vernacular and only then, if at all, to introduce a European language.

Another element of considerable importance in mission teaching was training in industrial crafts such as furniture-making, house-construction, timber-milling, boat-building and repair, printing and bookbinding. All missions shared in some kinds of industrial training. The strongest advocate for industrial missions in Papua was the Rev. C. W. Abel [q.v.] of the L.M.S. station of Kwato, near Milne Bay. Abel argued that industrial training would strengthen the Christianity of Papuans, would make them an example of industrious behaviour, and would allow them to face with confidence the challenge of the great influx of Europeans. The Rev. J. Flierl [q.v.] of the Neuendettelsau mission in New Guinea also emphasized the great need for training in agriculture and animal husbandry to lift the productivity of village subsistence farming. Lay brothers were recruited to give training in these skills as well as in printing, bookbinding and sawmilling.

Missions were compelled, both by the principles of their calling and by economic necessity, to depend upon mission staff and relatively untrained native teachers for the bulk of their work and they employed very few professional teachers. The Protestant missions used South Sea Island (Fiji, Samoa, Tonga, Rarotonga) teachers and pastors recruited from their earlier established Pacific mission stations. The Lutherans employed some lay brothers. The Catholic missions had the assistance of missionary brothers and sisters and Filipino teachers. In addition to expatriates, all missions trained indigenous teachers and preachers in advanced training institutions. The quality of those so trained, and of the Pacific Island teachers, varied considerably. Wallace Deane, of the Methodist Mission Society, wrote fulsomely of the South Sea Islanders who worked as missionary teachers in New Britain villages; 'Right nobly did they respond to the trust imposed on them, shrinking not from the shock of that onset, nor wavering in the fiercest conflicts'. With more restraint, the Rev. James Chalmers [q.v.], of the L.M.S., wrote with gratitude of the work of Pi, a Rarotongan teacher, who did much of the translation of Saint Mark's gospel into the Suau language of Papua. A. K. Chignell, writing of schools and teachers in the Anglican mission area in 1911, refers to good schools conducted by white teachers or by a 'thoroughly well-trained Papuan headmaster', and of a school 'where the admirable work of a South Sea Island teacher is having wonderful results'. He goes on to say that these schools are few, that the majority are staffed by men who, though full of missionary ardour, frequently have 'the very scantiest formal education' and that 'on the whole they are probably as ill-instructed and incapable as any body of men who ever handled a piece of chalk or flourished a duster'. Chignell's balance of the few well-trained and the many poorly-trained is probably representative of most areas in both Papua and New Guinea.

The emphasis given to religious instruction and the limited time available for formal schooling of any kind, left little time for secular education. Although the distinction between religious and secular education is to some degree false at the level of basic literacy, there was no full exploitation of the potential of students in secular education.

Some aspects of the secular education which was given were alien and inappropriate, being based on English and Australian models. In some schools pupils learned by rote the names of the different Australian colonies with their principal cities, or transcribed into copy-books such moral gems as 'Withstand every Inducement to Iniquity' or learned how to perform money sums in a coinage most would probably not use in their lifetime. Writing of schooling generally, Chignell questioned the view that an education suited to English children 'must also of course be suitable for children in Papua', thus expressing a point of view shared by many observers since.

The evaluations of mission educational work in official comments were not so critical. Sir William MacGregor [q.v.], Lieutenant-Governor of British New Guinea, in a farewell visit to the Anglican mission area in 1898, spoke highly of the standards achieved by pupils in the schools at Dogura and Wedau, and concluded, 'I wish that some of those that question the utility of mission work could or would come here and judge for themselves'. In the annual reports of German New Guinea and of Papua, references to education in mission work are approving in the German reports and laudatory in the Papuan reports. The German reports are primarily factual and statistical but mention that school work 'succeeded though under great difficulties', that schools 'developed satisfactorily', and that in the Methodist mission's schools 'the real desire, not only of the boys, but also of the girls, to learn reading, writing and arithmetic is a good sign'. The Papua reports refer to 'the growing influence and value . . . [of] educational effort', record that the school at Kwato 'is a revelation of what may be done in the direction of the civilisation, education and refinement of Papuan children' and that at Daru there was 'a most efficient native school in which English is taught, and is even the usual medium of instruction'.

The uniformly approving comments of the governments, both German and Australian, were not only fair praise for the best work done, but also recognition that the missions were doing what was a responsibility of the government. It would have been impolitic, as well as churlish, for the administrations to disparage the efficiency of the conduct of the educational responsibility they were avoiding.

PAPUA TO 1941

The early administrators made no attempt to introduce any form of native education policy except to encourage the teaching of English. The Royal Commissioners of 1906 found that English was inadequately taught and that for this the missionaries and administrators were culpable. The Commissioners completely neglected the opportunity to suggest that a general education policy should be formulated and the means to finance it be provided. Only one missionary witness before the Commissioners, the Rev. E. Baxter Riley (L.M.S.), encouraged the Commissioners to believe that there was a need for government involvement in native education. It was left to J. H. P. (later Sir Hubert) Murray [q.v.], Chief Judicial Officer from 1904, Acting Administrator from 1907 and Lieutenant-Governor from January 1909 until his death in February 1940, to create the needed educational policy. The Commonwealth's insistence upon pacification before education, the slow growth of the local economy and the meagre Commonwealth annual grants both delayed and determined the policy ultimately introduced. By a process of trial and error from 1911 to 1917 a policy was evolved which had as its key features the financing of native education from the proceeds of native taxation, the use of the missions as the agents of education and the gaining of some control over the nature of the education provided by the granting of educational subsidies to missions fulfilling prescribed conditions.

By a Native Taxes Ordinance which became effective from July 1919, taxable natives, that is males approximately sixteen to thirty-six years old and not otherwise exempted, were required to pay an annual tax of £1 or 10s. Those exempted were the Armed Native Constabulary, Village Constables, natives unfit for work, fathers of four or more children by one wife, and mission teachers and students. The money so raised was to be applied to a Native Education Fund, first 'for the general and technical education of the natives of Papua' and secondly, 'for such purposes having as their object the direct benefit of the natives of Papua as may be prescribed'. These latter purposes were at first described by Murray as providing for native sanitation and the medical treatment of villagers. The scope of benefits was subsequently enlarged very considerably to include the payment of salary of the government anthropologist, subsidies to missions for medical work and hospitals, payments of a family bonus to mothers of four or more children by one husband, and village improvements and provision of sporting equipment in villages. From 1925 these benefits were financed from a separate Native Benefit Fund but with moneys still supplied from the Native Taxation Account.

The Native Education Fund provided money for three main educational purposes: for establishment grants to 'assisted schools' and *per capita* subsidies for passes gained in government syllabus examinations, for the promotion of technical education and for general educational needs. Grants of £50 in the first school year and £5 (£10 from 1925) in each subsequent year were given for books and equipment in schools where English was taught, and sums of 10s or £1 for each child passing respective prescribed examinations (later 5s, 10s, 15s, 20s and 25s for passes at Standards 1 to 5), to a limit of £250 to any one mission. Because returns from native taxation were higher than at first anticipated, the government offered in 1920, £1,000 per annum for five years to missions which presented acceptable additional schemes of native education, and in 1921 this offer was limited by the proviso 'that no scheme would be approved that did not provide for technical education'. Technical subsidies proved a boon to the missions and all the large missions provided facilities to attract grants. The best-developed technical programme was at the Kwato Industrial Mission, Milne Bay, but the Methodists established a large centre at Salamo on Fergusson Island, the L.M.S. at Aird Hills and elsewhere, the Congregation of Missionaries of the Sacred Heart (M.S.C.) at Yule Island and the Anglicans at Boi-ani, the Mamba and Dogura. Apart from the institution at Kwato the technical education [q.v.] given was most probably meagre as the technical centres were more commonly workshops for the production of needed furniture and fittings for the missions or of articles for sale in Port Moresby and elsewhere.

The largest proportion of educational subsidies was paid to support general and technical educational work. It is a common misunderstanding of Murray's scheme to believe that it consisted almost solely of *per capita* subsidies paid for examination passes. In fact only 3 per cent of moneys paid from the Native Taxation Fund went towards *per capita* subsidies, whereas 26 per cent was distributed to missions for their technical and general educational work. Grants were given towards the salaries of European, Papuan and South Sea Island teachers, and towards the cost of provisioning boarding students, of school materials, of building maintenance and of living quarters for students and staff. These general subsidies were of great assistance. In the case of the L.M.S., for example, in the period 1920 to 1941, over £20,000 was received for general and technical subsidies and only approximately £3,500 for *per capita* subsidies. Of the large missions only the Anglican mission chose not to take advantage of the general subsidies. Strong Anglo-Catholic conservatism created the fear of loss of autonomy if too much reliance was placed upon government assistance.

Although it was not part of Murray's original intention the greatest proportion of taxation receipts, 36 per cent, was paid for medical benefits of various kinds. These included the erection and servicing of native hospitals and the salaries and supplies for the government's European and Papuan medical officers and their medical patrols. Missions received 40 per cent of the total spent on medical benefits in grants for their medical work.

The educational subsidies received by the various missions from the Native Taxation Fund are indicated in the table. Medical subsidies paid from the same fund are included for comparison.

SUBSIDIES TO MISSIONS, 1920–41 £

Mission	Per capita	Special Industrial	General and Technical	Medical
Anglican	3,045	1,550	—	9,202
London Missionary Society	3,546	8,640	20,035	11,130
Methodist	1,673	—	7,185	12,477
Missionaries of the Sacred Heart	1,471	—	17,000	1,714
Kwato	—	—	16,000	1,009
Seventh Day Adventist	353	—	—	1,134
Unevangelized Fields Mission	—	—	—	224
Bamu River Mission	18	—	—	5

Throughout the period of operation of the Native Taxation Fund a comparatively healthy balance was retained. At its lowest point in 1936 it stood at £15,816 and in the last year of the scheme, 1941, the balance was £26,200. Annual costs of the scheme held close to an average of about £14,000 and receipts averaged about £15,000 per annum. The argument in defence of the large balance was the uncertainty of assured receipts from taxation, but as the lowest return was £13,329 in 1935, the Administration appears to have been unduly pessimistic. In the light of the great educational needs in Papua and the relative poverty of the missions, the retention of such a large balance appears obtuse. There were ways in which the subsidies scheme could have

been extended helpfully or reorganized and in either case the unexpended balance could have been usefully drawn upon.

In general, the subsidies system was directed toward achieving greater literacy in English and in fostering technical education through the missions, while the Government itself organized agricultural education [q.v.] through the Native Plantations Scheme, and in a hopeful venture on Kiriwina. As an exercise in education, the Native Plantations Scheme barely deserves mention here. In the absence of trained agriculture teachers the scheme became a compulsory plantations extension programme rather than one of education. The agricultural school established with the assistance of the Methodist mission on Kiriwina (1935-40) was a failure—the Kiriwinans were not prepared to learn new ways of doing what they already did well.

To the extent that statistics are revealing there is evidence of academic growth under the subsidies system. In the first examination in 1921, Standard 2 was the highest pass awarded and at this level 28 passed of the 63 examined. By 1927 pupils were tested to Standard 4 and 95 of the 102 examined at this level passed. In 1936 pupils were tested to Standard 5, and 53 of 63 examined at this level passed. The total number of pupils examined in all grades increased from 130 in 1921 to 3,002 in 1940, in which year 91 passed at the highest level, Standard 5. Such figures as these reveal development but indicate how few were receiving an education equivalent to that in Australian primary schools. There are no published figures of total enrolments in Papuan schools, but data from various missionary sources suggest a total of 12,000 to 14,000 by 1941, though most of these pupils would have been in elementary classes receiving mainly religious instruction in the vernacular.

There were some advances in providing material appropriate to the local environment. Books designed for children of a primarily urban culture in Queensland and New South Wales were used in schools until 1927 when the Rev. W. J. V. Saville produced a *Papuan School Reader* which contained lessons in simple English related to the Papuan environment. This book proved too advanced for pupils and in 1932 a series of *Papuan Junior Readers*, nos 1, 2 and 3, together with instructions to teachers on their use, were issued. These readers were written by visiting Queensland Inspectors of Education and local teachers and, with two later volumes, nos 4 and 5, remained the basis of instruction in English until after 1945. In 1929 the government anthropologist, F. E. Williams [q.v.], produced a monthly simple-English newspaper, *The Papuan Villager*, (1929-41) which was more widely read than its circulation of 700-1,000 suggests. This newspaper was a source of information about the local and the wider world. Not until after 1945 was any other secular English-language material available for Papuans. Reading *The Papuan Villager* became the only justification for the learning of English for many school graduates.

The quality of instruction was, in general, low. The deeply entrenched system of teaching in the vernacular and the lack of sufficient well-trained English-speaking teachers, and of adequate reading material in English, made this inevitable. Reports of examiners drew constant attention to these inadequacies and especially to their effects in the poor command of conversational English, as distinct from rote-learned responses, of the majority of pupils. Examiners frequently commented that there were too few teachers for the number of children in their charge, and referred to the outstanding ability of some expatriate and a few indigenous teachers, the zeal but limited training of other expatriates, and the generally inadequate training of some indigenous and most South Sea Island teachers. Both Colonel John Hooper and T. Inglis, of the Queensland Department of Public Instruction, reported as examiners that there was great aptitude for teaching among intelligent Papuans and advocated professional training. Following the repetition of this suggestion in 1939, the Government Secretary admitted that neither the government nor the missions had sufficient funds to provide proper professional training schools.

The subsidies system was open to severe criticism. As subsidies were paid on the basis of successful examination passes, education was often limited to examined subjects and there was 'cramming', even to the extent of holding extra classes at night, in the weeks prior to examinations. These two criticisms were levelled by D. H. Barbe Smart, the headmaster of the school for European children in Port Moresby, who was the examiner in 1923.

There was little equity in the system. For a variety of stated reasons, the examiner was unable to visit some centres, and schools unvisited, presumably, earned no examination subsidy. Further, missions often presented many more successful students than earned subsidies because of the $250 limitation to any one mission.

Physical demands upon the pupils were also, in some cases, excessive; to attend the schools where examinations were conducted some pupils were forced to walk 25 or 50 miles.

The most serious criticism, however, is that the subsidies system did not promote the building of better schools or the better equipping of schools and did not encourage the development of training schools for teachers. L. P. Mair compares the educational work of missions in the British Crown Colonies and says, 'the basis on which grants are made in these colonies is one that has been a genuine stimulus to efficiency—namely, that they are proportionate to the number of certificated teachers employed, and that approval depends not on the marks earned in examinations but on the results of inspection of the actual school work and premises'. Barbe Smart in 1923 proposed as an alternative to the examinations system 'an inspection of the whole school on the year's work'. The proposal was not heeded by Murray but perhaps evoked the distant echo of the 1940 inspector's somewhat forlorn hope that when there is 'an army of intelligent, trustworthy, and thoroughly trained Papuan teachers . . . then inspection may usurp the place of the examination'.

Government assistance of £50 per annum was provided for the Anglican mission to run a school for the children of expatriates at Samarai. There were usually fewer than fifteen pupils in the school. A government school for the children of European residents at Port Moresby was opened in 1911. There were forty pupils in grades ranging from Infants to Standard 5. A similar school was established at Woodlark Island with about twenty pupils. In neither school did numbers vary significantly over years. Murray considered establishing a government technical school in 1925. Following the investigations of a visiting technical-education expert, the proposal was rejected on the grounds of inadequate revenue to support it and because of the superior claims of agricultural education.

Murray and Education. Murray's leadership in Papua traverses the quite unusual period of thirty-three years. Throughout this period his attitude to education changed little. He remained liberal within limits. From the beginning he was conscious that the provision of education was a government responsibility and was disappointed and irritated by the Commonwealth government's insistence upon the principle of pacification before education. He saw education as the important means of elevating Papuans to a higher standard of civilization—in fact 'to the highest state of civilisation which they are capable of obtaining'. He did his best to understand, by personal contact, reading and reflection, the Papuan people he served and he won their affection and respect. Yet, in spite of the search for understanding, Murray was unable fully to accept the notion of Papuan-European equality. In a statement of 1912 he saw the possibility that Papuans might in time reach 'a fairly high standard' but argued that a higher education should not be offered and warned of the dangers of considering Papuans socially and politically equal with Europeans. Warnings against the introduction of democratic procedures were given in 1929 and in 1935. In one of his last public statements on the question, in 1938, Murray faced the social and intellectual problems posed by the ordination of the Roman Catholic priest Fr Louis Vangeke [q.v.] and argued that as a Papuan had become a priest so could one become a doctor or a lawyer. But Murray could not fully accept the logic of this argument and fell back on the traditional view of the innate superiority of Europeans though admitting some overlap in ability. In this 1938 statement, however, Murray showed himself sufficiently free of his conservatism to note that one of the great obstacles to Papuan intellectual advancement was the presence of the 'colour bar' in the community, and sufficiently prescient to observe that the removal of the colour bar would make the higher education of Papuans 'perhaps even a burning question'.

It is this liberal-conservative background that gave Murray's education system its distinctive quality. The missions were encouraged by subsidies to provide a limited intellectual education in English, arithmetic and geography at the primary level only. No emphasis was given to teacher training and no grades above Standard 5 were assisted by subsidies even though this standard was introduced in 1930 and the unexpended balance in the Native Education Fund could have supported higher grades. As late as 1938 Murray argued privately that to establish secondary schools in the next generation would be 'soon enough'. The unpreparedness of the bulk of the Papuan people for the responsibilities demanded of them in the post-war world is in large part the legacy of the conservative educational policies of the period to 1941.

Murray's limited educational provision did not derive wholly from his own attitude. There is sufficient evidence that he would have provided more had the Commonwealth government not pursued economic policies which severely limited Papuan productivity or had the Commonwealth been less niggardly in its annual grants. The support of education and other welfare objectives by native taxation was determined by necessity, not principles. Murray was also influenced in what he could provide by the force of public attitudes. There is evidence in his annual reports that he had to work hard to convince Europeans that Papuans could be accepted as responsible and intelligent employees and it is to Murray's credit that the attitudes of some employers did improve even though racial prejudice generally continued. More subtly Murray was influenced by the paternalism of the well-disposed. The pervading concept of Pacific people as 'child-races' affected some scholars, many missionaries and, one suspects, most of those others who did not hold harsher views.

In general Murray's record in providing education is not bright but he created a system which established a base, however limited, for future development. If in doing so he was hampered by an unsympathetic Commonwealth government and a racially prejudiced and paternalist public, he was not dominated by either and thus his record stands higher than that of his compatriots over the border.

NEW GUINEA TO 1941

The attitude of the Administration in German New Guinea [q.v.] was similar to that in early Papua; the missions were praised and allowed to carry the burden alone. The reluctance of the missions to abandon or limit their teaching in the vernaculars forced the Administration to take some independent action. In 1907 a government school was opened at Namanula, near Rabaul, to teach the elementary years in Kuanua, the Blanche Bay vernacular, and later to introduce German as a language of study and then as the language of instruction. The school was small, only ninety-two pupils being enrolled in 1912, and employing two European and two native teachers. The Administration also encouraged the teaching of

German in mission schools, praised the Catholic mission for its success in teaching German and, by implication, was critical of the exclusive use of the vernaculars by the Neuendettelsau and Marist missions. This criticism appears to have been a less effective stimulus to the introduction of German than fear of competition for government positions from graduates of the Catholic mission's schools, where German was being successfully taught.

Government education. The change of governing authority after World War I led to an expression of some interest in education by the Australian Administration. By the Education Ordinance, 1922-38, the Administrator was authorized to establish schools, to prescribe the nature and standard of instruction, to make provision for teachers and to control expenditure from the Native Education Trust Fund. An elementary school was planned to provide general education and to train selected pupils for teaching or for the lower grades of government service, or to take positions in the industry and commerce of the Territory. A technical school and a school of domestic economy were also planned.

After 1924 the three schools, separate at inception in 1922, were brought together at Malaguna, outside Rabaul, and the school of domestic economy was soon closed. The elementary and technical schools were continued and by the end of the mandate period there were additional elementary schools at Kavieng (New Ireland), Nodup, Tavui, Pila Pila (near Rabaul) and Chimbu (Highlands). Enrolments in all government schools ranged from 146 in 1924 to 588 in 1940. The average yearly enrolment for fourteen years between 1924 and 1940 (there are no figures published for 1932-4) was 312.

Expenses for the provision of government education were met from the Native Education Trust Fund which was financed at first by a tax of up to 10s per year on natives living in prescribed taxation districts. This was later changed to a tax of 6s per year on all indentured labourers, payable by their employers. The Native Education Trust Fund was allowed to be exhausted after 1933 and the taxes were paid into general revenue, expenditures on education (which were not affected by the change) being met from general revenue. Annual expenditures on education ranged from £18,955 in 1923-4, when new schools were being built and equipped, to £3,903 in 1934-5. Average annual expenditure in the period 1923-40 was £7,753. This expenditure on an average yearly enrolment of 312 pupils represents a very much greater outlay per pupil than was made available to mission pupils in New Guinea, or in Papua under Murray's subsidy scheme.

The curriculum followed in the elementary schools was of the general Australian academic pattern with English as the language of instruction. There was some native craftwork and the usual Australian sporting activities were introduced. Teachers were recruited from Australia and were assisted in later years by a few graduates from the schools. Progress in academic subjects was consistently reported as very good. Two pupils were sent to Australia in 1928 and their Australian headmaster gave a highly laudatory report in 1929. Graduates from the elementary schools found positions as clerks in government offices, as telephone assistants and as trainee teachers. These trainees in time gained positions in government schools as assistant teachers, the numbers reported being two in 1932, two in 1937, three in 1938, five in 1940 and three in 1941. Two teachers, F. Boski Tom and Joseph Ritako graduated from Malaguna and started teaching in 1927 as the first teachers employed by the Administration. They retired in 1967 after having completed between them 78 years of service.

At the technical school the trades of carpentry, joinery, wood-machining, plumbing, driving and motor mechanics, and printing were taught. Trainees constructed saleable articles and were also engaged in government work of various kinds such as building a bungalow, manufacturing water tanks, or printing and bookbinding in the Government Printing Office. After graduation, some returned to their villages but most were able to find employment, especially carpenters, plumbers and drivers. From the judgment of the standard of students given by teachers in various official reports it would seem that the quantitative meagreness of government education was not an indication of the believed and demonstrated intellectual and technical capacity of native pupils.

If a satisfactory response was being gained from pupils, what were the policy decisions which determined the inadequate record of government in education in the mandate period? After the burst of activity implementing the Education Ordinance in 1922-4, the history of policy-making on education is a record of reports, conferences, references to committees and postponement of decisions. Prior to World War II, there was no major extension of the work begun in 1922, nor was any major alternative to it decided upon, nor was there even an officer appointed for anything but a very short period to deal exclusively with the problems of education.

Colonel John Ainsworth, a former Native Commissioner in Kenya Colony, reported on the administration of the mandate generally in 1924. He strongly advocated concentration on agricultural education even if this required the Administration 'to scrap the "educational" scheme' just begun. No great change came from the Ainsworth recommendations on education even though there was criticism in Australia in 1928 that education as practised was 'ridiculously specialised', there being 'undue emphasis on trade education . . . [but] no trace of agricultural education'. In 1928-9 an agricultural school was established on the Keravat River, twenty-eight miles from Rabaul, and a three-year course in the essentials of tropical agriculture was introduced. The stimulus behind this venture does not appear to have come from either the Ainsworth report or from Australian criticisms.

The promise of expansion was given in 1927 when it was announced that government schools would be established in every District and that the elementary school at Malaguna would be converted into a secondary school receiving good graduates from District elementary schools. In fact, by 1941 only two government schools were set up outside the Rabaul area, one at Kavieng and one at Chimbu.

A possible extension of education through subsidies to missions was discussed at the Mission Conference of 1927, but this was not welcomed by the missions and was abandoned. Seeking inspiration elsewhere, the Administration announced in 1928 that it was examining native education in other countries and would appoint a committee to examine New Guinea needs and recommend an adequate educational system. An educational expert to chair the committee could not be obtained. Instead, the Administration invited B. J. McKenna, Director of Education, Queensland, to enquire into and report on the educational system. This was done in July and August 1929. McKenna was critical of the Administration's failure to carry out the educational policy previously determined and made several important recommendations designed to widen and to improve education. The Administration claimed that McKenna's reports had been accepted as the basis of the future educational policy of the Territory. In fact, the only subsequent changes reflecting McKenna's recommendations were the adoption of the Torres Strait Islands syllabus and the recruitment of three Queensland teachers in 1931.

Another line of approach altogether was suggested in 1933 when the Administration explored the possibility of the missions undertaking entirely the education of natives. There were no developments in 1934 save for the appointment of a committee 'further to examine the proposals'. In 1935 the whole idea was abandoned.

In 1936 the above-mentioned committee was replaced by a special committee appointed by the Legislative Council. After conducting some enquiries and recommending Administration control of education, the special committee 'was granted further time to study the matter in greater detail before submitting any further recommendations'. The special committee did not continue its work in the next year because of the absence from the Territory of four of its members and in 1938 it lapsed with the expiry of the term of appointment of the Legislative Council. No new committee was formed by the new Legislative Council.

No doubt concerned at its continued failure to provide positive policy direction in education the Administration presented, in 1938, an unusually full account of the difficulties it faced, in the course of which it stated, 'Having regard then, to all the local conditions, it is not the purpose of the Administration to formulate a definite policy in connexion with native education before the matter has been fully investigated. It is essential that true foundations be laid if success is to attend any policy so formulated.' No further statement on native education policy was made in the mandate period.

A review of the record of the Administration in New Guinea in this period makes one seriously doubt the validity of its concern for 'true foundations'. The foundations were provided in the Education Ordinance as early as 1922, as McKenna pointed out. What was lacking, to continue the Administration's metaphor, was a building to match the foundations, workers to erect the building and money to be expended on both. Criticism of the lack of positive policy and of a far wider spread of native education was general. S. W. Reed, a sociologist and diplomatic critic of the Australian Administration's general record in the Mandated Territory, says that 'native education has proved to be probably the most sterile of all the Australian Government's undertakings'. Other post-war observers have been equally critical.

A contemporary critic and later Director of Education in the combined Territories, W. C. Groves [q.v.], published in 1936 a book based on educational research in New Guinea in which he condemned the formalism and lack of professional leadership of the system and its failure to provide a realistic programme for the great majority of the people. The most consistent contemporary criticism came from the Permanent Mandates Commission. The Commissioners blamed the Administration for leaving the bulk of education in the hands of the missions without any subsidies or inspections and frequently commented on the lack of positive independent action. The Australian representatives before the Commission were sometimes inadequately informed, frequently vague and evasive, and occasionally defensive and self-righteous. The strongest condemnation of the Administration's record was given in 1939 by a Commissioner, Mlle Dannevig, who related the small number of native officials working in New Guinea to the poor educational opportunities provided and added the stinging rebuke that she 'knew of no territory under mandate in which native education progressed so slowly'.

An important reason for the failure of the Administration to implement an adequate education system was the attitude of the white population to the indigenous people generally and to their education in particular. The term 'kanaka' was the common label for all indigenous people and was usually, though not always, given derogatory overtones. Low-status occupations were believed to be the only ones for which an indigene was, or could be, fitted. Education was looked upon as developing evil qualities in the native mind. On one occasion, in the hysteria produced by the Rabaul strike [q.v.] of January 1929, the local newspaper openly exulted that a citizens' committee had prevented the sending of adolescents to Australia for further education.

The missions did little to encourage the Administration to action. Their concern in education remained primarily religious. During a conference with the Administration in 1927, the mission representatives stated frankly their unwillingness to accept subsidies because they would not be able to meet the educational standards the Administration would rightly set. An important problem the missions would have had to face was that of teaching English. The language of instruction was primarily the mission-imposed vernacular or Pidgin English [q.v.] and it would have been extremely difficult to find sufficient teachers for English-language instruction among a white missionary population over 80 per cent of whom came from non-English-speaking countries.

Mission schools. It is difficult to comment generally on the mission schools in Mandated New Guinea. In the absence of Administration control and of any agreement among the missions on standards, there is no adequate reference point for evaluation. Agreement on the general picture may be found in the comments and descriptions of anthropologists, educationists, administrators and even of missionaries, given during the period and since. As in Papua the quality was very uneven. A few schools at head-stations were of superior standard and some outside observers compared them favourably with Australian schools. The vast majority were village schools in which little secular education was given and where the standards of hygiene, discipline and scholarship were very low. Village teachers, poorly educated themselves and who had additional responsibilities as village pastors, could not hope to achieve desirable educational levels. In fact, they were not expected to do this. The village school was an extension of the church. Only in the larger institutions was anything like a thorough educational programme attempted. These matters must be kept in mind when considering the 1940 mission educational statistics listing 35 training centres; 44 high, intermediate or technical schools; 158 elementary schools; 2,329 village schools; and their (approximately) 65,000 pupils.

While the generally poor standard of mission schooling must be noted it should be remembered that the missions came voluntarily to make converts, not scholars. For the majority, the missions were concerned to provide sufficient literacy to allow reading, in the vernaculars or Pidgin, of the scriptures, hymns, church history and other works necessary to the foundation and consolidation of Christian faith. For the minority they provided advanced secular training to prepare teachers, possible priests and other mission workers. But their responsibility was not believed to include supplying the needs of the secular community at large. The great weakness of the missions is that they did not put pressure upon the Administration to help them to raise the standards of their schools. In fact, as noted above, the missions in New Guinea deliberately opposed government subsidies. Whatever view is taken of their motives, the native people were educationally deprived by their parochialism.

THE NEW DEAL

The work of religious missions and of civil government almost ceased during the Japanese invasion and repulse. The missions in battle areas lost men, women and property, and their educational work was abandoned. In other areas it was drastically curtailed. White missionaries were forced to evacuate forward areas and white women missionaries left the Territories from late 1941 to late 1944. Civil government was replaced by military government from 14 February 1942, and a special Army unit, the Australian New Guinea Administrative Unit (Angau [q.v.]) was created to carry out those functions of civil government considered essential. Although native education was one of those functions other tasks rated higher priority. Little was done by Angau during 1942 and 1943 except to provide some basic materials for schools in the Port Moresby area. In 1944 a central training school was established at Sogeri. During 1944 and 1945, the Hon. Camilla Wedgwood [q.v.], an anthropologist and educationist in the Army Directorate of Research and Civil Affairs, visited schools in all mission areas in Papua and made recommendations on the many problems associated with the introduction of a comprehensive programme of native education.

The Australian Labor government introduced the 'new deal' for the indigenous people of the Territories in the Papua-New Guinea Provisional Administration Act 1945-46. The concept of a new deal had been discussed in Australia since 1943 in books, periodicals, pamphlets, newspapers and public lectures by priests, anthropologists, politicians and the public generally. While all wanted change, some missionaries were apprehensive about the possible secularizing tendency of change. The Minister for External Territories, E. J. Ward [q.v.], indicated the government's attitude by announcing that education was to be 'controlled and directed by the administration', although the missions were acknowledged as having a specific part to play. The days of mission autonomy were over.

Possible friction in this new relationship was avoided by the diplomatic choice of the first Director of Education and the inauguration of missions conferences. W. C. Groves [q.v.] was appointed Director on 17 June 1946. He was then forty-eight and had behind him a long experience in teaching in Victoria and New Guinea (he was the first teacher appointed to the government school at Kokopo in 1922); in educational and anthropological research in New Guinea, 1932-4; and as Director of Education on Nauru, 1937-8. Groves' experience in these years had brought him into close contact with missionaries and he had developed the strong conviction that the education of native people required the close co-operation of government and missions. At missions conferences arranged by the Minister for Territories in Sydney and Port Moresby in 1946, Groves set out his plans for educational development based on the need for cultural adaptation. His personality and his words revealed that the missions had no need to fear a prejudiced secularist, and the mission representatives voiced their gratitude.

In 1946 the prospects seemed good that the long era of inadequacy or neglect on the part of the government and near or complete autonomy of the missions could be succeeded by a period of educational development and government and mission co-operation.

D. J. DICKSON

POST-WAR POLICY

Educational work of missions had been disrupted by the war. A clear policy for the Administration was needed. Surveying the lack of resources and the inadequacy of teachers as Papua and New Guinea emerged from the war, Wedgwood drew up a thirty-year plan for educational development. She also recommended the appointment of a Director of Education. The structure of schooling followed her pattern to a considerable extent in the immediate post-war years. Concern for girls' education was stimulated by her writings. European teachers recruited to the new Department were guided by her experience, but there her direct influence ended. It was the appointment of Groves as Director that determined policy in these formative years until objectives were detailed by the Minister for Territories in 1955.

In his second-reading speech to the House of Assembly in October 1952, the Director of Education said 'the present Department of Education was established presumably by the appointment of a Director of Education in 1946. No detailed policy was laid down. In this and in all other respects, the Department started virtually from scratch.' As a critic of education policy in New Guinea during the pre-war period Groves had argued that departments of education in native communities should have wide scope beyond the task of running schools. The extent of his commitment to the needs of social welfare and community development may be gauged from the fact that in 1947 the Department of Education opened a hostel providing board and lodging for girls and married women in Port Moresby at a time when only five Administration schools were operating in Papua. The Special Services Division of the Department was already engaged in broadcasting (in English and vernacular languages), visual education, the organization of a library service (supplying twenty-five to thirty out-stations from a central library) and the provision of adult-education evening classes at Hanuabada, Kila, Samarai and Kokoda. By 1950 two special sections of the Department were established to survey forms of native music and to study the weaves and dyes used for native handicrafts. Conducting occupational therapy lessons at a Hansenide settlement, assisting the Boy Scouts Association or encouraging the activities 'of such bodies as the Photographic Society, the Arts Council and the Scientific Society', were regarded as much a responsibility of the Department of Education as the task of organizing schools.

This range of activity elicited much criticism from the committee appointed in 1954 to investigate the administration, organization and method of the Department of Education. 'The obvious main feature of the Committee's Report', as Groves commented, 'is that the range of operations of the Department should be limited to the establishment and running of schools.' Defending his policy Groves acknowledged that some of the wider services provided did not necessarily belong to a Department of Education, 'but had been made the responsibility of his Department since there was none other to organize them'. In an earlier debate of the Legislative Council he had described how after his appointment 'requests flowed in from all directions for educational services of various kinds on the assumption that, a Department having been established, it was in a position to handle effectively the variety of matters involved'.

To some extent this lateral extension had indeed occurred for administrative convenience but it represented also the logical outcome of Groves' educational beliefs. In 1955 a policy decision had to be made by the Minister for Territories. 'Looking more narrowly to the means by which the Department of Education will achieve its objectives,' wrote Hasluck, 'I think that the distinctive nature of its work (as contrasted with the work of, say the Department of Native Affairs or the Department of Labour) is the conducting of schools.'

School organization. In 1944 Wedgwood outlined a structure of school organization for the Territory. It provided for a total of nine years of elementary education at first in village primary schools and later in area schools from which the academically able would move to three years' schooling at an intermediate level. Above this level technical training, teacher training or medical training courses would continue for a further three years. As a long-range objective she proposed that right from the bottom of the system there should be sufficient government schools established so that native children were not dependent on the missions for schooling.

The five-year plan for native education produced by the Department in 1948 was broadly similar to that proposed by Wedgwood in the stages of educational progress but different in its allocation of responsibility between mission and government. In line with the existing situation Groves proposed that most of the village schools providing the first four years of education would be mission-run. From this basic vernacular education, children of sufficient merit would transfer to area schools or in places where geographical conditions made this impracticable to village higher schools.

Groves' description of the area school links several aspects of his original policy. 'Draw together a number of village Primary Schools into one suitable consolidated unit, with consequent wide range of teaching subjects and extra-curricular activities as well as better trained and specialist teachers, link the programme of such a school with the interests of the local community through its activities for adults as well as its syllabus for the children; organize and develop such an institution as the focal point of new interests for the people of the locality and as the radiating centre of developmental stimuli for the area; arrange for its management by a local people's

committee; at the same time, develop the teaching of English progressively through the grades partly to prepare selected students for entry into the District central school, and partly to widen the literary horizon of the people as a whole; and you have the general framework of the proposed Area School for Papua and New Guinea.'

District central schools were envisaged as the basic type of native school for post-primary general education. They led to vocational courses, technical and non-technical training centres preparing entrants for Administration departments or for teacher training courses.

Expansion in the immediate post-war years was restricted by the limitations of finance and especially of staff and buildings. In this situation, as Groves explained, it was accepted that 'the claims of the Europeans were undeniable (on the principle that these children belonged to a civilization which entitled them to the form of education normally provided for European communities) whereas the need for Native Schools was not considered of the same urgency in view of the lack of tradition of schooling for natives in the Territory'. Thus in June 1948 three-quarters of the expatriate teachers employed by the Administration were teaching in thirteen schools for European and mixed-race children with an enrolment of 690, while nine expatriate and sixty-six indigenous teachers worked in twenty-eight schools with 2,108 indigenous children. Some imbalance persisted as expatriate public servants were regarded as having, by right of employment, a prior claim to educational facilities comparable with those in Australia.

Another difficult decision in the ordering of priorities lay between primary and secondary education. Since government schools were virtually starting from scratch in the post-war period, priority had to be given to primary education until sufficient students had worked through to the top of that level. By 1955 Groves believed that priority could be given to the secondary level to support the training of soundly educated teachers, but in that year a policy directive from Hasluck, the Minister for Territories, reaffirmed the priority for primary education.

Under this directive of February 1955, the existing structure of school organization was retained, but the immediate tasks were seen to be as follows:

'(a) First attention to be given to primary schools with the goal of teaching all children in controlled areas to read and write in English.

(b) For the above purpose, efforts to be made to ensure the cooperation of the Christian missions; and, special attention to be given to teacher-training.

(c) Manual training and technical training to be developed both in conjunction with the primary schools and in special schools in response to the developing needs of the people.'

These tasks were to be given priority in order of time, and to be done well before the Department shouldered other tasks.

Plans for extension from 1955-7 proposed the establishment of 102 new schools, 82 of them at the primary level, raising the total enrolment in Administration schools from 6,200 to 22,630, made up of: primary 17,400; post-primary (including central schools and their teacher training courses) 3,650; secondary (including teachers' college) 780; and technical 800.

Three basic problems were involved in the implementation of this plan: relationship with missions, curriculum content (including the language of instruction) and the training of indigenous teachers. Since these were problems with which Groves had already been grappling they will be examined in relation to his whole period of office.

Mission relations. Wedgwood had recommended that the Administration should set up a complete system in parallel to the missions, and canvassed the proposal that missions could leave education to government. At the other extreme, the idea that education should be handed over entirely to missions was revived in 1953.

Between these two views Groves developed a more pragmatic approach building an upper level of Administration schools on the existing layer of mission primary schools and hoping that 'in their general educational outlook [the missions] will allow themselves to be guided by the government'. The work of the Administration, he originally believed, would lie primarily in research and in its role as a pace-setter, 'to test and to demonstrate the manner of interpretation of these principles so that other agencies may follow'. A series of conferences between missions and the Administration beginning in Sydney in 1946 and later in Port Moresby strengthened the co-operation on which this policy depended.

Its weaknesses were apparent in practice. Firstly the supply of ex-mission students to the more advanced Administration schools was never sufficient to meet the required output for government service and especially teacher training. In the long term this could only be met by the development of government primary schools. Secondly, the fragmented nature of mission education would require stronger powers to achieve co-ordination. An Education Ordinance to provide this was approved by an inter-departmental committee in November 1949. Subsequently revised in consultation with the missions and Department of Territories, it was eventually passsed in 1952.

Among the provisions of the Ordinance were the establishment of the Education Advisory Board, the authorization of District Education Committees and the enactment of regulations for the compulsory registration, recognition or exemption of mission and voluntary-agency schools. The Ordinance empowered the Director to determine language usage in schools. It empowered the Administrator to enforce compulsory school attendance and to make grants in aid to missions in respect of all registered mission teachers. It also authorized the issue of regulations regarding the standards of education, the secular curriculum, discipline, inspection, teachers, qualifications and training.

Curriculum content. In the forties no syllabus was laid down by the Department of Education for the schools, since Groves believed that each teacher should choose and adapt his subject matter for his local situation. In the European schools children studied the curriculum of their different home states in Australia until it was decided to standardize on the Queensland syllabus in English and arithmetic in order to reduce the confusion. A locally based social-studies syllabus was produced but this was replaced by the New South Wales syllabus.

The vast majority of the children in native schools lived in a traditional village environment. To relate their education to their daily life and needs Groves determined that schooling must have a rural bias. This would help to make the school a centre of community development. If the Department's wide activities outside the formal school system had to be reduced, the idea of rural bias in the school needed to be emphasized more strongly.

Vunamami Education Centre provided an outstanding example to copy. Begun in 1952, the Village Higher School was officially opened by the Administrator in 1955 when it was part of a larger institution including a central school and teacher training group specializing in education with a rural bias. The dormitories and rooms of the central school had been built by the students themselves and the school became self-supporting in rations after the first four months. Academic teaching was based on the farming cycle with lessons in arithmetic, English and social studies devised to illustrate and support the outdoor activities.

Visiting the school Groves remarked, 'This looks like one of my Native Education dreams coming true'. Following his suggestion the third meeting of the Education Advisory Board recommended the extension of the Vunamami type of education throughout the Territory and the establishment of similar institutions by missions.

Groves envisaged language policy as another aspect of the adaptation of education to the local environment. In the pre-war situation he had observed that 'The average European actually does not want the native to know English well; and it is certain that relations would not be improved if English were widely used by the natives. In any case, educationally the aim is the development of the native along his own lines. And if the scope of education is to be restricted, and its wider aims subordinated to the teaching of English simply for the doubtful advantage of facilitating intercourse between the native and the occasional European, the gain will be incommensurate with the loss.' This line of argument led to the remarkable conclusion that 'when English is widespread in New Guinea villages, they will no longer be New Guinea villages. And a sorry day that indeed will be.'

As Director of Education, Groves was therefore prepared to compromise the Administration's preference for the use of English by allowing the missions to continue with the vernaculars and

Pidgin. Expert opinion supported the use of Pidgin as an easier medium of learning for the indigenous child, but the Trusteeship Council of the United Nations was forthright in urging the Administration to eradicate Pidgin from all instruction given within the Territory. In this conflict of opinion, evidence was cited from the Ilo Ilo experiment with languages of instruction in the Philippines. The issue was partially resolved by Hasluck's instruction in 1955 that first attention was to be given to teaching children to read and write in English. But of course the linguists could still argue that the vernacular or Pidgin provided the quickest road to that goal. Although the transfer of a vernacular from one area to be used as the medium of instruction in another was officially banned from 1959, the use of a local vernacular or Pidgin is still permitted.

Teacher training. The limited supply of teachers constituted the greatest constraint on educational expansion throughout the post-war period. Teacher training became the main purpose of the existing institution at Sogeri to which was added the output from Dregerhafen for mainland New Guinea and Keravat for the islands from 1950 and 1952 respectively. From these education centres 179 teachers had entered the schools by 1954. In that year seventeen completed the course at Sogeri with the new entry requirements of two years' secondary education before admission to the teacher training course.

The consequent restriction of intake could not be maintained in the face of local pressure for more schools and of pressure by the 1953 United Nations Visiting Mission for the 'creation of a large and competent corps of elementary-school teachers'. As a result teacher training courses for 1954 were divided into three categories of shorter length and with lower standards of entry.

The normal teacher training course, already established, was combined with the second year of secondary education as a temporary measure, and became known as course C. An emergency B course was introduced in 1955 as an extension of six central schools. This one-year course with an intermediate level of entry qualified teachers for work throughout the village higher schools. An A course was provided originally for mission institutions with entry from primary level to qualify trainees to teach the first two years in village schools.

These courses emphasized method and classroom technique, the syllabus for the A course specifying that 'no time whatever is allowed for the study of general school subjects'. Supervised teaching practice was regarded as the 'central core of the whole programme of teacher training'.

Expansion. From 1946 to 1954 an average of 11 new Administration schools were opened per year. The total of 104 in operation at the later date consisted of 14 schools for European children, 5 for Asians and mixed races, and 85 schools for indigenous children. If this was only a fraction of the total proposed under the five-year plan in 1948, the shortfall was due to a lack of staffing and the frustrations of a building pro-

gramme in which only 27 of the 104 proposed projects were completed. These two factors were often interrelated as lack of suitable accommodation was a major cause of staff wastage. Whereas the 1948 plan envisaged 490 European officers employed in the Department by 1954 and an increasing number of indigenes, the staffing classification for that year shows only 188 European positions, and an actual teaching strength of 76 Europeans with 230 indigenes.

In 1957 the primary enrolment at 12,363 in 186 Administration schools was approaching the plan target for that year. But above that level enrolments were only a quarter of those proposed in 1955—in post-primary institutions 669, in secondary and teacher training 178 and in technical training 218. Another plan was drawn up in 1957-8 proposing more modest targets, but by this time Groves had reached retirement to be succeeded by G. T. Roscoe.

INDIGENOUS REACTION

The development of village councils (later known as Native Local Government Councils) in the post-war period helped to make local opinion articulate about education. In many cases, as at Vunamami near Rabaul, an early act of the council was to allocate a sum of money for an Administration school subsidized by the council. The Department welcomed on principle 'the active and practical participation of the community itself . . . in the provision and management of the educational enterprise designed to serve them'. Acceptance of financial liability by the council, while the Department retained substantial control, assisted expansion, but the pressure of such requests proved embarrassing when no new teachers were available.

Requests for schools indicated a growing hunger for education, but it was not always an unselective demand. When Roscoe met a deputation of local leaders at Buin and answered their request for an Administration school with the reply that they already had mission schools at hand, their comment was curt and to the point, 'Tok bilong God, tasol'.

Not surprisingly the missions did not always welcome the appearance of council-supported schools. The ruling that councils could not vote money to support mission schools provoked the Catholic bishop of Rabaul to make a strong protest and he formally proposed 'that the Native Local Government Councils withdraw from all educational activities'. But the councils retained their powers and expressed views as much in criticism of the type of education provided by the Administration as in respect of mission education.

As in East Africa the societies which were the most eager for education were the earliest to criticize its provision. At Vunamami the Administration teacher was convinced by his experience that greater emphasis needed to be placed on the outdoor work of the centre if students were to grasp the relationship between agricultural theory and practice. He argued that 'instead of a school with a few farming activities attached what is required is a farm where most of the learning takes place, together with a classroom to assist the practical learning on the farm'. But local opinion was moving in the other direction.

At a meeting of the Education Committee of the Vunamami Council in 1959, a number of bitter complaints were brought forward by Vin To Baining, President of the Council. Quoting a large number of the parents, he complained that:

'(1) There was far too much gardening work done at this Centre and that this was interfering with the quality of the school work.

(2) That the gardening work was much too hard for the younger boys.

(3) That it was too much to expect small boys to live in a boarding school.'

The protest was interpreted as questioning the suitability of a boarding system for pupils of that age, but a more fundamental principle was at stake in the first complaint.

A striking African parallel emerges from the comment made by N. Sithole, an African leader, on the mission school he attended in Rhodesia in 1932. 'To us education meant reading books, writing and talking English, and doing arithmetic . . . [and not] ploughing, planting, weeding and harvesting . . . We knew how to do these things. What we knew was not education; education was what we did not know.'

The educational philosophy of insistence on adaptation and relevance risked frustrating indigenous aspirations. In the Territory, this was implicit in Groves' philosophy 'of the possibility and value of devising an education which will belong truly to New Guinea; an education which will be bound up with the people's past and which will provide for their future progress in directions that will not bring the native into competition or rivalry with the European'. Before the war an educationist in New Guinea could legitimately aim 'to build a new cultural structure upon the real and solid foundations of existing native institutions and ideals'. War-time experience had shaken that foundation; widening contact with European culture and the desire for possessions used by expatriates outdated the ideas of differential development.

In Manus District, where the impact of war had been revolutionary, the followers of Paliau and his New Way or cargo cult [q.v.] would attend neither government schools nor that run by the Seventh Day Adventists. A former Roman Catholic catechist, who taught them counting and simple addition, provided their only formal education until a primary school was started at Baluan in 1951 under the control of the council Paliau had established. Even then the children of Paliau's home village would not attend before he returned again from Port Moresby.

Whether in criticism of content or through the provision of council subsidies, indigenous influence was showing that it could become effective in the partnership of education.

UNIVERSAL PRIMARY EDUCATION

G. T. Roscoe was appointed the second Director of Education in September 1958. A month later he had drafted for the Minister for Territories a plan for the development of universal primary education in the Territory, confident that it could be achieved within ten to fifteen years.

The consequent declaration of universal primary education as the objective of the Department of Education did not mark a change in policy direction. Universal literacy in English had been established by Hasluck in 1955 as the task to receive highest priority. Roscoe brought new vigour to the project by proposing detailed measures for its realization in a given time scale, but this provided for acceleration of the process rather than any change in the objective. It was in the form and content of the education to be provided that a fundamental change was made.

Groves had illustrated his policy of differential development by a reported conversation with a group of local people, one of whom concluded, 'I don't think we shall ever be like the white man and live the same kind of life as he does, because, you see our country is not like his. We must not hope ever to be like the Europeans.'

A conversation related by Roscoe in 1959 sets the contrast. Roscoe had been listening to a long speech by Sivi, a local leader in the Chimbu Sub-District, at the opening of Gena School. Afterwards he asked Sivi why he gave such emphasis to higher education and particularly to the learning of English. Sivi replied, 'We want our children to be exactly like you'. The concept of the blending of the cultures was rejected. No mention of rural bias was made anywhere in Roscoe's plan for universal primary education.

Again the Rhodesian comparison is illuminating. Harold Jowitt, appointed as first Director of the Department of Native Education in Southern Rhodesia in 1924, went 'imbued with the idea that education should uplift village life'. School activities, he maintained, 'should be built around centres of interest based on the African's environment'. When Jowitt was succeeded by Stark in 1935 he listed as the primary object of African education, mastery of the three R s and character training. Parker's description of the transition between the first and second Directors of Education in Southern Rhodesia is closely parallel to the Papua and New Guinea situation some twenty years later: 'the attempt to help the African adapt to his rural environment gave way before the pressures to educate the African in much the same way as the European was educated'.

Strategy. In 1958 the base for expansion was provided by the following enrolments:

Administration native schools: 200, enrolment 15,000.
Mission schools registered or recognized: 500, enrolment 18,000.
Mission schools provisionally recognized but not inspected: 1,500, enrolment 30,000.
Exempt schools: 2,000, enrolment 100,000.

Success of the plan to raise total enrolments

to 400,000 in ten to fifteen years depended *inter alia* on the fullest co-operation of the missions. The standard of exempt schools would have to be raised to a level acceptable for recognition and the opening of more exempt schools would be discouraged after an agreed date. Rapid expansion of the mission primary system was essential as Roscoe believed that the Department would never be able to educate more than 25 per cent of the potential school population from its own resources.

Equally vital was the expected mission contribution to the teacher training programme. A subsidy of £100,000 was recommended for the erection of teachers' colleges by missions. This policy was urged on grounds of greater speed and economy of construction of mission buildings. Increased grants for trainees and certified indigenous teachers would support the proposed expansion and provide an additional incentive for mission efforts.

A rapid increase in the number of inspectors constituted the first priority for the Administration in assisting missions to raise school standards. Over the period of the plan, Administration school enrolments would increase to 100,000. The cost of expansion would require an immediate doubling of the education vote to £2.2 million in 1959-60. It was estimated that annual expenditure would reach about £10 million when school enrolment reached 400,000.

Problems. The calculation of over-all needs was originally underestimated on the assumption that the school-age population would probably increase at 1 per cent per annum. A later estimate by the Director of Public Health suggested a rate of growth rising above 3.5 per cent per annum, approximately doubling the population in twenty years, and inevitably postponing the achievement of universal literacy.

Problems of implementing the plan, however, centred as before on staffing. In the original 1958 draft it was proposed that training of teachers by missions could rise from 300-400 to 1,000 per annum. A fortnight later the target was revised to 2,000. After ten years, total enrolments in mission teachers' colleges were just half this figure and, because of the change-over from a one-year to a two-year course of training, the output of mission teachers from pre-service courses was barely 500.

In the early years of the plan a limitation on expansion was imposed by several constraints. The high wastage rates at lower levels of education and the limited accommodation available after Standard 6 restricted the flow of suitable candidates for teacher training. High capital and recurrent costs of boarding schools made it difficult to increase this flow. Recruitment of staff for teachers' colleges could scarcely have been expanded at the rate required even if the buildings had been available. Finally the Administration grant of £30 for trainees offset only half their maintenance costs.

The supply of teachers was supplemented by an emergency A course run for indigenous trainees at Administration centres with an output averaging 150 from 1960 to 1966. Another innovation which met with remarkable success in recruitment from Australia was an emergency E course for expatriates. Instituted during the directorship of Roscoe, this course attracted a very wide range of recruits, most of whom were posted to bush schools. They had a significant effect on the standard of English-language teaching in those areas and remained as teachers in Papua and New Guinea for longer periods of service than was common among expatriate officers. The E courses were terminated in 1966 but strength of popular support (and the continuing shortage of teachers) encouraged the recommencement of these courses from 1969.

Discussing his plan in October 1959, Roscoe had forecast that 'under the most favourable circumstances, circumstances which are more favourable than we are likely to have, at the end of ten, fifteen, or twenty years we might have 100,000 children in Government schools'. Ten years later enrolments in Administration primary schools reached 80,000 but even with 132,000 children in church schools the target of universal primary education remained far distant. For the immediate future attention had shifted to the development of secondary and tertiary education which it was hoped would eventually produce enough teachers to make universal education a reality.

EMPHASIS ON QUALITY

The education system of which L. W. Johnson took over directorship in 1962 had an extensive primary base but its only secondary element was in classes added to the top of primary schools or run as part of the teacher training process. Most primary schools were small, staffed by one or two teachers, and operating only with classes at the lower grade levels. Less than a third of the children who began primary school could expect to complete that stage of education. The vast majority of teachers had not progressed beyond the sixth grade of primary schooling themselves before taking a year's course of teacher training.

The laying of a broad foundation was a creditable achievement but the urgent task of the nineteen-sixties was to raise the quality of the system. This required a rapid expansion of secondary and later tertiary education; a higher level of professional development in the teaching force, including the replacement or retraining by 1970 of the unqualified teachers in primary schools; and reorientation of the curriculum using material from Papua and New Guinea while introducing modern approaches to the teaching of mathematics, English, science and social studies. These qualitative needs had priority in the strategy of education for this period but it was essential to satisfy or at least contain the simultaneous pressures for expansion of numbers at the base of the primary system. Growth of the primary-school-age population was estimated to exceed 4 per cent per annum in some Districts and there was strong pressure from the Highlands electorates to expand their schools much faster in order to reach equality of educational opportunity with the coastal regions. The expatriate population, although relatively small, added to the strains on the education system through the build-up of army families during the period of Indonesian confrontation, and later with workers for the Bougainville copper project [q.v.].

Educational statistics give some indication of the extent to which these various objectives were met. At the primary level unqualified permit teachers had been replaced by the end of the decade, and enrolment of children in Standard 6, the top level of primary schools, had expanded by over 200 per cent in the government and non-government schools between 1964 and 1970. Enrolments at Standard 1 level had remained static in the non-government sector where the simultaneous efforts of building up schools to the higher grades and improving the quality of teachers had absorbed all the effort put into primary education. In government schools expansion in the Highlands contributed significantly to the 50 per cent growth in Standard 1 enrolments in the same period.

Expansion at the secondary level was far more dramatic as external pressures and changes within the Territory combined to make for rapid development at this level. From 1954 the Administration had operated a scholarship scheme to enable selected indigenous students to receive secondary education in Australian schools. Historically it was an important development but in numerical terms a scheme with an intake of less than 20 students per year had negligible effect. As African nations achieved independence and Australia's record of Administration came under closer scrutiny at the United Nations there was mounting criticism of the inadequacy of secondary and higher education for Papua and New Guinea. At the same time within the Territory the cohort completing primary school was expanding to provide the base for a higher level of education and employment opportunities increased as expatriate opinion was changing in regard to the professional role of Papuans and New Guineans. Secondary education in the early 1960s was mostly limited to the lower forms and output of indigenous students at Form IV level was only 66 in 1964. By 1970 high-school output at Form IV level had risen to over 1,700 with a total enrolment of 20,000 pupils in secondary and technical courses.

Of all the recommendations of the United Nations' Visiting Mission in 1962, the most radical in the field of education was the insistence that not only should secondary schools be expanded but also that planning for a university should commence urgently. A Commission on Higher Education was established in 1964 and teaching of a preliminary year for the University of Papua and New Guinea [q.v.] and higher institute of technology [q.v.] commenced two years later. Indigenous enrolments in post-secondary education grew from 290 in 1966 to 1,236 in 1970 (in addition to primary trainees at teachers' colleges). The mushroom growth of post-secondary training institutions in this period presented further problems, and the need for some co-ordination of activities was recognized in the appointment of a second commission in 1970.

Changes in the balance of education provide one index of qualitative improvement in the over-all system. It is much harder to evaluate the contribution of curriculum innovation and the improvement of teaching and learning materials. Substantial changes were made during the sixties in all subject areas. In some instances the pace of curriculum change appeared to outrun the practicality of retraining teachers, but secondary and tertiary institutions widely acknowledged a rising standard in their student intakes. Changes in the approach to language teaching are considered basic to this improvement although it is impossible to assess separately the contribution of better qualified teachers, improved materials, a new course structure, and a growing minority of parents whose children are the second generation to learn English.

A large investment of money has been needed in education to provide for qualitative and quantitative development. By the mid-sixties it was becoming evident that the educational effort of the missions would break down unless basic changes were made in the financial structure. Following on from a resolution in the House of Assembly an advisory committee on education was appointed in 1969 with W. J. Weeden, C. E. Beeby and G. B. Gris as its three members. The recommendations of this committee and the resulting establishment of a Territory Education System with a single employer of teachers in the Territory Teaching Service began a new era in education for Papua and New Guinea.

GEOFFREY SMITH

H. K. Colebatch, 'Educational Policy and Political Development in Australian New Guinea', in *Melbourne Studies in Education 1967*, ed. R. J. W. Selleck. Melbourne, 1968.

Department of External Territories, *Report of the Advisory Committee on Education in Papua and New Guinea* [W. J. Weeden, C. E. Beeby and G. B. Gris]. Canberra, 1969.

Department of Territories, *Report of the Commission on Higher Education in Papua and New Guinea* [G. Currie, J. T. Gunther and O. H. K. Spate]. Canberra, 1964.

D. J. Dickson, 'Murray and Education: Policy in Papua, 1906-1941', *New Guinea and Australia, the Pacific and South-East Asia*, vol. 4, 1969-70.

W. C. Groves, *Native Education and Culture Contact in New Guinea*. Melbourne, 1936.

K. R. McKinnon and others, 'Education in Papua and New Guinea', in a special issue of *Australian Journal of Education*, vol. 12, no. 1, 1968.

L. P. Mair, *Australia in New Guinea*. Melbourne, 1970.

J. A. Miles, 'The Development of Native Education in Papua and New Guinea', *South Pacific*, vol. 10, 1959.

R. C. Ralph, 'Some Notes on Education in German New Guinea, 1884-1914'. *Papua and New Guinea Journal of Education*, vol. 3, 1965.

——— 'Government Education under the Australian Mandate', *Papua and New Guinea Journal of*

Education, vol. 4, 1966.

C. D. Rowley, *The New Guinea Villager*. Melbourne, 1965.

O. H. K. Spate, 'Education and its Problems', in *New Guinea on the Threshold*, ed. E. K. Fisk. Canberra, 1966.

(*See also* EDUCATION, MISSIONS; MISSIONS)

EDUCATION, MISSIONS.

EDUCATION, MISSIONS. Immediately before World War II there were approximately eighty thousand pupils in mission schools throughout Papua and New Guinea. At the same time there were fewer than six hundred indigenous pupils in Administration schools in New Guinea and no Administration schools at all for indigenous children in Papua. For a long period the operation of schools in Papua and New Guinea was almost entirely entrusted to Christian missions [q.v.] and when missions entered the new Territory Education System in 1970 the majority of pupils were still in their schools.

Since Administration control of education for the combined Territories was officially introduced in August 1946, the policy of the government had been generally to get as much as possible out of the missions for as small an outlay as possible. Problems resulting from the low rates of pay for mission teachers precipitated the 1969 Weeden, Beeby and Gris Committee of Inquiry into Education. Their report acknowledged the great contribution churches and missions had made to education in the Territory in the past and their conviction of the vital role they still have in it.

In the first place missionaries were interested in giving the people a primary education to enable them to read the scriptures and become catechists, pastors and teachers within the church. The vernacular was generally used for instruction and standards were on the whole quite low. Missions and churches were inclined to overreach themselves. They responded in a practical way to the demand for education even in isolated villages, and established new schools for which they did not have the money or the trained teachers and supervisors to support at a reasonable level of educational efficiency. When the 1952 Education Ordinance came into force, village-centred mission schools had to begin adapting themselves to new national demands. However, the grass-roots involvement of churches in the life of the people at village level continues and through their representation on District and national boards under the 1970 Ordinance the churches will continue to contribute to planning and policy at all levels.

ANGLICAN

The Anglican mission commenced its work in British New Guinea [q.v.] in 1891 at Dogura, on the shore of Goodenough Bay. Under the agreement made between the Methodists, London Missionary Society and the Church of England missionaries, urged on by the Administrator, Sir William MacGregor [q.v.], the three groups defined the areas in which they would work. The Anglican mission was allotted the area north and east of the main range, from Cape Ducie on Goodenough Bay to the boundary with German New Guinea [q.v.].

The purpose of the mission was the inculcation of the Christian faith, the winning of converts to the Christian religion and the training of the people in Christian living. It was obviously desirable to begin this training in the children. Accordingly, a school was started as soon as the missionaries had mastered the local language sufficiently to be able to make contact with the children and to begin to teach them. A prime function of the school was moral and religious instruction, but it was also felt that the children should be taught some secular subjects, so lessons were given in simple arithmetic, and what could be classed as general knowledge, as an attempt was made to give the children some idea of the world of which they were part but from which they were so isolated. As the language became better known and committed to writing, there were lessons in reading and writing.

The murder of a government officer in the Mamba River area in 1897 brought an urgent appeal from the government to establish a mission station in that region. This posed a difficulty for the mission, as it meant having centres of work at each end of its area and a long stretch of untouched coast in between. However, a station was set up on the Mamba River and gradually the gap was filled as more stations were started. The pattern of opening a school as soon as possible was followed, and it became a tradition that where there was an Anglican mission station there would be a school.

At the time the mission was expanding other developments were taking place. Government activity was being extended, trading posts and plantations were being opened up and so there was increasing contact with the outside world. This called for greater efforts in the educational field in order to fit the people to take part in new activities. A start was made on the teaching of English. This was necessarily very elementary, but it did have the effect of introducing some of the children to the language of the government and the business world, providing a knowledge which could be built on. A result was that young men from the mission schools were in demand for jobs of minor responsibility in government and business.

The early European missions were assisted by men from the Solomon Islands. These men had spent some time working in Queensland and there had become Christians and learned a little of the English language. As the number of children attending school increased, it was impossible for the European missionaries to cope with them all, and Solomon Islanders were brought in to help in the schools, usually under the supervision of a white missionary.

Compared with what is achieved now, it cannot be claimed that the standard of the schools was high. However, under the conditions of that time it would not have been possible to reach today's standards, even if the means to attempt it had been available. Further, there were not the same incentives then for the education of children. Little employment was available and it was thought that a European type of education would make young men dissatisfied with village life. It was held that what was needed most was a thorough grounding in Christian principles with a view to the welfare of the individual and his community.

In the beginning it was difficult to get children to go to school in a village other than their own, but in time it became possible to bring boys to live at a mission station. As boarders they lived a regular life, had close contact with Europeans and as they reached adulthood many of these men emerged as leaders amongst their own people or became trusted employees in government and private enterprise.

It was not long before Papuan men who had passed through the schools became teachers themselves. Their duties included the work of evangelism as well as the imparting of secular knowledge, and it was found that many were able to exert strong influence on the people to change their old way of life. In 1917 St Aidan's Teachers' Training College was set up at Dogura for the training of teacher-evangelists. It was basic to the mission's thinking on education that secular and spiritual training should not be divorced.

One factor that limited educational development was paucity of resources. The early missionaries set their minds against any money-making activity. Their view was that their prime function was the spread of the Christian Gospel and they did not want to have their work confused with other interests. The Administration of the pre-war years had little money to work with and government assistance was small. However, by the time World War II began the mission had covered the coastline with a series of schools and in some parts, particularly inland from the government station of Buna, had penetrated into the interior. The mission area was divided into districts, each with a head station where the white missionary who was in charge of the district lived. At the head station was the main school of the district, usually with a white teacher in charge. There were also several out-stations under the care of Papuan teacher-evangelists, many of whom had been trained at St Aidan's College and who carried out both evangelistic and school work. The white teacher supervised the work of the schools on the out-stations, visiting them from time to time to examine their progress. Promising pupils, mostly boys, were brought into the head-station school as boarders to advance their educational standard. In the pre-war years out-stations generally reached Standard 2 and head stations Standard 4, with a slightly higher level at St Paul's School at Dogura.

The coming of the war to Papua had profound effects. The first Japanese landings in Papua took place in July 1942 at the Anglican mission station of Gona, on the shore of Holnicote Bay. Their advance inland to Kokoda was rapid, and soon the whole area was under Japanese control. There were several mission stations in the area. The white missionaries had stayed at their posts and seven of them were killed. These included two teachers, Mavis Parkinson of Gona, and Lilla Lashmar of

Sangara. With them was a young Papuan teacher, Lucian Tapiedi, who stayed with the missionaries and helped them when they attempted to escape from the invaders. The whole work of the mission was disrupted and not until the war was over was it possible to re-establish the work.

After the Japanese had been driven out a great Allied supply base was developed at Oro Bay. This meant the indigenous people had much greater contact with Europeans than ever before; one of the results of this was a desire for higher standards of education.

In 1947 a great gathering of native representatives of all mission districts met at Dogura and plans were made for rebuilding the mission work. It was unanimously decided that the memorial to the martyred missionaries should be a school to provide the opportunity for further education for those who had passed through the district schools. Martyrs' Memorial School came into being at the beginning of 1948, at Sangara, on the site of the old mission station and near the new government station at Higaturu. It was intended for boys (and in the early years, girls) who had completed the course at a head-station school and were considered capable of further study. At first it was attended almost exclusively by boys from the surrounding area, the then Northern Division. Parents in more distant places were reluctant to send their children to what was to them still an unknown land. The school raised standards year by year and had reached Standard 6 when it was destroyed by the Mt Lamington volcanic eruption in January 1951. It was soon re-established and has since grown in numbers as well as in standard attained, and now draws boys from the many parts of the Territory where the Anglican mission is working.

At about the same time St Christopher's Manual Training School was established at Popondetta to provide technical training for boys in manual trades. At Dogura the Sisters of the Community of the Holy Name started a girls' school.

The three institutions, Martyrs' School, St Christopher's School and Holy Name School, all started at upper primary level but have developed into secondary schools. Since World War II the mission's work has extended to the Trust Territory of New Guinea, and primary schools have been established on the south coast of New Britain, in the Siane Valley south-west of Goroka, and in the Simbai and Jimi River valleys.

The establishment of the Administration's Department of Education and the introduction of the 1952 Education Ordinance brought great changes. In the early days mission schools had had to provide their own syllabus, but now they followed that produced by the Department and prepared children for the Primary Final Examination set by the Department. Success in that examination was required for entry to one of the secondary schools. Whereas St Aidan's College previously prepared students for the dual role of teacher and evangelist, the emphasis was now transferred to teacher training and students were prepared for the examinations set by the Department of Education for the registration of teachers in the Territory.

The effect of negotiations for a new Education Ordinance in 1969-70 was equally profound. For some years the process had been going on of either closing schools which could not be adequately staffed as recognized schools for subsidy by the Department of Education, or of maintaining them as exempt schools with unqualified staff. The Weeden Report forced a decision as to the style of school the Church should try to maintain. It was decided to apply for membership of the new system for all schools and registered teachers. What had been exempt schools under the 1952 Ordinance were to be removed from the Education Division of the Diocese, and regarded primarily as places for evangelism, to be in the charge of evangelists responsible for imparting religious knowledge but free to give instruction in other subjects if they were willing and able and the people wished it. On 1 July 1970 all the recognized primary schools, Martyrs' Memorial School and Holy Name School became member schools of the new Education System.

The development of a higher standard of education with higher qualifications required for teachers had other effects. There were three possibilities for St Aidan's College, all strongly urged by their supporters: to rebuild on its site at Dogura; to build a new college in the Northern District; to join with another church or churches in the provision of a teachers' college. As it became clear that St Aidan's was unlikely to have the numbers required for a college with a large staff, big library and other facilities, an approach was made to the Lutheran Church to permit Anglican participation with them in Balob College near Lae. The overtures were warmly received and in 1969 the first Anglican students commenced their studies at Balob. Until the end of 1969 St Aidan's continued to allow those who had commenced their course there to complete it and conducted a special up-grading course for some senior teachers who had done their training at lower standards. The first Anglican students who did their full course at Balob graduated at the end of 1970.

St Christopher's Manual Training School had served a very useful purpose for a number of years, but the Department of Education decided that all secondary schools should follow the same course for two years, and that technical schools should then take over and provide courses at Form III and Form IV levels. The Church considered it was not their task to provide, from limited resources, the qualified staff and equipment needed for this level of technical education [q.v.], so St Christopher's was closed at the end of 1970.

The Anglican Church has welcomed the changes brought about by the adoption of the Weeden Report, especially its aim to involve the whole community in the field of education. The Church hopes, through its influence in boards of management, District education boards and especially in the training of teachers, to continue to exercise its function of leavening education with Christian principles and so help in the task of building a strong and upright nation.   B. R.

ROMAN CATHOLIC

An integral part of the process of establishing the Catholic Church in any country is the establishment of schools, and this was true of the Catholic mission work in the Territory of Papua and New Guinea.

Initially, the purpose of these schools is to contact the indigenous population to instruct them in the tenets and rituals of the Catholic Church. Though formal education is never excluded from these centres of instruction religious education is usually the main objective. Such centres for children provide an automatic and smooth involvement with the parents and adults of recently contacted peoples. Gradually, the centres first established introduce secular subjects and more and more elements of formal education as the initial contacts are consolidated and as the needs of the newly formed Catholic communities develop.

In both Papua and New Guinea before 1914 the Catholic Church established schools wherever missionaries settled. As the number of settlements increased, children with academic promise were sent to the longer-established stations to attend a boarding school. In contrast to the day schools at the village level, the boarding schools had longer hours of instruction per day; more secular subjects were included in the curriculum; qualified overseas teachers formed the staff; and a world language was both taught as a subject and used as the medium of instruction. In some instances this language was German and in others English. This second type of school brought pupils through to the completion of a primary course. Pupils of promise who graduated from the boarding-type school were often recruited to pursue further studies for vocational training to prepare the students for service in the Church.

Before World War I the Catholic Church in both Papua and New Guinea was engaged in the type of education just described. The Administration at that time, and especially the business people in the Territories, did not concern themselves with the education of the populace. Consequently, schools were virtually the sole domain of missions.

This pattern of education was continued and expanded by the Catholic Church. Formal secondary education was added, usually at the headquarters of the Catholic missions. During World War II students who had completed their secondary education and were training for the priesthood in seminaries had to interrupt their studies. Thus the Catholic Church was engaged in secondary education and beyond before World War II.

When the missionaries returned after the war, the former pattern of education was followed, but with differences. The personnel available for mission work was seriously depleted. Many missionaries were victims of the war and recruitment to missionary orders was seriously hampered during the war years.

Another difference was that the Central Highlands of New Guinea had been explored and a large and concentrated population discovered. Missionaries were compelled to spread their personnel even more thinly in the established stations in order to extend the work of the Church to the Highlands. Hence the school structure did not develop as fully as before the war and the pattern of the Catholic school system retained a very broad base with a narrow top.

By the late 1940s the Catholic Church was operating hundreds of schools that retained children for three or four years only. These schools attempted to expose the children to the basic tenets of the Catholic Church, train them in Church etiquette and drill them in needed prayers and singing. Central schools provided a post-primary education for some of the children capable of further learning. Pupils who were old enough and had learned enough were then encouraged to be catechists or teachers.

In the late forties and early fifties the Catholic Church realized that it was faced with the decision of whether to remain involved in general secular education as well as in education for specific Church needs and religious purposes. It is hard to pinpoint the exact time because the Church in all areas of the Territory did not come to the realization at the same time.

The Australian Administration was an effective catalytic agent. It recognized that it must start a concerted effort to provide indigenous people with the education needed for them to assume responsibilities in the public service and civic life at large, and admitted that the combined efforts of government and churches would be required to achieve this.

Through a series of changes in grants-in-aid to mission education, the Administration was able to encourage the Catholic Church to examine its role and programmes in general secular education. By the adoption of new syllabuses, by the teaching of English as a subject in all grades of all primary schools and using it as a medium for instruction in all subjects, and by the expansion of teacher training, the Catholic Church was able to keep pace with the Administration in providing schools suited to the current needs of the Territory.

By the mid-1960s the Church had virtually reached the limits of the available financial and personnel resources. It recognized that schools gave natural and traditional opportunities for instructing adherents, and confirmed its desire to educate citizens who were to become leaders in both public and private sectors of the community. However, there was a danger of concentrating on the field of general education at the expense of other areas of Church activity. Unless considerable financial assistance in addition to the Church's own funds was found, the Catholic Church's contribution to education would soon reach its limit.

The recommendations of the Weeden Committee on Education gave promise of a new financial basis for educational work conducted by churches. With mission teachers recognized as professionals on the same basis as those in Administration schools, and with full participation in a national education system, the Catholic Church entered a new phase of educational activity in 1970.

There are fifteen autonomous dioceses of the Catholic Church in Papua and New Guinea, coinciding for the most part with the Administration District boundaries. To use its resources to the best possible advantage the Catholic hierarchy established a National Education Office in Port Moresby. The office advises each diocese on its own educational matters and on education in the Territory as a whole. It also provides liaison with the Department of Education and helps to bring unity to the educational activity of all the dioceses.

Schools operated by the Catholic agency enrol approximately one-third of the total number of students at primary and secondary schools and teachers' colleges in the Territory. In over-all enrolments the Catholic system is nearly equal to the Administration education system and provides one-half of the education being given by missions and voluntary agencies. As a school system, the Catholic Church is not expanding horizontally at the primary level. Many smaller schools are being combined to form one larger, more economical and efficient school. Existing schools are being developed vertically so that each primary school offers a full range of primary classes with qualified teachers. In 1970, 75,424 children were enrolled in 526 Catholic primary schools.

The Catholic Church conducts secondary schools in all but four of its dioceses. While there are seven civil Districts in which the Church does not conduct secondary schools, in some Districts its operates more than two. Again, the pattern of development to be expected in secondary education will be vertical rather than horizontal. While very few new secondary schools are planned for the Catholic Church, the existing secondary schools all plan for expansion. In 1970 4,884 secondary students were enrolled in a total of twenty-one high schools.

Four new teacher training institutions have been established to serve regional areas. Vunakanau Teachers' College opened in Rabaul in 1969 to serve the New Guinea islands. Teachers' colleges are established at Mount Hagen and Wewak on the New Guinea mainland, and the Papua area is served by the Yule Island Teachers' College. In 1970 student enrolments in the five Catholic teachers' colleges totalled 551.

Three minor seminaries have been established to prepare men for the priesthood. Apart from a few courses, such as Latin, these schools follow the syllabus for secondary schools used by purely secular secondary schools. In point of time the minor seminaries preceded the establishment of senior high schools by the Administration at Form V and VI levels and run largely parallel to them.

Upon completion of Form VI successful students enter the major seminary which offers a six-year course at the tertiary level. There are two such tertiary schools of divinity, both at Bomana, near Port Moresby. One prepares students for the diocesan clergy; the other is for students who join the religious order of the Missionaries of the Sacred Heart. These are the only tertiary institutions the Church is conducting, although it is hoped that the teacher training colleges will develop to tertiary level.

With very few exceptions, all the secondary schools are staffed by expatriate teachers; expatriate teachers are found also in many primary schools although the number of indigenous teachers is far greater. No set pattern determines where in the primary system these overseas teachers work. One diocese may feel that they are best employed as full-time supervising, non-teaching headteachers. Another may value the services of its overseas teachers most at the preparatory class level, whereas another may use them in primary schools as subject or specialist teachers.

The Catholic Church lags behind the Administration in providing positions for the local or indigenous teachers. In 1970 there were no plans for the Church to train its local teachers as secondary-school teachers. Applicants for either headteachers' courses or pre-service courses for teachers will for the time being be trained in Administration colleges. The process of localization of the teaching service has been accepted in principle, though the rate at which it can proceed is problematical. The services of expatriate teachers, many of whom are members of religious communities, deserve much appreciation. Recently they have been joined by many lay teachers.

The curriculum used in all the Catholic schools is the syllabus prepared by the Department of Education. English is taught in all classes as a second language and used as the medium of instruction in all classes of primary and secondary schools.

As the number of children completing their primary education in Catholic schools increases and places in Catholic secondary schools become more competitive, many Catholic children are attending Administration secondary schools. The Catholic Church encourages this and plans to provide chaplains for the religious and spiritual needs of its students at Administration schools. As a matter of policy the Church favours co-educational secondary schools but some of the secondary schools in the Catholic school system are not co-educational because of the traditions and regulations of the religious communities conducting them.

The Catholic Church works as a partner with other church agencies and with the Department of Education under the 1970 National Education System, and Catholic personnel are members of education committees at local, District and national levels.   P. McV.

EVANGELICAL ALLIANCE

The Evangelical Alliance agency is responsible for the educational work carried out by a number of smaller missions and churches in the Territory. All member missions of the Alliance involved in education are members of the agency. They are Bamu River Mission, Asia Pacific Christian Mission, Christian Missions in Many Lands, Wesleyan Methodist Mission, Nazerene Mission, Australian Baptist Missionary Society, Gospel Tidings Mission, Apostolic Church Mission (New Zealand Administration), South Seas Evangelical Mission, New Guinea Gospel Mission, Assemblies of God Mission, Evangelical Mission of Manus, Australian Church of Christ Mission, Christian Radio Missionary Fellowship and the Christian Leaders' Training College. There are other missions and churches of the evangelical tradition who, although not members of the Alliance, have sought to be linked with the education agency. These are the Swiss Evangelical Brotherhood Mission, Evangelical Bible Mission, Christian Union Mission, Independent Christian Mission and the Bible Missionary Church. In 1970-1 other small groups were negotiating to join the agency.

The agency has a national education secretary whose main task is a co-ordinating one, ensuring that the work of the agency members does not overlap and encouraging co-operation wherever possible. He also represents all agency members at the national level and liaises with national groups on their behalf.

The agency has schools in nine of the eighteen administrative Districts, with the greatest concentration in the Western and Southern Highlands Districts. Educational work by missions in the Evangelical Alliance commenced early in the 1950s in the Western District and in the late 1950s in other Districts. The agency is thus young, and works mainly in areas where development has only recently begun.

The agency's main concern is the primary field where it had ninety-eight schools in 1970 with an enrolment of approximately 10,000; this figure rises annually and there is planned growth and development for the coming years. Evangelical Alliance enrolments have for several years been an increasing proportion of the total school enrolments in the Territory.

The agency's one fully developed high school is an established inter-District school with students from agency primary schools in six administrative Districts. There are usually thirty or more language groups and up to twelve churches represented in the student body. The agency has plans to expand its secondary facilities.

The Alliance conducts a primary teachers' college in the Southern Highlands, reasonably central to all member missions and churches, from which approximately forty teachers graduate annually.

A unique education service is provided by the Christian Radio Missionary Fellowship. The School of the Air commenced in 1963 at Rugli, seventeen miles north of Mount Hagen in the Western Highlands. It assists children receiving education through correspondence schools in Australia, New Zealand or the U.S.A. Enrolment fluctuates between forty and fifty. All grades are covered in two hours' broadcasting each day.

                                                    A. N.

LUTHERAN

From the inception of Lutheran missionary activity on mainland New Guinea the education of the people has been a major concern. Shortly after the arrival in 1886 of Johannes Flierl [q.v.], the first missionary in Finschhafen, a classroom was built. Initially the children would not stay overnight at the mission station, but eventually a group of boys agreed to stay for several months in a boarding school. A morning of instruction and an afternoon of work in the gardens and around the station was the programme. The missionaries who later joined Flierl in New Guinea also opened schools at their stations. Because it was impractical to teach in all the local vernaculars, three languages of instruction were adopted as the number of schools increased: Kâte and Yabem (Jabim) in Finschhafen, Graged in Madang. The purpose of this programme was to make people literate in the agreed vernacular, to help them to read their Bibles, to teach them to do simple arithmetic and to help them adopt good hygiene practices. A few girls were taught sewing, hygiene and cooking in a practical way by missionaries' wives.

Two central schools for training teacher-preachers were established in Finschhafen about 1905, and graduates established schools in the villages. The initial difficulties of the new teachers resulted from their own limited schooling and their poor methods. They were paid a small amount by the mission, while the communities helped them with their gardens and houses. In this pre-World War I period, a system of four years of village school, two years of station school, and two years of teacher training developed. In the Yabem district, in 1915, there were twenty-eight teachers with 850 pupils.

In the inter-war period there was a slow but steady growth of the system. The Lutheran churches and mission societies of Australia, the United States and Germany all contributed staff and finance to the programme. As more students finished the station schools, the area school was introduced as another two-year step prior to teacher training. The system attempted to provide four years of universal education in those areas where the mission was active. The upper levels of the system provided more teachers and leaders for the Church. By 1926, the Yabem district had fifty-six teachers with 1,360 students in village schools, 112 students in higher schools, and 57 in teacher training. Comparable growth was occurring in the Kâte and Madang districts. The Madang district established two teacher training centres in 1924. In the mid-1930s the Lutheran missionaries moved into the central Highlands. As schools were established, Kâte was adopted as the common language.

To assist in the educational programmes, printeries were established at Madang and Finschhafen. The Finschhafen plant did not continue after World War II, but the Madang plant is now a major printing establishment.

At a conference in 1935 missionaries discussed whether the Church's educational system should serve only the Church itself or whether it should prepare students for other kinds of work too. Before World War II, the missionaries had been influenced very little by the German or Australian Administrations in the operation of their schools.

In 1945 and 1946 the returning missionaries found that the physical facilities of the mission had been destroyed, and the display of goods from overseas during the war had created in the population a new motivation for education, including a desire to learn English. The lack of qualified English teachers resulted in the school system going ahead again in the vernaculars. By 1951, the Yabem district had 4,895 children in village schools, 371 in higher schools and 50 in teacher training. Throughout the mission, 19,464 children were in the village schools.

As the Australian Administration accepted responsibility for education, it offered subsidies to churches to assist them in their educational efforts. In 1950 Lutheran Mission New Guinea decided to accept these subsidies.

Within Lutheran Mission New Guinea there were those who recognized that some students should have an opportunity to study English thoroughly. The Rev. M. Heist opened the first all-English Lutheran school at Bumayong near Lae in 1952. In 1955 the first Lutheran students went to Australia for secondary schooling. Also in 1955 the Lutheran Conference agreed to start the teaching of English in the third year of village school. This agreement followed a discussion in which it was warned that this kind of education would not serve the real needs of the people.

In 1959, the Administration announced its intention to close, in 1960, all schools teaching in a foreign vernacular. The Evangelical Lutheran Church of New Guinea responded to this announcement through its Bishop, Dr J. Kuder, who had had a strong positive influence in the shaping of Lutheran educational policies and practices in New Guinea. In a lengthy reply, he expressed regret at the Administration's new policy and noted that closing vernacular schools would not thereby create English schools. So the number of children being taught in the church vernaculars decreased. The number of children being taught in English slowly increased but the quality of instruction was often poor. Parents soon realized that many children were not gaining literacy [q.v.] in either English or a vernacular. By the mid-1960s there was again an increase in the number of children being taught in one of the church vernaculars or in Pidgin English [q.v.]. The numbers of children in English primary schools and in vernacular village schools become comparable, totalling about 35,000 in 1970.

Several small teacher training colleges which had been changing from vernaculars to English were replaced by one central institution, Balob Teachers' College near Lae, founded in 1965. Some area schools developed into high schools and by 1966 there were seven. Staff shortages have allowed only four to continue.

Other significant educational institutions not receiving Administration subsidies include one English and three vernacular seminaries, two vernacular teacher training institutions, a commercial school, an agricultural school and a vocational-technical school.

In 1970 the English language schools of the Lutheran missions and churches joined the Territory Education System. While meeting the demands of the Territory System, the schools are also expected to educate the children for membership and participation in the Lutheran Church.

R. T. B.

SEVENTH DAY ADVENTIST

The work of the Seventh Day Adventist Mission in Papua and New Guinea is controlled by the Australasian Division and administered in the Territory by the Coral Sea Union Mission at Lae, and by the Bismarck Solomons Union Mission at Rabaul. The former administers work on the mainland, and the latter in the New Guinea islands. Local work is under supervision of fourteen mission presidents whose territory largely coincides with government Districts. There is an education secretary at Lae and at Rabaul.

In 1908 S. W. Carr, the first Adventist missionary, came to Papua and leased land at Bisiatabu about twenty-seven miles inland from Port Moresby. He was accompanied by Bennie Tavodi, a Fijian teacher, and in 1909 a small school was opened for the indigenous people. In 1932 a training school was opened at Merigeda, about sixteen miles east of Port Moresby. By this time schools had been established in the Vailala and Marshall Lagoon areas on the coast, and inland in the Efogi (Kokoda Trail) area.

During World War II Papuan leaders kept the mission work going. In 1948 a school was set up at Bautama about twelve miles east of Port Moresby. This replaced Merigeda which was demolished during the war. In 1952 the chief school in the Vailala area was established at Belepa about four miles from the mouth of the Vailala, and later resited on the banks of the Kikori River. A boarding school at Vilirupu on the shores of Marshall Lagoon was moved to a site at Madana about four miles west of the Lagoon in 1965 and in 1966 the Ramaga school in Milne Bay was built by volunteers from Australia.

Seventh Day Adventist mission work was commenced on Bougainville in 1924 and schools were started by Solomon Island teachers on the southeast coast, and a few years later at Inus to the north. In 1936 a school was opened at Rumba, several miles west of Kieta.

Two Solomon Island teachers, Oti and Salan, began work in New Britain in 1929. They started to operate a school on Matupi Island in Rabaul harbour, under the direction of G. F. Jones. In 1936 Put Put training school was established at Kambubu, forty miles south-east of Rabaul. During the war, this school was occupied by the Japanese and completely destroyed. The Jones Missionary College was established on the site after the war and became a secondary and training school for the Bismarck Archipelago and Solomon Islands. The well-known Kambubu male choir toured the eastern States of Australia in 1964.

In the New Ireland District, Seventh Day Adventist schools are all on the small adjacent islands. By 1932 nine schools had been established on the islands of Mussau and Emirau to the north. During 1931 and 1932 the people of these islands

became Christians as a result of Seventh Day Adventist mission work and remarkable changes took place. In 1970 mission schools were providing education for the children of Mussau, Emirau and the small island of Tench to the east. Many Mussau Islanders have worked on the New Guinea mainland as missionaries and teachers.

Schools were started in Manus on Tong Island in 1935 and on Lou and Baluan Islands in 1938. The largest school is at Pisik on Lou Island.

Seventh Day Adventist mission work on the New Guinea mainland commenced at Kainantu in 1934 and at Bena Bena, near Goroka, in 1935, where schools were opened by teachers from Mussau Island and New Britain. Early in the fifties a school was started at Kabiufa, near Goroka. This school developed into the senior Seventh Day Adventist school and training centre for the New Guinea and Papua mainland. In the late forties mission work spread to the Madang, Sepik and Western Highlands areas, and schools in each area were opened. Adventist missionaries were the first into the Wabag Valley and a health education school was established at Sopas, near Wabag, where nurses and medical assistants are trained.

Through the years the basic unit of Seventh Day Adventist education has been the village school. This caters for approximately the first three years of schooling. Pupils continuing then attend District schools which, in many cases, are situated at an area headquarters of the mission, and cater for the next two years' schooling. Next is the central school, catering for the full range of primary classes. Usually overseas teachers are in charge of the central schools. It has been mission policy to use English as the language of instruction. High schools are operating at Kambubu and at Kabiufa. In 1970 a total of 615 students were enrolled in these two schools. All pupils attending Seventh Day Adventist schools pay fees and in addition all pupils at boarding schools are asked to work for a stated period each school day to help in agricultural work to provide the food they eat. This fee and work programme is characteristic of the Adventist boarding system in all countries. Until 1967 two teacher training colleges operated, at Kambubu and Kabiufa. In 1968 the Kabiufa College was transferred to Kambubu and then two years later to Sonoma, near Kokopo. Seventy-one students were in training in 1970.

The Seventh Day Adventists operate several other educational institutions in the Territory including an agricultural course at Kabiufa and a building construction course at Kambubu. A marine maintenance department at Put Put Harbour, New Britain, trains boat captains and crew. Indigenous missionaries are trained for work in primitive areas at a Bible School at Omaura near Kainantu.

The Seventh Day Adventist Church does not accept payment of teachers' salaries by the Administration and operates its schools as permitted schools under the Education Ordinance, having elected to remain outside the Territory Education System.

R. W. R.

UNITED CHURCH

The United Church of Papua, New Guinea and the Solomon Islands was created in January 1968 by the union of the Papua Ekalesia (formerly London Missionary Society), the Methodist United Synod of Melanesia and the Port Moresby United Church. The London Missionary Society (L.M.S.) in Papua and the Methodists in the New Guinea and Papuan islands have been involved in education from the time of first European settlement in the 1870s.

London Missionary Society. In 1871 the L.M.S. sent South Sea Island pastor-teachers, together with two European missionaries, to start missionary work in New Guinea. They settled at a base station in the Cape York area of Australia and worked northwards through the islands establishing pastor-teachers in residence until they reached the Fly River area, where they found the climate too rigorous and the people too fierce. They tried on several occasions to settle, living there for a few months at a time, and it was probably then that the very first attempts at schooling occurred in the Territory.

In 1872 six pastor-teachers settled at Manumanu, but here too the stay was short, for they were evacuated because of disease. In 1873 pastor-teachers Anederu, Rau, Ruatoka and Eneri and the wives of two of them settled in the first permanent establishment at Elevala and Hanuabada in Port Moresby harbour, and it is here that the first real continuous school started. Many of the missionary society's records were destroyed in London during World War II and the earliest existing record of this school says, 'the teachers . . . try to do a little in the way of teaching the children to read, but of course not much can be done since they have nothing in print in the native language. This difficulty will be met . . . ere a great while.' The quotation illustrates two important principles of the work of the L.M.S. Firstly they were concerned to educate right from the beginning and secondly they felt that the people should be able to read their own language—and have something to read in it. In 1876 the Rev. W. G. Lawes [q.v.] commented that attendance at the Port Moresby school was fairly regular and several children had learned to read. By 1889 the Rev. F. W. Walker was able to describe the flourishing school, its curriculum and methods and listed one of its objectives as to teach as many people as possible the alphabet, spelling and reading. The Rev. James Chalmers [q.v.] had earlier (1885) said 'Only by a thorough system of education will they ever rise above their superstitions and shake off for ever the fear of sorcerers and sorceresses. . . . Educated . . . there is nothing to prevent . . . the rise to a worthy national life.'

Another main principle in early L.M.S. education was the emphasis on the teaching of English. Chalmers early insisted on the need for a school teaching only in English and official reports in the last decade of the nineteenth century commented favourably on the use of English in schools at both Port Moresby and Kwato. A further main principle was that Papuans were trained to take over the schools in the villages, and in 1889 Sir William MacGregor [q.v.] made the first official mention of a Papuan headmaster, a Suau man, trained at Port Moresby, who taught at Logia with three Logia assistants.

From 1871 the L.M.S. spread along the Papuan coastline, and wherever a pastor-teacher or a missionary went a school grew up. In 1890 the number of children in L.M.S. schools was given as 3,500. Seven languages had been reduced to writing and printed in elementary books. In addition the four Gospels were published in the Motu language, and Acts, Romans and 1 Corinthians were shortly to be printed. Toward the end of the century there were eighty day schools in operation with a total attendance of 3,600 children.

Until the establishment of the Department of Education fifty years later, the L.M.S. continued these four main themes in its education programme: education as an important aspect of mission work; literacy in the vernacular for as many as possible; the teaching of English; and the training of Papuan teachers. Today large numbers of Papuans in commerce and government service, the House of Assembly [q.v.] and Local Government Councils, owe their education, including their knowledge of English, to the voluntary efforts of the L.M.S.

In 1961 the L.M.S. handed over its work, staff, property and finance to the Papua Ekalesia. The policy of the Papua Ekalesia in education was to continue to assist the Administration by operating Primary-'T' schools until the Administration could offer a full primary education for all children in Papua; to offer what limited form of education it could to as many children as possible who were not within the Primary-'T' school system; to press for the place of the vernacular as well as English in education, and to continue with both in its own schools; to provide Christian secondary schools as far as its limited budget would allow; and to train Christian teachers at Ruatoka College, sixty miles east of Port Moresby.

The 1967 Papua Ekalesia annual assembly strongly affirmed the importance of the vernacular (but never to the exclusion of English), and the right of every child to have an education, even if only a limited education was possible because of staffing difficulties. At the time of Church Union, 1968, as well as having 8,547 students and 284 teachers in 127 recognized schools, the Papua Ekalesia conducted almost the same number of exempt schools with unqualified teachers giving a limited education to a further 2,164 children.

Methodist. The Methodist mission has concentrated its missionary activity in certain geographical areas in accordance with agreements with other major denominations. Each of the four regions, New Guinea islands, Papuan islands, Buka/Bougainville and the Highlands have separate histories of development.

In 1875 the Rev. George Brown [q.v.] landed at Molot in the Duke of York Group with eleven South Sea Islanders who had been trained as pastors and teachers. This marked the commencement of Methodist activity in the New Guinea district which spread across to the Gazelle Peninsula and Nakanai coast of New Britain, New Ireland, and New Hanover. By 1877 schools had been established in several villages, basically to promote Biblical literacy, but also teaching hygiene and simple computation. As local people were trained as church workers it became the pattern for the younger children to be taught by catechists and the older ones by native ministers in the village schools. The most able students were sent to a circuit training institute on the head station of each circuit as boarders and there they were taught each morning by the European missionary. All education was in the Blanche Bay dialect until 1939 when English was taught as a subject. Not until 1948 was English used in the instruction of arithmetic for classes above Standard 3.

As early as 1932 a group of the most able native teachers were set aside as demonstrators and after a period of training worked in village schools as teacher advisers on methods and the administration of schools. These demonstrators functioned until the 1950s when gradually a European was appointed to each circuit training institute to relieve the minister of teaching duties. For a number of years circuit schools taught only to Standard 4, with Standards 5 and 6 being taught at the District Training Institute at Vatnabara (Duke of York) where the more able students were trained for the dual role of pastor-teachers. With improvement in standards of teaching and increased European staff Methodist primary schools were able to teach the full seven primary grades by 1965.

In 1961 pastor and teacher training had separated with teacher education moving to Halis, New Ireland, and later to Gaulim, New Britain. Students continuing in secular studies attended the George Brown College which had been founded in 1956 and was moved from Vatnabara to Vunairima in New Britain in 1960.

Special Methodist educational efforts in New Guinea have included a school for mixed-race and orphaned children at Raluana from 1906 to 1919 and a school for Chinese [q.v.] children and later Ambonese children which was run by the church in Rabaul from 1930 until World War II. Both World Wars and the changes in administration from German to Australian resulted in setbacks to the mission. In 1915 there had been 389 day schools with 406 teachers and 10,976 scholars and nine training institutions with 543 students. Many of the staff were experienced teachers who, as Germans, had to leave the country in 1919. World War II again completely disrupted schools. All organized teaching ceased, records were lost and none of the expatriate teaching staff survived this period. Among those who died was the Superintendent of Methodist Education in 1937 who had been working on a syllabus in all subjects from village schools through to secondary. Post-war progress was hampered by lack of staff and resources and the pressing problems of rehabilitating the Church. It was not until the mid-1960s that the whole position of village schools was reviewed and

there was a complete reorganization of the mission's education system. In 1964 a full-time education officer was appointed and in 1966 some of the European teachers were relieved of classroom duties to become supervisors of schools in their circuits. The number of schools was severely restricted, the posts of teacher and pastor were separated, a grading scheme for teachers was introduced and permit staff gradually withdrawn. All education posts were opened to New Guinea staff and correspondence courses and retraining encouraged. New Guinea region entered the United Church in 1968 with fifty-eight primary schools, 5,004 primary students, one high school of 226 students and a teaching staff of 195 including 22 expatriates.

The history of Methodist education in the Papuan islands commenced in 1891 when the Rev. W. E. Bromilow [q.v.], together with thirty South Sea Islanders from Fiji, Samoa and Tonga, began building the head station at Dobu, the populous centre of Normanby and Fergusson Islands. Teachers were established in nearby villages and by 1892 there were eight schools operating with 240 scholars. Samoan teachers started schools in Ware and Tubetube and a settlement was made at Panaete in the Louisiade Archipelago. In 1894 the Kiriwina station in the Trobriand Islands was established followed by schools at Woodlark in 1897 and at Bwaidoga on Goodenough Island.

At the village schools boys and girls were given a simple education and promising students sent on to the central training institution for more advanced training. Ubuya was the first site for the central institution, but in 1921 this was shifted to Salamo on Fergusson Island where there was an excellent landlocked harbour, fresh water, room for building and good soil for cultivation. The vision of the Gilmours who established the centre was to make the white missionaries and South Sea Islanders unnecessary. In 1926 there were eighty men in training using an elementary but practically oriented curriculum including Bible knowledge, methods of teaching, station management, writing, reading, arithmetic, hygiene and general knowledge. Specific skills taught were woodwork, boatbuilding and repair, sawmilling, carpentry, cabinet-making, sailmaking, simple mechanics and modern methods of agriculture. A particular feature of Salamo was its training of women who were instructed in cleanliness and simple hygiene, the care of children, the art of teaching, mat and basket making and dressmaking.

The work of education was considered next in importance to preaching the Gospel and the aim was to have a school in every village or group of villages. However, not many schools taught English and in 1925 only £35 was received from the government as subsidy for passes in English, although there were 6,314 day school scholars, twenty-two South Sea Island teachers, and sixty-seven Papuan teachers in the schools. The first trained teachers from Australia arrived in the 1930s.

World War II caused great disruption to the education programme. All schools were closed and teachers evacuated. Salamo was re-established after the war and in 1952 the first secondary teacher was appointed to commence secondary classes. The Wesley high school at Salamo had been developed to Form IV level and was the only secondary school in the D'Entrecasteaux group in 1971. Although English was made compulsory in central schools in the 1950s, a large number of vernacular schools still operated throughout the Papuan islands region, and in 1968 at the time of Church Union it was decided to continue operating these schools outside the recognized school system.

The Methodist work in Bougainville began because of the Siwai people's interest in education. They visited their relatives in the Mono (Treasury Islands) group and as early as 1905 saw the educational work of the Methodist mission. After repeated requests, four teachers from the British Solomon Islands were placed in southern Bougainville in 1916. From then on the work of the Methodist mission was bound up with the work of education and in every village where an agent was stationed one of his tasks was to conduct a school, however elementary, in the local vernacular. A handful of young men were sent to the British Solomon Islands after 1936 to be trained as pastor-teachers, and some of them had already begun work before World War II.

In the post-war era a serious attempt was made to do two things: firstly to broaden education with the financial aid that was available from the Commonwealth Reconstruction Training Scheme and secondly to establish a reasonably strong base of academic education. An education officer for Buka/Bougainville was appointed to supervise the two hundred schools and to train teachers. In the late 1940s small village schools were combined into larger central schools serving a number of villages. These provided four years of formal education, at least two of which were conducted entirely in the vernacular with English introduced as a subject in the third year. Station schools taught Standards 5 and 6.

Early attempts to provide technical education in the form of short periods of training in carpentry, mechanics, domestic science and agriculture failed. Agricultural training was replaced by a farm project in 1950 where the emphasis was on production rather than training. Domestic training was reviewed in 1956 with the establishment of Kihili Girls' School. Teacher training transferred from the south of Bougainville to Kekesu in 1952 and in 1963 was combined with teacher training for the New Guinea region at Halis and later at Gaulim.

Methodist educational work in the Highlands region is of much more recent origin than the work in the other three regions. The first Methodist schools were commenced at Mendi in 1951 and Tari in 1953. From the beginning Papuan and New Guinean teachers from coastal areas staffed the schools with the assistance of supervisory Australian teachers. A programme of two years' vernacular literacy followed by six years of the standard Administration curriculum in English was followed. Absenteeism was high and by the end of 1963 only about twenty children had completed primary education from the twelve village schools in operation. The Administration opened six new schools in the Mendi circuit in 1961 so the mission closed its schools in this area and expanded its educational effort in the more isolated areas of Tari, Nipa and the Lai Valley.

At the first Assembly of the United Church in 1968 an Education Board was established and a full-time national education secretary was appointed and stationed in Port Moresby to direct the education work of the former Methodist and Papua Ekalesia churches in both the Territory of Papua and New Guinea and the British Solomon Islands Protectorate. Annual conferences for regional education officers have been initiated and the total education work of the whole Church planned on a national basis. Ruatoka College was closed in 1969 and primary teacher training consolidated at Gaulim where 130 students were enrolled in 1971. Selected students are sponsored by the Church to train either as secondary teachers at Goroka or for administrative positions at the University of Papua and New Guinea [q.v.]. The high schools at Salamo and Vunairima have been built up and an additional high school commenced at Mangai on New Ireland. European staff are gradually being withdrawn from most primary teaching positions and in 1971 the majority of Standard 6 classes were staffed by local teachers with expatriate staff employed in supervisory, secondary and teacher education positions. Since the Weeden Report, the United Church has been clarifying and developing its philosophy of education. Schools operated by the United Church have come within the Territory Education System and staff are members of the National Teaching Service. The 1970 Assembly called for an increased effort in leadership training, for the localization of all teaching positions and has set up committees to investigate community education programmes, education for physically handicapped children and school leavers, and pilot schools for syllabus development.

Running parallel to the Board of Education are the Board of Ministerial Studies and the Christian Education Council. Four-year, two-year and short courses are conducted in theological and Christian education at Laranga Theological College and the Malmaluan Christian Education Centre for students from all over the Pacific.

R. B., H. C. AND S. R.

OTHER MISSIONS

A number of other missionary societies working in the Territory are involved in education, but some are independent of the Territory Education System and conduct only a small number of schools.

The Salvation Army became a full member agency of the Territory Education System in 1970 and has from the beginning provided education for a cross-section of the community. In 1970 it conducted schools in three Districts for approximately eight hundred children and was still heavily dependent on expatriate teaching staff and finance from overseas for its sponsored student system.

New Tribes Mission, Highlands Christian Mission, Independent Christian Mission, Evangelical Wesley Church of North America, and Sovereign Grace Baptist Mission had also become full members of the Territory Education System in 1970, while the Faith Mission, World Mission Incorporated and Four Square Gospel Mission had elected to remain independent. It is expected that these smaller agencies will associate with one or other of the major church agencies as the Territory Education System develops.

(*See also* EDUCATION, HISTORY AND DEVELOPMENT; EDUCATION, ORGANIZATION AND MANAGEMENT; EDUCATION, STATISTICS; MISSIONS)

EDUCATION, ORGANIZATION AND MANAGEMENT.

Up to World War II, education in Papua and New Guinea was in the hands of Christian missions [q.v.]. Churches are still responsible for the largest part of the primary-school system and teacher education, and they conduct

approximately half the high schools in the Territory as part of a national education system (*see* EDUCATION, MISSIONS).

The establishment of a Department of Education in 1946 and its subsequent development in the post-war period led to a fairly authoritarian, centralized system with control from Konedobu (the Papua and New Guinea Administration centre) and indirectly from Canberra itself. In contrast, the Education Ordinance 1970 has made possible a consultative, decentralized system by setting up a united structure for education managed through a series of local, District and national boards. With a majority of indigenous members on each board at every level of decision-making, control of the education system is being transferred to Papuans and New Guineans (*see* EDUCATION, HISTORY AND DEVELOPMENT).

STRUCTURE OF THE TERRITORY EDUCATION SYSTEM

The Territory Education System consists of three categories of schools: member schools (including

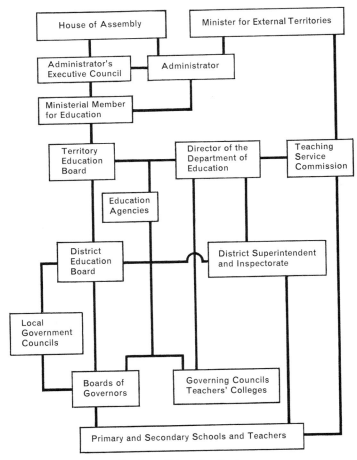

Territory Education System.

vocational centres and colleges), associate member schools and affiliated schools. Associated with these schools is a Territory Teaching Service. A fourth category, permitted schools, covers schools electing to remain outside the System.

The objects of the System are to develop a system of education fitted to the requirements of the Territory and its people, to improve standards of education and to make the benefits of education available as widely as possible. The System recognizes the rights of parents to obtain the education they want for their children, allowing a reasonable diversity of education methods and the preservation of the identity and character of particular schools and colleges. The principle of religious freedom is established, with no school or college entitled either to exclude a child solely on the grounds of religious or doctrinal affiliation or to compel a child to attend religious instruction.

The administration of the Ordinance and the Territory Education System is vested in the following authorities:

the Territory Education Board,
the Director and the Department,
the Teaching Service Commission,
District Education Boards,
Local Government Councils,
educational agencies,
the governing bodies of member schools, associate member schools and affiliated schools.

The lines of authority and communication within the Territory Education System are set out in the diagram.

Ministerial Member. The Papua and New Guinea Act 1949-68 made no provision for the House of Assembly [q.v.] to pass an ordinance giving powers to a ministerial member. Therefore in the 1970 Education Ordinance, power is vested in the Administrator [q.v.] or the Administrator-in-Council. However, the Administrator delegated these powers to the Ministerial Member for Education in 1970 and it is anticipated that direct power will be conferred on the Ministerial Member once legislative machinery is established to allow this.

The Ministerial Member approves the establishment, maintenance and development of all schools and colleges and makes decisions regarding policy, planning, finance and priorities to be observed in allocating staff and financial resources to Districts.

Territory Education Board. The fourteen-member Board has wide representation from many sectors of the community. Besides the Director and three representatives of the Administration there are representatives of churches and missions, Local Government Councils, business and civic interests, tertiary institutions and two members representing the interests of teachers. The majority of members of the Board are indigenous.

The Territory Education Board is responsible for keeping the economy and efficiency of the Territory Education System under continuous review. Its functions include advisory and supervisory duties. The Board advises the Ministerial Member on education, planning, development of schools, expansion of teacher education facilities,

school charges and any policy recommendations including final educational objectives. It co-ordinates and approves District plans for expansion and development. In addition, the Board advises the Teaching Service Commission, District Education Boards and education agencies on administrative matters affecting the efficiency of schools and welfare of teachers. The allocation of staff to Districts and students to teachers' colleges as well as the establishment of national criteria for the selection of students for secondary schools and colleges are important functions. The Director is the chairman of the Board which meets at least four times each year and is required to submit an annual report to the House of Assembly.

The Territory Education Board has authority to appoint specialist committees as the need arises. A Teacher Education Committee has been appointed to advise the Board on standards of admission, improvement of courses and facilities and the appointment of staff for all teachers' colleges. It will co-ordinate the work of teacher education institutions. A Planning Committee has also been appointed to advise the Board on overall education planning.

The Director and the Department. Although many of his powers have been transferred to the Territory Education Board, the Director retains authority to determine curricula, subjects, languages of instruction and standards of education to be adopted within the Territory Education System. He also remains responsible for the inspection of all schools, the certification and assessment of teachers and for fixing standard ratios between pupils and teachers.

The Department fulfils two functions. Not only is it the executive and inspectorial branch of the Territory Education System but it also acts as an agency in charge of all Administration schools and colleges. In its former capacity it is responsible for all finance and the supervision and implementation of approved plans and policies in relation to education. Thus at the District level the District Superintendent of Education is both the chairman and executive of the District Education Board and at the same time the senior representative of the Administration education agency. At the national level, the Director of Education is chairman of the Territory Education Board and head of the Administration agency.

District Education Boards. There are eighteen District Education Boards coextensive with Administration Districts. Membership of the Boards includes the District superintendents and representatives from the Administration, churches and missions, Local Government Councils, teachers and the community.

The Boards must consult with Local Government Councils and education agencies in plans for the establishment and development of schools in the District and submit these to the Territory Education Board for approval. The supervision and carrying out of approved plans is also the responsibility of the Territory Education Board. Other functions include selecting entrants for primary, secondary and technical schools, appointing staff, determining school fees, administering education funds and co-ordinating education activities within the District. The Boards report annually to the Territory Education Board.

Local Government Councils. Under the Ordinance, Local Government Councils have the authority to act as education agencies conducting their own schools. In practice very few have either the resources or expertise to do so. However the Councils have particular responsibilities in relation to all schools in their areas, undertaking some financial responsibility for the construction and maintenance of school buildings and teachers' houses as well as organizing self-help at a local level. The Councils have representation on both the Territory Education Board and District Education Boards.

Education agencies. Church, mission or voluntary education agencies operating before the 1970 Ordinance are included in this category. The Department of Education is the agency for Administration schools. An education agency may establish, maintain and conduct schools and colleges within the Territory Education Board's national plans for education. The agency is responsible for establishing a governing body for each of its schools and colleges, and nominates an education secretary to represent the agency at a national level and to communicate between the agency and other education authorities. As there are more than sixty missions involved in education the grouping of education agencies has been encouraged for representation at the national level.

Governing bodies. There is provision in the Ordinance for each school and college in the System to operate under a governing body. An education agency is responsible for establishing a board of management for each primary school and vocational centre or group of schools and centres. The agency may choose to act as a governing body or it may appoint a board, which must consist of at least five members representative of the community served by the school and include a teacher from the school. The board of management is immediately responsible for the planning, provision and maintenance of school buildings and teachers' houses, for the enrolment of pupils and for determining the aims and goals of the school.

Similarly each secondary and technical school must have a board of governors, appointed by the agency in consultation with the District Education Board. The school board consists of at least eight members representative of the District Education Board, the Local Government Council, teachers, pupils and the parents' and citizens' association of the school. Besides the finance and provision of school buildings, the board is responsible for the enrolment and discipline of pupils and the nomination of teachers for appointment. Governing councils, of widely representative membership, are also appointed for each teachers' college and technical college in the Territory. Each council appoints a board of studies to supervise the academic and professional instruction given in the college.

Schools and colleges. The Education Ordinance provides for four different categories of schools and colleges.

Full-member schools are those which conform to the standards of staffing and curricula laid down by the Director of Education. They may reserve up to one-third of their teaching positions for their own appointments and must guarantee places at Standard 6 level for 60 per cent of their Standard 1 intake. On 1 July 1970 approximately 90 per cent of non-government agencies joined the new system as full members.

Associate-member schools must conform to the same staffing and curricular standards as full-member schools but they are allowed to reserve more staffing positions and have less strict requirements on student progression. Agencies may elect to run affiliated schools where they are solely responsible for appointing staff. There is no condition on the proportion of places to be made available in the upper levels of these schools.

A fourth category of schools, known as permitted schools, may be run outside of the Territory Education System.

THE TERRITORY TEACHING SERVICE

The Territory Teaching Service consists of almost all teachers engaged in teaching in schools, vocational centres and colleges within the Territory Education System. Member schools can have additional staff who are not members of the Service. A temporary ordinance was passed in 1970 to provide for initial terms and conditions of appointment and service within the System and this was expected to be revised for adoption as a permanent ordinance by the end of 1971. There are two categories of teachers within the Service, full members and associate members. Full members staff full-member schools, whereas associate members teach in associate-member schools at a lower salary. Outside the Teaching Service there are two further categories: affiliated teachers and permitted teachers. Affiliated teachers may only teach in affiliated schools, and agencies receive nominal financial assistance from the Administration for them in the form of a grant-in-aid. Permitted teachers attract no subsidy.

Under the Ordinance teachers will be able to apply for schools of their own choice in Districts of their own choice. Although no final decision concerning procedure for appointments had been made in 1970 it was expected that individual teachers would make application to District Education Boards for individual positions advertised in the *Education Gazette*. Appointments would be finalized by matching up the District Education Boards preferences with teachers' preferences for positions but teachers would have to be prepared to serve anywhere in the Territory if necessary.

The Teaching Service Commission. The Minister has appointed a commissioner and associate commissioner to the Teaching Service Commission and provision exists for the appointment of additional associate commissioners and acting members for the Commission. The functions of the Commission are to be the employing authority of the members of the Territory Teaching Service, to determine the establishment of teachers in schools and colleges and the conditions of appointment, promotion, transfer, discipline, suspension, dismissal and conditions of service for all members of the Service.

DEPARTMENT AND SCHOOL ORGANIZATION

The Department of Education is administered from Port Moresby and contains six divisions: Management Services, Primary Education, Secondary Education, Technical Education, Teacher Education and Educational Services. Field officers of the various divisions work throughout each District.

The District superintendents, stationed in each District with supporting staff, are responsible for the implementation of educational policy and for the inspectorate at District level. A regional inspectors' and senior officers' conference is convened each year. It is attended by District superintendents, inspectors and headquarters professional staff and is usually held in a different Territory centre each year. The conference discusses educational policy and professional and administrative matters. It enables regular personal contact between the Director, headquarters staff and District inspectors in the field.

Tertiary and other institutions, apart from the teachers' and technical colleges, are administered by the public service departments or other bodies which established them, but all maintain varying degrees of liaison with the Department of Education.

Management Services. The Management Services Division provides personnel services, administrative services and office services at headquarters and District level. It is responsible for finance, property and buildings and for salaries, recruitment and development of administrative and clerical personnel.

Primary Education. Primary schools in the Territory have a multi-curricular policy using various curricula related to the individual needs of pupils. A Territory syllabus has been designed for pupils for whom English is a second language. The six-year curriculum anticipates an enrolment age of seven years. Other schools, using an Australian curriculum, are designed for expatriate children or indigenous children competent in English and follow the New South Wales syllabus. Children enrol in the year they turn six years of age and complete seven years of schooling.

A compromise has been developed in dual-curriculum schools, where both local and overseas children attend classes in the same buildings, amalgamating lessons and teachers in the same curriculum where appropriate, but using either the Territory syllabus or the New South Wales curriculum for core subjects like English. An experiment, still in its infancy, explores the advantages of using a variable curriculum. Waigani School, attached to the campus of the University of Papua and New Guinea [q.v.], opened in 1970 with an enrolment of 50 per cent local and 50 per cent overseas children in integrated classes. They work on one curriculum drawn from several sources which emphasizes small-group activity and individualized methods of instruction.

The proportion of children reaching school age who, in fact, enter school varies from District to District. Where there are insufficient places at Preparatory or Standard 1 level for all children of school age to commence schooling, the Board of Management decides the method of selection for entry to each school. At Standard 6 level indigenous children sit for the Primary Final Examination, which is an external examination in English, mathematics and general studies. Every child receives a certificate of assessment on the completion of his primary schooling.

In isolated parts of the Territory where schooling facilities are not available, the Administration assists expatriate children to undertake correspondence courses of instruction with the Departments of Education of the Australian States.

Secondary Education. Approximately 40 per cent of pupils completing primary education pass on to Form I at high school, while about a further 14 per cent enter vocational schools. Approximately one-half of the high-school entrants are selected on their results in the Primary Final Examination and their headteachers' assessments. District Education Boards decide on entrance standards for the remainder of students according to District needs; for instance, weighting may be given to female students, to urban or rural children, or to undeveloped Sub-Districts rather than the advanced areas.

The high schools follow a specially designed Territory syllabus offering all students a two-year course of study which completes the first stage of secondary education. About 60 per cent of Form II students continue to the second two-year stage of general education within the high-school system, some enter technical schools for further education and the remaining children leave school for employment or to return to the community. A Territory School Certificate is awarded at the end of the fourth year of high school recording the student's attainment over the secondary course. Selected students proceed to a third two-year stage offered at senior high schools in the Territory, while the remaining students graduate to courses in specialized tertiary institutions or to seek employment.

Multi-racial high schools follow the New South Wales syllabus and enrol Australian children and selected indigenous children on scholarships. Competitive scholarships are also available to enable outstanding indigenous children to attend secondary schools in Australia, and there is a subsidy-sponsorship scheme where some costs can be met by sponsors. The children of expatriates are also eligible for subsidies to attend high schools in Australia.

The syllabus for Territory high schools is designed in the first two-year stage to give a general and practical education that is a complete unit. In the second stage students continue with English, mathematics and science and a free choice of other subjects including social science, history, geography, agriculture, commerce, art, music, manual arts and home economics. The third two-year stage is specifically designed to prepare students for entry to tertiary institutions. The majority of high schools are co-educational boarding schools although present policy is to increase, where possible, the number of day students enrolled.

Technical Education [q.v.] is aimed at preparing students for careers in industry and commerce and is organized at several different levels.

Vocational training centres provide an additional year of training for selected students who have completed Standard 6 and who will not be proceeding to secondary education. Courses are designed to concentrate on teaching skills appropriate to local needs and include simple building and mechanical skills, crop and vegetable growing, fishing, sawmilling, trade store management, home management, baby care and community studies.

Students who have successfully completed Form II at a high school can become indentured to employers as apprentices. These students must attend a technical college for a concentrated course of specialized training during each year of the apprenticeship and also complete a series of correspondence assignments. Other Form II students who wish to continue full-time schooling can follow a composite course of general education and trade training at a technical college before gaining on-the-job experience.

For girls who have completed Form II secretarial training is available with courses in typing, simple bookkeeping, shorthand, business mathematics, English and community studies. Certificate level courses in engineering, commerce and building are being developed to provide above-average trained apprentices with further training for middle-level career positions in industry and commerce.

A variety of part-time courses are conducted by the Technical Division to meet the specific training needs of various organizations and departments. Courses include typing, institutional cooking, supervision and management and store control.

Teacher Education. Primary-teacher education courses are offered at twelve Administration and mission institutions. The courses are of two years' duration and have three different levels of entry: Form II, Form III and Form IV. The Administration provides scholarship allowances for all students at teachers' colleges according to their educational qualifications at entry and the year of the course.

Goroka Teachers' College offers a three-year training course for secondary-school teachers, who must have above-average results in the Territory School Certificate to be eligible for entry. Students are given the opportunity to specialize in science, agriculture, English, mathematics, art, social science, physical education, home economics or manual arts and some students are able to undertake university courses.

Expatriates may be trained in a special six-month 'E' course, two of which are offered in the Territory each year. The University of Papua and New Guinea offers post-graduate diplomas as well as education units to be included in a Bachelor of Arts or Bachelor of Science degree and a full four-year Bachelor of Education degree for both expatriate and indigenous students.

In-service training is of particular significance to teacher education [q.v.] as a large number of teachers hold only one-year trained certificates and primary syllabuses are being extensively changed with constant innovation. Six- or twelve-month in-service courses are offered at most colleges and special short courses are provided in particular subject areas on a regional basis. A senior officers' course is offered at several colleges to train senior indigenous teachers for wider responsibilities as headmasters and for administrative positions. Correspondence courses and overseas tours are also part of the in-service programme.

Educational Services. A number of non-teaching branches offering professional services to teachers, pupils and parents were amalgamated in 1969 to form the Educational Services Division. Sections include curriculum, planning, publications and broadcasts, research and statistics, libraries, adult education, examinations and guidance.

The curriculum branch employs curriculum officers, specializing in various learning areas, whose services are available to each division. The planning of educational development in accordance with national needs and the likely resources available is the responsibility of the planning branch working in conjunction with the Planning Committee of the Territory Education Board.

The basic function of the publications and broadcasts branch is to provide communication between the Administration and schools, teachers and administrators, teachers and pupils and, most importantly, between the Administration and parents in the community. The use of the mass media of broadcasting and publications have made a considerable contribution to the process of raising the general level of education of the people. Various school magazines, broadcast booklets, the *Education Gazette* and educational pamphlets are published through this branch. The educational materials section provides a lending and advisory service on educational materials, particularly audio-visual aids, to all schools in the Territory.

The research and statistics branch conducts research projects, collects and publishes statistics relating to the Territory Education System and provides information about all aspects of education to assist those who have to make policy decisions. The schools librarian, attached to the schools libraries branch, is concerned with establishing libraries in primary and secondary schools and assisting in the recruitment and pre-service training of library assistants.

The adult education [q.v.] section includes the School of External Studies which offers correspondence courses in secondary-school subjects to thousands of people throughout the Territory and plans special programmes for adults in literacy classes and vocational courses. Responsibility for setting external examination papers and overseeing printing, marking and processing requirements is in the hands of the examinations branch. Other functions of this branch include the provision of professional expertise in testing and evaluation procedures.

Finally, the guidance branch provides a service, covering the overlapping fields of educational and vocational guidance and clinical guidance, dealing with the atypical child. The major part of branch activities in the field is in secondary and technical schools.

HIGHER EDUCATION

The University of Papua and New Guinea began operations with a preliminary-year course in 1966. It now has students undertaking degree and post-graduate courses in arts, law, science, education and medicine. The Institute of Technology [q.v.], which was established in 1967, has diploma courses in civil engineering, mechanical engineering, accountancy and business studies.

There are several specialized institutions in Papua and New Guinea particularly catering for the needs of the public service, but also training people from other Pacific islands and for private enterprise. The major specialized institutions are the Papuan Medical College, Dental College [q.v.], Vudal Agricultural College, Forestry College [q.v.], Vunadidir Local Government Training Centre, Police Training College and the Administrative College [q.v.]. The Department of Education works in co-operation with these institutions.

S. K. RANDELL

(*See also* EDUCATION, POLICY AND PLANNING)

EDUCATION, POLICY AND PLANNING. Papua and New Guinea is virtually unique in that, until recently, there was very little articulate, local public opinion shaping educational policy. Since 1970, the policy of decentralization in educational management, and representation by indigenous majorities on education boards has brought local pressures to bear more closely on the education system. Until then, Australia, as trustee for the Territory, had to develop policy largely in the absence of informed indigenous comment. It is not the place here to discuss whether development of educational policy in that way was a good thing. What is important is that the absence of many of the forces which go to shape educational policy in most countries led the government to express educational policy in cautious general terms. The sentiments expressed in the policy are unexceptionably liberal and humanistic, but in the nature of things such statements are not fruitful guides to the daily operations of the education system. The details of policies emerge from day to day in decisions made as much to resolve diverse currents of opinion at the local level as to give practical expression to lofty philosophical considerations.

A major policy statement on education in 1956 by the then Minister for Territories, the Hon. P. M. C. Hasluck, defined the aims of the education programme in Papua and New Guinea as:

(1) The political, economic, social and educational advancement of the peoples of the Territory.
(2) A blending of cultures.
(3) The voluntary acceptance of Christianity by the indigenous people in the absence of any indigenous body of religious faith founded on indigenous teaching or ritual.

The Minister further directed that in attaining these aims it was necessary to foster a common language, which was to be English and that all educational facilities were to be available to both sexes.

The government of the day and subsequent governments have considered it necessary, in order to realize these aims, to establish a system of primary, secondary and technical schools and teachers' colleges, similar in many ways to educational institutions which have developed elsewhere in the Western world.

The second of the general objectives listed above merits some comment. The term 'blending of cultures' was developed before World War II by the Papuan government anthropologist, F. E. Williams. An essay he wrote in 1935 became widely known in Papua and New Guinea and was used as a cornerstone of educational thinking post-war. In that essay, the general aims of education were suggested as maintenance and strengthening of those elements of traditional society worth preserving, expunging elements like cruelty and sorcery which are incompatible with modern society and, finally, adding to the blend elements of Western culture which would make for a fuller and richer life.

The theory of blending cultures was attractive but there were and are a number of limiting factors which make it something of a will-o'-the-wisp as a practical education programme. There is, for example, the difficulty of altering or eliminating one element of culture without having some effect on other elements. Art and dance forms arise from magico-religious rituals and suppression of the latter removes the occasion for the former. Another difficulty is that of setting oneself up as a judge of which parts of culture should be maintained and strengthened and which parts ought to be suppressed. There might be common judgment about things like sorcery, but increasingly the value systems come into conflict. A major problem is the difficulty of finding teachers who can carry out this programme. Few teachers from another district or from overseas could usefully teach about the culture of a particular area.

Insolubility of the problems has led to abandonment of the notion that the education programme can actively blend cultures. What has been done is to accede to the wishes of the people where they seek the introduction of modern Western culture. It has not been possible to refuse to introduce parts of modern technology, or even Western art, craft or music, no matter how inferior to the indigenous traditional forms any of them may seem to be.

Accepting the inevitability of the onslaught of modern civilization neither precludes nor obviates the necessity at the same time to strengthen and renew traditional forms of expression so that individuals will have a choice. Each will make a choice of ideas and values; hopefully in such a way that he will develop an integrated, harmonious personality and be able to live successfully in the society in which he will be an adult. The future society must develop in its own way as a result of the individuals in that society freely selecting customs, values and attitudes which suit them.

Perhaps the most important consideration in developing a school programme based on these general considerations is the shape of the future society in which today's children will live as adults. It is not known what the organization or characteristics of this society will be. Any attempt to predict the details would be wrong in at least some major aspects. Papua and New Guinea are changing so rapidly that the course of their future social development cannot be accurately predicted. The number and complexity of technological changes is increasing rather than decreasing and change is likely to be the most pervasive feature of the lives of most people in Papua and New Guinea for a long time ahead.

A major objective of the education system must be to provide for this change. There is little use teaching a particular body of facts which will have no relevance in a few years. Children must be taught skills, attitudes and behaviour which will enable them to adapt to change and to extract order and stability from the world in which they live. Changes are crowding in upon the people so quickly that there are many dangers for them. If not rooted in a stable system of values, excessive change can lead to personality confusion, apathy and irresponsibility. Teachers must ensure that a school programme has strong links with the everyday life and surroundings of the children; that is, ensure that change leads to evolution not revolution.

CURRICULUM

The policy implies a pattern of curriculum development which shares many common elements with all other modern curricula, but one in which the subject areas and emphasis are related to the special needs of Papua and New Guinea.

This curriculum philosophy has developed through some very clear stages. W. C. Groves, who was Director of Education immediately after World War II, had the utopian vision of each teacher developing his own curriculum and so in the early post-war years there was no organized curriculum. Groves' vision was more that of an educator involved in all facets of community development than that of a school teacher. His approach and his strategy of placing the slender resources of manpower in all parts of the Territory allowed differences from area to area but also, very frequently, resulted in diffuse effort without satisfactory results.

Australians coming to this situation were, with rare exceptions, in difficulties. Thus there emerged the need for a curriculum sponsored by the Department of Education. The first effort was the work of one man, G. T. Roscoe, who was appointed Director of Education in 1958. Because it was a one-man effort it necessarily leaned very heavily on the Australian syllabus with which he was most familiar, the Queensland syllabus.

The next phase in development occurred around 1960 when a committee of the best available people in all fields of primary education produced a substantial document in which there was a conscious attempt to plan in sequence the content and approach to teaching. Likewise it was an attempt to map out for teachers the kinds of adaptation of their assumptions which would be necessary if they were to teach effectively in the Territory environment.

Few were satisfied with this for long and during the decade of the sixties the development effort in the primary curricula changed to a subject-by-subject approach. High-level expertise was brought to bear on the special problems of each area in turn. Through this period concentration of effort on English, mathematics, science and, latterly, health has produced a considerable volume of syllabus and teaching material.

Similarly, at the secondary level, there has been a cycle in the use of metropolitan syllabuses, heavily derivative syllabuses, locally produced committee-type syllabuses, and, more recently, redevelopment of individual subject areas using high-level expertise. Important to this development has been the internal control of the Papua and New Guinea examination system, obviating the necessity to work to unrealistic and unrelated syllabuses. Moreover, innovations have been introduced (e.g. social science) which are absolutely essential if students are to be provided with the insights and techniques to handle the problems of social development, but which would not be possible without a vigorous curriculum programme and control of testing and evaluation.

The curriculum development programme has thus in a short span of years progressed from no curriculum at all to subject development by committees of experts. Integrated syllabuses are unlikely unless a great deal more personnel and finance become available, since finance required for effective curriculum development has been grossly underestimated even in developed countries of the Western world. It is intended to maintain the curriculum improvement programme, but it must be expected that as more educational decisions are taken in the political arena, the pressure for expansion of numbers and hence restriction of resources applied to this programme will rise. Curriculum and materials improvement have a subtle effect on educational returns for money invested, much more profound than increases in the numbers of schools, but not nearly as obvious.

Language policy has been and continues to be a

vexing problem. There have been some practical considerations which determined language policy in Papua and New Guinea and which will continue to be of importance. The small number of people who speak each of the very many vernaculars would make the publication of vernacular material prohibitively expensive. No vernacular has won political acceptance for even a region, let alone the whole country. The task of a government to devise a language policy in such a complicated situation is not an enviable one. If the people of Papua and New Guinea are to be brought into a modern world, they need a national language, and preferably one which does not belong to any one group. Moreover, it ought to be a language which simplifies access to knowledge and technical information.

English has many of these advantages. It is one of the two or three languages into which the accumulated and new knowledge of the world is always translated. It is a status language throughout the world and the nearest equivalent at the present time to a lingua franca. Its adoption in Papua and New Guinea should not cause dissension since it does not favour any one group.

On the other hand, there are substantial disadvantages in promoting English. It is a relatively difficult language to learn, especially since most Oceanic people need to learn many of the concepts involved in English as well as the language itself. Practical evidence demonstrates that the people of Papua and New Guinea find it easier to learn other indigenous vernaculars or Pidgin English [q.v.] than to learn English.

The use of English is promoted vigorously throughout the school system. English is used as a medium of instruction from the child's first day at school. Notwithstanding the fact that policy has been to promote English as the common language with all possible speed, there has been no suppression of vernaculars. The language policy does not state that English is to be used exclusively. The Administration is perhaps open to the charge that it has not financed development of some of the vernaculars, and this is true, for the available finance has not been sufficient even to realize the policy of promoting a common language. Even if there had been more finance it is a fair conclusion that it would have gone into a better English programme though the school curriculum specifically states that vernaculars may be used and taught in schools initially. The restrictions are professionally defensible, for there is insistence that there be an organized vernacular syllabus, suitable material with which to learn reading and teachers competent in the particular vernacular. To date, none of the education agencies has taken up the possibility of teaching the vernacular under these conditions.

The urge to speak English has been strong. Until recently, there was no questioning of the policy of promoting English as the common language for there was no obvious alternative and promotion of any one vernacular seemed impracticable.

A major new factor has been added to the situation through the use of Pidgin as the common language of the House of Assembly [q.v.]. At first Pidgin was scorned, but since 1966 there has been a complete transformation to the point where most members now use Pidgin and it is being used increasingly in broadcasting when the speaker wishes to establish a point with as many people as possible. Simultaneously, there have been moves, enthusiastically backed by some anthropologists, to promote the respectability of Pidgin by reviving suggestions that it be called Neo-Melanesian.

The establishment of English as a common language could only be expected to take place gradually over several generations. The first signs of success of the policy are now evident in the second-generation children reaching the upper levels of primary schools and high schools. Given a little more time, the increasingly wide use of English would have reached the point where its growth and spread became, at least in part, self-sustaining and the job of teaching English considerably easier. With the respectability of Pidgin recognized and its spread, through the greater mobility of the Territory's population, the situation is now changing.

Pidgin is undoubtedly easier than English for Papuans and New Guineans to learn, but as a common language it has many drawbacks. It would require much effort and finance before it became a language of technology and commerce but, more importantly, the finance required to sustain a translation programme would continually impoverish the Territory.

It is possible that English will win through in the long run because of its international practicality. On the other hand, it is possible that Pidgin will increase in status and be used at the primary level regardless of the expense.

Innovation. Curriculum and teaching materials are constantly being developed. Until recently there has been emphasis on supplying poorly qualified teachers with pre-organized materials for use in their classes. That effort continues but now attention is being given to materials from which students, even early in their school careers, can learn with the minimum of supervision from the teacher. Examples may be cited from two subject areas.

The English-teaching programme has been devised around a modern systematic statement of the structure of English, and the concepts inherent in that structure. Special techniques have been developed to present syntactic patterns in realistic situations and these are drilled until they become second nature to the children. The techniques evolved have necessarily been tailored to the teachers' limited mastery of English. All aspects of the English programme have been systematically graded and integrated.

The development of abstract mathematical concepts is very difficult at any time and particularly difficult in a foreign language. It is easy for teaching whether by expatriates or local teachers, to degenerate into a rote process. A new curriculum with two special features has recently been intro-

(top) A rural Territory-curriculum primary school, Afore, Northern District.
(bottom) An urban demonstration primary school, Madang.

duced into primary-school mathematics. It extends the conceptual basis of the curriculum to cover modern ideas including logic and geometry. Children whose languages cover a variety of counting systems are, in fact, less likely to have difficulties with number bases other than ten than are, say, Australian children who have learned no other system. The second aspect of the mathematics curriculum is that it is based on the use of blocks of various shapes with which the children learn by discovering the principles inherent in the shapes. That they do learn is amply demonstrated by the encouraging results already achieved.

PRIMARY EDUCATION

Primary schools are of two types. The majority of children (over 200,000) are enrolled in Territory-curriculum schools. The syllabus used in these schools has been devised by educators within the Territory, specifically for Papuan and New Guinean children.

A small number of schools use Australian (N.S.W.) syllabuses. Enrolments in Australian dual- and variable-curriculum primary schools totalled 8,853 in 1970. These schools were originally established to cater for the children of expatriate residents whose language is English and whose background is largely Australian. The schools were set up in the knowledge that many Australians would not work in Papua and New Guinea unless their children could be educated in a way that would enable them to fit back into Australian life. Papuans and New Guineans may enrol in these schools if they are already fluent in English when they reach school age and if their background is not dissimilar to that of Australian children. For most Papuan children, however, Territory-curriculum schools are more suitable because of their orientation towards local needs.

Added to the problems of the different background and different initial learning of the two sets of children, there is the fact that one group are at home in the language of instruction whereas the other group has to learn a foreign language. Each syllabus presumes many things not presumed by the other. There are however increasing pressures to amalgamate the two types of schools and remove what appears to many as discrimination.

All the policy options have drawbacks. One option would be to increase vastly the enrolment of Papuan and New Guinean students in Australian-curriculum schools to the point of even racial representation. If this were done under the existing staff restrictions, all the Australian certificated primary teachers in the Territory would be diverted to Australian-curriculum schools, and would be removed from their present appointments at Territory-curriculum schools where they are providing specialist teaching in English. Another option would simply arrange appointments so that there was a mixture of Australian and Territory teachers in amalgamated schools. Most of the Papuans and New Guineans would, however, have lesser qualifications than the Australians. The original promise of the Australian

government to her public servants and others that their children's education would not suffer if they came to the Territory could not be sustained and this option could only be taken if the promise was felt to be no longer necessary.

Another option would be to make the Australian-curriculum schools private and to charge the fees necessary to keep them going. However, since much of the Territory's tax is raised from the expatriate population, they naturally expect tax-supported schools. Another possibility would be to have the Australian government pay for these schools from Commonwealth grants. This policy would also have many drawbacks and would certainly obviate the possibility of future absorption of these schools into the overall system. A further possibility would be to have two types of schools, one with high fees open to any who could afford them and the other free; that is better schools for the economically well to do and poorer schools for those without a high income. Although this is the Kenya solution, it would create a class structure in the Territory where none at present exists.

The policy currently adopted (1971) is a multi-curricular policy. The buildings provided for schools in urban areas have been standardized at one level and the children in an area attend school on the one campus. Within this one site, the school offers various curricula suited to the children. Both curricula with a mainly Territory approach and curricula with a mainly Australian approach are taught and lessons are amalgamated wherever appropriate and convenient. Considerable progress has been made towards realization of this policy since it was introduced and the pace will probably accelerate over the next two or three years. Certainly, Australian children in the Territory could benefit from more Territory-oriented teaching and some of the Territory children are gaining sufficient proficiency in English to take a syllabus which presumes an English-speaking and urban middle-class background.

Enrolment. At present, approximately one child of school age in every two has access to a primary school. These schools are not evenly spread throughout the Territory. Some places have 90 per cent or more of their children at school (Rabaul, Manus), while in the Highland areas the figure may be as low as 15 per cent. The disparity principally reflects the order of development of the areas and thus the readiness for formal schooling. The current objectives of the government are to quickly bring enrolments in the lagging areas up to 50 per cent of the school-age children, while maintaining the enrolment in areas which already have more than 50 per cent. The ideal of providing universal primary education has not been altogether discarded but sober assessment makes it a distant vision and current policies are statements of what seem to be attainable goals.

Nevertheless these enrolment policies are very difficult to sustain. In the Gazelle Peninsula, for example, the birth-rate is such that the population is increasing at the extraordinary rate of nearly

(top) Anglican mission primary school, Gona, Northern District.
(bottom) Waigani school on the campus of the University of Papua and New Guinea.

6 per cent per annum. To maintain the current enrolment ratio quite substantial expansion of facilities must be provided. Similarly, in the Highlands, even where there is only 25 per cent of the population enrolled at present, health services have reduced the child mortality rate and increased the birth-rate, so that the number in each age group is expanding dramatically. It will be difficult to maintain the percentages quoted unless there is a greater increase in enrolments than is envisaged at present.

Within this programme there is still the special problem of enrolment of girls. Many people of the Highlands still feel that the education of girls is best carried out at home, the limited places available being reserved for boys. There is still a sex imbalance; consequently there will be fewer educated girls than boys. Efforts are being made to improve these ratios by propaganda, persuasion and even by coercion through not providing school facilities if a substantial proportion of girls are not allowed to enrol. There is no indication that the problem will disappear although it does diminish as each area develops.

The difference between urban and rural areas creates another problem of enrolment policy. Is it better to put resources into towns or into rural areas? The need for teachers in rapidly growing towns receives much attention; in rural areas, teachers are provided in proportion to population. This approach may not continue to be accepted by a House of Assembly with a majority of members from the large rural population of the Highlands.

The average age of children entering Territory-curriculum primary schools has been steadily decreasing. In the early post-war years many children began their primary education at the age of 9 or 10 and, with frequent repeat years, it was not uncommon to find quite old students in primary-school classes. Most children now emerge from primary school at about 12-14 years of age. Recent consideration of the age pattern has led to a recommendation that the starting age be raised by one year so that children would emerge at an age when they could begin employment.

A developing country cannot afford to take all primary children into secondary school and so, for a large number of children, completion of a primary education is the end of their opportunities for formal education. There is real agony in this situation because a primary education is no longer adequate for jobs in the modern sector of the economy at any but the most menial levels and because the children are heartbreakingly young. They are certainly too young for positions of responsibility, even if they do have a better education than their parents. They are also physically too immature to take on whatever labouring jobs are available. What exacerbates the problem in Papua and New Guinea is that until very recently most school leavers could get a job without much difficulty. Within the memory of most people a primary education was sufficient for a good job, but as the number of better educated people increases rapidly, so the availability of positions will de-crease. Many of those who leave at the end of primary school do not want the kinds of jobs that are offering. There is a difficult period ahead of them in which many must lower their aspirations and come to terms with the realities of what is available.

Education planning might suggest only taking into primary schools the number of children who can be taken on to high schools, with some excess for those who do not complete the course successfully. But a democracy allows citizens to make decisions and must live with the result. In Papua and New Guinea the people would not tolerate a contraction of primary places in order to finance expansion of secondary education. They would prefer to have some education for many, than increased opportunity for a smaller number.

At the end of the sixth year of primary education an examination is conducted for a Primary Final Certificate. Selection for entry into high school is made in each District on the basis of this examination and the headteacher's assessments.

SECONDARY EDUCATION

In the secondary field, enrolments have increased at a great rate. In 1960 there were only 1,800 children in secondary school and in 1970 there were 17,785, a tenfold increase. When it is realized that nearly all of these children are in boarding schools, something of the practical problems and cost of such expansion will be appreciated.

The first secondary schools were closely modelled on Australian schools and were highly selective. A problem with the Australian-type curriculum, apart from its other shortcomings for Papua and New Guinea, was that it presumed all children would complete the first four-year cycle. Many children leave school before completing the first cycle and, in fact, the country could not afford to have too many at school so long. Also a four-year curriculum made it more difficult for children with limited backgrounds to relate their learning, especially in such subjects as science, to their own environment. Therefore the curriculum was changed to one of two-year cycles.

All schools provide a general curriculum which includes core subjects and, wherever possible, one of agriculture, commerce, or manual arts. It is probably more accurate to call the curriculum multilateral, although the point of commentary is that the accent is on all students having some part of their school period devoted to practical subjects. Since they are boarding schools, extracurricular practical projects have become quite a feature. It is important for students to continue to work with their hands, and to have experience in planning and executing self-help projects, thus increasing their capacity to take the initiative and carry projects through to completion.

Secondary enrolments will soon reach the level when there are more children enrolled than there are likely to be job openings available. Only a proportion of students will stay on for a second two-year cycle so it is essential for those who com-

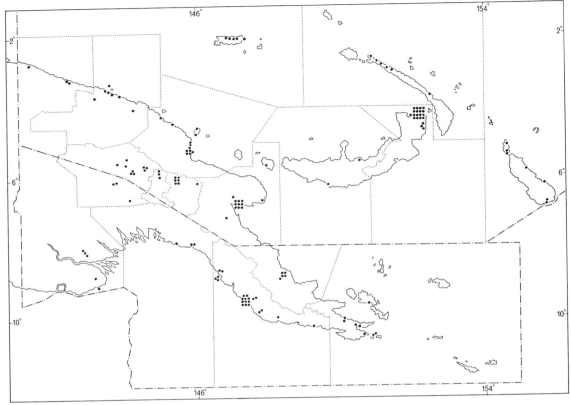

Post-primary schools, Administration and mission, in 1969.

plete their education at the end of the first two years that their course is complete in itself, and will give them sufficient to become competent citizens in a modern Papua and New Guinea.

There is still much to be done to strengthen staffing as there is a lack of experienced secondary teachers. It will be the policy over the next few years to build up facilities for the training of indigenous secondary teachers to the point where the needs of Papua and New Guinea can be supplied from its own training institutions.

Most government schools, but only a few non-government schools, are co-educational. More church authorities are moving towards co-educational schools, although there are still a few who prefer separate schools for boys and girls.

There is considerable pressure within the Territory for extension of the secondary-school course. A third two-year cycle is being developed in selected high schools. Students graduating from Form VI will then commence first-year studies at tertiary institutions. At present these institutions conduct preliminary-year courses which act as a matriculation year for Form IV graduates. It is expected that as the number of Form VI graduates rises, preliminary-year courses will no longer be required.

Boarding and day schools. Two significant devel-

opments in secondary education are bound-up with economics. In areas where it is possible, a much larger number of day students is being encouraged. Boarding schools have for so long been customary in Papua and New Guinea, that both teachers and parents have difficulty accepting the idea that a secondary school can be a day school. Boarding fees are currently $30 per year, which is less than half the cost of providing food for a student, and there is no charge for equipment, capital costs or tuition. All other costs are borne by the government or the agency conducting the school. Although many children must be resident because of the distance of their homes from the school, there is room for considerable increase in the number of day students.

There are good reasons why day attendance should be favoured, particularly at a time when there is such rapid social change. Students taken away from home for four or five years loosen their ties more quickly and more drastically than those who remain at home. It is probably true that teachers have more difficulty teaching day students, particularly as few of them have suitable home study facilities but, on the other hand, it is not merely intellectual development that is needed. Social integration and development may well rest on the integrity of the family group, so it is important that family relationships are maintained as much as possible even at the risk of cost to intellectual development.

Another issue of secondary policy is the problem of placement of high schools. A high school is now one of the most, if not the most, expensive prizes a District can win, and there is growing competition for them. A high school sets up a community of some forty families of teachers and over 600 students, and supplies and services to keep this community going have a significant impact on the area. The departmental policy of placing high schools so that there is equal opportunity for primary-school students to get into a secondary school in their local district seems to have general acceptance, even if the precise location is frequently contested.

TECHNICAL EDUCATION

In the field of technical education [q.v.] the policy has been to organize apprenticeship training around a combination of full-time and block-release courses. In the latter, apprentices are released from employment for 5-8 weeks' intensive training. The apprenticeship system had a slow start and even in 1970 had only 1,700 apprentices in training. Up to that date, approximately 300 apprentices had completed their training under the scheme.

A particular problem of providing skilled training is the inherent limitation of an apprenticeship scheme for a developing country. Historically the apprenticeship system was, among other things, a way of limiting the number of

entrants to a trade. The reverse of this situation is desirable in a developing country. What happens now is that the companies working in the Territory take on apprentices in proportion to the current level of their effort. The apprentices are in training for approximately five years, by which time, if the plans of the government have come to fruition, the economy will have greatly expanded. It needs little arithmetic to show that the number of skilled tradesmen becoming available at that point would always be far less than the demand. Since the country has few or no skilled tradesmen to start with, a policy based exclusively on apprenticeship is self-defeating.

Expansion is not easily planned. One of the essential components for a good trade-training scheme is the provision of industrial experience. It would be possible for the government to continue to expand its technical schools and so provide the institutional part of trade training, but unless some counterpart can be found for industrial experience the training would be incomplete. In an effort to overcome this problem, the government is currently subsidizing employers who provide skilled training through apprenticeship. This may prove insufficient. Another possibility being investigated is the provision of trade testing centres to allow tradesmen to get the industrial element in their training wherever they can outside the formal apprenticeship scheme. This would allow for the self-taught and for the itinerant worker who moves from employer to employer. It would also permit unlimited expansion of technical schools.

Vocational centres. For the students who do not

Technical education (left) Motor vehicle maintenance, Port Moresby Technical College; (right) Drying hides, Kamaliki Vocational Centre.

win places in secondary schools, a number of vocational centres are being developed to enable them to gain some practical skills with which to bridge the gap between school and the outside world. Present policy is to adapt each centre to the needs of its area and to provide short courses, one year for most students and two years for some. The centres are not expected to be expensively equipped, but should have facilities in keeping with those available to the people in the area. An essential part of the course is to show trainees how to start small enterprises without heavy investment of capital. The centres have been carefully placed and as far as possible staff transfers are avoided, since a centre takes its spirit and effectiveness from the ingenuity of the man in charge. It takes some time for him to secure the confidence of the people of an area, and it is essential that he remain at the one centre for a substantial period.

There is criticism of the whole system, principally from those who have seen ineffective centres or who are sceptical of the concept of effective elementary training in skilled trades. The centres vary in quality depending on the ingenuity and enterprise of the man in charge. To run one is a difficult task, requiring a man of special skills not usually recognized or rewarded by the public service system.

Another criticism is the history of failure of this kind of enterprise in other parts of the world, such as the village school in India. Likewise, the departmental policy of requiring local adaptation of the syllabus can lead to diffuse effort with few results. In order to overcome these problems, the centres are under continuous and intensive supervision by vocational centre advisers attached to the Department of Education.

TEACHER EDUCATION

The training of teachers is a major battleground in all developing countries. The urgent need for more teachers means pressure to shorten or at least not lengthen the training period of teachers. On the other hand, the need for quality demands resistance to these pressures and consistent moves to raise the standard of entry and to lengthen and improve teacher education [q.v.]. The tension existing in this area requires the government to maintain pressure for quality without being so unresponsive to practical needs as to cause unrest.

From the beginning of teacher education in Papua and New Guinea, in small one-man centres at widely dispersed locations, there has been a gradual development towards larger institutions providing longer training. At one stage, there were over twenty-six different centres, now there are twelve colleges and even that is too many for the number of teachers in training; too many because it is not possible to adequately staff and equip all the colleges.

Effort and persuasion have been used to restrict the number of centres through consolidation. This policy is working fairly well, although it is a long-term matter unless immediate consolidation is made mandatory. That could only be accomplished if the government were willing to provide enough money for new facilities.

In common with many other countries doubts have been expressed as to whether pre-service training is the best form. In a sandwich course which was tried recently, students were sent to the field after one year and returned after three years' teaching for a second year of training. The purists of teacher training insist that sandwich courses are wrong in principle, but the teachers who returned to the field after the second year's training were remarkable for their increased insight. The question of whether sandwich training should be attempted on a more systematic basis is under review.

In-service training has been provided as and when possible. For the last three years schools have closed for one week every year while the teachers participate in a national in-service training week. This was done to emphasize the necessity for in-service training and to provide an opportunity for all teachers to come together. In addition, in-service training is provided in vacation courses for science teachers and others.

The inadequacy of this policy has become increasingly obvious and a 'notional' teachers' college for in-service training is required. This college will have a principal and registrar's staff, but no buildings or permanent teaching staff, and will be in charge of all in-service courses wherever held throughout the Territory. The lecturing staff will be those pressed into service by the in-service college for the duration of each course and will be supervised by the college. The advantages of such an arrangement will be that the college can maintain records of all teachers and provide them with regular and systematic in-service training. A start on this scheme was made in 1970 but much remains to be done.

One problem in Papua and New Guinea not paralleled to the same extent in developed countries is the necessity to carry forward the general education of teachers, who have often had less than two years' secondary education. In the past, it was the professional training of teachers that was emphasized, on the assumption that this is what they most needed. Now it is becoming clearer that it is a general education that is required, for until teachers themselves are capable of focusing on a problem, analysing the variables and testing possible courses of action, it is not possible for them to teach students to do the same. New policies are needed in this area.

Trainee teachers may, at present, commence courses at any of four levels; Form II, Form III or Form IV, with in each case two years' training for primary teaching, and Form IV with three years of professional education for junior secondary teachers. The last mentioned course was initiated in 1967 and may well, through a developing relationship with the University, allow accumulation of university credits, with a few students going on direct to degrees and possibly postgraduate qualifications before entering service as teachers. As locally-trained secondary teachers enter the service it is desirable that some go into specialist positions as well as junior secondary positions.

For some years young expatriates undertook professional courses for primary teaching in the Territory at the Australian School of Pacific Administration [q.v.] at Mosman in New South Wales. In recent years there has been a change to secondary-teacher courses. A post-graduate diploma course is also conducted at the University of Papua and New Guinea [q.v.].

TERTIARY EDUCATION

Twelve small teachers' colleges in different parts of New Guinea, none of them with more than 200 students, together with an agricultural college with about the same enrolment, a forestry college [q.v.] with a smaller enrolment, an institute of technology [q.v.] with a small but rapidly growing enrolment, and the University of Papua and New Guinea, are part of a tertiary network which has grown up over the last few years. None of the institutions share a common governing body, there is no interchange of staff and there is no co-ordination between them except perhaps in the standards of teachers graduating from teachers' colleges.

The Topsy-like growth of tertiary institutions means that liberal arts faculties are duplicated in all of them; each has a library, science facilities (sometimes used as little as one-tenth of the time), separate student facilities and each has an administration. Generally small tertiary institutions are expensive and uneconomical and the present system can only become more expensive as time goes by. On the positive side, the spread of these institutions around the country is politically attractive and avoids concentration of expenditure in one area. On the academic side, most of the institutions are so small that staff crises occur when one key member of staff leaves. There is not the strength to ensure continuity of courses.

There is also the problem of standardization of academic qualifications. There is as yet no clear correlation between degrees, diplomas, certificates and subsidiary qualifications. It is possible under the present circumstances that a certificate given in one institution would merit a diploma in another and vice versa. It is also possible for salary scales to be in reverse order to qualifications. To ensure the value of qualifications it is necessary that rewards and status have an organized basis.

Independent growth of these institutions could also lead to a shortage of different types of skilled people. Faculties and departments, once established, have a way of going on for ever, irrespective of a decline in need after the first requirements have been met. They may use finance which might be better spent on other courses if there were effective co-ordination of enrolment patterns. Thus there is need for an over-all plan covering growth for the next five, ten or even fifteen years. Future plans for the development of tertiary institutions could be worked out to ensure that they adjust to the needs of the country in turning out enough people with the skills required. Realization of this goal is at present hampered by lack of data, and this underlines the inadequacy of present effort to collect data and co-ordinate their use. Co-ordination over the last few years would, for example, have avoided the problem of a secondary teachers' college at Goroka, 200 miles from the University. An arrangement with the University will have to be established if secondary teachers are not to be relegated to a sub-professional status. One possibility is for Goroka Teachers' College to be absorbed by the University as part of a Faculty of Education.

A new Commission on Post-Secondary and Higher Education was convened at the end of 1970 to study developments since the Currie Commission Report, and to plan the development of tertiary education for the 1970s.

ACKNOWLEDGMENT

Map after J. Rumens in *An Atlas of Papua and New Guinea*, ed. R. G. Ward and D. A. M. Lea. Glasgow, 1970.

K. R. McKinnon

(*See also* EDUCATION, HISTORY AND DEVELOPMENT; EDUCATION, ORGANIZATION AND MANAGEMENT)

EDUCATION, STATISTICS. The following tables have been compiled from the *Annual Reports of the Territories of Papua and New Guinea*, Canberra, and the T. P. N. G. Department of Education, *Official Bulletin of Statistics*, Port Moresby, 1970. Population estimates are estimates based on 1966 census data and information from the Department of District Administration.

Table 1

SCHOOLS AND ENROLMENTS BY CONTROLLING AUTHORITY FOR 1970

Controlling Authority	Primary		Secondary		Technical		Vocational		Teachers' Colleges	
	School	Enrolment	School	Enrolment	School	Enrolment	School	Enrolment	School	Enrolment
Administration	501	82,233	29	10,771	6	1,398	46	2,477	3	666
Anglican	62	7,522	2	559	1	94	—	—	*	—
Catholic	526	75,424	21	4,884	1	58	9	360	5	551
Evangelical Alliance	98	9,722	1	286	—	—	2	59	1	68
Lutheran	150	17,319	4	1,014	—	—	1	36	1	229
Seventh Day Adventist	107	7,137	2	615	1	25	—	—	1	71
United Church	165	14,868	3	584	—	—	—	—	1	121
Other	11	1,033	—	—	—	—	3	208	1	—

* Anglican students trained at the Lutheran College.

Table 2

POPULATION AND SCHOOL ENROLMENTS BY DISTRICT FOR 1970

District	Total Indigenous Population		Indigenous Children 7–12 Years			Total Indigenous Enrolments in Recognized Primary Schools, Including Over-age and Under-age Children
	Estimated Population	Percentage Enrolled at Recognized Schools, Vocational Centres and Technical Colleges	Estimated Population	Enrolments at Primary Schools	Percentage Enrolled	
Western	67,600	11.7	10,400	5,153	50	7,135
Gulf	58,400	12.0	9,150	4,739	52	6,691
Central	150,600	16.2	22,700	15,746	69	20,757
Milne Bay	107,200	11.9	15,200	8,159	54	11,547
Northern	63,900	11.7	10,550	4,891	46	6,603
Papuan Coastal	447,700	13.3	68,000	38,688	57	52,733
Southern Highlands	207,300	4.4	36,700	6,729	18	8,893
Eastern Highlands	230,300	4.8	34,050	7,588	22	9,635
Chimbu	186,600	5.3	25,900	7,059	27	9,436
Western Highlands	331,700	5.3	47,050	11,444	24	16,420
Highlands	955,900	5.0	143,700	32,820	23	44,384
West Sepik	113,500	6.4	16,250	4,951	30	6,853
East Sepik	178,300	9.0	25,300	10,539	42	14,775
Madang	162,800	11.6	22,350	11,673	52	17,090
Morobe	228,600	7.9	34,800	11,633	33	16,265
New Guinea Coastal	683,200	8.9	98,700	38,796	39	54,983
West New Britain	51,800	16.5	8,100	6,036	75	8,467
East New Britain	125,600	19.0	18,000	15,195	84	20,336
New Ireland	58,700	17.2	7,450	7,147	96	9,220
Bougainville	86,400	17.7	12,350	9,623	77	13,958
Manus	23,700	21.1	3,700	3,308	90	4,339
New Guinea Islands	346,200	18.2	49,600	41,309	83	56,320
Total	2,433,000	9.5	360,000	151,613	42	208,420

Table 3

PRIMARY SCHOOLS AND ENROLMENTS BY DISTRICT AND CONTROLLING AUTHORITY 1970

District	Administration		Anglican		Catholic		Evangelical Alliance		Lutheran		Seventh Day Adventist		United Church		Other	
	School	Enrolment	School	Enrolment	School	Enrolment	School	Enrolment	School	Enrolment	School	Enrolment	School	Enrolment	School	Enrolment
Western	18	3,185	—	—	7	899	17	2,726	—	—	5	330	7	370	1	40
Gulf	16	2,815	—	—	7	998	—	—	1	77	10	963	29	2,485	2	310
Central	53	13,204	1	164	42	6,402	—	—	—	—	3	106	32	2,971	—	—
Milne Bay	31	3,387	13	1,813	37	3,351	—	—	—	—	3	193	29	2,391	—	—
Northern	17	2,437	33	4,061	—	—	—	—	—	—	—	—	—	—	—	—
Papuan Coastal	135	25,028	47	6,038	93	11,650	17	2,726	1	77	21	1,592	97	8,217	3	350
Southern Highlands	30	3,836	—	—	18	2,083	17	1,799	4	511	2	65	5	524	2	149
Eastern Highlands	39	5,860	1	108	3	476	5	687	14	1,425	10	945	—	—	6	534
Chimbu	29	3,774	4	521	23	4,023	1	28	8	868	3	261	—	—	—	—
Western Highlands	34	5,179	3	292	32	6,734	17	1,523	19	2,442	11	621	—	—	—	—
Highlands	132	18,649	8	921	76	13,316	40	4,037	45	5,246	26	1,892	5	524	8	683
West Sepik	17	1,959	—	—	31	4,301	8	607	—	—	8	565	—	—	—	—
East Sepik	37	5,451	—	—	45	7,506	16	1,500	—	—	6	330	—	—	—	—
Madang	29	5,861	4	383	35	6,922	7	258	29	3,690	3	127	—	—	—	—
Morobe	47	8,182	—	—	4	720	—	—	75	8,306	—	—	—	—	—	—
New Guinea Coastal	130	21,453	4	383	115	19,449	31	2,365	104	11,996	17	1,022	—	—	—	—
West New Britain	13	1,457	3	180	39	5,994	—	—	—	—	3	291	3	584	—	—
East New Britain	29	9,184	—	—	56	9,558	—	—	—	—	4	287	21	2,263	—	—
New Ireland	23	2,652	—	—	47	4,188	—	—	—	—	14	874	21	1,661	—	—
Bougainville	17	1,862	—	—	80	9,965	—	—	—	—	10	617	18	1,646	—	—
Manus	22	1,948	—	—	20	1,304	10	594	—	—	12	562	—	—	—	—
New Guinea Islands	104	17,103	3	180	242	31,009	10	594	—	—	43	2,631	63	6,154	—	—
Total	501	82,233	62	7,522	526	75,424	98	9,722	150	17,319	107	7,137	165	14,895	11	1,033

Table 4(a)
PRIMARY-'T' SCHOOL ENROLMENTS BY STANDARD: GOVERNMENT

Year	Preparatory	1	2	3	4	5	6	Total
1964	10,216	9,085	8,841	8,385	6,389	4,209	3,056	50,181
1965	11,124	10,851	9,378	9,573	7,763	5,677	3,815	58,181
1966	11,142	12,200	10,787	10,018	8,760	7,285	5,063	65,255
1967	10,007	11,815	11,667	10,636	9,318	8,242	6,297	67,982
1968	11,781	10,828	11,521	11,263	10,092	8,772	7,655	71,912
1969	7,193	16,251	10,953	11,466	10,846	9,487	8,508	74,704
1970	3,849	14,523	15,105	10,909	10,807	10,134	9,160	74,487

Table 4(b)
PRIMARY-'T' SCHOOL ENROLMENTS BY STANDARD: NON-GOVERNMENT

Year	Preparatory	1	2	3	4	5	6	Total
1964	34,668	30,564	23,016	13,895	8,799	4,970	2,945	118,857
1965	31,077	30,656	25,207	16,309	10,442	6,465	3,644	123,800
1966	30,374	29,335	26,397	19,088	11,774	7,722	4,610	129,300
1967	26,889	29,587	25,577	20,584	14,183	8,761	5,718	131,299
1968	22,258	28,539	25,814	20,922	16,126	11,252	6,995	131,906
1969	19,533	27,323	25,187	21,812	16,941	12,819	8,467	132,082
1970	11,473	29,775	25,201	22,403	18,270	14,110	10,686	131,918

Table 5
INDIGENOUS HIGH-SCHOOL* ENROLMENTS: GOVERNMENT AND NON-GOVERNMENT

Year	Standard 7	Form I	II	III	IV	V	VI	Total
1964	1,519	2,310	1,354	365	66	34	—	5,648
1965	281	3,731	1,983	923	151	44	—	7,113
1966	—	4,310	2,865	1,468	496	14	—	9,153
1967	—	4,901	3,539	2,084	727	39	10	11,300
1968	—	5,560	4,343	2,665	982	51	30	13,631
1969	—	6,046	5,092	2,897	1,336	142	38	15,551
1970	—	6,848	5,581	3,335	1,731	168	122	17,785

* Includes junior high schools 1964.

Table 6(a)
ENROLMENTS BY LEVEL AND BY YEAR: GOVERNMENT

Year	Primary-'T'	Primary-'A'	Intermediate Junior High	High*	Technical Vocational	Teachers' College
1954	3,990	1,062	900	58	262	98
1958	14,515	1,834	817	131	333	102
1962	34,217	2,643	1,314	609	679	253
1966	65,255	3,859	—	5,888	2,879	376
1970	74,487	7,746	—	10,771	3,875	666

* Includes multi-racial high schools.

Table 6(b)
ENROLMENTS BY LEVEL AND BY YEAR: NON-GOVERNMENT

Year	Primary-'T'	Primary-'A'	Intermediate Junior High	High*	Technical/ Vocational	Teachers' Colleges
1954	† ——32, 119——		† ——————736——————			
1958	58,813	1,147	522	72	92	464
1962	93,619	1,422	1,301	110	171	536
1966	129,300	887	—	3,751	415	750
1970	131,198	1,107	—	7,942	840	1,040

* Includes multi-racial high schools.
† No separate figures available.

Table 7

ENROLMENTS IN POST-SECONDARY TRAINING (NOT INCLUDING PRIMARY-TEACHERS' COLLEGES)

Institution	Indigenous			Non-Indigenous			Total		
	1966	1968	1970	1966	1968	1970	1966	1968	1970
University (full-time students in 1st semester)	58	199	327	1	30	56	59	229	383
Institute of Technology	—	93	202	—	4	9	—	97	211
Papuan Medical College	45	54	63	11	13	12	56	67	75
Dental College	13	22	21	—	—	—	13	22	21
Vudal Agricultural College	46	84	116	10	13	14	56	97	130
Forestry College	—	31	51	—	7	12	—	38	63
Administrative College	63	76	176	—	—	—	63	76	176
Lae Technical College	32	53	14	—	2	3	32	55	17
School of Valuation	—	15	23	—	—	2	—	15	25
Warder Training Centre	—	6	25	—	—	—	—	6	25
Co-operative Education Centre	33	24	35	—	—	—	33	24	35
Goroka Teachers' College (Secondary)	—	87	183	—	1	5	—	88	188
Total	290	744	1,236	22	70	113	312	814	1,349

Table 8

STAFF BY LEVEL AND YEAR

Staff	1960	1962	1964	1966	1968	1970
Primary						
Indigenous	1,449	2,308	4,079	4,948	5,397	5,429
Non-Indigenous	469	738	1,226	1,258	1,189	1,022
Secondary*						
Indigenous	20	15	19	37	79	197
Non-Indigenous	82	141	297	419	596	735
Technical/Vocational						
Indigenous	1	10	33	56	59	141
Non-Indigenous	36	55	87	274	183	232
Teachers' Colleges						
Indigenous	3	2	4	12	23	78
Non-Indigenous	36	65	93	87	150	205
Total						
Indigenous	1,473	2,335	4,135	5,053	5,558	5,845
Non-Indigenous	623	999	1,703	2,038	2,118	2,194
Total	2,096	3,334	5,838	7,091	7,676	8,039

* Includes junior high schools.

EDUCATION, WEST IRIAN. Responsibility for education in West Irian lies, as with all other matters, with the Governor of the Province. The Governor is appointed by the President of the Republic to whom he is responsible through the Department of Home Affairs. The relation therefore between the West Irian branch of the Department of Education and Culture and the central office of the Department in Djakarta is a purely technical one. Money voted for education in West Irian is made available through the Department of Home Affairs to the provincial Governor. The head of the Department of Education in West Irian, like all other heads of department, is responsible to the Governor. The financing of education therefore depends on funds being released for that purpose by the Governor in West Irian to the amount intended when the original allocation was made in Djakarta.

A multiplicity of different government authorities is involved in educational matters in West Irian. Because of the political history of West Irian and the government's particular interest in the development of this province, a special office in Djakarta concerns itself with all West Irian affairs. The various bodies to which questions of education may be referred therefore include the Department of Education and Culture, the Department of Finance, the Department of Development (BAPPENAS), the Department of Home Affairs, the Sector for West Irian Affairs and the Governor's Council.

The structure of the educational system in West Irian is similar to that of the other provinces of Indonesia and is based historically on the system which was left by the Dutch. There are, however, a number of significant differences between education in West Irian and in the rest of Indonesia. These are partly caused by the fact that Indonesian rule is more recent in West Irian, and partly because an attempt has been made to adapt curricula to local conditions which are unique in Indonesia. It is also true that some types of schools which have been abolished or are being altered in the rest of Indonesia, are still in operation in West Irian; but it is probably only a question of time before the province conforms to the general Indonesian system.

The principal difference between West Irian education and that of the rest of Indonesia is in its administration. In West Irian it is a joint undertaking of the government and of the educational offices of the various religious missions which operate some 90 per cent of all schools in the country. In 1958 the churches organized educational foundations (Jajasan), of which the largest is the Christian School Foundation (JPK), followed by the Catholic Foundation (FPPK), and the Christian Alliance (JPPGR). A combination of Catholic and Protestant missions (JBMBS) operates a secondary school in the provincial capital, Djajapura. All these foundations receive subsidies from the Department of Education and Culture to operate schools. The receipt of a subsidy implies that certain conditions have to be met, principally the acceptance of the government curricula, including the teaching of Bahasa Indonesia and its use as the medium of instruction.

It should be noted that, in common with most activities in Indonesia, the various parts of the educational system are always referred to by the initials of Indonesian words. It is impossible for any student of education in West Irian, or for that matter in Indonesia as a whole, to understand any written work or conversation on the subject without a knowledge of the meaning of these initials. The more common abbreviations are listed at the end of this article.

The provincial office of the Department of Education and Culture in West Irian is divided into two. The local branch concerns itself with primary education only; theoretically this is part of the autonomy afforded to every province as they are responsible for raising their own money for primary education. In practice, many provinces are unable to raise sufficient money for this purpose and are dependent on a grant from the Department of Home Affairs. Thus, the financing of elementary education is a separate item from the rest of education. The second branch of the provincial office concerns itself with all other educational matters, except Tjenderawasih University [q.v.] which is nominally independent, although the head of the provincial department and the Vice-Governor are members of its governing body. The university is also financed from the provincial budget and its relations with the Division of Higher Education in Djakarta are purely technical. This second branch of the provincial department is subdivided according to the usual activities—personnel, statistics, training, secondary, technical, building and sport.

It is the policy of the Department of Education and Culture to provide all school children with six years of elementary education and therefore to establish an adequate number of primary schools of six grades. However, the process of realizing this aim is still in an early stage; the majority of primary schools in the Province have only four classrooms or fewer; in the central Highlands schools of one or two rooms are common. In many areas, especially in the Highlands, the sparseness of the population does not justify the operation of a six-classroom school; but it is the policy of the government to establish in each district at least one elementary school offering all six grades. After six years of primary education there are three years of junior secondary (SMP) and three years of senior secondary (SMA). There are various take-off points for professional and technical education, and the completion of the senior secondary course, i.e. twelfth grade, permits entrance to the university.

FINANCE

The government's allocations for education in West Irian were Irian Barat rupiah 63 million in 1969-70 and 72 million in 1970-1. (Twenty Irian Barat rupiah equal one U.S. dollar.) The main heads of expenditure are shown in Table 1.

It should be borne in mind that these are allocations and that the actual expenditure may be different, sometimes to a considerable extent. The total, however, represents about $U.S.4.50 per head of the population, which is above the average for Indonesia as a whole. This is chiefly because salaries of teachers in West Irian are higher than in the rest of Indonesia, owing to the separate and differently valued currency, and to the desire to encourage teachers from other parts of Indonesia to go to West Irian and to stay there for a reasonable period. A teacher, according to his qualification, will receive between 500 and 1,000 Irian Barat rupiah a month. These rates of pay are

Table 1

EDUCATION ALLOCATIONS 1970–1971
Irian Barat rupiah

Purpose	Allocation
Salaries	
Government	18,708,334
Grants	34,123,666
	52,832,000
Equipment, courses, vehicles and buildings	
Government	12,371,706
Grants	6,578,223
	18,949,929
Total	71,781,929

roughly twice as much as those in the remainder of Indonesia. It is possible that the separate currency of West Irian may cease to exist, but even if the normal Indonesian currency is applied to West Irian salaries will probably remain higher than elsewhere as an incentive to attract and retain teachers (and other professions) in West Irian.

ENROLMENTS

The population of West Irian is about 800,000; educational facilities are fairly evenly spread throughout the urban and coastal areas but thinly spread in the largely unexplored valleys of the central Highlands, where some 300,000 tribesmen still live in a neolithic culture, affected by Western material culture only through the government and mission stations. The population of West Irian is shown in broad age groups in Table 2.

Table 2

POPULATION OF WEST IRIAN BY AGE GROUP
Hundreds

Region	0–4	5–9	10–14	15–19	20–24	25–34	34–65+
Djajapura	198	128	98	51	75	117	153
Tjenderawasih	222	145	122	65	77	136	206
Manokwari	119	77	59	31	45	70	91
Sorong	153	106	95	56	51	99	175
Fak Fak	80	54	39	30	36	56	104
Paniai	307	250	179	122	95	200	381
Djajawidjaja	324	265	189	129	100	212	429
Merauke	280	229	163	111	87	182	369
Total	1,683	1,254	944	595	566	1,072	1,908

NOTE: The total of Table 2 is 802,200, but these figures are only indicative not precisely accurate.
SOURCE: Estimate based on the European Economic Community Demographic Survey 1959–62.

Tables 3a, 3b and 3c give enrolments at primary and secondary levels. Table 3b shows that wastage is high.

Table 3a

PRIMARY SCHOOLS, PUPILS AND TEACHERS 1968–1969

Region	Schools	Enrolment			Teachers
		Male	Female	Total	
Djajapura	110	5,846	5,044	10,890	286
Tjenderawasih	176	11,221	8,915	20,136	493
Manokwari	73	1,654	1,375	3,029	138
Sorong	150	4,798	4,034	8,832	355
Fak Fak	113	4,088	3,367	7,455	226
Paniai	83	5,073	3,229	8,302	208
Djajawidjaja	52	3,503	857	4,360	82
Merauke	215	12,981	9,285	22,266	613
Total	972	49,164	36,106	85,270	2,401

SOURCE: UNESCO-FUNDWI Survey, May 1969, from figures supplied by the Department.

Table 3b

PRIMARY ENROLMENT BY GRADES 1968–1969

Grade	Enrol-ment	Approximate Percentage
1	28,241	33
2	18,615	22
3	13,878	16
4	11,028	13
5	8,429	10
6	5,079	6
	85,270	100

Table 3c

ENROLMENT AT SECONDARY LEVEL, 1968–1969

Grade	Junior High School (SMP)	Technical, Home Economics, Business	Senior High School (SMA)	Technical, Home Economics, Business
7	2,542	652		
8	1,293	451		
9	902	245		
10			467	109
11			389	71
12			256	63

NOTE: These figures exclude teacher-trainees.

Of these figures, roughly half the total enrolment in technical, home economics, and business schools consists of girls in home economics. Of those in the SMP and SMA, the proportion of boys to girls is two to one. About 40 per cent of the teaching staff at secondary level is full-time and the remainder, part-time, frequently civil servants from other areas of Indonesia and their wives, who teach after government offices close at 1.30 p.m. The number of teachers in 1969 was:

SMP	181 full-time	134 part-time
SMA	58 full-time	78 part-time

There are thirty-one junior high schools (SMP), of which eleven are operated by the government, eight by the Protestant churches and twelve by the Catholics. Of the seven senior high schools (SMA) four are operated by the government, while the Catholics and Protestants operate one each and a third jointly.

TECHNICAL EDUCATION

There are ten junior technical schools, which in 1969 had an enrolment of 936, and seventy-three full-time and twenty-eight part-time staff. The senior technical schools are situated at Djajapura and Kotaradja; the enrolment in 1969 was 201, with ten full-time and twenty-six part-time staff.

There is a shortage of skilled instructors capable of meeting the development needs of the Province. Instruction based on the sophisticated machine tools left by the Dutch is largely ineffective, partly no doubt because many of these tools no longer function correctly. Teaching in the technical schools is further handicapped by shortages of power and materials. Efforts are being directed towards the reorientation of technical education for the teaching of skills which will be needed in the probable development of the province, e.g. woodwork, building, plumbing, auto-mechanics, electrical wiring and training for clerical and accounting occupations.

Home economics has developed in a number of centres in West Irian, partly because of the interest of mission societies, and partly because of encouragement by the department. The courses in home-making are, in the circumstances, practical and effective; in the last two years UNESCO has supplied a large amount of home-making equipment. There are eight home-making schools in West Irian, and one high school for home economics situated in Djajapura.

TEACHER EDUCATION

The training of primary teachers is carried out at two levels, in the junior institutes (SGB) and in the senior (SPG). The former, which have disappeared from the rest of Indonesia and which are slowly being closed in West Irian, give three years' training to pupils who have completed the primary course, i.e. six years of education. The entrance level to the SPG is after completion of the junior secondary course, i.e. nine years of education; the course is also of three years. It is now not uncommon for graduates from the SGB to go on to the SPG. Teacher training institutions are conducted both by the government and by mission societies. In January 1971 there were fifteen SGB spread throughout the Province, and six SPG (at Djajapura, Fak Fak, Merauke, Sorong and two at Biak). The syllabus in the teacher training institutions is inclined to the academic and theoretical; some observers believe that more attention should be paid to methodology and teaching practice. Thus, sociology, psychology and philosophy of education are subjects which largely owe their origin in Indonesian education to Dutch theories imported a good many years ago, but which are only slowly becoming less preponderant in the syllabus. In this regard West Irian is trailing behind the rest of Indonesia where experimental work on new curricula is already being carried out. Attempts to make the syllabus and training more practical have been begun in West Irian, where the lower standards of teacher trainees make this even more desirable. As is not unusual in developing countries, the number of teachers with the stipulated qualifications is always below the increasing number necessary to meet expansion; thus, it is common for teachers who have been trained in the SPG for the higher primary classes to be used in junior secondary classes (SMP).

The number of students in SGB in 1969-70 was 1,257, of whom 253 were girls. However wastage is heavy; of the total, 724 were first-year, 311 were second-year and 222 were third-year students.

The enrolment at SPG was 292, of whom 62 were girls. Wastage is not as heavy as in SGB, but is still considerable (128, 95 and 69). The training of secondary teachers is carried out at Tjenderawasih University, situated at Abepura about ten miles from Djajapura, in the Faculty of Teacher Training. This faculty provides a degree course in the normal academic subjects such as Indonesia, English, mathematics, science, history and geography. During the three-year course a small amount of theoretical education is also given, but no practical training. This again is a matter which international experts are attempting to modify.

A school for training teachers of home economics exists in Djajapura. The training of teachers in technical subjects is not yet undertaken in West Irian, though it is hoped to start. Teachers have to be imported from other parts of Indonesia.

QUALITY OF EDUCATION

The majority of primary teachers have completed nine or twelve years of education including three years of professional training; but there are still between 200 and 300 who have completed only the primary course with either no professional training or with one year's training. Wastage amongst primary teachers is heavy, not so much because of the salaries, but because of the difficult conditions, isolation and lack of contact with the Department of Education and Culture. In this last regard, it is to be noted that UNESCO is establishing a radio programme for teachers amongst its development activities. At the second level about two-thirds of the 240 full-time teachers have some graduate status.

Thus there are many hindrances to effective education: poorly trained teachers, lack of equipment, shortage of specialist teachers and restricted activity on the part of the inspectorate because of the difficulties of travelling. These hindrances require energetic practical effort and effective administration. Perhaps Indonesians show a tendency to prefer the philosophical to the concrete. The result is that factual subjects, especially the sciences, tend to be superficially taught; partly because of this and partly because of a lack of facilities very little is done in art and crafts. Similarly the teaching of science is handicapped by the absence of science rooms and equipment.

CURRICULUM

The curriculum of schools in West Irian is similar to that of the other provinces of Indonesia, except that some attempts have been made to adapt the syllabus to local conditions. It is a normal curriculum but it should be noted that at all levels it contains a number of hours each week in the national language, Bahasa Indonesia, and in the national subjects; the latter are based on *pantjasila*, the five principles upon which the Indonesian state is founded. These are belief in God, fellowship of man, nationalism, democracy and social justice.

In West Irian the departments carry out much of their own professional training at the middle and lower levels. There are schools for fishery, community development, agriculture, business administration; and at Manokwari there is the agricultural high school which provides a three-year course, and from which many middle-grade workers in agriculture are drawn for the Department of Agriculture. The Department of Domestic Services conducts a school of government administration. The Department of Manpower has opened two vocational training centres, at Djajapura and Manokwari; these are aided by the International Labour Organization. There are also nurses' schools, and training is provided for health supervisors.

EDUCATIONAL ATTAINMENT

The percentage of literacy varies greatly from area to area, with a probable maximum of 80 per cent in Teluk Tjenderawasih region and a probable minimum of 35 per cent in the Djajawidjaja and Paniai regions. The figure for West Irian as a whole in 1970 was estimated to be 58 per cent. It may be said that of 200,000 males between 15 and 60 years, about 84,000, 42 per cent, were illiterate; 74,000, 37 per cent, had three to six years of education; 8,000, 4 per cent, had more than elementary schooling; and 34,000, 17 per cent, were attending some form of literacy classes. The higher percentage of illiteracy is mainly due to the fact that only a very small part of the central Highlands has been opened up by the Administration; and education in that area is only just at the take-off point; where schools exist, absenteeism and drop-out are frequent. It would also be unwise to assume that all of the 37 per cent who have had three to six years of schooling will retain, or have retained, their literacy as follow-up material is lacking. Attempts are being made to remedy this, and the Department of Education and Culture has established forty libraries with simple material for new literates. The language of literacy is Bahasa Indonesia, although some not unsuccessful attempts have been made to teach literacy in Dhani, the language of one of the tribes in the central Highlands. It may be noted that there are reputed to be 125 languages in West Irian, so the government's insistence on Bahasa Indonesia is appropriate.

UNITED NATIONS' ASSISTANCE

When the Dutch left in 1962 they donated a sum of $U.S.30 million for the development of West Irian. This could not be used until Indonesia resumed membership of the United Nations in 1966. In the following year the Secretary-General instituted the Fund of the United Nations for the Development of West Irian (FUNDWI). The object of the fund is the social and economic development of the Province. UNESCO is responsible for the education projects, which may be summed up:

(1) to improve the quality of, and to expand, the educational system as a whole;
(2) to assist in educational planning and administration;
(3) to provide, and to supply training in the use of, technical and scientific equipment at the secondary level;
(4) to improve and develop teacher training with special emphasis on new curricula and teaching aids;
(5) to strengthen existing community development programmes, mainly through emphasis on literacy linked to basic skills in a local setting;
(6) to strengthen the provincial university in the fields of secondary teacher training and anthropology; emphasis on the latter has the aim of promoting understanding between sections of the community;
(7) to develop education in the central Highlands.

The implementation of this programme was begun in 1969, and is scheduled to finish in 1973.

ABBREVIATIONS IN COMMON USE

S. Dasar	Six-year primary school
SMP	Junior secondary (general)
SMA	Senior secondary (general)
SGB	Junior training college
SPG	Senior training college
SKKP	Home-making school
SKKA	Home economics school
ST	Junior technical school
STM	Senior technical school

The Department of Education and Culture (Pendidikan dan kebudijaan) is known as P.D.K.

ELECTRIC POWER. Before 1939 public supplies were established at Port Moresby and Samarai in Papua.

The first major electrical installation in New Guinea was a hydro-electric scheme constructed on the Bulolo River by Bulolo Gold Dredging Ltd (now Placer Development Ltd) in about 1928. This scheme was used to power the Company's gold dredges. Because of extreme erosion problems this site was abandoned and a new installation commissioned on the Baiune River, a tributary of the Bulolo. This was later supplemented by a second station which re-used the water to bring the total output to 5.5 MW (megawatts). The Company holds a franchise for public supply within the area.

In 1932, a public company, Rabaul Electricity Limited, was granted a franchise to supply the township of Rabaul. Diesel engines were the source of power.

During World War II the plants at Bulolo and Rabaul were destroyed. After the war the Bulolo equipment was replaced with identical equipment from the manufacturers in the United States.

The post-war Administration of the Territory of Papua and New Guinea took over various installations operated by the armed forces, and

these have since been augmented or replaced with modern equipment.

ADMINISTRATION CONTROL OF SUPPLY

Immediately after World War II public electricity supply was controlled by the Electrical Undertakings Branch of the Public Works Department of the Territory. In the early 1950s, the Commonwealth Department of Works moved into the Territory to assist in the reconstruction work and it assumed responsibility for the technical side of the maintenance and operation of the electricity supply. The Department was responsible for most of the reconstruction and augmentation work, and built the hydro-electric installations at Port Moresby and Goroka.

In June 1957 control of the Branch, then headed by an engineer-manager, was returned to the Territory Administration.

The Papua and New Guinea Electricity Commission was created by Territory Ordinance in 1961 and assumed control on 1 July 1963. It took over the assets in the main centres of Port Moresby, Samarai, Lae, Goroka, Madang, Wewak, Kavieng, Kokopo and Rabaul, as these were considered to form a workable commercial group.

The assets in some 126 minor centres remained the property of the Administration, with the Commission providing the technical services required for the construction, operation and maintenance of the plant, and the Administration providing the necessary funds and collecting the revenue.

The Commission consists of a full-time chairman/general manager and four part-time associate commissioners.

HYDRO ELECTRIC DEVELOPMENT

The Port Moresby scheme. The Laloki River Scheme for Port Moresby was developed by the construction of the first stage of Rouna No. 1 Station, some twenty miles from Port Moresby. Three 1,000 kW machines and a 33 kV transmission system were commissioned early in 1957.

In 1961 the second stage was commissioned, consisting of a 2.5 MW machine, a second penstock and diurnal storage pond at the head of the penstock. A second transmission line was also constructed, designed to operate at 66kV.

In 1963 the Sirinumu Dam was completed, regulating the Laloki River to give a minimum flow of 200 cusecs (cubic feet per second). The dam wall was 470 feet long, 76 feet high, 300 feet thick at the base and 15 feet at the top, and contains more than 75,000 cubic yards of rock filling. When storage demands increase the height will be raised to 96 feet. The lake formed by the dam has an area of 3,000 acres, a shoreline of 60 miles and contains 57,000 acre feet of water (15,500 million gallons).

In June 1964 a 54-inch concrete pipeline was constructed, parallel to the existing flumeline, and this augmented the flow of water to the station from 125 to 200 cusecs, matching the regulated flow of the river, and providing a firm continu-

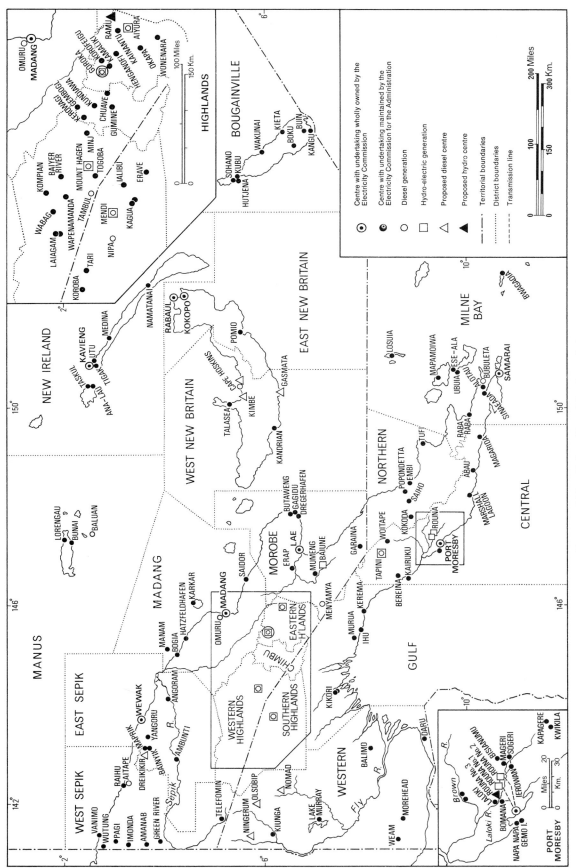

Papua and New Guinea Electricity Commission.

Inset map (Highlands)

OMURU ⊙ MADANG ⊙

RAMU ▲ AIYURA □
GOROKA ◎ KAINANTU KAMALIKI
HENGANOFI KOROFEIGU OKAPA
KEROWAGI GERUKANDAMA WONENARA
KUNDIAWA CHUAVE
MINJ
KOMPIAN GUMINE
BAIYER RIVER MOUNT HAGEN
TOGOBA
WABAG TAMBUL JALIBU ERAVE
WAPENAMANDA MENDI □
LAIAGAM NIPA ○ KAGUA
TARI
KOROBA

HIGHLANDS

Legend

⊙	Centre with undertaking wholly owned by the Electricity Commission
◉	Centre with undertaking maintained by the Electricity Commission for the Administration
○	Diesel generation
◎	Hydro-electric generation
□	Proposed diesel centre
△	Proposed hydro centre
▲	(Proposed hydro centre - filled)
─·─	Territorial boundaries
⋯⋯	District boundaries
─ ─ ─	Transmission line

Main map regions

BOUGAINVILLE
SOHANO KUBU KIETA BOKU BUIN
HUTJENA WAKUNAI KANGU

NEW IRELAND
NAMATANAI MEDINA KAVIENG ⊙ LITU TABAR
TASKUL ANA-LAVA TIGAK

EAST NEW BRITAIN
RABAUL ⊙ KOKOPO
POMIO

WEST NEW BRITAIN
TALASEA CAPE HOSKINS KIMBE GASMATA KANDRIAN

MANUS
LORENGAU BUNAI BALUAN

WEST SEPIK
VANIMO WUTUNG PAGI AITAPE IMONDA AMANAB GREEN RIVER RAIHU

EAST SEPIK
DREIKIKIR MAPRIK WEWAK ⊙ YANGORU BAINYIK ANGORAM AMBUNTI

MADANG
MANAM BOGIA HATZFELDHAFEN KARKAR SAIDOR OMURU ○ MADANG ⊙

MOROBE
ERAP LAE ◎ BUTAWENG GAGIDU DREGERHAFEN MUMENG BAIUNE

CHIMBU
EASTERN H'LANDS ◎

WESTERN HIGHLANDS ◎

SOUTHERN HIGHLANDS ◎

GULF
KIKORI IHU MURUA KEREMA BEREINA MENYAMYA GARAINA

WESTERN
TELEFOMIN NINGERUM OLSOBIP NOMAD KIUNGA LAKE MURRAY BALIMO MOREHEAD WEAM DARU

NORTHERN
POPONDETTA EMBI SAIHO KOKODA WOITAPE TUFI

CENTRAL
TAPINI KAIRUKU ROUNA □ PORT MORESBY ⊙ ABAU RABARABA MAGARIDA MARSHALL LAGOON

MILNE BAY
LOSUIA MAPAMOIWA UBUIA ESE-ALA ALOTAU BUBULETA SAMARAI SINEADA BWAGAOIA

Port Moresby inset

PORT MORESBY
LALOKI No. 3 ▲ ROUNA No. 2 ROUNA No. 1 ◎ BISIANUMU □ SOGERI MAGERI IEROWARI BOMANA ⊙ NAPA NAPA GEMO I. KAPAGERE KWIKILA
Brown R.
Laloki R.

Scales

100 Miles / 150 Km.

200 Miles / 300 Km.

Miles 0 20 / Km. 0 30

ous output of the station of 5,200 kW, and permitting peaks of up to 5,800 kW.

These works cost approximately:

Rouna No. 1 Stage 1	$1,200,000
Rouna No. 1 Stage 2	900,000
Sirinumu Dam Stage 1	1,470,000
Flume Augmentation	320,000
	$3,890,000

giving a cost of about $700 per kW.

In June 1965, construction of Rouna No. 2 Station began, two miles upstream from Rouna No. 1. The station, constructed in two stages of 18 and 12 MW, was finally completed in April 1968 at a cost of $8.5 million.

Water from a weir across the Laloki River is diverted 550 feet down an eight-foot diameter vertical pressure shaft to the five 6 MW machines below. Power is transmitted through two 66 kV lines to three substations in Port Moresby.

Early in 1970, contractors began raising the level of the Sirinumu Dam by 22 feet. This will increase the effective storage area to 280,000 acre feet. The wall length will be increased to 420 feet, the base thickness to 320 feet and top thickness to 17.25 feet. The project will cost about $2.3 million and will provide a regulated flow of 325 cusecs year-round. With this assured flow in the river below the dam, plans are being finalized to construct a Rouna No. 3 Station adjacent to Rouna No. 1.

It is estimated that this will lower the cost of the Laloki Scheme to about $400 a kW.

Goroka hydro scheme. A small scheme has been constructed near Goroka, with 2 × 100 kW and 1 × 200 kW machines. The cost of this work was $240,000 or $600 per kW.

The maintenance charges on this scheme have been very high owing to the unstable nature of the ground. For the first six years the flumeline, excavated in the natural ground, was constantly being carried away by small local landslides, caused largely by the cutting of the bench in the hillside for the flumeline. Most of the areas concerned have now been encased in Armco piping and the landslides permitted to settle on top of the pipeline, thus producing some stability.

Other small schemes. Small installations exist at Mount Hagen and Tapini. Both had high initial costs, and the Mount Hagen one seems likely to experience the same teething troubles as the Goroka scheme. Considerable expenditure will be needed to achieve stability of the flumeline. In the Tapini scheme the cost per kW was nearly $1,800; however, owing to the high cost of the alternative of air-freighting diesel fuel, the installation has proved economic.

PRIVATE SUPPLIES

Many missions and plantations, and some industrial undertakings, have their own power generators; most are diesel driven, there being only one or two small private hydro-electric units.

The normal supply to the consumer throughout the Territory is 240/415 volts, 3 phase, 50 cycle.

In general, the Commission has adopted the Standards Association of Australia 'Wiring Rules' as a minimum standard of wiring.

By-laws covering the approval of electrical appliances and the licensing of electrical contractors and electricians were drawn up in 1967.

TRANSMISSION AND DISTRIBUTION

Two transmission voltages are used, 66,000 and 33,000; distribution is either 22,000 or 11,000 volts, 3 phase, 50 cycle system; reticulation is at 240/415 volts.

Figures of the generation of electrical energy; charges for supply; kWh generated; power station plant, demand, and consumers; additional plant 1969-70; and hydro-electric power potential, are given in Tables 1-6.

In 1967 the Commonwealth Department of Works on behalf of the Papua and New Guinea Electricity Commission began investigations into the proposed Upper Ramu Hydro-electric Scheme. The first Ramu Power Station may have an ultimate capacity of 72 MW with an initial installed capacity of about 45 MW. This system is intended to supply the seaport towns of Lae and Madang; in the Highlands, the towns of Goroka and Mount Hagen, and intervening areas of the Eastern and Western Highlands; and the Markham and Ramu River valleys. The preliminary estimate for the first stage with an installed capacity of 45 MW is about $36 million.

Other preliminary investigations have been made by the Department of Works into the hydro-electric potential of other major river systems; these are listed in Table 4.

The rate of future development of electric power will depend on the amount of overseas finance available from both government and private funds. From July 1963 to June 1970 the average rate of growth increased from 11 per cent per year to over 22 per cent. Table 3 shows that six centres had a growth rate of 20 per cent or higher.

TRAINING

The Papua and New Guinea Electricity Commission, along with other government and private bodies, has been developing a complete training programme for local officers at its Training Centre, coupled with other part-time general education courses open to all employees.

Full-time courses at present include those for power station operators, linesmen, clerks, meter readers and drivers.

Apprentices are employed in the following fields; diesel mechanics, electricians, welders, draughtsmen, motor mechanics and printing machine operators.

The Commission also has a number of sponsored students attending technical colleges and universities, who will fill professional and sub-professional positions in the Commission. In January 1971 there were thirty trainee technical and commercial officers, and twenty-five cadets at tertiary institutions in the Territory and six cadets studying at universities in Australia.

WEST IRIAN

In the report on potential hydro-electric works in West Irian, by A. R. H. Brouwer of Amersfoort, some nineteen potential hydro-electric sites are listed. The report was published at The Hague in 1959. It is not known to what extent these potential sources of power have been developed since that time.

Table 1

GENERATION OF ELECTRICAL ENERGY
Year ended 30 June

	1963	1964	1965	1966	1967	1968	1969	1970
Installed Capacity	*Megawatts*							
Hydro-electric	11.43	11.43	11.55	11.55	11.55	23.90	35.90	35.90
Thermo-electric	10.08	12.80	14.26	17.15	21.72	10.33	13.37	17.93
	21.51	24.23	25.81	28.70	33.27	34.23	49.27	53.83
Production	*Million kWh*							
Hydro-electric	47.48	46.60	46.95	47.27	52.20	71.78	99.92	119.44
Thermo-electric	20.08	26.81	27.95	40.64	52.74	38.25	31.30	40.93
	67.56	73.41	74.90	87.91	104.94	110.03	131.22	160.37

Table 2

MONTHLY TARIFF SCHEDULES INTRODUCED 1 JULY 1968
Cents per unit

	Zone					
	1	2	3	4	5	6
Domestic Tariff						
First 10 Units	12.50	12.50	12.50	12.50	13.25	13.25
Next 30 Units	6.67	6.67	7.56	7.56	8.11	9.05
Next 150 Units	3.75	4.38	4.74	5.50	6.55	7.31
Balance	2.50	3.00	3.75	4.50	5.25	6.00
General Tariff						
First 50 Units	12.50	12.50	12.50	12.50	13.25	13.25
Next 200 Units	6.67	6.67	7.62	7.62	8.44	9.31
Next 400 Units	5.00	5.34	6.00	7.14	7.78	8.64
Next 4,000 Units	3.05	4.10	4.91	5.72	6.42	7.22
Balance	3.05	3.35	3.75	4.50	5.25	6.00

NOTES: Tariff Zone 1 applies at Port Moresby.
Tariff Zone 2 applies at Rabaul, Goroka, Lae and Madang.
Tariff Zone 3 applies at Kavieng, Wewak and Samarai.
Tariff Zones 4, 5 and 6. No consumers connected at these tariff rates.
As the Commission takes over minor centres from the Administration, Zones 4, 5 and 6 will come into effect.
A special tariff rate applicable to water pumping is in operation.
Zone 1, General Tariff consumers are eligible to apply for a two part Maximum Demand tariff, subject to meeting the following requirements:
a monthly consumption of over 21,000 kWh,
a maximum demand of 100 kW or over.

Table 3

KILOWATT HOURS GENERATED 1969–70

Centre	Hydro kWh	Percentage Increase Over 1968–9	Diesel kWh	Percentage Increase Over 1968–9	Total kWh	Percentage Increase Over 1968–9
Port Moresby	90,837,350	22.07			90,837,350	22.07
Lae	*25,668,500	13.11	4,945,220	328.7	30,613,720	28.37
Rabaul			15,731,290	21.38	15,731,290	21.38
Madang			9,357,220	11.54	9,357,220	11.54
Wewak			6,244,120	20.18	6,244,120	20.18
Goroka	2,930,964	4.38	2,669,990	58.85	5,600,954	24.78
Samarai			827,249	3.72	827,249	3.72
Kavieng			1,153,263	23.81	1,153,263	23.81
Total	119,436,814	19.54	40,928,352	30.77	160,365,166	22.22
Excluding Baiune	93,768,314	21.43			134,696,666	24.12

* Purchased under the Lae–Baiune agreement with Placer Development Ltd

Table 4

HYDRO-ELECTRIC POWER POTENTIAL

Centre	Source of Water	Capacity in MW	Load Factor	Availability in %
Planned				
Rouna No. 3	Laloki River	12	.6	100
Rouna No. 4	Laloki River	9	.6	100
Ramu No. 1	Upper Ramu River	75	.44	100
Sirinumu	Laloki River	1.5	.5	90
Feasible				
Wabo	Purari River	1,000	1.0	95
Pio	Purari River	450	1.0	95
Ramu No. 2	Upper Ramu River	180	.55	100
Safia	Musa River	400	.60	100
Mount Hagen	Nebelyer River	5	.5	85
West New Britain	Lake Hargy	6	.5	Approaching 100
Bougainville	Laluai River	50	.9	100
Vanapa	Lower Vanapa River	150	.6	85
Angabunga	Lower Angabunga	80	.6	100

Table 5

ADDITIONAL PLANT 1969–70

Location	No. and Size in kW
Lae	1 × 2,400 Diesel
	1 × 530 Diesel
Madang	1 × 1,340 Diesel
Goroka	1 × 392 Diesel

Table 6

POWER PLANT AS INSTALLED AT 30 JUNE 1970

Papua and New Guinea Electricity Commission

Diesel Stations

Location	No. and Size in kW	Make of Machines		Total MW	Maximum Monthly Demand MW	No. of Consumers 30.6.70
		Engine	*Alternator*			
Lae	2 × 840 2 × 320 1 × 320 1 × 2,400 1 × 530	English Electric Blackstone Blackstone Ruston English Electric	English Electric ASEA Lanc. Dyn. Crypto English Electric G.E.C.	5.57	5.87	2,722
Rabaul	2 × 840 4 × 320 1 × 1,200	English Electric Blackstone Fuji	English Electric ASEA Fuji Electric	4.16	3.13	2,155
Madang	1 × 1,340 2 × 530 1 × 500 3 × 240	English Electric English Electric English Electric Blackstone	English Electric G.E.C. G.E.C. Lanc. Dyn. Crypto	3.62	1.85	1,093
Wewak	3 × 530 2 × 250 1 × 210	English Electric National Mirrlees	G.E.C. Brush Brush	2.3	1.2	691
Goroka	1 × 392 4 × 250	Blackstone Dorman	Brush MacFarlane	1.392	1.415*	1,032
Samarai	1 × 140 2 × 150	Mirrlees Blackstone	G.E.C. Elect. Const. Co.	0.44	0.255	181
Kavieng	3 × 150	Blackstone	Elect. Const. Co.	0.45	0.24	293
			Total	17.932		8,167

Hydro Stations

Location	No. and Size in kW	Make of Machines		Total MW	Maximum Monthly Demand MW	No. of Consumers 30.6.70
		Engine	*Alternator*			
Rouna 1 Rouna 2	1 × 2,500 3 × 1,000 5 × 6,000	Boving Boving Voest	Bruce Peebles ⎫ Metro Vick ⎬ Elin Union ⎭	5.5 30.0	18.0	7,972
Goroka	1 × 200 2 × 100	Gilkes Gilkes	G.E.C. G.E.C.	0.4		
			Total	35.9		7,972

*Diesel and hydro combined.

ELEMA. People of Orokolo Bay, Gulf District.
References:

H. A. Brown, 'The Folklore of the Eastern Elema People', Papua and New Guinea Scientific Society, *Annual Report and Proceedings*, 1954.
———— 'Elema Traditional Art', Papua and New Guinea Scientific Society, *Annual Report and Proceedings*, 1959.
———— 'The Elema in Present-day Papua and New Guinea', Papua and New Guinea Scientific Society, *Annual Report and Proceedings*, 1962.
F. E. Williams, 'Trading Voyages from the Gulf of Papua', *Oceania*, vol. 3, 1932-3.
———— 'Seclusion and Age Grouping in the Gulf of Papua', *Oceania*, vol. 9, 1938-9.
———— 'A Cycle of Ceremonies in Orokolo Bay, Papua', *Mankind*, vol. 2, 1936-40.
———— 'The Kaiamunu-Ebiha-Gi Cult in Papua', *Man*, vol. 39, 1939.
———— *Drama of Orokolo*. Oxford, 1940.

EMPLOYERS' ORGANIZATIONS. Such associations are usually established when groups of employers feel that there is a need for a formal organization through which they can safeguard their common interests. Before 1960 the local Chambers of Commerce and regional planters' associations performed this function of protecting the mutual interests of the commercial undertakings in the Territory of Papua and New Guinea.

However, a series of events in the Territory led a number of leading employers to question whether the Chambers of Commerce were equipped to look after their interests in labour relations. With the proclamation of the Native Employment Board Ordinance in 1958 and the possibility of further government regulation of employment relations, there was a growing recognition, particularly among the large urban employers, that they would need to keep themselves informed of developments in this sphere.

The significance of the new industrial legislation for employers was further emphasized in 1959 when the Native Employment Board commenced its first enquiry into wage scales for native employees. As the Board indicated it would take evidence from all interested sections of the community some of the local employer groups felt it was necessary to be represented at the hearing. Mr J. P. Coneybeer, a well known industrial advocate in Brisbane, was employed on an *ad hoc* basis to represent a number of urban and rural employer groups. The problems of deciding on a joint policy for such an advocate and of his control and payment provided a further impetus to the formation of a specialist organization to look after employers' industrial interests.

The next important impetus was the formation of workers' organizations [q.v.]. In 1958 the Kerema Welfare Association in Port Moresby was formed with an interest in employment as well as welfare activities. Out of this association grew the Papua and New Guinea Workers' Association. In 1960 the Madang District Workers' Association was formed, and together with the Ambenob Local Government Council started negotiating terms of employment with the Madang Chamber of Commerce. The strong probability of workers' associations developing in other areas also was becoming apparent.

The passing of the Industrial Organizations Ordinance and the Industrial Relations Ordinance in 1962 provided the final impetus for the formation of a separate organization to look after employers' interests in the industrial relations field. There was a growing realization that the increasing complexity of industrial regulations, and the growth of workers' associations throughout the Territory, meant that in future it would not be possible to handle industrial relations matters adequately on a regional basis and in an *ad hoc* manner.

FORMATION OF THE EMPLOYERS' ORGANIZATION

In September-October 1960 a tripartite mission of government, employer and union representatives from Australia visited the Territory. This enabled employers to make personal contact with officials of Australia's two most important national employers' organizations, the Australian Council of Employers' Federations and the Associated Chambers of Manufactures of Australia. Subsequently Mr George Polites, the executive director of A.C.E.F., was asked to assist in the formation of an employers' organization in Papua and New Guinea. A.C.E.F. had previously advised in the development of an employer organization in Singapore. The president of the Port Moresby Chamber of Commerce arranged for a meeting of employers there in 1961 at which a decision was made that in principle an employers' organization was desirable. Mr Polites was asked to suggest ways of establishing an association and given authority to prepare a draft constitution and other documents.

Mr Polites was also asked to find a suitable person for the secretaryship of the proposed association. He recruited Mr Jack Henry, an industrial officer with Comalco at Bell Bay in Tasmania, whose previous industrial experience included a period as federal secretary of the Federated Clerks' Union of Australia. Mr Henry came to the Territory early in 1963, engaged by a provisional committee of employers acting in anticipation of the actual formation of the proposed employers' federation.

In June 1963 a meeting of employers was held which resulted in the formation of the Employers' Federation of Papua and New Guinea. The eight foundation members represented at the meeting were the B.N.G. Trading Company, Burns Philp (New Guinea), Hornibrook Constructions, E. A. James and Company, The Port Moresby Freezing Company, South Pacific Brewery, Steamships Trading Company, and John Stubbs and Sons. The foundation members were mainly large Australian-owned and -controlled firms with central offices in Port Moresby. Mr B. C. Goodsell of Burns Philp (New Guinea), the main driving force behind the formation of the Federation, became the Federation's first president. The Federation was one of the first four organizations registered on 27 August 1963 under the provisions of the Industrial Organizations Ordinance. It remains the only registered industrial organization of employers with eligibility for membership covering 'any trade, business, profession and calling' in the Territory.

GROWTH OF THE EMPLOYERS' FEDERATION

The Employers' Federation quickly grew from its eight foundation members in June 1963 to twenty-three members at the end of 1963 and forty-nine members at December 1970.

The formation of local workers' associations and their demands for increased wages assisted considerably in the Federation's recruitment of members. Also the Chambers of Commerce, which had traditionally provided a forum for local employers on mainly trade matters, realizing they did not have the specialist knowledge to meet the growing number of industrial relations issues, began requesting assistance from the Federation. This provided the Federation with sources of contact with potential members under the auspices of well established organizations. At first some employers thought Jack Henry, the secretary of the Federation, was an Administration employee. However, the members of the Federation are still predominantly the larger expatriate-controlled firms based in urban centres. However three non-European concerns have joined. In general the rural employers still favour independent regional organizations such as the Planters' Association of New Guinea, the Planters' Association of Papua and the Highland Farmers and Settlers' Association. It should be noted however that three of the largest members of the Federation—Burns Philp, Steamships Trading Company and W. R. Carpenter —have the largest plantation holdings in the Territory. It would be only reasonable to assume that should industrial troubles develop in their rural interests, these organizations will turn to the Federation for assistance.

FINANCE

The Federation is financed from members' subscriptions, which are calculated as a percentage of the members' payroll. The main advantage of this method is that the subscriptions are automatically adjusted to changes in money values.

The early rapid growth in membership allowed the original subscription rates to be reduced as from 1 July 1964. The rates in 1971 were based on the size of a member's annual payroll and ranged from 20c per cent per annum to 40c per cent per annum, with a minimum subscription of $40 and a maximum of $4,000 per annum.

This financial position of the Employers' Federation provides a sharp contrast with the financially embarrassed workers' associations. The Federation is able to employ trained staff and back them up with the necessary technical and travel resources to service a variety of industries in widely separated urban communities. The full-time professional staff of the Federation consists of a secretary with considerable industrial relations experience and an assistant secretary. The workers' associations in 1967 had no full-time national officials.

RELATIONS WITH EXTERNAL ASSOCIATIONS

The A.C.E.F. was instrumental in founding the Federation and has continued to assist in a number of ways. The Executive Director of A.C.E.F. still advises the Federation and occasionally visits the Territory. He also selected and negotiated the appointment conditions of the assistant secretary appointed by the Federation in 1967. When requested the A.C.E.F. sends up an adviser who is well versed in the particular industry involved in negotiations. While the professional staff of the association remains small it is likely this service will continue to be essential as two men cannot be expected to be specialists in all the industries in the Territory. At the Annual General Meeting of A.C.E.F. in April 1966 the Federation was admitted as an associate member.

The other major employers' organizations in Australia such as the Associated Chambers of Manufactures and the Metal Trades Employers' Association have not sought to be involved in the Territory.

Although not a member of the International Organization of Employers or the Organization of Employers' Federations and Employers in Developing Countries, the Federation is able to arrange through A.C.E.F. for the liaison services of these organizations. The Federation, also through A.C.E.F., has access to the I.L.O.

G. W. FORD

(*See also* WORKERS' ORGANIZATIONS)

ENGA. People of the Western Highlands District.
References:
N. Bowers, 'Permanent Bachelorhood in the Upper Kaugel Valley of Highland New Guinea', *Oceania*, vol. 36, 1965-6.

R. N. H. Bulmer, 'Hagen and Wapenamanda Open Electorates: the Election among the Kyaka Enga' (New Guinea's First National Election), *Journal of the Polynesian Society*, vol. 73, 1964.

A. P. Elkin, 'Delayed Exchange in Wabag Sub-district, Central Highlands of New Guinea', *Oceania*, vol. 23, 1952-3.

W. H. Goodenough, 'Ethnographic Notes on the Mae People of New Guinea's Western Highlands', *Southwestern Journal of Anthropology*, vol. 9, 1953.

M. J. Meggitt, 'The Valleys of the upper Wage and Lai Rivers, Western Highlands, New Guinea', *Oceania*, vol. 27, 1956-7.

———— 'House Building among the Mae Enga, Western Highlands', *Oceania*, vol. 27, 1956-7.

———— 'Enga Political Organization', *Mankind*, vol. 5, 1954-62.

———— 'The Enga of the New Guinea Highlands', *Oceania*, vol. 28, 1957-8.

———— 'Mae Enga Time-Reckoning and Calendar, New Guinea', *Man*, vol. 58, 1958.

———— 'Growth and Decline of Agnatic Descent Groups among the Mae Enga of the New Guinea Highlands', *Ethnology*, vol. 1, 1962.

———— 'Dream Interpretation among the Mae Enga of New Guinea', *Southwestern Journal of Anthropology*, vol. 18, 1962.

———— 'The Kinship Terminology of the Mae Enga of New Guinea', *Oceania*, vol. 34, 1963-4.
———— 'Male-Female Relationships in the Highlands of Australian New Guinea', *American Anthropologist*, vol. 66, Special Publication, 1964.
———— *The Lineage System of the Mae-Enga of New Guinea*. Edinburgh, 1965.
———— 'The Mae Enga of the Western Highlands', in *Gods Ghosts and Men in Melanesia*, ed. P. Lawrence and M. J. Meggitt. Melbourne, 1965.

ENVIRONMENT AND HEALTH. In a biological sense the environment may be defined as the sum of all the external conditions and influences affecting the life and development of an organism, so that any reasonably comprehensive examination of all the potentially harmful factors in the New Guinea environment might seem a very formidable undertaking. However, most of the more important continuing problems associated with life there have some part 'of their origin in the climate. An examination of the effects of the climate on the inhabitants will serve, therefore, not only to identify the major problems but also to suggest ameliorative measures.

THE PHYSICAL ENVIRONMENT

The climate of New Guinea is dealt with in another article (see CLIMATE AND WEATHER), so that it is sufficient to consider here only the high temperature and humidity, and the little diurnal and seasonal variation. The prevailing climate is determined primarily by the fact that New Guinea is an island lying just south of the equator—most of the Territory of Papua and New Guinea lies between 3°S. and 9°S.—so that the temperature is warm to hot, the days are of uniform length with only a brief twilight, and the seasons which occur in higher latitudes are unknown, except in the extreme south where there is some slight change. Lack of variation to the point of monotony is one of the chief characteristics of the New Guinea climate. The temperature is however not excessively high; at coastal stations the mean maximum is about 90°F. but diurnal and seasonal variations are small and warm nights provide little relief from day-time heat.

Inland the climate is modified by the presence of a massive cordillera stretching roughly from east to west throughout the length of the island. Air temperature decreases by about 1°F. for every 300 feet above sea-level, so that altitudes above 3,000 feet provide welcome relief, indeed the only relief, from the high temperature prevailing at sea-level. However, at high altitudes, the air being clearer and drier and the cloud cover less, the sunlight is stronger and more continuous and, though the diurnal variation in temperature is greater, there is still but little seasonal variation. There are no extensive areas in New Guinea where the physiological effects of altitude alone are important.

Besides being hot the New Guinea climate is also moist, which adds greatly to the burden of the prevailing temperature. Most areas receive in excess of 80 inches of rain per year but there are wide variations. Some receive as much as 250 inches but in the rain shadow around Port Moresby the annual rainfall is only 40 inches, confined almost entirely to the period December to March. Despite these variations the air is nowhere dry in the physiological sense and high levels of absolute humidity are the rule.

Although there are no seasons in the accepted sense it is nevertheless customary in New Guinea to recognize two 'seasons'—that of the SE. trade wind, December to March, and that of the NW. monsoon, May to October, with transition periods between—the product of the changing position of the intertropical convergence as it moves north and south in the wake of the sun. Local topography is largely responsible for determining with which of these two seasons the heavier rainfall is associated.

CLIMATE AND HEALTH

It would be wrong to say that New Guinea's climate is necessarily unhealthy, even though medical problems of great magnitude, such as endemic malaria, are associated with it. One can go further and say that for a man not supported by artificial aids it is an excellent climate, far kinder than that which prevails for example over the greater part of Europe. However, it is characteristic of this area that at heights of less than 5,000 feet above sea-level many, if not most, people will be uncomfortably hot at some time of the day throughout the entire year and suffer inconvenience and loss of efficiency as a result.

It is important to bear in mind, when assessing the extent of this discomfort or inconvenience, that the stress imposed by the thermal environment depends not only on the prevailing temperature and humidity but also on the radiant-heat level—for example, the intensity of the sun, and the prevailing air speed—at the moderate temperature of the humid tropics increasing the air speed mitigates the effect of the temperature and humidity. Furthermore the physiological strain produced in a person will vary with a number of factors, the most important of which are the amount of clothing worn by him and, especially, his rate of energy expenditure.

The preferred temperature for those engaged in sedentary occupations indoors and wearing ordinary office clothing is, in south-eastern Australia, approximately 73°F. In New Guinea it has been shown that in these circumstances the preferred temperature is 78°F., the difference being due in the main to differences in clothing. It seems that acclimatization, though it improves the capacity to withstand high temperatures, does not materially change the preferred temperature. At the temperatures prevailing in New Guinea, therefore, those engaged in sedentary occupations indoors can expect to be uncomfortable for at least some part of the day and heavy outdoor labour in full sunlight could prove for some an intolerable burden. Nevertheless, despite this discomfort and inconvenience the classical major heat disorders—acute heat exhaustion, miners' cramp (salt-deficiency heat exhaustion), and the grave medical emergency of heat stroke—are very rare or non-existent.

Disorders of the skin are, however, common. Discomfort due to heat is always accompanied by the presence of unevaporated sweat upon the skin. This softens the epidermis, renders it susceptible to damage from the slightest abrasion thus facilitating its invasion by bacteria and fungi and providing conditions favourable to their growth and multiplication. As a result, bacterial and mycotic dermatoses are among the most common illnesses. Continuous profuse sweating also deranges the sweating mechanism itself. The sweat ducts become occluded and the result is the familiar prickly heat (see SKIN DISEASES) which, in extreme cases, may proceed to the complete suppression of sweating on large areas of the body, which in turn can interfere with the regulation of the body temperature.

Indirectly, the warm climate does create medical risks. High temperatures favour the multiplication of pathogenic organisms, the problem of food spoilage is much greater than in cold climates and bowel disorders tend to flourish. For these reasons, infants and small children are at special risk. The danger of 'summer diarrhoea' is always present and in hot climates, especially in the presence of diarrhoea and vomiting, they can dehydrate with alarming rapidity. Special care must always be taken in the preparation of their food, their fluid intake watched over at all times and they should be burdened with the absolute minimum of clothing indoors but adequately protected from the danger of sunburn out of doors.

In speaking of the medical and physiological effects of heat it is unnecessary to distinguish between the expatriate and the indigenous inhabitants. No differences have as yet been demonstrated in the ability of the various races of mankind to tolerate unaccustomed heat when adequate time has elapsed for adaptation. It is not to be expected, therefore, that the degree of discomfort experienced by the indigenous population will in any way differ from that of Europeans in the same circumstances. The apparent disregard of the indigenous people for conditions found irksome by Europeans is to be explained partly in terms of clothing, rate of energy expenditure and perhaps in such physical characteristics as the ratio of body weight to surface area, and partly in a willingness to accept a greater degree of discomfort without complaint.

One advantage, however, which the indigenes do possess is their heavier skin pigmentation. This provides protection from the neoplastic effects of exposure of the skin to tropical sunlight. The danger of malignant disease of the skin in Europeans in the tropics has long been recognized, but it has also recently come to be known that strong sunlight induces a premature ageing of the skin by provoking degenerative changes in the connective tissue of the dermis. It would be of interest to determine whether the indigenous inhabitants enjoy a similar immunity to this disorder.

ADAPTATION TO THE ENVIRONMENT

It has long been known that a newcomer to a hot climate undergoes with time a process of adaptation—acclimatization—as a result of which the hardships imposed by the climate are diminished. Part of this adaptation is behavioural—he discards excessive clothing, reduces his food intake, increases his consumption of fluids, walks at a more leisurely pace on the shadier side of the street and avoids excessive activity in the hottest part of the day, but there are also profound physiological changes as a result of which he can better withstand the stress of the environment. In other words, the physiological strain produced by the stress of the environment is diminished. The greater part of this physiological change appears to occur within the first few weeks of exposure to the environment but there is evidence to suggest that these initial adjustments are replaced in the course of months or even years by a more efficient form of adaptation involving somewhat different mechanisms. It is important to note that there is no way except exposure to heat by which these changes can be induced.

Apart from the physiological changes which will inevitably occur, to a greater or lesser degree according to the willingness of the individual to encourage them by active exercise in the heat, there are two ways of achieving a successful modus vivendi with the New Guinea climate: the adjustment of behaviour, or behavioural adaptation, and the application of technology. The relative importance of these two methods is largely determined by circumstances. The office worker can have resort to air-conditioning, a technological aid. The labourer out of doors, on the other hand, is forced to have recourse to a slower rate of working, behavioural adaptation, although even he can exploit simple artificial aids; for instance, the erection of a temporary shelter or the wearing of a shady hat.

Adjustment of the working hours is one form of behavioural adaptation that has been widely exploited in different forms in different countries. Whether this can be done successfully depends largely upon its compatibility with the existing social, commercial or industrial framework. One method is to commence the working day so early that the day's work can be accomplished before the occurrence of the maximum daily temperature which usually occurs early in the afternoon.

Another device commonly adopted is the siesta. This achieves some measure of success in hot, dry desert climates in sub-tropical latitudes but seems to have much less to recommend it in equatorial regions. Wherever it is practised it has the inherent disadvantage of disturbing the circadian (diurnal) rhythm of the body in that each day has to be commenced twice. If the siesta is devoted to sleep or recumbency the temperature regulating mechanism of the body is placed at a great disadvantage as only half the body surface is available for the evaporation of sweat, a matter of considerable importance in hot moist climates. Furthermore, if the same amount of work has to be done in each day the day must either start early or end late or both. This means that the cooler part of the day which should be available for rest or recreation must be devoted to work. This is of less significance in the subtropics where daylight is longer and consequently more time is available for outdoor recreation than in equatorial regions with a short twilight.

Even in the hottest part of the day the temperature in equatorial regions is seldom so high that even moderate physical work is impossible, so that the extreme solution employed in the most hostile desert climates where man becomes a semi-nocturnal animal would seem quite inappropriate in New Guinea. One sure escape from heat stress, which may be considered under the heading of behavioural adaptation, is provided in New Guinea by the Highlands and this may well have an important bearing on the distribution of the population in the future.

It is unfortunate that many people, through ignorance, imperfect understanding or an unquestioning acceptance of popular beliefs, cause themselves unnecessary hardship and hinder their physiological adjustment. Nowhere is this more evident than in matters relating to salt and water requirements in the tropics. It is absolutely obligatory, if the temperature-regulating mechanism of the body is to function correctly, that water lost in the sweat should be replaced. Some degree of water deficit is tolerated by the body but at the cost of loss of efficiency. Nevertheless, it is still believed by many that drinking water, especially cold water, when hot is harmful and that efficiency is improved by abstinence. Water discipline, as it is called, is still held to be a virtue to be cultivated in some sections of the armed forces. This is quite false. No harm, indeed only good, can come from drinking freely and the water can with advantage be as cold as is palatable.

Similarly, salt lost in the sweat must be replaced, but with this difference—it must be done in accordance with the need. The taking of an ordinary Western type of diet will ensure the ingestion of some 10 gm. of sodium chloride per day and the concentration of salt in sweat, the only inescapable salt loss from the body, is such that this is sufficient in almost all circumstances. If it is thought desirable to supplement the salt intake for any reason this is best done by adding salt to the food. It is only in the most exceptional circumstances that this will be inadequate to provide sufficient salt. The exceptions are unacclimatized men engaged in heavy and prolonged work out of doors (one of the effects of acclimatization is to reduce the salt concentration in sweat so that the need for salt tends to diminish with time) or workers in hot industries such as glass-making or iron-founding when quite exceptional amounts of sweat may be lost—up to twenty or more pints per day. In these cases salt should be added to the drinking water at the rate of one teaspoonful per gallon (0.1 per cent NaCl)

and the necessarily large intake of water will ensure sufficient salt to replace losses. The foregoing applies only to healthy people taking a normal solid diet. In the case of the sick, especially in the presence of diarrhoea and vomiting, the usual rules for the replacement of water and electrolytes will apply. Under no circumstances should additional salt be taken when the water intake is restricted for any reason. Salt should never be taken in large doses or as a concentrated solution. The taking of salt tablets should be discouraged. They are usually taken unnecessarily and with quite inadequate amounts of water.

There will always be some would-be residents of tropical climates who are unable to adapt to the environment, probably more often for emotional than for physiological reasons. Such people are perhaps ill-advised to persist. The decision should, nevertheless, not be made hastily, as it is only after the lapse of a considerable time that inability to adapt becomes unequivocal. Socio-cultural adaptation is often a longer and more difficult process than physiological acclimatization and is often accompanied by an urgent desire to escape from the apparently hostile environment.

The expatriate public servant of colonial days established the tradition of a tour of duty, usually of two to five years, with a long period of home leave at the end of each tour. The reason advanced—the restoration of the officer's physical health undermined by repeated bouts of tropical diseases—may well have been fully justified one hundred or even fifty years ago but, as the result of advances in medicine, there is now little real justification on this score. However, the practice has continued—it is a privilege not lightly to be surrendered—and the ostensible reason, grounds of health, has remained the same. It is perhaps time that the practice was examined carefully, rather than condemned out of hand, as it may be essentially sound even if justified on fallacious grounds. The recent more careful study of immigrant behaviour in Australia has shown that a nostalgic desire to return home is a universal phenomenon among expatriates. Serious consideration is now being given to the contention that it would be an economically sound measure if, in order to satisfy this desire and thereby prevent the loss of valuable settlers, they were financially assisted to re-visit their homeland at intervals. An understanding of these facts might help to remove an unwarranted slur on the climate of New Guinea and still permit the granting of leave to expatriate officers on a more rational basis.

COUNTERACTING THE CLIMATE

It was technological advances—the invention of fire, shelter and clothing—which enabled man, a tropical animal, to establish himself in temperate and cold climates and this suggests that the logical approach to living with the New Guinea climate is a similar use of the resources of modern technology.

There can be no doubt of the importance of fire to primitive man in a cold climate and the analogous role of air-conditioning is at once apparent, but there are difficulties. Heating is a simple, inexpensive process, possible with the most primitive apparatus. Air-conditioning is a sophisticated process requiring complicated apparatus which is expensive to install and run, and requires skilled maintenance that is not always available. Its use is restricted—it cannot be used out of doors or in industrial buildings in which large quantities of heat are liberated—and to function efficiently it requires a special type of building which, should the air-conditioning fail, is less inhabitable than a building designed to exploit natural means of ventilation.

Although the air-conditioning of public buildings, especially hospitals, is now coming to be accepted as desirable standard practice, the domestic use of full air-conditioning is unlikely to be widely adopted in the foreseeable future, largely because of the expense and the unsuitable nature of existing housing. But these objections should not be permitted to discourage the compromise of using small units to condition part of a house. The maximum physiological benefit is likely to be derived from its use in bedrooms where it would ensure sound sleep at night. Though no immediate reduction in running costs is to be expected there is every reason to believe that this will come with time, possibly by the exploitation of solar energy. The use of solar energy for such purposes as water heating is rapidly increasing in New Guinea and, though the high proportion of cloudy days presents difficulties, its wider use in the future seems inevitable.

Air-conditioning is not the only means available for reducing the level of heat stress indoors. Correct architectural design, good ventilation and the use of fans are perhaps even more important. In a warm, moist climate the use of fans is particularly successful but the large slow ceiling type, fitted with a speed regulator so that the resulting air movement can be adjusted with nicety to existing requirements, is much to be preferred to the small high-speed table model. It should perhaps be added in passing that evaporative coolers, which provide a satisfactory substitute in arid climates for refrigerated air-conditioning, cannot, because of the high humidity, be used successfully in New Guinea. Emphasis on reducing the air temperature should not be permitted to obscure the fact that in many parts of the Highlands the nights are sufficiently cold to require some form of heating, and there is no doubt that inadequate warmth at night is a source of much unnecessary discomfort for the indigenous population. Here again the exploitation of solar energy would seem to be indicated.

The devices so far mentioned have no application out of doors and the whole gamut of external activities must be pursued without their aid. There are, however, other means of reducing the level of heat stress and even the most unpromising situation can be improved; the important thing is that there should be the desire to do so. Among the means available are the erection of temporary shelters wherever possible, the avoidance of the hottest hours of the day for the performance of heavy labour and the wearing of suitable clothing, but the real solution, again technological, would appear to be the replacement wherever possible of muscular energy by mechanical energy —the pick and the shovel by the bulldozer.

One of the strongest defences against a hostile climate is the provision of suitable shelter, in the form of appropriately designed buildings. As a result of intensive research over the past twenty years, in which Australian architects and building scientists have played a notable part, the formula for successful building in the moist tropics is now well established. It includes correct orientation with respect to the sun and the prevailing breeze, the proper use of insulation in walls and ceilings, the use of reflective finishes on surfaces exposed to sun, the provision of adequate shading to protect walls and windows, restriction in the use of glass, suitable arrangements for the disposal of large quantities of rain water from roofs, the use of flyscreens, and the protection of the fabric from the ravages of insects and fungi and from disfiguring algal growths. These things are well understood although the best architectural solutions may yet have to be found, more particularly with respect to the resolution of conflicting needs. For example, freedom of ventilation must not be allowed to result in loss of privacy or of protection from intruders or permit the ingress of rain or dust. But though it is true to say that this knowledge is readily available the public conscience and the building industry have lagged sadly behind in its application. One of the most acute social problems at present in Papua and New Guinea is the provision of suitable low-cost housing for an expanding urban indigenous population. It is important also that buildings should be aesthetically acceptable and have an air of permanence and solidity. This applies both to public and domestic buildings so that the one fosters civic pride and the other pride of ownership.

Besides its basic function of providing shelter a building must also provide certain facilities for its occupants, the nature of which varies with the purpose of the building. In a house the basic requirements are space for living and eating and for sleeping; but in addition to these there must be provision for the storage and cooking of food, for bathing and washing of clothes and, above all else, acceptable sanitation. This latter group of requirements are apt to be more exacting and in consequence more expensive than in temperate climates. Food is more difficult to protect from spoilage so that a refrigerator is essential. Cooking can result in an unacceptable rise in temperature in the kitchen; the stove must, therefore, not be a simple device which will radiate wild heat. Bathing is more important and there are more clothes to wash so that both a hot water system and washing machine are indicated. In fact in order to reduce the burden of the climate on the housewife the free use of labour-saving devices in general is indicated.

Whilst there is no doubt that the adoption of clothing suited to the climate is a matter of importance, the achievement of that end is by no means simple. For much of the day in most parts of New Guinea, if the wearer is not exposed to the direct rays of the sun, any clothing whatever constitutes a physiological handicap. In the privacy and the safe environment of the home the minimum which satisfies current standards of decency may be worn but, in general, this simple solution is not acceptable.

As well as providing protection from the cold clothing gives protection from the sun, from mechanical trauma and from insect bites, an important matter in malarious areas. In crowded communities it serves not only to protect the wearer from the environment but also to protect the environment from contamination by the wearer. But besides these primary functions, clothing has come with time to perform a whole range of important secondary functions. It provides a means of personal adornment; it can be used to conceal physical defects and the ravages of age; it distinguishes the cleric from the layman and the soldier from the civilian. It may even stand as a symbol of rebellion against conventional society. In the humid tropics the clothing worn must meet all these requirements, with the exception of protection from cold, and at the same time provide the minimum interference with cooling by convection and evaporation.

Temperate zone standards of clothing are so unsuitable for tropical man that it is tempting to advocate that such standards should be ruthlessly disregarded. This is clearly impossible. Nevertheless if sudden innovations are impossible there is no reason why a process of slow evolution should not be encouraged. An appeal is therefore made to those in authority to adopt a liberal attitude and to use their good sense to lead the way along the narrow path between what is socially acceptable and that which gives offence to current standards of behaviour.

The wearing of hats in the tropics has fallen into disrepute, probably as a reaction against the absurd notions current some fifty years ago of the dangers to the brain of the 'death-dealing' rays of the tropical sun. An unventilated hat does impede the evaporation of sweat from the scalp, but a hat does provide considerable shade to the whole of the body in a land where in the heat of the day the sun is directly overhead and, in an uncomfortably bright environment, protects the eyes from glare. In view of the dangers to the skin, especially of fair-haired individuals, of long exposure to strong sunlight, the wearing of suitable hats, especially by children, should be encouraged.

SOCIO-ECONOMIC PROBLEMS

There was a time, and that not so long ago, when life for many Europeans in New Guinea was an unhappy frustrating experience abounding in difficulties. Loneliness, uncertain communications, lack of social amenities, poor educational facilities, the remoteness of skilled medical attention, inadequate housing, poor water supplies, defective sanitation, inability to communicate—in the widest sense—with the indigenous inhabitants, lack of recreational facilities, an enforced change in dietary patterns—all these things combined to produce a sense of frustration and, in parents, a deep anxiety for the continued health and well-being of their children. Life was not made easier by the existence of a tropical folklore now known to be largely fallacious—that tropical foods were deficient in essential vitamins and minerals; that the pallor of the children was due to anaemia; that exercise in the heat of the day was to be avoided, especially by women; that puberty in girls occurs earlier in the tropics (thought to be specially undesirable for no very clear reason); and that alcohol was necessary for reasons of health. Many, if not most, of these problems were attributed to the climate whereas in fact they were the inevitable accompaniments of life in a primitive or isolated community.

Much of this now belongs in the past. It is doubtful whether anyone believes now that there is such a thing as tropical neurasthenia or that continuous residence for more than two years in the tropics will result in permanent physical deterioration or that European children fail to thrive in the area. Better communications, an increase in cultural amenities, improvements in the standard of housing, more accessible medical care, have now eased the burden of frustration and hardship of earlier days. Whatever social changes may take place in the future the climate and its problems will remain.

R. K. MACPHERSON

ERI, Vincent (1936-   ), public servant, was born in 1936 at Moveave in the Gulf District. He was educated at Catholic mission schools and, after a brief time with the co-operative movement at

Vincent Eri.

Kerema, entered Sogeri High School in 1951. Later he was trained as a teacher and from 1956 to 1962 taught in various Gulf District schools while continuing his studies. In 1962 he became acting District Inspector of Schools. He has travelled to Australia, Malaysia and Iran. In 1965 he started the Local Teachers' Association and was its first and only president. He entered the University of Papua and New Guinea in 1967 and graduated B.A. three years later. Among other things, he is now acting Superintendent of Primary Education and vice-president of the Papua and New Guinea Society. He is the author of the first novel to be written by a Papuan or New Guinean, *The Crocodile* (Brisbane, 1970).

ETHICS.   The term ethics as here used means the system of morals of a particular group, including not only the current ideals of right and wrong but also the sanctions that secure conformity with those ideals.

In the first half of the nineteenth century, prior to the emergence of anthropology as a special study, the peoples to whom we now apply the term primitive were regarded simply as immoral or uncivilized. Later, under the influence of the theory of evolution, there was an attempt to show that they were rather pre-moral or, perhaps, amoral, and the slaves of custom. This attitude resulted in the neglect of ethics or morality as a field of inquiry. The reaction against evolutionism, the so-called functional movement of the 1920s, although demonstrating convincingly that primitive peoples were not in fact slaves of custom and that their lives were less simple than had been supposed, did little to stimulate work on ethics *per se*. The tendency was now to regard morality as part of religion, and where moral rules were not backed by supernatural sanctions of some sort, as is sometimes the case in primitive societies, they were omitted from study. If on the other hand there were such sanctions, morality was discussed under the general heading of religion instead of being treated as an independent subject.

A revival of interest in ethics and values occurred in the late 1930s, particularly in the United States, and since that time extensive studies of particular moral systems have been undertaken. Although these have restored consideration of ethics to a legitimate place in anthropology and stimulated much interest, there has been as yet no intensive investigation of the subject in New Guinea. Such information as is available is usually embedded in some more general ethnographic text or is marginally covered in a treatment of social control, law, or politics. Nevertheless, certain facts are known, and it is now possible to perceive important variations in the moral systems of New Guinea as well as certain features that appear to be universal.

One aspect of variation concerns the presence or absence of supernatural sanctions for breaches of the moral code. Among the Huli of the Southern Highlands, according to Glasse (1965),

there is a specific supernatural being, Datagaliwabe, whose particular function is the supervision of ethical conduct: 'Datagaliwabe is no ordinary deity and indeed the Huli never call him a *dama* [a class of invisible deities possessing supra-physical powers to control the weather, cause sickness and infertility, etc.] but refer to him only by name. His special province is punishing breaches of kinship and for this purpose he continually observes social behaviour. One man described him as a giant who, with legs astride, looks down upon all and punishes lying, stealing, adultery, murder, incest, breaches of exogamy and of taboos relating to ritual. He also penalizes those who fail to avenge the deaths of kin slain in war. He has no concern, however, with the behaviour of unrelated persons'.

But in general the belief in supernatural beings who validate morality is relatively uncommon. Sanctions of a supernatural type, where they exist, are more commonly associated with ghosts. Perhaps the best example is to be found among the Manus of the Admiralty Islands, recorded by Mead (1937): 'Each Manus household is governed by a ghost of a recently dead male relative. In conception this ghost is a father, but a son may actually be raised to this position after death. The skull of the ghost is kept in the house and presides over the moral and economic life of the household. He punishes sex offenses, scandalmongering, obscenity, failure to pay debts, failure to help relatives, and failure to keep one's house in repair. For derelictions in these duties, he sends illness and misfortune'.

Still another form of supernatural sanction, noted by Berndt (1965), perhaps a more indirect and less efficacious one, is related to mythology (*see* MYTHS AND TALES). Here mythological non-humans of various kinds, as well as humans in some cases, are held up as examples of how human beings should behave: 'Each [myth] ends with a moral injunction, to the effect that "we, story characters, have done this; you, men, should not." In many cases men behave as the story characters do, and not as the moral dictates. But generally speaking this type of myth deals (negatively) with what people should not do, rather than (positively) with what they should'.

Wagner comments similarly for the Daribi near Mount Karimui: 'Models of correct courteous action are given by a pair of stock characters in Daribi legends, generally portrayed as two cross-cousins . . . the *bidi mu*, or "true man," and the *peraberabidi*, or "man who breaks things" '.

The above comments by no means account for the complexity of belief and action regarding supernatural sanctions. Nor are the types ever found in pure form. Among the Huli, for example, it is not only Datagaliwabe who is concerned with the moral affairs of the living but also, albeit to a lesser degree, the *dama*, as well as the ghosts of both recent and distant ancestors. Among the Fore, Kamano, and others is found, along with the mythology, a belief in ghosts, although how functional these are in the moral sphere is not entirely clear. In looking at New Guinea as a whole, one finds a remarkable complexity of belief regarding supernatural beings: gods, ghosts, spirit-beings, sky-dwelling creatures, demons, and others. And in each case the limits of action for any specific supernatural, as well as the limits for all supernaturals, can vary. Sometimes the ghosts are concerned only with the morality of their surviving kinsmen and not that of others; sometimes a god is concerned only with violations of incest rules but not with stealing; sometimes the supernaturals intervene only upon the failure to perform certain rituals, and so on. The distribution of various types of supernaturals and the specifics of their influence upon the moral behaviour of the living are not well known (*see* RELIGION AND MAGIC).

In contrast with the above, there are many societies in which there is no relationship between moral rules and supernatural sanctions, or, indeed, between religion and morality. Even where a belief in ghosts exists, for example, such things are not necessarily believed to affect the moral affairs of the living. The Gururumba of the Highlands are a good case in point: 'In other words, ghosts are not moral agents punishing the living for acts of wrongdoing. Neither are they thought of as vengeful. Wrong between living individuals is not made right by ghostly attack when the wronged individual dies and becomes a ghost. In general terms, ghosts act because of affronts to their physical person, as in the case of wanting their bones cleaned; to their esteem, as in the case of not wanting to be forgotten; or to express some strong personal desire, as in the case of not wanting to have one's name spoken'.

The Enga, as noted by Meggitt (1965), with a similar belief in ghosts, also do not associate them with morality. Enga dogmas about other types of supernaturals likewise do not associate them with morality. The sky beings, conceived of as the 'causal and originating people', responsible for good and bad luck, are not concerned with the ethical conduct of their putative descendants: 'Although some people assert that a dishonest man is more likely to experience bad luck than is an honest man, they do not believe that the sky beings are concerned consistently to punish the evil and reward the good. The popular tendency is to define right and wrong behaviour in terms of what currently serves the particular interests of corporate groups in the lineage hierarchy'.

The Wogeo (Hogbin, 1938) and the Orokaiva (Reay) appear to be even clearer examples of societies in which there is no connection between morality and religion. This situation, and many more examples could be cited, has given rise to obvious questions, the most fundamental being what sanctions do exist to maintain the moral order. A number of explanations have been offered. For convenience these can be classified as follows: 1. retaliation, 2. group identification, 3. self-regulation, and 4. quasi-legal sanctions. As will become obvious, these are not precise

categories. Each can be subdivided, and one category tends to merge into the next.

Retaliation is a widespread sanction and expresses itself in at least two different ways. In its simplest form, retaliation takes the character of direct physical violence. Among most groups, for example, a woman found guilty of adultery would simply be beaten by her husband. He might beat the guilty man also or, as among the Bena Bena, shoot him in the thigh with a special arrow kept for this purpose. Likewise, to avenge a death, either by sorcery or through some physical act, the relatives of the deceased must kill someone in the group presumed responsible. Thus the knowledge that reprisals of this kind can be expected encourages observance of the moral prescriptions.

As Reay has shown for the Orokaiva, retaliation can also take the form of withdrawal, as in the case of a woman who leaves her adulterous husband to fend for himself. There is also the withholding of goods and services as, for example, when an uncle refuses to contribute to a youth's bride-price.

A more indirect form of retaliation involves sorcery, the threat of which can act as a sanction for proper conduct (*see* SORCERY AND WITCHCRAFT). This was apparently of some significance among the Busama at one time, as recorded by Hogbin (1963): 'In earlier days sorcery was another factor to be reckoned with. The fear of black magic spurred people to overcome temptation and meet the legitimate claims of their kin; and, in addition, it served as an innocuous outlet for feelings of irritation. By this means the man harbouring a grievance obtained satisfaction without jeopardizing his position, hurting his enemy, or upsetting the life of the village'.

Although sorcery beliefs exist almost universally throughout Melanesia, sorcery is not always employed as a sanction, nor is it always associated with morality. The Bena Bena, with strong beliefs about sorcery, view it as emanating only from enemies, and, as such, it is an activity having nothing to do with their own moral conduct, either right or wrong. Nor does there appear to be any clear-cut relationship between the presence of beliefs about sorcery and the presence or absence of religious sanctions for moral behaviour, according to Lawrence and Meggitt.

In the category of group identification must first be placed what F. E. Williams defines as group sentiment. This phenomenon, he believed, accounts for much of the conformity found in primitive societies, including conformity to moral rules. In brief, Williams argued, there is a basic 'sentiment of fellowship', which is strong in men, and particularly strong among primitives, who characteristically live in relatively small groups. This is not something of which people are aware and it is related to what Williams regarded as an 'unconscious imitativeness'. But it is much more than merely imitativeness, it is also 'an often-expressed desire, even duty, to do things in the approved manner, in the "way of our fathers"'. Although Williams was aware that there was a limited range of choice for primitives, and that there were practical reasons as well for conformity, he did not believe these were sufficient to explain the degree of conformity he observed: 'It may be claimed that there are ample reasons of a more practical kind why a man should behave with special consideration towards his own group-members—e.g. the prospect of mutual assistance, the necessity for co-operation and mutual restraint, etc., which the individual is supposed to keep in mind. But to lay all the stress on this aspect seems to the present writer to embody the intellectualistic error. It is not to be supposed that the native is so calculating in his conduct, so keen a student of self-interest. Without unduly discounting this factor in his motives, the writer is disposed to believe that the native acts, or refrains from acting, with less intellectual finesse than it implies. At any rate it can hardly be denied that the group sentiment which we have called that of fellowship exists; and if it exists, it does not exist for nothing. It must influence conduct, and we need not entirely disbelieve such oft-repeated statements as "I would not do so and so an injury because he is my brother, my kinsman, my neighbor, etc." '.

Although 'group sentiment' is a difficult concept to define and work with, and although Williams himself only asserts its existence, the basic position is part of a wider tradition that still exists in sociology and anthropology. Many scholars would agree that among primitives there is a kind of mystique or sense of solidarity that is not present in more complex societies.

In the same category, group identification, can be justifiably placed attempts to explain moral behaviour in terms of 'shame'. Shame is an apparently universal concept among the peoples of New Guinea, but it should be made clear that this is not shame in precisely the sense that Europeans are accustomed to think of it. The feeling as an emotional experience is perhaps more akin to what Europeans would call intense guilt. It is unlike guilt, however, in that it is related to the fear of being found out, rather than to purely private pangs of conscience over having sinned or committed an unpardonable offence. There is no doubt that it has an effect on the personalities of those who experience it, driving them to extremes of behaviour and even to suicide.

In the most intensive account of shame to date, Hogbin (1946-7) has shown both its overwhelmingly social character and its relationship to morality. The Busama, with whom he deals, clearly regulate much of their conduct in terms of the avoidance of shame. This regulation extends from the most fundamental of daily interpersonal relations, to sexual behaviour, to magic, and even to legal and political behaviour. In this particular case, paradoxically, shame also operates at times to inhibit the punishment of those who do wrong. Hogbin cites the case of a man, obviously unsuitable for office, being appointed because the people were ashamed to say anything about him once his name had been submitted.

Hogbin maintains that the content of shame is similar everywhere but that the actions that arouse it vary with the moral code. While this may be true, it is of less importance as a sanction in some areas than in others. Burridge, for example, reports that shame, although present, is relatively unimportant among the Tangu.

Self-regulation can also be considered from more than one point of view. First, it is implicit in the notion that primitive folk act only in terms of custom. Indeed, it is implicit in the concepts of society and of culture, for no matter how these are defined, the definitions always imply some regularity of behaviour. But beyond this are usually enumerated characteristics of small-scale societies that automatically constrain action within narrow limits. There is the relative absence of choice so often noted; the need to help others if a person is to expect help in his turn—in some cases at least, co-operation is a necessity for survival in an inhospitable environment with only a crude technology; and the psychological and social limits imposed by kinship as the primary principle of organization. But to see self-regulation in this way it is necessary to make one of two extreme assumptions about human behaviour. Either, as Williams noted, people must be seen as acting always in terms of conscious self-interest—I will help him only because I expect something in return; or else they are seen as acting with virtually no conscious awareness at all—this is the way people have always acted so I will act in this way; neither a very satisfactory view of human nature.

Nadel has offered a more penetrating explanation of the process of self-regulation by adding the concepts of value and maximization as necessary conditions for even customary behaviour to occur: 'Rather, traditional or customary behaviour operates reliably only when two other conditions apply and derives its force and apparent self-propulsion from them. Either acting in accordance with tradition (i.e. in accordance with old inherited models) is as such considered desirable and good; or, this way of acting happens also to be safe, known routine. In the first case the traditional action is also value-oriented, being indeed short-lived without this support, as is instanced by changing fashions and fads. In the second case the custom remains such because its routinized procedure affords maximum success with least risk. It is, I suggest, in these two conditions that we find the true elements of self-regulation'.

He then goes on to show that any activity that is socially important is, simply by virtue of its importance, automatically protected from violation. This is so, he argues, from two different points of view. From the point of view of the participant in the action, an important activity is one that is valued and, as people do not readily give up their values and convictions, that which is important is by that measure protected. More important for Nadel's argument is that from the point of view of the observer, the social importance of an activity is determined by its focal position among all other social activities. This is because an action can, of course, serve many ends or interests other than those for which it is primarily intended. If it is truly focal, the failure to perform it will result in more undesirable consequences and greater dislocation of the system than if it is not a focal activity. This works as follows: 'Consider for example, a society, patrilineally organized, where marriage is prohibited between agnatic kin, is contracted by the payment of bride price, and entails specific duties towards the offspring on the part of both father's and mother's kin. If any man married in disregard of the first rule, the others would fail to work also. The bride price would have to be paid within the same descent group, while in the people's conception it is a payment suitable only between such groups, being meant (among other things) to indemnify the bride's group for the loss of her prospective progeny. The offspring of such an irregular union would forfeit the double assistance from two kin groups since the father's and mother's kin now coincide, and would be less advantageously placed than the offspring of customary marriages. And there would be various other, minor but no less confusing, complications; for example, rules of avoidance (obligatory towards in-laws) and intimacy (towards blood relations) would now apply to the same people. In short, one breach of routine disrupts routine all round, and the individual is faced with a wide loss of social bearings'.

That this is self-regulation can be seen in that the punishment for the violation of the marriage rule is intrinsic in the situation rather than extrinsic. That is, no formal or legal sanction is necessarily involved—the man does not face a jail sentence or execution—he simply cannot get satisfaction from the social system.

The process here cannot be separated from the values of the society, for the self-regulation implied in the notion of multiple consequences is part of a system that continuously feeds back upon itself. That is, any conduct that conforms to the norm stimulates further positive actions which keep the system going, becomes a model exhibiting its efficacy, and thereby gets its positive value reinforced.

Nadel believed that self-regulation was characteristic of small primitive societies: 'In more general terms, the regulative effects must vary inversely with the separation of social roles, with the specialization of offices and tasks, and, implicitly, with the size of groups (since only small groups can function adequately without considerable internal differentiation). It is precisely the small scale and lack of internal differentiation which characterize the societies we commonly call primitive and hence enable them to lean more heavily on such machinery of self-regulation'.

Thus, following Nadel, it would be unusual to find highly developed legal institutions or procedures of law enforcement in the traditional societies of New Guinea (see LAW, INDIGENOUS). This is precisely the case; and hence the last category, quasi-legal sanctions. Here are found various forms of institutionalized behaviour, other than simple retaliation, that can be used against those who violate the moral rules. Often these come into play only when the principle of retaliation threatens to become overly disruptive. Hogbin (1963) reports that among the Busama, for example, it is up to the individual to secure redress by personal retaliation. However, if serious argument ensues and it appears that someone may be hurt, formal machinery is brought into play. This consists of a headman, preferably not a relative of either party to the dispute, and a council of elders who are empowered to suggest punishments in the form of fines. They seem to have had no power to impose punishments if the weight of public opinion behind them was not sufficiently strong and if one or both of the disputants did not defer to their judgment. This situation appears to have been fairly uniform over New Guinea. Leadership was characteristically based more upon strength of personality, success, and knowledge, rather than upon inheritance or election; and, although leaders could influence and suggest, they could not command. They held little or no authority over individuals who did not wish to obey. Thus, although leadership and authority are present, as they must be in all societies, intervention in the moral or legal sphere occurs only under certain conditions. It is, as Nadel suggests, only when self-regulation fails to operate that quasi-legal or legal sanctions appear.

There are other mechanisms for dealing with violations of moral rules. These are sometimes built into the economic life of the community. Kaberry records that among the Abelam, for example, a man who suspects his wife of adultery can challenge the accused man to an exchange of yams: 'The husband, with the object of shaming the other man, sends yams and pigs to him, with the challenge that he make an equivalent return. The implication is that the adulterer is more interested in sexual intercourse than in growing yams, and that he will not be able to meet the challenge. An avoidance is established between them and they no longer sit and talk together. They are *wauna-ndu*, men who mock and abuse one another on public occasions. Such quarrels have wide repercussions, for unless a man can exonerate himself he is placed in the position where his relations become strained with a number of individuals in the village, and he has also to make additional efforts as a gardener if he is to meet his adversary's challenge and produce yams to vindicate his reputation. Thus the yam cult, with its taboos on sexual intercourse during part of the year, ambition and a jealous regard for prestige act as sanctions to preserve marital fidelity'.

Here, then, is an institutionalized way of punishing a breach of morality without unnecessarily disrupting the foundations of social life through physical assault or murder. This method of maintaining the moral system through exchange and equivalence is fundamental to many societies. It is so basic to the Tangu, for example, that Burridge reports there would be no amity without it: 'The critical axiom which governs all Tangu relationships through a variety of contents, bases and motives is amity. No vague and emotional goodwill, amity depends on and is expressed by equivalence, a principle of moral equality which must be continually reaffirmed and reiterated lest someone become dominant. Without equivalence there can be no amity in Tangu. The focal assertion of equivalence is at food exchanges at every level whether the exchange is completed in a day, weeks or months'.

The principle here, which Burridge refers to as a 'principle of moral equality', operates not only at the level of individual behaviour but is also invoked at a level of action more properly termed political (see, for example: Berndt, 1962; Glasse, 1954-62; Read, 1959). This merely emphasizes the difficulty of distinguishing between such concepts as morality, law, and politics in societies of this type, a distinction always more analytical than real.

Contained in the above remarks are hints, at least, as to the contents of the various moral codes found in the area. Some moral prescriptions are probably universal: those dealing with stealing, adultery, murder, incest, rape, bad behaviour towards kinsmen and friends, etc. But there is variation, of course, and what is considered ethical conduct by one group is not necessarily so considered by another. Among the Bena Bena, for example, consuming the dead bodies of certain kinsmen is considered right and proper, whereas among the peoples further to the west such conduct would be horrifying; premarital intercourse is the rule among the Bena Bena, whereas among the Enga it is improper, and so on. The extent of this variation has not been determined.

Beyond the specific universal content of the codes, whatever that may prove to be, there are certain universal features of the moral systems *qua* systems. Shame, as noted, is probably universally present. In that sense they can be categorized as 'shame cultures' as opposed to 'guilt cultures' (Piers and Singer) assuming that is a valid distinction. Another universal feature is that the moral code, along with whatever sanctions support it, is always group specific. That is, the moral rules do not apply beyond some known and finite boundary—the clan, the parish, an alliance of parishes, or perhaps at most a language group. K. E. Read (1954-5) has made by far the most cogent and penetrating analysis of this aspect of tribal morality. Although he is speaking only of the Gahuku-Gama, his remarks would apply to all known peoples in New Guinea prior to European contact: 'We may note, however, that people do not assert that "it is wrong to kill," or that "it is right to love everyone," while of the other universal commands of Christianity a large number are conspicuously absent. The Gahuku-Gama, for example, do not say that one should practise forbearance in all circumstances; indeed, their injunctions against adultery, against

lying, thieving and slander should not be accepted as applying to all the situations in which the individual may find himself. There is nothing unusual in this. It is simply another way of saying that we are dealing with a tribal morality as distinct from the universal morality of Christian teaching. In other words, Gahuku-Gama assertions of what is right or wrong, good or bad, are not intended to apply to all men; they are stated from the position of a particular collectivity outside of which the moral norm ceases to have any meaning'.

Still another universal feature is that moral rules are not abstracted from their social context or their locus in the system. The people themselves do not think of a category morality as opposed to other aspects of behaviour. They have thus no theology and no ethics, if we restrict this latter term to its strictly philosophical meaning. The moral rules are simply part of social life itself as are the accompanying sanctions.

Retaliation, group identification, self-regulation, and quasi-legal sanctions are, of course, merely convenient categories for outlining different mechanisms working to ensure conformity with moral, and other, rules. No society exhibits only one of these, and, indeed, it is likely that their presence and mixture in all societies of New Guinea is a further universal feature of their moral systems.

R. M. Berndt, *Excess and Restraint*. Chicago, 1962.
———— 'The Kamano, Usurufa, Jate and Fore of the Eastern Highlands', in *Gods Ghosts and Men in Melanesia*, ed. P. Lawrence and M. J. Meggitt. Melbourne, 1965.
K. O. L. Burridge, 'Tangu, Northern Madang District', in *Gods Ghosts and Men in Melanesia*, ed. P. Lawrence and M. J. Meggitt. Melbourne, 1965.
R. M. Glasse, 'Revenge and Redress among the Huli', *Mankind*, vol. 5, 1954-62.
———— 'The Huli of the Southern Highlands', in *Gods Ghosts and Men in Melanesia*, ed. P. Lawrence and M. J. Meggitt. Melbourne, 1965.
H I. Hogbin, 'Social Reaction to Crime', *Journal of the Royal Anthropological Institute*, vol. 68, 1938.
———— 'Shame: A Study of Social Conformity in a New Guinea Village', *Oceania*, vol. 17, 1946-7.
———— *Kinship and Marriage in a New Guinea Village*. London, 1963.
———— *The Island of Menstruating Men: Religion in Wogeo*. San Francisco, 1970.
P. M. Kaberry, 'Law and Political Organization in the Abelam Tribe, New Guinea', *Oceania*, vol. 12, 1941-2.
L. L. Langness, 'Sexual Antagonism in the New Guinea Highlands', *Oceania*, vol. 37, 1966-7.
P. Lawrence and M. J. Meggitt, 'Introduction', to *Gods Ghosts and Men in Melanesia*. Melbourne, 1965.
M. Mead, *Growing Up in New Guinea*. New York, 1930.
———— 'The Manus of the Admiralty Islands', in *Co-operation and Competition among Primitive Peoples*, ed. M. Mead. New York, 1937.
M. J. Meggitt, 'Male-Female Relationships in the Highlands of Australian New Guinea', *American Anthropologist*, vol. 66, Special Publication, 1964.
———— 'The Mae Enga of the Western Highlands', in

Gods Ghosts and Men in Melanesia, ed. P. Lawrence and M. J. Meggitt. Melbourne, 1965.

S. F. Nadel, 'Social Control and Self-Regulation', *Social Forces*, vol. 31, 1952-3.

P. L. Newman, *Knowing the Gururumba*. New York, 1965.

G. Piers and M. B. Singer, *Shame and Guilt: A Psychoanalytic and a Cultural Study*. Springfield, Ill., 1953.

K. E. Read, 'Morality and the Concept of the Person among the Gahuku-Gama', *Oceania*, vol. 25, 1954-5.

────── 'Leadership and Consensus in a New Guinea Society', *American Anthropologist*, vol. 61, 1959.

M. Reay, 'Social Control amongst the Orokaiva', *Oceania*, vol. 24, 1953-4.

M. Spiro, 'Social Systems, Personality and Functional Analysis', in *Studying Personality Cross-Culturally*, ed. B. Kaplan. Evanston, Ill., 1961.

R. Wagner, *The Curse of Souw*. Chicago, 1968.

F. E. Williams, 'Group Sentiment and Primitive Justice', *American Anthropologist*, vol. 43, 1941.

                                                    L. L. LANGNESS

ETHNOBOTANY. This may be defined as the study of the interrelationships between plants and man. As Barrau (1966) indicated, changes in the interpretation of the word have occurred since it was coined in 1895. The earlier reference was to the distribution and dispersal of species and their uses by prehistoric or aboriginal populations. The present application of ethnobotany to contemporary indigenous peoples has been occasioned by the realization of the role plants play in social organization and behaviour.

The geographic diversity of New Guinea provides a fertile field for investigation. Most of the inhabitants are subsistence agriculturalists, and many of the cultivated plants come from elsewhere, as do the people themselves. The region therefore affords unique opportunities for the study of the adaptation of man and plants over some sharply contrasting environments. The modification of these environments by agriculture means technological advancement. This is on a modest scale in comparison with what has been attained by other civilizations but is of high significance in places marginal for agriculture, such as the coastal saline swamps and the higher areas up to 9,000 feet.

MODIFICATION OF THE NATURAL ENVIRONMENT

S. Bulmer cited archaeological evidence for the occupation of the Highlands before 8000 B.C. The settlement of some coastal areas and offshore islands must have been even earlier. With the coming of man the artificial change of the environment began. Thus, taking the sequence of cultural phases proposed for Highlands prehistory by S. and R. Bulmer, the first settlers were palaeolithic hunters and gatherers who probably did not much alter their surroundings. In the second phase, *c.* 4-3000 B.C., the artefact yield indicates agriculture and a more significant effect on the flora; and in the third phase the tools were

elaborated, and hence agricultural development must have continued, resulting in further effects on the wild plants. The recent investigations of ecologists, using pollen analysis, of the possible floristic sequences in the Highlands may well elucidate the nature and times of significant changes in both eastern and western areas of the Territory of Papua and New Guinea. That signs of human intervention will be forthcoming can be confidently forecast; the direct evidence of substitution of cultivated plants from outside for the wild flora through the identification of the actual species may not be so likely, for most of the staples produce few flowers to yield pollen deposition. On the other hand, some of the native plants originally wild and now cultivated do have more flowers.

Another ecological approach to the problem of the influence of man has been the use of survey techniques of the composition of current vegetation (Robbins, 1960, 1963). Grasslands occur up to the highest areas of occupation. Gardening after clearing the original rain forest may produce tall grassland with immigrant shrub species, succeeded by short grassland, generally unused for cultivation. Such sequences, together with certain ethnological evidence, has led to the view that the main settlement of the Highlands was from east to west. The theory has, however, been questioned, and Robbins (1963) suggested other routes following the great river systems.

If the early Austronesians came from the Asian mainland, as is generally agreed, allowance must be made for an hypothesis of early modification of New Guinea environments. In a recent review of the prehistory of Formosa Chang and Stuiver demonstrated that an agriculture based on tree and root crops probably existed as long ago as 9000 B.C. It is an open question whether the earlier settlers brought to New Guinea the idea of a shifting slash-and-burn agriculture based on root crops not native to the area but growing spontaneously, with supplementary hunting and gathering of local resources. If so, the process of degrading the local flora must have begun soon after the arrival of these immigrants.

USE OF THE NATURAL FLORA

Many ethnographers have recorded the use of native plants in diet, ritual, and medicine. Barrau (1958) listed coastal and montane herbaceous and arboreal species that yield food in the form of seeds, fruits, inflorescences, and vegetative parts. In the swampy coastal areas a new type of agriculture based on endemic species of the sago palm may have evolved, and Keleny has suggested that the earliest Highlands economy may have been based on gathering the nuts of mountain *Pandanus*. Even if the first human penetration of the Highlands brought in new species for cultivation and rudimentary techniques, a possibility not eliminated by S. and R. Bulmer, the largest plant contribution to the food supply was most likely to have been gathered. This, for smaller populations, would have allowed for an experimental stage in agricultural development in strange but productive surroundings.

According to Lawrence and Meggitt the ritual connotations of wild plants appear to be unimportant. In most plant cults, especially among coastal and island peoples, the emphasis is on the main crop, either yam or taro. Few identifications of wild plants or inquiries about their special significance in ceremonial have been made. Likewise, not much material is available on the native pharmacopoeia, although Webb (1955) provided chemical information of extracts from wild plants in a survey of flora. He subsequently (1959) collected information, over a wide area of New Guinea and Queensland, on native uses of plants as abortifacients, contraceptives, and febrifuges and in the alleviation of skin lesions, muscle pains, dysentery, snake bite, and colds. The plants are mostly native, though a few introduced species are included.

ORIGINS OF THE INTRODUCED CULTIVATED PLANTS

Most of the staple food plants came from outside the New Guinea area, but there are some notable exceptions. The starch-producing staple of the coastal swamp-dwellers is the *Metroxylon* sago palm, with specific forms, *M. sagus, M. rumphii,* though other wild forms of the *Eumetroxylon* section of the family, as well as the *Coelococcus,* are represented in New Guinea and New Britain (Barrau, 1959). The concentration of different species in the area and the divergence of species to the east, together with the possibility that the palm was transported to the fringes of the Highlands (S. and R. Bulmer) suggest local domestication. Barrau's statement (1958) about the Marind Anim is relevant here. These people say they transfer from the forest to the village any thornless sago seedlings found among the thorny sago palms.

Malaysia is the place of origin of the banana, *Musa* spp., which spread west to India and east to New Guinea. Of the two cultivated groups, *Eumusa* and *Australimusa,* the latter is regarded as the product of parallel independent evolution centralized in the Moluccas, New Guinea, and the Solomons. Simmonds stated that the wild *Australimusa* species *M. maclayi,* a native of New Guinea, is significant in the evolution of the form found in Polynesia, known locally as *fe'i.*

One of the most important Pacific contributions to modern agriculture is the sugar-cane, *Saccharum officinarum,* which is not only the basis of the early varieties of pan-tropic adaptation but according to Warner is a parental contributor, along with *S. barberi* and two wild species found in New Guinea, *S. spontaneum* and *S. robustum,* in many varieties of modern commerce. The theory, if proven, that *S. barberi* and another form widely cultivated in Asia, *S. sinense,* are prehistoric derivatives of *S. officinarum* and a related species, probably *S. spontaneum* (Artschwager and Brandes), would add strength to the claims of New Guinea as a nuclear area for the sugar-

producing canes. The range of adaptation of the native forms of *S. officinarum* in New Guinea is unmatched elsewhere. Plants are found in gardens as high as 7,000 feet above sea-level.

The least known of the cultivated plants are the green vegetables. They are often cooked with wild grass. Barrau (1958) gave the most comprehensive list. Among those with south-east Asian affinities but not known to have been introduced in recent times are species of *Hibiscus, Amaranthus, Psophocarpus,* and *Setaria.* There is a wild form of the last species, *S. palmifolia,* suggesting that the domestication was effected in New Guinea. Another example of possible domestication is *Saccharum edule,* valued for its unopened flower. This species is used in Fiji, and was described by Parham as almost certainly an aboriginal introduction. A member of the Acanthaceae family, *Rungia klossii,* is recorded through most of the Highlands areas, including West Irian, as a common green-leaf vegetable. It appears as a wild plant in many wooded areas, where it may be a natural form or a garden escape.

These examples of likely domestication in New Guinea are significant. With the exception of the sago and the banana, they are not used as basic foods. If the plants were not domesticated in a period when the main subsistence was provided by hunting, they must have been accompanied by some staple yielding a bulk food, probably starch; if they were, then we have to think of an agriculture initiated by the domestication of low-energy food plants, and the subsequent introduction of tuberous crops. It is notable that all these species are vegetative in reproduction, as are the root crops; and in all cases except *Psophocarpus* this is the method used in cultivation.

The staples other than sago and banana are root crops of genera distributed throughout the Pacific—yams, taro, and sweet potato. The first two are Asiatic in origin. Several species of yams are represented in New Guinea, such as *Dioscorea alata, D. esculenta, D. bulbifera, D. pentaphylla, D. nummularia,* and *D. hispida.* While all may be seen in native gardens, the first two are the most common. Forms of *D. alata* are the subject of competition and ceremonial in many parts of New Guinea. *D. esculenta* appears to be more adaptable to varying environments and is cultivated at levels up to 4,000 feet. Some of the varieties grown at higher elevations (Meggitt) have not been identified. Taro, *Colocasia esculenta,* is cultivated at levels up to 7,000 feet. There are numerous varieties. Yams and taro provide the chief food in a few areas in the Highlands, including Telefomin (Brookfield) and the country in the east occupied by the Awa, but elsewhere the staple is sweet potato, *Ipomoea batatas.* This plant is of American origin. Its introduction to the Pacific has been attributed to Spanish and Portuguese voyages to the East Indies during the sixteenth century.

Watson (1964), from his experience in the eastern Highlands, put forward the hypothesis that the leguminous root plant *Pueraria lobata* was formerly the dominant crop throughout the

entire Highlands region. Bowers (1964) also recorded its cultivation in the Kaugel Valley in the
west and also among the Buang of the Snake
Valley, Morobe District. Barrau (1965) reviewed
the literature on the origin of the plant. Its distribution in India, the Philippines, China, and Japan
places it as probably Asiatic. The uncertainty of
some identifications and the lack of agronomic
information make speculation on its antiquity in
New Guinea futile. The same applies to some
plants of the Asian aroid family, *Amorphophallus
campanulatus* and *Cyrtosperma chamissonis*,
found growing in coastal areas in most of Melanesia, and *Alocasia macrorrhiza*, a species that
grows up to at least 7,000 feet. Generally these
are untended, but here and there they may be
cared for in established cultivations.

The *Cordyline terminalis*, *tangket* [q.v.] in Pidgin English, produces a large edible tuber seldom
used in New Guinea, although a few peoples are
aware of its potential. The plant is conspicuous
everywhere. It has ornamental value and serves
as a border marker. The leaves are also used for
personal decoration, as food wrappings, and for
ceremonial purposes. Possible medicinal qualities
are not recognized. The wide range of morphological variation of the species in the eastern
Highlands suggested to Ridley that the plant
might be native to New Guinea.

There is also a group of plants that may be
termed semi-domesticated in the sense that
although they mostly grow wild they may also
be cultivated. Included are the fibre-bearing
species of *Ruellia*, *Broussonetia*, the condiment
ginger *Zingiber* (a common ingredient in magic),
and the *Pandanus*. On the coast the leaves of the
last provide material for thatch, mats, and canoe
sails; in the areas of middle altitude the fruit of
P. conoideus is prized; and higher up the nuts of
P. guillianettii and *P. brosimos*.

The origin of two other important plants, the
coconut *Cocos nucifera*, which grows everywhere
on the coast and in the lower river valleys, and
the bottle gourd *Lagenaria siceraria*, used widely
as a water vessel and a penis cover, is unknown.

The speed with which foreign plants of recent
introduction can become part of the local agricultural scene is indicated by the number of those
of American origin now visible in native gardens.
They include maize *Zea mays*, tobacco *Nicotiana*
spp., *Xanthosoma* spp., and the *Solanum* potato.
The identification of tobacco with native cultivation has been so complete that Merrill (1946) was
moved to rebut assertions of the independent New
Guinea origin of the species.

The bulk of the foreign plants cultivated in
New Guinea support the common view that the
inhabitants and their basic cultural materials came
from Asia. But allowance must be made for some
movement during prehistoric times in the opposite
direction. Warner showed that sugar-cane was
recognized in India from the time of Alexander
the Great, and its cultivation in Persia and south
China can be dated at least as early as A.D. 600
and A.D. 200 respectively. Its presence in Polynesia in the eighteenth century, when Europeans

first reported it, indicated a prehistoric transfer
in the opposite direction. The *Cordyline* may
prove to have travelled along similar pathways.

AGRICULTURAL METHODS

Brookfield, in discussing contemporary types of
cultivation, associated the degree of technical
elaboration with ecological factors. The range is
from simple slash-and-burn clearing with periods
of fallow, through complete digging over with or
without drainage or mounding, to erosion-control
practices, the creation of permanent banks or
walls, crop fertilization, and the controlled grazing and feeding of livestock. Concentrating on the
Highlands, he picked out the three areas of
highest population density (those of the Chimbu,
Enga, and Dani) as the centres from which agricultural techniques spread. But there must also
have been local developments in response to
special environments. Bowers (1965) pointed out
that the correlates suggested did not apply in the
high-rainfall and low-seasonality area of the
Kaugel Valley, Hagen, and Chimbu. She regarded
the mounding technique of the Kaugel as a
superior method of cultivation to gridiron-ditching
drainage and hence thought the technique must
have moved eastwards from there. Knowledge of
the distribution of such practices is still far from
complete.

Highlands cultures may also have been influenced from the coast. The presence of marine
shells in a site in the eastern Highlands during the
earliest and also the latest phases of human occupation clearly indicates continuous trade with
peoples living near the sea (S. and R. Bulmer).
Immigrant plants such as the tobacco and sweet
potato, and also improved agricultural methods,
may have travelled in the same direction. Certainly there are a number of lowland peoples who
practise elaborate techniques, including the Abelam of the Sepik (Lea) and the Frederik Hen-
drik Islanders, with their composting, raising of
artificial islands, and crop rotation (Serpenti).

AGRICULTURAL SYSTEMS

Few contemporary agricultural systems of New
Guinea have been studied intensively. From such
data as are available it may be concluded that
lowland regions exhibit three broad forms of subsistence with several sub-types:
1. Essentially gathering economies, common
among swamp-dwellers, with technological development in the preparation of starch from the
sago palm. The people exploit the stands of palms
in a cyclic manner. They nurture both the vegetative shoots from cut trees and also the wild and
planted seedlings. Barrau (1959) estimated the
interval between propagation and cutting the palm
at eight to fifteen years. This provides a cycle
similar to that of the shifting agriculturalists with
their eight to fifteen years of fallow. The
economics of these groups are little known, but
the fact that the people survive in such an inhospitable environment suggests some depth of horticultural knowledge.

2. Shifting cultivation, with clearing usually by fire. Several methods of soil preparation are practised, from the rudimentary (including simple hole planting) to the building of small mounds and complete digging over the garden area. Shallow drainage may be a feature. The duration of the fallow period tends to follow a formal cycle determined by the rate of growth of the secondary forest.

3. Shifting cultivation but with partial dependence also on permanent or semi-permanent garden areas. The proportions of the more intensive cultivation vary but are characterized by modified or artificial soils built up with composting. Earthworks, whether by the heaping up of mounds or the excavation of drains, are more comprehensive. The pattern is of crop rotation, with considerable reshaping of the ground before each replanting.

Only a few of such systems in areas of low altitude have been described. Representative of the second type are the Trobriands (Malinowski) [qq.v.] and the Abelam (Lea) and of the third the Kiman (Serpenti).

In the Highlands, although gathering, hunting and fishing are practised, nowhere is the economy of the purely gathering type. The planting of perennial trees like *Pandanus* and *Casuarina* may be comparatively recent practice, although with the ability of both genera to undergo vegetative propagation, there is no reason to exclude the possibility of such practices in earlier agricultural patterns. Commonly the systems fit into types 2 or 3 and thus resemble categories of Philippine shifting agriculture that Conklin called 'integral and partial'. It is tempting to apply some form of simple ecological correlation, such as the association of shifting cultivation with slope. The Maring (Rappaport), occupying a hilly terrain with no cultivable flats, are exclusively shifting cultivators; and the Kakoli (Bowers, 1965) use shifting techniques on slopes, independent of altitude, and semi-permanent techniques on the flat areas of the Kaugel river-bed. The Chimbu, however, practise shifting agriculture on both flats and slopes (Brookfield and Brown).

In New Guinea and the Solomon Islands, in contrast with Indonesia and eastern Melanesia, there is no evidence, past or present, of agricultural terracing. Complex irrigation and drainage in New Caledonia, with ridge and valley development (Barrau, 1956), may be a reflection of isolation from New Guinea; but perhaps the ecological necessity did not arise in other places. The relative immobility of agricultural systems incorporating irrigation contrasts with the highest technical levels of attainment noted by Brookfield in the Baliem Valley. These may be regarded as semi-permanent or long rotational only. The extensive grasslands on the river flats above and below the areas of cultivation show definite signs of former gardening.

SWEET POTATO IN NEW GUINEA AGRICULTURE

The comparatively recent arrival of the sweet potato and its wide use, especially in the Highlands, led Keleny and others to speculate about the demographic effects. Watson (1965a) took the argument further and suggested major changes in agricultural patterns and in social institutions, such as the development of large-scale warfare. But his hypothesis remains unproven. The other crops have had a long history, and, besides, these are also adaptable to variation in environment, with lower yields at higher elevations. The ritual connected with taro and yam as reported by R. Bulmer for the Karam, Reay for the Kuma, and Malinowski for the Trobriand Islanders is not matched with anything comparable for the sweet potato, although Reay has described the associations between this crop and the ideas about disease. The taro and the cultivated yam are not naturalized in the Highlands and are unlikely to have survived without cultivation. They are true domesticates, unfitted for exploitation by gatherers or casual itinerant planters. The cultivators must therefore have been already sedentary.

This does not mean that the introduction of the sweet potato was without quantitative effects. Its superior yield and the ease with which it can be cultivated must have allowed of greater production at lower levels and an extension of the areas under cropping at levels higher than 5,000 feet. An increase in population was thus probable. Further, the suitability of the sweet potato as feed for animals would have been early recognized, with the result that the pig herds could have been expanded. At present archaeological investigation has been largely confined to the excavation of early rock shelters, which S. and R. Bulmer have found reveal few pig remains. When research is extended to the later building sites a sudden rise in the number of pig bones may well be indicative of the approximate date of the arrival of the sweet potato (*see* PREHISTORY).

E. Artschwager and E. W. Brandes, *Sugar Cane*. U.S. Department of Agriculture, Agricultural Handbook 122. Washington, 1958.
J. Barrau, *L'Agriculture Vivrière Autochtone de la Nouvelle-Calédonie*. South Pacific Commission, Technical Paper no. 87. Noumea, 1956.
—— *Subsistence Agriculture in Melanesia*. Honolulu, 1958.
—— 'The Sago Palms and Other Food Plants of Marsh Dwellers in the South Pacific Islands', *Economic Botany*, vol. 13, 1959.
—— 'Witnesses of the Past: Notes on Some Food Plants of Oceania', *Ethnology*, vol. 4, 1965.
—— An Ethnobotanical Guide for Anthropological Research in Malayo-Oceania. UNESCO Science Corporation Office for Southeast Asia, Preliminary Draft, 1966 (mimeographed).
N. Bowers, 'A Further Note on a Recently Reported Root Crop from the New Guinea Highlands', *Journal of the Polynesian Society*, vol. 73, 1964.
—— 'Agricultural Practices and Successional Vegetation in the Upper Kaugel Valley, Western Highlands, Australian New Guinea', paper read at Northwestern University Anthropological Conference, held at Evanston, Ill., 1965 (mimeographed).
H. C. Brookfield, 'Local Study and Comparative Method: An Example from Central New Guinea', *Annals of the Association of American Geographers*, vol. 52, 1962.

———— and P. Brown, *Struggle for Land*. Melbourne, 1963.

R. N. H. Bulmer, 'Why is the Cassowary not a Bird? A Problem of Zoological Taxonomy among the Karam of the New Guinea Highlands', *Man*, new series, vol. 2, 1967.

S. Bulmer, 'Radiocarbon Dates from New Guinea', *Journal of the Polynesian Society*, vol. 73, 1964.

———— and R. N. H. Bulmer, 'The Prehistory of the Australian New Guinea Highlands', *American Anthropologist*, vol. 66, Special Publication, 1964.

I. F. Champion, *Across New Guinea from the Fly to the Sepik*. London, 1932.

K. C. Chang and M. Stuiver, 'Recent Advances in the Prehistoric Archaeology of Formosa', *Proceedings of the National Academy of Sciences*, vol. 55, 1966.

H. C. Conklin, *Hanunoo Agriculture in the Philippines*. F.A.O., Forestry Development Paper no. 12. Rome, 1957.

C. D. Darlington and A. P. Wylie, *Chromosome Atlas of Flowering Plants*. 2nd ed., London, 1955.

I. Dyen, *A Lexicostatistical Classification of the Austronesian Languages*. Supplement to *International Journal of American Linguistics*, vol. 31, 1965.

J. Golson, R. J. Lampert, J. M. Wheeler and W. R. Ambrose, 'A Note on Carbon Dates for Horticulture in the New Guinea Highlands', *Journal of the Polynesian Society*, vol. 76, 1967.

H. I. Hogbin, 'Tillage and Collection: a New Guinea Economy', *Oceania*, vol. 9, 1938-9.

———— *Transformation Scene*. London, 1951.

G. P. Keleny, 'Notes on the Origin and Introduction of the Basic Food Crops of the New Guinea People', paper read at Symposium on the Impact of Man on Humid Tropics Vegetation, held at Goroka, T. P. N. G. 1960. Canberra, 1960.

P. Lawrence and M. J. Meggitt (eds), *Gods Ghosts and Men in Melanesia*. Melbourne, 1965.

D. A. M. Lea, 'The Abelam: A Study in Local Differentiation', *Pacific Viewpoint*, vol. 6, 1965.

B. Malinowski, *Coral Gardens and their Magic*. 2 vols, London, 1965.

M. J. Meggitt, 'The Enga of the New Guinea Highlands', *Oceania*, vol. 28, 1957-8.

E. D. Merrill, 'Further Notes on Tobacco in New Guinea', *American Anthropologist*, vol. 48, 1946.

———— 'The Botany of Cook's Voyages', *Chronica Botanica*, vol. 14, 1954.

Great Britain, Naval Intelligence Division, *Pacific Islands*, vol. 4. London, 1945 (Geographical Handbook Series).

J. W. Parham, *Plants of the Fiji Islands*. Suva, 1964.

L. Pospisil, *Kapauku Papuan Economy*. New Haven, 1963.

R. A. Rappaport, 'Ritual Regulation of Environmental Relations among a New Guinea People', *Ethnology*, vol. 6, 1967.

M. Reay, *The Kuma*. Melbourne, 1959.

H. N. Ridley, *The Flora of the Malay Peninsula*, vol. 4. London, 1924.

A. Riesenfeld, 'Tobacco in New Guinea and the Other Areas of Melanesia', *Journal of the Royal Anthropological Institute*, vol. 81, 1951.

R. G. Robbins, 'The Anthropogenic Grasslands of Papua and New Guinea', paper read at Symposium on the Impact of Man on Humid Tropics Vegetation, held at Goroka, T. P. N. G. 1960. Canberra, 1960.

———— 'Correlation of Plant Patterns and Population Migration into the Australian New Guinea Highlands', in *Plants and the Migrations of Pacific Peoples*, ed. J. Barrau. Honolulu, 1963.

L. M. Serpenti, *Cultivators in the Swamps*. Assen, 1965.

N. W. Simmonds, *The Evolution of the Banana*. London, 1962.

W. C. Sturtevant, 'Studies in Ethnoscience', *American Anthropologist*, vol. 66, Special Publication, 1964.

J. N. Warner, 'Sugar Cane: An Indigenous Papuan Cultigen', *Ethnology*, vol. 1, 1962.

J. B. Watson, 'A Previously Unreported Root Crop from the New Guinea Highlands', *Ethnology*, vol. 3, 1964.

———— 'From Hunting to Horticulture in the New Guinea Highlands', *Ethnology*, vol. 4, 1965a.

———— 'The Significance of a Recent Ecological Change in the Central Highlands of New Guinea', *Journal of the Polynesian Society*, vol. 74, 1965b.

L. J. Webb, 'A Preliminary Phytochemical Survey of Papua-New Guinea', *Pacific Science*, vol. 9, 1955.

———— 'Some New Records of Medicinal Plants Used by the Aborigines of Tropical Queensland and New Guinea', *Proceedings of the Royal Society of Queensland*, vol. 71, 1959.

D. E. Yen and J. M. Wheeler, 'Introduction of Taro into the Pacific', *Ethnology*, vol. 8, 1968.

D. E. YEN

(*See also* AGRICULTURE, INDIGENOUS)

EXHIBITIONS AND TRADE FAIRS.

During the past few years the value of exports from the Territory of Papua and New Guinea has more than doubled, increasing from $33 million in 1960-1 to over $70 million in 1967-8. A further increase in the value of exports is expected to result from new plantings of cash crops as part of the current five-year development programme. New markets have to be found for the rapidly increasing exports, and existing markets must be expanded. The Administration has participated in trade fairs and displays in countries which are already importing Territory products and which offer favourable opportunities for increased penetration of the market, as well as in areas which do not at present import from the Territory but which, according to market studies, could well become important buyers. Trade fairs and exhibitions provide a convenient and effective means of contacting trade circles in these market areas and of drawing attention to the availability of export commodities.

The displays are arranged with the assistance of the Department of External Territories. In recent years the Territory participated in a number of fairs and exhibitions, e.g. the A.N.U.G.A. (Allgemeine Nahrungs- und Genussmittel Ausstellung) Food Fair at Cologne in 1964; the Australian Trade Displays at Milan in 1965 and 1966, and Los Angeles in 1967; the S.I.A.L. (Salon International de l'Alimentation) Food Fair at Paris in 1966; the International Trade Fairs or Australian Trade Displays at Osaka and Tokyo in 1964, 1965, 1967 and 1968; the Sydney International Trade Fair in 1965 and 1967; and in 1968, the Queensland Industries Fair at Brisbane, the International Consumer Goods Fair at Melbourne and the Australian Trade Display at Stockholm. During 1969 the Territory was represented at the Australian Trade Displays in San

Francisco and Vancouver, and at the International Trade Fair in Sydney.

The stand at trade fairs and displays is usually built of timbers from the Territory and is itself an exhibit of an important export commodity. Most stands have a coffee bar, where free cups of New Guinea coffee are served. Most of the Territory's export commodities, such as coffee, cocoa, tea, timber, plywood, pyrethrum, palm oil, rubber, copra and other coconut products, are featured. Tourist attractions, artefacts, and other handicrafts are also shown, and add colour and interest to the exhibit.

The displays are usually staffed by at least one Administration officer with a wide knowledge of the Territory and its products. Trade inquiries are recorded and referred to exporters' and producers' organizations.

Participation in trade fairs and exhibitions is an important part of the Territory's trade promotion programme, facilitating contacts with the trade in importing countries.

(*See also* OVERSEAS TRADE)

EXPLORATION. Few countries offer such obstacles to the explorer as does New Guinea. The hazards of swamp, jungle, high mountains, tropical diseases, dearth of food and the hostility of the native inhabitants made the effective penetration of the main island in particular a slow and painful process. The most striking explorations have been the achievements of intrepid individuals or small parties, though some ambitious expeditions were conducted with large scientific staffs and equipment, especially in German times (*see* GERMAN NEW GUINEA). Some pioneering journeys by private individuals, often mining prospectors, have never been fully recorded. Even now it cannot be said that New Guinea has been explored in detail on the ground although through the use of aerial surveys no part remains wholly unknown.

The navigators who sailed the coasts of the island of New Guinea had limited contacts with coastal peoples (*see* DISCOVERY) but the exploration of the interior, apparently filled with high mountain ranges, only began in the late nineteenth century. Nicolai Miklouho-Maclay [q.v.], a Russian biologist who stayed at Astrolabe Bay in north-east New Guinea in 1871, walked in the mountains behind the Rai Coast and the Finisterre Range, and one of the first London Missionary Society men, James Chalmers [q.v.], visited the south-eastern coast, but the interior was still an unknown place where literary fantasies could be set by authors like Captain Lawson and Louis Trégance. The real penetration inland began with journeys up the Fly River in western Papua, especially the journeys of London Missionary Society parties and then the Italian Luigi d'Albertis [q.v.]. The Rev. Samuel MacFarlane had gone 150 miles up the Fly; d'Albertis looked for its source in 1876, penetrating by his own extravagant estimate 580 miles along the river and its tributary the Palmer. He

tried again in 1877, but broke no new ground, missing the junction of the Strickland and the opportunity to travel up that great river; nor was his exploration quickly followed up. A Dutch vessel sailed 50 miles up the Mamberamo River in 1884 and in the following year Dr Otto Finsch [q.v.] sailed 30 miles up the Sepik River in German New Guinea [q.v.] from the north coast of the island. The Rev. James Chalmers walked into the country behind Port Moresby. But the interior of the island was still largely blank on the map.

In 1883 the Melbourne newspapers the *Age* and the *Argus* both sent expeditions. The former, organized by G. E. (Chinese) Morrison [q.v.] went from Port Moresby towards the Goldie River, a tributary of the Laloki, but was stopped by native hostility; the latter, led by Captain W. E. Armit, set off for the Astrolabe Range from Port Moresby. Neither got more than forty miles inland, and both failed to reach the foot of the Owen Stanley Range; although H. O. Forbes in 1886 tried to go inland and Cuthbertson in 1887 climbed Mt Obree, it was left to Sir William MacGregor [q.v.] to make an effective start upon the exploration of the mountains of the interior.

BRITISH NEW GUINEA

Exploration was a major part of MacGregor's work in British New Guinea from 1888 to 1898. He thought it was essential for efficient rule to locate and count as many as possible of Britain's new Papuan subjects. In contrast with the Germans in the north, who tended to concentrate control over the areas around coastal stations, MacGregor believed government exploration should cover as much of the territory as was practicable. Hence his patrols went far beyond the areas which he could hope to administer in detail with his limited field staff.

Most exploration was carried out by MacGregor himself, and he severely restricted private expeditions. He wanted to supervise contacts between Europeans and Papuans and particularly distrusted explorers entering new areas. He knew he had too few government officers to protect explorers from attacks by Papuans, especially considering the difficulties caused in the eastern end of the colony by the recruiting in the early 1880s of Papuans to work on Queensland sugar plantations. The return by the Queensland government of some of these men in 1885 had not ended the hostility. MacGregor declared several areas to be 'unsafe', closed to all Europeans. Protests came from private explorers such as Theodore Bevan [q.v.]. These restrictions were progressively relaxed, and Bevan later explored the mouths and courses of the Aird, Purari and surrounding rivers in the Gulf of Papua. The Royal Geographical Society and learned societies of Australia also conducted some expeditions in the territory.

MacGregor went up all the important rivers, reached the central mountain chain and climbed its major peaks, crossed British New Guinea twice, and explored many of the islands off shore.

He could not have hoped to control all the villages he contacted, and he spent time in uninhabited territory, such as the tops of some of the central mountains, so that his journeys were often adding to geographical knowledge rather than aiding the expansion of government.

MacGregor's longest river exploration was in 1890 up the Fly in a 37-foot steam launch. He travelled for 535 miles, further than d'Albertis, until his way was blocked by rapids. He then launched a whale-boat and proceeded another seventy miles until he was stopped by rocks. His attempt to reach on foot a range only six miles ahead was foiled by thick bush, fear of hostile natives, and thunderstorms. As the party had used most of their provisions they hoped for a rapid return journey. An engine breakdown five hundred miles from the Fly mouth was mended in a couple of hours and they swept straight past a hundred surprised warriors fully armed with bows and arrows and decked out in war dress.

MacGregor's ascent of the major rivers gave access to only part of the colony, and he was faced with the constant challenge of the mountain chain in the centre of the island. In 1889 he set out to climb one of the highest peaks, Mt Victoria. With a party of forty-two, including three other Europeans, he first ascended the Vanapa River. He had difficulty with his carriers but managed to persuade them to keep going. The party spent some days crossing the ridges in front of the high mountains. Eventually, after dropping to the head of the Vanapa, MacGregor moved on to the central ridge of the Owen Stanleys at 11,882 feet. His party then crossed the top of Mt Winter, 11,880 feet and Mt Douglas, 11,796 feet, and on to the final climb up Mt Victoria, reaching its north-west peak, 13,120 feet, on 11 June.

This was probably MacGregor's main purely exploratory journey. His two crossings of northeast Papua, in 1896 and 1897, were both associated with clashes between prospectors and Papuans, and more closely associated with the extension of government control. Likewise his journeys towards and over the boundary of Dutch New Guinea were to subdue raids made by the Tugeri people upon natives on the British side of the border, and to ensure peace in his colony.

Other exploration was carried out by some members of MacGregor's small staff. For example, John Green, who became the first government agent in the mountainous north-west, and C. A. W. Monckton [q.v.] who served in the Eastern and Northern Divisions. After MacGregor left New Guinea, Monckton was the officer most interested in exploration. In 1906 he climbed Mt Albert Edward; and later he went from Kokoda to the headwaters of the Waria, then over the central ranges and down the Lakekamu. His journeys were criticized by Hubert Murray [q.v.], who preferred consolidation of existing areas to exploratory expeditions. The work of MacGregor and of men like Monckton had, however, pioneered the way for later expansion.

MacGregor's expeditions were also significant in gathering scientific specimens. He collected many Papuan artefacts now in the Brisbane Museum, many plants sent to and identified by Baron Ferdinand von Mueller in Melbourne, as well as geological and other specimens. MacGregor sincerely believed that any administrator of New Guinea should explore, and said at the end of his term that he should leave because he was too old to climb mountains any more.

PAPUA

During Sir Hubert Murray's long term of office most of Papua was explored. In his early years, however, he had neither the desire, money nor men to encourage exploration. He discouraged Monckton's 1906-7 journey and disapproved even more of Staniforth Smith's [q.v.] abortive exploratory trip in 1910.

Smith, who became acting administrator while Murray was on leave, hoped to create a favourable impression by undertaking a large-scale journey to the west. He wanted to go beyond the limit reached by the prospectors, Little and Mackay, who had searched the Purari to locate the coal deposits reported by MacGregor. With four Europeans, twenty-five native police and fifty carriers Smith left Goaribari Island, travelled up the Kikori River, then went inland to Mt Murray. From this previously explored area he planned to cross the unexplored interior to the Strickland River. He discovered the Samberigi Valley before he became lost and eventually, after surviving the capsizing of the party's rafts, he circled back to the Kikori. Although Murray wrote that 'the expedition cannot be looked upon as otherwise than disastrous' Smith had penetrated some new territory, and so did the search parties under W. N. Beaver which went to look for him.

After 1912 Murray had more money available for exploration, and gradually many of the villagers near European centres, particularly in the Central Division, were contacted. In 1913 a patrol officer, Henry Ryan, continued Smith's exploration in the west. He left Kikori, travelled west rather than north as Smith had done, and crossed the headwaters of the Turama, Abavi and Wawe Rivers—surviving an attack although hit by four arrows—and then came down the Aworra River. Ryan did not reach the Strickland River, but, far more than Smith did, understood where he had been. Some of the significant patrols after Ryan's were those led by W. R. Humphries in 1917 linking Nepa on the Lakekamu River with Kerema in the south and Ioma on the Mambare River; and that led in 1917 by E. W. P. Chinnery [q.v.], who found the source of the Waria River; and another led in 1918 by R. W. Grist which explored the Goilala Valley near the German boundary. Murray himself was to cover a great deal of Papua on foot, his most important trip being a 200-mile journey in 1913 from Biatu, opposite Yule Island, through Mafulu and the Kambisi villages back to Port Moresby. This gradual extension of knowledge of the territory by patrol became typical of Papuan exploration. Murray's idea was 'to keep hammering away at the north-west corner of the

Territory until the country on our side was fairly
well known, and then to send a party to attempt
a crossing to the other [German] coast'. So from
the headwaters of the Fly patrols gradually penetrated further. In 1920 A. P. Lyons and L. Austen
searched for the murderers of two bird of paradise hunters in the neighbourhood of the Alice
River and the boundary of Dutch New Guinea.
In 1922 Austen and L. Logan further explored
the Alice area; in 1924 Austen and W. H. Thompson penetrated to the limestone ridges some six
hundred miles from the sea. Then in 1927-8, on
their second attempt, Ivan Champion [q.v.] and
C. Karius in four months crossed New Guinea
from the Fly to the Sepik in a nightmare journey.
The limestone barrier proved tremendously difficult to cross, and after they had passed it Champion injured his knee and had to be carried for
ten days.

This long journey linked the great rivers of the
west of the island but left large areas unexplored
further east. The land between the Strickland and
the Purari Rivers remained little known. Earlier
patrols had reached some way inland; for instance in 1922 L. Flint and H. M. Saunders had
penetrated into the Samberigi Valley and gone
on to the Erave River, while in 1929 Champion
and R. W. Faithorn had followed the Turama
and Erave Rivers before returning down the
Purari. Patrols in the 1930s were to go much
further.

The first important expedition was led by J. G.
Hides [q.v.] and L. J. O'Malley in 1935. They
followed the Strickland up into the southern
Highlands, returning eventually down the Purari
and Kikori. Hides found, as he described in
Papuan Wonderland, much difficulty with the
limestone; 'the rock is honeycombed . . . it forms
fissures and craters, large and small, and every
step has to be watched, for the limestone edges
are as sharp as broken glass'. Although he over-
estimated, at 250,000, the number of the grasslands population his journey had uncovered many
new British subjects. Relationships between Hides
and the Highlanders were bad, Hides shooting
frequently, alleging that he was often attacked.
Murray, although deploring the bloodshed, said
that no previous expedition had 'called for higher
qualities of leadership'.

The other major expeditions in this area were
led by Ivan Champion. His patrols were far more
peaceful than that led by Hides and caused no
loss of life. Champion, with Hides, flew over the
country first, and planned his land route. In 1936
Champion with C. J. Adamson went up the Bamu
and across the mountains to Lake Kutubu which
had been sighted from the air, then north-east-
ward to Mount Hagen before returning to the
Purari. In 1937 Champion, this time with F. G. W.
Andersen, established a base camp at Lake
Kutubu. When Murray visited this lake in 1938 he
boasted that 'the whole of Papua had been explored'. He was broadly correct, although post-war
patrols in Papua, notably by S. S. Smith and
D. Clancy, explored the unknown Southern Highlands region of Papua in the 1950s.

THE MANDATED TERRITORY

In 1914 the Australians took over from the Germans an area explored around the coastal centres
of German influence and along the major rivers.
The most dramatic discoveries of the period before World War II followed the finding of gold
and the penetration of the Highlands.

The Australian government in its first decade
made few attempts to extend its influence. In 1924
Ambunti station was opened which allowed for
extension of control over the middle Sepik area,
and there were some exploratory patrols in the
Morobe District.

Gold had been discovered before 1914 but not
until the 1920s were major strikes made. About
1922 William, 'Shark-eye', Park [q.v.] found rich
deposits on Koranga Creek off the Bulolo River
and other finds followed. In 1926 a rush to Edie
Creek followed a discovery by W. G. Royal. Soon
the new township of Wau became the centre of
the highly profitable industry dominated by companies such as New Guinea Goldfields Limited
which used the then revolutionary method of aerial
transport. Subsequent exploration was much facilitated by aerial sightings.

Prospectors continued searching for new fields
and made some finds mainly in the central unexplored area. N. Rowlands, for instance, found
payable gold on the upper Ramu River near Kainantu in 1930. The same year M. J. Leahy [q.v.]
and M. Dwyer crossed the island. They followed
the Markham River westward, crossed the Bismarck Range to the upper Ramu, then went
southwards over the boundary into Papua and on
to the Purari River. Such was the lack of geographical knowledge even at this comparatively
recent date that they did not know, as related in
The Land That Time Forgot, what river they had
been following. These men then recrossed the
island from Port Moresby and explored more of
the waterways, such as the Bena Bena River, of
the upper Purari system. Early in 1931 on another
of their prospecting trips for New Guinea Goldfields Limited they were attacked by Kukukuku
pygmies while in the country east of the upper
Purari. Another prospector, H. Baum, associated
with their exploration, was killed by the same
people nearby. Government exploration usually
followed prospecting trips. In 1933, after two
other prospectors had been killed, three patrols
were sent into the area, the leader of one of the
three, J. K. McCarthy, being wounded after arrest-
ing some of the suspected murderers. Missionaries
also were sometimes active ahead of the government; in 1927 a Lutheran, L. Flierl, ascended the
Asaro and Bena Bena Rivers into previously un-
penetrated territory.

Prospectors and government in combination
were to penetrate the Highlands. The Leahy
brothers, still financed by the same gold company,
built an airstrip at Bena Bena which was first used
at Christmas 1932 when the Assistant District
Officer at Salamaua, J. L. Taylor [q.v.] arrived.
Soon after it was decided that a joint party should
explore a valley seen from the mountains above.

In March 1933 Ian Grabowsky flew the Leahy brothers and the general manager of New Guinea Goldfields Limited over the new valley, and then in April the land patrol reached the Chimbu and Wahgi Valleys. After this initial penetration Taylor and the Leahys spent over three months exploring from a base camp at Mount Hagen. Taylor had begun the gradual process of bringing the inhabitants under Australian control. Patrol posts were set up in the 1930s at Kainantu, Bena Bena, Kundiawa, Gogme and Mount Hagen.

Missionaries soon followed the early explorations. The Roman Catholic mission at Alexishafen set up a station at Bundi, on the Ramu side of the Bismarck Range, and in October 1933 three missionaries of the Society of the Divine Word reached the Chimbu and Wahgi Valleys. By January 1934 the society had a station at Kundiawa, and later at Mount Hagen. The Lutherans followed and as mission stations increased so did knowledge of the Highlanders. Much of the exploration of New Guinea was done by isolated Europeans, whether patrol officers, prospectors, or missionaries, rather than by the first spectacular patrols.

Prospectors, although disappointed by the lack of gold in the Highlands, continued their search into the unknown country beyond. In 1933 M. J. Leahy, again with Taylor, went north from Mount Hagen around the Baiyer and Jimmi Rivers; later in 1933 and in 1934 the Leahy brothers went south from Mount Hagen into the area of the Nebilyer and Gauil Rivers; and in the latter year they went west from Mount Hagen to the Lai River. L. Schmidt went even further west into the unexplored territory towards the Sepik following the Jimmi, Yuat and the Maramuni Rivers. Schmidt was hanged in 1936 for the murder of four New Guineans during this journey. Later in 1934 the Ashton and McKee brothers walked from Lae to Kainantu, and explored to the south-west of this patrol post. In the same year the Fox brothers [q.v.] went west from Mount Hagen to Wabag, then to the Strickland River and, by their own account, well over the Dutch boundary, then back on a more southerly route in the north of Papua through the Tari Valley and Mt Giluwe. They were pessimistic about the area which held, they thought, 'not enough gold . . . to fill a tooth'.

Even if this report ended much of the prospecting hopes in the area the government still had the task of contacting all Highlanders. Another motive for exploration, scientific curiosity, was to incite further patrols into the unknown west. The ethnologist A. C. Haddon [q.v.], who had encouraged Hides' explorations in Papua, urged that all the area between longitudes 142° and 144° should be explored. In 1938 the New Guinea administration decided to examine the ten thousand square miles of mountainous country between Mount Hagen, the Papuan-Dutch borders, and the Sepik River. The expedition led by J. L. Taylor and J. Black was 'easily the largest, longest-lasting and best equipped ever mounted in New Guinea or Papua'. Three Europeans, twenty police and 230 carriers were on this Mount Hagen-Telefomin patrol which, aided by aircraft and wireless, was in the field for over fifteen months in 1938-9. Taylor's technique was to use 'existing tracks by making friendly contact with the people and using them as guides'.

After reaching Hoiyevia, near the Papuan border, Black divided the patrol into two; Black was to follow the southern side of the range and try to reach Telefomin, having to cross the limestone country of the Strickland River which had so nearly stopped Champion and Karius. Taylor was first to establish a radio camp and airstrip at Wabag and then to follow the northern side of the range to Telefomin along the Strickland and to pass through the Sepik watershed. Neither Black nor Taylor had an easy journey. Black was slow, particularly because of the limestone, while Taylor was almost drowned crossing the Logaiyu River, one of the headwaters of the Strickland, and he found it very difficult to cross the Victor Emanuel Range. After meeting at Telefomin the two men went on to the May River and then returned separately to Wabag. Black went through Telefomin, and the Strickland and Sepik watersheds, while Taylor went down the May to the Sepik where the government steamer took him to its mouth. He was then towed back to the headwaters of the Karawari, a tributary of the Sepik, from where his party walked for eight weeks through high mountains to Wabag. Taylor then went west again to Hoiyevia and recrossed the central range to meet Black, who was investigating reported gold discoveries, before both men finally returned to Mount Hagen.

This long patrol had covered much of the area previously uncontacted, though shorter patrols were to be needed for years to contact and control all villages. As in Papua no large blank space existed on the map of New Guinea at the outbreak of the Pacific war, but also, as in Papua, some hitherto unknown country was explored in detail by post-war patrols of officers such as J. P. Sinclair, chiefly in the Western Highlands.

British New Guinea, *Annual Report* 1884-5 to 1905-6.
Commonwealth of Australia, *Annual Report, Territory of Papua 1906-7* to *1939-40*. Melbourne and Canberra, 1908-41.
———— *Report to the League of Nations on the Administration of the Territory of New Guinea 1914-21* to *1939-40*. Melbourne and Canberra, 1922-41.
T. F. Bevan, *Toil, Travel, and Discovery in British New Guinea*. London, 1890.
I. F. Champion, *Across New Guinea from the Fly to the Sepik*. London, 1932.
J. G. Hides, *Papuan Wonderland*. London, 1936.
R. B. Joyce, *New Guinea*. Melbourne, 1960.
M. J. Leahy and M. Crain, *The Land that Time Forgot*. London, 1937.
W. MacGregor, *Diary*, 4 vols, 1890-2 (N.L.A.)
J. A. K. Mackay, *Across Papua*. London, 1909.
C. A. W. Monckton, *Some Experiences of a New Guinea Resident Magistrate*. London, 1921.
J. H. P. Murray, *Papua or British New Guinea*. London, 1912.
———— *Recent Exploration in Papua*. Sydney, 1923.
G. Pilhofer, 'Eine Durchquerung Neuguineas vom Waria-zum Markhamfluss', *Petermanns Mitteilungen*, vol. 61, 1915.
J. P. Sinclair, *Behind the Ranges*. Melbourne, 1966.

G. Souter, *New Guinea: The Last Unknown*. Sydney, 1963.

J. Strachan, *Explorations and Adventures in New Guinea*. London, 1888.

J. L. Taylor, 'Interim Report on the Hagen-Sepik Patrol, 1938-39', in 'Report to the League of Nations on the Administration of the Territory of New Guinea 1938-9', *C. P. P. 1940*, vol. 6.

———— Hagen-Sepik Patrol 1938-39 (roneoed; copy in Library of Papua and New Guinea; 194?).

J. P. Thomson, *British New Guinea*. London, 1892.

F. J. West, *Hubert Murray: The Australian Pro-Consul*. Melbourne, 1968.

R. B. JOYCE

(*See also* DUTCH NEW GUINEA)

EXPLORATION, BOTANICAL. In 1526 Portuguese mariners reached the shores of New Guinea. Botanical results from these very early contacts were meagre. Some 300 years after the first Portuguese, Zipelius participated in the expedition of the ship *Triton* to the coasts of southwest New Guinea. This was the only expedition made by Zipelius: he died in Koepang during the return voyage to Batavia. His extensive manuscripts and drawings have been published by C. L. Blume and also incorporated in the writings of F. A. W. Miquel and Spanoghe. It would appear that Zipelius as *the* pioneer plant collector of New Guinea has not been justly treated.

The latter years of the nineteenth century saw active botanical exploration of New Guinea emanating from the Dutch botanical centre at Buitenzorg. Teysmann visited western New Guinea and made extensive collections including the famed 'flame of the forest' (*Mucuna novoguineensis*). Beccari [q.v.] made three visits, in 1871, 1875 and 1876, exploring in particular the Arfak Mountains and Vogelkop peninsula. *Malesia*, a three-volume work, records his discoveries. By the turn of the century such was the interest of Dutch scientists in the natural history of the island that a journal, *Nova Guinea*, commenced publication to receive the results of the Dutch expeditions in the fields of ethnography, geography, zoology and botany. A long series of volumes in numerous parts appeared between 1909 and 1936. A new series which commenced publication in 1937 contains a conglomeration of papers on the natural science of New Guinea. In 1949 editorial policy and the membership of the board was revised so that the ensuing volumes contain either botanical, zoological, ethnographic or geological papers. With declining interest by Dutch scientists the series ceased publication in the early 1960s. Other journals such as *Blumea*, *Reinwardtia* and *Annales Bogoriense* cater for the continuing output of scientific botanical papers from Holland.

In north-east New Guinea German botanists from the late 1800s were exploring the coast and hinterland of Kaiser Wilhelmsland. They included U. M. Hollrung (1885-8), F. C. Hellwig (1888-9), C. Lauterbach (1896-9), G. Bamler (1898-9), F. R. R. Schlechter (1901-3, 1906-10), G. Peekel (1908-49) and Chr. Keysser (1909-19). To cope with the flood of writings emanating from the botanists who studied the many collections a series of papers, Beitrage zur Flora Papuasiens, commenced appearing under the editorship of C. Lauterbach and L. Diels in *Engler Botanische Jahrbucher*. Over 100 papers were published between the years 1912 and 1939.

World War II saw the loss of the main collections of plants from north-east New Guinea when the Berlin herbarium was bombed during 1943-5. Since then there has been only a small degree of interest in the plants of New Guinea by German botanists.

In 1886 H. O. Forbes was appointed Deputy Commissioner in Samarai in British New Guinea, now the Territory of Papua. In 1887 he resigned to undertake exploration of the Goldie River. He returned to England in 1888, but his collections from the Sogeri plateau added much to the knowledge of Papuan botany.

Papua was first explored botanically by Sir William MacGregor [q.v.], administrator and later lieutenant-governor between 1888 and 1898, who collected plants himself during the course of his administrative patrols and encouraged others to do likewise. Government officers and missionaries collected specimens which were sent to F. von Mueller in Melbourne. Mueller's descriptions of these collections are to be found in a host of little-known journals, together with his 'Descriptive Notes on Papuan Plants'. Following Mueller's death in 1896, F. M. Bailey in Queensland carried on describing collections of plants, particularly in the *Queensland Agricultural Journal*.

The dawn of the modern era of botanical exploration occurred in 1925 when L. J. Brass came to Papua for the Arnold Arboretum expedition, thereby beginning a lifetime association with New Guinea and more than a quarter of a century of active work by the Arnold Arboretum. After his first visit Brass returned under the auspices of the Archbold Expeditions [q.v.]. Many of the Brass collections were described by C. T. White and W. D. Francis. Lane-Poole in 1925-6 made extensive botanical collections during the course of forest surveys in Papua and the Mandated Territory of New Guinea for the Australian government.

C. E. Carr, a rubber planter from Malaya with a lifelong interest in orchids [q.v.], came to Papua in 1935. His extensive collections of about 7,000 numbers have not been properly worked up. He died in Port Moresby in 1936.

Mary Strong Clemens, indefatigable plant collector, arrived in New Guinea in 1935 with her missionary husband. When she was evacuated from Lae as the Japanese were preparing to land, she left plant collections which were in all probability destroyed but which could, just conceivably, have reached Japan. Most of her earlier collections went to Berlin where some were described. Mary Strong Clemens did not return to New Guinea after the war; she died in Brisbane some years ago.

Brass and the Archbold Expeditions had set the pattern for the future botanical exploration of New Guinea before the outbreak of World War II. Aircraft had been used for transport, large carrier lines had been employed for logistic support, composite multi-disciplinary scientific parties had penetrated the previously inaccessible hinterland. Then came the war.

By 1944 the need for timber supplies for the Allied forces opened the door for J. B. McAdam, pre-war forester at Wau, to commence the forest resource surveys. McAdam obtained the services of L. S. Smith, a young botanist from Queensland, together with support from C. T. White and H. E. Dadswell. The nucleus of the botanical unit of the first Australian Army Forest Company was formed and established at Lae. Collections were made in various parts of mainland New Guinea and the Bismarck Archipelago. With demobilization in 1945-6, McAdam became Secretary for Forests in the Provisional Administration. One of the first professional appointments made was that of J. S. Womersley as forest botanist, and thus began the Division of Botany.

From collections of fewer than 2,000 numbers there has grown a herbarium of at least 120,000 specimens with annual accessions totalling, in a good year, 10,000 sheets. Botanists who have contributed to this are A. G. Floyd (1953-6), E. E. Henty (1957 ——), D. G. Frodin (1965-6), C. E. Ridsdale (1966-8), M. J. E. Coode (1966——), D. Foreman (1969——), J. Vandenberg (1967-70), P. F. Stevens (1970——) and many technical assistants. Visiting botanists from all over the world come to Lae to participate in the botanical programme and use the facilities now available.

The University of Papua and New Guinea [q.v.] is now training students in botany to degree level. The day is coming when the successors of the nomadic dwellers who lived by their sense of practical botany will take their place with colleagues from other countries to further the study of the plant life of New Guinea.

'Cyclopaedia of Collectors and Collections' and 'Supplement', *Flora Malesiana*, series I, vols 1 and 5, 1950 and 1958; O. Beccari, *Malesia*. Genoa and Florence, 1877-90; *Nova Guinea*, pub. E. J. Brill, Leiden. Vols 1-18, 1907-26. New series, vols 1-10, 1937-60. Then separate series: anthropology parts 1-3, botany parts 1-24, geology parts 1-6, zoology parts 1-35. Ceased publication December 1966; H. C. de Wit, 'Recent phytography of New Guinea', part of 'Short History of the Phytography of Malaysian Vascular Plants', *Flora Malesiana*, series I, vol. 4, 1949, pp. cxlix-clii.				J. S. WOMERSLEY

EXTERNAL RELATIONS. During World War II Papua and New Guinea were both under Australian military administration; their international status was however quite distinct. The Territory of Papua, under Australian administration since 1902, was not formally subject to the provisions of article 22 of the Covenant of the League of Nations. The Territory of New Guinea, on the other hand, was a 'C' class mandate administered by Australia under article 22. Joint administration was continued after the war under the Papua-New Guinea Provisional Administration Act 1945-46. The Act was provisional because legally the administration of New Guinea was subject to the provisions of the League of Nations and its successor, the United Nations.

The international principles concerning non-selfgoverning territories were broadly outlined by the Allied Powers in the Atlantic Charter in 1941, the Cairo Declaration in 1943 and at the Yalta Conference in 1945. It was agreed at Yalta that a system of trusteeship would be established and that existing mandated territories would be covered by the trusteeship system, as well as those non-selfgoverning territories which were placed voluntarily under trusteeship by administering powers. The war-time conferences did not specify the terms of the future trusteeship system; this was left to the United Nations' conference in San Francisco.

The Australian government, and especially its chief spokesman Dr H. V. Evatt, the Minister for External Affairs, played a leading role in formulating the principles of trusteeship. The government whole-heartedly endorsed the principles of the Atlantic Charter and other agreements dealing with the protection and advancement of non-self-governing peoples. Australia and New Zealand sought to initiate the promotion of the principles of trusteeship in the Pacific in the Australia-New Zealand Agreement of 1944. This affirmed that the principles of the Atlantic Charter also applied to the Pacific and that the provisions of trusteeship applied in principle to colonial territories not mandated and called for the establishment of a regional advisory body to promote the welfare and advancement of non-selfgoverning peoples; this initiative led to the formation of the South Pacific Commission.

THE UNITED NATIONS TRUSTEESHIP SYSTEM

The trusteeship system, as devised in San Francisco, was purely voluntary. However, with the exception of South Africa, all administering powers placed their mandated territories under trusteeship. Chapter XI of the Charter of the United Nations deals with all non-selfgoverning territories; chapters XII and XIII set out the trusteeship system. The differences between chapter XI and chapters XII and XIII are considerable. While chapter XI only deals broadly with the principles that should direct non-selfgoverning territories, chapters XII and XIII set out in considerably more detail the objectives of trusteeship, the role and authority of the United Nations and its agencies with regard to trust territories and the obligations of administering powers towards the United Nations and the peoples under trusteeship. Chapter XIII sets out the composition, functions, powers and procedure of the Trusteeship Council, which is the United Nations' major agency concerned with trust territories. While chapters XII and XIII apply only to those states who have voluntarily concluded trusteeship agreements, chapter XI applies automatically to all members of the United Nations. Thus the provisions of chapters XI, XII and XIII apply to New Guinea, while only chapter XI applies to Papua.

Australia, along with other powers holding

mandated territories except South Africa, concluded trusteeship agreements. The Trusteeship Agreement for the Territory of New Guinea was approved by the General Assembly in 1946 and approved by the Commonwealth Parliament in the Papua and New Guinea Act in 1949. Thus Australia as a trust-administering power holds a seat in the Trusteeship Council, is obliged to submit annual reports on the Territory of New Guinea based on a comprehensive questionnaire drawn up by the Trusteeship Council, and to receive in the Territory periodic (three-yearly) Visiting Missions of the Council.

ADMINISTRATIVE UNION

The difference in international status between the two Territories is blurred as far as Australia is concerned by the administrative union (*see* PROVISIONAL ADMINISTRATION 1945-1949). The union was first established unilaterally in 1945-6 on a temporary basis, but subsequently approved by the General Assembly as article 5 of the Trusteeship Agreement for New Guinea. The Papua and New Guinea Act expressly states the intention of the Commonwealth government to maintain the separate identity of New Guinea as a trust territory. Separate statistics are compiled for each territory and the national status of the indigenous inhabitants is also separate; however, from the administrative standpoint, the two Territories are a single unit. Since the administrative union all international treaties contracted by Australia apply to both Territories. While the General Assembly has accepted the administrative union, it was, especially in earlier years, somewhat apprehensive that the identity and status of the two Territories might merge. In more recent years the emphasis has changed; the United Nations has called on Australia to take measures to encourage a sense of nationhood by adopting a national flag, anthem, and a single name for the Territories.

The administrative union enabled the government to concentrate a single administrative structure in Port Moresby, Papua, where the jurisdiction of the United Nations was considerably more limited than in New Guinea. This meant that the government was in a position to dilute the limitations placed by the Charter (article 84) and the Trusteeship Agreement (article 4) on defence installations. While defence establishments are limited in the Trust Territory to broadly defensive types, no such legal restrictions apply to Papua. By creating a single defence establishment under the administrative union, with personnel recruited from both Territories, the government retains the option of building defence forces, dictated by its own judgments, which are largely outside the scrutiny of the Trusteeship Council. This was a particularly significant consideration in the early post-war years, when the results of the limitations on armaments in mandated territories was freshly imprinted in the minds of Australians. It was generally felt that the Territories fell easily under Japanese occupation largely because of the military limitations placed on mandated territories. Indeed

the Labor government was subject to more domestic criticism for not seeking to place New Guinea under strategic trust than for any other aspect of the Trusteeship agreement. Strategic trust territories are not subject to the same degree of scrutiny as non-strategic trusts, largely because they fall within the purview of the Security Council instead of the General Assembly. The Japanese mandated territories which came under United States control after the war were placed under strategic trust.

THE UNITED NATIONS AND THE TERRITORIES
1945-1962

Until December 1960 when the General Assembly adopted its declaration on the granting of independence to colonial peoples (resolution 1514) the attention of the United Nations was primarily focused on the administration of the Territory of New Guinea through the Trusteeship Council.

The following categories of states are members of the Trusteeship Council (article 86): administering states; permanent members of the Security Council who are not administering trust territories; and sufficient members, elected by the General Assembly, to ensure an even balance between administering and non-administering states. Largely because of this form of selection the Trusteeship Council, in earlier years, tended to assume a milder attitude towards the administering powers than the General Assembly. The Trusteeship Council was the main source of information on colonial matters prior to 1962 and thus tended to act as a modifying influence on the General Assembly.

The Trusteeship Council (article 88) is responsible for formulating a comprehensive questionnaire on the political, economic, social and educational development of trust territories. Australia, as the administering authority, submits an annual report to the Trusteeship Council which is largely, though not completely, based on the questionnaire approved by the Council in 1952 and amended in 1958 and 1961. For administrative convenience, the annual report on Papua follows much the same format. The annual reports of the administering powers are the major source of information on the territories for both the General Assembly and the Trusteeship Council. A second source of information available to the United Nations are the reports of the Visiting Missions of the Trusteeship Council (article 87) who have visited the Territory of New Guinea every three years since 1950. The Visiting Missions have no legal authority to report or inspect developments in Papua, though partly because of the administrative centralization in Port Moresby, they do visit parts of Papua as well. The annual reports of the administering powers and the reports and recommendations of the Visiting Missions are examined by the United Nations, which passes resolutions on the reports. The interaction between reports and resolutions constitutes the main cycle of communications between the United Nations and the administering powers. Thus prior to the report of the first Visiting Mission in 1950, the resolutions of the Trusteeship Council were mild, accepting almost wholly the broad framework of the Administration's development policies. After the report of the 1950 Visiting Mission, resolutions were still sympathetic, but firmer than before.

Visiting Missions. The early reports accepted the basic framework, assumptions and priorities of the Administration and sought to stimulate progress by recommending further changes along the course already set. Generally the reports acknowledged progress and urged further steps in indigenous participation in decision-making, economic development and the extension of public services and education. The Administration was urged to take measures that would have a unifying effect on the Territories; the construction of roads, the teaching of English as the common language and the acceleration of administrative control over the Territory were among those recommended. The Missions were critical of practices relating to racial discrimination, such as curfews and corporal punishment. Target dates, first in non-political fields of development and subsequently in all fields, were recommended. From the outset Missions commented on the lack of over-all planning which would facilitate the establishment of target dates. Generally the Administration was receptive to the recommendations of the Trusteeship Council, especially in areas which called for acceleration in those aspects of development which it had already established such as target dates and planning and somewhat more reluctantly on those recommendations which called for changes or additions to ongoing programmes such as policy on racial discrimination.

The first Visiting Mission noted that despite the generous grants given by the Commonwealth, development in the social and economic fields would have been accelerated if the resources of the United Nations were tapped for further assistance. Though the Commonwealth government acknowledged a policy of co-operation with multilateral bodies in accordance with the Charter and the Trusteeship Agreement, it had from the outset shown reluctance to involve the Territories with the outside world. From 1946 to 1962 the government was usually reluctant to seek multilateral assistance or to recruit professional and technical personnel from outside the British Commonwealth. There were limited contacts with external non-political bodies such as religious missions [q.v.], the International Red Cross, and the Boy Scouts, and also some co-operation with multilateral organizations such as the World Health Organization. The only multilateral body that the government encouraged was the South Pacific Commission, which is advisory and non-political.

Throughout the first fifteen years of trusteeship, the Commonwealth government was able to pursue its policies and priorities in the Territories without significant challenge or criticism from external sources. With virtually a bipartisan policy at home, criticism was scattered and piecemeal. The only political international body with access to the Territories was the Trusteeship Council through its Visiting Missions. Neither the members of the Missions nor the Council itself had the resources and expertise to examine thoroughly and comment on government policy, and the main source of information available to the Council was the Administration. Although the Council has a well-equipped secretariat which can supply a great deal of information, it acts basically as a research agency rather than a source of expert advice. The Council chooses its Visiting Missions with a number of considerations in mind and expertise is by no means an overriding consideration. This situation is in contrast to the mandate system under the League, which attempted to emphasize expertise rather than political considerations.

Entry of all external visitors was and is closely controlled by the Administration. The nationals of those countries which have adopted hostile attitudes to Australian administration—most notably the Soviet bloc—were, and to a large extent still are, not admitted into the Territories. Even in the case of Visiting Missions, the government can exercise informal control over composition. The concentration of expertise and the control of access to the Territories put the government into a position where it could effect the political isolation of the Territories.

THE UNITED NATIONS AND THE TERRITORIES SINCE 1962

No report from a Visiting Mission had more impact on the development of the Territories than the report of the 1962 Mission sometimes called the 'Foot report' after the leader, Sir Hugh Foot. Though more forceful and far reaching, it was still within the tradition of its predecessors. The impact of the report was partly due to its contents and partly due to its timing. The Mission made its report at a time when the government was re-evaluating its policies in the Territories and on colonial matters at the United Nations. For some years the criticism of colonial powers in the United Nations had been increasing and Australia was finding itself more and more isolated on colonial questions. Thus the Foot report was read receptively, and it was still within a framework acceptable to the government.

The report made a number of far-reaching recommendations. It noted the lack of planning and suggested a full review of the economy by the International Bank for Reconstruction and Development (World Bank) which would be used as the basis for a concerted development plan. It recommended accelerated steps to train indigenous leaders and suggested that until a university was established, a minimum of one hundred indigenous students be placed in universities abroad. Despite the recently announced reforms in the Legislative Council, the report called for the fostering of democratic, representative, central government by the establishment of a parliament of about one hundred members, elected directly from single-member constituencies by the end of 1963. The report acknowledged the developmental achievements of the Administration and suggested that a level of progress had been reached where a kind of 'take-off' could be stimulated in the political, economic and social fields.

In October 1963 the Hon. P. M. C. Hasluck, Minister for Territories, introduced amendments to the Papua and New Guinea Act which transformed the Legislative Council into the House of Assembly [q.v.] along lines recommended by the report. A number of reforms in other governmental organs and the judiciary were also introduced by the amendments to the Act. The government changed its standing policy on planning and external assistance. A World Bank Mission was invited to make a comprehensive survey of the Territories' resources early in 1963 and its report was presented to the government in June 1964.

The more assertive tone of the Foot Mission was continued by subsequent Missions, though their recommendations were not as far reaching nor their impact as apparent. These Missions continued to accept the framework laid down in government policies and mostly recommended accelerated progress in areas where the government initiated activity. The Missions of 1965 and 1968, like their predecessors, were mainly composed of delegates from countries not especially critical of Australian administration. They enjoyed one advantage not possible prior to 1964; they could draw on the World Bank report which is the most comprehensive document on the Territory not drawn up by the Administration. As in the case of previous Missions, the members of the 1965 and 1968 Missions were not experts and their report reflected the biases and interests of the members. Thus the 1965 report showed more than usual interest in discriminatory practices, while the 1968 report showed considerable interest in the land problem. Partly because of progress in the Territories and partly because of changing climate and interests in the United Nations on colonial matters, the recommendations and emphasis of the seven Visiting Missions changed with time. The earlier Missions were more concerned with the administrative union, territorial control and social and educational progress while later ones emphasized economic viability, increased indigenous participation in decision-making and national unity.

The Committee of Twenty-four. In December 1960, the General Assembly adopted resolution 1514 (XV) calling for the independence of all colonial peoples. The resolution urged that immediate steps be taken to transfer all power to peoples in trust and non-selfgoverning territories. It stated that inadequacy of political, economic, social or educational development should never serve as a pretext for delaying independence.

Resolution 1514 was a major victory for the anti-colonial countries at the United Nations. It rejected a basic argument put forward by Australia and other administering states, which had been maintained throughout the previous decade (Australia still largely holds this view), that independence is only a meaningful question when non-selfgoverning territories have reached a largely viable social, economic and political stage of development. In fact Australian official statements still rarely refer to independence, preferring rather to discuss 'self-determination'. Resolution 1514 put the General Assembly on record as holding the position that good government is not a substitute for, or preferable to, self-government. Two considerations have, in the eyes of the Commonwealth, diluted the implications of resolution 1514. Firstly, the resolutions of the General Assembly are not legally binding on member states and, secondly, resolution 1514 (XV), also passed in December 1960, sets out guiding principles on the transmission of information on non-selfgoverning territories which could assist the United Nations in determining when territories are ready for independence.

The General Assembly has sought to press for compliance with resolution 1514 by passing a number of subsequent resolutions reaffirming resolution 1514 and calling on administering powers to take a number of steps which would bring them into compliance with the objectives of resolution 1514. In November 1961, the Assembly established a special committee of seventeen members, including Australia, to study the application of resolution 1514 and to make suggestions and recommendations on the progress of its application. In December 1962, the Assembly enlarged the membership of the special committee to twenty-four members; it is now commonly referred to as the 'Committee of Twenty-four'. The Assembly requested the Committee to continue to seek suitable ways of implementing resolution 1514 and to propose specific measures concerning territories still not independent.

The Committee deals with all Australian non-selfgoverning external territories. Thus it regularly reviewed developments in Papua and the Cocos (Keeling) Islands which previously were not subject to the special attention of an agency of the United Nations. No special reports are compiled by Australia for the Committee of Twenty-four. The main sources of information are the annual reports on Papua, New Guinea and the Cocos Islands.

The Committee of Twenty-four makes no attempt to balance the composition of its membership between states sympathetic towards and states critical of the administering powers and hence has been more critical of the administering states than the Trusteeship Council. Sub-committee II, of the Committee of Twenty-four, has in recent years made separate reports on Australian non-selfgoverning territories and, on their recommendation, the General Assembly has passed a number of resolutions noting Australia's reluctance to implement the objectives of resolution 1514. For a number of years Australia has been unhappy about the text of certain resolutions and reports drafted by the sub-committee and about the tone of many of the Committee's debates. While it is evident that the Committee of Twenty-four has become a forum for the anti-colonial members of the United Nations, who have at times drafted resolutions that were ill informed and hostile, it should also be noted that the Committee's criticisms were primarily focused not on Australia, but old enemies such as South Africa and Portugal. The strongest criticism of Australia has persistently come from the Soviet delegate with only partial support from other, non-communist, quarters.

Defence Review. In April 1968, the Committee decided to examine, as a separate issue, the military activities and arrangements of administering states which might impede the implementation of resolution 1514. By focusing on defence arrangements the Committee struck a nerve centre of the Administration. The government was less concerned about what the Committee would report than that the Committee had assumed defence interests in the Territory. The response of the government can largely be explained in terms of its traditional apprehension in which the Territories are seen as being within the ambit of Australia's vital defence interest. Thus 'interference' by the United Nations could lead to a situation which existed before World War II, when New Guinea was left vulnerable because the government, due to its mandate obligations, could not take defence precautions.

The Committee noted a defence expansion in the Territories since 1963, the reactivation of the naval facilities on Manus Island and the use of these in SEATO exercises. The report, however, also acknowledged Australia's defence responsibilities towards the Trust Territory (articles 4 and 7), did not challenge sections of the Defence Act relating to the Territories and noted the limitations on the terms of service of indigenous personnel in the armed forces. They are not subject to active service outside the Territories.

The conclusions and recommendations of the Committee were generalized and thus not all of them can be interpreted as applicable to Papua and New Guinea. The more extreme conclusions such as those concerning the use of the armed forces to repress national movements and support foreign exploitation clearly are directed at other colonial powers and especially Portugal. The Committee found that military arrangements in non-selfgoverning territories impeded the objectives of resolution 1514 and that armed forces in some territories had been used to deny human freedoms. It recommended that, in the interests of implementing resolution 1514 and of international peace, administering powers cease to deploy further military installations and dismantle existing ones.

The Committee was much more critical of Portugal, South Africa and Rhodesia than of Australia. The Soviet Union and Poland were the most hostile to Australia, noting especially the use of Manus Island in SEATO exercises and the integration of the Territories in Australia's alliance systems. The Committee's recommendations, in so far as they can be applied to the Territories, were relatively mild; not altogether consistent—for example, there is a contradiction between acknowledging Australia's defence responsibilities on the one hand and requesting the abolition of all military installations on the other; and not especially perceptive—for example, the Committee failed to comment on existing military arrangements which put virtually all defence responsibilities outside the purview of the House of Assembly, the Department of External Territories and the Trusteeship Council.

The government has consistently made a distinction between the Committee of Twenty-four and the Trusteeship Council; it has recognized its legal obligations towards the Council under the Charter and the Trusteeship Agreement. On the other hand, the government has been more reserved towards the Committee, though it was a member from its formation to February 1969. As it became apparent that the Committee was becoming increasingly critical, so the government became less willing to co-operate. Legally the Committee's position is not as well entrenched as that of the Trusteeship Council, as it was formed simply by decision of the majority of the General Assembly. As the anti-colonial fervour of the Council grew, so did Australia's defensive reaction to it. Australia's position has become more legally based; it has become more reluctant to make extra efforts to submit information requested by the Committee. For some years now, the Committee has sought permission to send a Mission to visit Australian territories. The government has not permitted this although the Visiting Missions of the Trusteeship Council have been given some access to Papua to which they have no legal claim. The question of access to the Territories has been a major point of difference and reflects the attitude of Australia to the Committee.

In February 1969, Australia withdrew from the Committee of Twenty-four. She has continued to supply information on her territories and attends the meetings of the Committee when requested for discussion of the Australian territories. The decision to withdraw was the result of increasing dissatisfaction with the activities and tone of the Committee. Whether the decision was in the best interests of the territories or of Australia is at least open to doubt. Withdrawal has not censured the Committee sufficiently to alter its attitude towards Australian territories; it has however limited the opportunities to influence the deliberations of the Committee and has, to some extent, weakened the position of those members of the Committee who have shown increasing sympathy to Australia's position.

THE FUTURE OF THE TRUSTEESHIP COUNCIL

To some extent the Committee of Twenty-four has been overlapping with and even usurping the functions of the Trusteeship Council. The Committee was born out of the dissatisfaction of the General Assembly with the Trusteeship Council, which was considered to be too sympathetic to administering powers. Australia by readily co-operating with the Trusteeship Council in contrast to its attitudes towards the Committee, was attempting to reinforce the primary role of the Trusteeship Council. As previously noted the attitude of the Council differs from that of the Committee largely because of its composition. However, with the ever-decreasing number of trust territories, the composition and the existence of the Trusteeship Council are becoming increasingly doubtful. As more trust territories gain independence so the number of seats held by administering powers declines. Whether the Trusteeship Council will continue to exist in its present form after self-government is granted to American strategic trust territories in the Pacific is very much open to doubt. The Trust Territory of New Guinea is already the last of its category. It is therefore likely that after the American territories reach self-government, the Committee of Twenty-four will become more involved in New Guinea on behalf of the United Nations. In the light of these developments the present policies of the government have made for a situation where the agency succeeding the Trusteeship Council will be one towards which Australia has already shown its dissatisfaction.

In December 1969 the General Assembly adopted a resolution on New Guinea which amounts to a compromise between Australia and the Committee of Twenty-four on the question of visiting the Territories. The resolution noted the previous requests of the Committee that Australia reconsider its position concerning Visiting Missions and allow a Mission from the Committee into the Territory. It requested that the Trusteeship Council include non-members of the Council in future Visiting Missions after consulting the Committee and Australia. The resolution is a compromise which attempts to admit members of the Committee without totally revising Australia's previous policy of excluding Missions from the Committee. The specific arrangements of the compromise have not yet been worked out. Australia has accepted the resolution in principle as a holding operation. Whether the compromise will satisfy the Committee for long and whether Australia will be able to muster sufficient support to block the Committee from sending its own Missions in the future is still open to doubt.

INTERNATIONAL AID

The World Bank report of 1964 is the most comprehensive and authoritative review made by a multilateral body on Papua and New Guinea. The report was mainly concerned with economic development, but its recommendations had far-reaching implications for the political, social and educational development of the Territories. Some recommendations were implemented piecemeal in the years following and in 1968 a five-year development programme was drawn up based on the World Bank report.

A number of points arising out of the report and its conclusions had international implications. The report served as an independent source of information to the United Nations agencies concerned with the Territories and subsequent recommendations of the Trusteeship Council referred to it frequently. The five-year programme estab-

lished a more cohesive framework for development to which the Council could refer, thus facilitating continuity of reference. The World Bank report and the 1968 development programme went some way towards satisfying the standing request of the United Nations for the establishment of target dates. As the World Bank report and the development programme covered both Territories, they effectively brought the Territory of Papua under the purview of the Trusteeship Council.

The report also had the effect of legitimizing the assumptions and policies of the government at the United Nations. It supported the standing position of the government which held that the Territories were backward in the social, economic and political fields and thus necessarily reliant on Australian assistance and guidance, that the road to economic and political independence was decades away and that development would be best stimulated by increased Australian assistance and participation on both the official and private levels. The report however did not endorse all aspects of Australian policy; for example, it described the treatment of the indigenous peoples as 'benevolently paternalistic'.

Volunteers. The World Bank report suggested that in order to facilitate development, the Commonwealth consider various forms of international assistance and finance. Both the World Bank report and the 1968 Visiting Mission of the Trusteeship Council recommended the use of volunteer assistance to overcome shortages of skilled and professional personnel in the Territories. The Administration was initially reluctant to use volunteer service because of its lack of continuity, the problems of controlling volunteers, the tendency of the home governments to interfere and a tendency of some volunteers to interfere in local government. Volunteers have been used in health, education and development work; they have come from both Britain (Volunteer Service Overseas) and Australia (Australian Volunteers Abroad). Volunteer lay-workers have also been recruited by various Christian mission organizations from such countries as Germany, Canada and the United States.

FOREIGN INVESTMENT

The policy on investment of external capital is formally uniform for all sources outside the Territories. The government has encouraged foreign investments, but also seeks to ensure that these are in accord with development programmes. The Administration has reserved the right to approve specific investment proposals put forward by private companies. Current arrangements with Bougainville Copper Pty Limited are an example of the Administration holding equity in investments on behalf of the people of the Territories (*see* BOUGAINVILLE COPPER PROJECT). No political party in the Territories has expressed opposition to external investments. The House of Assembly has twice affirmed the Development Capital Guarantee Declaration which welcomes external capital and guarantees that such capital will not be expropriated, that no unreasonable limitations will be placed on its repatriation and that no discriminatory trade legislation will be introduced. A number of incentives have also been introduced to attract capital to the Territory.

Foreign aid. Since 1964 the policy on international aid has been to seek maximum assistance from international agencies. Australia has entered into a number of Basic Agreements covering the terms and conditions under which aid is to be provided. Current projects involving international aid are shown in the table.

Project	Agency	Aid ($U.S. million)
Telecommunications project	World Bank	7.0
Oil palm project	IDA	1.5
Teachers' College, Goroka	IDA	1.2
Transport survey	UNDP	0.5
Science education	UNICEF	0.3
Agricultural development project	IDA	4.8
Total		15.3

IDA, International Development Association.

UNDP, United Nations Development Programme.

UNICEF, United Nations International Children's Emergency Fund.

Further projects to the approximate value of $U.S.110.6 million are being considered. Present aid from multilateral assistance is only a fraction of the Commonwealth grants made annually to the Territories, but if the projects under consideration materialize, multilateral assistance will contribute a sizeable portion of the resources and funds available to the Territories. While the Commonwealth contribution is in the form of a grant, only a small portion of the multilateral assistance comes in the form of non-repayable grants from the United Nations. Funds from the World Bank are repayable on a commercial basis, while International Development Association (IDA) loans are non-interest bearing.

THE HOUSE OF ASSEMBLY IN FOREIGN AFFAIRS

For a number of years the United Nations has been urging the Administration to help make the indigenous population of the Territories more aware of the outside world and the United Nations. This has been recommended in order to assist in stimulating a sense of unity and nationhood in the Territories, and thus as a preparation for independence. It was also believed that greater international participation would enable the people of the Territories to view their position in a wider perspective and make them better acquainted with other social, economic and political systems.

The government responded to this recommendation and has increasingly sought to involve the indigenous people of the Territories in international activities for the past five years. This policy is a partial change from the previous practice of the government which amounted to virtual isolation of the Territories. Early in 1970 two cadets from the Territories were appointed as diplomatic trainees at the Department of External Affairs in Canberra; indigenous advisers have been attached to the Australian delegation at the United Nations. The advisers have generally been drawn from the House of Assembly and spend only a limited time at the United Nations. In past years arrangements have been made to enable returning advisers to visit other developing countries. The Select Committee of the House of Assembly, as of March 1970, is also scheduled to visit overseas countries in order to study other forms of government. Representatives of the Territories have been included in Australian delegations to a number of United Nations' specialized agencies, whose work is of interest to the Territories. It has also been the policy of the government to send indigenous delegates to the sessions of the South Pacific Commission and its advisory body, the South Pacific Conference. With the exception of the Select Committee and the partial exception of advisers to the United Nations, indigenous representatives have only attended nonpolitical meetings. Under the Trusteeship Agreement and the present interpretation of the Papua and New Guinea Act, the external interests of the Territories remain with the Commonwealth; Australia still represents the Territories in substantive international matters. The inclusion of indigenous members in Australian delegations serves two main purposes; it enables the people of the Territories to become acquainted at first hand with the outside world and it enables Australia to demonstrate to the world that the peoples of the Territories are satisfied with their present status and relationship with Australia.

Defence and foreign affairs are the primary responsibility of the Commonwealth under article 84 of the Charter, articles 4 and 7 of the Trusteeship Agreement and the Commonwealth Defence Act. However there is nothing set out in the Papua and New Guinea Act which restricts the House of Assembly from passing resolutions or ordinances in the fields of foreign affairs and defence, although section 55 (d and e) requires that ordinances in these fields be reserved for the approval of the Governor-General and that such ordinances must not be contrary to Australia's international treaty obligations. Under articles 11 (2), 73 and 76 of the Charter both Territories may petition the General Assembly. Article 87 enables the Territory of New Guinea also to petition the Trusteeship Council. The operative articles of the Charter make no restrictions on the range of subjects on which petitions can be made.

In practice, the House of Assembly has not passed legislation in the fields of defence and foreign affairs and has no budgetary control over this area. There have been debates in the House on related issues and three resolutions passed.

The right of the House to pass such resolutions has now been recognized and procedures have been worked out whereby the government transmit these resolutions to external states or the United Nations.

Resolutions of the House of Assembly. The first resolution of the House concerned the Soviet intervention in Czechoslovakia in 1968. It expressed sympathy for the people of Czechoslovakia and stated its concern over Soviet interference in the internal affairs of another state. At the request of the House, the resolution was transmitted to the Soviet Embassy in Canberra by the Department of External Affairs. The resolution was not unwelcome to the Australian government partly because it shared similar views regarding Czechoslovakia, and partly because Soviet delegates at the United Nations have been the toughest critics of Australia's policies in the Territories. The second resolution of the House was also one that coincided with Australia's position. In March 1969 the House passed a resolution after noting resolution 2427 (XXIII) of the General Assembly which called for free elections in the Territories under United Nations supervision and for early independence. The resolution of the House stated that free elections had been carried out in the Territories, that the people of the Territories were best able to judge when they were ready for self-government and that in the meantime they were satisfied with the Australian Administration. The resolution was transmitted to the United Nations by the Department of External Affairs.

In June 1969 the House passed its third resolution on foreign affairs, on the act of free choice in West Irian. The House commended the Administration for its handling of the West Irian border incidents, expressed concern over the conduct of the act of free choice, and mildly censured the United Nations for not ensuring a more equitable referendum. Unlike the previous resolutions of the House, the West Irian resolution was embarrassing to the government, mainly because it was thought to be at cross purposes with the government's policy of building closer relations with Indonesia. Largely on the advice of the Department of External Affairs, the government at first hesitated to convey the resolution to the United Nations. It was finally conveyed early in September after the act of free choice was concluded, thus reducing the impact of the resolution on the United Nations.

The West Irian resolution brought to light two problems that have still to be resolved. Firstly, the latent contradiction existing in the present arrangements on foreign affairs, that when the people of the Territories become concerned with outside events, they are reliant on Canberra for channels of communication. This can create a problem when the wishes of the Territories do not coincide with the interest of the Australian government.

The second problem is related to West Irian itself. There is considerable sentiment and concern over events in West Irian. The division of administrative control of the island between Indonesia and Australia is not very meaningful to most people on either side of the border. An unsuccessful resolution in November 1969, requesting the Administration to treat West Irian refugees with every consideration, gives expression to the concern which is felt in the Territories about West Irian problems. There is little evidence to suggest that in the event of further disturbances in West Irian there will not be pressure on the Administration to handle matters sympathetically.

The present policies of the Administration with regard to West Irian refugees reflects the dual pressures on a government which seeks to build co-operation with Indonesia and to be responsive to the sympathies of the people of the Territories. During the border incidents of 1969 the government sought to be formally neutral. However, as a result of co-operation with Indonesian authorities in early June 1969 in Djajapura, and subsequently for a time at regular intervals, Australian and Indonesian authorities were able to reduce the number of border crossings. Indonesian officials have also been permitted to visit refugee camps in the Territories to induce refugees to return. It has been estimated that over 1,000 refugees have crossed the border, but only about 276 have been granted temporary entry permits as permissive residents.

With an increasing sense of nationhood and growing awareness of the outside world and its ways, whether the people of the Territories will accept the recent practices of the Administration towards political refugees, is open to doubt. The case of two political refugees, Wilhelm Zonggonao and Clemen Runaweri, sheds some light on present practices. On crossing the border, both men stated their intention to ascertain Australian attitudes to the act of free choice and to travel on to New York to state their case at the United Nations. A member of the House of Assembly guaranteed their travel expenses to New York. The Administration, however, did not issue them with travel documents and made it a condition of entry that they be settled in refugee camps. The application for permissive residence requires applicants to agree, *inter alia*, that they will not engage in any political activity in connection with their country of origin and that they accept resettlement wherever the Administration designates. These requirements are in part contrary to the International Convention Relating to the Status of Refugees (1954) to which Australia is a party, as are therefore the Territories. Article 26 of the Convention gives lawful refugees the right to choose their own place of residence and free movement within the receiving territory. Article 28 calls on parties to the Convention to issue travel documents to refugees who wish to go abroad; the Convention calls for especially sympathetic consideration for those refugees who are unable to obtain travel documents from their country of origin. Australia reserved its position on a number of articles in 1954 (articles 17, 18, 19, 26, 28, 32) but has removed its objections to all except article 28, and that mainly because of its present implications for the Territories.

CONCLUSION

Australia's foreign policy is influenced, to a considerable extent, by New Guinea. The policies of the government at the United Nations may well have been more acceptable to its regional neighbours had New Guinea not been a major consideration. In explaining and justifying its administrative policies abroad, the government tended to be defensive and legalistic. Until about 1965, Australia faced a mostly critical General Assembly whose resolutions might have been more irritating but for the moderating influence of the Trusteeship Council. The task of administering the Territories was generally a thankless one abroad.

In the face of mounting pressure from the international community, the government changed many of its standing policies relating to non-self-governing territories. It has also recently changed its defensive position. Australian diplomats, especially in Africa and Asia, were instructed to actively publicize and explain the conditions in the Territories and the goals of the Administration. Because of these attempts, of the greater contact between the Territories and the rest of the world and because of a general decline in the emotive power of colonial issues, most members of the United Nations, with the exception of the Soviet bloc, have come to understand and even sometimes to accept Australia's policies.

It is not easy to evaluate the extent to which the United Nations has influenced the development of the Territories, though it does not appear to have been a primary mover in the first fifteen years of trusteeship. Over this period, the United Nations was hindered by lack of authoritative independent information, which also enabled the Administration to carry on its tasks in relative insulation. With the Foot report, which coincided with major policy re-evaluations in Australia, the impact of the United Nations increased. The United Nations was a major factor in reducing the isolation of the Territories, in stimulating awareness in the outside world and hence in increasing external assistance. It would seem that in time the government has come to accept the involvement of the Trusteeship Council, if only because of the negative effect of the Committee of Twenty-four. Beyond the next few years, the future of the Council is uncertain. It seems that at least the General Assembly's influence over it will increase with its changing composition. The compromise resolution of December 1969 suggests that the government realizes this and is taking steps to accommodate the Assembly's vociferous body, the Committee.

It is more than likely that West Irian will replace the United Nations as the major point of interest for the Territories in the outside world. Interest in external affairs will increase and become more salient as political development progresses. The present situation is one where the interests of the people in the Territories and the government differ in emphasis and the divergence is likely to increase in time. The people in the Territories continue to look with concern and sympathy on the progress of events in West Irian. On the other hand, the government sees Indonesia as its closest Asian neighbour and fellow administrator. To avoid potential strain some formula might be worked out which permits Australia to pursue its foreign interests without having to compromise the sympathies of the people of the Territories. One answer might be to develop procedures which would enable the Territories to articulate their external interests with greater independence.

F. A. MEDIANSKY

F

FILARIASIS is a very common condition in New Guinea but for the most part it produces no detectable manifestations of disease. Essentially it is an infestation by the nematode worm *Wucheria bancrofti*; infection takes place through the mosquito and once established lasts for many years. In 1-2 per cent of infected people the condition results in blockage of lymph channels with the development of elephantiasis or varicocele. It should be emphasized that such effects of filariasis in New Guinea are rarer and less severe than in other Pacific areas such as Samoa and Tahiti.

In the established condition, adult worms lodge in the veins or larger lymph vessels of the pelvis and for fifteen or twenty years the females produce successive broods of microfilaria, microscopic worms which are found in large numbers in the blood during the night hours—when mosquitoes are most likely to bite—but at other times disappear from the superficial vessels of the skin and lodge mainly in the lungs. The microfilaria in the blood cannot develop to adults unless they are taken up by a mosquito. The worm taken into a mosquito's stomach penetrates the stomach wall and in the tissues of the insect develops into an infective larva. This moves to the mosquito's mouth parts and when next it bites, the larva moves on to the skin of the individual bitten and makes its own way into the blood. On reaching a suitable site in vein or lymph vessel it develops to the adult form.

The mosquito concerned in New Guinea is *Anopheles punctulatis* and the infection is mainly one of rural areas. Most of the regions up to an altitude of 1,500 feet have an infestation rate of about 30 per cent and a low incidence of clinical manifestations. There are patches of infection at higher altitudes, and here and there at lower levels regions with higher parasite rates and more clinical disease can be recognized.

Prevention of filariasis. The disease is transmitted by the same group of mosquitoes as malaria [q.v.] so that anti-mosquito measures directed at the control of malaria are equally relevant to filariasis. It is not difficult, therefore, to protect Europeans from infection.

It has not yet been found practical to initiate serious attempts to eradicate the condition in New Guinea. In theory, control of mosquitoes and the administration of a drug to prevent the appearance of microfilaria in the blood should stop any new infections and eventually eliminate the disease. Unfortunately, campaigns elsewhere, in Tahiti and Samoa, using the drug diethylcarbamazine have only had moderate success. This drug can greatly reduce the numbers of microfilaria appearing in the blood but only while its administration is continued. The use of the drug has its dangers, some individuals have severe reactions to the drug as such while others may suffer from complications associated with the killing of large numbers of parasites.

Control of mosquitoes in rural areas is still too expensive a proposition to be undertaken in New Guinea. It has, however, been the general experience that with general improvement in living standards, there is relatively rapid disappearance of filariasis. Queensland's experience has been outstanding in this respect and holds out hope for steady automatic improvement in New Guinea.

FINANCIAL INSTITUTIONS (Other than Banks). At any point of time there are some people or institutions within a country—or overseas—with funds in excess of their immediate needs, and others who could make profitable use of more funds were they available. This is true of both the government and private sectors. An institutional framework is required to act as a bridge between those with surplus financial resources and those with a deficit. This framework is the financial system, made up of a wide range of financial institutions.

An effective financial system is essential for economic advancement. It ensures that financial resources are made available in an efficient and orderly manner to those who require them. Financial resources represent ownership or control of real resources: land, minerals, capital equipment, labour. Development depends on an adequacy of real resources at the right time and in the right place.

In most developing countries the financial system has at first consisted mainly of branches or agents of overseas financial institutions. Papua and New Guinea is no exception. The major part of its financial system originated in Australia and still consists largely of Australian institutions. However, in the long run the financial system of a country should grow out of the needs of that country. Institutions and practices, whether their origins be foreign or local, must be suitable and acceptable to the needs of the local populace.

Since 1960 there have been a number of changes in the financial system. The range of financial institutions has widened in response to the expansion of trade, the increased urban population and the growing sophistication of the local community. Overseas-based institutions have taken an increasing interest in the Territory and several new local institutions have been established by government and private enterprise.

A particular feature of the Papua and New Guinea economy in the 1960s has been the growing involvement of the indigenous people with financial institutions. This applies particularly to banking institutions but also to insurance companies, hire purchase organizations, savings and loan societies and, to a lesser extent, investment agencies. In considering the impact of financial institutions upon the indigenous sector it should be borne in mind that until 1963 financial transactions involving Papuans and New Guineans were restricted by law. The Transactions with Natives Ordinance 1958—and its predecessors—provided that contracts in excess of $100 were unlawful and void 'as against a native unless the contract is in writing and contains the full names of every party thereto and what is to be done under the contract by each of those persons and unless the contract is approved by an authorized officer'. In practice the authorized officer was usually a District Officer, and there was provision for the then Director of Native Affairs to exempt certain classes of indigenous people.

Non-bank financial institutions may be classified according to their major functions and according to whether they are organs of government or private enterprise. In Papua and New Guinea government agencies have tended to cater more for the indigenous sector while private enterprise has concentrated predominantly on the non-indigenous sector. This division is being gradually eroded.

NATIVE LOANS BOARD

In 1955 the Native Loans Fund Ordinance established a Native Loans Board to make loans to indigenous individuals or groups for a wide range of economic or welfare purposes. The Native Loans Fund was established as a revolving fund, initially by transfer of $113,444 from the Commonwealth. This represented the profits earned by the Production Control Board from local trade store operations at the time of the Angau administration of the Territory during and immediately after World War II. Further appropriations have since been made by the Administration, $74,000 in all, to supplement the Fund.

The Native Loans Fund was intended as a lender of last resort, to provide loans to indigenes or to indigenous organizations not able to obtain funds from other sources. It was not intended to replace or compete with existing credit facilities. However, this meant little, since opportunities for Papuans and New Guineans to obtain credit from other institutions in the 1950s were almost non-existent.

In the first seven years of the Fund's operations no loan could exceed $10,000 and there tended to be an emphasis on welfare projects. The restriction on amount was removed in 1962 when the Board was reorganized, and economic projects were given priority.

The majority of loans made were to Papuans and New Guineans granted land under Administration-sponsored land settlement schemes. Other loans were for the purchase of trucks, tractors and outboard motors, to assist in the establishment of trade stores and other small indigenous business projects, and for community development through Local Government Councils. Throughout the life of the Fund, interest was levied on loans at 4.75 per cent per annum.

Under section 14 (2) of the Papua and New Guinea Development Bank Ordinance 1965 the functions, assets and liabilities of the Native Loans Board were transferred to the Papua and New Guinea Development Bank. The transfer was effected in early 1969 when 713 accounts with outstanding balances totalling over $300,000 were taken over by the Development Bank.

EX-SERVICEMEN'S CREDIT BOARD

This Board was set up under the Ex-Servicemen's Credit Ordinance 1958 and commenced operation in November of that year. Essentially, it was an extension of the arrangements in operation in Australia for settlement of returned servicemen on the land. The Board's main purpose was to make loans to assist ex-servicemen—Australian, Papuan, and New Guinean—residing in the Territory since their discharge to establish themselves as farmers. Requirements for obtaining a loan were satisfactory military service and residence in the Territory for at least five years prior to 1958. Applicants were also expected to have had some previous agricultural experience.

Funds for the Board's operations have been provided by the Commonwealth through the Territory Administration, and almost $6 million have been advanced since 1958. At first loans were granted to a maximum of $50,000 at 3.75 per cent a year for up to twenty-five years. In practice, since loans were based on the budgeted needs of the applicants, the amounts provided for indigenous borrowers were substantially below those provided for Australians. The average loan to Papuans and New Guineans was around $1,700, to Australians $44,000.

Applications for loans under the scheme were open for four years and formally closed in November 1962. Since then, however, some additions to existing loans, at a higher interest rate of 5 per cent per annum, have been granted by the Board.

At 30 June 1967, 138 Australian ex-servicemen and 128 indigenous ex-servicemen had received loans from the Board; several had already repaid in full. Loans were made for development of all of the main cash crops: coconuts, cocoa, coffee, rubber and peanuts.

The 1963 Mission from the International Bank for Reconstruction and Development recommended that the Board's functions and assets should be transferred to the Papua and New

Guinea Development Bank when formed. This was done in early 1969 when the Development Bank took over 244 current loans with a total debt of almost $7 million.

HOUSING COMMISSION

The Housing Loans Ordinance, No. 40 of 1953, established a Commissioner for Housing to advance moneys to individuals for the purchase or lease of land and the erection or modification of a dwelling. The maximum loan in respect of any one property was 90 per cent of valuation or $4,000, later raised to $7,000, whichever was the lesser. To 30 September 1967, 718 applications for loans were dealt with, of which 428, involving almost $2 million, were approved. Funds for the operation of the scheme were provided from two Administration loans together with loans from the Commonwealth Savings Bank of Australia and the Bank of New South Wales Savings Bank.

In 1967, under the terms of the Housing Commission Ordinance, No. 27 of 1967, a Housing Commission of five members was established. Part of its role was to take over the functions, assets and responsibilities of the previous Commissioner for Housing. The new Commission followed recommendations of the 1963 Mission from the International Bank for Reconstruction and Development. Its main functions are to improve the housing situation by providing houses for sale or lease to private individuals or government employees; to develop land for housing; and to make advances to eligible borrowers to enable them to erect, purchase or improve a dwelling.

The enabling legislation provides for the Commission to obtain funds through Treasury advances, by negotiating private treaty loans from the public or from the Commonwealth, or by borrowing on overdraft. Housing loans may be made for a maximum period of forty years and for an amount up to 90 per cent of the value of the property.

In his Second Reading speech on 28 February 1967 on the Housing Commission Bill the Treasurer commented that the government hoped that 'the establishment of the Housing Commission will give impetus to the growth of co-operative building and loan societies; and the formation of land development companies'.

SUB-BANKING (SAVINGS AND LOAN SOCIETIES)

In under-developed countries it is usually difficult to provide facilities to mobilize the small savings of the village people and to meet their needs for small-scale credit. Particularly where communications are inadequate, language barriers exist, and the bulk of the populace has scant familiarity with money and credit, the orthodox financial system is not geared to these tasks. Special 'grass-roots' sub-banking institutions are required. In Papua and New Guinea this role is filled by savings and loan societies and savings clubs.

Savings and loan societies are credit societies of limited liability, based on capital contributed solely by members, with limited powers to borrow from outside sources, and with loans restricted to members only. In operation, they are similar to the credit unions which operate in many countries of the world. In essence, they are very small-scale co-operatively run banks. As the only widespread grass-roots financial institutions in Papua and New Guinea they form an integral part of the financial system, serving mainly, but not solely, the indigenous people.

Savings and loan societies in Papua and New Guinea were started on the initiative of the Reserve Bank of Australia. The Reserve Bank, with the support of the commercial banks, accepted responsibility for assisting societies until the movement was strong enough to handle these tasks itself. The Registry of Savings and Loan Societies is staffed by the Reserve Bank.

Under the Savings and Loan Societies Ordinance 1961-69, any group of twenty or more people with a common membership bond may apply for registration as a savings and loan society. Most groups who apply come from the same village or belong to the same clan or extended family; some have a common employer or attend the same mission. Rural groups predominate. Members elect officers to manage the affairs of each society.

The first savings and loan society was registered in May 1962. At 30 June 1969 there were 221 societies throughout the Territory with over eleven thousand members and total funds of $781,481. Most of these funds had been saved from members' current incomes.

SAVINGS AND LOAN SOCIETIES

	No. of Societies	Membership	Funds ($)
1962	1	80	592
1964	23	1,161	48,058
1966	139	7,523	392,507
1968	208	10,781	695,978
1969	221	11,238	781,481

Societies use their funds to make loans to members or to invest in approved securities. The remainder is held on interest-bearing deposit with a bank. During the early period of societies' existence loans accounted for only a minor part of total funds. However, demand for loans has grown

SAVINGS AND LOAN SOCIETIES
Classification of Loans by Purpose, 1962 to 1969

	No. of Loans	Amount Approved ($)
Building materials	1,159	113,732
Trading	1,410	143,026
Motor vehicles	455	133,703
Agriculture	1,014	74,644
Durable consumer goods	250	14,173
Education	58	2,709
Miscellaneous	550	51,487
	4,896	533,474

significantly. At 30 June 1969, of total funds of $781,481, loans accounted for $317,712; another $116,360 was invested, mainly in Territory Administration securities; and $347,409 was on deposit with banks.

Up to 30 June 1969 almost five thousand loans had been made for $533,474.

Most loans are made on the basis of the borrower's personal standing; the advantage of a closely knit membership group is that the 'personal equation' can be assessed reasonably accurately. In some cases, however, guarantees are sought from other members of the society, and provisions exist for taking other forms of security.

In March 1966 societies throughout Papua and New Guinea formed a Territory-wide Federation of Savings and Loan Societies. The Federation conducts a contributory Loan Protection Fund used to pay the outstanding balance of any loan due from a deceased borrower to a member society. It also acts as a central supplier of stationery and generally deals with matters of common interest to societies.

In addition to the Federation district leagues of savings and loan societies have been formed. At the end of 1969, two such leagues were in existence: in the Gazelle Peninsula of New Britain, formed March 1966; and in the Eastern Highlands District, formed August 1967. These deal with matters of a more local nature, perform some auditing and clerical functions, and generally assist member societies with financial and management problems.

Section 12 of the Savings and Loan Societies Ordinance 1961-69 requires that the Registrar shall, before registering any group as a savings and loan society, be satisfied that registration is advisable and that the proposed society is viable. To facilitate a decision on this, groups wishing to form societies are asked to complete a probationary period as a savings club. This is an informal association which provides for members to save regularly in a common fund, but does not make loans. Each club member retains full rights to any funds he has submitted. This procedure gives the Registrar an indication of the likely strength of the group and the keenness of its members; at the same time the members are enabled to test their own enthusiasm, to train their future office-bearers, and to build up the level of their funds. Most clubs eventually become registered as savings and loan societies.

LIFE ASSURANCE AND GENERAL INSURANCE

Insurance is a way of sharing risks. Insurance institutions operate to pool risks of a similar nature faced by a wide range of people or groups, and to convert these risks into monetary terms. It is usual to distinguish between those institutions providing cover against death or advancing age—life assurance, and those insuring against other contingencies—general insurance. Even where the one institution handles both types of business, it is usually done through separate subsidiaries with separate financial reserves.

SAVINGS CLUBS

	No. of Clubs	Membership	Funds ($)
1962	1	40	100
1964	111	5,156	57,712
1966	346	14,783	224,787
1968*	298	12,142	298,263
1969*	253	9,713	281,180

* Reflects increased rate of registration as Societies.

Eight major life assurance companies are registered in Papua and New Guinea. All are overseas institutions which operate through branches or accredited agents. They provide a full range of life policies—whole of life, endowment, temporary and annuity. Most life policies written have been for non-indigenous policy holders though indigenous business has been increasing, particularly since 1966. A major difficulty with indigenous policies has been the lack of accurate life tables on which to assess risks and base premiums. This is being gradually overcome and several companies are now actively pursuing indigenous business among employees of government or large commercial organizations.

Apart from general provisions of the Companies Ordinance 1963, the only Territory legislation covering life assurance is the Life Policies Protection Ordinance, No. 49 of 1951, which protects the interest of the insured in certain cases. Provisions of the Life Insurance Act 1945-66 of the Commonwealth can be extended by proclamation to Papua and New Guinea, but such a proclamation has yet to be made. Accordingly, no special control measures are laid down for the local operations of assurance companies; there is no local Insurance Commissioner for example, nor are there any special provisions relating to the investment of funds collected in the Territory. However, some life assurance companies have subscribed to Territory Administration securities. The first such investments took place in 1963, and in the period from 1 July 1963 to 31 December 1969, life assurance companies had subscribed a total of almost $6.8 million.

Over twenty firms write general insurance business in the fire, accident and marine fields. About half of these are registered locally as foreign companies, and the rest operate either through local agents or directly from one of their Australian offices.

The Insurance Act of 1932-66 of the Commonwealth extends to Papua and New Guinea, and this requires general insurance companies to lodge certain deposits with the Commonwealth Treasurer and also to supply him regularly with prescribed information. In some fields, particularly in the fields of workers' compensation and motor vehicle third party insurance, companies are bound also by provisions of specific Territory legislation.

Co-operative societies in Papua and New Guinea have established their own insurance institution, the Co-operative Security Society Limited, which has a risk-sharing arrangement with the Territory subsidiary of an Australian insurance company under which it carries part of the risk on insured marine vessels owned by co-operative societies and part of societies' fire insurance. It is intended that the proportion of the risk borne by the Co-operative Security Society Limited will gradually increase as it builds up its reserves and its experience in the insurance field.

HIRE PURCHASE

Hire purchase finance provides a means whereby a person may obtain possession of goods upon payment of a first instalment, but does not acquire ownership until the final instalment is paid. Instalments are legally regarded as hiring fees. If they fall in arrears the lender may regain possession of the goods; on the other hand, the hirer may elect to terminate the hiring and return the goods at any time.

A number of institutions provide hire purchase facilities in Papua and New Guinea. The three private trading banks hold equity capital in Australian finance companies which operate in the Territory, the Papua and New Guinea Development Bank provides hire purchase finance, and a number of Australian hire purchase companies and some small local companies also operate. Most large trading firms have arrangements with one or more hire purchase companies to provide facilities in association with their retailing activities.

Apart from general provisions of the Companies Ordinance 1963 hire purchase activities are controlled by the Hire Purchase Ordinance 1966. This came into operation in January 1969, replacing earlier cumbersome legislation.

Statistical information on the extent of hire purchase approvals and outstandings is not available, but the level of debt has been growing in importance in recent years. Motor vehicles, agricultural plant and equipment, and consumer durables have been the major items financed. Increasing use is being made of hire purchase finance by Papuans and New Guineans.

Australian hire purchase companies operating in the Territory accept money on deposit from the public. This applies also to some of the small local ventures which pay interest at about 6 per cent a year for money repayable on demand.

TRADE CREDIT

Most wholesale and retail firms provide credit on an extensive scale to their customers, and trade credit between suppliers is also common. Most accounts are nominally payable in thirty days though there is a tendency for the period to lengthen unless a firm's credit supervision is efficient. Statistics on the amount of trade credit are not collected.

STOCK EXCHANGE

No stock exchange has yet developed in Papua and New Guinea. Pressure for the establishment of an exchange so far has been restricted to a very limited number of the non-indigenous community.

A stock exchange provides a valuable service in helping to promote economic development in an organized society. It is difficult to say, however, just when a developing country should acquire one. There are certain prerequisites. There must be a sufficient number of companies whose shares qualify for listing on an exchange; there must be a sufficient number of buyers and sellers to trade in these shares; and there must be people able and willing to act as brokers. Papua and New Guinea does not yet meet these minimum conditions.

There are over fifteen hundred companies registered as 'local' companies with nominal capital in excess of $300 million; paid-up capital would be much less. However, most of these are small concerns whose shares would not be suitable for trading on a stock exchange. In addition there are about two hundred companies registered in the Territory as 'foreign' companies. A great number of these are branches or subsidiaries of companies listed on Australian or overseas stock exchanges. It is doubtful if the volume of trade in most of their shares among Territory residents would persuade them to seek listing on a Territory exchange.

Residents who wish to deal in shares or other securities are able to deal locally on Australian stock exchanges. Two members of Australian stock exchanges operate branch offices in Port Moresby, and agents in the other main towns have arrangements with Australian brokers. The total volume of transactions does not seem sufficient to justify the establishment of an exchange at any centre.

Securities issued by the Territory Administration so far have not been suitable for public trading. Public loan issues have consisted of premium securities redeemable at face value on one month's notice, and the only other securities on issue are for private treaty loans. If in the future the Administration varies the types of securities it issues, a market for them could develop and this could become the forerunner of a full stock exchange.

OTHER FINANCIAL INSTITUTIONS

Other institutions operate as part of Papua and New Guinea's financial system, meeting specialized needs. For the most part these institutions are branches of Australian concerns, and the Territory is a very small part of their operations.

The Territory has not yet developed any specialized money market institutions but there are local agents for several dealers in the Australian short-term money market. The use made of these facilities is growing. Australian unit trust companies also attract funds from the Territory.

Some Australian and overseas merchant banking firms, more correctly termed development corporations, have interests in Papua and New Guinea. The three main firms involved are Australia and New Guinea Corporation Limited, Commonwealth Development Finance Company Limited, and Development Finance Corporation Limited.

Co-operative societies operating in Papua and New Guinea are planning to establish a central finance society to mobilize funds within the co-operative movement and lend them for new co-operative ventures.

A number of superannuation, pension and trust funds exist and these will form an important part of any local securities markets which may develop. The Papua and New Guinea Superannuation Board which administers the public service fund, at 31 December 1969 had more than $2.2 million invested in Territory Administration securities.

Commonwealth of Australia, *Annual Report, Territory of Papua 1927-8, 1948-9, 1951-2* —. Canberra, 1929, 1950, 1953 —.
———— *Report to the League of Nations on the Administration of the Territory of New Guinea 1936-7.* Canberra, 1938.
———— *Report to the United Nations on the Administration of the Territory of New Guinea 1947-8* —. Canberra, 1949 —.
R. R. Hirst and R. H. Wallace (eds), *Studies in the Australian Capital Market.* Melbourne, 1964.
International Bank for Reconstruction and Development, *The Economic Development of the Territory of Papua and New Guinea,* pp. 354-61 and ch. 8. Baltimore, 1965.
M. J. Phillips, 'The Introduction of Savings and Loan Societies in Papua-New Guinea', in *Proceedings, Regional Technical Meeting on Economic Development and Capital Formation,* South Pacific Commission. Noumea, 1962.
———— 'Unsatisfactory Trash—Monetary Transition in Papua and New Guinea', paper to Papua and New Guinea Society of Victoria. Melbourne, 1969 (roneoed).
———— and P. S. Ferguson, 'Savings Clubs and Savings and Loan Societies in Papua and New Guinea', in *Credit Unions in the South Pacific,* ed. N. Runcie. London, 1969.
Reserve Bank of Australia, *Report and Financial Statements.* Sydney.
T. P. N. G. House of Assembly, *Debates,* vol. 1, nos 1-15, 1964-7.
———— *Registrar of Savings and Loan Societies, Annual Report 1961-2* —. Port Moresby, 1962 —.

M. J. P.

(*See also* BANKING; CO-OPERATIVES)

FINSCH, Friedrich Hermann Otto (1839-1917), ornithologist and ethnographer, was born at Warmbrunn in Silesia on 8 August 1839, and died at Brunswick, Germany, on 31 January 1917. Although educated for a business career he was a self-taught naturalist and achieved great distinction in that field. He travelled extensively in pursuit of his scientific interests and spent two lengthy periods in the Pacific area. During the years 1879-82 he visited Australia, New Zealand, Polynesia, and eastern New Guinea and near-by islands. In 1881 he visited the Astrolabe Bay region of New Guinea in the capacity of a natural history collector but apparently was also examining the economic potential of the area on behalf of German business interests. By claiming friendship with N. Miklouho-Maclay [q.v.] he won the confidence of the natives, which facilitated German

Otto Finsch.

occupation three years later. About this time German trading firms had established stations at several points around New Britain and adjacent islands. While they traded in copra their main interest was in recruiting labour for their Samoa plantations.

Finsch's second visit to New Guinea in 1884-5 was of a very different character and its real purpose was surrounded with the greatest secrecy. After arriving from Germany he left Sydney in the trading ship *Samoa* ostensibly on a scientific trip to the Phoenix Islands. In fact he had been commissioned by Adolph von Hansemann [q.v.], a prominent German financier and leader of a new consortium, the Neuguinea-Kompagnie, to lead an expedition charged with the selection of harbours, establishment of trading posts, and acquisition of land for colonial development on the north-eastern coast of New Guinea. During November 1884 the German flag was raised at a number of points in the Bismarck Archipelago and the north-eastern New Guinea mainland. These proceedings had the approval of Bismarck and the German protectorate was proclaimed in December.

On his travels Finsch made extensive collections of birds, other natural history specimens, and ethnographical material. During his second expedition to New Guinea he had no spare time for his scientific interests but purchased a collection of bird specimens from Carl Hunstein, a German collector who had gone originally to New Guinea as a gold-seeker but having failed in that enterprise, had obtained employment in the Neuguinea-Kompagnie.

Finsch was one of the leading systematic ornithologists of his time and during his career held curatorial appointments in museums at Leyden in Holland, Bremen and Brunswick. He published a large number of papers on birds in European and British scientific journals, besides some large works including important monographs on the parrots, and the birds of central Polynesia and east Africa. He described for the first time many genera and species of birds. Several birds, a couple of mammals, and the plant genus *Finschia*, from New Guinea, were named after him. He is also commemorated in the name of the township of Finschhafen, and a part of the north-eastern coast was known at one time as the Finsch Coast. In 1868 he was given an honorary degree of D.Phil. by the University of Bonn.

During the latter part of his life Finsch largely gave up ornithology and concentrated on ethnography, and for the last twelve years of his life was Curator of Ethnography at the Municipal Museum in Brunswick.

O. Finsch, *Samoafahrten. Reisen in Kaiser Wilhelms-Land und Englisch-Neu-Guinea in den Jahren 1884 u. 1885 an Bord des deutschen Dampfers 'Samoa'*. Leipzig, 1888; *Otto Finsch: Systematische Übersicht der Ergebnisse seiner Reisen und schriftstellerischen Tätigkeit, 1859-1889*. Berlin, 1899; M. G. Jacobs, 'Bismarck and the Annexation of New Guinea', *Historical Studies Australia and New Zealand*, vol. 5, 1951; J. D. Legge, *Australian Colonial Policy*. Sydney, 1956; Obituary, *Ibis*, 10th series, vol. 6, 1918; *An Ethnographic Bibliography of New Guinea*. 3 vols, Canberra, 1968.

J. H. CALABY

(*See also* EXPLORATION; GERMAN NEW GUINEA)

FISHES. Published records show that 1,392 species occur in New Guinea, Admiralty Islands, Bismarck Archipelago, Waigeo, Buka and Bougainville. Additional species recorded from the remainder of the Solomon Islands raise this number by 6 per cent. The number appears too low, considering the geographical position of New Guinea within the Indo-West Pacific faunal area, and the fact that local speciation has occurred freely, especially amongst freshwater and fluviatile families. Lists published respectively in 1953 and 1964 attribute the Philippines with 2,176 and Australia with 2,447 species. Knowledge of this fauna has been built from collections made by individuals, scientific and exploratory expeditions, and hydrographical surveys since late in the eighteenth century. These collections are stored in museums in England, France, Holland, Belgium, Germany, Switzerland, Italy, U.S.A. and Australia.

Apart from *Scleropages* the fauna is composed entirely of marine families. Even those species which now occupy fresh and brackish water have been derived from marine ancestors in fairly recent geological times. The fauna is typically that of the Indo-West Pacific, combining elements of the Indian Ocean, the western part of Oceania and tropical Australia.

Sharks (order Lamniformes). Six families and twenty-one species. The whale shark, which belongs to family Rhincodontidae, grows to forty-five feet, is pelagic (lives in the open sea) and gregarious in off-shore waters and feeds on plankton and small fish, but is harmless. Family Orectolobidae is represented by a pelagic tawny shark (*Ginglymostoma*) and, in reef areas, sluggish ground forms including two small harmless catsharks

(*Hemiscyllium* and *Chiloscyllium*) and two rather large carpet-sharks or wobbegong (*Orectolobus* and *Eucrossorhinus*) which may attack man. The swift ferocious hammerhead shark belongs to the family Sphyrnidae, attains fifteen feet and is very dangerous. Ten pelagic species constituting the family Carcharhinidae include the small smooth-fanged shark (*Aprionodon*), Maclot's shark (*Hypoprion*), the large man-eating tiger shark (*Galeocerda*) and whaler sharks (*Carcharhinus*). One whaler may be a permanent resident of freshwater lakes but the best known is the black-tip shark which schools in shallow coastal waters. The family Scyliorhinidae is represented by a small marbled catshark (*Atelomycterus*) and the family Triakidae by two small dog-sharks (*Triaenodon*). Pelagic species frequent coastal waters and inlets but some penetrate rivers even to considerable distances from the sea.

Rays (order Myliobatiformes). Four families and nine species. Characteristically they have flattened discoid bodies with the mouth and gill openings below. More typical species live close to the bottom in muddy areas close inshore, especially in lagoons and near river mouths, and feed on tidal flats. The family Urolophidae is represented by an imperfectly known short-tailed stingray, and the family Dasyatidae embraces fantail-rays (*Taeniura* and *Dasyatis*), coachwhip-rays (*Himantura*) and a blue-spotted ray (*Amphotistius*). An eagle-ray (*Aetobatus*) with wide wing-like flaps and a duckbill-shaped head belongs to the family Myliobatidae. In the family Mobulidae is the giant, horned devil-ray (*Manta*) which swims at the surface in the open sea and may exceed twenty feet across its disc.

Shovelnose-rays (order Rhinobatiformes). One species in each of families Rhynchobatidae and Rhinobatidae. Their form is shark-like but with a tapering flat shovel-like snout. The mouth and gill openings are below. The white-spotted and green species are harmless sluggish bottom-dwellers in sandy areas inshore. They grow to seven feet.

Sawfishes (order Pristiformes). Family Pristidae with two freshwater species of *Pristiopsis*. There may also be saltwater species. They have shark-like bodies with gill openings below and with the snout extended into a long toothed blade. This saw is used to grub in mud for food. Sawfishes are sluggish but dangerous when cornered.

Herring-like fishes (order Clupeiformes). Fifty-seven species arranged in seventeen families grouped in five suborders. The largest group is the Clupeoidei with eight families. The family Alepocephalidae is represented by one small bathypelagic (inhabiting the deep sea) species but the members of the other families are inhabitants of coastal shallows, estuaries and rivers. In the family Dorosomidae are three gizzard-shads or bony-bream including the marine *Anodontostoma* and *Nematalosa* and a freshwater *Fluvialosa* endemic to the Fly River. They feed in muddy places and have gizzard-like stomachs. The family Engraulidae is represented by seventeen species of anchovies including the small transparent *Stolephorus* which forms large schools in coastal shallows. Larger forms with backward prolongation of the upper jaw bones include *Scutengraulis*, *Thrissina* and *Thrissocles*. *Setipinna* has the uppermost rays of the pectoral fin greatly prolonged and the endemic *Papuengraulis* has the dorsal fin vestigial. All have protruding pig-like snouts. Round herrings of the family Dussumieridae include two small blue sprats (*Spratelloides*) and two larger sprats (*Dussumieria*). Herrings and sardines comprise seventeen species in the family Clupeidae. The more typical kinds which school in shallow waters are *Harengula*, *Sardinella*, *Macrura* and *Kowala*. Brackish and freshwater species belong to the genus *Clupeoides*. Two pilchard-like species belong to *Amblygaster*. *Pellona* and *Euplatygaster* are aberrant forms with long-based anal fins and modified jaw structure. Amongst the larger members of the suborder are the families Albulidae (bonefish), Megalopidae (ox-eye herring) and Elopidae (giant herring) each with a single species. The suborders Chanoidei, Chirocentroidei and Osteoglossoidei are represented each by a single species. Milkfish (family Chanidae) inhabit coastal waters and rivers. They are vegetarian and extensively cultured in ponds throughout South-east Asia. Wolf-herring (family Chirocentridae) are voracious carnivores with strap-like bodies and large fangs. The family Osteoglossidae, which has a few living freshwater representatives on the continental land masses, is an archaic group of which a subspecies of *Scleropages* (barramundi) is found in southern New Guinea. The suborder Stomiatoidei embraces nine species of deep-water fishes representing six families. These exhibit various modifications for life in the lightless ocean depths. They are generally black or silvery and many have luminous glands and series of photophores. The families are Idiacanthidae (sea-dragons), Chauliodontidae (viperfish), Stomiatidae (boafish), Malacosteidae (hinged-heads), Gonostomidae (porthole-fish) and Sternoptychidae (hatchetfish).

Lizardfish, lanternfish, barracudinas (order Myctophiformes). Thirty-four species arranged in four families. All have an adipose second dorsal fin. The family Myctophidae includes sixteen small lanternfish of the genera *Centrobranchus*, *Hygophum*, *Symbolophorus*, *Myctophum*, *Diaphus*, *Lepidophanes* and *Lampanyctus*. All are bathypelagic in ocean depths but move up into the surface layers at night. They are characterized by series of light-emitting photophores. The family Paralepidae contains eleven species of small sharp-nosed slender fishes of the genera *Stemonosudis*, *Paralepis* and *Lestidium*. They are called barracudinas because of their superficial resemblance to the barracudas or sea-pike. They are restricted to deep waters and thus are seldom seen. The family Synodontidae (lizardfish or saurys) contains five shallow-water species in the genera *Synodus*, *Saurida* and *Trachinocephalus*. They are elongate bottom-dwellers with lizard-like heads and dentition. There are two translucent ghost-grinners or Bombay ducks (*Harpodon*) in the closely related family Harpodontidae.

Pelican-eels (order Saccopharyngiformes). One species in family Eurypharyngidae. It has an extremely large head and slender tapering tail and is bathypelagic in ocean waters.

Tapetails (order Miripinniformes). One species in family Eutaeniophoridae. It is a deep-water pelagic form which trails a long streamer-like appendage from its tail during its larval phase.

Catfish (order Siluroidiformes). Forty-five species arranged in three families. The family Plotosidae has twenty species including coastal and estuarine *Plotosus*, *Paraplotosus*, *Cnidoglanis* and *Euristhmus*. Freshwater genera include *Oloplotosus*, *Prochilus* and *Neosilurus*. All have the vertical fins continuous around the tail and many saltwater genera have a preanal dendritic gland. The family Tachysuridae comprises twenty-four fork-tailed species distributed through coastal, estuarine and fresh waters. *Cinetodus*, *Brustiarius*, *Tachysurus*, *Cochlefelis*, *Hexanematichthys*, *Netuma*, *Nedystoma*, *Tetranesodon* and *Hemipimelodus* are represented. A single species in the family Doiichthyidae and many species in the other two families are endemic. All have barbels (elongated fleshy projections, usually on the head) around their mouths and some are nest builders.

Eels (order Anguilliformes). Fifty-eight species arranged in eight families. The family Synaphobranchidae has one species in deep water. There

(1) Wobbygong *Eucrossorhinus dasypogon* (family Orectolobidae); (2) Catshark *Hemiscyllium freycineti* (Orectolobidae); (3) Whale shark *Rhincodon typus* (Rhincodontidae); (4) Hammerhead shark *Sphyrna lewini* (Sphyrnidae); (5) White-tip shark *Triaenodon apicalis* (Triakidae); (6) Tiger shark *Galeocerda cuvieri* (Carcharhinidae); (7) Catshark *Atelomycterus marmoratus* (Scyliorhinidae); (8) Coachwhip-ray *Himantura uarnak* (Dasyatidae); (9) Sawfish *Pristiopsis microdon* (Pristidae); (10) Eagle-ray *Aetobatus narinari* (Myliobatidae); (11) Devil-ray *Manta birostris* (Mobulidae); (12) Shovelnose-ray *Rhynchobatus djiddensis* (Rhynchobatidae); (13) Shovelnose-ray *Rhinobatos batillum* (Rhinobatidae); (14) Black-head *Xenodermichthys schmidti* (Alepocephalidae); (15) Bony-bream *Nematalosa come* (Dorosomidae); (16) Milkfish *Chanos chanos* (Chanidae); (17) Ox-eye herring *Megalops cyprinoides* (Megalopidae); (18) Bonefish *Albula neoguinaica* (Albulidae); (19) Giant herring *Elops hawaiensis* (Elopidae); (20) Sardine *Sardinella perforata* (Clupeidae); (21) Anchovy *Stolephorus devisi* (Engraulidae); (22) Sprat *Dussumieria acuta* (Dussumieridae); (23) Wolf-herring *Chirocentrus dorab* (Chirocentridae); (24) Barramundi *Scleropages leichardti leichardti* (Osteoglossidae); (25) Hinged-head *Malacosteus niger* (Malacosteidae); (26) Viperfish *Chauliodus sloanei* (Chauliodontidae); (27) Sea-dragon *Idiacanthus fasciola* (Idiacanthidae); (28) Boafish *Stomias nebulosus* (Stomiatidae); (29) Porthole-fish *Cyclothone microdon* (Gonostomidae); (30) Barracudina *Lestidium nudum* (Paralepidae); (31) Lanternfish *Hygophum macrochir* (Myctophidae); (32) Saury *Trachinocephalus myops* (Synodontidae); (33) Bombay duck *Harpodon translucens* (Harpodontidae); (34) Hatchetfish *Sternoptyx diaphana* (Sternoptychidae).

are six species of catadromous (i.e. that live in fresh water but go to sea to spawn) freshwater eels in family Anguillidae. The family Ophichthyidae comprises eleven species which are mostly nocturnal and burrow tail first in mud and sand. These snake-eels (*Myrichthys*, *Achirophichthys*, *Leiuranus*, *Pisodonophis*, *Zonophichthus* and *Caecula*) are slender, have a free pointed tail-tip and are often strikingly banded. Four species of worm-eels (*Muraenichthys*) represent the family Echelidae. They are small, plain coloured, and burrow. The family Muraenidae includes twenty-four species of reef-eels or morays. The genera *Arndha*, *Echidna*, *Thyrsoidea*, *Uropterygius*, *Enchelynassa*, *Pseudechidna*, *Priodonophis*, *Sideria* and *Gymnothorax* make up this group. They are robust eels with strong caninoid dentition and are usually brightly coloured and patterned. They are extremely voracious and inhabit crevices in reefs. Eight species of thrush-eels (*Moringua*) constitute the family Moringuidae. They are small, degenerate, thread-like forms inhabiting shallow water and burrowing in the bottom. A voracious pike-eel of coastal waters and rivers is the sole member of family Muraenesocidae. Conger-eels (family Leptocephalidae) are represented by three species including the littoral and nocturnal *Conger*, and deeper water *Congrellus* and *Brachyconger*.

Swamp-eels (order Symbranchiformes). One species in the family Symbranchidae is an eel-like inhabitant of fresh and brackish water swamps. The gills open into a single transverse slit ventrally.

Half-beaks, garfish, flyingfish (order Beloniformes). Forty-seven species arranged in three families grouped in two suborders. The Scomberesocoidei includes twelve garfish or long-toms in the family Belonidae. These are elongate surface fishes with both jaws prolonged and studded with needle-like teeth. *Stenocaulus* is freshwater but *Tylosurus* and *Strongylura* are marine. The coastal genus *Thalassosteus* has a short keel on its lower jaw. The remaining families belong to the Exocoetoidei. There are sixteen half-beaks in the family Hemirhamphidae. These have the lower jaw produced forwards into a rod-like beak. The very elongate *Euleptorhamphus* has enlarged pectoral fins and inhabits open waters. The genera *Labidorhamphus*, *Rhynchorhamphus*, *Hemirhamphus* and *Hyporhamphus* are primarily coastal. The short-bodied *Zenarchopterus*, in which males have enlarged feather-like rays in the dorsal and anal fins, inhabit fresh and brackish waters. In coastal and adjacent oceanic waters are nineteen flyingfish of the family Exocoetidae. *Oxyporhamphus*, *Parexocoetus*, *Exocoetus*, *Prognichthys*, *Hirundichthys* and *Cypselurus* are represented. Members of this family have their paired fins enlarged and wing-like enabling gliding flights to be made above the water surface.

Cod-like fishes (order Gadiformes). Four species in family Bregmacerotidae. All are small pelagic forms in coastal and deeper waters. They are named unicorn-cod because of the single filamentous ray on the nape.

Thread-tails (order Lampridiformes). A single abyssal species in family Stylephoridae. It swims vertically with head uppermost, has projecting telescopic eyes and an elongate thread-like extension to its tail.

Flatfishes (order Pleuronectiformes). Thirty-one species arranged in five families grouped in two suborders. These highly modified forms are greatly flattened and swim on their sides close to the bottom. Both eyes are on the same side which according to family may be either left or right. Most occur in shallow coastal waters and estuaries but a few live in deeper waters and others penetrate into freshwater. The suborder Psettodoidei has one species in the family Psettodidae. This is a robust halibut with large needle-like teeth and may be left- or right-handed. The remaining families are grouped in the suborder Pleuronectoidei. In the family Bothidae are eleven species of left-hand flounders with distinct tails, *Taeniopsetta*, *Pseudorhombus*, *Bothus*, *Arnoglossus* and *Engyprosopon*. The family Pleuronectidae is represented by two species of right-hand flounders with tails, *Nematops* and *Brachypleura*. Males in the last genus are crested. Twelve species of right-hand soles make up the family Soleidae. They include *Heteromycteris*, *Achirus*, *Aseraggodes*, *Aesopia*,

(35) Catfish-eel *Plotosus papuensis* (family Plotosidae); (36) Salmon-catfish *Hemipimelodus papillifer* (Tachysuridae); (37) Spoon-snouted catfish *Doiichthys novaeguineae* (Doiichthyidae); (38) Tapetail *Eutaeniophorus festivus* (Eutaeniophoridae); (39) Pelican-eel *Eurypharynx pelecanoides* (Eurypharyngidae); (40) Snake-eel *Myrichthys maculosus* (Ophichthyidae); (41) Moray *Echidna nebulosa* (Muraenidae); (42) Freshwater eel *Anguilla interioris* (Anguillidae); (43) Worm-eel *Muraenichthys schultzei* (Echelidae); (44) Thrush-eel *Moringua bicolor* (Moringuidae); (45) Conger-eel *Conger cinereus* (Leptocephalidae); (46) One-gilled eel *Symbranchus bengalensis* (Symbranchidae); (47) Pike-eel *Muraenesox cinereus* (Muraenesocidae); (48) Unicorn-cod *Bregmaceros nectabanus* (Bregmacerotidae); (49) Half-beak *Hemirhamphus commersoni* (Hemirhamphidae); (50) Thread-tail *Stylephorus chordatus* (Stylephoridae); (51) Flyingfish *Cypselurus oligolepis* (Exocoetidae); (52) Long-tom *Tylosurus melanotus* (Belonidae); (53) Queensland halibut *Psettodes erumei* (Psettodidae); (54) Tongue-sole *Cynoglossus puncticeps* (Cynoglossidae); (55) Left-hand flounder *Bothus pantherinus* (Bothidae); (56) Sole *Brachirus orientalis* (Soleidae); (57) Right-hand flounder *Brachypleura novaezeelandiae* (Pleuronectidae); (58) Squirrelfish *Holocentrus caudimaculatus* (Holocentridae); (59) Headlight-fish *Anomalops katoptron* (Anomalopidae); (60) Midnight-fish *Melamphaes crassiceps* (Melamphaidae); (61) Ghost pipefish *Solenichthys cyanopterus* (Solenichthyidae); (62) Pipefish *Corythoichthys intestinalis* (Syngnathidae); (63) Razorfish *Centriscus scutatus* (Centriscidae); (64) Winged dragonfish *Pegasus volitans* (Pegasidae); (65) Pipefish *Syngnathoides biaculeatus* (Syngnathidae); (66) Flutemouth *Fistularia petimba* (Fistulariidae); (67) Trumpetfish *Aulostoma chinensis* (Aulostomidae); (68) Seahorse *Hippocampus histrix* (Syngnathidae).

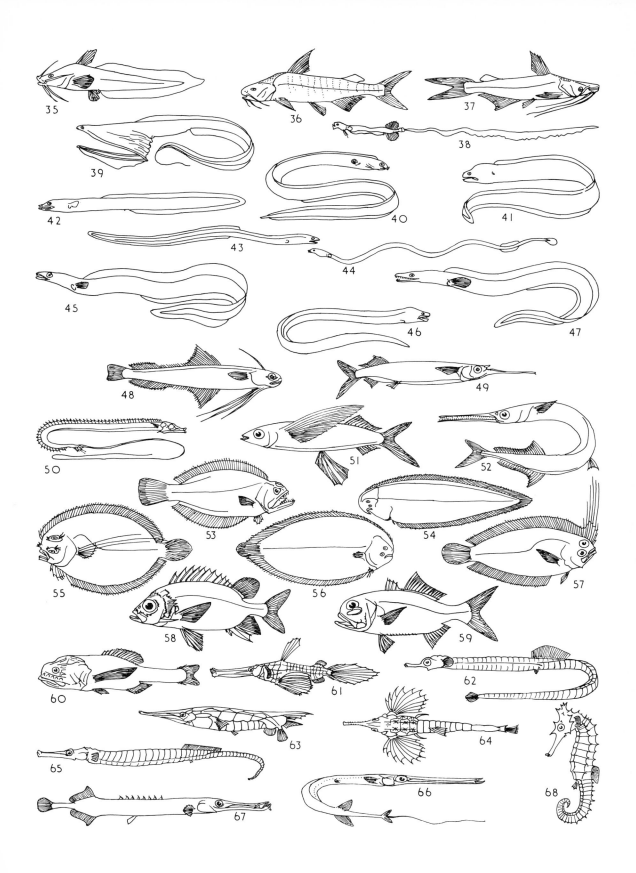

Dexillichthys and *Brachirus*. The tail fin is free in some of these but not in others. Some are strikingly banded or ocellated (having eye-like spots) and others have tufts of dermal filaments. The family Cynoglossidae comprises five species of tongue-soles, *Cynoglossus* and *Paraplagusia*. These are elongate, end in a sharp point and have a hooked flap around the mouth.

Squirrelfish (order Beryciformes). Twenty-three species arranged in three families. Deep-water forms include one species in each of the families Anomalopidae and Melamphaidae. The remainder belong to the family Holocentridae (squirrelfish) which are marine nocturnal forms retreating into crevices in reefs during the day. They have hard scales with sharp jagged margins and spiny heads. The colour of most is bright red. Genera include *Kutaflammeo, Holocentrus, Myripristis* and *Ostichthys*. The first two have the preoperculum (membrane bone between cheek and operculum forming the front part of the gill cover) armed with a long sharp spine.

Tuft-gilled fishes (order Syngnathiformes). Thirty-four species arranged in five families grouped in two suborders. They are curiously specialized and degenerate and have a tiny mouth at the end of a tubular snout. The suborder Aulostomoidei has three families in coastal waters. The family Centriscidae with one species each in *Aeoliscus* and *Centriscus* are the razorfish or wafers. They have extremely compressed bodies encased in a hard transparent cuirass. They swim in small platoons in a vertical attitude with the snout pointing downward. There is one species of trumpetfish (family Aulostomidae) and this is the least specialized of the group, retaining normal scales and a low dorsal fin. Two species of flutemouth in the family Fistulariidae are pelagic in coastal waters. They have elongate depressed bodies with elongate flute-like snouts and a whiplash-like filament protruding from the middle of the forked tail. The suborder Syngnathoidei comprises two coastal short-bodied ghost pipefish in the family Solenichthyidae and twenty-seven highly modified forms in the family Syngnathidae. The last consists of seahorses (*Hippocampus*) and pipefishes of the genera

Stigmatophora, Syngnathoides and *Haliichthys* with prehensile tails, and *Ichthyocampus, Choeroichthys, Doryrhamphus, Dunckerocampus, Halicampus, Coelonotus, Oostethus, Doryichthys, Bombonia, Micrognathus, Syngnathus* and *Corythoichthys* which have small caudal fins. The Syngnathoidei are sluggish and poor swimmers and seek protection through camouflage in vegetation, using colour, shape and weed-like dermal appendages to blend with their surroundings. All are encased in an armour of bony rings which permit limited body movement. Eggs are carried on the trunk or abdomen of the males, sometimes enclosed in a pouch. They inhabit shallow coastal waters, some penetrating through brackish into fresh waters.

Winged-dragonfish (order Pegasiformes). Two small pelagic species (*Pegasus* and *Zalises*) in family Pegasidae. These resemble pipefish in having the body encased in bony rings but which are fused solidly in the head and thorax. The mouth is overhung by a rod-like rostrum and the pectoral fins are enlarged and wing-like.

Barracuda, mullet, silversides (order Mugiliformes). Fifty-nine species arranged in six families grouped in two suborders. The six species of barracuda or sea-pike (*Sphyraenella, Sphyraena, Agrioposphyraena* and *Callosphyraena*) represent the family Sphyraenidae and suborder Sphyraenoidei. They are voracious, fast-swimming fishes with slender bodies and canine teeth. They are carnivorous, the larger ones frequenting reefs and the smaller species schooling in estuaries. The remaining families constitute the suborder Mugiloidei which is characterized by reduced dentition. The best known are eighteen species of grey mullet (family Mugilidae). Some are important food fishes. They ingest mud and travel in schools in coastal waters, entering rivers and in some cases penetrating into fresh water. *Liza, Mugil, Valamugil* and *Crenimugil* are basically marine. *Rhinomugil* has a shark-like snout and protruding eyes. *Cestraeus* is strictly resident in fresh water. Hardyheads or silversides (family Atherinidae) are small, slender, silverbanded fishes which congregate in schools. There are fourteen species. *Atherion, Stenatherina, Alla-*

(69) Mullet *Liza dussumieri* (family Mugilidae); (70) Rainbowfish *Nematocentris rubrostriatus* (Melanotaeniidae); (71) Hardyhead *Hypoatherina lacunosa* (Atherinidae); (72) Blue-eye *Pseudomugil novaeguineae* (Pseudomugilidae); (73) Sea-pike *Sphyraenella flavicauda* (Sphyraenidae); (74) Threadfin-salmon *Polydactylus plebeius* (Polynemidae); (75) Little beauty *Charisella fredericki* (Telmatherinidae); (76) Rake-gill mackerel *Rastrelliger kanagurta* (Scombridae); (77) Wahoo *Acanthocybium solandri* (Acanthocybiidae); (78) Spanish mackerel *Scomberomorus commersoni* (Scomberomoridae); (79) Tuna *Neothunnus macropterus* (Thunnidae); (80) Skipjack *Katsuwonus pelamis* (Katsuwonidae); (81) Snake-mackerel *Gempylus serpens* (Gempylidae); (82) Sailfish *Istiophorus orientalis* (Istiophoridae); (83) Ravenfish *Tetragonurus pacificus* (Tetragonuridae); (84) Ruffe *Mupus paucidens* (Centrolophidae); (85) Eyebrowfish *Psenes cyanophrys* (Nomeidae); (86) Broadbill swordfish *Xiphias gladius* (Xiphiidae); (87) Hairtail *Trichiurus haumela* (Trichiuridae); (88) Nurseryfish *Kurtus gulliveri* (Kurtidae); (89) Pomfret *Collybus drachme* (Bramidae); (90) Dolphinfish *Coryphaena hippurus* (Coryphaenidae); (91) Black pomfret *Parastromateus niger* (Parastromateidae); (92) Black kingfish *Rachycentron canadus* (Rachycentridae); (93) Kingfish *Zonichthys nigrofasciata* (Carangidae); (94) Pennantfish *Alectis ciliaris* (Carangidae); (95) Dart *Trachinotus russelli* (Carangidae); (96) Trevally *Caranx ignobilis* (Carangidae); (97) Milk trevally *Lactarius lactarius* (Lactariidae); (98) Moonfish *Mene maculata* (Menidae); (99) Soldierfish *Lovamia fasciata* (Apogonidae); (100) Ponyfish *Leiognathus splendens* (Leiognathidae); (101) Flagtail *Kuhlia rupestris* (Kuhliidae).

netta, *Hypoatherina* and *Pranesus* are coastal genera but *Craterocephalus* inhabits fresh water. One diminutive freshwater species, *Charisella*, from the Vogelkop Peninsula appears to belong to the family Telmatherinidae which has relatives in Celebes. Three other diminutive species with brilliant blue or green eyes belong to the family Pseudomugilidae. Members of this family inhabit brackish or fresh waters and the males have elaborate finnage. The family Melanotaeniidae which is endemic to freshwater systems of New Guinea and Australia has seventeen species. These small deep-bodied rainbowfish belong to the genera *Glossolepis*, *Chilatherina*, *Centratherina*, *Melanotaenia* and *Nematocentris*. Being attractively coloured they are of interest to aquarists.

Threadfins (order Polynemiformes). Twelve species in family Polynemidae. These are highly-esteemed food fishes which inhabit sandy shores and muddy estuaries. Some grow to a large size. They have protruding putty-like noses, adipose eyelids and the lower rays of the pectoral fins are produced into elongated free filaments as tactile organs. *Polynemus* is represented by one small species with streamer-like extensions to its fins. The genera *Eleutheronema* and *Polydactylus* include larger species. These have three to eight free pectoral filaments.

Mackerel-like fishes (order Perciformes, suborder Scombroidei). Nineteen species arranged in seven families. Most are large, powerful, swift-swimming, predatory forms which inhabit coastal, reef or oceanic waters. Generally they congregate in schools and are pelagic at the surface or in moderate depths. As a group they have great commercial importance. The family Scombridae includes the shark-mackerel, *Grammatorcynus*, which has two lateral lines, and three smaller rake-gilled mackerels, *Rastrelliger*. The wahoo, sole member of the family Acanthocybiidae and famous as a sporting fish, is taken around reefs. The family Scomberomoridae includes two species of Spanish mackerel; the narrow-barred one is commercially exploited, being trolled for around reefs and headlands. Well-known tunas include the northern bluefin (*Kishinoella*), yellowfin (*Neothunnus*), albacore (*Thunnus*)

and bigeye (*Parathunnus*). They are grouped as the family Thunnidae, but dogtooth (*Gymnosarda*), skipjack (*Katsuwonus*) and mackerel tuna (*Euthynnus*) belong to the family Katsuwonidae. Larger sporting fish with the snout prolonged into a sword include sailfish (*Istiophorus*) and two marlins (*Makaira* and *Istiompax*) in the family Istiophoridae and the broadbill swordfish (*Xiphias*) in the family Xiphiidae.

Snake-mackerel, hairtail (order Perciformes, suborder Trichiuroidei). Four species arranged in two families. Both have strong canine teeth and are predatory on other fishes. The family Gempylidae is represented by the deep-water *Gempylus* (snake-mackerel) and *Promethichthys* (conejo). Two hairtails (*Trichiurus*) of the family Trichiuridae are silvery ribbon-like forms with pointed tails that inhabit shallow coastal waters and enter rivers.

Pomfrets (order Perciformes, suborder Stromateoidei). Three small species arranged in two families. The family Centrolophidae is represented by a small toothless ruffe (*Mupus*) and the family Nomeidae by two small eyebrowfish (*Psenes*). These live at the surface in open coastal waters, some taking cover in the tentacles of jellyfish.

Square-tails (order Perciformes, suborder Tetragonuroidei). A single species in family Tetragonuridae. It is an oceanic pelagic form with a torpedo-shaped body, keeled scales and a box-like mouth.

Nurseryfish (order Perciformes, suborder Kurtoidei). One species in family Kurtidae. This small fish is endemic to New Guinea and northern Australia but a related species occurs in India. It schools in the lower parts of rivers, preferring brackish water but it penetrates into fresh water. The male has a hook on the forehead to which the female attaches her eggs.

Typical perch-like fishes (order Perciformes, suborder Percoidei). This enormous assemblage comprises 581 species arranged in sixty-two families. Although the basic shape and fin arrangement is perch-like, many families have become specialized and have diverged from the typical pattern. The majority are shallow-water shore fishes but some are inhabitants of brackish and fresh waters. In

(102) Giant perch *Lates calcarifer* (family Latidae); (103) Rock-cod *Epinephelus fasciatus* (Epinephelidae); (104) Six-lined perch *Grammistes sexlineatus* (Grammistidae); (105) Perchlet *Ambassis agrammus* (Chandidae); (106) Dottyback *Pseudochromis fuscus* (Pseudochromidae); (107) Sea-perch *Anthias squammipinnis* (Anthiidae); (108) Pink lady *Pseudoplesiops typus* (Pseudoplesiopidae); (109) Long-fin *Plesiops coeruleolineatus* (Plesiopidae); (110) Two-banded perch *Diploprion bifasciatum* (Diploprionidae); (111) Bullseye *Priacanthus tayenus* (Priacanthidae); (112) Triple-tail *Lobotes surinamensis* (Lobotidae); (113) Jobfish *Aprion virescens* (Lutjanidae); (114) Sea-perch *Lutjanus ehrenbergi* (Lutjanidae); (115) Fusilier *Caesio chrysozonus* (Caesiodidae); (116) Paradisefish *Pentapodus setosus* (Nemipteridae); (117) Jobfish *Aphareus rutilans* (Aphareidae); (118) Monocle-bream *Scolopsis margaritifer* (Scolopsidae); (119) Butterfly-bream *Odontoglyphis tolu* (Nemipteridae); (120) Sweetlips *Spilotichthys pictus* (Plectorhynchidae); (121) Grunter *Autisthes puta* (Theraponidae); (122) Javelinfish *Pomadasys hasta* (Pomadasyidae); (123) Emperor *Lethrinus nebulosus* (Lethrinidae); (124) Tarwhine *Rhabdosargus sarba* (Sparidae); (125) Goatfish *Upeneus vittatus* (Mullidae); (126) Beach-salmon *Leptobrama mulleri* (Pempheridae); (127) Silver-biddy *Gerres abbreviatus* (Gerridae); (128) Silver batfish *Monodactylus argenteus* (Monodactylidae); (129) Jewfish *Sciaena macroptera* (Sciaenidae); (130) Blanquillo *Malacanthus latovittatus* (Malacanthidae); (131) Whiting *Sillago maculata* (Sillaginidae); (132) Sweeper *Pempheris vanicolensis* (Pempheridae); (133) Archerfish *Toxotes jaculator* (Toxotidae); (134) Drummer *Kyphosus lembus* (Kyphosidae).

marine environments pelagic, demersal (living on the sea bottom) and reef-dwelling forms are represented. The families Coryphaenidae (dolphinfish), Bramidae (pomfrets), Parastromateidae (black pomfret), Rachycentridae (black kingfish), Lactariidae (milk trevally) and Menidae (moonfish) have each a single species. These are related to members of the family Carangidae with thirty-eight species including scads (*Megalaspis*, *Decapterus*, *Selar* and *Alepes*), pennantfish (*Alectis*), trevally (*Selaroides*, *Ulua*, *Gnathanodon*, *Caranx* and *Carangoides*), leatherskins (*Chorinemus*), darts (*Trachinotus*), runner (*Elegatis*), pilotfish (*Naucrates*) and kingfish (*Seriola* and *Zonichthys*). These species are mainly pelagic in the marine littoral zone. Ponyfish of the family Leiognathidae with ten representatives in the genera *Gazza*, *Secutor*, *Equula*, *Equulites* and *Leiognathus* are demersal and school in shallow water. There are forty-one cardinalfish in the family Apogonidae including representatives of the genera *Paramia*, *Cheilodipterops*, *Cheilodipterus*, *Siphamia*, *Archamia*, *Sphaeramia*, *Apogon*, *Pristiapogon*, *Gronovichthys*, *Lovamia* and *Apogonichthys* in shallow coastal waters and around reefs, and *Glossamia* in fresh water. Seventeen species of chanda-perch constitute the family Chandidae with *Ambassis*, *Parambassis* and *Priopidichthys* in salt, brackish and fresh waters. *Tetracentrum*, *Xenambassis* and *Synechopterus* are endemic freshwater genera. Related to these are the larger representatives of the families Kuhliidae and Latidae with respectively three and two species in coastal and fresh waters. The last family includes the commercially important barramundi or giant perch (*Lates calcarifer*). The family Epinephelidae has thirty-six species of commercial importance in the genera *Cromileptes*, *Anyperodon*, *Plectropoma*, *Cephalopholis* and *Epinephelus* in addition to *Centrogenys* which superficially resembles a scorpionfish. The reef-cods and gropers of this family are most abundant around coral reefs. Related families include Grammistidae with the sole six-lined perch, Anthiidae with five species, Pseudochromidae with two species of small dottybacks, and the roundheads comprising one species in Pseudoplesiopidae

and three in Plesiopidae. All are likewise reef-dwelling forms. Four species of bullseyes (family Priacanthidae) are demersal in deeper waters but some come further inshore. The small two-banded perch representing the family Diploprionidae also inhabits coral reefs. Three species of triple-tail (*Lobotes* and *Datnioides*) penetrate into fresh water from the sea. A very important group is the sea-perch or bass (family Lutjanidae) which are mainly brightly coloured inhabitants of reefs although some enter rivers. The thirty species belong to the genera *Symphysanodon*, *Aprion*, *Pristipomoides*, *Macolor* and *Lutjanus*, principally the last named. The chinamanfish (*Symphorus nematophorus*) is poisonous at times. A close relative is a jobfish representing the family Aphareidae. Five species of small pelagic fusiliers including the bananafish represent the family Caesiodidae. All are brilliantly coloured and school near coral reefs. Monocle-bream (family Scolopsidae) and sea-bream (family Nemipteridae) are represented respectively by thirteen and fifteen species. Both groups are brightly coloured coastal forms, some being demersal and others inhabiting reefs. Amongst the sea-bream representatives of the genera *Monotaxis*, *Symphorichthys*, *Gnathodentex* and *Gymnocranius* grow quite large, but *Odontoglyphis*, *Nemipterus* and *Pentapodus* seldom exceed a foot in length. Three or four species of javelinfish (family Pomadasyidae) inhabit coastal shallows and rivers along with ten species of closely related round-headed sweetlips (family Plectorhynchidae). Some members of both families attain large size and are important food fishes. Grunters (family Theraponidae), of which there are thirteen species, include plain and banded inhabitants of coastal, brackish and fresh waters. Genera represented are *Pingalla*, *Helotes*, *Pelates*, *Eutherapon*, *Autisthes*, *Therapon*, *Papuservus*, *Mesopristis*, *Madagania* and *Amphitherapon*. Some of the brackish and freshwater species are endemic. Another important group is the emperor or pigface-bream (family Lethrinidae) of which there are fourteen reddish or greenish species in the genera *Lethrinus* and *Lethrinella*. The family Sparidae is represented in rivers and estu-

---

(135) Batfish *Platax orbicularis* (family Platacidae); (136) Thread-fin scat *Rhinoprenes pentanemus* (Rhinoprenidae); (137) Spotted batfish *Drepane punctata* (Drepanidae); (138) Coralfish *Anisochaetodon auriga* (Chaetodontidae); (139) Scat *Scatophagus argus* (Scatophagidae); (140) Angelfish *Euxiphipops sexstriatus* (Pomacanthidae); (141) Boarfish *Histiopterus typus* (Histiopteridae); (142) Demoiselle *Pomacentrus ambionensis* (Pomacentridae); (143) Clownfish *Premnas biaculeatus* (Premnidae); (144) Anemone-fish *Amphiprion percula* (Amphiprionidae); (145) Sergeant-major *Abudefduf curacoa* (Abudefdufidae); (146) Puller *Chromis dimidiatus* (Chromidae); (147) Wrasse *Hemipteronotus pentadactylus* (Coridae); (148) Pigfish *Bodianus oxycephalus* (Labridae); (149) Half-toothed parrotfish *Calotomus spinidens* (Sparisomidae); (150) Parrotfish *Callyodon blochi* (Scaridae); (151) Hawkfish *Cirrhitichthys aprinus* (Cirrhitidae); (152) Smiler *Opistognathus papuensis* (Opistognathidae); (153) Hairfin *Trichonotus setiger* (Trichonotidae); (154) Schindler's fish *Schindleria praematura* (Schindleriidae); (155) Weaver *Parapercis hexophthalma* (Parapercidae); (156) Sabre-gill *Champsodon guentheri* (Champsodontidae); (157) Blenny *Istiblennius edentulus* (Blenniidae); (158) Eel-blenny *Congrogadus subducens* (Congrogadidae); (159) Weedfish *Petraites roseus* (Clinidae); (160) Hair-tail blenny *Xiphasia setifer* (Xiphasiidae); (161) Snake-blenny *Notograptus guttatus* (Notograptidae); (162) Ass-fish *Acanthonus armatus* (Brotulidae); (163) Messmate-fish *Onuxodon margaritiferae* (Carapidae); (164) Moorish idol *Zanclus canescens* (Zanclidae); (165) Threadfish *Disparichthys fluviatilis* (Disparichthyidae); (166) Spinefoot *Siganus guttatus* (Siganidae); (167) Dragonet *Synchiropus lineolatus* (Callionymidae); (168) Unicornfish *Naso unicornis* (Acanthuridae).

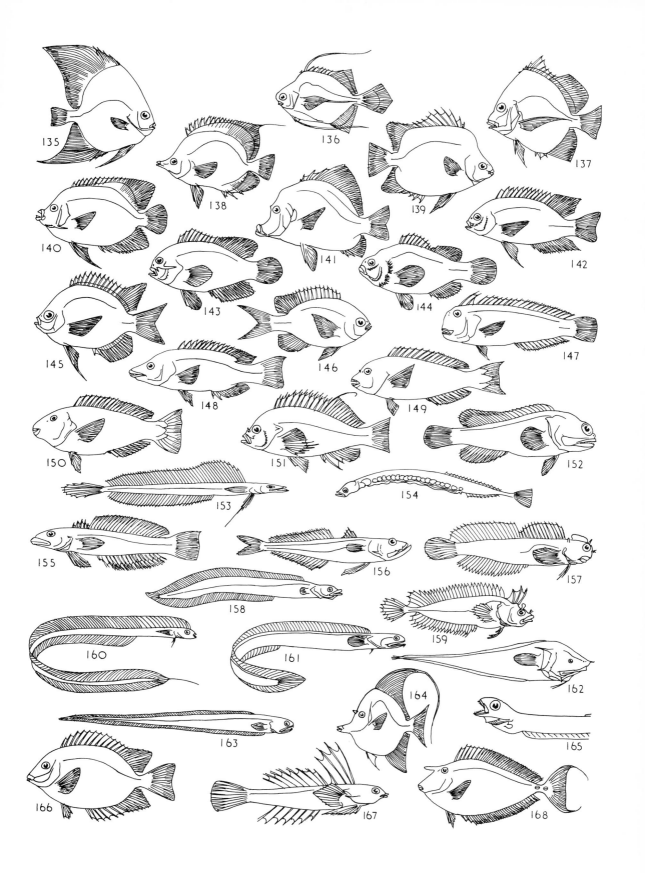

aries by two species of silver-bream or tarwhine (*Rhabdosargus* and *Acanthopagrus*). Essentially coastal, but entering rivers, are ten species of silver-biddies of the family Gerridae. They have deciduous scales but resemble ponyfish in having greatly protrusible mouths. Sixteen species of goatfish (family Mullidae) are distinguished by possession of a pair of barbels on the chin. Representatives of *Upeneus*, *Mulloidichthys* and *Parupeneus* are all brightly coloured carnivorous bottom-dwellers. Jewfish which live in coastal waters and rivers produce a drumming noise. Larger ones are commercially important and this family (Sciaenidae) has twelve species representing the genera *Sciaena*, *Johnius*, *Pseudosciaena*, *Collichthys* and the sharp-toothed *Otolithes*. Other ground fish include seven species of whiting (family Sillaginidae) and two blanquillos (family Malacanthidae). The following eight families of deep-bodied fishes form a close-knit group. There is one species of silver batfish (family Monodactylidae) in brackish and fresh waters. The family Pempheridae includes the beach-salmon (*Leptobrama*) of coastal waters and rivers and three sweepers (*Pempheris*) from deeper waters. Archerfish (family Toxotidae) which shoot down insects with a spurt of water, are represented in fresh and brackish waters by four species (*Toxotes* and *Protoxotes*). Three species of drummer (family Kyphosidae) feed on algae around reefs. The family Platacidae is represented in coastal waters and harbours by three species of large orbicular (round or shield-shaped) batfish renowned for their foul feeding habits. A single species of silver-batfish with sickle-shaped pectoral fin belongs to the family Drepanidae. Three scats (*Selenetoca* and *Scatophagus*) represent the family Scatophagidae and are estuarine but enter fresh water. The family Rhinoprenidae has a single endemic species in the Gulf of Papua. Some of its fin rays are produced into long free filaments. Coralfish or butterflyfish (family Chaetodontidae) comprise thirty-five species in the genera *Forcipiger*, *Chelmon*, *Heniochus*, *Parachaetodon*, *Hemitaurichthys*, *Coradion*, *Gonochaetodon*, *Megaprotodon*, *Tetrachaetodon*, *Chaetodon* and *Anisochaetodon*. These are small, agile and extremely colourful inhabitants of coral formations. The larger angelfish (family Pomacanthidae) include fifteen species representing the genera *Chaetodontoplus*, *Pomacanthus*, *Euxiphipops*, *Genicanthus*, *Holacanthus*, *Pygoplites* and *Centropyge*. These also are brilliantly ornamented denizens of coral reefs. One species of boarfish (family Histiopteridae) lives in deeper waters. Also amongst inhabitants of coral reefs is a complex of five families which in common have a single nostril on each side. The families Premnidae with one species and Amphiprionidae with ten species constitute the clownfish or anemone-fish. They have a curious habit of swimming unharmed amongst tentacles of sea anemones. Demoiselles and their close relatives comprise twenty-two species of *Eupomacentrus* and *Pomacentrus* (family Pomacentridae), nineteen species of *Hemiglyphidodon* and *Abudefduf* (family Abudefdufidae) and nine species of *Chromis*, *Hemichromis* and *Dascyllus* (family Chromidae). Most are small, colourful or strikingly banded, and very active, thus contributing to the decoration of coral communities. A few are known to penetrate into fresh water. Also amongst inhabitants of coral reefs is a large complex of bigger and even more colourful species. Eleven species of tuskfish or pigfish including *Cirrhilabrus*, *Pseudodax*, *Bodianus* and *Choerodon* make up the family Labridae. Assorted parrotfish and wrasses of the family Coridae account for sixty-eight species in the genera *Cymolutes*, *Epibulus*, *Pseudochelinus*, *Thalliurus*, *Cheilinus*, *Iniistius*, *Novaculichthys*, *Hemipteronotus*, *Hypselonotus*, *Cheilio*, *Gomphosus*, *Thalassoma*, *Anampses*, *Hologymnosus*, *Labroides*, *Coris*, *Duymaeria*, *Hemigymnus*, *Xenojulis*, *Stethojulis*, *Macropharyngodon* and *Halichoeres*. The half-toothed parrotfish of the family Sparisomidae add three species (*Leptoscarus* and *Calotomus*) and the true parrotfish of the family Scaridae total twenty-eight species. The last named have teeth fused into bony plates reminiscent of a parrot's beak and belong to the genera *Xanothon*, *Bolbometopon*, *Scarops*, *Callyodon*, *Cetoscarus*, *Hipposcarus* and *Chlorurus*. The remaining but atypical members of

(169) Goby *Paragobiodon histrio* (family Gobiidae); (170) Bearded goby *Scartelaos viridis* (Apocrypteidae); (171) Mud-skipper *Periophthalmus vulgaris* (Periophthalmidae); (172) Burrowing goby *Ctenotrypauchen microcephalus* (Taeniodidae); (173) Gudgeon *Mogurnda mogurnda* (Eleotridae); (174) Goby *Bathygobius fuscus* (Gobiidae); (175) Cleft-lipped goby *Sicyopterus cynocephalus* (Sicydiaphiidae); (176) Loach goby *Rhyacichthys aspro* (Rhyacichthyidae); (177) Searobin *Peristedion liorhynchus* (Peristediidae); (178) Flathead *Cociella quoyi* (Platycephalidae); (179) Stonefish *Synanceichthys verrucosus* (Synanceiidae); (180) Stingfish *Dendroscorpaena cirrhosa* (Scorpaenidae); (181) Flying-gurnard *Dactyloptena orientalis* (Dactylopteridae); (182) Velvetfish *Adventor elongatus* (Aploactidae); (183) Velvetfish *Caracanthus maculatus* (Caracanthidae); (184) Suckerfish *Remora remora* (Echeneidae); (185) Sharp-nosed puffer *Canthigaster valentini* (Canthigasteridae); (186) Toadfish *Gastrophysus spadiceus* (Lagocephalidae); (187) Toadfish *Arothron aerostaticus* (Tetrodontidae); (188) Porcupinefish *Dicotylichthys punctulatus* (Diodontidae); (189) Triggerfish *Balistoides conspicillum* (Balistidae); (190) Tripodfish *Triacanthus indicus* (Triacanthidae); (191) Leatherjacket *Paramonacanthus oblongus* (Aluteridae); (192) Boxfish *Lactoria cornuta* (Ostraciidae); (193) Frogfish *Pseudobatrachus dubius* (Batrachoididae); (194) Prickly anglerfish *Centrophryne spinulosa* (Centrophrynidae); (195) Two-rod anglerfish *Diceratias bispinosus* (Diceratiidae); (196) Horned anglerfish *Cryptosaras couesi* (Ceratiidae); (197) Goosefish *Chirolophius moseleyi* (Lophiidae); (198) Smooth anglerfish *Oneirodes eschrichti* (Oneirodidae); (199) Abyssal anglerfish *Melanocetus murrayi* (Melanocetidae); (200) Fishing-frogfish *Antennarius chironemus* (Antennariidae); (201) Handfish *Halieutaea stellata* (Ogcocephalidae).

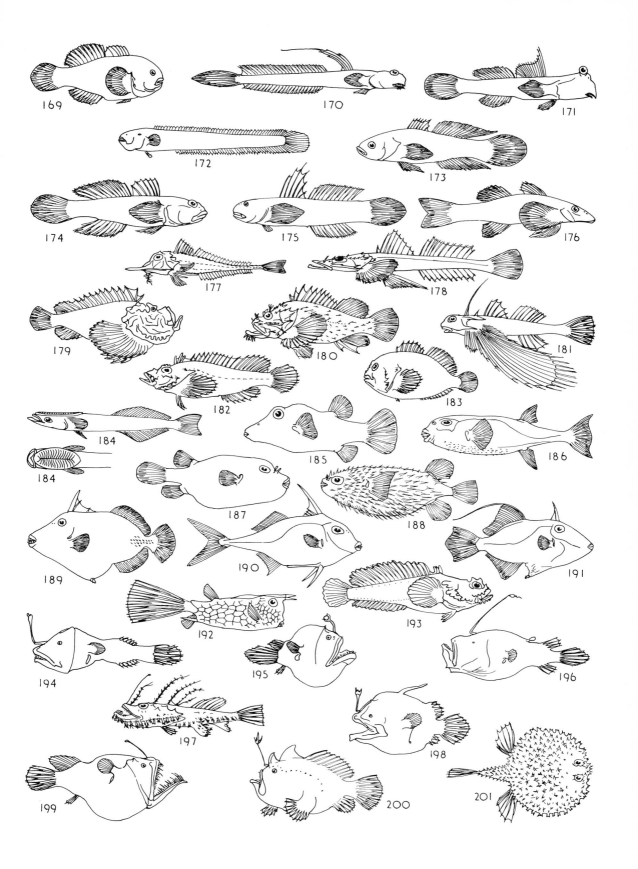

this suborder are three species of hawkfish (family Cirrhitidae), one goggle-eyed cod or smiler (family Opistognathidae), four weavers (family Parapercidae), two sabre-gills (family Champsodontidae), a slender sand-eel or hairfin (family Trichonotidae) and the tiny pelagic Schindler's fish (family Schindleriidae) of uncertain affinities.

Blennies (order Perciformes, suborder Blennioidei). Thirty-five species arranged in six families. Generally these are small naked forms with the ventral fins reduced to a few rays and inserted at the throat. The family Blenniidae has thirty species in several genera including *Petroscirtes*, *Aspidontus*, *Runula*, *Omobranchus*, *Dasson*, *Meiacanthus*, *Rhabdoblennius*, *Cirripectes*, *Andamia*, *Alticus*, *Salarias*, *Negoscartes*, *Istiblennius* and *Halmablennius*. These include inhabitants of coral crevices and tide pools on rock platforms. The remaining families are represented each by a single species. They are the Xiphasiidae (hair-tail blenny), Xenocephalidae (armoured blenny), Congrogadidae (eel-blenny), Notograptidae (bearded snake-blenny) and Clinidae (crested weedfish).

Eel-pouts, messmate-fish (order Perciformes, suborder Ophidioidei). Ten species arranged in three families. The family Brotulidae has five species of which *Brotula* is a reef-dweller but *Aphyonus*, *Acanthonus*, *Bassozetus* and *Porogadus* are abyssal. The family Carapidae (messmate-fish) has four species representing *Jordanicus*, *Onuxodon* and *Carapus*, these being slender forms which are symbiotic in the intestines of holothurians and starfish as well as molluscs and sea-squirts. One thread-like species from fresh water may also be a member of the same family but is usually held as distinct in the family Disparichthyidae.

Dragonets (order Perciformes, suborder Callionymoidei). Eight species in family Callionymidae. Members of the genera *Eleutherochir*, *Callionymus* and *Synchiropus* are small bottom-dwellers from the continental shelf or inhabitants of rock pools. They have flattened heads and characteristic preopercular spines and superficially resemble flathead.

Spine-feet (order Perciformes, suborder Siganoidei). Fifteen species in family Siganidae. Most of these are rabbitfish of the genus *Siganus*. The snout is tubular in *Lo*. All are littoral, some entering rivers and penetrating into fresh water but others frequent reefs. They are characterized by having two spines in the pelvic fins and seven spines in the anal fin. Some are brilliantly coloured.

Surgeonfish, unicornfish (order Perciformes, suborder Acanthuroidei). Twenty-eight species arranged in two families. The family Zanclidae has a single species, the Moorish idol, which superficially resembles a coralfish. The remainder belong to the family Acanthuridae. Unicornfish include *Callicanthus*, *Cyphomycter*, *Naso* and *Axinurus* and the more typical ones have a bump or horn on the forehead. *Paracanthurus*, *Zebrasoma*, *Ctenochaetus* and *Acanthurus* are the tang and surgeonfish, of which one characteristic is the fixed bucklers or erectile spine laterally placed on the caudal peduncle (stalk or basal support of the tail). They inhabit coastal waters, usually around reefs.

Gobies, gudgeons (order Perciformes, suborder Gobioidei). Ninety-nine species arranged in seven families. Most of these are small forms of the littoral zone, some inhabiting coral formations, others estuaries and rivers. Some are permanent inhabitants of fresh waters. There are forty-seven true gobies (family Gobiidae) grouped in the genera *Paragobiodon*, *Gobiodon*, *Aloricatogobius*, *Oplopomus*, *Gladiogobius*, *Stenogobius*, *Paraoxyurichthys*, *Oxyurichthys*, *Callogobius*, *Acentrogobius*, *Cryptocentrus*, *Stigmatogobius*, *Zonogobius*, *Amblygobius*, *Awaous*, *Bathygobius*, *Glossogobius*, *Cryptocentroides* and *Ctenogobius*. All these have the ventral fins united into a sucking disc. The family Apocrypteidae includes three elongate species representing *Apocryptodon*, *Boleophthalmus* and *Scartelaos* which inhabit mud flats and river mouths. Also on the mud flats and penetrating up rivers into fresh waters are five species of mud-skippers of the family Periophthalmidae. The mud-skippers *Periophthalmus* and *Periophthalmodon* have projecting eyes and limb-like paired fins. They spend most of their time out of water or in burrows. There are six species in the family Sicydiaphiidae including *Sicyopterus*, *Stiphodon*, *Pleurosicya* and *Sicyopus*. These have teeth embedded in their lips and are mainly fluviatile inhabitants. The family Taeniodidae is represented by three species of burrowing gobies including the barbelled *Taeniodes* and the near-blind *Ctenotrypauchen*. In the family Eleotridae are thirty-four species of sluggish gudgeons or sleepers, all of which have their ventral fins separated. Brackish and freshwater genera include *Bostrichthys*, *Eleotris*, *Prionobutis*, *Butis*, *Hypseleotris*, *Odontoeleotris*, *Ophiocara*, *Bunaka*, *Oxyelotris*, *Belobranchus*, *Tateurndina* and *Mogurnda*. Pelagic littoral forms include hoverers *Ptereleotris* and *Parioglossus*. Reef inhabitants are *Asterropteryx*, *Eviota* and *Eleotroides*. The family Rhyacichthyidae is represented by a single species of *Rhyacichthys* which has a flat head and curiously modified ventral fins as adaptations for life in mountain torrents. Superficially it resembles the Asian homalopterid loaches.

Mail-cheeked fishes (order Perciformes, suborder Cottoidei). Forty-two species arranged in six families. The suborder is characterized by a bony stay across the cheek. The family Platycephalidae (flathead) have depressed bodies and flat broad heads. There are thirteen species of them inhabiting the sea floor of the littoral zone. The genera *Platycephalus*, *Rogadius*, *Cymbacephalus*, *Onigocia*, *Suggrundus*, *Levanaora* and *Cociella* are represented. In deep waters is a species of the family Peristediidae (searobin) which is characterized by its grotesque armour. Stingfish (family Scorpaenidae) are represented by nineteen species occupying reef outcrops, weed beds and muddy bottoms. These comprise roguefish (*Tetraroge*, *Gymnapistes* and *Richardsonichthys*), waspfish (*Paracentropogon*, *Sibogapistus*, *Amblyapistus* and *Apistops*), butterfly-cod (*Pteropterus*, *Pterois*, and *Dendrochirus*) and other spiny stingers including *Notestes*, *Scorpaenodes*, *Scorpaenopsis*, *Dendroscorpaena*, *Parascorpaena* and *Sebastapistes*. The family Aploactidae has one small velvetfish (*Adventor*) inhabiting bottoms off river mouths. Coral heads are occupied by two small orbicular velvetfish (family Caracanthidae). The family Synanceiidae has six grotesque misshapen species including ghoulfish (*Inimicus* and *Minous*), the dangerous stonefish (*Synanceja* and *Synanceichthys*) and a sluggish relative of muddy rivers (*Leptosynanceia*).

Flying-gurnards (order Dactylopteriformes). One species in family Dactylopteridae. This is a littoral form with its body encased in hard armour and possessing enlarged, colourful, wing-like pectoral fins.

Suckerfish (order Echeneiformes). Four species in family Echeneidae. All are elongate blackish fish with an oval sucker on top of the head. This sucker is used to attach the fish to turtles and large fish such as sharks, barracuda and marlin. *Phtheirichthys*, *Echeneis* and *Remora* are the genera.

Leatherjackets, filefish, boxfish, toadfish, porcupinefish (order Tetrodontiformes). Seventy-four species arranged in eight families grouped in three suborders. The suborder Tetrodontiformes includes the rounded inflatable fish whose teeth are fused together like a parrot's beak. The family Diodontidae (porcupinefish) has the teeth in each jaw fused into a single plate, and large erectile spines. Its six species belong to the genera *Dicotylichthys*, *Cyclichthys*, *Chilomycterus* and *Diodon*. The toadfish or puffers have shorter spines and the teeth are divided by a median suture in each jaw. There are three sharp-nosed puffers representing the family Canthigasteridae, seven toadfish species with two nostrils on each side (family Lagocephalidae) including *Gastrophysus*, *Takifugu*, *Torafugu* and *Amblyrhynchotes*, and ten species with a single nostril on each side (family Tetrodontidae) including *Chelonodon* and *Arothron* in littoral and brackish waters and *Monotretus* in fresh water. The suborder Balistoidei includes three families. The tripodfish (family Triacanthidae) have the first spine of the dorsal fin and that of each of the pelvic fins enlarged and erectile. The genera *Triacanthus* and *Pseudotriacanthus* are represented by six species. Filefish or triggerfish (family Balistidae) have a body casing of hard scales and the first dorsal fin reduced to a mechanism for locking the first enlarged spine in an erect position. Seventeen species, some very colourful, belong to the genera *Xanthichthys*, *Canthidermis*, *Odonus*, *Abalistes*, *Balistoides*, *Sufflamen*, *Hemibalistes*, *Melichthys*, *Pseudobalistes*, *Balistapus* and *Rhinecanthus*. The family Aluteridae includes nineteen species of leatherjackets. These have a finely spinose leathery skin and a single erectile dorsal spine. Their shape varies from almost circular to extremely elongate. Some have a well-developed ventral flap while others have dermal filaments or enlarged bristle-like spines on the caudal peduncle. The genera are *Acreichthys*, *Pervagor*, *Paramonacanthus*, *Chaetoderma*, *Arotrolepis*, *Monacanthus*, *Pseudalutarius*, *Alutera*, *Paraluteres*, *Brachaluteres*, *Nelusetta*, *Oxymonacanthus*, *Scobinichthys*, *Pseudomonacanthus*, *Amanses* and *Cantherines*. The remaining suborder Ostracioidei has six species in the family Ostraciidae. These boxfish have a hard bony casing of fused plates, are triangular, square or pentagonal in cross-section and have only the pectorals and unpaired fins free to provide limited propulsion. *Rhinesomus*, *Ostracion*, *Rhynchostracion* and *Lactoria* are represented.

Frogfish (order Batrachoidiformes). Two species in the family Batrachoididae. *Pseudobatrachus* and *Halophryne* are robust forms with smooth skin and frog-like mouths. They are sluggish bottom-dwellers inhabiting littoral waters and entering estuaries. Their spines are venomous.

Anglerfish (order Lophiiformes). Twenty-one species arranged in eight families grouped in three suborders. The suborder Ceratioidei has two species in each of the families Melanocetidae and Oneirodidae and one species in each of Ceratiidae, Diceratiidae, and Centrophrynidae. This group are abyssal in oceanic depths and the males are degenerate and ectoparasitic on the larger females. The suborder Lophioidei includes two deep-water species of goosefish in the family Lophiidae. These demersal forms are less specialized than other anglerfish, but fish for prey in the same manner using a modified fin ray on the head as a baited rod and line. The suborder Antennarioidei is represented by one species of handfish in the family Ogeocephalidae and eleven species of fishing-frogs in the family Antennariidae. The handfish has a much flattened trunk and short tail and is studded with spiny tubercles. The fishing-frogs have flabby misshapen bodies, have a fishing rod on their heads, and the paired fins are limb-like to provide a mechanism for crawling. The genera are *Tetrabrachium*, *Histrio*, *Golem*, *Triantennatus*, *Antennatus* and *Antennarius*. They are bottom-dwellers in shallow coastal waters and estuaries.

L. F. de Beaufort, 'Fishes of the eastern part of the Indo-Australian Archipelago, with remarks on its zoogeography', *Bijdragen tot de Dierkunde*, vol. 19, 1913.

P. Bleeker, 'Vischsoorten van Nieuw-Guinea, verzameld door F. G. Beckman', *Natuurkundig Tijdschrift voor Nederlandsch Indie*, vol. 22, 1860.

——— *Atlas ichthyologique des Indes Orientales Néerlandaises*. Amsterdam, vols 1-9, 1862-77.

——— 'Quatrième mémoire sur la faune ichthyologique de la Nouvelle-Guinée', *Archives Néerlandaises des Sciences exactes et naturelles*, vol. 13, 1878.

G. Duncker and E. Mohr, 'Die Fische der Südsee-Expedition der Hamburgischen Wissenschaftlichen Stiftung, 1908-1909', *Mitteilungen Zoologisches Museum Hamburg*, vol. 41, 1925; vol. 42, 1926; vol. 44, 1931.

H. W. Fowler, 'The Fishes of Oceania', *Memoirs of the Bernice P. Bishop Museum*, vol. 10, 1928; vol. 11, 1931-4; supps 1 and 2, 1931 and 1934; vol. 12, 1949; supp. 3, 1949.

——— 'Contributions to the biology of the Philippine Archipelago and adjacent regions', United States National Museum, *Bulletin*, series no. 100, vols 11-13, 1931-40.

——— and B. A. Bean, 'Contributions to the biology of the Philippine Archipelago and adjacent regions', United States National Museum, *Bulletin*, series no. 100, vols 7, 8, 10, 1928-30.

A. Günther, *Catalogue of the Fishes in the Collection of the British Museum*. London, vols 1-8, 1859-70.

——— 'Andrew Garrett's Fische der Südsee', *Journal of the Museum Godeffroy*, vols 1-9, 1873-1910.

J. D. F. Hardenberg, 'Fishes of New Guinea', *Treubia*, vol. 18, 1941.

A. Hase, 'Die Fische der Deutschen Grenzexpedition 1910 in das Kaiser-Wilhelms-Land, Neu Guinea', *Jenaische Zeitschrift für Naturwissenschaft*, vol. 51, 1914.

A. W. Herre, 'A check list of the fishes from the Solomon Islands', *Journal of the pan-Pacific Research Institution*, vol. 6, 1931.

——— 'A check list of the fishes known from Madang, New Guinea', *Journal of the pan-Pacific Research Institution*, vol. 8, 1933.

——— 'New fishes obtained by the Crane Pacific Expedition', *Publications of the Field Museum of Natural History*, no. 335, zoological series vol. 18, 1935.

——— 'Fishes of the Crane Pacific Expedition', *Publications of the Field Museum of Natural History*, no. 353, zoological series vol. 21, 1936.

D. S. Jordan and A. Seale, 'The Fishes of Samoa', *Bulletin of the Bureau of Fisheries*, Washington, vol. 25, 1906.

W. Macleay, 'Contribution to a knowledge of the fishes of New Guinea. Parts I-IV', *Proceedings of the Linnean Society of N.S.W.*, vol. 7, 1882; vol. 8, 1883.

I. S. R. Munro, 'The Fishes of the New Guinea Region', *Papua and New Guinea Agricultural Journal*, vol. 10, 1956.

——— 'Additions to the Fish Fauna of New Guinea', *Papua and New Guinea Agricultural Journal*, vol. 16, 1964.

——— *The Fishes of New Guinea*. Port Moresby, 1967.

J. T. Nichols, 'Results of the Archbold Expeditions. Nos. 15, 30 and 71', *American Museum Novitates*, no. 922, 1937; no. 1093, 1940; no. 1735, 1955.

——— 'A new *Collichthys*, with remarks on this genus of fishes', *American Museum Novitates*, no. 1445, 1950.

——— 'Four new gobies from New Guinea', *American Museum Novitates*, no. 1539, 1951.

——— 'A new Blenny from Bali and a new threadfin from New Guinea', *American Museum Novitates*, no. 1860, 1954.

——— and H. C. Raven, 'Two fresh-water fishes (Percesoces) from New Guinea', *American Museum Novitates*, no. 755, 1934.

J. R. Norman, 'A new Percoid fish from Papua', *Copeia*, 1935.

J. D. Ogilby and A. R. McCulloch, 'A Revision of the Australian Therapons with notes on some Papuan species', *Memoirs of the Queensland Museum*, vol. 5, 1916.

A. Perugia, 'Viaggio di Lamberto Loria nella Papuasia orientale. Pesci d'acqua dolce', *Annali del Museo civico di Storia Naturale Giacomo Doria*, vol. 14, 1894.

E. P. Ramsay and J. D. Ogilby, 'A Contribution to the Knowledge of the Fish-Fauna of New Guinea', *Proceedings of the Linnean Society of N.S.W.*, second series, vol. 1, 1886.

C. T. Regan, 'Descriptions of four new freshwater fishes from British New Guinea', *Annals and Magazine of Natural History*, vol. 1, 1908.

——— 'Note on *Aristeus goldiei* Macleay and on some other fishes from New Guinea', *Proceedings of the Zoological Society of London*, 1914.

——— 'Report on the fresh water fishes collected by the British Ornithologists' Union Expedition and the Wollaston Expedition in Dutch New Guinea', *Transactions of the Zoological Society of London*, vol. 20, 1914.

R. R. Rofen, 'The marine fishes of Rennell Island', *The Natural History of Rennell Island British Solomon Islands*, vol. 1, 1958.

E. Tortonese, 'Contributo allo Studio sistematico e biogeografico dei Pesci della Nuovo Guinea', *Annali del Museo Civico di Storia Naturale Giacomo Doria*, vol. 75, 1964-5.

M. Weber, 'Süsswasserfische von Neu-Guinea', *Nova Guinea*, vol. 5, 1908.

——— 'Die Fische der Aru- und Kei-Inseln', *Abhandlungen hrsg. von der Senckenbergischen naturforschenden Gesellschaft*, vol. 34, 1911.

——— 'Die Fische der Siboga-Expedition', *Siboga-Expedition*, vol. 57, 1913.

——— 'Süsswasserfische aus Niederländisch Süd- und Nord-Neu-Guinea', *Nova Guinea*, vol. 9, 1913.

——— and L. F. de Beaufort, *The Fishes of the Indo-Australian Archipelago*, vols 1-11, 1913-62.

G. P. Whitley, 'Descriptions of some New Guinea Fishes', *Records of the Australian Museum*, vol. 20, 1938.

——— 'The fishes of New Guinea', *Australian Museum Magazine*, vol. 8, 1943.

——— 'A new shark from New Guinea', *Proceedings of the Royal Zoological Society of N.S.W.*, 1947-8.

——— 'A new Papuan Trevally', *Proceedings of the Royal Zoological Society of N.S.W.*, 1947-8.

——— 'Fish Doctor in Papua', *Australian Museum Magazine*, vol. 9, 1949.

——— 'A new catfish from New Guinea', *Proceedings of the Royal Zoological Society of N.S.W.*, 1954-5.

——— 'Fishes from inland New Guinea', *Records of the Australian Museum*, vol. 24, 1956.

IAN S. R. MUNRO

(*See also* FISHES, FLUVIATILE; FISHES, FRESHWATER; FISHES, MARINE)

FISHES, FLUVIATILE. A complex of ninety-six species inhabits fresh waters in addition to the 111 marine derivatives which have become strictly freshwater residents (*see* FISHES, FRESHWATER). Members of this complex penetrate into fresh water but are not permanent residents. Most are marine or estuarine forms which migrate upstream to above tidal influence. They not only occupy fresh waters in the lower reaches of rivers and lakes near the sea but often penetrate hundreds of miles inland from the coast. Some species appear to make only brief excursions into fresh waters but others, notably the catadromous eels of the family Anguillidae which return to the sea to spawn, may remain up to several years. Possibly some may be anadromous in that they descend rivers into estuaries or the sea but return to fresh water to spawn. Some catfishes may be of this type. In the absence of information on spawning habits, the only criterion that distinguishes permanent residents of fresh water from visitors is that the latter occur in salt and brackish water as well as in fresh water. Probably all the fluviatile species discussed here, with the exception of catadromous eels, are basically saltwater forms which make only temporary excursions into fresh water.

Of the six species of catadromous eels only *Anguilla interioris* is endemic to mainland New

Guinea. The distribution of *A. celebesensis* is essentially the Philippines and the Indonesian Archipelago but the species extends into north-west New Guinea. Where the term 'New Guinea' is used without any qualification such as region it means the whole main island. *A. bicolor pacifica* extends from the Philippines and Borneo through New Guinea to the Bismarck Archipelago and the Solomon Islands. *A. megastoma* and *A. obscura* are South Pacific forms which extend westward, the first only to the Solomon Islands and the second through New Guinea to the Bismarck Archipelago and Halmahera in Indonesia. *A. marmorata* is widely distributed throughout most of the Indo-West Pacific area.

Fluviatile species endemic to New Guinea, with the exception of the snake-eel *Caecula gjellerupi* from the Hollandia coastal plain, inhabit river systems whose fresh waters are occupied by the Riechian fluvifauna (*see* FISHES, FRESHWATER). Thus they occur in rivers which flow southward across low swampy areas comprising the Fly-Digul Depression westward through the Mimika Coast to the Vogelkop Peninsula. This group consists of eleven species comprising a herring *Clupeoides multispinis*, catfishes *Cinetodus froggatti, Hexanematichthys danielsi, H. acrocephalus* and *Hemipimelodus aaldereni*, half-beak *Zenarchopterus novaeguineae*, sole *Brachirus villosa*, goby *Oxyurichthys jaarmani*, gudgeon *Bostrichthys zonatus* and mud-skippers *Periophthalmus weberi* and *P. cantonensis novaeguineaensis*.

In addition there are seven species jointly endemic to New Guinea and Australia. The catfish *Hexanematichthys stirlingi*, sole *Aseraggodes klunzingeri* and nurseryfish *Kurtus gulliveri* are confined to rivers whose fresh waters are occupied by the Riechian and Leichhardtian fluvifaunas. The green shovelnose-ray *Rhinobatos batillum*, catfish *Hexanematichthys leptaspis* and gudgeon *Prionobutis microps* occur, in addition, in rivers whose fresh waters are occupied by the Gaimardian fluvifauna. The flag-tailed grunter *Amphitherapon caudovittatus* ranges from south-west Australia through the Leichhardtian Province into the Riechian Province.

A whaler shark *Carcharhinus leucas* occurs in Jamoer Lake and possibly other freshwater lakes and rivers. It is regarded as fluviatile because its breeding habits are unknown and it has been taken elsewhere in brackish water. It has extraordinarily wide distribution through the fresh waters of Atlantic drainage of North, Central and South America, Africa, South-east Asia, the Philippines and Australia.

Most of the remaining seventy fluviatile species have wide general distributions throughout the Indo-West Pacific. They belong to a wide variety of families and many of these families have representatives that have taken up permanent residence in fresh water. The order Clupeiformes is represented by the ox-eye herring *Megalops cyprinoides*. Eels include the anguilliform snake-eel *Caecula mindora*, worm-eel *Muraenichthys schulzei*, moray *Gymnothorax polyuranodon*, pike-eel *Muraenesox cinereus* and symbranchiform one-gilled swamp-eel *Symbranchus bengalensis*. Beloniformes is represented by the long-tom *Strongylura urvilli* and half-beaks *Zenarchopterus kampeni* and *Z. brevirostris*. In the order Syngnathiformes are the pipefishes *Doryichthys retzi, Oostethus manadensis, O. brachyurus, Coelonotus liaspis, Bombonia djarong* and *B. spicifer*. Mullets *Mugil cephalus, Liza tade, L. macrolepis* and *L. dussumieri* represent the order Mugiliformes. Typical perch-like fishes include cardinalfish *Pristiapogon frenatus, Apogon hyalosoma* and *A. amboinensis*, flagtails *Kuhlia marginata* and *K. rupestris*, the palmer or commercial barramundi *Lates calcarifer*, chanda-perch *Priopidichthys gymnocephalus, Ambassis interruptus, A. nalua, A. buruensis, A. macracanthus* and *A. commersoni*, tripletail *Datnioides quadrifasciatus*, cod *Epinephelus summana*, grunters *Therapon jarbua, Eutherapon theraps, Mesopristes cancellatus* and *M. argenteus*, sea-perch *Lutjanus fulviflamma* and *L. argentimaculatus*, jewfish *Johnius belengeri*, silver batfish *Monodactylus argenteus*, scat *Scatophagus argus*, archerfish *Toxotes chatareus* and demoiselles *Abudefduf melas* and *A. anabatoides*. The percoid suborder Siganoidei includes the rabbitfishes *Siganus javus* and *S. vermiculatus*. There are nineteen Gobioidei including gobies *Glossogobius celebicus, G. giurus, Stenogobius genivittatus, Stigmatogobius hoeveni* and *Callogobius hassellti*, tooth-lipped goby *Stiphodon elegans*, gudgeons *Butis butis, B. amboinensis, Bunaka gyrinoides, Awaous grammepomus, Eleotris fusca, E. melanosoma, E. macrolepis, Belobranchus belobranchus, Ophiocara aporos* and *O. porocephala*, burrowing-goby *Brachyamblyopus brachysoma*, goggle-eyed goby *Boleophthalmus boddarti* and mud-skipper *Periophthalmodon schlosseri freycineti*. The remaining migrants into fresh water are scorpionfishes *Tetraroge barbata, Gymnapistes niger* and *Leptosynanceia asteroblepa* and a pufferfish *Monotretus erythrotaenia*.

The extensive waterways of the numerous large rivers have provided an additional habitat for those saltwater species which have osmoregulatory powers sufficient to permit free movements between saline and fresh waters. It is not surprising that a large number of saltwater species have availed themselves of these waterways and extended the range of their environment. This procedure surely represents a trend in the direction of those species which have evolved comparatively recently from marine ancestors and permanently colonized fresh waters. In common with other Indo-West Pacific areas the majority of species penetrating upstream are either catfishes, typical percoids or gobioid fishes. In parallel with the strictly freshwater species, there has been some comparatively recent speciation resulting in the establishment of endemic forms. This process is noticeable particularly in the catfish genera *Hexanematichthys* and *Hemipimelodus*. The genus *Cinetodus* is endemic to the Riechian Province. In spite of the fact that the gobioid species dominate numerically, very few in this group have evolved locally to establish endemic species.

M. Boeseman, 'Marine Fishes in Fresh Water', *Science*, vol. 123, 1956; ——— 'Notes on the fishes of Western New Guinea III. The fresh water shark of Jamoer Lake', *Zoölogische Mededeelingen Leiden*, vol. 40, 1964; V. Ege, 'A Revision of the Genus *Anguilla* Shaw. A systematic, phylogenetic and geographical study', *Dana Report*, no. 16, 1939; A. W. Herre, 'Distribution of Fresh-Water Fishes in the Indo-Pacific', *Scientific Monthly*, vol. 51, 1940; ——— 'Sharks in fresh water', *Science*, vol. 122, 1955; ——— 'Marine fishes in fresh water', *Science*, vol. 123, 1956; ——— 'Marine fishes in Philippine rivers and lakes', *Philippine Journal of Science*, vol. 87, 1958.

IAN S. R. MUNRO

(*See also* FISHES)

FISHES, FRESHWATER. Although 207 species have been recorded from freshwater habitats, only 111 appear to qualify as permanent residents which breed in fresh water. These are the inhabitants of upper freshwater reaches of rivers and tributaries above tidal influence, mountain torrents, coastal brooks, lakes, marshes, ponds and ditches. Mainland New Guinea and adjacent islands including Waigeo share a common continental plateau with Australia, the islands of Torres Strait and the Aru Islands. Where the term 'New Guinea' is used without any qualification such as region it means the whole main island. This is isolated by deep water on the west from the Philippines and the Indonesian Archipelago, and on the east from the Bismarck Archipelago, Solomon Islands and Oceania. The land masses on the tropical part of this continental plateau have a freshwater fish fauna which is basically homogeneous as regards genera. Zoogeographical barriers have brought about speciation within these genera. Presumably the fresh waters have been colonized in comparatively recent geological times by ancestral fishes originating in salt water. The components are representatives of the orders Pristiformes (sawfish), Clupeiformes (herring-like fishes), Siluroidiformes (catfish), Beloniformes (gars and half-beaks), Syngnathiformes (pipefish), Mugiliformes (hardyheads and rainbowfish), Perciformes (chanda-perch, cardinalfish, grunters, archerfish, scats, gudgeons and gobies) and Pleuronectiformes (flatfish). All have close relatives inhabiting estuaries and coastal waters today.

The New Guinea region completely lacks elements of the characteristic, true freshwater fauna of South-east Asia. This comprises a numerically large assemblage of genera and species in the orders Cyriniformes (homalopterid catfish, loaches, carps, barbs and rasboras), Cyprinodontiformes (top-minnows), Masticembelliformes (spiny-eels), Ophiocephaliformes (murrels and snakeheads) and the perciform suborder Anabantoidei (gouramys and air-breathing perch). Except for very few species this Asian fauna is confined to the west of the zoogeographical boundary known as Wallace's Line [q.v.]. Exceptions include cyprinids and ophiocephalids extending east to Halmahera and cyprinodonts extending into Celebes and Timor. Some zoogeographers prefer to recognize the boundary as being along Weber's Line which includes Timor and Celebes in the Asian fauna.

The only freshwater species which New Guinea shares with the general Indo-West Pacific are the sawfish *Pristiopsis microdon*, a mullet *Cestraeus goldiei* which extends to the Bismarck Archipelago, Timor and the Philippines, and two gobies. *Rhyacichthys aspro* inhabits mountain torrents and occurs also in the Solomon Islands, the Indonesian Archipelago and the Philippines. *Sicyopterus ouwensi* extends from west New Guinea to the Sunda group and reputedly to the Marquesas Islands.

The New Guinea mainland is divided into two major fluvifaunal provinces. Zoogeographically these are separated by a land barrier in the form of the massive central mountain range, or cordillera, which traverses practically the whole length of the island from the Vogelkop Peninsula to Milne Bay. The Gaimardian Province comprises the catchment basins of rivers that originate on the northern slopes of the dividing range and discharge into the sea along the northern coastline. The Riechian Province comprises the catchment basins of rivers that originate on the southern slopes of the dividing range and discharge into the Arafura Sea, Gulf of Papua and the Coral Sea. The Riechian fluvifauna has much in common with that of the Leichhardtian Province which embraces rivers on the Australian continent that flow north into the Timor and Arafura Seas, and the Gulf of Carpentaria.

Of eighty-four species endemic to New Guinea thirty-six are confined to the Gaimardian Province. There appear to be at least three divisions of this province. The eastern division comprises the basins of the Sepik, Ramu and Markham Rivers. Its specific components are catfishes *Neosilurus gjellerupi*, *N. ater sepikensis*, *Brustiarius nox*, *Tachysurus solidus*, *T. kanganamanensis* and *Hemipimelodus papillifer*, garfish *Stenocaulis perornatus*, half-beak *Zenarchopterus sepikensis*, pipefish *Doryichthys spinachoides*, tripletail *Datnioides campbelli*, threadfish *Disparichthys fluviatilis* and goby *Acentrogobius bulmeri*. The western division comprises the basin of the Mamberamo River and its tributaries, the Rouffaer and Idenburg Rivers. Its specific components are catfishes *Neosilurus idenburgi*, *N. novaeguineae niger*, *Netuma microstoma* and *Hemipimelodus bernhardi*, rainbowfishes *Melanotaenia vanheurni*, *Nematocentris praecox* and *N. multisquamata* and a goby *Ctenogobius tigrellus*. The third division is the coastal plain of Hollandia and Aitape which is isolated from the Mamberamo-Idenburg and Sepik basins by the series of ranges stretching from the Gauttier to the Prince Alexander Mountains. Its specific components are the pipefish *Doryichthys caudocarinatus*, rainbowfishes *Glossolepis incisus* and *Chilatherina sentaniensis*, cardinalfish *Glossamia wichmanni wichmanni*, goby *Paroxyurichthys laterisquamatus* and gudgeon *Odontoeleotris nesolepis*. Also there is some overlap from the other divisions. The rainbowfish *Chilatherina lorentzi* is common to all. The catfish *Hemipimelodus velutinus*, rainbowfishes *Centratherina crassispinosa* and *Melanotaenia affinis* and chanda-perch *Parambassis confinis confinis* are shared with the Sepik-Ramu basin. *Parambassis confinis occidentalis* is shared with the Mamberamo-Idenburg basin. *Glossamia wichmanni gjellerupi* is common to the eastern and western divisions but absent from the coastal Hollandia-Aitape division.

The Markham River basin appears to be strictly Gaimardian because it shares species with the Sepik-Ramu basin. East of where the Kuper and Bowutu Ranges intrude to the coast the fluvifauna may change. Specialized chanda-perch *Xenambassis honessi* and *X. simoni* inhabit lowland streams near Buna, and *Synechopterus caudovittatus* inhabits highlands at Kokoda. Their nearest relatives are from the southern slopes of the Owen Stanley Range between Kerema and Port Moresby. Rainbowfishes *Charisella fredericki* from the Wa Samson River in northern Vogelkop Peninsula and *Melanotaenia catherinae* from Waigeo are also not typically Gaimardian.

Sixty-nine species inhabit the Riechian Province and of these forty are strictly endemic and twenty more jointly endemic to it and the Leichhardtian Province of Australia. There are three divisions of the Riechian Province. By area the largest part is occupied by the low-lying swampy lands of the Fly-Digul Depression with extensions east to the Aird River delta and west through the Eilanden and Lorentz Rivers to the narrow swampy Mimika coast. The fluvifauna changes in the headwaters of the Kikori and Purari Rivers in the central highlands, and also in the area east of Kerema where ranges and foothills come close to the coast.

The fluvifaunula of the great Fly-Digul Depression is better known than that of the other sections. It contains the species which are common to the Riechian and Leichhardtian fluvifaunas. Topographically there is no reason to expect other than homogeneous distribution throughout the swamplands but apparently there is some variation from east to west. The hardyhead *Craterocephalus nouhuysi*, blue-eye *Pseudomugil novaeguineae* and grunter *Amphitherapon habbenami* range along the Mimika coast to the Lorentz basin, and the cardinalfish *Glossamia sandei* reaches as far east as the Digul River. The herring *Kowala venulosus*, catfishes *Plotosus papuensis*, *Oloplotosus mariae*, *Neosilurus equinus*, *Doiichthys novaeguineae*, *Tetranesodon conorhynchus* and *Hemipimelodus macrorhynchus*, and cardinalfish *Glossamia trifasciata* are restricted to the Lorentz basin. A herring *Clupeoides papuensis*, catfishes *Cochlefelis spatula*, *Hexanematichthys carinatus* and *Nedystoma dayi*, and grunter *Pelates romeri* are common to the Lorentz and Fly-Digul basins together with the catfish *Hexanematichthys latirostris* which extends further east. Bony-bream *Fluvialosa papuensis*, catfishes *Neosilurus meraukensis*, *Hexanematichthys digulensis* and *Hemipimelodus crassilabris*, hardyhead *Craterocephalus annator*, archerfish *Protoxotes lorentzi* and gudgeon *Bostrichthys strigogenys* are confined to the Fly-Digul system together with a rainbowfish *Nematocentris sexlineatus* which ranges east to the Goldie River.

In the central Highlands gobies *Aloricatogobius asaro* and *Glossogobius brunnoides* inhabit the headwaters of the Kikori and Purari Rivers. Lacustrine species inhabiting elevated Lake Kutubu include the hardyhead *Craterocephalus lacustris*, rainbowfish *Melanotaenia lacustris*, grunter *Madagania adamsoni* and gudgeon *Mogurnda variegata*.

Inhabitants of streams east of Kerema including the Laloki River are catfishes *Neosilurus bartoni* and *N. perugiae*, hardyhead *Craterocephalus randi*, blue-eye *Pseudomugil furcatus*, chanda-perch *Xenambassis lalokiensis* and *Tetracentrum apogonoides*, and gudgeons *Hypseleotris moncktoni* and *Tateurndina ocellicauda*.

Few species are common to the Riechian and Gaimardian Provinces. A rainbowfish *Chilatherina campsi* occurs in Highland streams on both sides of the Sepik-Wahgi divide. Seven species appear to have crossed the neck of the Vogelkop Peninsula in the Jamoer Lake district. The catfish *Neosilurus novaeguineae novaeguineae* is possibly basically Gaimardian but has penetrated the Mimika coast and the gudgeon *Oxyeleotris urophthalmus novaeguineae* has reached the Lorentz River. The cardinalfish *Glossamia beauforti* and the gudgeon *Oxyeleotris fimbriatus* occur also in the Aru Islands and are probably basically Riechian. Other gudgeons *Bunaka herwerdeni*, *Oxyeleotris lineolatus* and *Mogurnda mogurnda mogurnda* extend from the Gaimardian through the Riechian into the Leichhardtian Province. The last named is probably Australian, extending to the Aru Islands and to south-eastern fluvifaunal provinces on the Australian continent.

The remaining species share the marshy lowlands of the Lorentz-Digul-Fly basins with those of rivers flowing north in the Leichhardtian Province of Australia. This complex consists of sawfish *Pristiopsis leichhardti*, barrumundi *Scleropages leichardti leichardti*, anchovy *Scutengraulis scratchleyi*, catfishes *Neosilurus ater ater*, *N. brevidorsalis*, and *Prochilus obbesi*, garfish *Stenocaulis kreffti*, tongue-sole *Cynoglossus heterolepis*, rainbowfish *Melanotaenia nigrans*, *M. goldiei*, *Nematocentris ogilbyi*, *N. rubrostriatus* and *N. maculatus*, cardinalfish *Glossamia aprion aprion*, chanda-perch *Parambassis gulliveri*, *Ambassis macleayi* and *A. agrammus*, grunters *Pingalla lorentzi* and *Papuservus trimaculatus* and gudgeon *Hypseleotris compressus*. Some of these also extend into streams east of Kerema.

The barramundi *Scleropages leichardti leichardti* is a more archaic form and its colonization of the Fly-Digul Depression and the Gulf of Carpentaria drainage probably antedates Wallace's Line. Another subspecies occupies a few coastal streams in central Queensland separated from the Gulf drainage by the watershed of the Great Dividing Range. More distant relatives occur in the central Indo-Pacific, Africa and South America.

An important endemic element is the complex of mugiloid forms derived from the marine family Atherinidae. The genus *Craterocephalus* has three species in the Riechian Province and ten others, including estuarine forms, in Australia. Specialization in the family Melanotaeniidae is expressed in dentition. The genus *Nematocentris* is the simplest. This genus has respectively three and one species endemic to the Gaimardian and Riechian Provinces, three common to the Riechian and Leichhardtian Provinces and five others elsewhere in Australia. *Melanotaenia* has respectively three and one species endemic to the Gaimardian and Riechian and two common to the Riechian and Leichhardtian Provinces. The most specialized *Chilatherina, Centratherina* and *Glossolepis* are Gaimardian. The family Pseudomugilidae has two species in the Riechian Province, one common to the Aru Islands and Australia, and four others in Australia. *Charisella fredericki* from the Vogelkop Peninsula and four species of *Telmatherina* from Celebes constitute the family Telmatherinidae which is probably an independent derivative from marine atherinids. The main centre of evolution of these mugiloid fishes appears to be northern Australia or southern New Guinea. *Pseudomugil* and *Craterocephalus* have not reached the Gaimardian Province but the Melanotaeniidae have become more specialized there.

The Asian catfish families Clariidae, Siluridae, Chacidae, Pangasidae, Bagridae, Bagariidae and Akysidae are unknown east of Wallace's Line but there has been considerable speciation in New Guinea of the widespread Indo-West Pacific family Tachysuridae. Seven and eight species respectively are endemic to the Gaimardian and Riechian Provinces but none of these are shared with tropical Australia. Endemic genera are Gaimardian *Brustiarius* and Riechian *Tetranesodon, Cochlefelis* and *Nedystoma*. The family Doiichthyidae is endemic to the Riechian Province. Local speciation has occurred also in the family Plotosidae. The widespread Indo-West Pacific genus *Plotosus*, although basically marine, has an endemic freshwater species in the Riechian Province. The genera *Oloplotosus, Prochilus* and *Neosilurus* are endemic to New Guinea and Australia. The genus *Neosilurus* contains four species endemic to each of the New Guinea provinces, two common to the Riechian and Leichhardtian Provinces, and others on the Australian continent.

Other groups exhibiting local speciation are the families Apogonidae, Chandidae, Theraponidae, Eleotridae and Gobiidae. One section of the large Indo-West Pacific family Chandidae (*Xenambassis, Synechopterus* and *Tetracentrum*) has modified fin structure. Its distribution is restricted to the south-east corner of mainland New Guinea.

In addition to the species discussed above, a complex of ninety-six others penetrate into fresh water but are not regarded as permanent residents (*see* FISHES, FLUVIATILE).

L. F. de Beaufort, 'Notes on the distribution of freshwater fishes', *Copeia*, 1964; D. F. McMichael, 'New Guinea: Physical Geography and Environment', *Australian Museum Magazine*, vol. 12, 1958; —— and I. D. Hiscock, 'Monograph of the freshwater mussels (Mollusca: Pelecypoda) of the Australian Region', *Australian Journal of Marine and Freshwater Research*, vol. 9, 1958; G. P. Whitley, 'The freshwater fishes of Australia', *Monographiae biologicae*, vol. 8, 1959.   IAN S. R. MUNRO

(*See also* FISHES)

FISHES, MARINE. The habitats of marine fauna are classified mainly as coastal pelagic (living in the open sea) or demersal (living on the sea bottom), deep-water pelagic, bathypelagic (inhabiting the deep sea) or abyssal (ultra deep). Coastal forms include those which live on the continental plateau and also many that enter bays, harbours, river estuaries and lagoons. Some marine species pass through brackish water into fresh water (*see* FISHES, FLUVIATILE). Other coastal habitats include tide pools in rock outcrops and tidal flats fringing the shoreline, the surf zone of beaches, and submerged rock or coral reefs. The fauna of coral reefs is generally different from that of river estuaries. An estuarine environment normally is characterized by mangroves, tidal mud flats and periodic reduction in water salinity. A description of the fauna and the preferred habitat is given in the general article FISHES. All but a few families have representatives in the sea.

The marine fauna is composed primarily of elements characteristic of the wide Indo-West Pacific area, especially the Indo-Malayan, Western Pacific and Australian zones.

Forty-six species are distinctive in that they occur only in New Guinea and the tropical parts of Australia. The white-tip shark *Triaenodon apicalis*, half-beak *Labidorhamphus caudovittatus* and unicorn-cod *Bregmaceros nectabanus* are pelagic. The shark-mullet *Rhinomugil nasutus*, beach-salmon *Leptobrama mulleri* and banded scat *Selenetoca multifasciata* are basically estuarine, and blennies *Halmablennius meleagris* and *Petraites roseus* prefer rock pools. The remainder are basically demersal on the floor of the open sea or congregate around reefs. These are the wobbegong *Orectolobus ornatus*, shovelnose-ray *Rhinobatus batillum*, catfish-eels *Euristhmus nudiceps* and *E. lepturus*, ghost-grinner *Harpodon translucens* and weedy pipefish, *Haliichthys taeniophorus*. Flatfish include *Dexillichthys muelleri, Paraplagusia guttata* and *Pseudorhombus elevatus*. Typical perch-like forms include trevally *Carangoides laticaudis* and *C. diversa*, ponyfish *Equulites novaehollandiae*, reef-cods *Cephalopholis coatesi, Epinephelus slacksmithi* and *E. australis*, red bass *Lutjanus coatesi*, threadfin-bream *Pentapodus vitta*, emperor *Lethrinus fletus*, coralfish *Chaetodon aureofasciatus*, demoiselle *Pomacentrus sufflavus* and goggle-eyed cod *Opistognathus papuensis*. Others include the snake-blenny *Notograptus guttatus*, dragonet *Synchiropus calauropomus*, flathead *Inegocia parilis*, stingfish *Apistops caloundra, Notestes robustus* and *Minous versicolor*, pufferfish *Takifugu pleurostictus* and *T. meraukensis*, leatherjackets *Arotrolepis filicauda, Monacanthus mylii, Brachaluteres braueri, Nelusetta ayraudi, Scobinichthys granulatus* and *Pseudomonacanthus maynardi*, boxfish *Rhinesomus reipublicae*, frogfish *Pseudobatrachus dubius* and fishing-frog *Tetrabrachium ocellatum*.

In addition forty-two species appear to be endemic to New Guinea and its associated islands and the Bismarck Archipelago and Admiralty Islands. Amongst pelagic forms are a whaler shark *Carcharhinus tufiensis*, flyingfish *Cypselurus fur-*

catus and unicorn-cod *Bregmaceros rarisquamosus*. Deeper water forms include an eel *Congrellus neoguinaicus*, flounder *Taeniopsetta ocellata*, blenny *Xenocephalus armatus* and ass-fishes *Aphyonus gelatinosus* and *Porogadus gracilis*. Reef species include a wobbegong *Eucrossorhinus dasypogon*, squirrelfish *Kutoflammeo angustifrons*, butterflyfish *Anisochaetodon dahli*, demoiselle *Abudefduf bimaculatus*, wrasse *Anampses neoguinaicus* and blenny *Petroscirtes periophthalmoides*. The remainder are mainly residents of the shallower parts of the continental plateau and situations close inshore. These include a stingray *Urolophus armatus*, anchovies *Setipinna papuensis* and *Papuengraulis micropinna*, catfishes *Tachysurus armiger* and *Netuma sagaroides*, and eels *Achirophichthys kampeni*, *Caecula misolensis*, *Priodonophis angusticauda* and *Brachyconger platyrhynchus*. Flatfish *Aseraggodes persimilis* and *Brachirus dicholepis*, pipefishes *Solenichthys armatus* and *Doryichthys brevidorsalis*, Spanish mackerel *Scomberomorus multiradiatus* and threadfins *Polynemus intermedius* and *Polydactylus nigripinnis* also occupy shallow coastal waters. Amongst the typical perch-like fishes are a ponyfish *Leiognathus rapsoni*, cardinalfishes *Siphamia argyrogaster* and *Apogon dammermani*, butterfly-perch *Chelidoperca margaritifer*, jewfishes *Johnius pacifica*, *Pseudosciaena pamoides* and *Collichthys novaeguineae* and a threadfin-scat *Rhinoprenes pentanemus*. The dragonet *Synchiropus picturatus* and gobioid fishes *Stigmatogobius reticularis*, *Pleurosicya boldinghi* and *Apocryptodon wirzi* are also endemic shallow water species.

IAN S. R. MUNRO

(*See also* FISHES; FISHES, FLUVIATILE)

FISHING. In many coastal parts of New Guinea and the islands fishing is of the greatest economic importance, though most fishing communities also cultivate. The same is true of many peoples on the lower and middle courses of the larger rivers, but not of those who live in the mountains. Fish are few or absent in many mountain streams; and eels, crayfish, and tadpoles, though present, are rarely of great significance in the diet.

Most of the fishing methods practised in Oceania can be illustrated from New Guinea: hook fishing with baited hooks or spinners; the gorge; nets and traps of several kinds; plungebaskets; spearing and shooting with the bow; drugging; and a few specialized methods of local distribution.

Hooks used with bait seem to be of most importance in the Massim area and in some of the islands. The Massim, the Torres Strait islanders, and the people of New Britain all make one-piece hooks of turtle-shell, which can be cut or shaped by heating (Fig. 1c). The Massim made two-piece hooks of palm wood, with the pieces lashed at an angle (Fig. 1b). One-piece hooks of pearl-shell are typical of the Bismarck Archipelago, where in some cases the snood, a short length of line permanently attached to the hook, is protected from the

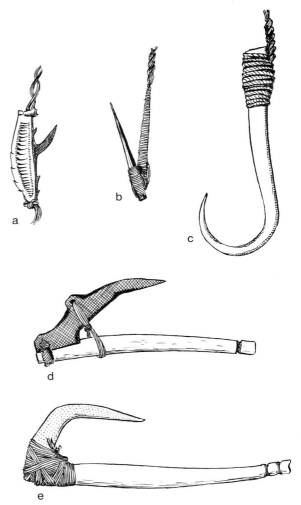

Fig 1. Fish hooks (a) Hook made from an insect's leg, Goodenough Island; (b) Hook made from two pieces of palm wood, Collingwood Bay; (c) Turtle-shell hook, Torres Strait; (d) Bonito spinner with bone shank and turtle-shell point, Morobe District; (e) Bonito spinner with pearl-shell shank and turtle-shell point, Bougainville.

teeth of the fish by means of a split stick (Fig. 2b). The Massim use a large baited hook of wood for catching sharks. It is usually cut from a fork, which gives maximum strength since the grain follows the form of the hook. Sometimes a separate incurved point is lashed on (Fig. 2a).

Two peculiar local forms may be mentioned. In the Redscar Bay area of Papua a short length of pandanus cortex with a few of the curved thorns served as a hook; and in Goodenough Island fish were caught in mountain streams with part of the leg of an insect which bears a hooked spur (Fig. 1a).

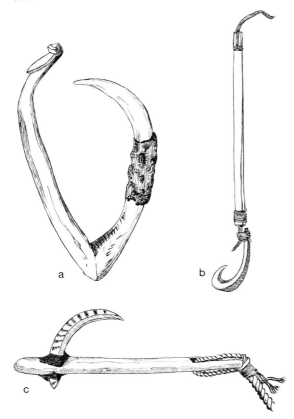

Fig 2. Fish hooks (a) Wood shark hook with separate wood point, Trobriand Islands; (b) Shell hook with wood guard for the snood, Hermit Islands; (c) Shark hook with wood shank and shell point, Admiralty Islands.

Spinning hooks, mainly for catching bonito, are used in Bougainville and parts of northern New Guinea. They consist of a shank, usually of bone or shell, to which is lashed a point of the same materials or of turtle-shell. They are towed behind a moving canoe and, turning and glinting in the sun, resemble a small fish. No bait is therefore necessary (Fig. 1d, e). A much larger hook, perhaps a spinner, is used in the Admiralty Islands for catching sharks. It has a straight wood shank with a curved point, usually of shell, set in gum in a hole cut in one end of it (Fig. 2c).

The gorge, a straight or angled piece of wood or bone about an inch long, is reported from the Gulf of Papua area and some of the northern islands. It is held parallel to the line, which is tied to the middle of it, with a lump of bait, and turns across the fish's gullet when taken.

Hand nets—often used one in each hand—are widely employed for fishing on reefs or in shallow water. The seine net, a long net with wood floats along the top edge and sinkers along the bottom, is especially typical of eastern Papua.

It is used from canoes or from the beach, and is shot round a shoal or to enclose an area, and dragged in from the ends. The casting net has been recorded only in a few localities: it has weights round the perimeter and is thrown so as to fall over a fish or a shoal.

The plunge-basket, open-ended and usually conical, is used by people wading in shallow water for catching fish by plunging it down over them.

Traps are nearly always made of basketry. There are two main types: long tapering cylindrical traps, often set in fast-flowing water or in weirs, in which the fish is held by the force of the water or because it is unable to back out; and traps with entrances formed by converging slats which open when the fish pushes inwards but close behind it and prevent its escape. These are usually baited. Both types have an almost world-wide distribution. A much more specialized form, found sporadically from New Britain to the south coast of Papua, is the thorn-lined trap. This is conical in outline and is made from lengths of a creeper with strongly curved thorns, set with the thorns pointing inwards. The trap is often suspended from a float, and bait is placed at the apex of the cone. The set of the thorns allows a fish to push inwards to reach the bait but prevents its backing out by catching in the scales (Fig. 3).

At various points along the north coast, from the Trobriands to the Admiralty group, garfish are caught by means of a kite—a method practised in the Solomons and further west in Indonesia. The bait is a mass of dense cobweb, in which the fish's teeth become entangled. The kite is flown from a canoe, and a cord from its tail trails the bait along the surface. The kite is usually made from palm leaf stiffened with mid-rib slats.

In New Ireland sharks are captured with nooses, a practice found widely in Polynesia. The shark is attracted to the vicinity of the canoe by means of a coconut rattle. A noose is then lowered into the water, attached to a wood float

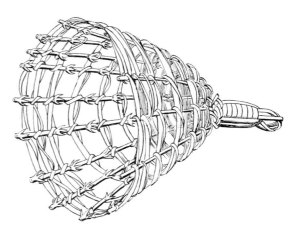

Fig 3. Thorn-lined fish trap, Gulf of Papua.

or marker shaped rather like a propeller. The shark is attracted by a bait and induced to pass its head through the noose, which is tightened round its gills. The float tires the fish by preventing diving; and it also marks the position. Eventually the shark is drawn alongside and killed with a club.

The practice of drugging (poisoning) fish is widespread. Roots or stems of plants of the legume family (*Derris* spp.) are most commonly used. They are crushed so that the juice runs into a pool. The stupefied fish rise to the surface and are easily caught.

Spears and arrows and harpoons have been described elsewhere (*see* MATERIAL CULTURE). It is sufficient here to say that fish spears and arrows have clusters of three or more barbed points.

Many of the methods and devices described are still in use. In some parts steel trade hooks have been adopted, and often European materials are incorporated in devices of traditional form.

B. Anell, *Contribution to the History of Fishing in the South Seas.* Uppsala, 1955; H. Balfour, 'Kite-Fishing', in *Essays and Studies Presented to William Ridgeway on his Sixtieth Birthday.* Cambridge, 1913; H. G. Beasley, *Pacific Island Records: Fish Hooks.* London, 1928; B. A. L. Cranstone, *Melanesia: A Short Ethnography.* London, 1961; A. B. Lewis, *Ethnology of Melanesia.* Chicago, 1932.

B. A. L. CRANSTONE

FISHING INDUSTRY. In the report of a survey made in 1961-2 it was estimated that about one million people in the Territory of Papua and New Guinea, about one-half of the total population, are partly or wholly dependent on fishing. Many ingenious methods for catching fish and other aquatic animals have been developed (*see* FISHING). There is a rich fishing tradition in many coastal areas and along the larger rivers. Modern methods of transport and modern types of fishing gear have greatly increased the potential of the industry in most areas.

Because of the wide distribution and primitive nature of indigenous fisheries it is impossible to obtain accurate statistics on the landed catch, but it is certainly not less than 10,000-15,000 tons per annum, and possibly as much as 30,000 tons. When crustaceans, shellfish, turtles, dugong and other aquatic animals are included, the latter figure is probably closer, since these items form an appreciable part of the catch in many marine areas and some inland fisheries. No information is available for West Irian, but the proportion of the population involved in fishing and the relative catch are probably about the same.

Little is known about the amount of the catch consumed in the village compared to the quantity sold or used for trade purposes, but the proportion probably varies considerably from place to place and with seasonal and other factors. The proportion sold is certainly rising rapidly and will continue to rise as individuals specialize in fishing and acquire gear, vessels and handling equipment. Significant markets exist at all major centres

and many minor ones, and the supply of local fish seldom exceeds the demand. Prices are high, nearly equal to the equivalent in red meat in some centres. It is estimated that 150-200 tons of local seafoods are sold annually through Koki Market in Port Moresby and at least 100 tons through other Port Moresby outlets. The total marketed catch in Papua and New Guinea is probably about 1,000-2,000 tons per annum, or only about 5 per cent of the total estimated possible catch of 30,000 tons.

Statistics are available for fisheries exports. Shell and shell products have always been by far the most important in quantity and value, and retain this position despite a recent decline in demand. Quantities of exported bêche-de-mer and turtle-shell have also declined, but the value of exported seafoods has risen rapidly in recent years, owing to the increased catch of barramundi and crayfish. The gross annual value of exported marine products reached about $30,000 for Papua before World War I; there was little increase before World War II, when it did not much exceed $80,000 for Papua and New Guinea. In the post-war period there was a strong demand for shell, and the enforced resting of the beds allowed a significant increase in production. The peak value reached almost $1,000,000 in 1956.

On the other hand, fish imports have increased steadily in the post-war period, and the total value exceeds $2,000,000 per annum, mainly as cheap tinned fish. This represents more than 10 per cent of the value of all imported foods.

SCALEFISH

There are probably over two thousand species of fish in New Guinea waters, and most kinds that can be caught are eaten. It is usual for over two hundred species to pass through the larger markets in a year. The principal groups taken are shark, ray, trevally, mullet, threadfin, Spanish mackerel, tuna, seapike, garfish, longtom, catfish, snapper, sweetlip, reef cod, barramundi, surgeon fish, wrasse, parrot fish and eel. The importance of a particular species in the catch-composition varies in each area and season, depending on local habitats and fishing methods. For example, in the Western and Gulf Districts barramundi are very important, and mullet, threadfin and tripletail are taken by the same inshore netting methods; but barramundi are absent from the north coast, the New Guinea islands and the Papuan eastern islands.

Throughout New Guinea Spanish mackerel, seapike and tuna are taken by surface trolling in deeper waters, and tuna is also taken by poling techniques which are essentially the same as the overseas commercial method. In reef areas, snapper, reef cod, parrot fish, sweetlip, triggerfish and many other types are taken by hand-lining. Shark and trevally of various species are taken everywhere. In different areas and seasons special traps and nets are used for species ranging from eels to runners, others are still hunted by spear and bow, and others are caught by hand. Poisoning is still employed in suitable localities. With the advent of trawling, exploitable stocks of jewfish, flatfish and other demersal species have been located, together with large quantities of small species, notably ponyfish and grunters, which are suitable for processing.

A number of the inshore species are diadromous, and they are found in fresh water as well as in the sea and estuaries. They include barramundi, mullet, longtom, some snapper, tarpon, catfish and freshwater eels. There are relatively few purely freshwater species large enough to be important as food, and the freshwater eels are the only diadromous species which are able to penetrate to higher altitudes. Several species, including tilapia, gourami and carp have been introduced to both coastal and Highland waters. Tilapia from local swamps now form a significant proportion of the Port Moresby market. Carp are widely used for fish culture—there are about seven thousand fish ponds in the Highlands region—and they form important stocks in natural waters at higher altitudes.

SHELLFISH

The important export species are mother-of-pearl, both black-lip and gold-lip, trochus and green snail. Because of the low demand gold-lip pearlshell [q.v.] is no longer fished by suit-divers. This species was extensively used for trade in pre-European times, and is still important for ornaments in the Highlands. Black-lip pearl-shell, which occurs in shallow water, is still fished extensively for export, as are trochus and green snail. Many other types of molluscs are used locally for food. They are usually consumed fresh-cooked but some are smoked for local trade. Apart from marine species, large freshwater mussels are eaten where they occur. In the Admiralty Islands the giant clam (*Tridacna*) has been traditionally 'farmed' by carrying small shells to suitable fattening grounds. Local species of oysters are amenable to cultivation as practised overseas and are considered scarcely inferior to Australian and New Zealand products. In recent years cultivation of pearls has been undertaken in Papua with encouraging results. There is a small trade in ornamental shells for tourists and collectors: certain species (*Conus gloriamaris*, *Cypraea guttata*, etc.) are worth from $1,000-$2,000 each on the specialist market. Many species of shellfish equally handsome and colourful occur in favourable environments. Small tropical scallops have been taken by trawling and dredging, but not so far in commercial quantities.

CRUSTACEANS

There are over forty species of penaeid prawns in New Guinea waters, of which at least a dozen occur in commercial quantities. The most important are the banana prawn and the giant tiger-prawn. Stocks of estuarine and inshore prawns and shrimps, and of freshwater shrimps, have always been used locally for food. The first small-mesh trawling survey was carried out in 1955, and prawns have now been found in places along the whole coastline. One small fleet began exploiting these resources commercially in 1967. No significant quantities have yet been exported, but this is likely in the near future. Small quantities of shovelnose lobsters ('bugs') are also taken by trawling.

Six species of tropical crayfish (*Panulirus*) occur in New Guinea, at least three of them in commercial quantities in the appropriate habitat. One species (the painted crayfish) makes a seasonal run into shallow water on the Papuan central coast; the reason for this phenomenon is unknown, but it has been traditionally exploited and is now the basis of a small but vigorous export industry. The method used in this fishery is hand capture, and the other species are taken in the same way or by spearing or trap-netting. Research is being undertaken to extend these fisheries by the use of pots, traps, tangle-nets and ring-nets.

Several species of freshwater and diadromous river prawns (*Macrobrachium*) are found in New Guinea to an altitude of 3,000 feet. These are eaten wherever they occur, but are not taken in commercial quantities because the main method of capture is in traps. The same applies to the various local species of freshwater crayfish.

Many species of crabs are used as food, notably the large mud crab. Sand crabs are also taken by trawling and gill-netting in suitable areas (*see* CRUSTACEA).

BÊCHE-DE-MER

There are many species of holothurians in New Guinea, but only a few are in demand on the Asian market. At one period bêche-de-mer was exported in small but significant quantities; although the demand remains, interest in production has generally declined, partly owing to the difficulty of processing and changes in the type of product required. Bêche-de-mer is used locally for food in many areas, but is generally less important than other marine products.

OTHER AQUATIC VERTEBRATES

Marine turtle, freshwater tortoise and turtle, dugong and dolphin [qq.v.] are all traditional local foods. They are still hunted extensively and turtle eggs are eaten wherever nests are found. There has been an apparent decline in the numbers of dugong, and of turtles in some areas, probably due to over-fishing. Dolphin-hunting appears to have declined rather than otherwise, and dolphins are no longer killed for their teeth (used for brideprice) in Bougainville. Turtle-shell has been exported in small quantities, but this trade has declined. There is a small trade in curio shells and stuffed turtles.

SEAWEEDS

There is an overseas demand for agar-producing seaweeds, but resources in New Guinea appear to be limited and none has so far been produced commercially.

FISHERIES ADMINISTRATION

Administration of fisheries laws is vested in the Department of Agriculture, Stock and Fisheries. The Division of Fisheries was established in 1954 to promote the development of commercial fishing. It engages in research on the distribution, abundance and biology of important species, as well as on the adaptation of modern fishing, handling and processing methods to local use. Information is disseminated through example, formal and informal fisheries schools, and training programmes. At the same time, internal and external markets for fish and sea products are investigated by the Department of Agriculture, Stock and Fisheries and by the Department of Trade and Industry. The latter department also promotes co-operative societies, several of which are based partly or wholly on the fishing industry.

There are nearly forty commercial fishermen licensed under the existing legislation, which refers explicitly to fishing boats. Licences are required only for fishing boats engaged in full-time commercial fishing, and the number of licences does not in any way reflect the number of people involved in fishing; most of the catch is landed by unlicensed subsistence and part-time fishermen.

FACILITIES

The main difficulty in the development of the industry is limitation of facilities and equipment. The bulk of the catch is landed by wading, and from canoes. Although there are more than one hundred motorized canoes in Papua alone, they are not used exclusively for fishing and some are used entirely for transport. In any case canoes are not suitable for most types of commercial fishing and petrol-driven outboard motors are not economic except for high-priced seafoods.

Further commercial development depends on an increase in the number of large and small fishing boats which are more reliable, more economical to maintain and run, less dependent on weather conditions, and capable of carrying more complex fishing gear and greater payloads over greater distances. Commensurate improvements are needed in port and shore facilities, both for maintenance of vessels and handling of fish.

There are a few small privately owned refrigerators used mainly for fish, and the Administration has installed fish-rooms at Daru, Port Moresby, Loupom, Samarai, Madang and Rabaul. There are extensive rooms at Kairuku, the centre of the crayfish export industry. A few private boats are equipped with built-in refrigeration, and two boats owned by the Federation of Native Associations have a total freezer capacity of eight shipping tons. The use of insulated ice-boxes is increasing, but the supply of ice is limited and often expensive. The Administration produces flake ice at Daru and Rabaul, and block ice in some other centres where supplies are otherwise unobtainable or inadequate.

Some types of imported fishing equipment are readily available, although often expensive, but ancillary equipment is often difficult to obtain.

Measures to meet these problems are constantly under investigation and review. The relatively high costs of capital equipment, maintenance, and transport are by no means confined to the fishing industry and the problem is being met on a broad front. The peculiar need of the fishing industry is for widespread refrigeration, which is costly both to install and to maintain. In general, the larger the installation and the greater the volume of fish handled, the more economical it becomes.

There has already been some development in crayfish and barramundi fishing and there is a decided interest in both tuna and prawn resources. It is expected that, as these fisheries expand, subsidiary ones will become important seasonally until the majority of exploitable stocks are utilized in an integrated industry.

T. P. N. G. Bureau of Statistics, *Survey of Indigenous Agriculture and Ancillary Surveys 1961-1962*. Port Moresby, 1963.   L. W. C. FILEWOOD

(*See also* FISHING)

FLAG AND CREST. A flag for Papua New Guinea has been widely and keenly considered. By resolution on 14 March 1971 the House of Assembly adopted the design shown below, as

The flag (above) and crest (below) adopted by the House of Assembly as the national flag and official crest of Papua New Guinea. The flag features a yellow bird of paradise on a red background above a white Southern Cross on a black background.

proposed in a report from the Select Committee on Constitutional Development. The design was based on one submitted by Susan Kanike, aged about 15, from the Catholic mission school at Yule Island in the Central District. Details of the design will be incorporated in a Bill to be submitted to the House.

The crest of the Territory is also shown.

The Gazette Extraordinary of 1st July 1971 in which the flag and crest are given their full official descriptions appears facsimile as an appendix in Volume 3.

FLIERL, Johann (1858-1947) and Wilhelm (1892-1966) were Lutheran missionaries. Johann was born on 16 April 1858 at Fürnried, near Munich, Germany, and in 1878 was consecrated at Neuendettelsau and sailed for Australia. He served at Cooper's Creek and then in 1885 moved to Cooktown en route for New Guinea. He had to wait there for a considerable time and founded the mission station at Elim, north of Cooktown. At last, on a boat chartered by the New Guinea Company, he arrived at Finschhafen on 12 July 1886, establishing the first station at Simbang. Another was founded at Sattelberg in 1892. He finally left New Guinea in 1930 and retired to the Mission House in Tanunda, South Australia. Later he returned to Germany and died at Neuendettelsau on 30 September 1947. His son Wilhelm was born on 30 June 1892 at Finschhafen, educated at a mission seminary in Bavaria and the Colonial Institute in Hamburg, returning to work in New Guinea in 1914. He served in the United States 1922-7 and in the latter year returned to Finschhafen. He retired in 1963 and returned to Germany in 1964, though still continuing his translation work. He died at Neuendettelsau on 16 August 1966. A third generation of the family is represented in New Guinea today by the missionary Helmut Flierl.

J. Flierl, *Forty-Five Years in New Guinea*, tr. M. Wiederaenders. Columbus, Ohio, 1931.

FRANCIS WEST

(*See also* GERMAN NEW GUINEA)

FLIES. The term 'fly', in its technical sense, refers to the Diptera, one of the larger orders of insects with a world total of about 150,000 species. As adults, almost all can be immediately recognized by the presence of only a single pair of wings (the fore wings). The hind wings are reduced to small, club-like structures (the halteres), which are believed to act as gyroscopic organs of balance. The mouth-parts are also characteristic; they are usually more or less elongated to form a proboscis adapted for sucking either free moisture via a pair of fleshy, apical lobes, or the body fluids of vertebrates or other insects via a sharp, piercing proboscis. The latter habit is exemplified by the blood-sucking mosquitoes, midges, etc., which, as pests or vectors of disease, take an enormous toll of human health and comfort.

Diptera, like other 'higher' insects, develop first as an active, feeding larva, then as a more or less quiescent pupa, before the adult is formed. All larvae are legless; the more 'primitive' families (e.g. mosquitoes) have a distinct head, but in 'higher' families the head is reduced, culminating in the headless 'maggot' that typifies blowflies and related families. Most larvae are either aquatic, living in free water (e.g. mosquitoes) or saturated mud (e.g. certain midges); or terrestrial, living in soil or, very commonly, in decomposing organic matter; or parasitic within plants or other animals, particularly insects (e.g. Tachinidae). Quite a few free-living forms are predators. Pupae are generally found in the soil or litter but may be aquatic. Most are either free or, in 'higher' families, enclosed in a puparium, an oval or barrel-shaped container formed from the unshed larval skin. They may also be enclosed in a cocoon.

Adults are typically found in moist situations, particularly on vegetation, and are commonly seen on blossom, feeding on nectar. In some families, in addition to the familiar blood-suckers, they are mainly or entirely predators (e.g. Asilidae, Empididae, Dolichopodidae), while some highly specialized forms are ectoparasites (Hippoboscidae, mainly on birds; Nycteribiidae and Streblidae, on bats).

COMPOSITION AND EXTERNAL RELATIONS OF
THE FAUNA

With a few notable exceptions, serious study of the New Guinea Diptera is only just commencing. At present, therefore, it is difficult to make valid generalizations. However, at least 65 families have been recorded and about 10 others possibly occur there (world total about 118, with 86 in Australia). The number of species is possibly around 5,000, but that is a mere guess. All the families so far recorded probably occur in the Oriental region also, and only the Diopsidae do not reach Australia. However, by comparison with the Australian fauna, it seems that some families are poorly represented (e.g. Therevidae, Bombyliidae, Apioceridae), others are of comparable size (e.g. Culicidae, Ceratopogonidae) or, as in Psychodidae, the New Guinea fauna is by far the greater. As elsewhere in the wet tropics, there is a noticeable tendency for species-rich families to include strikingly divergent, even bizarre forms.

As regards external relations of the fauna, the evidence, such as it is, is consistent with Cheesman's generalizations about the whole insect fauna: (a) the dipterofauna is 'harmonious', with few marked lacunae not explicable on purely climatic grounds; (b) there is a marked degree of endemism; (c) there are distinct resemblances at all levels to both the Oriental and Australian faunas, the proportions varying with the group. It is perhaps noteworthy that Mackerras' analysis of ancestral origins of the Tabanidae indicates about 50 per cent early migrants via Asia, 35 per cent more recent Oriental forms and 15 per cent more recent Australian forms; Cheesman's figures for all insects are 60, 30 and 10 per cent respectively.

Some families (e.g. Psychodidae, Ceratopogonidae) show a small but distinct group related to Oceanian forms. Also, although most resemblances to the Australian fauna are found in groups distributed in the wet tropics of that area, there are also (mostly unpublished) records of 'Bassian' or 'Antarctic' elements in New Guinea; i.e., with their closest relatives in cool-temperate Australia, and, in some cases, southern South America. Such records are few, and mainly from high elevations, but no doubt more will turn up and their implications, perhaps as regards continental drift, will become clearer.

SYNOPSIS OF FAMILIES

It is impossible here to deal in detail with all recorded families. Only salient points are mentioned about those better known, better represented or otherwise of most interest. References are given only to major studies or entries in the literature, but many families are dealt with in lesser fashion in other works listed in the bibliography.

Tipulidae Crane-flies. Over 200 species and subspecies have been recorded probably representing only a minor part of those present. The fauna is essentially Oriental, but includes many elements with resemblances to the Australian fauna; some of the latter (e.g. *Gynoplistia, Erioptera* (=*Molophilus*), *Amphineurus*) seem to comprise an 'Antarctic' element.

Tanyderidae. Six large and ornate species of *Radinoderus* have been recorded.

Psychodidae Moth-flies, sandflies. Two hundred and twenty-eight species have been recorded, representing probably less than half of an extremely rich fauna. All major genera are present, dominated by *Psychoda* with 80 species. Their affinities are divided about equally between the Oriental and Australian regions.

Culicidae includes 335 species, 63 per cent of which are apparently endemic. The dominant genera (subgenera in brackets) are *Anopheles* (*Cellia*), *Tripteroides* (*Rachisoura*), *Aedes* (*Finlaya* and *Verrallina*), and *Culex* (*Culex* and *Lophoceraomyia*). Faunal relationships indicate derivation from both the Orient and Australia. Some major groups (e.g. *Lophoceraomyia*, Group A) seem to have originated in the New Guinea area.

Chironomidae. Surprisingly few have been recorded in view of the apparently rich fauna; species of *Polypedilum* and *Chironomus* are common pests around lights.

Ceratopogonidae. Some 232 species of biting midges and sandflies in twenty-one genera have been recorded. The dominant genera are *Culicoides, Stilobezzia, Forcipomyia* and *Atrichopogon*, and to a lesser extent *Palpomyia, Bezzia* and *Alluaudomyia*. The majority of species are endemic and resemblances are perhaps rather greater to the Oriental than to the Australian fauna. The apparent rarity of *Dasyhelea* is surprising, as is the occurrence of 6 species of the Australian and Neotropical *Echinohelea*.

Simuliidae Blackflies. Fifty-two species of *Simulium* have been reviewed; the typically Australian *Cnephia* and *Austrosimulium* have not been found,

but elevations above 8,000 feet remain to be investigated. Most species (32) belong in a typically Australasian subgenus, *Morops*, but 9 others fall in the typically Oriental *Gomphostilbia*.

Anisopodidae. Apart from several species of the cosmopolitan *Sylvicola*, there is one (undescribed) of the extremely rare, pan-tropical *Mesochria*. The three known specimens of the latter comprise 25 per cent of the world collection as recorded in 1962.

Bibionidae. Fourteen species of the largely tropical *Plecia* have been recorded and 3 of *Dilophus*.

Sciaridae. Very numerous but apparently unrecorded in the literature. A surprise is the unpublished record of the aberrant *Colonomyia* from high elevations, otherwise known only from cool-temperate Australia.

Mycetophilidae Fungus-gnats. Few species have been recorded, but available collections indicate a rich and harmonious fauna including most of the major genera and some new ones. The dominant genera appear to be *Epicypta, Leia, Orfelia* and *Neoempheria*, and at high elevations *Mycetophila* (and related genera), *Macrocera* and *Mycomya*. Amongst the surprises are *Diadocidia* (typically cool-temperate, but found in the *lowlands*), *Eumanota* (very rare; Borneo and Queensland) and the 'Antarctic' *Stenophragma*.

Rhagionidae. Only *Chrysopilus* is known to occur and that not very abundantly.

Tabanidae Horse-flies, march-flies. The fauna is quite well studied; 119 species in eleven genera (three, and one subgenus, endemic) have been reviewed.

Stratiomyidae. Many species have been described, but the family still awaits a comprehensive review.

Asilidae Robber-flies. Records suggest a relatively small fauna, certainly much smaller than the Australian. Dasypogoninae, so abundant in temperate areas, seem conspicuously rare. Recorded species belong mostly to *Ommatius* and *Laphria* (or its close relative the metallic *Maira*, an obvious link with the Oriental fauna).

Bombyliidae. Only a few species have been recorded, so the fauna is presumably small; but large, handsome flies of two wide-ranging species of *Ligyra* are not uncommon.

Empididae. Scattered records and available material suggest a fairly large fauna, but almost completely lacking in subfamily Empidinae (perhaps commoner at very high altitudes). Hemerodromiinae are not common and seem to resemble Australian forms. Hybotinae are well represented by species, some very handsome, of *Syneches, Hybos*, and related genera; two species of Ocydromiini closely resemble others known from south-eastern Australia. Small Tachydromiinae make up the bulk of the fauna (*Tachydromia, Elaphropeza, Drapetis*, etc.).

Dolichopodidae. Most of the usual tropical genera are represented. As is common in the tropics the fauna is dominated by the larger metallic-green or blue Sciapodinae, mostly described under *Psilopus* or *Chrysosoma*. There are also many species of small obscure Campsicneminae, particularly at high altitudes.

Pipunculidae. The genera *Pipunculus*, *Tomasvaryella* and *Achalarus* are known to be represented.

Syrphidae Hover-flies. The fauna seems quite a rich one, with over 50 species so far recorded in at least fourteen genera; there is a notable predominance of *Eristalis* and *Syrphus*.

Platystomatidae. Some 130 species in twenty-eight genera have been recorded, which is no doubt only a small portion of the fauna. There is a resemblance to the Australian fauna in the large number of species of *Euprosopia* and *Lamprogaster* (the latter a purely Australian-New Guinean genus); but the considerable radiations in *Achias* and *Cleitamia* seem to be endemic developments. There are many bizarre species, including the males of *Achias* with long-stalked eyes (Fig. 1).

Pyrgotidae. Few species are recorded, but there is a significant fauna, including the typically Australian *Epicerella*.

Tephritidae Fruit-flies. There seems to be a rich fauna, particularly of the fruit-breeding Dacinae. The curious, aberrant *Phytalmyia* (Fig. 2) is endemic and notable for the long, forked 'horns' arising from below the male eyes. More than 70 species in over thirty genera have been described and no doubt many remain.

Diopsidae. In this largely Oriental family of curious, small flies, both sexes have their eyes at the apices of long stalks; one species is known to reach New Guinea.

Lauxaniidae. At least 50 species are recorded and the family is clearly well represented, but it remains unreviewed in detail.

Muscidae. Detailed review of the family was only begun in the early 1970s, but it is clear that many species are present. Amongst those most commonly seen are the metallic-green or blue members of *Orthellia*. The ubiquitous house fly (*Musca domestica*) and stable-fly (*Stomoxys calcitrans*), and the wide-ranging bush fly (*M. vetustissima*) are all present, but at most only locally abundant. There are some distinct links with the Australian fauna in, for instance, species of *Dichaetomyia*.

Calliphoridae Blowflies. The fauna, as far as known, seems small by comparison with the Australian. A notable feature is the radiation in *Euphumosia* with 33 species, mostly restricted to New Guinea.

Tachinidae. The family is quite well represented but not yet reviewed. The tribe Rutiliini is represented mainly by the large, handsome, metallic species of *Formosia*.

Nycteribiidae Bat flies. At least 23 species occur in six genera, most in *Basilia*, sub-genus *Tripselia*, and in *Cyclopodia*; the latter occur exclusively on the large fruit bats.

Other families recorded are listed below; a double asterisk indicates an apparently rich fauna and a single asterisk a smaller but at least significant one.

Scatopsidae*, Cecidomyiidae**, Xylomyidae (*Solva*), Acroceridae (*Ogcodes*), Therevidae, Nemestrinidae, Scenopinidae, Platypezidae, Phoridae**, Conopidae, Otitidae, Cypselosomatidae (*Formicosepsis*), Neriidae, Micropezidae*, Tanypezidae (*Strongylophthalmyia*), Psilidae (*Chyliza*), Sepsidae, Sciomyzidae (*Sepedon*), Chamaemyiidae (*Acrometopia*), Sphaeroceridae*, Lonchaeidae, Piophilidae, Clusiidae*, Agromyzidae**, Anthomyzidae (*Stenomicra*, *Amygdalops*), Asteidae, Curtonotidae (*Axinota*), Milichiidae, Ephydridae*, Drosophilidae**, Cryptochetidae, Canaceidae, Chloropidae**, Sarcophagidae**, Hippoboscidae**, Streblidae.

This bibliography is not exhaustive; the most important works dealing with the New Guinea fauna are either given here or in the works given here.

C. P. Alexander, 'Undescribed Species of Nematocerous Diptera. Part VI.', *Bulletin of the Brooklyn Entomological Society*, vol. 54, 1959.

———— 'New or little-known crane-flies from New Guinea (Diptera: Tipulidae). Part 1.', *Pacific Insects*, vol. 3, 1961.

T. Becker, 'Dipterologische Studien, Dolichopodidae der Indo-Australischen Region', *Capita Zoologica*, vol. 1, 1922.

E. M. Beyer, 'Neue und wenig bekannte Phoriden, zumeist aus dem Bishop Museum, Honolulu (Diptera: Phoridae)', *Pacific Insects*, vol. 8, 1966.

M. Bezzi, '*Empididi* Indo-australian raccolti dal Signor L. Bíro', *Annales Musei Nationalis Hungarici*, vol. 2, 1904.

T. Borgmeier, 'Studies on Indo-Australian Phorid Flies', *Studia Entomologica*, vol. 9, 1966.

L. E. Cheesman, 'Old Mountains of New Guinea', *Nature*, vol. 168, 1951.

D. H. Colless, 'Notes on Australasian Tanyderidae, with Description of a New Species of *Radinoderus* Handl. (Diptera)', *Proceedings of the Linnean Society of N.S.W.*, vol. 87, 1963.

E. T. Cresson, Jr., 'A Systematic Annotated Arrange-

Fig 1. Fly with long-stalked eyes, *Achias* sp., male (Platystomatidae).

Fig 2. Horned fly *Phytalmyia* sp., male (Tephritidae).

ment of the Genera and Species of the Indo-Australian Ephydridae (Diptera). II', *Transactions of the American Entomological Society*, vol. 73, 1947.

R. W. Crosskey, 'The Classification of *Simulium* Latreille (Diptera: Simuliidae) from Australia, New Guinea and the Western Pacific', *Journal of Natural History*, vol. 1, 1967.

D. E. Hardy, 'Studies in Pacific Bibionidae (Diptera), Part II: Genus *Philia* Meigen', *Proceedings of Hawaiian Entomological Society*, vol. 14, 1951.

——— 'The *Plecia* of the Pacific and Southeast Asia (Bibionidae-Diptera)', *Pacific Science*, vol. 12, 1958.

K. Kertész, 'Verzeichniss einiger, von. L. Biró in Neu-Guinea und am Malayischen Archipel gesammelten *Dipteren*', *Természtrajzi Füzetek*, vol. 22, 1899.

E. Lindner, 'The Diptera of the Territory of New Guinea. VI. Family Stratiomyiidae', *Proceedings of the Linnean Society of N.S.W.*, vol. 63, 1938.

——— 'Results of the Archbold Expeditions. Statiomyiiden von Neu-Guinea', *Nova Guinea*, new series, vol. 8, 1957.

T. C. Maa, 'Records and descriptions of Nycteribiidae and Streblidae (Diptera)', *Pacific Insects*, vol. 4, 1962.

——— 'Partial revision of the Cyclopodiinae (Diptera: Nycteribiidae)', *Pacific Insects*, vol. 8, 1966.

——— 'Studies in Hippoboscidae (Diptera)', *Pacific Insects Monograph 10*, 1966.

D. K. McAlpine, 'Description and biology of an Australian species of Cypselosomatidae (Diptera)', *Australian Journal of Zoology*, vol. 14, 1966.

I. M. Mackerras, 'The Tabanidae (Diptera) of New Guinea', *Pacific Insects*, vol. 6, 1964.

J. R. Malloch, 'Papuan Diptera. I. Family Diopsidae', *Proceedings of the Linnean Society of N.S.W.*, vol. 63, 1938.

——— 'The Diptera of the Territory of New Guinea. VII. Family Otitidae (Ortalidae)'; 'IX. Family Phytalmyiidae'; 'XI. Family Trypetidae', *Proceedings of the Linnean Society of N.S.W.*, vol. 64, 1939.

E. N. Marks, 'Faunal relationships of some Australian and Papuan Culicidae', *Verhandlungen XI. Internationaler Kongress für Entomologie*, 1961.

J. C. H. de Meijere, 'Studien über südostasiatische Dipteren XIV', *Tijdschrift voor Entomologie*, vol, 60, 1917.

O. Parent, 'The Diptera of the Territory of New Guinea. VIII. Dolichopodidae', *Proceedings of the Linnean Society of N.S.W.*, vol. 64, 1939.

L. W. and S. H. Quate, 'A monograph of Papuan Psychodidae, including *Phlebotomus* (Diptera)', *Pacific Insects Monograph 15*, 1967.

M. Sasakawa, 'Papuan Agromyzidae (Diptera)', *Pacific Insects*, vol. 5, 1963.

——— 'Studies on the Oriental and Pacific Clusiidae (Diptera). Part 1. Genus *Heteromeringia* Czerny, with one new, related genus', *Pacific Insects*, vol. 8, 1966.

J. Smart and E. A. Clifford, 'Simuliidae (Diptera) of the Territory of Papua and New Guinea', *Pacific Insects*, vol. 7, 1965.

W. A. Steffan, 'A Checklist and Review of the Mosquitoes of the Papuan Subregion', *Journal of Medical Entomology*, vol. 3, 1966.

B. Theowald, 'Results of the Archbold Expeditions. Notes on Calliphoridae of New Guinea. I', *Nova Guinea*, new series, vol. 8, 1957; 'Part II', *Nova Guinea*, new series, vol. 10, 1959.

M. Tokunaga, 'New Guinea biting midges (Diptera: Ceratopogonidae), 3', *Pacific Insects*, vol. 5, 1963; 'Biting midges of the genus *Ceratopogon* from New Guinea (Diptera: Ceratopogonidae)', *Pacific Insects*, vol. 6, 1964; 'Biting midges of the Palpomyiinae from New Guinea (Diptera: Ceratopogonidae)', *Pacific Insects*, vol. 8, 1966.

R. L. Torgerson and M. T. James, 'Revision of the world species of *Euphumosia* (Diptera: Calliphoridae)', *Pacific Insects*, vol. 9, 1967.

F. M. van der Wulp, '*Dipteren* aus Neu-Guinea in der Sammlung des Ungarischen National-Museums', *Természetrajzi Füzetek*, vol. 21, 1898.

DONALD H. COLLESS

FLORISTICS. The flora of Papua New Guinea is rich and varied, with habitats ranging from tidal swamps at sea-level to truly alpine conditions where snow falls. Knowledge of this flora is far from complete; both collecting in the field and systematic description of specimens already gathered still have much to contribute before a comprehensive treatment of the flora is possible. The selection of plants illustrated in Figs 1-8 on the following pages shows the wide range of types and the curious nature of some species.

FOOD. The great majority of peoples in New Guinea live directly off the resources of the land and adjacent waters, and in most parts of the country each family produces the major part of its own food. Everywhere the bulk of the diet comes from one or more staple starchy foods: sweet potatoes, taro, yams, bananas, or sago. Sago in the form prepared locally can be stored for two to three months, and yams may be harvested annually and stored, but the other three crops keep for only a few days. Usually they are brought from the garden and eaten the same day. Rough terrain and poor communications hinder trade in food. Diet thus largely depends on what foods are produced locally, and that is determined to a great extent by the physical environment (*see* AGRICULTURE, INDIGENOUS).

Varieties of sweet potatoes grow at all altitudes but are the characteristic staple of the cooler upland areas. At 8,000 feet they take eighteen months to mature, compared with six months at 5,000 feet; yields are greatest between 5,000 and 6,500 feet. They are the main food for at least half the population. It is estimated that annual production is about 1.2 million tons, a quantity far in excess of any other food crop.

Taro is usually the staple in lowland rain forest areas where soils are only moderately fertile, though in parts of the Highlands it is as plentiful as the sweet potato and often it is the main subsidiary root crop. There is some possibility that taro was the staple in the Highlands prior to the introduction of sweet potatoes some time after the fifteenth century. Present annual production throughout the Australian Territory is about 460,000 tons.

Small quantities of yams are grown in most parts of the country, but they do best in well drained soils of high mineral fertility. They are the staple in areas with new volcanic soils such as the Prince Alexander and Torricelli Mountains, and also in the richer soils derived from coral limestone, as in the Trobriand Islands. Annual production is estimated at about 230,000 tons.

FLORISTICS

Fig 1. (a) *Humelacanthus* (family Acanthaceae). A native plant found usually in the swamp forests. The brilliant red flower heads, 6 inches long, make this a worthy introduction to horticulture; (b) *Semecarpus* (family Anacardiaceae). This genus of plant has very poisonous sap in all parts. As can be seen from the photograph of the fruit there is a striking resemblance to the cashew nut. Another related plant is the poison ivy in America. People who become sensitized to the poison in the sap of all these suffer increasingly each time they come in contact. In New Guinea the traveller should learn to recognize and avoid *Semecarpus*. The fruit spike may be up to 15 inches in length and the nut 1¼ inches long; (c) *Amorphophallus* (family Araceae). This relative of the arum lily is a common plant in regrowth forest in lowland New Guinea. The large leaf arises on a thick leaf stem and may last for two or more years. The leaf eventually dies down and the enormous flower head, 18 inches wide and 15 inches high, comes up from the underground tuber. The flower has a most unpleasant odour. It attracts and is pollinated by blowflies; (d) *Hoya* (family Asclepiadaceae). This fine species of *Hoya* comes from the Wantoat region of the Finisterre Range. It has been brought into cultivation and may now be seen in several botanic gardens throughout the world. The flowers may be 2 inches across.

a

b

c

d

FLORISTICS

Fig 2. (a) *Octomeles sumatrana* (family Datiscaceae). This large river bank tree is widely used for canoes as the wood is easily worked and the logs are long and straight. The tree may grow to 120 feet; (b) *Tecomanthe* (family Bignoniaceae). There are several species of *Tecomanthe* or native tecoma in New Guinea. All are very beautiful flowering vines. The flowers, 4 to 6 inches long, vary from pale to deep pink and some, as in the species illustrated here, have yellow tips to the corolla; (c) *Balanophora* (family Balanophoraceae). This curious plant is parasitic on the roots of trees in the mountain forests. Plants are separately male or female. The underground stem produces a short erect leafy branch. The leaves are brown because the plant lacks chlorophyll. The separate male and female spikes, 4 to 6 inches tall, emerge just above the leaf litter on the forest floor; (d) *Helichrysum bracteatum* (family Compositae). The flowers of this small grassland plant are frequently used as shown here as ornamentation for head-dresses.

c   d

FLORISTICS

Fig 3. (a) *Nothofagus pullei* (family Fagaceae). The antarctic beech trees of New Guinea are very significant for plant geographers. This is one of some seventeen or eighteen species which occur throughout the mountainous regions of the country. This species grows to 60 feet; (b) *Rhododendron womersleyi* (family Ericaceae). A very common species adjacent to the lakes on Wilhelm where it is seen by many visitors. It apparently does not occur other than on this mountain. The flowers are 1 inch in length; (c) *Dimorphanthera womersleyi* (family Ericaceae). A robust vine which produces long trailing shoots upon which the white flowers, 1 inch long, are produced; (d) *Dichrotrichum* (family Gesneriaceae). The family Gesneriaceae includes many colourful small shrubs and creepers. One of the latter is *Dichrotrichum*. The stem clings by means of roots to the bark of trees of the mountain forests. The flower heads, 4 inches across, are produced on long stems that stand out almost at right angles from the tree trunk.

FLORISTICS

Fig 4. (a) *Macropsychanthus lauterbachii* (family Leguminosae). A climber which has been wrongly
identified as a blue form of the d'Albertis creeper. In fact, the flower heads are produced high in
the crowns of the supporting trees and only a few blossoms are open at a time. The flower
spikes are 8 inches tall and the flowers 2 inches in length; (b) *Bauhinia acuminata* (family Leguminosae). The pure white flowers, 3 inches across, of this fine species of *Bauhinia* are distinctive.
There are many other species with pink to purplish flowers including *Bauhinia blakeana* which
is being increasingly grown as an ornamental; (c) *Abutilon* (family Malvaceae). A relative of
hibiscus which may be seen growing in the drier areas of the Bulolo Valley and round Port
Moresby. The flowers are 4 inches across; (d) *Thespesia* (family Malvaceae). One of several
forest trees also related to the hibiscus, which are seen by the traveller through the jungles of
New Guinea. The flowers are 2½ inches across.

FLORISTICS

Fig 5. (a) *Ficus dammaropsis* (family Moraceae). A native fig common throughout the Highlands. The corrugated leaves are used for wrapping meat before cooking but the large fruits, 5 to 6 inches diameter, are not eaten; (b) *Ensete calosperma* (family Musaceae). A banana-like plant which may be readily distinguished by the bracts which are persistent like a crinoline round the fruit bunch. There are several species of wild banana also in New Guinea; (c) *Eugenia versteegii* (family Myrtaceae). A curious species which produces the large pink flowers, 2½ to 3 inches long, on the twigs and branches well below the leaves. A tree of the swamp forests; (d) *Eugenia nutans* (family Myrtaceae). One of many species of Eugenia which take the place of the flowering gums in New Guinea. This small shrub is found wild in swamp forests. The flowers, up to 2 inches long, always droop.

FLORISTICS

Fig 6. (a) *Calanthe veratrifolia* (family Orchidaceae). A common forest orchid with snow-white flowers in a head 12 inches or more in height on a 3-foot stalk. If bruised, the flowers turn black; (b) *Dendrobium anosmum* (family Orchidaceae). This fine species is strongly scented reminiscent of raspberry or rhubarb. A common plant in the low-lands where it is frequently seen growing on tree branches and flowering on long pendulous shoots. The flowers are 4 inches across; (c) *Dendrobium ostrinoglossum* (family Orchidaceae). The so-called 'Sepik blue', found only in the Sepik River basin, belies its name by having flowers which vary from pale to dark purple in colour with a violet lip. The flower spike is 8 to 10 inches; (d) *Dendrobium goldii* (family Orchidaceae). This species comes in many forms varying in colour from pure white through blues to a yellow and brown form from Guadalcanal. The flower spikes are 18 to 20 inches long and commonly called the shower orchid.

FLORISTICS

Fig 7. (a) *Phaius tancarvilliae* (family Orchidaceae). The 'nun orchid' is common in grasslands where the flower spikes, 12 inches high, with their showy white and brown flowers are often conspicuous; (b) *Dendrobium auricolor* (family Orchidaceae). This is one of the 'one day wonder' species of *Dendrobium*. The flowers last but a single day. In full bloom the plants, 10 to 12 inches across, appear to be covered in crystalline stars; (c) *Freycinetia kanehirae* (family Pandanaceae). Of the several species of *Freycinetia* this one is quite colourful. Bright orange and yellow bracts, 6 to 8 inches between the points, surround the flowers; (d) *Nepenthes* (family Nepenthaceae). The pitcher plants are curious in that the leaf tip develops into a specialized cup-shaped organ, 6 inches or more deep, in which insects fall into the liquid and are digested and absorbed by the plant as a source of nitrogen.

a

b

c

d

FLORISTICS

Fig 8. (a) *Pandanus brassii* (family Pandanaceae). Many species of Pandanus occur in New Guinea. Some are important as a source of food, others provide leaf material which is sewn together for raincapes, house roofs, floor mats or canoe sails; (b) *Helicia* (family Proteaceae). Related to the Australian banksias and waratahs are many species of *Helicia*. Nearly all are forest trees. The flower buds are often tipped with electric blue colour. The flower spikes are 8 inches long; (c) *Banksia dentata* (family Proteaceae). This is the only species of *Banksia* native to New Guinea. In distribution it is rather local being confined mainly to Papua, but occurring also in the Bulolo Valley. The flower head is 4 to 6 inches high; (d) *Rhizophora* (family Rhizophoraceae). Mangrove forest includes several species of the genera *Rhizophora* and *Bruguiera*. This fine stand is on the mouth of the Fly River where the trees are over 100 feet in height.

Bananas are an important staple in those parts of the country that experience a pronounced dry season, e.g. the coastal strip near Port Moresby and the Markham Valley. Elsewhere they are grown in smaller quantities. Some 610,000 tons are harvested each year.

A sizeable minority of the indigenous people derives most of its subsistence from naturally occurring products. The main item in their diet is starch extracted from the trunk of the sago palm. Wild and cultivated stands are widely distributed in the extensive lowlying swampy areas associated with the larger river systems. For many agriculturalists around the coast sago is a reserve to be eaten when taro is in short supply. It is estimated that about 115,000 tons are produced annually.

In addition to the staples, an extensive variety of fruit, vegetables, and nuts is grown. Others are collected from the bush.

In some parts of the world tapioca (cassava) and maize are staple foods. Both have been introduced into New Guinea and at present some 50,000 tons of tapioca and 60,000 tons of maize are grown annually, but they still rank as subsidiaries. Tapioca is tolerant of salt and so is often cultivated extensively in estuarine areas.

Roughly 80 per cent of the population grow bananas and sugar-cane. Papaws are available to about 60 per cent, breadfruit to about 50 per cent, pineapples to some 30 per cent, and citrus fruits to roughly 25 per cent. Other fruits are grown in smaller quantities. Many varieties of native spinach, wild and cultivated, and the leaves of taro, cucurbits, beans and several bush trees are eaten as supplements. Cabbages, onions, leeks, tomatoes, Irish potatoes, and other European vegetables are grown at higher altitudes. Cucurbits—pumpkins, squashes, cucumbers—and legumes—winged, lima, and field beans, peas, peanuts, etc.—are popular but usually are available only at certain periods. *Pitpit*, a tall cane-grass, is grown for its inflorescence, and banana flowers are sometimes eaten. The growing shoots of palms and tree-ferns are highly prized. Fungi are eaten in small quantities.

The native people own about 24 million coconut palms, of which some 10 million are mature. Much of the crop goes into the production of copra, but nuts at various stages of development are consumed by people in the lowlands. In the cooler parts of the country several species of wild and cultivated pandanus are the most important nut-bearing palms. Although harvested annually, the bulk of the crop in some regions is preserved by drying for distribution at feasts throughout the year.

It is estimated that there are approximately forty fowls and sixty pigs [q.v.] for every hundred people, but the livestock are not distributed uniformly among the population. The fowls are small and lean, with a very low egg production and are kept mainly for their feathers. They contribute virtually nothing to the diet. Pigs are the only important domestic animals. The methods of husbandry are primitive. The beasts are usually enclosed at night and let out to forage by day. In many lowland villages they are fed irregularly; keeping them domesticated seems to be the main purpose. The people living in the higher regions appear to have more pigs per family and usually give them a substantial feed of sweet potatoes each day. Pigs are only slaughtered on important social occasions.

Along the coast many different types of sea foods are available. Women and children net small fish in the creeks and collect shellfish, shrimps, etc. Men fish with hook and line, spear, net and trap (*see* FISHING); occasionally they may catch a crocodile. In the coastal rain forest they hunt wild pig and a large phalanger (*see* HUNTING). Both adults and children consider the grub that lives in the sago palm a delicacy.

In the interior, especially in grasslands at higher altitudes, men hunt wallabies and other marsupials, rodents, snakes, and lizards, commonly firing the grass to drive out the animals for spearing or netting. Traps and snares are set in forested hunting grounds. Everywhere men and boys try to spear birds, though usually without much success. The women and children catch and eat field rats, frogs, grubs, and any small animals they find in the gardens.

TRADE IN FOOD

In many parts of the country trade in foodstuffs between neighbouring areas adds variety to the diet but has little if any effect on nutritive values. Often the foods exchanged are nutritionally equivalent; or, as is probably true of much of the fish that goes to inland villages, the quantities are too small to make much difference. However, in a few areas appreciable supplies of the staple food are obtained by trade. A well-known example is the exchange of fish for yams between coastal and inland villages in the Trobriand Islands [q.v.], where some of the coastal people rely heavily on those from the interior for their vegetables. Here a common language facilitates the barter. Another example is the trade by which, traditionally, the Motu people near Port Moresby obtained a considerable part of their food needs by exchanging cooking pots for sago with villagers from the Gulf of Papua several hundred miles away (*see* HIRI).

Seasonal shortages in some marginal food-producing areas may be overcome by importing food.

QUANTITIES

During the last twenty years food consumption surveys in different regions have shown clearly how heavily the rural people depend on starchy staples. Every day an adult eats up to five pounds of tubers. These supply from 70 to 95 per cent of his calories. In some lowland villages there are two or three staples, each predominating at a different time of the year, but many of the mountain people eat sweet potato as their main food every day. A similar dependence on one food characterizes many sago eaters and some other lowland groups. New Guinea diets are by no means unique in respect of this high degree of reliance on one or two foods; it is a feature they share with many in under-developed countries. Probably another is the wide fluctuation from day to day in the amount of food eaten. The report of the first survey in 1947 drew attention to the differences both between households and between successive visits to the same household.

There is considerable range in the quantity and variety of supplementary foods. In parts of the central Highlands adults eat as much as a pound of spinach a day, though supplies are irregular and much reduced in the dry season. Intakes are often less at lower altitudes and fall to quite small amounts in some coastal villages. Yet even where the total quantity of accessory foods is small they may contain a considerable number of items that help to balance the diet and provide variety.

The main nutrition problems in the rural areas are protein and calorie deficiencies. These take an acute form in infants and toddlers with clinical kwashiorkor and marasmus (see MALNUTRITION), but chronic shortages throughout childhood lead to retardation of growth rates after the age of four or five months. New Guinea children are not only substantially shorter and lighter than Australian children of the same age, they also weigh less than their Australian counterparts of the same height.

Adults, too, show signs of calorie and protein shortages, but the ages at which these become manifest differ for men and women. The progressive decline in the weight/height ratio for women over twenty-five years and in men over thirty is probably the result of chronic protein deficiency. The amount of subcutaneous fat, measured by skinfold thickness, indicates adequacy of calorie intakes. Few New Guinea people except adolescents who are exempted from routine work have any surplus fat. In women there is a continual decrease in skinfold thickness from the age of twenty, reflecting a strenuous physical life. In contrast, men show only a slight decrease up to about fifty.

It seems likely that daily fluctuation in the amount of food contributes to the low average calorie intakes, but this is unlikely to be the only cause. Low figures are reported also for people who grow enough surplus to be able to feed substantial quantities to pigs. This suggests that the physical nature of the foods may also be relevant. Both staples and supplements are bulky foods containing much water and often considerable amounts of fibre. For a given weight the yield of calories is small compared with many foods in the Australian diet. Consequently a much larger volume is needed to provide the same amount of energy. But there is a risk that appetite may be satisfied before enough food is eaten to meet the body's optimal requirements, especially with children whose needs relative to body weight are much higher than an adult's. It is more difficult to assess the effects of monotony in reducing intakes. Unlike cereals, such as rice and maize flour, which require a tasty side-dish to make them palatable, New Guinea staples have sufficient flavour to be eaten alone, with the

possible exception of sago. People recognize differences between the many varieties of each kind of tuber and often have marked preferences. They seldom complain of monotony even when a meal consists solely of the staple, as is often the case. Nevertheless, it is possible they would eat more on a diet with a wider range of flavours.

All the staples are rich in carbohydrate, low in protein and practically devoid of fat. Samples collected in 1947 show the following order when arranged in a series of decreasing protein content expressed in grams per 100 calories—calculated from edible portion—yam 1.8, taro 1.0, banana 0.9, sweet potato 0.6, and sago nil. The comparable figures for rice, white flour, and wheat are 1.6, 2.8, and 3.5 grams of protein respectively. Some varieties of yam, taro, and sweet potato which have been analysed since 1947 have less protein, others almost twice as much. When the quality of the different proteins is taken into account yams and taro on average are comparable with cereals as a source of protein, but sweet potato, banana, and sago are inferior.

In coastal villages marine foods partly offset the protein shortage for all except the small children, who are not usually given fish. Despite the wide range of animal species available to the inland people, meat is eaten so rarely and in such small quantities that it makes no substantial contribution to the diet. Supplementary vegetables supply most of the additional protein. As with calories, the bulk of the diet makes it difficult for those with relatively high protein needs, small children and women, to obtain their requirements from traditional vegetables. Clinical evidence shows that children fare worse than their mothers.

Vitamin and mineral deficiencies are rare in the rural areas. The yellow varieties of sweet potatoes are the only staple that contains the precursor of vitamin A, but the indigenous leafy vegetables are rich sources. In general the diets supply adequate amounts of the vitamin B complex. All staples except sago provide an abundance of vitamin C, not because they are rich sources but because such large quantities are eaten. Vitamin C intake is further augmented by many other vegetables.

The calcium and iron contents of the main foods range from low to moderate, but many of the greens are good sources of these minerals. In a number of localities goitre is common because of iodine deficiency in the soil.

KITCHEN

To some extent climate determines where food is prepared and cooked. In the lowlands it is usually on the ground just outside the house. If there is not enough space under the eaves a fireplace on the verandah or on the floor is used in wet weather. In the mountains even the large oven for cooking fifty or sixty pounds of potatoes may be made on the earth floor of the small one-roomed house where a woman lives with her daughters, young sons, and the family pig herd. But in parts of the Highlands groups of relatives prepare and eat their food in special kitchens built close to the house. Others cook small quantities inside and make their ovens in the open near by.

FOOD PREPARATION AND COOKING

Tubers are washed on the way home from the garden. If they are to be boiled they are usually peeled and sometimes cut into slices. The introduction of European cooking vessels, tin cans, and drums has extended the practice of boiling food to regions like the central Highlands, where formerly there were no clay pots. In lowland areas boiling appears to have been the most common method of cooking tubers and bananas as well as most supplementary vegetables. Along the coast a mixture of fresh water and sea water is often used. The pot is sealed with non-edible leaves, and in some places it is also lined with them. Cooking time varies from twenty minutes to an hour, depending on the size of the tubers and the heat of the fire.

In the early morning, and sometimes for snacks during the day, tubers are roasted in a bed of fine ash over which a small fire is burning. They may be peeled first.

There are several varieties of native oven, but the principle is the same in all of them. Cooking is effected by steam under pressure. Food is piled on red hot stones and the oven is tightly sealed to prevent the escape of steam. Water is usually sprinkled over the food but this is not essential; sufficient steam may be generated from the food itself. Cooking time is usually about an hour, but there is considerable variation. In the central Highlands heated stones are lifted into an upright hollow log, a depression in the ground, or, nowadays, a metal drum. Tubers may first be peeled and wrapped in leaves. Alternating layers of food and stones are separated by banana leaves or grasses that keep the food from direct contact with the stones. Water is poured into the oven prior to sealing it, and more may be inserted through a bamboo at intervals during cooking. The oven is sealed with grass and banana leaves. A slightly different type of oven is made in the mountains to the north of Port Moresby. There a single layer of stones is heated *in situ*, and food is piled directly on top. It is covered with layers of banana and fern leaves, and the oven is sealed with pandanus leaves. Earth may be packed tightly around the base.

Sago. Men fell a sago palm, and when the trunk is lying on the ground the bark is removed to expose the pith, which is dug out from the trunk. The men or their wives then carry the pith to a washing trough set up at the edge of the nearest stream. In the trough the pith is kneaded with water to release flour from the fibre. Suspended in water, the sago flour passes through a crude filter lower down the trough into a container below. It settles to the bottom, and the water flows away over the sides. The flour is wrapped in leaves, then baked or smoked prior to being stored.

Dumplings are made from sago or a mixture of sago and grated coconut moistened with water. They may be wrapped in leaves for baking or dropped into boiling water, usually a mixture of fresh and salt water, and cooked for 30 to 40 minutes. Sago may also be baked in the form of sticks in a casing made from nipa palm leaves. Gruel is prepared by adding crumbs of sago to the water in which green leaves, nuts, bananas, and other foods are boiling.

Coconuts. The meat of mature coconuts is shredded with a shell or a metal scraper. It may be mixed with sago, grated tuber, and the like; or it is treated further to make coconut cream. The grated meat is first squeezed alone, then water is added, and it is squeezed again. The process may be repeated several times until the emulsion becomes watery. The cream is made with fresh water, a mixture of fresh water and sea water, or the coconut water contained in the kernel. Coconut cream is added to boiled foods, especially greens. Banana and pumpkin soups are prepared by adding coconut cream to the boiled vegetable which has been mashed in cooking water. Coconut oil is prepared by slowly evaporating the cream.

Supplementary vegetables. Many greens are washed and cooked without more treatment. Some leaves may be plucked from their stalks and the veins of a large coarse leaf like taro are removed before cooking.

Supplementary vegetables are often cooked together with the staple food in a pot or oven. For cooking beside the fire they are wrapped in leaf or bark packets. They may be boiled separately in a small pot or steamed with a small quantity of water in a bamboo tube which is turned slowly by hand over a low fire for 15 to 20 minutes. A plug prevents the escape of steam.

Many foods, including corn, *pitpit*, breadfruit and nuts, are roasted for a snack between meals.

Pandanus. The large mountain pandanus is eaten raw, cooked in an oven, or boiled. If well dried immediately after cutting it can be stored in a rack above a hearth for many months. No further cooking is required.

A relish is made from the long red-fruited pandanus. Strips of fruit are cut from the core and boiled. An oily extract squeezed from the seeds is served with tubers or greens, generally at feasts.

Animal foods. Grubs, rats, birds, snakes, lizards, etc., are roasted over coals or cooked with greens in a bamboo tube. Sometimes phalangers, bandicoots, and other small game are partly roasted and smoked to preserve them until enough have been accumulated for a feast. Usually they are served with vegetables.

In the mountains pigs are cooked in an oven with special leaves (especially *Ficus dammaropsis*) and often tubers and the principal supplementary vegetables. In some lowland areas it is more usual to cut up a carcass for boiling. In either case the only parts not eaten are the bladder and gall bladder. All other organs are washed thoroughly, and the blood is mopped up with edible leaves. Cooking pork is men's work.

Shrimps, crabs, oysters, and other shellfish are roasted or boiled with tubers or in sago soup. Fish are boiled with tubers or soup or wrapped in leaves for roasting.

ASSESSMENT OF COOKING METHODS

No quantitative studies have been made to assess nutrient losses. They are probably minimal when food is steamed under pressure in an oven or in bamboo. Greater losses are likely in boiling, especially if vegetables are peeled, if there is an excess of liquid, if cooking water is discarded, the lid is not well sealed, and cooking time is prolonged. Significant differences on these matters have been recorded from various parts of the country.

MEAL PATTERN

The main meal is cooked at the end of a day's work, usually between mid and late afternoon. Most of the preparation falls to women working alone or in small groups according to the custom of the people, though in some societies men do not accept food from a menstruating woman and bachelors must cook all their own food. In the lowlands men sometimes assist their wives by grating coconuts. Children are frequently called on for small chores like fetching fuel, water, or leaves, attending to the fire, and so on. As people wait for the meal a woman may roast a few tubers in the ashes or boil some of the supplementary vegetables as a snack for herself and the children.

When everything is ready portions are allotted to visitors, members of the family and often a gift is set aside for a relative. The distribution is usually made by the housewife, but in a few societies it is the prerogative of the husband.

In many parts of the country it is rare for all family members to sit down together. A man normally eats at his wife's house unless there are visitors at his men's house, he and the neighbours have important matters to discuss, or his wife has a visitor whom he must avoid. Then his food is sent to him. He is always given the best. Young children are fed immediately. Boys are usually occupied elsewhere with their own affairs and eat when they return home. An older girl may have to help her mother feed the pigs and tidy up before they eat their meal.

Any food left from the evening is kept for breakfast or fed to the pigs; nothing is wasted. It is usual practice in many lowland villages not to cook again before setting out for the gardens. Many people say they work better after only a light snack. Others roast a few tubers in the coals, and a few boil a pot of food. In the cooler parts of the country a substantial breakfast is cooked, generally in the ashes, for many of these people have few or no pots. Food consumption surveys suggest that energy intakes are at least 20 per cent higher in the mountains than on the coast, matching corresponding increases in energy expenditures, in large part the result of the climate and the rough terrain. An extra meal may

well be necessary to reach the higher levels of intake.

During the day women take an occasional rest from work in the garden to tend their infants and prepare a snack for themselves and the children. Coconuts, sugar-cane, cucumbers, bananas, papaw, and pineapple are eaten when available. Cold leftovers from breakfast are eaten about midday, especially by children, but sometimes a few tubers are freshly cooked. Corn, *pitpit*, peanuts, and small animals are roasted over a fire. Men rarely seem to carry food when they go into the forest for firewood or building materials, but they are likely to take a snack if they are working in the garden.

Snacks are estimated to contribute on average between 5 and 10 per cent of the food eaten each day, though in a few places it rises as high as 25 per cent.

SOCIOLOGY OF FOOD

Malnutrition is not recognized as such by village people. They are, of course, aware that a person needs a certain amount of food to be able to live a normal life, and they realize that they become thin and lethargic during periods of food shortage. Women recognize that they lose weight as a result of prolonged breast feeding. But while people in some societies believe that particular foods have specific beneficial effects, like 'making strong blood', there is no general notion that food affects health. This is hardly surprising for the connection is not immediately obvious. The physique and capacity for work of most rural people are likely to impress a casual observer more than any signs of diet deficiency. Admittedly children are small and thin, and though many die more survive.

In addition, as observers have noted from societies in all parts of the country, food is the focus of many different interests. Some of these are given precedence over nutritional considerations. In subsistence societies the production, distribution, and consumption of food are an integral part of the fabric of social life. Inevitably it is an important element in most relationships between people, and often it is linked with the supernatural. Relatively few other goods are produced or traded, and none in comparable quantity. Food is thus one of the main forms of wealth, and consequently one of the most significant items in the competition between men for prestige and status. As might be expected, all rural people have an intense emotional attachment to food.

The production of food to satisfy daily needs is not the sole or even the main objective. Without a surplus there can be no feasts or ceremonies and all the pleasures these make possible. Few things delight people more than the sight of large quantities of food arranged to satisfy local aesthetic standards even if some of it is already deteriorating by the time it is eaten. The amount of food displayed and later given away is an important criterion for judging the success of a feast or ceremony. An abundance of food is tangible evidence of success and a fit subject for boasting. Conversely a shortage is considered disgraceful and humiliating, where possible to be concealed from others, especially enemies. Little wonder then that hardships resulting from a shortage of food are usually expressed in terms of a restricted social and emotional life. Compared to these the pain of hunger is unpleasant but bearable. In some societies a person expresses his sorrow after the death of a relative by voluntarily refusing some delicacy for a period of months or years.

Often the staple becomes the focus for yet other sentiments. It alone is the real food that makes people strong and capable of hard work. Myths frequently explain how it came into their possession and specify the rules about how it must be planted, harvested, prepared, and eaten. Yams and taro in particular are considered in many places to be a gift of the creator or a culture hero; in a few societies they are sacred because of their intimate association with traditional deities. Yams are often endowed with human characteristics; they are believed to be able to smell, to hear, and to react to heat and cold.

Eating is considered primarily a social event and only secondarily a means of satisfying hunger. To eat with people is to show confidence in them, an indication that sorcery is not suspected. Bride and groom share food to celebrate their marriage; their relatives may also eat together. Similarly the parties to a dispute sometimes partake of a feast to indicate an end to hostilities. In eating together people express their common interests. Conversely, there is a ban on sharing food by those who must by custom avoid each other.

Persons in a special social or ritual state, such as pregnant women, initiates, and magicians, usually observe food taboos to mark themselves off from others. The foods prohibited vary from one society to another but usually do not materially affect normal diet.

Frequently little or no food is actually eaten at a feast or ceremony by those who organize it. In many societies people do not eat meat from pigs they or their close relatives rear. The ban is buttressed by a belief that dire consequences will afflict any who ignore it. Pork, the most highly valued food, must therefore be given away. In every society there are rules about how many pigs should be killed and for which occasions. A man disposes of his herd with these in mind, but the result is not always the most rational use of resources. His wife may continue to feed pigs long after they are fully grown so that she and her husband will have one available to be killed for some event of significance to them. At the big pig ceremonials in the central Highlands people who are starved for pork and fat stuff themselves even to the extent of vomiting so that they can eat more. Then after this orgy they may not eat meat again for two or three years.

Other rules lay down who should be presented with pork, vegetable foods, and such other goods as are available. Recipients differ according to the occasion that prompts the feast or ceremony. They may be kinsmen or affines of the donor or people chosen because they dwell in a particular village or because they fight against their hosts. Often they live so far away that the donor does not see them frequently. In the process of making gifts of food to them at ceremonies he is doing more than simply providing them with a few delicacies to eat. He is maintaining a relationship that otherwise might lapse.

To present a gift is to place the recipient under an obligation to return a countergift of equivalent value. In these transactions the man who gives on one occasion receives a similar amount at a later date to cancel the debt. The relationship is symmetrical. Failure to reciprocate gives rise to an asymmetrical relationship in which the debtor accepts a subordinate status. In other words, the debt is paid not with goods but with deference and respect. In New Guinea a man acquires prestige by giving away wealth, of which food is a major item. In this way he puts others in his debt. Unless they can pay him back in kind they have to recognize his superior status. This situation in turn is the basis for the system of leadership. To be prominent in his community a man must produce or control large quantities of food, not to hoard but to give away.

Village people often talk about the responsibilities between relatives in these same terms. A child loves and respects his parents, it is said, because they fed him. Rarely is much importance attached in this context to begetting a child; the emphasis is rather on providing food, especially pork, to enable him to grow and develop. Many relatives contribute in this way. In doing so each creates a debt that the youngster discharges when, in due course, he helps support them in their old age.

RATION AND URBAN DIETS

The Native Employment Ordinance includes a ration scale which is intended to ensure that indigenous workers and their families receive an adequate balanced diet. Alternative local and imported foods can be supplied under each food item. For many years most workers received such rations as part of their remuneration, but today, especially in the urban areas, the majority are paid a cash wage from which they buy their food. Unfortunately very little research has been carried out to determine which foods people at different income levels are selecting from what must be to many of them a bewildering variety. Consequently we do not know with any certainty how adequate their diets are, nor whether, nutritionally speaking, they are getting value for the money they are spending on food. Reliable information on these matters is needed for an education programme to correct any bad food habits among newcomers to the towns.

Everywhere rice seems to be very popular with people from the rural areas when they go to live on plantations, government stations, or in the towns. Their preference for rice is probably partly due to its novelty, but, and perhaps more important, it is a symbol of a sophisticated way of life. However, there is ample evidence that established urban residents like to eat their traditional staples for a change; many complain that they find rice meals too dry. Because of inadequate supplies or relative costs they are not always able to indulge this preference, especially in Port Moresby. Since most of the rice is imported it would seem good sense to encourage the consumption of locally produced food.

Townspeople also eat bread and biscuits as snacks and with their meals. Jam is probably the most common spread; the consumption of butter and margarine is low. Probably an important part of the attraction of bread and biscuits, especially for those in homes with limited cooking facilities, is that no preparation is needed.

There is considerable variation between towns in the quantities of fresh fruit and vegetables, other than the staples, which are available in the markets. In addition some urban people plant vegetable gardens if land is available and if conditions are suitable. Those living near enough receive gifts from their relatives in the country. Supplies are probably adequate in most towns, but in Port Moresby there is an urgent need for a programme to overcome the serious shortage of fresh fruit and vegetables.

Supplies of fresh meat and fish are limited in most towns, but in any case they are too expensive for the majority of urban workers to buy regularly. Tinned fish and meat, to which an earlier generation became accustomed as part of their rations, remain the most commonly eaten animal foods. Town dwellers probably eat considerably more animal foods, and eat them more regularly, than do most rural people.

K. V. Bailey, 'Nutrition in New Guinea', *Food and Nutrition Notes and Reviews*, vol. 20, 1963.
———— 'Nutritional Status of East New Guinean Populations', *Tropical and Geographical Medicine*, vol. 15, 1963.
———— and J. Whiteman, 'Dietary Studies in the Chimbu', *Tropical and Geographical Medicine*, vol. 15, 1963.
F. L. S. Bell, 'The Place of Food in the Social Life of the Tanga', *Oceania*, vols. 17-19, 1946-9.
R. F. Fortune, *Sorcerers of Dobu*, pp. 94-132, 189-200. London, 1932.
E. H. Hipsley and F. W. Clements (eds), *Report of the New Guinea Nutrition Survey Expedition 1947*. Sydney, 1950.
———— and N. E. Kirk, *Studies of Dietary Intake and Expenditure of Energy by New Guineans*. South Pacific Commission, Technical Paper no. 147. Noumea, 1956.
H. I. Hogbin, 'Tillage and Collection: A New Guinea Economy', *Oceania*, vol. 9, 1938-9.
———— *Transformation Scene*, pp. 39-78, 118-30. London, 1951.
P. M. Kaberry, 'The Abelam Tribe, Sepik District, New Guinea', *Oceania*, vol. 11, 1940-1.
B. Malinowski, *Coral Gardens and their Magic*. 2 vols, London, 1935.
D. L. Oliver, 'Studies in the Anthropology of Bougainville, Solomon Islands', *Papers of the Peabody Museum, Harvard University*, vol. 29, 1949.
H. A. P. C. Oomen and S. H. Malcolm, *Nutrition and the Papuan Child*. South Pacific Commission, Technical Paper no. 118. Noumea, 1958.
———— W. Spoon, J. E. Heesterman, J. Ruinard, R. Luyken and P. Slump, 'The Sweet Potato as the Staff of Life of the Highland Papuan', *Tropical and Geographical Medicine*, vol. 13, 1961.
F. E. Peters, *The Chemical Composition of South Pacific Foods*. South Pacific Commission, Technical Paper no. 115. Noumea, 1958.
K. E. Read, The Relationship between Food Production and Social Structure in Simple Societies. Ph.D. thesis, University of London, 1948.
M. Reay, *The Kuma*, pp. 18-24, 86-95, 102-12. Melbourne, 1959.
Survey of Indigenous Agriculture and Ancillary Surveys 1961-1962. Bureau of Statistics, Port Moresby, 1963.
P. S. Venkatachalam, *A Study of the Diet, Nutrition and Health of the People of the Chimbu Area (New Guinea Highlands)*. Department of Public Health, Monograph no. 4. Port Moresby, 1962.
J. Whiteman, 'A Study of the Dietary Habits of a North Wosera Village in the Territory of Papua-New Guinea', *Food and Nutrition Notes and Reviews*, vol. 22, 1965.
———— 'Customs and Beliefs Relating to Food, Nutrition and Health in the Chimbu Area', *Tropical and Geographical Medicine*, vol. 17, 1965.
F. E. Williams, *Drama of Orokolo*, pp. 11-19. Oxford, 1940.
———— 'Natives of Lake Kutubu, Papua', *Oceania*, vol. 11, 1940-1.

MARGARET MCARTHUR

(*See also* MATERIAL CULTURE)

FORE. People of the Eastern Highlands District. References:

S. Lindenbaum and R. Glasse, 'Fore Age Mates', *Oceania*, vol. 39, 1968-9.
Ruth Nicholson, 'Introductory North Fore Verb Paper', Summer Institute of Linguistics, New Guinea, *Workshop Papers*, 1961 (roneoed).
———— and Ray Nicholson, 'Phonemes of the Fore Language', Summer Institute of Linguistics, New Guinea, *Workshop Papers*, 1961 (roneoed).
———— 'Fore Phonemes and their Interpretation', in 'Studies in New Guinea Linguistics', *Oceania Linguistic Monographs*, no. 6, 1962.
K. L. Pike, 'Theoretical Implications of Matrix Permutation in Fore (New Guinea)', *Anthropological Linguistics*, vol. 5, 1963.
———— and G. K. Scott, 'Pitch Accent and Non-accented Phrases in Fore (New Guinea)', *Zeitschrift für Phonetik, Sprachwissenschaft und Kommunikationsforschung*, vol. 16, 1963.
G. K. Scott, 'The Dialects of Fore', *Oceania*, vol. 33, 1962-3.
W. Stöcklin, 'Medizin und schwarze Magie bei den Fore im östlichen Hochland Neuguineas', in *Festschrift Alfred Bühler*, hrsg. von C. A. Schmitz und R. Wildhaber, *Basler Beiträge zur Geographie und Ethnologie*, Ethnologische Reihe, 2. Basel, 1965.

(*See also* KAINANTU)

FORESTRY. The whole area of Papua and New Guinea comprises some 183,540 square miles of land and internal waterways. Of the 140,625 square miles estimated to be forested, some 83,400 square miles are regarded as unproductive at present, chiefly because of steepness and inaccessibility, leaving some 57,200 square miles of forest classed as potentially productive.

Because it lies in the equatorial region, the relatively high rainfall and uniformly high temperatures which occur over much of the Territory result in generally prolific vegetative growth. The considerable altitudinal range ensures a wide variety of vegetation types, and the climax type—that which has reached equilibrium with climate, soil, etc.—in most of the country is, or should be, closed forest. Natural variation from this only occurs in certain limited areas where rainfall is 40 inches or less and distribution is very unevenly balanced, or above 10,000 feet, which represents the limit of tree growth. Below this limit most of the savannah and grassland areas are the result of man's activities.

The more important forest communities, ranging from sea-level to 10,000 feet, are:
(1) mangrove forest, subject to tidal inundation;
(2) swamp forest, temporarily or permanently inundated;
(3) strand or littoral vegetation, usually a narrow strip;
(4) drained tropical-lowland forest, somewhat restricted in extent;
(5) monsoon forest, localized in particular climatic areas;
(6) rain forests, covering the bulk of the country;
(7) montane forests, from 6,500 feet to the upper tree limit.

Throughout the centuries these forests have provided the native peoples with many of the necessities of life, but their demands on the resources have been comparatively small. Round timbers of various sizes provide the framework of houses, bound with vines, split rattan or fibrous bark. Walls and roofs are made of leaves of palms. Bamboo has many uses. Vast quantities of fuel are consumed daily. Canoes are made from large trees. Sago palms provide a staple food item for many natives, and many other items of foodstuffs come from the forest, including fruits, nuts and leaves, as well as the animal life it shelters. Various types of clothing are by-products of trees.

Perhaps the most important part played by the forest in the lives of the people was, and is, as a source of fertile land for their gardens (see AGRICULTURE, INDIGENOUS). The shifting cultivation cycle of clearing, burning, cultivating, followed by abandonment after a few years, and then a gradual regrowth of tree cover, has formed the pattern of subsistence farming throughout the country. With an abundance of forest land and a paucity of people the effect of shifting cultivation has been relatively slight. That some 75 per cent of the total land area is still estimated to be forest covered is evidence of this. Serious degradation of the vegetation has occurred only in marginal climatic areas and in a few localities where high population density resulted in a short fallow period and repetitious burning.

Undoubtedly, over extensive areas the climax forest type has been replaced by secondary subclimax bush but the latter is not necessarily less important economically.

All the forest types listed have timbers that are valuable economically, but in some the quantity

per acre or overall extent of the stand do not justify large-scale utilization. These forests are better suited to small-scale commercial operations or for local consumption.

In parts of the mainland there are extensive mangrove forests, but unfortunately the nature of most of the species is such that no worthwhile large-scale economic utilization has been developed.

The montane forests have considerable economic potential but occur in difficult country and are comparatively inaccessible to markets. Intensive utilization of such forests will have to await favourable conditions and will require careful control because of the risk of soil erosion.

The forests with the greatest potential for economic development are those grouped as rain forest. Ranging from sea-level to 6,500 feet where rainfall is high, there are a number of specific floristic types each having its own range of valuable economic trees. One or two species are confined to a particular forest community; others appear in several.

The tropical rain forests contain a typically wide variety of species with varying qualities and characteristics. This complicates harvesting and marketing if there is to be maximum utilization of forest resources and not merely selective logging. Nevertheless, with extensive areas of readily accessible high-quality forests and a growing demand in the Pacific area for forest produce, plus suitable conditions for rapid regeneration by natural or artificial means, the economic possibilities of sustained high yield are extremely good. Forestry undoubtedly has a major part to play in the future development of Papua and New Guinea and in the employment of its people both in management and utilization.

HISTORY

1908-1937. The first specific forest resources investigation was made in 1908 when, at the request of the Papuan Administration, Gilbert Burnett, District Forest Inspector of Queensland, attempted to assess the timber potential of the region. The survey lasted only a few months and the difficulties of access limited inspection to eight main areas accessible by river. The chief result was a printed catalogue of commercial timbers and a description of the areas visited.

In 1921 a New Guinea Expedition which included H. W. Haynes, a forestry expert, visited the Territory to study the natural resources. Nine hundred miles of coastline and river were investigated but, apart from proceeding 162 nautical miles up the Ramu River, there was no great penetration inland. Because of Haynes' ill-health no forestry report was written, but the general report included notes and comments on forest resources and utilization, and a recommendation that a forestry department be established to conserve resources and encourage and control utilization.

During 1923 and 1924 C. E. Lane-Poole, Australian Commonwealth forestry adviser, carried out a fairly extensive survey of the forest resources of

(top) Extension nursery, Highland areas. A variety of species suitable for local planting are grown for distribution to villages and towns.
(bottom) A teak (*Tectona grandis*) plantation seven years after planting, Mt Lawes Forest Station.

Papua and New Guinea. In Papua he inspected areas in the Central and North-eastern Divisions, the Delta and Gulf Divisions, and in New Guinea north-east New Britain, north-west New Ireland and the Morobe, Madang and Sepik areas. He penetrated deeply inland both by river and on foot, made extensive collections of botanical and timber specimens, and carried out a considerable number of enumeration surveys which gave a good picture of forest composition and resources.

Lane-Poole's report recommended the creation of a forest authority and outlined a policy and ordinance. No forestry officer was appointed to establish a forest service until 1938.

1938-1947. The outbreak of World War II slowed down forestry development, and the Japanese attack stopped all activity for a year but thereafter stimulated development.

In 1943 the Australian New Guinea Administrative Unit (Angau [q.v.]) reopened the two sawmills which had operated pre-war in Papua. The Allied military forces also commenced timber-getting operations and in a short while Australian, American and New Zealand units were all producing increasing volumes of round and sawn timber.

In 1944 the Australian Engineers formed two Forest Survey Companies, headed by J. B. McAdam, the first Forestry Officer. These units were to record the utilization activities, and to make surveys of forest resources using all the available military resources of aerial photography, operational mapping and transport.

Two years of intensive work in resource inventory was carried out. Using aerial photographs and criteria evolved from field correlation studies, vegetation types were mapped over an area of some 56,000 square miles, about 30 per cent of the total land area, on one inch to the mile military maps. By the end of the war nearly a quarter of the vegetation mapping had been ground checked. This work provided an excellent base for post-war forestry development.

Effective forestry work resumed in 1946 under the newly constituted Department, and in the Report of the Economic Development Committee, 1948, the lines of forestry development were laid down, with an estimate of staff requirements and funds.

1948-1957. The two main problems facing the department were reorganization and staffing. For ten years after the war shortage of staff limited the scope of activity. The urgent need for timber for rehabilitation work and new construction dictated expansion of production. Resources assessment and inventory work practically ceased. To meet the demand, emergency timber permits were issued; pre-war permit-holders were encouraged to mill as well as log the forests, and mostly field staff were engaged in exploitation.

Two war-time sawmills, at Keravat and near Lae, were taken over by the Administration and operated by the Department to supply sawn timber and to acquire factual information on local timbers which would be of practical benefit in the development of a local commercial timber industry. One sawmill closed in 1960 and the other in 1961.

By that time private commercial enterprises were more than capable of filling local timber requirements. There were more than some sixty private sawmills, two veneer mills and one plymill in operation, and log production had increased from 11 million super feet true volume (26,000 cubic metres) in 1947-8 to some 65 million super feet, sufficient not only for local needs, but also for the start of a growing export industry. (The super foot is a volume measurement, the equivalent of 144 cubic inches.)

With a somewhat improved staff position at the end of the first post-war decade, more diversified and constructive forestry work was undertaken in resource survey, management, silviculture, utilization and botanical investigation. Allied with training to build up a resources survey team for renewal of extensive resource survey and inventory work, a detailed management survey was undertaken in the Bulolo area. Management surveys were also made at Port Moresby, Keravat and Lae.

By 1958 preliminary surveys had been made over extensive areas leading to the acquisition of 400,000 acres of timber rights. Reconnaissance investigations covered over 25,000 square miles. However, although considerable areas were annually covered by aerial photography for the CSIRO Land Research and Regional Survey team, the maps did not show topography and their usefulness for forest management was therefore restricted.

In silviculture a good start had been made in regeneration and reforestation work at Bulolo-Wau, Keravat and Mt Lawes. Starting with small experimental plantations, work gradually expanded and by 1958 planting had reached 1,000 acres per annum and the total close on 4,000 acres. The Utilization Division at first worked the two Administration sawmills but gradually expanded its functions to include training, investigations in logging and sawmilling problems and, in conjunction with the CSIRO Division of Forest Products in Melbourne, investigations into wood properties and utilization. From 1953, with the appointment of a Chief of Division of Utilization, there was a reorganization of sawmilling activities, the Yalu mill being rebuilt and modernized at Lae, and the Keravat milling operation expanded. A well-equipped workshop was also established.

1958-1967 saw great progress. In December 1957 the Minister for Territories, the Hon. P. M. C. Hasluck, approved a programme for forestry development and management which included continuation of land and forest resources survey; the acquisition and reservation for sustained forest management of 4 million acres of permanent forest within ten years; creation of a training centre; establishment of a research institute; a reforestation programme; extended timber utilization research; and continuation of activities of the botanical section.

In 1962 a five-year programme was approved which envisaged an increase in log production from 80 million super feet in 1962-3 to 120 million super feet in 1966-7; acquisition of land and timber rights over 2.3 million acres of forest land;

Teak (*Tectona grandis*) plantations, Mt Lawes Forest Station, Papua. Mosaic of lowland monsoon forest and rain forest with areas of eucalypt savannah forest (lower left and ridges) and teak plantation (right and centre).

300,000 acres of permanent forest reservations; an annual reforestation programme of some 2,000 acres plantation plus substantial natural regeneration operations; establishment of a timber research unit and workshops to step up timber utilization research and training; increased botanical and ecological activity; and the establishment of a training school of a fairly elementary level.

In 1964 the five-year plan of the International Bank for Reconstruction and Development (World Bank) recommended a utilization programme well above that of the Department's proposals, plus the increases in other forestry activities necessary to support this.

Achievement, while not matching up to everything programmed, has been substantial. By the end of the decade staff had increased from around 200 to over 400. The main increase was in local subordinate staff, but there was a reasonable improvement in the professional and technically-skilled categories. The closing of the two Administration sawmills during this period and the release of staff for other work helped to increase forest activities. Steady but slow progress in resources survey work was made with limits set by staff availability and by problems of mobility and accessibility, which were partly solved, however, by the introduction of helicopters.

By 1967 permanent Administration forest estate totalled 1.6 million acres of which only 183,000 acres had been bought outright. Extensive areas are under negotiation for acquisition. Despite the paucity of land classed as Territory Forest, management of forest areas has been extended by the establishment of forest stations or the posting of forestry officers at some thirty locations throughout the Territory to control and supervise utilization and provide extension services.

Utilization has expanded from 51 million super feet of log extracted in 1957 to 156 million super feet in 1969. Timber exports in all forms rose from about $2.6 million to $4.8 million.

The three main reforestation centres—Bulolo-Wau, Keravat and Mt Lawes—together with other areas being developed, have an annual planting of 2,000 acres, and some 1,000 acres of natural regeneration work per annum.

The Division of Botany at Lae is pursuing its activities steadily. The Division of Utilization which has a new research building and workshops at Hohola, Port Moresby, and which works in conjunction with the CSIRO Division of Forest Products, is equipped to play a major part in the expansion of conversion, utilization and marketing activities of all forest produce.

Training is now on a sound footing with the opening in 1965 of the first stage of a permanent training centre at Bulolo.

FOREST POLICY

Forestry is a long-term activity and needs unusual vision to determine over-all policies in advance of the pressure of events. This is particularly so in an under-developed country where basic information is lacking, machinery for implementing policy is non-existent or inadequate, and short-term needs are given priority.

Burnett's visit to Papua in 1908 resulted only in the passing of the Timber Ordinance (Consolidated) in 1909, intended mainly to encourage utilization. Lack of demand prevented any major destructive consequences.

Neither the 1921 Expedition nor the Lane-Poole report bore fruit.

In the 1930s gold mining in the Bulolo area, with concomitant timber-cutting activities, and a growing export trade in walnut (*Dracontomelum*) log to North America stimulated some action.

A new ordinance, the Forestry Ordinance 1936-37, was adopted for the Mandated Territory of New Guinea. It gave more effective control, and provided for a professional forestry authority and a forest estate. Two trained foresters were appointed, but World War II prevented development.

In 1948 J. B. McAdam, then acting Secretary for Land, Mines, Survey and Forests, recommended a forest resource survey associated with:

a vigorous programme of forest reservation;

the need for utilization and silvicultural research;

controlled working of all forested areas and preparation of working plans for Territory forests;

the proper protection of forest areas where necessary;

harvesting and marketing inspection services;

provision for publicity, technical advice and publication;

training of staff.

These objectives were approved by the Administrator.

In 1951 the Minister for External Territories, the Hon. P. C. Spender, made a statement to the House of Representatives on forest policy. The main features can be summarized:

to locate, assess and regulate the availability of the natural forest resources of the Territory to bring them within the reach of development;

to afford all reasonable encouragement for the investment of private capital in the development of these resources;

to ensure that the native peoples of the Territory are enabled to participate to an ever-increasing extent in the fruits of this development.

The main emphasis was on the provision of sufficient local timber for reconstruction and expansion by developing a timber industry. This was achieved by concentrating activity in areas of major European development and where timber lands were to be cleared for agricultural development, again mainly European. Other desirable objectives received less attention.

In December 1957 the Minister for Territories made a policy statement which has provided the basis for subsequent forestry development. This has included an increase of activity in most fields including forest resources inventory, reforestation and regeneration work, and the creation of a permanent forest estate. There has also been improvement in staffing, both in numbers and quality, extension of research work in utilization and silvi-

Hoop pine (*Araucaria cunninghamii*) plantation near Bulolo. Centre is the forest reserve of klinkii pine (*Araucaria hunsteinii*). This area is reserved from logging.

culture, an increase in botanical and ecological work, and greater activity in all forms of extension work whether related to tree growing or timber utilization.

The timber industry, which was expanding at a reasonable rate, received an added stimulus in 1964 following the visit of the Mission from the World Bank which reported on the economic development of the Territory. Impressed by the forestry potential and its contribution to the economy, and relating this to probable demand in the South-east Asia and Pacific region within the next ten years, the Mission recommended a considerable increase in target production figures from 80 million super feet in 1962-3 to 300 million super feet in 1968-9 (programmed departmentally at 180 million super feet). The Mission appreciated that to achieve this other aspects of forestry must correspondingly increase and made recommendations regarding land acquisition, timber concessions, the necessary infrastructure in the way of roads, etc., to service greater utilization, and for more staff and better training facilities, including the upgrading of the Forestry College to diploma level.

The proposed production figures were accepted by the Australian government.

FOREST LAW

The earliest forest law applicable to the Territory was the Timber Ordinance 1909 enacted for Papua. This was an adaptation of an old Queensland ordinance and provided among other things:

for purchase from native owners of timber lands, and the vesting of such lands in the Crown; and the creation of timber reserves;

for the granting of permits and licences (in timber reserves) to cut timber;

for protection of certain areas of timber and of certain species from cutting;

provision for royalty on timber exported;

for granting of agricultural and pastoral leases within a timber reserve, whether licensed or not;

for the making of regulations.

This ordinance was amended by Timber Ordinance 1917 and Timber Ordinance 1920 and the Forestry (Papua) Ordinance 1950.

Under the Timber Ordinance 1909-20 nine areas of land were proclaimed timber reserves between 1912 and 1922, and two areas proclaimed protected areas.

In New Guinea a Timber Ordinance 1922 was enacted, similar to that of Papua, and amended by Timber Ordinance (No. 2) 1922, Timber Ordinance 1926 and Timber Ordinance 1931. These were repealed in 1937.

In the mid-1930s a growing interest in both logging and export of timbers and an appreciation of the need for a professional controlling organization led to the introduction of a new ordinance —Forestry Ordinance 1936-37—incorporating Forestry Ordinance 1936 and Forestry Ordinance 1937. Both came into operation on 15 September 1937. Forestry Regulations were also enacted under this ordinance at the same time.

This ordinance applied to the Territory of New Guinea only, but was adopted for Papua by the Forestry (Papua) Ordinance 1950 as amended by the Forestry (Papua) Ordinance 1951. The title 'Forestry Ordinance 1936-37' has been retained for the Papuan ordinance.

In New Guinea, however, amending ordinances —Forestry (New Guinea) Ordinance 1951 and Forestry (New Guinea) Ordinance 1962—were reflected in changes of title, firstly to Forestry Ordinance 1936-51 and then to Forestry Ordinance 1936-62. However, the context of both Territories' ordinances and the regulations framed thereunder are identical and are those at present in force.

The ordinances make provision for the appointment of an administering authority and of forest officers and inspectors, and define the powers of both these latter.

There is provision for the purchase of timber rights from indigenous owners. Once rights have been acquired the land may be declared Administration land for the purposes of the ordinance. Provision is made to proclaim Administration land as Territory forest or a timber reserve. Any trees or any species or classes of trees may be declared to be reserved trees.

The conditions covering the issue of permits or licences to take forest produce from Administration land are defined. Permits may be granted for a period up to ten years but, in the case of Administration land declared to be a special area, may be issued for up to twenty-five years. A permit grants exclusive harvesting right. A licence is valid for only one year and confers no exclusive rights.

There is provision for the control of export of timber species or classes; forest offences are defined and penalties prescribed; and finally there is provision for the making of regulations covering all aspects of forest conservation, management and protection, for the control and recording of forest produce, and for prescribing any fees or royalties that may be payable.

The regulations detail all matters relevant to the issue and usage of permits and licences, and of native timber authorities (for small, local dealing). There is provision for the establishment of Administration timber depots and the conditions of use of such. There is a section dealing with Administration brands and private brands for marking trees, timber and other forest produce and the use of such brands. There is a section governing the construction of forest tramways and sawmills in a permit area.

Finally there is a general section making provision for the drawing up of working plans for Territory forests; for the agistment of cattle in a timber reserve; for controlling the felling of trees by establishing girth limits; for conditions of removal of forest produce; for measurement of forest produce; for treatment of logs prior to export unless exempted; for maintenance and production of specified records, and penalties for failure to do so. It also makes provisions relating to

Lowland rain forest, Mt Lawes Forest Station, near Port Moresby, Papua.

the loss of a permit; to the destruction of forest produce and penalty therefor; and there is a general penalty clause for breach of regulations where no penalty is specifically provided.

Special legislation. In 1952 a special piece of legislation entitled New Guinea Timber Agreement Act 1952 was enacted by the Australian parliament. This covered the agreement between the Commonwealth of Australia and Bulolo Gold Dredging Ltd to form a company—Commonwealth New Guinea Timbers Ltd—with the object of acquiring timber rights in the Territory, and harvesting, converting and marketing timber and timber products. The Commonwealth held a majority of the initial issue of shares. This agreement led to the establishment of a new industry with the opening of a plywood mill at Bulolo in 1954. A permit for ten years was issued to the new company with provision for a further ten-year extension, and consideration of a further extension.

LAND TENURE AND THE FOREST ESTATE

Generally speaking, ownership of land in the Territory, other than land occupied by the Administration by purchase or lease, or land proclaimed by the Administration to be waste or vacant land, is vested in the indigenous inhabitants. Such indigenously owned land may only be alienated to the Administration.

Ownership is a vague definition, obscured by the fact that tribes, groups and individuals have or claim various rights. It is further complicated by the fact that boundaries in most areas are still undefined and there are competing claims to many areas. However, the vast bulk of the land is held by the indigenous inhabitants.

To people who have always lived off the land, it is a symbol of immense significance, the sheet anchor of their existence, and there is great reluctance, even stubborn refusal, to part with titles.

This is the main problem in the creation of a permanent forest estate. Forestry is a long-term enterprise and security of tenure is necessary before substantial capital expenditure and management effort are worth investing.

Yet it is vital to both the economic and physical well-being of the country that a considerable proportion of the land remains permanently under forest cover and, wherever feasible, under as intensive management as is economically worthwhile.

In a country such as Papua and New Guinea the forests provide, and will for a long time, many of the basic necessities of life for the local peoples. Secondly, they can provide employment and economic benefit both to individuals and the country if a permanent forest industry, local and export, is established. Thirdly, the protective value of forest cover is of vital importance. Soil and water conservation and local amelioration of climatic conditions are heavily dependent on the proper distribution and management of forest coverage. Finally, there are the many other fields in which forests play an important part—recreation and hunting activities, fauna and flora protection, and conservation.

A rapid global survey indicates that, broadly, either on a country or community scale at comparable levels of development, standards of living are lower and living conditions harsher where forests are non-existent than where they are abundant.

It is impossible to be dogmatic about the desirable size of the permanent forest for any particular country. In general terms the greater the area under forest the better, but topography, geographical location, climate, population pressures, industrial, agricultural and forestry development, government and popular attitudes, and land tenure will all influence this.

The following table gives an indication of the variation in extent of permanent forest estate compared with total land area and available forest in a range of countries at different levels of development.

Table 1

Country	Population per Square Mile	Forest as Per Cent of Total Land Area		Permanent Forest Estate	
		All Forest	Accessible Forest	Per Cent of Total Land Area	Per Cent of Accessible Forest
Ghana	51	59	59	9.1	15
Kenya	27	3.4	3.4	3.3	100
India	287	24	15	14.7	96
Japan	630	63	59	25	43
Philippines	196	44	34	34	100
Sweden	—	56	56	56	100
Greece		20	20	20	100
Papua New Guinea	12	76	31	0.16	0.5
Fiji	71	51	—	3.4	—
Sarawak	15	76	76	23	30

While the Territory is far from unique in the small area of forest land dedicated to permanent forestry, it ranks very low. Even Fiji, with somewhat similar problems of land tenure and acquisition and with 51 per cent of forested land, has managed to set aside 3.4 per cent of the total land area compared to the 76 per cent and 0.16 per cent, respectively, of Papua and New Guinea. Undoubtedly the forest estate is far too small.

Of the examples given Sarawak, in terms of population density, forested land, climate, geographical location and degree of development, could be compared to the Territory and it would not be unrealistic to consider that the forest estate in the latter should be of comparable extent. As a short term target therefore 11 million acres of the 36 million classed as accessible forest should be dedicated to forestry.

Another approach to the same question, based on estimates of population growth to the year 2000, *per caput* consumption of forest produce, productive capacity of managed forests and a component for an export industry, suggests a forest estate of 10 million acres of which 4 million would be commercially productive on a sustained-yield basis. The Department aims at such a target.

However, the reluctance of indigenous owners to part with the title to their land has created a bottle-neck. By 1967 some 6.6 million acres of forest land had been classed as suitable for inclusion in the forest estate, but full title had only been attained for 0.18 million acres, and timber rights for periods ranging from one to forty years purchased for approximately 1.5 million acres.

Since the purchase of timber rights confers no rights other than those related to harvesting the forest crop during the period of tenure, there is little incentive to sustain and improve yields. Such areas can therefore be regarded only as temporary components of the forest estate.

Failing a change in attitude, other approaches will have to be considered. Under the Lands Ordinance land may be compulsorily acquired for a public purpose, and forests essential for soil and water conservation purposes could well be included within such a definition. An alternative would be compulsory dedication under a soil and water conservation ordinance. The application of compulsory acquisition powers to the creation of a forest estate to support a forest industry would require very strong economic pressures.

For this latter purpose some form of long-term lease agreement or dedication on a share-cropping basis is possible. A forest estate could thus be created without loss of title to the owners.

FOREST MANAGEMENT AND RESOURCES

A primary function of the Department of Forests is a forest resources survey with two main objectives; to provide a base on which to develop and expand forest utilization, and to enable a permanent forest estate to be established which will ensure the continuity of the forest industry and will perform other functions essential to proper land use such as soil, water and wild-life conservation, and climatic amelioration.

The resources inventory undertaken by the military provided an effective beginning. Because of the impossibility of a detailed survey of all the forested land within a reasonable time, certain topographical criteria were selected to divide the forest cover in air photos into three broad categories. These were forests on slopes less than 10°, 10° to 30°, and greater than 30°. The forests in the first category were considered to be accessible and potential agricultural land; those in the second primarily protection forest but with utilization potential and could be made into permanent forest estate; the third category of forests were classed as inaccessible and purely protective.

This classification reduced considerably the work of the resources survey. Of an estimated 90 million acres of forested land, 53.4 million acres have been classified as protection reserves leaving 36.6 million acres classed as productive and therefore meriting investigation. Of this area 17 million acres have been classified as potential agricultural land and the balance as potential permanent forest. Detailed work has been concentrated on these productive forests.

After the war the resources survey was carried out by field parties, often in undeveloped regions with scanty populations. Parties were small and surveys long, limited and expensive.

The helicopter has made a tremendous impact and unproductive travelling and transportation have been cut to a minimum. Larger field teams, efficiently serviced and transported, have led to far greater output of results. Between 1946 and 1963, using conventional methods, 1.5 million acres of forest were assessed. In the four years 1964 to 1967 with helicopter transportation 7 million acres have been investigated. A brief description of a helicopter-assisted survey follows.

A potential survey area is chosen by use of air photographs and ground reconnaissance. Basic preliminaries are agreement of the indigenous owners, preparation of topographical maps, delineation of approximate boundaries of the survey area, and determination of vegetation and forest types from air photographs.

Natural or artificial helicopter pads throughout the area provide the bases and temporary camps for field teams from which traverse lines are run in predetermined directions to secure a representative sampling intensity of up to 0.5 per cent. Data collected along these lines include forest and vegetation types and boundaries, topographical information, volume assessment by species, log length, girth measurement and form class, and soil characteristics. With six to ten assessment teams of four persons serviced by a single helicopter 200-300 acres per week can be sampled.

The chief limiting factor in the use of helicopters is the availability of road, water or airstrip access to the main base camp within thirty miles of the proposed survey area—the effective working range for a helicopter transporting and supplying the survey teams.

Current resources surveys seek areas of forested land mainly suitable for agricultural development and bearing economic stands of forest, and all necessary pre-investment data about the timber potential, and the infrastructure to support a utilization project.

Because of relatively low population density forest degradation has been limited. In most types of forest the variety of timber trees is extensive and this complicates utilization. However, in many of the better-timbered areas a limited number of acceptable market species (*see* TIMBER, COMMERCIAL SPECIES) make up the bulk of the mature stand. For example, in the Vanimo area one hundred species were identified in the 600,000 acres of timbered land, but twenty-five species made up over 80 per cent of the total estimated volume. A further favourable factor is that many of the major species are trees of large size, in both height and girth, and of good form enabling high recovery rates.

In the mixed lowland rain forests which comprise the bulk of the forested areas readily suitable for utilization the main economic species include taun (*Pometia* spp.), *Terminalia* spp., kwila (*Intsia* spp.), pencil cedar (*Palaquium* spp.), malas (*Homalium foetidum*), *Celtis* spp., *Planchonella torricellensis*, erima (*Octomeles sumatrana*), water gum (*Eugenia* spp.), walnut (*Dracontomelum mangiferum*), rosewood (*Pterocarpus indicus*), *Canarium* spp., *Sterculia* spp. and *Endospermum* spp. Many of these are suitable for veneer production.

In certain areas of lowland forest one species predominates, such as *Anisoptera polyandra*, kamarere (*Eucalyptus deglupta*), *Terminalia brassii*, taun and kwila.

In the mid-montane region from 1,500 to 7,000 feet there are extensive areas of good economic forest but, except for forests in the Bulolo-Wau area, most of these are at present relatively inaccessible. In these forests the best species include the conifers klinkii (*Araucaria hunsteinii*), hoop (*A. cunninghamii*), *Podocarpus* spp., *Papuacedrus* and *Phyllocladus*, and amongst the hardwoods *Cedrela*, *Flindersia* spp., *Vitex*, *Geijera salicifolia*, *Dysoxylum* spp., *Amoora* and *Nothofagus*, together with other species occurring in the lowland forests.

Many of the major hardwoods exceed 100 feet in height, kamarere reaches 200 feet, and have girths up to 20 feet. With klinkii and hoop pine, trees 150-200 feet high with girths of up to 18 feet are common.

The density of stands varies considerably, but merchantable yields of up to 30,000 super feet per acre are not uncommon. The average, over some 6.5 million acres inventoried and classified as bearing economic forest, is 3,000 super feet per acre.

The major areas assessed and available for industrial development include Vanimo with an area of 750,000 acres, of which 595,000 acres are classed as productive, containing an estimated 4,500 million super feet; Open Bay, New Britain, 420,000 acres in area of which 306,000 acres are productive, containing 4,500 million super feet; Ania-Kapiura, New Britain, 460,000 acres in area and containing 2,400 million super feet; and Toiru-Pandi, New Britain, 297,000 acres in area of which 176,000 acres are productive, containing an estimated 2,000 million super feet. Major forest areas which have been investigated and assessed are shown on the map.

UTILIZATION AND THE FOREST INDUSTRY

Apart from shifting cultivation, most of the demands made on the forest by the indigenous people have had little effect. But the clearing of forest, cultivation of the soil and raising of food crops, followed by abandonment and repeated burning, have drastically altered forest composition or even denuded the land of forest cover over extensive areas.

With the advent of the European, 'utilization' in the modern sense was introduced. Small mills were established by missions, on plantations and in the Bulolo goldfields area, mainly to supply their own needs. In the depression years of the late 1930s copra planters began to export logs and flitches of New Guinea walnut (*Dracontomelum mangiferum*) to America and by 1940 some 7.5 million super feet had been exported.

Utilization during the war was entirely for military purposes. The sawmills operated by the Allied services and Angau are estimated to have produced 80 million super feet of sawn timber, plus large quantities of round timber.

Since 1946 there has been a steady expansion of the timber industry [q.v.]. Initially there was an embargo on export of sawn timber to ensure that all production served local needs for rehabilitation and development. This was gradually relaxed, first to supply urgently required hoop and klinkii pine battery separator material to Australia, and later other sawn produce, as local production exceeded demand.

There was no post-war restriction on log exports, but shipping difficulties and other factors kept exports low for some years. Table 2 shows the rate of development of logging activities from 1947 to 1969.

Table 2

TOTAL LOG VOLUME HARVESTED

Year	Super Feet True Volume in Thousands	Cubic Metres
1947–8	10,985	26,000
1951–2	19,600	46,200
1956–7	50,985	120,000
1961–2	66,629	157,200
1965–6	135,144	318,900
1966–7	154,949	365,000
1968–9	155,833	367,800

Log exports have increased from 757,550 super feet to 33.5 million super feet over the same period, and export of sawn timber from some 144 super feet to almost 7 million super feet.

The New Guinea Timber Agreement Act of 1952 paved the way for the establishment of a plymill in the Bulolo area which commenced operations in 1954. In 1966-7 this mill and two other veneer plants in the Morobe District, besides supplying local needs, had built up an export trade in veneer and plywood totalling some 23.4 million square feet of plywood (³⁄₁₆ inch) and 19.8 million square feet of veneer (¹⁄₁₆ inch) in 1968-9 (*see* PLYWOOD INDUSTRY). Besides the ply and veneer mills there were some eighty-one sawmills operating throughout the Territory in 1969.

Shortly after the war twenty-seven permits covering 274,000 acres were in operation; by June 1969 this had increased to seventy-two permits and fifty-two timber licences covering 1,339,181 acres.

Timber permits over large new areas are now let by tender or negotiation. Following a recommendation made by the World Bank during its Mission in 1964, the Administration engaged consultants to carry out feasibility studies of extensive areas of forested land with potential for integrated large-scale utilization. It is hoped thus to attract operators with adequate finance, experience and market connections to develop such areas.

Based on resources surveys carried out up to that time the World Bank Mission estimated that an annual cut of not less than 500 million super feet on a permanent basis was possible. Further surveys and assessments since then indicate that, as of 1967, no less than 6.5 million acres of forested land offered potential for economic devel-

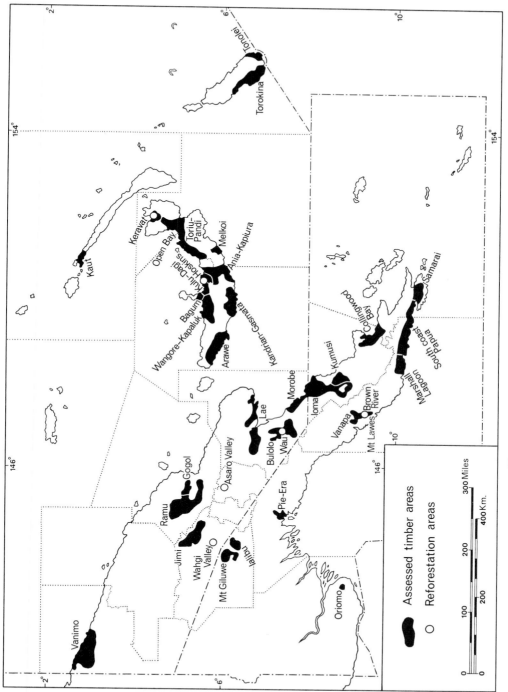

Forest resource surveys and reforestation centres.

opment. This is five times the area on which the Mission's estimate was based and indicates the tremendous potential of the industry.

For the year ended June 1969 the impact of the forest industry on the local economy is shown in the following table.

Table 3

	No.	Persons Employed	Salaries and Wages $m.	Value of Output $m.	Value of Land, Buildings, Plant and Machinery, $m.
Sawmills Plywood and Veneer Mills	81* 2	} 2,827	2,032	9,990	5,140
Joinery	69	1,105	1,115	4,893	1,830
Total	152	3,932	3,147	14,883	6,970

*Includes one mill producing veneer.

The total value of forest products exported for the year ended June 1969 was $4,813,539. Plywood and veneer represented $2.5 million of this total.

The timber conversion industry is the largest employer of labour among secondary industries in the country. To the nearly 4,000 employees can be added another 1,350 who are employed by the Department of Forests, together with a considerable number employed in logging.

SILVICULTURE

While there is still a vast reserve of forest produce it is essential to ensure continuity of supplies. There are two ways of achieving this. One is by natural regeneration of the indigenous forest, attempting if possible to improve both quality and quantity. The second is by the establishment of plantations either in exploited forest or in treeless areas. The Department of Forests is doing both.

Natural regeneration. There are a number of problems with regeneration by natural means. A major one is the difficulty of obtaining adequate tenure to suitable forest land. Secondly, many of the more valuable trees are either pioneer or sub-climax species whose regeneration is dependent on conditions often difficult or impossible to reproduce. And thirdly, in the typical climax rain forest of the Territory, there is a tremendous diversity of species, a large proportion of which are not readily marketable.

In the hope that the primary problem of land tenure will eventually be overcome pilot plots have been established in a number of forest types to obtain data from which prescriptions of treatment may be worked out to regenerate and improve the natural stands.

In the limited areas where title is assured silvicultural management is more advanced. At Keravat, one of the few territorial forests (41,800 acres) two lowland rain-forest types are recognized. One contains desirable pioneer or sub-climax species— *Eucalyptus deglupta, Octomeles sumatrana, Pometia tomentosa, Dracontomelum mangiferum* and *Terminalia* spp.—classed as 'intolerant' species (i.e. seedlings will not grow in the presence of the adult trees). The second is the typical rain-forest climax type with a wide range of tolerant species capable of reproducing themselves on the same site. In the normal course of ecological succession the second type would in all probability take over the first.

Treatment is directed towards regeneration of the intolerant-species forest through the generally prolific seedling regeneration of the commercially desirable intolerant species. Once all the merchantable species above the minimum girth limit have been logged, all non-desirable species, defective stems of desirable species and large vines are poisoned. Advance growth of desirable intolerants is retained. Removal or 'brushing' of small vines and undergrowth is carried out until regeneration is well advanced. By this means adequate regeneration and growth of desirable intolerant species have been achieved, primarily of *Pometia tomentosa*. A follow up treatment of thinning allows crown space to encourage growth of selected stems.

By 1967 some 2,500 acres have received initial treatment and 100 acres the follow up treatment. Subsequently about 1,000 acres per year received the initial treatment, but by 1970 this work was abandoned due to uncertainty about the future of the natural forest areas at Keravat.

Eucalyptus savannah forest makes up 20 per cent of the Mt Lawes Territorial forest of 46,500 acres, twenty miles north of Port Moresby. The main species are *Eucalyptus confertiflora, Eucalyptus alba* and *Eucalyptus papuana*. None is particularly valuable for milling, but they are useful for posts and as firewood. Two forms of treatment have been applied; one is clear felling (removal of all trees of any size) in strips and the other consists of retention of seed trees at specified spacing, allied with thinning of dense sapling and pole stands. The aim is to improve the density and quality of the stand by both natural seedling regeneration and coppice shoots.

Artificial regeneration. There are three main and a number of subsidiary areas where plantation forestry is being practised or tested. The main areas are Keravat, Mt Lawes and Bulolo-Wau.

At Keravat artificial reforestation is effected in rain forest containing the very diverse tolerant species. After logging, these areas are clear felled, burned and planted. The main species used are teak (*Tectona grandis*), kamarere (*Eucalyptus deglupta*), balsa (*Ochroma lagopus*) and *Terminalia brassii*. Trial plantings of other species have been made. By June 1969 3,312 acres had been planted and the current rate of planting was 400 acres a year, mainly of teak. Teak and kamarere comprise some 90 per cent of the plantation.

At Mt Lawes the main reforestation is in the monsoon forest where 2,100 acres have been planted, again mainly teak (94 per cent). Trial plantings of twenty-five species have been made.

Bulolo-Wau is the chief planting centre. The main species used are klinkii pine (*Araucaria hunsteinii*) and hoop pine (*Araucaria cunninghamii*). Logged areas are clear felled, burned and planted. Within the past few years experimental underplanting of logged forest with klinkii has been done with gradual removal of the overhead canopy by

Kamarere (*Eucalyptus deglupta*) plantation at Keravat, New Britain. Thin understorey of *Alpinia* spp. and broad-leafed trees.

poisoning. The primary aim is to improve the survival rate of klinkii in the early establishment period. To mid-1969 15,226 acres had been planted, including some 10,400 acres of hoop pine, 2,500 acres of klinkii, and miscellaneous species including pines. The current planting programme was then 1,250 acres a year.

Pine planting. With considerable areas of grassland available as potential afforestation areas, extensive trials of tropical and subtropical species of *Pinus* have been made in a wide range of soil and altitudinal sites from sea-level up to 9,000 feet. Several are showing promise but considerable data have yet to be accumulated before full-scale pine afforestation can be undertaken. By mid-1969 some 550 acres had been planted in the Bulolo-Wau area with an annual target of around 400 acres. In the Highlands pine plantations totalled 750 acres with the annual planting also at 400 acres.

Seed collection and nursery practice. *Araucaria*—both klinkii and hoop—seed is collected locally in cone form when the cones are nearing maturity. If left too long, they disintegrate and the seed is dispersed and lost. Collecting is done either from felled trees in logging areas if the operations can be suitably synchronized or by climbing standing trees. The cones are dried, they disintegrate, and the seed is placed in containers and kept under refrigeration. In the case of klinkii seed containers must be air-tight.

Both species are germinated by broadcast sowing in seed beds in permanent nurseries with overhead shade, and are transplanted into metal tubes when 6 to 9 inches in height.

Teak seed is collected from selected betterquality stands specially prepared for seed production and collection, pending large-scale production from seed orchards. When the major seed flush is ready, the trees are climbed and branches shaken. Fallen seed is collected from the cleared ground under the trees, dried, dehusked, and stored under cover in sacks.

Generally teak plants are raised in temporary nurseries without shade adjacent to planting areas. Following pregermination treatment with water to promote rapid and even germination, seed is broadcast sown in beds and covered with sawdust. For planting out the seedlings are lifted and stumped, the stem cut to $\frac{1}{2}$ to 1 inch above ground level and the root 7 to 8 inches below ground level.

Kamarere capsules are collected from wellformed trees before they open, are sun dried, the major debris removed and the residue sieved through two grades of very fine mesh. The larger mesh removes the larger particles of waste; the smaller catches the seed but allows dust through. This is necessary because of the extremely small size of the seed—5.5 million per pound. The seed is sterilized, sealed in small containers in quantities large enough for annual sowings, and stored under refrigeration. Seed is germinated in seed flats (trays) under weather-proof shelters to prevent over-wetting. Seedlings are tubed when two to three pairs of leaves develop.

Extension work is an important aspect of forestry in various Districts. Besides the main reforestation centres a number of stations have been established throughout the country. Amongst their functions are political contact at village level and education on the value of forests; encouragement of conservation, afforestation or reforestation projects in areas of existing or probable timber shortage for village needs; research to test species and sites; the provision of stock for commercial plantings; and provision of amenity species.

In 1969 these services were provided from thirty-three centres.

TRAINING

Training policy is governed by the need to train local personnel to standards and in sufficient numbers to fill gradually all echelons of the Department. The three main categories required are forestry assistants—subordinate sub-professional officers trained in a specific branch of forestry work; technical assistants and technical officers; and professional staff—fully qualified university graduates.

The establishment of a training centre was approved in principle in late 1957 and provision was made for it in the 1962 five-year programme. The first short course commenced at Bulolo Forestry School in 1962 and by 1967 a three-year diploma course was established. The Forestry College [q.v.] offers several short courses in specialized branches in addition to the diploma course.

Some extension training work is carried out by Departmental staff among local people, chiefly in the Highlands and elsewhere where shifting cultivation and fires have denuded the country of trees. Villagers are encouraged to learn how to raise, plant and tend trees suitable for fuel, building and fencing material.

The Division of Botany at Lae periodically runs short training courses on horticulture and arboriculture.

At present training at the professional level is carried out at Australian universities under a cadetship scheme. However, proposals are under consideration for training Papuans and New Guineans locally, in conjunction with the University of Papua and New Guinea, to meet current and future requirements for trained professional foresters.

RESEARCH

Research within the Department is divided between the Divisions of Silviculture, Botany, and Utilization and Marketing.

Utilization and marketing. The Pacific war stimulated the first intensive and organized research project. Large collections of botanical and wood specimens, made by the field parties of the Forest Survey Companies of the Australian Army Engineers, were identified by the Queensland government botanist, C. T. White, and the CSIRO Division of Forest Products, under Dr H. E. Dadswell. The latter produced a card-sorting key for rapid identification of 140 timbers from macroscopic characteristics and this has been expanded and revised since the war. The CSIRO Division of Forest Products has also undertaken research into the following aspects of New Guinea species:

physiology and microstructure;
pulp- and paper-making properties;
physical and mechanical properties;
seasoning;
preservation.

The Division of Utilization and Marketing has been engaged in a variety of projects. Practical aspects of seasoning, preservation and insect attack have been studied. Problems of recovery and quality of sawn produce, and working properties of species are being investigated. Interim grading rules for sawn timber have been established, and interim log-grading rules proposed. Work has been done on the harvesting and economics of a number of minor forest products including gum, resin, tannin and rattans. Potential markets for a developing forestry industry have been studied.

Botany. This Division has its headquarters at Lae at the botanic gardens where an air-conditioned herbarium was opened in 1965. Housed there is a collection which, in 1971, included more than 120,000 specimens. The collection and classification of the extensive Papua and New Guinea flora continues steadily with duplicates deposited at a number of major herbaria throughout the world. Ecological studies have been carried out in various vegetation communities. A series of booklets forming a manual of forest trees of Papua and New Guinea has been published. The botanic gardens are the responsibility of the Division.

Silviculture. In 1971 there was no established research centre although a building to house forest entomology was built at Bulolo in 1968. Research, formulated and co-ordinated at headquarters, is carried out at the main centres of silvicultural activity and the Forestry College. Early research was directed to species trials and the development of techniques applicable to local conditions. This work was based to a considerable extent on the adaptation of research done elsewhere on the same or closely related species. The Germans had introduced teak (*Tectona grandis*) as early as 1911 and established it at Madang, Kokopo and Rabaul, and the performance of these plantings was a useful guide. The results of the early research are seen in the extensive plantations at Bulolo, Wau, Keravat, Mt Lawes and Goroka, and in the naturally regenerated forest at Keravat.

Current work is concerned with further species trials and cultivation techniques (particularly of *Pinus* species), plant nutrition, improved nursery techniques and forest-tree improvement. In this last field work is presently concentrated on teak, hoop pine, klinkii pine, kamarere, and *Pinus* spp., using selected trees, vegetative propagation, seed orchards, controlled pollination and progeny testing. Trials in thinning to improve productivity are under way in hoop pine and other plantation areas to determine optimum management schedules.

Entomological investigations seek to control a leaf scolatid, *Hylurdrectonus araucariae*, which is causing considerable damage in hoop pine plantations, and the termite, *Coptotermes elesae* (see

INSECT PESTS OF AGRICULTURE AND FORESTRY). Preliminary pathology studies have been initiated with the collection, identification and culturing of known and potential pathogens.

FIRE

Burning of bush and grass, which forms a regular feature of native life, presents a major hazard to plantations. A fire-fighting unit equipped with tankers, portable pumps, knapsack sprays and other equipment has been established in the Bulolo area. This unit, besides having the responsibility for protecting the plantations, has initiated research into fire protection problems, commencing with work on a fire-danger meter based on variables of local significance.

'The Bulolo stand in perpetuity', *Australian Timber Journal*, vol. 25, 1959.
'Regeneration experiments in Papua', *Australian Timber Journal*, vol. 29, 1959.
International Bank for Reconstruction and Development, *The Economic Development of the Territory of Papua and New Guinea*. Baltimore, 1969.
C. E. Lane-Poole, 'The Forest Resources of the Territories of Papua and New Guinea', *Commonwealth Parliamentary Papers*, vol. 2, 1925.
R. Levingston, 'Reafforestation with teak', *South Pacific Bulletin*, vol. 17, 1967.
J. B. McAdam, 'Forestry in New Guinea', *Papua and New Guinea Scientific Society: Annual Report*, 1952.
W. R. Suttie, 'Forestry in Papua and New Guinea: A transition period 1951-61', *Papua and New Guinea Scientific Society: Annual Report and Proceedings*, 1962.
K. J. White, 'Forestry Activity (in the Territory of Papua and New Guinea)', *South Pacific Bulletin*, vol. 15, 1965.
T. P. N. G. Bureau of Statistics, *Quarterly Summary of Statistics, no. 43*. Port Moresby, 1971.
—— *Secondary Industries, 1968-69*. Port Moresby, 1971.
T. P. N. G. Department of Forests, 'A Dictionary of Generic and Family Names of Flowering Plants for the New Guinea and Southwest Pacific Region', *Botany Bulletin*, no. 3, 1969.
—— *The Forests and Forest Conditions in the Territories of Papua and New Guinea*. Port Moresby, 1957.
—— *Manual of the Forest Trees of Papua and New Guinea: I Combretaceae*. 1964; *II Sapindaceae*. 1964; *III Sterculiaceae*. 1964; *IV Anacardiaceae*. 1964; *V Himantandraceae, VI Magnoliaceae, VII Eupomatiaceae, VIII Dipterocarpaceae*. 1965; *IX Apocynaceae*. Port Moresby, 1966.
—— *Papua and New Guinea Forestry College Handbook*. Port Moresby (annual).
—— *Properties and Uses of New Papua and New Guinea Timbers*. Port Moresby, 1970.
—— 'Silvicultural techniques in Papua New Guinea forest plantations', *Bulletin*, no. 1, 1965.

R. J. B. ANGUS

(*See also* PLYWOOD INDUSTRY; TIMBER, COMMERCIAL SPECIES; TIMBER INDUSTRY)

FORESTRY COLLEGE. The Papua and New Guinea Forestry College is situated within the Bulolo township some 2,500 feet above sea-level. There are vast natural forests accessible to the school for training purposes, including the humid lowland rain forests near Lae, the rich and productive hoop and klinkii pine forests of the Bulolo and Watut Valleys and the cool temperate oak and beech forests of Edie Creek at altitudes of over 7,000 feet. In the Bulolo Valley there are forest industries of wide diversity operating which provide employment to many people in a wide range of skills. Actual studies are carried out on sawmill, veneer and plywood techniques, and problems associated with these industries.

Forestry [q.v.] training commenced in 1962 in temporary accommodation at Bulolo with a brief one-year course for in-service staff. In 1963 two-year certificate courses covering elementary silviculture, forest survey and engineering and forest botany were initiated for in-service staff and external recruits with a nominal entry level of Form II. A three-year diploma course was established in 1967 with a level of entry set at Form IV, although Form III graduates were accepted in the initial years. The course covers the major subject areas of forest biology, forest management, forest economics, policy and administration, and wood technology and utilization. There is a strong emphasis on practical work, but administrative and managerial aspects are included to produce graduates capable of being sub-professional forest managers. Special training in the handling of explosives and extension work is given by other departments during the course. Lecturing staff are encouraged to undertake research projects in which students can co-operate.

In addition to the certificate and diploma courses in forestry, a three-year diploma course in cartography was commenced in 1969 to train draughtsmen for the departments of Forests, Lands, Surveys and Mines, and Agriculture, Stock and Fisheries. Six-month artisan courses, mainly practical work, are offered each year in particular branches of forestry such as silviculture, survey or harvesting and marketing. Shorter in-service refresher or up-grading courses are provided as required. With the establishment of fully equipped and staffed workshops and research facilities available in the Utilization Division, training has been extended into the timber utilization field covering conversion, seasoning, preservation and grading. Plans for future expansion include the provision of facilities for the training of national park rangers.

The Forestry College provides centralized training for English-speaking Pacific Islanders through the South Pacific Commission. Students from the Solomon Islands, Fiji, Tonga, Western Samoa and the Caroline Islands have undergone training at Bulolo.

In 1970 63 students were undertaking diploma and certificate courses at the College. Accommodation was provided for 105 residential students with plans completed for an expansion to 150 students.

K. J. W.

FORSAYTH, Emma Eliza, 'Queen Emma' (1850-1913), was born in Samoa in 1850, the daughter

Emma Forsayth, 'Queen Emma'.

of Jonas Coe. She was educated in Sydney and San Francisco, and married James Forsayth, but had affairs with others, including the American Colonel Steinberger. In 1878 with Captain Thomas Farrell she left Samoa for Mioko in the Duke of York Group, where they lived as man and wife, and established themselves as traders. They were joined by Emma's sister Phoebe who had married Richard Parkinson [q.v.] and bought land for plantations extensively around Blanche Bay and in the Mortlocks. When the German government annexed the north-eastern section of New Guinea Emma and her clan were numerous, wealthy and socially prominent colonists. Farrell died in 1886, leaving the property to Emma who lived at Gunantambu with an Austrian sailor, Captain Agostino Stalio, until he was killed by natives on Nuguria Island. In 1893 she married a former Prussian officer, Captain August Karl Paul Kolbe. Her commercial empire continued to grow but in 1907 she sold all the Forsayth interests with the exception of those transferred to her son, Coe Forsayth, and lived in Sydney. She was then a sick woman, but in 1913 followed her husband to Monte Carlo. They both died there, Kolbe on 19, Emma on 21 July of that year, in circumstances which led to gossip about murder and suicide but the deaths were in fact accidental and natural.

R. W. Robson, *Queen Emma.* Sydney, 1965.

FRANCIS WEST

(*See also* GERMAN NEW GUINEA)

FOSSIL MAMMALS were first discovered on the island of New Guinea during the 1930s by alluvial gold-miners who sluiced the auriferous gravels and terrace deposits in the valleys of the

Watut and Bulolo Rivers. The gold-bearing gravels mantled rocks of the Otibanda formation which had been deposited in lakes and restricted flood plains during middle to late Pliocene time (8 to 3 million years ago). Collections of the fossil animals accumulated slowly in the Australian Museum, Sydney, and the Queensland Museum. However, apart from Anderson's description in 1937 of the heavy quadrupedal herbivore *Nototherium watutense*, no systematic study of the fossils was made until 1964. During 1964 and 1965 all the material which had accumulated, together with new collections found during intensive investigations in 1962 and 1963, were assembled, examined, evaluated and described.

Two other sites are known in eastern New Guinea. The first, discovered in 1960, is at Kiowa, about three miles south-east of Chuave government station in the Eastern Highlands. This site is an archaeological excavation and to date the only fossil mammal recorded from it is a *Thylacinus* (Tasmanian wolf or tiger). Work on the fauna which was found with the thylacine mandible is in progress. The age of the layer in which the jaw was found is known to be about ten thousand years, from associated material dated by the 'radiocarbon' method. The second site, discovered in 1967, is at Pureni, a small mission station near Tari in the Southern Highlands, and was found during the excavation for the extension of the airfield. The site has been under investigation since early 1968 and the only animal so far recognized is a member of the family Diprotodontidae. It seems likely that this site is of Pleistocene age; however, there is a possibility that it may be late Tertiary.

There are then only three known areas which contain fossil mammals of any antiquity. Only one area has been studied intensively and the fossil mammals which come from rocks of the Otibanda formation are formally designated the 'Awe fauna'. It contains fossil gastropods, crocodiles, snakes, birds, both placental and marsupial mammals, and plant material.

The marsupials are represented by the families Dasyuridae (marsupial mice and cats), Macropodidae (wallabies and kangaroos), and Diprotodontidae (extinct herbivores), while the only placentals are the Muridae (rats and mice).

The dasyurid is a small animal closely resembling the living genus *Parantechinus*, the insectivorous, forest-dwelling, freckled marsupial mouse which is known from the south-west of Western Australia.

Three types of macropodids are known. Two have been referred to the genus *Protemnodon*, large wallaby-like animals which flourished on the Australian mainland during the Pleistocene epoch and which are characterized by a low crowned molar dentition and a short, broad hind foot. The two species from the Otibanda formation, *Protemnodon otibandus* and *Protemnodon buloloensis* are the smallest members of the genus known. They are well represented by cranial and, to a lesser degree, post-cranial material. The third macropodid is a small animal with similarities to

Side view of left lower jaw of *Kolopsis rotundus*, ¼ times natural size.

the living genera *Dorcopsis* and *Dendrolagus*, the forest wallaby and the tree kangaroo. It is rather poorly represented by cranial material and some limb bones.

The last, and to some the most interesting group, are the diprotodontids. These large extinct animals roamed Australia in considerable numbers during the Tertiary and co-existed with the earliest Aborigines in the late Pleistocene. The forms of Pliocene age found in New Guinea are medium-sized, comparable with young rhinoceroses, and closely related to forms found in Australia belonging to late Miocene to early Pliocene time, 14-10 million years ago. The largest species was named *Nototherium watutense* by Anderson in 1937. The others are *Kolopsis rotundus* and *Kolopsoides cultridens*.

Nototherium watutense is related to diprotodontids found in the Pliocene and Pleistocene of Australia. *Kolopsis rotundus* is very closely linked with *Kolopsis torus* from the late Miocene deposits of Central Australia; while *Kolopsoides cultridens* is clearly derived from a *Kolopsis*-like form but is extremely specialized in its premolar dentition. To date, no descendants of this animal have been found in New Guinea or Australia.

The placental mammals are members of the Muridae and attest to the entry from Asia of this group during late Tertiary time.

C. Anderson, 'Palaeontological Notes. No. IV. Fossil Marsupials from New Guinea', *Records of the Australian Museum*, vol. 20, 1937-40; S. Bulmer, 'Radiocarbon Dates from New Guinea', *Journal of the Polynesian Society*, vol. 73, 1964; M. D. Plane, 'Two new diprotodontids from the Pliocene Otibanda Formation, New Guinea', Australian Bureau of Mineral Resources, Geology and Geophysics. *Bulletin*, no. 85, 1967; —— 'Stratigraphy and Vertebrate Fauna of the Otibanda Formation, New Guinea', Australian Bureau of Mineral Resources, Geology and Geophysics. *Bulletin*, no. 86, 1967; H. M. Van Deusen, 'First New Guinea Record of Thylacinus', *Journal of Mammalogy*, vol. 44, 1963; M. O. Woodburne, 'Three new diprotodontids from the Tertiary of the Northern Territory, Australia', Australian Bureau of Mineral Resources, Geology and Geophysics. *Bulletin*, no. 85, 1967.   M. D. PLANE

(*See also* MAMMALS)

FOX, John (1892-   ) and Thomas (1892-1952), prospectors and explorers. Identical twins, they were born in Rayleigh, Essex, England, on 12 November 1892, and arrived in Australia in

Jack and Tom Fox, c. 1934.

August 1914. They served first with the Australian forces in New Guinea, and later with the A.I.F. in France. They returned to the Mandated Territory of New Guinea in 1922, working as officers of the Expropriation Board until 1926, and as prospectors. They went gold-mining at Edie Creek and continued prospecting. After a visit to England in 1933 they went to Lae in February 1934, and thence to the central Highlands, meeting the Leahy brothers [q.v.] at Mount Hagen. From here they prospected through Wabag towards and almost certainly over the Dutch border. They found no gold, but were the first white men to have traversed much of this rugged country when they returned to Mount Hagen on Christmas Eve 1934.

Until World War II they were engaged in mining and farming in the Sepik District. Upon the Japanese invasion they walked from Vanimo back to Madang to Kainantu and across the country into Papua down the Purari River to the Gulf of Papua, and saw active war service again with Angau [q.v.]. After the war they were employed by the Department of Agriculture, Stock and Fisheries.

Thomas died in Port Moresby on 15 August 1952 and John settled near Mount Hagen, where he still lives.

John Fox kept a diary of the 1934 journey and a copy is in the Library of the University of Papua and New Guinea.

(*See also* EXPLORATION)

FROGS. Of the three major groups of amphibians —caecilians, salamanders and frogs—only the last is found in New Guinea. The peculiar, legless caecilians, widespread in tropical areas in other parts of the world, occur no nearer than Java and Borneo. Salamanders, especially in the eastern hemisphere, are essentially animals of north temperate regions. They live no closer than the Indo-Chinese peninsula.

COMPOSITION OF THE FAUNA

New Guinea, as defined for the purposes of this encyclopaedia, follows political boundaries and includes areas with quite different faunas. Therefore, the frogs must be considered in three geographic units: New Guinea itself—with satellite islands; Bougainville and Buka Islands; and the intermediate region of the Bismarck Archipelago.

The frog fauna of New Guinea proper is diverse; at least 160 species live there, and many areas of the island have not yet been adequately explored for these animals. In contrast, the large island of Borneo has fewer than 100 species, and Australia supports only a few more than 100. The New Guinean species are distributed unequally among four families and fifteen genera.

Only five species in three genera represent the family Leptodactylidae, in contrast to its prominent position in the Australian fauna. Three species are Australian forms, known from New Guinea only in the southern region opposite Cape York Peninsula. One is known only from a single specimen, and one is widely distributed though confined to New Guinea.

Frogs of the family Ranidae are individually extremely abundant in some parts, but only two genera and possibly ten species occur. *Rana grisea* (Fig. 1), a typical member of the genus, is usually associated with streams from near sea-level to high altitudes in the mountains. It lays its eggs in water and the young develop in the conventional tadpole fashion. In contrast, frogs of the genus *Platymantis* deposit their eggs in moist places on land and have eliminated the free-living tadpole stage; a fully formed, miniature frog hatches from the egg. *Platymantis papuensis* (Fig. 2) lives on the floor of lowland rain forest throughout much of New Guinea and the surrounding islands.

The treefrogs, family Hylidae, include about 40 per cent of the frog species known to live in New Guinea, and thus share dominance with the family Microhylidae. Most treefrogs are long-legged, large-eyed frogs with webbed toes, and sometimes webbed fingers as well, and prominent enlarged discs, helpful in climbing, on the tips of the fingers and toes. As the common name implies, many hylid frogs are largely arboreal, and their abundance reflects the predominance of forest habitats. Only two genera of treefrogs are present, *Litoria* (formerly *Hyla*) and *Nyctimystes*. The largest treefrog in the world, *Litoria infrafrenata*, which reaches a body length of 140 mm., is a common species throughout the lowlands. Other treefrogs such as *Litoria nigropunctata* (Fig. 3), with a body length of about 30 mm., are small frogs, conspicuous only by their voices. Frogs of the genus *Nyctimystes* closely resemble *Litoria*. One of the distinguishing characteristics of *Nyctimystes*, the cat-like, vertical pupil—horizontal or diamond-

Fig 1. *Rana grisea.*
Fig 2. *Platymantis papuensis.*

shaped in *Litoria*—is indicated in the illustration of *Nyctimystes papua* (Fig. 4), though in this specimen the pupil is dilated because the frog is in a darkened situation.

About half of the species of frogs known from New Guinea belong to eleven genera of the family Microhylidae. Unlike the treefrogs, the microhylids cannot readily be characterized, either morphologically or ecologically. Some species resemble treefrogs in being arboreal with enlarged toe discs, but rarely with webbed toes. Others are fat-bodied, short-legged frogs that burrow in leaf litter and humus, and still others are adapted to different modes of life. An arboreal species common in coastal and foothill regions is *Oreophryne biroi* (Fig. 5), a frog only about 20 mm. in length that calls at night from bushes or from low in trees; banana plants, which hold moisture in the leaf axils, are a favourite site. The other microhylid species illustrated (Fig. 6), a large 70 mm. member of the genus *Phrynomantis*, is typical of the terrestrial microhylids. As far as is known, all microhylid frogs of New Guinea and the Bismarck Archipelago have direct development. That is, the eggs are laid in moist places, but not directly in water, and a fully formed frog rather than a tadpole hatches.

The frog fauna of Bougainville and Buka Islands, and of the rest of the Solomons, is almost totally different. Of twenty-six species known to live on Bougainville, only three live also in New Guinea. All frogs native to the Solomon Islands except two species of *Litoria* are members of the family Ranidae, which has diversified extensively. Among the six genera on Bougainville are species that in external appearance, and probably in habits, resemble frogs of hylid, leptodactylid, and microhylid genera. Here again, direct reproductive development is the rule.

The Bismarck Archipelago, which lies between New Guinea and Bougainville, has a fauna that is to some extent a mixture derived from both east and west. The best-known island of the Archipelago is New Britain, but knowledge is scanty even there. Three species of *Litoria*, at least ten frogs of the family Ranidae in three genera, and two or three microhylids in two genera make up the known fauna. This is a small number for such a large island, and undoubtedly more species await discovery.

There is one introduced species. The giant tropical American toad *Bufo marinus* was introduced into Queensland and many islands in the Pacific, including New Guinea, in an effort to control insect pests of sugar-cane. These toads are extremely prolific and eat large numbers of insects, but they have not had any noticeable effect on those pests. They are a mixed blessing though. The toad's skin contains poison glands, the most prominent of which are the large parotoid glands above the ears. The venom these glands secrete is capable of killing such small animals as dogs or cats that might bite a toad, and it can cause irritation in a human being if it gets into the eyes or the blood stream, which might happen if a person with an open cut on

the hand picked up a toad. Ordinarily though, these toads pose no threat to people.

A species of animal successfully introduced into a foreign habitat may succeed by displacing a native species. Inasmuch as New Guinea lacked native species with habits closely resembling those of the toad it may fill a formerly empty ecological niche. What effect *Bufo* may have on the native fauna remains to be seen, however.

DISTRIBUTION

Most of the species of frogs found in New Guinea are restricted to the island. The faunas to the north-west and west in the Philippines, Borneo and the other Indonesian islands are totally different. They include families not represented by species native to New Guinea: the Bufonidae, Pelobatidae, and Rhacophoridae; one record for *Rhacophorus* requires substantiation. The different faunas of the Bismarck Archipelago and Solomon Islands have been mentioned. Australia and New Guinea, despite their closeness and connection in the recent geologic past, share only about fifteen species. The uniqueness of the New Guinean fauna results from the isolation of the region, and its diversity from the wide variety of habitats that mountainous islands offer.

Frogs do not easily cross salt water. Evidently many millions of years have elapsed since land connected South-east Asia and New Guinea, if it ever did. Consequently the frogs isolated in New Guinea evolved essentially free from competition with the rich fauna to the west. A similar situation prevails to the east. A distance of less than sixty miles separates New Britain and New Guinea, but few members of the New Guinean fauna have crossed the gap. The islands off the south-eastern 'tail' present a different picture. Though some species here are unknown on the mainland the fauna is wholly derived from species that originated there. At one time most of these insular areas must have been part of a larger mainland mass.

Australia and New Guinea evidently were connected by a land bridge rather recently, but this connection failed to promote a large exchange of frog faunas. Perhaps the habitats on the land bridge were unfavourable. Most of the amphibians of the New Guinean fauna are adapted to rain-forest conditions, whereas the Australian frog fauna evolved under much more arid circumstances. Typically Australian forms living in New Guinea are largely limited to the drier parts of the south; both leptodactylid and hylid species exhibit this pattern. Similarly, forms now found in Australia that have their closest relatives in New Guinea are confined largely to rain forests of the Cape York Peninsula; included are species of *Rana*, *Litoria* and *Nyctimystes*, as well as several microhylids.

Relatively little is known of the distribution of species in New Guinea. Some patterns are evident, such as the general restriction of Australian forms to the south and the broad distribution of many species of lowland and foothill regions. Of

3

4

Fig 3. *Litoria nigropunctata.*
Fig 4. *Nyctimystes papua.*

5

6

Fig 5. *Oreophryne biroi.*
Fig 6. *Phrynomantis* sp.

particular interest is the distribution of species confined to high elevations. When populations of a species are isolated on two or more mountains, it may be inferred that the climate was once sufficiently cool to permit dispersal through the lower areas between the mountains.

HABITATS

Frogs inhabiting the rugged mountainous topography have become adapted to a wide variety of habitat conditions. Such topography also promotes the separation of populations that underlies speciation.

The habitats of frogs may be considered in three major categories: aquatic, terrestrial, and arboreal. Frogs do not necessarily confine their activities to a single habitat though. Some may use different habitats at different times of the day, and when breeding others may shift temporarily.

Aquatic habitats customarily are divided into those of running water and those of still water such as swamps, lakes, and temporary rain pools. Swampy lowland areas, where not strongly influenced by tidal waters—none of the New Guinea frogs tolerate sea water—support large numbers of frogs. A common species in these situations, *Rana papua*, closely resembles the *Rana* illustrated. Where forests border swamps many species of *Litoria* resort to the water for breeding, the males advertising their sex to the females by croaking loudly. The giant treefrog, *Litoria infrafrenata*, contributes much to this din. The introduced giant toad, *Bufo marinus*, also favours still waters for breeding, though it is strictly terrestrial at other times.

In much of the country the only aquatic habitats are mountain streams. In similar situations in other parts of the world many species are adapted to such habitats. Here, however, few species restrict their activities to such streams following their metamorphosis. The mouth-parts of the stream-dwelling larvae of *Nyctimystes* have become adaptively modified as suction discs that permit the tadpoles to cling to rocks. Larvae of some *Litoria* are similarly adapted, and even though males of both genera call at night from bushes and trees overhanging streams, the adults seldom enter water except when they are breeding. At least two microhylid frogs of the genus *Sphenophryne* occur in streams, and both adults and tadpoles of *Rana grisea* are commonly found there, although no special adaptations are evident.

A wide variety of microhylid frogs are purely terrestrial. They burrow in the leaf litter or live in holes dug by other animals. Because these frogs lay their eggs on the forest floor they do not form breeding choruses in water, and consequently are seldom seen. The only evidence of their presence may be the disembodied calls that issue intermittently from indefinable spots beneath the leaf litter. Most of the terrestrial microhylids are confined to habitats in the forest but a few range into alpine grasslands, where they are the only frogs to be found. The ground-dwelling ranid, *Platymantis papuensis*, is more conspicuous

than most of the microhylids not only because the males call repeatedly at night but also because both males and females are less secretive.

Little is known about the species more highly specialized for life in the forest crown, to which some of the least frequently captured species of *Litoria* may restrict their activities. In other parts of the world such specialized frogs breed in the cavities in trees or in epiphytic plants that catch and retain water. If this is what the hylids of New Guinea do, it remains to be demonstrated. However, the cavities of ant plants, *Hydnophytum*, serve as breeding sites for arboreal microhylid frogs, and for lizards [q.v.] as well. Many frogs divide their time between arboreal and terrestrial habitats. Small microhylids, for example, may hide in the leaf litter during the day and at night climb into low bushes to call and feed.

W. C. Brown, 'The Amphibians of the Solomon Islands', *Bulletin of the Museum of Comparative Zoology at Harvard College*, vol. 107, 1952; P. N. van Kampen, *The Amphibia of the Indo-Australian Archipelago*. Leyden, 1923; A. Loveridge, 'New Guinean Reptiles and Amphibians in the Museum of Comparative Zoology and United States National Museum', *Bulletin of the Museum of Comparative Zoology at Harvard College*, vol. 101, 1948; M. J. Tyler, 'Microhylid Frogs of New Britain', *Transactions of the Royal Society of South Australia*, vol. 91, 1967; —— 'Papuan Hylid Frogs of the Genus *Hyla*', *Zoologische Verhandelingen*, no. 96, 1968; R. G. Zweifel, 'Results of the Archbold Expeditions. No. 72. Microhylid Frogs from New Guinea, with Descriptions of New Species', *American Museum Novitates*, no. 1766, 1956; —— 'Results of the Archbold Expeditions. No. 78. Frogs of the Papuan Hylid Genus *Nyctimystes*', *American Museum Novitates*, no. 1896, 1958; —— 'Results of the 1958-1959 Gilliard New Britain Expedition. 3. Notes on the Frogs of New Britain', *American Museum Novitates*, no. 2023, 1960; —— 'Frogs of the Genus *Platymantis* (Ranidae) in New Guinea', *American Museum Novitates*, no. 2374, 1969; —— 'Results of the Archbold Expeditions. A Revision of the Frogs of the Subfamily Asterophryinae, Family Microhylidae', *Bulletin of the American Museum of Natural History* (forthcoming).

RICHARD G. ZWEIFEL

FUEL SUPPLY AND DISTRIBUTION. The various fuels in common use in the Territory are wood, electricity (*see* ELECTRIC POWER), petroleum derivatives and liquefied petroleum gas. In parts of the Southern Highlands and in areas bordering the Gulf of Papua crude oil obtained from seeps has been a traditional fuel and is still used today. Vegetable wastes such as coconut husks and shells have been used as fuel on plantations since their inception. Some small, scattered deposits of low rank coal have been noted but they are of no significance commercially.

Wood. Although the popular conception of the Territory is of lush jungle covered country, wood is not available everywhere in unlimited quantities. In the Highlands and in the vicinity of the main towns there is a marked scarcity of wood for fuel and in other parts of the country, such as the delta regions, such wood as is available is usually of poor quality. In the Highlands fast growing Casuarina groves are planted for fuel purposes and form an economic crop for the owner. Neatly squared piles of firewood stacked ready for sale are a common sight along the roads in the upland areas. Offcuts from sawmills are always readily saleable (*see* TIMBER INDUSTRY).

Petroleum derivatives. Two oil companies at present supply the Territory market. Both have bulk terminals in the major coastal towns. Overseas tankers call at Port Moresby, Lae, Madang and Rabaul. Small inter-island tankers service Wewak, Kavieng and Samarai.

Distribution is effected by the companies themselves as well as through direct purchasing agents who resell on their own invoice. Most of the distribution in inland centres is undertaken by direct purchasing agents.

Prices are controlled by the Oil Industry Prices Committee in conjunction with the Treasurer. The base price is the main port price, to which freight costs are added. Road freight is charged at a flat rate per drum, regardless of the contents. Air freight is calculated according to the weight of the fuel. The all-up weights of a forty-four gallon drum of each of the three principal fuels are: motor spirit 366 lb., diesoline 426 lb., and lighting kerosene, 396 lb. Airfreight costs vary greatly from one airstrip to the next since technical considerations limit not only the types of aircraft permitted to land but also the maximum payload permissible for each aircraft.

The following table illustrates the effect of freight costs on liquid fuel prices:

INFLUENCE OF TRANSPORT COSTS ON LIQUID FUEL PRICES IN SELECTED CENTRES IN PAPUA AND NEW GUINEA

	Prices per gallon at July 1967		
	Motor Spirit	Diesoline	Lighting Kerosene
At main ports			
Port Moresby, Lae, Madang, Rabaul	28.3c	22.5c	25.6c
Centres serviced by road transport from Lae			
Goroka	45.8c	40.0c	43.1c
Mount Hagen	60.3c	54.5c	57.6c
Centres serviced by aircraft			
Mendi, from Madang	$1.00	$1.03	$1.01
Tapini, from Port Moresby	94.5c	98.3c	96.9c
Centre serviced by coastal shipping			
Bougainville—bulk	36.3c	30.5c	—
—drums ex Rabaul	43.8c	38.0c	41.1c

Wholesale prices are controlled for sales by drum lots, but retail sales through dealer outlets are controlled only in Port Moresby, Lae, Madang and Rabaul. Prices for lubricants are controlled only in the main ports. A $10 deposit is charged on forty-four gallon fuel drums, which are returnable if in good condition.

Liquid petroleum gas. This fuel has shown itself to be increasingly popular with domestic and commercial consumers. Bulk supply facilities are now available at Port Moresby, Lae and Rabaul and extensions are at the planning stage.

Prices are not controlled, but suppliers charge a standard price of $22.50 per 100 lb. of gas in coastal centres and Highland centres accessible by road. The necessity to return bottles for refilling renders this fuel too expensive for most consumers without road access to main centres.

Natural gas. This fuel is as yet untapped. Estimates of natural gas reserves discovered in 1958 vary from 40,000 million cubic feet to 530,000 million cubic feet. Analysis of this gas showed its constituents to be 80 per cent methane, 1 per cent ethane and heavier hydrocarbons and 19 per cent hydrogen. The reservoir pressure is more than 2,000 p.s.i. (pounds per square inch). At the present stage of development within the Territory there is no market for this gas, although an export potential may exist.

G. L. CORFIELD

(*See also* ELECTRIC POWER)

FUNGI are a group of living organisms which lack chlorophyll and, therefore, are incapable of utilizing the sun's energy to build up carbohydrate foods as do green plants. They obtain their food either parasitically from living organisms or saprophytically from dead organic matter. The food is absorbed in solution, often over the whole fungal body, this being a highly effective method of exploiting the resources of the environment.

The fungus body (or thallus) consists of very fine filaments which permeate the soil or other substrate on which they grow, and is seldom visible to the naked eye. Only when fungi produce their fruiting bodies or their spores is it usually possible to identify them. The fruiting bodies may be macroscopic (visible to the naked eye) or microscopic (only seen with the aid of a lens or microscope). The macroscopic forms, which include mushrooms and toadstools, are often the fungi most well known to the public because they are conspicuous.

The fungal propagating units, the spores, form directly on the hyphae or in the fruiting bodies, and after germination grow into hyphae which multiply apically and with lateral branches and form the new thallus or fungal colony. The spores may be colourless or coloured, spherical, ovoid, snake-like, star-shaped or coiled, with or without lateral or longitudinal cross walls, and with or without surface ornamentations such as roughenings, spikes, warts or appendages.

Some spores are ejected forcibly into the air from the fruiting body; others are distributed mainly by wind, sometimes for many miles, while other kinds are distributed by water or rain splash or by adherence to or passive carriage on insects, other animals and materials.

Spores of some fungi such as agarics (mushrooms) and some bracket fungi may be produced in millions. As well as the spores which are distributed in space by wind, water and other means, some fruiting bodies and spores are more resistant to adverse changes of environment, such as desiccation, and so could be said to be distributed in time; that is, many of them are capable of surviving for relatively long periods during conditions unfavourable for their germination and growth.

Fungi are world-wide except perhaps in regions of perpetual ice or in deserts. They abound, however, in areas of abundant moisture, being particularly prolific in the rain-forest areas of the tropics and on other substrates in conditions of high humidity and temperature. About 100,000 species of fungi have been described in the world, although some of these may be synonyms, and many more species will no doubt be described in the years to come.

Since the first known published record of a fungus in Papua New Guinea by Berkeley in 1842, knowledge has been accumulating on the species present. The records have been mainly of macroscopic fungi such as brackets on old logs, these being conspicuous in rain forests, and of plant pathogenic fungi, these being economically important. Records of other fungi on specialized substrates or of special importance for various reasons have also been made, including medical and veterinary fungi, entomogenous fungi (parasitizing insects), fungi causing deterioration of materials or foodstuffs, mycorrhizal fungi, (i.e., growing in a close benign association with plant roots), and fungi of other ecological niches such as the sooty moulds, and species found in soil or water, or parasitic on other fungi. As well as fungi known elsewhere in the world, species and even genera not previously known have been recorded and without doubt more species have still to be described.

The 'true' fungi, those which form sexual states, are divided into three main groups, the Phycomycetes, the Ascomycetes (sac fungi) and the Basidiomycetes (club fungi). They are well represented in Papua New Guinea, as are species in the Fungi Imperfecti, an artificial grouping of fungi whose sexual states have not as yet been discovered.

Phycomycetes. Species in the Phycomycetes, the group which does not have an elaborate fruiting body, have been recorded and include a *Synchytrium* on a higher plant, species in the family Saprolegniaceae (water moulds), species of *Entomophthora* (often occurring on insects), as well as many species of *Pythium* (often causing 'damping-off' of seedlings), and species of *Phytophthora*. Some *Phytophthora* live in the soil and may cause root rot and others are pathogenic on above-ground parts of plants; for example *P. palmivora* causes pod rot, canker and chupon wilt of cacao (*Theobroma cacao*), and *P. colocasiae* causes leaf blight of taro (*Colocasia* spp.), one of the native subsistence crops. Downy mildews, caused by other species in this group, have been recorded on various plant hosts.

Ascomycetes (sac fungi). Many species of the sac fungi or Ascomycetes have already been recorded in Papua New Guinea, and others are at present being described. The group includes species of *Aspergillus* and *Penicillium*, some of which are antibiotic producers, found widely in the soil and on decomposing and dead organic matter. Special studies have been carried out on the species found on stored brown rice and other stored native foodstuffs.

The powdery mildews, also Ascomycetes, have been recorded on many hosts, including rubber (*Hevea brasiliensis*) on which *Oidium heveae* causes secondary leaf fall and blossom loss, which in turn affects seed production.

Some of the fungal species of importance in human pathology are Ascomycetes, while others, still classified in the Fungi Imperfecti, may have ascomycetous states as yet undiscovered. To date only a few fungi causing disease in vertebrates have been recorded in Papua New Guinea, but they include several records of *Cryptococcus neoformans*, *Sporotrichum schenkii*, *Trichophyton megatrophytes*, *T. terrestre*, *Epidermophyton floccosum*, *Microsporum gypseum* and *Chrysosporium* species. Special studies have been carried out on tinea imbricata, a body tinea said to affect about 150,000 people in the lowlands and islands of the country and caused by the fungus *Trichophyton concentricum* (see SKIN DISEASES).

Some keratinophilous fungi, either human dermatophytic or skin pathogens or possible pathogens, have also been recorded in local soils.

The only fungi recorded to date as causing diseases of higher animals are *Aspergillus fumigatus* and *Candida albicans* on fowl, *Microsporum canis* on dog and *Rhiosporidium seeberi* (clinical diagnosis) on cattle.

Sooty moulds occur abundantly on insect honey dew on plant surfaces, especially in the high rainfall areas, and many species have already been recorded.

Hyperparasites, or fungi parasitic on other fungi, also occur, those recorded so far being mainly hyperparasites of fungi found on plants. particularly on plant pathogens.

Some of the Ascomycetes form large fruiting bodies on rotting logs and dead organic matter and are commonly encountered in the rain forest. Others are pathogenic on plants, causing leaf spots and other symptoms on the above-ground parts.

Various lichens have also been recorded in Papua New Guinea. Each colony is a self-supporting symbiotic association of a fungus and an alga, the fungi mainly belonging to the Ascomycetes group. They occur very commonly on the upper surface of some leaves and on the bark of trees.

Basidiomycetes (club fungi) include the smuts and rusts, some of which are among the most economically important fungi in the world. In Papua New Guinea one probable and two confirmed outbreaks of coffee rust, caused by *Hemileia vastatrix*, have been recorded since 1892. The successful eradication campaign of 1965 was assessed as costing $70,000, a non-recurring sum, but the rust was prevented from reaching the main coffee areas, which probably prevented losses of millions of dollars per annum. Many other rusts, including two species on maize, and some smuts, including two other species on maize and one on rice, have been recorded on crop plants and on indigenous plant hosts.

Another group in the Basidiomycetes includes the agarics, or mushrooms and toadstools. The indigenous people eat some of the naturally occurring mushrooms, and a few cases of deleterious effects after eating have been attributed to some species. In the Wahgi Valley the Kuma people attribute a local temporary 'madness' to several species of mushroom. The mushrooms cultivated in Australia and other temperate countries have been imported into Papua New Guinea as spawn, but to date mushroom cultivation has not been attempted on a commercial scale. Some of the native mushrooms are luminous, and a special study has been made of these species.

Other members of the Basidiomycetes abound in the rain forest, including puff-balls, stinkhorns, bird's nest fungi, coral fungi and fungal brackets. The great majority of the bracket fungi help to break down logs and other decomposing organic matter, but a few are plant pathogens causing root rots of economically important tree species such as rubber, cacao and coffee.

Some of the thread blights on the upper parts of plants, and root and plant collar-attacking fungi, belong to the Basidiomycetes, as does the reputed cause of the die back in cacao, one of the most serious diseases in the plantations (*see* COCOA INDUSTRY).

Some of the mycorrhizal fungi belong to the Basidiomycetes, although one of the genera (*Endogone*) found to be widespread in other countries is a Phycomycete.

Some of the most commonly encountered entomogenous fungi are species of *Septobasidium*. These fungi form grey felt-like growths covering colonies of scale insects from which they derive their nutrients.

'Imperfect' fungi. Many species of Fungi Imperfecti, which have no known sexual states (they reproduce vegetatively by means of conidia or asexual spores), occur in a wide variety of habitats. It is believed that most of these species are conidial states of Ascomycetes whose ascus (or sac) states no longer exist or have not yet been discovered. Some species recorded in this group occur as plant pathogens on the major plantation and cash crops (coconut, cacao, coffee, rubber, tea, pyrethrum, peanuts and vegetables), on subsistence crops (sweet potato, yams, tapioca, bananas, etc.), and on pasture and shade species, forest trees, ornamentals and other plants; many other species live saprophytically on decomposing or dead organic matter.

Cellular and 'true' slime moulds. No species of cellular slime moulds (Acrasiales), which form an aggregated cellular mass or pseudoplasmodia and live in the soil or on dung, have been recorded as yet in Papua New Guinea. Species of 'true' slime moulds (Myxomycetes), however, have been found on various substrates.

Quarantine restrictions against the importation of pests and diseases of plants, man and other animals are rigorously policed. This practice has excluded many of the fungal diseases of plants such as witches broom (*Crinipellis perniciosa*), Ceratocystis wilt (*Ceratocystis fimbriata*), and some pod diseases (including *Monilia roreri*) of cacao, South American leaf blight of rubber (*Microcyclus ulei*), blister blight of tea (*Exobasidium vexans*) and Panama disease of bananas (*Fusarium oxysporum* f. *cubense*), which cause considerable damage in other countries. Coffee rust (*Hemileia vastatrix*), one of the most devastating diseases known, has breached the quarantine barrier twice for sure and probably three times since 1892, but has been successfully eradicated. Many plants and animals are still free from other fungal diseases recorded overseas, and it is probable that lack of records for some of these at least indicates absence of the fungi and not merely undiscovered occurrence.

Export restrictions on fauna and flora including fungi operate under Papua New Guinea laws; export is only allowed under permit, this measure having been introduced to prevent the exploitation of the country's wildlife and other natural resources. Permits to export fungi are issued to *bona fide* collectors for scientific institutions, with certain provisos, mainly that portion of the collections will be returned to the country after study.

National fungal collection. The national fungal collection is lodged in the Department of Agriculture, Stock and Fisheries at Konedobu near Port Moresby, and consists of dried and preserved specimens of both macro- and micro-species. Portions of some of the collections have also been lodged with the Commonwealth Mycological Institute and the Royal Botanic Gardens in England, and with overseas specialists of various fungal groups.

J. R. Edgerton and T. L. W. Rothwell, 'The distribution of infectious and parasitic diseases of animals in Papua and New Guinea', T. P. N. G. Department of Agriculture, Stock and Fisheries, *Research Bulletin*, Veterinary Science Series, no. 1, 1964; D. Frey, 'Isolation of keratinophilic and other fungi from soils collected in Australia and New Guinea', *Mycologia*, vol. 57, 1965; R. Heim and R. G. Wasson, 'La folie des Kuma', *Cahiers du Pacifique*, no. 6, 1964; M. Reay, 'Mushrooms and Collective Hysteria', *Australian Territories*, vol. 5, 1965; D. E. Shaw, 'Plant pathogens and other microorganisms in Papua and New Guinea', T. P. N. G. Department of Agriculture, Stock and Fisheries, *Research Bulletin*, no. 1, 1963; —— 'Coffee Rust Outbreaks in Papua from 1892 to 1965 and the 1965 eradication campaign', T. P. N. G. Department of Agriculture, Stock and Fisheries, *Research Bulletin*, Plant Pathology Series, no. 2, 1968.

DOROTHY E. SHAW

G

GAB-GAB. People of West Irian. Reference:
J. van Baal, 'Een reis naar het Gab-Gab-gebied (Midden-Fly-rivier)', *Tijdschrift voor Indische taal-land- en volkenkunde*, vol. 80, 1940.

GADSUP. People of the Eastern Highlands District. References:
B. M. du Toit, 'Filiation and Affiliation among the Gadsup', *Oceania*, vol. 35, 1964-5.
———— 'Gadsup Culture Hero Tales', *Journal of American Folklore*, vol. 77, 1964.
M. M. Leininger, 'Kainantu Open Electorate: (2) A Gadsup Village Experiences its First Election' (New Guinea's First National Election), *Journal of the Polynesian Society*, vol. 73, 1964.
J. B. Watson, 'Loose Structure Loosely Construed: Groupless Groupings in Gadsup?', *Oceania*, vol. 35, 1964-5.

(*See also* KAINANTU)

GAHUKU-GAMA. People of the Eastern Highlands District. References:
K. E. Read, 'The Gahuku-Gama of the Central Highlands', *South Pacific*, vol. 5, 1951-2.
———— 'Missionary Activities and Social Change in the Central Highlands of Papua and New Guinea', *South Pacific*, vol. 5, 1951-2.
———— 'Nama Cult of the Central Highlands, New Guinea', *Oceania*, vol. 23, 1952-3.
———— 'Marriage among the Gahuku-Gama of Eastern Central Highlands, New Guinea', *South Pacific*, vol. 7, 1953-4.
———— 'Cultures of the Central Highlands, New Guinea', *Southwestern Journal of Anthropology*, vol. 10, 1954.
———— 'Morality and the Concept of Person among the Gahuku-Gama', *Oceania*, vol. 25, 1954-5.
———— 'Leadership and Consensus in a New Guinea Society', *American Anthropologist*, vol. 61, 1959.
———— *The High Valley.* New York, 1965.

GAIAS, Simon, bishop, was born about 1920 in a Valuana village in East New Britain. He had just completed his training at the Theological College and was working in the Baining region when the Japanese landed in New Britain. He remained working among the Baining people until after the war, when he went to Leigh Theological College in Sydney. Two years later he returned to the Baining area and first served as an ordained Methodist minister in Gaulim village. He was ordained bishop on the formation of the United Church. He now lives at Maleguna in Rabaul.

He has travelled to Fiji, India, Britain, America and Africa on Church affairs.

GAMBLING. The variety and multi-racial character, though not the extent, of gambling in the Territory of Papua and New Guinea may be gauged from the following extract from the Gaming Ordinance 1959, in which 'unlawful games' are defined as including *inter alia*: 'the games known as or called respectively "fan tan", "fan-tan-troy", "troy", "pak-a-pu", "two-up", "heading them", "sin-ki-loo", "tray-bit peter", "yankee grab", "hazard", "pitch-and-toss", "banker", "red-and-white", "roulette", "baccarat", "crown and anchor", "ace of hearts", "ins-and-outs", "mina dina", "back-gammon", "laki", "satu" and "kuk"'. At least five of these are of Chinese origin; 'crown and anchor' and 'two-up' or 'heading them' are principally Australian, as against the general European character of most of the remainder; and the last three are adaptations by indigenes of common card and dice games.

Expatriate gambling. Europeans and Asians brought with them the gambling games of their homelands and continued—and continue—to play them, legally and illegally, in much the same way and under much the same conditions as in those homelands. The alien environment, the loneliness, adventurism, and the relatively short arm of the law in the early days, may all have played a part in intensifying the extent of gambling and the amount of the stakes, and gambling games still provide one of the most successful sources of funds for charity, but otherwise there is nothing remarkable about European and Asian gambling in Papua and New Guinea.

Indigenous gambling. Among the local peoples the picture is rather different. Little enough is known of the pre-European games, but there seem to have been none that depended solely on luck for appeal. In fact, the concept of luck seems foreign to societies that are regulated by man's attitude to his neighbours and to the spirit world. Accidents, death, disease, and disaster occur through non-observance of taboos, and through enmity on the part of man or the ancestors. The attitude suggests fate rather than luck.

On the other hand, competition on the individual level is emphasized in many societies, both in the form of games—archery contests, canoe races, and much of the warfare—and in the very fabric of life: the 'big man' syndrome. Though luck—the accident of hereditary status, the failure of a rival's yam crop—may play a part in the creation of a 'big man', the attainment of such status is attributed by the achiever to the possession in himself of the necessary personality attributes. This is reflected in the rationalization affected by many native gamblers: the winner is likely to boast and believe that he has won, not from luck, but because he has the psychological attributes necessary for success— because in fact he is, at least in this one aspect and at this time, a 'big man'. The loser, on the other hand, may attempt to acquire or salvage prestige by boasting of the money he has lost, how much he has been able to afford to throw away on this pursuit. The use of talismans and other magic to ensure success is also widespread.

Native gambling is basically a product of the contact situation. Its causes and extent have not yet been studied, but some of the factors can be determined. To begin with, gambling, like drinking, is one of the easily accessible means of imitating European behaviour. But it would be misleading to imply that it has cargo-cult overtones, though the element of obtaining quantities of cash or 'cargo' for a small outlay lies at the base of cargo cults [q.v.] and all gambling. Though gambling has been common in well contacted areas since the early days of settlement—just how early has not been determined—the Territory-wide gambling at present in evidence is almost certainly a reflection of the extreme disruption of native society and of extensive contact with Europeans during and in the period subsequent to World War II. The gambling habits of Allied troops may well have played no small part, especially in providing the models for the games.

An important prerequisite for gambling is ample leisure. Time for non-productive pursuits, whether these are talking or playing games, has always been a feature of native society—especially for the men, who are normally exempt from unending household tasks. Wage labour has not made serious inroads on native time. In fact, European employment away from the village may provide increased leisure, and often a great deal of concomitant boredom, by freeing the employee from the numerous small jobs and obligations entailed by village life.

A second prerequisite is an economy based on cash or some other recognized medium of exchange. While gambling may be carried out with goods, the difficulty of finding equivalent stakes, and of giving and receiving 'change', soon becomes apparent. In some unsophisticated areas, gambling is still carried on with non-monetary stakes such as pieces of betel pepper, lime sticks, shells, pocket knives, or lengths of string; but these are often merely tokens, redeemable for cash at some later stage, in areas where actual coins are short; or else games of this type may be played for amusement only and the stakes

returned to participants at the conclusion of play. There are stories of unsophisticated natives who have staked a watch against a betel-nut and lost; but such incidents cannot have been common.

With increasing opportunities for employment, and increased marketing facilities, cash in reasonable quantities has been available for some time now to natives of almost all areas—and not only to the young labourers. Increased cash income, however, has not always brought with it increased opportunities for spending. Little cash is required for life in a village, even where money payments are replacing traditional goods for bride-price, compensation, and feast contributions; and trade-store goods account for only a relatively small proportion of these cash resources—though it must be admitted that drinking in town areas accounts for a great deal more. Thus, apart from money saved for a special purpose, a bride or an outboard motor, there is much fluid cash in native hands to circulate through gambling.

Economic consequences. An 'easy-come-easy-go' attitude to cash is strengthened by the fact that loss on the part of natives living close to their own gardens, or on plantations with rations supplied, is not fraught with serious economic consequences, at least at the level of sustenance. At the same time, the loss of a few dollars can be a serious blow to a household in a migrant community wholly or largely dependent on a cash income; and it is just the migrant-labour communities that are most prone to gamble, for a number of reasons—greater association with Europeans, regular income (contrasted with crop producers, with sporadic incomes paid into a bank account rather than as cash), need for social contacts with fellow villagers and for competition with strangers, younger average age, and the irresponsibility and contempt for authority apparent in many people away from the home environment. Nevertheless, the economic consequences of gambling at present are far from being as serious as those of drinking, and many police and religious authorities appear to regard gambling, in the economic rather than the moral aspect, as a nuisance rather than as a menace.

The mechanics of gambling. Card games are definitely the preferred form of gambling. Dice games (*satu*) are also widely known, however, and in some areas, such as the West Sepik District, play at dice is more frequent than play at cards. The dice themselves are sometimes manufactured locally, from the woody fruit of a variety of sago palm or similar materials. Two-up has not been adopted, except by native ex-servicemen, who sometimes follow the Australian tradition of playing two-up once yearly, on Anzac Day. Betting on competitive games, such as golf-putting, is reported to be popular in some parts of the Highlands, but it is not common elsewhere.

Card games most favoured include *kings*, *mani*, *kuk*, *swip*, *siaman-rais* or *sewenlip*, and *laki*; only the last three, based on the European games of casino, rummy, and baccarat, are normally played for stakes. Other European games such as poker and pontoon are played by some but are not widely known. By far the most important game, in terms of popularity and distribution, is *laki* (Lucky). It is played in many variants through the Territory, and disputes about rules are not uncommon. The account below describes the game prevalent in Rabaul in 1967.

Laki may be played, in theory, by any number of players from two to seventeen, but the usual number is around eight. Three cards are dealt to each player, who places a stake in the centre. Stakes are usually of ten cents per player, but dollar stakes are frequently played. Games with unit stakes of ten and twenty dollars have been reported. At any stage any player may call for doubling (standard two) or tripling (standard three) of unit stakes. After the placing of the stakes, the hands are examined, and the player who holds the highest hand takes all the stakes.

The hierarchy of hands is as follows—aces count as one, picture cards as ten: three aces; three threes; three kings; three queens; three jacks; three tens; any other combination of picture cards and/or tens; any three cards whose added value is ten or a multiple of ten; any three cards whose added value is a figure whose last digit is nine; any three cards whose added value is a figure ending in eight, seven, six, etc.

If two players have equal hands, the stakes are usually left for a further round; if three or more players have equal counts, the stakes may be divided evenly among the winning players. There is no bank and no betting. The stakes and odds are even for all, with the result that men who play consistently neither win nor lose. With ten cent stakes, the individual loss from an evening's play is rarely more than three dollars, while wins can range up to ten times that amount, depending on the number of players.

Play is usually at night, and clandestinely because of the illegality; however, games may be played at any time players have leisure and reasonable freedom from interruption. The location may be a house in a village, a bush area near the village, behind a building, or in native servants' quarters. The players are usually men, although only very unsophisticated male players object to women playing, provided they have the means. Factors operating against extensive participation in gambling games on the part of women include their lower social and economic status and the fact that they tend to be more interested in security than in chance, especially when there are children. Where these factors are not apparent, as among single girls in sophisticated urban areas, women can often be found gambling against each other and against men.

Normal social and kin obligations remain unchanged in the gambling context, and gifts and loans between relatives and friends are common. Credit is extended, and losers will often pledge a high-value article, such as a bicycle, if they do not have the cash to cover a loss. Fights are not uncommon, but they usually stem from tensions, aggravated by alcohol, unrelated or only marginally related to the gambling situation. Cheating occurs but is rare, less because of natural honesty than because of lack of sophistication on the part of many players, because the game of *laki* affords few opportunities for cheating, and because the cheap and worn packs of cards normally used do not lend themselves readily to marking or manipulation. The commonest method of cheating consists of secreting extra cards behind the knee, an easy feat in a squatting position.

Gambling and the law. Gambling in Papua and New Guinea is covered in the first place by the basic provisions of the criminal code, supplemented by a number of Gaming Ordinances and certain provisions of the Native Administration and Native Regulation Ordinances. European and Asian gambling are penalized principally according to the various Gaming Ordinances, which prohibit, in general, all forms of playing for money except certain approved types of lotteries, betting on horse-races, and lotto (bingo, housie-housie), and similar games when conducted for charity or under carefully defined conditions, specifying, for example, the way in which stakes are to be divided up into prize-money, expenses, profit and gifts to charity. The Gaming Ordinance 1959-1962 provides a penalty of $50 for participation in a gambling game, and $200 or six months' imprisonment for running a gaming house or non-approved lottery. According to the usual practice of British and Australian law, cheating is regarded as intent to defraud, and gaming contracts are null and void.

Natives are usually charged under the Native Administration Ordinance 1921-1963, which provides lower penalties; section 103 allows for a penalty of $6 or six months' imprisonment for 'any native who . . . plays cards for money or gambles in any way'.

The most recent legislation is the controversial Gaming (Playing Cards) Ordinance 1965, assented to 28 September 1966, which prohibits the importation of playing cards into Papua and New Guinea, the manufacture of playing cards, and the adaptation of 'anything for use as or in substitute for playing cards'; penalty $200. The Commissioner of Police may license a 'hotel, club, mess hall or other building or institution' for the playing of cards, at a fee of $5 (Gaming (Playing Cards) Regulations 1966), and play is legal anywhere with cards hired or borrowed from such licensed premises, provided the cards are returned as soon as practicable after play has finished. Otherwise, as the Ordinance blankly states, 'a person shall not play at cards', penalty: three months' imprisonment, but under the provisions of the Local Courts Ordinance 1963-1966 magistrates have the option of imposing a fine of up to $50. Contrary to popular European and native opinion, neither the Ordinance nor any later Regulation prohibits the possession, purchase, or sale of playing cards.

The Gaming (Playing Cards) Ordinance was passed through the Papua and New Guinea House of Assembly principally by native members, against strong but by no means unanimous European opposition, on 2 September 1965; an immediate attempt to repeal the bill before it became law was heavily defeated on 23 November 1965. The bill was intended to curb native gambling, but because of loopholes and deficiencies it has to date, late 1967, largely failed. Further modifications will no doubt give the legislation the desired force, and after present stocks of cards are used up the playing of *laki* and other card games may well be brought to a virtual standstill. But it is not likely that gambling will totally cease; probably other forms of gambling will become more popular and usurp the place now held by card-playing.

H. I. Hogbin, *Transformation Scene*. London, 1951; D. C. Laycock, 'Three Native Card Games of New Guinea and their European Ancestors', *Oceania*, vol. 37, 1966-7; ——— 'Three More New Guinean Card Games, and a Note on "Lucky" ', *Oceania*, vol. 38, 1967-8.

TERRITORY OF PAPUA AND NEW GUINEA LEGISLATION

The Criminal Code (Queensland, adopted), continued by the Papua and New Guinea Act 1949-50.
Gaming Ordinance 1959-62.
Gaming Regulations 1961-62.
Gaming (Playing Cards) Ordinance 1965.
Gaming (Playing Cards) Regulations 1966.
Local Courts Ordinance 1963-66.

TERRITORY OF PAPUA LEGISLATION

The Criminal Code (Queensland) 1899 adopted by The Criminal Code Ordinance 1902.
Gaming Ordinance 1912-50.
Native Regulation Ordinance 1908-63.
Native Regulations 1939-62.

TERRITORY OF NEW GUINEA LEGISLATION

The Criminal Code (Queensland) 1899, adopted by The Laws Repeal and Adopting Ordinance 1921-39.
Gaming Ordinance 1922-50.
Native Administration Ordinance 1921-63.
Native Administration Regulations 1924-62.

HOUSE OF ASSEMBLY DEBATES RELATING TO THE GAMING (PLAYING CARDS) BILL
1965: sessions of 21 May, 25 August, 2 September, 23 November.
1966: sessions of 7 March, 8 March, 14 June, 15 June.

D. C. LAYCOCK

GARIA. People of the Madang District. References:
P. Lawrence, Social Structure and the Process of Social Control among the Garia, Madang District, New Guinea. Ph.D. thesis, University of Cambridge, 1951.
——— *Land Tenure among the Garia.* Canberra, 1955; republished in *Studies in New Guinea Land Tenure*, by I. Hogbin and P. Lawrence. Sydney, 1967.
——— 'Cargo Cult and Religious Beliefs among the Garia', *Internationales Archiv für Ethnographie*, vol. 47, 1954.
——— 'The Garia of the Madang District', *Anthropological Forum*, vol. 1, 1963-6.
——— *Road Belong Cargo*. Melbourne, 1965.

GEOLOGY of New Guinea is complex, and to enable the reader to follow the detailed geological account given later, a simplified account will be given here first. The most significant features are shown in Fig. 1.

A 60-mile-wide belt containing metamorphic and intrusive igneous rocks runs through the centre of mainland New Guinea and the islands to the south-east. The metamorphic rocks consist mainly of altered sedimentary and volcanic rocks of Jurassic and Cretaceous age, and to a lesser extent of lower Tertiary age. The intrusive rocks are predominantly Tertiary in age. This metamorphic belt can be conveniently divided into three geographical units, which are, from west to east, the central Highlands, the Owen Stanley Range, and the line of islands from Goodenough Island to Rossel Island.

The watershed of the central Highlands coincides with a transition from unmetamorphosed sediments in the south to highly deformed, often metamorphosed sediments and volcanics with many igneous intrusions to the north.

To the south of the metamorphic belt of the central Highlands there is a belt of unmetamorphosed Mesozoic rocks, and in one area, the Kubor anticline, a small area of Palaeozoic metamorphic and igneous rocks is exposed.

North and south of the central mountain chain lie widespread Tertiary deposits, derived in part from erosion of the central core, in part by accumulations of limestone and volcanic products. The igneous component increases to the north and east. The West Papuan shelf has long been a fairly stable area, and the Mesozoic and Tertiary rocks preserved there have experienced little folding. The area is devoid of igneous activity or mineralization.

The area called here the 'Papuan geosyncline' is a much more mobile zone than the West Papuan shelf. Throughout Mesozoic and Tertiary times deep sedimentary basins existed here, not always on the same site, and great thicknesses of sediment accumulated. These deposits have been subjected to considerable thrusting, folding and faulting.

The south-east Papua region is a complicated area of Tertiary rocks, containing many basic igneous rocks and also some folded sedimentary strata, some possibly as old as Cretaceous.

The mountain ranges along the north and northeast coasts of New Guinea are geologically different from the rest of the island. The Torricelli Range consists of folded upper Tertiary sediments (mainly upper Miocene and Pliocene) on a basement of metamorphic rocks (possibly Oligocene). The Adelbert Range differs from the Torricelli in that the folded upper Tertiary sediments overlie unmetamorphosed lower Tertiary sediments and volcanics. In the Finisterre Range the lower Tertiary volcanic 'basement' is overlain by upper Tertiary sediments in which middle Miocene limestone predominates.

North of the Owen Stanley Range ultramafic

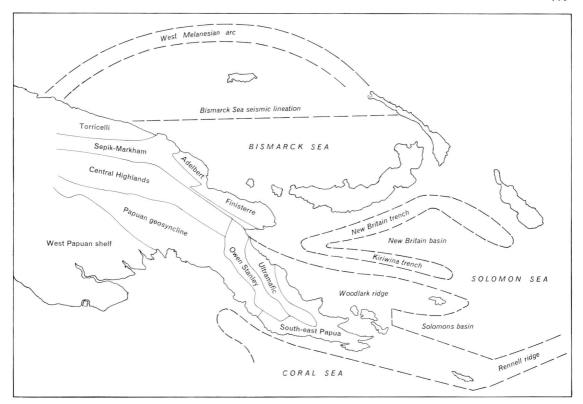

Fig 1. The principal geological features.

and basic igneous rocks constitute the Papuan ultramafic belt. This is believed to be a slice of old sea floor and mantle that has been thrust over the continental rocks of the Owen Stanley Range. Ultramafic rocks north of the central Highlands may have been similarly faulted into position.

Tertiary sediments and volcanics bordering the Papuan ultramafic belt in the Cape Vogel area, are largely masked by Quaternary alluvium and volcanics.

Apart from the metamorphic islands of the D'Entrecasteaux-Louisiade group, all the main islands—New Britain, Bougainville, New Ireland and Manus—are built entirely of Tertiary materials, some having a volcanic basement going back to Eocene time and others having a more recent origin.

GEOLOGICAL HISTORY OF MAINLAND PAPUA NEW GUINEA

Palaeozoic rocks form the basement beneath the south-western corner of the mainland, extending as far north as the central Highlands and as far east as the Gulf of Papua. The rocks crop out in the Kubor and Muller anticlines in the central Highlands, and on the south-west coast, and are known from boreholes. Igneous, sedimentary and metamorphic rocks are represented. The term 'Oriomo

spur' has been applied to an area of granitic rocks that extends from Cape York beneath Torres Strait to the south coast of Papua.

The south-west corner of mainland Papua New Guinea can be regarded as a peripheral part of the Australian continent, unlike the rest of New Guinea.

Mesozoic rocks of the mainland were formed by sedimentation from the Australian proto-continent, from the Kubor landmass which was emergent at that time, and by accumulation of volcanic products and limestone.

In the area of the West Papuan shelf the Mesozoic sediments are less than 5,000 feet thick. Much greater thicknesses were deposited in the various troughs that made up the Papuan geosyncline, and the main trough has over 23,000 feet of Mesozoic sediments, mainly Upper Cretaceous.

North of the Papuan border Jurassic shales are discontinuously exposed along a belt extending from Telefomin to Kundiawa in which Mesozoic sediments attain thicknesses of 2.5-5 miles. In Lower Cretaceous time vulcanism developed in the north of the basin of deposition, providing submarine volcanic rocks, tuffs and material for greywacke deposition. Virtually no Mesozoic rocks are known north of the Sepik River and the geosyncline possibly never extended beyond this.

In eastern Papua the Mesozoic sediments are all

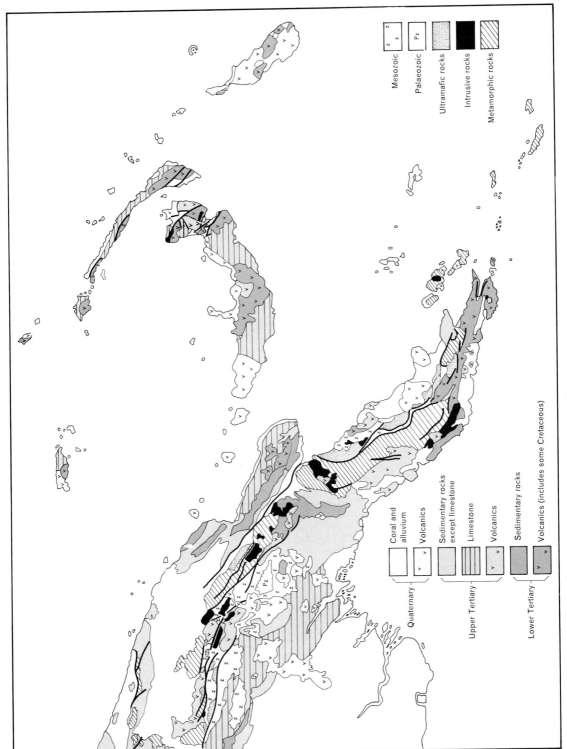

Fig 2. Geological map.

Mesozoic

Palaeozoic

Ultramafic rocks

Intrusive rocks

Metamorphic rocks

Quaternary
- Coral and alluvium
- Volcanics

Upper Tertiary
- Sedimentary rocks except limestone
- Limestone
- Volcanics

Lower Tertiary
- Sedimentary rocks
- Volcanics (includes some Cretaceous)

metamorphosed, so ideas on the original conditions of deposition are rather speculative. There was probably a trough containing 6-7 miles of sediment of overall sialic composition but with some limestone and basalt. This appears to be of Cretaceous age and geosynclinal rocks of Jurassic or older age have not yet been proved.

The Papuan ultramafic belt consists of three layers: 2.5-5 miles of peridotite at the base; 2.5 miles of gabbro in the middle; and 2.5-4 miles of basalt at the top. These rocks are of Jurassic and/or Cretaceous age, although they were emplaced against the metamorphic core only in lower Tertiary time.

Tertiary. Intermittent marine deposition occurred during Eocene and early Oligocene time in the Gulf area and regions to the east. Western Papua was an emergent area. The basalt pillow lavas which make up much of south-east Papua are partly Cretaceous and partly Eocene. In the south Sepik area Upper Cretaceous and lower Tertiary marine clastics and volcanics were deposited.

Deposition continued into upper Oligocene time and transgressed onto the West Papuan shelf but regressed from the emergent Papuan peninsula. The maximum thickness of upper Oligocene sediments, mainly mudstones and greywackes, was deposited in the Aure trough (north of the Gulf of Papua). The oldest rocks in the Torricelli Range are probably Oligocene, and in the Adelbert-Finisterre Ranges the oldest rocks are lower Oligocene volcanics, followed by upper Oligocene volcanics and sediments.

In Miocene times there were two areas of dominantly clastic sedimentation south of the ranges, the Aure trough and the Mendi basin, where mudstones and greywackes (largely turbidites) were deposited. Miocene limestones are extensively developed in the western part of the Papuan geosyncline, on the West Papuan shelf, and in the Finisterre area where they overlie lower Miocene sediments and volcanics. In the Cape Vogel basin middle Miocene and younger clastic sediments, limestones and pyroclastics were deposited. A thick succession of subaerial pyroclastic rocks and lava flows of upper Tertiary age were deposited on the southern flanks of the Owen Stanley Range, and were the source of much of the volcanic greywacke in the Papuan geosyncline.

Volcanics of Miocene and Pliocene age cover large areas south of Tapini and east of Port Moresby. A thousand feet or so of Pliocene sediments cover much of the Miocene limestone on the West Papuan shelf, but thick Pliocene sedimentation occurred in the areas of the Strickland River basin and the Kikori delta. Pliocene marine and terrestrial clastic sedimentation was extensive in the Torricelli and Adelbert region.

Quaternary. Thick deposits of Quaternary marine sediments were laid down in a gulf on the site of the Sepik-Ramu depression, interdigitating with fans and sheets of terrestrial sediment. These sediments now make a large bench above the Sepik swamps, which contains Pleistocene to Recent sediments. Other vast areas of Quaternary alluvium are the Fly River basin and the delta country around the Gulf of Papua. Coral grows around many parts of the coast, and uplifted coral benches are found at Milne Bay, Cape Vogel and especially in the Finschhafen area.

Considerable volcanic activity occurred in the Quaternary and continues to the present day in many places, but mainly on the islands, though a few active volcanoes such as Mt Lamington are on the mainland. The volcanic region of central New Guinea, extremely active in Pleistocene times, is now almost extinct (see LANDFORMS).

GEOLOGICAL HISTORY OF THE ISLANDS

Bougainville and Buka. The oldest rocks are probably upper Oligocene to lower Miocene and consist of subaerial andesitic and basaltic volcanics and water-laid sedimentary rocks of volcanic origin. These rocks are overlain by a lower Miocene reef limestone, which is in turn overlain by unnamed volcanics of Miocene to Pliocene age. Dioritic intrusions occur, and the important copper mineralization on Bougainville is associated with two porphyritic microdiorite bodies intruding agglomerate (see BOUGAINVILLE COPPER PROJECT).

Most of Bougainville is covered by the Bougainville group of Pliocene to Recent volcanics which consists of predominantly andesitic lavas, agglomerates and tuffs, and derived sediments.

Apart from the Oligocene to Miocene andesitic volcanic rocks of the Parkinson Range, Buka consists of the Sohano limestone, a Pleistocene reef complex which also crops out on the north coast of Bougainville.

New Ireland has an origin in Oligocene vulcanicity, with numerous basic to intermediate stocks and dykes intruding the volcanics. These rocks were intensely folded and faulted in the lower Miocene. Upper Tertiary limestones were deposited in the north of the island and now form cappings over large areas. In central New Ireland these limestones give way to sediments of volcanic origin of the same age.

In late Pleistocene times New Ireland was rapidly uplifted, with maximum movement at the southern end and along the west coast.

Southern New Ireland is cut by a major northwest trending fault, which has possibly moved a mile or two by left-lateral strike-slip faulting.

New Hanover consists of a single mountain range of probably Oligocene volcanics, which rises steeply from the south and has extensive dissected alluvial fans to the north.

Admiralty Islands. Manus Island has a nucleus of Oligocene volcanics, flanked on the north and east by Miocene limestone and other sediments. The western third of the island consists of basaltic and dacitic flows and tuffs of Pleistocene or Recent age. There is an active submarine volcano south of the Quaternary volcanic Lou Island.

New Britain originated with Eocene vulcanism, the deposits of which were folded and faulted and then covered unconformably by upper Oligocene volcanics. Basic to intermediate plutons intruded these deposits. In Miocene times considerable thicknesses of reef limestone were deposited over much of the island. Vulcanism resumed in the upper Miocene.

Much of the present mountainous topography of New Britain results from block faulting and regional uplift which started in late Pliocene times. The south coast bears much evidence of uplift continuing to the present day, but the north coast is not raised. Pleistocene to Recent volcanics occur at Rabaul, along the north coast and at the western end of the island.

The Gazelle Peninsula is structurally more akin to the islands of the Solomon-Bougainville-New Ireland group; structures trend north-west, unlike the general north-easterly strike of the southern part of New Britain. Possibly the Gazelle Peninsula has been grafted on to New Britain by strike-slip faulting.

Volcanic Islands consisting of little more than an active or recently active volcano form a long arc which runs along the northern edge of the mainland from the Sepik delta and is continuous with the line of volcanoes in northern New Britain. These islands include Manam, Karkar and Long Islands.

A chain of extinct volcanic islands with fringing reefs exists off the northern coast of New Ireland.

D'Entrecasteaux Islands. Goodenough Island consists of a central dome of metasediments and Pleistocene granodiorite, separated by clear fault boundaries from surrounding younger volcanics and coral limestone. Fergusson Island has a similar structure.

Normanby Island has a core of metamorphic rocks covered by limestones, and active basaltic volcanoes in the Esa'ala area.

Louisiade Archipelago. Many reefs and low coral islands occur in this group, but the larger islands, Misima Island, Tagula and Rossel Island, have a core of metamorphosed Mesozoic rocks.

Trobriand Islands are entirely coral islands. All the islands are low except for Kitava, which is about 500 feet high and has at least five terraces indicating intermittent uplift.

Woodlark Island is a deeply eroded lower Miocene andesitic volcanic complex with granitic and gabbroic intrusives. It is almost entirely covered by a coral reef cap. This isolated island is of interest for diverse mineralization of gold, silver, lead, zinc, copper and manganese.

SUBMARINE GEOLOGY

Bathymetry, seismic data and some sea-floor sampling reveal features of the submarine geology essential to an understanding of the total geology of the country.

The Bismarck Sea is an oval region bounded by the north New Guinea coast, the New Britain arc and the Bismarck ridge. The interior depression is over 6,500 feet and divided into the New Ireland basin and the New Guinea basin by a central rise. A well-defined earthquake zone runs east-west across the Bismarck Sea, but no topographic feature follows this line.

The Solomon Sea is divided into several ridges and trenches by structural units. The New Britain basin is over 13,000 feet with marginal depressions even deeper, and Planet Deep in the New Britain trench is 29,970 feet. The Kiriwina trench is shallower, 17,739 feet at deepest, and runs along the foot of the Kiriwina slope. The Kiriwina slope appears to be continuous with the Ramu-Markham fault zone, and is the northern boundary of a strip of continental rock called the Woodlark ridge. The Solomons basin separates the Woodlark ridge from the Rennell ridge which connects south-east Papua to the Solomon Islands.

The Coral Sea south of New Guinea is underlain by oceanic crust and may be an area of sea-floor spreading.

EARTH MOVEMENTS

Earth movements took place throughout Tertiary time, but there were two great culminations. In Eocene-Oligocene times the rocks of the ultramafic belt were thrust over the sialic rocks to the south-west, and some of the metamorphism of the Owen Stanley Range, the central Highlands and the Torricelli Range probably occurred at this time. The second great earth movement reached a peak at the end of the Pliocene and start of the Quaternary. The Tertiary sediments south of the Highlands moved southwards by gravity sliding resulting in roughly parallel zones of equal intensity of deformation which range from intense folding and thrusting in the north, through gentle folding, to a stable zone on the West Papuan shelf. These movements probably followed vertical uplift of the Highland belt.

In the northern ranges a period of folding was followed by a period of vertical movements which continue to the present day. A network of anastomosing faults is associated with uplift, and some fault-bounded strips of land have sunk between uplifted blocks. The largest depression of this kind is the Sepik-Ramu-Markham trough which separates the northern mountain ranges from the central Highlands, and in Pleistocene time was a marine gulf. It is probable that considerable strike-slip faulting (sideways movement) has also occurred, though positive proof is lacking.

Earth movements continue to the present day. Uplift is especially prevalent on the northern coast, with tilting to the south. In many ranges short steep rivers drain to the north while longer and gentler streams flow south. Uplift occurs along the north coast from the Torricelli Range to the Finisterre Range. From Lae to Morobe the coast is drowned but the remaining north coast of east Papua is uplifted while subsidence is general along the southern coast.

EARTHQUAKES

Earthquakes are concentrated in northern New Guinea (extending under the central Highlands), around the New Britain arc, along the Solomon-Bougainville-New Ireland trend, and along a distinct east-west line from near Wewak called the Bismarck Sea seismic lineation. Two minor lines of

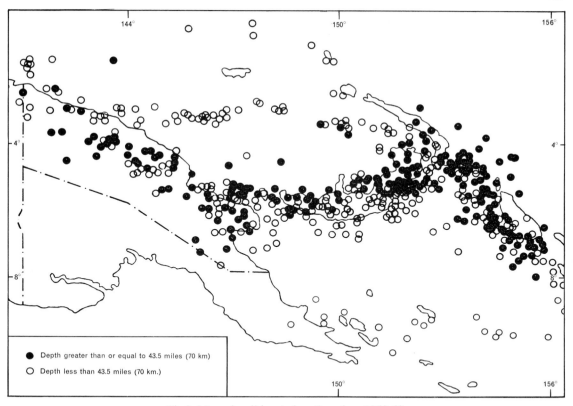

Fig 3. Map of well-located earthquakes, 1958-68.

earthquakes are located along the West Melanesian arc, which runs from New Hanover to the mainland coast near the West Irian border with a convex side to the north, and a line along the Woodlark ridge.

Earthquakes result from movement along fault planes, and by plotting the depth and location of earthquakes it is possible to determine the direction of inclination of fault planes. By a study of first movements in earthquakes it is possible to determine whether underthrusting or overthrusting is actually occurring.

It is found that the New Ireland-Buka zone dips steeply towards the Pacific, which is consistent with underthrusting towards the Pacific. The trend changes in Bougainville and the earthquake zone plunges almost vertically, consistent with strike-slip faulting. In the New Britain arc the seismic zone dips steeply to the north under the line of volcanoes, consistent with underthrusting from the south. In the Finisterre area a continuation of the New Britain seismic zone has become almost vertical, and a second seismic zone appears that dips steeply to the south, suggesting overthrusting from the south. In the western part of northern New Guinea, only this south-dipping trend is present. The Bismarck Sea seismic lineation appears to be along a fault with left-lateral strike-slip movement.

In an average year about five hundred New

Guinea earthquakes are in the magnitude range 4.5 to 5.5 on the Richter scale, but earthquakes over magnitude 8 are known. Most earthquakes occur at depths between 20 and 70 miles and deep earthquakes occur down to and exceeding 300 miles behind the New Britain trench.

TECTONIC SYNTHESIS

The present structure and the structural history of New Guinea can be explained in terms of plate tectonics, whereby the surface of the earth is considered to consist of several plates which move around and interact with one another, with occasional new patches of oceanic crust appearing at widening cracks called spreading sites. The plates move at velocities of about an inch per year, and seismic activity occurs where they interact.

On this hypothesis, when plates collide, one may override or thrust beneath the other to produce an island arc, either an arcuate island or a line of islands. The overriding plate rises at the front, and there may be indications of backward tilting as the front goes up. A deep ocean trench commonly occurs in front of the rising block, on the convex side of the arc. A line of volcanoes occurs on the inner, concave side, and earthquakes record a sloping seismic zone high on the convex side and low on the concave side. Strike-slip faulting, when plates

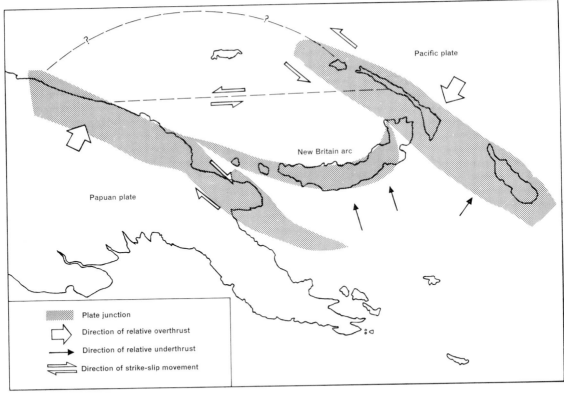

Fig 4. Summary of the tectonic synthesis of New Guinea.

move sideways past each other, may be indicated by vertical seismic zones. If these ideas are applied to New Guinea the following synthesis emerges.

The south-west part of the mainland, the West Papuan shelf and the Papuan geosyncline, are now almost free of seismic activity and can be regarded as stable.

New Britain is an island arc with most of the distinguishing features well represented except that there is no continent behind the arc. First movements of earthquakes indicate underthrusting from the south-east.

Although the New Ireland-Buka sector is not arcuate, the presence of an inclined seismic zone, volcanoes and an ocean deep suggest relationship to an island arc. First movements of earthquakes indicate underthrusting from the south-west. However in this area an oceanic plate is underthrusting another oceanic plate, not a continental one. Furthermore most ocean deeps are on the ocean side of the arc, but the New Britain trench is on the mainland side.

In northern New Guinea mountain ranges rise to the north, there is a southerly dipping seismic zone, and first movements suggest overthrusting to the north. The volcanic islands off the coast of northern New Guinea appear to be related more to the New Britain arc than to any tectonic movements of the mainland.

It appears therefore that there are three areas of thrusting—the New Ireland-Buka sector, northern New Guinea, and the New Britain arc. However, in both the northern mountains and in the New Ireland-Gazelle Peninsula-Bougainville area there is topographic, geological and seismic evidence for strike-slip movements along fault zones striking north-west.

The total situation is summarized in Fig. 4.

Two outer plates defined by seismic zones, bound a central strip which is itself divided into two parts by the New Britain arc. The southern or Papuan plate is sialic; the outer or Pacific plate, and both parts of the central strip are basically oceanic. The two outer plates appear on general grounds to be thrusting towards each other and overriding the central strip; however first movement solutions indicate that only the Papuan plate is overthrusting, the Pacific plate is being underthrust. General observations suggest that the central strip as a whole may be moving south-east relative to the two outer blocks, with strike-slip faulting where blocks meet. The New Britain arc divides the central strip. Where the oceanic rocks of the Solomon Sea are thrust beneath New Britain a volcanic arc divides the central strip into two.

Minor shearing is occurring along the Bismarck Sea seismic lineation, and movements as yet unresolved occur around the Woodlark ridge.

ECONOMIC GEOLOGY

Gold is the only metal won in substantial quantities so far. The principal gold areas were the Morobe goldfield (Wau, Bulolo, Edie Creek), the Kainantu goldfield and Misima Island, but small occurrences were worked throughout most of Papua New Guinea with the exception of the West Papuan shelf and the Papuan geosyncline. A large porphyry copper orebody now being mined on Bougainville contains an estimated 900 million tons of ore containing 0.5 per cent copper. The search for nickel has concentrated on the ultramafic belt, but the topography is not generally favourable for lateritic nickel enrichment. Many other minerals have been found and worked in small amounts and nowadays non-metallic deposits such as limestone and clay are beginning to assume economic importance.

Despite extensive exploration, commercial quantities of oil have not yet been proved in New Guinea, although substantial quantities of natural gas are known to occur. Oil exploration is continuing, both on shore and off shore.

The terrain of New Guinea makes exploration difficult and early work was severely hampered by transport difficulties, quite apart from problems of deep weathering and thick vegetation cover. The increasing application of air photo interpretation and the use of helicopters as a routine means of transport has revolutionized mapping techniques and provided a wealth of new information in recent years; knowledge of New Guinea is still growing very rapidly.

The Bureau of Mineral Resources, Geology and Geophysics in Canberra is the main repository for geological information from New Guinea, and their records and maps are of special value.

Australasian Petroleum Company Proprietary Limited, 'Geological results of petroleum exploration in Western Papua, 1937-1961', *Journal of the Geological Society of Australia*, vol. 8, 1961.

J. H. C. Bain, D. E. MacKenzie and R. J. Ryburn, 'Geology of the Kubor Anticline, Central Highlands of New Guinea', Australian Bureau of Mineral Resources, Geology and Geophysics, Record 1970/79 (unpublished).

D. H. Blake and Y. Miezitis, 'Geology of Bougainville and Buka Islands, New Guinea', Australian Bureau of Mineral Resources, Geology and Geophysics, *Bulletin*, no. 93, 1967.

Australian Bureau of Mineral Resources, Geology and Geophysics, '1 : 1,000,000 Geological Map of the Territory of Papua and New Guinea' (forthcoming).

H. L. Davies, 'Peridotite-gabbro-basalt complex in Eastern Papua: an overthrust plate of oceanic mantle and crust', Australian Bureau of Mineral Resources, Geology and Geophysics, *Bulletin*, no. 128, 1971.

———— and I. E. Smith, 'Geology of Eastern Papua: a synthesis', Australian Bureau of Mineral Resources, Geology and Geophysics, Record 1970/116 1970 (unpublished).

F. de Keyser, 'Misima Island: Geology and gold mineralization', Australian Bureau of Mineral Resources, Geology and Geophysics, *Report*, no. 57, 1961.

D. Denham, 'Distribution of Earthquakes in the New Guinea-Solomon Islands region', *Journal of Geophysical Research*, vol. 74, 1969.

D. B. Dow, J. A. J. Smit, J. H. C. Bain and R. J. Ryburn, 'Geology of the South Sepik region', Australian Bureau of Mineral Resources, Geology and Geophysics, *Bulletin* (forthcoming).

M. Ewing, L. V. Hawkins and W. J. Ludwig, 'Crustal structure of the Coral Sea', *Journal of Geophysical Research*, vol. 15, 1970.

R. W. Fairbridge, 'Coral Sea', 'Bismarck Sea' and 'Solomon Sea', in *Encyclopedia of Oceanography*, ed. R. W. Fairbridge. New York, 1966.

N. H. Fisher, *Catalogue of the Active Volcanoes of the World including Solfataric Fields. Pt. V. Melanesia*. International Volcanological Association, Naples, 1957.

J. V. Gardner, 'Submarine Geology of the Western Coral Sea', *Geological Society of America Bulletin*, vol. 81, 1970.

P. Hohnen, 'Geology of New Ireland', Australian Bureau of Mineral Resources, Geology and Geophysics, Record 1970/49 (unpublished).

D. C. Krause, 'Submarine geology north of New Guinea', *Geological Society of America Bulletin*, vol. 76, 1965.

R. P. Macnab, 'Geology of the Gazelle Peninsula, T. P. N. G.', Australian Bureau of Mineral Resources, Geology and Geophysics, Record 1970/63 (unpublished).

W. Manser and C. Freeman, 'Bibliography of the geology of eastern New Guinea (Papua-New Guinea)', Australian Bureau of Mineral Resources, Geology and Geophysics, *Report*, no. 141, 1971.

R. W. Page, The Geochronology of Igneous Rocks in the New Guinea Region. Ph.D. thesis, Australian National University, 1971.

F. K. Rickwood, 'The Geology of Western Papua', *APEA Journal*, vol. 8, 1968.

J. E. Thompson, 'A Geological History of Eastern New Guinea', *APEA Journal*, vol. 7, 1967.

———— and N. H. Fisher, 'Mineral deposits of New Guinea and Papua and their tectonic setting', *Proceedings of the Eighth Commonwealth Mining and Metallurgical Congress, Australia and New Zealand, 1965*, vol. 6. Melbourne, 1967.

ACKNOWLEDGMENT

Fig. 3 was kindly prepared by D. Denham.

C. D. Ollier and J. H. C. Bain

GERMAN NEW GUINEA. Although some German traders and others had been active in the area earlier, official German interest in New Guinea began in 1884. It continued until World War I, when Australian forces occupied Rabaul [q.v.] and other centres in September 1914.

ADMINISTRATION

The early years of German rule in New Guinea were dominated by an attempt to revive an outmoded conception of government which delayed the beginning of effective development in the colony by at least fifteen years. Germany in 1884, having abruptly joined the ranks of the colonial powers, had neither an accumulated fund of colonial doctrine and experience nor the metropolitan machinery for the government of an overseas empire. It had traders and missionaries reprieved from the danger of eclipse under foreign rule, a few influential bankers eager for new openings overseas, colonial propagandists who had whipped up substantial public enthusiasm for an overseas empire, critics of the whole venture on the grounds of expense or humanity—and a Chancellor whose determined stance on the question of acquiring colonies in Africa and the Pacific in 1884 was offset by reluctance to involve the home government in a large administrative and financial outlay.

The New Guinea Company (die Neuguinea-Kompagnie). A way out of the dilemma of having colonies without the embarrassment of having to govern them was suggested to Bismarck by some of the bankers and traders and their sympathizers in the Foreign Office. Chartered companies on the model of the East India companies of the seventeenth and eighteenth centuries were, in return for economic concessions, to undertake the administration. Bismarck seems to have accepted the scheme as suddenly as he agreed to annexations and to have believed that those who devised it knew enough about the colonies to make it workable.

From the first the weaknesses in the scheme were apparent. The chartered companies in Africa soon ceased to exercise public functions. But the company in New Guinea lingered on as the administering authority until 1899. Its failures bequeathed to the colony a forbidding reputation which was not totally dispelled even by 1914.

The New Guinea Company was closely linked with one of the largest of the private banking companies in Berlin, the Disconto-Gesellschaft, the president of which, Adolph von Hansemann [q.v.], had taken an interest in investment opportunities outside Europe for many years. In 1880 he hit upon the island of New Guinea as a completely unopened area where German investment could be profitable. His early overtures for official assistance were rejected by Bismarck, but when the colonial agitation mounted in 1884 he founded a consortium of Berlin financiers to acquire land on the New Guinea mainland as a prelude to a request for German annexation. His plans were rewarded when the German flag was raised in 1884. The consortium transformed itself into a company and applied to Bismarck for a charter, granted in May 1885. By its terms the New Guinea Company was to exercise rights of sovereignty for an indefinite period. Control over foreign relations and the administration of justice, and a vague right of supervision over measures affecting the indigenous people were reserved to the Imperial government. Otherwise this company, dominated by Berlin financiers who had never seen a Pacific island, was to administer the colony in return for the exclusive right to acquire land.

The colony acquired by Germany in 1884 comprised two distinct areas, the north-eastern portion of the mainland, known in German times as Kaiser-Wilhelmsland, and the adjacent islands to the north and north-east, known as the Bismarck Archipelago. The latter area had been frequented by German and other traders and labour recruiters for almost a decade. In the Gazelle Peninsula of New Britain (Neupommern) and the adjacent Duke of York islands (Neulauenburg) a tiny nucleus of settlers, white and part-Samoan, had grown up. They were traders in coconuts in the islands, recruiters of labour for the German plantations in Samoa and a few missionaries. Some planting of coconuts had started on the land at Ralum of Emma Forsayth [q.v.], also known as 'Queen Emma'.

What little they knew of these settlers did not appeal to von Hansemann and his associates. Their venture was to be planned on a different scale. Spurning the barter trade and the rather motley group which participated in it they looked to the mainland, where orderly, well equipped stations were to be the nucleus of a plantation economy. They were encouraged by reports sent back by their agent, the explorer Dr F. H. O. Finsch [q.v.], who had marked on his map a substantial part of the hinterland behind Finschhafen as suitable for plantations. There was promise, it was assumed in Berlin, of 'a second Java', where introduced crops such as tobacco, coffee and cocoa would flourish.

From the first the Company planned its venture on a generous scale. Even before the first administrator, Admiral von Schleinitz, arrived in 1886, Finschhafen had been selected as the capital, and additional stations had been opened at Konstantinhafen (Melamu) on Astrolabe Bay and at Hatzfeldthafen, near Bogia, where experimental crops of tobacco, cotton and coffee were soon planted. Kerawara, in the Duke of York Group, was added shortly afterwards as a base for recruiting labour in the Bismarck Archipelago. By March 1887 the Company was said to have spent two and a half million marks (about £125,000) on staff, supplies, shipping, and the importation of Javanese servants. But the directors soon had a foretaste of the difficulties that were eventually to overwhelm the chartered company. From the colony came a depressing tale of oppressive climate, disease, shipping losses, labour problems and an intractable land, which convinced von Hansemann that early estimates of the possibilities of combining administration with economic exploitation had been too optimistic. Temporary relief was obtained in 1889, when the Imperial government agreed to appoint an Imperial Commissioner to handle the administration at the Company's expense. Von Hansemann then sought further capital for investment in plantations and in 1891 launched a subsidiary company under his presidency, the Astrolabe Company (die Astrolabekompagnie), which embarked on the growing of tobacco in the vicinity of Astrolabe Bay.

Believing that the way to prosperity was now clear, the New Guinea Company resumed direct responsibility for the administration in 1892. From that year until it surrendered its charter in 1899 its activities were largely dominated by the tobacco venture. Four plantations in fairly close proximity to Stephansort (Bogadjim), managed by the Astrolabe Company, produced leaf that sold quite well on the Bremen market. But it was produced at a grievous cost in men and money.

Not surprisingly, labour was the most intractable problem. From the first the New Guinea Company had difficulty in persuading local people to work and had had recourse to the more familiar recruiting areas in the Archipelago, bringing Melanesians to the mainland under three-year contracts. The decision to grow tobacco posed new problems. Some of the managers employed by the Astrolabe Company were familiar with the Javanese and the imported Chinese workers of the Dutch tobacco plantations in Java and Sumatra. It was decided, therefore, to supplement unskilled Melanesian labour by importing Asians. Von Hansemann was able to use his contacts with the Foreign Office to organize the recruitment of Chinese in Singapore and Javanese in the Dutch East Indies. For six years from 1891 an average of a thousand or so Asian labourers a year worked on the plantations at Astrolabe Bay.

But the experiment created more problems than it solved, and in the end ruined the Astrolabe Company. Inefficient recruitment through agents provided the colony with Javanese and Chinese who appeared to have had experience of every type except tobacco cultivation. Many were physically unfit. With the Chinese came smallpox, and a high death rate which soon brought the Company into disrepute in Java and Singapore. Further recruitment was banned by the Dutch and British colonial governments in 1893. Although it was later resumed after inspections on the spot had shown that the charges of neglect were exaggerated, the interruption in recruitment and production was disastrous for the Astrolabe Company and in 1896 it was merged with the parent company.

Nevertheless, von Hansemann was reluctant to forsake his 'second Java', and the venture in tobacco was not completely abandoned until his death in 1903. But common sense prevailed to the extent that the New Guinea Company began in the late nineties to lay out coconut plantations at Berlinhafen, near Aitape, and in the Gazelle Peninsula, and to engage in the barter trade for native-grown coconuts. Its financial position was now seriously impaired. By 1898 it had spent 11 million marks in New Guinea. Exports, which had risen in the heyday of the tobacco plantations, dwindled in value to 115,400 marks in that year. As early as 1896 von Hansemann had started to negotiate with the Imperial government for the surrender of the charter. He found the Reichstag reluctant to grant compensation for all losses incurred in administration, and it was not until 1898 that the New Guinea Company found relief from the embarrassment of its charter. By an agreement with the Imperial government in that year, which took effect on 1 April 1899, it surrendered its rights of sovereignty in return for the sum of 4 million marks to be paid over ten years and the right to add 50,000 hectares of land in Kaiser-Wilhelmsland to the extensive areas it claimed to have previously acquired under its charter.

The Company, in fact, had found New Guinea impossible to administer. Its officials were inexperienced and often could not adapt themselves to the harshness and strangeness of their new environment. Death from tropical disease, illness or resignation after a short term of service led to rapid changes in personnel. Men on the spot were subjected to a barrage of instructions from Berlin, for von Hansemann's enthusiasm for the new colony was not confined to its plantations. 'In the morning hours before he left for the bank', wrote a biographer, 'Adolph Hansemann ruled New Guinea'.

Relations with the indigenous people were theoretically well intentioned and in practice haphazard. Confident that work for the Company could not fail to benefit the people, the directors took steps to check abuses by legislating for control over the employment of labour, the alienation of land and the administration of justice. Observance of laws was another matter in a colony which was conceived primarily as a business proposition, and it was inevitable that they should be evaded when those responsible for enforcing them were themselves the main employers of labour and buyers of land.

It would, however, be easy to exaggerate the impact of the Company's administration on indigenous society on the mainland. The area of contact was small. Apart from an occasional exploring thrust into the interior, German activity in this period did not extend more than a few miles inland from the coastal stations. This meant that up to 1900, except for small pockets at Finschhafen and Berlinhafen, where missionaries were also active, the main effects of Company rule were felt in the vicinity of the tobacco plantations at Astrolabe Bay. Here villagers tended to keep uneasily aloof, ignored by officials and baffling the proselytizing efforts of the Lutheran missionaries. But the period of Company rule had one major consequence for them. Beguiled by the attractions of trade goods, Astrolabe Bay people signed away land, to which their customary rights seem often to have been dubious, to German officials who were indifferent to, or lacked understanding of, the complexities of ownership rights. The small amount of clearing done at the time left the villagers in occupation and delayed the emergence of a land problem until later years.

In the Archipelago, on the other hand, relations between white settlers and indigenous people were more varied. The New Guinea Company, having no staff or shipping to spare, could not patrol the islands regularly and relied on occasional punitive expeditions to quell unruly coasts. In 1895 it handed over responsibility for administering the Archipelago to the Imperial Judge (Kaiserlicher Richter) appointed by the home government.

Government administration. Despite its slow start German New Guinea was beginning to prosper when the Australian troops arrived in 1914. Most of the small islands of the Archipelago and the coasts of the large islands and the mainland had been brought under some degree of control and were administered from a series of district offices and government stations. Rabaul, which had become the capital in 1910, with its good wharves, botanic garden and well planned streets, over-

looked by the governor's house on Namanula
Hill, bore little resemblance to the struggling,
fever-stricken stations of the New Guinea Company. Hope for the future of German New
Guinea was high in 1914. Exports were increasing
rapidly as palms on the plantations reached
maturity. A series of scientific expeditions, equipped by German museums and societies, had paved
the way for the penetration of the mainland interior. There was much speculation about the
mineral resources of the colony and a scramble
for concessions for oil, of which traces had just
been found near the Dutch border.

These changes were the more remarkable because they occurred in the main in the last six
years or so of German rule. In 1899 little was expected of the colony. Remoteness, the difficult
terrain, the fiasco of the New Guinea Company
and the greater resources of the African colonies
left it for some years 'the stepchild of the German
Empire'. At first the home government was interested in establishing little more than a nominal
administration. The colony was placed under a
governor, who was responsible in law to the Kaiser and in practice to the Chancellor. He was
charged with the implementation of laws and instructions issued in Berlin and had power to legis-
late on matters of local concern. After 1903 he
had a Government Council (Gouvernementsrat),
consisting of nominated senior officials and private
settlers, whose functions were advisory. Much was
left to the discretion of the governor, but his scope
for local initiative was strictly curbed by the
funds and personnel at his disposal, which were
at first meagre. As late as 1908 there were only
fifty-six officials in German New Guinea. This
fact alone accounted for the slow extension of
German administrative control up to that time.

In 1899 the administrative division into two
major areas—the mainland and the Archipelago—
was retained. The greater accessibility of the latter for commercial purposes was acknowledged
when the capital was transferred immediately to
Kokopo (Herbertshöhe). For some years after that
time the white population of the mainland consisted of employees of the New Guinea Company,
now a private concern, and missionaries. A district office (Bezirksamt) at Madang (Friedrich-
Wilhelmshafen), staffed by a few officials, catered
for their needs, with a nominal responsibility for
German administration on the mainland.

The problems of government in the Archipelago
could not be so lightly dismissed. By the turn of
the century the economic frontier of the white
settlers reached out to the maritime fringes of the
colony. Traders in coconuts and labour recruiters
paid irregular visits to coastal villages from the
Solomons to New Ireland (Neumecklenburg), protected and supervised only by an occasional naval
patrol or punitive expedition. Regular administration in 1899 was confined to the Gazelle Peninsula, where an official of unusual ability, Dr
Albert Hahl [q.v.], had been stationed as Imperial
Judge from 1896 till 1899. In this time he had
managed to reverse the Company's record of in-
difference to administrative contact with the in-

digenous people about Blanche Bay, and had
created the rudiments of a system of government
which was to be followed in the colony until 1914.
Hahl's interest in the indigenous people was undoubtedly motivated by sympathy, but sprang also
from a realistic appraisal of Germany's future in
what appeared in 1896 to be a forlorn outpost,
for he had no doubt from the beginning that the
native as producer and labourer was indispensable
to the colony's material progress.

At Kokopo in 1896 Hahl encountered in micro-
cosm the typical tensions and frustrations of the
early years of contact between an aggressive white
community and primitive villages. By this time the
original nucleus of settlers at Blanche Bay had
grown. Catholic missionaries had joined the earlier
Methodists and were competing with them for
the souls of the villagers of the coastal plateau. A
few primitive settlers and the New Guinea Company had extensive claims to land, some of them
going back to the time before annexation, which
the Company had registered in the ground books
(Grundbücher) without proper survey. Labour recruiting in the inland villages and fears that the
plantations would spread from the coast had em-
bittered relations between whites and the indigenous people. Equally, these new conditions, in
upsetting traditional patterns of behaviour and
alignments in the villages, had intensified the endemic feuds and warfare of the Peninsula.

The means at Hahl's disposal in 1896 were
meagre: a secretary and a police force of thirty
or forty natives were the sum of the human resources he could command. Convinced by his
observations on the spot and his study of local
institutions that stability within each of the small
villages and hamlets was a prerequisite for a more
general peace in the peninsula, he decided to
create a link with the villages by recognizing
headmen, who were to be responsible for law and
order within their respective communities. It was
difficult to find such leaders and impossible to find
men who commanded a following wider than that
of the single village. Hahl's solution to the problem of dispersed authority was to require each
village to nominate a leading man as headman, or,
using one of the local terms for village leader,
luluai. The luluais were to adjudicate and impose small fines in village disputes and report
more serious cases and breaches of the peace to
the German courts.

Hahl had no illusions about the gap between his
luluai system and traditional notions of leadership
in the villages. He recognized that he was not reinforcing an indigenous pattern of authority so
much as manipulating it in order to create village
leaders with whom the government might deal.
Despite its inadequacies, the system worked well.
By the time the Reich took over, Hahl had reduced overt friction in the villages and created
points of contact between them and himself. From
the first he tried to strengthen his hold by requiring roads to be built to the inland plateau, for
which the luluais had to furnish quotas of unpaid
labourers, and by reducing some of the friction
over land. Settlers were encouraged to define more

precisely the areas that they intended to plant. Where the lands they claimed included areas actually occupied or used by the villages he created a small number of reserves by persuading settlers to surrender their more dubious titles or accept compensation elsewhere. It was clearly a temporary and piecemeal remedy for a land problem that was to endure. Hahl's own dissatisfaction with it was expressed in the recommendation that he made in 1899 to the home authorities for legislation to provide for confiscation when settlers refused to negotiate.

For several years after 1899 the Germans were slow to build on this foundation. Hahl was transferred to the Micronesian islands north of the equator, which were acquired from Spain in 1899 and administered jointly with New Guinea. The task of extending German control beyond the Gazelle Peninsula fell to the first governor, Rudolf von Benningsen. Hampered by shortage of personnel and tied to the capital for long periods by lack of transport, von Benningsen viewed his role mainly as that of patron of the white settlers and guarantor of their safety. He extended the appointment of *luluais* in the Gazelle Peninsula and the Duke of York Group and attempted, when opportunity offered, to patrol the outer islands. But he had to deal with a series of scattered attacks on settlers, and his response was a succession of punitive expeditions conducted with a ruthlessness unusual even at a time when such expeditions were accepted as a normal method of chastisement in the Western Pacific.

The only effective extension of control under von Benningsen was on New Ireland, where a government station (Regierungsstation) was opened at Kavieng (Käwieng) in 1900. It was from the first in charge of a former employee of the New Guinea Company, Franz Boluminski [q.v.], who remained there until his death in 1913. Forceful and energetic, Boluminski found his personal dominance as effective as his small police troop in establishing control on the north coast of the island. *Luluais*, subject to his firm control, were installed and used to organize the labour required for the construction of the north coast road. Peace and the road led shortly to the first white plantations on New Ireland.

Von Benningsen's uneasy tenure of office ended with his resignation in 1901. Hahl became Acting Governor, but six months later he contracted blackwater fever. A slow recuperation was followed by leave in Germany, from which he returned as governor in 1903. He remained in office until June 1914.

On the administrative side Hahl's most obvious achievement as governor was the extension of the area of effective control. Convinced that the old expedient of relying on irregular patrols and occasional punitive expeditions would have to be replaced by regular administration along the lines of that already in operation in the Gazelle Peninsula, he planned to work out from permanent government stations located at strategic points in the colony. Two conditions governed their establishment. On the one hand, the selection of sites was more or less predetermined by the existing pattern of white settlement, for up to 1914 the settlers continued to move out in advance of the administration, and the latter strove to overtake or keep up with them.

On the other hand, the need for the most strict economy set limits to the pace of administrative advance up to 1908. In this period customs duties provided the main source of internal revenue. It was supplemented by annual subsidies granted by the home government. The Reichstag's reluctance to approve more than a minimum expenditure from Imperial funds and the burden of paying from the subsidies the annual sum of 400,000 marks in compensation to the New Guinea Company meant that the colonial government had to work within a restricted budget. Consequently, stations at first were opened at long intervals and operated with skeleton staffs. By 1908 four had been added: Namatanai (1904), Kieta (1905), Aitape (1906) and Simpsonhafen (1906), which was later converted into the district office of Rabaul.

Each station had two or three officials and a detachment of the police troop, which was used for patrols of the pacified villages and penetration of new areas. Using his early experience in the Gazelle Peninsula, Hahl made the appointment of *luluais* the regular method of extending and maintaining control over the villages. Inevitably, as its range widened, the system lost some of the intimacy of contact between officials and headmen that had been sought in the Gazelle Peninsula. The *luluais* continued to be regarded as village magistrates dispensing local justice in accordance with indigenous custom, but increasingly they were assigned duties as minor administrative functionaries, responsible to the station officer for seeing that their people kept the peace, extended their gardens, worked on the roads or paid the head tax of 5 to 10 marks a year, which was introduced in 1907. To overcome the shortcomings of village leaders who had no experience outside their communities, Hahl appointed assistants, known as *tultuls*, who were usually men who after service in the police troop returned to their villages with a smattering of Pidgin English [q.v.].

After 1908 the financial resources of the government began to improve. This was due in the main to the export duty on copra imposed for the first time in that year. The steady increase in revenue it afforded pointed to the sudden acceleration in commercial activity in the last few years of German rule. Coconut planting of earlier years began to pay dividends as the palms reached maturity. Improved communications with Europe and rising prices for copra were incentives to the older companies to plant more, and to new settlers to take up land or extend the substantial trade in native-produced copra. Between 1908 and 1914 the white population almost doubled. Exports, mainly of copra, rose in value from 1,707,393 marks in 1908 to just over 8 million marks in 1913. Internal revenue, amounting to 381,900 marks in 1908 was up to an estimated 2,095,810 marks in the budget for 1914. Promise of greater economic development in turn broke down some of the resistance at home to financial aid to the colony and, coupled with rumours of mineral resources awaiting exploitation in the mainland, led to enlarged subsidies from the home government. From 1900 to 1909 the Reichstag granted 9,452,928 marks in subsidies for New Guinea, from which a sum of 4 million marks was drained off for the New Guinea Company. In the five years from 1910 to 1914, with the subsidies totalling 5,738,421 marks, the colonial government had slightly more made available for its use than in the preceding ten years. Moreover, the sum allocated each year increased. In 1914 it amounted to 1,717,022 marks and it was expected that the allocation in the three-year period from 1915 to 1917 would reach a total of seven and a half millions.

Freed from some of the more crippling restrictions imposed by shortage of money and personnel, Hahl was able to plan development on a more ample scale. Two major gaps in the coastal network were closed when stations were opened at Morobe in 1909 and at Manus in 1911. The first approaches to the penetration of the mainland interior by means of the rivers were made with stations at Angoram on the lower Sepik in 1913 and at Lae (Burgberg) on the Markham in 1914. By 1914 there were three district offices—Madang, Kavieng and Rabaul—and eight government stations. Nominally control extended over the coasts of the colony, although in fact it depended on shipping facilities and diminished in direct proportion to the distance of a particular locality from the headquarters of the district or station.

Perhaps the most impressive aspect of German rule in its last years was not so much what was accomplished, although that was considerable, as what was envisaged. Early in 1914, before he left the colony, Hahl laid before the Government Council a blueprint for the next three years. A systematic extension of control was contemplated, particularly into the interior. The new stations at Angoram and Lae were to serve as bases for a chain of posts to connect the Markham and the lower Sepik and open up the area behind the coastal ranges of the eastern mainland. New stations on the coast west of Madang and in southern New Britain and the Solomons were to strengthen the administration on the coasts and lead to the penetration of their respective hinterlands.

At the same time Hahl planned to widen the range of the administrative services within the opened area. Between 1908 and 1914 the number of officials in German New Guinea increased from fifty-six to about a hundred, approximately the same number as in Papua at the time. Where the German colony differed markedly from Papua was in the professional qualifications possessed by its officials. Most of its senior administrative officers held university degrees. About one-third of the entire staff was made up of men qualified to provide specialist services: among them were doctors, medical assistants, agricultural officers, a veterinary officer and various technical and engineering experts. In 1914 Hahl gave high priority to technical development, particularly in the extension of health services and the promotion of indigenous agriculture. Well informed and wide ranging, his planning in this respect was not matched again until after World War II.

EXPLORATION

German exploration in New Guinea began with Finsch's coastal surveys at the time of annexation. Between October 1884 and March 1885 he located the main harbours and anchorages of the mainland coast and went a few miles up the Sepik River, to which he gave the name that it retained in German times, the Kaiserin-Augusta-Fluss. Details were filled in by the first administrator, Admiral von Schleinitz, who discovered the mouth of the Markham River, and the mouth of a large river just east of the Sepik to which he gave the name Ottilienfluss (the Ramu). In a remarkable voyage in 1886 von Schleinitz travelled up the Sepik to a point just beyond Ambunti.

At first the New Guinea Company envisaged an easy conquest of the unknown mainland of its territory. The instructions to the first exploring expedition that it dispatched were as remote from the facts of the colony as was the rest of its administration. The expedition was to 'examine the general geographic, climatic and meteorological as well as the geological conditions of the country, ascertain the nature of the soil, the physical, psychic and social conditions of the natives, all with a view to the possibility of settlement and development of the area and the peaceful winning of the natives for civilization'. It was 'to advance from the coast to the interior, where possible to the border of the English territory, and then return by another route to the coast and after replenishing its equipment set off again from another coastal point for the interior and so gradually open up the whole territory'. The expedition was led by an astronomer, C. Schrader, who had been with von Schleinitz on the Sepik. With him were a botanist, M. Hollrung and a geologist, C. Schneider. In 1887 they went up the Sepik beyond the point reached by von Schleinitz and spent a few months on land near Malu, where the difficult terrain and the hostility of the local people posed insuperable barriers to exploration on foot. Their departure for Europe in 1887 put an end to von Hansemann's grandiose designs. There was no further exploration on the Sepik for twenty years.

The next area to be tackled was the coastal strip inland from Astrolabe Bay and thence to the mountains. In 1888 a journalist, H. Zöller, was commissioned by the Kölnische Zeitung to work his way from the coast. Starting from Astrolabe Bay he followed the Kabenau River to the Finisterre Ranges and climbed to a height of over 8,000 feet. Glimpsing the distant Bismarck Range, he bestowed on their peaks Christian names of the Chancellor and his family.

The death of the explorer Otto von Ehlers in a reckless attempt to walk overland from the present Salamaua south to the Papuan coast in 1895 brought private ventures into the mainland interior to an end for many years. One last attempt to go inland was made by the Company.

A botanist, Dr Carl Lauterbach, had undertaken a private journey by land in 1889, in which he followed the course of the Gogol River, near Madang, for some 70 kilometres. In 1896 he was commissioned by the Company to lead an expedition to the interior. Accompanied by a doctor, Dr H. Kersting, and E. Tappenbeck, the brother of a noted African explorer, he made his way inland from Astrolabe Bay and came to a large river, which he followed downstream for thirteen days before returning via the same route to the coast. Lauterbach's suspicion that the river he had discovered and called the Ramu was identical with the Ottilienfluss of the coast was proved correct in 1898, when Tappenbeck, later joined by Lauterbach, led an official, well equipped expedition upstream from the mouth of the Ottilienfluss to a point which was recognized as the scene of Lauterbach's previous journey. Thus the course of the middle and lower Ramu was charted.

The collapse of the New Guinea Company's administration was followed by a lull in exploring activity; private explorers and sponsors were discouraged and the colonial government had no finance for the equipment of expeditions. Exploration was confined to minor journeys inland from coastal stations, undertaken mainly as an adjunct to missionary or administrative activity, of which the most important were those of the Neuendettelsauer Mission in the Huon Gulf area. Hahl, when time permitted, found an outlet for his energy and curiosity in treks into the unexplored hinterland of the Gazelle Peninsula. In 1903, with Father Rascher of the Sacred Heart Mission, he travelled overland through unexplored territory from Toriu to Weberhafen. In 1905 he crossed the mountainous interior of New Hanover with several officials, and in 1908 he was a member of the first party to cross over the mountains from coast to coast in Bougainville.

A remarkable revival of interest in exploration and scientific research occurred after 1907. It was due partly to the need to participate with the British and the Dutch in defining the frontiers, partly to the great impetus given by scientific bodies in Germany, which provided funds for anthropological, botanical and geographical research. In their view discovery of new land was not an end in itself; they wanted as well an assessment of its human and natural capabilities. Consequently, in this period the German expeditions, stationed for months on end in the area they were studying, were usually elaborately equipped and comprised scientists with varied qualifications. As one of the most noted of them, Walter Behrmann, said later, the thrust of an adventurous individual unencumbered by equipment and companions might yield more in distance covered, but its output, measured in additions to scientific knowledge, was less than that of the expedition with a range of qualifications and skills.

The first of the large expeditions was financed by the Deutsche Kolonialgesellschaft and the government. Its object was to introduce a rational scheme for evaluating the resources of wild guttapercha on the mainland and for training the indigenous people in its collection. Dr F. R. Schlechter, a botanist who had studied the area about the lower Ramu in 1902, was in charge. Its labours extended over three years; in this time Schlechter worked inland from Astrolabe Bay, on the upper Ramu and the lower ranges of the Bismarck mountains, and at Aitape, and in the Huon Gulf area. Gutta-percha was found in considerable quantities, although tests in Germany showed that much of it was unsuitable for the industrial purpose for which it was intended, the manufacture of submarine cables. More important in extending geographical knowledge was the journey made by W. Dammköhler in 1907 overland from the mouth of the Markham River to the Ramu and thence over the Finisterres to the Kabenau River and Astrolabe Bay. In an attempt to follow the same route in a reverse direction in 1909 Dammköhler was killed by natives only a few days before he expected to reach the Huon Gulf.

The first of the expeditions whose purpose was scientific research rather than geographical discovery was sent out by the German Navy in 1907. It was led, until his death in May 1908, by a Navy doctor, Emil K. Stephan, and then by Dr A. Krämer, already famed for his work as an anthropologist in Samoa and the Caroline Islands. The expedition, which included an anthropologist and an ethnologist in addition to its directors, spent over two years in New Ireland, engaged in the studies of social behaviour and art which even today make their books standard works of reference. In the later stages of their stay in New Ireland they joined forces with another expedition launched by the Landeskundliche Kommission of the Reichskolonialamt. It was led by Karl Sapper, Professor of Geography at Tübingen, and Carl Friederici, who spent the year 1908 in New Ireland and New Hanover. The popularity of this type of work in scientific circles in Germany and rivalry between museums as collectors of New Guinea art and artefacts stimulated yet another expedition to the Archipelago, this time supported by the Hamburgisches Museum für Völkerkunde, whose Director, Professor G. C. Thilenius, had worked in the Pacific at the turn of the century. The Hamburgische Südsee Expedition was divided into two sections: one, under Dr Krämer, worked in the Carolines; the other, under a doctor of medicine, Dr F. Fülleborn, an authority on tropical diseases, worked in New Britain, the Hermit Islands and the Admiralty Islands before it shifted its attention to the mainland and travelled about 416 kilometres up the Sepik River in 1909. The expedition left the colony at the beginning of 1910 with a rich scientific booty, including 6,667 items in its ethnographic collection and 1,700 photographs, together with recordings of languages.

The investigation of the Sepik and its tributaries was the major geographical objective of the last years of German rule. The immediate incentive was the joint Dutch and German plan for defining the boundary in 1910. The German team was led by a geographer, Professor L. Schulze of Jena, and included among others a mining engineer A. Stollé who had led the German section of the English-German border expedition to the Waria in the previous year. The expedition made its way up the Sepik for 970 kilometres, crossed into Dutch New Guinea and proved that the Sepik turned south-east again, towards the central mountain chain on the German side.

Its sequel was the largest expedition undertaken in German times. The Kaiserin-Augusta-Fluss-Expedition of 1912-13 was sponsored jointly by the Colonial Office, the Königliches Museum of Berlin and the Deutsche Kolonialgesellschaft. Led by Stollé, it included among its scientists the anthropologist R. Thurnwald and Professor W. Behrmann of Berlin University as geographer. Its purpose was to explore the Sepik basin, work up the main tributaries and penetrate the adjacent mountains. The expedition made significant contributions to geographical and anthropological knowledge and Thurnwald studied the Sepik people and explored widely between the Dörper River (Yuat River) and the coast. Behrmann explored both sides of the April River and penetrated the mountain ranges to its south to a height of about 6,000 feet, whence he looked across low country to the central mountains and what he took to be the Victor Emanuel Range, discovered in Papua by d'Albertis [q.v.].

It was the last of the German expeditions and one of the last of its kind, for exploration thenceforth was to be in the Papuan style, undertaken by the adventurous amateur, either in the course of, or as a diversion from, administrative duties, or in search of gold.

NATIVE POLICY AND ADMINISTRATION

Whether the administrative competence of German officials was matched by success in dealing with the indigenous population is a difficult question. The men who passed judgment on German rule in 1919 were satisfied that the Germans had treated the indigenes badly. Murray [q.v.] whose opinions about German officialdom were to influence subsequent attitudes, deprecated what he took to be the German habit of viewing the native population only as an 'asset' in the exploitation of the country. There was evidence from German times to support his view. But there was much that he overlooked, or misunderstood because he could not envisage any criteria other than those on which his own administration was based.

However, there were resemblances between the two colonies in 1914. Both governments professed benevolent intentions, holding themselves to be responsible for the protection and 'civilization' of the indigenous people; both relied on indigenous officials in their contacts at the village level. The German system was less cautious than that of Murray, less dedicated to conservatism, for Hahl believed that adaptation in village life was a necessary concomitant of colonial rule, to be encouraged rather than deplored. German rule was often harsher and more self-interested than its counterpart in Papua at the time. On the other hand, Hahl looked more hopefully to the possibilities of development in indigenous society and to the positive role of the administration in promoting change. In this respect his ideas had slowly developed. By 1914 experience and greater resources permitted him to envisage a planned advance that was to have started in 1915. Its main features were speedier pacification of unopened areas, and within the administered districts improved health and educational services, greater attention to indigenous agriculture and more control over the employment of native labour.

While it is not difficult to establish the broad outlines of Hahl's policies or to recognize the unusual closeness of his ties with the indigenous people with whom he was in direct contact, it is quite clear that he did not control the full range of German relations with the local people. His views were not always shared by subordinate officials, some of whom were more prone to connive at injustice or behave arrogantly. Moreover, Hahl was subject to strong pressure from commercial interests. The larger firms could make direct representations to the Colonial Office through their directors at home. Acrimonious debates over some years in the Government Council showed how widely private and official attitudes to the employment of native labour diverged. On the other hand, Hahl's plans for development in 1914 found fairly general acceptance.

The harsher aspects of German rule were sometimes evident in the methods by which control was extended. Hahl deplored the barbarousness of the early punitive expeditions and under his administration most of the pacification was in fact accomplished by peaceful contact. But every year brought its crop of armed advances by the police troop, which the Germans seem to have publicized rather more than their contemporaries in other colonies. Resistance to the police troop, attacks on European life and property, and fighting between villages were punished promptly and often severely. Nor was it anticipated that the advance into the interior would be without such incidents, for the Germans planned to move forward quickly. Hahl summed up his view shortly before he left, when he said that peaceful advance was the aim, but 'force would have to be met by force'.

There was harshness, too, on the plantations. Under Imperial control the system of indentured labour, initiated by the Company, was freed from its more obvious abuses. Labour laws, revised in 1901 and 1909, contained in a precise form the conventional safeguards in regard to recruitment, pay, maintenance and medical care. Where official supervision could reach employment was policed fairly strictly. But the popularity of the islands of the Archipelago as recruiting grounds meant that supervision had to extend over vast expanses of ocean and was often impossible. In more remote places recruiters could cajole or bribe village headmen into conscripting quotas of young men. Strict conditions of housing and

medical care could be enforced on the plantations, where the death rate was remarkably reduced, but the licence granted to planters to flog
their labourers inevitably led to maltreatment.

Moreover, by 1912 it was clear that recruitment was pressing heavily on certain areas. While
Hahl accepted 10 per cent as the maximum number of young men who should be absent from
their villages at the one time, in popular recruiting areas like New Ireland, the Gazelle Peninsula
and the coast of Bougainville this figure had been
exceeded. The demand for labour was expected to
rise sharply and accounted in part for Hahl's insistence on opening the mainland. Apart from
finding new reservoirs for recruitment, Hahl envisaged two remedies. A new Labour Ordinance,
which, subject to the approval of the Colonial
Office, was to have come into operation in 1915,
tightened up conditions of recruitment and employment considerably. The second remedy, to
which Hahl gave a high priority, was to revive
the importation of contract labour from China
and South-east Asia. Arrangements for this, undertaken by the Imperial government, had just
been completed in 1914.

Except in the areas of the early alienations, it
was easier to give priority to indigenous interests
in land policy. After 1899 the exclusive right to
take possession of unowned land or to buy land
from natives was vested in the government, from
which it might be bought by private settlers. A
prospective purchaser might negotiate directly
with the owners and agree to a price, but as a rule
the purchase was made by officials, who had the
land surveyed, examined indigenous rights and
saw to it that the regulations prohibiting the purchase of land inhabited or used by the natives
were observed. The area reserved for the use of
the village was usually calculated on the basis of
one hectare per head of the population, and these
regulations seem to have been observed fairly
strictly. Inquiries for the purchase of land were
not great between 1900 and 1909. Even after
1909, with an influx of new settlers and older employees of the companies branching out for themselves, the demand was not excessive. In the
Archipelago, where most of the plantations were
located, the area held by planters increased from
67,672 hectares in 1905 to 108,000 in 1913. The
total plantation land in the colony in the latter
year, excluding that which had not been surveyed
and registered, was 180,000 hectares, of which
29,290 hectares were under cultivation.

The land problem of New Guinea in German
times lay not in the total area of land alienated
but in its location. Most of the plantations were
in the Gazelle Peninsula and near Madang on
land that had been acquired either before annexation or under the New Guinea Company's administration. The laxity with which the Company
observed the land regulations has already been explained. The lands it had conferred on itself and
the claims of settlers in the Archipelago had been
given formal recognition as freehold by 1899, but
although entered in the ground books, the
majority had not been properly surveyed or tested

against indigenous titles. In this respect the New
Guinea Company was the principal offender. In
1899 it claimed 105,620 hectares on the mainland
coast and in the Gazelle Peninsula, and had the
right, under the terms for the surrender of the
charter, to take up another 50,000 hectares on the
mainland.

The method of re-examining titles and defining
small reserves, which Hahl had tried to get the
settlers to accept voluntarily before 1899, was
given legal recognition in 1903. An Imperial law
of that year provided for the review of titles
which had already been registered and for confiscation when claimants refused to negotiate over
disputed titles. A circular issued by the Chancellor explained that rights were to be restored to
the natives by converting into Crown land for
their use land that had been illegally acquired by
Europeans. In practice, this meant that in cases of
obvious hardship or injustice to natives titles were
not to be confirmed until lands actually occupied
or used by the villages had been excised. The review was still in progress in 1914. It was virtually
completed in the Archipelago, where the surrender of disputed sites in exchange for compensation elsewhere and the excision of reserves still
left the settlers with substantial holdings in the
Blanche Bay area. On the mainland the review of
old claims was tedious and protracted. Survey
staff was inadequate; the New Guinea Company
was often unwilling to negotiate and Hahl was
anxious not to have recourse to confiscation. Instead, he adopted the expedient of postponing a
final decision until planting was contemplated,
leaving the villages to use the land in the meantime. Accordingly, when German rule ended,
there were still large unsettled claims especially
in the vicinity of Astrolabe Bay. Of the total area
of 137,144 hectares claimed by the New Guinea
Company in the colony in 1913, 56,685 hectares
had not been surveyed or registered in the ground
books, a fact which seems to have escaped the
Australian military administration when it credited
the Company with the whole area as freehold.

In the settled areas Hahl stressed the value of
encouraging villages to make better use of their
lands. In part, self-interest dictated such a course,
for the long wait for the coconut plantations to
bear created a demand from the planters for
native-produced copra, which even in 1914 accounted for almost half of the copra export. But
Hahl seems to have anticipated some advantage
for the native people in the possession of cash
incomes, and to have believed that they would
make a useful contribution to the territory's production. Officials went to great pains to get people
to grow more coconuts, collect wild gutta-percha
on the mainland or grow vegetables for the urban
market in the Gazelle Peninsula. Despite strong
criticism from planters who felt that opportunities
for earning independent cash incomes discouraged
indentured labour, the budget of 1914 confirmed
this trend in official policy with its provision for
the appointment of five agricultural experts to
assist indigenous producers.

Greater participation of the indigenous people

in the European economy was one aspect of Hahl's plan for development in 1914. The others were education and medical services. Until 1914 education was mainly in the hands of the missions [q.v.], which were left free to follow their own methods and curricula subject to increasing pressure from the government to teach German, for which a small subsidy was paid. The abandonment of this policy was contemplated in 1914. Hahl intended to extend government supervision of the mission schools. His plan, which had been discussed with the missions, envisaged a six-year course of elementary education, in which a minimum of twelve hours a week were to be devoted to subjects other than religion. Teaching was to be in the language of the locality or in German, which was to be a compulsory subject from the earliest year and the medium of instruction at the secondary level. The missions were to have had increased subsidies, but the sums mentioned in preliminary discussions were small, so that a rapid implementation of the programme could not have been contemplated.

Much more ambitious were his plans for the extension of government schools. Since 1907 there had been a government school for indigenous boys near his own house on Namanula Hill. It had a six-year curriculum, which stressed the teaching of German, and a technical branch. Pupils were brought from different parts of the colony, their number—130 in 1914—being limited by the accommodation and staff available. Four schools of this type were to have been opened between 1915 and 1917, one at Madang in 1915, the others at Kieta, Kavieng and Aitape. The ablest boys in them were to have gone on to an advanced school at Rabaul, from which recruits for the clerical ranks of the government departments were to have been drawn.

No matter affecting the indigenous people received more earnest attention in German times than medical services and medical research. In 1913 about one-fifth of the officials employed in the colony were doctors or qualified medical assistants. They were supplemented by medical staff employed by the large firms and the missions. Even after allowance has been made for the fact that care of Europeans occupied part of their time and that a high priority was given to indentured labourers and villages in the vicinity of administrative centres, the German record was unusual for its time. Patrols of more distant villages were regularly undertaken and some provision was made for village hygiene and first aid by training young men at the hospitals for indigenous people located at Rabaul and Namatanai. After a few months' instruction they were sent back to their villages as 'medical *tultuls*' (Heiltultul). A greater extension of health services in the villages was planned in 1914, when it was intended within a few years to have medical stations at Morobe, Manus, Buin, the Ramu and south New Britain.

Because the emphasis on developing the indigenous communities was new in 1914 and virtually untried, it is difficult to predict the direction in which German administration would have moved had it not ended in 1914. One fact alone is clear: the Germans did not envisage a static relationship with New Guinea people. The discovery of gold and of the Highlands, which would almost certainly have come more quickly under German rule, might have produced sharpened conflict in interests between the German firms and the indigenous communities in which the latter would have been the losers. It might, on the other hand, have provided resources for more rapid implementation of the policies initiated by Hahl.

MISSIONS

By 1914 mission stations were widely dispersed on the coasts of German New Guinea. The Gazelle Peninsula and the Duke of York Group had been the scene of intensive missionary effort for over thirty years. On the mainland mission outposts studded the coast from near the Dutch border to the Waria, with a concentration of activity at three points, the Huon Gulf, Astrolabe Bay and the Aitape area. The baptized Christians in the indigenous population numbered about 33,000 in 1914; almost two-thirds of them belonged to the Catholic mission at Vunapope. A far greater number had been in touch with the missions without having been accepted for baptism. The Methodist Missionary Society of Australasia, for example, having only 4,768 baptized Christians, reported that its services, conducted by native helpers in several hundred village churches, were attended by 30,000 worshippers. Nor can the work of the missions be measured only in terms of their successes and failures in winning converts. Missionaries had often, particularly in the early years, been pioneers in entering new areas, and their scholarly studies of language and customs had been major contributions to anthropology. Education, apart from that in the government school in Rabaul, was in their hands.

The German administration at first attempted to segregate the different denominations. On the Gazelle Peninsula in 1890 a line was drawn to separate the areas of the Catholic and Methodist missions but neither adhered to it and the division was abandoned in 1899. Less formally on the mainland, the first missionaries of the Society of the Divine Word, on their arrival in 1896, were encouraged to move on from the area they initially contemplated on Astrolabe Bay, where the Lutheran Rheinische Mission was already active. Here, too, the delimitation of areas was abandoned when Hahl permitted the Catholic mission to move to Alexishafen in 1905.

With the exception of the Methodist Mission the societies were financed in the main from Germany and the staffs of the missions were predominantly German. In this they reflected both the impetus that the acquisition of colonies gave to missionary interest in Germany and the official policy of encouraging the teaching of German in schools. Preference for German-speaking missionaries created problems only for the Methodist Missionary Society of Australasia, which sought help from the Methodist Episcopal Church of Germany. By 1914 four of its eight ordained missionaries came from this source, although its work continued to be controlled and financed from Australia.

There were six missions in 1914. The Methodist Missionary Society of Australasia had been the first in the field, having commenced its work in 1875 when the Rev. George Brown [q.v.] reached the Duke of York Group with some Fijian and Samoan teachers. By 1914 it had a network of stations about Blanche Bay and in New Ireland. Often pitifully short of funds, the mission had spread through the extensive use of indigenous assistants, who conducted services in village churches. There were 197 native teachers and 276 native preachers in 1914. The use of indigenous workers spread the mission's teachings widely but it explains the relatively small number of adherents actually baptized. This was also the reason for the predominance of elementary teaching in the educational programme. In 1914, 7,327 children were attending, often irregularly, 224 village schools conducted by indigenous teachers. On the other hand there were only 269 pupils in the seven station schools, conducted by the missionaries at a higher level than the village schools, and 158 pupils in the four boarding schools. German was taught regularly only at Raluana.

The first Catholic missionaries were a few French priests who reached the Gazelle Peninsula in 1882 after the failure of the Marquis de Rays' [q.v.] expedition. They belonged to the Missionaries of the Sacred Heart, founded at Issoudun in France in 1854. In 1889 a separate vicariate of New Britain was created and in the following year a French priest, Louis Couppé, was consecrated as bishop. He was in charge of the mission until 1923. Of imposing presence, autocratic, practical, Couppé planned the extension of the mission in a systematic way. He had ample assistance, especially after the opening of a German province of the society at Hiltrup in 1897 facilitated the recruitment of German-speaking priests.

The Gazelle Peninsula was the first area of the mission's work. By 1903 it had twenty-six stations, often located at quite short distances from one another, each with a priest in charge and a school. New Ireland was the next target. A few stations on the south coast and at Namatanai were the prelude to a more determined move into the Kavieng district in 1911. In 1913 the first station was opened in the Admiralty Islands and work on the southern and northern coasts of New Britain was planned when German rule ended. By that time the mission had 32 main stations, 130 sub-stations, with 37 priests, 43 brothers, 34 sisters and 132 native catechists.

Couppé paid particular attention to the educational work of the mission. Vunapope had a school for catechists, a boarding school, a technical school, orphans' houses and a school for mixed race children. Elsewhere, there were schools conducted by missionaries at all the stations, and at most of the sub-stations, where they were often entrusted to indigenous catechists. By 1914 there

were 135 schools, with 4,825 pupils. As well as at Vunapope, German was taught in all schools where missionaries were teachers. The expansion had been financed in the main from local sources. Couppé had made it a policy from the beginning to buy land, partly for stations, and partly in large blocks for planting. By 1914 the mission already held about 32,000 acres, with substantial areas under coconuts.

In the German Solomons the missionaries of the Society of Mary, operating from the German province of the order at Meppen in Hanover, opened a station at Kieta in 1901. Their numbers depleted by disease and death, they struggled against the hostility of the villages until the establishment of a government station at Kieta gave some security. By 1914 the Society had five stations in the colony: Buin (1905), Koromira (1908), Bononi (1912) on Bougainville and a station on Buka, which was opened in 1910. By 1912 they had twelve schools, attended by 443 pupils and had 480 baptized adherents.

Three missions divided the coast of the mainland between them. To the east, about the Huon Gulf, the Lutheran Neuendettelsauer Mission was active. Founded in Bavaria in 1849, it began work in New Guinea in 1886 when Johannes Flierl [q.v.] opened the first station at Simbang near Finschhafen. The early years of the mission's activities were arduous and results slow. Two separate languages had to be mastered, Yabem for the coast and Kâte for the villages accessible from its inland station at Sattelberg. The rigorous methods of Flierl, with his strict insistence on individual repudiation of indigenous customs as a prerequisite for baptism, made the mission hesitant about claiming converts, and it was not until 1899 that the first baptism occurred.

By 1914 many of the difficulties had been overcome. Languages had been mastered, and notable work in geographical exploration had been completed. Methods, too, had varied. Flierl's emphasis on individual conversion had been modified in the inland villages by Keysser's approach to the group and his conception of the village as a vital Christian community with its own leaders. The mission was still reluctant, however, to entrust its work to indigenous preachers, and there were only forty native assistants at that time. The number of baptized Christians was correspondingly small, 3,637 in 1913. In that year there were twenty-six ordained missionaries, nine lay missionaries, and two women mission assistants. They had spread the work of the mission on stations that extended from Zaka at the mouth of the Waria to Sio on the north coast and inland to the slopes of the main mountain ranges.

In education Flierl stressed intensive work with limited numbers in station schools conducted by the missionaries themselves. There were thirteen of these schools in 1913, with 1,193 pupils. Two training centres, for native assistants, at Longaueng and Heldsbach near Finschhafen, were the only schools at which German was taught.

The record of the other Lutheran mission on the mainland, the Rheinische Mission, was disappointing, despite the dedicated efforts of its members. Established at Barmen in Germany in 1828, and drawing its support largely from the Evangelical Church of the Rhineland and Westphalia, the Rheinische Mission opened its first New Guinea station in 1887 at Bogadjim on Astrolabe Bay. More stations followed at Siar, north of Madang (1889), Karkar Island (opened in 1890 and abandoned in 1895) and Bongu, on Astrolabe Bay (1896). Language problems were serious; even for stations only a short distance apart it was necessary to learn two distinct languages. Malaria [q.v.] and other diseases took heavy toll of the staff; by 1906 ten missionary wives and five of their children had died in the colony.

The mission was unfortunate in the location of its stations, which were in the vicinity of the New Guinea Company's plantations. The influx of alien labourers and the clearing of land caused unrest and suspicion in the villages in which the mission was working. Twice, in 1904 and 1912, there were conspiracies to attack the German settlement at Madang, the second of which was followed by the banishment of the people of Siar and the adjacent islands to the Rai Coast. It is not surprising that the total number of converts stood at only eighty-one in 1912, the twenty-fifth anniversary of the mission's arrival in the colony, or that attendance at its schools did not exceed five hundred.

Just before the outbreak of the war the tide began to turn. Samoan teachers sent by the London Missionary Society and more flexible methods, especially on new stations at Nobonob, near Madang (1906) and Kurum on Karkar (1911), helped to make the mission more popular. Early in 1913 candidates for baptism began to come forward in hundreds in Bogadjim, Bongu and the villages inland from these stations. With the beginning of conversions *en masse* in the next year the way opened for the expansion of Lutheran influence that was to follow in the next decade.

The third mission on the mainland was that conducted by a Catholic society, the Steyler Gesellschaft or Society of the Divine Word, which was founded at Steyl in Holland in 1875. Its first representative, Father Eberhard Limbrock, reached the colony as Apostolic Prefect for the mainland in 1896. The mission was at first active on the coast towards the Dutch border, where it had its first stations on the small islands of Tumleo and Aly not far from where the government station of Aitape was later opened and on the mainland at Monumbo. From the first a distinctive aspect of its work was the emphasis given to the teaching of German in its schools in an attempt to overcome linguistic fragmentation and to forestall Pidgin English. Following the example of the missionaries of the Sacred Heart, Limbrock stressed the value of financing the mission's work from local income, and in 1900 he obtained land from the government for a coconut plantation at Bogia. A request shortly afterwards for a compact area of 10,000 hectares for the mission's use found the governor less compliant.

In 1905 the mission moved its headquarters to Alexishafen to be closer to the administrative centre. By 1914 a chain of stations filled the gap between Astrolabe Bay and the earlier posts to the west. Extensive land purchases along the coast had made it a major landowner by this time. On its plantations, a Lutheran missionary observed in 1914, there was more land under coconuts than the New Guinea Company cultivated in this district.

At Alexishafen the mission had a school for catechists, boarding schools for boys and girls, various industrial establishments and a timber mill. Seventeen stations were scattered along the coast from Alexishafen to Tumleo. In 1913 the first move inland occurred with the opening of an outpost at Marienberg on the lower Sepik, from which the mission planned to move with the government into the interior. There were twenty-seven priests, twenty-four brothers and forty-four sisters in 1914. The Christian flock had not grown as rapidly as the Catholic population in the Archipelago, probably because it required a more thorough preparation for baptism than was usual in the early years at Vunapope. Baptized Christians numbered 4,200. The mission's twenty-seven schools were attended by 1,550 pupils.

EUROPEAN ENTERPRISE

Despite the failure of its early attempts to introduce plantation crops the New Guinea Company dominated the colonial economy up to 1914. In that year it held nearly half the alienated land and employed about one-third of the German planters and traders in the colony. Its network of plantations and trading stations was evidence of cautious planning since 1899, made possible by funds received in compensation for its charter or raised in the form of additional capital. Following the death of von Hansemann in 1903, the Company's Berlin management was taken over by two of the ablest of its directors, Carl von Beck and Professor Paul Preuss, a noted authority on tropical agriculture. Economic programmes were adapted to New Guinea's resources and the opportunities of the world market.

Fortunately for the colony the export that required least effort on the spot was in demand in Europe. Copra could be sold well in Germany, with the result that there was little incentive to grow crops that demanded more skilled labour. Of the total area of 29,290 hectares under cultivation in the colony at the beginning of 1913 all but about 3,000 hectares were under coconuts. Both the government and the New Guinea Company attempted to diversify production, the former by sponsoring scientific research in tropical agriculture, the latter by growing rubber at Astrolabe Bay. But the good prices for copra and a market assured by regular subsidized shipping services to Europe meant that diversification was far from a compelling necessity.

By 1914 the New Guinea Company's plantations were spread over the coasts from the Gazelle Peninsula across the Vitu Islands to the mainland coast at Madang and Potsdamhafen (Bogia). They were grouped under three headquarters, each of which was responsible directly to Berlin. Kokopo was the centre from which were managed fourteen plantations located in New Britain, the Duke of York Group and New Ireland; Madang controlled thirteen plantations on the mainland coast, while Peterhafen was the centre of eleven plantations in the Vitu Islands which the Company valued highly. Rabaul was the headquarters of its trading operations. With the payment of its first dividend in 1913 and the prospect of a vast increase in the copra output as palms reached maturity, the Company was confident of its future. An increase in its capital to eleven million marks in 1914 made it the largest of the plantation companies in the German colonies.

Dwarfed by the New Guinea Company but substantial enterprises nevertheless, were two Hamburg companies whose activities were built on foundations laid before the establishment of the German colony. The firm of Hernsheim & Co., more concerned with trade than planting, operated a complex of stations which had grown out of the early ventures of the brothers Hernsheim, pioneer traders at Matupi in the 1870s. The other Hamburg company was founded much later, after the death of the first planter at Blanche Bay, Emma Kolbe (formerly Forsayth). Fears that her extensive lands and plantations in the Archipelago would fall into Australian hands had long been entertained by the Germans. They were set at rest in 1910 when Heinrich Rudolph Wahlen, a planter with interests in the Hermit and Admiralty Islands, managed to form a company in Hamburg to buy up her entire holdings. On her death it was converted into the Hamburgische Südsee-Aktiengesellschaft (Hasag) and operated coconut plantations at Blanche Bay and on small islands to the north-east.

A number of minor companies, among them several British firms operating in the Solomons, and the missions made up the complement of large enterprises in the colony. Small settlement by individual planters, on the other hand, grew more slowly. At the beginning of 1901 there were only 301 whites in German New Guinea, of whom 77 were missionaries; by 1908 the number had grown slowly to 647. After that date the buoyant state of the copra market and an official policy of encouraging small settlement brought in a trickle of new settlers who helped to bring the white population up to 1,137 in 1914. Small settlement was favoured by Hahl, who was reluctant to accept the dominance of the large companies and looked, too, to the immigration of industrious settlers of modest means to reinforce the German element in the colony. The normal price for land purchased from the government was 5 marks per hectare until 1914, when it was raised to 20 marks; together with this the purchaser was required to meet the costs of survey and registration and to pay to the government the sum due to the native owners. Under the land laws a prospective purchaser was required to have capital of at least 20,000 marks for every 100 hectares of land pur-

chased in freehold, to start clearing within a year and to have three-fourths of his land under cultivation in fifteen years. Since these terms were too rigorous to attract small settlers, Hahl offered blocks of about 100 hectares at one mark per hectare, without additional charges, to men who had been two years in the colony or had experience in tropical agriculture elsewhere. By 1914 he had attracted about a hundred such settlers mainly to New Ireland, the Baining coast of New Britain and the mainland coast west of Madang.

But the experiment, in conjunction with the expansion of the older companies and the compulsion to start immediate planting, aggravated the old problem of finding adequate labour. By 1914 it was clear that the future of German settlement in New Guinea depended on the availability of additional sources of labour. In part, this accounted for Hahl's plans for opening the inland of Kaiser-Wilhelmsland. It also caused him to reopen the question of large scale importation of Asiatic contract labour.

By this time the colony had a Chinese population of 1,377 and 163 Malays. Many of the Chinese were transitory residents, coming mainly from Hong Kong, which was connected to the colony by a regular subsidized shipping service operated by Norddeutscher Lloyd. Such people stayed long enough to accumulate savings in European employment. But there were also more stable elements in the Chinese population. Some of the Chinese traders had been in the colony continuously for twenty years or so, having stayed on after the failure of the New Guinea Company's experiment with Asiatic labour. There were about a hundred Chinese women residents in 1914, and there were Chinese farmers on the sparsely populated south coast of New Ireland, where Hahl had encouraged them to settle on land leased from the government. Most of the Chinese, whether transient or settled, were traders, and artisans. In Rabaul the Chinese quarter housed about one-third of the total Chinese population of the colony, the skilled workers, small traders, cooks and laundrymen of the capital.

In contrast to the steady German investment in the plantations little interest was taken in the discovery and development of mineral resources until the last years of German rule. At first, the New Guinea Company's dominance of the mainland discouraged prospecting. Reluctant to admit private prospectors from British New Guinea in the days of its chartered rule, it attempted to maintain its monopolistic position after 1899 by obtaining the sole right to search for precious metals on the upper Ramu when the charter was surrendered. This was reinforced by a further concession to von Hansemann in 1901 when a syndicate that he organized through the Disconto-Gesellschaft secured exclusive rights in the Huon Gulf area. Expeditions in both areas failed to locate more than unpromising traces of gold in the rivers, and it was not until the Huon Gulf concessions lapsed in 1908 that the way was open for private prospecting and close investigation. By 1914 prospecting, both licensed and illegal, was under way on the Waria, where the miners were mainly from Papua.

Although the major gold deposits were not found in German times, there was a marked change in the attitudes of officials and settlers towards mineral development just before German rule ended, and a growing conviction that the colony would at last flourish when its suspected mineral riches were uncovered. Long negotiations in Berlin over concessions in the area between the Waria and the Markham reached fruition in 1914 with the decision to grant mining rights to Rudolph Wahlen. But oil discoveries near the Dutch border aroused more interest in Berlin than any previous report from New Guinea. To the members of the Reichstag, who supported a grant of 500,000 marks for oil exploration in 1914 and to the Acting Governor, Eduard Haber, who was to have succeeded Hahl, oil and gold were major components in the enticing picture that New Guinea presented in 1914.

The major records relating to German New Guinea are in the Deutsches Zentralarchiv at Potsdam in the German Democratic Republic. In addition to the archives of the Reichskolonialamt, the Deutsches Zentralarchiv has useful records of the Kolonialrat and the Reichstag.

The Australian National Archives holds the surviving records of the German government brought from New Guinea. They relate mainly to the courts but here and there the files contain some general administrative papers.

PRINTED OFFICIAL SOURCES

Neu Guinea Compagnie, *Nachrichten über Kaiser Wilhelms-Land und den Bismarck-Archipel.* Berlin, 1885-98.

The annual reports on the colonies, which were prepared for the Reichstag and subsequently printed for general circulation. Until 1908 they appeared under the title *Jahresbericht über die Entwicklung der deutschen Schutzgebiete in Afrika und der Südsee.* From 1909 to 1913 the annual reports were published with the title *Die deutschen Schutzgebiete in Afrika und der Südsee.*

Deutsches Kolonialblatt, 1890-1914.

Amtsblatt für das Schutzgebiet Deutsch-Neuguinea, 1909-14.

Mitteilungen aus den deutschen Schutzgebieten, 1888-1914.

PERIODICALS

Deutsche Kolonialzeitung, 1884-1914.

Koloniale Zeitschrift, 1900-14.

Beiträge zur Kolonialpolitik und Kolonialwirtschaft, 1899-1903.

Zeitschrift für Kolonialpolitik, Kolonialrecht und Kolonialwirtschaft, 1904-12.

Koloniale Monatsblätter, 1913-14.

Jahrbuch über die deutschen Kolonien, ed. K. Schneider. 1910-14.

Koloniale Rundschau, 1909-34.

BOOKS

H. Blum, *Neu-Guinea und der Bismarckarchipel; Eine wirtschaftliche Studie.* Berlin, 1900.

A. Hahl, *Deutsch-Neuguinea.* Berlin, 1936.

——— *Gouverneursjahre in Neuguinea.* Berlin, 1937.

J. Hüskes (ed.), *Pioniere der Südsee. Werden und Wachsen der Herz-Jesu-Mission von Rabaul zum goldenen Jubiläum, 1882-1932.* Salzburg, 1932.

C. Mirbt, *Mission und Kolonialpolitik in den deutschen Schutzgebieten.* Tübingen, 1910.

R. Neuhauss, *Deutsch Neu-Guinea.* 3 vols, Berlin, 1911.

R. Parkinson, *Dreissig Jahre in der Südsee.* Stuttgart, 1907.

D. G. Pilhofer, *Die Geschichte der Neuendettelsauer Mission in Neuguinea.* 3 vols, Neuendettelsau, 1961-3.

H. Schnee, *Bilder aus der Südsee.* Berlin, 1904.

G. Souter, *New Guinea: The Last Unknown.* Sydney, 1963.

A. Wichmann, *Entdeckungsgeschichte von Neu-Guinea.* 3 vols, Leyden, 1909-12.

H. Zöller, *Deutsch-Neuguinea und meine Ersteigung des Finisterre-Gebirges.* Stuttgart, 1891.

MARJORIE JACOBS

(*See also* NEW GUINEA, MANDATED TERRITORY)

GIMI. People of the Eastern Highlands District. References:

L. B. Glick, Foundations of a Primitive Medical System: the Gimi of the New Guinea Highlands. Ph.D. thesis, University of Pennsylvania, 1963.

——— 'Categories and Relations in Gimi Natural Science', *American Anthropologist*, vol. 66, Special Publication, 1964.

GIREGIRE, Sinake (1937-   ), Ministerial Member for Posts and Telegraphs, M.H.A. for Daulo open electorate, was born about 1937 at Asaro, Eastern Highlands District. He owns a coffee plantation, runs a market garden and trade store, and prospects for gold. He is president of the Asaro Native Local Government Council and director of the Highlands Commodity Exchange. Before taking up his present ministry he was Under-Secretary to the Assistant Administrator and later Under-Secretary for Agriculture.

GOGODARA. People of the Western District. References:

A. C. Haddon, 'The Kabiri of Girara District, Fly River, Papua', *Journal of the Royal Anthropological Institute*, vol. 46, 1916.

——— 'Note on the Gogodara (Kabiri or Girara)', *Man*, vol. 17, 1917.

GOITRE AND CRETINISM. Goitre is now known to be widely distributed throughout Papua and New Guinea and recent studies from Papua, New Guinea and West Irian indicate an associated wide distribution of endemic cretinism.

Goitre is an enlargement of the thyroid gland in the neck—it has various causes but is usually due to iodine deficiency in the diet. Severe iodine deficiency affects people living in remote Highland villages who eat almost exclusively sweet potato and taro which provide a diet of high carbohydrate, low salt and low protein content. These vegetables are grown in grossly iodine-deficient soil around the villages. This soil has been denuded of iodine over many thousands of years by the high rainfall on the steep slopes characteristic of the mountainous areas of the region.

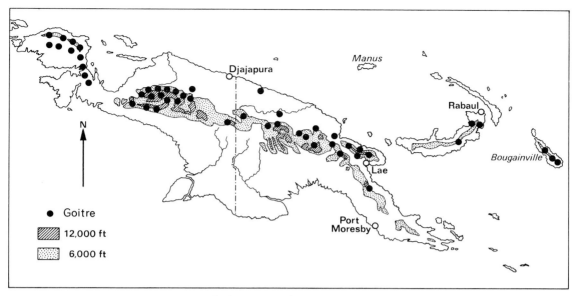

Endemic goitre in New Guinea.

The correction of severe iodine deficiency in New Guinea has been approached in a novel way. In Australia, New Zealand and the United States of America, the use of iodized salt along with wider distribution of foodstuffs has been moderately successful in the control of goitre. However, distribution of iodized salt (or iodide tablets weekly as in Tasmanian schools) could hardly be effective with people living in remote villages in New Guinea. Hence the intramuscular injection of iodine in oil as iodized poppyseed oil was introduced by McCullagh in 1957 following the suggestions of Gunther and Jamieson. The effect of injection of a dose of 2-4 ml. of iodized oil was followed up by studies of body iodine content as revealed by urine measurement and radioactive iodine uptake in the neck. These studies showed substantial correction of severe iodine deficiency for nearly five years after a single injection of iodized oil (Buttfield and Hetzel, 1967).

Injection of iodized oil to people with established goitre was followed by subsidence of long-standing goitre within one to three months. This experience has led to widespread demand for the injection by the people and the virtual abolition of surgical removal of goitre for symptoms due to pressure or for cosmetic reasons.

The condition of endemic cretinism is characterized by multiple neurological defects including deaf mutism, incoordination in walking, spasticity (a state similar to that of spastic children in Australia), squint and varying degrees of mental deficiency. However, neither these subjects nor those with goitre suffer from clinical hypothyroidism due to deficient secretion of the thyroid hormone by the thyroid gland. Endemic cretinism has also been described in other mountainous areas of the world such as the Himalayas and the Andes. It is found in association with the highest incidence of goitre with more severe iodine deficiency; 2.5 per cent of 10,000 people surveyed in the mountainous Huon Peninsula were classified as endemic cretins.

A controlled trial of the effect of iodized oil in the Western Highlands of New Guinea by Buttfield, Pharoah and Hetzel has now demonstrated that endemic cretinism can be prevented by injection of the iodine deficient mother prior to pregnancy. Injection after pregnancy has commenced will not be effective. These findings indicate that the condition probably results from the effects of severe iodine deficiency on brain development during the first three months of pregnancy—an effect similar to that of rubella (German measles).

I. H. Buttfield and B. S. Hetzel, 'Endemic goitre in Eastern New Guinea with special reference to the use of iodised oil in prophylaxis and treatment', *Bulletin of the World Health Organization*, vol. 36, 1967; —— 'Endemic cretinism in Eastern New Guinea', *Australasian Annals of Medicine*, vol. 18, 1969; B. S. Hetzel, 'The Control of Iodine Deficiency', *Medical Journal of Australia*, vol. 2, 1970.   B. S. HETZEL

GOLDFIELDS. The idea that New Guinea was a land of gold originated with an imaginative account of the region by the Spaniard, Antonio Pigafetta, in 1525. More than three centuries later, in 1852, a scientific basis for this belief was provided by John MacGillivray, naturalist with Captain Owen Stanley's [q.v.] cartographical expedition in H.M.S. *Rattlesnake*, who noticed traces of gold in native pottery at Redscar Bay, and other indications on the nearby islands. He predicted that a rich lode would be found in the mountains of the interior.

The actual development of gold extraction followed the trend sketched by MacGillivray. In 1873 Captain Moresby [q.v.] of H.M.S. *Basilisk* unwittingly began the prospecting era by locating gold traces near Fairfax Harbour. Thenceforth small miners, often men disappointed on the Australian diggings, spread out along the eastern coast and off-shore islands. Their activities had some bearing on the annexation of British New Guinea in 1884.

In the 1890s the islands of the Louisiade Archipelago supported several hundred miners, most of whom got modest returns from simple boxing and sluicing. In the period 1888-98 gold constituted 54 per cent of the total value of exports from British New Guinea.

By this time prospecting had shifted to the Mambare River area of the mainland, adjoining the German colony. Here the Administration officially proclaimed the Yodda field in 1901; but yields were nowhere spectacular, so that prospectors were continually moving further north-east into the ranges. The Waria River, on the border between the two colonies, carried much alluvial gold, but in concentrations too low to be profitably extracted.

The northern side of the Waria watershed fed the Watut-Bulolo River systems. A few men penetrated this area before World War I and reported gold indications, but did not live to explore further. After the war the area came under Australian control, and prospecting increased. The first significant finds on the Watut were made by William, 'Shark-eye', Park [q.v.] in 1922, after which more prospectors poured in overland from Salamaua, despite the difficulties of crossing steep ranges and obtaining supplies by porter.

At this time several under-capitalized Australian companies were also engaged in gold prospecting, mainly on the Waria. In 1924 B. V. Barton and J. C. Coldham prepared encouraging reports on the alluvial prospects of the Bulolo River. But extraction appeared impossible until a road was built to the area and neither the companies nor the Administration could afford this.

Early in 1926 a further stimulus was provided by an extremely rich strike at Edie Creek near Wau by W. Royal and R. Glasson, who seemed to have found the major gold source feeding the Bulolo-Watut river system. The lucky few made quick fortunes here from simple surface sluicing; but gold extractable by these methods was soon exhausted.

Ultimately the major effect of the brief Edie Creek boom was to enable Australian and overseas companies to raise substantial capital for further investigation, with a view to large-scale working. The leader of this trend was C. J. Levien [q.v.], a former administrative officer who had quietly been surveying the Bulolo flats. He was responsible for floating in Adelaide a company called Guinea Gold No Liability, which commissioned further drilling of the flats to confirm Levien's estimate of their value.

In 1928 Guinea Gold, lacking adequate working capital, sold the options on its Bulolo leases to Placer Development Limited, a Canadian company managed by C. A. Banks [q.v.]. The following year extensive drilling by Placer revealed auriferous alluvial reserves sufficient to pay substantial dividends for at least twelve years. The big obstacle, however, remained the lack of any method of getting heavy equipment to the field. Banks determined to examine the practicability of air transportation.

Guinea Airways Limited, a subsidiary of Guinea Gold N.L., had pioneered a successful biplane service to the Wau-Bulolo area in 1926. Other companies were already experimenting with the regular use of aircraft to bring in equipment (*see* CIVIL AVIATION). Daydawn Limited, which operated near Wau, broke down its equipment into sections of size suitable for the available aircraft. The Ellyou Corporation, backed by the massive Mining Trust of London, imported a big Handley-Page machine which crashed shortly afterwards.

Banks planned air transportation on an unprecedented scale. He learned that the Junkers factory in Germany was producing the G31, an aircraft capable of lifting 7,000 lb. on short hauls. Placer engineers calculated that careful sectionalizing would enable dredges, hydro-electric turbines, and building materials to be flown in to Bulolo from Lae. On this understanding Bulolo Gold Dredging Limited (B.G.D.) was floated as an operating company in February 1930, under Canadian registration but open to Australian investors.

The operations of this company during the 1930s were an unqualified success, and resulted from detailed planning on a scale unusual at that time in the mining industry. B.G.D.'s three Junkers aircraft carried 40,000 tons to Bulolo between 1931 and 1942 without a single serious accident, a feat which demonstrated the practicability of opening up the whole New Guinea Highlands. The company steadily found greater alluvial reserves, so that expansion was continuous. Eventually eight dredges were working in the Bulolo-Wau Valleys, the two largest weighing 2,500 tons each. Three separate hydro-electric power stations were built, to drive the dredges and other technical equipment and to supply power to Bulolo township, also constructed by the company.

By increasing the scale of dredging B.G.D. was able to hold costs steady and thus treat progressively poorer gravels, to the benefit of the Mandated Territory as well as its own shareholders. Through gold royalties, at 5 per cent, and other charges this one company supplied 18.14 per cent of all government revenue in the ten years before the war. Royalties from gold-mining as a whole accounted for 25.7 per cent of total revenue.

As this indicates, smaller companies and some individual miners were also involved in gold-mining at the same time, almost all of them in the Wau-Bulolo area. The era of quick profits from small-scale methods was over by the time that B.G.D. and other companies began operating, and relations between individual self-employed miners and the companies were generally good.

The other gold-mining companies were not as successful as B.G.D., primarily because they had concentrated on trying to locate and exploit the mother lode which, they felt, must have been enriching the Bulolo alluvium. The biggest of these was New Guinea Goldfields Limited (N.G.G.) successor to the Ellyou Corporation, which undertook tunnel mining in the ranges above Edie Creek. This company had faced serious financial and operating problems from the beginning: the original Corporation had announced initial capitalization of some £4 million sterling, a figure not justified by the actual scale or quality of underground ores. Operations had to be drastically pruned and the company remained relatively unproductive and unattractive financially. A steady lowering of costs, notably that of air freight, largely due to the scale of B.G.D.'s operations, contributed to the survival of N.G.G. and other companies in the Edie Creek area. N.G.G. had the additional problem of maintaining a working site over 6,000 feet above sea-level, cold and damp, and in steep terrain which made the provision of adequate accommodation difficult. The result was a succession of labour disputes with both Europeans and natives.

On the other hand, B.G.D. had the benefit of above-ground working in a warm, pleasant valley, where the company was able to provide excellent housing and recreational facilities for its employees. The provisions of the Native Labour Ordinance were regularly policed by the Administration and were amply met by B.G.D., whose health services in particular were the best in the Territory. For a mining area—especially one in the tropics—B.G.D.'s overall staff morbidity rate of 1.8 per cent—compared with 4.3 per cent at Edie Creek—was exceptionally low.

The Japanese invasion of New Guinea in February 1942 stopped mining, although the Wau-Bulolo area was never actually occupied; but most of the machinery was destroyed by the Australian Army to prevent its use by the enemy. The result was that the gold-mining companies, especially B.G.D., faced virtually total reconstruction in 1945-6. Commonwealth war damage compensation did not make up for the loss of experienced personnel and the need for overall re-planning. Nevertheless, B.G.D. was fortunate in retaining its original management team of 1929, which displayed remarkable ingenuity in improvising equipment and cannibalizing dredges in order to get production under way again; the incoming funds then permitted an acceleration of the rehabilitation process.

B.G.D., however, like other gold-mining interests, was seriously affected by steeply rising post-war labour and equipment costs in relation to the world price of gold, which remained pegged —as it has since—at the 1934 price of $U.S.35.00 per fine ounce. As a result, gold never again reached its pre-war position in New Guinea's economy. B.G.D. eventually rebuilt all its dredges, but some pre-war marginal reserves proved uneconomic, and the company began phasing dredges out of production from 1949 on.

Owing to the successful operation of the two biggest dredges, 1953 was the most productive post-war year for gold-mining in New Guinea, a total of 138,781 fine ounces being refined, after which—principally due to B.G.D.'s run-down— there was a rapid decline.

Facing this situation, and wishing to use the capital and maintain the community at Bulolo, B.G.D. entered into a unique partnership with the Commonwealth government to establish a successful plywood-manufacturing factory in the valley. This venture might not have been possible at all without the contribution of the facilities and equipment originally installed to service the gold industry.

B.G.D. finally brought gold dredging to an end in 1965. Such gold extraction as continues—the Territory produced 33,760 fine ounces in 1965— depends largely on a reversion to the early small-scale methods; though sluicing in particular is now practised more effectively, often by groups of indigenous miners in partnership. Low overheads and small expectations enable these people to extract gold profitably.

But the stagnant world price of gold has forced modern mineral exploration companies, including the parent Placer Development Limited, to concentrate on the location of high-demand industrial metals like copper or high-priced exotic ones like osmiridium.

D. R. Booth, *Mountains, Gold and Cannibals*. Sydney, 1929; E. Demaitre, *New Guinea Gold: Cannibals and Gold-seekers in New Guinea*. London, 1936; I. L. Idriess, *Gold-dust and Ashes: The Romantic Story of the New Guinea Goldfields*. Sydney, 1933; A. M. Healy, 'Bulolo: A History of the Development of the Bulolo Region, New Guinea', *New Guinea Research Bulletin*, no. 15, 1967; S. W. Reed, *The Making of Modern New Guinea*. Philadelphia, 1943; G. Souter, *New Guinea: The Last Unknown*. Sydney, 1963.

A. M. HEALY

GORE, Ralph Thomas (1888-), judge, was born at Glen Innes, N.S.W., on 4 October 1888, son of F. D. C. Gore of Goondiwindi, Queensland. He was educated at Brisbane Grammar School, and called to the Queensland Bar in 1915. He served in the A.I.F. 1916-19. He practised at the Queensland Bar from 1919 to 1924 and became Crown Law Officer of Papua in 1924, Judge of the Supreme Court of Papua 1928-42, and of Papua and New Guinea 1945-62. He was Deputy Commonwealth Crown Solicitor, Adelaide, 1942-5. C.B.E. 1953; published *Justice versus Sorcery* 1965.

FRANCIS WEST

GRASSES. Large areas of New Guinea are covered by grassland, rich in grass flora with about 130 genera and over 300 species. These grasslands may be separated into two broad categories: natural grasslands, developed where soil and climatic conditions inhibit the growth of woody vegetation, and anthropogenic grasslands, brought about by the interference of man with the natural forest cover (*see* AGRICULTURE, INDIGENOUS). Where the term 'New Guinea' is used without qualification such as region it refers to the whole main island.

Natural grasslands fall into three distinct and easily recognized types, savannah, swamp and subalpine, with minor gradations which are here disregarded.

Savannah grasslands occur mainly along the southern coast of mainland New Guinea, in a climate characterized by a long and severe dry season. The natural savannahs include and border upon tracts of anthropogenic grassland and boundaries are indefinable. Fire and climate influence the development and maintenance of the savannahs. The dominant grasses are tussocky, mostly of medium height (2 to 4 feet) and include *Themeda australis*, *Cymbopogon globosus*, *Elyonurus citreus* and *Heteropogon contortus*, with several, usually shorter, species of *Dichanthium* and a few taller species, including *Saccharum spontaneum* and *Themeda novoguineensis*. *Imperata conferta* and *I. cylindrica* occur in some more favoured spots or where the soil has recently been disturbed. In the savannahs of the Trans-Fly region of the Western District of Papua, where the land is flat and soil-moisture variations extreme, *Themeda* is not a feature of the grassland; most of the species are shorter, fine-stemmed grasses such as *Ectrosia leporina*, *Digastrium fragile* and *Aristida macroclada*. More robust species are *Vetiveria filipes* and *Heteropogon triticeus*.

Swamp grassland covers a wide range of conditions, deep or shallow, permanent or temporary flooding, low to high altitude, and consequently a wide range of species.

Partly floating, dense, tangled grass mats of plants with long culms, or stems, develop on deeply flooded swamps and along the margins of slow moving streams at low altitudes as in the valleys of the Fly and Sepik Rivers. Important species are *Echinochloa stagnina*, *Hymenachne amplexicaulis*, *Oryza rufipogon* and *Panicum paludosum*; several other species of *Oryza* occur, and *Coix* and *Polytoca* are sometimes present. At times, masses of this vegetation become detached, to form floating islands.

Shallower swamps support species of *Ischaemum* and *Isachne* and usually *Leersia hexandra*; the last named is very common at altitudes above 3,000 feet. Sedges compete more or less successfully with these grasses.

Phragmites karka, a reed with erect culms up to

Saccharum spontaneum, roadside and swamp grass near Port Moresby, but Territory wide.

15 feet high, forms almost pure stands on shallow permanent swamps, from low levels (e.g. in the lower Markham Valley) to at least 6,000 feet. An extensive stand, now partly drained, occupies part of the Waghi Valley.

Saccharum robustum, a coarse-stemmed cane-grass, with culms up to 1 inch in diameter and up to 20 feet long, often decumbent and interlaced, occurs conspicuously as dense brakes along stream banks and in shallow swamps, from sea-level to at least 6,000 feet. It actively colonizes exposed sand banks in river-beds, and broken ground and new clearings in wet localities. At Sagarai River in southern Papua, *S. spontaneum*, a smaller species, has been observed colonizing river-beds in the same way.

Subalpine grasslands are those above the mountain (cloud) forests; they extend upward from about 10,000 feet. Conditions are cool and usually wet. On the better-drained soils, tussock grasses from 1 to 4 feet high, including *Deschampsia klossii*, *Danthonia archboldii*, *Anthoxanthum angustum*, *Hierochloe redolens* and species of *Poa* and *Deyeuxia*, are dominant. On boggy areas, small creeping grasses, such as *Poa epileuca* and *Monostachya oreoboloides* form mats and cushions. The mountain grasses belong to the festucoid group in contrast to the species of the lowland grasslands, which are panicoid, with Andropogoneae predominating.

Patches of grassland occur in mountain areas well below the upper level of the cloud forest, but above the upper level of cultivation at about 7,500 feet. These may be due to 'frost-pocket' effects.

Fire plays a part in the maintenance of mountain grassland. The grasses and other species produce inflammable material and hunting parties make a practice of firing any area which will burn. The burning modifies the herbage and inhibits regeneration of woody plants.

Anthropogenic grassland. Large areas of grassland in New Guinea appear to have developed as a result of the activities of man. Gardening is traditionally practised in forest clearings which, after a few years, are abandoned and permitted to revert to forest. This is called shifting cultivation or, if more systematic, bush fallow. Given adequate soil fertility and a rest period long enough to permit forest regeneration, this system is well adapted to humid tropical conditions. If, however, the fallow period must be shortened (e.g. when more cultivation is required to support an increasing population) the forest is degraded and finally grass becomes dominant. Anthropogenic grassland extends from sea-level to the upper limit of gardening.

The first grasses to become established in abandoned gardens are tall species such as *Polytoca macrophylla*, *Pennisetum macrostachyum*, *Imperata cylindrica* and *I. conferta*, often with the rampant decumbent grass, *Eulalia leptostachys*. In highland areas above 5,500 feet *Miscanthus floridulus*, a cane-grass, colonizes abandoned gardens and often forms extensive, almost pure stands.

In lowland grasslands on the better soils, *Im-perata* species usually become dominant, with *Polytoca* and *Pennisetum* confined to forest edges. Two tall species, *Coelorhachis rottboellioides* and *Ophiruos tongcalingii*, may occur as scattered clumps. *Saccharum spontaneum* is often found in deeper soils under a strongly seasonal climate and is usually gregarious in dense brakes. On gravelly and degraded soils *Themeda australis* becomes dominant, often forming almost pure stands on eroded hillsides. Some *Themeda* grassland covers soil just deep enough for cultivation; after disturbance *Imperata* will establish itself for a time but eventually *Themeda* will again become dominant.

In highland grasslands (3,000 to 7,500 feet) *Themeda australis* is usually dominant, with *Imperata* in varying proportions and a variety of other species including *Arundinella setosa*, *Alloteropsis semialata*, *Capillipedium parviflorum*, *Hyparrhenia filipendula* (particularly on dry ridges), *Arthraxon ciliaris* (with or without creeping and scattered clumps of *Ophiuros*). *Ischaemum polystachyum* and *I. barbatum* appear in wetter areas which are often hillside soaks.

Fire is the main factor in the maintenance of anthropogenic grassland, but whether, under a humid climate, the grassland is extended much by fire alone is debatable. The margins are usually clear-cut with an abrupt transition to closed-canopy forest which will not, or only very rarely, burn.

A few fire-resistant trees grow in the grassland; lowland species are *Nauclea coadunata*, *Albizia procera*, *Antidesma ghaesembilla* and *Cordia dichotoma*. *Alphitonia incana* is found from near sea-level to 6,000 feet and *Dodonaea viscosa* is sometimes common in highland grassland.

Small leguminous shrubs and sub-shrubs of numerous genera, with *Crotalaria*, *Desmodium* and *Indigofera* well represented, occur throughout the grassland from low levels to about 7,000 feet. A number of species range widely under varied climates; others are confined to climatic zones determined by the length and severity of the dry season.

Native grasslands as pasture. The grasslands have been little affected by grazing animals during their development, and the main grass species are tolerant of fire rather than grazing. Both *Imperata*- and *Themeda*-dominant grasslands give adequate grazing after an initial burn, but the herbage soon becomes fibrous. Grazing, if long-continued, is likely to result in the suppression of the major species and the entry of small prostrate grasses and weeds. In mixed highland grasslands with *Arundinella*, the proportion of this species has been seen to increase after moderate grazing (possibly due to relative unpalatability) while *Alloteropsis* (often abundant in this type of grassland) has, in places, disappeared altogether. In general, the grazing of native grassland is attended by deleterious changes; if any kind of intensive grazing is projected, improvement with introduced species becomes necessary.

Forest grasses. A number of grasses grow only under forest shade; their leaves are usually broad and flat, often with characteristically prominent cross-veins. The fruits of several species are armed with hooked hairs or spines to aid in dispersal. *Leptaspis urceolata* and *Centotheca lappacea* are widely spread as are several species of *Oplismenus*.

Beach grasses. A few species inhabit the zone between foreshore shrubbery and wave-swept sand. These are creeping grasses, and their roots and stems help to stabilize the foreshore. A widespread, prominent species is *Ischaemum muticum* with short broad leaves on the erect flowering stems which rise 1 to 2 feet from the prostrate main-stem. Two superficially similar, but not taxonomically alike, grasses are *Lepturus repens* and *Stenotaphrum micranthus* with fine leaves and the flowers in slender spikes up to 1 foot high. *Thuarea involuta*, a small creeping grass with broad leaves, is notable for its seed disposal. The erect rachis is broad and flat with one or two fertile flowers below and several male flowers above; after anthesis the male flowers fall. The edges of the lower rachis then fold over to embrace the developing fruit, while the upper part bends down to join the lower to form a watertight fruit case; corky material develops in the rachis at the same time. Meanwhile the flowering stem bends over to thrust the fruit case into the sand. If washed out again it is well adapted for water-dispersal. The genus *Spinifex*, often found behind Australian beaches, is represented in New Guinea by *S. littoreus* which occurs in a few places along the southern coast.

Bamboos differ in habit from other grasses and cannot conveniently be treated with them. The bamboo culm is woody and perennial; the leaf-blade narrows to a petiole which is jointed to the leaf-sheath, so that the old leaves are shed while the sheaths persist. In New Guinea, they are essentially plants of the forests and forest-margins.

The genera represented here are *Bambusa*, *Schizostachyum*, *Racemobambos* and *Nastus*. The only large erect native bamboo so far discovered is *Nastus elatus*; this is common at median altitudes, often planted, and is used for a variety of purposes. *Schizostachyum lima*, often found at low levels, has an erect thin-walled culm of about 2 inches diameter at the base. The introduced *Bambusa vulgaris*, with large strong culms, is now widespread; it is easily propagated from culm cuttings. The native species of *Bambusa* are much smaller with slender culms.

Climbing bamboos are most common in the cloud-forest zone between 8,000 and 10,000 feet. The tangle of stems at ground level is often difficult to penetrate. *Nastus productus*, a well-known species, and numerous other species in *Schizostachyum*, *Racemobambos* and *Nastus* are climbing.

Use of grasses by man. *Imperata* is used throughout for thatch. Patches are maintained by judicious burning as it is considered that the durability of the grass decreases after flowering. *Saccharum robustum* is used for fencing in the Eastern Highlands. Flattened culms of the bamboo *Nastus elatus* are woven to make house-walls, and pieces of culm are used as water vessels and cooking-pots, and carved into various utensils. *Bambusa vulgaris*, which is much stronger, cannot be woven

but is used for various types of construction and in other ways as *Nastus elatus*. *Nastus* or *Schizostachyum* (or both) are used as water-pipes in a few areas.

Bamboos (unidentified, ? *B. vulgaris*) are used as bows in some areas. Strips of the culms of *Nastus* and *Schizostachyum* species serve as bowstrings, culms of *Phragmites karka* and *Miscanthus floridulus* make arrow-shafts, and pieces of *Nastus* wall are shaped into the broad points of pig-killing arrows.

Saccharum edule (possibly derived from *S. robustum*) is cultivated for the non-mature inflorescence which is eaten; another food plant is *Setaria palmifolia* of which the tender growing shoots are used. Bamboo shoots from *Nastus elatus* are eaten in the central Highlands.

The false fruits of *Coix lacryma-jobi* (Job's tears) are used as beads. A 'soft shelled' form of this species has been reported in cultivation in West Irian for food. *Coix gigantea* has been extensively cultivated for the manufacture of salt [q.v.], which is obtained by burning and crude extraction of the ash (see SALT).

Cereals as such are not a traditional food but rice is now cultivated to some extent as a cash crop in suitable areas. Maize is widely grown; the ears are eaten roasted slightly before maturity.

M. Bromley and J. Barrau, 'Présence d'un *Coix* cultivé dans les montagnes de la Nouvelle Guinee', *Journal d'Agriculture Tropicale et de Botanique Appliquée*, vol. 12, 1965.

N. T. Burbidge, 'Grass Systematics', in *Grasses and Grasslands*, ed. C. Barnard. London, 1964.

A. P. H. Freund, E. E. Henty and M. A. Lynch, 'Salt making in inland New Guinea', *Transactions of the Papua and New Guinea Scientific Society*, vol. 6, 1965.

A. N. Gillison, 'Plant succession in an irregularly-fired grassland area—Doma Peaks region, Papua', *Journal of Ecology*, vol. 57, 1969.

C. O. T. Grassl, 'Saccharum robustum and other wild relatives of "noble" sugar canes', *Journal of the Arnold Arboretum*, vol. 27, 1946.

J. J. Havel, 'Factors influencing the establishment of ligneous vegetation in mid-mountain pyro- and anthropo-genic grasslands', paper read at Symposium on the Impact of Man on Humid Tropical Vegetation, held at Goroka, T. P. N. G. 1960. Canberra, 1960.

E. E. Henty, 'A manual of the grasses of New Guinea', T. P. N. G. Department of Forests, *Botany Bulletin*, no. 1, 1969.

D. C. Heyligers, 'Vegetation and Ecology of the Port Moresby–Kairuku Area', in 'Lands of the Port Moresby–Kairuku Area, Territory of Papua and New Guinea', CSIRO, *Land Research Series*, no. 14, 1965.

R. E. Holttum, 'The Bamboos of New Guinea', *Kew Bulletin*, vol. 21, 1967.

C. W. E. Moore, 'Distribution of Grasslands', in *Grasses and Grasslands*, ed. C. Barnard. London, 1964.

R. G. Robbins, 'The anthropogenic grasslands of Papua and New Guinea', paper read at Symposium on the Impact of Man on Humid Tropical Vegetation, held at Goroka, T. P. N. G. 1960. Canberra, 1960.

N. W. Simmonds, 'Archery in South East Asia and the

Pacific', *Journal of the Malayan Branch Royal Asiatic Society*, vol. 32, 1959.

C. G. G. J. van Steenis and others, 'Preliminary review of some genera of Malaysian Papilionaceae', *Reinwardtia*, vol. 5, 1961, pp. 419-29.

E. E. HENTY

GRIFFITHS, Thomas (1865-1947), Administrator of New Guinea, was born at Presteigne, Radnorshire, South Wales, on 29 September 1865. He came to Australia at an early age. In 1886 he enlisted as a gunner in the Victorian Permanent Artillery, and in 1895 he gained warrant rank. At federation in 1901 he transferred to the Commonwealth Defence Department. For three years he was on the staff of the Inspector-General of the Army. In October 1908 he gained an honorary commission. He had married Delia, daughter of William Macnamara, of Kew.

When the Military Board was instituted in 1909 Griffiths, an honorary lieutenant of the Corps of Military Staff Clerks, became its first secretary. In the same year he was promoted to captain. This was his appointment at the outbreak of war in August 1914.

General Bridges, who raised the A.I.F., well knew Griffiths' ability and experience, and was determined to get him into his division. Griffiths was deputy assistant adjutant-general at the time of the Gallipoli landing. In June 1915 he was promoted to major. He was chiefly concerned with personnel, and one of his principal nightly duties was to supervise the landing of reinforcements on the beach, which was often shelled. For his work on the peninsula he was awarded the D.S.O.

Early in 1916 Griffiths, now assistant adjutant-general and a lieutenant-colonel, was closely concerned with the major reorganization of the A.I.F. in Egypt. From May 1916 he served in France as assistant adjutant-general at H.Q., A.I.F. His work was recognized with the C.M.G. In April 1917 he became Commandant of administrative headquarters A.I.F. in London, with the rank of colonel. On 1 January 1918 he was promoted to brigadier-general.

Back in Australia in March 1920 he became, very briefly, Inspector-General of Administration. In April he was appointed Administrator of German New Guinea.

On 1 May 1920 Griffiths took over from Brigadier-General G. J. Johnston [q.v.]. The incoming Administrator was a very different sort of person, a staff officer rather than a commander, more interested in the details of administration than in the policy decisions that governed these details; more tolerant, less credulous, perhaps less imaginative. His reputation stood high. The Australian government must have known that here was a man who would implement its decisions capably and without question.

The major decision had already been reached, and Griffiths' first few months were largely taken up with preparations for the coming expropriation of German interests. The ordinance giving effect to this came into force on 1 September.

Thereafter for several years, as C. D. Rowley points out, the post of administrator lost much of its significance. Griffiths felt obliged to refer many matters for the opinion of W. H. Lucas [q.v.], the chairman of the Expropriation Board. He concerned himself with the details of army administration, with illegal migration, with abuses of labour recruiting, and with unrestrained proselytizing by religious missions. But he followed no particular line on questions of native interests, or the control of the interior; and he did not take the same interest in the districts as Johnston had.

In October 1920 Griffiths was an applicant for the appointment of administrator in the coming civil government, but he was placed second to Brigadier-General E. A. Wisdom [q.v.]. He then successfully applied for the administratorship of Nauru. He handed over to Wisdom on 21 March 1921.

Griffiths took office as Administrator of Nauru in June 1921. In his six years the island made steady progress. Compulsory education was introduced, and in 1923 the government took over responsibility for native education from the missions. During 1927 a new agreement was negotiated between the native landowners and the Phosphate Commission. The traditional ascendancy of the chiefs was maintained. Contract labour continued to be be recruited from Hong Kong. The Nauruans 'do not care for any kind of sustained work', as Griffiths reported, but they were 'a gentle, law-abiding, and pleasant-mannered people'. He claimed, with some justice, that they were 'being taught to think for themselves and to initiate schemes for their own advancement'. He relinquished his post in June 1927.

In 1929 Griffiths came out of retirement to be Deputy Chairman of the War Pensions Entitlement Appeal Tribunal. Then, after three years, he was commissioned to act as Administrator of the Mandated Territory of New Guinea during the absence of General Wisdom on long leave.

When he arrived at Rabaul for the second time, on 11 July 1932, Griffiths was nearing sixty-seven years of age. Seaforth Mackenzie·[q.v.] had said of his first term: 'His administration of New Guinea was marked by the same qualities of thoroughness and industry that he had shown in his previous career'; but no one should have expected these qualities to have remained unimpaired. In fact by now Griffiths was inclined to take the easy way out. He initiated no new policies—except the proposal, not accepted by the Australian cabinet, that responsibility for all native education should be handed over to the missions—and he spent most of his time at his Rabaul headquarters. The reorganization of the public service, the proclamation of the New Guinea Act, and the inauguration of the Executive and Legislative Councils, all of which came to pass in Griffiths' time, stemmed from the initiatives of the Wisdom era. When Wisdom retired in June 1933 Griffiths had been appointed Administrator for a two-year term, but he did not see his time out; early in 1934 he let it be known that an earlier relief would be acceptable. He departed on 12 September 1934, being succeeded by Brigadier-General W. R. McNicoll [q.v.].

He was to have one more active connection with the Mandated Territory. In February 1938 he led the committee which investigated new sites for the capital in place of Rabaul, which was no longer considered safe. The committee's recommendation of Lae was rejected by the Minister of the day, but most people recognized the choice as sound, and Lae did indeed become the capital, briefly, in 1941.

Griffiths died in Melbourne on 10 November 1947.

In his prime he was an exceedingly able staff officer. In Nauru, a minuscule world, he showed up well as a commander. Would he have made his mark in New Guinea if he had stayed there in 1921? It seems more likely that he would have become the passive instrument of distant and capricious policy makers. When he did come to New Guinea in 1932 it was too late for him to shine. But late or not, he received there, as he did throughout his life, the esteem and affection due to a modest and unassuming person; coupled, now, with the approbation of all defenders of established practices.

COMMONWEALTH RECORD SERIES

In the Commonwealth Archives Office, Canberra
CRS A 518 Territories Branch, Prime Minister's Department
    Appointment of Administrator, G 800/1/3
    Education of Natives, C 818/1/3
    Transfer of Administrative Headquarters, AK 800/1/3

Commonwealth of Australia, *Report to the League of Nations on the Administration of the Territory of New Guinea, 1914-21, 1931-2* to *1933-4*. Melbourne and Canberra, 1923, 1933-5.
——— *Report to the League of Nations on the Administration of Nauru, 1920-1* to *1927*. Melbourne and Canberra, 1922-8.
S. S. Mackenzie, *The Australians at Rabaul (Official History of Australia in the War of 1914-1918*, vol. 10). Sydney, 1927.
McNicoll Papers, (N.L.A.)
'Report of Committee Appointed to Investigate New Site for the Administrative Head-Quarters of the Territory of New Guinea', 27 April 1938. *C. P. P. 1937-40*, vol. 3.
'Report by the Minister of State for Defence on the Military Occupation of the German New Guinea Possessions'. *C. P. P. 1922*, vol. 2.
C. D. Rowley, *The Australians in German New Guinea 1914-1921*. Melbourne, 1958. Rowley made use of correspondence between Griffiths and the Department of Defence, Melbourne, which is in the library of the Australian War Memorial, Canberra.
                                    R. R. McN.

(*See also* NEW GUINEA, MANDATED TERRITORY).

GRIMSHAW, Beatrice Ethel (1871-1953), author, was born at Cloona, County Antrim, Ireland, in 1871 and educated at Caen, at Victoria College, Belfast, and at Bedford College, University of London and Queen's College, Belfast. She travelled extensively in the Pacific and South-east Asia, as well as other areas, writing novels, travel books and journalism, and in 1907 was commissioned by the Australian government to write a pamphlet on Papua, where she lived for many years and became a close friend and admirer of Hubert Murray [q.v.]. She died in 1953 at Bathurst, N.S.W.

B. Grimshaw, *The New New Guinea*. London, 1910; ——— *When the Red Gods Call*. London, 1911; ——— *Guinea Gold*. London, 1912; ——— *Red Bob of the Bismarcks*. London, 1915.   FRANCIS WEST

GROVES, William Charles (1898-1967), educationist, was born on 18 August 1898 at Ballarat, Victoria, educated at Ballarat High School and the universities of Melbourne and Sydney. In 1922 he became Supervisor of Education in the Mandated Territory of New Guinea, then in 1926 lecturer at the Teachers' College in Melbourne. As a research fellow of the Australian National Research Council he did anthropological work in the western Pacific area, including New Guinea, during 1931-6, and then became Director of Education in Nauru 1937-8, Adviser on Education, British Solomon Islands Protectorate 1939-40. He had served with the A.I.F. 1915-19 and from 1941 to 1946 he served as major with the Second A.I.F. After World War II he became Director of Education in the Territory of Papua and New Guinea. He died in 1967. A son, Murray Groves, is an anthropologist part of whose work has been among the Motu people of Papua.

W. C. Groves, *Native Education and Culture-Contact in New Guinea: A scientific approach*. Melbourne, 1936.   FRANCIS WEST

GUISE, John (1914-   ), Speaker of the House of Assembly and M.H.A. for Alotau open electorate, was born on 29 August 1914 at Gedulara near Dogura, Milne Bay District. He first worked

Dr John Guise.

in private enterprise but during World War II served with Angau [q.v.] as a clerk in Signals. He joined the police in 1946 and reached the rank of sergeant-major. In 1961 he was elected to the Legislative Council as member for Eastern Papua. He has represented the government and the Anglican Church on several overseas delegations and at conferences, and was chairman of the Select Committee on Political and Constitutional Development in 1967. In 1970 the University of Papua and New Guinea conferred the degree of Doctor of Laws, *honoris causa*, upon him.

GULF DISTRICT. The popular conception of the Gulf District is of vast sago swamps which offer no opportunities for economic development. The presence in the towns of large numbers of 'Keremas', as all coastal people from this District are generally called, lends credence to this popular view. At the time of the 1966 Census it was estimated that 7,051 persons, some 15.2 per cent of those people born in the Gulf District, were resident elsewhere. The examination of the District which follows will be set against this 'outside' view.

PHYSICAL FEATURES

From Bell Point in the west to Cape Possession in the east more than 350 miles of shoreline of the Gulf of Papua forms the southern land limit of this District of some 13,700 square miles. Between the northern boundary and the coast is a small section of the high mountains that form the central spine of the island; extensive foothills flank these central ranges and two lowlying embayments separated by a southward-sweeping lobe of the foothills.

Delta and Lakekamu embayments. The great delta embayment extends from the Fly River in the Western District [q.v.] to The Bluff about eight miles west of Kerema. This is the depositional area for vast quantities of alluvial material transported by the Turama, Kikori, Purari and Vailala Rivers, the distributaries of which form an intricate network through their outward-growing deltas. For more than twenty miles inland from the mouth of the Purari, the largest of the rivers, are tidal flats which have an almost imperceptible gradient inland. These have been described as littoral plains and in the salt-water tidal area are colonized by various species of mangrove. Where the tidal flats are inundated with brackish water nipa palms replace mangroves. Further inland again stands of sago begin where the water is fresh.

Beyond the limit of tidal influence in the delta embayment are alluvial plains which extend up to forty miles inland. They offer a variety of environments ranging from permanent stagnant swamps containing herbaceous material to well-drained alluvial terraces supporting tall forest.

To the east of Cape Cupola is the smaller Lakekamu embayment which, as it rises more steeply, is subject to tidal influences for only about seven to ten miles inland. Large seasonal freshwater swamps which flank the Tauri and Lakekamu Rivers are the major feature of this embayment.

Foothill zone. In the north-west of the District the foothills are largely limestone. *The Resources of the Territory of Papua and New Guinea* (1951) describes the area north of Kikori: 'the limestone ridges rise to 300 feet on the lower Sirebi (a tributary of the Kikori River), then to 2,000 feet on the middle Sirebi, and so progressively to ridges of 3,000 feet near Mount Murray', which lies just over the border in the Southern Highlands [q.v.]. So rugged is this country, in which the limestone has weathered into rough pinnacles, that it has been called 'broken bottle' country. Rapid percolation of water through the limestone makes travel even more difficult as, in spite of the high rainfall, surface water is noticeably absent. This area is such a barrier to movement that it helps explain the late contact made with the Southern Highlands, where Erave Patrol Post, a mere sixty air miles from Kikori, was not opened until 1963.

The twin peaks of Mt Duau and Mt Faveng in the upper Purari are volcanic cones and surrounding mantles, which overlie the limestone to the north-west. The only prominent feature in the great flat expanse of the Kikori Delta is the volcanic remnant, Aird Hills, which rises to 1,100 feet.

The southward-sweeping Kukukuku lobe of the foothill zone interposed between the delta and Lakekamu embayments is a complex of at least four ranges rising to about 7,500 feet at Mt Eruki. Cape Cupola and The Bluff, rocky coastal prominences to the east and west of Kerema respectively, are outlying arms of this system. Fringing the Kukukuku lobe are low hills, seldom exceeding 500 feet in height, enclosing basins such as those occupied in the west by the Vailala and in the east by the Tauri upstream from a breach in a low hill series named Rim Ridge by CSIRO workers.

Moving inland the Kukukuku lobe becomes progressively more rugged with precipitous slopes, and the water courses, entrenched in canyon-like valleys, have numerous waterfalls.

Between the eastward-flowing segment of the Purari and the District border in the north-east the foothill zone merges into the main ranges.

CLIMATE

In terms of rainfall there is a pronounced west to east gradient both in amount and distribution. In the west of the District Kikori has an average annual rainfall of 227 inches while at Kukipi in the east the average annual rainfall is 46 inches.

In *An Atlas of Papua and New Guinea* (1970), Hart has classified that portion of the District west from Kerema as continuously wet. This climate is the result of a bank-up of the south-easterlies against the barrier of the southern face of the central cordillera during the May-October period and from westerly-moving vortical circulations from December to March.

From May to October, when the south-easterly

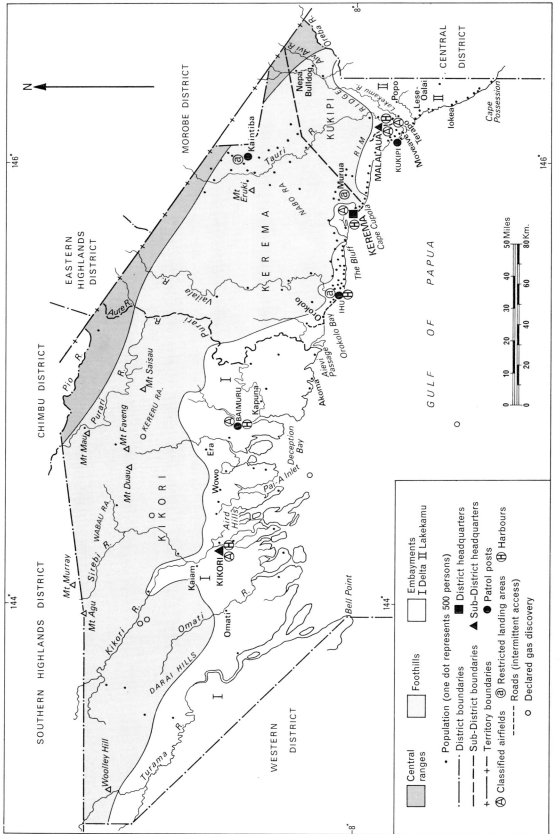

Gulf District.

system is operating, Kukipi receives little rain as these air masses move parallel to the coast and general lines of relief in that area. Thus most of the eastern area's rain falls in the period December to March.

The average temperature at Kerema of 79.1°F. with a small annual range is typical of coastal areas. No data is available on temperatures at higher elevations such as the moderately populated locality surrounding Kaintiba Patrol Post. However normal lapse rate suggests a decline in average temperatures of 3°F. per 1,000 feet increase in elevation. Average monthly humidity is uniformly high throughout the year, averaging 83 per cent at 9 a.m. and 74 per cent at 3 p.m.

VEGETATION

The natural vegetation of most of the District is rain forest, but drainage is a major factor determining the type of vegetation in any locality. The coast is fringed with mangrove forest, while extensive areas of nipa palm occur in the brackish environments. The freshwater swamps contain sago palms and an upper storey of trees of varying density. In the seasonally inundated areas of the lower Tauri-Lakekamu basin, *Melaleuca* (paperbark) trees and mixed grasses are the main components of the extensive swamp savannah.

The original tall forest vegetation on the well-drained, fairly densely populated coastal areas east of Kerema has been widely disturbed by human activities such as gardening and coconut planting. Abandoned garden sites carry secondary forest or grassland. Sparsely populated lowland areas that are well drained have dense forest of very mixed composition, including some valuable timber species such as *Pometia* and *Terminalia*.

Much of the foothill zone between 1,000 and 3,000 feet has also been disturbed by gardening activities, and the original forest has been replaced by secondary growth over considerable areas. In the lower montane zone, between 3,000 and 9,000 feet, where such trees as southern beech and laurels occur, the original forest has been removed in the area administered from the Kaintiba Patrol Post.

MINERALS

The Gulf District attracted gold prospectors whose short-lived rush to the upper Lakekamu brought this sparsely populated area into prominence and led to the establishment of a patrol post in 1910 at Nepa. The working out of the gold led to the departure of the miners and the withdrawal of Administration personnel by 1921. Interest in the area then lapsed until World War II when the need to move large quantities of material to the Wau area resulted in the construction of a road link between Papua and New Guinea. The road commenced at Bulldog on the Aiv Avi River, a major tributary of the Lakekamu, and was driven ninety-one miles through to Wau. An important consequence of this wartime project was that many people from the lower

Lakekamu-Tauri area were drawn into war service, thus gaining non-village experience and skills which accelerated change in the area: for example the establishment of a co-operatively owned sawmill by the people of Moveave village and the considerable emigration to urban areas in the post-war years.

Petroleum is the mineral most keenly sought in the Gulf District, which lies within the geological area known as the Papuan Basin. Discovery of oil seepages near the mouth of the Vailala in 1911 sparked off exploratory work which has continued with varying intensity ever since. More than $70,000,000, about three-quarters of total expenditure on petroleum exploration in Papua and New Guinea, have been spent in the Gulf District. The geological conditions, massive sedimentary deposits, are favourable for petroleum occurrences and no less than nineteen oil or gas seepages have been recorded in the District. By 1969 some fifteen dry holes had been sunk on shore and seven off shore. Even though commercial quantities of crude oil have not been located, other holes have resulted in gas discoveries, both on shore and off shore. No agreement has yet been concluded for the sale of gas, which is principally methane, a type that requires very low temperatures (−260°F.) for transportation as a condensate. However, the potential of these reserves as a source of energy for refining and manufacturing purposes is appreciated by mining companies. One company, which has a 15 per cent interest in one of the declared off-shore gas discoveries, is now searching in the District for limestone and clay, raw materials required for the manufacture of cement.

THE PEOPLE

In April 1970, the District's population [q.v.], including 260 non-indigenes, was estimated to be 67,400, distributed as follows: Kerema Sub-District 22,660, Kikori Sub-District 17,940 and Kukipi Sub-District 26,770. The extremely uneven population distribution shows as a marked concentration along the coast from Cape Possession westwards to Ihu, with the delta embayment and foothill zone having a sparse, scattered population. The only exception is the mountainous country to the east of the upper Tauri where some 8,000 people are in the area surrounding the Kaintiba Patrol Post. CSIRO officers estimate that population densities on usable land in some coastal localities, such as Orokolo, may rise to over 600 persons per square mile.

The population consists of four broad groups. From the western border, Bell Point, to Aievi Passage at the eastern end of the Purari Delta live the Delta people who form one broad ethnic group of approximately 16,000. The largest of the groups identified, the Elema, number about 40,000. They are found along the coast in settled villages from Aievi Passage to Cape Possession and as far inland as Malalaua.

The major inland population concentration, around the headwaters of the Tauri River, belongs to a widespread ethnic group to whom the general name Kukukuku has been applied. They inhabit a large area, straddling the Papua-New Guinea border, which is administered from Marawaka in the Eastern Highlands District [q.v.], and Aseki in the Morobe District [q.v.] as well as from Kaintiba in the Gulf District. In the western inland section of the District are small numbers of a semi-nomadic people who are related to the Highlanders.

Rates of increase in population [q.v.] in the District are not known precisely, but van de Kaa (1970) suggested that a rate in excess of 2.2 per cent per annum is likely in coastal areas.

TRADITIONAL SETTLEMENT PATTERNS AND SUBSISTENCE ACTIVITIES

Nucleated settlements, quite large by local standards, occur along the coastal and embayment areas, while in the foothills and mountains dispersed settlements consist of single houses, or hamlets of three or four dwellings.

In the CSIRO report on the Kerema-Vailala area four associations or subsistence patterns of land use with land form are identified. The largest proportion of the District's population, the Elema, occupy beach ridges and beach plains. Their villages are located on the stable beach ridge nearest the sea, and on this and inland beach ridges are coconut groves, breadfruit trees and gardens containing bananas, yams, taro and sweet potatoes. These supplement the major food item, sago, which is collected from the intervening swampy depressions. The relative importance of the gardens, which are worked on a short fallow cycle in the areas of high population density, declines from west to east as rainfall decreases. Consequently sago gathering and fishing become even more important in the east. The inland beach plains, such as those to the east and west of the Vailala River, support a similar subsistence pattern but carry a lower population density and rivers replace the sea as a source of fish.

In the mangrove-nipa environment of the tidal flats from Bell Point in the west to the eastern edge of the Purari Delta the land available for gardening is extremely limited, and sago collecting and fishing, especially for crabs, are of even greater importance than in the beach ridge environment. The small gardens that do exist occupy mounds that have been thrown up above high water by crabs. The people move quite frequently, spending a great deal of time living in small sago-making settlements.

The inhabitants of scattered settlements in the alluvial swamps away from the beach ridges and beach plains depend on sago collecting and the cultivation of narrow levees and terraces.

The reported form of subsistence agriculture practised by the Kukukuku people in the foothills and mountains is unusual in that undergrowth cleared from the garden site is not burned and the felling of larger trees follows, rather than precedes, planting. In some ridge areas gardening has resulted in anthropogenic grasslands.

MODERN INFLUENCES ON THE DISTRICT

The coastal portion of the Gulf District is an area which has had long contact with Europeans. Representatives of the London Missionary Society are reported to have been in contact with the Elema people from Cape Possession to Orokolo from as early as 1884. Since that time the missions [q.v.] have constituted one of the most continuing and pervasive influences, introducing healing and educational services in the coastal areas. The London Missionary Society was for long the only mission west of Kukipi with the Roman Catholics to the east. Today a greater number of mission groups operate in the District and the spheres of influence of each mission are no longer so clearly defined. The activities of the Roman Catholic Mission of the Sacred Heart overlap with those of the United Church (which has absorbed the London Missionary Society), and the Seventh Day Adventist and Salvation Army missions have entered the coastal areas. Missionary penetration of the populous interior around Kaintiba occurred in the 1960s as a result of Lutheran expansion from Menyamya in the Morobe District, and Catholic expansion from the mission headquarters on Yule Island.

Government influence dates from the 1880s, but until 1906 the eastern portion was administered from the Central Division. In 1906 a station was established at Kerema to administer the area from Cape Possession to the Western Division. In 1912 a station was established at Kikori, and the Delta Division was brought into existence and Kerema was left to administer the area from the Purari to Cape Possession, known as the Gulf Division.

Before World War II the only other administrative stations opened were Nepa Patrol Post and a temporary police station at Omati in 1926.

During World War II the Gulf Division was administered from Kairuku in the Central Division and was known as the Lakekamu Division. The number of administrative centres increased in this period. In 1942 Waroi substation, about twelve miles east of the present station at Baimuru, was opened. It was replaced by Beara, about three miles to the west, in 1947. During the same year Ihu Patrol Post was opened. A co-operative office and post office were the first Administration facilities established at Kukipi in 1950. A patrol post followed in 1952.

The present broad outlines of the District were created in 1951 when the two Divisions, Delta and Gulf, were combined to form the Gulf District with headquarters at Kikori. District headquarters moved from Kikori to Kerema in 1958.

Several changes occurred in 1961. Beara Patrol Post was closed down and replaced by the present station at Baimuru, and a patrol post was opened at Kaintiba. In 1960 the Kaintiba area was visited by contact patrols from Kerema, a solid six days' walk away. The establishment of this inland patrol post meant the Administration had a fairly comprehensive network of stations from which to administer the main population concentrations in the District.

In 1967 the Administration opened a Sub-District Office at Malalaua with a view to providing a centre around which resettlement could occur. The site chosen is located in an area of fairly extensive, well-drained and sparsely populated plains and foothills which offer opportunities to the coastal people for development of cash cropping not available on the limited areas of well-drained land near the coast.

Prospectors, traders, planters and timber millers have all had some influence on the people of the District. Of these the petroleum exploration companies have been the most dramatic. Over a long period they have employed large teams of workers, often for only short engagements. These workers have been paid relatively high wages and some have acquired artisan-type skills. In part, the high rate of migration from the District could be a consequence of such an introduction to the modern economy.

Large-scale modernization and participation in the cash economy have not occurred in the Gulf District. The low non-indigenous component in the population, only 260 in April 1970, is an indication of the limited amount of development that has occurred. Two corroborative statistics from the 1966 Census, the percentages of population in urban areas, 3.3 per cent, and rural non-village settlements, 5.7 per cent, are substantially lower than those for Districts where greater economic development has occurred.

At the time of the 1966 Census, when urban areas were defined as those having a population of more than 500 (excluding separately located schools, hospitals, missions, plantations, rural settlements and villages of whatever size), Baimuru, Kerema and Kikori qualified as urban places. The main functions of these centres, where most of the non-indigenous population lives, are administrative. Kerema, the largest town, with a population of 820 at the 1966 Census, is the administrative centre of the District. Representatives of most government departments, and users of facilities such as the hospital and high school located at Kerema to serve the District, form the bulk of its population. It is the only town with an official post office and telephone exchange, to which fifty-two subscribers were connected in mid-1969. A government radio station providing programmes in five languages is also located in Kerema. Outstation radio links, four non-official post offices and one agency complete the limited communications network.

In addition to these towns there are four other administrative centres: Ihu, Malalaua, Kukipi and Kaintiba which are difficult to conceive as being incipient 'central places'. Their location is in reasonable accord with the present population distribution.

Further confirmation of the limited development is the reported 30 per cent of the work force, that is population aged from ten to sixty-four, in the money-raising category; this stands well below the Territory average of 54 per cent. Only 11 per cent of the indigenous work force is involved in wholly or mainly money-raising activities.

EDUCATION

The limited impact of education was revealed in the 1966 Census which showed that a mere 245 of the District's indigenes had obtained any secondary education and for 135 of them it was of only Form I level. By May 1969 the District possessed sixty-three primary schools, forty-six mission and seventeen Administration, and three post-primary schools, two Administration and one mission, which catered for approximately 50 per cent of school-age children. Of the post-primary educational institutions two are vocational schools, which teach useful skills to a small number of primary-school leavers. Only one is a full-scale high school, with a 1970 enrolment of 285, including 52 females. Thus the high-school population in the District is equal to approximately 5 per cent of primary-school enrolments.

History perhaps more than population distribution determined the location of schools. The quite large population concentration in the Kaintiba area, first subject to serious contact from 1960, has not yet obtained an Administration school and the two missions present have established only one school each.

HEALTH SERVICES

As with all services these are concentrated in coastal areas, and expansion is most needed in the Kaintiba area. The District is served by two hospitals with doctors, one run by the Administration at Kerema and the other by the United Church at Kapuna, and three minor Administration hospitals at Ihu, Kukipi and Kikori. These institutions provide accommodation for up to three hundred in-patients.

In 1970 there were forty-five aid posts of which eight were controlled by Local Government Councils and fifteen by the missions. Although infant welfare and maternity clinics, mainly provided by missions, are held monthly throughout most of the District, 75 per cent of mothers still choose to have village deliveries (see COMMUNITY MEDICINE).

The three most important diseases are malaria, leprosy and tuberculosis [qq.v.]. There are no malaria-control activities in the District. It has been estimated that one-quarter of the children in coastal areas have enlarged spleens, a symptom of malarial infection. Tuberculosis, also a big problem in the coastal areas, was systematically assessed in 1970 when a three-month survey and vaccination campaign was undertaken. There are over 800 registered leprosy patients, mainly coming from the three areas: East Kerema, Orokolo and Ihu.

LOCAL GOVERNMENT

The local government movement, introduced to Papua and New Guinea in 1950, first reached the Gulf District in 1960. By 1966 seven councils had been formed to cover the coastal population. The goals of local government are twofold; first, to encourage participation in decision-making in a wider context than the village. In this respect they are designed as an educative bridge between village and national-level decision-making. The other aspect is economic. Councils are expected to accept some of the responsibilities for provision of items of social overhead capital, such as school buildings and aid posts, and of economic infrastructure, such as roads (*see* URBAN ADMINISTRATION).

The limited development and the consequent high rate of emigration severely limits the tax-raising capacity of the councils. Recent patrol reports mention 47 per cent of male members of the work force being absent from some coastal villages. A report on the District compiled in April 1970, states that at least 30 per cent of the nominal population of 50,100 in the council areas is living outside the Gulf District. Thus there is only scope for provision of a limited range of services by these councils. In the 1969-70 financial year their total overall revenue was only $80,000.

The hoped-for long-term ideals of local government, of increasingly large council units which can reap the benefits of economies of scale and have integrative effects, favourable in nation-building, by fostering identification with wider units of authority, have not emerged in the Gulf District. In the Kerema Sub-District where three councils were originally created, there are now four with populations ranging from 4,500 to 6,000. Smaller, rather than increasingly larger units, have developed.

CO-OPERATIVES AND TRADE STORES PRIVATELY OWNED BY PAPUANS

At present these institutions, together with cash cropping, are the main vehicles for entrepreneurial participation in the cash economy by Papuans and New Guineans. In the Gulf District the level of indigenous activity as measured by these indices declines from east to west. In the Kukipi Sub-District in the year ended 30 June 1969 it was estimated that there were fifty indigenously owned trade stores with an annual turnover of $64,000. The Kerema Sub-District estimates showed forty stores with a turnover of $35,000, whilst Kikori Sub-District was estimated to possess ten stores with a turnover of $3,000.

There was a similar distribution of co-operatives [q.v.] in the year ended 31 March 1969. For administrative purposes three areas, which more or less coincide with Sub-Districts, are identified by the Registrar of Co-operatives. These are the Kukipi-Moveave, Ihu-Kerema and Baimuru areas.

In the Kukipi-Moveave area there are twenty co-operative societies all of which are members of the Toaripi Association of Co-operative Societies. These are mostly dual purpose; the Moveave Co-operative Society also runs a sawmill.

The Ihu-Kerema area is administered from Ihu, where a co-operative association, which carries out wholesaling and supervisory functions on behalf of co-operatives in the area, has its headquarters. There are thirteen co-operative societies in this area, all of which are dual purpose.

In the Baimuru area the societies are for the most part unregistered and uneconomic units. There are five societies of which only one has sought registration.

There was a low rate of growth in co-operative activities during the 1960s, and the problems encountered in the District are common to the movement throughout Papua and New Guinea. Absence of skilled management has resulted in extension of credit to society members but little repayment, leading to financial difficulties. Further, increasing knowledge of business seems to lead to a decline in participation in the co-operative movement. For reasons of prestige and profit many individuals start their own trade stores which compete with the co-operatives. The more successful of these stores develop a substantial trade at the expense of the co-operatives.

The difficulties of establishing business enterprises in areas far removed from major urban centres and with poor transport were highlighted by an attempt to produce hand-woven wall matting from the mid-ribs of sago palm fronds. This project was initiated by Tommy Kabu, a well-known leader in the Purari Delta area. By 1966 two looms were operating, one at Aerava village on a distributary of the Purari and another in Akoma village on the coast. Initially Administration vessels picked up the woven sheets at Aerava.

In 1966 sales were made to the Department of Public Health which used the matting in a low-cost housing programme it undertook in the District in 1966-7. In late 1967 the Administration ceased to pick up the finished sheets and a substantial sale to an oil-prospecting firm in 1967 was the last major business done by the Kabu group. The major problem was transport. Very few motorized canoes are found in the Purari Delta area, and movement of the sheets

CO-OPERATIVE ACTIVITIES FOR YEAR ENDED 31 MARCH 1969

Area	Members	Capital $	Total Turnover $	Store Turnover $	Copra $	Timber $	Other $
Kukipi–Moveave	3,570	132,977	401,804	253,321	90,828	41,413	16,242
Ihu–Kerema	1,555	54,888	134,295	102,138	32,157		
Baimuru	872	13,381	35,201	22,152	12,124		925

to Baimuru where they could be loaded on coastal vessels required eight to twelve hours of paddling. This was a strong disincentive in itself and, coupled with the difficulty of organizing the marketing side of the operation, ultimately led to the failure of this project.

CASH CROPPING

Cash cropping is not a dominant activity in the District. In the year ended 30 June 1969 an estimated three thousand indigenous growers produced 2,156 tons of copra, 5 tons of rubber and 2.5 tons of Robusta coffee. Non-indigenous landholders produced 580 tons of copra and approximately 350 tons of rubber. This non-indigenous output amounted to about 25 per cent of the District's marketed rural output and came from sixteen rural holdings, which is fewer than in any other Papuan District except the Western District.

All coastal settlements possess some coconut palms, and thus copra can be a source of cash income for many villagers—provided transport can be arranged to one of the major centres (see COCONUT INDUSTRY). Rubber production on the other hand is concentrated in the Kerema Bay area. About six miles east of Kerema township is an Australian-owned plantation which with almost 2,000 acres under rubber is the major producer in the District. One of the two significant rubber plantings controlled by Papuans lies between the town and the Australian plantation, the other is at Murua. Neither of these schemes has been an unqualified success. The so-called Cupisi scheme close to the Kerema station initially used a government estate as its basic production unit with subsequent new plantings on traditionally owned land. The Murua scheme is based on re-settlement of individual families on blocks leased from the government. This latter involves forty-six families who have planted 250 acres of high-yielding rubber. Robusta coffee is also being incorporated in the planting scheme at Murua. The problems encountered in endeavouring to achieve self-sustaining operations have been compounded by falling prices for rubber (see RUBBER INDUSTRY).

The total area devoted to tree crops in the District is estimated to be 14,200 acres. No reliable estimates have been made of the area required for subsistence production, but there are considerable areas of unused land which would be suitable for commercial production as some 380,000 acres, 4 per cent of the total area of the District, has been assessed as suitable, with various restrictions, for cropping. It is to be noted that the CSIRO land research officers did not consider any portion of the District surveyed suitable for all cropping. A further 81,000 acres is thought to be suitable for grazing under natural or improved pasture. The bulk of these lands of known agricultural potential are the better-drained alluvial plains of the Vailala, Lakekamu and Tauri Rivers, together with the narrow coastal fringe east from Orokolo Bay and some inland pockets with more gentle topography. Effective utilization of these areas is bedevilled by constraints among which difficulties of access and resolution of land rights loom large.

In the Kikori area there are several small settlement schemes: Omati, Kaiam and Wowo, in which 15- to 20-acre blocks are being planted with coconuts or rubber.

Rice is a crop which has been tried over a long period in the District and in 1969 about twenty tons was produced in the Malalaua area where there is Catholic mission interest in the crop. Increased acreages do not seem likely in the near future.

Provisional development plans for the District drawn up by the Office of the Economic Adviser envisage fairly limited increases, in the short term, in the acreages of cash crops. The main proposals are for about 350 acres of new coconut plantings per year, some undefined but clearly limited expansion of rubber and a rise in the number of Papuan-owned cattle from 8 in June 1969 to 250 by June 1975. Difficulty of transport to markets is the major inhibiting factor in the development of the cattle industry [q.v.].

Fish have been mentioned as being an important source of protein in the subsistence economy, and the resources of the delta region and the Gulf of Papua appear considerable. The most commercially attractive fish of the area is the seasonally available barramundi, which has been airfreighted to Port Moresby by a company at Baimuru. In late 1970 an expatriate company obtained land at Kerema in order to establish a factory to process fish, especially prawns. Local fishing groups however lack easily accessible urban markets in which to sell their catch and consequently have not exploited this resource.

FORESTRY

A comprehensive District-wide survey is planned by the Department of Forests for 1971. However, the forest potential of the Gulf District is at present assessed at 483,000 acres. In addition, some 2,283,000 acres are believed to have economic potential but require much more detailed assessment to indicate the volume, nature and extent of the resource. The possible area of potential forest is therefore of the order of 2,766,000 acres, of which 121,000 acres are at present controlled by the Department of Forests through purchases of timber rights.

Four sawmills operate in the District: Baimuru and Era in the Kikori Sub-District, Ihu in the Kerema Sub-District and Moveave in the Kukipi Sub-District. They have an annual output of approximately 2,500,000 super feet of sawn timber valued at $300,000. The first three of these mills are expatriate business ventures, while Moveave sawmill is a co-operatively owned venture established by the people of the Moveave villages in 1963.

This last enterprise, the largest co-operative business in the District, has been the subject of close examination by research workers, who believe that it could be a prototype for large-scale village industries. The considerable management and technical problems of this enterprise (R. K. Wilson, 1968) still persisted in 1970. This may be due in part to the large-scale emigration of school leavers sufficiently educated to acquire the management and technical skills required. This drift of the younger generation to the larger urban areas, leaving the milling operation in the hands of the middle-aged and elderly, has probably had an adverse effect on the standard of management. What are reported to be some of the best stands of New Guinea walnut in the country occur in the Tauri River area being logged by the Moveave co-operative sawmill. Should an export market be developed for this valuable furniture timber, the Co-operative Society would obtain a substantial increase in its revenue.

The bulk of timber produced in the District is shipped to Port Moresby where the tremendous building programme of the 1960s provided a strong demand. Expansion of the industry does not appear likely in the near future (*see* FORESTRY; TIMBER INDUSTRY).

COMMUNICATIONS

Movement of goods and people is mainly by sea and air.

All major movement of goods, inter- and intra-District, is by shallow-draught coastal vessels. Kerema, as the main centre, has three coastal vessels call each week from Port Moresby. Vessels of up to eight-feet draught can enter Kerema at nearly all times of the year. The four other ports, Kikori, Baimuru, Ihu and the landing for Malalaua, each receive at least one coastal vessel per week. Both Kikori and Kerema have watering facilities and it is planned to provide bunkering at Kerema. The Administration operates three small vessels in the District, one of which is used for medical work.

Nine airstrips serve the District, none of which can accommodate large aircraft such as the DC3. Kerema, Malalaua, Kikori, Baimuru and Ihu have strips which can take aircraft such as the Twin Otter, of up to 12,500 pounds all-up weight. The other airfields, for example at Kaintiba, are restricted to light aircraft. However, these airfields are a vital link in the communications network of the District as they make possible the rapid movement of people, mail, etc. Increasingly villagers are placing a premium on greater mobility and the people of Iokea and Lese-Oalai villages in the East Kerema area are constructing authorized landing areas so that chartered aircraft can move people in and out. There is one aircraft stationed in the District for charter work and Kerema has seven services per week to Port Moresby.

Very little road development has taken place in the District. Approximately 55 miles, mainly in the Ihu and Kerema areas, had been completed by April 1970. However, roads are now being accorded a higher priority and work is under way on a series of them, three of which radiate from Kerema. The centres to be linked, and mileages involved, are: Kerema–Malalaua, 55 miles; Kerema–Vailala, 25 miles; Kerema–Kaintiba, 50 miles; and Kaintiba–Menyamya, 30 miles. During 1971-2 it is intended to begin two other roads, namely Malalaua–Terapo, 10 miles and Cape Possession–Popo, 44 miles. These roads will have an important integrating effect when completed. The oft-mentioned Papua to New Guinea road link appears to be materializing in the proposed Kerema–Kaintiba–Menyamya–Wau link, portions of which were being constructed in late 1970.

CONCLUSION

The impression emerging from a survey of the Gulf District is that little economic development has occurred. Even though considerable areas of land with moderate to high potential for arable or tree crops are at present unused, social and economic barriers, such as problems of unresolved land ownership and difficulties of access, preclude a dramatic surge forward in the immediate future. Only a major crude-oil discovery would give significant impetus to the slow rate of development.

In 1959 Brookfield said of the delta area: 'A more practical line of thinking might be along the lines of complete removal of some population to wage-employment areas.' This has not been Administration policy but nevertheless a major migration has occurred to Port Moresby and other major urban centres. The recent estimate of a 30 per cent absentee rate from the coastal areas is a most significant revelation of how many people of the Gulf District perceive the opportunities in their own area in comparison with opportunities elsewhere. It also seems to confirm, in economic terms, the popular conception of the District.

Australasian Petroleum Company Proprietary Limited, 'Geological Results of Petroleum Exploration in Western Papua 1937-61', *Journal of the Geological Society of Australia*, vol. 8, 1961.
H. C. Brookfield, 'Two Population Problem Areas of Papua-New Guinea', *South Pacific*, vol. 10, 1959.
CSIRO, 'Lands of the Kerema-Vailala Area, Territory of Papua and New Guinea', *Land Research Series*, no. 23, 1969.
Department of National Development, Division of Regional Planning, *The Resources of the Territory of Papua and New Guinea*, 2 vols, Canberra, 1951.
G. R. Hogbin, 'A Survey of Indigenous Rubber Producers in the Kerema Bay Area', *New Guinea Research Unit Bulletin*, no. 5, 1964.
J. H. Holmes, *In Primitive New Guinea*. London, 1924.
R. F. Maher, *New Men of Papua*. Madison, 1961.
D. Ryan, 'The Toaripi Association: Some Problems of Economic Development in Papua', *Mankind*, vol. 6, 1963-7.
T. P. N. G. Bureau of Statistics, *Population Census 1966; Preliminary Bulletin, No. 22, Gulf District*. Port Moresby, 1969.
—— *Transport and Communications Bulletin, No. 8, 1969.* Port Moresby, 1970.
—— *Rural Industries Bulletin 1968-69.* Port Moresby, 1970.
T. P. N. G. Department of Agriculture, Stock and Fisheries, *Indigenous Crop and Cattle Statistics, No. 3, 1968-69.* Port Moresby, 1970.

T. P. N. G. Department of District Administration, *Village Directory*. Port Moresby, 1968.
——— 'An Introduction to the Gulf District of the Territory of Papua and New Guinea', paper prepared for the visit by the Administrator's Executive Council to the Gulf District 1970.
T. P. N. G. Department of Information and Extension Services, *Districts of Papua and New Guinea*. Port Moresby, 1969.
D. J. van de Kaa, 'The Future Growth of Papua-New Guinea's Population', paper presented to the Population Growth and Economic Development Seminar, University of Papua and New Guinea, 1970. *New Guinea Research Bulletin* (forthcoming).
R. G. Ward and D. A. M. Lea (eds), *An Atlas of Papua and New Guinea*. Glasgow, 1970.
——— 'Internal Migration and Urbanization in Papua and New Guinea', paper presented to the Population Growth and Economic Development Seminar, University of Papua and New Guinea, 1970. *New Guinea Research Bulletin* (forthcoming).
F. E. Williams, 'The Vailala Madness and the Destruction of Native Ceremonies in the Gulf Division', Territory of Papua, *Anthropology Report*, no. 4. Port Moresby, 1923.
——— 'The Natives of the Purari Delta', Territory of Papua, *Anthropology Report*, no. 5. Port Moresby, 1924.
——— *Drama of Orokolo*. Oxford, 1940.
R. K. Wilson, 'Village Industries in Papua-New Guinea', *New Guinea Research Bulletin*, no. 20, 1967.
——— and R. Garnaut, 'A Survey of Village Industries in Papua-New Guinea', *New Guinea Research Bulletin*, no. 25, 1968.

J. RUMENS

GUNTHER, John Thomson (1910-   ), vice-chancellor, was born in Sydney on 2 October 1910, and graduated in medicine from the University of Sydney. He was a medical officer in the British Solomon Islands in the 1930s, led an investigation into lead poisoning in Queensland 1938-41, and served in the Royal Australian Air Force in the Pacific war, with special responsibilities in matters of tropical medicine. In 1949 he became Director of Public Health in the Territory of Papua and New Guinea, and Assistant Administrator of the Territory in 1957. In 1966 he accepted appointment as first vice-chancellor of the University of Papua and New Guinea [q.v.] and began the task of supervising the creation of a new institution, literally from its foundation upwards. He was made C.M.G. in 1965.

GURURUMBA. People of the Eastern Highlands District. References:

P. L. Newman, Supernaturalism and Ritual among the Gururumba. Ph.D. thesis, University of Washington, 1962.
——— ' "Wild Man" Behaviour in a New Guinea Highlands Community', *American Anthropologist*, vol. 66, 1964.
——— 'Religious Belief and Ritual in a New Guinea Society', *American Anthropologist*, vol. 66, Special Publication, 1964.
——— *Knowing the Gururumba*. New York, 1965.

H

HABER, Eduard (1866-19??), German administrator, was born on 1 October 1866 at Riesa in Prussia. After qualifying as a mining engineer in 1893 he joined the Colonial Section of the Foreign Office in 1900. He was posted to German East Africa as a mining expert in 1901 but was soon involved in general administrative duties and became the senior administrative assistant to the governor in October 1903. He was decorated by the Kaiser for devotion to duty during the East African uprising against the German government in 1905-6. At the end of 1906 he returned to Berlin and became a senior official of the Colonial Office.

Haber's professional interest in mining directed his attention to New Guinea and accounted for his acceptance of an appointment there as acting Governor when Hahl [q.v.] went on leave in April 1914. He left Berlin in January of that year expecting to succeed Hahl, but the announcement of his appointment had not been made when war broke out. Consequently it was as acting Governor that he signed the terms of capitulation in September 1914. He was repatriated to Germany in 1915 and in the later stages of the war served in the German Red Cross on the Romanian Front. His appointment as Governor of German New Guinea was officially announced in December 1917.

Haber appears to have had great difficulty in finding a new career after the war. Finally in 1930 he became a lecturer on colonial and industrial affairs at the university at Tübingen. The date of his death is not known. MARJORIE JACOBS

HADDON, Alfred Cort (1855-1940), anthropologist, was born in London on 24 May 1855, elder son of John Haddon, head of a printing firm. His mother published children's books under the name of Caroline Hadley, and Alfred never lost this early interest. After a broken schooling he went up to Christ's College, Cambridge, in 1875 where he took a first in natural sciences and became curator of the Zoological Museum and university Demonstrator in Zoology. In 1880 he was appointed Professor of Zoology at the Royal College of Science in Dublin. In 1889 he went to the Torres Strait and there became interested in recording native custom before it was affected by European contact, and after his return to England he accepted a part-time lectureship in physical anthropology at Cambridge, organizing in 1898 the famous Cambridge Torres Strait expedition which brought him to British New Guinea. He was elected F.R.S. in 1899. In 1909 he became Reader in Ethnology at Cambridge where he remained until 1925. He died on 20 April 1940.

A. C. Haddon, *The Races of Man and their Distribution*. Cambridge, 1924; *The Dictionary of National Biography 1931-1940*. London, 1949. FRANCIS WEST

HAGEN, MOUNT. People of the Western Highlands District. References:
M. Reay, 'The Minj Open Electorate', in *The Papua-New Guinea Elections 1964*, ed. D. G. Bettison, C. A. Hughes and P. W. van der Veur. Canberra, 1965.
A. Strathern, 'Despots and Directors in the New Guinea Highlands', *Man*, new series, vol. 1, 1966.
———— 'Finance and Production', *Oceania*, vol. 40, 1969-70.
———— and M. Strathern, 'Minj Open Electorate: the Campaign in the Dei Council Area' (New Guinea's First Election), *Journal of the Polynesian Society*, vol. 73, 1964.
———— 'Marriage in Melpa', in *Pigs, Pearlshells, and Women: Marriage in the New Guinea Highlands*, ed. R. M. Glasse and M. J. Meggitt. Englewood Cliffs, N.J., 1969.
H. Tischner, 'Eine ethnographische Sammlung aus dem östlichen Zentral-Neuguinea (Hagen-Gebirge, Wagi-Tal, Ramu)'. Hamburg, Museum für Völkerkunde, *Mitteilungen*, vol. 21, 1939.
G. F. Vicedom, 'Ein neuentdecktes Volk in Neuguinea. Völkerkundliche Beobachtungen an der Bevölkerung des Hagen-Berges im ehemals deutschen Teil von Neuguinea', *Archiv für Anthropologie*, vol. 24, 1937-8.
———— and H. Tischner, *Die Mbowamb*. 3 vols. Hamburg, 1943-8.
F. E. Williams, 'The Natives of Mount Hagen, Papua: Further Notes', *Man*, vol. 37, 1937.

HAHL, Albert (1868-1945), German administrator, was born at Gern in Lower Bavaria on 10 September 1868. He attended the gymnasium at Freising until 1887 when he went to the University of Würzburg to study law and economics. After passing the state examination in 1894, he was immediately employed in the Department of the Interior in Bavaria. In 1895 he went to Berlin to enter the Colonial Section (Kolonialabteilung) of the Foreign Office and six months later left for New Guinea as Imperial Judge (Kaiserlicher Richter) in the Bismarck Archipelago.

Hahl was appointed Vice-Governor of the East Caroline Islands in 1899. He returned to Kokopo in May 1901 as acting Governor and after a severe illness left in June of the following year to spend his leave in Germany. He was appointed Governor of German New Guinea on 20 November 1902. In this capacity he was responsible for the administration of the Micronesian Islands as well as the Bismarck Archipelago, the German Solomon Islands and the north-eastern part of the mainland of New Guinea. He published a number of articles on New Guinea while he was in office.

Hahl's term as governor terminated in May 1914, when he was on leave in Germany. He was contemplating a career outside the government when the outbreak of war led to his retention in the service of the Colonial Office until 1916; he then went to Constantinople as adviser to the Turkish Ministry for Trade and Agriculture.

After the war Hahl was invited to join the New Guinea Company as a director, and was associated with it until World War II. In this period the Company attempted to compensate for the loss of its holdings in New Guinea by investment in the Cameroons and Venezuela. Although he did not again visit New Guinea, he retained his interest in the former German colonies throughout the 1920s and the Nazi period. He belonged to the group of 'ex-colonials' who supported the Deutsche Kolonialgesellschaft in its bid to keep German interest in colonies alive. In the late 1930s he wrote several books, including his autobiography *Gouverneursjahre in Neuguinea*, for which he had been collecting material for several years. They were clearly intended to publicize the colonial past in Hitler's Germany, but there is no evidence in them of adherence to Nazi doctrines. On the contrary, their unadorned prose, strict adherence to facts, and reiteration of the views about the indigenous people that he had held before 1914 suggest that Hahl was not at ease in his association with Nazi colonial propaganda, although he did in 1938 accept an appointment to the Kolonialrat of the Reichskolonialbund.

Albert Hahl.

He was one of the most successful of all the German colonial governors. Physically courageous, humane and resourceful, he combined common-sense with intellectual curiosity in his approach to New Guinea. An unpretentious ease of manner won him the respect of the rather bizarre community of whites and part-Samoans at Kokopo in 1900; it made him equally at home in the villages of the Gazelle Peninsula, where he learned to talk to the leading men in their own language. He was no theorist in colonial relations.

In February 1903 Hahl married Luise Freiin von Seckendorff-Aberdar. They had two daughters and one son. He died on Christmas Day 1945, his wife having died ten years previously.

A. Hahl, *Gouverneursjahre in Neuguinea.* Berlin, 1937.

MARJORIE JACOBS

(*See also* GERMAN NEW GUINEA)

HANDICRAFTS INDUSTRY. The New Guinea villager traditionally made many handicrafts from stone, wood and fibre for utilitarian, ritual and decorative purposes. In some areas, particularly those with long contact, the missions frowned on ritual and art died out as ritual declined; but today the general attitude of missionaries is much more permissive, with one or two exceptions amongst the fundamentalist sects, while a minority of missions actually engage in the handicrafts trade. Utilitarian handicrafts are still made for everyday use; these include bags, baskets, mats, plaited walling, pottery, woven roofing, vine ropes, nets, fish traps, bowls, canoes, grass skirts, walking sticks, lime spatulas, gourds, hats, bows and arrows, and spears. Some of these find a market as curios, but most trade is in carvings of ritual and decorative objects from only a few of the many regions of the Territory of Papua and New Guinea. Carvings and art forms of many other regions are now to be found only in museums. The trade in handicrafts is a fairly recent development, supported partly by the growing tourist trade and partly by the expansion of the foreign market for curios and exotic art forms.

The main areas in which handicrafts are made are the Sepik, Madang, and Western Highlands Districts, the Vitiaz Straits, the Trobriand Islands [q.v.], Bougainville, and the coast of the Central District around Port Moresby. Sepik artefacts that are traded include traditional drums, masks, stools, statues and food hooks, some of them made for use in the yam ceremonies connected with the house *tambaran*. Traditional items may be sold after their ceremonial use is finished but most carvings are made specifically for sale and include figurines, crocodiles and other animals, food bowls and carved tables. Some are aged artificially by hanging in smoke or by submerging in water before sale. Although carving may be the only source of cash income in some areas and is invariably a part-time occupation, it has spread more widely than in traditional times when there were reservations about the art. Hospital patients in towns along the Sepik River and at Wewak carve full-time and from these centres styles of one district have spread to another and now there is great stylistic confusion.

Artefacts from Maprik are highly coloured in red, white, yellow and black, particularly the masks which are often made of wicker daubed with coloured clay. Preservation of these items is difficult as the clay tends to crack. Pottery is made at Wosera, near Maprik, on islands off Wewak and at Aibom and other places along the Sepik, but Aibom has adopted exotic styles, including mugs with faces reminiscent of German beer mugs but, because the pottery is fragile, little is exported. More durable pots are made at Yabob village, near Madang, and considerable numbers are sold both for village use and as curios.

In the Wewak-Sepik area the handicrafts trade is largely in the hands of either river traders, who bring in trade goods and send out artefacts and crocodile skins, or missionaries who, with their many posts and contacts with village people, are in a good position to buy. Purchases are forwarded to wholesale depots in Wewak and elsewhere and from there are sold mainly overseas to meet the orders of curio dealers in Europe and North America, and of private collectors and museums. The value of exports of native curios in 1965-6 was given as $92,000, of which $75,000 went through Madang and Wewak. This figure greatly understates the value of the whole trade, as much is taken by tourists in person and much is posted as ordinary postal articles and not assessed. The total value was, probably, twice the official export figure and is rising rapidly.

There is no doubt of the predominant position of the Sepik in the recorded trade. Of this it has been estimated that traders and missions have about equal shares, and a minor position is held by sales by Local Government Councils and direct sales by carvers to visitors. Should the tourist trade of the Sepik expand as may be expected, sales directly to tourists can be expected to rise, but this would probably be additional to, rather than competitive with, the trade passing through existing sales outlets.

In the Morobe District the most distinctive carving is that of the Tami Islanders, a small community now shifted to the mainland but in command of a special technique and design for making wooden tableware, particularly bowls, which have superb balance and decoration. On the Siassi Islands in the Vitiaz Strait, canoes are made for sale, and other carvings, including tableware, are being produced. Lae probably surpasses Port Moresby as a retail outlet for curios, because it is a tourist crossroads. In Manus, New Ireland and most of New Britain handicrafts are not made for sale and famous art forms, such as the carved wooden figures of New Ireland *malanggan* [q.v.], have practically disappeared. On Bougainville, the basketware of Buin constitutes perhaps the most distinctive utilitarian handicraft of New Guinea. The raw material is a thin vine which is pliable when woven and hardens to form a very sturdy basket. Many hundreds of people now make the basketware part-time, and wholesaling is in the

hands of two large co-operatives. The ware is retailed in Rabaul and through trading firms in Australia, but demand generally exceeds supply. The technique was also taken to Karkar Island off Madang, where a product little inferior is now made.

The Western Highlands District is famous for Mount Hagen stone axes but the process is time-consuming, relatively few are produced, and all are assured of ready sale. Spears and bows and arrows are the other artefacts traded from the Highlands, but otherwise the curio trade is little developed. In the Northern District of Papua many handicrafts such as pottery, tapa cloth, pandanus bags and mats, carved wooden figures and other carvings are made, but trade is little organized and most of it is sold through retailers in Lae. The Trobriand Islands have become a tourist centre, and regular charter flights bring tourists from all main towns to a hotel on Kiriwina. Carving has increased very greatly under the stimulus of tourism and partly because of a lack of other sources of cash income due to relative over-population. It has been estimated that in 1966 the Trobriand income from carvings was at least $27,000, mostly from direct sales to tourists, a minor part from purchases by traders for export, and from a small amount bought by missions. Quality of carving has shown a drastic decline in face of the great rise in demand and in the volume of production. Grass skirts, shells, beads and pearls of low value are offered to tourists as well as all types of carved fish, reptiles, bowls, paddles, walking sticks, figurines, stools and many other objects of non-traditional design. In the remainder of Papua there is little handicraft trade except around Port Moresby itself, where the people make model canoes, shell beads, pandanus mats and bags, and a limited amount of pottery from Porebada village which is mainly sold as flower pots. In most of the main towns immigrant workers carve in their spare time and hawk around a certain amount of carving mainly of Sepik or imitation Sepik design, though often finished in inappropriate modern materials such as glossy varnish.

The National Cultural Property (Preservation) Ordinance 1965 operates to protect and preserve objects of cultural or historical importance and all items to be exported require a permit signed by the District Commissioner. If it is felt that the items should be preserved the permit may be refused and the item sold to the Papua and New Guinea Museum and Art Gallery. Most contemporary carving is unaffected by the provision but stone carvings, which are generally not contemporary, are not usually permitted to be exported, though there is no provision for inspecting individual parcels in the post, and much ancient art is undoubtedly exported in this manner.

The expansion of the handicraft trade has been strongly encouraged by the great rise in price and in volume demanded in North America and very great profits are commonly made. The dealer in the Sepik and the wholesaler there may each have a mark-up of 100 per cent and a retail dealer in

Australia the same, but this margin is small compared with retail prices in the U.S.A. The supply of items more than twenty years old is now declining, but demand for contemporary pieces is still buoyant and the trade may come to be based on these, except for serious collectors who may still be able to recover the art of earlier generations by assiduous searching. Overall, the handicrafts industry has brought a new source of income to villagers as well as to traders, missions and retailers and, while the effect on quality has been adverse, much of this art would otherwise have died out.

A. McBean, 'Handicrafts of the South Seas', *South Pacific Bulletin*, vol. 14, 1964.

R. K. W.

(*See also* ART)

HANNETT, Leo Joseph (1941-   ), author, was born on Nissan Island in 1941. He spent his infancy during World War II in the British Solomon Islands. He was educated at Rigu, Bougainville, at Catholic seminaries in Rabaul and Madang and at the University of Papua and New Guinea. He was the first Papuan or New Guinean to matriculate within the country and he graduated B.A. in 1971.

At the seminary in Madang he produced a small magazine called *Dialogue*, which was the first indigenous publication. He criticized the 'troika of exploiters' (the Administration, the planters and the missions) and was subsequently asked to leave the seminary. He was a prominent defender of the land rights of the Rorovana people in Bougainville in 1969. He has written and lectured widely on New Guinean nationalism at home and in Australia, and has had two plays successfully produced, *Road Bilong Cargo* and *The Ungrateful Daughter*.

HANSEMANN, Adolph von (1827-1903), German banker, was born at Aachen on 27 July 1827, the eldest son of a prosperous wool merchant, David Hansemann. The latter, after a brief venture into politics as a Liberal deputy and then Finance Minister in the Prussian National Assembly of 1848, moved to Berlin, where in 1851 he founded a private bank, the Disconto-Gesellschaft. Meanwhile the son, who had been taken from school at the age of sixteen to gain experience in commerce, had built up a flourishing textile factory in Eupen. In 1857 he yielded to his father's wish that he should move to Berlin to join him in the Disconto-Gesellschaft. The death of David Hansemann in 1864 left Adolph in control of the bank, a position that he was retain until his death in 1903. Expansion under his management made it for a time the largest private bank in Germany.

Adolph von Hansemann's success owed much to his own astuteness and energy, and much to the opportunities created by German industrial and commercial expansion after 1871. The activities of the Disconto-Gesellschaft included loans to the German and foreign governments, investment in various branches of industry, railways and real estate in Berlin, and, towards the end of the century, ventures in South America, China and the Pacific. Von Hansemann's part in helping to finance the war of 1870 established him in political circles in Berlin, where Bismarck thought well of him. His company played a leading part in financing the rapid development of the coal and iron industries of the Rhineland and Westphalia and German railways. In Europe the Disconto-Gesellschaft was prominent in loans to foreign governments, especially to the Austro-Hungarian Empire and Romania, where it was associated with the Rothschilds.

In the 1880s von Hansemann, like other bankers in Germany, began to look further afield for investment opportunities. South America attracted him, then China, where he played a leading part in launching the Deutsch-Asiatische Bank in 1889 and in establishing a large German company for railway development in Shantung province in 1899.

His enthusiasm for German colonial ventures seems to have sprung partly from anticipation of profitable investment, partly from a personal conviction that the possession of colonies would enhance Germany's status in the world. He was in a strong position to advance his views. Not only was he personally known to Bismarck, but in his brother-in-law, Heinrich von Kusserow, he had an ally who shared his views and gave him a voice in the Foreign Office, where von Kusserow was a prominent official in the 1880s. Von Hansemann was interested in German South-west Africa; he was a strong supporter of the Colonial Society (Deutsche Kolonialgesellschaft) and a member of the official Advisory Council on the Colonies (Kolonialrat) from 1891 till his death.

But New Guinea seems to have absorbed most of the attention that he directed to the colonies; it was his hobby as well as his investment. Furniture was made from New Guinea timber for his house in the fashionable Tiergarten; his cigars were made from New Guinea tobacco. Despite heavy financial loss to himself and the Disconto-Gesellschaft, he retained his enthusiasm for the colony till his death.

Adolph von Hansemann married Ottilie von Kusserow in 1860. They had one son and one daughter. He was ennobled in 1872. Later in his life he was reputed to be one of the richest men in Germany. He had large estates and a country residence at Dwasieden in the province of Posen. It was here that his private papers were probably destroyed during World War II. Those of the New Guinea Company and the Disconto-Gesellschaft were lost simultaneously with Hahl's private papers in the bombing of Berlin in 1945.

MARJORIE JACOBS

(*See also* GERMAN NEW GUINEA)

HANUABADA. The name, meaning 'big village', is now applied to the settlement largely built on piles over the water a mile or so north of the shopping centre of Port Moresby [q.v.]. The population in 1966 was almost four thousand. Originally there were three villages separated by

Hanuabada today.

stretches of open beach: Hanuabada itself, Tanobada and Elevala. Most of the people belong to
the Motu group [q.v.], but a Koita minority
occupy two sections, one in the original Hanuabada, the other in Tanobada. All now speak the
Motu language. Before 1942 the dwellings were
built of native materials, but the population was
evacuated in that year and the place turned over
to the labourers conscripted by the Army. By the
end of the war so many houses had been destroyed, and the rest were in such disrepair, that
the Administration rebuilt the village, using sawn
timber and corrugated iron. The usual house
measurements are forty feet by fifteen feet, with
a verandah in front. The sand fireplace has been
replaced by a kerosene stove.

The basic social unit is ostensibly the patrilineage, though sometimes a man takes up a permanent residence with his wife's relatives, and
the children then become full members of their
mother's group rather than of the father's. Till
recently each of these so-called patrilineages occupied a line of houses joined by a gangway extending from the shore out into the bay. Nowadays,
however, more than a third of the people prefer
to live ashore, and the traditional pattern is becoming blurred. At the same time, the rule of
patrilineage exogamy is still observed.

In pre-European times the economy was based
chiefly on fishing, hunting, pot-making, and trading. The soil in the neighbourhood is poor and
the rainfall low, and the yield from yam gardens
and banana groves was insufficient to support the
population. Every year therefore expeditions
called *hiri* [q.v.] were fitted out to take a cargo
of pots to the far side of the Gulf of Papua and
exchange them for supplies of sago, which then
for months became the staple diet.

Modern Hanuabadans, by contrast, are almost
completely dependent upon cash income. All the
children attend school, and many go on to further education in secondary and even tertiary
institutions like the Administrative College and
university. Most of the males over the age of
seventeen have constant employment as clerks in
the public service, school teachers, artisans, and
mechanics; and a few work on their own as building contractors or traders. The unmarried girls
also are trained as typists, shop assistants,
teachers, or nurses. No trading voyage across the
Gulf has taken place for years; fishing and hunting—with shot-guns in place of spears—are carried on mainly at weekends for the sport; and
the cultivations have shrunk in acreage. Pot-making is virtually a lost art, and although the women
still make grass skirts in quantity, the reason is
that tourists from Australia provide a market
ready to hand.

C. S. Belshaw, *The Great Village*. London, 1957; R. B. Dakeyne, *Village and Town in New Guinea*. Melbourne, 1969; M. Groves, 'Dancing in Poreporena', *Journal of the Royal Anthropological Institute*, vol. 84, 1954; N. Oram, 'The Hula in Port Moresby', *Oceania*, vol. 39, 1968-9; C. G. Seligman, *The Melanesians of British New Guinea*. Cambridge, 1910.

R. B. DAKEYNE

HASLUCK, Sir Paul Meernaa Caedwalla (1905-), author, cabinet minister and Governor-General, was born in Fremantle, Western Australia, on 1 April 1905. He is a graduate of the University of Western Australia, and worked as a journalist, a university teacher and a senior officer of the Department of External Affairs. He entered the Commonwealth Parliament in 1949, having won the Western Australian seat of Curtin. He has held the portfolios of Defence (1963-4), Territories (1951-63) and External Affairs (1964-9). In 1969 he was created G.C.M.G. and was appointed Governor-General of Australia.

The extended period during which he was the minister responsible for Papua and New Guinea saw vast changes in the Territory, the virtual completion of its exploration and great expansion in government services and economic development. While the merits of some of Sir Paul's policies were warmly debated, there is no question that he brought to the administration of his Territory portfolio the force of a trained mind and a seriousness of purpose that were something quite new. Until then the Department of Territories had been something of a backwater. The Australian government, during Hasluck's ministry, was obliged to set Papua and New Guinea in the forefront of its attention, and to increase the funds allocated to it to more realistic dimensions.

His books include *Black Australians* (Melbourne, 1942; reprinted 1970) and two volumes, *The Government and the People, 1939-41* and *The Government and the People, 1942-45*, in the official history 'Australia in the War of 1939-1945', which deal with political and civil affairs during World War II.

HAY, David Osborne (1916-), administrator and public servant, was born at Corowa, New South Wales, on 29 November 1916. He is a graduate of Oxford and Melbourne Universities, and served in the Australian army in the Middle East, Greece and New Guinea for almost the whole of World War II. He was awarded the D.S.O. and later, in 1963, was created C.B.E.

After some seventeen years in senior diplomatic posts, he was appointed Administrator of Papua and New Guinea on 9 January 1967, and held the appointment until 22 July 1970. His term as Administrator saw the rapid acceleration of political development in New Guinea, and significant unrest, especially in the Gazelle Peninsula of New Britain. From the Administratorship he moved to become Secretary of the Australian Department of External Territories.

HEALTH EDUCATION. Health education of an informal or personal sort was given from the earliest days of Christian missions and European governments in Papua and New Guinea, and important work was done by individuals for the health and welfare of the indigenous communities in which they worked. However, health education as a discipline or as an organized service has been developed only in recent years. Three main influences in the setting up of newer health education services were: the efforts of the Director of Public Health; the influence of the South Pacific Commission; the professional guidance and practical assistance of the World Health Organization. Recently, through its Western Pacific Regional Office, W.H.O. has played an important role in the establishment of health education services upon a satisfactory professional basis in Papua and New Guinea.

To 1966. The following are the more important developments up to 1966, in which year health education services entered a new phase.

In 1957-8 W.H.O. fellowships were granted to two officers of the Department of Public Health to study health education in London. Upon their return both were posted to duty with the malaria services, and one, Mr L. Tomlinson, came to Port Moresby in 1959 to set up a health education section in the Department of Public Health. In 1961 the other London trained officer, Mr R. Carlaw, took over the management of the health education services.

From April 1959 until 1964 a Health Education Council was in operation. It was a co-operative committee whose members represented the Departments of Public Health, Education, Native Affairs, and Agriculture, Stock and Fisheries. One of its important achievements was the organization of a Territory-wide survey of beliefs and attitudes in health and related matters.

A system of health education orderlies was begun, in which aid post orderlies were given six weeks training in elementary health education methods, and then detailed for field work in the districts. Between 1962 and 1965 six such training courses were held, and 105 orderlies received instruction.

From 1964 to 1966 the health education section was under the control of the Assistant Director of Medical Training, Dr W. Symes. Activities expanded in such fields as health broadcasts, health education 'workshop' activities and health publications. Uses of radio include the 'Radio Doctor' series from Administration broadcasting stations and schools broadcasts produced with the Department of Education and the Australian Broadcasting Commission, and transmitted to schools over the A.B.C. network. Both are successful programmes; the 'Radio Doctor' series has run for three years, and school health broadcasts cover one year of primary school health education, the series being repeated each year.

By the end of 1966 ten Administration officers had received health education training overseas, and five of them were working in the health education services. The end of the first phase of development of health education services was marked by visits by the W.H.O. Regional Adviser in 1965 and 1966, and by a W.H.O. Consultant on Health Education from January to March 1966.

After 1966. Following the W.H.O. visits, Dr E. J. Wright was appointed to plan and organize the health education services of the Territory. He was assisted by Mr K. Riggall, who was later seconded to the Department of Education for school health education work, and by Miss J. Abijah, a Papuan with two years overseas training who showed outstanding ability. She was the forerunner of several competent Papuan and New Guinean officers well able in the near future to assume full responsibility for the Territory's health education services and training.

In June 1968 a W.H.O. Consultant on Health Education, Teodora V. Tiglao, visited the Territory for four weeks to assist the Administration to review developments since the previous visits of W.H.O. staff in 1966. Her report, dated 13 September 1968, provides a good review of progress in health education.

The Mission from the International Bank for Reconstruction and Development which surveyed Papua and New Guinea in 1963 suggested that expenditure on health education services should be increased, and the Administration of Papua and New Guinea has taken the view that a certain standard of health education, apart from its personal and social value, is a prerequisite for economic development. Such education trains ordinary men and women to maintain and promote health, so that they are fit to do their work in the community. By self-help and community responsibility, it mobilizes great latent manpower resources and prevents some of the costly mistakes which may occur in major health projects when educational and social science aspects are not fully taken into account.

Acting on the advice of the W.H.O. consultants four papers were prepared by E. J. Wright which laid down in detail the structure of the health education programme. By the end of 1968 many of the objectives set out in those papers had been achieved.

The health education section has three main functions: training, services and research. Training is carried out largely through the Institute of Health Education in Port Moresby, and its work may be summed up in the following way.

(1) Post-basic training through the course for the Diploma of Health Education. About one hundred persons applied for the first course in 1967, twenty-nine were admitted, twenty-four completed the course, ten qualified for the Diploma of Health Education and eight for the certificate. The curriculum provides 1600 hours of study and experience, divided equally between principles and practice of health education; methods and media; basic biological science as a foundation of health education; social science as a foundation of health education.

(2) Pre-service training of doctors, medical assistants, health inspectors, nurses, dental officers and teachers.

(3) In-service training courses for teachers, social welfare officers, ministers and pastors of the Christian missions.

(4) Training of village teachers and village people. Services will be extended through health educators in the various administrative Districts. Their chief concern will be secondary health education, and the development of all governmental and community health education resources.

Much progress has been made, and Tiglao's report of 1968 states: 'One cannot but be impressed by the developments . . . in the past two years . . . by and large sound principles of planning are reflected in the development of the total health education programme'.

T. V. Tiglao, *Assignment Report*, by Short-term Consultant on Health Education. W.H.O. Regional Office for the Western Pacific, 1968 (roneoed, WPR/ 324/68); E. J. Wright, *Diploma in Health Education.* Port Moresby, 1967 (roneoed); ——— *District Health Education Services in Papua-New Guinea.* Port Moresby, 1967 (roneoed); ——— *Professional Health Education Services for Papua-New Guinea.* Port Moresby, 1967 (roneoed); ——— *From the Outside: A Discussion on School Health Education.* Port Moresby, 1968 (roneoed).

E. J. WRIGHT

HERBERT, Charles Edward (1860-1929), judge and administrator, was born at Strathalbyn, South Australia, in 1860. Called to the Bar in 1883 he became Government Resident and Judge in the Northern Territory after four years as a member of the South Australian Parliament. In 1906 Herbert was appointed one of the three Royal Commissioners into the existing state and future prospects of Papua under Australian rule, and Hubert Murray [q.v.] thought of him as a possible appointment to the lieutenant-governorship. When Murray himself was appointed while still retaining the post of Chief Judicial Officer, the convenience of a deputy judge soon became apparent and in 1910 Herbert was appointed Deputy Chief Judicial Officer. He remained in this office, occasionally acting as Administrator during Murray's absences, until 1927 when he was appointed Administrator of Norfolk Island. He died in 1929.

F. J. West, *Hubert Murray: The Australian Pro-Consul.* Melbourne, 1968. Herbert's official papers are in the Commonwealth Archives Office.

FRANCIS WEST

HIDES, Jack Gordon (1906-1938), government officer, was born at Port Moresby on 23 June 1906, the second of the seven children of Horace Herbert and Helena Marie Hides. His formal education was limited: Port Moresby European School 1911-17; State school Einasleigh (Q'ld) 1917; private tuition 1918-19; State school Maleny (Q'ld) 1920. He left school at fourteen and for several years his mother assisted him to educate himself privately. A fine swimmer and runner, Hides was six feet tall and thinly built. He joined the Papuan Public Service in July 1925 as a Cadet Clerk, was appointed Cadet Patrol Officer in May 1926 and Patrol Officer in February 1928. He was promoted to Assistant Resident Magistrate in February 1934. He served at Kambisi Police Camp, Cape Nelson, Kairuku, Kerema, Kikori, Daru, Buna Bay, Mondo Police Camp and Misima, making his field reputation with patrols from Kerema north into the so-called Kukukuku country, and on patrols to arrest murderers from Daru, and from Kikori and Mondo into the mountains of the Central Division. In September 1934 Hides was chosen by Sir Hubert Murray [q.v.] to undertake the exploration of the last remaining unexplored country in Papua, between the Strickland and Purari Rivers. Patrol Officer L. J. O'Malley was his companion. The patrol left Daru on 1 January 1935 by launch and canoes and ascended the Strickland River to the junction with the Rentoul, then proceeding up the Rentoul. Leaving the river, Hides and O'Malley, with ten police and twenty-eight carriers, crossed the Great Papuan Plateau and the dreaded limestone barrier and were the first to see the wig-wearing peoples of the present Southern Highlands District, discovering in turn the Tari Basin, and the Wage and Nembi Valleys with populations exceeding in density any hitherto encountered in Papua; thence to the Erave and through the Samberigi Valley to Kikori, arriving there on 17 June 1935. The patrol came into conflict with newly discovered populations on at least nine occasions; at least thirty-two attackers were shot dead; the patrol suffered no casualties but one carrier and one police constable died from cold and exhaustion. Sir Hubert Murray called this Strickland-Purari Patrol the most difficult and dangerous ever carried out in New Guinea. The patrol completed the investigation of the grassed Highland valleys of the interior first discovered by the Leahys and J. L. Taylor [qq.v] in the then Mandated Territory of New Guinea, and proved that the dense Highland populations extended south well into Papua. It was the last exploratory patrol to be carried out in the old way, without radio or aerial assistance.

Hides resigned from the Papuan Service in July 1936 and in February 1937, with David Lyall, led an expedition up the Strickland River to exploit gold deposits that he claimed to have discovered during the Strickland-Purari Patrol. The expedition was sponsored by the Sydney company, Investors Limited. In early August Lyall became dangerously ill, forcing Hides to abandon the expedition and make a dash for the coast. Five carriers died of beri-beri on this march and Lyall himself died at Daru on 16 September 1937. Hides returned to Sydney shattered in health and died of pneumonia on 19 June 1938.

He married Marguerite Montebell Priestley on 20 September 1932. There were two children: Marguerite, born February 1935, and John Fairfax, born November 1938.

Hides wrote four successful books based on his personal experiences: *Through Wildest Papua, Papuan Wonderland, Savages in Serge, Beyond the Kubea*, the last published posthumously. All are out of print.

COMMONWEALTH RECORD SERIES

In the Commonwealth Archives Office, Canberra
G 91 Items 97, 148-9, 212, 302-4, 346, 383-4, 559-60
AS 13/26 Items 1, 3, 5, 7
A 518 C 251/1/3/1 Parts 1-2, Item 852/4/100

J. G. Hides, *Through Wildest Papua*. London, 1935.
———— *Papuan Wonderland*. London, 1936.
———— *Savages in Serge*. Sydney, 1938.
———— *Beyond the Kubea*. Sydney, 1939.
J. P. Sinclair, *The Outside Man: Jack Hides of Papua*. Melbourne, 1969.
G. Souter, *New Guinea: The Last Unknown*. Sydney, 1963.
                                                J. P. SINCLAIR

(*See also* EXPLORATION)

HIRI. Until recently an overseas trading expedition known as *hiri* significantly shaped the lives of the Motu people [q.v.] who live on the Papuan coast near Port Moresby. Each year in October or November, before the south-east trade wind faded, Motu seamen sailed vessels called *lagatoi* (the word is usually but incorrectly spelt *lakatoi*), specially built for the occasion, north-west for several hundred miles across the Gulf of Papua, sometimes beyond sight of land, to exchange pottery manufactured by Motu women for sago produced in the west. In late December or January they sailed home on the north-west monsoon. These voyages were part of a larger cycle of activities that linked the people of many different villages and several different linguistic groups in a network of ceremonial and economic exchanges, and at the same time conferred differential prestige within their own communities upon the entrepreneurs who participated. In scale and complexity the *hiri* rivalled the Trobriand Islanders' *kula* [qq.v.], which in some ways it resembled.

The *hiri* was a conspicuous feature when the first English missionary settled at Port Moresby in 1874. Barton, who published a detailed account of it in 1910, suggested that the institution had existed 'for many generations'. It continued to flourish until 1941, when World War II disrupted traditional customs. Motu from villages close to Port Moresby did not resume the *hiri*, but the people of Manumanu, the Motu village furthest west from Port Moresby, sailed regularly each year until 1958, when they built their last *lagatoi*, and several other Motu villages sponsored *hiri* sporadically after the war. In 1957 two communities, Boera and Porebada, conducted a modernized version of the *hiri* in chartered motor vessels. It appears that no Motu village has sent any vessel westward on a *hiri* since 1961 when some people at Porebada organized a traditional voyage.

The following account is based upon observation of three expeditions from Manumanu: in 1954, when two vessels known as *hakona*, smaller than true *lagatoi*, sailed west; in 1957, when again two *hakona* sailed; and in 1958, when the people of Manumanu built a true *lagatoi* with all

Ready to sail on the trial run.

the many ritual appurtenances, ceremonies, and restrictions traditionally required. Despite the change of time and place, these expeditions were identical in almost every detail with those described by Barton fifty years earlier.

A man who intends to sponsor a *hiri* must start the planning at least a year in advance, but he keeps the information to himself and his closest associates. One of these is normally his partner. During the year he and his family plant larger gardens than usual to provide food both for the feasts that accompany each stage in the *lagatoi*'s construction and for the voyage itself. At harvest time in April or May, if his gardens are successful, he finally decides to proceed. From now onwards he must observe certain ritual restrictions, such as avoiding his wife, so that he may keep himself *helaga*, 'sacred', 'charged with ritual potency', and thus 'set apart'. When ready to begin construction of the vessel the sponsor (*baditauna*), who has control of the forward half of the vessel, is expected to open the enterprise with a small ceremony in the village street. At this point first his partner (*doritauna*), who has control of the stern half of the vessel, and then all those who wish to sail as crew under either man, smoke a pipe together.

It takes many weeks to build a *lagatoi*. First the sponsor must assemble the required number of large dug-out hulls. He may use old hulls brought back from the west in previous *lagatoi*, as Barton described, but at Manumanu several additional hulls were shaped from trees felled in the rain forest on the banks of the Vanapa River and floated downstream to the river mouth. Otherwise, the completion of the vessel followed exactly the stages described by Barton: floating the hulls in the water, lashing them together, and constructing the deck, with accompanying magic; building the deck-houses; cutting the mast from a mangrove tree; stepping the mast; hoisting the sail; and finally testing the craft in a trial run. At each stage before the last a small feast was held for those who participated. Meantime, the women of the village spent all their spare hours making earthenware pottery, each one firing five or six pots at a time in an open fire of fast-burning dry softwood.

Every member of the crew takes his own consignment of pots. In addition to those made by women of his household, he customarily volunteers to take one for each of his female kin in other households, to whom ultimately he returns a package of sago. This practice provides a means of maintaining exchange relationships with female kin and their households. On the day set aside for loading the pots each man lays his consignment out on the ground in front of the house, and brushes the whole collection with a sprig of leaves in a magical rite to ensure the success of his overseas exchanges. The women then carry the pots to the beach, from where they are ferried to the *lagatoi*, which lies at anchor some distance off shore. The crew load the pots in the *lagatoi* hulls with dry banana leaf packing to prevent breakage on the voyage.

On the day of departure women and children take tearful farewell of their men on the beach. The men are then paddled out to the *lagatoi* in small canoes, the sail is set, and the anchor raised. With a good wind and no mishap the party can reach the nearer villages on the far side of the Gulf within two or three days.

Upon arrival at their destination the crew pole the *lagatoi* into a sheltered river mouth near the host village and drop anchor. The senior hosts then lead a ceremonial visit to the *lagatoi*. The *baditauna* greets his exchange partner, with whom he has usually made arrangements on a previous *hiri*, announces that he has brought the *lagatoi* for him, and makes him a gift of armshell ornaments. Other men then seek out old exchange partners, or solicit new ones, and each gives his partner an armshell. A day or so later each man lays out the pots intended for his partner. Together they make a count, using tally sticks.

For every item the Motu man expects a fixed return. In 'presenting the *lagatoi*' to his partner the *baditauna* is in fact presenting neither the vessel itself nor its contents, but the social role of principal entrepreneur among the men of the host village for that particular *hiri*. In return for this honour the partner presents a pig to the crew. For certain large armshells the fixed return is a log from which the recipient shapes a *lagatoi* hull. For other armshells and ornaments, the return is a large conical package of sago, which has special ceremonial value in Motu villages. For each pot the return is a smaller package of sago. Exchange rates are fixed and have remained constant for half a century.

It takes many weeks for the hosts to prepare the sago. During this time the Motu dismantle their *lagatoi*, fell and shape a number of new dug-out hulls, and then rebuild the craft with sufficient additional ones to carry the return cargo of sago, which is heavier than pottery and therefore requires a larger vessel. During their stay in the west the Motu also fish and sometimes supply fish to their partners for other food. They also engage in 'hidden' barter trade, exchanging additional pots which they have concealed from their exchange partners, tobacco, and other trade goods, for sago or betel-nut at the best rates they can get by bargaining. All this time they camp on the beach a short distance from the village, maintain a formal relationship with the local men, and scrupulously avoid any undue familiarity with the women. When all the sago is ready the regular bundles are packed in the hulls and the conical ceremonial bundles lashed between the beams so that the top half of each stands a foot or so above the deck.

When the weather seems favourable the *lagatoi* sets sail for home. The return journey is more hazardous than the forward voyage, for with a heavier cargo the vessel has less freeboard, and the north-west monsoon is less reliable than the south-east trade wind, often giving way to sudden violent squalls. One of the two vessels that went on the *hiri* from Manumanu in 1954 broke up in heavy seas during a fierce northerly squall, with

(top) Firing clay pots.
(bottom) Conical parcels of sago protruding above the deck of a *lagatoi*.

the loss of one life, all the cargo, and all the personal possessions of the men.

Once the *lagatoi* has safely crossed the Gulf it drops anchor inshore at a point some distance west of its home village. Here the men adorn themselves with perfumed leaves, facial paints, and various items of festive apparel. Then some of the crew pole the vessel slowly towards its home anchorage while others sing special *hiri* songs to the accompaniment of a bamboo percussion instrument. At the approach of the vessel, the wives, sisters, and daughters of the crew, wearing brightly coloured grass skirts and other adornments, dance on the beach in welcome. The day is then given over to festive reunion.

During 1954-8 Doura and Gabadi people from inland and Koita from villages along the coast gathered at Manumanu. They came to receive sago in return for gifts of food made to the people left behind while the breadwinners were away. Formerly at Motu villages in the Port Moresby area Hula men assembled in the same way to receive payment for fish supplied to the women while their men were away and for armshells given to members of the crew before departure. At Manumanu the sponsor of a *lagatoi* invited his Gabadi or Doura exchange partners to bring a party of dancers, and then the *hiri* terminated in a large-scale feast with dancing. In payment for the dance the exchange partners received one or more large conical sago packages, each equivalent to a pig in the currency of ceremonial exchange.

Traditionally the *hiri* was a major link in a maritime trading network extending along the Papuan coast from the Vailala River in the west to the eastern extremity of the New Guinea mainland and even further to the Trobriand Islands and the other islands of the *kula* ring. The *hiri* at the western extremity and the *kula* at the eastern extremity were the two most spectacular institutions in this system. Armshells and other ornaments were the major item of ceremonial currency. The centre of manufacture lay in the villages of the Hula, Aroma, and Mailu peoples east of Port Moresby. The *kula* carried these armshells into the eastern archipelagoes; the *hiri* carried them west to the head of the Gulf of Papua, from where they were taken along inland trade routes into the mountains.

A major function of the *hiri*, Motu themselves insist, was economic. Without it they could not have subsisted, for in the frequent poor seasons neither their gardens nor their inland exchanges of fish for bananas and tubers yielded sufficient staple food to tide them over the months immediately preceding the annual harvest. Yet they valued the institution also for other reasons. It sustained their links with regular exchange partners among their immediate neighbours. It provided one of the two great festive occasions of the year, when for days or even weeks they gave themselves up entirely, as the early missionaries indignantly complained, to feasting and dancing. Finally, it conferred prestige upon those who participated. Acquiring prestige, or as the Motu put it, having a 'name' (*mai ladana*), was traditionally the major objective of almost all Motu householders. Each man strove to gain advantage over others in a continual battle for prestige. The heads of village sections competed at the highest level, but lesser men competed also at lesser levels, all attempting to outshine their rivals in certain public enterprises that particularly conferred prestige: small-scale distributions of food at various stages in the cycle of mortuary rites; bride-price payments; the *hiri*; and the great feast with dancing that closed the cycle of mortuary rites.

It was ultimately in political disputes and debates that prestige became most important to the Motu, for discussions of relative prestige constituted the major idiom of political discourse. A man of higher prestige could usually silence a lesser man completely, causing him to withdraw in shame, by referring to their relative performances in those enterprises that particularly confer prestige. Ultimately, most serious public issues were traditionally settled by consensus among the two or three men of highest prestige.

Each man valued his reputation, not because in itself it gave him political power but because it directly reflected his command of those resources upon which political power rested. These happened to be the same as those required for economic enterprises carrying high prestige: a large personal following—comprising his family, his village section, and the kin and affines who were his clients in reciprocal exchange relationships; character, physical strength, and managerial skill; and wealth in the form of capital assets, such as land, canoes, nets, armshells, and armshell credits, rather than perishable foodstuffs which he gave away when possible. A large personal following gave a man the numbers to win a political struggle; character, strength, and skill gave him influence; and wealth provided him with economic sanctions to ensure the continued political support of his followers.

The *hiri* was one of the two major enterprises—the other was the feast with dancing known as *turia*—in which Motu entrepreneurs at all social levels publicly displayed the cards they held in the power game.

F. R. Barton, 'The Annual Trading Expedition to the Papuan Gulf', ch. 8 in *The Melanesians of British New Guinea*, by C. G. Seligman. Cambridge, 1910; F. E. Williams, 'Trading Voyages from the Gulf of Papua', *Oceania*, vol. 3, 1932-3.   MURRAY GROVES

HOLMES, William (1862-1917), Administrator of New Guinea, was born in Sydney on 12 September 1862. He was educated at public schools and privately. He joined the Sydney Metropolitan Board of Water Supply and Sewerage and by 1895 had become its secretary. He married in 1887 Susan, daughter of Henry Green, a former artillery officer.

He had joined the volunteer forces in N.S.W. at an early age, and on the outbreak of the South African War gained a commission in the N.S.W. Mounted Rifles and sailed in the first contingent in October 1899. He was at the relief of Colesburg and took part in the advance to Bloemfontein. His regiment formed part of the force which advanced into the Transvaal, fighting actions at Kroonstad and Doornkop and capturing Johannesburg. On 12 June 1900, at the battle of Diamond Hill, the last major engagement of the war, Holmes was wounded. He was invalided to Australia, a major, having won the D.S.O.

He returned to his appointment with the Water Board, but continued to take an active part in the Citizen Military Forces. At the outbreak of World War I in August 1914 he held the rank of colonel and commanded the 6th Infantry Brigade.

On 10 August Holmes was offered, and at once accepted, the command of the Australian Naval and Military Expeditionary Force, which it had been decided to raise for the purpose of seizing the German possessions in the Pacific. Recruitment began the next day, and one week later the force sailed from Sydney. This was a notable feat by any standards. Holmes's orders from the Minister for Defence, Senator Pearce [q.v.], were to seize all German wireless stations in the Pacific, to occupy German territory as soon as possible, to make suitable arrangements for temporary administration, but not to proclaim any formal annexation. On the morning of 11 September Holmes landed his leading elements at Kabakaul Bay, five miles east of Herbertshöhe (Kokopo). There was a brisk skirmish during the advance to the wireless station at Bitapaka, which was captured that afternoon. Another landing was made at Herbertshöhe on the 12th. By now all organized resistance had ceased. The force disembarked at Rabaul [q.v.], where Holmes proclaimed a military occupation.

The terms of capitulation, signed by Holmes and Eduard Haber [q.v.], the German Acting Governor, on 17 September covered all the German possessions administered from Rabaul, and hence the islands north of the equator. Military resistance was to cease and the armed forces were to surrender. It was agreed that while regular officers and men would become prisoners of war, militiamen in most cases would be free, on signing an oath of neutrality, to return to their businesses and plantations. German laws and customs were to remain in force, and a number of German officials were to be retained in office by the military administration. These latter provisions were attacked in Australia, where anti-German feeling was strong, by people who did not know or care that Holmes was under orders not to annex the territory, and that a military occupation leaves local law unimpaired. Holmes's chief concern, having captured the territory quickly and cheaply, was to return it to normal commercial prosperity, largely because he believed that after the war it would become an Australian colony. He saw the release of the Germans as necessary not only for economic reasons but to bring the indentured labourers back under control.

On 20 September Holmes was appointed Administrator of German New Guinea. He extended the occupation from Rabaul to the outstations as rapidly as his shipping resources allowed. At the same time he was engaged in supporting the monetary system, importing supplies and trade goods, and arranging the export of copra. By early October he had organized most departments of the military administration.

His plans received a set-back at the end of November, when he took reprisals against three Germans and a Belgian who had beaten an Australian missionary at Namatanai during the interregnum before the district was occupied. Holmes regarded the offence as a deliberate defiance of the authority of the Administration and a slight to British prestige; and ignoring the advice of his German judge and his own legal adviser he had the offenders publicly flogged. This was illegal as well as injudicious, and there were repercussions in Australia and in Europe. Of more importance at the time was the action of the German officials, who all resigned in protest. This deprived Holmes of impartial advisers on native policy, and must have contributed to the somewhat reactionary attitude to the indigenous people which tended to persist in the Mandated Territory.

Holmes's efforts to occupy the German possessions north of the equator were thwarted by shortages of shipping. Finally a separate expedition, under S. A. Pethebridge [q.v.], was mounted for the task. Holmes, believing that Pethebridge was to supersede him, asked for permission to return to Australia with his troops at the end of their six months' engagement. He sought an appointment in the A.I.F. The Minister had not meant to relieve him, but in view of his request, coupled, perhaps, with public discontent over various supposed shortcomings of Holmes, he decided to do so. Holmes handed over to Pethebridge on 8 January 1915.

Holmes was appointed to command the 5th Infantry Brigade of the A.I.F., which was raised in N.S.W., and many of his officers and men of the A.N.M.E.F. joined it. In August the brigade was on the Gallipoli Peninsula, and at the end of that month Holmes, now a brigadier-general, took over command of the important sector of Russell Top. In November he was appointed to the temporary command of the 2nd Division, which he still held at the time of the evacuation in December.

He commanded the 5th Brigade in France in 1916, when it was heavily engaged at Pozières and again at Flers.

In January 1917 Holmes was promoted to major-general and appointed to the command of the 4th Division. Under his command the division took part in the first battle of Bullecourt, in April, and was then engaged on the Messines front. It was when Holmes was showing a distinguished visitor over the Messines battlefield, on 2 July 1917, that he was mortally wounded by a chance German artillery salvo. He died the same day.

C. E. W. Bean has noted Holmes's 'fine moral qualities, transparent sincerity, energy, and courage'. Again, he was 'of a hearty and cheerful disposition, but he enforced a high standard of duty'. There is no doubt that Holmes was a good commander. In New Guinea he made one major error of judgment. But his handling of the operation of seizing the territory was highly competent; and the principal terms of the capitulation, viewed in retrospect, are unassailable. The defects which some have found in Holmes's policies during his four months of office should be attributed to the absence of direction from the government of the day.

Commonwealth of Australia, *Report to the League of Nations on the Administration of the Territory of New Guinea, from September 1914 to 30th June, 1921.* Melbourne, 1922; S. S. Mackenzie, *The Australians at Rabaul (Official History of Australia in the War of 1914-1918,* vol. 10). Sydney, 1927; 'Report by the Minister of State for Defence on the Military Occupation of the German New Guinea Possessions', *Commonwealth Parliamentary Papers 1922,* vol. 2; C. D. Rowley, *The Australians in German New Guinea 1914-1921.* Melbourne, 1958. Rowley made extensive use of the correspondence between Holmes and the Minister for Defence and the Chief of the General Staff, which, with many other contemporary papers, is in the library of the Australian War Memorial, Canberra.

R. R. McN.

HOMOSEXUALITY. This is the term commonly applied to latent or overt sexual relations between persons of the same sex. A wide spectrum of incidence and range of manifestations is likely to be encountered in a country with such a multitude of diverse cultures as New Guinea. Precise information on the subject, however, is difficult to find.

The work of Malinowski [q.v.] is of special interest. He doubted whether homosexuality existed at all among the Trobriand Islanders [q.v.] in their natural setting. This he ascribed to their freedom from inhibition in a culture where heterosexual experience is related to biological maturity. On the other hand, Williams described an institutionalized form of homosexuality universally practised among a group of peoples of western Papua. In this area boys are initiated in a group at the bullroarer ceremony. Homosexual relations with an older man have a specific purpose as part of the *rites de passage* and are considered essential for the lads' growth. Later when they leave home to work in a large town where the norms and values are vastly different they may run into difficulties.

In the unnatural conditions of life in jails, mission stations, plantations, army and police barracks, and hospitals an atmosphere favourable to an acquired form of homosexuality is created, as in comparable institutions among any people. In these circumstances it is largely a response to deprivation of contacts with members of the opposite sex and disappears as soon as those concerned return to a normal environment.

Bateson describes a cultural tranvestitism of homosexual type among the Iatmül people of the Sepik River. In this society each sex has its own consistent ethos which contrasts with that of the other. When women take part in spectacular ceremonial they may imitate the behaviour of the men. Actual lesbianism is seldom reported.

The cause of homosexuality is still a matter for debate. The extent of the biological component, if it exists at all, is not known. There is much learned behaviour in the patterns to be observed in New Guinea, and these depend in large measure upon the traditions of the particular society concerned. Homosexuality appears to be uncommon among individuals who have adopted Western habits, but when it occurs the form resembles that of European society.

G. Bateson, *Naven.* 2nd ed., Stanford, 1958; E. M. Lemert, *Social Pathology*, New York, 1951; B. Malinowski, *The Sexual Life of Savages in North-Western Melanesia.* London, 1929; —— *Sex and Repression in Savage Society.* London, 1927; M. Mead, *From the South Seas.* New York, 1939; —— *Male and Female.* Pelican ed., London, 1962; F. E. Williams, *Papuans of the Trans-Fly.* Oxford, 1936.

B. G. BURTON-BRADLEY

HONEYEATERS. The birds commonly called honeyeaters, family Meliphagidae, belong to the order Passeriformes, suborder Oscines. There are about 160 species in some thirty-eight genera; of these, sixty-five species are found in New Guinea, five in New Britain, four in New Ireland, and two in Bougainville. It is the largest family of birds in the New Guinea region. Where the term 'New Guinea' is used without any qualification such as 'region' it means the whole main island.

Australia (66 species) and New Guinea share the greatest number of species. Elsewhere they are thinly distributed from Bali (1), east to New Zealand (3), Samoa (3), Hawaii (5, 1 extinct), and north to the Marianas (2). One genus, *Promerops*, doubtfully related to true honeyeaters, is isolated in South Africa.

Honeyeaters, except the New Guinea genus *Melipotes*, are distinguished anatomically by their brush-like tongue—an adaptation to nectar feeding. The tongue is long and protrusible; it is tube-like at its root and deeply cleft at the tip into four parts which are 'frayed' on their edges, forming the brush used to gather the nectar. This type of tongue is structurally quite unlike that of other nectar-feeding birds such as the lorikeets.

Honeyeaters range in length from three inches —the pigmy honeyeater, *Oedistoma*, of New Guinea—to about fourteen inches—the wattle-birds, *Anthochaera*, of Australia. The plumage is green, grey, brown, often red in one genus, *Myzomela*, or black and white. Coloured ear-tufts are a prominent feature of the head pattern in the genus *Meliphaga*, and can be a useful field-mark in their identification. The friar-birds, *Philemon*, and some others have patches of naked skin on the head; some species of *Anthochaera* and *Melidectes* have coloured pendant flaps of skin (wattles) around the bill.

The bill is generally slender, nearly always down-curved, and varies in length from about ten millimetres—*Oedistoma*—to forty-seven milli-

Endemic genera of New Guinea honeyeaters (a) *Melipotes*; (b) *Ptiloprora*; (c) *Pycnopygius*; (d) *Timeliopsis*; (e) *Melilestes*; (f) *Toxorhamphus*; (g) *Melidectes*; (h) *Oedistoma*; (i) *Vosea* (New Britain only).

metres—*Melidectes princeps*. The wings are rather long and rounded; the tail is short to long. The sexes are mostly alike but sometimes strikingly different, as in the genus *Myzomela*.

Nearly all honeyeaters are arboreal in habit, but a few descend to the ground for feeding. In New Guinea they range altitudinally from sea-level to about 13,000 feet and are the most ubiquitous members of the island's avifauna.

Some Australian honeyeaters, for example *Meliphaga chrysops*, are highly migratory; other, inland species are nomadic, but very little is known about the seasonal and altitudinal movements of honeyeaters in New Guinea. Specimen records at present only indicate the altitudinal range of some species.

With the exception of one species, *Ramsayornis modestus*, of New Guinea and Cape York, which has a dome-shaped nest with side entrance, all honeyeaters build cup-shaped nests, often slung in branches at a considerable height. Some New Guinea species nest in tree-ferns. In New Guinea species the clutch is normally one, but breeding data for many species are still meagre. The eggs are generally white or pinkish with some darker spots at the larger end.

Honeyeaters feed on nectar, pollen, insects and other small arthropods, fruits and, rarely, seeds. All species of the New Guinea genus *Melipotes* appear to specialize in eating berries, the bill and tongue being modified accordingly; the tongue has no brush.

There are eighteen genera of honeyeaters in the New Guinea region, of which eight are confined to the New Guinea mainland and off-shore islands: *Timeliopsis, Oedistoma, Toxorhamphus, Melilestes, Melipotes, Melidectes, Ptiloprora,* and *Pycnopygius*. One genus, *Vosea*, is known only from the Whiteman Range in western New Britain. The remaining nine genera, *Glycichaera, Melithreptus, Entomyzon, Ramsayornis, Conopophila, Myzomela, Lichmera, Meliphaga,* and *Philemon* also occur in Australia. One species of *Myzomela, M. lafargei*, is found only on Bougainville, Buka, Shortland Islands, Choiseul, and Ysabel in the Solomons; *Myzomela erythromelas* is confined to New Britain, and a third, *M. sclateri*, occurs only on small islands off the northern coasts of New Guinea and New Britain. One species of *Meliphaga, M. bougainvillei*, is endemic in the mountains of Bougainville and may have affinities with the genus *Vosea*. One *Myzomela, M. pulchella*, and one friar-bird, *Philemon eichhorni*, are endemic on New Ireland.

It is of interest to note briefly the ecological distribution of the endemic New Guinea species. Three species, *Myzomela sclateri, M. albigula,* and *Lichmera argentauris*, are confined to small islands. Fifteen species are essentially birds of lowland rain forest: *Timeliopsis griseigula, Oedistoma pygmaeum, Myzomela eques, Toxorhamphus novaeguineae* and *T. iliolophus, Melilestes megarhynchus, Meliphaga obscura, M. polygramma* and *M. aruensis, Pycnopygius stictocephalus* and *P. ixoides,* and *Philemon meyeri. Myzomela nigrita* occurs from sea-level to 4,000

feet, inhabiting coastal vegetation, savannah, and lowland forest; *Philemon novaeguineae* is widespread in the lowlands in a similar range of habitats. *Philemon brassi* is known only from the lowlands of the Idenburg River where it lives, according to Rand and Gilliard, in 'tall open cane grass and dense second growth trees around the end of one of the lagoons'.

Twenty-one species are essentially birds of the montane rain forest, from about 4,000 to 8,000 feet. In this zone most honeyeaters live in the primary oak and beech forests (*Lithocarpus-Castanopsis* and *Nothofagus*), but there is much secondary tree and grass (e.g. *Miscanthus floridulus*) regrowth following cultivation, burning, and timber-cutting, and some species, such as *Myzomela rosenbergii*, commonly feed in and around cultivated areas. Two species of *Meliphaga, M. montana* and *M. mimikae,* also occur sparsely in the lowland forests of the Fly River. *Melidectes belfordi, Meliphaga subfrenata,* and *Myzomela rosenbergii* also occur in the higher zone of cloud forest and alpine shrubbery. *Ptiloprora perstriata* replaces *Pt. guisei* at about 8,500 feet in south-east New Guinea but in western New Guinea it is a bird of the lower montane zone.

Four species only are restricted to the cloud forests and alpine vegetation above 9,000 feet. These are: *Melidectes princeps, M. fuscus,* and *M. nouhuysi,* and *Meliphaga chrysogenys*. All are sombre-plumaged birds with rather specialized diets, and they blend well with the cold and dark environment of the cloud forests.

E. Mayr, *List of New Guinea Birds*. New York, 1941; ——*Birds of the Southwest Pacific*. New York, 1945; A. L. Rand and E. T. Gilliard, *Handbook of New Guinea Birds*. London, 1967.

W. B. HITCHCOCK

HOUSE OF ASSEMBLY is the legislature of Papua New Guinea and in 1964 replaced the Legislative Council which first sat in 1951. (Before 1942 the two Territories had separate Legislative Councils.) Under the Papua and New Guinea Act (section 52), it is empowered to make ordinances for the peace, order and good government of the country, subject to that Act. The House has a total membership of ninety-four and a quorum of thirty-two, including the member presiding (sections 36(i) and 42). Questions are determined by majority vote of those present and the Speaker or other member presiding has *only* a casting vote (section 46). Ordinances passed by the House do not have any force or effect unless or until assent has been given. Such assent may be given by the Administrator or the Governor-General of the Commonwealth (sections 53-57A).

The House of Assembly is a 'subordinate legislature' since Papua New Guinea is not yet independent. This means that

(1) Ordinances passed by the House cannot affect the application of Acts of the Commonwealth Parliament which apply directly to Papua

New Guinea. In particular, the present 'constitution' of Papua New Guinea is such a Commonwealth Act: the Papua and New Guinea
Act 1949-68.

(2) The Administrator must reserve for the Governor-General's pleasure (i.e. he cannot assent to)
any ordinance
    (a) that relates to divorce;
    (b) that relates to the granting or disposal of
        lands of the Crown or of the Administra-
        tion;
    (c) whereby a grant of money or of an interest
        in land is made to the Administrator;
    (d) that may not, in the opinion of the Ad-
        ministrator, be fully in accordance with the
        treaty obligations of the Commonwealth
        or with the obligations of the Common-
        wealth under the Trusteeship agreement;
    (e) that relates to naval, military or air forces;
    (f) that relates to the sale of, or other disposi-
        tion of or dealing with, land;
    (g) that relates to the employment of persons;
    (h) that relates to arms, ammunition, explo-
        sives, intoxicating liquor or opium;
    (i) that relates to immigration, emigration or
        deportation;
    (j) that relates to the public service;
    (ja) that removes any matter or class of mat-
        ters from the jurisdiction of the Supreme
        Court;
    (jb) that makes provision affecting the practice
        or procedure of the Supreme Court;
    (jc) that establishes, or provides for the estab-
        lishment of, a court; or
    (k) that contains a provision having substan-
        tially the same effect as a provision in an
        ordinance, or in a part of an ordinance,
        to which the Governor-General has with-
        held his assent or which the Governor-
        General has disallowed.

(3) The Administrator, an official appointed by the
Commonwealth, has the power to withhold his
assent to other ordinances or to return ordinances with amendments that he recommends.

(4) Even if the Administrator assents to an ordinance, the Governor-General may within six
months of that assent disallow the ordinance in
whole or in part. Similarly, the Governor-
General may within six months recommend
amendments to 'the laws of the Territory'
which he considers to be desirable in consequence of the ordinance. In such a case, the
period within which he may disallow the
ordinance is extended for a further six months
after the date of his recommendation.

(5) A vote, resolution or proposed law for the
appropriation of revenue or moneys of the
Territory shall not be passed unless the purpose of the appropriation has in the same
session been recommended by message of the
Administrator to the House (section 50).

(6) It is the Administrator who has the power to
dissolve the House 'at any time', although elections must be held at intervals not exceeding
four years (section 40).

It can thus be seen that the House of Assembly
is a subordinate legislature in a double sense.
Firstly, it is subordinate to the Commonwealth
government. Secondly, within the country, it is
subordinate to a non-elected executive in the
person of the Administrator.

It should be noted that the above restrictions
on the House are 'constitutional'. Politically, given
the overall climate of opinion since 1964, the
Commonwealth would have found it difficult to
insist on its 'rights' in the face of determined
opposition from a majority of the House and on
occasions has clearly recognized this. Secondly,
since July 1970, the Commonwealth has made it
clear that it does not intend to exercise its powers
of intervention in certain specified areas and that
these specified areas are to be progressively extended. Within the country, it seems probable that
the Administrator's executive powers will be transferred to a cabinet responsible to the House. The
1971 Report of the Select Committee on Constitutional Development did not make any recommendation contrary to such an evolution. Nevertheless, writing at the same time, Mr Justice Kerr
felt that it was still an open possibility that the
Administrator's powers might be transferred to a
strong president; in which case the executive would
be independent of the legislature, rather than responsible to it. There is certainly support for such
a change of direction amongst some indigenous
people.

Major constitutional changes involving amend-
ment to the Papua and New Guinea Act are the
responsibility of the Commonwealth government.
To date, no attempt has been made to implement
the suggestion made in 1963 by the present
Speaker of the House, Dr John Guise [q.v.], that a
broad-based constitutional convention, independent of the Administration and with its own expert
advisers, should assume this responsibility. Since
1960, however, the opinions of local people have
become increasingly influential. In that year, the
Minister for Territories consulted urban groups in
Papua New Guinea before introducing a major
reform of the Legislative Council, including the
first provisions for (indirectly) elected indigenous
members. The introduction of the House of
Assembly was clearly a consequence of both the
recommendations of the 1962 United Nations
Visiting Mission, under the chairmanship of Sir
Hugh Foot, and the work of a Select Committee of
the Legislative Council, which sat from March
1962 to February 1963 and began the practice of
touring the country to elicit the views of the
people. Select Committees of the House of
Assembly followed in May 1965 to June 1967 and
June 1969 to March 1971, each recommending
further changes of an essentially incremental kind
in the general direction of a 'Westminster' system
of representative and responsible government. The
last Select Committee also split up so that its
members could visit various tropical states in
Africa and the Pacific. After it made its final
report, a 'parliamentary delegation' from the
House made an official visit to Indonesia. Other,
less formal, overseas contacts are gradually in-

creasing in number and it should not be assumed that the people of Papua New Guinea are unaware of alternatives to the Westminster system.

MEMBERSHIP OF THE HOUSE

The ninety-four members are selected in the following ways:
(1) There are ten official members: office holders or officers of the public service, who are appointed by the Governor-General on the nomination of the Administrator.
(2) Sixty-nine of the elected members are returned from 'open' constituencies, which means that candidates are not required to have any educational qualifications.
(3) Fifteen of the elected members are returned from 'regional' constituencies, for which candidates are required to possess educational qualifications equivalent to the Territory Intermediate certificate.

Since 1964, the total membership of the House has been increased and altered. Further changes have been proposed for 1972 by the Select Committee on Constitutional Development (see Table 1). Regional electorates should, in the Committee's view, be increased to eighteen and their boundaries ought to coincide with those of the administrative Districts. At present, they do for the most part coincide with Districts in twelve cases and in the

Table 1

CATEGORIES OF MEMBER
Actual 1964 and 1968; proposed 1972

Category	1964	1968	1972 (proposed)
Official	10	10	4
Special	10	0	0
Regional	0	15	18
Open	44	69	82
Nominated	0	0	up to 3
Total	64	94	104–7

other three they embrace two adjoining Districts (Gulf and Western; East and West New Britain; Manus and New Ireland). The original intention was that they should coincide, but the number of Districts was increased from fifteen to eighteen between the decision to have fifteen regional electorates and the actual determination of boundaries for the 1968 elections. They were introduced in 1968 and replaced the ten 'special' constituencies of the 1964 House, for which candidature was reserved to non-indigenes. In 1968 twenty Papuans and New Guineans contested the regional seats and four were successful. The Select Committee also recommended that in 1972 the House should have the power, if it wished, to nominate up to three additional members. Defeated candidates in the 1972 elections would not be eligible; public servants would be required to resign their positions before accepting nomination; and nomination would be restricted to those 'who had lived in the Territory continuously for not less than five years'. The process of selection proposed comprises three stages: (i) the House agrees by a two-thirds vote of the total membership to set up a seven-member selection committee; (ii) this committee chooses a person or persons, in consultation with the Administrator; and (iii) their choice is then endorsed, or otherwise, by a simple majority of the members of the House present and voting. Once nominated, a person would have the same status as an elected member and in particular be eligible for ministerial office. Finally, it proposed that the number of official members be reduced to four.

Contrary to expectations, some Europeans did secure election from open electorates in 1964 and again in 1968. The composition of the House in terms of the membership of indigenous people is shown in Table 2.

Candidates must be over twenty-one years of age. If public servants they must resign before nomination, but if unsuccessful they may apply for reinstatement. The Australian practice of securing leave to campaign and resigning if elected is not followed. Undischarged bankrupts or those who are insolvent may not stand nor may those who

Table 2

COMPOSITION OF THE LEGISLATIVE COUNCIL AND HOUSE OF ASSEMBLY, 1951–68

Nature of Appointment	Category of Member	Legislative Council				House of Assembly			
		1951–60		1961		1964		1968	
		Total	Indigenous	Total	Indigenous	Total	Indigenous	Total	Indigenous
Ex officio	Administrator	1	0	1	0	0	0	0	0
Nominated	Official	16	1*	14	0	10	0	10	0
	Non-official	9	3	10	6	0	0	0	0
Elected	Separate rolls	3	0	12	6	0	0	0	0
	Special	0	0	0	0	10	0	0	0
	Regional	0	0	0	0	0	0	15	4
	Open	0	0	0	0	44	38	69	61
Totals		29	4*	37	12	64	38	94	65

* In October 1960, Dr Reuben Taureka was appointed to fill a vacancy.

have been convicted and are undergoing sentences of one year or more. In addition, candidates are required to have lived in the Territory for five years and to have lived in the electorate for which they are seeking nomination for a period of at least twelve months continuously or to have a 'home' (as defined by the Electoral Ordinance 1963-67) in the electorate. This frequently gives candidates some choice between electorates, but they are not entitled to nominate for more than one. A $50 deposit must accompany nomination papers. This deposit is returnable provided the candidate polls one-eighth of the winning candidate's first preference votes.

No restrictions based on sex, race, property or education are placed on candidates for open electorates. In 1964, a racial qualification did prevent indigenes standing for the special electorates. Candidates for regional electorates (which replaced special electorates in 1968) are required to have an educational qualification equivalent to the Territory Intermediate certificate. This requirement debarred a number of expatriates from standing, while permitting a number of local people to stand in at least eleven of the fifteen electorates in 1968, and considerably more will be eligible in 1972. Before 1964 it was widely assumed that no expatriate would be returned for an open electorate and the reservation of ten special seats probably helped to reconcile European opinion in the country to what was a very dramatic change. The other justification for special electorates, ensuring that some elected members would be literate, is now achieved by the educational qualification for the regional electorates.

WORKING OF THE HOUSE

The House elects its own Speaker and conducts its business in the tradition of British and Australian parliaments, with a Mace, Serjeant-at-Arms, Clerk of the House and so on. Members wear coats, ties and in general long trousers rather than lap-laps, which when worn are of a suitably dark colour. Some emphasis is placed on being suitably dressed and behaving with decorum. Bills are introduced, 'read' for a first, second and third time, with the usual general debate at the second reading and movement into committee of the whole House for the third reading stage.

It is not certain that Papuans and New Guineans wished things otherwise, but expatriate members in the first House certainly encouraged the notion that making the House 'a proper parliament' involved modelling its symbols, practices and procedures very closely on those current in Canberra. The extent to which this was a desirable goal, a necessary first step, or a constraint on indigenous political development (and if so, how serious a constraint) has been the subject of some debate. As a legislature the House has operated efficiently in the sense that bills have been passed and the smooth flow of proceedings has rarely been interrupted (i.e. interruptions have not been more noticeable than in Westminster or Canberra). Other criteria for evaluation are notoriously diffi-

cult to apply. How does one judge 'the quality of debate'—by the beauty of the language employed, by the loftiness of the sentiments or principles invoked? Most indigenous members do concern themselves very largely with parochial issues, but this is an important part of a representative's job and a common feature of elected assemblies which are not dominated by political parties. Even the claim that members do not always understand what they are voting for is not peculiar to the House of Assembly.

Still, it is clear that certain matters could be improved. A deliberate decision was made not to impose educational qualifications for membership, on the grounds that this would restrict the representative nature of the House, given the uneven distribution of education in the country. This is a reasonable position, but one which would seem to imply that members deserve rather more and different consideration from that normally accorded by an executive to members of a legislature. In this respect, the Administration has attempted to do more than it is credited with, while still achieving less than it might have. A simultaneous translation service in English, Police Motu and Pidgin English [qq.v.] has been provided, but numerous complaints have been made that too little has been done to assist the translators, by insisting that speeches be made slowly and as simply as is possible in the particular circumstances. Action on these lines would not be easy, but what is at issue is a question of priorities.

A basic conflict exists between the House of Assembly as a working part of government and the House as part of the overall educative preparation for independence. Put at its crudest, the need of the Administration to secure the passage of legislation often conflicts with its wish that members should be fully informed. On occasion, the Administration has sought to ensure that members are briefed as fully as possible, but the potential conflict is inherent in the situation.

One problem is posed by the existence of Standing Orders which are perhaps modelled too closely on *current* practices in Australia. The first reading of a bill was once quite literally that, a reading of a bill. With the growth of literacy, the practice of reading the entire bill was curtailed at Westminster to a mere reading of its title. Yet only the title is read in Papua New Guinea, where most members find reading difficult and many are not literate in English. Summaries of bills are often provided in Pidgin English and Police Motu, the two other languages of the House; but demands for more complete translations have generally been resisted on the grounds that the technical terms involved cannot be accurately translated into these languages. Some informal assistance is often available for members prepared to seek it and some departments offer lengthy briefing sessions on bills in which they have a strong interest. Since 1969, the practice has developed of setting aside a day for briefing and discussions on the Appropriations Bill or Budget. Three further significant developments occurred in this area in 1970. What may become a legislative reference service was inaugurated with the appointment of a legal counsel to the House of Assembly, whose duties include advising elected members in legal matters and drafting legislation for them. Second, Fiji was included in the itinerary of members whose 'political education' tours had previously been confined to Australia and its parliaments. Third, the House voted to introduce a system of subject committees covering works and services, land and industries, finance and public service, and welfare and social service.

One classical means by which an executive keeps the legislature quiet is to keep meetings short and legislators busy. On the average, the House meets four times a year for a total period of about ten weeks. The introduction of subject committees and the continuation of departmentally sponsored 'briefing' sessions may lead to longer meetings. In 1971 there were some demands to extend the length of the meeting. Other members have, however, argued for fewer meetings, since they are already away from their electorates too much.

THE FRONT BENCH

The bulk of the tasks usually associated with a government in the legislature: the introduction of legislation, answering questions and making official statements was initially undertaken by the ten official members, with increasing assistance from several of the under-secretaries. The Parliamentary Under-Secretaries Ordinance 1963 provided for not more than fifteen of these to be appointed by the Administrator from amongst the elected members. Ten were appointed in 1964 and an eleventh late in 1967. Under-secretaries received £1,300 per annum, rather than the £950 per annum of an ordinary member. The first appointees were all literate or more or less fluent in English and their appointments were seen by some critics as an attempt to deprive the less educated members of leadership. The Administration regarded them as being in training, and took some care to draw them from the various parts of the country. What they were in training for was never entirely clear, but possibly this was left fluid because few people had any clear expectation of the situation which would emerge after the 1964 elections. In the event, several departments went to some trouble to explain to their under-secretaries how policies were made, executive decisions were taken, and departments were organized. Others did not. A few were latterly briefed to represent their departments in the House. Only one actually resigned in the first year, but there was a certain measure of discontent amongst the under-secretaries, which they eventually expressed to the Minister, and some minor adjustments followed. The departments or branches of the Administration with which under-secretaries were associated were: Information and Extension Services; Forests; Lands, Surveys and Mines; Police; Public Health; Public Works; Treasury; Education and Local Government; Agriculture, Stock and Fisheries; Trade and Industry; and Labour. Probably the main significance of the experiment was that it

clarified demands for the introduction of a ministerial system in 1968. This was recommended by the Select Committee on Constitutional Development in June 1967. What was actually introduced in 1968, however, was a system of ministerial members and assistant ministerial members (ministerial office holders) which was to be reviewed after two years. Seven ministerial members were appointed (including one expatriate) and eight assistant ministerial members. All seven were appointed to the Administrator's Executive Council, a much more significant body than the Administrator's Council to which five of the under-secretaries had been appointed. The departments with which ministerial members are associated are Trade and Industry; Public Works (the one expatriate); Education; Posts and Telegraphs; Agriculture, Stock and Fisheries; Public Health; and Labour. Assistant ministerial members are associated with Forests; Lands and Surveys; Local Government; Social Development and Home Affairs; Transport; Treasury; Business Development; and Rural Development. The selection process for ministerial office holders requires that they should first be nominated by a special nominations committee of the House and that the Administrator should concur, before the Minister for External Territories appoints them. If the House resolves that an appointment should be terminated the Minister 'may' terminate it. Also, after report by the Administrator to the Minister, the Governor-General may terminate an appointment 'in the public interest'. The Minister has the power to decide which ministerial offices are to be held by appointees and may change these. Once again, in terms of actual politics, the position is potentially much more fluid than the Papua and New Guinea Act suggests. Several ministerial office holders are known to occupy the positions which they sought, although the exact process by which this occurred is not known.

As in the case of the under-secretaries, the ministerial office holders between them represent most regions of the country. Taking the present eighteen administrative Districts as a guide, under-secretaries were drawn initially from all these Districts except Gulf, Madang, West Sepik, Western Highlands, Chimbu, Southern Highlands, Manus, and West New Britain. (In 1964, the West Sepik, Chimbu and West New Britain Districts had not been created. The eleventh position went to the Western Highlands in 1967.) Ministerial office holders are drawn from all Districts except Northern, East Sepik, Southern Highlands, Manus and New Ireland. When an assistant ministerial member resigned late in 1969 he was replaced by a member from the same District. In effect, this means that only Manus (the smallest District) and the Southern Highlands (the least contacted) have never been represented at this level. Some attempt seems to have been made to recognize other criteria, such as size of population and overall levels of development. Thus both the Western Highlands and the Central District have a ministerial member and an assistant ministerial member. Put at its crudest, in terms of regions, there are two Papuan ministerial members, two Highlanders, one from the New Guinea coast, one from the New Guinea islands, and one expatriate, also from the New Guinea islands. There are three Papuan assistant ministerial members, two from the Highlands, two from the New Guinea coast and one from the New Guinea islands. It is scarcely possible to offer any judgments concerning capability, but ministerial office holders are less clearly the best educated than were the under-secretaries. One possible factor, and explanation of their 'relatively conservative' tinge, is that the Pangu Party decided that its members should not accept ministerial office. Whether they would have been selected is, of course, another question; but this certainly meant that some of the better educated, more articulate, and 'relatively radical' members were not available for nomination.

It has also meant that some attempt has been made to institutionalize the concept of a responsible opposition. Pangu members, on the whole, 'do their homework' and try as far as is possible (given constituency pressures and the state of party organization in the villages) to vote as a group. They have initiated bills and they have supported or opposed Administration bills, in accordance with what they see as the national interest.

The introduction of ministerial office holders in 1968 meant that there was less need for public service departmental heads to be appointed as official members. Only four departments are so represented, Lands, Surveys and Mines; Law; Treasury; and the Department of the Administrator. This last department is responsible for field or District administration and is represented by no less than five official members: the Director, three District commissioners and a District inspector. Critics have regarded these appointments as attempts to provide the front bench with 'whips'. Since there is no majority party the Administration, from the inauguration of the House, has been forced to find majorities for its bills, as best it could. In default of party organization and party whips it has been suggested that these officials seek to build up support amongst less sophisticated members by appealing to their diffuse loyalties to the Administration rather than by emphasizing the merits of particular legislation. If their role has been as vital in this respect as critics have alleged, 1972 will represent something of a leap in the dark, for the Select Committee has recommended reducing the number of official members to four, and there is no certainty that a majority party will emerge.

Overall then, ministerial office holders have been responsible for most of the representation of departments and departmental policies since 1968. Initially, ministerial members shared responsibility for running 'their' departments and making departmental policy with the public service heads, with the Administrator resolving any disputes which might arise. In October 1969 they were given sole responsibility for approving expenditures of up to $20,000 and in July 1970 their powers, and those of assistant ministerial members, were substantially increased. In effect, these changes resemble the

introduction of 'dyarchy', an attempt to provide self-government in certain scheduled areas only. The initial areas are listed in the annexures to the Minister's Speech at Port Moresby, 6 July 1970, but the stated intention is progressively to increase them. For the moment, Canberra retains control over the judiciary, police, security, foreign affairs, including trade, and large-scale developmental projects. Within the scheduled areas, therefore, the power of initiative now lies clearly with Papuans and New Guineas, and the Commonwealth has undertaken not to use its veto powers on legislation passed by the House within these areas in which 'full authority' has been transferred. Attempts have also been made to convert the Administrator's Executive Council into something more closely resembling a cabinet. The early practice of holding sittings in various parts of the country, for the mutual education of members and local people, has been supplemented by the encouragement of individual members to raise issues beyond their area of responsibility and by the Administrator's increasing referral of issues to the Administrator's Executive Council, collectively, beyond constitutional requirements. Further, official members now have 'second class' status in the Council in the sense that they can no longer vote on matters which fall within the scheduled areas. Finally, the Council now has a spokesman and deputy spokesman to represent it in the House.

However, the problem of linkage between ministerial office holders and the House has still to be clarified. The presumption appears to be that a majority party will soon emerge in the House and that the mechanics of responsible government will in consequence solve themselves. There appears to have been no consideration given to alternatives, such as minimal fixed terms for ministers, and limitations on the number of no-confidence motions or circumstances in which they can be moved. A second area of obscurity concerns the Select Committee's proposal to have ten ministers in 1972. This is significantly less than the fifteen present ministerial office holders, who in turn are less than the existing number of departments. Even if the proposed four official members are all departmental heads, some departments will still not be represented in the House. This is of some significance in view of the select committee's opinion that there may be full internal self-government before 1976.

THE BUDGET

A major factor in the evolution of the House of Assembly has been the existence of Australian financial grants on such a scale that they have accounted on the average for some two-thirds of the expenditures by the local Administration, excluding further sums expended by Commonwealth departments operating directly in the Territory (see PUBLIC ADMINISTRATION). In an interim report the 1965-7 Select Committee suggested the introduction of a split budget, whereby local revenues could be locally allocated and Canberra would continue to allocate its own grants. This was associated with one of the rare confrontations between the House and the Administration when in 1966 the House voted (28 to 25) to reduce the budget by $50,000. Behind this lay a growing discontent amongst members that insufficient funds were being allocated for local development and a recognition of the link between this and their own prospects for re-election. The split-budget proposal was dropped from the Select Committee's final report, but in the interim the Administration had proposed to involve members far more, although only by consultation, in the preparation of the budget. Although occasional discontent continued to be expressed, these measures were apparently of some consequence and no further 'revolts' occurred on this issue.

A major feature of the reforms announced in July 1970 by the Prime Minister (the Rt Hon. John Gorton) was the introduction of a form of split budget. Four ministerial members went to Canberra in 1970 as a committee of the Administrator's Executive Council, to negotiate with the Minister and his officials. Later that year, the Commonwealth estimates itemized expenditures on New Guinea, distinguishing for the first time between (i) the special allowances paid to overseas officials, i.e. the visible differences in cost between employing overseas as against local officers; (ii) loans for special developmental projects; (iii) a general developmental grant; and (iv) a grant-in-aid for recurrent expenses and minor works. This last sum, together with the internal revenues of the country was placed at the disposal of the Administrator's Executive Council to whom 'the various "Ministries" . . . will put in claims in the way Ministers put in claims to the Cabinet in Canberra'. Having received an allocation in this way, ministers now have authority to decide how to spend it without reference to Canberra. The availability of further funds in these areas depends on the willingness of the House of Assembly to increase local taxation. In 1970-1 estimated internal revenue was $73.5 million and the relevant portion of the Australian grant was $33 million. Thus ministerial members have a sum in excess of $106 million at their disposal, although much of this will be difficult to reallocate in view of existing programmes and expectations. Nevertheless, the fact that the Australian grant still accounts for almost 60 per cent of total expenditure no longer prevents Papuans and New Guineans from having any effective voice in the budget. It may not be coincidental that the announcement of these changes was followed by an unusually strong attempt to organize a majority party within the House. In the event, the Compass (later United) Party failed by a small margin to achieve this.

THE FRANCHISE AND THE ELECTIONS

The Electoral Ordinance 1963-67 provides for adult suffrage. The voting age is twenty-one. There is considerable support for lowering the voting age to eighteen, the age for voting in local government elections. Many voters have a choice between electorates in which they are entitled to enrol, which can either be the electorate in which they have lived continuously for the last twelve months or an electorate in which they have had 'a home'. This provision permits a migrant to continue to vote with his home village should he so desire. Voting is not compulsory. In 1964, the turn-out was just over 72 per cent and in 1968 it was 63 per cent of the total eligible voters. Registration or enrolment is compulsory, but is undertaken by the Administration.

In the more developed areas the commercial press offered all local candidates space to state their policies. Some private associations also provided forums for all local candidates. There was no official attempt to disseminate the views of candidates, either through special publications or by organizing patrols and meetings for all candidates as a group. This was regarded as an obligation which rested on the candidates themselves. Given the late emergence and minimal organization of political parties, this meant that many people had less information concerning at least some candidates than might otherwise have been the case. The customs of the country continued to give candidates access to official transport already scheduled for official business, but instructions were issued to the effect that all candidates must have equal access, and no special facilities were provided. Thus the policy of endeavouring to remain politically neutral clashed with the hope that the election itself would have an educational effect.

The Administration has assumed the responsibility for compiling a common roll of all eligible voters for each electorate. This is an arduous undertaking which absorbs a considerable amount of the Administration's resources. At the polling place, voters identify themselves, a line is drawn through their name on the roll, and they are issued with two ballot papers, one for the regional electorate and one for the open, in which they are enrolled. (In 1964 some confusion arose because the candidates for both the special and the open electorates were listed on the same ballot paper.) Each paper lists the names of the candidates in order determined by ballot, with a box drawn to the left of each name in which voters should list their preferences by number. There has been no indication of party affiliation on the ballot papers, because political parties emerged too late in 1967 to be officially recognized for election purposes. The use of symbols has frequently been considered, but results elsewhere (as in the Tanzanian General Election of 1965) seem to confirm the view that it is extremely difficult to devise a collection of symbols which will not give an advantage to some candidates and a disadvantage to others. Literate voters are able to mark their papers in privacy. Partitions and limitations on the numbers permitted to be in the polling place at any one time ensure that for them the ballot is secret. Preliterates, the majority of voters, are obliged to use the *whisper ballot*, communicating their preferences out of general earshot to the presiding officer. To safeguard this officer, and the voter's intentions, it is further provided that a third person must be present, either a person appointed by the voter or the poll clerk. In some areas it is also necessary to involve interpreters in this process. Marked ballot papers are folded and placed in a locked ballot box. The fact that some people in Papua New Guinea use several names or the same names in different combinations poses a problem for polling clerks. In general, difficult cases are treated much the same way as absentee votes. The papers are placed in an envelope, which is placed inside another envelope indicating the nature of the problem. These envelopes are placed in a second ballot box, for later checking and allocation. A record is kept of the number of such votes. Absentee votes are often very high because of the provision which permits voters, if they so desire, to enrol for their home electorates rather than the electorate in which they are living. Unfortunately, absentee voters often change their names as well. This very largely accounts for the fact that of the 26,000 absent votes cast in 1968, for example, less than 11,000 were finally admitted to scrutiny. In an attempt to assist voters, arrangements were made to photograph all candidates and to provide printed enlargements at all polling places. It was not possible to have all candidates' photos at all polling places so that often the absentee voters, who perhaps had the most need, were unable to see their candidates. In some cases also, arrangements broke down so that photographs were not everywhere available. The fact that voting is supervised by the Administration also accounts for the fact that polling is extended over a four-week period (thirty-three days in 1964 and twenty-nine days in 1968). Polling teams move from polling place to polling place, sometimes by helicopter or other mechanical means, often by walking. The objective is to provide a polling place within a few hours walk of every significant group of voters. Ensuring that people know their day for voting is an important part of the pre-election educational patrols carried out by the Administration.

THE PROBLEM OF REPRESENTATION

The original Papua and New Guinea Act suggested very vaguely that indigenous members for the central legislature might eventually be selected through a tiered system of direct and indirect election. At the base, local governments would be directly elected by the people generally, on adult franchise. The councils would then elect representatives for an intermediary body, District or regional. In the event, the experimental stage of local councils lasted for most of the fifties. The few councils initially introduced were widely dispersed and no intermediary bodies were set up, although the existing councils did begin to hold Territory-wide conferences in 1959.

When the Legislative Council was reorganized in 1960 the Minister for Territories announced (22 September 1960) that in due course universal franchise would be introduced. For 1961, however, an electoral college system was employed to elect indigenous members. New Guinea was divided into six electorates, each with its own electoral college of some sixty to seventy 'electors',

who were chosen by existing Local Government Councils (which often chose non-councillors) and by direct election from certain gazetted groups, such as town residents and those about to have a council in the near future. In all some 250,000 persons could be said to have been involved directly or indirectly in the process of selecting the electors. The electoral colleges sat for three days, listening to candidates' speeches, questioning candidates and discussing matters, before casting their final ballots for a 'first past the post' or simple plurality vote. The results showed evidence of regional bloc voting and only one candidate won with a majority vote. Nevertheless, it was clear that narrow parochialism had often been surmounted and that considerable aggregation of votes did occur. It is possible that this process might have been taken further had the ballot been more exhaustive and a majority vote been demanded. This had been the case in some of the direct elections of electors, where it was clear that some local politicians had recognized both the real pressures which led to an initial vote for 'a favourite son' or 'wantok' and the importance of second preferences. In Port Moresby, for example, the voters for defeated candidates were speedily deployed behind the survivors in a way which indicated prior organization and agreement.

It seems likely that this experience, together with its widespread use in Australia, was responsible for the adoption of preferential voting in the House of Assembly elections of 1964. Subsequent official reviews of voting procedures have adamantly insisted that the preferential system is understood by the indigenous people, and there seems little reason to doubt that in principle this is so. Difficulties exist, however, as a result of the size of electorates and possibly as a consequence of the central counting of votes. Thus in many electorates voters simply do not know enough about candidates to allocate all their preferences meaningfully. This has been recognized by accepting as valid ballot papers which only indicate one or a few preferences. Together with the central counting of votes, however, this fails to make clear to the voter the essential linkages in the process. Electorates are not 'natural' units. Although consideration is given to existing patterns of social organization, the principle of 'one man one vote' biases them in the direction of equality in terms of mere numbers. Boundary changes have introduced a destabilizing factor in more advanced areas and have not materially resolved the problem elsewhere. Traditionally, life in New Guinea is lived on a much smaller scale and more publicly than the electoral system assumes. If the House of Assembly should be limited in size (and there are arguments for this), such processes as direct election, the secret ballot, and central counting of votes must be seen as means rather than ends. As in so many other spheres, the gap between the introduced model and existing behaviour is so great that serious consideration may need to be given either to bridging the gap imaginatively or to modifying particular, less essential, features of the model. So far the Administration has been reluctant to modify, but it has recently accepted responsibility for a political education programme. Unfortunately this is a particularly difficult task for an administration. By its nature, the problem seems to demand concrete rather than abstract treatment, but it is difficult for officials to be concrete, explicit, and communicate effectively on such matters, without incurring accusations of seeking to exercise political influence. As a result, previous campaigns have tended to concentrate on neutral aspects such as the mechanics of voting. Whether the present campaign can find an imaginative solution, or any solution, remains to be seen. Essentially, the task of political education is one more easily performed by parties, but so far in Papua New Guinea they have lacked the resources to reach many people. The possibility of 'sterilized assistance' to parties has been raised, but to date attention has focused on the problems and difficulties in such a course rather than the basic problem which the proposal is designed to meet.

What is at stake, firstly, is the willingness of people to vote. The former Chief Electoral Officer was disposed to blame the near 10 per cent decline in the popular vote (from 72 per cent in 1964 to 63 per cent in 1968) very largely on generalized disappointment with the results of 1964: in particular, the man 'they all' voted for did not win and the material consequences of the election were insignificant. Secondly, there is the question of the visibility of sitting members, which applies particularly to ministerial office holders, who are expected to spend the better part of three weeks in every month on official duties. To what extent electors' complaints in 1968 (that 'we never see our member') were a cover for other grounds for opposition (this was certainly true in some areas) is not clear; but it does seem likely that the electorates require nursing, and this is no simple matter. Special assistance to sitting members raises the question of undue advantage in the elections of 1972, but once again at a deeper level the real question is one of establishing clear priorities. Office holders are in a different situation since official demands on their time are great. The parallel with under-secretaries is not in this respect an exact one. In 1968, nine of the under-secretaries stood for re-election and five were successful. In the other four cases there is little reason to believe that merely being an under-secretary was a significant ground for rejection. (Five out of nine was in fact the general success ratio of the thirty-six members from open electorates who stood again.) Given their responsibilities it was reasonable to give ministerial members the means to employ electorate secretaries, but so far the requests of ordinary members (and a resolution of the House) have only been recognized by the provision of office space at District headquarters.

Perhaps, as several indigenous members have suggested, the real problem is the gap between village concerns and the central legislature. What is required, they suggest, is some intermediary assembly, although not as an electoral device. Thus by meaningful analogy, the significance of

the House might become better understood. This view has been endorsed by the 1969-71 Select Committee, which suggested that the administrative District might be the appropriate level. The Administration has proposed the creation of Area Authorities, which would operate at approximately that level and would be concerned with the allocation of rural development funds, amongst

UNDER-SECRETARIES 1964-8

Name	Electorate	Under-secretary to
Matthias Tutanava Toliman	Rabaul	Dept of the Administrator; Education & Local Government (late in 1966)
Nicholas Brokam	New Ireland	Assistant Administrator (Economic Affairs); Dept of Information and Extension Services (1965)
Sinake Giregire	Goroka	Assistant Administrator (Services); Dept of Agriculture, Stock and Fisheries (late in 1966)
Paul Lapun	Bougainville	Dept of Forests
John Guise	Milne Bay	Dept of Information and Extension Services (resigned 1964)
Edric Eupu	Popondetta	Dept of Lands, Surveys and Mines
Simogen Pita	Wewak-Aitape	Dept of Police
Dirona Abe	Rigo-Abau	Dept of Public Health
Robert Tabua	Fly River	Dept of Public Works
Zure Makili Zurecnuoc	Finschhafen	Dept of Treasury
Lepani Watson (appointed to replace John Guise)	Esa'ala-Losuia	Assistant Administrator (Economic Affairs); Dept of Trade and Industry (late in 1966)
Tei Abal (appointed late in 1967)	Wabag	Dept of Labour

MINISTERIAL MEMBERS 1968 ——

Name	Electorate	Department
Angmai Bilas	Mabuso	Trade and Industry
O. I. Ashton	New Britain (regional)	Public Works
Matthias Tutanava Toliman	Gazelle	Education
Sinake Giregire	Daulo	Posts and Telegraphs
Tei Abal	Wabag	Agriculture, Stock and Fisheries
Tore Lokoloko	Kerema	Public Health
Toua Kapena	Hiri	Labour

ASSISTANT MINISTERIAL MEMBERS 1968 ——

Name	Electorate	Responsibilities
Andagari Wabiria	Koroba	Lands, Surveys and Mines
Joseph Lue	Bougainville (regional)	Technical Education and Training; Transport (early 1970)
Kaibelt Diria	Wahgi	Local Government
Lepani Watson	Kula	Co-operatives; Business Development (early 1971)
Meck Singiliong	Finschhafen	Rural Development
Oala Oala-Rarua	Central (regional)	Treasury
Paul Langro (resigned late 1969)	West Sepik (regional)	Information and Extension Services
Siwi Kurondo	Kerowagi	Forests
Wesani Iwoksim (appointed to replace Paul Langro)	Upper Sepik	Social Development and Home Affairs

ADMINISTRATOR'S EXECUTIVE COUNCIL 1971

Official members	A. P. J. Newman	Assistant Administrator (Economic Affairs)
	H. P. Ritchie	Treasurer
	T. W. Ellis	Department of the Administrator
Ministerial members	Angmai Bilas	Trade and Industry
	O. I. Ashton	Public Works
	Matthias Toliman	Education
	Sinake Giregire	Posts and Telegraphs
	Tei Abal	Agriculture, Stock and Fisheries
	Tore Lokoloko	Public Health
	Toua Kapena	Labour
Administrator's nominee	T. J. Leahy (Markham open)	
Spokesman for the A.E.C.	T. J. Leahy	
Deputy Spokesman	Tore Lokoloko	

SPEAKERS OF THE HOUSE OF ASSEMBLY

1964-8	H. L. R. Niall
1968 ——	John Guise

other things. Such an innovation would, of course, profoundly affect the existing system of District administration and the existing position of District Commissioners. It does seem, however, to contain the possibility of (i) relating the voter more adequately to the House of Assembly and (ii) providing an opportunity for co-ordinating the developmental activities of members of the House: as for example in party organization; the various departments, particularly District Administration; Local Government Councils; and possibly other interested parties, groups and individuals.

C. E. Barnes, 'Increased Responsibility for Ministerial and Assistant Ministerial Members', speech by the Minister for External Territories in Port Moresby, 6 July 1970 (bound with Gorton, 1970).

D. G. Bettison, C. A. Hughes and P. W. van der Veur (eds), *The Papua-New Guinea Elections 1964*, chs 1-5, 18-21. Canberra, 1965.

J. Gorton, 'Steps Towards Self-Government in Papua and New Guinea', speech by the Prime Minister in Port Moresby, 6 July 1970. Canberra, 1970.

I. Grosart, 'Native Members in the Legislative Council of the Territory of Papua and New Guinea: 1951-1963', *Journal of Pacific History*, vol. 1, 1966.

J. Kerr, 'A Constitutional Suggestion', *New Guinea and Australia, the Pacific and South-East Asia*, vol. 5, 1971.

N. Meller, 'Papers of the Papua-New Guinea House of Assembly', *New Guinea Research Bulletin*, no. 22, 1968.

R. S. Parker, 'The Advance to Responsible Government', in *New Guinea on the Threshold*, ed. E. K. Fisk. Canberra, 1966.

T. P. N. G. Chief Electoral Officer, *Report of the Chief Electoral Officer on the House of Assembly Election, 1964*. Port Moresby, 1964.

—— *Report of the Chief Electoral Officer on the House of Assembly Election, 1968*. Port Moresby, 1968.

T. P. N. G. House of Assembly, Select Committee on constitutional development (Chairman John Guise), *Interim report 1965. Second interim report 1966. Final report 1967*. Port Moresby, 1967; Canberra,

1968; *Commonwealth Parliamentary Papers*, session 1, vol. 7, 1967-8.

—— Select Committee on House of Assembly procedures, *Interim report. Final report. Supplementary report*. Port Moresby, 1969.

—— Select Committee on constitutional development (Chairman Paulus Arek), *First interim report 1969. Second interim report 1970. Final report 1971*. Port Moresby, 1971.

T. P. N. G. Legislative Council, Select Committee appointed to inquire into and report upon the political development of the Territory (Chairman J. T. Gunther), *Interim report 1962. Second interim report 1963*. Canberra, 1963; *Commonwealth Parliamentary Papers*, vol. 13, 1962-3.

T. P. N. G., *Report of the electoral Commission of Inquiry into electoral procedures, 1970*. Port Moresby, 1970.

COMMONWEALTH OF AUSTRALIA LEGISLATION

Papua and New Guinea Act 1949-68.

TERRITORY OF PAPUA AND NEW GUINEA LEGISLATION

Electoral Ordinance 1963-67.

IAN GROSART

HULI. People of the Southern Highlands District.
References:
R. M. Glasse, 'The Huli Descent System', *Oceania*, vol. 29, 1958-9.

—— 'Revenge and Redress among the Huli', *Mankind*, vol. 5, 1954-62.

—— *The Huli of Papua*. Paris, 1968.

—— 'Bingi at Tari', *Journal of the Polynesian Society*, vol. 72, 1963.

—— 'The Huli of the Southern Highlands', in *Gods Ghosts and Men in Melanesia*, ed. P. Lawrence and M. J. Meggitt. Melbourne, 1965.

HUMAN GENETICS. It is difficult to make a sharp distinction between physical anthropological characteristics and the genetics of man, because most of man's measurable features are at least partly determined by his ancestry. Height, hair form, eye colour and skin pigmentation are examples. The reader interested in genetics is, therefore, advised to refer to the article on Physical Anthropology.

Human genetic studies in New Guinea have been mainly concerned with population characteristics but a few have been involved with rare clinical disorders of special interest such as kuru [q.v.] or albinism.

POPULATION GENETICS

Until recently most of the population of New Guinea was relatively isolated. Marital horizons were limited because there were geographic barriers to easy movement, and warfare between groups restricted communications. Males generally sought their partners either within their own community or within those in the surrounding neighbourhood. These and other factors responsible for the formation of isolates are now disappearing with the recruitment of labour, the building of roads and the liberal use of aircraft. However, many population studies were made of isolated groups before economic and cultural advances changed the traditional way of life, using a limited number of readily observed characteristics (gene markers) known to be inherited according to the standard rules of genetics. These studies have been concerned mainly with the blood groups; but more recently the serum protein types have also been determined. The findings are given in the article on Physical Anthropology.

The relative isolation of the groups studied has encouraged speculation concerning the factors producing the genetic pattern, especially the blood groups. Some factors possibly involved are mutation, random genetic drift, migration and disease selection.

Mutation. In stabilized populations the blood group mutation rate is low but two fairly definite mutations have been found in localized areas in New Guinea. The first, described by Watson and others, Simmons and others (1961), Giles and others (1966) and Dowell and others, is the D^u variant of the Rh factor. People with this gene give a weak type of Rh positive reaction which is sometimes confused with an Rh negative reaction. It has been found only in the Kainantu-Markham Valley area in the Eastern Highlands, at the mouth of the Crora River in the Northern District and in New Britain, although it has been specifically sought amongst many thousands of blood samples tested from other areas. Giles and others (1965-6) point out that twenty-seven out of the twenty-eight known D^u individuals in the Eastern Highlands came from an area roughly twenty-five by twenty-five miles in area. The second mutation was also found in the Eastern Highlands when Simmons and others (1961) described a family in which two members had the A_2 gene, a variant which has not been found elsewhere.

Localization of both mutations to restricted areas suggests that they may have occurred after migrants from Asia were well established in isolated areas. This would apply to the disease kuru, if this proves to be a genetically determined disease. Some other genetic conditions which are probably the results of mutation, such as albinism, are widespread and could have been produced by frequent local mutations or by the spread of a mutant gene present in the founding population.

Random genetic drift. The frequency of blood group genes varies greatly between villages in the same geographic area and even between village units within the same linguistic area. For example, in the Markham River Valley and surrounding hills Giles and others (1965-6) showed that the frequency of the A gene varied from 7.6 per cent to 36.3 per cent and of the M gene from 0.4 per cent to 18.6 per cent. It is thought that random genetic drift, defined by Dobzhansky as 'random fluctuations in gene frequencies in effectively small populations', is principally responsible for these variations. Expressed in another way, the variations are thought to have occurred mainly because the people from whom isolated populations developed were few in number and by random chance differed in gene frequency from the parent population.

Migration. Haddon and Seligman both drew attention to the obvious physical and cultural differences between the inhabitants of the eastern part of the Papuan peninsula and those of the remainder of the island. Seligman suggested that the Papuans were probably the original inhabitants and the Melanesians were later arrivals. This hypothesis supposes that genetically different populations mixed in varying proportions in different geographic regions. Macintosh and others reviewed the blood group gene frequencies then available and found that they were consistent with the hypothesis of an earlier population driven to the Highlands by a series of migratory waves along the rivers from the north and the south and from the eastern peninsula.

The use of gene markers as an ethnographic tool in a country whose inhabitants have been subjected to the extremes of environmental stresses for generations is likely to produce inconclusive results. Theories often gain support from other disciplines, such as linguistics, but can rarely be proved.

Selection. Most geneticists believe that the susceptibility or resistance of an individual to some diseases is to a certain extent dependent on the genetic endowment of the individual.

This presumably holds as much for the people of New Guinea as for others but so far no established example of undue susceptibility to disease, of genetic origin, is known.

CLINICAL CONDITIONS OF GENETIC ORIGIN

It is possible that their general genetic constitution may render some individuals susceptible to various diseases, but there are a number of disorders which are genetically determined and are easily recognizable in individuals with the appropriate genes.

Dermatology. The degree of skin pigmentation can now be objectively measured by reflectance spectrometry (see PHYSICAL ANTHROPOLOGY). It is a genetic characteristic undoubtedly controlled by several genes (multi-factorial inheritance), but the genes responsible have not been defined.

There are, however, at least two related abnormalities of skin pigmentation due to recessive inheritance.

Albinism. Many writers have referred to the presence of albinos but there has not been an accurate survey of the prevalence of the condition. The victims obviously have a selective disadvantage in tropical areas and they all develop hyperkeratosis and optical disorders. Carcinoma of the skin is common amongst them. They are apparently not sought or accepted in marriage.

Albinos of the classical type with complete absence of pigmentation of the skin, hair and eyes have been seen by the author. Pearson was the first to observe albinos who showed large numbers of pigmented spots, especially on the exposed parts of the skin. The spots are not raised, there is considerable variation in their size and shape, and the degree of pigmentation is approximately equal to that of subjects from the same population who are not albinos. Examples of this variant form of albinism have been observed at Port Moresby, in the Madang area and on the Trobriand Islands. It seems likely that all were born without the pigmented areas and that an increasing number of spots developed during childhood. It has been suggested that the pigmented areas represent changes or mutations induced by ultra-violet light in pigment-producing cells of certain parts of the skin, so that the altered cells function in the normal manner. As the changes apparently do not affect the gametes, the mutations are called somatic mutations.

Red skins. This condition is characterized by deficient production of melanin but is easily recognized because of the presence of a reddish-brown pigment which is not normally present. It is particularly striking in childhood but persists throughout life. The hair fibres contain some pigment and are usually light brown in colour. Ocular symptoms similar to those seen in true albinism are present. A high incidence of the condition has been observed in the Western Highlands near Wabag and in the Maprik area in the East Sepik District but examples have been seen in most parts of the Territory.

A study of family pedigrees suggests that, like albinism, the condition of red skin is due to autosomal recessive inheritance; this means that its occurrence is not associated with the sex of the subject, and that both parents carry the responsible gene without symptoms. The condition results only when two genes, one from each parent, are present in the subject. Since some areas show a relatively high incidence of the condition carriers must be common. Unlike albinos, affected subjects seem to be at no marital disadvantage and are not unusually susceptible to any form of illness. If the genes which produce albinism and red skins arose by mutation, the changes must have occurred either before the ancestors of the present inhabitants reached New Guinea or the mutant genes must have spread freely throughout the country. The situation contrasts with that seen with the other mutant genes, A_2 and D^u.

Ophthalmology. Mann and Loschdorfer conducted an ophthalmic survey and tested 7,043 subjects for colour vision. They found 2 per cent of 4,077 males to be colour-blind by the Ishihara Chart Method. This can be compared with 5.5 per cent colour-blind males amongst 464 Australian Aborigines and between 6 per cent and 22 per cent in different European populations.

Haematology. Abnormal haemoglobins are rarely found in the blood of New Guinea subjects and only occasional examples of haemoglobins E, H and Lepore have been reported, by Curtain and others; Ryan and others; and Booth. Sickle cell haemoglobin has never been encountered although it has been sought in several surveys in which techniques adequate to detect it were used. Its absence is significant because New Guinea is one of the few tropical countries with a high incidence of malaria but without sickle cell haemoglobin. Thalassaemia (Mediterranean anaemia) was first

reported in a patient from Port Moresby by Ryan and the trait has since been found in four widely separated regions of New Guinea and New Britain. Again, the frequency is not as great as in other malarial countries but Curtain and others claim that the trait is more common in the coastal regions of the Gazelle Peninsula of New Britain than in the Eastern and Western Highlands.

An important enzyme concerned with the metabolism of glucose in red cells, known as glucose-6-phosphate dehydrogenase (G-6-P-D) is sometimes deficient or absent from red cells. This deficiency is determined by a sex-linked recessive gene. Affected subjects are often susceptible to drugs, especially anti-malarial drugs and certain vegetable toxins. Gorman and Kidson found a high incidence of G-6-P-D deficiency in several coastal groups in New Guinea and New Britain but the enzyme was present in normal amounts in all except three of 343 males tested in the Eastern Highlands. The distribution of enzyme deficient subjects in malarial areas has provoked speculation that there may be some selective force in the distribution of the deficient subjects.

Haemophilia, with Factor VIII deficiency in the blood, was found in a boy aged six years from the Vitu Islands off New Britain by Champness. This is the only family known to contain the haemophilia gene in the Territory, but it is likely that the condition has been fatal in other sufferers without being recognized as haemophilia.

Hypertension. Most workers believe that there is a genetic component in the causation of high blood pressure but there has been dispute about the relative parts played by genetic and by environmental factors. The rarity of hypertension in New Guinea is, therefore, of considerable interest to geneticists, especially as socio-economic changes will introduce environmental factors comparable with those now found in European populations.

Other issues. Isolated examples have been found of such conditions as neurofibromatosis, brachydactyly, polydactyly, syndactylism, achondroplasia, Madelung's deformity, cleido-dysostosis and nail-patella syndrome. A diabetic survey in Hula and Kalo, rural Papuan villages, disclosed no cases of diabetes among 852 subjects examined and a similar survey in four suburban groups in Port Moresby found two affected among 2,383 people tested. No condition has been seen with sufficient frequency to suggest that it has a selective advantage in New Guinea and no condition often seen in other populations is notably absent in New Guinea.

K. Booth, 'Haemoglobin H in a Papuan Family', *Papua and New Guinea Medical Journal*, vol. 9, 1966.

L. T. Champness, 'Haemophilia in New Guinea', *Medical Journal of Australia*, vol. 1, 1962.

C. C. Curtain, C. Kidson, D. C. Gajdusek and J. G. Gorman, 'Distribution Pattern, Population Genetics and Anthropological Significance of Thalassemia and Abnormal Hemoglobins in Melanesia', *American Journal of Physical Anthropology*, new series, vol. 20, 1962.

Th. Dobzhansky, *Genetics and the Origin of Species.* 3rd ed., New York, 1951.

M. F. Dowell, P. B. Booth and R. J. Walsh, 'Blood Groups and Haemoglobin Values amongst the Ewa Ge and Orokaiva People of the Northern District of Papua', *Archaeology & Physical Anthropology in Oceania,* vol. 2, 1967.

E. Giles, E. Ogan, R. J. Walsh and M. A. Bradley, Blood Group Genetics of Natives of the Morobe District and Bougainville, Territory of New Guinea', *Archaeology & Physical Anthropology in Oceania,* vol. 1, 1966.

E. Giles, R. J. Walsh and M. A. Bradley, 'Micro-Evolution in New Guinea: The Role of Genetic Drift', *Annals of the New York Academy of Sciences,* vol. 134, 1965-6.

J. G. Gorman and C. Kidson, 'Distribution Pattern of an Inherited Trait, Red Cell Enzyme Deficiency, in New Guinea and New Britain', *American Journal of Physical Anthropology,* new series, vol. 20, 1962.

A. C. Haddon, *The Decorative Art of British New Guinea,* 1894. Quoted by C. G. Seligman.

N. W. G. Macintosh, R. J. Walsh and O. Kooptzoff, 'The Blood Groups of the Native Inhabitants of the Western Highlands, New Guinea', *Oceania,* vol. 28, 1957-8.

I. Mann and J. Loschdorfer, *Ophthalmic Survey of the Territories of Papua and New Guinea.* Port Moresby, 1955.

K. Pearson, E. Nettleship and C. H. Usher, *A Monograph on Albinism in Man,* 1913; quoted by N. A. Barnicot, 'Albinism in south-western Nigeria', *Annals of Eugenics,* vol. 17, 1952-3.

B. Ryan, 'Thalassaemia: Report of a Case in Papua', *Medical Journal of Australia,* vol. 1, 1961.

B. P. Ryan, A. L. Campbell and P. Brain, 'Haemoglobin H Disease in a Papuan', *Medical Journal of Australia,* vol. 2, 1961.

C. G. Seligman, *The Melanesians of British New Guinea.* Cambridge, 1910.

R. T. Simmons, D. C. Gajdusek and L. C. Larkin, 'A Blood Group Genetical Survey in New Britain', *American Journal of Physical Anthropology,* new series, vol. 18, 1960.

R. T. Simmons, J. J. Graydon, V. Zigas, L. L. Baker and D. C. Gajdusek, 'Studies on Kuru. V. A Blood Group Genetical Survey of the Kuru region and other parts of Papua-New Guinea', *American Journal of Tropical Medicine and Hygiene,* vol. 10, 1961.

J. B. Watson, V. Zigas, O. Kooptzoff and R. J. Walsh, 'The Blood Groups of Natives in Kainantu, New Guinea', *Human Biology,* vol. 33, 1961.

J. Wolstenholme, P. B. Booth and D. J. Basset, 'Cleido-Dysostosis in a New Guinea Family', *Journal of the College of Radiologists of Australia,* vol. 8, 1964.

R. J. WALSH

HUNT, Atlee Arthur (1864-1927), public servant, was born at Baroonda, Queensland, on 7 November 1864, son of Arthur Hunt, a manufacturer of Sydney. He was educated at Balmain Public School and Sydney Grammar School. In 1879 he joined the N.S.W. Lands Department but resigned in 1887 to study for the Bar, to which he was called in 1892. He became Secretary of the N.S.W. Federal Association in 1898 and in the following year General Secretary of the Federal League. With the foundation of the Commonwealth he became private secretary to Sir Edmund Barton, the Prime Minister, and then Secretary and permanent head of the Department of External Affairs—which was to administer Papua—in May 1901.

Hunt visited British New Guinea, then in the process of becoming the Australian colony of Papua, in 1905 and wrote a report upon policy which was laid before the Commonwealth Parliament. He advocated a policy of development by European enterprise as the surest way to benefit the natives, in the belief that the administration of a colony was in many ways a communal undertaking and his views in general constituted the 'official' mind in Australia. Hunt also tried to keep himself informed about Papuan affairs by an extensive, semi-official, correspondence with officers of the administration of the territory. His relations with Hubert Murray [q.v.] were not particularly cordial; they disagreed over details of policy and personally disliked each other, but Hunt remained responsible for Papuan affairs when they were transferred to the Department of Home and Territories in 1916, becoming Secretary and permanent head of that department. In 1919 he was one of the three Royal Commissioners on the former German colony of New Guinea, under Murray's chairmanship, with Walter H. Lucas [q.v.] as the other member. He and Lucas reported against amalgamation with Papua, in the face of Murray's strong dissent, and their view prevailed. But Hunt's connection with the territory ended soon afterwards when in 1921 he became Public Service Commissioner. He died in 1927.

He was a shrewd and able lawyer who, until the end of World War I, provided the constant and informed part of metropolitan views of Papua. But he was never wholly liked or trusted by those who, like some of his ministers and like Murray, had to deal with him.

J. D. Legge, *Australia's Colonial Policy.* Sydney, 1956; F. J. West, *Hubert Murray: The Australian Proconsul.* Melbourne, 1968. Hunt's private papers are in the National Library, Canberra, and his official ones in the Commonwealth Archives Office.

FRANCIS WEST

HUNTING. To the majority of New Guinea peoples hunting and collecting wildlife—excluding fish and other aquatic creatures (*see* FISHING)—are subsidiary to horticulture, pig husbandry, and, for coastal or lake-side populations, fishing. However, in sparsely settled regions hunting provides a great part of the animal protein in the diet; and even among the densely settled sweet potato cultivators of the Highlands small vertebrate and invertebrate animals are significant in the diet of women and children. It is also striking that in many parts of New Guinea where hunting and collecting are economically marginal, animal lore and hunting are still prominent themes in mythology, cosmology, ritual, and art.

The only pre-European big game animals in New Guinea are feral pig, *Sus scrofa papuensis,* descended from stock introduced by man prior to 3000 B.C., and three species of cassowary, *Casuarius*. With crocodiles and pythons, these are the only terrestrial creatures that grow as large as man and, apart also from a few venomous snakes, are the only ones capable of maiming or killing a hunter.

Other wildlife utilized as food includes wallabies, tree-kangaroos, and many smaller marsupials; echidnas; giant rats and many smaller rodents; bats; a very rich bird fauna; monitor lizards and many smaller reptiles; many species of frogs; and a very large number of invertebrates, of which the larvae of certain longicorn beetles and moths found in sago and timber are the most significant.

Plumes of many species of birds, especially birds of paradise, parrots, hornbills, hawks, and cassowaries, and pelts of mammals, especially tree-kangaroos and certain cuscuses, provide highly valued ornaments. Bone, teeth, claws or bills of many mammals and birds, including cassowary, dog, pig, wallaby, tree-kangaroo, giant rat, and the larger fruit bat, have many uses for tools and ornaments. Skins of monitor lizards and of possums, *Pseudocheirus* spp., are used as drum-skins.

Bird plumes and to a lesser extent mammal pelts, live animals, smoked mammal and reptile carcasses, and other animal products are important in traditional local trade or gift exchange.

Hunting and trapping also serve to protect gardens from depredations of wild pigs, rodents, fruit bats, and other fauna. In many societies game is also periodically required for ritual consumption or ceremonial distribution; in some instances live animals must be captured for ritual slaughter. Where success in hunting is socially as well as economically significant, associated ritual observances and magic are often highly elaborated.

In general, hunting and trapping are activities for men and boys, and women and children collect or capture small mammals, frogs, and other small vertebrates and invertebrates.

WEAPONS

The main traditional weapons of the hunt are the bow and arrow and the spear. Clubs and throwing sticks are less widely used. Blowpipes are known only in limited areas of West Irian and of New Britain and New Ireland, slings only in restricted areas of the Bismarck Archipelago. In any one region many categories of arrows are used. Typically these fall into three or four functional classes: with a single palmwood or bone point for medium-sized mammals and large birds; three- or four-pronged, with prongs often barbed, for small birds and mammals; bird bolts with a blunt hardwood tip, especially for birds with valuable plumes; and bamboo-bladed for large game, especially pigs.

METHODS

Collective methods, various forms of drive, are characteristic of grassland and savannah areas, especially at lower altitudes, and are only employed sporadically in forest zones, where most hunting is by individuals or groups of two or three men. Both collective hunting, especially grassland drives with fire, and intensive individual hunting tend to be seasonal, reflecting climatic conditions, but also occupying slack periods in annual horticultural cycles and often related to periodic ceremonial activities for which game is required. The extensive use of traps and snares is related both to the fact that most New Guinea peoples are relatively sedentary horticulturists and only part-time hunters, and to the necessity for horticultural populations to protect their crops.

The drive. In the simplest form of drive a group of hunters co-ordinates its efforts in flushing and chasing game, generally in a restricted area from which escape is impeded by natural barriers. In seasonally flooded localities in southern and western New Guinea advantage is taken of the concentration of wallabies and other animals in limited areas above flood level, and of the creatures' impeded movements under marshy conditions.

More frequently, hunters surround game and either close in on it or force it to attempt to escape by use of fire or dogs. This is a general lowland method of pig hunting, but the occasional cassowary and many smaller grassland animals are taken by this strategy. Of all hunting methods in New Guinea the fire-drive has the greatest ecological significance, as the repeated burning of grasslands prevents regeneration of forest.

In some lowland savannah areas combined use of hunters in ambush and of beaters is the largest-scale form of hunting, with pig, wallaby, and cassowary the main game. The same technique is more rarely used in lowland forest. In coastal and lowland south-east New Guinea and in scattered parts of northern New Guinea and the Bismarck Archipelago nets are used. In other regions ambushers wait behind screens or fences. In large drives women and boys frequently participate as beaters. Dogs are also sometimes employed. To create noise, rattles and trumpets may be used, as well as the human voice. On a smaller scale this strategy is employed in wallaby hunting in Highlands forests.

A special device used in parts of southern New Guinea is the pig-fender—a loop of rattan, with or without a net, attached to a pole. This enables dangerous beasts to be kept at a distance and animals to be captured alive for domestication or ceremonial slaughter.

One reported method of crocodile hunting is a form of drive. The freshwater crocodile, *Crocodylus novaeguineae*, smaller and less dangerous than the estuarine species, *C. porosus*, is taken in the Sepik during the dry season by lines of men walking through shallow water and feeling for sleeping beasts with their feet. A hunter who finds a crocodile seizes it with fingers under the jaw and thumbs in its eyes, which he gouges out. His companions then lift him and the reptile from the water.

Individual methods. In open country stalking and the chase are the main strategies employed by individual hunters, but in forest areas most game is taken by diverse forms of ambush and by besetting quarry at its lair, roost, or nest. Luring is also of some importance. Successful use of these methods requires detailed knowledge of animal behaviour and ability to interpret correctly the evidence of tracks, droppings, food remnants, browsed foliage, etc.

Pigs and cassowaries are ambushed at their feeding places, sometimes by a hunter safely out of reach in a tree; cassowaries are also beset at the nest, pigs at their regular sleeping places. In lowland areas of West Irian a sago palm is felled and split as a bait for pigs, which are then ambushed. Pigs are also widely hunted with dogs to run them down.

Wallabies are individually stalked in the southern grasslands and in some areas are attracted by stamping on or striking the ground and by calling. Dogs are used to run down both grassland and forest species.

Arboreal forest mammals are mainly nocturnal. They may be stalked on moonlit nights, but a particularly frequent method of obtaining them is by besetting them at their lairs. Some, such as the giant rat *Mallomys rothschildi*, which have lairs in tree hollows, are difficult to extract and capable of injuring the hunter if tackled by hand. Smoke may be used to force them out, or hooked and pointed sticks to extract them. Trees adjacent to that in which the quarry is located may be felled or lopped to prevent escape overhead. Dogs are used to run down or tree arboreal mammals that feed on the ground.

Although birds are frequently stalked with bow and arrow, in forest areas the greatest numbers appear to be taken by ambush strategies. Frugivorous and blossom-feeding birds—doves, small parrots, honeyeaters, flower-peckers, and certain birds of paradise—are shot or in some lowland areas taken with hand-nets at their food trees. Hides are often constructed either in the branches or under the trees. Adult male birds of paradise are similarly obtained at their display trees or display grounds, or taken by hand at their roosts. Birds are also shot from hides at drinking or bathing pools, or they may be shot, hand-snared, or captured by hand at the nest. In some lowland areas bird-lime, prepared from viscous sap of breadfruit or certain other trees, is spread on perches, or on sticks manipulated by the hunter.

Hunters attract certain birds by imitating their calls. In parts of West Irian, whistles of hollowed-out fruits are used. Captive chicks or fledglings of many species are used to decoy their parents. The use of captive adult or tame birds as decoys, however, seems to be rare. There are a few records of birds being taken with baited lures or gorges, the latter technique also being employed to capture crocodiles.

Switches or brushes are used to knock down small birds and bats in their flight lines, sometimes by a hunter concealed behind a screen. In restricted areas of mainly northern New Guinea nets are hung in flight lines. At night fire is sometimes used to attract birds or bats or to dazzle them so that they hit nets.

Bats are shot or struck in daytime at their roosts in caves or trees or knocked down in caves or cave entrances with switches or brushes. Fruit bats are also shot or struck while feeding at bananas or papaws.

Reptiles, both terrestrial and arboreal, are probably captured in the main by *ad hoc* stalking or chase. Hand-operated pole-snares are used to capture pythons and lizards in some areas.

Trapping. Spring-snares of many varieties are the most generally and frequently used trapping devices, particularly for birds, fruit bats, and smaller terrestrial and arboreal mammals, but also on occasion for wallabies, cassowaries, and even pigs and crocodiles. For smaller creatures they are sometimes baited, for crocodiles they are baited with carrion, and for fruit bats they are set over bunches of ripening bananas; but for larger terrestrial and arboreal game the usual technique is to place them in runs. Spring-snares are also set at the entrances to mammals' lairs, at birds' nests, at bower-birds' bowers, and at the display grounds of certain birds of paradise. Simple snares are widely but less intensively employed to take birds. Baited tube-snares are used for small rodents. Baited deadfalls and log-traps are widely used for pigs, and smaller versions of the same for rodents, bandicoots, and ground-feeding birds. Baited box-traps, with and without clap-doors, and funnel-traps, are used in some areas for pigs and smaller mammals. Spring-spears or spring-poles are used in limited areas of West Irian for pigs. Simple pitfalls are constructed for pigs and in some Highlands areas for wallabies. Shallow pitfalls baited with carrion, are used to trap crocodiles. Spiked pitfalls are commonly used for pigs, and in some areas for cassowaries. Spikes, of wood or bamboo, are also set in the ground, beside a lowered portion of fence, to wound and capture pigs breaking into gardens. Nets and hand-operated snares and lures have been mentioned above.

EFFECTS OF EUROPEAN CONTACT

The main effects on wildlife and hunting of European penetration and administration are indirect and hard to evaluate. A decrease in game in many areas may be assumed on account of increasing human pressure on forest resources. Social and economic changes of many kinds are also altering the methods and extent of hunting. The introduction of shot-guns, though on a relatively small scale, has led to intensified indigenous hunting of birds of paradise and possibly also of such large game as pigs, cassowaries, and wallabies, while the earlier introduction of steel axes and bush knives has significantly modified hunting practices in many forest areas.

Since 1900 rusa deer (*Cervus timorensis*) have been introduced in West Irian and New Britain, and they are now common in the southern lowlands of West Irian and western Papua. There are small numbers of other introduced deer species, feral cattle, and water buffalo in some regions.

In western and northern New Guinea trade in bird of paradise plumes with collectors from the

Indonesian islands has a great antiquity. External trade in plumes increased enormously during the early colonial period until it was declared illegal in the Australian Mandated Territory in 1922 and in Netherlands New Guinea in 1931. In many regions, however, internal trade in bird of paradise plumes continues unabated and has apparently intensified since the central Highlands were brought under administration in the 1930s.

Crocodile hunting has become commercially important since World War II, and the value of skins exported from the Territory of Papua and New Guinea rose to a peak of over $1 million in 1965-6. The industry is almost entirely in the hands of Europeans, who themselves hunt and also purchase skins from villagers. The main method is night shooting from a boat with a spotlight.

Apart from crocodile hunting and bird of paradise collecting, now illegal, hunting with firearms by, or on behalf of, Europeans has concentrated on the creatures which Europeans consider to be edible, notably pig, pigeons, and wild-fowl.

B. Anell, *Hunting and trapping methods in Australia and Oceania.* Lund, 1960; R. N. H. Bulmer, 'The strategies of hunting in New Guinea', *Oceania,* vol. 38, 1967-8.   R. N. H. BULMER

(*See also* FISHING; MATERIAL CULTURE)

I

IATMÜL. People of the Sepik River. References:
G. Bateson, 'Social Structure of the Iatmül People of the Sepik River', *Oceania*, vol. 2, 1931-2.
—— *Naven*. Cambridge, 1936; 2nd ed., Stanford, 1958.
—————'The Naven Ceremony in New Guinea', in *Primitive Heritage*, ed. M. Mead and N. Calas. London, 1954.
H. Damm, 'Eine "Totenfigur" aus dem Gebiete der Jatmül, Sepik, Neuguinea', Leipzig, Museum für Völkerkunde, *Jahrbuch*, vol. 11, 1953.
M. Mead, 'Research on Primitive Children', in *Manual of Child Psychology*, ed. L. Carmichael. New York, 1946.
P. Staalsen, 'Brugnowi Origins: the Founding of a Village', *Man*, vol. 65, 1965.
K. H. Wolff, 'A Critique of Bateson's "Naven" ', *Journal of the Royal Anthropological Institute*, vol. 74, 1944.

INDUSTRIALIZATION. Manufacturing industries in the Territory of Papua and New Guinea were set up originally to process primary products, to maintain and repair boats and road vehicles, and to provide a few consumer services. Slipways, garages, sawmills, joineries, desiccated coconut factories, bakeries, and one or two workshops for repair of mining equipment were amongst the few facilities established before World War II and these were mainly in or near Rabaul, or on the goldfields. Official statistics include cacao fermentaries and coffee mills, as the definition of 'factory' used is a broad one.

In 1965-6 (Table 1) 10,786 workers—less than a tenth of the paid work force—were employed in 407 factories. Of the 180 factories in Class 1, 128 are essentially engaged in serving forms of transport: garages and motor body building (93 and 1); slipways (22); aircraft workshops (13). The remaining fifty-two factories are concerned with: general engineering (25); sheet metal (11); electrical machinery, radio apparatus and cables (12); machinery manufacture and related activities (3). This class thus performs predominantly a service function for the domestic market, and only a minority of factories are manufacturing goods for first sale. But the growth of this class is particularly important for industrialization in the broad sense, as it is the training ground for the most advanced skills of industry, the electrical and metal-working trades.

The sixty-five factories in Class 2 cover: coffee mills and cacao fermentaries (19); bakeries (18); soft drink factories (11); freezers (6); breweries (2); some recently established plants packing or processing tobacco and cigarettes; fruit, meat, spices, nuts and roasting coffee. Class 3 consists largely of sawmills (64), and joineries (41), with two other mills making plywood or veneers. All other industries are placed in Class 4. Among the fifty-five factories included in this class are: power stations (15); printeries (14); cement goods (6); furniture (5); the remainder process paints or

Table 1

FACTORY STATISTICS 1965–6

	Class 1 Industrial Metals, Conveyances, etc.	Class 2 Food, Drink, Tobacco	Class 3 Sawmills, Joinery, etc.	Class 4 Other Industries	Total
	Number				
Factories	180	65	107	55	407
Employees	3,042	2,445	4,014	1,285	10,786
	$	$	$	$	$
Salaries and wages paid	3,809,624	1,090,893	2,585,530	1,300,899	8,786,946
Value of:					
Output	11,784,348	13,005,831	11,672,351	11,871,697	48,334,227
Materials and power	5,201,030	7,767,818	5,490,433	8,327,726	26,787,007
Land, buildings, plant, machinery	5,133,294	4,750,179	5,612,547	7,918,115	23,414,135
Production	6,583,318	5,238,013	6,181,918	3,543,971	21,547,220

Table 2

NUMBERS AND PERCENTAGE OF FACTORIES AND EMPLOYMENT IN CLASSES 1960–1 AND 1965–6

| | Factories | | | | Employment | | | |
| | 1960–1 | | 1965–6 | | 1960–1 | | 1965–6 | |
	No.	%	No.	%	No.	%	No.	%
Class 1	83	39.7	180	44.2	1,237	25.3	3,042	28.2
Class 2	36	17.2	65	16.0	845	17.3	2,445	22.6
Class 3	64	30.6	107	26.3	2,240	45.9	4,014	37.3
Class 4	26	12.5	55	13.5	562	11.5	1,285	11.9
Total	209	100.0	407	100.0	4,884	100.0	10,786	100.0

vegetable oils, make bedding, or are tailoring, dry cleaning or similar establishments. Class 3 is the largest employer, but Class 1, with about one thousand fewer workers, recorded a higher value added. These two, then, are the leading sectors, and while Class 2 is not much less important, Class 4 is a minor employer, and contributed only about one-sixth of the value added by all industry.

Table 2 shows the trends in number of factories and employment in each class between 1960-1 and 1965-6. Both workers and numbers of factories approximately doubled over the period, but as some of the increase was due to widening the statistical collection, the real rate of increase was probably about 12 per cent per annum. The greatest growth in employment and in numbers of factories was in Class 1, in which garages are prominent. Employment increased by almost as much in Class 3 (sawmills and joinery) but less than half as many factories were added, so the scale of operations increased. Additional employment was almost as great in Class 2 (food, drink and tobacco) but even fewer new factories were established, pointing again to increase in scale. Growth in Class 4 was small. Overall there was a relative displacement of sawmills and joinery from the position of providing nearly a half of industrial employment to that of providing little more than a third, and there was an increase in the importance of Class 1, garages, etc., which uses modern skills and serves the domestic market only.

Ownership of industry in Papua and New Guinea largely reflects the business structure; half a dozen merchant firms are also of considerable manufacturing importance and much enterprise is carried on by local Chinese traders; smaller firms are owned by single entrepreneurs, many of whom came first as tradesmen and later established a factory; some large overseas firms have established branches or subsidiaries in the Territory. The merchant firms are important in garages, engineering, freezers, aerated waters and coffee and cacao processing, and they have interests in sheet metal working, joinery, vegetable oils, dry cleaning and electric power. There are many Chinese with interests in garages, shipbuilding, bakeries, soft drinks, and some minor services such as tailoring. The Administration owns slipways, garages and joineries, while the Australian government has a half interest in a major plywood

factory. Individual entrepreneurs are involved in some sawmills, metal-working, garages and engineering, while overseas firms are important in engineering, aircraft repair, brewing, cigarette manufacture and cement goods. Missions own many small sawmills, joinery works, bakeries, garages and printing presses to meet church and school needs and to provide technical training facilities. The largest such industrial complex is owned by the Roman Catholic mission at Vunapope, near Kokopo in the Gazelle Peninsula.

As would be expected, industrialization is largely an urban phenomenon and both the Territory of Papua and New Guinea and West Irian face somewhat the same problems in the location of industry, though to judge from the numbers employed the scale of industry is ten times greater in the former. In both the market is fragmented, as there are at least half a dozen main port towns considerable distances apart. For many types of services and for perishable products an enterprise may be set up to serve only one town, but in other cases, an efficient unit would perforce be large enough to serve the whole market and would thus have to bear transport costs to every other port from the chosen location of the factory. In the Territory inter-port freights are generally little below freights from overseas, thus eliminating the manufacturer's advantage of nearness to his market. In West Irian inter-port freights have been deliberately kept low, but this is part of the reason for infrequent and inadequate coastal shipping services, an equal handicap to the would-be manufacturer.

Lae is the most centrally located port town in Papua and New Guinea, but Port Moresby [q.v.] is usually the largest single market for all but indigenous consumption goods, and it is also the most accessible to regular services from Australia. Thus to reserve the whole market for, e.g. a flour mill, would probably require protection to cover the costs of shipping the largest part of production from the mill to other ports. Lae is not a well-sheltered port and has practically no waterfront sites available for industries which need such a situation. Madang is well supplied with waterfront sites but is a small market and has no road connection with the Highlands. In West Irian Djajapura is the largest market with a population of sixteen thousand and some hinterland, but it is the most off-centre of the ports, except for

Merauke. Thus in setting up some industries a choice might have to be made, for example, between a number of small plants serving separate towns and one large plant at Sorong, which could serve most of the market if there were a reliable coastal shipping service.

The would-be manufacturer in Papua and New Guinea is not allowed to buy land and can only apply for a leasehold from the Administration. This may mean a delay of up to a year or even more, as the effect of government policy has been to make land available only after the need arises. However, moves are now being made to set up industrial estates with sites serviced before occupation. In part the delay in obtaining land is due to the difficulty the Administration faces in buying it from the indigenous owners and in getting it surveyed. In the town of Rabaul [q.v.] hardly any land is available for leasing. Owners of adjoining land will not sell to the Administration and others are questioning its title to the present town land. Development in other towns is hindered partly by land shortage but generally the delay is caused by slowness in survey.

Towns in Papua and New Guinea are zoned for heavy, light and noxious industry. Apart from Port Moresby few have reticulated water and industrialists who require large quantities of water must generally expect to obtain it from underground; this is not usually difficult but adds to the expense of establishment. Power charges—above a small minimum—are lower in Port Moresby and Goroka than elsewhere, though rates generally are becoming negotiable when a large uninterrupted supply is required. So far cheap power is not one of Papua New Guinea's industrial attractions but the position may change if or when the Ramu River hydro-electric scheme is completed (*see* ELECTRIC POWER).

Though Port Moresby has most factories Lae has attracted many of the significant new industries, while factories have been set up in both places for some products such as paint and industrial gases and roofing iron.

Of the four hundred factories in Papua and New Guinea almost a quarter are located in Port Moresby, over sixty in Lae, over fifty in Rabaul, twenty-eight in Madang, eighteen in each of Goroka and Mount Hagen, sixteen in Wewak, eight in Samarai and six in Lorengau. Sawmills are the most widely dispersed plants and are located mainly in rural areas, though some are to be found in Lae, Port Moresby, Mount Hagen, Madang and near Rabaul. In some Districts such as Gulf, West Sepik, and West New Britain the only factories are sawmills, but in quite small centres such as Buka Passage on Buka Island one may find a soft drink factory, or as in Buin on Bougainville, a bakery. In many isolated centres the Administration provides facilities for overhauling Administration vehicles or sawing timber for out-station buildings; for instance, in the Southern Highlands where all three sawmills are operated by the Public Works Department. This is the pioneering phase of development; it is only when roads develop and cash cropping becomes

important that the small towns attract garages, bakeries and joineries.

As air transport to and from the Highlands and Madang has been replaced recently by road transport from Lae to the Highlands, the position of Lae as the premier industrial location has been confirmed, and it will be a long time before new road connections challenge this position.

A significant factor for growth is building and construction, probably the most rapidly growing sector of the economy. Factories whose output goes entirely to building and construction are those working sheet metal, making cement goods, joinery, metal louvres and plumbing fixtures, while most of the output of the sawmill industry and about a third of the plywood produced at Bulolo are consumed locally. Many builders' workshops prefabricate metal for construction. In total, factories supplying the building industry account for about a third of all factories. The needs of this industry are met locally rather than from imports, either because the products are bulky, fragile or perishable, or because the customer requires on-the-spot fabrication to ensure that specifications are met.

Some consumer goods are also made locally because they are perishable—bread or newspapers, or because they are bulky and heavy but of low value—cheap furniture or soft drinks, or because the service can only be performed on the spot, as with maintenance of transport. These factories may be called 'residentiary' as they tend to grow fairly readily and on the spot, in proportion to the market, and they make up about 40 per cent of all factories. With those whose output is tied to the building industry, these account for about 73 per cent.

The remaining 27 per cent do not become established so spontaneously, and it is in this relatively small group that industrial promotion can be influential. Industries of this type already established include some shipbuilding—as distinct from overhaul, manufacture of steel drums, nails, barbed wire, woven wire mesh, paints, coconut oil, pyrethrum, canvas goods, louvre frames, rolled roofing iron, cigarettes and trade tobacco, plantation machinery and implements. Also foundry work and the assembly of electrical goods, batteries, trucks and trailers. Amongst them are a few, such as coconut oil and plywood, set up primarily to serve export markets, though not themselves an essential part of export processing.

Though it is government policy to encourage secondary industry not much has yet been done; some incentives are offered but they apply to few cases. Nor has the Administration seriously tackled those disabilities which it could abolish or mitigate. Incentives offered by government include special tax concessions for approved pioneer manufacturing and service industries, if they are the first in the field. Companies approved under the Industrial Development (Incentives to Pioneer Industries) Ordinance 1965 gain complete exemption from income tax, and dividends are also exempt, while there are complementary provisions, in some cases, for those paying tax in Australia.

Income tax is also lower in the Territory than in Australia. Excise concessions have been used in one case to encourage industry—cigarette making, and tariff protection has been accorded some local products. Papua and New Guinea has been in general a low tariff country and official policy to date has been to keep it so, though this is coming under review. Most factory plant and raw materials are permitted duty-free entry (*see* OVERSEAS TRADE). The Papua and New Guinea Development Bank was established by ordinance in 1965 and commenced business on 6 July 1967, with power to provide funds not otherwise available for industry (*see* BANKING).

Disabilities of local manufacturers include higher costs of the following items: buildings; power and water supply—most towns do not have reticulated water; expatriate managers, supervisors and skilled workers, who must be supplied with expensive housing and leave privileges; provision of housing for workers; need to carry larger stocks; delay in supply of imported materials, and loss through breakage; delay in provision of industrial land, and of services to sites. These difficulties have had a considerable deterrent effect on the growth of a local manufacturing industry and require to be offset by government intervention more effectively than has been done in the past.

In only a few cases are these disabilities offset by the lower costs of indigenous labour, for though the unskilled wage rate is only about a quarter of that for labour in Australia, labour is often only a small share of costs and low labour wages are themselves partly offset by the costs of training workers. Most of the semi-skilled and skilled workers have, perforce, been trained on the job, though the success of the apprenticeship system is now easing the shortages to a small extent. On-job training has been quite successful, and manufacturers generally find that they can replace a considerable proportion of their skilled expatriate employees, but they cannot be replaced as easily at the foreman or supervisor level. To augment skilled labour supply the Administration has supported and expanded the apprenticeship system through the technical schools, and sometimes gives assistance with the initial selection and training of labour for new factories.

So far the role of indigenous people in industry has been that of worker, rather than owner or manager. Trading and transport provide easier entry points to management and ownership of modern business than does manufacturing, and such indigenous capital and entrepreneurship as have developed outside agriculture have favoured trade stores and transport businesses. Village industries, often concerned with timber or woodworking, have been set up in scattered parts of the country. Village bakeries are widespread, and Local Government Councils own sawmills, freezers and cacao fermentaries, as well as facilities for brick-making and servicing vehicles. Even in village industries, a missionary, trader or the co-operative system has generally provided some expatriate oversight. The aspirations of village people to own their own sawmills, joineries,

freezers and similar facilities are rising, and present a challenge to the Administration. A small industry development corporation, or at least an advisory bureau, could do much in this field, which is at present the responsibility of the Department of Trade and Industry. Much could be learned from the recent experience of neighbouring Asian countries. Up to 1969, no steps had been taken to implement the suggestion of the Mission from the International Bank for Reconstruction and Development that indigenous entrepreneurs should be helped to set themselves up as manufacturers on rented sites in industrial estates.

There is scope for more industrial development through expansion of existing industry. This could do much to reduce the heavy reliance on imports. Such possibilities include biscuits, aerated waters, cigarettes, metal and wooden furniture, fibre-glass products, electrical equipment and batteries, wire products, building materials, machinery, printing and publishing, paper products and ships. New industries are likely to include: a glass bottle factory at Lae, with an associated carton-making plant; a desiccated coconut factory at Rabaul, reviving an industry which has begun twice before; coir processing; mixing of chemical preservatives; a flour mill; a soap factory. Coir and desiccated coconut would be for export.

There are also bigger possibilities, based on natural resources of forest, natural gas, hydropower, limestone and other minerals, but these require more deliberate planning and promotion by government than has hitherto been provided. Forest-based industries could include wallboard, particle board, paper and pulp; natural gas could be converted to fertilizers and plastics, and used to make cement; hydro-power could be used to refine bauxite to aluminium, or possibly to refine Bougainville copper. The use of New Guinea fuel or power to process northern Australia's minerals has long been a possibility. Canning—which would require reliable supplies of fish, fruit, vegetables or meat as raw materials—and clothing manufacture, are possibilities in light industry; by-products of slaughtering could be rendered to make glue, fertilizer or meat meal; tanning could become established and a sugar industry cannot be far away. Few are likely to eventuate, however, without more government help. An industrial development corporation with its own funds would do much to assist the many prospects which Papua New Guinea offers.

Manufacturing industry has developed in West Irian mainly to meet consumer needs and to maintain transport. In 1967 between 7 and 8 per cent of wage-earners, or about 1,300 workers in all, were employed in manufacturing enterprises, ranging from garages to bakeries. The numbers of privately owned plants of different types in eight main towns are shown in Table 3 and total employment in them at full capacity would have been over six hundred workers in 1967, though many were inoperative. Apart from sawmills, few factories are located outside the urban areas. About half of the enterprises shown in Table 3 supply food and drink, mainly bread, soy products and

Table 3

NUMBER AND TYPE OF PRIVATE FACTORIES IN MAIN TOWNS OF WEST IRIAN 1967

Industry or Product	Number of Factories								
	Sorong	Biak	Djajapura	Merauke	Manokwari	Fakfak	Kaimana	Serui	Total
Bread and/or cake	15	5	2	6	1	1			30
Soy products	1	6	1	2	3	1			14
Noodles or ice-cream	3	1	1	1		1			7
Soft drinks		1	2		2				5
Coconut oil	1	1		1			1	1	5
Tailoring		1	1						2
Shirts		1	1	1	1				4
Shoe repair			1		1				2
Furniture	2	2	3	2	1				10
Printing			1	1					2
Soap	2	1	1	1					5
Oxygen					1				1
Concrete products	1	1	2		1				5
Clay products				1					1
Vehicle repair	2	4	3	2	3				14
Jeep tops			1						1
Mattresses			2						2
Knapsacks			1						1
Laundry					1				1
Sawmills				1					1
Hand tools		1				4			5
Slipway	1								1
Total	28	25	23	19	15	7	1	1	119

soft drinks. There are ten furniture factories, eight making apparel or repairing shoes, and five making soap. Most are thus concerned with consumer needs. On the transport side there is one slipway and there are fourteen garages listed in the official statistics, though more than this number are known to operate. Sawmills and enterprises making concrete and clay products serve mainly the needs of building and construction.

In the official statistics industries are classified into three groups on the basis of employment and technology: small industry employs less than ten full-time workers and does not use mechanical power; medium industry from ten to fifty workers and/or uses mechanical power; large industry has over fifty workers. Most enterprises are medium and a significant number are large. West Irian has skipped the handicraft stage in small industry and gone straight to mechanization. The largest individual employers are slipways, garages and furniture factories. The pattern of ownership is indicated by information collected in 1967 relating to fifty-one enterprises: 30 per cent were Chinese-owned; 28 per cent government; 22 per cent owned by indigenous people; 14 per cent Indonesian; 4 per cent Dutch; and 2 per cent unknown. Some of these enterprises were set up before 1962 and in a few cases still belonged to the original Dutch owners. Some government-owned enterprises had been set up recently and others had been inherited from the former administration. Government operation is particularly important in transport: one large slipway at Manokwari has the capacity to build sizeable steel vessels and there is a smaller one at Merauke. Most towns have one or two government-operated vehicle workshops, and aircraft maintenance is undertaken by the public corporation which runs the airline. There are publicly-owned sawmills at Merauke and Manokwari and a pre-cut housing factory at the latter place. In one or two places missions operate sawmills, furniture and joinery factories and printing presses.

While Sorong and Biak have more private industrial enterprises than other towns (Table 3) the scale of operations is generally larger in Djajapura. Djajapura also has the most industrial workers. Biak is an important industrial centre, but is generally exceeded in total employment by Manokwari, where there are large numbers of workers at the government slipway and at the sawmill and pre-cut housing factory. Sorong has long been an important industrial centre, partly because it was the terminal to the oil pipeline from the Klamono oilfield and partly because it had a strategic situation being so far west and because of the large shipyard there. With a decline in these activities the town has to some extent been eclipsed by centres further east.

In 1967 industry suffered from a number of problems. Short supplies of raw materials and essential parts caused many factories to close or to work below capacity. Supplies were short partly because of a shortage of foreign exchange, and partly because of irregular and deficient shipping services from Indonesia and overseas. Information regarding the level of output of fifty-one enterprises in 1967 showed that 40 per cent were at full capacity, 20 per cent part capacity, 10 per cent were not fully installed and 30 per cent were shut down. However, the shipping problem had also spared industry the competition of Javanese goods in some cases, for when these are available they may often displace local products. This is partly because the wage level of West Irian was still in 1967 as much as two to three times higher than that of Indonesia.

The West Irian government has assisted industry in the past by sending workers and managers to Indonesia for training, by itself investing in necessary projects and by making loans to industry. Some experimental small projects begun before 1962 have been continued, such as the salt and tree oil experiments near Merauke, and new techniques, such as the mechanical scraping of sago, are being tried. The utilitarian handicrafts have disappeared from sale, and there is no export trade in artefacts, though it could possibly be encouraged. Carvings, pottery, palm leaf bags, mats, rattan furniture and stone implements are still made for village use, especially in the central Highlands, but none are marketed commercially.

R. K. W.

Since the above was written there have been a number of important changes in the position regarding industrialization in Papua New Guinea, although in many respects the structure of industry remains the same. Employment in factories had risen to 13,287 persons by 1968-9. Class 1 industries referred to in Table 1 (industrial metals, machines and conveyances) have superseded Class 3 (sawmills and joinery, etc.) as the largest employer of labour. While there has been a drop in the number employed in the latter sector, this is not expected to continue with the opening up of large timber leases in the Madang, Sepik and West New Britain areas.

There has been a further broadening of the industrial base. Additional new industries that have been established include fibre glass products, prawn processing plants, abattoirs in a number of centres, a tannery, coir and coconut shell by-products, a large-scale tyre retreading plant, gaseous oxygen, roof-metal rolling, transport equipment, steel furniture, glass bottles and fibre-board containers, clothing manufacture, a heavy welding plant and an ice cream factory. Existing industries in which the number of factories increased included bakeries, cement goods, the establishment of a third brewery, a large aerated water factory, a cigarette factory along with a large number of service industries associated with the Bougainville copper project. This project has also stimulated demand for producer goods from local manufacturers and has increased demand for locally produced consumer goods.

Industry on the whole remains expatriate orientated with most larger scale ventures being financed from overseas. However, there are moves being made both by the Papua and New Guinea Development Bank, and the newly created Department of Business Development to sponsor the establishment of Papuans and New Guineans in small-scale industry. This has included a joinery, metal fabrication and shoe repairs.

The Pioneer Certificate incentive scheme still remains the main instrument for attracting new industry to the Territory. To June 1971, fifty industries had been declared under the Ordinance. Other incentives apart from tariffs that have been introduced mainly centre around subsidies associated with the training of Papuans and New Guineas both within the Territory and overseas.

It is still true that the Administration has not attempted to provide serviced industrial estates in the major centres, although several private companies have entered this field and established small serviced estates in both Lae and Port Moresby.

While Lae and Port Moresby have remained the major industrial centres, the prospect of a highway linking the Highlands and Madang should ensure that town's position for new industry in the years to come, bearing in mind its added advantage of being a deep-sea port and having adequate waterfront space. There is a possibility that a large-scale fully integrated fishing complex based in Madang could be established in the near future.

The decision to proceed with the Upper Ramu hydro-electricity scheme, with a capacity on completion of 255 megawatts, will greatly improve the electricity supply on the New Guinea side of the mainland, and will be sufficient to meet foreseeable future demand. Stage 1 of the project with a capacity of 45 megawatts is expected to be completed and on line by January 1975. It is also planned to increase the capacity of the Rouna system that supplies power to Port Moresby.

In accordance with its policy of securing greater participation of Papuans and New Guineans in industry the government has undertaken two direct measures. It has established an Investment Corporation which is principally charged with taking up equity in major overseas enterprises for eventual sale to Papuans and New Guineans. Secondly, during 1971 the government introduced a Bill whereby expatriate workers in certain unskilled and semi-skilled positions will not be allowed entry into the Territory if it is considered by the government that there are sufficient Papuans and New Guineans to fill such vacancies.

C. C. WILSON

(*See also* ECONOMIC POLICY)

INITIATION. This term is commonly used to refer to two distinct forms of ritual: individual *rites de passage* associated with an important change in status or assumption of office, and group rites performed by the members of closed, and in many cases secret, associations when these admit new members into their company. In the small-scale and predominantly egalitarian communities of pre-contact New Guinea, initiations of the first type were relatively uncommon, whereas the group rites were widely practised and of major importance in the secular and religious life of the people.

During the past half-century European investigators, most of them trained anthropologists, have published reports on approximately fifty New Guinea societies, forty-two of which are in sufficient detail to be used in a survey of initiation ritual. Though as many as half of these are located in two areas, twelve in the Highlands and nine in the Sepik River region, the remainder are so distributed that they may be taken to provide examples of the main varieties of social systems found within the rest of the Territory of Papua and New Guinea.

A notable feature of the incidence and distribution of group rites was that there were only eleven societies in which they were not practised and ten of these were located east of a line drawn between the Huon Gulf on the north coast and the eastern part of the Gulf of Papua on the south. The one western society without the rites was Mbowamb in the Central Highlands; the ten eastern were Mekeo, Roro (with the exception of the Waima group), Koita and Mafulu of central Papua, and Wagawaga, Wedau, Tubetube Island, Dobu Island, Trobriand Islands, and Rossel Island, all in the Massim area. Of the thirty-one societies in which the rites were practised, twenty-one were located west of the line and ten east. Although the rites in certain well-defined socio-geographical areas had many features in common, such as the Eastern Highlands and Sepik River sacred flute, male secrecy, and blood-letting complex, there were also major differences between neighbouring communities and striking similarities in the rites of widely separated peoples.

WOMEN'S RITES

In most parts of New Guinea the men believed that women, especially during their menstrual periods and when giving birth, were possessed of a kind of sanctity or supernatural power that was different from, and indeed opposed to, the power that they themselves acquired by the performance of ritual. Though there was much variation in the extent to which men feared and took precautions against the dangers of feminine ritual pollution, there were few societies in which menstruating women were not required to retire from social intercourse during the period of bleeding and for a few days afterwards. The usual procedure was for the husband or father of the woman to build a special hut well isolated from residential areas. When the bleeding began she retired to the hut where she either cared for her own needs or had her food and other necessities brought to her by female relatives. Even in those few societies where seclusion was either not practised or laxly observed, it was usual for the woman to avoid any close contact with men, to refrain from cooking and to keep away from the gardens. The people generally believed that if a man came into contact, even in the most indirect manner, with menstrual blood, he would sicken and perhaps die. The growth of plants was believed to be endangered in the same way.

In those societies in which male fear of feminine pollution was especially strong (for example, throughout most of the Highland and Sepik River areas) a girl's first menses were marked by the performance of secret female rites. Among the Arapesh, a Sepik River people who live on the north bank and not far from the coast, a girl was usually living in her husband's village at the time of her first menses. She informed her brother, who then built a hut in the bush where she retired for about a week with an elderly female relative in attendance. During her seclusion she fasted for as long as she could and refrained from drinking and smoking. Her attendant regularly rubbed her body with nettles and taught her how to thrust a roll of the weed in and out of her vulva. The stinging was believed to make her breasts large and low-hanging and in general further her physical development. Her attendant told her she must keep her knowledge of the nettles secret from men. The men learnt their 'secret' when they were taught how to incise the penis when initiated into the *tambaran* cult; the women likewise had their secret which was known as 'women's *tambaran*'.

In Wogeo and Manam Islands in the Schouten group off the Wewak coast, a girl's first menstruation was made the occasion for elaborate and publicly performed ritual. The Wogeo girl, instead of being secluded in a special hut, celebrated her first period by working a few hours in every garden in the village and then visiting the other villages on the island. She thus performed the very acts that in most New Guinea societies were strictly prohibited. The ritual attributes of menstruation were still emphasized and placed in a special relationship with the gardens, but a danger that in other societies was literally shut up and guarded against was treated by the Wogeo as a force that could yield positive results. In the concluding stages of the rites the women gathered on a mountain top and amidst much lewd jesting ritually burned the girl's old skirt, the symbol of her youth now past. The men then stormed the mountain top and chased the women back to the village with sticks and stones. Later in the evening the women held a dance of their own from which men were excluded.

The Manam rites differed in that though they were performed when the girl first menstruated, they had no real connection with menstruation as a physiological event, with ideas about menstrual blood, or with the dangers that were elsewhere believed to be inherent in such overt manifestations of a girl's sexual maturity. For a period of seven days the girl was made the centre of much attention. Four or five young girls were appointed as attendants to care for her needs, especially to prepare her food. Each afternoon the older women took her to bathe in the sea and, though the rite was clearly purificatory in intent, it was performed with much light-hearted enjoyment and laughter. On the first day she discarded her old petticoat and was dressed in new ones made of shredded banana leaf. Her attendants washed her face with leaves and beautified her body with oil. Each day a female specialist added to her beauty by making small cuts to raise decorative keloids on various parts of her body. On the final day, after the usual bathing and oiling and donning of new petticoats, the girl was placed on a mat in front of her parents' house, and male relatives plaited ornaments on her body. A large gathering of kinsfolk attended this important ceremony and were feasted by the girl's parents. Early in the afternoon, when most of the visitors had departed, a woman shaved the girl's head. The women then returned to the beach for a final washing, and while still in the water the girl donned an ornamental waistband and the type of coloured petticoat worn by adult women. Back in the village she was painted, dressed in yet more petticoats, and redecorated with ornaments. Her father sat in front of her, and after the women had ritually wailed she ate food presented by various relatives. The next day she returned to normal life.

The Manam, Wogeo, and Arapesh rites can be regarded as initiations only in so far as they conferred on the girl a new status as potential wife and mother—they did not make her a member of an exclusive group of initiates.

GROUP RITES

Initiations into closed ritual associations differed from the menstrual rites of women in that, instead of being performed separately for each individual at a specific stage in the life cycle, a number of novices were jointly admitted at periodic intervals. Rites of this type were practised in thirty-one societies and in only three were girls included amongst the novices.

The Orokaiva and the Koko of the Northern District of Papua initiated girls as well as boys, but whereas the boys went through the rites in full and learned all the secrets, the girls went through only a modified version and could not themselves subsequently act as initiators. Every few years the men of the village, disguised as ancestral spirits, took all the uninitiated children from their homes and assembled them on the ceremonial ground. They proceeded to terrify the novices by performing masked dances and representing the voices of the spirits with bull-roarers and flutes. At the end of the day the boys, but not the girls, were shown the instruments and had their significance explained. They were told that though these were truly sacred objects they were also used by the men to impersonate the voices of the spirits (see MUSICAL IN-STRUMENTS IN RITUAL). The ceremony was followed by a period of seclusion that lasted for some months; the boys stayed in the men's club where the sacred instruments were also kept, the girls in a separate building specially erected for the occasion.

The Mundugumor, a Sepik River people, also initiated girls into a cult that centred on the possession of sacred flutes and bullroarers. Mun-dugumor social structure differed radically from that found elsewhere in New Guinea, especially in the unique descent categories which they so aptly termed 'ropes'. According to this system, a son belonged to his mother's rope, and a daughter to her father's, and so on down the generations. Given such a system, it was not surprising to find that the largest corporate and enduring groups were autonomous families living in widely separated homesteads.

Instead of a lineage, village, or phyle cult (see ANTHROPOLOGICAL DEFINITIONS) there were innumerable small cults, each owned by one individual and each passed down a separate rope. In each family group at least two cults were represented, and father and son necessarily belonged to different ones. The holding of a ceremony depended solely on the ambition and influence of the twenty or so adults who qualified for the title of 'big man'. When such a person decided to initiate new members into his personal cult he sounded his flutes, and the men of neighbouring homesteads came to help build a small ceremonial house. The men rounded up all the youths who had not yet been initiated into this particular cult, showed them the sacred objects, and subjected them to the particular torture that went with the rope concerned. Girls were given the choice of joining or not, and as they were exempted from the physical ordeals most of them agreed on at least one occasion. The boys had no choice, and by the time they were sufficiently strong to resist capture, most of them had been initiated into the cults of four or more 'big men'.

MALE RITES

Exclusively male rites of initiation were practised in twenty-eight societies, and normally all males were initiated by the time they reached adulthood. However, in New Britain and in the neighbouring island of Tanga the rites were performed by the members of secret societies—the *dukduk* and *ingiet* in New Britain and the *sokapana* in Tanga, and though most adult men belonged to one and frequently to many, membership was voluntary, could be acquired at any age, and was subject to the payment of a fee. The initiating men subjected the novices to numerous and harsh ordeals and hoaxes during a long period of seclusion in an isolated lodge. They also disguised themselves as supernatural beings by wearing elaborate masks and cloaks and rampaged through the neighbourhood destroying the property of non-members and terrifying the women and children.

The rites practised in the remaining twenty-six societies differed in that they united all men as members of a single ritual association. Within each area of social and cultural uniformity, which varied in scale from the five hundred or so residents of Busama village in the Huon Gulf to the sixty thousand Chimbu of the Eastern Highlands, all adult men went through similar initiatory experiences prior to marriage [q.v.]. In Busama and similar small-scale societies, mostly found in coastal areas, all the adult men jointly initiated their youths in ceremonies held at intervals that varied from two or three to as many as ten years. In larger-scale societies, such as those found throughout the Highlands, separate rites were held by the members of important constituent units such as lineages, sub-clans, or even, as among the Gahuku-Gama, sub-tribes. By contrast with the New Britain and Tanga rites, which stressed lines of cleavage and antagonism between men, the great majority of the compulsory pre-marital rites reflected the community of male interests and their essential opposition to the sphere of women. This was especially true of those societies in which male fear of feminine pollution was extreme. In such cases the rites were primarily intended to mark the end of the lad's former close association with his mother and other female members of the household, cleanse him of the polluting effects of such contact, and make him grow into a strong and healthy adult by acquiring specifically male ritual powers. Though the boys were usually required to undergo various unpleasant and painful experiences, these were seldom so harsh or cruel as in the secret society rites and were mostly intended to have beneficial effects.

The Gahuku-Gama of the Eastern Highlands provide a good example of a people who performed rites of this type. They are a congeries of tribes numbering about eight thousand persons, and they all speak the same language and share a common cultural heritage. The component tribes, about a dozen, united in offence and defence, and the great *idza nama* festivals were an expression of tribal unity. Each tribe was divided into two sub-tribes which in turn consisted of a number of named patrilineal clans. The clan was ideally exogamous, and most of the male members lived in a single palisaded village.

The men of each sub-tribe periodically initiated their youths into an exclusively male association based on the possession of sacred flutes. The separation of the sexes, and their opposition, was clearly expressed in the symbolic content of the rites, the ideology of the flutes, and the institution of the male club. The rites were divided into three separate stages spread over approximately four months and were usually so timed that the final and most important stage coincided with the holding of a tribal pig-exchange festival. Each novice participated on three successive occasions, the first during early childhood, the second as an adolescent, and the third shortly before marriage.

In the first stage the men led the novices to a stream and allowed them to witness ritual vomiting and nose-bleeding. The sacred flutes were sounded continuously and the men threatened to kill any women who saw either the boys or the flutes. When the men returned to the villages they were set upon by armed women.

In the second stage the novices were secluded in the men's club for about two months. They were admitted into the secret of the flutes and also taught how to play them. The third stage marked the end of seclusion and the formal return of the youths to everyday life.

The five- and six-year-old boys who took part for the first time were brought to the river to witness the nose-bleeding and vomiting. They were also made to bathe, and as they came out of the water the men greeted them with mock triumphant shouts. At the end of the day they rejoined their mothers in the family dwellings and took no further part in the rites.

The intermediate grade of novices had their noses bled and were shown how to make themselves vomit by swallowing a length of cane. They lived in the club for a few months, practising nose-bleeding and vomiting and avoiding any direct contact with women. However, the rules were lax, and they spent much of the time roving in bands. They were also taught the secret of the flutes, but were not yet allowed to play them.

The senior novices, after participating in the purificatory ceremony at the stream, entered a two-year period of seclusion. They had to avoid all forms of contact with women and could not even eat food cooked by them. They were taught how to play the flutes and received much instruction in the traditions of the tribe and the expected behaviour of adult males.

The men told the women that the flute tunes were produced by large birds, that the birds appeared in the club during the course of the rites, and that they tended them during this period. The men agreed that the tale was invented for the express purpose of deceiving the women and keeping them in a position of inferiority. The men believed that in physiological endowment they were inferior to women and that in order to overcome this handicap it was necessary for them to resort to such an elaborate achievement as the sacred flute cult and its associated rites of admission. Read wrote, 'A girl's growing breasts and her first menstruation are signs of a maturing process which is without obvious parallel in the boy, a fact that the men resent. . . . The challenge of the physiological processes of growth and sexual maturity in women is met by men's initiation rites and, thereafter, the practice of regular self-induced bleeding and magical acts'.

The people of Wogeo Island, the most northerly of the Schouten group, initiated boys into a sacred flute cult in four stages which resembled those of the Gahuku-Gama. The first took place at about four years of age when the boys had their earlobes pierced and were permitted to hear, but not see, the flutes. The second was performed three years later when the boys were carried to the beach where they were shown the flutes and had their significance explained. The third stage took place when the novices were about ten. The men cut the lads' tongues and taught them how to play the flutes. The tongue-cutting was said to release the mother's blood with which children were born, and in addition, all those contaminating influences acquired through contact with women. The final rites took place at about the age of eighteen when the youths were shown how to incise the penis and were dressed in adult fashion.

The men told the women and children that the flutes were the voices of supernatural beings, *nibek*, and they referred to initiation as being eaten by a *nibek*. Though the women were not deceived by the men's tale, they nevertheless believed that they would die if they should see the flutes. The men themselves, despite regarding their deception of the women as a joke rather than as a means of maintaining their superior status, firmly believed that they could only become strong and healthy adults by seeing the flutes and by releasing bad blood through tongue-cutting and penile incision. Like the Gahuku-Gama, the Wogeo men continued periodically to bleed the penis, an act which they explicitly referred to as 'men's menstruation'.

The Gahuku-Gama and Wogeo rites were, with only minor variations, typical of those practised by the Kamano, Fore, Siane, and Chimbu in the Highlands, and by the Abelam, Arapesh, and Kwoma of the Sepik. In each of these societies the men maintained elaborate ceremonial houses which no woman or child was permitted to enter. The rites of initiation conferred on boys the right to use these buildings as eating places and dormitories and to share in the secret of the flutes, masks, and carved objects stored in them. The uninitiated were supposed to believe that the sound of the flutes was really that of spirits come to visit the men in their club, and that the spirits disliked women, especially during menstruation and childbirth. In some societies the men also told the women that the spirits bit or devoured the novices. The men performed rites with at least three aims in mind: to cleanse the boys of the polluting effects of past feminine contact; to make them grow into strong and healthy adults; to hoax, impress, and sometimes frighten the women. The three were related in that they derived from anxieties experienced by the men in their relationship with women, and especially from fear of menstrual blood and childbirth.

The compulsory rites practised in the remaining nineteen societies differed in that though they were performed with some, and in a few cases all, of the above goals, additional considerations were of equal if not greater importance. They fall into two broad classes: those in which status differences amongst the men directly cut across and hence reduced the basic sex dichotomy between adult initiated men and uninitiated women; those in which the participants were at least as much concerned with political, economic, or entertainment functions of the rites as with status differentiation.

All the compulsory rites, including those in which the sex division was of paramount importance, divided the men into two main categories—the initiators and the initiands. When the rites were held at widely spaced intervals and the novices were secluded together for long periods during which they underwent numerous unpleasant experiences, strong bonds that persisted for many years were formed between the members of each initiatory set. But in the great majority of such rites—for example, those performed by the Gahuku-Gama—the boys were first and foremost initiated into a relatively undifferentiated adult male cult group and only secondarily into discrete age grades. The men shared the same secrets, resided in the same clubhouse and were members of the same patrilineal descent group.

The Busama of the Huon Gulf and the Iatmül of the Sepik were the only New Guinea societies in which the social gulf separating the novices from the initiators was as great if not greater than that separating both from the uninitiated women and children. As in the New Britain and Tanga secret society rites, the senior men subjected the boys to numerous ordeals and appeared to do so in order to make them suffer rather than to further their growth or cleanse them of feminine pollution.

In Busama the rites were held at intervals of about a decade, and the age of the novices varied from about fifteen to twenty-five. When the day came each novice was carried by a kinsman who had been initiated on a previous occasion to a hut specially prepared in the bush. Throughout the journey the older men beat the novices with firebrands, sticks tipped with obsidian, and nettles. They arrived covered in blood and were handed to two men who were to act as guardians and tormentors during their long period of seclusion. They were beaten, starved, deprived of sleep, partially suffocated, and almost roasted. Water was prohibited, and if thirsty they had to chew sugarcane. Only the coarsest of foods were allowed, and even these were left raw. The guardians also repeatedly instructed the boys about their kinship responsibilities and duties to elders. At length, after some months, a priest summoned supernatural beings from underground while the other men sounded bullroarers. The guardians then taught their charges how to incise the penis. As in the Eastern Highlands and Sepik River communities, all initiated men were expected to repeat the operation regularly on their own penis, especially after sexual intercourse and before undertaking any difficult or dangerous task. The period of seclusion ended when a series of great feasts was held and the initiands emerged richly decorated.

Hogbin, who studied both the Wogeo and the Busama, concluded his account of the Busama rites with the following observation: 'The question to be decided is whether the youths were introduced primarily into an age group or primarily into a sex group. . . . My impression is that a dual purpose was aimed at but with slightly greater emphasis on age. This conclusion is backed up by negative evidence from Wogeo, in the Sepik district, where the sexual side receives the stress. The Wogeo men when initiating a youth concentrate on hoaxing the women and refrain from inflicting hardships upon him; . . . The behaviour of the Busama was the direct opposite. They ignored the women's reactions and the initiation of girls and devoted their energy to making the youths suffer' (*Kinship and Marriage in a New Guinea Village*).

The Iatmül, a Sepik River people whose social

structure was notable for its complex series of age grades based on alternating generations and half-generations, emphasized the hoaxing and bullying of the novices to an even greater extent than the Busama. Instead of ritual purification by means of incision, circumcision, nose-bleeding, or nettle-stinging, the boys were cruelly scarified. In the second stage of the rites the men taught the novices to play the sacred flutes kept in the ceremonial house, fed them meat to make them grow big, and at the end decked them with finery and paraded them before the women. But the ethnographer Bateson made no mention of the men attempting to deceive the women with tales of devouring monsters. In fact, a number of girls even went through a modified version of the rites in which they too saw the flutes and were scarified.

Bateson described the spirit in which the ceremonies were carried out as that of irresponsible bullying and swagger on the part of the men: 'In the process of scarification nobody cares how the little boys bear their pain. If they scream, some of the initiators go and hammer on the gongs to drown the sound. The father of the little boy will perhaps stand by and watch the process, occasionally saying in a conventional way "That's enough! that's enough!" but no attention is paid to him . . . When pain is inflicted in other parts of initiation, it is done by men who enjoy doing it and who carry out their business in a cynical, practical-joking spirit. The drinking of filthy water is a great joke and the wretched novices are tricked into drinking plenty of it . . . In the first week of their seclusion, the novices are subjected to a great variety of cruel and harsh tricks'.

There were no New Guinea societies in which initiation was the exclusive concern of an hereditary aristocracy. There were, however, two communities, Manam Island in the Schouten group and Möwehafen in southern New Britain, in which the sons of high-ranking fathers went through the rites in full, while commoner boys were excluded from the final and most important ceremonies.

The Manam rites, like those of all the Sepik River peoples, were closely associated with a cult of sacred flutes kept hidden from women in the men's houses. Each village possessed a pair of the flutes, one male and the other female, and though every youth was instructed in their use during initiation, they were blown only for a member of the high-ranking *tanepwa* class. The rites themselves were performed in three stages that closely resembled those of the Wogeo, but instead of ritually reinforcing the sex dichotomy, the ceremonies emphasized the rights and privileges of the aristocrats. It is significant that they did not include incision or any other form of blood-letting operation. The ethnographer Wedgwood noted that only the *tanepwa* went through the rites in full, though she did not specify which stages were omitted for the commoner boys.

The geographical position of Möwehafen is of particular interest in that the people maintained regular contact with the Huon Gulf area of New Guinea via Siassi Island. The Huon Gulf ceremonies, which formed part of a secret male cult similar to that found in the Eastern Highlands and parts of the Sepik area, were recently introduced into Möwehafen. The people, however, radically altered the rites by initiating boys and girls together and excluding all commoners. The operation of circumcision, which in the Huon Gulf area was a carefully guarded male secret, was performed shortly after birth by an old woman. During the course of the rites proper, which were performed some years after circumcision, the initiates, both girls and boys, were shown bullroarers and then secluded for a short period. The Möwehafen, like the Manam, thus transformed a ritual complex usually associated with male solidarity and fear of women into one associated with an hereditary status distinction between men.

The Tchambuli (Chambri) are yet another Sepik River people who initiated their boys into a male cult that centred on the possession of sacred musical instruments, including flutes, and a tale told to the women that sounds of the instruments were really the voices of supernatural beings come to visit the men in their ceremonial houses. But the Tchambuli showed little interest either in the efficacy of their deception of the women or in making the boys suffer. The boys were initiated, not because they had reached an important stage of physiological or social development, nor as a ritual reinforcement of their separation from women and incorporation into a world of male secrets and exclusively male activities, nor again as a means of maintaining and reinforcing male status differences based on age, generation or rank, but rather as an excuse to hold an elaborate and beautiful ceremony providing entertainment and amusement for the entire community, women included. The rites were simply one of the many occasions on which the men displayed the magnificence of their masks, their skill as dancers, the size and ornateness of their ceremonial houses, and the sumptuousness of their feasts.

Each boy was initiated individually at the whim of his father's ceremonial ambitions, and age was a matter of little importance. As with the Iatmül, the boy was scarified, but every effort was made to reduce his suffering to the minimum. The operation, which was intended to make him beautiful, was performed in the men's house by one of the boy's classificatory mother's brothers, and far from being a carefully guarded male secret, the lad's mother attended so that she might comfort him. He was secluded for a short period but did not have to undergo any unpleasant experiences.

The flutes, gongs, and masks were supposed to be male secrets, but the women knew everything, and the men knew that they knew. The women said they perpetuated the pretence so that the men would not be embarrassed and also to ensure their own enjoyment of the dances and masked dramas. During these latter the women joined in and threatened the younger men who wore masks representing the opposite sex.

All the compulsory pre-marital male rites so far discussed shared at least one characteristic—the initiated men, regardless of the degree of internal status differentiation, continued throughout their lives as members of the cult group. In three societies—the Enga and west Kyaka of the New Guinea Highlands, and the Huli of the Papuan Highlands—the rites, though having many features in common with those found elsewhere, differed in that they were for bachelors only. So long as a man remained a bachelor, regardless of how old he might be, he retained membership of a closely knit ritual association and participated in the initiation of new members. The strict exclusion of married men was a consequence of their close association with women, and did not have anything to do with their having reached a certain age category.

In all three societies the sex relationship was characterized by strict residential separation from an early age, acute male anxiety concerning the dangers of feminine pollution, and the performance of rites, including the initiation ceremonies, from which women and children were excluded. Amongst the Enga, when a boy was about six he left his mother's house to sleep in his lineage club. At about fifteen he first participated in group rituals which the bachelors of his sub-clan performed in order to nullify the unavoidable contacts with clanswomen. The bachelors maintained cult grounds, forbidden to women and married men, where they cultivated a type of bog iris to ensure the health and welfare of their fellows. The withering of a plant was taken as evidence that someone had broken the taboo on associating with women. It was thought that such a person would fall ill or suffer other misfortune. The iris was connected in myths with female blood and was thought to protect the young men from the dangers of menstruation. The iris was also employed in magic having to do with wealth, pigs and war.

When a new member joined the group he faced seclusion for about two years in a special house on the cult ground. During this period various rites were performed including regular body- and eye-washing, rubbing with potent leaves, singing of spells, cultivation of the iris plants, observances of regulations concerning dress, diet, conversation and general behaviour, interpretation of dreams, and final emergence in full regalia at a public festival.

G. Bateson, *Naven*. 2nd ed., Stanford, 1958.

F. L. S. Bell, 'Sokapana: A Melanesian Secret Society', *Journal of the Royal Anthropological Institute*, vol. 65, 1935.

R. M. Berndt, *Excess and Restraint*, pp. 232-68. Chicago, 1962.

B. Blackwood, *Both Sides of Buka Passage*, pp. 102-40. Oxford, 1935.

R. N. H. Bulmer, 'The Kyaka of the Western Highlands', in *Gods Ghosts and Men in Melanesia*, ed. P. Lawrence and M. J. Meggitt. Melbourne, 1965.

E. W. P. Chinnery and W. N. Beaver, 'Notes on the Initiation Ceremonies of the Koko, Papua', *Journal of the Royal Anthropological Institute*, vol. 45, 1915.

W. C. Groves, 'Secret Beliefs and Practices in New Ireland', *Oceania*, vol. 7, 1936-7.

H. I. Hogbin, 'Puberty to Marriage: A Study of the Sexual Life of the Natives of Wogeo, New Guinea', *Oceania*, vol. 16, 1945-6.

———— 'Pagan Religion in a New Guinea Village', *Oceania*, vol. 18, 1947-8.

———— *Transformation Scene*, pp. 216-21. London, 1951.

———— *Kinship and Marriage in a New Guinea Village*, pp. 29-31. London, 1963.

———— *The Island of Menstruating Men: Religion in Wogeo*. San Francisco, 1970.

P. M. Kaberry, 'The Abelam Tribe, Sepik District, New Guinea', *Oceania*, vol. 11, 1940-1.

P. Lawrence, 'The Ngaing of the Rai Coast', in *Gods Ghosts and Men in Melanesia*, ed. P. Lawrence and M. J. Meggitt. Melbourne, 1965.

S. Lehner, 'The Balum Cult of the Bukaua of Huon Gulf, New Guinea', *Oceania*, vol. 5, 1934-5.

M. Mead, 'The Marsalai Cult among the Arapesh', *Oceania*, vol. 4, 1933-4.

———— 'Tamberans and Tumbuans in New Guinea', *Natural History*, vol. 34, 1934.

———— *Sex and Temperament in Three Primitive Societies*. London, 1935.

———— *The Mountain Arapesh, II; Supernaturalism*. Anthropological Papers of the American Museum of Natural History, vol. 37. New York, 1939-41.

M. J. Meggitt, 'Male-Female Relationships in the Highlands of Australian New Guinea', *American Anthropologist*, vol. 66, Special Publication, 1964.

J. Nilles, 'Eine Knaben-Jugendweihe bei den östlichen Waugla im Bismarckgebirge Neuguineas', *Internationales Archiv für Ethnographie*, vol. 38, 1940.

———— 'The Kuman of the Chimbu Region, Central Highlands, New Guinea', *Oceania*' vol. 21, 1950-1.

H. Powell, 'Competitive Leadership in Trobriand Political Organization', *Journal of the Royal Anthropological Institute*, vol. 90, 1960.

K. E. Read, 'Nama Cult of the Central Highlands, New Guinea', *Oceania*, vol. 23, 1952-3.

M. Reay, 'Social Control amongst the Orokaiva', *Oceania*, vol. 24, 1953-4.

———— *The Kuma*, pp. 170-80. Melbourne, 1959.

R. F. Salisbury, 'The Siane of the Eastern Highlands', in *Gods Ghosts and Men in Melanesia*, ed. P. Lawrence and M. J. Meggitt. Melbourne, 1965.

J. A. Todd, 'Report on Research Work in South-west New Britain', *Oceania*, vol. 5, 1934-5.

C. H. Wedgwood, 'Girls' Puberty Rites in Manam Island, New Guinea', *Oceania*, vol. 4, 1933-4.

———— 'Report on Research in Manam Island, *Oceania*, vol. 4, 1933-4.

J. W. M. Whiting, *Becoming a Kwoma*. New Haven, 1941.

———— and S. W. Reed, 'Kwoma Culture', *Oceania*, vol. 9, 1938-9.

F. E. Williams, 'Pairama Ceremony in the Purari Delta', *Journal of the Royal Anthropological Institute*, vol. 53, 1923.

———— 'Sex Affiliation and its Implications', *Journal of the Royal Anthropological Institute*, vol. 62, 1932.

———— 'Bull-Roarers in the Papuan Gulf', Territory of Papua, *Anthropology Report*, no. 17. Port Moresby, 1936.

———— 'Seclusion and Age Grouping in the Gulf of Papua', *Oceania*, vol. 9, 1938-9.

———— *Drama of Orokolo*. Oxford, 1940.

MICHAEL ALLEN

INSECT PESTS OF AGRICULTURE AND FORESTRY.

Although the study of insect pests in Papua New Guinea began early in the twentieth century, little was published on crop pests and their control in the first three decades. Research on insects of economic importance began in the 1930s, and especially since 1954, many papers have been published on the systematics, distribution, ecology and control of the insect pests of agriculture. The number of papers on forest insects, however, is still very small.

Close to 1,400 insect pests of cultivated plants and stored products have been found in the Territory, and it is of interest that a list of the insect pests known in 1954 recorded only 194 species from the Territory. Less than 40 can be considered major pests, and with the exception of one or perhaps two all are indigenous species of the rain forest. More than half of the major pests are endemic species which have adapted to the mostly introduced economic crops.

PESTS OF AGRICULTURE

Coconut palm (*Cocos nucifera*). One of the most important agricultural pests in the Territory is the Asiatic rhinoceros beetle, *Oryctes rhinoceros*, a black scarab beetle of the subfamily Dynastinae. It was introduced to New Britain during World War II, probably about 1942. So far it has not spread to the eastern half of the New Guinea mainland, although it occurs in some parts of western New Guinea. It is abundant on New Ireland but has been found only once in the Admiralty Islands.

Damage to palms is caused by the adult beetle, which bores into the soft parts of the central spike in an area near the growing point. Then the beetle usually bores downward through the white centre, where the new fronds are folded into semicylinders. This results in loss of leaf area, a reduction in growth and, if the meristem is destroyed, the palm dies. Similar damage to that of *Oryctes rhinoceros* is caused by indigenous rhinoceros beetles, such as *Scapanes australis* (New Guinea mainland), *Scapanes grossepunctatus* (Bismarck Archipelago and Bougainville), and more rarely by the large species *Oryctes centaurus* and species of the genera *Oryctoderus*, *Trichogomphus*, *Xylotrupes* and *Papuana*.

The crowns of young palms are sometimes treated with residual insecticides. However the only widely used method of control of dynastine beetles is the individual collection and destruction of the adult insect. Rhinoceros beetle populations can also be reduced to a large extent by maintaining proper plantation hygiene to eliminate the breeding sites of the larvae, such as dying or dead palms, refuse heaps, coconut husks and refuse from sawmills. The control of rhinoceros beetles has been tried by the introduction of various beneficial insects, such as the wasps *Scolia oryctophaga* and *S. ruficornis*, the predacious beetles *Pachylister chinensis* and *Leionota* spp. (Histeridae), the click-beetles *Pyrophorus* spp., the large ground beetle *Neochryopus savagei* (Scaritidae),

and the assassin bug *Platymerus rhadamanthus*. Only three of these, *Scolia ruficornis*, *Neochryopus savagei* and *Pachylister chinensis*, are known to have become established and all on the Gazelle Peninsula of New Britain.

The palm weevil, *Rhynchophorus bilineatus*, usually appears as a secondary pest after damage by the rhinoceros beetle. The adult weevil lays its eggs in a beetle bore-hole or in an area of other mechanical damage. The larvae feed voraciously and most young palms die if they are attacked by a large number of palm-weevil grubs. Palms can be treated by cutting a hole above the infested part of the stem and pouring a residual insecticide into it.

Other major beetle pests are the Hispidae, *Brontispa longissima* and *Promecotheca papuana*. *Brontispa* attacks the surfaces of the leaflets and it damages young palms. It has a Territory-wide distribution. The larva of *Promecotheca* is a true leafminer and it attacks palms of all ages. Both species can cause severe damage; however, *Brontispa* is easy to control with insecticides because it attacks mainly young palms. *Promecotheca* has been recorded from New Britain, New Ireland, Manus and north-east New Guinea and from time to time causes serious damage in some parts of New Britain and Manus. Both *Brontispa* and *Promecotheca* have local parasites but these do not seem to exert efficient control. The egg-parasite *Pediobius parvulus* was introduced from Fiji for the control of *Promecotheca* and another egg-parasite, *Tetrastichodes brontispae* (Eulophidae) was introduced from Java for the control of *Brontispa*; both became established. The 'kurukum ant', *Oecophylla smaragdina* reduces *Promecotheca* populations to a certain extent.

Important pests of the coconut palm are long-horned grasshoppers of the subfamily Mecopodinae, species of the genera *Eumossula*, *Segestidea* and *Sexava*, which attack the fronds. Serious damage is caused by these insects in the Admiralty Islands, in the New Ireland District and on Misima Island. Chemical, biological and mechanical control methods have been studied since the 1930s. A wasp parasite, *Leefmansia bicolor* (Encyrtidae), was successfully introduced from Amboina in 1933 but does not always seem able to keep Mecopodidae populations below the level of economic damage. The Strepsipteron *Stichotrema dallatorreanum* or a related species probably controls coconut Mecopodidae in some parts of the New Guinea mainland.

Other pests of the coconut palm are bugs of the genus *Amblypelta* (family Coreidae); *A. cocophaga* on Bougainville and *A. lutescens* in Papua, which cause premature nutfall; the spathe moth *Tirathaba rufivena* (Pyralidae) and the flower bug *Axiagastus cambelli* (Pentatomidae) which damage coconuts mainly in the New Ireland District; and the larvae of the coconut skipper *Cephrenes moseleyi* which has a Territory-wide distribution and feeds on the fronds. During an outbreak of the gregarious phase of the migratory locust (*Locusta migratoria*) on Goodenough Island in 1966 coconut palms were completely defoliated.

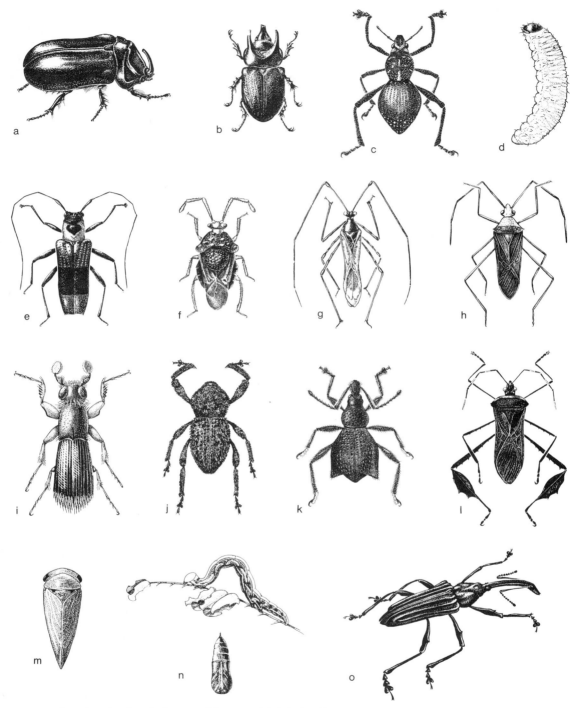

Insect pests of agriculture and forestry (a) Asiatic rhinoceros beetle *Oryctes rhinoceros*; (b) An indigenous rhinoceros beetle *Scapanes grossepunctatus*; (c) Weevil *Pantorhytes szentivanyi*; (d) Weevil larva *Pantorhytes batesi*; (e) Longicorn borer *Glenea lefebueri*; (f) *Pseudodoniella typica*; (g) *Helopeltis clavifer*; (h) Tip-wilt bug *Amblypelta lutescens papuensis*; (i) *Platypus selysi*; (j) Stem-girdler weevil *Meroleptus cinctor*; (k) Weevil *Apirocalus cornutus*; (l) *Leptoglossus australis*; (m) Leafhopper *Batrachomorphus szentivanyi*; (n) Semi-looper (larva and pupa) *Pericyma cruegeri*; (o) Stemborer weevil *Vanapa oberthuri*.

Cacao (*Theobroma cacao*) is attacked by more than 240 recorded pests in Papua and New Guinea but only 12 of these can be considered major pests. The stems and the branches of the cacao tree are attacked by weevils of the genus *Pantorhytes* and by longicorn beetles belonging to several genera of the subfamily Lamiinae. Ten species of *Pantorhytes* have been recorded as cacao pests in Papua New Guinea. The most serious are *Pantorhytes plutus* on New Britain, *P. batesi* in the Morobe District and *P. szentivanyi* in the Northern District. The larvae, by boring into the inner bark, cause severe weakening and even death of trees, especially if *Pantorhytes* damage is followed by secondary pests or diseases. The spread of the weevils is promoted by the fast growth of their indigenous host plants, especially *Pipturus argenteus* which is one of the main regrowth trees in forest clearings. A chemical control method which has been successful so far requires individual treatment of the bore-holes. Among the longicorn borers, *Glenea aluensis* and *G. lefebueri* are considered major pests; species of the genera *Dihammus*, *Heteroclytomorpha* and *Tmesisternus* are of minor importance.

Other major pests of cacao are bugs of the family Miridae *Pseudodoniella typica*, *P. pacifica*, *P. laensis* and *Helopeltis clavifer*, and *Amblypelta theobromae* of the family Coreidae. A fifth species of Miridae, *Pseudodoniella duni* is of minor importance. Although Miridae occasionally attack young shoots and flush growth, and one species (*P. laensis*) was observed even attacking the trunk and laterals, the main part damaged by these insects is the pods. Both the Miridae and *Amblypelta theobromae* make roundish or irregular shaped punctures, the scars of which are usually infected by secondary fungi. The *Pseudodoniella* species have a relatively short life cycle and in the case of *P. typica* it was observed that individual insects are able to cause up to eighty scars in twenty-four hours. *Amblypelta theobromae* occurs in the Milne Bay, Northern and Morobe Districts. The other three species found on cacao, *A. ardleyi* (in the Markham Valley), *A. madangana* (in the Madang District) and *A. costalis szentivanyi* (on New Britain), are considered minor pests. Miridae and *Amblypelta* are controlled with residual insecticides, preferably dusts or mists, applied at regular intervals.

Other wood-feeding insects of cacao are the branch-borer moth *Pansepta teleturga* (family Xyloryctidae), the leopard moth *Zeuzera* sp., and the large termite *Neotermes* sp.

About 1960 the caterpillars of various moths, which were considered minor pests for many years, became important in two districts where large areas of rain forest were converted to cacao plantations in a relatively short time. The most serious of these pests is *Tiracola plagiata* (Noctuidae) in the Northern District where almost continuous outbreaks occurred for five years. During this period various chemical, biological and cultural control trials were carried out. Eventually a cultural method, the partial removing or thinning of the *Leucaena leucocephala* shade trees,

was found to reduce the population density of the pest; and this together with the increase of local and introduced parasites (especially the fly *Winthemia? diversa*, family Tachinidae) has put an end to the long series of severe outbreaks of *Tiracola plagiata* in the Northern District. Much leaf damage has been caused to cacao on the Gazelle Peninsula of New Britain by the larvae of *Achaea janata* (Noctuidae) and the loopers *Ectropis sabulosa* and *E. bhurmitra*, all of which can be controlled chemically.

Among the minor pests there are leaf-beetles (Chrysomelidae) of the genera *Rhyparida*, *Cleoporus* and *Deretrichia*, weevils of various subfamilies, many species of leafhoppers, mealy bugs and scales, Lepidoptera larvae (Lymantriidae, Limacodidae, Psychidae, Lycaenidae), the large stick insect *Anchiale maculata*, the leafcutter bee *Megachile frontalis*, and the cockchafer *Dermolepida noxium* which is a pest of the roots of young cacao trees.

Rubber (*Hevea brasiliensis*) suffers from only one major pest, the tip-wilt bug *Amblypelta lutescens papuensis* mentioned earlier as a coconut pest. This polyphagous insect was first found to damage rubber seedlings in 1957. It feeds on the soft bark tissue close to the growing point. The result is tip-wilt, serious set-back in growth, and in some cases the death of the seedling. The three egg-parasites found in the Central District do not seem to control this pest but chemical control can be effected with residual insecticides. The weevils *Idiopsis grisea* and *I. coerulea* and the owlet moth *Tiracola plagiata* occasionally cause defoliation of young rubber trees. Among the wood-eating pests the termite *Coptotermes elisae* and the beetles *Platypus selysi* and *Xyleborus perforans* are of some importance.

Coffee (*Coffea canephora*, *C. arabica*). Lowland coffee (*Coffea canephora*) has no major pests. Green scale *Coccus viridis*, the leopard moth *Zeuzera* sp., the mealy bugs *Pseudococcus* sp., *Planococcus citri*, *Ferrisia virgata* and *Paraputo leveri*, and the weevils *Apirocalus cornutus* and *Oribius cruciatus* are some of its recorded minor pests.

All major pests of highland coffee (*Coffea arabica*) can be satisfactorily controlled by chemical means or by biological control methods. For many years the most serious pest of *C. arabica* in the Highlands was the stem-girdler weevil *Meroleptus cinctor*. It can be controlled by brushing the trunks of the coffee bushes once a year with a residual insecticide. All major defoliating weevils, such as *Oribius destructor*, *O. inimicus*, *Aulacophrys facialis* and *Apirocalus cornutus* as well as the leafroller *Homona coffearia* (Tortricidae) and the leafhopper *Batrachomorphus szentivanyi* (Cicadellidae) can be controlled with one or other of the residual insecticides. *Paraputo leveri* caused considerable damage to coffee roots in a plantation in the Morobe District during 1959 to 1963. A severe outbreak of *Planococcus citri* in the Wau Valley was successfully controlled by the introduction of the ladybird *Cryptolaemus affinis* from the Markham Valley. Damage to seedlings is sometimes caused by the black cricket *Achetus commodus*. The larvae of cutworms *Agrotis* spp. and the large brown cricket *Brachytrypes achatinus* were observed in 1955-6 causing damage to coffee stems at ground level in the Western Highlands.

Tea (*Camellia sinensis*). The tea bush is free of serious pests in Papua New Guinea. Minor damage is caused by *Homona coffearia*, the leopard moth *Zeuzera* sp., by weevils of the genus *Oribius*, the green scale *Coccus viridis* and the mealy bug *Planococcus citri*.

Crops of subsistence agriculture. Sweet potato (*Ipomoea batatas*) is attacked by three major pests: the hawkmoths *Hippotion celerio* and *Herse convolvuli*, and the sweet potato weevil *Cylas formicarius*. The larvae of the hawkmoths feed on the leaves, and those of the weevil on the tubers. Minor pests are the weevil *Apirocalus cornutus* and the tortoise beetle *Aspidomorpha adhaerens*. The most serious pest is *Cylas formicarius* which causes up to 60 per cent reduction in yield in village gardens during extreme droughts and 100 per cent loss of crop in large blocks where sweet potato is planted during several growing seasons. Chemical control of the weevil is very difficult; but it is successful against the four other pests. In 1939 the giant toad *Bufo marinus* was introduced to New Britain for the control of *H. celerio*.

Taro (*Colocasia*, *Xanthosoma*) suffers from two major pests, the small rhinoceros beetles *Papuana huebneri* and *P. woodlarkiana*, the adults of which damage the roots and stems. Control is effected by spraying the soil around the taro plants at planting time with a residual insecticide which kills the larvae.

Sugar cane (*Saccharum officinarum*) is damaged by three major pests: the stemborer weevil *Rhabdoscelus obscurus* which is probably controlled in many areas by the fly *Carcelia sphenophori* (Tachinidae), the stemborer moth *Sesamia grisescens* (Noctuidae), and the mealy bug *Saccharicoccus sacchari*. A serious outbreak of *Locusta migratoria* on Goodenough Island in 1966 resulted in the complete defoliation of every *Saccharum* plant growing in village gardens. Other grasshoppers observed feeding on sugar cane were *Atractomorpha crenaticeps*, *Gesonula mundata sanguinolenta*, *Heteropternis obscurella*, *Oxya gavia*, *O. vittigera*, *Stenacatantops angustifrons*, *Phaneroptera brevis* and *Valanga irregularis*.

The sago palm (*Metroxylon rumphii*), an important food crop in some parts of Papua and New Guinea, is attacked by various rhinoceros beetles *Oryctes centaurus* and *Scapanes* spp., and by the palm weevil *Rhynchophorus bilineatus*. Cassava (*Manihot esculenta*) has one major pest *Amblypelta lutescens papuensis* which causes tip-wilt, and in most cases death of the plant. It causes similar damage to papaw (*Carica papaya*). The only major pest of yam (*Dioscorea alata*) is the mealy bug *Planococcus dioscoreae*, which attacks yams in the ground and in storage houses, where the termite *Schedorhinotermes dimorphus* has also been found damaging roots.

The most important pests of banana (*Musa paradisiaca* subsp. *sapientum*) are the scabmoth *Nacoleia octasema* (Pyralidae) and the fruit fly *Dacus musae*. The banana weevil *Cosmopolites sordidus* is relatively rare in Papua and New Guinea.

Fruit trees. Citrus is damaged by various scale insects, the aphis *Toxoptera citricidus*, leaf-eating weevils, the leafroller *Homona coffearia*, the leafmining moth *Phyllocnistis citrella* and the orchard butterfly *Papilio aegeus*. On one occasion the bug *Leptoglossus australis* was observed causing fruitfall of mandarines in the Morobe District. This bug is also a pest of passionfruit, pumpkin and cucumber.

Temperate climate field crops. Potato (*Solanum tuberosum*), cabbage (*Brassica oleracea*) turnip (*B. rapa*) and strawberry (*Fragaria* sp.) are attacked in the Highlands by the adults of a small dynastine beetle of the genus *Papuana*. *Brachylybas dimorphus*, a smallish brown bug of the family Coreidae was found to be a serious local pest of potato in the Goilala Sub-District in 1963. Tobacco (*Nicotiana tabacum*) is sometimes defoliated by the army worm *Spodoptera litura*, which also causes severe damage to cabbage, spinach, cauliflower and other garden crops. The larvae of the cutworm moth *Heliothis armigera* cause severe local damage to maize in some areas, and moths of the Pyralidae *Ostrinia nubilalis* and *O. salentialis* are of minor importance as pests of this crop in Papua and New Guinea.

Experimental crops. Rice suffers from less than 20 recorded pests of which 12 were found before World War II. The most important species are the moth borers *Chilo auricilia* and *Ostrinia salentialis* (Pyralidae), the leafrollers *Marasmia bilinealis*, *M. hexagona* and *M. poeyalis* (Pyralidae), and the flower bugs *Leptocorisa* spp. (Coreidae). The Pyrrhocoridae *Dysdercus cingulatus*, *D. decussatus* and *D. sidae*, the shield bug *Tectocoris diophthalmus*, and the moths *Earias fabia* (Noctuidae) and *Pectinophora gossypiella* (Gelechiidae) are the most important pests of cotton (*Gossypium* spp.). Damage to kenaf (*Hibiscus cannabinus*) is caused by 17 recorded pests. The cupmoth *Scopelodes dinawa* causes complete defoliation to Manila hemp (*Musa textilis*) in some years.

Pastures. The only major pest, the cockchafer *Lepidiota vogeli* is known from both highland and coastal areas but it has appeared only in the Highlands as a pest of pastures, airstrips, garden lawns and golf courses. It can be controlled with various residual insecticides. Sporadic outbreaks of the grassmoths *Spodoptera exempta* and *S. mauritia* (Noctuidae) occur in some districts.

Ornamentals. The larvae of the semi-looper *Pericyma cruegeri* cause severe defoliation to the ornamental legumes *Delonix regia* ('flamboyant tree') and *Peltophorum pterocarpum*. Cassia trees suffer from attacks of the larvae of the butterfly *Captopsilia pomona* which has been observed migrating during severe outbreaks. The most important pest of *Hibiscus rosa sinensis* is the mealy bug *Maconellicoccus hirsutus*; the worst affected areas are the Central, Madang and New Britain

Districts. Raintrees (*Samanea saman*) in the Port Moresby area are severely damaged by the branch-borer moth, *Cryptophasa setiotricha* (Xylorycti-dae).

Pests of stored products and household pests. Most pests of stored rice, peanuts, wheat meal, copra, cacao beans, chocolate, biscuits and other stored products found in Papua and New Guinea are moths or beetles which are cosmopolitan or have a very wide area of distribution. Such are the Pyralidae *Cadra cautella* and *Corcyra cephalonica*, and the beetles *Lasioderma serricorne* (Anobiidae), *Rhizopertha dominica* (Bostrychidae), *Ahasverus advena*, *Cryptolestes pusillus*, *Oryzaephilus surinamensis* (Cucujidae), *Sitophilus oryzae* (Curculionidae), *Tribolium castaneum* (Tenebrionidae) and *Tenebroides mauritanicus* (Trogositidae). Common household pests are the cockroaches *Blattella germanica* and *Periplaneta australasiae*, and the ants *Monomorium destructor* and *Pheidole megacephala*. These two ants sometimes damage the polythene cover of cables and other electric installations.

PESTS OF FORESTRY

Pests of living commercial trees. The most important pests are the stemborer weevil *Vanapa oberthuri*, the needle-borer *Hylurdrectonus araucariae* (Scolytidae) and the termite *Coptotermes elisae*, which attack the hoop pine (*Araucaria cunninghamii*). *Coptotermes* is also found as a pest of klinkii pine (*Araucaria hunsteinii*) in primary forest. It is a serious pest of young hoop pines in the Bulolo area. *Vanapa oberthuri* is a large slender weevil with a long snout, the larvae of which often attack and kill pines up to 30 feet tall and 10 inches diameter. It is probably widely distributed in the Highlands. Most severe damage is caused to hoop pine in the Kainantu, Goroka, and Bulolo areas. The tiny needleborer *H. araucariae* appeared for the first time in plague proportions in 1963 and, as with so many major phytophagous pests of the Territory, it was found to be an undescribed species. The ecology, natural enemies, and methods of control are currently being studied by forest entomologists.

The teak moth *Hyblaea puera* causes severe defoliation to seedlings in the nursery and to plantation grown trees. It is indigenous to mainland New Guinea. Further study is needed to find its local host plants. *Hyblaea* can be controlled in teak nurseries by frequent spraying with a residual insecticide.

Some other recorded pests of forest trees are the looper *Milionia isodoxa*, and the weevils *Oribius* spp. on hoop pine, the beetle *Diapus pusillimus* (Platypodidae) on klinkii pine, the giant silk-moth *Syntherata janetta*, the polyphagous bug *Leptoglossus australis*, the Scolytidae *Hypothenemus eruditus*, *H. hispidus* and *Xyleborus cognatus*, the leaf-beetles *Arsipoda* sp. and *Rhyparida coriacea*, and the leafcutter bee *Megachile frontalis* on *Eucalyptus deglupta*.

Timber pests. The most important pests are the termite *Mastotermes darwiniensis* introduced acci-dentally from Australia during World War II and three platypodid beetles, *Platypus jansoni*, *P. selysi* and *P. solidus*. The termite has so far been restricted to the town area of Lae and is being checked by an eradication programme developed by the CSIRO and the Department of Agriculture, Stock and Fisheries. *P. jansoni* and *P. solidus* were found to be active in chemically preserved *Anisoptera* and *Antocephalus* logs. The beetle *Heterobostrychus aequalis* was found attacking timber floors (of *Pometia pinnata*), wooden cases and furniture. Various drywood termites *Incisitermes* and *Cryptotermes* damage structural timber and wood-carvings. The larvae of the moth *Herculia nigrivitta* (Pyralidae) cause severe damage to sago palm roofs of village houses in the Maprik Sub-District and in the New Ireland District.

E. Ballard, 'Some Insects associated with Cotton in Papua and the Mandated Territory of New Guinea', *Bulletin of Entomological Research*, vol. 17, 1925.

J. H. Barrett, 'The Occurrence of Termites in the New Guinea Highlands', *Papua and New Guinea Agricultural Journal*, vol. 17, 1965.

—— 'Insect Pests of *Coffea arabica* in the New Guinea Highlands', *Papua and New Guinea Agricultural Journal*, vol. 18, 1966.

T. V. Bourke, 'Further records of insects collected from *Saccharum officinarum* in the Territory of Papua and New Guinea, with notes on their potential as pest species', *Proceedings of the 12th Congress of the International Society of Sugar Cane Technologists* (forthcoming).

—— and G. L. Baker, 'The occurrence and control of *Locusta migratoria* on Goodenough Island, Milne Bay District, Territory of Papua and New Guinea', *Papua and New Guinea Agricultural Journal* (forthcoming).

A. Catley, 'Parasites and predators of some insects recorded from the Territory of Papua and New Guinea', T. P. N. G. Department of Agriculture, Stock and Fisheries, *Research Bulletin*, no. 2, 1966.

L. J. Dumbleton, *A list of insect pests recorded in South Pacific Territories*, Technical Paper—South Pacific Commission, no. 79. Noumea, 1954.

G. S. Dun, 'Economic Entomology in Papua and New Guinea 1948-1954', *Papua and New Guinea Agricultural Journal*, vol. 9, 1955.

T. L. Fenner, 'Plantation Pests in Papua and New Guinea', *South Pacific Bulletin*, vol. 17, 1967.

J. L. Froggatt, 'Insect pests of rice', *New Guinea Agricultural Gazette*, vol. 5, 1939.

B. Gray, 'Forest tree and timber insect pests in the Territory of Papua and New Guinea', *Pacific Insects*, vol. 10, 1968.

J. L. Gressitt, 'Entomology in the Pacific Area with Special Reference to Agriculture', *Proceedings, Tenth International Congress of Entomology*, vol. 3, 1958.

—— 'The Coconut Leaf-Mining Beetle, *Promecotheca papuana*', *Papua and New Guinea Agricultural Journal*, vol. 12, 1959.

—— 'Economic Chrysomelid Beetles from New Guinea, with New Species', *Papua and New Guinea Agricultural Journal*, vol. 16, 1963.

—— 'The weevil genus *Pantorhytes* (Coleoptera), involving cacao pests and epizoic symbiosis with cryptogamic plants and microfauna', *Pacific Insects*, vol. 8, 1966.

G. A. K. Marshall, 'Some injurious Curculionidae

(Col.) from New Guinea', *Bulletin of Entomological Research*, vol. 48, 1957.

K. E. Schedl, 'On some Coleoptera of economic importance from New Guinea and Australia', *Pacific Insects*, vol. 6, 1964.

R. T. Simon Thomas, 'De Plagen van enkele Cultuur Gewassen in West Niew Guinea. Checklist of pests of some crops in West Irian', *Mededelingen van Economische Zaken*, Landbouwkundige Series, vol. 1, 1962.

L. Smee, 'Insect Pests of *Hevea brasiliensis* in the Territory of Papua and New Guinea: Their Habits and Control', *Papua and New Guinea Agricultural Journal*, vol. 17, 1964.

———— 'Insect pests of *Cocos nucifera* in the Territory of Papua and New Guinea: Their Habits and Control', *Papua and New Guinea Agricultural Journal*, vol. 17, 1965.

———— 'Insect Pests of Sweet Potato and Taro in the Territory of Papua and New Guinea: Their Habits and Control', *Papua and New Guinea Agricultural Journal*, vol. 17, 1965.

J. J. H. Szent-Ivany, 'New insect pest and host plant records in the Territory of Papua and New Guinea', *Papua and New Guinea Agricultural Journal*, vol. 11, 1956.

———— 'Insects of Cultivated Plants in the Central Highlands of New Guinea', *Proceedings, Tenth International Congress of Entomology*, vol. 3, 1958.

———— 'Host plant and distribution records of some insects in New Guinea', *Pacific Insects*, vol. 1, 1959.

———— 'Insect pests of *Theobroma cacao* in the Territory of Papua and New Guinea', *Papua and New Guinea Agricultural Journal*, vol. 13, 1961.

———— 'The zoogeographical factor in economic entomology on Pacific islands with special reference to New Guinea', *Verhandlungen, 9. Internationaler Kongress für Entomologie*, vol. 1, 1961.

———— 'Further records of insect pests of *Theobroma cacao* in the Territory of Papua and New Guinea', *Papua and New Guinea Agricultural Journal*, vol. 16, 1963.

———— 'An annotated list of phytophagous insect pests of the Territory of Papua and New Guinea with host plant and distribution records', T. P. N. G. Department of Agriculture, Stock and Fisheries, *Research Bulletin* (forthcoming).

———— and J. H. Ardley, 'Insects of *Saccharum* spp. in the Territory of Papua and New Guinea', *Papua and New Guinea Scientific Society, Transactions*, vol. 3, 1962.

———— and J. H. Barrett, 'Some Insects of Banana in the Territory of Papua and New Guinea', *Papua and New Guinea Agricultural Journal*, vol. 11, 1956.

———— and J. H. Barrett, 'Major Insect Pests in the Highlands of New Guinea', *Highlands Quarterly Bulletin*, vol. 1, 1960.

———— and R. M. Stevens, 'Insects Associated with *Coffea arabica* and Some other Crops in the Wau-Bulolo area of New Guinea', *Papua and New Guinea Agricultural Journal*, vol. 18, 1966.

J. J. H. SZENT-IVANY

INSECTS AND RELATIVES. The fauna of New Guinea is to be compared with those of the major humid tropical areas of the world, such as those of the Amazon Basin, Central America, the Congo Basin, Southern Asia, and certain tropical parts of Australia. Though New Guinea is smaller in area than most of these regions, in general it appears to compare favourably in terms of wealth of fauna, even though it is an island. Where the term 'New Guinea' is used without qualification such as region it refers to the whole main island.

The mountain ranges of New Guinea have provided isolation of varying degrees to foster the development of separate species in the different mountain areas. There are some fascinating aspects to the history of many of these ranges, and the isolation of some has probably been more decisive in the past than it is at present. It has been stated that many of these ranges were separate islands in the late Tertiary period, and there appears to be good evidence for this in the form of not very ancient marine deposits now located at considerable altitudes in the mountain ranges. An archipelago would have fostered the development of separate species of different genera or species-groups on the different islands. Now many young or incipient species appear to be evolving with changes in topography, vegetation, altitude or climate. Thus topographical, geohistorical and ecological diversification has engendered extensive speciation producing a rich and highly varied fauna.

The fauna of New Guinea is semi-insular, or slightly 'disharmonic' in the sense of unbalanced representation, in comparison with the principal continental areas, suggesting that the long insular history kept out certain elements. But this is much more true of the mammals than of the insects, since Asian mammals could not cross the water barriers (while Australian marsupials and monotremes moved back and forth over the occasional land connections across Torres Straits or from the Northern Territory area through Timor and the southern part of the Moluccas when these were connected), but insects could fly or be blown from the Indonesian islands. This certainly happened extensively, for the New Guinea insect fauna is in general more closely related to that of Indonesia than to the typical Australian fauna. In the rain forests of Queensland there are many New Guinea region types, and in the savannah country of southern New Guinea the species are primarily of Australian types. To most insect zoogeographers New Guinea is part of South-east Asia, or the Oriental region, but to the mammalogist New Guinea is part of the Australian region. The birds are intermediate.

The fauna of New Guinea is in some respects young and in other respects old. It appears to have been evolving over a long period in isolation; some genera or higher groups are not found elsewhere, some segments of the fauna have close ties in Indonesia or the Philippines, and others are affiliated with elements in tropical Australia. The associations with Australia are recent, apparently involving the exchange of species in both directions over the low Pleistocene land connection. There is a theory that much earlier Australia was farther from New Guinea, and drifted north and eastwards nearer New Guinea. However, this remains to be proven. New Guinea is said to have been preceded by a Melanesian land mass, situated a little farther north, with the Bismarck Archipelago and the Solomons forming remnants of the land mass. At any rate, the Papuan and Australian faunas have evolved for long periods in isolation. The recent proximity and connection has given them elements in common and rendered them to some extent superficially similar, whereas the principal endemic elements of each are generally quite unrelated. New Guinean insects appear to have more relationships with South-east Asia and Indonesia than with Australia, and many close ties with the Philippines through, or independent of, Celebes.

Probably a rather high percentage of the insect species of New Guinea as a unit may prove to be endemic to the island. New Britain has many species closely related to others on the New Guinea mainland, with perhaps rather few in common. Many of the species on New Ireland are a little more different from those of New Guinea, but often close to, or the same as, those of New Britain. Some elements on New Ireland are somewhat intermediate between those of New Britain and Bougainville, though usually closer to the former. Bougainville, faunistically, is definitely part of the Solomon Islands, and has many genera absent in New Guinea and the Bismarck Archipelago, and vice versa.

The New Guinea insect fauna is a striking one, with many conspicuous aspects. It boasts the largest butterfly in the world and one of the very largest moths. Also, it has some of the largest stick insects, some over 8 inches long, and some of the largest grasshoppers, as well as very large beetles such as the long-horned beetle, rhinoceros beetle and others. In addition to the striking size of many New Guinea insects, some are exceedingly beautiful. The *Ornithoptera* (*Troides*) butterflies are not only large, but most of them are outstandingly beautiful in the males with a brilliant green, gold, blue or orange metallic lustre.

No adequate analyses have been made of entomological inhabitants of the various vegetation types, but it can be said that many species of insects are characteristic of a certain type of vegetation, or of a particular plant species. A simplified classification of vegetation zones is as follows:

Nipa swamps. Tidal zone. Very poor in insects.

Mangrove swamps. Tidal zone. Relatively poor in insects.

Sago swamps (*saksak*). Generally flat coastal plain fresh-water swamps, but extending up streams into low mountains. Fauna specialized, richer than it might first appear to be.

Lowland swampy rain forest with extensive rattans. Very rich insect fauna.

Savannah and savannah forest, *Eucalyptus* or *Melaleuca*, 0-5,600 feet. Usually rich fauna, Australian elements.

Kunai–*Pitpit*, 0-9,000 feet. Grass, often man-induced, with wild *Saccharum* species dominating swamps to ridges. Certain insects abundant.

Monsoon forest, 0-1,500 feet. Relatively dry; in areas with a dry season. Fairly rich, mixed fauna.

Upland rain forest (merging with lowland swampy forest), 1,000-7,900 feet. Very rich fauna with tendency towards local endemism.

Mid-mountain forest (*Castanopsis–Quercus* association), 1,600-7,700 feet. A dominant type fairly rich in its canopy and fringes.

Araucaria zone, 2,500-5,000 feet. This grows mixed with upland rain forest. Rich in insects, including some peculiar to *Araucaria*.

Nothofagus (beech) forest, 2,800-10,200 feet. Very rich in endemic insects.

Montane cloud forest (mossy forest), 4,900-10,500 feet. Insects often not in evidence, but with conspicuous endemics.

Subalpine forest (often shrubbery), 9,850-13,300 feet. Rich in endemics, but some genera even the same as in lowlands.

Alpine grassland, 9,500 feet to summits or glaciers. Fewer insects, but at least spiders and flies to highest altitudes.

In general, groups of species are characteristic of a given altitude range, which may in turn be dependent upon the range of a certain plant or animal host species or vegetation type. There are considerable differences in the vegetation on the north and south sides of the main east-west backbone of New Guinea. These differences are certainly reflected in the fauna, but the contrast is poorly documented.

By and large, with increase in altitude there are narrower limits on the range of a species. Thus, species occurring at low altitudes may be very widely distributed for great distances along the north or south coastal areas and on off-shore islands. Conversely, many species inhabiting high altitudes may be closely related to, but actually different from, those in similar environments at the same altitudes on different (but even nearby) mountain ranges. The isolation of breeding populations permits the course of evolution to proceed in different directions, dependent upon a number of variable factors. The genetic factors produce various changes (mutations), some of which are perpetuated by successful reproduction and inheritance, and others not. The isolation of related populations may result from dispersal of individuals to new areas, the spread of populations upward or downward in altitude with changes in the environment, and with other gradual or sudden changes in topography, vegetation, or other external factors.

Actually, many species described from New Guinea are still only known from a single locality, so it is difficult to generalize regarding distribution of species. Some kinds recorded as the same species from widely separate areas may actually prove different, and many cases of the reverse may also come to light.

Faunal representation. Some groups of insects are remarkably well developed in the New Guinea region, and others are very poorly represented. Among groups particularly well represented are many of the plant-feeding groups in general, which include many of the hoppers, true bugs, grasshoppers, stick insects, moths, butterflies and beetles. Some predacious insects, such as arboreal carabid beetles, dragon-flies and damsel flies, are numerous in species, although tiger beetles, scorpion flies and some other predators are poorly represented. Water insects are scarce in general. This is particularly noticeable in the mayflies and stone flies and to a lesser extent in the caddisflies, water bugs and water beetles.

INSECT RELATIVES

Onychophora (*Peripatus* and relatives) are the most primitive land arthropods and are more worm-like than insect-like. They have short fleshy legs and occur in damp forest under logs and litter. New Guinea and New Britain have several species of this rare group.

Arachnida. This large group, the spiders, Opiliones (harvestmen), scorpions (Fig. 1e), false-scorpions (Fig. 2e), mites, ticks and many others, is richly represented in New Guinea. Few have been collected and studied. Spiders and mites occur in very large numbers of species and individuals, but are still largely unknown. Scorpions are not as much in evidence, and generally not as large, in New Guinea as in South-east Asia. Bites from them, and from spiders, do not seem to be especially common here. Some of the spiders [q.v.] are quite large, with bodies 2 inches long and legs 4½ to 6 inches long, but even these do not commonly bite people. Their large orb webs may be very strong, and sometimes catch small birds and very large insects. Spiders are useful predators, feeding on many kinds of insects.

Mites [q.v.] inhabit nearly every type of environment, from the highest mountain peaks to ocean bottoms. They are mostly minute, very rarely as much as 2 inches long, and include scavengers, plant-feeders, parasites and predators. Ticks [q.v.] are a subdivision of mites having larger and tougher bodies.

Myriopoda. The Chilopoda (centipedes) and Diplopoda (millipedes) are abundant in New Guinea. Some of each attain very large proportions, 8 inches or more in length, and are dangerous. The large centipedes (one pair of legs per body segment which is more or less flattened) have a poisonous bite inflicted with the jaw-like structures on the underside of the head. People commonly believe they sting with all their legs, since these, particularly the long last pair, are equipped with needle-like claws. Centipedes are often useful predators of agricultural pests. The millipedes (two pairs of legs per body segment which is more or less cylindrical) have poison glands which squirt a red-brown fluid from the sides of the body. Small species merely make the fingers brown when handled, but larger ones may squirt the poison for some distance and seriously burn eyes or tender skin. Millipedes are primarily scavengers, reducing leaf-mould and old stumps and logs, but some may do damage to leafy vegetables.

INSECTS

Apterygota are primitive wingless insects. These include Thysanura, the silver-fish and its relatives, which are scaly insects with filament-bearing tails.

They are generally found in dark places, such as under old bark, and are probably mostly scavengers.

The Collembola (spring-tails) are quite small, cylindrical or subglobose, and generally jump by means of a structure like a spring under the abdomen. They live in damp places, particularly under forest litter and logs, and probably feed largely on algae. According to most modern authorities, this and the preceding groups are not true insects.

Isoptera. The termites are well represented, as in most tropical areas. These are primarily inhabitants of the lowland forest and often build their nests on the trunks of trees. They can be observed as black masses on coconut trunks. There are probably no extremely tall termite ground nests as in northern Australia.

Blattaria. The cockroaches are a large group in the tropics and numerous in New Guinea. Size ranges from one-quarter to several inches in length. Most are flat, they are of all colours, and many are wingless as adults. Several heavy-bodied types, some black and some brown, are abundant in old logs and stumps and contribute to breaking down the forest refuse.

Mantodea. The praying mantids are famous predators which eat many insects, and even small frogs, lizards and birds. They have a slender body, a long thorax and spiny raptorial front legs. The largest species may give the fingers quite a pinch, and even draw blood. There is a great range in size, from about 1 to 6 inches or so in length, and also a range of colour, though they are usually green or brown. Some species, particularly those living on tree trunks, have short wings or are wingless as adults. But most of them can fly, and they are attracted to light.

Phasmida (Phasmatodea). The stick insects are very well represented in New Guinea. They include the longest insects, some nearly a foot long not counting the long slender legs. Most of them are extremely slender and resemble dead twigs, but two types in New Guinea are quite heavy-bodied. Those of the genus *Eurycantha* are somewhat armoured, with very strong spines on the hind legs in the male. When approached closely, these males jump backward and snap their hind legs shut, causing a wound if within range. The other heavy-bodied type, *Extatosoma*, has wide fringes on parts of the body and legs, and looks quite grotesque. They can change colour and may vary from chalky white through mottled to black. Many stick insects are wingless or short-winged, but some have large folded wings and can fly. They feed on leaves, mostly of trees, palms and pandanus.

Orthoptera. The locusts and other short-horned grasshoppers, tetrigids (slender short-horned grasshoppers found in damp places, Fig. 1d), long-horned grasshoppers (katydids), grouse-locusts, crickets and their relatives are extremely abundant and varied. In particular the long-horned grasshoppers and grouse-locusts are extremely numerous in species. Some grasshoppers reach 6 inches or more in length and may have a very heavy body and with a toothed shield on their back. Many of

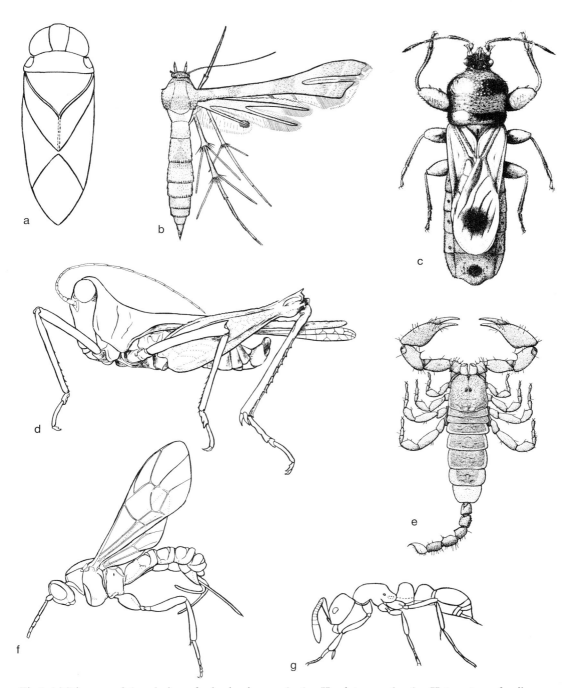

Fig 1. (a) Diagram of dorsal view of a backswimmer (order Hemiptera, suborder Heteroptera, family Notonectidae), 13 times; (b) *Nippoptilia spinosa* (order Lepidoptera, family Pterophoridae) from north-west New Guinea, 10 times; (c) *Dentisblissus venosus* (order Hemiptera, suborder Heteroptera, family Lygaeidae) from north-east New Guinea, 9 times; (d) *Palaioscaria frenatum* (order Orthoptera, family Tetrigidae), 5.5 times; (e) *Hormurus australasiae* (order Scorpionidae, family Ischnuridae), 1.6 times; (f) *Lycorina cornigera* (order Hymenoptera, family Ichneumonidae) from south-east New Guinea, whole insect (except apical part of antenna and fore and mid-legs) in lateral view, 5 times; (g) Worker caste of a cerapachyine ant, *Cerapachys opaca* (order Hymenoptera, family Formicidae), from north-east New Guinea, 10 times.

them have wings resembling leaves. Generally they look like a leaf in side view, but some flatten their wings and look like a leaf from above. The grouse-locusts have the peculiar habit of rapidly vibrating and ruffling their wings when disturbed, making a loud squeaky or rattling noise at the same time. Crickets vary in size; some are quite stout and strong jumpers. Most of the Orthoptera are leaf-feeders, though some eat roots, tubers or stems. A few are occasionally carnivorous. In houses built near forests, some long-horned grasshoppers make temporary resting places in curtains, umbrellas or clothing, chewing an arc which they fold over to make their protective enclosure, as they are accustomed to doing with leaves.

Hemiptera. These are all sucking insects, mostly feeding on plants. The suborder Homoptera includes the cicadas, leafhoppers, tree-hoppers (Figs 2c and 2d) and their relatives. The cicadas are mostly large and the rest small to medium-sized. Some male cicadas have very loud songs, particularly one type which sings in upland forest at dusk. Also included in the Homoptera are the scale insects, flattish, inconspicuous and seemingly legless, and the aphids (plant-lice) and white-flies (aleyrodids). All of these last three are small and usually inconspicuous or rare in New Guinea forests. When abundant, they may do great damage to crops. The females are generally wingless and the males often minute and with very thin delicate wings. They are generally green, brown, black, pink or white. Among the hoppers are some serious pests of agriculture, particularly of sugar cane (*see* INSECT PESTS OF AGRICULTURE AND FORESTRY).

Heteroptera, the 'true bugs', are mostly plant-suckers, but a few, the bedbugs and their relatives, feed upon birds, bats and man, sucking blood. The reduviids are predacious on other insects, and may pierce human skin with their beaks, or even suck blood. The Gelastocoridae (Fig. 2b) and others are also predacious. The various families of plant bugs (Lygaeidae, Fig. 1c; Tingitidae; and others) have more or less characteristic shapes, some slender, some broad, and many of them have a large triangle (scutellum) between the wing-bases which may cover the wings. Some of the larger plant bugs are more than 1 inch long, very broad, and make a noise when they fly. They are primarily diurnal, but some come to lights at night. The Aradidae (Fig. 2f) live under bark and feed on fungi. The water bugs are poorly represented and not particularly conspicuous in the mountains. The family Naucoridae is highly developed in New Guinea, but rarely seen unless searched for in·streams. The Notonectidae (Fig. 1a) are often found in semi-stagnant water.

Anoplura. The sucking lice are ectoparasites living only on the bodies of mammals and sucking blood. They are found primarily on rats in New Guinea.

Mallophaga. The biting lice are ectoparasites of mammals and birds, but primarily on birds. Often there are two or more different species of lice on each bird species. Many in New Guinea have not yet been studied. One would expect a very rich and unusual mallophagan fauna, since the New Guinea bird fauna is very rich.

Thysanoptera. Thrips are slender, usually very small insects with narrow feathery wings. They are mainly plant-suckers and often agricultural pests. There are a few large black species in the southern savannah country.

Plecoptera. Stone-flies are extremely rare and few in species in New Guinea. The young (nymphs) are generally in streams; the adults have two pairs of wings, though there might be wingless adults as in New Zealand.

Trichoptera. Caddisflies are rather poorly represented in New Guinea. Most of the species are slender and many are pale in colour. The larvae construct cases of various materials, in streams, for protection. The adults have four wings and usually very long slender antennae.

Lepidoptera. The moths, skippers and butterflies make up one of the four major orders of insects. They are extremely well represented in New Guinea. The many families of small moths (Microlepidoptera) are numerous and little studied. Diakonoff has described a large number from the Third Archbold Expedition to north-west New Guinea. The major families of pyralids, noctuids, geometrids, giant silk-worm moths and sphinx moths are very well represented. The moth caterpillars feed upon leaves of all sorts of plants; some are wood-borers. The hercules moth (*Coscinocera*), the larva of which feeds on *Homalanthus*, is one of the largest moths in the world. The skippers are moderately represented in New Guinea. Their caterpillars are generally hidden in a roll of leaves. The Pterophoridae (Fig. 1b) are small and have divided and fringed wings. The butterfly species are very rich and include the world's largest, *Ornithoptera (Troides) alexandrae* of the Northern District, Papua. Swallow-tails are numerous and beautiful. The large metallic blue *Papilio ulysses* is widespread. *P. (Graphium) weiskei*, a remarkably coloured species, fast-flying and generally at higher altitudes near small streams, is featured on one of the recent Territory of Papua and New Guinea stamp series, as is *P. ulysses*. The Amathusiidae are represented by many large, broad-winged species with large 'eye-spots' of pale buff or white with black rings or round spots (*see* MOTHS AND BUTTERFLIES).

Coleoptera. Beetles [q.v.] are extremely richly represented. Probably there are over 30,000 species in New Guinea. Only a small fraction have been named. The Carabidae (ground beetles) are mostly arboreal, living under moss on trunks of trees. Tiger beetles are not as conspicuous as in some other regions, but one in the lowlands is a flightless, elongate kind living on tree trunks and resembling a huge ant. Among the water beetles are many minute species, but few large ones. Rove-beetles, with short wing-covers, are numerous and include some very large metallic species. These are very active fliers and suggest wasps as they fly over the ground. Many of the smaller families of beetles have been little studied. The lycids are very richly represented, particularly in the high mountains. Some are of unusual colours such as blue, green and purple, and some closely mimic

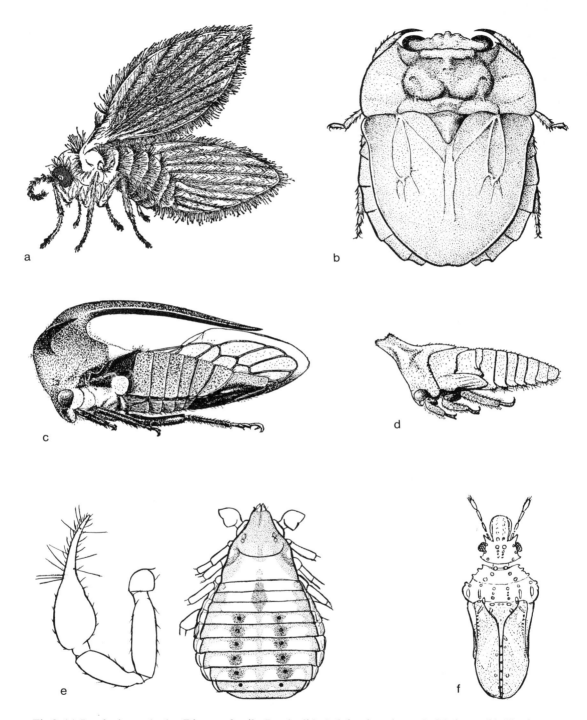

Fig 2. (a) *Psychoda* sp. (order Diptera, family Psychodidae), left wing elevated, 25 times; (b) *Nerthra macrothorax* (order Hemiptera, suborder Heteroptera, family Gelastocoridae), type locality Woodlark Island, Milne Bay District, 9 times; (c) *Leptocentrus taurus* (order Hemiptera, suborder Homoptera, family Membracidae), side view of adult and (d) nymph, both 10 times; (e) *Geogarypus sagittatus* (order Pseudoscorpionida, family Garypidae) from north-west New Guinea. Leg, 37 times, body, 29 times; (f) *Calisius montanus* (order Hemiptera, suborder Heteroptera, family Aradidae) from Wissel Lakes, West Irian, 15 times.

(or are mimicked by) various other beetles like leaf-beetles, long-horned beetles, click-beetles and others. Fire-flies are rather few in species, but their relatives the cantharids, like the lycids, are numerous. Elateridae, the click-beetles, are also numerous. Scarabs are not so well represented although there are a number of kinds of rhinoceros beetles and cetoniids. The latter are active day-fliers, mostly metallic and often fairly large. They make quite a noise when flying, as the wing-covers are only slightly raised, permitting fast flight with much less wind-resistance than with most beetles which, in flight, spread their wing-covers more or less at right angles to the body. Stag beetles are rather few in species, but some are quite large with long toothed mandibles. Leaf-beetles are extremely numerous in kind, and feed on leaves of all sorts of plants including cacao (particularly the new leaves), coconut, sugar cane and other crops. Long-horned beetles (cerambycids) are also very richly represented with many types characteristic of New Guinea. They have a somewhat buprestid-like shape, relatively short antennae and often metallic colouring. Buprestids are somewhat scarce, but some are large and beautiful. They are active day-fliers. Weevils are extremely numerous in species and numbers of individuals. Some of the high-altitude weevils have developed an interesting ecological association (epizoic symbiosis) involving the growth of many groups of cryptogamic plants (fungi, algae, lichens, liverworts, moss). Among the plants on the backs of the weevils are plant-feeding mites, rotifers and nematodes. The association seems to involve special modifications on the backs of the weevils to protect the plants, and some benefit, such as protective resemblance to plants or chemical protection, for the weevils. The Strepsiptera, or twisted-winged insects, are parasites of mainly grasshoppers, leaf hoppers and wasps. They are now included in the Coleoptera by many authorities.

Diptera. The flies [q.v.] represent one of the largest orders of insects. They inhabit almost all types of environments, from the inter-tidal zone to the tops of high mountains. They breed in almost everything from rotting fruit to ponds, streams, soil and bark, and feed on juices, decomposition products, micro-organisms, leaves, roots, and such like. The mosquitoes are of the greatest importance to man particularly in New Guinea, where there are virulent strains of malaria. The various related families of midges include some biters, like the minute ceratopogonids, and the slightly larger simuliids, both called 'sandflies', but more strictly biting midges and blackflies, respectively. There are also the minute biting phlebotomines, belonging to the Psychodidae (Fig. 2a). Most midge larvae are aquatic. Tabanids (horseflies, march-flies) are numerous in species, some quite large. Other families of flies are too numerous to mention in detail, but include flower-flies (Syrphidae), bee-flies (Bombyliidae), vinegar-flies (*Drosophila*), fruit-flies (Trypetidae) (usually found in fruit still on the tree, and not in rotting fruit like the much smaller vinegar-flies), and the

various filth flies (blowflies, flesh flies, house flies, etc.) and many others. Among the largest and most colourful flies in New Guinea are tachinids of the *Rutilia* group, parasites of unknown insect hosts.

Siphonaptera. The fleas are not usually as conspicuous in New Guinea as in many other countries, at least in the lowlands. However, there are some peculiar ones in the mountains, and new species, and even new genera, are being discovered. There is a theory that because flea larvae live primarily in the ground nests of their hosts, the wet lowland environment may be less favourable.

Hymenoptera. This again is one of the largest orders of insects. The ants (Fig. 1g), bees and larger wasps (hornets) are familiar to all, but the great majority in this order are minute to medium-sized wasps (Ichneumonidae, Fig. 1f, and other families) parasitizing nearly every other type of insect. Most of them develop inside the body of the host, often in the larvae (caterpillar) stages. New Guinea is very rich in ants, but is poorer in variety of bees. Most of the parasitic species have not been studied. Sawflies, the larvae of which eat leaves, are scarce, but more numerous in the Highlands. Some of the largest wasps (scoliids) parasitize rhinoceros beetles and other large insects, and are beneficial. In fact, most members of the order are useful, unless they parasitize or prey upon useful insects. Many are hyperparasites, feeding on other parasitic wasp larvae parasitizing other insects. Thus when the primary host is a pest, the hyperparasite is also a pest. Sometimes there are tertiary parasites.

Many articles on New Guinean insects and other arthropods have appeared since 1959 in the journal *Pacific Insects* and the associated monograph series.

C. P. Alexander, 'New or little-known crane-flies from New Guinea (Diptera: Tipulidae), Part 1', *Pacific Insects*, vol. 3, 1961.

M. Beier, 'Die Mantodeen Neu-Guineas', *Pacific Insects*, vol. 7, 1965.

——— 'Die Pseudoscorpioniden Neu-Guineas und der benachbarten Inseln', *Pacific Insects*, vol. 7, 1965.

R. B. Benson, 'Some new pergid sawflies from New Guinea (Hymenoptera: Symphyta)', *Annals and Magazine of Natural History*, vol. 8, 1965.

R. Bielawski, 'A review of the New Guinean species of the genus *Harmonia* Muls. (Coleoptera: Coccinellidae)', *Pacific Insects*, vol. 6, 1964.

H. C. Blöte, 'The genus *Baeturia* Stål as represented in New Guinea (Homoptera, Cicadidae)', *Zoologische Mededeelingen*, vol. 37, 1960.

J. Bonne-Wepster, 'Synopsis of a hundred common non-anopheline mosquitoes of the Greater and Lesser Sundas, the Moluccas and New Guinea', *Documenta de Medecina Geographica et Medica*, vol. 6, 1954.

S. Breuning, 'Revision der Gattung *Glenea* Newm. (Coleoptera: Cerambycidae)', *Entomologische Arbeiten Museum G. Frey*, vol. 9, 1958.

W. L. Brown, Jr., 'Contributions towards a reclassification of the Formicidae. II. Tribe Ectatomini (Hymenoptera)', *Bulletin of the Museum of Comparative Zoology*, vol. 118, 1958.

M. Cameron, 'Results of the Archbold Expeditions. New species of Staphylinidae (Col.) from New Guinea and Misool', *Treubia*, vol. 21, 1952.

G. D. H. Carpenter, 'The genus *Euploea* (Lep. Danaidae) in Micronesia, Melanesia, Polynesia and Australia. A zoogeographical study', *Transactions of the Zoological Society of London*, vol. 28, 1953.

L. E. Cheesman, 'Megachiline bees of New Guinea', *Annals and Magazine of Natural History*, vol. 1, 1938.

———— 'Ropalidia of Papuasia', *Annals and Magazine of Natural History*, vol. 5, 1952.

Fr. Chrysanthus, 'Spiders from South New Guinea', I-VIII, *Nova Guinea*, n.s. vol. 9, 1958; zoological series, vol. 37, 1967.

R. W. Crosskey, 'A revision of the genus *Pygophora* Schiner (Diptera: Muscidae)', *Transactions of the Zoological Society of London*, vol. 29, 1962.

P. J. Darlington, 'The carabid beetles of New Guinea. Part 2. The Agonini', *Bulletin of the Museum of Comparative Zoology*, vol. 107, 1952.

———— 'The carabid beetles of New Guinea. Part 1. Cicindelinae, Carabinae, Harpalinae through Pterostichini', *Bulletin of the Museum of Comparative Zoology*, vol. 126, 1962.

———— *Biogeography of the southern end of the world: Distribution and history of far-southern life and land, with an assessment of continental drift.* Cambridge, Mass., 1965.

A. Diakonoff, 'New Guinea Microlepidoptera', Koninklijke Nederlandse Akademie van Wetenschappen, *Proceedings of the Section of Sciences*, series C, vol. 56, 1953; vol. 59, 1957.

———— 'Microlepidoptera of New Guinea. Results of the Third Archbold Expedition (American-Netherlands Indian Expedition 1938-39)', *Verhandelingen der Koninklijke Nederlandse Akademie van Wetenschappen, AFD Natuurkunde Tweede Reeks*, vols 49-50, 1952-5.

P. H. van Doesburg, 'On some Syrphidae from New Guinea and Australia', *Entomologisk tidskrift*, vol. 87, 1966.

C. J. Drake and F. A. Ruhoff, 'Lacebugs from New Guinea, Borneo, Solomons and other islands of the South Pacific and Indian Oceans (Hemiptera: Tingidae)', *Pacific Insects*, vol. 7, 1965.

J. W. Evans, 'Some New Eurymelids from Australia and New Guinea (Homoptera, Jassoidea)', *Transactions of the Royal Society of South Australia*, vol. 71, 1947.

E. F. Gilmour, 'Revision of the genus *Rosenbergia* Ritsema (Coleoptera, Cerambycidae, Lamiinae, Batocerini)', *Idea*, vol. 12, 1959; *Reichenbachia*, vol. 6, 1966.

J. L. Gressitt, 'Entomological Investigations in New Guinea Mountains', *Proceedings of the Hawaiian Entomological Society for 1955*, vol. 16, 1956.

———— 'Longicorn beetles of New Guinea, I (Cerambycidae)', *Pacific Insects*, vol. 1, 1959.

———— 'Papuan-West Polynesian Hispine beetles (Chrysomelidae)', *Pacific Insects*, vol. 2, 1960.

———— 'Problems in the zoogeography of Pacific and Antarctic insects', *Pacific Insects Monograph 2*, 1961.

———— 'Hispine beetles (Chrysomelidae) from New Guinea', *Pacific Insects*, vol. 5, 1963.

———— 'Chrysomelid beetles from the Papuan Subregion, Parts 1-5', *Pacific Insects*, vols 7-9, 1965-7.

———— 'Epizoic symbiosis: The Papuan weevil genus *Gymnopholus* (Leptopiinae) symbiotic with cryptogamic plants, oribatid mites, rotifers and nematodes', *Pacific Insects*, vol. 8, 1966.

———— 'The weevil genus *Pantorhytes* (Coleoptera), involving cacao pests and epizoic symbiosis with cryptogamic plants and microfauna', *Pacific Insects*, vol. 8, 1966.

———— J. Sedlacek and J. J. H. Szent-Ivany, 'Flora and Fauna on Backs of Large Papuan Moss-Forest Weevils', *Science*, vol. 150, 1965.

———— and J. J. H. Szent-Ivany, 'Bibliography of New Guinea entomology', *Pacific Insects Monograph 18*, 1968.

K. Günther, 'Acrydiinen (Orthoptera, Acrididae) von Neu Guinea hauptsächlich aus den Ausbeuten von Professor Dr. Bürgers (Deutsche Kaiser Augusta Fluss-Expedition 1912/13), Dr. E. Mayr (1928), G. Stein (1931) und Miss L. E. Cheesman (1933/34)', *Nova Guinea*, n.s. vol. 2, 1938.

D. E. Hardy, 'The Walker types of fruit flies (Tephritidae-Diptera) in the British Museum collection', *Bulletin of the British Museum (Natural History), Entomology*, vol. 8, 1959.

K. M. Heller, 'Neue papuanische Rüsselkäfer', *Arbeiten über Morphologische und Taxonomische Entomologie aus Berlin-Dahlem*, vol. 4, 1937; vol. 9, 1942.

W. Hennig, 'Revision der Tyliden (Dipt., Acalypt.)', *Konowia*, vols 14-15, 1935-6.

———— 'The Diptera fauna of New Zealand as a problem in systematics and zoogeography', *Pacific Insects Monograph 9*, 1966.

E. M. Hering, 'Results of the Archbold Expeditions. Fruchtfliegen (Trypetidae) von Neu-Guinea (Dipt.)', *Treubia*, vol. 31, 1953.

J. L. Herring, 'The genus *Halobates* (Hemiptera: Gerridae)', *Pacific Insects*, vol. 3, 1961.

G. F. Hill, *Termites (Isoptera) from the Australian region (including Australia, New Guinea and Islands South of the equator between 140° E Longitude and 170° W Longitude)*. Melbourne, 1942.

W. D. Hincks, 'Notes on Passalid Coleoptera from New Guinea with the description of two new species', *Proceedings of the Royal Entomological Society of London*, vol. B 25, 1956.

H. E. Hinton, 'On some new and little-known Indo-Australian Diaperini (Coleoptera, Tenebrionidae)', *Annals and Magazine of Natural History*, vol. 14, 1947.

Y. Hirashima, 'Metallic forms of *Nomia* (*Mellitidia*) of New Guinea in the collection of Bishop Museum (Hymenoptera, Halictidae)', *Journal of the Faculty of Agriculture, Kyushu University*, vol. 14, 1967.

J. Hlisnikowsky, 'Neue Liodidae (Coleoptera) aus Neu-Guinea I', *Annali Historico-Naturali, Museo Nationali Hungarici*, vol. 55, 1963.

H. John, 'Eine Übersicht über die Familie Propalticidae (Col.)', *Pacific Insects*, vol. 2, 1960.

———— 'Pazifische Discolomidae (Coleoptera)', *Pacific Insects*, vol. 9, 1967.

J. J. Joicey and G. Talbot, 'Notes on some Lepidoptera, with descriptions of new forms', *Annals and Magazine of Natural History*, vol. 16, 1925.

K. Jordan, 'On the oriental Anthribid genus *Xenocerus* Germar 1833, with descriptions of new species and sub-species (Coleoptera)', *Proceedings of the Royal Entomological Society of London*, vol. B 14, 1945.

Z. Kaszab, 'Einige neue Tenebrioniden aus den papuanischen Inseln (Coleoptera)', *Idea*, vol. 11, 1958.

D. K. McE. Kevan, 'The tribe Nereniini: With additions to the Pyrgomorphidae (Orthoptera: Acridoidea) from the South Pacific', *Pacific Insects*, vol. 8, 1966.

D. E. Kimmins, 'Miss L. E. Cheesman's expeditions to New Guinea, Trichoptera', *Bulletin of the British Museum (Natural History), Entomology*, vol. 11, 1962.

W. V. King and H. Hoogstraal, 'New Guinea species of mosquitoes of the genus *Aedes*, subgenus *Aedes*', *Journal of the Washington Academy of Science*, vol. 37, 1947.

R. Kleine, 'Bericht über die von Miss Cheesman in Britisch Neu-Guinea gesammelten Brenthiden und Lyciden', *Nova Guinea*, vol. 17, 1935.

N. Kormilev, 'Aradidae in the Bishop Museum, Honolulu (Hemiptera-Heteroptera)', *Pacific Insects*, vol. 9, 1967.

K. V. Krombein, 'The Scoliidae of New Guinea, Bismarck Archipelago and Solomon Islands (Hymenoptera, Aculeata)', *Nova Guinea*, zoological series, vol. 22, 1963.

V. Lallemand and H. Synave, 'Description des Cercopides nouveaux recuillis en Nouvelle Guinée durant les années 1938 et 1939. Results of the Archbold Expeditions', *Treubia*, vol. 23, 1955.

I. Lansbury, 'Notes on the genus *Anisops* in Bishop Museum (Hemiptera: Notonectidae)', *Pacific Insects*, vol. 4, 1962.

M. A. Lieftinck, 'The Dragonflies (Odonata) of New Guinea and neighbouring islands', *Nova Guinea*, vols 15-17, n.s. vols 1-2 and 5, 1932-49; *Treubia*, vol. 18, 1942.

————— 'Revision of the Carpenter-bees (*Xylocopa* Latr., subgenus *Maiella* Michener) of the Papuan Region (Hymenoptera, Apoidea)', *Nova Guinea*, n.s. vol. 8, 1957.

————— 'Revision of the Indo-Australian species of the genus *Thyreus* Panzer (= *Crocisa* Jurine) (Hym., Apoidea, Anthophoridae) Parts 1, 2', *Nova Guinea*, n.s. vols 9-10, 1958-9.

T. C. Maa, 'A review of the Machaerotidae (Hemiptera: Cercopoidea)', *Pacific Insects Monograph 5*, 1963.

————— 'Genera and species of Hippoboscidae (Diptera): Types, synonymy, habitats and natural groupings', *Pacific Insects Monograph 6*, 1963.

————— 'A review of the Old World Polyctenidae (Hemiptera: Cimicoidea)', *Pacific Insects*, vol. 6, 1964.

————— 'Studies in Hippoboscidae (Diptera)', *Pacific Insects Monograph 10*, 1966.

I. M. Mackerras, 'The Tabanidae (Diptera) of New Guinea', *Pacific Insects*, vol. 6, 1964.

E. N. Marks, 'Taxonomy and biology of some Papuan Culicidae. 1. Genus *Topomyia*', *Pacific Insects*, vol. 2, 1960.

G. A. K. Marshall, 'Curculionid genus *Gymnopholus* (Coleoptera)', *Occasional Papers of the Bernice P. Bishop Museum*, vol. 22, 1959.

W. B. Mather, 'Chromosomal polymorphism in *Drosophila rubida* Mather', *Genetics*, vol. 46, 1961.

C. D. Michener, 'A classification of the bees of the Australian and South Pacific regions', *Bulletin of the American Museum of Natural History*, vol. 130, 1965.

S. J. Paramonov, 'Notes on Australian Diptera', *Annals and Magazine of Natural History*, series 12, vol. 4 to series 13, vol. 6, 1951-63.

W. Peters, 'Mosquitoes of New Guinea', *Proceedings of the Royal Entomological Society of London*, vols B 27-8, 1958-9; vols B 31-3, 1962.

L. B. Prout, 'New species of Indo-Australian Geometridae', *Bulletin of the British Museum (Natural History), Entomology*, vol. 6, 1958.

L. W. Quate and S. H. Quate, 'A monograph of Papuan Psychodidae, including *Phlebotomus* (Diptera)', *Pacific Insects Monograph 15*, 1967.

W. K. J. Roepke, 'Results of the Archbold Expeditions. The butterflies of the genus *Delias* Hübner (Lepidoptera) in Netherlands New Guinea', *Nova Guinea*, n.s. vol. 6, 1955.

E. S. Ross, 'The Embioptera of New Guinea', *Pan-Pacific Entomologist*, vol. 24, 1948.

G. A. Samuelson, 'Alticinae of New Guinea, Parts I and II', *Pacific Insects*, vols 7-8, 1965-6.

M. Sasakawa, 'Papuan Agromyzidae (Diptera)', *Pacific Insects*, vol. 5, 1963.

————— 'Studies on the Oriental and Pacific Clusiidae (Diptera), Part 1. Genus *Heteromeringia* Czerny, with one new related genus', *Pacific Insects*, vol. 8, 1966.

B. J. Selman, 'A revision of the genus *Deretrichia* Weise (Coleoptera: Eumolpidae)', *Bulletin of the British Museum (Natural History), Entomology*, vol. 14, 1963.

J. A. Slater, 'A revision of the subfamily Pachygronthinae of the world (Hemiptera: Lygaeidae)', *Philippine Journal of Science*, vol. 84, 1955.

J. Smart and E. A. Clifford, 'Simuliidae (Diptera) of the Territory of Papua and New Guinea', *Pacific Insects*, vol. 7, 1965.

W. A. Steffan, 'A Checklist and Review of the Mosquitoes of the Papuan Subregion (Diptera: Culicidae)', *Journal of Medical Entomology*, vol. 3, 1966.

J. J. H. Szent-Ivany, 'Report of the Chairman of the Standing Committee on Pacific Entomology', *Proceedings of the Tenth Pacific Science Congress*, 1964.

————— 'Notes on the vertical distribution of some beetles in New Guinea with new locality data and host plant records of some high altitude species', *Papua and New Guinea Scientific Society, Transactions*, vol. 6, 1965.

G. Talbot, *A Monograph of the Pierine Genus* Delias. London, 1928-9, 1937.

E. L. Todd, 'Results of the Archbold Expeditions. The Gelastocoridae of Melanesia (Hemiptera)', *Nova Guinea*, vol. 10, 1959.

M. Tokunaga, 'New Guinea biting midges (Diptera: Ceratopogonidae)', *Pacific Insects*, vol. 1, 1959.

————— 'Biting midges of the genus *Culicoides* from New Guinea (Diptera: Ceratopogonidae)', *Pacific Insects*, vol. 4, 1962.

R. L. Torgerson and M. T. James, 'Revision of the world species of *Euphumosia* (Diptera: Calliphoridae)', *Pacific Insects*, vol. 9, 1967.

L. J. Toxopeus, 'The geological principles of species evolution in New Guinea (a study of parallelisms in geological and lepidopterological development)', *Proceedings, 8th International Congress Entomology*, 1950.

R. L. Usinger and others, *Monograph of the Cimicidae*. Washington, D.C., 1966.

————— and R. Matsuda, *Classification of the Aradidae (Hemiptera–Heteroptera)*. London, 1959.

R. H. Van Zwaluwenburg, 'Some Elateridae from the Papuan region (Coleoptera)', *Nova Guinea*, Zoological series, vol. 16, 1963.

J. van der Vecht, 'Studies on Indo-Australian and East-Asiatic Eumenidae (Hymenoptera, Vespoidea)', *Zoologische Verhandlungen*, vol. 60, 1963.

A. Watson, 'A revision of the genus *Tridrepana* Swinhoe (Lepidoptera: Drepanidae)', *Bulletin of the British Museum (Natural History), Entomology*, vol. 4, 1957.

J. T. Wiebes, 'Indo-Malayan and Papuan fig wasps (Hymenoptera, Chalcidoidea), 2. The genus *Pleistodontes* Saunders (Agaonidae)', *Zoologische Mededeelingen*, vol. 38, 1963.

C. Willemse, 'Tettigonoidea of the Papuan subregion (Orthoptera). I. Mecopodidae', *Pacific Insects*, vol. 3, 1961.

E. O. Wilson, 'Studies of the ant fauna of Melanesia. VI. The tribe Cerapachyini', *Pacific Insects*, vol. 1, 1959.

———— 'The true army ants of the Indo-Australian area (Hymenoptera: Formicidae: Dorylinae)', *Pacific Insects*, vol. 6, 1964.

W. Wittmer, 'Neue Malacodermata aus Neu Guinea', *Nova Guinea*, Zoological series vol. 30, 1964.

E. C. Zimmerman, '*Imathia* and *Amblycnemus* (Coleoptera: Curculionidae: Cryptorhynchinae)', *Pacific Insects*, vol. 9, 1967.

ACKNOWLEDGMENTS

The figures are reproduced from *Insects of Micronesia*: Chapin, 1957, vol. 3 (1e); Quate, 1959, vol. 12 (2a); Kato, 1960, vol. 6 (2c, d); *Pacific Insects*: Wilson, 1959, vol. 1 (1g); Todd, 1960, vol. 2 (2b); Slater, 1961, vol. 3 (1c); Yano, 1963, vol. 5 (1b); Beier, 1965, vol. 7 (2e); Momoi, 1966, vol. 8 (1f); Grant, 1966, vol. 8 (1d); Kormilev, 1967, vol. 9 (2f).

J. L. GRESSITT

(*See also* BEETLES; INSECT PESTS OF AGRICULTURE AND FORESTRY; MEDICAL ENTOMOLOGY; MITES; MOTHS AND BUTTERFLIES; SPIDERS; TICKS).

INSTITUTE OF HUMAN BIOLOGY. The Institute of Human Biology is an independent research organization whose aims are to conduct and foster research in any branch of medical science or biology, including the anthropological aspects of health and ill-health. In 1967 the formation of the Institute was authorized by the approval of an Ordinance by the House of Assembly and in 1968 became a reality with the appointment of Dr R. W. Hornabrook as Director.

The Institute is governed by a council of eleven members representing various Papua and New Guinea organizations and including four distinguished Australian medical scientists. The Chairman of the Council, Professor R. J. Walsh, succeeded Sir Macfarlane Burnet who retired from the position at the end of 1969.

An annual grant from the Administration provides the financial basis for the Institute's activities. The value of this grant has been related to an establishment of a certain size, and any expansion of the activities of the Institute must be financed by endowments from other non-government sources.

The headquarters of the Institute are situated in Goroka, where several buildings previously occupied by the Goroka Hospital, have been converted into staff residences, laboratories and offices. A residential suite and small laboratory is maintained in Madang, and field stations are sited on Karkar Island and at Okapa.

Early staff appointments were designed to provide a cadre of technical officers whose experience of local field conditions would provide a sound basis for scientific work. An active training programme will result in an increasing number of indigenous members of staff. The professional staff comprises a haematologist, Dr G. G. Crane, and an epidemiologist, Dr J. M. Stanhope. Additional staff have been seconded from the Department of Public Health to undertake research into special problems such as goitre and chronic chest diseases.

The Institute has a programme of scientific research which includes investigation of human biology as well as research in purely medical problems. Along with its own projects, collaborative studies with overseas workers have been developed wherever possible. In the field of human biology, the Institute was a participant in the Human Adaptability Section of the International Biological Programme [q.v.], and it contributed administrative and logistic support for both the Karkar and Lufa phases of this project. In association with several overseas laboratories, studies of the distribution of blood group genetic markers and the influence of a changing nutrition and environment on health and growth are being undertaken. New Guinea, with its very extensive range of ecological niches, provides enormous scope for investigating man's adaptation to his environment. Although there is known to be a great variety of spoken languages and social groupings, little is known of the nature of the biological variations among the population. There is an urgent need to identify the characteristics of the people before these have been obscured or altered by the changing world.

In medical research, attention is concentrated on certain conditions which are unique, or have a singular importance in the region. The Institute succeeded to the role previously occupied by the Medical Research Division of the Department of Public Health, and it inherited certain established projects which had been initiated by this Division (*see* MEDICAL SERVICES, HISTORY). The best known of these was, probably, kuru [q.v.]. An office and residence is maintained at Okapa in the centre of the kuru region, and a field officer is stationed there. He is responsible for the maintenance of accurate records of kuru cases. He also participates in annual census patrols which are maintained by the Department of District Administration. As a result of this work detailed records of the demographic background to kuru are obtained. The kuru office provides a base for various specialized investigations which are from time to time undertaken in the area.

The Haematology Section of the Institute had its origins in the Haematology Research Unit at the Angau Memorial Hospital, Lae. This unit was established at the instigation of Dr W. R. Pitney, and was supported by the Wellcome Trust and the Department of Public Health. With the development of the Institute laboratories at Goroka, the unit was transferred there. It is involved in the investigation of an unusually heavy incidence of tropical splenomegaly in the Watut Valley of the Morobe District. The disorder, which is characterized by a gross enlargement of the spleen and severe anaemia, makes its appearance in children and has been found to involve some 80 per cent of the adult population. The view that this disorder may be the result of an abnormal immunological response to malaria [q.v.] is being investigated by a programme which includes controlled treatment of malaria and laboratory studies of immunity. The Haematology Unit is also involved in the study of anaemia, which is found almost universally among villagers, both in the Highlands and on the coast.

Research into a number of other medical problems has been initiated. These investigations include the study of goitre and its relationship to damage to the nervous system and mental deficiency (*see* GOITRE AND CRETINISM). Chronic respiratory disease, which is perhaps the commonest cause of death in the older age groups, is also under investigation. In association with the Institute of Clinical Pathology and Medical Research of New South Wales, investigations of the presence of antibodies to the organisms responsible for yaws [q.v.] have been conducted in various areas in the Highlands, and the Institute is becoming more involved in the investigation of the epidemic of syphilis [q.v.]. A social anthropologist is employed in the study of the social and anthropological background to this epidemic, and clinical studies are also under way. In association with Dr Bruce McMillan of the School of Public Health and Tropical Medicine, Sydney, a variety of surveys of intestinal parasites in various New Guinea societies are in progress.

With these studies as a background, surveys of the incidence of disease in areas not previously studied are undertaken from time to time. These are usually combined with investigations of genetic and other biological characteristics so that the maximum amount of information can be obtained from each study.

The Institute is required to supply the House of Assembly with an annual report which describes progress over the preceding twelve months. Institute workers are encouraged to publish the results of their investigations in the appropriate specialist journals. The Institute council has also resolved to publish the results of some studies in monograph form. The first such work, *Growth and Development in New Guinea* by L. A. Malcolm, was published in 1970.

R. W. Hornabrook, 'The Institute of Human Biology of Papua-New Guinea', *Science*, vol. 167, 1970; R. W. Hornabrook, 'International Biological Programme Investigation on Kar Kar Island', *South Pacific Bulletin*, vol. 20, 1970; Institute of Human Biology, *Annual Report*. Goroka, 1970; L. A. Malcolm, *Growth and Development in New Guinea—A Study of the Bundi people of the Madang District*. Institute of Human Biology, monograph series no. 1. Madang, 1970.

R. W. HORNABROOK

INSTITUTE OF TECHNOLOGY. The Papua and New Guinea Institute of Technology (previously known as the Papua and New Guinea Institute of Higher Technical Education) and the University of Papua and New Guinea were set up as a direct result of recommendations made in the *Report on Higher Education in Papua and New Guinea, 1964*. This report was produced by a commission of enquiry established in February 1963 by the then Australian Minister for Territories, the Hon. P. M. C. Hasluck. The Commissioners were Sir George Currie (chairman), Dr J. T. Gunther and Professor O. H. K. Spate.

The Commission was required to give particular attention to 'the establishment in the Territory at the earliest practicable date of an institution or institutions to provide education at or near the university level; and the range of courses, the degrees or diplomas to be awarded, the standards of entry and of graduation and the staff and facilities likely to be required in successive stages of the development of such an institution or institutions'. The Currie Report, as it has come to be known, recommended that a university should be established in Port Moresby and also that what the Commissioners termed 'an institute of higher technical education' should be established at the same time and in the same place.

Two institutions on the same campus were envisaged, to share facilities and costly amenities such as a library, and to facilitate the co-ordination of higher education in the Territory. The institute was established by the Institute of Higher Technical Education Ordinance of the House of Assembly dated 26 May 1965, and the Institute Council under the chairmanship of Sir Herbert B. Watkin met for the first time on 30 September 1965 to begin detailed planning.

The new Council soon found that some of the proposals made by the Currie Commissioners were not feasible. Their report had made it clear that the Commission had in mind for the Territory an institute of technology which would initially at least operate at a level somewhat lower than that of the university. But three critical factors conspired to alter this plan. First, it was not envisaged that there would be any course duplication in the two institutions planned. This would have meant that the only institution that could supply professional manpower for instance, in engineering, would have been unable to train engineering students to degree level. Second, the Currie Commissioners had suggested that entry standards for the institute should be lower than those for the university. This was seen to be impractical, however, since entry to the university preliminary year was recommended after four years of secondary school, and thus students from Form III would have formed the initial intake to the institute. Such students would have been unable to cope with the courses proposed, since they lacked a thorough grounding in both mathematics and science. Thus, when the two institutions began to admit their first students, they both demanded the same entry qualifications and standards.

Finally, it was soon realized that if students were to achieve the necessary technical competence the institute courses needed to be five years, since even with Form IV entry standard the students were still ill-equipped in mathematics and the applied sciences.

More changes were to follow. Although the two institutions did operate side by side in Port Moresby in 1967 their separation was imminent, since in mid-1966 the House of Assembly introduced a Bill separating the two. It was then decided to move the institute to Lae on the north coast, and in 1967 a five-hundred acre campus area was obtained approximately six miles from the town centre.

This site was an overgrown coffee and cocoa plantation and extensive clearing, draining, road-

A view of the campus showing the first academic building.

making, sewerage works, and the provision of water, electricity and telephone services had to be undertaken in addition to an extensive building programme. Nevertheless by February 1968 sufficient preliminary work had been accomplished, and the move from Port Moresby to Lae took place in time for the start of the 1968 academic year.

Early in 1966 Dr J. A. L. Matheson, Vice-Chancellor of Monash University, Melbourne, had been appointed chairman of the Institute Council following the death of Sir Herbert B. Watkin. In August of the same year, the first Director of the Institute, Dr W. E. Duncanson, took up his duties and the first academic staff were appointed soon afterwards. The problems facing this early staff were largely those associated with the different kinds of skill and the different levels of academic training needed for the three major classes of tradesmen, technicians and professional personnel.

Professional staff are those who plan, design (in over-all terms) and organize the construction, production and maintenance processes in any industry or government department. It must be assumed that some of them will rise to the highest posts directing major policy in these fields. They must therefore be trained in the analytical basis of their discipline, as well as in the practical aspects of design and execution of schemes, and further, be trained to formulate policy in technical matters, and to manage and administer staff working under them. Professional staff therefore require a full tertiary education leading to a degree or equivalent

and eventually, with appropriate experience, a professional qualification.

The functions and training of a technician are more difficult to define but between tradesman and professional technologist there must be a range of staff to deal with details of planning and design, and to control those actually engaged on the work.

It is common in both developed and underdeveloped countries for the technician to be trained at technical institutes or colleges of technology, but in a new society there is always a danger that with the more obvious need for professional staff, institutions training the latter alone may be developed in advance of those training technical staff. Such staff, at what might be termed near-professional level, are in fact needed in considerably greater numbers—between two and four to each professional man—to fill posts with titles such as 'technical officer', 'architectural assistant', or 'works superintendent'.

In planning the pattern of higher technical education in the Territory, it was apparent that the technical colleges would be able to train a good, practical craftsman, but it was also clear that they would not for some time be able to provide the more extensive facilities and specialized staff required to produce men at near-professional levels. The institute therefore saw its task as providing training at two levels—the professional level and the semi-professional or technician level. Moreover it was also seen that by far the greatest number of students would be needed at the technician level. In fact the first students accepted by the institute were enrolled for courses in civil engineering and surveying, some students in the latter course having previously spent one year on a survey training programme organized by the Department of Lands, Surveys and Mines. With the move to Lae in 1968 a course in accountancy and business studies was introduced and further courses have been added as the institute continues its programme of rapid expansion. Courses in mechanical and electrical engineering commenced in 1969 and courses in architecture and building technology were commenced in 1970.

In all cases the courses have been designed to meet the needs of the Territory. In accountancy and business studies the immediate needs were at the near-professional level. For this reason diploma courses began in 1968 and the end of the 1971 academic year saw the first diplomates ready to take up positions in the commercial sector of the Territory's economy. The decision to establish courses at diploma level has been vindicated by the support received from commercial enterprise. In 1971 over 90 per cent of the students reading courses in the School of Accountancy and Business Studies were being supported financially by private firms or statutory organizations, and there is a steadily growing demand for these graduates.

In engineering a somewhat different pattern has emerged. It was recognized quite early that a growing number of civil engineers would be required for the design and construction of roads and bridges, and a host of related developmental activities. Accordingly, the first school established by the institute was in engineering and a Professor of Civil Engineering was among the first of the academic staff to be appointed. However, in planning civil engineering courses it was expected that for every professionally trained graduate a number of supporting staff trained to near-professional levels would be needed. Courses were therefore planned to produce a relatively small number of students at full professional level and a much larger number who would supply the necessary ancillary services.

To provide for this two-stream pattern, the Institute Ordinance was amended in 1970 to allow the institute to award degrees as well as diplomas. A similar two-stream pattern of development exists in mechanical and electrical engineering courses, and also in architecture and building. In surveying it was felt that a four-year diploma course would be most appropriate and already nine students have successfully completed this programme and are serving two years under articles to licensed surveyors. They will then be eligible for full professional status.

A student at work in the mechanical engineering laboratory.

The first consideration in designing courses has been the needs of the Territory, and as the institute develops and extends into such fields as mining engineering, chemical technology and other related areas, this approach will remain. The institute's function must continue to be the training of people capable of using modern techniques. This entails a firm theoretical knowledge backed by sound practical experience related specifically to Territory conditions. For example, a large proportion of New Guinea's civil engineers will be engaged in the design and construction of roads, often in mountainous country. The course should take account of this, and provide advanced study in soil mechanics, road surfacing materials and drainage problems. Moreover many of these topics need to be considered in more depth and detail than would be the case in engineering degree courses in other parts of the world. The institute believes that it is only by constantly checking course design against practical needs in this way that the appropriate type of graduate will be produced.

The Ordinance establishing the institute also charged it to provide 'for research into technical branches of learning and to assist in its practical application'. It is invaluable for students to observe and participate in advanced research, and such activities ensure that optimum use is made of expensive teaching equipment, and also helps to attract high quality staff. Research projects include studies of the effects of earthquakes on structures, analysis of the engineering properties and strength characteristics of New Guinea timbers, studies of the engineering properties and structure of residual volcanic soils, investigations of methods of providing low-cost river crossings, the effects of humidity on the mechanical properties of materials, and a number of other projects. In addition the institute provides facilities for local industry to test timber, concrete, cement, steel, soil, rock and bituminous material. Another important service provided by the institute is in mineral sample analysis, and there is a well-equipped water analysis laboratory.

In 1971 there were 308 students at the Institute of Technology in the following schools: Accountancy and Business Studies, 104; Engineering, 185; Architecture and Building, 19.   P. BOTSMAN

INTERNATIONAL BIOLOGICAL PROGRAMME.
This is an attempt on the part of biologists throughout the world to investigate 'the biological basis of productivity and human welfare'. It began with a two-year planning phase followed by a period of five years of active work. Although it officially closes in 1972, its effects are likely to continue long after that year.

There are seven sections, each concerned with a specific aspect of biology; that which deals directly with humans is the Human Adaptability or H.A. section, in which research is designed to elucidate the nature and mechanisms of Man's adaptations to his environment in all parts of the world, and involves studies of genetical, physical, physiological, nutritional and psychological factors.

The H.A. project in New Guinea is a collaborative undertaking between the United Kingdom H.A. Committee, the Australian H.A. Committee, the Institute of Human Biology of Papua and New Guinea [q.v.], and various institutions and laboratories in Australia, the United Kingdom and New Guinea. It is a multidisciplinary study of two contrasting populations, one in the village of Kaul on Karkar Island, and the other at Lufa in the Eastern Highlands. The first population consists of people resident at sea-level, many of whom work on coconut and cocoa plantations and who are undergoing rapid socio-economic changes. The second consists of people living at an altitude of 5,000 feet above sea-level, who to date have been less exposed to European civilization.

The Director of the Institute of Human Biology has been responsible for the direction and co-ordination of the project. It has been necessary to construct laboratories and houses in both areas, to obtain special equipment and to negotiate with the local communities for volunteers for the many experiments. The work was originally divided between the principal participants as follows:

Institute of Human Biology: medical examination, socio-demographic survey, growth and development studies.

United Kingdom H.A. Committee: nutrition and energy expenditure studies, work capacity physiology and respiratory functions investigations.

Australian H.A. Committee: genetics, anthropometry, thermal tolerance studies, parasitology and salt and water metabolism.

Department of Public Health: provision of personnel to assist the nutrition and physiology studies and generally to provide administrative assistance.

The thermal tolerance studies were later made a joint responsibility of the School of Public Health and Tropical Medicine of the University of Sydney, and the United Kingdom Committee in collaboration with the Medical Research Council of the United Kingdom. The statistical analysis of the data will be undertaken by the Department of Clinical Science of the Australian National University, Canberra.

Workers and technical assistants in every aspect of the studies have resided in the areas for varying periods of time and they have been visited for shorter periods by consultants from Australia and the United Kingdom. The studies have been extensive and a few are mentioned to give some idea of the scope. Aliquots of blood samples obtained during the medical and genetical surveys have been tested in Port Moresby, Sydney, London and Cambridge for blood groups, serum groups, abnormal haemoglobins, electrolytes and biochemical components. The anthropometric work has included photographs, standard anthropometric measurements, skin colour measurements, dermatoglyphs, hair samples, colour vision and the ability to taste P.T.C. (phenylthiocarbamide). The nutrition workers have obtained extensive data on dietary intake and energy expenditure, and in addition have obtained samples of every common food for analysis at the University of Strathclyde. They have also measured mean body mass by underwater weighing of subjects. The laboratory studies of thermal tolerance and respiratory physiology were performed in special air-conditioned laboratories. The reactions of subjects to cooling and heating were measured with the subjects in double plastic suits so that air which had been cooled or heated could be blown into the space between the bags. A number of measurements were made to evaluate functional aspects of the lungs and the circulatory apparatus, and to measure physical fitness.

It is premature to make any attempt to assess the significance of the results which have been obtained during the International Biological Programme in New Guinea. It is, however, expected that they will provide some understanding of the biological reaction of members of the two populations with their contrasting environments.

R. J. WALSH

J

JABGA. People of West Irian. Reference: H. Nevermann, 'Die Jabga auf Südneuguinea', *Baessler-Archiv*, new series, vol. 1, 1952.

JOHNSON, Leslie Wilson (1916-   ), Administrator, was born at Tambellup, Western Australia, on 2 April 1916. He is a graduate (M.A.) of the University of Western Australia. After service as an officer of the Western Australian Education Department, and war service, he became Director of Education for the Territory of Papua and New Guinea in 1962 and Assistant Administrator of the Territory in 1966. In 1970 he was appointed Administrator, in succession to D. O. Hay [q.v.].

JOHNSTON, George Jameson (1869-1949), Administrator of New Guinea, was born in East Melbourne on 24 October 1869, the son of Charles Johnston and believed to be a descendant of the Major Johnston who deposed Governor Bligh. He entered the family firm of Charles Johnston & Co., furniture manufacturers and warehousemen, of Fitzroy. At an early age he joined the Victorian militia, and in 1889 he gained a commission in the artillery. In 1894 he married Margaret, daughter of Charles Hobson of Melbourne.

When the South African War started in 1899 Johnston, a captain of artillery, joined the first Victorian contingent as one of the 'special service officers' attached for instruction. He served with various artillery units of the British Army, taking part in the operations in Cape Colony, including the advance on Kimberley. He later commanded the 4th Australian Commonwealth Horse during the operations in the Transvaal in the closing stages of the war. He returned in 1902 to the family business.

In 1914 he joined the A.I.F. and left Australia in command of the 2nd Field Artillery Brigade. He led this unit throughout most of the Gallipoli campaign. For a brief period late in 1915, as a colonel, he commanded the 3rd Infantry Brigade. For his services he was awarded the C.B. When the 2nd Australian Division was formed at the end of 1915 he was appointed to command the artillery and promoted to brigadier-general. He commanded the 2nd Divisional Artillery in France throughout 1916 and most of 1917, participating in the battles of Pozières, First Bullecourt and Third Ypres. He was awarded the C.M.G. for his work.

On 16 March 1918 he was appointed Administrator of German New Guinea. He reached Rabaul [q.v.] on 21 April.

Johnston took over from S. S. Mackenzie [q.v.], who had been acting as administrator for six months, and who had continued Pethebridge's [q.v.] organization with few changes. The incoming Administrator was not favourably impressed. This, he understood, was a military administration; but almost no attention was being paid to defence. At the time, the Germans were achieving major successes on the Western Front. He set about forming a mobile force which could be sent to any threatened place, but he had such difficulty in getting men of a high enough physical standard that he was obliged to give up the project. He reverted to Pethebridge's plan of depending on the same individuals for both normal administrative duties and defence in emergency. He did, however, cause a coastal battery to be installed at Raluana Point commanding the approach to Rabaul.

In the absence of a directive from the Australian government Johnston had to reach his own conclusions about the objects of the military administration. According to C. D. Rowley, he saw his duty as empire building in the traditional fashion. He wanted the country opened up. He observed with disapproval the sedentary habits which district staffs had acquired under Pethebridge's regime; he called for a policy of active patrolling, and he provided additional staff to make this possible. He visited the outstations. He established posts at Buka Passage and Vanimo and a new district headquarters at Gasmata. It was his object to extend administrative control to every area which recruiters and missionaries had penetrated. He was the first administrator to propose a scheme of training for New Guinea district officers.

His attitude to the native people was paternal, and he was less disposed than his predecessors to regard them as mere economic assets. He certainly accepted without question the necessity for corporal punishment for labour offences, and when in 1919 the Australian government abolished flogging in such cases it was his strong reaction, followed by his search for alternatives such as irons and field punishment, that must have cast the first doubts on his suitability for his appointment; but in other respects his administration of the labour law was enlightened, as when he insisted that labourers should be returned to their villages for a period before signing new contracts.

And although he was obliged to order punitive expeditions from time to time he was at pains to avoid bloodshed.

Johnston was a proponent of closer settlement of New Guinea land by Australians, but when the post-war expropriation of German enterprises was mooted he came out in favour of allowing the German owners of smaller plantations to remain.

His expectation of remaining in office until the end of the military administration was not fulfilled. His appointment was terminated early in 1920, perhaps because of public criticism of his attitude to penalties for labour offences, perhaps because of newspaper attacks on high living and high jinks at Government House, but more likely because of the government's doubts whether he could accommodate his firmly held opinions to the coming expropriation of German interests.

He handed over to Brigadier-General T. Griffiths [q.v.] on 1 May 1920, having been two years in office. He was appointed C.B.E. in recognition of his work.

Johnston returned to his furniture business in Melbourne. He continued his association with the Citizen Military Forces, and commanded the 3rd Division from 1922 to 1927. He died in Melbourne on 23 May 1949.

C. D. Rowley, having studied Johnston's official correspondence, says: 'He had neither the background nor the intellectual capacity to adapt himself to the task of colonial administration'. Also, 'He was a foolish and headstrong person, of rather coarse and insensitive fibre, one guesses; but there is an impression also of honesty'. And again, 'His statements were often so self-condemnatory that one does not know whether to impute them to foolishness or to a rough honesty'. But these judgments reflect only the written record. People who knew Johnston recall his sturdy independence of mind, his frankness, his hearty good nature, his kindness and generosity.

One must conclude that in New Guinea Johnston conscientiously did his best in an appointment for which he was suited by neither temperament nor training.

Commonwealth of Australia, *Report to the League of Nations on the Administration of the Territory of New Guinea, from September 1914 to 30 June, 1921*. Melbourne, 1922; S. S. Mackenzie, *The Australians at Rabaul (Official History of Australia in the War of 1914-1918*, vol. 10). Sydney, 1927; 'Report by the Minister of State for Defence on the Military Occupation of the German New Guinea Possessions', *Commonwealth Parliamentary Papers 1922*, vol. 2; C. D. Rowley, *The Australians in German New Guinea 1914-1921*. Melbourne, 1958. Rowley made use of the correspondence between Johnston and the Department of Defence, Melbourne, which is in the library of the Australian War Memorial, Canberra.

R. R. McN.

(*See also* NEW GUINEA, MANDATED TERRITORY)

K

KAINANTU. People of the Eastern Highlands District. References:

C. H. Berndt, 'Socio-cultural Change in the Eastern Central Highlands of New Guinea', *Southwestern Journal of Anthropology*, vol. 9, 1953.

—— 'Translation Problems in Three New Guinea Highland Languages', *Oceania*, vol. 24, 1953-4.

—— Myth in Action: a Study of Oral Literature in the Eastern Highlands. Ph.D. thesis, London School of Economics, 1955.

—— 'Social and Cultural Change in New Guinea: Communication and Views about "Other People"', *Sociologus*, vol. 7, 1957.

—— 'Ascription of Meaning in a Ceremonial Context, in the Eastern Central Highlands of New Guinea', in *Anthropology in the South Seas*, ed. J. D. Freeman and W. R. Geddes. New Plymouth, N.Z., 1959.

R. M. Berndt, 'A Cargo Movement in the Eastern Central Highlands of New Guinea', *Oceania*, vol. 23, 1952-3.

—— 'Reaction to Contact in the Eastern Highlands of New Guinea', *Oceania*, vol. 24, 1953-4; vol. 25, 1954-5 (errata).

—— 'Kamano, Jate, Usurufa and Fore Kinship of the Eastern Highlands of New Guinea', *Oceania*, vol. 25, 1954-5.

—— 'A "Devastating Disease Syndrome"; *Kuru* Sorcery in the Eastern Central Highlands of New Guinea', *Sociologus*, vol. 8, 1958.

—— *Excess and Restraint: Social Control among a New Guinea Mountain People*. Chicago, 1962.

—— 'Warfare in the New Guinea Highlands', *American Anthropologist*, vol. 66, Special Publication, 1964.

—— 'The Kamano, Usurufa, Jate and Fore of the Eastern Highlands', in *Gods Ghosts and Men in Melanesia*, ed. P. Lawrence and M. J. Meggitt. Melbourne, 1965.

R. F. Fortune, 'The Rules of Relationship Behaviour in One Variety of Primitive Warfare', *Man*, vol. 47, 1947.

—— 'Law and Force in Papuan Societies', *American Anthropologist*, vol. 49, 1947.

—— 'New Guinea Warfare: Correction of a Mistake Previously Published', *Man*, vol. 60, 1960.

R. M. Glasse, 'Marriage in South Fore', in *Pigs, Pearlshells, and Women: Marriage in the New Guinea Highlands*, ed. R. M. Glasse and M. J. Meggitt. Englewood Cliffs, N.J., 1969.

—— and S. Lindenbaum, 'South Fore Politics', *Anthropological Forum*, vol. 2, 1967-70.

J. B. Watson, 'A New Guinea "Opening Man"', in *In the Company of Man*, ed. J. B. Casagrande. New York, 1960.

—— 'Krakatoa's Echo?', *Journal of the Polynesian Society*, vol. 72, 1963.

—— 'A Previously Unreported Root Crop from the New Guinea Highlands', *Ethnology*, vol. 3, 1964.

—— 'Anthropology in the New Guinea Highlands', *American Anthropologist*, vol. 66, Special Publication, 1964.

—— 'Kainantu Open Electorate: (1) A General Analysis of the Elections at Kainantu' (New Guinea's First National Election), *Journal of the Polynesian Society*, vol. 73, 1964.

—— 'From Hunting to Horticulture in the New Guinea Highlands', *Ethnology*, vol. 4, 1965.

—— 'The Significance of a Recent Ecological Change in the Central Highlands of New Guinea', *Journal of the Polynesian Society*, vol. 74, 1965.

—— 'The Kainantu Open and South Markham Special Electorates', in *The Papua-New Guinea Elections 1964*, ed. D. G. Bettison, C. A. Hughes and P. W. van der Veur. Canberra, 1965.

—— and others, 'The Blood Groups of Natives in Kainantu, New Guinea', *Human Biology*, vol. 33, 1961.

V. Watson, 'Pottery in the Eastern Highlands of New Guinea', *Southwestern Journal of Anthropology*, vol. 11, 1955.

(*See also* GAHUKU-GAMA)

KANUM. People of West Irian. Reference:

H. Nevermann, 'Die Kanum-irebe und ihre Nachbarn', *Zeitschrift für Ethnologie*, vol. 71, 1939.

KAPAUKU. People of the Wissel Lakes, West Irian. References:

L. F. B. Dubbeldam, 'The Devaluation of the Kapauku-cowrie as a Factor of Social Disintegration', *American Anthropologist*, vol. 66, Special Publication, 1964.

L. Pospisil, 'Social Change and Primitive Law: Consequences of a Papuan Legal Case', *American Anthropologist*, vol. 60, 1958.

—— 'Kapauku Political Structure', in *Systems of Political Control and Bureaucracy in Human Societies*, Proceedings of the 1958 Annual Spring Meeting of the American Ethnological Society, ed. V. F. Ray. Seattle, 1958.

—— *Kapauku Papuans and Their Law*. New Haven, 1958.

—— 'The Kapauku Papuans and their Kinship Organization', *Oceania*, vol. 30, 1959-60.

—— *The Kapauku Papuans of West New Guinea*. New York, 1963.

—— *Kapauku Papuan Economy*. New Haven, 1963.

—— 'A Formal Analysis of Substantive Law; Kapauku Laws of Land Tenure', *American Anthropologist*, vol. 67, Special Publication, 1965.

KAPENA, Toua (1920-), Ministerial Member for Labour and M.H.A. for Hiri (open) electorate. He was born in September 1920 in Hanuabada village, Port Moresby. His education, interrupted by the war, was completed by a six months' medical course at Sydney University. During the war he served with Angau Medical Services and was awarded the Loyal Service Medal. From 1946 to 1965 he was a clerk for the Education Department. At present he is president of the Hiri Local Government Council and chairman of the Local Government Association of Papua and New Guinea. He has involved himself in the Boy Scout movement and parents' and citizens' associations. He was awarded the C.B.E. in 1971.

KAPUTIN, John Rumet (1939-   ) was born at Matupit Island on 7 July 1939, a member of the Tolai group. He was educated in New Guinea and Australia; he played Rugby football and was an outstanding athlete, representing Papua and New Guinea at the 1962 Empire Games. He began training as a school teacher; he was self-employed, and then joined the staff of the House of Assembly. In 1966 he was the first Papuan or New Guinean to be awarded a scholarship by the East-West Centre to the University of Hawaii. He spent two years there, and after returning to New Guinea was appointed manager of a Savings and Loans Society. He is not now employed by the Society. He became an active spokesman for the Mataungan Association and sponsored the development of a finance corporation to give the Tolais a larger measure of investment in business and property. He is considered a radical supporter of independence.

J. T. GUNTHER

KARAM. People of the Schrader Mountains. References:
B. Biggs, 'The Phonology of Karam, a "Pygmy"-language of the Schrader Mountains', Tenth Pacific Science Congress, Honolulu, *Abstracts of Symposium Papers*, 1961.
———— 'A Non-phonemic Central Vowel Type in Karam, a "Pygmy"-language of the Schrader Mountains, Central New Guinea', *Anthropological Linguistics*, vol. 5, 1963.
R. N. H. Bulmer, 'Beliefs Concerning the Propagation of New Varieties of Sweet Potato in Two New Guinea Highlands Societies', *Journal of the Polynesian Society*, vol. 74, 1965.
———— 'Why is the Cassowary not a Bird?' *Man*, new series, vol. 2, 1967.

KEREWA. People of the Gulf District, including Goaribari Island. References:
A. C. Haddon, 'The Agiba Cult of the Kerewa Culture', *Man*, vol. 18, 1918.
D. E. Newton, 'Multiple Human Figures in Western Papuan Art', *Man*, vol. 63, 1963.
P. Wirz, 'Kopfjagd und Trophäenkult im Gebiete des Papuagolfes', *Ethnologischer Anzeiger*, vol. 3, 1933.

KEVERI. People of the Central District. Reference:
F. E. Williams, 'Mission Influence amongst the Keveri of South-east Papua', *Oceania*, vol. 15, 1944-5.

KEWA. People of the Southern Highlands District. References:
K. J. Franklin, 'Kewa Ethnolinguistic Concepts of

Body Parts', *Southwestern Journal of Anthropology*, vol. 19, 1963.
———— 'Kewa Verb Morphology', Summer Institute of Linguistics, New Guinea, *Workshop Papers*, no. 2, 1963 (roneoed).
———— 'Kewa Clause Markers', *Oceania*, vol. 35, 1964-5.
———— 'Kewa Social Organization', *Ethnology*, vol. 4, 1965.
———— and J. Franklin, 'The Kewa Counting Systems', *Journal of the Polynesian Society*, vol. 71, 1962.
———— 'Kewa 1: Phonological Asymmetry', *Anthropological Linguistics*, vol. 4, 1962.

KIKI, Albert Maori (1931-   ), author and politician, was born on 21 September 1931 at Orokolo village, Ihu Sub-District, Gulf District, Papua. He was educated at the London Missionary Society school in Orokolo village from 1940 to 1945. The course was interrupted by the war, and he did not go on to Sogeri High School until 1948. He took a teacher training course in 1949, and was at Suva Medical College from 1952 to 1956. He received the Laboratory Technician's Diploma at the Administrative College [q.v.], Port Moresby, in 1965.

He worked as a school teacher from 1950 to 1951, as a laboratory technician at Port Moresby General Hospital from 1956 to 1961 and from 1961 to 1963 was posted to Buka as a welfare assistant with the Hahalis Welfare Society. In 1967 he resigned to become National Secretary of Pangu Pati. He unsuccessfully contested the House of Assembly elections for the Kikori open electorate, but was elected to the Port Moresby Urban Council in 1971. He was president of the Kerema Welfare Association from 1958 to 1960 and is now a member of the Port Moresby Town Council and of the Territory Education Board, president of the Miscellaneous Workers' Union, secretary of the Building and Construction Industry Workers' Union, and honorary vice-president of the University Rugby Union Association. His *Kiki: Ten Thousand Years in a Lifetime* (Melbourne, 1968) is the first autobiography by a Papuan or New Guinean. A second book is *Hohao* and he has had articles published in several journals.

KINGFISHERS. Mythical harbingers of peaceful times, kingfishers (family Alcedinidae) are perhaps the most easily recognized group of birds in the world with their squat bodies, short tails, long straight bills, syndactylic toes and preponderance of blue-green plumage. The family, though cosmopolitan in distribution, is richer in the New Guinea region than anywhere else. Where the term 'New Guinea' is used without any qualification such as 'region' it refers to the whole main island. Represented there are not only two of the three kingfisher subfamilies, namely the Alcedininae or 'true' river kingfishers and the Daceloninae or 'wood' kingfishers, but also seven of the family's fourteen genera and twenty-eight of the approximately one hundred species.

Of the five 'true' kingfishers found in the region, one is a representative of the widely known palaearctic river kingfisher (*Alcedo atthis*) which, living entirely on fish, is found throughout the smaller islands. The other four (genus *Ceyx*) resemble the river kingfisher in size and general colour pattern but differ in having two front toes instead of three. They live largely in forest where they feed on insects as well as crustacea and small fish caught in streams. Two of these species, the solitary (*C. lepidus*) and little (*C. pusilla*) kingfishers, iridescent in brilliant blues and barely larger than a humming bird, shine out like tiny jewels in the dark lowland jungles.

'Wood' kingfishers differ from 'true' kingfishers in having stouter bills, longer tails and, commonly, brown plumage, and in the mode of moulting the primaries. Their diversity in the New Guinea region is unparalleled elsewhere in the world. Five of the subfamily's eight genera and twenty-three of its approximately fifty-nine species occur there, including the three endemic or sub-endemic genera *Clytoceyx*, *Melidora* and *Tanysiptera*. The single species of *Clytoceyx*, the shovel-billed kingfisher, is perhaps the most bizarre of all kingfishers. About the size of a kookaburra and similar in colour pattern, it has a remarkably short and flattened bill which it uses to dig worms and other food out of the ground on the forest floor. It is also said to be crepuscular in habits. Monotypic *Melidora* has a strongly hooked bill which it apparently uses similarly to dig in the forest floor. The eight species of *Tanysiptera* are among the most beautiful of kingfishers in their iridescent blues, whites and soft reds and streaming central tail feathers (rackets). They occur, usually as solitary individuals, in the substage of the primary lowland and hill rain forests throughout the region and feed chiefly on insects. Kookaburras (*Dacelo*), the largest kingfishers in the world, also belong to the Daceloninae. They are represented in New Guinea by three species, one of which, the blue-winged kookaburra (*D. leachii*), is found also in northern Australia. This and a second New Guinean species, the mantled kookaburra (*D. tyro*), inhabit the eucalypt savannah woodlands of southern New Guinea. The third species, Gaudichaud's kookaburra (*D. gaudichaud*), is a smaller and darker bird of the lowland rain forests throughout the island. The remaining ten New Guinean kingfishers belong to the large genus *Halcyon*. Included here are a number of exquisitely blue endemics, such as the purple (*H. nigrocyanea*) and ultramarine (*H. leucopygia*) kingfishers, the widespread and polymorphic white-collared kingfisher (*H. chloris*), and a well-known Australian migrant, the sacred kingfisher (*H. sanctus*).

Despite their morphological diversity, the New Guinean kingfishers are, like all kingfishers, remarkably alike in their behaviour. Either solitary or in pairs, all perch motionless on horizontal branches usually at low levels in forest or woodland, with their heads pointed downward watching the ground or streams for food for most of the day. On seeing their prey, most species dart swiftly down to seize it in the bill and return to the same or another similar perch. Their calls are discordant to a lesser or greater extent, varying from prolonged trills in the case of the yellow-billed kingfisher (*Halcyon torotoro*) to sharp ejaculations in

the 'true' kingfishers (*Ceyx*) and hysterical cacklings in the kookaburras, often given in dawn and dusk choruses. Nests are placed in dug-out burrows, either in a stream bank by the 'true' kingfishers or in an arboreal termite mound or tree hollow by the 'wood' kingfishers. The eggs of all species are uniformly white and the clutch size varies with the species from two to about five, rather more than is usual in New Guinea land birds.

Nearly all kingfishers are confined to low altitudes in the New Guinea region, and most of them occur in the primary lowland and hill rain forests. Only two endemic species range above 4,000 feet to approximately 6,500 feet above sea-level, namely the mountain (*Halcyon megarhyncha*) and the shovel-billed kingfishers; the immigrant sacred kingfisher is occasionally recorded also at these altitudes in areas cleared by human habitation. Most species occupy particular ecological niches: open coastal forest by the beach kingfisher (*H. saurophaga*), the substage of primary lowland rain forest by the species of *Ceyx* and *Tanysiptera*, cleared areas by immigrant species of *Halcyon*, and eucalypt savannah by two of the kookaburras. An exception is the white-collared kingfisher which is found in different habitats in different parts of its range, i.e. coastal mangrove forest in New Guinea and hill and lowland rain forest in the eastern archipelagoes.

The evolutionary and adaptational relationships between the genera and species of 'wood' kingfishers in the Australian-New Guinea region have not yet been fully elucidated. Preliminary assessments indicate firstly that the group may have arrived and radiated relatively recently in the region because so few are found in the montane rain forests of New Guinea, a major source of austral avifaunal elements. Secondly, it seems likely that monotypic *Melidora*, one of the larger brown kingfishers, represents a neotenic derivative from *Tanysiptera* stock because of its similarity to juveniles of *Tanysiptera* species. These interpretations and their implications contradict the widely held belief that the large dull-coloured palaeotropic 'wood' kingfishers are primitive in the family while the small, brilliantly plumaged, cosmopolitan 'river' kingfishers (Alcedininae, Cerylinae) represent derived forms. It seems likely that the solution to this dilemma will be found in the polymorphic Malaysian-centred *Halcyon* stock, from which both the specialized 'river' and large brown 'wood' kingfishers may have sprung.

A. Landsborough Thomson (ed.), *A New Dictionary of Birds*. London, 1964; E. Mayr, *List of New Guinea Birds*. New York, 1941; A. L. Rand and E. T. Gilliard, *Handbook of New Guinea Birds*. London, 1967.

RICHARD SCHODDE

KIWAI. People of the Western District. References:
G. Landtman, 'The Poetry of the Kiwai Papuans', *Folklore*, vol. 24, 1913.
————'Cat's Cradles of the Kiwai Papuans, British New Guinea', *Anthropos*, vol. 9, 1914.
————'The Magic of the Kiwai Papuans in Warfare',

Journal of the Royal Anthropological Institute, vol. 46, 1916.
———— 'The Folk-tales of the Kiwai Papuans', *Acta Societatis Scientiarum Fennicae*, vol. 47, 1917.
———— 'The Origin of Images as Objects of Cult', *Archiv für Religionswissenschaft*, vol. 24, 1926.
———— *The Kiwai Papuans of British New Guinea*. London, 1927.
———— *Ethnographical Collection from the Kiwai District of British New Guinea, in the National Museum of Finland, Helsingfors (Helsinki); a Descriptive Survey of the Material Culture of the Kiwai People*. Helsinki, 1933.
———— 'The Origins of Sacrifices as Illustrated by a Primitive People', in *Essays Presented to C. G. Seligman*, ed. E. E. Evans-Pritchard and others. London, 1934.
———— 'Initiation Ceremonies of the Kiwai Papuans', in *Primitive Heritage*, ed. M. Mead and N. Calas. London, 1954.
W. H. R. Rivers, 'Contributions to Comparative Psychology from Torres Straits and New Guinea: 1. General Account and Observations on Vision &c.', in British Association for the Advancement of Science, *Report of the Sixty-ninth Meeting, 1899*. London, 1900.
———— 'The Regulation of Marriage', in *Reports of the Cambridge Anthropological Expedition to Torres Straits*, ed. A. C. Haddon, vol. 6, 1908.
———— and A. C. Haddon, 'A Method of Recording String Figures and Tricks', *Man*, vol. 2, 1902.

KOITA. People of the Central District. Reference:
R. W. Firth, 'Notes on the Social Structure of Some South-eastern New Guinea Communities. Part 1: Mailu; Part 2: Koita', *Man*, vol. 52, 1952.

KOMBA. People of the Morobe District. References:
H. Wagner, 'Mythen und Erzählungen der Komba in Nordost-Neu-Guinea', *Zeitschrift für Ethnologie*, vol. 88, 1963.
———— 'Beschneidungswiten und die damit verbundenen Moral-Lehren der Komba in Nordost-Neuguinea', *Zeitschrift für Ethnologie*, vol. 90, 1965.

KONDOM (*c.* 1917-1966), Highlands native leader. He was born in Chimbu District, and by the traditional method of making alliances through several marriages and the acquisition and manipulation of wealth made himself a 'big man' in his tribal area. Though he worked briefly for the Catholic mission he was never converted to Christianity.

He was enthusiastic in embracing all the new ways brought by the government, and was appointed a *luluai*, or government headman. He assisted in the opening up of the Highlands, in road construction, the introduction of cash crops and of local government councils.

In 1961 he was appointed to the Legislative Council in Port Moresby, representing the most populous constituency in the Territory. He was not elected to the House of Assembly which succeeded the Legislative Assembly. Although he did not speak English, using either his local language or Pidgin English, he held many positions of local influence and importance, and was chairman of the Kundiawa Coffee Co-operative.

He was an impressive example of that generation of indigenous people who bridged the gap between old and modern times, his roots in primitive life and his aspirations in a civilized future. He died in a motor accident on Daulo Pass in August 1966.

KORIKI. People of the Gulf District. References:
R. F. Maher, 'Tommy Kabu Movement of the Purari Delta', *Oceania*, vol. 29, 1958-9.
———— 'Social Structure and Cultural Change in Papua', *American Anthropologist*, vol. 62, 1960.
———— 'Varieties of Change in Koriki Culture', *Southwestern Journal of Anthropology*, vol. 17, 1961.
———— *New Men of Papua: a Study in Culture Change*. Madison, Wisc., 1961.
F. E. Williams, 'The Pairama Ceremony in the Purari Delta, Papua', *Journal of the Royal Anthropological Institute*, vol. 53, 1923.
———— 'The Natives of the Purari Delta', Territory of Papua, *Anthropology Report*, no. 5. Port Moresby, 1924.

KOROFEIGU. People of the Bena Bena Valley, Eastern Highlands District. References:
L. L. Langness, 'Notes on the Bena Council, Eastern Highlands', *Oceania*, vol. 33, 1962-3.
———— 'Some Problems in the Conceptualization of Highlands Social Structures', *American Anthropologist*, vol. 66, Special Publication, 1964.
———— 'Sexual Antagonism in the New Guinea Highlands', *Oceania*, vol. 37, 1966-7.
———— 'Bena Bena Political Organization', *Anthropological Forum*, vol. 2, 1967-70.
———— 'Marriage in Bena Bena', in *Pigs, Pearlshells, and Women: Marriage in the New Guinea Highlands*, ed. R. M. Glasse and M. J. Meggitt. Englewood Cliffs, N.J., 1969.

KOROWORI. People of a tributary of the Sepik River. Reference:
E. Haberland, 'Kulturverfall und Heilserwartung am oberen Korowori (Sepik-Distrikt, Neuguinea)', *Sociologus*, vol. 14, 1964.

KUKUKUKU. People of the Eastern Highlands and Morobe Districts. References:
B. Blackwood, 'Life on the Upper Watut, New Guinea', *Geographical Journal*, vol. 94, 1939.
———— 'Use of Plants among the Kukukuku of Southeast-Central New Guinea', Sixth Pacific Science Congress, California, *Proceedings*, vol. 4, 1939.
———— 'Folk-stories of a Stone Age People in New Guinea', *Folklore*, vol. 50, 1939.
———— *The Technology of a Modern Stone Age People in New Guinea*. Oxford, 1950.
H. Fischer, *Watut: Notizen zur Kultur eines Melanesierstammes in Nordost-Neuguinea*. Braunschweig, 1963.

KULA. This is the system of ceremonial gift-exchange found among the small islands off the south-eastern coast of Papua. It is the best-known example of the cycles of ceremonial exchange and trade that exist, or formerly existed, over many parts of Australia and Melanesia. It was first described by Malinowski [q.v.] in a classic monograph and has since been extensively treated comparatively in English and French by others. As the exchange of gifts, in the wide sense, is now recognized as a particularly important way of expressing and maintaining social relations between individuals and groups, the *kula* is of considerable interest in theoretical social anthropology.

The *kula* is a form of alliance by the ceremonial exchange of gifts in public. There are two kinds of valuable objects, red shell necklaces and white armshells, the supreme symbols of wealth and prestige, that form the customary gift and countergift in the *kula*. Each kind of valuable is handed from one man to another—it is a men's affair only—in a series of gift-givings that recur annually so that the valuables are kept in perpetual circulation around a fixed ring of islands. All localities of the *kula* ring are fixed in relation to their immediate neighbours in such a way that the exchanges between them have the effect of circulating the necklaces clockwise and the armshells anti-clockwise. The islands of the *kula* ring are: Trobriands, Amphletts, Dobu-speaking parts of the D'Entrecasteaux Islands, Tubetube, Wari, Misima and Panaete (Panayati), Woodlark, Marshall Bennett, and some others (*see* TROBRIAND ISLANDS).

The *kula* relationship between two men is a lasting partnership, often life-long. A man has some partners in his home district, usually his relatives-in-law and friends, and some partners abroad. A man owes to his visiting partner from oversea, who comes to solicit his gift, the important duty of being the 'host, patron, and ally in a land of danger and insecurity' (Malinowski). One must not be 'slow' or 'hard' in making *kula*, i.e. one should pass on the valuables one holds sooner rather than later. The *kula* contains therefore the morality of the relay race as well as the values of hospitality and reciprocity.

The men of each island in the *kula* ring make two oversea expeditions annually, one to each island on either side, the first to receive one kind of valuable and the second to receive the other. Gifts received from the adjacent neighbours are matched by countergifts, armshell for necklace and necklace for armshell, given them when they come oversea in their turns some months or a year later. All giving of both kinds of the valuables takes place at home, and all the receiving abroad. Home and abroad, which are normally wholly opposed conceptions, are brought by the *kula* into a complementary and reciprocal relation like that of giving and receiving, or like that of red shell necklace and white armshell that must be exchanged one for the other. Oversea exchange is necessarily a delayed exchange of the long term; in exchanges within one island the gift given is matched by a return gift almost immediately.

A great deal of magic, ritual, and mythology is associated with the *kula*. An oversea expedition must, for example, be punctuated by two ritual halts, a preliminary one when magic is performed over the canoes, and a later one when self-beauti-

fication magic is performed to aid in wooing the *kula* partner.

An oversea expedition is a collective, ceremonial, and competitive affair. Its organization brings together men of the different local and kin groups of each island as contestants for prizes held for the moment by men of the neighbouring island. In this way rivalries and differences existing within a group and between the groups inhabiting an island are turned outward and made to affirm and renew the oversea alliances. Every oversea *kula* partnership marks a formal friendship between two individuals belonging to separate and potentially hostile islands, and all such partnerships taken together serve to establish, maintain, and regulate relations between a series of autonomous communities. The fundamental political separateness of the islands is recognized in symbolic expression in the *kula*, its ceremonies and myths, and bridged over without being annulled.

In former times, before the imposed peace of European power, it was the *kula* that established peace where otherwise there was war. It was the peace of the market place. All inter-island trade was conducted under the umbrella of *kula* expeditions, the rule being that the individual visitor traded and bartered (*gimwali*) not with his own *kula* partner but with other men. This trade was of vital importance not merely to those islands, like Tubetube and the Amphletts, that were short of food, but also to others whose necessary needs were less apparent. The otherwise rich Trobriand Islands, for example, were obliged to import stone for making axes along the route Woodlark to Marshall Bennett Islands to Kitava to Kiriwina, and to polish it with special sand imported from Fergusson Island to Kaileuna (Kayleula) to Kavataria. They also had to import pottery from the Amphletts and sago from Dobu. Every island had extensive trade connections via its neighbours so that all of them were interwoven by a network of traffic in the special products, and to suit the particular needs, of each.

The practice of the *kula* has declined in recent years, the institution having lost some of its functions for the islanders under the British and later the Australian Administration and being replaced partly by pearling and other new activities, but the lesson that Mauss, following Malinowski, drew from it is still valid. The *kula*, he wrote, 'takes the whole tribe out of the narrow circle of its own frontiers. The same holds also for the clans and villages within the tribes, which are bound by links of the same sort'. It is in ways such as this that individuals, groups, and whole peoples learn to 'succeed in substituting alliance, gift, and commerce for war, isolation, and stagnation'.

W. H. Alkire, *Lamotrek Atoll and Inter-island Socioeconomic Ties.* Urbana, Ill., 1965; C. S. Belshaw, 'Changes in Heirloom Jewellery in the Solomon Islands', *Oceania,* vol. 20, 1949-50; Raymond Firth (ed.), *Man and Culture.* London, 1957; R. F. Fortune, *Sorcerers of Dobu.* London, 1932; B. Malinowski, *Argonauts of the Western Pacific.* London,

1922; M. Mauss, *The Gift;* tr. I. Cunnison. London, 1954; M. D. Sahlins, 'On the Sociology of Primitive Exchange', in *The Relevance of Models for Social Anthropology,* ed. M. Banton. London, 1965; R. F. Salisbury, *From Stone to Steel.* Melbourne, 1962; J. P. Singh Uberoi, *Politics of the Kula Ring.* Manchester, 1962.
                                             J. P. SINGH UBEROI

KUMA. People of the Western Highlands District. References:

M. Reay, 'The Sweet Witchcraft of Kuma Dream Experience', *Mankind,* vol. 5, 1954-62.
———— 'Two Kinds of Ritual Conflict', *Oceania,* vol. 29, 1958-9.
———— *The Kuma: Freedom and Conformity in the New Guinea Highlands.* Melbourne, 1959.
———— 'Individual Ownership and Transfer of Land among the Kuma', *Man,* vol. 59, 1959.
———— ' "Mushroom Madness" in the New Guinea Highlands', *Oceania,* vol. 31, 1960-1.
———— 'Present-Day Politics in the New Guinea Highlands', *American Anthropologist,* vol. 66, Special Publication, 1964.
———— 'Women in Transitional Society', *Australian Territories,* vol. 5, 1965.
———— 'Mushrooms and Collective Hysteria', *Australian Territories,* vol. 5, 1965.

KUNIMAIPA. People of the Central District. Reference:

M. McArthur, The Kunimaipa: the Social Structure of a Papuan People. Ph.D. thesis, Australian National University, Canberra, 1961.

KURU is an invariably fatal disease of the nervous system prevalent in the Fore people of the Eastern Highlands of New Guinea and to a smaller extent in adjacent linguistic groups. Symptoms and the pathological changes found post mortem indicate that the disease is essentially a degenerative process in the cerebellum with relatively minor changes in other parts of the brain.

Symptoms. In adult women, the group most commonly affected, the initial symptom is an increasing clumsiness and inability to carry out finely co-ordinated movements. This ataxia steadily increases in severity and eventually makes walking impossible. Associated with the inco-ordination of movement is a variable tendency to tremors usually accentuated by cold or exertion, and in the early stages hardly distinguishable from physiological shivering. In the early and intermediate stages there is emotional instability, sometimes with excessive hysterical laughter—hence the unfortunate name of 'laughing sickness' —but the more usual appearance is that of depression and withdrawal. In from three to six months from the onset the women are unable to walk without support and there is progressive loss of muscular control without clear evidence of paralysis. Eventually the patient cannot sit up or feed herself. Death results from a variety of disabilities and accidents associated with complete ataxia which in effect is a functional paralysis not only of limb and body movement but also of speaking and swallowing. Terminal infection of decubitus ulcers, 'bed-sores', or death as a result of inhalation pneumonia, is common. The symptoms and course of the disease in children follow the same general pattern.

Incidence of the disease. The region of major incidence is among the North and South Fore peoples, with a population of about 11,000 in 1961. Over the period 1957-66 the annual death rate per 1,000 was 32 and 11.8 for women and 5.0 and 1.3 for men, for South Fore and North Fore respectively. Everywhere there is a ratio of four to eight female to one male death. The importance of kuru as a cause of death in the combined region can be gauged from the fact that 1,079 females and 245 males died from the disease in the ten years 1957-66.

The age incidence of death from kuru differs characteristically according to sex. In general, deaths are seen only in young males while female deaths range over all ages from relatively early childhood to late middle age. According to Mathews the average age at death has risen strikingly between 1960 and 1966 from 14 to 22 in males, 29 to 38 in females. No cases are on record in any child born since 1954.

The first cases of kuru were observed by Europeans in 1952 and by 1953 it was known to be the major cause of death in the Fore region. Questioning of older indigenes and analysis of pedigrees and deaths by Glasse, Mathews and others indicates that kuru was unknown in the area before 1920 and that it spread roughly from north to south like a slow moving epidemic making its full impact on the South Fore only in the 1940s.

The investigation of kuru. The first studies of kuru are due to V. Zigas who visited the area in 1956 and obtained blood for tests to exclude the possibility that the condition might have been a sequel to virus infection of the brain. In 1957 D. C. Gajdusek joined Zigas in the first extensive study of the disease and most of our knowledge of the disease must be ascribed to Gajdusek. He made extensive field investigations of the symptomatology and incidence of the disease, recognizing the characteristic sex and age incidence and collecting family histories. He also tried several types of drug treatment none of which had any influence on the course of the disease. The two papers published by Gajdusek and Zigas in November 1957 gave a clinical account of the disease which has not been significantly altered by subsequent work.

It was evident from the limitation of the disease to one area of the Eastern Highlands, the failure of immigrants from other regions ever to contract the disease and the very high incidence of a disease known nowhere else in the world, that genetic factors were almost certainly involved. The next significant work, in 1958, was by Bennett, Rhodes and Robson, who concentrated on the genetic aspect. They postulated that the condition was due to a dominant gene K present in a relatively high proportion of people in the region. When present in double dose KK it gave rise to kuru in either sex and at an early age. If only one K gene was present, Kk, the disease could only be expressed in females and at a later age. This, of course, gave no enlightenment as to what determined the actual age at which the disease process was initiated or what was the nature of the pathological changes.

The next significant investigation was a report by the Glasses that the existence of kuru as a disease dates only from about 1920. This immediately implied that an environmental as well as a genetic factor must be involved and Glasse's suggestion was that this may have been the development of cannibalism in the area. This suggestion has been much discussed. Some, like the present writer, initially found the suggestion incredible but must confess now to at least an open mind on the matter. Glasse is specific that among the South Fore people kuru victims were regularly eaten by the female kinswomen of the deceased. Adult males had a firm taboo against eating women. If kuru were a slow virus disease conveyed from one person to another only by eating half-cooked brain, it would obviously be extremely difficult to differentiate its epidemiology from that of a genetically transmitted disease. If the verbal information about cannibalism and kuru in the past obtained by the Glasses from elderly indigenous informants was not distorted to fit a preconceived idea associating cannibalism with guilt and punishment (kuru), then it fits the hypothesis reasonably well.

The most recent discovery and so far the only one that has been obtained by experimental work was the transmission of a disease with most of the qualities of kuru to chimpanzees by Gajdusek and his associates. Chimpanzees were inoculated into the brain with material from the brains of kuru victims. Seven out of eight developed the picture of kuru from 18 to 30 months after inoculation. Transfer of brain material from one animal to other chimpanzees gave a similar picture with a shorter incubation period of 10 to 12 months.

Hornabrook's main contribution was to establish that clinically the disease is a progressive cerebellar degeneration, other aspects being secondary.

There has been continuing interest in the field enumeration of cases and accurate statistics are available for 1957 to the present as well as several compilations of past incidence from native informants. This has allowed further epidemiological studies including those by Alpers and Gajdusek and by Mathews. These agree that the incidence is falling and the average age of death rising. Superimposed on the general trend, Mathews finds some accumulations of cases suggesting an additional factor which could be related to rainfall presumably working through a seasonal food shortage.

The interpretation of kuru. There is no adequate interpretation of the causation of kuru yet available. Kuru is unique to New Guinea but elsewhere there are rare cases of cerebellar degeneration in man usually associated with malignant disease, e.g. cancer of the stomach, which show much the same symptoms and pathological changes as kuru. Amongst animal diseases, scrapie of sheep, which is relatively widespread in some lines of British sheep breeds, has some remarkable resemblances to kuru. It is genetically determined, shows cerebellar symptoms and tissue changes, and a virus-like agent can be obtained from the brains of diseased sheep. The incrimination of a virus is, however, complicated by the fact that the 'agent' has none of the physical or chemical qualities of conventional viruses and there is no evidence that scrapie is ever transmitted from sheep to sheep by any other means than genetic inheritance.

It is too early, therefore, to take the chimpanzee results at their face value as indicating that they are being infected with 'the virus' which caused kuru in the Fore and not in the rest of humanity, either because the Fore were the only people whose women regularly ate their dead kinswomen's brains or because the Fore had a unique genetically based susceptibility to the virus.

The chief argument against the cannibalism theory is the limitation of kuru to this one region of New Guinea, although cannibalism has been a widespread custom in many peoples elsewhere in New Guinea and throughout the world for millennia. Why did kuru arise only once and at a time when European entry to the area was beginning? The alternative is still that kuru is a genetic anomaly that only became lethal when some environmental factor—a virus brought by Europeans or a new food plant are two possibilities—came into prominence.

The future of kuru. In our ignorance of the real nature of kuru the only guide we have to the future is the really striking decrease in incidence in the last seven years and the absence of any cases in children born since 1954. This offers the heartening possibility that the environmental factor which initiated kuru in 1920 or thereabouts has now disappeared or been counteracted by some change associated with governmental control. My own belief is that kuru will burn itself out in the next twenty years, perhaps without our ever knowing what was the nature of the disease. It is very important, however, that a close epidemiological scrutiny be maintained in the Fore region for the next ten years at least. Any recurrence of juvenile kuru would obviously eliminate the cannibalism hypothesis and call for a renewed attack on the nature of the environmental agent.

FIRST DESCRIPTION
D. C. Gajdusek and V. Zigas, 'Degenerative Disease of the Central Nervous System in New Guinea', *New England Journal of Medicine*, vol. 257, 1957.
V. Zigas and D. C. Gajdusek, 'Kuru: Clinical Study of a New Syndrome resembling Paralysis Agitans in Natives of the Eastern Highlands of Australian New Guinea', *Medical Journal of Australia*, vol. 2, 1957.

GENETICS
J. H. Bennett, F. A. Rhodes and H. N. Robson, 'Observations on Kuru: I. A Possible Genetic Basis', *Australasian Annals of Medicine*, vol. 7, 1958.

TRANSMISSION TO CHIMPANZEES

E. Beck and others, 'Experimental "Kuru" in Chimpanzees: A Pathological Report', *Lancet*, vol. 2, 1966.

D. C. Gajdusek, C. J. Gibbs and M. Alpers, 'Transmission and Passage of Experimental "Kuru" to Chimpanzees', *Science*, vol. 155, 1967.

SCRAPIE

H. B. Parry, 'Scrapie: A Transmissible and Hereditary Disease of Sheep', *Heredity*, vol. 17, 1962.

D. C. Gajdusek, C. J. Gibbs and M. Alpers (eds), *Slow, Latent, and Temperate Virus Infections*. National Institute of Neurological Diseases and Blindness, Monograph no. 2. Washington, 1965.

CANNIBALISM IN RELATION TO KURU

R. M. Glasse. 'Cannibalism in the Kuru Region of New Guinea', *Transactions of the New York Academy of Sciences*, Series II, vol. 29, 1966-7.

J. D. Mathews, R. M. Glasse and S. Lindenbaum, 'Kuru and Cannibalism', *Lancet*, vol. 2, 1968.

F. M. BURNET

KUTUBU. People of the Southern Highlands District. References:

F. E. Williams, 'Report on the Grasslanders, Augu-Wage-Wela', in *Annual Report of the Territory of Papua 1938-9*. Canberra, 1940.

———— 'Group Sentiment and Primitive Justice', *American Anthropologist*, vol. 43, 1941.

———— 'Natives of Lake Kutubu, Papua', *Oceania*, vols 11-12, 1940-2 (republished as *Oceania Monograph* no. 6).

KWOMA. People from north of the Sepik River near Ambuntí.
References:

J. W. M. Whiting, *Becoming a Kwoma: Teaching and Learning in a New Guinea Tribe*. New Haven, 1941.

———— 'The Frustration Complex in Kwoma Society', *Man*, vol. 44, 1944.

———— and S. W. Reed, 'Kwoma Culture: Report on Field Work in the Mandated Territory of New Guinea', *Oceania*, vol. 9, 1938-9.

KYAKA. People of the Western Highlands District. References:

R. N. H. Bulmer, Leadership and Social Structure among the Kyaka People of the Western Highlands District of New Guinea. Ph.D. thesis, Australian National University, Canberra, 1960.

———— 'Political Aspects of the Moka Ceremonial Exchange System among the Kyaka People of the Western Highlands of New Guinea', *Oceania*, vol. 31, 1960-1.

———— 'Hagen and Wapenamanda Open Electorates: the Election among the Kyaka Enga' (New Guinea's First National Election), *Journal of the Polynesian Society*, vol. 73, 1964.

———— 'The Kyaka of the Western Highlands', in *Gods Ghosts and Men in Melanesia*, ed. P. Lawrence and M. J. Meggitt. Melbourne, 1965.

———— 'Beliefs Concerning the Propagation of New Varieties of Sweet Potato in Two New Guinea Highlands Societies', *Journal of the Polynesian Society*, vol. 74, 1965.

———— and S. Bulmer, 'Figurines and Other Stones of Power among the Kyaka of Central New Guinea', *Journal of the Polynesian Society*, vol. 71, 1962.